PRAISE FOR *AMERICAN CONSTITUTIONAL LA* *SELECTED CASES*, 18TH EDITION

In its 18th edition, Mason and Stephenson's *A* [illegible] disappoint. It *continues* the authors' tradition of publishing a well-edited, lucidly written, accessible text for undergraduate audiences that is ideal for a single-semester course. The case selection is complete and up to date and the authors' introductory essays are crisp and comprehensive. I've used Mason and Stephenson throughout my teaching career and I look forward to using the new edition.

Mark Rush, *Washington and Lee University*

Mason and Stephenson's *American Constitutional Law* remains the leader among single-volume undergraduate constitutional law casebooks. The new edition has been updated to cover cases through the most recent Supreme Court term; examine the changes in the Court's composition and the less-than-statesmanlike confirmation battles that preceded those changes; consider the early jurisprudential results of Donald Trump's three appointees—Neil Gorsuch, Brett Kavanaugh, and Amy Coney Barrett; and explore the effects of a global pandemic, a presidential impeachment, and an incredibly contentious 2020 presidential election on the work of the Court. The cases are masterfully edited, and meticulously written introductory essays place them in their proper context. The engaging part of a course on constitutional law comes from the professor, not the textbook. But Mason and Stephenson certainly make the job easier.

Richard A. Glenn, *Millersville University*

PRAISE FOR PREVIOUS EDITIONS

Mason and Stephenson's *American Constitutional Law* continues to be the gold standard. The book introduction immediately intrigues the reader and offers a rich historical background. The cases are thoughtfully selected, introduced with clear and engaging explanations.

Robert J. Bresler, *Pennsylvania State University*

In *American Constitutional Law*, Mason and Stephenson provide an illuminating look into the institutional tensions inherent in the Constitution. This single-volume introduction to Constitutional Law covers both the structure of government as well as the people's rights and liberties. By integrating the latest in Supreme Court politics and electoral politics, this text provides students with the latest perspectives on constitutional developments.

Kati Mohammad-Zadeh, *University of Minnesota*

American Constitutional Law

This book is a collection of comprehensive background essays coupled with carefully edited Supreme Court case excerpts designed to explore constitutional law and the role of the Supreme Court in its development and interpretation. Well-grounded in both theory and politics, the book endeavors to heighten students' understanding of this critical part of the American political system.

NEW TO THE 18TH EDITION

- An account of the Trump impeachments and a full discussion of the recent Supreme Court transitions, including the fraught Kavanaugh hearings, the death of Ruth Bader Ginsburg, and the nomination process surrounding Amy Coney Barrett.
- Fourteen new cases carefully edited and excerpted, including *Chiafalo* v. *Washington* (2020) on the Electoral College, *Masterpiece Cakeshop* (2018) on gay rights, and three Trump cases as well.
- Thirty-four new cases discussed in chapter essays.
- Tips on reading a Supreme Court decision now appear as a box in Chapter One.

Alpheus Thomas Mason (late) was McCormick Professor of Jurisprudence Emeritus at Princeton University.

Donald Grier Stephenson, Jr. is Charles A. Dana Professor of Government, Emeritus, at Franklin and Marshall College where he taught from 1970 until 2017. Reared on a farm near Covington, Georgia, he is a graduate of Davidson College (1964) and received the M.A. and Ph.D. degrees from Princeton University in 1966 and 1967, respectively. Between 1968 and 1970 he was in the United States Army, completing his service at the rank of captain. He is author of *Campaigns and the Court: The U.S. Supreme Court in Presidential Elections* (1999), *The Waite Court* (2003), and *The Right to Vote* (2004), and is coauthor of *American Constitutional Law* (17th ed. 2018) and *Introduction to American Government* (11th ed., 2021). He writes "The Judicial Bookshelf" for the *Journal of Supreme Court History.*

American Constitutional Law

Introductory Essays and Selected Cases

Alpheus Thomas Mason and
Donald Grier Stephenson, Jr.

Routledge
Taylor & Francis Group
NEW YORK AND LONDON

Eighteenth edition published 2022
by Routledge
605 Third Avenue, New York, NY 10158

and by Routledge
2 Park Square, Milton Park, Abingdon, Oxon, OX14 4RN

Routledge is an imprint of the Taylor & Francis Group, an informa business

Sixteenth edition published by Pearson Education Inc., 2021 and by Routledge, 2016
Seventeenth edition published by Routledge, 2018

Library of Congress Cataloging-in-Publication Data
A catalog record for this book has been requested

ISBN: 978-0-367-75866-0 (hbk)
ISBN: 978-0-367-75863-9 (pbk)
ISBN: 978-1-003-16434-0 (ebk)

DOI: 10.4324/9781003164340

Typeset in Garamond
by Apex CoVantage, LLC

Access the Support Material: www.routledge.com/9780367758639

In honor of
Barbara and Ed Lucas and Peg and Ron Langenberg

BRIEF CONTENTS

CONTENTS

PREFACE

Few will quickly forget the searing and shocking pictures from January 6, 2021, after remarks by President Donald Trump to supporters at a "Stop the Steal" rally on the Ellipse were quickly followed by a rampage and breach of the U.S. Capitol—a deadly assault during which rioters attempted to hunt down some elected leaders and which delayed by nearly 12 hours completion of the congressional count and certification of the electoral vote and the official end of the 2020 presidential election.

That attack on the democratic process sadly joined a list of horrific events and developments that had already marked 2020, particularly the COVID-19 scourge with its staggering death toll and its widespread, upending, and enduring hardships and effects. Moreover, as it reached the Supreme Court, the pandemic closed the Supreme Court Building, caused the justices to announce decisions and opinions virtually, and in May 2020, for the first time, necessitated oral arguments via teleconferencing with real-time public audio streaming. Wholly unrelated to the virus, the nation had already experienced something akin to only three previous occasions in American history: impeachment by the House of Representatives in December 2019 of the president of the United States and a subsequent trial by the Senate in January and February 2020 that ended in acquittal. The riot on January 6 then led to yet a second impeachment of Trump a week later, only seven days before the end of his term. On February 13, after a trial at which Senator Patrick Leahy, president pro tempore of the Senate, presided in place of the chief justice, the Senate vote of 57–43 fell short of the two-thirds margin needed to convict the former president. In contrast, Trump's first trial in early 2020 had called for application of one of the Constitution's unequivocal provisions: "When the President of the United States is tried, the Chief Justice shall preside."

Yet, the chief justice's presence at the raised rostrum in the Senate chamber for the earlier trial remained a visual reminder of one of the major themes of this book: that the Supreme Court has rarely been far from the cauldron of politics since it opened for business in 1790. At first glance that may seem a surprising statement, in that the Constitution appears to wall off the Court from politics. Justices never face the voters in an election, and they effectively enjoy life tenure. Even their salaries may not be reduced. Yet some of the Court's decisions directly shape public policy by determining what government may or may not do. Other decisions clarify the boundaries of political authority, focusing not so much on what government may do as on what part of government may act or how government is supposed to do something. Still other rulings affect the electoral process itself, as happens in cases on voting rights, representation, and campaign finance. On other occasions the Court itself may sometimes become an issue in elections or be a target of criticism by candidates, presidents, and members of Congress because of unpopular decisions. In each of these situations, the Court is using its authority or is having its authority questioned and challenged. The Court's proximity to politics therefore poses a question. Are the women and men who sit on its bench judges, partisans, or a combination of both?

While the Court in the modern era has enjoyed substantially higher approval ratings than the elected branches of the national government, public opinion polls more recently have revealed a modest but nonetheless noticeable decline of confidence in the Court. A Quinnipiac University poll in May 2019 found that 55 percent of respondents thought that the Supreme Court is "motivated mainly by politics," a 5-point increase from 2018. Slightly more than half also believed that the Court should be "restructured" in order to "reduce the influence of politics." A year later, the same poll reported that the Court's overall approval rating stood at 52 percent, a drop of 6 points from 2007. In a period of heightened political polarization in the United States, some observers have attributed such numbers to statements by journalists, pundits, and elected officials suggesting that the justices are partisan agents, not judges. Thus, when those on one side of a political divide believe a justice has not voted as expected, the justice is reproached for falling short. Similarly, when the Court appears poised to issue a ruling opposed by another side, its advocates go beyond arguments against a particular outcome and instead threaten the Court with corrective retribution. Either situation may suggest that justices are perceived by many not as judges but as robed agents for one political dogma or another.

Chief Justice John Roberts candidly addressed this concern during a question-and-answer session at Rensselaer Polytechnic Institute in 2018, soon after Justice Neil Gorsuch's confirmation. "It is a real danger that the partisan hostility that people see in the political branches will affect the nonpartisan activity of the judicial branch," warned Roberts.

> It is very difficult I think for a member of the public to look at what goes on in confirmation hearings these days, which is a very sharp conflict in political terms between Democrats and Republicans, and not think that the person who comes out of that process must similarly share that partisan view of public issues and public life.

Abundant examples soon followed suggesting that the Court was in a partisan crossfire. In November 2019 President Trump spoke disparagingly of a member of the federal bench as an "Obama judge." The reference prompted a rebuke from the chief justice. "We do not have Obama judges or Trump judges, Bush judges or Clinton judges. What we have is an extraordinary group of dedicated judges doing their level best to do equal right to those appearing before them." Two months prior to this exchange, a remarkable friend of the court brief was filed in the Supreme Court by U.S. Senators Sheldon Whitehouse, Mazie Hirono, Richard Blumenthal, Richard Durbin, and Kirsten Gillibrand concerning *New York State Rifle & Pistol Association, Inc.* v. *City of New York*, a gun rights dispute then before the Court. It was a case that the senators did not want the justices to decide. "The Supreme Court is not well," their brief concluded. "And the people know it. Perhaps the Court can heal itself before the public demands it be 'restructured in order to reduce the influence of politics.' Particularly on the urgent issue of gun control, a nation desperately needs it to heal." (The Court in an unsigned opinion, with two justices dissenting, later avoided the issue by dismissing the case as moot.)

Such language may have been on the mind of the chief justice when he released his year-end report for 2019:

> We should celebrate our strong and independent judiciary, a key source of national unity and stability. But we should also remember that justice is not inevitable. We should

> reflect on our duty to judge without fear or favor, deciding each matter with humility, integrity, and dispatch.

Yet barely three months later, Senate Minority Leader Charles Schumer took two justices to task while addressing a crowd in front of the Supreme Court Building: "I want to tell you, Gorsuch. I want to tell you, Kavanaugh," he shouted. "You have released the whirlwind, and you will pay the price. You won't know what hit you if you go forward with those awful decisions." Schumer's threat of reprisal again pushed the chief justice into a defensive mode:

> Justices know that criticism comes with the territory, but threatening statements of this sort from the highest levels of government are not only inappropriate, they are dangerous. All members of the Court will continue to do their job, without fear or favor, from whatever quarter.

Thus, while Trump was the first president in a long time to be so naked in his attack on judicial independence, Democratic politicians matched his tone.

However, Trump had more to say. Through his Twitter account he fired a volley shortly before the 2020 elections. "If Sleepy Joe Biden is actually elected President," he declared on October 30, "the 4 Justices (plus1) that helped make such a ridiculous win possible would be relegated to sitting on not only a heavily PACKED COURT, but probably a REVOLVING COURT as well." His language became even more reckless once it was certain that he would be a one-term occupant of the White House. "The fact that the Supreme Court wouldn't find standing in an original jurisdiction matter between multiple states, and including the President of the States, is absurd," he insisted on December 13 after the justices turned away Texas Attorney General Ken Paxton's challenge to the election results in four states. "They just 'chickened out' and didn't want to rule on the merits of the case." Seemingly forgetting that three members of the Court were on the bench by his choosing, he tweeted on December 26 that the justices were "totally incompetent and weak."

Such comments and verbal exchanges have been a reminder that the Court's continuing power and influence in American government rests upon its legitimacy—a recognition among the people and political elites that it is entitled to make decisions and to have those decisions obeyed. Yet, on what does that legitimacy rest? While the legitimacy of members of Congress and the president derives from the consent of the governed by way of elections, justices of the Supreme Court and other federal judges enjoy no identical popular underpinnings. At most they may claim that their link with the people is indirect in that they hold their positions through appointment by officials who themselves are elected.

That recognition, however, poses a second question. Why has the general public along with its elected officials nonetheless been mainly content, with notable exceptions, to accept the Court's authority? Does acceptance of the Court's authority stem mainly from the usefulness of the Court's referee or conflict resolution function, or perhaps from something else? Some have suggested that acceptance has historically rested on a perception that most of the time, the justices do their work of deciding cases not as partisans or agents of various factions but as judges who strive to subordinate their own personal preferences in an effort conscientiously to safeguard, construe, and apply the Constitution and acts of Congress. Thus, as Alexander Hamilton anticipated in what proved to be classic understatement at the founding, the Court's power consists of "neither force nor will but merely judgment." Or as Justice Robert H. Jackson suggested in 1953, "We are not final because we are infallible, but we are infallible only because we are final." Yet it is precisely this civic understanding that today appears increasingly to be in some doubt. Justices, after all, succeed at their task of deciding cases to the extent that their decisions convincingly appear to rest not on their personal predilections but on what the law of the land requires. Achieving that goal is challenging, because the judicial selection process places on the bench individuals who possess not only contrasting personal values and partisan backgrounds but contrasting theories of constitutional and statutory interpretation as well. The resulting mix then leads to case outcomes that often favor one side but not the other in a political storm, meaning that even in the best of circumstances the Court may unavoidably appear to fall short in reaching a goal of principled decision making.

The inauguration of Joe Biden as the nation's 46th chief executive on January 20, 2021 has hardly quieted controversy over the Court. Making good on a campaign position, Biden on April 9 announced creation of a 36-person commission to study possible changes to the Court and to issue a report within six months of its first meeting. Barely a week later, House lawmakers introduced legislation to add four seats to the Court's membership, raising it to 13. These moves followed a speech Justice Stephen Breyer gave at Harvard Law School on April 6 where he warned against tampering with the Court, noting that he hoped "to make those whose initial instincts may favor important structural (or other similar institutional) changes, such as forms of 'court-packing,' think long and hard before embodying those changes in law." "It is wrong to think of the Court as another political institution. And, it is doubly wrong to think of its members as junior-league politicians," he continued. "Structural alteration motivated by the perception of political influence can only feed that perception, further eroding that trust. There are no shortcuts to it." Such developments were more indications of the possibly substantial influence that any president or Congress may have, not only on the makeup of the Court but therefore also on the future of American constitutional law. Supreme Court justices, after all, are not merely lawyers who wear robes but major players whose distinctive work in interpreting the Constitution and statutes helps to shape American government, individual freedom, and the political life of the nation. With those realities in mind, the Introduction retains its distinctive focus on institutional development and the politics of judicial selection.

This edition, following the pattern set in earlier editions, is rooted in the conviction that constitutional law is an intricate blend of politics, history, and competing values. Even though judicial decisions are couched in the language and method used by lawyers, constitutional cases are proper turf for students of politics and government. This is because the judiciary is the place where law and politics meet.

Accordingly, the book emphasizes the ongoing importance of constitutional interpretation. Interpretation embodies choices about the meaning of the Constitution. These choices in turn affect the operation of the political system, help to define individual rights and freedoms, and influence the quality of life that Americans enjoy. Constitutional interpretation has thus made the justices participants in the governing process. Their decisions embody selections among hard (and consequential) alternatives rather than the easy dictates of a cold mechanical process. The book invites students to become party to the dialogue that the Court has maintained with the American people for over two centuries, a dialogue that reflects a historic attraction to, and suspicion of, majority rule—on the part of both the people and the Court.

NEW TO THIS EDITION

- Throughout: New material in both essays and excerpted cases reflects recent developments, especially from the 2016–2017, 2017–2018, 2018–2019, 2019–2020, and 2020–2021 terms. Moreover, all data in tables have been updated.
- This edition contains 14 newly added excerpted cases, as detailed in the list of chapters.
- The chapter essays contain discussion of 31 additional cases.
- The Constitution of the United States is now located between the Preface and the Introduction, rather than at the back of the book as part of an appendix. The text of the Constitution does not resolve most matters of constitutional law, but it is always the place to start. Placing the document up front sends a helpful message: "This is the document we are studying. Get used to consulting it." The Constitution, after all, is central to this book, not merely "additional" matter.
- The Introduction, which is the first substantive chapter of the book, includes new material on the appointments to the Supreme Court of Justices Gorsuch, Kavanaugh, and Barrett. Moreover, the chapter concludes with a table showing comparative data on federal judicial appointments for presidents from Carter through Trump.
- Chapter One includes the most recent data on the Supreme Court's caseload. In addition, as a way of illustrating the Court at work, the chapter includes a brief excerpt from the courtroom argument in *Minnesota Voters Alliance* v. *Mansky* (2018). Tips on reading a Supreme Court decision now appear as a box in Chapter One.
- Chapter Two includes the most recent data on state and federal laws declared unconstitutional.
- Chapter Three reviews recent military actions abroad as well as Senate Joint Resolution 68 and adds three cases: *Trump* v. *Hawaii* (2018), *Trump* v. *Mazars* (2020), and *Trump* v. *Vance* (2020).
- Chapter Five adds two cases: *Rucho* v. *Common Cause* (2019) and *Chiafalo* v. *Washington* (2020).
- Chapter Six adds *South Dakota* v. *Wayfair, Inc.* (2018).
- Chapter Nine adds *Timbs* v. *Indiana* (2019).
- Chapter Ten, recognizing the heightened salience of race in law enforcement and criminal justice, restores *McCleskey* v. *Kemp* (1987). Moreover, the essay has been updated with the most recent data on electronic surveillance and on stop-and-frisks in New York City.
- Chapter Eleven adds *Janus* v. *AFSCME* (2018).
- Chapter Twelve adds three cases: *Masterpiece Cakeshop* v. *Colorado Civil Rights Commission* (2018), *American Legion* v. *American Humanist Association* (2019), and *Espinoza* v. *Montana Department of Revenue* (2020).
- Chapter Thirteen adds *June Medical Services* v. *Russo* (2020), depicting the Court's change in how it reviews regulation affecting abortions.
- Chapter Fifteen has been partly renamed and shows how government responses to the COVID-19 pandemic have posed constitutional questions. With the pandemic in mind, the chapter adds *Roman Catholic Diocese of Brooklyn* v. *Cuomo* (2020).
- The Glossary adds 15 new terms that draw from the Key Terms feature that follows each chapter essay.
- The Appendix section of the book is now organized into three parts: Appendix A displays a table of all justices of the Supreme Court arranged by natural or discrete court. Appendix B displays a table of the justices arranged by presidential term. Appendix C displays a table depicting American constitutional development as reflected in a

chronology of cases reprinted in this book. Also organized by presidential term, it can be viewed as a chronological table of contents. Moreover, as noted above, the Constitution of the United States is no longer located in the Appendix, but is now placed so that it immediately follows this Preface.

FEATURES

- **Essays**. A distinctive feature of the book remains the essay preceding the cases in each chapter. These essays supply the historical and political contexts and trace the meandering thread of constitutional doctrine across major decisions.
- **Case Excerpts**. The case excerpts that follow the essays—essential for learning and in depicting constitutional interpretation at work—are as generous as space allows. As shown in the contents, cases in each chapter are grouped by subtopic within that chapter, loosely corresponding to the organization of the essay itself.
- **Unstaged Debates**. Chapters Two and Eight each contain an "unstaged debate" that highlights a topic covered within the chapter.
- **Views Inside the Court**. Chapters Eight and Twelve each contain an example of a justice's attempt to persuade one or more colleagues as opinions were being drafted. In addition, as noted above, Chapter One includes a brief excerpt from the oral argument in *Minnesota Voters Alliance* v. *Mansky* (2018).
- Tips on reading a Supreme Court decision are presented in Chapter One.
- Court-related publications and the abundant Court-related resources available on the Internet are surveyed in Chapter One.
- **Glossary**. Complementing both the essays and case excerpts is the glossary, which contains a definition of every term that is set in boldface in the essays and listed among the key terms at the conclusion of each chapter essay.
- **Selected Readings**. To complement both the essays and excerpted cases, each chapter essay concludes with a short and updated list of suggestions for further reading.
- **Boldface Italics**. Names of cases discussed in the essays that are also reprinted in the book appear in boldface italics.
- **Headnotes**. Each case headnote features not only a summary of the background of the case but also the voting alignment for that case. The case citations above each headnote identifying print sources also include the URL for online access to the case.
- Throughout, the book's few footnotes scattered are numbered consecutively by chapter. In every instance, text appearing within excerpted opinions is the Court's, except for brief insertions within brackets for dates or case names or unless specially marked "—Ed." as having been inserted for this book.
- **Web Page Support Material**. The online materials complement the eighteenth edition and facilitate teaching and learning in at least three ways. (1) The site contains important decisions handed down after this edition went to press, which are edited in the same manner as cases excerpted in the book. (2) The site retains cases from previous editions that were displaced by new material and so may be used as a case archive. Faculty designing syllabi thus have a larger number of edited cases from which to choose. (3) Finally, the site contains useful noncase material as well as links to other Court-related sites.

ACKNOWLEDGMENTS

Any new edition of this book necessarily brings to mind the legacy of Professor Alpheus Thomas Mason—great man, teacher, scholar, mentor, and friend—who through more than six decades of teaching in the Department of Politics at Princeton University and elsewhere following his retirement literally touched thousands of students, undergraduates and graduates alike.

Through the years since publication of the first edition of *American Constitutional Law* in 1954, general readers, faculty, and students have contributed to its betterment. Their suggestions, reflected in both deletions and additions, indicate the measure of my indebtedness. I am especially grateful to those scholars who thoroughly reviewed the seventeenth edition and made recommendations for the eighteenth. These include Laura N. Bell, West Texas A&M University; Richard A. Glenn, Millersville University; and Mark Rush, Washington & Lee University, among several others who offered constructive comments for the revision. Special thanks are due also to Tom Karel, Associate Librarian for Collection Management at the Franklin & Marshall College Library, who ably assisted in ferreting out sometimes obscure sources, as well as to Robert Bresler of Pennsylvania State University who provided helpful feedback especially on my summations of the Kavanaugh and Barrett appointments. I am also indebted to my students, past and present, in Government 314 and 315 who over many years have helped me realize what works and does not work in the classroom.

As always, deserving of much credit for their wisdom, guidance, and forbearance are the many people at Routledge who have supported this book. In particular, my thanks go to senior politics editor Jennifer Knerr, editorial assistant Jacqueline Dorsey, and senior production editor Emma Harder. I would also like to thank our copy editor, Jen Fester, and project manager Kate Fornadel. Much gratitude is owed also to family—my son Todd and his wife Stacy; my daughter Claire and her husband Michael; my grandsons Jackson, Everett, and Benjamin; and especially Ellen, my wife for well over half a century. Their love, patience, and devotion have been both sustaining and reassuring.

Finally, and sadly, I note the passing in early 2021 of Stanley J. Michalak, the Honorable John C. and Mrs. Kunkel Professor of Government Emeritus at Franklin & Marshall and a colleague for 34 years. Throughout his long career Stan had a remarkable impact in all the best ways as teacher, scholar, and mentor.

Questions, suggestions, and comments about the book are welcomed via e-mail: grier.stephenson@fandm.edu.

D. G. S., Jr.

Prelude to the U.S. Constitution

What is known today as the Constitutional Convention began its work in Philadelphia, Pennsylvania, on May 25, 1787, and adjourned on September 17. Although state legislatures had selected 74 delegates, only 55 from 12 states—Rhode Island having declined to send any—eventually took their seats, and fewer than a dozen delegates did the bulk of the work. Among them, 29 were college graduates and 34 were lawyers, while others were farmers and merchants. Ten had been members of Congress under the Articles of Confederation. Eight were signers of the Declaration of Independence, and the signatures of six appeared on the Articles of Confederation. Five were under the age of 30. On balance, however, the convention was not a reassembling of the generation that had set the American Revolution in motion in 1776. The delegates instead came from a pool of individuals who were fast gaining a wealth of practical experience in the political life of the young nation. Most were also committed to making changes in the Articles of Confederation—otherwise they would not have sacrificed the time and effort to attend.

THE CONSTITUTION OF THE UNITED STATES OF AMERICA

We the people of the United States, in order to form a more perfect Union, establish Justice, insure domestic Tranquility, provide for the common defence, promote the general Welfare, and secure the Blessings of Liberty to ourselves and our Posterity, do ordain and establish this CONSTITUTION for the United States of America.

ARTICLE I

Section 1

All legislative Powers herein granted shall be vested in a Congress of the United States, which shall consist of a Senate and House of Representatives.

Section 2

The House of Representatives shall be composed of Members chosen every second Year by the People of the several States, and the Electors in each State shall have the Qualifications requisite for Electors of the most numerous Branch of the State Legislature.

No Person shall be a Representative who shall not have attained to the Age of twenty-five Years, and been seven Years a Citizen of the United States, and who shall not, when elected, be an Inhabitant of that State in which he shall be chosen.

[Representatives and direct Taxes shall be apportioned among the several States which may be included within this Union, according to their respective Numbers, which shall be determined by adding to the whole Number of Free Persons, including those bound to Service for a Term of Years, and excluding Indians not taxed, three fifths of all other persons.][1] The actual Enumeration shall be made within three Years after the first Meeting of the Congress of the United States, and within every subsequent Term of ten Years, in such Manner as they shall by Law direct. The Number of Representatives shall not exceed one for every thirty thousand, but each State shall have at least one Representative; and until such enumeration shall be made, the State of New Hampshire shall be entitled to chuse three, Massachusetts eight, Rhode Island and Providence Plantations one, Connecticut five, New York six, New Jersey four, Pennsylvania eight, Delaware one, Maryland six, Virginia ten, North Carolina five, South Carolina five, and Georgia three.

When vacancies happen in the Representation from any State, the Executive Authority thereof shall issue Writs of Election to fill such Vacancies.

The House of Representatives shall chuse their Speaker and other Officers; and shall have the sole Power of Impeachment.

Section 3

The Senate of the United States shall be composed of two Senators from each State, chosen by the Legislature thereof,[2] for six Years; and each Senator shall have one Vote.

Immediately after they shall be assembled in Consequence of the first Election, they shall be divided as equally as may be into three Classes. The Seats of the Senators of the first Class shall be vacated at the Expiration of the second Year, of the Second Class at the Expiration of the fourth Year, and of the third Class at the Expiration of the sixth Year, so that one-third may be chosen every second Year; and if Vacancies happen by Resignation, or otherwise, during the Recess of the Legislature of any State, the Executive therefore may make temporary Appointments until the next Meeting of the Legislature, which shall then fill such Vacancies.

No Person shall be a Senator who shall not have attained to the Age of thirty Years, and been nine Years a Citizen of the United States, and who shall not, when elected, be an Inhabitant of that State in which he shall be chosen.

The Vice President of the United States shall be President of the Senate, but shall have no vote, unless they be equally divided.

The Senate shall chuse their other Officers, and also a President pro tempore, in the absence of the Vice President, or when he shall exercise the Office of President of the United States.

The Senate shall have the sole Power to try all Impeachments. When sitting for that Purpose, they shall be on Oath or Affirmation. When the President of the United States is tried, the Chief Justice shall preside; And no Person shall be convicted without the Concurrence of two thirds of the Members present.

Judgment in Cases of Impeachment shall not extend further than to removal from Office, and disqualification to hold and enjoy any Office of honor, Trust or Profit under the United States; but the Party convicted shall nevertheless be liable and subject to Indictment, Trial, Judgment, and Punishment, according to Law.

Section 4

The Times, Places and Manner of holding Elections for Senators and Representatives, shall be prescribed in each State by the Legislature thereof; but the Congress may at any time by Law make or alter such Regulations, except as to the Places of chusing Senators.

The Congress shall assemble at least once in every Year, and such Meeting shall be on the first Monday in December, unless they shall by Law appoint a different Day.[3]

Section 5

Each House shall be the Judge of the Elections, Returns and Qualifications of its own Members, and a Majority of each shall constitute a Quorum to do Business; but a smaller Number may adjourn from day to day, and may be authorized to compel the Attendance of absent Members, in such Manner, and under such Penalties, as each House may provide.

Each House may determine the Rules of its Proceedings, punish its Members for disorderly Behavior, and, with the Concurrence of two thirds, expel a Member.

Each House shall keep a Journal of its Proceedings and from time to time publish the same, excepting such Parts as may in their Judgment require Secrecy; and the Yeas and Nays of the Members of either House on any question shall, at the Desire of one fifth of those Present, be entered on the Journal.

Neither House, during the Session of Congress, shall without the Consent of the other, adjourn for more than three days, nor to any other Place than that in which the two Houses shall be sitting.

Section 6

The Senators and Representatives shall receive a Compensation for their Services, to be ascertained by Law, and paid out of the Treasury of the United States. They shall in all Cases, except Treason, Felony, and Breach of the peace, be privileged from Arrest during their Attendance at the Session of their respective Houses, and in going to and returning from the same; and for any Speech or Debate in either House, they shall not be questioned in any other Place.

No Senator or Representative shall, during the Time for which he was elected, be appointed to any civil Office under the Authority of the United States, which shall have been created, or the Emoluments whereof shall have been encreased during such time; and no Person holding any Office under the United States shall be a Member of either House during his continuance in Office.

Section 7

All Bills for raising Revenue shall originate in the House of Representatives; but the Senate may propose or concur with Amendments as on other Bills.

Every Bill which shall have passed the House of Representatives and the Senate, shall, before it become a Law, be presented to the President of the United States; if he approve he shall sign it, but if not he shall return it, with his Objections to that House in which it shall have originated, who shall enter the Objections at large on their Journal, and proceed to reconsider it. If after such Reconsideration two thirds of that House shall agree to pass the Bill it shall be sent, together with the Objections, to the other House, by which it shall likewise be reconsidered, and if approved by two thirds of that House, it shall become a Law. But in all such Cases the Votes of both Houses shall be determined by Yeas and Nays, and the Names of the Persons voting for and against the Bill shall be entered on the Journal of each House respectively. If any Bill shall not be returned by the President within ten Days (Sundays excepted) after it shall have been presented to him, the Same shall be a Law, in like Manner as if he had signed it, unless the Congress by their Adjournment prevent its Return, in which Case it shall not be a Law.

Every Order, Resolution, or Vote to which the Concurrence of the Senate and House of Representatives may be necessary (except on a question of Adjournment) shall be presented to the President of the United States; and before the Same shall take Effect, shall be approved by him, or being disapproved by him, shall be repassed by two thirds of the Senate and House of Representatives, according to the Rules and Limitations prescribed in the Case of a Bill.

Section 8

The Congress shall have Power To lay and collect Taxes, Duties, Imposts and Excises, to pay the Debts and provide for the common Defence and general Welfare of the United States; but all Duties, Imposts and Excises shall be uniform throughout the United States;

To borrow money on the Credit of the United States;

To regulate Commerce with foreign Nations, and among the several States, and with the Indian Tribes;

To establish an uniform Rule of Naturalization, and uniform Laws on the subject of Bankruptcies throughout the United States;

To coin Money, regulate the Value thereof, and of foreign Coin, and fix the Standard of Weights and Measures;

To provide for the Punishment of counterfeiting the Securities and current Coin of the United States; To Establish Post Offices and Post Roads;

To promote the Progress of Science and useful Arts, by securing for limited Times to Authors and Inventors the exclusive Right to their respective Writings and Discoveries;

To constitute Tribunals inferior to the supreme Court;

To define and punish Piracies and Felonies committed on the high Seas, and Offenses against the Law of Nations;

To declare War, grant Letters of Marque and Reprisal, and make Rules concerning Captures on Land and Water;

To raise and support Armies, but no Appropriation of Money to that Use shall be for a longer Term than two Years;

To provide and maintain a Navy;

To make Rules for the Government and Regulation of the land and naval Forces;

To provide for calling forth the Militia to execute the Laws of the Union, suppress Insurrections and repel Invasions;

To provide for organizing, arming, and disciplining the Militia, and for governing such Part of them as may be employed in the Service of the United States, reserving to the States respectively, the Appointment of the Officers, and the Authority of training the Militia according to the discipline prescribed by Congress;

To exercise exclusive Legislation in all Cases whatsoever, over such District (not exceeding ten Miles square) as may, by Cession of particular States, and the acceptance of Congress, become the Seat of the Government of the United States, and to exercise like Authority over all Places purchased by the Consent of the Legislature of the State in which the Same shall be, for the Erection of Forts, Magazines, Arsenals, dock-Yards, and other needful Buildings;—And

To make all Laws which shall be necessary and proper for carrying into Execution the foregoing Powers, and all other Powers vested by this Constitution in the Government of the United States, or in any Department or Officer thereof.

Section 9

The Migration or Importation of such Persons as any of the States now existing shall think proper to admit, shall not be prohibited by the Congress prior to the Year, one thousand eight hundred and eight, but a tax or duty may be imposed on such Importation, not exceeding ten dollars for each person.

The privilege of the Writ of Habeas Corpus shall not be suspended, unless when in Cases of Rebellion or Invasion the public Safety may require it.

No Bill of Attainder or ex post facto Law shall be passed.

No capitation, or other direct Tax shall be laid, unless in Proportion to the Census or Enumeration herein before directed to be taken.[4]

No Tax or Duty shall be laid on Articles exported from any State.

No Preference shall be given by any Regulation of Commerce or Revenue to the Ports of one State over those of another: nor shall Vessels bound to, or from one State, be obliged to enter, clear, or pay Duties in another.

No Money shall be drawn from the Treasury, but in Consequence of Appropriations made by Law; and a regular Statement and Account of the Receipts and Expenditures of all public Money shall be published from time to time.

No Title of Nobility shall be granted by the United States:—And no Person holding any Office of Profit or Trust under them, shall, without the Consent of the Congress, accept of any present, Emolument, Office, or Title, of any kind whatever, from any King, Prince or foreign State.

Section 10

No State shall enter into any Treaty, Alliance, or Confederation; grant Letters of Marque and Reprisal; coin Money; emit Bills of Credit; make any Thing but gold and silver Coin a Tender in Payment of Debts; pass any Bill of Attainder, ex post facto Law, or Law impairing the Obligation of Contracts, or grant any Title of Nobility.

No State shall, without the Consent of the Congress, lay any Imposts or Duties on Imports or Exports, except what may be absolutely necessary for executing its inspection Laws: and the net Produce of all Duties and Imposts, laid by any State on Imports or Exports, shall be for the Use of the Treasury of the United States and all such Laws shall be subject to the Revision and Controul of the Congress.

No State shall, without the Consent of Congress, lay any duty of Tonnage, keep Troops, or Ships of War in time of Peace, enter into any Agreement or Compact with another State, or with a foreign Power, or engage in War, unless actually invaded, or in such imminent Danger as will not admit of delay.

ARTICLE II

Section 1

The executive Power shall be vested in a President of the United States of America. He shall hold his Office during the Term of four Years, and, together with the Vice-President, chosen for the same term, be elected, as follows.

Each State shall appoint, in such Manner as the Legislature thereof may direct, a number of Electors, equal to the whole number of Senators and Representatives to which the State may be entitled in the Congress; but no Senator or Representative, or Person holding an Office of Trust or Profit under the United States, shall be appointed an Elector.

The Electors shall meet in their respective States, and vote by Ballot for two persons, of whom one at least shall not be an Inhabitant of the same State with themselves. And they shall make a List of all the Persons voted for, and of the

Number of Votes for each; which List they shall sign and certify, and transmit sealed to the Seat of the Government of the United States, directed to the President of the Senate;—The President of the Senate shall, in the Presence of the Senate and House of Representatives, open all the Certificates, and the Votes shall then be counted. The Person having the greatest Number of Votes shall be the President, if such Number be a Majority of the whole Number of Electors appointed; and if there be more than one who have such Majority, and have an Equal Number of Votes, then the House of Representatives shall immediately chuse by Ballot one of them for President; and if no Person have a Majority, then from the five highest on the List the said House shall in like Manner chuse the President, but in chusing the President, the Votes shall be taken by States, the Representation from each State having one Vote; a quorum for this Purpose shall consist of a Member or Members from two-thirds of the States, and a Majority of all the States shall be necessary to a Choice. In every Case, after the Choice of the President, the Person having the greatest Number of Votes of the Electors shall be the Vice-President. But if there should remain two or more who have equal Votes, the Senate shall chuse from them by Ballot the Vice-President.[5]

The Congress may determine the Time of chusing the Electors, and the Day on which they shall give their Vote; which Day shall be the same throughout the United States.

No person except a natural born Citizen, or a Citizen of the United States, at the time of the Adoption of this Constitution, shall be eligible to the Office of President; neither shall any Person be eligible to that Office who shall not have attained to the Age of thirty-five Years, and been fourteen Years a Resident within the United States.

In Case of the Removal of the President from Office, or of his Death, Resignation, or Inability to discharge the Powers and Duties of the said Office, the same shall devolve on the Vice-President, and the Congress may by Law provide for the Case of Removal, Death, Resignation, or Inability, both of the President and Vice-President, declaring what Officer shall then act as President, and such Officer shall act accordingly, until the Disability be removed, or a President shall be elected.

The President shall, at stated Times, receive for his Services, a Compensation, which shall neither be encreased nor diminished during the Period for which he shall have been elected, and he shall not receive within that Period any other Emolument from the United States, or any of them.

Before he enters on the Execution of his Office, he shall take the following Oath or Affirmation: "I do solemnly swear (or affirm) that I will faithfully execute the Office of President of the United States, and will to the best of my Ability, preserve, protect and defend the Constitution of the United States."

Section 2

The President shall be Commander in Chief of the Army and Navy of the United States, and of the Militia of the several States, when called into the actual Service of the United States; he may require the Opinion in writing, of the principal Officer in each of the executive Departments, upon any subject relating to the Duties of their respective Offices, and he shall have Power to grant Reprieves and Pardons for Offenses against the United States, except in Cases of Impeachment.

He shall have Power, by and with the Advice and Consent of the Senate, to make Treaties, provided two-thirds of the Senators present concur; and he shall nominate, and by and with the Advice and Consent of the Senate, shall appoint Ambassadors, other public Ministers and Consuls, Judges of the supreme Court, and all other Officers of the United States, whose Appointments are not herein otherwise provided for, and which shall be established by Law: but the Congress may by Law vest the Appointment of such inferior Officers, as they think proper, in the President alone, in the Courts of Law, or in the Heads of Departments.

The President shall have Power to fill up all Vacancies that may happen during the Recess of the Senate, by granting Commissions which shall expire at the End of their next Session.

Section 3

He shall from time to time give to the Congress Information of the State of the Union, and recommend to their Consideration such Measures as he shall judge necessary and expedient; he may, on extraordinary Occasions, convene both Houses, or either of them, and in Cases of Disagreement between them, with Respect to the Time of Adjournment, he may adjourn them to such Time as he shall think proper; he shall receive Ambassadors and other public Ministers; he shall take Care that the Laws be faithfully executed, and shall Commission all the Officers of the United States.

Section 4

The President, Vice-President and all civil Officers of the United States, shall be removed from Office on Impeachment for, and Conviction of, Treason, Bribery, or other high Crimes and Misdemeanors.

ARTICLE III

Section 1

The judicial Power of the United States, shall be vested in one supreme Court, and in such inferior Courts as the Congress may from time to time ordain and establish. The Judges, both of the supreme and inferior Courts, shall hold their offices during good Behaviour, and shall, at stated Times, receive for their Services a Compensation, which shall not be diminished during their Continuance in Office.

Section 2

The judicial Power shall extend to all Cases, in Law and Equity, arising under this Constitution, the Laws of the United States and Treaties made, or which shall be made, under their Authority;—to all Cases affecting Ambassadors, other public Ministers and Consuls;—to all Cases of admiralty and maritime Jurisdiction;—to Controversies to which the United States shall be a Party;—to Controversies between two or more States;—between a State and Citizens of another State;[6]—Between Citizens of different States;—between Citizens of the same State claiming Lands under Grants of different States, and between a State, or the Citizens thereof, and foreign States, Citizens or Subjects.

In all Cases affecting Ambassadors, other public Ministers and Consuls, and those in which a State shall be a Party, the supreme Court shall have original Jurisdiction. In all the other Cases before mentioned, the supreme Court shall have appellate Jurisdiction, both as to Law and Fact, with such Exceptions, and under such Regulations as the Congress shall make.

The trial of all Crimes, except in Cases of Impeachment, shall be by Jury, and such Trial shall be held in the State where the said Crimes shall have been committed; but when not committed within any State, the Trial shall be at such Place or Places as the Congress may by Law have directed.

Section 3

Treason against the United States, shall consist only in levying War against them, or, in adhering to their Enemies, giving them Aid and Comfort. No Person shall be convicted of Treason unless on the Testimony of two Witnesses to the same overt Act, or on Confession in open Court.

The Congress shall have Power to declare the Punishment of Treason, but no Attainder of Treason shall work Corruption of Blood, or Forfeiture except during the Life of the Person attainted.

ARTICLE IV

Section 1

Full Faith and Credit shall be given in each State to the public acts, Records, and judicial Proceedings of every other State. And the Congress may by general Laws prescribe the Manner in which such Acts, Records and Proceedings shall be proved, and the Effect thereof.

Section 2

The Citizens of each State shall be entitled to all Privileges and Immunities of Citizens in the several States.

A person charged in any State with Treason, Felony, or other Crime, who shall flee from Justice, and be found in another State, shall on demand of the executive Authority of the State from which he fled, be delivered up, to be removed to the State having Jurisdiction of the Crime.

No Person held to Service or Labour in one State, under the Laws thereof, escaping into another, shall, in Consequence of any Law or Regulation therein, be discharged from such Service or Labour, but shall be delivered up on Claim of the Party to whom such Service or Labour may be due.[7]

Section 3

New States may be admitted by the Congress into this Union; but no new States shall be formed or erected within the Jurisdiction of any other State; nor any State be formed by the Junction of two or more States, or parts of States, without the Consent of the Legislatures of the States concerned as well as of the Congress.

The Congress shall have Power to dispose of and make all needful Rules and Regulations respecting the Territory or other Property belonging to the United States; and nothing in this Constitution shall be so constructed as to Prejudice any Claims of the United States, or of any particular State.

Section 4

The United States shall guarantee to every State in this Union a Republican Form of Government, and shall protect each of them against Invasion; and on Application of the Legislature, or of the Executive (when the Legislature cannot be convened) against domestic Violence.

ARTICLE V

The Congress, whenever two-thirds of both Houses shall deem it necessary, shall propose Amendments to this Constitution, or, on the Application of the Legislatures of two-thirds of the several States, shall call a Convention for proposing Amendments, which, in either Case, shall be valid to all Intents and Purposes, as part of this Constitution, when ratified by the Legislatures of three-fourths of the several States, or by Conventions in three-fourths thereof, as the one or the other Mode of Ratification may be proposed by the Congress; Provided that no Amendment which may be made prior to the Year One thousand eight hundred and eight shall in any Manner affect the first and fourth Clauses in the Ninth Section of the first Article; and that no State, without its Consent, shall be deprived of its equal Suffrage in the Senate.

ARTICLE VI

All Debts contracted and Engagements entered into, before the Adoption of this Constitution, shall be as valid against the United States under this Constitution, as under the Confederation.

This Constitution, and the Laws of the United States which shall be made in Pursuance thereof; and all Treaties made, or which shall be made, under the Authority of the United States, shall be the supreme Law of the Land; and the Judges in every State shall be bound thereby, any Thing in the Constitution or Laws of any State to the Contrary notwithstanding.

The Senators and Representatives before mentioned, and the Members of the several State Legislatures, and all executive and judicial Officers, both of the United States and of the several States, shall be bound by Oath or Affirmation, to support this Constitution; but no religious Test shall ever be required as a Qualification to any Office or public Trust under the United States.

ARTICLE VII

The Ratification of the Conventions of nine States shall be sufficient for the Establishment of this Constitution between the States so ratifying the Same.

Done in Convention by the Unanimous Consent of the States Present the Seventeenth Day of September in the Year of our Lord one thousand seven hundred and eighty-seven and of the Independence of the United States of America the Twelfth. In Witness whereof We have hereunto subscribed our Names. [Names of signatories omitted.—Ed.]

AMENDMENTS[8]

Amendment I

Congress shall make no law respecting an establishment of religion, or prohibiting the free exercise thereof; or abridging the freedom of speech, or of the press; or the right of the people peaceably to assemble, and to petition the Government for a redress of grievances.

Amendment II

A well regulated Militia, being necessary to the security of a free State, the right of the people to keep and bear Arms, shall not be infringed.

Amendment III

No Soldier shall, in time of peace be quartered in any house, without the consent of the Owner, nor in time of war, but in a manner to be prescribed by law.

Amendment IV

The right of the people to be secure in their persons, houses, papers, and effects, against unreasonable searches and seizures, shall not be violated, and no Warrants shall issue, but upon probable cause, supported by Oath or affirmation, and particularly describing the place to be searched, and the persons or things to be seized.

Amendment V

No person shall be held to answer for a capital, or otherwise infamous crime, unless on a presentment or indictment of a Grand Jury, except in cases arising in the land or naval forces, or in the Militia, when in actual service in time of War or public danger; nor shall any person be subject for the same offense to be twice put in jeopardy of life or limb, nor shall be compelled in any criminal case to be a witness against himself, nor be deprived of life, liberty, or property, without due process of law; nor shall private property be taken for public use, without just compensation.

Amendment VI

In all criminal prosecutions, the accused shall enjoy the right to a speedy and public trial, by an impartial jury of the State and district wherein the crime shall have been committed, which district shall have been previously ascertained by law, and to be informed of the nature and cause of the accusation; to be confronted with the witnesses against him; to have compulsory process for obtaining witnesses in his favor, and to have the Assistance of Counsel for his defence.

Amendment VII

In suits at common law, where the value in controversy shall exceed twenty dollars, the right of trial by jury shall be preserved, and no fact tried by jury, shall be otherwise reexamined in any Court of the United States, than according to the rules of the common law.

Amendment VIII

Excessive bail shall not be required, nor excessive fines imposed, nor cruel and unusual punishments inflicted.

Amendment IX

The enumeration in the Constitution, of certain rights, shall not be construed to deny or disparage others retained by the people.

Amendment X

The powers not delegated to the United States by the Constitution, nor prohibited by it to the States, are reserved to the States respectively, or to the people.

Amendment XI (1798)

The Judicial power of the United States shall not be construed to extend to any suit in law or equity, commenced or prosecuted against one of the United States by Citizens of another State, or by Citizens or Subjects of any Foreign States.

Amendment XII (1804)

The Electors shall meet in their respective states and vote by ballot for President and Vice-President, one of whom, at least, shall not be an inhabitant of the same state with themselves; they shall name in their ballots the person voted for as President, and indistinct ballots the person voted for as Vice-President, and they shall make distinct lists of all persons voted for as president, and all persons voted for as Vice-President, and of the number of votes for each, which lists they shall sign and certify, and transmit sealed to the seat of the government of the United States, directed to the President of the Senate; The President of the Senate shall, in the presence of the Senate and House of Representatives, open all the certificates and the votes shall then be counted;—The person having the greatest number of votes for President, shall be the President, if such number be a majority of the whole number of Electors appointed; and if no person have such majority, then from the persons having the highest numbers not exceeding three on the list of those voted for as President, the House of Representatives shall choose immediately, by ballot, the President. But in choosing the President, the votes shall be taken by states, the representation from each state having one vote; a quorum for this purpose shall consist of a member or members from two-thirds of the states, and a majority of all the states shall be necessary to a choice. And if the House of Representatives shall not choose a President whenever the right of choice shall devolve upon them, before the fourth day of March next following, then the Vice-President shall act as President, as in the case of the death or other constitutional disability of the President.—The person having the greatest number of votes as Vice-President, shall be the Vice-President, if such number be a majority of the whole number of Electors appointed, and if no person have a majority, then from the two highest numbers on the list, the Senate shall choose the Vice-President; a quorum for the purpose shall consist of two-thirds of the whole number of Senators, and a majority of the whole number shall be necessary to a choice. But no person constitutionally ineligible to the office of the President shall be eligible to that of Vice-President of the United States.

Amendment XIII (1865)

Section 1

Neither slavery nor involuntary servitude, except as a punishment for crime whereof the party shall have been duly convicted, shall exist within the United States, or any place subject to their jurisdiction.

Section 2

Congress shall have power to enforce this article by appropriate legislation.

Amendment XIV (1868)

Section 1

All persons born or naturalized in the United States and subject to the jurisdiction thereof, are citizens of the United States and of the State wherein they reside. No State shall make or enforce any law which shall abridge the privileges or immunities of citizens of the United States; nor shall any State deprive any person of life, liberty, or property, without due process of law; nor deny to any person within its jurisdiction the equal protection of the laws.

Section 2

Representatives shall be apportioned among the several States according to their respective numbers, counting the whole number of persons in each State, excluding Indians not taxed. But when the right to vote at any election for the choice of electors for President and Vice-President of the United States, Representatives in Congress, the Executive and Judicial Officers of a State, or the members of the Legislature thereof, is denied to any of the male inhabitants of such State, being twenty-one years of age, and citizens of the United States, or in any way abridged, except for participation in rebellion, or other crime, the basis of representation therein shall be reduced in the proportion which the number of such male citizens shall bear to the whole number of male citizens twenty-one years of age in such State.

Section 3

No person shall be a Senator or Representative in Congress, or elector of President and Vice-President, or hold any office, civil or military, under the United States, or under any State, who, having previously taken an oath, as a member of Congress, or as an officer of the United States, or as a member of any State legislature, or as an executive or judicial officer of any State, to support the Constitution of the United States, shall have engaged in insurrection or rebellion against the same, or given aid or comfort to the enemies thereof. But Congress may by a vote of two-thirds of each House, remove such disability.

Section 4

The validity of the public debt of the United States, authorized by law, including debts incurred for payment of pensions and bounties for services in suppressing insurrection or rebellion, shall not be questioned. But neither the United States nor any State shall assume or pay any debt or obligation incurred in aid of insurrection or rebellion against the United States, or any claim for the loss or emancipation of any slave; but all such debts, obligations, and claims shall be held illegal and void.

Section 5

The Congress shall have power to enforce, by appropriate legislation, the provisions of this article.

Amendment XV (1870)

Section 1

The right of citizens of the United States to vote shall not be denied or abridged by the United States or by any State on account of race, color, or previous condition of servitude.

Section 2

The Congress shall have the power to enforce this article by appropriate legislation.

Amendment XVI (1913)

The Congress shall have power to lay and collect taxes on incomes, from whatever source derived, without apportionment among the several States, and without regard to any census or enumeration.

Amendment XVII (1913)

The Senate of the United States shall be composed of two Senators from each State, elected by the people thereof, for six years, and each Senator shall have one vote. The electors in each State shall have the qualifications requisite for electors of the most numerous branch of the State legislatures.

When vacancies happen in the representation of any State in the Senate, the executive authority of such State shall issue writs of election to fill such vacancies: Provided, That the legislature of any State may empower the executive thereof to make temporary appointments until the people fill the vacancies by election as the legislature may direct.

This amendment shall not be so construed as to affect the election or term of any Senator chosen before it becomes valid as part of the Constitution.

Amendment XVIII (1919)[9]

Section 1

After one year from the ratification of this article the manufacture, sale, or transportation of intoxicating liquors within, the importation thereof into, or the exportation thereof from the United States and all territory subject to the jurisdiction thereof for beverage purposes is hereby prohibited.

Section 2

The Congress and the several States shall have concurrent power to enforce this article by appropriate legislation.

Section 3

This article shall be inoperative unless it shall have been ratified as an amendment to the Constitution by the legislatures of the several States, as provided in the Constitution, within seven years from the date of the submission hereof to the States by the Congress.

Amendment XIX (1920)

The right of citizens of the United States to vote shall not be denied or abridged by the United States or by any State on account of sex.

Congress shall have power to enforce this article by appropriate legislation.

Amendment XX (1933)

Section 1

The terms of the President and Vice-President shall end at noon on the 20th day of January, and the terms of Senators and Representatives at noon on the 3rd day of January, of the years in which such terms would have ended if this article had not been ratified; and the terms of their successors shall then begin.

Section 2

The Congress shall assemble at least once in every year, and such meeting shall begin at noon on the 3rd day of January, unless they shall by law appoint a different day.

Section 3

If, at the time fixed for the beginning of the term of the President, the President elect shall have died, the Vice-President elect shall become President. If a President shall not have been chosen before the time fixed for the beginning of his term, or if the President elect shall have failed to qualify, then the Vice-President elect shall act as President until a President shall have qualified; and the Congress may by law provide for the case wherein neither a President elect nor a Vice-President elect shall have qualified, declaring who shall then act as President, or the manner in which one who is to act shall be selected, and such person shall act accordingly until a President or Vice-President shall have qualified.

Section 4

The Congress may by law provide for the case of the death of any of the persons from whom the House of Representatives may choose a President whenever the right of choice shall have devolved upon them, and for the case of the death of any of the persons from whom the Senate may choose a Vice-President whenever the right of choice shall have devolved upon them.

Section 5

Sections 1 and 2 shall take effect on the 15th day of October following the ratification of this article.

Section 6

This article shall be inoperative unless it shall have been ratified as an amendment to the Constitution by the legislatures of three-fourths of the several States within seven years from the date of its submission.

Amendment XXI (1933)[10]

Section 1

The eighteenth article of amendment to the Constitution of the United States is hereby repealed.

Section 2

The transportation or importation into any State, Territory, or possession of the United States for delivery or use of intoxicating liquors, in violation of the laws thereof, is hereby prohibited.

Section 3

This article shall be inoperative unless it shall have been ratified as an amendment to the Constitution by conventions in the several States, as provided in the Constitution, within seven years from the date of the submission hereof to the states by the Congress.

Amendment XXII (1951)

Section 1

No person shall be elected to the office of the President more than twice, and no person who has held the office of President, or acted as President, for more than two years of a term to which some other person was elected President shall be elected to the office of President more than once. But this Article shall not apply to any person holding the office of President when this Article was proposed by the Congress, and shall not prevent any person who may be holding the office of President, or acting as President, during the term within which this Article becomes operative from holding the office of President, or acting as President during the remainder of such term.

Section 2

This article shall be inoperative unless it shall have been ratified as an amendment to the Constitution by the legislatures of three-fourths of the several States within seven years from the date of its submission to the States by the Congress.

Amendment XXIII (1961)

Section 1

The District constituting the seat of Government of the United States shall appoint in such manner as the Congress may direct:

A number of electors of President and Vice-President equal to the whole number of Senators and Representatives in Congress to which the District would be entitled if it were a State, but in no event more than the least populous State; they shall be in addition to those appointed by the States, but they shall be considered, for the purposes of the election of President and Vice-President, to be electors appointed by a state; and they shall meet in the District and perform such duties as provided by the twelfth article of amendment.

Section 2

The Congress shall have power to enforce this article by appropriate legislation.

Amendment XXIV (1964)

Section 1

The right of citizens of the United States to vote in any primary or other election for President or Vice-President, for electors for President or Vice-President, or for Senator or Representative in Congress, shall not be denied or abridged by the United States or any State by reason of failure to pay any poll tax or other tax.

Section 2

The Congress shall have power to enforce this article by appropriate legislation.

Amendment XXV (1967)

Section 1

In case of the removal of the President from office or his death or resignation, the Vice-President shall become President.

Section 2

Whenever there is a vacancy in the office of the Vice-President, the President shall nominate a Vice-President who shall take the office upon confirmation by a majority vote of both houses of Congress.

Section 3

Whenever the President transmits to the President pro tempore of the Senate and the Speaker of the House of Representatives his written declaration that he is unable to discharge the powers and duties of his office, and until he transmits to them a written declaration to the contrary, such powers and duties shall be discharged by the Vice-President as Acting President.

Section 4

Whenever the Vice-President and a majority of either the principal officers of the executive departments or of such other body as Congress may by law provide, transmit to the President pro tempore of the Senate and the Speaker of the House of Representatives their written declaration that the President is unable to discharge the powers and duties of his office, the Vice-President shall immediately assume the powers and duties of the office as Acting President.

Thereafter, when the President transmits to the President pro tempore of the Senate and the Speaker of the House of Representatives his written declaration that no inability exists, he shall resume the powers and duties of his office unless the Vice-President and a majority of either the principal officers of the executive department or of such other body as Congress may by law provide, transmit within four days to the President pro tempore of the Senate and the Speaker of the House of Representatives their written declaration that the President is unable to discharge the powers and duties of his office. Thereupon Congress shall decide the issue, assembling within 48 hours for that purpose if not in session. If the Congress, within 21 days after receipt of the latter written declaration, or, if Congress is not in session, within 21 days after Congress is required to assemble, determines by two-thirds vote of both houses that the President is unable to discharge the powers and duties of his office, the Vice-President shall continue to discharge the same as Acting President; otherwise, the President shall resume the powers and duties of his office.

Amendment XXVI (1971)

Section 1

The Right of Citizens of the United States, who are eighteen years of age or older, to vote shall not be denied or abridged by the United States or any State on account of age.

Section 2

The Congress shall have the power to enforce this article by appropriate legislation.

Amendment XXVII (1992)

No law varying the compensation for the services of the Senators and Representatives shall take effect, until an election of Representatives shall have intervened.[11]

[Status of what could be Amendment XXVIII][12]

NOTES

1. This provision was modified by the Sixteenth Amendment. The three-fifths reference to slaves was rendered obsolete by the Thirteenth and Fourteenth Amendments.
2. This provision was modified by the Seventeenth Amendment.
3. See the Twentieth Amendment.
4. See the Sixteenth Amendment.
5. This paragraph was superseded by the Twelfth Amendment.
6. See the Eleventh Amendment.
7. Obsolete. See the Thirteenth Amendment.
8. The first ten amendments were adopted in 1791 as the Bill of Rights.
9. Repealed by the Twenty-First Amendment.
10. This is the only amendment to date to have been ratified not by state legislatures but by specially called conventions in the states.
11. This is the so-called Lost Amendment, proposed in 1789 along with 11 others submitted to the states. One of the 11 was never ratified; the other ten were ratified in 1791 as the Bill of Rights. With no limitation imposed on the time allowed for ratification, the remaining amendment was finally adopted more than two centuries later.
12. In March 1972, Congress proposed the following amendment to the Constitution, coupled with a seven-year deadline for ratification: "Equality of rights under the law shall not be denied or abridged by the United States or by any state on account of sex. The Congress shall have the power to enforce, by appropriate legislation, the provisions of this article." By 1977, 35 states had ratified the Equal Rights Amendment, three states short of the necessary 38. Even though Congress voted to extend the ratification deadline by an additional three years, no additional states ratified. Moreover, legislatures in five states—Nebraska, Tennessee, Idaho, Kentucky, and South Dakota—voted to rescind their earlier votes to ratify. After several decades of inactivity, however, Nevada (2017) and Illinois (2018) voted to ratify. Virginia's ratification in January 2020 meant that the threshold of 38 had been reached, but questions about the viability of the proposed amendment remain. First, given that the congressionally reset deadline has long passed, may Congress now lift the lapsed deadline? Second, may a state validly rescind its vote to ratify a proposed amendment before the amendment has officially been ratified? Third, aside from an important symbolic value, is there still a need for the amendment, given the Supreme Court's decisions on gender discrimination since 1972? According to statute, it is the responsibility of the archivist of the United States to certify when an amendment is to be added to the Constitution.

INTRODUCTION

A Political Supreme Court

There are two parties in the United States, most decidedly opposed to each other as to the rights, powers and province of the judiciary. . . . One party almost claims infallibility for the judges, and would hedge them round about in such a manner that they cannot be reached by popular opinion at all, and . . . the other would subject them to the vacillations of popular prejudice and seemingly require it of them to define and administer the law, and interpret the Constitution, according to the real or apparent expediency of things.

—NILES' WEEKLY REGISTER (1822)

It was one of George Washington's first concerns as president: Who would sit on the Supreme Court of the United States? "Impressed with a conviction that the true administration of justice is the firmest pillar of good government," he wrote future Attorney General Edmund Randolph in 1789, "I have considered the first arrangement of the judicial department as essential to the happiness of our country and the stability of its political system." Under the Articles of Confederation, which the recently ratified Constitution replaced, there had been no national judiciary, a "circumstance," insisted Alexander Hamilton, "which crowns the defects of the Confederation." The Court's role in the new political system was unclear, but Washington realized the impact the Court might have in the young Republic. This required, he told Randolph, "the selection of the fittest characters to expound the laws and dispense justice. . . ." As he selected the six justices Congress had authorized, Washington also made sure that each section of the nation was represented and that the six were strong supporters of the new Constitution.

The first session of the newly constituted Supreme Court was scheduled for February 1, 1790, in the Exchange Building at the foot of Broad Street in New York City. The occasion was inauspicious. Only three of the six justices were present, so the Court adjourned until February 2. By then a fourth justice had arrived. In contrast to the black robes worn today, the justices were dressed in black and red gowns. A newspaper account of the day reported, "As no business appeared to require immediate notice, the Court was adjourned."

DOI: 10.4324/9781003164340-1

Against the background of the Court's beginnings in 1790, anyone embarking on the study of constitutional law today is aided by an appreciation of three points. First, the justices have had an impact on American life that can scarcely be exaggerated. This reality is made possible by and is bound up with democratic politics and a written Constitution. Students of political science therefore pay attention to Supreme Court decisions because they matter. As Washington anticipated, what the Court does—or does not do—affects the allocation of power. Second, the Court of Washington's time was not the Court of today. Like Congress and the presidency, it has changed markedly as an institution. Third, even though people frequently think of the Court as being "above" politics, it is not. From the outset, the membership of the Supreme Court has consisted of politicians (all justices have had some experience in public affairs, and many were active in partisan politics before going on the bench) appointed by politicians (presidents) and confirmed by politicians (senators). The Court's decisions, therefore, have given the justices a hand in governing the nation. That fact alone makes the Court political. This introductory chapter considers these points in turn. Later chapters will explore the organization and jurisdiction of the federal courts and many of the constitutional issues that have bedeviled the justices and the nation for more than two centuries.

CONSTITUTIONAL INTERPRETATION AND POLITICAL CHOICE

"[W]e must never forget that it is a *constitution*[1] we are expounding." With this commanding reminder, Chief Justice John Marshall interrupted a closely reasoned argument in ***McCulloch* v. *Maryland*** (1819).[2] He did not pause to spell out what he had in mind. His meaning emerged from other passages in the opinion.

As Chapter Four will show, Marshall found in the Constitution a deep reservoir of congressional power and a subordinate place for the states in the federal system. Even without express authorization in the Constitution, Congress could charter a national bank. Furthermore, Maryland and other states could not tax it. The Supreme Court, as expounder of the Constitution, would correspondingly have a narrow but nonetheless important role, guarding national over state interests. The results of *McCulloch* have been far-reaching.

In *McCulloch*, Marshall made **constitutional law**.[3] Constitutional law or jurisprudence consists of the prevailing meaning of the Constitution as found mainly in decisions by the U.S. Supreme Court. As law, these decisions are "legal," to be sure, but the law they announce is not ordinary law. Because it deals with fundamental matters such as the organization of government and the authority of officials over the lives of citizens, constitutional law is a very special kind of law, fusing politics, history, and political philosophy. This art of interpreting the Constitution is a lawyer's art only in the narrow sense that all justices of the Supreme Court have been lawyers, even though some people are surprised to learn that the Constitution does not require that the justices be lawyers or even that they have judicial experience. But the justices have had to be more than mere legal technicians. Supreme Court justices succeed as credible constitutional authorities to the degree that they are persuasive that it is the Constitution, not their individual preferences, that speak.

A theme of this book is the continuing importance of constitutional interpretation. After some 230 years, the Constitution is far more than a historic relic on display for tourists visiting the National Archives in Washington. The Constitution is the vital foundation of our political system. Broad or narrow, the prevailing interpretation of the Constitution at different times has been a major influence on the kind of nation and society Americans have enjoyed. Interpretation requires choice and is always the product of contending values. Some of these ideas promote centralized power; others control by the states. Some enlarge or diminish the influence of one branch of the national government in relation to another. Some expand individual liberties; others expand the powers of government, state and national, at the expense of the individual. Still others allow government to protect minorities from majorities.

Constitutional interpretation occurs when the Supreme Court and other courts decide cases that require judges to give meaning to particular words and passages in the Constitution. **Cases** are disputes handled by a court. They may pit one individual against another, the government against an individual or corporation, and so forth. Cases are thus the raw material of the judicial process. Although many cases do not involve conflicting interpretations of the Constitution, those that do enable courts to apply the nation's fundamental law—largely crafted for an agrarian society near the end of the eighteenth century—to the needs of a technological nation in the twenty-first century.

The justices long ago established the Supreme Court as the oracle of the Constitution through the power of **judicial review**: the authority to set aside laws passed by Congress and the state legislatures as being contrary to the Constitution. Accordingly, judicial review is law steeped in politics. The development of judicial review has meant that two branches of the national government—Congress and the presidency—are preoccupied with partisan pressures. The third branch—the judiciary—is preoccupied with constitutional principles packed with political significance. Constitutional interpretation is political in the broadest sense because it makes courts, especially the Supreme Court, participants in the process of governing. American courts are therefore distinctive because they routinely speak the language of the fundamental values of the political system.

A CHANGING JUDICIARY

Understanding constitutional law today is helped by an awareness of the Court's institutional development.

Beginnings. The Court's first decade was characterized by obscurity, weakness, and uncertainty. To a degree, each was both a cause and an effect of a high turnover in membership, an absence of effective leadership, and relatively few cases to decide. After George Washington filled the six positions Congress had authorized, he and his successor, John Adams, encountered eight vacancies between 1790 and 1800. Moreover, the Court had three chief justices during the same period (John Jay, John Rutledge, and Oliver Ellsworth).

For some early jurists, other positions were more appealing. Washington's first choice for one of the initial appointments in 1789 was Robert Harrison. Five days after his confirmation by the Senate he was selected chancellor of Maryland, a position he preferred to the seat on the Supreme Court. Without having attended a single session of the Court, John Rutledge resigned as associate justice in 1791 to become chief justice of South Carolina. He would later return when Washington handed him a **recess appointment** to be the second chief justice, a nomination the Senate rejected a few months later. (A recess appointment allows the president to fill a vacancy when the Senate is not in session. It expires at the end of the next session unless the Senate has acted on the nomination.) Chief Justice Jay did not attend a session of the Court after 1793; accepted a diplomatic mission to England in 1794, which led to an accord that today bears his name; and resigned in 1795 to become governor of New York. Departing Treasury Secretary Alexander Hamilton then turned down Washington's offer of the chief justiceship so he could resume law practice in New York. Today, presidents are rarely rebuffed by prospective nominees. Moreover, a justice's tenure is usually long, with both the average and median length of service for justices appointed since 1900 equaling four presidential terms.

Detracting from the attractiveness of the high bench in the early years was the **circuit riding** Congress imposed on the justices, a duty not finally eliminated until 1891. In addition to sitting collectively as the Supreme Court, justices sat as judges of the circuit courts, one of the two types of lower federal courts established by the Judiciary Act of 1789. Though the act provided for three types of courts (district courts, circuit courts, and the Supreme Court), it authorized the appointment of judges only for the district courts and the Supreme Court. Except for a brief period in 1801–1802, no separate circuit judgeships existed until 1855 for California and then in 1869 for the rest of the nation. Each circuit court was at first staffed by two justices (a number soon reduced to one) and one district judge. As a result, the early justices spent far more time holding circuit court than they did sitting on the Supreme Court. Nonetheless, though small in number, some of the Court's decisions in this first decade—three of which are reprinted in this book—were instrumental in laying the foundations of an enlarged judicial power that emerged in the nineteenth century.

Whether a justice traveled by carriage or by boat, riding circuit was onerous. The rigors must have tested devotion to Court and country. Not only were the distances long, but justices paid expenses out of their salaries. Accommodations were rarely ideal. Justice Cushing once found himself with 12 other lodgers in a single room, and Justice Iredell reported encountering "a bed fellow of the wrong sort." While crossing the frozen Susquehanna River at Havre de Grace, Maryland, Justice Chase fell through the ice and almost drowned.

The Court Comes of Age. Although the Supreme Court had three chief justices in its first decade, the combined service of the next three chief justices (John Marshall, Roger Taney, and Salmon Chase) totaled 72 years. As an institution of American government, the Supreme Court owes much to John Marshall, sometimes called "the Great Chief Justice" as if no other occupant of that office could ever be his equal. Appointed in the last days of John Adams's term after former Chief Justice Jay had refused reappointment (in declining, Jay wrote Adams that the Court "would not obtain the energy, weight and dignity which are essential to its affording due support to the National Government"), Marshall served 34 years (1801–1835), longer than any other chief.

Marshall dominated the Court like no chief justice before or since, making the Court the institution Jay had doubted it could become. Some of the factors that contributed to Marshall's influence were his personality and political acumen, the issues embedded within the cases the Court decided, and his determination to use the federal judiciary as a means to reinforce constitutional principles he thought vital to the advancement of the nation. In addition, circumstances of life in Washington—the justices resided and took their meals at the same boardinghouse and traveled together across town to the small courtroom in the Capitol basement—made it easier for a strong-willed individual like Marshall to influence his colleagues. Marshall also ended the practice of **seriatim opinions** inherited from English courts whereby each judge gave his view of the case. Henceforth, the Court would speak with one voice—the opinion of the Court—and the voice was usually Marshall's.

Judicial Business in the Nineteenth Century. Despite Marshall's deserved reputation in constitutional law, the bulk of the Court's work in his time and for years afterward was nonconstitutional in nature. Private law cases vastly outnumbered public law cases. In fact, of the 1,121 cases the Court decided during Marshall's tenure, only 76 raised federal constitutional issues. The majority involved admiralty and maritime issues (these cases were numerous given the fact that most of the nation's commerce before the Civil War was waterborne), common-law matters, and diversity disputes. (Created by the Judiciary Act of 1789, **diversity jurisdiction** allows federal courts to hear some suits involving ordinary matters of state law when the parties are citizens of different states.) In 1825, for example, there were no constitutional cases decided at all, and 54 percent of the **docket** (a court's caseload or list of cases awaiting action) involved admiralty, common-law, and diversity matters. As late as 1875, such cases consumed 45 percent of the docket; constitutional cases amounted to but 6 percent of the total. The Court of the nineteenth century was still largely a tribunal for the final settlement of disputes between individual parties. Its role as policymaker was decidedly secondary.

Though secondary, policymaking was hardly unimportant. Congress recognized as much in a series of statutes that altered the number of justices. Between 1789 and 1869, Congress changed the number of justices from six to five, five to six, six to seven, seven to nine, nine to ten, ten to seven, and seven to nine (the number authorized today)—each time partly with an eye toward influencing the Court's constitutional decisions.

The Modern Court. The federal judiciary underwent important structural changes beginning in the late nineteenth century. By the 1880s, it had a case backlog of several years. A cartoon of the day depicted the justices wading about their courtroom in a sea of briefs and other documents, pleading for relief, but a docket in arrears was not simply the product of an expanding population. Congress had gradually enlarged the jurisdiction of the federal courts, meaning that a greater variety of questions confronted the justices. Through its cases, the Court could hardly escape embroiling itself in virtually every political movement of the day. Swollen dockets prompted Congress to act. First, in 1891 Congress authorized intermediate appellate courts called circuit courts of appeals. For the first time, the federal judiciary had appellate tribunals below the Supreme Court. For most cases, the old circuit courts had not been appellate tribunals; a case began in either the district or circuit court depending on the subject matter. The old circuit courts were soon merged into the district courts. Circuit riding by the justices, already reduced substantially in the latter half of the nineteenth century, came to an end (ironically just as interstate rail transportation had become faster, more reliable, and more comfortable).

Second, the 1891 statute introduced some certiorari, or discretionary, jurisdiction. This meant that there were fewer categories of cases the justices were legally obliged to hear and that the new courts of appeals became the courts of last resort for many cases.

Third, as a result of intense lobbying by Chief Justice William Howard Taft (the only president to have become chief justice), Congress in 1925 passed the Judges Bill, which expanded discretionary jurisdiction even further. Now, the Court was in control of most of its docket, not only in terms of the number of cases it would decide each year but also, for the most part, of the issues it would confront. Taft's political talents left another institutional legacy: the Supreme Court Building. With construction finished in 1935, five years after Taft's death, the justices finally had a home of their own.

Today, in contrast to the docket in the nineteenth century, public law consumes the Court's time. Roughly half of the Court's business now consists of constitutional cases, with statutory interpretation accounting for almost all of the rest. Moving beyond its dispute-resolution role, the Court has become mainly a maker of public policy for uniform application across the nation.

APPOINTMENT POLITICS, 1968–1984

The Constitution entrusts the selection of Supreme Court justices, as well as judges of the lower federal courts, to both the president and the Senate. The choice of the former requires the consent of the latter. Senatorial approval is usually forthcoming, but not always. As of May 2021, 115 individuals have served on the Court.[4] Of the 162 nominations presidents have submitted to the Senate, 37 have failed to pass, all but eight in the nineteenth century. Several confirmed persons have declined to sit. By contrast, the Senate has blocked only nine nominations to the Cabinet since 1789. In exercising their constitutional obligation to give "advice and consent," senators ordinarily employ greater scrutiny and more independence with the review of justices than with heads of executive departments. Enhanced attention to the former is explained by the Court's place in the political system, life tenure for justices, and the fact that the Court, unlike the Cabinet, is not part of the executive branch.

While most senatorial scrutiny today occurs during public hearings before the Judiciary Committee at which the nominee testifies, for most of American history, the practice was otherwise. As a standing committee of the Senate, the Judiciary Committee dates only from 1816, with nominations prior to that date being dealt with by the full Senate alone. Between 1816 and 1867 some two-thirds of the nominations were referred to the Judiciary Committee, with nearly all of them being processed in that way since 1868.

The modern practice began to take shape with President Woodrow Wilson's nomination of Louis Brandeis in 1916 when the committee first held an open hearing with outside witnesses testifying, although the nominee himself was not present. Supreme Court nominees did not appear before the committee to answer questions until 1925, when President Calvin Coolidge's nomination of Attorney General Harlan F. Stone ran into difficulty. Even here, however, Stone was present only to respond to specific allegations growing out of his work as attorney general. The second nominee to testify was Felix Frankfurter in 1939, who agreed to appear only when supporters informed him that he would probably be rejected if he did not. Indeed, Frankfurter was the first to take a variety of questions in a transcribed public hearing. Still, such appearances did not become routine until after 1954. Ever since, all nominees have been expected to appear, although concerns persist over the propriety of questions that senators ask and what obligation the nominee has to answer them. Moreover, hearings since 1965 have usually been both exhaustive and, for the prospective justice, often exhausting. Gone forever, apparently, are the days of the cursory Senate probing that Kennedy nominee Byron White experienced in 1962, when public hearings lasted a scant one hour and 35 minutes.

"The good that Presidents do is often interred with their Administrations," *The Nation* editorialized in 1939. "It is their choice of Supreme Court Justices that lives after them." Although the separate institutions mandated by the Constitution make possible the Court's considerable independence from outside political pressure, three factors thrust the Court into the partisan life of the nation: the role of interpretation the Constitution allows, the significance of the decisions the justices render, and the method of judicial selection the Constitution imposes. Little wonder the appointment of justices is of paramount concern to presidents, senators, and citizens alike, as events since 1968 illustrate.

From Warren to Burger. On June 26, 1968, President Lyndon Johnson announced Chief Justice Earl Warren's intention to resign. Appointment of a chief justice is a rare occurrence. There have been 46 presidents, counting Grover Cleveland's separated presidencies twice, but only 17 chief justices. During the 34 years John Marshall sat in the Court's center chair, there were six presidents. The contrast is significant substantively as well as statistically, a fact that prompted President John Quincy Adams to rate the office of chief justice as "more important than that of President." Chief justice since 1953, Warren's tenure had been one of the most active and remarkable in American history. By one count, in the approximately 150 years before Warren's appointment, the Court had overruled 88 of its precedents. In Warren's 16 years it added another 45 to the list. Hardly an aspect of life had gone untouched by landmark decisions on race discrimination, legislative apportionment, and the Bill of Rights. The **Warren Court** initiated a revolution that is measured by President Dwight Eisenhower's purported latter-day lament over Warren's appointment: "The biggest damn fool mistake I ever made."

On June 27, President Johnson nominated Associate Justice Abe Fortas, a close friend, to succeed the controversial chief. Accusing President Johnson of "cronyism," opposition formed immediately. Fortas was charged with various improprieties, including participation in White House strategy conferences on the Vietnam War and acceptance of high lecture fees raised by wealthy business executives who happened to be clients of Fortas's former law partner, Paul Porter. Some opposing senators that included both Democrats and Republicans insisted that "the appointment should be left to the next President, who will be elected in November." After four days of deliberation, the Senate voted 45–43 on October 1 to cut off debate, well shy of the margin necessary to end the anti-Fortas filibuster. Two days later, the ill-fated justice withdrew his name. For the first time, nomination of a Supreme Court justice had been blocked by a Senate filibuster.

It remains unclear why Johnson refused to submit another name to the Senate. The lame-duck president left this high-level appointment to President Richard M. Nixon, whose 1968 campaign for the White House had been in part a campaign against the Warren Court. President Nixon's first step toward fulfilling his 1968 campaign promise to strengthen the "peace forces as against the criminal forces of the country" was the selection of Warren Earl Burger, 61, chief judge of the U.S. Court of Appeals for the District of Columbia Circuit. Burger's confirmation came 18 days later on June 9, 1969, by a vote of 74–3.

Fortas Resigns. In the spring of 1969, *Life* magazine revealed that Justice Fortas had received a yearly $20,000 retainer from the Family Foundation of Louis Wolfson, then serving a prison term for selling unregistered stock. Once again the judicial fat was in the political fire. Fortas's resignation on May 16, 1969, the first by a justice because of public criticism, opened the way for Nixon's nomination of Clement F. Haynsworth, Jr., chief judge of the Court of Appeals for the Fourth Circuit. Because Haynsworth had taken a restrictive view of school desegregation and had been insensitive to proprieties in matters involving finance and conflict of interest, the Senate, still in Democratic hands, in a surprise vote rejected the new president's nominee 55–45.

Rejection of Haynsworth strengthened Nixon's determination to "pack" the Court with what he called "strict constructionists." His next nominee, G. Harrold Carswell, had served seven years as a federal district judge in Florida and six months on the Court of Appeals for the Fifth Circuit. In 1948, he had said, "I yield to no man as a fellow candidate [he was then running for political office] or as a fellow citizen in the firm, vigorous belief in the principles of White Supremacy, and I shall always be so governed." Quite apart from Judge Carswell's avowed racism (which he now disavowed), critics charged that President Nixon's nominee was mediocre. Accepting the criticism, Nebraska senator Roman Hruska tried to convert it into an asset:

> Even if he is mediocre, there are a lot of mediocre judges and people and lawyers. They are entitled to a little representation, aren't they, and a little chance? We can't have all Brandeises, Cardozos and Frankfurters and stuff like that there.

Carswell was rejected 51–45. Not since the second presidency of Grover Cleveland in 1893 and 1894 had the Senate refused to accept two nominees for the same Supreme Court vacancy. Nixon's third choice was Chief Justice Burger's longtime Minnesota friend, Harry A. Blackmun, age 61, of the Court of Appeals for the Eighth Circuit. Blackmun aroused little opposition and was promptly confirmed 94–0 and sworn in on June 9, 1970.

POWELL, REHNQUIST, AND STEVENS

In the fall of 1970, President Nixon was still determined to appoint a southerner to the Supreme Court. The most likely spot to be vacated was that occupied by 84-year-old Justice Hugo Black. Asked for his reaction, Black replied, "I think it would be nice to have *another* Southerner up here." The Alabaman, appointed in 1937, had moved into third place in length of service. The longevity goal was in sight, but fate defeated its realization. In September 1971, Justices Black and John Harlan, both ailing, resigned within days of each other. Black fell eight months shy of Justice Stephen J. Field's record of 34½ years.

Nixon now had an opportunity no president had experienced since 1940: that of simultaneously filling two Supreme Court vacancies. His choices were Lewis F. Powell, Jr., 64, a distinguished Richmond lawyer, and William H. Rehnquist, 47, law clerk (1952–1953) to Justice Robert H. Jackson and since 1969 assistant attorney general in charge of the Justice Department's Office of Legal Counsel.

Powell, arousing little or no objection, was confirmed 89–1 on December 6. Rehnquist ran into stormy waters, but ultimately received Senate approval on December 10, 1971, 68–26. Powell was sworn in on January 6, 1972, and Rehnquist on January 7.

On New Year's Eve 1974, Justice William O. Douglas suffered a stroke. Although seriously disabled, Douglas was reluctant to retire. "Even if I'm only half alive," he remarked, "I can still cast a liberal vote." But some of his colleagues questioned whether he should be casting any votes at all. "I should like to register my protest," Justice Byron White wrote Chief Justice Burger on October 20, 1975 (with copies to the other justices),

> against the decision of the Court not to assign the writing of any opinions to Mr. Justice Douglas. . . . [T]here are one or more Justices who are doubtful about the competence of Mr. Justice Douglas that they would not join any opinion purportedly authored by him. At the very least, they would not hand down any judgment arrived at by a 5–4 vote where Mr. Justice Douglas is in the majority. . . . That decision, made in the absence of Mr. Justice Douglas, was supported by seven Justices. It is clear that the ground for the action was the assumed incompetence of the justice.

White then reminded the "Brethren" (as the justices used to refer to themselves) that "nowhere" does the Constitution provide

> that a Justice's colleagues may deprive him of his office by refusing to permit him to function as a Justice. . . . If the Court is convinced that Justice Douglas should not continue to function as a Justice, the Court should say so publicly and invite Congress to take appropriate action.

Raised again was the thorny question of how to remove an incapacitated Supreme Court justice. The Constitution supplies no answer, but history does. On more than one occasion, the power of persuasion exerted on a faltering justice by colleagues has proved effective. In 1869, Justice Field convinced Justice Grier that he was too ill to continue. Later, according to one account, when Justice Field became incapacitated, the first Justice Harlan asked his colleague whether he remembered urging Grier to retire. "Yes," Field snapped, "and a dirtier day's work I never did in my life." Ignoring or eluding pressure from whatever source, Douglas reached his own decision to leave the Court on November 12, almost a year after he was stricken. He had served 36 years, surpassing the record long held by Justice Field.

For Douglas's seat President Ford nominated John Paul Stevens, a 55-year-old appeals court judge from the Seventh Circuit and a former clerk to Justice Wiley Rutledge. The Senate quickly confirmed 98–0, and on December 19, 1975, Stevens was sworn in.

THE FIRST WOMAN JUSTICE. The judiciary figured prominently in the presidential campaign of 1980. Five years had passed without a Supreme Court vacancy on a bench where more than half the justices were above 70 years of age. Moreover, the Court only seven years before had injected itself into the most divisive of contemporary moral issues by declaring abortion to be a constitutional right. Three Nixon appointees had voted with the majority, and one of them—Blackmun—had written the majority opinion. This case alone was reminder enough that Republican presidents Eisenhower, Nixon, and Ford had not been notably adept in picking nominees who accorded with their political views. Warren, Brennan, Blackmun, and Stevens had all proved to be "surprises" in various ways, lending credence to President Truman's lament: "Packing the Supreme Court simply can't be done. I've tried and it won't work." This time, Republicans wanted to try harder.

The Republican platform therefore called for judges "who respect traditional family values and the sanctity of innocent human life." The second part was code for opposition to abortion. Denounced by the National Organization for Women for "medieval stances on women's issues," Ronald Reagan confounded the campaign by promising to name a woman to fill one of "the first Supreme Court vacancies in my administration."

As president, Reagan soon had his chance. Potter Stewart, appointed by President Eisenhower in 1958, announced his retirement on June 18, 1981. Reagan's choice for a successor was Sandra Day O'Connor, 51, of the Arizona Court of Appeals. A law student with Justice Rehnquist at Stanford University (he finished first, she third, in the class of 1952), not only was O'Connor to be the first woman to sit on the High Court, she was the first since Brennan to have had experience on a state bench. Moreover, she was the first since Justice Harold Burton, Stewart's predecessor, to have served as a state legislator. Criticized by some for injecting gender into justice, Reagan's fulfillment of a campaign pledge placed him squarely in an established tradition in which other presidents considered region, religion, and race in making appointments to the Court. Despite concerns of right-to-life groups that she was "unsound" on abortion, the Senate, under Republican control for the first time since 1955, confirmed her 99–0 on September 21.

APPOINTMENT POLITICS, 1984–1992

On June 17, 1986, President Reagan announced Chief Justice Burger's retirement and his intention to nominate Rehnquist as chief justice. Rehnquist would become only the third chief to have been selected from the Court itself.

At age 78, Burger had served longer than any other chief justice nominated in the twentieth century. Although Nixon named Burger to the Court in 1969 to fulfill a campaign pledge against judicial activism, the Court during Burger's time did not overturn outright a single major decision of the activist Warren Court (1953–1969). The persistence of the Warren Court's jurisprudence was all the more remarkable when it is remembered that by 1986, only three members of the Warren Court were still serving, and of the three only two (Justices Brennan and Marshall) had been closely identified with the Warren Court's major accomplishments. Although some of the Warren Court's landmark rulings on criminal procedure were restricted—most notably the exclusionary rule (see Chapter Ten)—the Burger Court practiced its own kind of judicial activism, especially with respect to racial and sexual equality, abortion, and other privacy issues (see Chapters Thirteen and Fourteen). With the possible exception of Taft, Burger was the most active chief justice outside the Supreme Court. He treated his office like a pulpit from which to campaign energetically for changes in legal education, professional standards for bench and bar, criminal sanctions, prisons, and the administration of justice.

Also on June 17, 1986, Reagan nominated Antonin Scalia, 50, of the Court of Appeals for the District of Columbia Circuit as associate justice. Scalia would become the first Italian American to serve on the nation's highest court. Formerly a law school professor and an assistant attorney general in the Department of Justice, he, like Rehnquist, was widely regarded as a politically conservative legal thinker.

WHOSE SUPREME COURT IS IT? From the outset, Rehnquist's nomination encountered intense opposition, a "Rehnquisition," as Senator Orrin Hatch called it, even though Republicans still controlled the Senate. If the president took a nominee's views into account, should not the Senate do the same? Preferring to forget their party's opposition to Abe Fortas in 1968, Republican leaders wanted to limit the Senate to a consideration of character and merit, but some Democrats seemed intent on ensuring a coordinate role for the Senate. "The framers envisioned a major role for the Senate in the appointment of judges," argued Senator Edward Kennedy. "It is historical nonsense to suggest that all the Senate has to do is to check the nominee's I.Q., be sure he has a law degree and no arrests, and rubber stamp the President's choice." If Rehnquist's vision of the Constitution was properly the Senate's concern, how much should it matter? Neither the Constitution nor Senate tradition offered a conclusive answer.

Hearings by the Judiciary Committee on the Rehnquist nomination consumed four days, and Senate floor debate five. Confirmation, 65–33, came on September 17. Not since 1836, when the Senate confirmed Roger Taney, had a nominee for chief justice been approved by a ratio of less than 2–1.

Perhaps because the Senate's scrutiny of Rehnquist was so intense, Scalia's nomination generated only mild turbulence. The Judiciary Committee's hearings on Judge Scalia lasted only two days. Floor debate did not exceed five minutes. Following the vote on Rehnquist, the Senate confirmed Scalia, 98–0.

The Bork Debacle. At the end of Rehnquist's first term as chief, Justice Lewis Powell announced his retirement. For several years, Powell had held a pivotal seat on the Court, especially in abortion, privacy, church–state, and affirmative action cases. Reagan now had a chance to advance his social agenda judicially, much of which had been rebuffed by Congress.

Reagan's announcement on July 1, 1987, was no surprise. At his side was Robert H. Bork, age 60, of the Court of Appeals for the District of Columbia Circuit, who had been passed over in favor of Scalia the year before. A legal scholar and former solicitor general, Bork was also a prolific writer. Not since Felix Frankfurter's appointment in 1939 had the Senate considered a Supreme Court nominee with such a long paper trail. Of particular interest was a 1971 article in the *Indiana Law Journal* that, among other things, called into question the constitutional underpinnings of ***Griswold* v. *Connecticut***, the landmark 1965 ruling on a right of privacy and birth control. If *Griswold* rested on dubious ground, so did ***Roe* v. *Wade***, the 1973 abortion rights decision (see Chapter Thirteen).

Bork's nomination was therefore guaranteed to be rancorous. Indeed, before the Judiciary Committee began its record-setting 12 days of hearings on the nomination on September 15 (Bork would testify and be questioned on five of those days), the battle lines had already been drawn. The nomination had hardly been announced before Senator Kennedy fired one of the opening shots:

> Robert Bork's America is a land in which women would be forced into back alley abortions, blacks would sit at segregated lunch counters, rogue police could break down citizens' doors in midnight raids, schoolchildren could not be taught about evolution, writers and artists could be censored at the whim of government, and the doors of the federal courts would be shut on the fingers of millions of citizens for whom the judiciary is—and is often the only—protector of the individual rights that are the heart of our democracy.

Bork's supporters had gravely underestimated the nature and extent of the opposition. Democrats like Kennedy succeeded in demonizing Bork before he could define or defend himself. Not since Woodrow Wilson nominated Louis Brandeis in 1916 had a confirmation battle become so vitriolic. On October 23, Judge Bork's Senate opponents prevailed, 58–42, a larger negative vote than either Haynsworth or Carswell endured. The phrases "to Bork" or "to be Borked" consequently entered the American political lexicon.

In place of Bork, President Reagan's advisers recommended a conservative without a paper trail. Senate Minority Leader Robert Dole advised anyone with ambitions to sit on the Supreme Court not to "write a word. I would hide in the closet until I was nominated."

On October 29, Reagan selected Douglas H. Ginsburg, one of Bork's colleagues on the District of Columbia Circuit, but senators never got a chance to query Ginsburg. Problems surfaced almost instantly. Ginsburg acknowledged that he had used marijuana as a student in the 1960s and more recently as a member of the Harvard law faculty in the 1970s. On November 7, the nomination went up in a puff of smoke as he withdrew his name from consideration.

Not since 1970 had a president had to make a third nomination to fill a single vacancy. Time was critical. Reagan was nearing the start of his last year in office. "Lame-duck" talk abounded. Like Johnson with Fortas in 1968, the vacancy might carry over to his successor in 1989. On November 10, Reagan made his next move, nominating long-time acquaintance Anthony M. Kennedy, 51, who had been a judge on the Ninth Circuit Court of Appeals since leaving private practice in 1975. Democrats could find little wrong with the nominee. An hour's debate in the Senate on February 3, 1988, preceded the vote to confirm, 97–0. On February 18, Kennedy was sworn in on as the Court's 104th justice, ending a seven-month struggle over Justice Powell's successor.

The fight to replace Powell has had consequences apart from Kennedy's career on the Court. The tentative senatorial probing of ideology in the nominations of Rehnquist and Scalia in 1986 gave way to searching scrutiny with Bork in 1987. The Senate firmly reestablished the precedent that judicial philosophy is relevant and important. Two of President Reagan's contributions to American government were no doubt unintended: He helped to make the Senate a more equal partner in shaping the Supreme Court, and he and his staff demonstrated to successors how a Supreme Court nomination should not be managed.

End of the Brennan Era. On the evening of July 20, 1990, Justice William J. Brennan, Jr., sent a note to the White House informing President George H. W. Bush that he would step down. The most senior justice in age (84) and in length of service (34 years), Brennan had suffered a mild stroke several days after the Court's term ended on June 27. Brennan's career on the High Court began in 1956 when President Eisenhower offered him a recess appointment after Justice Sherman Minton retired, and his contribution to American constitutional law was substantial. Since the 1960s, he had been leader of the Court's liberal bloc and one of the driving forces behind the Court's major decisions on subjects as varied as racial justice, affirmative action, criminal procedure, access to the courts, privacy and abortion, religious freedom, free speech and press, and legislative districting.

Bush faced a Senate firmly in Democratic hands. Moreover, his previously high public approval ratings had fallen precipitously. In short, the president was in no position to force a contentious nominee on the Senate. Within 72 hours of Brennan's retirement, Bush picked David H. Souter, who had been appointed just three months before to the First Circuit Court of Appeals. The first justice to be named from New Hampshire since Levi Woodbury in 1845 and the first bachelor since Frank Murphy in 1940, Souter had been state attorney general and a trial judge before Governor John Sununu (later Bush's chief of staff) placed him on the New Hampshire Supreme Court in 1983. Yet this background yielded few clues to his thinking on the most divisive federal constitutional issues. For Alabama's senator Howell Heflin, Souter was "the stealth candidate." On national television Justice Thurgood Marshall harrumphed, "Never heard of him." The contrast with what had abundantly been known about Bork was stunning, deliberately so in the opinion of suspicious senators.

Bush disavowed the use of "any litmus test" on abortion or on any other specific matter. Was Bush heeding Abraham Lincoln's advice? Presented with the opportunity to name Roger Taney's successor as chief justice in 1864, Lincoln advised, "We cannot ask a man what he will do, and if we should, and he should answer us, we should despise him for it. Therefore, we must take a man whose opinions are known."

Members of the Senate Judiciary Committee unabashedly asked the questions President Bush had not, making it clear that abortion was the ever-present issue at the hearings. Democrats especially wanted to satisfy themselves that Souter passed the "not Bork" test. While Souter spoke to some issues, he remained silent on the abortion right. His reticence made it difficult for opponents to mobilize the kind of opposition that had worked so well in stopping Bork. On October 2, the Senate voted overwhelmingly (90–9) to confirm Souter, barely two weeks after his 51st birthday.

The appointment again demonstrated how both the president and senators have an interest in the views of the nominee. Yet Souter presented a dilemma. When the accessible record of nominees leaves their constitutional values shrouded in mystery, should they be expected publicly to lay bare their positions on current constitutional controversies? If they do, has their independence as justices been compromised? If they do not, does the Senate's approval amount to informed consent?

The Thomas Maelstrom. Souter's first term marked Thurgood Marshall's last. On June 27, 1991, five days shy of his 83rd birthday, Justice Marshall, citing the physical toll taken by age and ill health, sent President Bush his notice of retirement. "What's wrong with me?" he responded to a reporter, "I'm old! I'm getting old and coming apart." Despite his age, the announcement took some by surprise. Only recently, Marshall had been characteristically defiant about stepping down. "I have a lifetime appointment, and I intend to serve it." His attitude seemed not to have changed from the day in 1970 when President Nixon, upon learning that Marshall was ill with pneumonia at Bethesda Naval Hospital, asked to see his medical records. Marshall let the records be sent, but not before scrawling on the folder in large print, "NOT YET."

Marshall occupies a unique place in Supreme Court history. Not only was he the first black justice, but in a way equaled by few, he helped to shape constitutional law off the Court as well as on the bench. His appointment by President Johnson in 1967 was as much recognition of what he had accomplished as it was an expectation of what he would do as a justice. From 1938 until his appointment by President Kennedy in 1961 to the Court of Appeals for the Second Circuit, he was one of the leaders in efforts by the Legal Defense Fund of the National Association for the Advancement of Colored People (NAACP) to use the judiciary as a vehicle to combat racial discrimination. He argued 32 cases before the Supreme Court and won 29, including ***Brown* v. *Board of Education*** in 1954, reprinted in Chapter Fourteen. As a justice he remained a tenacious advocate of civil rights.

The irony created by Marshall's departure escaped few. As an outspoken opponent of racial quotas, would the president name a black person to the bench? The suspense was short-lived. On July 1, Bush turned to Clarence Thomas, 43, of the U.S. Court of Appeals for the District of Columbia Circuit. A 1971 graduate of Holy Cross with a law degree from Yale, Thomas had been an assistant attorney general in Missouri and a lawyer for the Monsanto Company before going to work for Senator John Danforth. He was assistant secretary for civil rights in the Department of

Education in 1981 and 1982 and then chaired the Equal Employment Opportunity Commission (EEOC) until his appeals court appointment in 1990.

Although African American like Marshall, the contrast between the two was striking. True, both had been reared in a racially segregated environment, but Marshall came from a middle-class Maryland home. Thomas had been born into abject poverty in the tiny coastal plain community of Pin Point, Georgia, and was deserted by his father at the age of two. More significant, Thomas rejected much of what Marshall had strived for. He had questioned the wisdom of busing to achieve racial integration and opposed preferences for racial minorities, among other things. During the five days Thomas appeared before the Senate Judiciary Committee in September, Democrats especially pressed him to reveal his position on abortion. Although acknowledging the existence of a constitutional right to privacy, Thomas rebuffed their entreaties, asserting that he had not formed an opinion on the subject and claiming that he could not maintain his impartiality as a judge if he had. He wanted to avoid testimony that would give senators reason to reject him. The Souter approach had been to come across as a compassionate person but to leave senators in doubt on constitutional particulars. Robert Bork, after all, gave forthright answers and was rejected.

Objections to what Thomas's constitutional values might be and concern over his qualifications, however, led to a 7–7 split when the Judiciary Committee voted on September 27. The nomination thus went to the Senate floor without a recommendation, as press accounts predicted that Thomas would be approved easily in a vote scheduled for October 8.

Events suddenly took an unexpected turn when a leak to the press during the weekend of October 5 placed the nomination in doubt. Several weeks before the committee's vote, Professor Anita F. Hill of the University of Oklahoma School of Law had notified the committee's staff, in confidence, that Thomas had sexually harassed her in 1981–1983 while she was his assistant, first at the Department of Education and later at the Equal Employment Opportunity Commission. Some members of the committee were aware of Hill's accusations prior to their vote on September 27. Thanks to the leak, virtually the entire nation knew about them.

Now senators were themselves on trial for failing to take sexual harassment seriously. Accordingly, they sent the nomination back to the Judiciary Committee. What followed was a television spectacle that left few satisfied: 28 hours of additional hearings marked by lurid details, bitter charges and countercharges, and equally bitter denials and counter-denials. Thomas told the committee that he was the victim of a "high-tech lynching for uppity blacks." Likened by some to a morality play or a psychodrama, the acrimonious hearings drew a larger viewing audience than the National League and American League baseball playoffs going on at the same time.

The charges were grave and were potentially fatal. Thomas had headed the agency responsible for enforcing the law against sexual harassment. Moreover, the charges undercut his principal strength. Without a record of legal scholarship or extensive judicial service, the merits of the nomination had rested all along on character—precisely what Hill called into question. On October 15, such doubts helped to make the Senate's vote to confirm, 52–48, one of the closest on record for a successful Supreme Court nominee. Only the approval of Stanley Matthews by a vote of 24–23 in 1881 had generated a higher percentage of negative votes.

Not since the controversy over membership in the Ku Klux Klan enveloped Hugo Black shortly after his confirmation had a justice begun work under such a cloud of suspicion.

APPOINTMENT POLITICS, 1992–2016

Bill Clinton's inauguration as the 42nd president in 1993 was soon followed by news of an impending vacancy on the Supreme Court, as Justice Byron White on March 19 announced his intention to retire. Placed on the Court in 1962 by President John F. Kennedy, White was by 1993 the sole justice to have been nominated by a Democrat. The length of his judicial career was itself a lesson in constitutional change. Some of the issues that occupied the Court's time near the end of his tenure were not even on the docket in the early 1960s. Similarly, some highly visible issues in White's first year on the Court had all but disappeared by his last.

Ginsburg and Breyer. During the 1992 campaign, Clinton had indicated a preference for Supreme Court nominees with stature in public life who had run for election, not just those with prior judicial service. On June 14, he revealed his choice: Ruth Bader Ginsburg, 60, of the Court of Appeals for the District of Columbia Circuit, and one of President Carter's last nominations to the federal bench in 1980.

Ginsburg had been turned down for a Supreme Court clerkship in 1960 by Justice Frankfurter, who explained to her Harvard professor that he "just wasn't ready to hire a woman." While she had never held public office, she had been in public life. As founder and director of the Women's Rights Project of the American Civil Liberties Union, she had participated in 35 cases in the Supreme Court, had argued six, and had won five, including ***Frontiero* v. *Richardson*** (see Chapter Fourteen). Significantly, perhaps, her work with the ACLU did not include direct participation in the litigation that spawned *Roe* v. *Wade*. Otherwise, her confirmation chances might well have been diminished. Of recent justices, only Thurgood Marshall had come to the Court with similar experience in the creative use of constitutional law to right social wrongs.

Ginsburg's record spawned few serious doubts when the Senate Judiciary Committee convened for four days of hearings on July 20. Cautious in discussing most issues except abortion, Ginsburg appeared to be a person of politically liberal views with a sense of limits to judicial power. On August 3, the Senate approved her by a vote of 96–3; on August 10, she took the constitutional and judicial oaths as the Court's 107th justice. The occasion was noteworthy. For the first time, a nominee to the Supreme Court had been forthright in presenting her views on abortion and had been confirmed.

In the public's mind, no justice has been more closely linked with abortion than Harry A. Blackmun, author of the Court's opinion in *Roe* v. *Wade*. On April 6, 1994, Blackmun, age 85, announced his forthcoming retirement. Although 20 justices (including White) since 1789 had served longer than Blackmun's 24 years, only two were older when they left the Court. Widely expected to practice judicial restraint and to harbor conservative judicial values when appointed, Blackmun soon left the reservation. Insisting at retirement that the Court, not he, had changed, he was only partly correct. He had changed as well. At the hearings on his nomination in 1970, for example, senators queried him on only a single specific constitutional issue: capital punishment. His position then on that question was the exact opposite of his position two decades later. While he still sided with the government on Fourth Amendment issues, in nearly every other category of constitutional law he had become by 1991 the Court's most consistently liberal voice.

Having called for a nominee who possessed a "big heart," the president revealed his choice for Blackmun's seat on May 13: Judge Stephen G. Breyer, 55, of the Court of Appeals for the First Circuit, who had been a contender for White's seat. Clinton's announcement was unprecedented. He publicly agonized over his decision, discussed reasons why he could not offer the seat to two others, and left the impression that Breyer was third best.

Breyer had clerked for Justice Arthur Goldberg, worked on the Watergate prosecution team, taught at Harvard Law School, and was chief counsel to the Senate Judiciary Committee before Carter named him to the federal bench in 1980. Well-known and highly regarded by both Democrats and Republicans in the Senate, the nominee encountered only minor resistance. On July 12, hearings convened for four days with confirmation, 87–9, following on July 29. With the addition of Breyer, when the Court convened on October 3, the bench contained two Jewish justices for the first time since 1938.

A New Chief Justice. As Democratic and Republican nominees John Kerry and George W. Bush campaigned for the presidency in the fall of 2004, both acknowledged that the future direction of the Supreme Court might well rest in the outcome of the election. This seemed true for two reasons. First, on a series of salient "hot-button" constitutional issues ranging from abortion and affirmative action to federalism and religious liberty, the Court early in the new century seemed divided 5–4 or 6–3. Second, the membership of the Court had remained unchanged since Breyer's arrival in 1994. This fact was unique. Since 1869, when Congress set the Court's roster at the current complement of nine justices, there had been no other period of at least ten years without the retirement or death of a justice.

That fact, however, did not mean that the politics of judicial selection took a vacation. In particular with respect to nominees to the courts of appeals, an ideological and political war seemingly with no end in sight had been raging between the White House and Senate Democrats over who becomes a judge ever since the Supreme Court had effectively handed the presidency to Bush following the electoral contest between Bush and challenger Al Gore in 2000. (See ***Bush* v. *Gore*** in Chapter Five.) Even after Republicans gained a one-vote majority in the Senate in the 2002 midterm elections and maintained control until after the 2006 elections, Democrats deployed or threatened to deploy the filibuster against certain nominees favorably reported by the Judiciary Committee. Most notably, on September 4, 2003, Justice Department attorney Miguel Estrada, whom Bush probably wanted to groom for the Supreme Court as the first Hispanic justice, asked the president to withdraw his name after his nomination to the court of appeals for the District of Columbia Circuit had languished in the Senate for nearly two years.

By early 2005, Republicans were determined to break the Senate logjam and threatened to resort to a parliamentary maneuver popularly called the "nuclear option" to make judicial nominees filibuster-proof. With potentially disruptive or destructive consequences for Senate procedures and traditions (hence the term "nuclear"), the Senate leadership, under this option, would seek a ruling from the chamber's presiding officer (then Republican Vice President Dick Cheney) that filibusters against judicial nominees were unconstitutional. It would then take only a simple majority to sustain the chair's ruling, a number far easier for Republicans to achieve than the 60 votes needed to break a filibuster or the 67 votes required to change Senate rules outright.

On May 24, a showdown was averted when a bipartisan group of 14 senators agreed neither to support the filibuster of a judicial nominee (except in "extraordinary circumstances"—a phrase left undefined), nor to support a rule change that would limit debate on future appeals court and Supreme Court nominees. The immediate effect of the agreement was the confirmation of several heretofore controversial nominees, but observers wondered whether the truce would hold once a seat on the Supreme Court became vacant. They did not have long to wait.

On July 1, 2005, Justice Sandra Day O'Connor notified President Bush of her retirement to become "effective upon the nomination and confirmation of my successor." The first woman justice had served the equivalent of six presidential terms. During that time she established a reputation as a "swing vote" on the bench, often making the difference in closely divided cases, especially those dealing with voting rights and social issues such as abortion, affirmative action, and religion in public life. Her stance on issues was so pivotal that attorneys frequently pitched their arguments mainly to her, since the positions of the other eight justices were all but apparent in advance. While news of the first retirement at the Court in 11 years took few by surprise, most thought Rehnquist would be the first to go after an announcement on October 25, 2004, that he was afflicted with thyroid cancer. Although present for Bush's inauguration on January 20, the enfeebled chief missed most sessions of Court thereafter, working from home instead. Anticipating a vacancy, interest groups were primed to mobilize the grass roots for or against practically anyone whom the president might choose. A March email alert from NARAL Pro-Choice America (formerly the National Abortion Rights Action League) was subtitled "Emergency instructions for a Supreme Court retirement" and urged supporters to "print, cut, and fold this card and keep it in your wallet. When a Supreme Court justice retires, you'll be READY for action." The same email referred recipients to a website "for more action instructions." Conservative organizations were in a similar campaign mode.

On July 19, 2005, disregarding First Lady Laura Bush's preference for a woman nominee, Bush announced his choice for O'Connor's seat: Harvard-educated and former Rehnquist law clerk John G. Roberts, Jr., age 50, and a judge on the U.S. Court of Appeals for the District of Columbia Circuit since May 2003. Roberts had worked in the Reagan White House, served as special assistant to the attorney general in 1981–1982, and had been principal deputy solicitor general during the presidency of George H. W. Bush. Both there and in private practice, he was widely regarded as a legal superstar, a "lawyer's lawyer" who, having argued 39 cases before the Supreme Court and prevailed in 25 of them, had become a member of a rarified inner circle of appellate advocates. Acknowledging his skill and brilliance, Democrats thought that his years in the White House and the Department of Justice might incline him to view claims of presidential power too generously. They were also troubled by a footnote in a brief he had signed in an abortion financing case where he argued that *Roe* v. *Wade*, the landmark abortion rights decision, should be overturned because it "finds no support in the text, structure or history of the Constitution." In short, they feared that he would tilt a closely divided Court to the right.

On September 3, however, shortly before hearings on the nomination were to begin in the Senate Judiciary Committee, Chief Justice William Rehnquist lost his struggle with cancer. For the first time since 1971, a president would have two Supreme Court seats to fill.

Rehnquist's tenure of nearly 19 years as chief ranked him fourth on the all-time list, behind John Marshall's 34, Roger B. Taney's 28, and Melville W. Fuller's 22. In early 1999, after the House of Representatives voted impeachment charges against President Clinton, Rehnquist became only the second chief justice to preside over the Senate trial of a president. (Rehnquist's successor, Chief Justice John Roberts, was the third.)[5] Although he often found himself in the minority in abortion, affirmative action, and church–state cases—particularly during his early years on the bench, when law clerks dubbed him the "Lone Ranger"—he was nonetheless viewed as an effective spokesperson for conservative judicial values. His most lasting legacy may prove to be the Court's recent decisions reemphasizing the role of states in the federal system. A vigorous defender of judicial independence, Rehnquist was held in affectionate high esteem by the other justices, especially with respect to such internal Court matters as the fairness he exhibited in the assignment of opinions and the efficiency which marked the dispatch of the Court's business. For Justice Brennan, hardly an admirer of Rehnquist's constitutional views, he was "the most all-around successful chief justice" he had known, including Earl Warren. The 16th chief justice also had a sense of humor, being known to pass trivia questions to his colleagues during oral argument, plot practical jokes, and to take wagers on nearly anything.

The president moved promptly to fill the Rehnquist seat. Bypassing a chance to make history by naming the first woman chief justice, Bush announced on September 5 that he would nominate Roberts for the chief justiceship. The decision surprised few. Four days of hearings by the Senate Judiciary Committee commenced on September 12. By most accounts, Roberts' performance was masterful. Like most recent nominees, he generally declined to address issues that would come before the Court for decision. Reflecting the values of the president who nominated him, he advocated a modest role for the judiciary in a democratic political system. "Judges and justices are servants of the law, not the other way around," said the nominee. "Judges are like umpires. Umpires don't make the rules; they apply them. And I will remember that it's my job to call balls and strikes and not to pitch or bat."

Yet being mindful of Democrats and others who were concerned lest cherished rights-friendly decisions be placed in jeopardy, he expressed a respect for precedent. In particular, he assured the committee that he recognized a constitutionally protected right to privacy. *Roe* v. *Wade*, he said, "is settled as precedent of the court, and is entitled to respect under the principles of *stare decisis*" (to stand by what is decided). "I do think that it is a jolt to the legal system when you overrule a precedent," he added. "It is not enough that you may think the prior decision was wrongly decided." After emphasizing that he had "no agenda" and "was not an ideologue," the committee voted favorably on the nomination 13–5 on September 22. On September 29, the full Senate confirmed Roberts as by a vote of 78–22, with exactly half the Senate's 44 Democrats voting in the affirmative. Roberts was sworn in a few hours later at the White House, as John Paul Stevens, senior associate justice, administered the constitutional oath to the 17th chief justice of the United States.

Attention then returned to a replacement for Justice O'Connor with Bush announcing on October 3 that her seat should go to White House Counsel Harriet Miers. A Bush confidante since his days as Texas governor and holding a law degree from Southern Methodist University, Miers, age 50, had been co-managing partner of one of the state's largest law firms and the first woman to be elected president of the State Bar of Texas. She also had experience in state and local electoral politics, having served a term on the Dallas City Council. Lacking any judicial experience, however, the nominee failed to generate enthusiasm, especially among Republicans and others who had been expecting someone in the Roberts mold or at least one more solidly grounded than Miers in conservative legal thinking. Some accused the president of "wasting" an opportunity to reshape the Court. Others wondered out loud whether she had the intellectual wherewithal to advance the president's agenda judicially. Rather than risk the embarrassment of an inadequate performance at the Senate hearings, especially following the flair Roberts had displayed or, worse still, rejection by the Senate, Bush withdrew the nomination on October 27. For the first time since the Grant administration in the 1870s, a Supreme Court nomination had effectively been scuttled by members of the president's own political base, and for the first time since 1987, a president would have to submit a second name for the same Court position.

On October 31, Bush turned to Judge Samuel A. Alito, Jr., age 55. The son of Italian immigrants, Alito since 1990 had been judge on the U.S. Court of Appeals for the Third Circuit and previously U.S. Attorney for New Jersey. Educated at Princeton and Yale Law School, the nominee, like Roberts, had experience in the Department of Justice during the Reagan presidency, although unlike Roberts he had no experience in private practice. Furthermore, he possessed the acumen, intellectual depth, and conservative credentials that Miers's detractors feared she lacked. Five days of hearings before the Judiciary Committee opened on January 9, 2006. As with Roberts, liberals suspected that Alito was hostile to abortion rights and, in light of revelations in late 2005 of massive warrantless electronic eavesdropping by the Bush administration (see Chapter Ten), too inclined because of his executive branch experience to look favorably on claims of presidential power. With respect to the latter, the nominee declined to offer an opinion on the legality of the eavesdropping policy but insisted that "Our Constitution applies in times of peace and in times of war." With respect to abortion, in what is now in the post-Bork era a mandatory ritual for Supreme Court nominees, Alito expressed support for a constitutionally protected right of privacy, one that encompassed access to contraceptives. When asked about a statement he once wrote on a Justice Department job application that there was no constitutionally protected right to abortion, Alito explained, "That was what I thought . . . from my vantage point in 1985 . . . as a line attorney in the Reagan administration." Since that time, Alito reminded the panel, as an appeals judge he had voted to uphold one law restricting abortion access and struck down two others. "If I had had an agenda to . . . uphold any regulation of abortion that came up in any case," he insisted that he would have voted differently. As for the sanctity of precedent, he echoed Roberts in saying, "There needs to be a special justification for overruling a prior precedent."

That he failed to assuage Democratic concerns was reflected by the straight party-line vote of 10–8 on January 14, when the committee acted favorably on the nomination. Republicans claimed that they had judged Clinton nominees Ginsburg and Breyer by more neutral and less ideological criteria in 1993 and 1994. Democrats countered that Bush was trying to stack the Court with staunch conservatives. Despite eleventh-hour attempts by Senators John Kerry, Edward Kennedy, and Barack Obama to block the nomination with a filibuster—and editorial advice from the *New York Times* that senators were "in need of spine"—Republicans mustered sufficient votes to end debate with the Senate confirming Alito 58–42 on January 31, whereupon Chief Justice Roberts administered the constitutional and judicial oaths to the 110th justice in a private ceremony at the Court an hour later. Notably, the Senate count reflected the smallest number of senators from the opposition party to support a Supreme Court nomination in modern times. Yet, the Roberts and Alito confirmations defied conventional wisdom of the day that Supreme Court nominees whose records cast doubt on the validity of abortion rights decisions were unconfirmable.

The Obama Appointments. As Chief Justice Roberts administered the oath of office to Barack Obama in January 2009, some spectators were surely mindful of the uniqueness of the event even beyond the fact that the new chief executive was also the nation's first African American president. The Obama inauguration also marked the first time that a chief justice administered the oath of office to a president who, as a U.S. senator, voted against the same chief justice's confirmation.

Although President George W. Bush had no opportunity to make a High Court appointment until well into his second term, Obama encountered his first Court vacancy just a few months into his presidency, as Justice Souter notified the White House on May 1, 2009, of his intention to retire when the Court recessed for the summer. In his place on June 1 Obama nominated Judge Sonia Sotomayor, age 55, of the U.S. Court of Appeals for the Second Circuit. Like Alito, she was a graduate of Princeton University and Yale Law School and had been a prosecutor and a judge on a U.S. court of appeals. Unlike Alito, she had served as a federal trial judge and had experience in private practice, but lacked his experience in the offices of the solicitor general and the attorney general of the United States. She was also the first Latina to be nominated to the High Court.

Despite a compelling life story that had begun with Puerto Rican–born parents in a housing project in the South Bronx of New York City, questions arose not about her resume but about her judicial temperament. In particular, some senators were concerned about a public statement at the University of California at Berkeley in 2001 that a "wise Latina woman with the richness of her experiences would more often than not reach a better conclusion than a white male who hasn't lived that life." Some senators were also troubled by her vote in a ruling by the Second Circuit rejecting a reverse-discrimination claim by firefighters in New Haven, Connecticut, a decision that the Supreme Court overturned in late June (*Ricci* v. *DeStefano*) while her nomination was pending. During four days of hearings in the Judiciary Committee, the nominee spoke competently throughout but revealed little about her constitutional philosophy. A positive 13–6 vote in committee on July 28 preceded a favorable confirmation vote of 68–31 by the full Senate, then in Democratic hands, on August 6. However, negative votes totaled more than any Democratic nominee had received since the Senate rejected President Grover Cleveland's nomination of Wheeler Peckham in 1894. Chief Justice Roberts swore in the 111th justice on August 8.

Obama's second opportunity to shape the Supreme Court came on April 9, 2010, when senior associate justice John Paul Stevens, just 11 days shy of his 90th birthday, announced his intention to retire when the Court "rises for the summer recess." In Stevens's place Obama named native New Yorker Elena Kagan, age 50, on May 10. As the first solicitor general to be elevated to the Court since Justice Thurgood Marshall, for whom she clerked, Kagan, former dean of Harvard Law School, was to become the first person in 38 years to reach the Court with no experience as a judge. Educated at Princeton University and Harvard Law School, she was associate counsel in the Clinton White House following two years in private practice and was a finalist in 2009 for the seat that became Sotomayor's.

Just as Democrats had thwarted John Roberts's nomination to the U.S. Court of Appeals in 1992, Kagan's nomination to the appellate bench had been blocked by Republicans in 2009. Now Republicans insisted that she lacked the requisite judicial temperament for service on the High Court. As four days of hearings began in the Senate on June 28, the irony was lost on few. In published comments in 1995, she had written that modern-day confirmation hearings had become "a vapid and hollow charade." In her view, the process had broken down not because nominees had been pressed too hard but because senators did not press them hard enough. With Democrats in firm control of the Senate, however, her confirmation, like Sotomayor's, was never in jeopardy. A favorable committee vote (13–6) on July 20 preceded three days of debate in the full Senate. On August 5, she was confirmed 63–37, with 58 Democrats and Independents and five Republicans in the affirmative, and 36 Republicans and one Democrat opposed. On August 7, in ceremonies at the Supreme Court, Chief Justice Roberts swore in the 112th justice.

The environment in the Senate for nominations changed in November 2013 when the Democratic majority, led by Senator Harry Reid, employed the "nuclear option," voting 52–48, with all Republicans and 3 Democrats voting against, to eliminate the use of the filibuster on executive branch and judicial nominees *other than to the Supreme Court*. At the time of the vote there were 59 executive branch nominees and 17 nominees to district and appeals courts awaiting confirmation. While Republicans left the altered practice in place when they regained control of the Senate in 2015, the situation spoke for itself: in the future, Senate tradition would now not be a hindrance to a determined majority.

JUSTICE SCALIA'S DEATH, A ROADBLOCK FOR GARLAND, AND THE TRUMP APPOINTMENTS

The significance for the Court of the occupant of the White House and a party's control of the Senate became dramatically salient after Justice Antonin Scalia, then in his 29th year on the Court, died unexpectedly on February 13, 2016.

His passing meant not only the loss of a rapier wit, critic of an imperious judiciary, and perhaps the most energetic questioner at oral argument but also one of the modern era's most dependable and enthusiastic judicial advocates of originalism as a method for interpreting the Constitution and textualism as a method for interpreting the laws passed by Congress. (Different approaches to constitutional interpretation are discussed in Chapter Two.) The departure of so distinctive a voice quickly made it apparent that not only had the Court's public sessions fundamentally changed but just as surely its internal dynamics as well. Also different was the public face that the institution's decisions and opinions project. Justice Scalia, after all, had been a large presence at the Court where in the give-and-take of deciding cases, his influence sometimes exceeded the weight of his single vote. Moreover, the Court faced the prospect of functioning for an indefinite and conceivably extensive period of time with a complement of only eight justices. The situation posed the question whether the justices would be hopelessly deadlocked or function effectively as a party of eight.

As the Court finished its work at the end of June 2016, the record pointed more to the latter than to the former, as only four of the term's 69 cases had been decided 4–4. (In such situations, the Court issues no opinion and merely affirms the decision of the court below). Of these, only two were decided after Justice Scalia's death, although each of these posed a question of major national importance that was thus left without an authoritative ruling.

If an even-numbered bench in the modern era has been both unusual and, for many observers, less than desirable, it is nonetheless hardly unprecedented, even aside from occasions when a justice has been absent because of illness. Eight months lapsed between the retirement of Justice Powell in June 1987 and the arrival of Justice Kennedy in February 1988. In recent Court history, so lengthy an interval has been exceeded only by the full year between Justice Fortas's resignation in May 1969 and the swearing in of Justice Blackmun in June 1970, although even that span fell short of the leave of absence Justice Robert H. Jackson had from the Court, at President Harry Truman's request, from May 1945 until October 1946 when Jackson was chief U.S. Prosecutor at the Nuremberg war crimes trials after World War II. (The circumstances of both the Fortas to Blackmun and the Powell to Kennedy gaps are explained earlier in this chapter.) Nonetheless, the even-numbered bench in 2016 created a totally novel situation for the remaining justices in that none of them was on the Court prior to Justice Kennedy's arrival.

On March 16, President Obama announced his choice of Merrick B. Garland, age 63, to fill Scalia's seat. Chief judge of the United States Court of Appeals for the District of Columbia Circuit since 2013, the Harvard-educated nominee had been named to the appeals bench in 1997 by President Bill Clinton and confirmed by the Democratic-controlled Senate 76–23, in a vote that included support from 30 Republicans. In 2016, however, President Obama faced a Senate controlled by Republicans whose leadership, reflecting the intense partisanship that gripped both parties, insisted that they would not act on any nomination for Scalia's seat—and hence on the future direction of the Court—until "after the people had spoken" in the November presidential election. For support of this block-then-wait-and-see strategy, majority leader Mitchell McConnell and Judiciary Committee Chair Charles Grassley referred to a speech in the Senate made by none other than Vice President Joseph Biden in June 1992 during the administration of President George H. W. Bush when then Senator Biden chaired the Judiciary Committee:

> [I]t is my view that if a Supreme Court Justice resigns tomorrow, or within the next several weeks, or resigns at the end of the summer, President Bush should consider following the practice of a majority of his predecessors and not—and not—name a nominee until after the November election is completed. . . . It is my view that if the President . . . presses an election-year nomination, the Senate Judiciary Committee should seriously consider not scheduling confirmation hearings on the nomination until after the political campaign season is over.

Biden insisted that Republicans were taking his words out of context, but Biden could not deny that the words were his and that the context had been appointments to the Court. As the Garland nomination continued to languish, Republicans had another reason not to accommodate the president. They had not forgotten that then Senator Obama had participated in an unsuccessful filibuster in early 2006 to block a vote on Judge Samuel Alito's nomination to the Supreme Court. In politics, memories sometimes run long as well as deep.

By July, inaction on the Garland nomination surpassed the previous record of 125 days between nomination and confirmation set in 1916 when President Woodrow Wilson named Louis Brandeis for Justice Joseph R. Lamar's seat on the bench. "If Republicans in the Senate refuse even to consider a nominee in the hopes of running out the clock until they can elect a president from their own party, so that he can nominate his own justice to the Supreme Court," cautioned President Obama in an op-ed essay in the *Wall Street Journal*, "then they will effectively nullify the ability of any president from the opposing party to make an appointment to the nation's highest court. They would reduce the very functioning of the judicial branch of the government to another political leverage point." Yet with Republican nominee Donald J. Trump's victory over Democratic nominee Hillary Rodham Clinton coupled with continued Republican control of the U.S. Senate, stalemate nonetheless persisted as the Garland nomination expired at noon on January 3, 2017, when the 115th Congress convened. It had languished for a total of 293 days. The contest between Hillary Clinton and Donald Trump once more served as a reminder—if one was needed—that elections truly have constitutional consequences. (As for Garland, three years later he became President Biden's choice for attorney general in 2021.)

As a candidate Trump had pledged to nominate a conservative jurist "in the mold of" Justice Scalia. On January 31—just eleven days after his inauguration—the new president announced his choice of Neil M. Gorsuch, age 49, for the long-vacant seat. A judge on the U.S. Court of Appeals for the Tenth Circuit since his nomination in 2006 by President George W. Bush and confirmation by voice vote without recorded opposition in the Senate, Gorsuch attended Columbia University and Harvard Law School, as well as Oxford University where he was a Rhodes Scholar. After a clerkship on the U.S. Court of Appeals for the District of Columbia Circuit, he clerked at the Supreme Court for both Justices Byron White and Anthony Kennedy. Five years in private practice with a law firm in Washington, D.C., preceded service in the Department of Justice, where in 2005–2006 he was principal deputy to the associate attorney general and acting associate attorney general.

Still smarting from the blockade on Garland's nomination, some Senate Democrats referred to the vacancy as a "stolen seat" and promised a robust debate on the nominee's fitness to serve on the Court. Minority Leader Chuck Schumer said he had "very serious doubts" about whether Gorsuch fell within the legal mainstream and whether he could protect the Constitution from potential abuses of power by the executive branch. After four days of hearings that began on March 20, the Senate Judiciary Committee, voting along party lines, approved Gorsuch 11–9. In the full Senate, Republicans invoked the so-called "nuclear option" to end a filibuster by Democrats. Gorsuch was confirmed 54–45 on April 7 and sworn in on April 9.

Justice Kennedy's retirement and the Kavanaugh Ruckus. On the afternoon of June 27, 2018, Justice Anthony Kennedy, age 81, went to the White House to deliver his letter of retirement to President Trump to become effective July 31. A pivotal figure in some of the Court's most consequential rulings on the rights of same-sex couples and campaign finance since his appointment by President Reagan in February 1988, he was often described as a "swing justice," a moniker Kennedy routinely resisted. "I hate that term," he said at Harvard Law School in 2015. "The cases swing. I don't." Ironically, Kennedy had succeeded Justice Lewis Powell, who was also considered a swing justice and whose departure in 1987 touched off a confirmation donnybrook that led to the Senate's rejection of Judge Robert Bork. Now, some three decades later, a swing-seat vacancy seemed ready to reignite partisan passions again, given continued political polarization combined with fears of Democrats that Kennedy's replacement might cement a conservative majority on the Court, particularly endangering abortion rights.

The president acted promptly to name Kennedy's successor when, in the East Room of the White House on the night of July 9, he introduced Judge Brett M. Kavanaugh, age 53, of the U.S. Court of Appeals for the District of Columbia Circuit. Born in the District and reared in suburban Bethesda, Maryland, the nominee graduated from Yale College and Yale Law School before clerking for two federal appeals court judges. After working for Solicitor General Kenneth Starr, he clerked for Justice Kennedy in 1993–1994 before returning to Starr, who by this time was independent counsel. It was during this time in Starr's office that Kavanaugh helped draft the report that outlined grounds for President Bill Clinton's impeachment. After work at the law firm of Kirkland & Ellis, he joined the administration of President George W. Bush, first as counsel to the president and then as staff secretary to the president. In 2003 Bush nominated him to the U.S. Court of Appeals for the District of Columbia Circuit, but Democrats blocked the vote. Renominated to the same court by Bush in 2006, Kavanaugh was confirmed 57–36. Moreover, at the outset of the Trump administration in 2017, Attorney General Jeff Sessions had considered him for solicitor general.

Most observers anticipated that while Kavanaugh would surely face opposition for confirmation, any resistance that arose would likely be no more serious than Gorsuch had encountered a year earlier. Democrats, after all, had hardly forgotten majority leader Mitchell McConnell's decision plainly to ignore President Obama's nomination of Judge Merrick Garland after Justice Antonin Scalia's death in early 2016. Still, few were prepared for the buzz saw that awaited Kavanaugh in the Senate where Republicans held a slim 51 to 49 majority. Indeed, had the nature and magnitude of opposition been foreseen, Trump might well have picked one of the other three finalists on the White House short list for Kennedy's seat, each of whom was awaiting the president's pleasure and had been advised to be available for the evening and to have prepared appropriate remarks.

Senator Charles Grassley, chair of the Senate Judiciary Committee, initially scheduled four days of hearings beginning September 4. At the start, however, order and decorum were displaced by chaos as Democratic members, some of whom had already announced their intention to vote against the nominee and their annoyance at the absence of perhaps probative documents from Kavanaugh's time in Bush administration, attempted to prevent the committee from proceeding. Indeed, over the following days more than 200 protesters—part of a self-styled "creative resistance"—would be arrested either in the committee's meeting room itself or in nearby corridors. Yet, even with the pandemonium and hostile questions from Democratic members—three of whom (Cory Booker, Kamala Harris, and Amy Klobuchar) had well-known ambitions for the 2020 presidential race—the nomination did not appear to be in jeopardy until September 13, a week before the committee planned to vote on whether to forward Kavanaugh's name to the Senate floor for final consideration. On that day Senator Dianne Feinstein, **ranking member** (or senior Democrat) on the committee, revealed that she had forwarded to the FBI an allegation that she had received from a constituent concerning sexual misconduct by Kavanaugh. On September 16, the *Washington Post* published details of this accusation as coming from Dr. Christine Blasey Ford, a research psychologist at Palo Alto University in California. According to her account, Kavanaugh, with the help of a friend, had sexually assaulted her at a party in a private home when both she and Kavanaugh were in high school. Given the **#MeToo movement** that had taken shape barely a year before, Ford's charge was hardly one the committee could ignore. The timing of her assertion, becoming public as it did after hearings had begun, reminded some of the workplace allegations of sexual misconduct made by Professor Anita Hill against Judge Clarence Thomas during his confirmation proceedings in 1991, when Joe Biden chaired the Judiciary Committee.

Feinstein apparently learned of the accusation in a July 30 letter from Ford that had also requested confidentiality. With the claim now in the public domain, both

Dr. Ford and Judge Kavanaugh appeared before the committee on September 27 in a combined eight hours of testimony, with Dr. Ford going first without the nominee being present in the room. Republican members of the committee, not wishing to interrogate Ford directly, instead enlisted Rachel Mitchell, a sex crimes prosecutor from Phoenix, Arizona, to question her on their behalf. Consequently, Mitchell questioned Ford in five-minute segments, alternating with five-minute segments for questions from Democratic members of the committee. While Dr. Ford could not recall certain details of the event, she nonetheless insisted that she was "100 percent certain" that Kavanaugh was the attacker.

In his statement to the senators, some of whom asked questions also about his drinking habits in high school, the nominee (who had already vigorously denied Ford's charges in an evening interview alongside his wife Ashley on Fox News three days earlier) was fired up with indignation and claimed that Democratic senators had orchestrated a partisan attack against him. Fighting back tears, he told the committee "you have replaced advice and consent with search and destroy." For some, his belligerent defense and robust denials themselves displayed a disqualifying lack of judicial temperament. Bizarrely, in contrast to the hearings for Neil Gorsuch, Kavanaugh's had transmuted from an expected debate over judicial ideology into a raucous, raw, and even riveting jumble of questions, statements, assertions, and counter assertions about victims' rights and personal attacks on nominees.

Although the committee voted 11–10 on September 28 to forward the nomination to the floor with a favorable recommendation, the vote in the full Senate was delayed so that the FBI could probe claims by three other accusers who had announced through various media and spokespersons that Kavanaugh had been sexually abusive with women in college and had engaged in wild, drunken behavior. After a report of that investigation was made available for examination by senators, the Senate voted 50–48 to confirm on October 6, five days after the start of the Court's new term. Within hours after this historically close confirmation, Kavanaugh was then sworn in as the 114th justice at a private ceremony in the justices' conference room at the Supreme Court, where Chief Justice Roberts administered the constitutional oath and retired Justice Kennedy administered the judicial oath.

JUSTICE GINSBURG'S DEATH AND JUSTICE BARRETT'S ARRIVAL

The news of Justice Ruth Bader Ginsburg's death from cancer on September 18, 2020, bolted across the nation. For many it was difficult to think of another justice in the modern era whose life had been as remarkable and consequential. As noted earlier in this chapter, this warrior for gender equality reached the Supreme Court in 1993 with enviable accomplishments already in hand. Aside from many cases she litigated and dozens of important Supreme Court opinions that bear her name—some of which are reprinted in this book—she is also remembered as having achieved folk hero status, as well as for maintaining a well-publicized friendship with her jurisprudential opposite, Justice Antonin Scalia, a relationship that demonstrated the importance of collegiality in the workings of the Court.

With a 53–47 Republican majority in the Senate, President Trump wasted no time in naming someone to fill the vacancy, announcing on September 26 his choice of Judge Amy Coney Barrett, age 48, whom Trump had named to the Court of Appeals for the Seventh Circuit in 2017. Born and reared in New Orleans, Barrett graduated from Rhodes College and Notre Dame Law School, where she finished first in her class. Following a clerkship with Judge Laurence Silberman of the Court of Appeals for the District of Columbia Circuit, she clerked for Justice Scalia at the Supreme Court. A year of private practice in Washington preceded her appointment to the law faculty at Notre Dame in 2002.

Yet even with splendid credentials, confluence of five considerations made her nomination problematical for some: an impending election, the Supreme Court's docket, the Court's ideological makeup, the president's own remarks, and the nominee herself. First, Justice Ginsburg's death occurred less than two months before the presidential election on November 3. Democrats especially needed no reminder that when Justice Scalia had died in early 2016, the Republican-controlled Senate—pointing to the presidential election some eleven months later—refused even to hold hearings on President Obama's nomination of Judge Merrick Garland. Now, with the 2020 election only weeks away, Republicans displayed no hesitation in moving ahead. Majority Leader McConnell explained that the situation in 2016, with a Democratic president and a Republican Senate, was different from 2020 when Republicans held both the White House and the Senate. Democrats insisted that such hypocrisy rested on a distinction without a true difference, especially since the 2020 election was so much closer. Still, with an eye toward November 3, both Democrats and Republicans hoped Trump's third Supreme Court nomination would help energize their electoral bases. Indeed, being wary of offending voters may have deterred Democratic senators from emphasizing the nominee's deeply held Catholicism, as had happened in her appeals court hearings in 2017 when Senator Dianne Feinstein judgmentally said to Barrett, "The dogma lives loudly in you," a remark that drew widespread criticism as approaching a religious test that Article VI of the Constitution expressly forbids.

Second, the Court was already scheduled to hear arguments in *Texas* v. *California* on November 10, a case that could determine whether the Affordable Care Act (ACA), which had survived a constitutional challenge in 2012 (see Chapter Six), would survive again. Moreover, the Justice Department had filed a brief in the case urging the ACA's demise. Were Judge Barrett confirmed before the 10th, she would be able to participate in the case.

Third and fourth, Democrats feared that a Justice Barrett would cement a 6–3 conservative majority on the Court, a concern magnified by the president's own comments that stressed the need for a fifth vote on the Court to decide any election-related disputes that might soon arise. "This scam that the Democrats are pulling—it's a scam—this scam will be before the United States Supreme Court. And I think having a 4–4 situation is not a good situation," Mr. Trump had said in September. Such statements by Trump moved some Democratic members of the Judiciary Committee to insist that, were she to be confirmed, Barrett, despite promises of independence, would be obliged to recuse herself in any case arising from the presidential election.

The fifth concern was the nominee herself, especially in connection with the upcoming ACA case. In an article in 2017 Barrett had been critical of Chief Justice John Roberts's position in 2012, when the Court had first considered the ACA and Roberts provided an essential fifth vote that had kept the ACA alive. In his opinion construing a central provision of the law, Roberts, she wrote, "had pushed the ACA beyond its plausible meaning to save the statute." Moreover, as a protégé of Justice Scalia, she believed that originalism and textualism were the correct interpretative tools to use when construing the Constitution or an act of Congress. For some, her approach put the future of *Roe* v. *Wade* and reproductive rights generally, among other issues, in question, particularly in light of an advertisement in 2006 that she had signed in Indiana that supported overturning "the barbaric legacy" of the 1973 decision.

The Senate Judiciary Committee, chaired by Lindsey Graham, held four days of hearings beginning on October 12. Questioning of the nominee was tough, but the proceedings lacked the disruptions, histrionics, and circus atmosphere that had marred Judge Brett Kavanaugh's in 2017. While she was willing to discuss her jurisprudential approach to cases, Barrett nonetheless deflected many questions from Democratic members, insisting, as most recent nominees had done, that she would not provide hints as to what position she might take in hypotheticals that could reach the Court in actual cases. Moreover, she insisted that she was "not here on a mission to destroy the Affordable Care Act."

On Thursday, October 22, in a session almost all Democratic members refused to attend but voted by proxy, the committee voted 12–10 to forward the nomination to the Senate floor. McConnell then kept the Senate in session through the weekend to guard against efforts by Democrats to derail the nomination. Then a rare vote on Sunday largely along party lines put the nomination in place for a vote by the full Senate. Senate Minority Leader Charles Schumer labeled the Republican action "a travesty. And it will be an inerasable stain on this Republican majority forevermore." Yet, unable to mount a convincing case against Barrett on her merits, the Democratic case against Barrett had been procedural, not substantive, from the start. A vote to confirm 52–48 followed early Monday evening, October 26, marking the first time since 1869 that a justice had been confirmed with no votes from the minority party. Less than two hours later, Justice Clarence Thomas administered the constitutional oath to Barrett at a ceremony on the South Lawn of the White House. "Federal judges don't stand for election," she reminded her audience. "Thus, they have no basis for claiming that their preferences reflect those of the people. This separation of duty from political preference is what makes the judiciary distinct among the three branches of government. A judge declares independence not only from Congress and the president, but also from the private beliefs that might otherwise move her," she continued. "The judicial oath captures the essence of the judicial duty the rule of law must always control." Chief Justice Roberts administered the judicial oath to Barrett at the Court in a private ceremony the following morning.

Judicial Legacies. As Chief Justice Roberts administered the presidential oath to Joe Biden on January 20, 2021, the 46th chief executive may have realized that his predecessor was leaving office with a significant judicial legacy, as illustrated by Table 0.1. Among the eleven other presidents who served only a single full four-year term, Donald Trump's three appointments to the Supreme Court were exceeded only by Benjamin Harrison's four, and William Howard Taft's six. Moreover, during his four years, Trump appointed 54 judges to the U.S. courts of appeals, one fewer than President Obama's total during eight years.

Yet, the inauguration of a new president has hardly quieted controversy over the Court. Making good on a campaign position, Biden on April 9 announced creation of a 36-person commission to study possible changes to the Court and to issue a report within six months of its first meeting. Barely a week later, House lawmakers introduced legislation to add four seats to the Court's membership, raising it to 13. These moves followed a speech Justice Stephen Breyer gave at Harvard Law School on April 6 where he warned against tampering with the Court, noting that he hoped "to make those whose initial instincts may favor important structural (or other

Table 0.1 Federal Judicial Appointments by Presidency (1977–2021)

President	Supreme Court Justices	Appeals Court Judges	District Court Judges	Total
Carter#	0	59	203	262
Reagan	4*	83	290	377
G. H. W. Bush#	2	42	148	192
Clinton	2	66	305	373
G. W. Bush	2	62	261	325
Obama	2	55	268	325
Trump#	3	54	174	231

# Denotes single-term president.
* Number includes Justice Rehnquist's appointment as chief justice.
Source: Federal Judicial Center.

similar institutional) changes, such as forms of 'court-packing,' think long and hard before embodying those changes in law." It is wrong to think of the Court as another political institution. And, it is doubly wrong to think of its members as junior-league politicians," he continued. "Structural alteration motivated by the perception of political influence can only feed that perception, further eroding that trust. There are no shortcuts to it."

KEY TERMS

constitutional law
constitutional interpretation
cases
judicial review
recess appointment
circuit riding
seriatim opinions
diversity jurisdiction
docket
Warren Court
ranking member
#MeToo movement

QUERIES

1. Does prior judicial experience make someone better qualified for the Supreme Court? The Court's roster in 2021 revealed that all justices but one arrived on the bench with previous service on one of the federal courts of appeals. By contrast, as late as 1963, five justices were sitting with no significant prior judicial experience at all. Justice Felix Frankfurter, who reached the bench in 1939 with no experience as a judge, flatly declared in 1957 that "the correlation between prior judicial experience and fitness for the Supreme Court is zero." What qualifications should a president consider when selecting a justice? Should there be a judicial experience requirement for appointment to the Supreme Court? What strengths might someone with no judicial experience bring to the bench? What challenges might that person encounter after joining the Court?

2. Review the Supreme Court appointments discussed in this chapter. How do you explain the fact that some proceeded without controversy whereas others were highly contentious?

3. Is there an acceptable way to combine judicial independence (made possible partly by life tenure) with political accountability? One proposal calls for a constitutional amendment to fix a term of 14 years for Supreme Court justices and other federal judges. In the 14th year, the president in office could choose to reappoint the individual for another term of 14 years, or not. As with the initial appointment, reappointment would be subject to approval by the Senate. What are the strengths and weaknesses of this proposal?

4. The roadblocked nomination of Merrick Garland in 2016 and the successful nomination of Amy Coney Barrett in 2020 fueled partisan debates about filling a Supreme Court vacancy during an election year. Given that the United States is never more than two years away from an election in which control of the Senate may be at stake and never more than four years from the next presidential election, should the timing of elections matter in the appointment of justices? Or is timing solely a matter of the exercise of political power?

SELECTED READINGS

Federal Judicial Appointments

Abraham, Henry J. *Justices, Presidents, and Senators: A History of the U.S. Supreme Court Appointments from Washington to Bush II*, 5th ed. Lanham, MD: Rowman & Littlefield, 2007.

Bronner, Ethan. *Battle for Justice: How the Bork Nomination Shook America*. New York: Doubleday, 1990.

Collins, Paul M., and Lori A. Ringhand. *Supreme Court Confirmation Hearings and Constitutional Change*. New York: Cambridge University Press, 2015.

Comiskey, Michael. *Seeking Justices*. Lawrence: University Press of Kansas, 2004.

Epstein, Lee, and Jeffrey A. Segal. *Advice and Consent: The Politics of Judicial Appointments*. New York: Oxford University Press, 2007.

Farganis, Dion, and Justin Wedeking. *Supreme Court Confirmation Hearings in the U.S. Senate: Reconsidering the Charade*. Ann Arbor: University of Michigan Press, 2014.

Frank, John P. *Clement Haynsworth, the Senate, and the Supreme Court*. Charlottesville: University Press of Virginia, 1991.

Goldman, Sheldon. *Picking Federal Judges*. New Haven, CT: Yale University Press, 1997.

Jefferson, Renee Knake, and Hannah Brenner Johnson. *Shortlisted: Women in the Shadows of the Supreme Court*. New York: New York University Press, 2020.

Maltese, John A. *The Selling of Supreme Court Nominees*. Baltimore, MD: Johns Hopkins University Press, 1995.

Massaro, John. *Supremely Political: The Role of Ideology and Presidential Management in Unsuccessful Supreme Court Nominations*. Albany: State University of New York Press, 1990.

Maveety, Nancy. *Picking Judges*. New Brunswick, NJ: Transaction Publishers, 2016.

Nemacheck, Christine L. *Strategic Selection: Presidential Nominations of Supreme Court Judges from Herbert Hoover through George W. Bush*. Charlottesville: University of Virginia Press, 2007.

Yalof, David Alistair. *Pursuit of Justices: Presidential Politics and the Selection of Supreme Court Nominees*. Chicago: University of Chicago Press, 1999.

The Supreme Court

Epstein, Lee, and Jack Knight. *The Choices Justices Make*. Washington, DC: CQ Press, 1998.

Finkelman, Paul. *Supreme Injustice: Slavery in the Nation's Highest Court*. Cambridge, MA: Harvard University Press, 2018.

Garraty, John, ed. *Quarrels that Have Shaped the Constitution*, rev. ed. New York: Harper & Row, 2009.

Jackson, Robert H. *The Struggle for Judicial Supremacy*. New York: Knopf, 1941.

Johnson, Herbert, gen. ed. *Chief Justiceships of the United States Supreme Court*. Columbia: University of South Carolina Press, 1995–. Volumes to date include William R. Casto, *The Supreme Court in the Early Republic: The Chief Justiceships of John Jay and Oliver Ellsworth* (1995); James W. Ely, Jr., *The Chief Justiceship of Melville W. Fuller, 1888–1910* (1995); Herbert A. Johnson, *The Chief Justiceship of John Marshall, 1801–1835* (1997); Melvin I. Urofsky, *Division and Discord: The Supreme Court under Stone and Vinson, 1941–1953* (1997); Walter F. Pratt, Jr., *The Supreme Court under Edward Douglass White, 1910–1921* (1999); Earl M. Maltz, *The Chief Justiceship of Warren Burger, 1969–1986* (2000); Michal Belknap, *The Supreme Court under Earl Warren, 1953–1969* (2005); William G. Ross, *The Chief Justiceship of Charles Evans Hughes, 1930–1941* (2007); Paul Kens, *The Supreme Court under Morrison R. Waite, 1874–1888* (2010); Jonathan Lurie, *The Chief Justiceship of William Howard Taft*, 1921–1930 (2019).

Kelly, Alfred H., Winfred A. Harbison, and Herman Belz. *The American Constitution*, 7th ed., 2 vols. New York: Norton, 1997.

Mason, Alpheus T. *The Supreme Court from Taft to Burger*. Baton Rouge: Louisiana State University Press, 1979.

McCloskey, Robert G. *The American Supreme Court*, 6th ed., rev. by Sandford Levinson. Chicago: University of Chicago Press, 2016.

Murphy, Walter F. *Elements of Judicial Strategy*. Chicago: University of Chicago Press, 1964.

O'Brien, David M. *Judges on Judging: Views from the Bench*, 5th ed. Thousand Oaks, CA: CQ Press, 2017.

O'Brien, David M. *Storm Center*, 11th ed. New York: Norton, 2017.

Renstrom, Peter G., gen. ed. *Supreme Court Handbooks Series*. Santa Barbara, CA: ABC-CLIO, 2000–. Volumes to date include Tinsley E. Yarbrough, *The Burger Court* (2000); Peter G. Renstrom, *The Stone Court* (2001) and *The Taft Court* (2003); Melvin I. Urofsky, *The Warren Court* (2001); Michael E. Parrish, *The Hughes Court* (2002); James W. Ely, Jr., *The Fuller Court* (2003); Timothy S. Huebner, *The Taney Court* (2003); Donald Grier Stephenson, Jr., *The Waite Court* (2003); Jonathan Lurie, *The Chase Court* (2004); Thomas R. Hensley, *The Rehnquist Court* (2006); Matthew P. Harrington, *Jay and Ellsworth* (2008).

Stephenson, Donald Grier, Jr. *Campaigns and the Court: The U.S. Supreme Court in Presidential Elections*. New York: Columbia University Press, 1999.

Ward, Artemus. *Deciding to Leave: The Politics of Retirement from the United States Supreme Court*. Albany: State University of New York Press, 2003.

Warren, Charles. *The Supreme Court in United States History*, 2 vols. Boston: Little, Brown, 1926.

Wiecek, William M. *Liberty under Law*. Baltimore: Johns Hopkins University Press, 1988.

BIOGRAPHIES

Brookhiser, Richard. *John Marshall: The Man Who Made the Supreme Court*. New York: Basic Books, 2018.

Budiansky, Stephen. *Oliver Wendell Holmes: A Life in War, Law, and Ideas*. New York: Norton, 2020.

Dunne, Gerald T. *Hugo Black and the Judicial Revolution*. New York: Simon & Schuster, 1978.

Ferren, John M. *Salt of the Earth, Conscience of the Court: The Story of Justice Wiley Rutledge*. Chapel Hill: University of North Carolina Press, 2004.

Ginsburg, Ruth Bader (with Nancy Hartnett and Wendy Williams). *My Own Words*. New York: Simon & Schuster, 2016.

Jeffries, John C., Jr. *Justice Lewis F. Powell, Jr.* New York: Macmillan, 1994.

Kens, Paul. *Justice Stephen Field*. Lawrence: University Press of Kansas, 1997.

Magrath, C. Peter. *Morrison R. Waite*. New York: Macmillan, 1963.

Mason, Alpheus Thomas. *Brandeis: A Free Man's Life*. New York: Viking, 1946.

Mason, Alpheus Thomas. *Harlan Fiske Stone: Pillar of the Law*. New York: Viking, 1956.

Mason, Alpheus Thomas. *William Howard Taft: Chief Justice*. New York: Simon & Schuster, 1964.

Morgan, Donald G. *Justice William Johnson: The First Dissenter*. Columbia: University of South Carolina Press, 1954.

Murphy, Bruce Allen. *Wild Bill: The Legend and Life of William O. Douglas*. New York: Random House, 2003.

Newton, Jim. *Justice for All: Earl Warren and the Nation He Made*. New York: Riverhead, 2006.

Paul, Joel Richard. *Without Precedent: Chief Justice John Marshall and His Times*. New York: Riverhead, 2018.

Smith, Jean Edward. *John Marshall*. New York: Henry Holt, 1996.

Sotomayor, Sonia. *My Beloved World*. New York: Knopf, 2013.

Stern, Seth, and Stephen Wermiel. *Justice Brennan: Liberal Champion*. New York: Houghton Mifflin, 2010.

Swisher, Carl B. *Roger B. Taney*. Washington, DC: Brookings Institution, 1935.

Thomas, Clarence. *My Grandfather's Son: A Memoir*. New York: Harper, 2007.

Thomas, Evan, *First: Sandra Day O'Connor*. New York: Random House, 2019.

Urofsky, Melvin. *Louis D. Brandeis: A Life*. New York: Schocken Books, 2012.

Wells, Catharine Pierce. *Oliver Wendell Holmes: A Willing Servant to an Unknown God*. New York: Cambridge University Press, 2020.

Yarbrough, Tinsley E. *John Marshall Harlan*. New York: Oxford University Press, 1992.

NOTES

1. Throughout the book, emphasis within quotations is in the original, unless otherwise indicated.
2. Boldface italic type is used throughout to indicate those cases reprinted in the book.
3. Key terms, boldfaced at the point in each chapter where they are first explained, also appear in a list at the end of each chapter, as well as in a glossary in the appendix.
4. Although both John Rutledge and Charles Evans Hughes served as associate justices, then resigned and were later named chief justice, each is counted only once.

Similarly, Edward Douglass White, Harlan Fiske Stone, and William H. Rehnquist—the only three chief justices to have been appointed from the ranks of associate justices—are counted only once.

5. The House of Representatives approved two articles of impeachment (abuse of power and obstruction of Congress) against President Donald J. Trump on December 18, 2019. Trial by the Senate began on January 22, 2020, and concluded with an acquittal for both articles on February 5.

1

Jurisdiction and Organization of the Federal Courts

[R]eversal by a higher court is not proof that justice is thereby better done. There is no doubt that if there were a super-Supreme Court, a substantial proportion of our reversals of state courts would also be reversed. We are not final because we are infallible, but we are infallible only because we are final.

—JUSTICE ROBERT H. JACKSON (1953)

American constitutional law represents only a tiny fraction of the entire corpus of the law. Routine litigation between private parties seldom falls into the category of "cases" to which the judicial power of the Supreme Court extends. Even cases involving constitutional questions may be sidestepped. The Supreme Court of the United States is not "a super legal aid bureau."

This chapter presents certain rules and procedures guiding the justices in choosing the cases they will decide and sketches the major steps leading to a decision. The rules governing jurisdiction and standing to sue vest in the justices' considerable discretionary power as to when they will act or refuse to act. The justices control their workload by selecting the cases that demand attention at the highest level. In the governing process, the Supreme Court has an important, if circumscribed, role to play.

THE JUDICIAL POWER

The Constitution in Article III makes possible the resolution of certain legal disputes in national, as opposed to state, courts. One significant difference between American government under the Articles of Confederation and the Constitution was the provision in the latter for a system of national courts. Under the Articles, there was not even a Supreme Court.

FIFTY-TWO JUDICIAL SYSTEMS. Civilian courts in the United States are spread across 52 separate judicial systems: the court systems of the 50 states plus the District of Columbia, and the court system of the national government. The latter are commonly referred to, somewhat misleadingly, as **federal courts** and exist because

DOI: 10.4324/9781003164340-2

of acts of Congress. By contrast, **state courts** derive their existence from the constitutions and statutes of their respective states. This dual system of federal and state courts means that almost everyone in any of the 50 states is simultaneously within the **jurisdiction**, or reach, of two judicial systems, one state and the other federal. Jurisdiction refers to the authority a court has to decide a case. The term has two basic dimensions: who and what. The first identifies the parties who may take a case into a particular court, or who may be brought before a court. The second, the "what," refers to the subject matter the parties may raise in their case.

According to Article III, federal judicial power extends to (1) cases arising under the Constitution, the laws of the United States, and treaties made under the authority of the United States; (2) admiralty and maritime cases; (3) controversies between two or more states; (4) controversies to which the United States is a party, even where the other party is a state; (5) suits between citizens of different states; and (6) cases begun by a state against a citizen of another state or against another country. (As explained in Chapter Four, the Eleventh Amendment modified Article III to bar suits brought against a state by a citizen of another state or country.) The Constitution vests this judicial power of the United States in "one Supreme Court and in such inferior courts as the Congress may from time to time ordain and establish." This provision is not self-executing, and Congress at the outset of the government in 1789 created a system of lower federal courts in addition to the Supreme Court.

As currently organized, this system consists of (1) a court of appeals for each of the 11 judicial circuits, plus one for the District of Columbia; (2) district courts, of which there are now 94 (89 in the 50 states, plus one in the District of Columbia and one in Puerto Rico, the Virgin Islands, the Northern Mariana Islands, and Guam); and (3) other courts, such as the Court of Appeals for the Federal Circuit. (See Figure 1.1.) Moreover, each district includes a bankruptcy court as a unit of the district court. Bankruptcy judges are appointed for renewable 14-year terms by the U.S. court of appeals for each circuit.

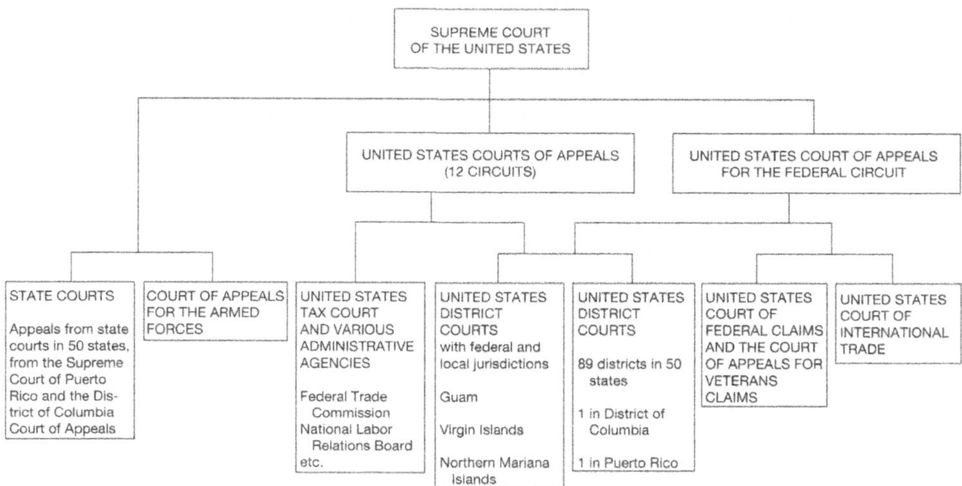

FIGURE 1.1 The National Court System

Cases in the federal courts usually originate in the district courts. Cases in state courts may qualify for review by the U.S. Supreme Court if they raise a federal question.

Source: Administrative Office of the U.S. Courts.

The Supreme Court, courts of appeals, and the district courts within the 50 states, District of Columbia, and Puerto Rico are known as constitutional courts, or **Article III courts**. Their judges are appointed by the president, confirmed by the Senate, and enjoy the constitutional assurances of tenure "during good behavior" (effectively lifetime appointment) and no reduction in salary. Specialized courts such as the Court of Federal Claims or the Court of Appeals for the Armed Forces are legislative courts, or **Article I courts**, meaning that they were created by Congress in furtherance of a power granted by Article I. In contrast to Article III courts, Congress has full power over the salaries and tenure of judges of these Article I courts and may assign administrative or legislative duties to them. The district courts in the territories of Guam, Northern Mariana Islands, and the Virgin Islands are also Article I courts. The distinction between Article III and Article I judges has real operational significance. In *Nguyen* v. *United States* (2003), the Supreme Court vacated two judgments of the Ninth Circuit Court of Appeals because the panel of three judges included the chief judge of the District Court of the Northern Mariana Islands (an Article I judge), who was sitting by designation with the Article III appeals court judges.

Jurisdiction of the District Courts. The district courts are the trial courts and workhorses of the federal judicial system. (See Figure 1.2.) Their original jurisdiction includes cases that raise a federal question and cases that involve more than $75,000

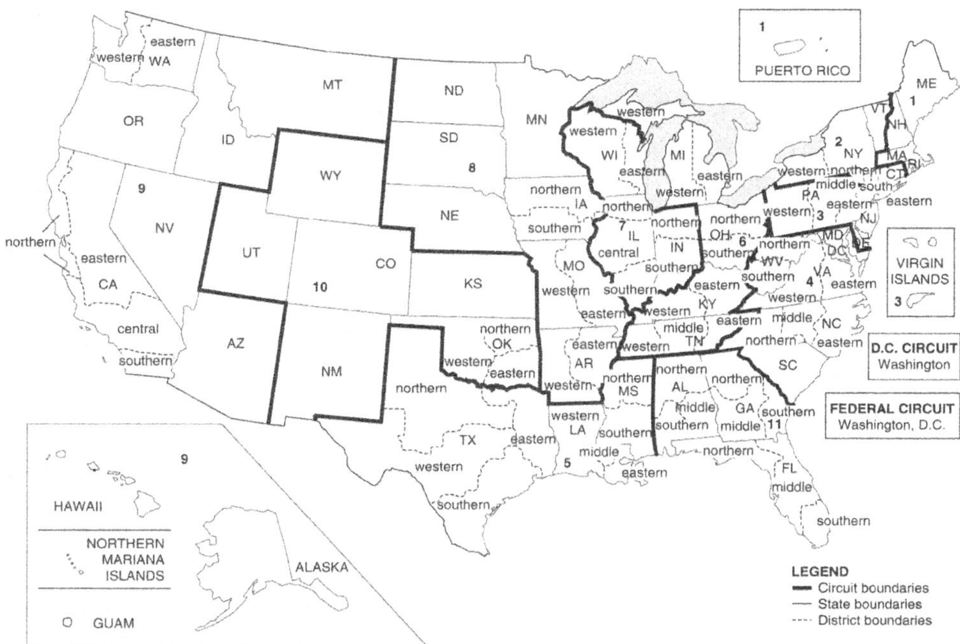

FIGURE 1.2 Geographic Boundaries of the U.S. Courts of Appeals and U.S. District Courts

This map shows how the 94 U.S. District Courts and the 13 U.S. Courts of Appeals exist with the court systems of the 50 states and the District of Columbia. The District Courts include 89 divided among the 50 states, plus one each for the District of Columbia, Guam, Puerto Rico, Northern Mariana Islands, and the Virgin Islands.

Source: Administrative Office of the U.S. Courts.

where the parties are citizens of different states. (A court has **original jurisdiction** when a case begins or originates there, and **appellate jurisdiction** when a case involves review of the decision of a lower court. A **federal question** is one that involves the meaning and/or application of the Constitution, a statute, or a treaty of the United States.) Two wholly independent bases of jurisdiction are thus provided: The first is defined by the nature of the question, and the second (**diversity jurisdiction**) by the citizenship of the parties and the amount at stake. Diversity jurisdiction allows cases presenting issues normally heard in state court to be tried in federal court. District courts also have supervisory powers over bankruptcy courts within each district and appellate jurisdiction with respect to a few classes of cases tried before U.S. **magistrate judges**. These judicial officers are appointed by majority vote of the active district judges of the court, with those in full-time positions serving eight-year terms. Magistrate judges issue search warrants, conduct arraignments of persons charged with federal crimes, and perform other duties assigned by their district court.

Jurisdiction of the Courts of Appeals. Congress has given the courts of appeals jurisdiction in appeals taken from the district courts within their respective circuits, from judgments of the Tax Court, and from the rulings of particular administrative and regulatory agencies such as the National Labor Relations Board and the Securities and Exchange Commission. In addition, courts of appeals may review cases from the district courts in the territories. (For example, Guam and the Northern Mariana Islands are part of the Ninth Circuit.) The Court of Appeals for the Federal Circuit has a more specialized jurisdiction. Unlike the other 12, it hears appeals in patent, trademark, and copyright cases and in certain administrative law matters from district courts in all circuits as well as from the Court of Federal Claims, Court of International Trade, Court of Appeals for Veterans Claims, and specified administrative bodies.

Jurisdiction of the Supreme Court. The Supreme Court's jurisdiction is in two parts: original and appellate. The Court's original jurisdiction is specified in Article III and can be neither diminished nor enlarged by Congress. It includes four kinds of disputes: (1) cases between one of the states and the national government; (2) cases between two or more states; (3) cases involving foreign ambassadors, ministers, or consuls; and (4) cases begun by a state against a citizen of another state or against another country. Only controversies between states qualify today exclusively as original cases in the Supreme Court. For the others, Congress has given concurrent jurisdiction to the lower federal courts. As a result, almost all of the Court's cases come from its appellate jurisdiction.

According to Article III, the Supreme Court has appellate jurisdiction "in all other cases both . . . as to law and fact, with such exceptions, and under such regulations as the Congress shall make." Congress, in other words, decides which categories of cases in the lower courts qualify for review by the Supreme Court. Not until 1889, for example, was there a right of appeal to the Supreme Court in some federal criminal cases. Perhaps Congress could even deprive the Court of all appellate review and make final the decisions of lower courts. An extreme example occurred in 1869 when Congress, fearing that the Court would invalidate the Reconstruction Acts, hastily withdrew the Court's jurisdiction under the Habeas Corpus Act of 1867. The Court thus became powerless to pass on a case in which argument had been heard (**Ex parte *McCardle***, in Chapter Two). A latter-day re-enactment of *McCardle* seemed to be in the making after Congress in the Military Commissions Act of 2006 withdrew federal court jurisdiction over challenges to detention by prisoners at

Guantanamo Bay. However, ***Boumediene* v. *Bush*** (2008; see Chapter Fifteen) held that the jurisdiction-stripping provision of the MCA was invalid.

The major change in the appellate jurisdiction of the Supreme Court since 1789 has been in the proportion of cases qualifying for obligatory as opposed to discretionary review. Although the Judiciary Act of 1789 allowed Supreme Court review of certain cases from the state and lower federal courts by way of a writ of error, it was not until 1891, with passage of the Circuit Courts of Appeals Act, that the justices gained some discretion over the cases they would decide.

The Judges Act of 1925 further reduced the mandatory jurisdiction. As a result, most cases raising a federal question reached the Court on **certiorari** (Latin for "to make sure"). Review in this category was plainly discretionary. The justices could select for decision those cases they considered most worthy of their time. A smaller number of cases came to the Court on **appeal**. As with the old writ of error, these cases qualified by statute for obligatory review without regard to the importance of the issue raised or its impact on the government or the general public. By the mid-1980s, the appeal category of the Court's appellate **docket** (the court's caseload or list of cases awaiting action) accounted for only 5 percent of the total filings but a full one-third of the cases the Court decided on the merits.

In 1988, Congress enacted a major overhaul of the Supreme Court's jurisdiction. With the start of the October 1988 term, the Court's appellate jurisdiction became almost entirely discretionary, meaning that nearly every case now comes to the Court on certiorari. The mandatory appeal category has been virtually abolished, except for decisions by three-judge district courts (required by Congress in a few instances), which reach the Supreme Court on **direct appeal**, bypassing the courts of appeals.

Self-Imposed Limitations on Judicial Power. In many cases where the federal courts, including the Supreme Court, would appear to have jurisdiction, one or more other requirements may prevent a court from accepting and deciding the case. Alexander Bickel once referred to such stipulations as the "passive virtues" that facilitate resolution of cases without actually rendering rulings on the merits. Some of these self-denying ordinances were set forth by Justice Brandeis, concurring, in *Ashwander* v. *TVA* (1936). Summarized briefly, these so-called **Ashwander rules** provide:

1. The Court will not issue a constitutional ruling in a friendly, nonadversary proceeding.
2. The Court will not anticipate a question of constitutional law in advance of the necessity for deciding it.
3. The Court will not formulate a rule of law broader than the facts of the case require.
4. If possible, the Court will dispose of a case on nonconstitutional grounds.
5. The Court will not pass upon the validity of a statute on complaint of one who fails to show injury to person or property.
6. The Court will not pass upon the constitutionality of a statute at the instance of one who has accepted its benefits.
7. Whenever possible, the court will construe statutes so as to avoid a constitutional issue.

Specifically, before a federal court will accept jurisdiction, there must be an actual **case or controversy**, in the language of Article III. That is, the conflict must be real, touching the parties who have adverse interests. This case or controversy requirement means, therefore, that a case must present a live dispute and not be moot. Thus, in *New York State Rifle & Pistol Association, Inc.* v. *City of New York*

(2020), firearms enthusiasts challenged the constitutionality of an administrative rule in New York City that restricted transport of licensed firearms outside the city. After the Supreme Court granted review, the city amended the rule, leading seven justices in an unsigned opinion to dismiss the case on grounds of **mootness**.

Similarly, a case must be "ripe for review." The **ripeness** requirement injects an element of timing in order to avoid premature adjudication. A controversy must have reached a certain stage of maturity before the Court will engage it.

The case or controversy requirement also means that the federal courts, unlike the courts of some states, will not render an **advisory opinion**—a statement about a hypothetical situation or a statement indicating how a court would rule were litigation to develop. This policy originated in 1793. Responding to a request from President George Washington and Secretary of State Thomas Jefferson, the justices declined to offer their views on "the construction of treaties, laws of nations and laws of the land, which the Secretary said were often presented under circumstances which 'do not give a cognizance of them to the tribunals of the country.'"

Closely related to the case or controversy stipulation is the rule requiring "standing to sue." **Standing** focuses attention on whether the litigant is the proper party to bring a lawsuit, not whether the issue itself is appropriate for courts to decide. Standing is a threshold question, for without it, litigants do not get to press the merits or substance of their dispute. In federal litigation, standing consists of three elements: (1) the plaintiff must have suffered an "injury in fact" (an invasion of a legally protected interest that is "concrete and particularized" and is "actual or imminent"); (2) "a causal connection between the injury and the conduct complained of;" and (3) it must be "likely," and not merely "speculative," that the injury will be redressed by a favorable decision (*Lujan* v. *Defenders of Wildlife* (1992)).

For example, *Frothingham* v. *Mellon* (1923) held that a federal taxpayer could not challenge the Federal Maternity Act because the taxpayer's interest was minute and indeterminable. In spite of this decision, the Court in 1968 conceded standing to a federal taxpayer who sought to challenge an alleged breach of the First Amendment's establishment-of-religion clause through federal expenditures under a 1965 act for textbooks and instructional costs in sectarian schools (*Flast* v. *Cohen*). The Court distinguished this situation from the typical taxpayer suit by viewing the establishment clause as itself a limitation on the taxing and spending power of Congress; hence, taxpayers could urge more than their general interest in the expenditure of federal funds. Yet in 1982, the Court denied standing in a case where surplus government property had been transferred to a sectarian school (*Valley Forge Christian College* v. *Americans United for Separation of Church and State*). The majority regarded the transfer as an executive action under the property clause of Article IV, not congressional action under the taxing and spending clause, as had been the case in *Flast*. So the easier standing rules of *Flast* did not apply.

Standing therefore can be not just a hurdle for litigation but also a barrier, as Wisconsin Democrats learned in 2018 when they challenged a legislative districting plan as a partisan gerrymander that violated the Constitution. A unanimous bench turned the plaintiffs away and dodged the issue because of a lack of standing (*Gill* v. *Whitford*). Yet, the Court chose to address the issue in ***Rucho* v. *Common Cause*** the following year (see Chapter Five).

Standing and ripeness combined in late 2020, when the Court in a 6–3 vote deflected ruling on the merits of a challenge brought by several states against President Trump's order to exclude undocumented immigrants from the decennial reapportionment figures from that year's census (*Trump* v. *New York*). "First, a plaintiff must demonstrate standing, including 'an injury that is concrete, particularized, and imminent rather than conjectural or hypothetical.' Second," advised the per curiam opinion, "the case must be ripe—not dependent on 'contingent future events that may not occur as anticipated, or indeed may not occur at all.'" Otherwise, "a case would be 'riddled with contingencies and speculation that impede judicial review.'"

Absence of a live controversy, ripeness, standing, or jurisdiction makes a case **nonjusticiable**, or inappropriate for settlement by a court. Justiciability in turn merges into the **political question doctrine** (discussed more fully in Chapter Two). A political question is one that the Court believes should be decided by the "political branches" of the government—Congress or the presidency. Today, political questions include certain foreign-policy matters, the Constitution's stipulation of a "republican form of government" for every state, and ratification of constitutional amendments. At one time, legislative apportionment and districting were deemed "political" and hence out of judicial bounds.

Modesty pervades these self-denials, and the justices differ markedly in defining their role. **Judicial activists** (those more eager to intervene and to substitute their views for those of other policymakers) tend to gloss over such matters as "technical." **Judicial restraintists** (those inclined to defer to decisions made elsewhere in the political system) can frequently avoid a decision on the merits by insisting that a litigant has run afoul of one or more rules.

SUPREME COURT DECISION MAKING

Article III of the Constitution establishes "the judicial power of the United States" in "one Supreme Court." Initially staffed by six justices, since 1869 the Supreme Court's size has been set by Congress at nine: eight associate justices and the chief justice. Also by statute, the Court's annual term opens on the first Monday in October and concludes when the justices have disposed of all argued cases, usually in late June or very early July.

Access to the Supreme Court. Having a case decided by a state or lower federal court by no means assures the losing litigant of eventual review by the U.S. Supreme Court. The justices reject many more cases for review than they decide—indeed, so many more that most of what the Supreme Court does is to say "no." In recent terms, the justices have annually denied review in about 7,000 cases and have given plenary treatment (consisting of oral argument and a signed opinion, as explained below) to fewer than 100. Another several dozen other cases may be decided summarily. Several hundred cases are usually carried over for action the following term. Indeed, despite a sizeable docket, the number of decided cases has actually fallen. (See Table 1.1.) Moreover, prisoner appeals, most of which are assigned to the "*in forma pauperis*" docket for indigents (where fees and other requirements are waived), are routinely granted review at a far lower rate than cases on the "paid" docket. In addition, some 1,200 applications of various kinds are filed each year that can be acted upon by a single justice or sometimes referred by that justice to the rest of the Court. This category of cases that does not move through the full process described below has been called the **shadow docket** by scholar William Baude.

The Justices at Work. The actual work of the Supreme Court proceeds through five stages: agenda setting, briefs on the merits, oral argument, conference, and opinions and decision.

Table 1.1 Caseload in the U.S. Supreme Court, 1929–2020

Term	Total Cases on Docket	Cases Decided with Opinion
1929–1930	981	156
1939–1940	1,078	151
1949–1950	1,441	122
1959–1960	2,143	132
1969–1970	4,172	126
1979–1980	4,781	155
1989–1990	5,746	146
1999–2000	8,445	81
2006–2007	10,256	78
2009–2010	9,302	72
2015–2016	7,535	69
2019–2020	6,534	53*

* The number of cases with opinions in 2019–2020 was the smallest number for a term since the 41 cases in 1862 during the Civil War.
Source: Clerk's Office, U.S. Supreme Court.

Throughout this decision-making process, justices are assisted by their **law clerks**. Congress authorized the first clerk or "secretary" (as the position was initially labeled) in 1886. Today, most justices annually employ four clerks, each a recent law school graduate usually with experience clerking on a lower federal court. With one aide to chambers (formerly called a messenger) and two secretaries for each justice (the chief justice enjoys a somewhat larger staff), the Court, as Justice Powell once remarked, resembles a collection of "nine small, independent law firms." Increased reliance by most members of the Court on their clerks—the "junior Supreme Court," in Justice Douglas's description—both in making recommendations on which cases to accept for review and in writing opinions, calls into question the observation made long ago by Justice Brandeis that "the Justices . . . are almost the only people in Washington who do their own work." Yet by congressional or White House standards, the Court's support staff remains very small. "[I]ndividual justices still continue to do a great deal more of their 'own work,'" Chief Justice Rehnquist once insisted, "than do their counterparts in the other branches of the federal government."

(1) *Agenda Setting*. Petitions for review from litigants and their counsel who lost in the court below arrive in the form of documents called **briefs** that demonstrate why the Court should accept the case for decision. Litigants and their counsel who won in the court below file briefs in opposition, explaining why the Court should not grant review. A minimum of four justices must vote to accept the case. This is the so-called **rule of four**. (However, in capital cases where the petition for review is also a petition for a stay of execution, the condemned prisoner needs five votes to prevail.) Deciding what to decide is therefore an important stage in the judicial process. At this and other stages in Supreme Court decision making, the U.S. government is represented by the **solicitor general**, the third-ranking official in the Department of Justice. Thus, when an agency of the national government such as the Federal Communications Commission (FCC) has lost a case in a court of appeals,

it is the solicitor general, not an attorney in the FCC, who makes the call whether to seek review in the Supreme Court.

When the justices meet in conference to act on petitions for review, the chief justice uses a "discuss list." This is a time-saving device. Any justice may add a case to the discuss list, but unless a case makes the list—and over 70 percent do not—review is automatically denied, without discussion. If the Court grants review, the case moves to the steps explained below. If the Court denies review, the case is ordinarily at an end. The decision of "the court below"—the last court to render a decision in the case—stands. As of 2021, all justices except for Alito and Gorsuch participate in a **cert pool**, a labor-saving device. Petitions for certiorari are first examined by a law clerk in one of the chambers, who then prepares a memorandum on the case with a recommendation on whether to grant or deny review. That memorandum is then circulated to the other chambers. Clerks for Justices Alito and Gorsuch review the petitions and send their analyses and recommendations directly to them.

Mystery surrounds selection of cases because the justices only very rarely publish their reasons favoring a grant or denial of review. Yet experience suggests that the presence of one or more of the following factors increases the likelihood that the justices will accept a case: (a) the United States is a party to the case and requests review; (b) courts of appeals have issued conflicting decisions on the question; (c) the issue is one some justices are eager to engage; (d) the court below has made a decision clearly at odds with established Supreme Court interpretation of a law or constitutional provision; (e) the case is not "fact-bound"—that is, of primary interest only to the parties to the case; and (f) the case raises an issue of overriding importance to the nation.

(2) *Briefs on the Merits*. Once the justices have accepted a case, opposing counsel submit yet another round of briefs. Like briefs seeking or opposing review, their length has been limited since 1980 to a maximum of 50 pages each. These briefs focus not on why the Court should hear the case but on the substantive issues the case presents. Sometimes the Court will have specified in its grant of review that it wants to limit consideration to a single question. Persons, governments, and organizations interested in but not parties to a case may file their own briefs as **amici curiae**, or "friends of the court." (Less frequently, an amicus may have already submitted a brief during stage one, thus alerting the Court to the national importance of a case.) Nongovernmental entities filing an amicus brief must obtain the permission of the opposing parties, although the Court itself may grant permission if a litigant refuses. The solicitor general and state attorneys general may file amici briefs without seeking permission. Most merit briefs and petitions for certiorari are now filed electronically in a word-searchable PDF format, although Court rules still require submission of a hard copy as well.

(3) *Oral Argument*. In addition to reading the briefs submitted by counsel, the Court listens to **oral argument**. During the chief justiceship of John Marshall (1801–1835), arguments were well-nigh interminable. Daniel Webster, a leading attorney of that day, used to run on for days. In 1849, the Court reduced the time for oral argument to two hours, one for each side. Opposing counsel now divide an hour between themselves, with additional time allotted only in exceptional circumstances. From October until the end of April, Mondays, Tuesdays, and Wednesdays of two consecutive weeks are set aside for oral argument, with at least two weeks following being reserved for the preparation of opinions. The justices hear arguments on those days from 10:00 A.M. until 3:00 P.M., with an hour recess at noon for lunch. This stage

of the decision-making process gives the justices an opportunity to ask questions to clear up uncertainties or other matters that they may have noticed in the briefs. Even for seasoned attorneys, the experience can be like a grueling oral examination.

Consider, for example, this exchange between Justice Alito and attorney Daniel Rogan when *Minnesota Voters Alliance* v. *Mansky* was argued on February 28, 2018. Attorney Rogan was defending a state ban on wearing political apparel in or near a polling place on primary or election day.

JUSTICE ALITO: How about a shirt with a rainbow flag? Would that be permitted?

MR. ROGAN: A shirt with a rainbow flag? No, it would—yes, it would be—it would be permitted unless there was—unless there was an issue on the ballot that—that related somehow to—to gay rights.

JUSTICE ALITO: How about a shirt that says "Parkland Strong"?

MR. ROGAN: No, that would—that would be—that would be allowed. I think—I think, Your Honor—

JUSTICE ALITO: Even though gun control would very likely be an issue?

MR. ROGAN: To the extent—

JUSTICE ALITO: I bet some candidate would raise an issue about gun control.

MR. ROGAN: Your Honor, the—the—the line that we're drawing is one that is—is related to electoral choices in a—

JUSTICE ALITO: Well, what's the answer to this question? You're a polling official. You're the reasonable person. Would that be allowed or would it not be allowed?

MR. ROGAN: The—the Parkland?

JUSTICE ALITO: Yeah.

MR. ROGAN: I—I think—I think today that I—that would be—if—if that was in Minnesota, and it was "Parkland Strong," I—I would say that that would be allowed in, that there's not—

JUSTICE ALITO: Okay. How about an NRA shirt?

MR. ROGAN: An NRA shirt? Today, in Minnesota, no, it would not, Your Honor. I think that that's a clear indication—and I think what you're getting at, Your Honor—

JUSTICE ALITO: How about a shirt with the text of the Second Amendment?

MR. ROGAN: Your Honor, I—I—I think that that could be viewed as political, that that—that would be—that would be—

JUSTICE ALITO: How about the First Amendment? [Laughter.]

MR. ROGAN: No, Your Honor, I don't—I don't think the First Amendment. And, Your Honor, I—

CHIEF JUSTICE ROBERTS: No—no what, that it would be covered or wouldn't be allowed?

MR. ROGAN: It would be allowed.

CHIEF JUSTICE ROBERTS: It would be?

MR. ROGAN: It would be. And—and I think the—I understand the—the idea, and I've—I've—there are obviously a lot of examples that—that have been bandied about here—

JUSTICE ALITO: Yeah, well, this is the problem. How about a Colin Kaepernick jersey?

MR. ROGAN: No, Your Honor, I don't think that that would be under—under our statute. And I think—

JUSTICE ALITO: How about "All Lives Matter"?

MR. ROGAN: That could be, Your Honor, that could be—that could be perceived as political.

A few months later, the Court ruled 7–2 that the ban's imprecision placed too much discretion in the hands of local officials and so impermissibly infringed the freedom of speech protected by the First Amendment.

Although oral argument has traditionally been open to the public on a first-come, first-served basis in the small courtroom, the COVID-19 pandemic caused major changes beginning in the spring of 2020. Not only was the Supreme Court Building itself closed to the public, but oral argument was switched from in-person to argument via teleconference, with the justices participating remotely. These conditions have continued into 2021, with the single positive change perhaps being live, rather than delayed, audio release of argument sessions.

(4) *Conference.* Wednesday and Friday ordinarily are **conference** days—the time set apart primarily for confidential discussion of and decision on cases argued during the week. Conference is held in a room adjoining the chambers of the chief justice, who begins the discussion of each case with a summary of the facts, his analysis of the law, and an announcement of his proposed vote whether to affirm, reverse, or modify. The discussion then passes to the senior associate justice, who does likewise. It then goes around the table to the junior associate justice. When discussion of one case is finished, the justices move to the next one until all the argued cases on the agenda for that particular conference have been disposed of. The Wednesday conference, which the justices refer to as a "mini-conference," proceeds like the longer Friday conference except that no petitions for certiorari are discussed. (Among the associate justices, "junior justice" and "senior justice" refer to length of service on the Court, not a justice's age. By Court tradition, the junior justice has special responsibilities, including answering the door if someone knocks during a conference and meeting with other staff on the committee that oversees operation of the cafeteria on the ground floor of the building. According to one report, Justice Kagan claims credit for having a frozen yogurt machine installed.)

In cases of greatest importance, discussion may take place at more than one conference before the justices are prepared to reach a decision. All cases are decided by majority vote, a fact that gives meaning to the question Justice Brennan routinely posed to his new clerks each year: "What is the most important rule around here?" After they offered various incorrect responses, Brennan would say, "It's the 'rule of five.' You need five votes to get anything done."

(5) *Opinions and Decisions.* On the Monday after a two-week argument session, the chief justice circulates an assignment list to the justices. If the chief justice is in the majority, the chief assigns the task of writing the opinion for the Court; if not, the senior associate justice in the majority makes the assignment. Preparation of the majority opinion requires much give-and-take, with an opinion going through as many as a dozen drafts. The goal is an **opinion of the Court** representing the consensus of the majority, not merely the views of the writer, which explains and applies the legal principles applicable to that case. In situations where a majority is unable to agree on a single opinion, a **plurality opinion** announces the "judgment of the Court" (the outcome of the case) and explains the views of the plurality. The justices' positions are fluid. Up to the moment—weeks or months after the opinion writing began—that the decision is announced in open Court, the justices are free to change their votes.

In contrast to a norm of consensus in the nineteenth century and early twentieth century Supreme Court that discouraged published dissents (even when justices disagreed with a decision), today in barely a third of the decisions each term is the Court unanimous. In the rest, dissenters file one or more opinions explaining their differences with the majority. According to Chief Justice Hughes, a **dissent** is "an appeal to the brooding spirit of the law, to the intelligence of a future day, when a later decision may possibly correct the error into which the dissenting judge believes the court to have been betrayed." Justices may also write a **concurring opinion** to indicate their acceptance of the outcome but either an unwillingness to adopt all the reasoning contained in the opinion of the Court or a desire to say something additional. Thus, a **regular concurrence** is a separate opinion filed by a justice who also joins the opinion of the Court, while a **special concurrence** is one filed by a justice who votes with the majority but does not join the opinion of the Court.

SOURCE MATERIALS

The Internet has transformed study of the judiciary. Today, with a computer properly connected, someone in even a remote location has easy access to many resources previously available only at law or other research libraries. What follows is a listing and annotation of essential source materials in both print and electronic form.

Supreme Court Decisions. The reported decisions and opinions of the Supreme Court form the basic material for the study of constitutional law. They appear in several printed editions and formats and are accessible on the Internet.

(1) *United States Reports*. This is the official edition published by the Government Printing Office. Until 1875, the reports were cited according to the name of the Reporter of Decisions, with the reporter's name usually abbreviated. Beginning with volume 91 in 1875, the reports have been cited only by volume and page number and the designation "U.S." For example, a case cited as 444 U.S. 130 is located in volume 444 of the *U.S. Reports*, beginning on page 130.

1789–1800 Dallas	(1–4 Dall., 1–4 U.S.)
1801–1815 Cranch	(1–9 Cr., 5–13 U.S.)
1816–1827 Wheaton	(1–12 Wheat., 14–25 U.S.)
1828–1842 Peters	(1–16 Pet., 26–41 U.S.)
1843–1860 Howard	(1–24 How., 42–65 U.S.)
1861–1862 Black	(1–2 Bl., 66–67 U.S.)
1863–1874 Wallace	(1–23 Wall., 68–90 U.S.)
1875–	(91– U.S.)

(2) *United States Supreme Court Reports, Lawyers' Edition* (until 1996 published by Lawyers' Cooperative Publishing Company; now published by LexisNexis). The advantage of this complete edition lies in the inclusion of summaries of briefs of counsel plus notes and annotations on various topics of constitutional law. *Lawyers' Edition* is cited as L.Ed. (e.g., 96 L.Ed. 954). Decisions since 1956 appear in a second series (e.g., 118 L.Ed. 2d 293).

(3) *Supreme Court Reporter* (until 1996 published by West Publishing Company, now Thomson Reuters). This is similar in concept to *Lawyers' Edition* but includes only decisions since 1882. Thus for cases in volumes 1–105 U.S., one must consult another edition. It is cited as S.Ct. (e.g., 58 S.Ct. 166).

(4) *United States Law Week* (published by the Bureau of National Affairs, another commercial publisher). This is both a loose-leaf and online service, one advantage of which is that decisions are published within a day of their release at the Court. Thus, decisions appear in printed form in *Law Week* well before even the advance issues distributed by the two other commercial publishers listed above (and long before the government's). *Law Week* also keeps track of all cases on the

Supreme Court's docket, whether ultimately accepted for decision or not. It is cited as U.S.L.W. (e.g., 71 U.S.L.W. 4263).

(5) Electronic access. Supreme Court decisions are accessible through Westlaw and LexisNexis (available through many college and university libraries or by subscription) as well as various Internet sites. At present, the sites listed below are available at no charge and were active at the time this book went into production. Be advised that any Internet address or URL (uniform resource locator) is subject to change.

(a) The LII and Hermes: The Legal Information Institute and Project Hermes provide decisions since May 1990 through Cornell University. Decisions are ordinarily accessible within hours of their announcement by the Supreme Court. Several hundred selected decisions prior to 1990 are available from LII at the second address.
www.law.cornell.edu/supremecourt/text
www.law.cornell.edu/supct/cases/topic.htm

(b) FindLaw: Includes decisions since 1791.
http://caselaw.findlaw.com/court/us-supreme-court

(c) The U.S. Supreme Court: This official site contains recent decisions, orders, the current docket, calendar, court rules, transcripts and audio recordings of oral arguments, press releases, a table of all justices since 1789, and some speeches by justices. The same site also contains the bound volumes of the *U.S. Reports* since 1991. Additional volumes are added as they appear in print form.
www.supremecourtus.gov

(6) Case record. The record of each decided case includes briefs of counsel, oral argument, proceedings in lower courts, and exhibits. Unfortunately, these are not nearly so widely available as the Supreme Court decisions themselves. LexisNexis now publishes *Landmark Briefs and Arguments of the Supreme Court of the United States: Constitutional Law*. With new volumes added annually, this set contains the complete extant record of major constitutional decisions of the Supreme Court, beginning in 1793, including many of the cases selected for this book. Briefs in current cases are available online at the Supreme Court's website. Briefs filed by the solicitor general may be accessed at www.usdoj.gov/osg.

Lower Federal Court Decisions. Decisions by the lower federal courts are published by Thomson Reuters. Decisions of the courts of appeals appear in the *Federal Reporter*, which is currently in its third series. Volumes are numbered successively, similar to the Supreme Court reporters, and each series is cited as F., F. 2d, or F. 3d. Selected decisions of the district courts appear in the *Federal Supplement*, similarly numbered and cited as F. Supp., F. Supp. 2d, or F. Supp. 3d.

State Court Decisions. The decisions of the highest state courts are published separately by either the state or a commercial publisher. A sectional reporter system, which combines selected decisions of the courts of several states in one publication, is also available in most law libraries. The National Center for State Courts maintains a directory of state court sites: www.ncsc.org/information-and-resources/state-court-websites.

Miscellaneous Judicial Resources Online. In addition to sites that make judicial decisions available, other Internet locations contain a variety of materials related to the courts.

1. Oyez: The Oyez Supreme Court Project of Cornell University and the Chicago Kent College of Law provides summaries of and access to recent decisions. Of great

importance, the site holds digital sound recordings of oral arguments at the Supreme Court for cases since 1955: www.oyez.org.

2. The Federal Judicial Center: Of particular interest is the "History of the Federal Judiciary." This online reference contains a biographical database of all justices and other federal judges since 1789, histories of the federal courts, and historical documents related to the judicial branch of government: www.fjc.gov.
3. The Federal Judiciary Home Page: Maintained by the Administrative Office of U.S. Courts, the site provides the text of both current and back issues of *The Third Branch* newsletter, various reports and other publications, and press releases: www.uscourts.gov.
4. *The Law and Politics Book Review*: Produced by the Law and Courts Section of the American Political Science Association this electronic journal is the best single source for timely reviews of recent books on constitutional law, the Supreme Court, and the judicial process generally: www.lpbr.net/.
5. SCOTUSblog: Established by journalist Lyle Denniston, this valuable blog features a variety of postings about developments at the Supreme Court: www.scotusblog.com.

Legislative and Administrative Materials. Acts of Congress may be found chronologically arranged in the *United States Statutes at Large*, of which a new volume appears annually and, for statutes currently in effect, are available in an analytical form in the *United States Code* (Government Printing Office), *United States Code Annotated* (West Group), and *United States Code Service* (LexisNexis). The *U.S. Code* is accessible online: www.gpo.gov/fdsys. Debates in Congress are available under the following titles and have been officially published since 1873: *Annals of Congress*, 1789–1824; *Register of Debates in Congress*, 1824–1837; *Congressional Globe*, 1833–1873; *Congressional Record*, 1873–. Text of the *Congressional Record* (as well as bills), beginning with the 101st Congress in 1989, is available online at www.gpo.gov/fdsys/.

Executive orders and proposed administrative rules and orders are published chronologically in the *Federal Register*; regulations in force are presented analytically in the *Code of Federal Regulations*. These publications are accessible online at www.gpo.gov/fdsys. Administrative and congressional activity is followed by *Congressional Quarterly Weekly Report* (published by Congressional Quarterly, Inc.) and by *National Journal* (published by Government Research Corp.).

General Reference Works. Bibliographic sources include the massive set compiled by Kermit L. Hall, *A Comprehensive Bibliography of American Constitutional and Legal History, 1896–1979*, 5 vols. (Millwood, NY: Kraus International Publications, 1984, with a supplement through 1987 issued in 1991), and Fenton S. Martin and Robert U. Goehlert, *The U.S. Supreme Court: A Bibliography* (Washington, DC: CQ Press, 1990). More concise is D. Grier Stephenson, Jr., *The Supreme Court and the American Republic: An Annotated Bibliography* (New York: Garland Publishing, 1981). The latter volume includes a guide to the location of the papers of Supreme Court justices.

Study of individual justices is aided by Linda A. Blandford and Patricia Russell Evans, eds., *Supreme Court of the United States 1789–1980: An Index to Opinions Arranged by Justice*, 2 vols. (Millwood, NY: Kraus International Publications, 1983). A supplement covering the years 1981–1991 appeared in 1994. Biographical essays are contained in Leon Friedman and Fred L. Israel, *The Justices of the United States Supreme Court 1789–1995*, rev. ed., 5 vols. (New York: Chelsea House, 1995). Somewhat briefer treatments appear in Clare Cushman, *The Supreme Court Justices:*

Illustrated Biographies, 3rd ed. (Washington, DC: CQ Press, 2012), and in the more inclusive Roger K. Newman, ed., *The Yale Biographical Dictionary of American Law* (New Haven, CT: Yale University Press, 2009).

General information on many aspects of the work of the Supreme Court is contained in Kermit L. Hall, ed., *The Oxford Companion to the Supreme Court of the United States*, 2nd ed. (New York: Oxford University Press, 2005); Lee Epstein et al., *The Supreme Court Compendium*, 6th ed. (Washington, DC: Congressional Quarterly, 2015); and David Savage, *Congressional Quarterly's Guide to the U.S. Supreme Court*, 2 vols., 5th ed. (2010). *The Constitution of the United States: Analysis and Interpretation*, originally authored by Edward S. Corwin and subsequently maintained by the Congressional Research Service, is accessible online at www.gpo.gov/fdsys.

Studies of the Court, its justices, and its decisions are featured in the *Journal of Supreme Court History*. Originally an annual publication of the Supreme Court Historical Society, the journal now appears three times each year. Some back issues are accessible at http://supremecourthistory.org/pub_journal_archive.html.

Reading a Supreme Court Decision

Every discipline has its own literature, and the literature of the study of the Constitution includes judicial opinions. It is essential, therefore, to acquire a talent for reading cases because they represent the medium through which a court speaks. Students of the Court will find it helpful to take careful notes in the form of an outline on the cases they read. Making the outline is called **briefing a case**. Thorough case briefing consists of a summary of at least four elements.

Litigants and the Facts

Always located at the beginning, the name or title identifies the parties to the case called the litigants. The name of the person or entity bringing the case to the Supreme Court appears first; the party being brought to the Court is listed second. The *v.* stands for "versus," or "against." In cases that reach the Supreme Court on certiorari (as almost all now do), the **petitioner** brings the case against the **respondent**. In cases on appeal, the **appellant** brings the case against the **appellee**. Cases are real, not hypothetical, controversies between parties. The issues of a case arise from circumstances or events that have prompted one or both parties to seek redress in court. The facts of a case may or may not be in dispute, but they are always a factor in how cases are decided.

Question(s)

The facts of a case present one or more issues or questions for decision. Most of a judicial opinion is an effort to answer those questions. Although even a relatively simple case may generate many questions, counsel in the Supreme Court seek review only of those of the gravest importance—to the parties involved and to the nation. Ordinarily, the Supreme Court decides questions of law, not fact. In reviewing a criminal conviction, for instance, the Court is rarely concerned with a defendant's actual guilt or innocence. Rather, the justices focus on procedural issues, such as the admissibility of evidence or the lawfulness of an arrest.

Decision

The answers to the questions that arise from the facts of a case lead to a decision. This is the result or outcome of a case. For example, a government agency has, or has not, exceeded its authority under the law or the Constitution. Typically in the Supreme Court, decisions take the form of **affirming** (accepting) or **reversing** (rejecting and setting aside) the judgment of the court below. When reversing, the justices will often **remand** (send back) a case to the lower court for action "consistent with" the Court's decision.

Reasoning of the Opinions

As explained in a previous section, the goal of the Court's decision-making process is a statement reflecting the consensus of a majority of the justices. This statement is the opinion of the Court—also called the majority opinion—that explains why a certain question requires a certain answer. An exercise in persuasion, the majority opinion attempts to justify the decision the Court has reached. Concurring and dissenting opinions should also be examined closely because they may shed light on what has been decided. Dissenting opinions attempt to highlight weaknesses in the majority's reasoning. Concurring opinions may indicate the limits to a line of reasoning beyond which certain members of the majority are unwilling to go. Both may highlight legal trends. Moreover, awareness of the votes of individual justices can alert the reader to shifts in a justice's position. Throughout this book, the headnote for each excerpted case displays the voting alignment.

KEY TERMS

federal courts
state courts
jurisdiction
Article III courts
Article I courts
original jurisdiction
appellate jurisdiction
federal question
diversity jurisdiction
magistrate judges
certiorari
docket
appeal
direct appeal
Ashwander rules
case or controversy
mootness
ripeness
advisory opinion
standing
nonjusticiable
political question doctrine
judicial activists
judicial restraintists
shadow docket
law clerks
briefs
cert pool
rule of four
solicitor general
amicus (or amici) curiae
oral argument
conference
opinion of the Court
plurality opinion
dissent
concurring opinion
regular concurrence
special concurrence
briefing a case
petitioner
respondent
appellant
appellee
affirming
reversing
remand

QUERIES

1. Review Table 1.1. What do the data suggest about the importance of state and lower federal courts in helping to shape American constitutional law?

2. In an interview published in the *New York Times* on July 10, 2016, just days before the Republican National Convention formally named Donald Trump as its candidate for president, Justice Ruth Ginsburg said, "I can't imagine what this place would be—I can't imagine what the country would be—with Donald Trump as our president. For the country, it could be four years. For the Court, it could be—I don't even want to contemplate that." In an interview aired on CNN the following day, she referred to Trump as "a faker. . . . He has no consistency about him. He says whatever comes into his mind at the moment. He really has an ego." Her words stirred up a flurry of criticism of Ginsburg from across the political spectrum. On July 14, she moderated her comments through a written statement released by the Court: "On reflection, my recent remarks in response to press inquiries were ill-advised, and I regret making them. Judges should avoid commenting on a candidate for public office. In the future I will be more circumspect." In its prohibition of political activity, Canon 5 of the Code of Conduct for United States Judges states: "A judge should not . . . make speeches for a political organization or candidate, or publicly endorse or oppose a candidate for public office." While not officially binding on Supreme Court justices, they generally adhere to the code that binds the rest of the federal judiciary. Were Justice Ginsburg's comments about Trump out of line? Wholly aside from the strictures of Canon 5, should justices feel free to express their political views like anyone else? Are some kinds of comments more appropriate or inappropriate than others?

3. Between 1800 and the 1940s, nonunanimous Supreme Court decisions were the exception, not the rule. Rarely did a published dissent appear in as many as 25 percent of the cases, and the dissent rate usually hovered near 10 percent. The pattern in the past 60 years has been sharply different. Nonunanimous decisions are the rule, not the exception. In some terms, published dissents routinely appear in as many as half the decisions. What factors might account for this change? Is the Court helped or hurt by dissenting opinions?

4. Fred Graham, former Supreme Court reporter for the *New York Times* and CBS News has said, "The only groups who don't appear on television are the Supreme Court and the Mafia." Although the Court's argument sessions are open to the public, the justices resolutely refuse to allow oral arguments to be telecast at all, and only in the pandemic have they routinely allowed live audio transmission of proceedings. Moreover, few justices grant interviews to journalists and, when they do, rarely speak about specific cases. Should oral arguments be telecast in the same way that the House and Senate allow televised coverage of their floor proceedings? How would increased exposure affect the Court?

SELECTED READINGS

Baum, Lawrence, *The Supreme Court*, 14th ed. Washington, DC: CQ Press, 2021.

Baum, Lawrence, and Neal Devins. *The Company They Keep: How Partisan Divisions Came to the Supreme Court*. New York: Oxford University Press, 2019.

Black, Ryan C. *Oral Arguments and Coalition Formation on the U.S. Supreme Court: A Deliberate Dialogue*. Ann Arbor: University of Michigan Press, 2012.

Black, Ryan C., and Ryan J. Owens. *The Solicitor General and the United States Supreme Court: Executive Branch Influence and Judicial Decisions*. New York: Cambridge University Press, 2012.

Corley, Pamela C., Amy Steigerwalt, and Artemus Ward. *The Puzzle of Unanimity: Consensus on the United States Supreme Court*. Stanford, CA: Stanford University Press, 2013.

Crowe, Justin. *Building the Judiciary: Law, Courts, and the Politics of Institutional Development*. Princeton, NJ: Princeton University Press, 2012.

Friedman, Barry, et al., *Judicial Decisionmaking: A Coursebook*. Eagan, MN: West Academic Publihing, 2020.

Peppers, Todd C. *Courtiers of the Marble Palace: The Rise and Influence of the Supreme Court Law Clerk*. Stanford, CA: Stanford University Press, 2006.

Perry, H.W., Jr. *Deciding to Decide: Agenda Setting in the United States Supreme Court*. Cambridge, MA: Harvard University Press, 1991.

Shapiro, Stephen, et al. *Supreme Court Practice*, 11th ed. New York: Bloomberg Law, 2019.

2

The Constitution, the Supreme Court, and Judicial Review

Judicial review represents an attempt by American Democracy to cover its bet.
—Professor Edward S. Corwin (1942)

The Constitution of 1787 and its 27 amendments, reprinted near the beginning of this book, can be read in about half an hour. One could memorize the written document word for word and still know little or nothing of its meaning. The reason is that the body of rules known as constitutional law consists primarily of decisions and opinions of the U.S. Supreme Court—the gloss that the justices have spread on the formal document. Charles Warren asked us not to forget that "[h]owever the Court may interpret the provisions of the Constitution, it is still the Constitution which is law and not decisions of the Court." But future justice and chief justice Charles Evans Hughes bluntly asserted that "[t]he Constitution is what the Judges say it is." Furthermore, recurrent declarations of reverence for the "ark of our covenant," as Chief Justice Taft called the Constitution, stand in sharp contrast to the reality that most Americans do not adequately understand the Constitution. Popular perceptions about the Constitution are frequently at odds with the document itself, making the American Constitution in its broadest sense greater than the sum of its parts. Myth wars with fact both within and without the Court.

GRANTING AND LIMITING POWER

In the United States, the Constitution alone is supreme. All agencies of government stand in the relationship of creator to creatures. There is, Woodrow Wilson observed, "no sovereign government in America." But Wilson was not blind to the fact that government means action. "Power belongs to government, is lodged in organs of initiative; control belongs to the community, is lodged with the voters"—and the courts.

Constitutionalism. American **constitutionalism—**the belief in limiting government power by a written charter—deals with the problem James Madison posed

DOI: 10.4324/9781003164340-3

in *The Federalist*, No. 51: "In framing a government which is to be administered by men over men, the great difficulty lies in this: you must first enable the government to control the governed; and in the next place oblige it to control itself." To achieve those twin objectives, the Constitution both grants and limits power; yet in ways both obvious and subtle, the Constitution appears to be more an instrument of rights and limitations than of powers. There are certain things Congress is expressly forbidden to do. It may not pass an ex post facto law or a bill of attainder; it may not tax exports from any state; and it may not—except in great emergencies—suspend the writ of habeas corpus. The Bill of Rights (Amendments I through VIII) contains a longer list of things government is powerless to do. (Almost all restrictions imposed by the Bill of Rights on the national government have now been "incorporated" into the Fourteenth Amendment as limits on the states, as Chapter Nine explains.) State governments are likewise forbidden to do specific things. Article I, Section 10, declares that a state may not enact ex post facto laws, impair the obligation of contracts, coin money, emit bills of credit, or enter into any treaty or alliance with a foreign state. Chief Justice Marshall called parts of this section, the only one in the original Constitution limiting state power, "a bill of rights for the people of the states." Nonetheless, the Constitution provides no definition of either powers or limitations, nor does the Constitution state how its words are to be interpreted.

Separation and Sharing of Powers. Government is also circumscribed in less specific ways. The Constitution divides power, even as it confers it. Congress is endowed with "legislative" power; it may not, therefore (except as a result of a specific grant or by implication), exercise executive or judicial power. The same restrictions apply to the other branches of the national government: the terms *judicial power* and *executive power*, like *legislative power*, have a technical meaning. In the exercise of their respective functions, neither Congress, nor the president, nor the judiciary may, under the principle of **separation of powers**, encroach on fields allocated to the other branches of government. Instead of requiring that the departments be kept absolutely separate and distinct, however, the Constitution mingles their functions. Congress is granted legislative power, but the grant is not exclusive. Lawmaking is shared by the president through the veto. The appointing authority is vested in the president, but for many appointments the Senate must give its advice and consent.

Federalism. The second power-limiting principle, **federalism**, means a constitutional system in which two authorities, each having a complete government system, exist in the same territory and act on the same people. In its American manifestation, federalism is a complicated arrangement whereby the national government exercises enumerated, implied, and inherent powers, with all others being "reserved to the States respectively, or to the people," in the words of the Tenth Amendment. Each government is supreme within its own sphere; neither is supreme within the sphere of the other. Federalism, like separation of powers and checks and balances, is a means of obliging government to control itself. None of these limiting principles is spelled out; they are either implicit in the organization and structure of the Constitution or, as with judicial review, deducible from "the theory of our government."

James Madison and other Founders generally called this intricate system **free government**. The power surrendered by the people is first divided "vertically" between two distinct governments (the national government and the states), and then the portion allotted to each is subdivided "horizontally" among distinct and separate departments. Hence, a double security is provided for the rights of the people. Distinct governments will exercise control over each other, and at the same time each will be checked by itself. "Vibrations of power" (the "genius" of free government, Alexander Hamilton called it) are inherent in this complexus of restraints. Just how such controls were to be enforced the Constitution does not specify.

THE DOCTRINE OF JUDICIAL REVIEW

For correctives against abuse of power, Americans have not been content to rely on **political checks** such as public opinion and the ballot box. The essential safeguards in most free societies, they have not sufficed here. In America, government is kept within bounds not only by the electoral process but also through separation of powers, federalism, and (as an adjunct to all these) **judicial review**—the authority of courts to set aside actions of another branch of government that, in the judges' view, conflict with the Constitution.

The Framers. The **supremacy clause** in Article VI of the Constitution declares that the Constitution (along with treaties and federal statutes) is "the supreme law of the land." This principle is essential to the operation of the federal system and makes explicit the doctrine that national law will prevail in situations where it conflicts with state law. The framers, however, left unanswered the question of who or what was to sustain this supremacy. Moreover, their Constitution did not expressly contain a method for resolving disputes concerning the constitutionality of specific acts of Congress. In the Philadelphia Convention debates of 1787, it was suggested that each house of Congress might, when in doubt, call on the judges for an opinion concerning the validity of national legislation. Madison declared that a "law violating a constitution established by the people themselves would be considered by the judges as null and void." It was repeatedly urged that Supreme Court justices be joined with the executive in a council of revision and be empowered to veto congressional legislation. Certain delegates objected to this proposal, contending that the justices would already have this power in cases properly before them. Any such provision, they argued, would give the Court a double check. It would compromise "the impartiality of the Court by making them go on record before they were called in due course, to give . . . their exposition of the laws, which involved a power of deciding on their constitutionality." Other members of the Convention, though not denying that the Court could exercise such power, asserted that it would violate the principle of separation of powers and have the effect, as Elbridge Gerry remarked, of "making statesmen of judges." In the end, the power of judicial review was not expressly authorized.

Professor Edward Corwin suggested that for the Constitution's framers, judicial review rested "upon certain general principles [government under law, separation of powers, federalism, Bill of Rights] which, in their estimation, made specific provision for it unnecessary." Indeed, James Wilson, Oliver Ellsworth, and John Marshall, all destined for appointment to the Supreme Court, subscribed to the doctrine of judicial review in their respective state ratifying conventions. As Ellsworth of Connecticut declared on January 17, 1788:

> If the United States go beyond their powers, if they make a law which the constitution does not authorize, it is void; and the judicial power, the national judges, who, to secure their impartiality, are to be made independent, will declare it to be void. On the other hand, if the States go beyond their limits, if they make a law which is an usurpation

> upon the general government, the law is void; and upright independent judges will declare it so.

Robert Yates, a Philadelphia Convention delegate from New York but a nonsigner of the Constitution, probed these realities and predicted that judicial review, which he took for granted, would enable the justices "to mould the government into almost any shape they please. . . . Men placed in this situation will generally soon feel themselves independent of heaven itself."

Yates leveled a serious charge. To answer it, Hamilton responded in *The Federalist*, No. 78, that judicial review does not suppose "a superiority of the judicial to the legislative power. It only supposes that the power of the people (whose will the Constitution embodies) is superior to both." Thanks to judicial review, the "intentions of the people" would prevail over "the intentions of their agents." Hamilton, apparently realizing that such reasoning bordered on duplicity, went the whole way toward legerdemain: "It may be truly said that the judiciary has neither force nor will, but merely judgment." For Hamilton, judges claim no supremacy in exercising this high authority; they claim only to administer the public will. If an act of the legislature is held void, it is not because judges have any control over legislative power but because the act is forbidden by the Constitution and because the will of the people, which is declared supreme, is paramount to that of their representatives. Hence the ideal of a "government of laws and not of men." Hence also the intriguing paradox of judicial review: while wearing the magical habiliments of the law and speaking the language of the Constitution, Supreme Court justices take sides on vital social and political issues. This unstaged debate between Yates and Hamilton is excerpted in this chapter.

The Written and Unwritten Constitution. The American Constitution, unlike that of the British, cannot be changed by an ordinary act of legislation; this is its distinctive feature, not the fact that it is written. No constitution, including our own, is either altogether written or altogether unwritten. The British Constitution, though supposedly made up of custom and tradition, is partly written: the Magna Carta, the Petition of Right, the Bill of Rights, the Act of Settlement, and the Parliament Act of 1911 are written. In the American Constitution, there is no mention of the president's cabinet and no reference to senatorial courtesy, to political parties, or to the national presidential nominating conventions. The Electoral College is expressly provided for in the written Constitution; usage has discarded it as an independent decision-making body. Thus, the Constitution is only the original trunk, and important new branches have been added through formal amendment, custom and usage, and above all, judicial interpretation. The American Constitution "in operation," Woodrow Wilson wrote, "is manifestly a very different thing from the Constitution of the books."

From William Marbury to Dred Scott. Several weeks before Thomas Jefferson's inauguration as the third president in 1801, Congress—lame-duck and Federalist-dominated—passed the District of Columbia Act, which authorized the appointment of 42 new justices of the peace. Outgoing President Adams made the nominations and the Senate confirmed them, but in the waning hours of the administration, Chief Justice John Marshall, also still serving as secretary of state, failed to deliver all of the commissions of office to the would-be justices of the peace. Upon assuming office on March 4, Jefferson held back delivery to some of Adams's appointees. Later that year, William Marbury and three others whom Adams had named filed suit in the Supreme Court against Secretary of State James Madison.

They wanted the Court to issue a **writ of mandamus**, commanding Madison to hand over the undelivered commissions. (A writ of mandamus is an order by a court to a public official directing performance of a ministerial, or nondiscretionary, act.)

When the Court heard argument in February 1803, it was apparent that the justices were in a predicament. Because of tense partisan differences between Federalists and Democratic-Republicans, Jefferson and Madison would probably disregard the writ. There would then be no one to enforce the order. Yet for the Court to rule that Marbury was not entitled to the judgeship would be an open and painful acknowledgment of weakness.

Marshall's opinion in ***Marbury* v. *Madison*** avoided both dangers and claimed power for the Court. He announced first that Marbury and the others were entitled to their jobs and that the Court in a proper case could direct a coordinate branch of government to comply with the law. However, the Court was powerless to act in this instance. Why? Section 13 of the Judiciary Act of 1789—the basis of Marbury's suit—had given the Court authority to issue writs of mandamus as part of the Court's original, as opposed to appellate, jurisdiction (see Chapter One). Marshall noted that the Court's original jurisdiction is spelled out in Article III, and Article III includes no mention of writs of mandamus. By enlarging the Court's original jurisdiction, Section 13 therefore conflicted with the Constitution. Was the Court to apply an unconstitutional statute? To do so would make the statute (and Congress) superior to the Constitution. Section 13 was, therefore, void. Judicial review was thus a necessary adjunct to both a written Constitution and a government deriving its power from the people. Nor does judicial power, he maintained, give the Supreme Court any practical or real omnipotence. The Court merely exercised judicial power conferred by the Constitution and sustained by the principle of separation of powers. "It is, emphatically, the province and duty of the Judicial department to say what the law is." The effect, in theory, was not to elevate Court over legislature, but rather to make "the power of the people superior to both."

John Marshall did not "invent" judicial review. Aside from Hamilton's defense of it in 1788, several earlier Supreme Court decisions assumed this power, as had some state supreme courts. Nonetheless, *Marbury* may have been Marshall's most important contribution as chief justice. He was the first to articulate a defense of judicial review in a U.S. Supreme Court decision. Moreover, as much as anyone, he "legalized" the Constitution, treating the nation's fundamental charter as *law*—a text whose meaning would be discerned in the process of deciding cases. That meaning, in turn, would resolve disputes over allocations of power. This transformation, however, did not take place overnight. Marshall's assertion and defense of judicial review in *Marbury* stated more possibility than reality. Still, it was in *Marbury* that the view of the Constitution as a juridical document began to take root.

Marshall's theory was not unanswerable, as Justice Gibson's trenchant criticism in ***Eakin* v. *Raub*** made clear 22 years later. "[T]o affirm that the judiciary has a right to judge of the existence of such collision [between the Constitution and a statute]," declared the Pennsylvania jurist, "is to take for granted the very thing to be proved." Nonetheless, in 1803, and for quite some time thereafter, *Marbury* aroused comment and criticism, not because the "great Chief Justice" asserted the power of judicial review, but because he went out of his way to read a lecture to President Jefferson and Secretary of State Madison concerning their official duties under the Constitution. Earlier, Jefferson and other Democratic-Republicans had severely criticized the Sedition Act of 1798 and incorporation of the national bank in 1791 as unconstitutional. Indeed, the principle of judicial review of congressional statutes was so widely accepted by 1830 that Gibson's opposition to it partly explained why he was passed over in favor of fellow Pennsylvanian Henry Baldwin when President Andrew Jackson picked a successor to Justice Bushrod Washington. Where the principle remained controversial was with Supreme Court review of *state* legislation, a practice which, ironically, Gibson accepted because of paragraph 2 in Article VI of the Constitution.

The "autocratic" potential of the judicial veto, at least in Marshall's time, was less onerous than is sometimes imagined. It was not until 1857 and the ill-fated decision in ***Scott* v. *Sandford*** did the Court adjudge a second act of Congress to run afoul of the Constitution. Rejecting Marshall's view of a constitution intended to endure, Chief Justice Roger B. Taney affirmed that the Constitution "speaks not only with the same words, but with the same meaning and intent" as when it came from the hands of the framers. Taney did not confine his opinion to the question of black citizenship and Dred Scott's right to bring suit in federal court but proceeded to discuss the extent of congressional power over the territories. Congress, Taney insisted, had no power to prohibit slavery in the territories, and therefore the Missouri Compromise of 1820 was invalid. In so doing, the Court declared as illegitimate the organizing principle of the new Republican Party.

Dred Scott marked a major expansion of judicial review. Unlike the statute in *Marbury*, the invalidated act did not pertain to the judicial system nor contravene a seemingly unambiguous provision of the Constitution. Indeed, the Court ruled as it did even though the Constitution contained express authority in Article IV for Congress to legislate concerning "the Territory . . . belonging to the United States." By vetoing a major legislative policy, the bench forestalled future congressional efforts to deal with the foremost political issue of the day. *Dred Scott*, not *Marbury*, foreshadowed future controversies concerning the scope of judicial review. For Marshall's doctrine of constitutional supremacy, Taney substituted judicial supremacy.

Supreme Court Review of State Court Decisions. More important than judicial review of acts of Congress is the control federal courts exercise over state laws and court decisions. During the formative period of our history, it was of first importance to establish an effective barrier against state action hostile to the Constitution and the Union it created. Jefferson had voiced the hope "that some peaceable means should be contrived for the federal head to enforce compliance on the part of the States." The Philadelphia Convention delegates, keenly aware of the necessity of establishing external control over state action, suggested various limitations. One proposal gave Congress a negative on state laws; another provided for federal appointment of state governors and gave the general government a negative on state acts. All these were rejected. In its final form, "this Constitution" and the laws "made in pursuance thereof, and all treaties made, or which shall be made, under the authority of the United States," are declared by the supremacy clause in Article VI to be "the supreme law of the land; and the judges in every state are bound thereby, anything in the Constitution or laws of any State to the contrary notwithstanding." The first Congress, apparently believing that the purpose of the clause was to make the judiciary the final resort for all cases arising in the states, enacted **Section 25** of the Judiciary Act of 1789, authorizing the Supreme Court to pass on the validity of state legislation and to review decisions of state tribunals in cases where constitutional questions had been answered in favor of the state or adversely to national power. Though Section 25 recognized the important role that state courts might play in interpreting and applying the Constitution, federal law, and treaties, it had the effect of strengthening

Table 2.1 Statutes Invalidated by the U.S. Supreme Court

Period	Chief Justice	U.S. Statutes	State Statutes and Local Ordinances
1789–1800	Jay, Rutledge, Ellsworth	0	0
1801–1835	Marshall	1	19
1836–1864	Taney	1	21
1864–1873	Chase	8	34
1874–1888	Waite	8	66
1888–1910	Fuller	14	91
1910–1921	White	12	175
1921–1930	Taft	12	138
1930–1941	Hughes	14	92
1941–1946	Stone	2	27
1946–1953	Vinson	1	47
1953–1969	Warren	23	188
1969–1986	Burger	32	308
1986–2005	Rehnquist	36	146
2005–	Roberts	20	38

Data include decisions through May 2021.
Source: Congressional Research Service.

national power by making explicit a function of the Supreme Court left to inference in the Constitution itself.

The number of congressional acts invalidated has been comparatively small, fewer than 190 not counting the potentially broad swath cut by ***Immigration and Naturalization Service* v. *Chadha*** (see Chapter Three) on legislative vetoes found in several hundred congressional statutes. (See Table 2.1.) Quite otherwise has been the effect of judicial review of state action. Since 1810, when the Court overturned the first state act on constitutional grounds in *Fletcher* v. *Peck*, some 1,388 state laws and local ordinances have been struck down.

The tension between the doctrine of judicial review of congressional legislation and the need for effective government did not become a serious public issue until the last quarter of the nineteenth century. Prior to 1900 the Court had invoked its authority against Congress so sparingly that Justice Oliver Wendell Holmes could predict that "the United States would not come to an end if we lost our power to declare an Act of Congress void." But Holmes added, "I do think the Union would be imperiled if we could not make that declaration as to the laws of the several states. . . . [H]ow often a local policy prevails with those who are not trained to national views."

INFLUENCES ON JUDICIAL DECISION MAKING

Even though the Supreme Court was already firmly an active part of American government by the late 1800s, Justice Brewer maintained that judges "make no laws, establish no policy, never enter into the domain of popular action. They do not govern." Instead, "All the court does, or can do," Justice Owen J. Roberts declared in 1936, "is to announce its considered judgment. . . . The only power it has, if such it may be called, is the power of judgment. This court neither approves nor condemns any legislative policy." Yet, as Justice Holmes insisted with respect to one ruling in 1905, "This case is decided upon an economic theory which a large part of the country does not entertain." Through the years, Supreme Court justices have continued to profess detachment and value-free adjudication, but hardly ever without arousing incredulity. In its dual role of symbol and instrument of authority—temple and forum—the Supreme Court has always been confronted with the difficult task of reconciling the claim of judicial neutrality with the reality of individual discretion and political power. "We are not final because we are infallible, but we are infallible only because we are final," Justice Jackson observed with refreshing candor in 1953.

Such statements suggest that a polarity of factors—legal and political—may influence judicial decision making. Legal ingredients include, among others, the text of the Constitution and statutes, precedents construing the text, and procedural rules about standing and other matters that can determine preliminarily whether certain issues may even be raised by a litigant. Political ingredients include public opinion, the personal values of a justice—that is, his or her predilections—as well as a justice's beliefs about the Court's role in the governmental structure, conclusions about the opportunities and limitations of judicial power, and the dynamics of decision making within a small group like the Court.

Thus, some political scientists subscribe to a **legal model** of judicial decision making, so that where text and precedent are determinate—that is, clear and largely uncontroverted—legal factors will often dictate the decision unless truly powerful emanations from the political axis exist. Other political scientists find decisions better explained by an **attitudinal model**. To the degree that the law appears indeterminate—as is frequently true in constitutional adjudication where cases may engage open-ended passages involving "commerce" or "due process of law"—judges have more latitude, and so elements from the political axis, including personal policy preferences, may become more influential in the outcome of a case. Still others lean toward a **strategic model** that focuses on the importance of the collegial environment of the Court, where justices may seek to achieve certain goals not merely by voting their own preferences but by taking the views and behavior of colleagues as well as the Court's internal decision-making procedures into account.

CHECKS ON JUDICIAL POWER

Supreme Court justices and other federal judges enjoy substantial independence from outside political control. Thanks to the Constitution, they never face the voters in an election and may not have their salaries decreased by Congress. Yet while the Court is a potent institution in American government, it does not have unlimited power.

External Checks. Like the judges on the lower federal courts, Supreme Court justices are appointed for life—or during "good behavior," in the language of the Constitution. They may be impeached, but impeachment has proved in practice to be not even a "scarecrow," as Jefferson said. Indeed, the Senate has held no impeachment trial for a justice since the Jefferson administration sought unsuccessfully to have Samuel Chase removed from the bench in 1805. Nevertheless, the Court is subject to various other direct and indirect controls. For instance, the number of justices on the Court is set by act of Congress, not by the Constitution. Thus, the dramatic repudiation of its own decisions in 1937, on the heels of President Franklin Roosevelt's audacious Court-packing plan, contradicted Justice Stone's self-effacing dictum that "the only check upon our own exercise of power is our own sense of self-restraint." Although FDR's proposal failed of enactment, it was not without effect. Justice Owen J. Roberts told a congressional committee in 1954 that he had been "fully conscious of the tremendous strain and threat to the existing court" (see Chapter Six). Most recently, some Democrats, unhappy with the failure by Republicans to act on the Garland nomination in 2016 and then moving ahead with Justice Barrett's pre-election appointment following Justice Ginsburg's death in 2020, threatened in April 2021 to add four seats to the Court's roster, barely a week after President Biden created a 36-member commission to study possible changes to the Court and then to issue a report. (The Garland nomination and the Barrett appointment are discussed in the Introduction.) Furthermore, decisions on constitutional issues may be changed by constitutional amendment, as happened following the Income Tax Case of 1895 (see Chapter Seven). Decisions involving statutory interpretation can be altered by an act of Congress, as was done by the Lilly Ledbetter Fair Pay Act, the very first piece of legislation that Barack Obama signed into law after becoming president in 2009. This statute overturned *Ledbetter* v. *Goodyear* (2007), which barred claims under Title VII of the Civil Rights Act of 1964 that were not filed within 180 days of an employer's discriminatory action. Amending the law in 2009, Congress made clear that the 180-day statute of limitations for filing a pay discrimination suit resets with each new discriminatory paycheck.

As Chapter One explained, the Constitution expressly gives Congress control over the Court's appellate jurisdiction. That is, Congress determines what categories of cases qualify for appeal to the High Court from state courts and lower federal courts. To prevent the Court from passing on the constitutionality of the Reconstruction Acts, Congress denied the Court's jurisdiction in a case then pending (**Ex parte *McCardle***, 1869). Moreover, a president—if a vacancy arises—may change the voting balance within the Court through discerning appointments. Ours is "a government of laws and not of men" only in a qualified sense.

The Political Question Doctrine. One important historical check on judicial power has not been external, but one that the Court has placed upon itself. "If judges can open it [the Constitution] at all," Chief Justice Marshall asked in *Marbury* v. *Madison*, "what part of it are they forbidden to read or obey?" A self-disabling answer, at odds with Marshall's inference, was given in *Luther* v. *Borden* (1849), when Chief Justice Taney attempted for the first time to explain why a case raising a federal question might nonetheless be off limits to the federal courts. The litigation stemmed from the Dorr Rebellion of 1841–1842 in Rhode Island, in which rival factions both claimed to be the lawful government of the state. Luther was a participant in the rebellion against the state's old charter government; Borden was a member of the militia who had forcibly entered Luther's house under martial law. Article IV of the Constitution guarantees "to every State in this Union a Republican Form of government." Luther relied on this **guarantee** (or guaranty) **clause** to claim that the old charter government was not "Republican" and therefore illegitimate, making Borden's entry a trespass. In the Court's view, however, whether a state maintained a "Republican Form of government" lay "beyond [the judiciary's] appropriate sphere of action." The matter was "political" in that it must be resolved not by the judiciary but either by Congress through its seating of representatives from the state or by presidential acts in response to requests for assistance in suppressing domestic violence. The Court was "not to involve itself in discussions which properly belong to other forums." This posture is called the **political question doctrine**. Seemingly a misnomer because it suggests that other decisions are not political, the term is used in a specific sense to designate a type of controversy that is **nonjusticiable**. A political question is thus an issue the resolution of which belongs to one of the "political" branches of government (executive and legislative) and is, for that reason, inappropriate for judicial decision.

Accordingly, most decisions made by Congress and the executive concerning the international relations of the United States are considered "political" and binding on the Court. Another political question is determination of whether a state has properly ratified a proposed constitutional amendment (*Coleman* v. *Miller*, 1939). The Court has also refused to decide whether use by a state of initiative and referendum is in conflict with the guarantee clause (*Pacific States Tel. & Tel. Co.* v. *Oregon*, 1912). And for years the Court declined to intervene in lawsuits challenging population imbalances in legislative districts (*Colegrove* v. *Green*, 1946). "It is hostile to a democratic system to involve the judiciary in the politics of the people," warned Justice Felix Frankfurter. "And it is not less pernicious if such judicial intervention in an essentially political contest be dressed up in the abstract phrases of the law."

Ironically, the Court has come closest to articulating a formula identifying a political question in the act of deciding that legislative apportionment and districting are *not* out of judicial bounds. ***Baker* v. *Carr*** (in Chapter Five) held in 1962 that numerically unequal legislative districts may constitute a violation of the Fourteenth Amendment's equal protection clause and that federal courts could provide a remedy. The political question doctrine was no obstacle. "Prominent on the surface of any case held to involve a political question," explained Justice Brennan,

> is found a textually demonstrable constitutional commitment of the issue to a coordinate political department; or a lack of judicially discoverable and manageable standards for resolving it; or the impossibility of deciding without an initial policy determination of a kind clearly for nonjudicial discretion; or the impossibility of a court's undertaking independent resolution without expressing lack of the respect due coordinate branches of government; or an unusual need for unquestioning adherence to a political decision already made; or the potentiality of embarrassment from multifarious pronouncements by various departments on one question.

Even this taxonomy yields no touchstone for deciding precisely what is and what is not a political question. Justices disagree among themselves as to when this discretionary tool should be invoked. Some have favored use of this self-imposed limitation as a way of steering clear of "inconvenient" cases or those fraught with partisan controversy. Others have viewed it as a cowardly evasion of the Court's duty to provide peaceful solutions to any and all issues arising in a constitutional system.

FINALITY OF SUPREME COURT DECISIONS

Closely related to external and internal checks on judicial power is the question of the finality of Supreme Court decisions. Is constitutional interpretation a uniquely judicial responsibility? To what degree are constitutional decisions by the Supreme Court binding on the rest of the political system?

Even though Jefferson often impugned his nemesis John Marshall for abusing judicial power—"a crafty chief judge, who sophisticates the law to his mind, by the turn of his own reasoning," the third president once said—Jefferson himself never denied the authority of the Supreme Court to pass on the validity of acts of Congress in the course of deciding cases. But he did deny that such a decision was binding on the president in the performance of his purely executive function. As Jefferson explained in 1804:

> The judges, believing the [Sedition] law constitutional, had a right to pass a sentence of fine and imprisonment, because that power was placed in their hands by the Constitution. But the Executive, believing the law to be unconstitutional, was bound to remit the execution of it, because that power has been confided to him by the Constitution. That instrument meant that its coordinate branches should be checks on each other. But the opinion which gives to the judges the right to decide what laws are constitutional, and what not, not only for themselves in their own sphere of action, but for the legislative and Executive also in their spheres, would make the Judiciary a despotic branch.

Jefferson accepted the finality of judicial decisions in cases where their effects were primarily on the judiciary, as in *Marbury*; he rejected their binding effect on coordinate branches of the government. Other presidents (notably Jackson, Lincoln, both Roosevelts, Nixon, Reagan, Clinton, George W. Bush, Obama, and Trump) and Congress too have also on occasion refused to accept Supreme Court decisions as foreclosing further debate on the meaning of the Constitution. Their view is that all constitutional officers, not the justices alone, play a part in constitutional interpretation.

Is their position supported by the Constitution itself? Section 5 of the Fourteenth Amendment empowers Congress to "enforce, by appropriate legislation, the provisions of this article." Those "provisions" offer broad protections against infringement of individual rights by state governments that the Court has never defined in any fixed way. Relying on Section 5, one part of the Voting Rights Act of 1965 directed that no person be denied the right to vote because of an inability to read and write English if that person had completed the sixth grade in a Spanish-language school in Puerto Rico. The law effectively nullified New York's English-language literacy test, even though the Supreme Court had upheld the constitutionality of literacy tests against a challenge on Fourteenth Amendment grounds only six years earlier (*Lassiter* v. *Board of Elections*). In upholding the 1965 legislation, Justice Brennan explained in *Katzenbach* v. *Morgan* (1966) that Section 5 was "a positive grant of legislative power authorizing Congress to exercise its discretion in determining whether and what legislation is needed to secure the guarantees of the Fourteenth Amendment." Either Congress might have reasoned that enfranchised Puerto Ricans would now be able to fight discrimination or, Brennan continued, Congress might have concluded that the English-language literacy test itself violated the amendment, despite the Court's stated position to the contrary. The first basis was remedial; the second basis was declaratory, elevating Congress to the role of constitutional expositor within the Fourteenth Amendment domain.

Some commentators claimed that *Morgan* stood *Marbury* on its head. Justice John Harlan declared later that "Congress' expression of [its] view . . . cannot displace the duty of this Court to make an independent determination whether Congress has exceeded its powers." To give Congress a free hand in construing the Fourteenth would contradict the "structure of the constitutional system itself" by allowing Congress effectively to amend the Constitution by a simple majority vote and the president's signature.

Controversy over Section 5 persists. Since 1940 the Supreme Court has agreed that the Fourteenth Amendment's due process clause "incorporates" within its meaning the First Amendment's guarantee of free exercise of religion. As will be explained further in Chapter Twelve, the Supreme Court in 1963 expanded the protections of the free exercise clause, requiring state and federal governments in many circumstances to grant religiously based exemptions in the application of otherwise valid laws that inhibited religious practice (***Sherbert* v. *Verner***). In 1990, however, the Court did a near about-face on its interpretation of the clause, announcing that when a law of general application conflicted with religious practice, the former would prevail (***Employment Division* v. *Smith***). In 1993, Congress responded with enactment of the **Religious Freedom Restoration Act** (RFRA), directing with its Section 5 powers that the free exercise clause meant what the Court deemed it to mean in 1963 (and arguably even more), not what the Court judged it to mean in 1990.

A test of RFRA soon materialized, and in ***City of Boerne* v. *Flores*** the Court invalidated the statute 6–3 as applied to *state* governments. Laudable though its objectives were, Congress had exceeded its constitutional authority. Conspicuously, the dissenting opinions took issue less with the Court's conclusion about Congress and Section 5 and more with the 1990 decision shrinking the free exercise clause. As a result, congressional power under *Morgan* survives only insofar as it is remedial, not declaratory. Yet, the Court remains willing to apply RFRA to congressional policies, as *Burwell* v. *Hobby Lobby Stores, Inc.* (2014) demonstrates. Concluding that RFRA applies not only to individuals but to closely held for-profit corporations, five justices allowed a religiously based exemption from the contraception mandate for employers under the Affordable Care Act. Excerpts from *City of Boerne* precede an "unstaged debate" on the finality of Supreme Court decisions at the end of this chapter.

APPROACHES TO CONSTITUTIONAL INTERPRETATION

A long-standing consensus that the Supreme Court is the chief if not the only expositor of the Constitution dissolves over the question of how judges are supposed to interpret the Constitution. The answer to this question partly determines the values the Constitution protects.

What Is "the Constitution"? There is first the matter of what is interpreted. To say that the answer is obvious, that the court interprets the Constitution, merely presumes a consensus on what "the Constitution" includes. One might suppose that it includes at least the text of the document of 1787, as amended. But even such a conventional statement needs qualification. The Constitution may be less than the text. There are, after all, parts of the text (the privileges and immunities clause of the Fourteenth Amendment or the guarantee clause, for instance) that the Court has largely neglected or forsworn. Moreover, tension exists between some provisions of the text. Chapter Twelve, for example, grapples with how one satisfies fully the First Amendment safeguards of both free exercise (freedom *for* religion) and nonestablishment (freedom *from* religion).

The Constitution may also encompass *more* than the document because judges may seek its meaning apart from the text itself. One justice may turn to the intent of those who drafted and ratified its provisions. Another might look to documents of the period that describe the kind of system the framers established. In speaking of "liberty" and the "consent of the governed," the Declaration of Independence certainly anticipated constitutional government to cure the evils of unchecked power.

Moreover, as did Justice Kennedy in *Roper* v. *Simmons* (2005), which invalidated state laws allowing the execution of juvenile offenders who were older than 15 but younger than 18 when they committed a capital crime (see Chapter Ten), members of the Court will sometimes refer to foreign and international law in construing the U.S. Constitution, although hardly ever without provoking strong objection from one or more other justices. The Court "should not," Justice Thomas insists, "impose foreign moods, fads, or fashions on Americans."

Should custom count as part of the Constitution? "Long settled and established practice is a consideration of great weight in a proper interpretation of constitutional provisions," the Court noted in 1919. Similarly, in ***Youngstown Sheet and Tube Co. v. Sawyer*** in 1952 (see Chapter Three), Justice Frankfurter argued that

> a systematic, unbroken, executive practice, long pursued in the knowledge of Congress and never before questioned, engaged in by Presidents who have also sworn to uphold the Constitution, making as it were such exercise of power part of the structure of our government, may be treated as a gloss on the "executive power" vested in the President. . . .

Sometimes interpretations of the Constitution become almost inseparable from the text. One thinks of judicial review itself, nowhere in the document expressly authorized for the Supreme Court but widely regarded today as an essential component of the "judicial power."

Deciding what the Constitution includes is therefore an important starting point for interpretation. Then one must consider the method to be used. Four of the most common approaches judges employ in constitutional interpretation include clear meaning, adaptation, original intent, and structuralism. These methods, however, are not mutually exclusive categories. More than one may appear in a single opinion.

Clear Meaning. For some, constitutional interpretation is a mechanical process, much like a sales clerk measuring fabric. "When an act of Congress is appropriately challenged in the courts as not conforming to constitutional mandate," explained Justice Roberts in ***United States v. Butler*** (1936), "the judicial branch of the Government has only one duty—to lay the article of the Constitution which is invoked beside the statute which is challenged and to decide whether the latter squares with the former." (As will be seen in Chapter Seven, Justice Roberts seemed oblivious to the fact that three of his colleagues had performed this "squaring" and had reached the opposite conclusion.) Approached in this way, the Constitution speaks for itself; the words emit clear meaning. The judge's task is to point out what is plainly there. John Jay seemed to suggest as much at the New York ratifying convention. The meaning of the Constitution would involve "no sophistry, no construction, no false glosses, but simple inferences from the obvious operation of things." Of course, some parts of the Constitution do have a clear meaning. The president's term is four years, a senator's six. Yet these are rarely, if ever, involved in litigation. More common and more troublesome are open ended provisions such as the "commerce" that Article I empowers Congress to regulate (see Chapter Six) and the "speech" that the First Amendment protects (see Chapter Eleven).

Adaptation. Even judges who sometimes rest on the Constitution's clear meaning will also employ adaptation. The judge reasons from the Constitution by first identifying principles or values the Constitution contains and then applying them to contemporary circumstances. As much as any other, this method, sometimes also called the "living Constitution" approach, enables the Court to accommodate the

Constitution to situations and problems the framers did not foresee, yet it opens the Court to charges that it has engaged in "lawmaking." A variation on adaptation resembles *majoritarianism*, meaning that judges construe the Constitution's limits to permit most policies the dominant opinion of the day deems necessary or desirable.

Original Intent. As this approach developed particularly in the 1980s, advocates searched for what drafters of a provision intended it to mean. More recently, originalists, who may have drawn some guidance from James Madison's admonition reprinted below, look for the original public meaning of a provision: what the words meant to the people of that day. Once ascertained, this meaning represents the supreme will of the people, which is the only authority by which a judge may invalidate an action taken by the people's representatives. Anything else amounts to lawmaking by judges and is illegitimate. This method thus combines historicity with contemporary application: applying what may be a very old principle to a current situation or issue. For some advocates of original intent, such as former Judge Robert Bork, the absence of an ascertainable intent is not an invitation for judges to create one but a reason for them to defer to the elected branches so that the people's will might prevail.

Perhaps relevant to the debate over interpretive approaches is the fact that the framers themselves had mixed feelings on publication of the record of their work. The official *Journal* of the Convention, which was entrusted to George Washington at the close of business in 1787 but which contains only the barest account of what transpired in Philadelphia, was not published until 1819—three decades after government under the Constitution began. James Madison's notes, the single most complete record of the Convention, were not published until 1840, four years after his death. "As a guide in expounding and applying the provisions of the Constitution," Madison wrote Virginia journalist Thomas Ritchie in 1821,

> the debates and incidental decisions of the Convention can have no authoritative character. . . . [T]he legitimate meaning of the Instrument must be derived from the text itself; or if a key is to be sought elsewhere, it must be not in the opinions or intentions of the Body which planned & proposed the Constitution, but in the sense attached to it by the people in their respective State Conventions where it rec[eive]d all the authority which it possesses.

The strengths and weaknesses of original intent are explored in the "unstaged debate" between Judge Bork and Professor Laurence Tribe later in this chapter.

Structuralism. Some cases are decided on principles drawn not so much from the words of single passages but from the design or framework the Constitution establishes or from the relation of one clause to another. Chief Justice Marshall's opinion in *Marbury* v. *Madison* is an example of structuralism at work. Examining the system of limited government created by the Constitution, Marshall found the basis of judicial review. Structuralism also lies at the heart of separation-of-powers decisions like ***Morrison* v. *Olson*** (1988), in Chapter Three.

With any interpretative approach, judges have considerable leeway. Agreement on the method to be used by no means assures agreement on the outcome in individual cases. Because it is the Constitution that is being applied, judges do something more than merely interpret its written provisions. The justices not only formulate the principles that govern the federal system and the relations of Congress, Court, and president; they sit in judgment on the policy that controls the social and economic life of the nation. There are limits to judicial review, to be sure, but many seem largely self-imposed. "Government by judiciary" is no idle phrase when applied to the politics of the United States.

JUDICIAL REVIEW: A DISTINCTIVELY AMERICAN CONTRIBUTION

The pervasiveness of judicial power is now one of the most conspicuous aspects of the American political system. It is hard to think of a feature of life left untouched by the Court's decrees. Its docket reads like a policy agenda for the nation. "The restraining power of the judiciary does not manifest its chief worth," Benjamin Cardozo observed, "in the few cases in which the legislature has gone beyond the lines that mark the limits of discretion." Its primary value has been in "making vocal and audible the ideals that might otherwise be silenced. . . ." Had this not been so, a document framed in the context of an agrarian country and largely unamended except by constitutional interpretation could not serve the expanding needs of government in a complex technological society.

In the Virginia ratifying convention of 1788, John Marshall envisioned judicial review as an alternative to revolution. "What is the service or purpose of a judiciary but to execute the laws in a peaceful, orderly manner, without shedding blood, or creating a contest, or availing yourselves of force?" Madison reinforced Marshall:

> A political system that does not provide for a peaceable and effectual decision of all controversies arising among the parties is not a Government, but a mere Treaty between independent nations, without any resort for terminating disputes but negotiations, and that failing, the sword.

Failure to lodge this power in the federal judiciary, he added in 1832, "would be as much a mockery as a scabbard put into the hands of a soldier without a sword in it."

Applying standards drawn from the Constitution, the Court is the ultimate guardian of individual rights and governmental prerogative alike. "The people have seemed to feel that the Supreme Court, whatever its defects," Justice Jackson concluded, "is still the most detached, dispassionate, and trustworthy custodian that our system affords for the translation of abstract into concrete constitutional commands." It is, Woodrow Wilson observed, "the balance-wheel of our entire system." Thanks largely to the Supreme Court, the Constitution has been more than "a mere lawyer's document." It has been "a vehicle of the nation's life." The justices have become keepers of American constitutional values. That reality is a source of and limit on their power.

KEY TERMS

constitutionalism
separation of powers
federalism
free government
political checks
judicial review
supremacy clause
writ of mandamus
Section 25
legal model
attitudinal model
strategic model
guarantee (or guaranty) clause
political question doctrine
nonjusticiable
Religious Freedom Restoration Act

QUERIES

1. Was *Marbury* v. *Madison* a usurpation of power by the Supreme Court? What did John Marshall mean when he insisted that the absence of judicial review would "subvert the very foundations of all written constitutions"?

2. Members of the contemporary Court will sometimes look to foreign courts or international bodies as authorities or guides in interpreting the Constitution. Is this appropriate? Should it matter that judges on courts abroad are not appointed by the president and confirmed by the Senate and that such judges do not take an oath of loyalty to the U.S. Constitution?

3. Constitutional scholars widely regard *Dred Scott* not only as a consequential decision but also as the worst decision ever rendered by the Supreme Court. Why?

4. On what points are Robert Yates ("Letters of Brutus") and Alexander Hamilton (*The Federalist*, No. 78) in agreement? Where do they disagree? Does Yates overstate the dangers to popular government posed by judicial power? Does Hamilton understate them? What are the safeguards against abuse of judicial power?

SELECTED READINGS

Corwin, Edward S. *The Doctrine of Judicial Review*. Gloucester, MA: Peter Smith, 1963; reissue of 1914 edition, published by Princeton University Press.

Fisher, Louis. *Reconsidering Judicial Finality: Why the Supreme Court Is Not the Last Word on the Constitution*. Lawrence: University Press of Kansas, 2019.

Graber, Mark A. "The Nonmajoritarian Difficulty: Legislative Deference to the Judiciary." *7 Studies in American Political Development* 35, 1993.

Greenawalt, Kent. *Interpreting the Constitution*. New York: Oxford University Press, 2015.

Maltz, Earl M. *Dred Scott and the Politics of Slavery*. Lawrence: University Press of Kansas, 2007.

Murphy, Walter F. *Constitutional Democracy*. Baltimore, MD: Johns Hopkins University Press, 2006.

Scalia, Antonin, and Bryan A. Garner. *Reading Law: The Interpretation of Legal Texts*. St. Paul, MN: Thomson/West, 2012.

Seddig, Robert G. "John Marshall and the Origins of Supreme Court Leadership." *36 University of Pittsburgh Law Review 785*, 1975; reprinted in *Journal of Supreme Court History* 63, 1991.

Sloan, Cliff, and David McKean. *The Great Decision: Jefferson, Adams, Marshall and the Battle for the Supreme Court*. New York: Public Affairs, 2009.

Snowiss, Sylvia. *Judicial Review and the Law of the Constitution*. New Haven, CT: Yale University Press, 1990.

Waltman, Jerold. *Congress, The Supreme Court, and Religious Liberty: The Case of City of Boerne v. Flores*. New York: Palgrave Macmillan, 2013.

Whittington, Keith E. *Repugnant Laws: Judicial Review of Acts of Congress from the Founding to the Present*. Lawrence: University Press of Kansas, 2019.

I. ESTABLISHING AND TESTING JUDICIAL REVIEW

Unstaged Debate of 1788: Robert Yates v. Alexander Hamilton

Robert Yates, *Letters of Brutus*[1]

No. XI
31 January 1788

. . . Much has been said and written upon the subject of this new system on both sides, but I have not met with any writer, who has discussed the judicial powers with any degree of accuracy. . . . The real effect of this system of government will therefore be brought home to the feelings of the people through the medium of the judicial power. It is, moreover, of great importance, to examine with care the nature and extent of the judicial power, because those who are to be vested with it, are to be placed in a situation altogether unprecedented in a free country. They are to be rendered totally independent, both of the people and the legislature, both with respect to their offices and salaries. No errors they may commit can be corrected by any power above them, if any such power there be, nor can they be removed from office for making ever so many erroneous adjudications.

The only causes for which they can be displaced, is, conviction of treason, bribery, and high crimes and misdemeanors.

This part of the plan is so modelled, as to authorize the courts, not only to carry into execution the powers expressly given, but where these are wanting or ambiguously expressed, to supply what is wanting by their own decisions. . . .

They [the courts] will give the sense of every article of the constitution, that may from time to time come before them. And in their decisions they will not confine themselves to any fixed or established rules, but will determine, according to what appears to them, the reason and spirit of the constitution. The opinions of the supreme court, whatever they may be, will have the force of law, because there is no power provided in the constitution, that can correct their errors, or control their adjudications. From this court there is no appeal. And I conceive the legislature themselves, cannot set aside a judgment of this court, because they are authorized by the constitution to decide in the last resort. The legislature must be controlled by the constitution, and not the constitution by them. They have therefore no more right to set aside any judgment pronounced upon the construction of the constitution, than they have to take from the president, the chief command of the army and navy, and commit it to some other person. The reason is plain; the judicial and executive derive their authority from the same source, that the legislature do theirs; and therefore in all cases, where the constitution does not make the one responsible to, or controllable by the other, they are altogether independent of each other.

The judicial power will operate to effect, in the most certain, but yet silent and imperceptible manner, what is evidently the tendency of the constitution:—I mean, an entire subversion of the legislative, executive and judicial powers of the individual states. Every adjudication of the supreme court, on any question that may arise upon the nature and extent of the general government, will affect the limits of the state jurisdiction. In proportion as the former enlarge the exercise of their powers, will that of the latter be restricted.

That the judicial power of the United States, will lean strongly in favor of the general government, it will give such an explanation to the constitution, as will favour an extension of its jurisdiction, is very evident from a variety of considerations.

1st. The constitution itself strongly countenances such a mode of construction. Most of the articles in this system, which convey powers of any considerable importance, are conceived in general and indefinite terms, which are either equivocal, ambiguous, or which require long definitions to unfold the extent of their meaning. . . . The clause which vests the power to pass all laws which are proper and necessary, to carry the powers given into execution . . . leaves the legislature at liberty, to do every thing, which in their judgment is best. . . . in this situation will generally soon feel themselves independent of heaven itself. . . .

2d. Not only will the constitution justify the courts in inclining to this mode of explaining it, but they will be interested in using this latitude of interpretation. Every body of men invested with office are tenacious of power; they feel interested, and hence it has become a kind of maxim, to hand down their offices, with all its rights and privileges, unimpaired to their successors; the same principle will influence them to extend their power, and increase their rights; this of itself will operate strongly upon the courts to give such a meaning to the constitution in all cases where it can possibly be done, as will enlarge the sphere of their own authority. . . .

3d. Because they will have precedent to plead, to justify them in it. It is well known, that the courts in England, have by their own authority, extended their jurisdiction far beyond the limits set them in their original institution, and by the laws of the land. . . .

This power in the judicial, will enable them to mould the government, into almost any shape they please. . . .

No. XV
20 March 1788

I do not object to the judges holding their commissions during good behavior. I suppose it a proper provision provided they were made properly responsible. But I say, this system has followed the English government in this, while it has departed from almost every other principle of their jurisprudence, under the idea, of rendering the judges independent; which, in the British constitution, means no more than that they hold their places during good behavior, and have fixed salaries, they have made the judges independent, in the fullest sense of the word. There is no power above them, to control any of their decisions. There is no authority that can remove them, and they cannot be controlled by the laws of the legislature. In short, they are independent of the people, of the legislature, and of every power under heaven. Men placed in this situation will generally soon feel themselves independent of heaven itself. . . .

The supreme court then have a right, independent of the legislature, to give a construction of the constitution and every part of it, and there is no power provided in this system to correct their construction or do it away. If, therefore, the legislature pass any laws, inconsistent with the sense the judges put upon the constitution, they will declare it void; and therefore in this respect their power is superior to that of the legislature. . . .

Had the construction of the constitution been left with the legislature, they would have explained it at their peril; if they exceeded their powers, or sought to find, in the spirit of the constitution, more than was expressed in the letter, the people from whom they derived their power could remove them, and do themselves right; and indeed I can see no other remedy that the people can have against their rulers for encroachments of this nature. A constitution is a compact of a people with their rulers; if the rulers break the compact, the people have a right and ought to remove them and do themselves justice; but in order to enable them to do this with the greater facility, those whom the people choose at stated periods, should have the power in the last resort to determine the sense of the compact; if they determine contrary to the understanding of the people, an appeal will lie to the people at the period when the rulers are to be elected, and they will have it in their power to remedy the evil; but when this power is lodged in the hands of men independent of the people, and of their representatives, and who are not, constitutionally, accountable for their opinions, no way is left to control them but with a high hand and an outstretched arm.

Alexander Hamilton's Reply to Brutus: *The Federalist*, No. 78[2]

We proceed now to an examination of the judiciary department of the proposed government. . . .

Whoever attentively considers the different departments of power must perceive, that, in a government in which they are separated from each other, the judiciary, from the nature of its functions, will always be the least dangerous to the political rights of the Constitution; because it will be least in a capacity to annoy or injure them. . . . The judiciary . . . has no influence over either the sword or the purse; no direction either of the strength or of the wealth of the society; and can take no active resolution whatever. It may truly be said to have neither FORCE nor WILL, but merely judgment; and must ultimately depend upon the aid of the executive arm even for the efficacy of its judgments.

This simple view of the matter suggests several important consequences. It proves incontestably, that the judiciary is beyond comparison the weakest of the three departments of power; that it can never attack with success either of the other two; and that all possible care is requisite to enable it to defend itself against their attacks. It equally proves, that though individual oppression may now and then proceed from the courts of justice, the general liberty of the people can never be endangered from that quarter; I mean so long as the judiciary remains truly distinct from both the legislature and the Executive. . . .

Some perplexity respecting the right of courts to pronounce legislative acts void, because contrary to the Constitution, has arisen from an imagination that the doctrine would imply a superiority of the judiciary to the legislative power. It is urged that the authority which can declare the acts of another void, must necessarily be superior to the one whose acts may be declared void. As this doctrine is of great importance in all the American constitutions, a brief discussion of the ground on which it rests cannot be unacceptable.

There is no position which depends on clearer principles, than that every act of a delegated authority, contrary to the tenor of the commission under which it is exercised, is void. No legislative act, therefore, contrary to the Constitution, can be valid. To deny this, would be to affirm, that the deputy is greater than his principal; that the servant is above his master; that the representatives of the people are superior to the people themselves; that men acting by virtue of powers, may do not only what their powers do not authorize, but what they forbid.

If it be said that the legislative body are themselves the constitutional judges of their own powers, and that the construction they put upon them is conclusive upon the other departments, it may be answered, that this cannot be the natural presumption, where it is not to be collected from any particular provisions in the Constitution. It is not otherwise to be supposed, that the Constitution could intend to enable the representatives of the people to substitute their will to that of their constituents. It is far more rational to suppose, that the courts were designed to be an intermediate body between the people and the legislature, in order, among other things, to keep the latter within the limits assigned to their authority. The interpretation of the laws is the proper and peculiar province of the courts. A constitution is, in fact, and must be regarded by the judges, as a fundamental law. It therefore belongs to them to ascertain its meaning, as well as the meaning of any particular act proceeding from the legislative body. If there should happen to be an irreconcilable variance between the two, that which has the superior obligation and validity ought, of course, to be preferred; or, in other words, the Constitution ought to be preferred to the statute, the intention of the people to the intention of their agents.

Nor does this conclusion by any means suppose a superiority of the judicial to the legislative power. It only supposes that the power of the people is superior to both; and that where the will of the legislature, declared in its statutes, stands in opposition to that of the people, declared in the Constitution, the judges ought to be governed by the latter rather than the former. They ought to regulate their decisions by the fundamental laws, rather than by those which are not fundamental. . . .

If, then, the courts of justice are to be considered as the bulwarks of a limited Constitution against legislative encroachments, this consideration will afford a strong argument for the permanent tenure of judicial offices, since nothing will contribute so much as this to that independent spirit in the judges which must be essential to the faithful performance of so arduous a duty. laws is one of the inconveniences necessarily connected with the advantages of a free government. To avoid an arbitrary discretion in the courts, it is indispensable that they should be bound down by strict rules and precedents, which serve to define and point out their duty in every particular case that comes before them; and it will readily be conceived from the variety of controversies which grow out of the folly and wickedness of mankind, that the records of those precedents must unavoidably swell to a very considerable bulk, and must demand long and laborious study to acquire a competent knowledge of them. Hence it is, that there can be but few men in the society who will have sufficient skill in the laws to qualify them for the stations of judges. And making the proper deductions for the ordinary depravity of human nature, the number must be still smaller of those who unite the requisite integrity with the requisite knowledge. These considerations apprise us, that the government can have no great option between fit character; and that a temporary duration in office, which would naturally discourage such characters from quitting a lucrative line of practice to accept a seat on the bench, would have a tendency to throw the administration of justice into hands less able, and less well qualified, to conduct it with utility and dignity. . . .

This independence of the judges is equally requisite to guard the Constitution and the rights of individuals from the effects of those ill humors, which the arts of designing men, or the influence of particular conjectures, sometimes disseminate among the people themselves, and which, though they speedily give place to better information, and more deliberate reflection, have a tendency, in the meantime, to occasion dangerous innovations in the government, and serious oppressions of the minor party in the community. . . .

But it is not with a view to infractions of the Constitution only, that the independence of the judges may be an essential safeguard against the effects of occasional ill humors in the society. These sometimes extend no farther than to the injury of the private rights of particular classes of citizens, by unjust and partial laws. Here also the firmness of the judicial magistracy is of vast importance in mitigating the severity and confining the operation of such laws. . . .

There is yet a further and a weightier reason for the permanency of the judicial offices, which is deducible from the nature of the qualifications they require. It has been frequently remarked, with great propriety, that a voluminous code of laws is one of the inconveniences necessarily connected with the advantages of a free government. To avoid an arbitrary discretion in the courts, it is indispensable that they should be bound down by strict rules and precedents, which serve to define and point out their duty in every particular case that comes before them; and it will readily be conceived from the variety of controversies which grow out of the folly and wickedness of mankind, that the records of those precedents must unavoidably swell to a very considerable bulk, and must demand long and laborious study to acquire a competent knowledge of them. Hence it is, that there can be but few men in the society who will have sufficient skill in the laws to qualify them for the stations of judges. And making the proper deductions for the ordinary depravity of human nature, the number must be still smaller of those who unite the requisite integrity with the requisite knowledge. These considerations apprise us, that the government can have no great option between fit character; and that a temporary duration in office, which would naturally discourage such characters from quitting a lucrative line of practice to accept a seat on the bench, would have a tendency to throw the administration of justice into hands less able, and less well qualified, to conduct it with utility and dignity. . . .

Marbury v. *Madison*
5 U.S. (1 Cranch) 137, 2 L.Ed. 60 (1803)

http://supct.law.cornell.edu/supct/cases/name.htm#Case_Name-M

Several weeks before the end of his term, President John Adams nominated William Marbury and others to be justices of the peace in the District of Columbia. Their nominations were confirmed and commissions signed by the president, but the secretary of state, John Marshall, had not delivered them by the time Thomas Jefferson became president on March 4, 1801. Jefferson's new secretary of state, James Madison, refused to deliver the commissions of Marbury and three others, claiming that delivery was necessary to complete the appointments. The four men asked the Supreme Court to issue a writ of mandamus ordering delivery under its original jurisdiction as authorized by Section 13 of the Judiciary Act of 1789. Mandamus was not sought from lower federal courts. Majority: Marshall, Chase, Paterson, Washington. Not participating: Cushing, Moore.

The opinion of the court was delivered by the Chief Justice [Marshall]. . . .

The first object of inquiry is—Has the applicant a right to the commission he demands? . . .

It is . . . decidedly the opinion of the court, that when a commission has been signed by the president, the appointment is made; and that the commission is complete, when the seal of the United States has been affixed to it by the secretary of state. . . .

Mr. Marbury, then, since his commission was signed by the president, and sealed by the secretary of state, was appointed; and as the law creating the office, gave the officer a right to hold for five years, independent of the executive, the appointment was not revocable, but vested in the officer legal rights, which are protected by the laws of his country. To withhold his commission, therefore, is an act deemed by the court not warranted by law, but violative of a vested legal right.

This brings us to the second inquiry; which is: If he has a right, and that right has been violated, do the laws of this country afford him a remedy? . . .

The very essence of civil liberty certainly consists in the right of every individual to claim the protection of the laws, whenever he receives an injury. One of the first duties of government is to afford that protection. . . . The government of the United States has been emphatically termed a government of laws, and not of men. It will certainly cease to deserve this high appellation, if the laws furnish no remedy for the violation of a vested legal right. . . .

By the constitution . . ., the president is invested with certain important political powers, in the exercise of which he is to use his own discretion, and is accountable only to his country in his political character, and to his own conscience. To aid him in the performance of these duties, he is authorized to appoint certain officers, who act by his authority, and in conformity with his orders. In such cases, their acts are his acts; and whatever opinion may be entertained of the manner in which executive discretion may be used, still there exists, and can exist, no power to control that discretion. The subjects are political; they respect the nation, not individual rights, and being entrusted to the executive, the decision of the executive is conclusive. . . .

The conclusion from this reasoning is, that where the heads of departments are the political or confidential agents of the executive, merely to execute the will of the president, or rather to act in cases in which the executive possesses a constitutional or legal discretion, nothing can be more perfectly clear, than that their acts are only politically examinable. But where a specific duty is assigned by law, and individual rights depend upon the performance of that duty, it seems equally clear, that the individual who considers himself injured, has a right to resort to the laws of his country for a remedy. . . .

The question whether a right has vested or not, is in its nature, judicial, and must be tried by the judicial authority. . . .

It is, then, the opinion of the Court: 1st. That . . . the appointment conferred on him a legal right to the office for the space of five years. 2d. That, having this legal title to the office, he has a consequent right to the commission; a refusal to deliver which is a plain violation of that right, for which the laws of his country afford him a remedy.

It remains to be inquired whether he is entitled to the remedy for which he applies [the writ of mandamus]. This depends on 1st. The nature of the writ applied for; and 2d. The power of this court.

1st . . . This, then, is a plain case for a *mandamus*, either to deliver the commission, or a copy of it from the record; and it only remains to be inquired, whether it can issue from this court.

The act to establish the judicial courts of the United States authorizes the supreme court "to issue writs of *mandamus*, in cases warranted by the principles and usages of law, to any courts appointed, or persons holding office, under the authority of the United States." . . . The constitution vests the whole judicial power of the United States in one supreme court, and such inferior courts as congress shall, from time to time, ordain and establish. This power is expressly extended to all cases arising under the laws of the United States; and consequently, in some form, may be exercised over the present case; because the right claimed is given by a law of the United States.

In the distribution of this power, it is declared, that "the supreme court shall have original jurisdiction, in all cases affecting ambassadors, other public ministers and consuls, and those in which a state shall be a party. In all other cases, the supreme court shall have appellate jurisdiction." . . . If it had been intended to leave it in the discretion of the legislature, to apportion the judicial power between the supreme and inferior courts, according to the will of that body, it would certainly have been useless to have proceeded further than to have defined the judicial power, and the tribunals in which it should be vested. The subsequent part of the section is mere surplusage—is entirely without meaning, if such is to be the construction. If congress remains at liberty to give this court appellate jurisdiction, where the constitution has declared their jurisdiction shall be original; and original jurisdiction where the constitution has declared it shall be appellate; the distribution of jurisdiction, made in the constitution, is form without substance. . . . To enable this court, then, to issue a *mandamus*, it must be shown to be an exercise of appellate jurisdiction, or to be necessary to enable them to exercise appellate jurisdiction. . . . It is the essential criterion of appellate jurisdiction, that it revises and corrects the proceedings in a cause already instituted, and does not create that cause. Although therefore, a *mandamus* may be directed to courts, yet to issue such a writ to an officer, for the delivery of a paper, is, in effect, the same as to sustain an original action for that paper, and therefore, seems not to belong to appellate, but to original jurisdiction. Neither is it necessary in such a case as this to enable the court to exercise its appellate jurisdiction. The authority, therefore, given to the supreme court, by the act establishing the judicial courts of the United States, to issue writs of *mandamus* to public officers, appears not to be warranted by the constitution; and it becomes necessary to inquire whether a jurisdiction so conferred can be exercised.

The question, whether an act, repugnant to the constitution, can become the law of the land, is a question deeply interesting to the United States: but, happily, not of an intricacy proportioned to its interest. It seems only necessary to recognize certain principles, supposed to have been long and well established, to decide it. That the people have an original right to establish, for their future government, such principles as, in their opinion, shall most conduce to their own happiness, is the basis on which the whole American fabric has been erected. The exercise of this original right is a very great exertion; nor can it, nor ought it, to be frequently repeated. The principles, therefore, so established, are deemed fundamental: and as the authority from which they proceed is supreme, and can seldom act, they are designed to be permanent.

This original and supreme will organizes the government, and assigns to different departments their respective powers. It may either stop here, or establish certain limits not to be transcended by those departments. The government of the United States is of the latter description. The powers of the legislature are defined and limited; and that those limits may not be mistaken, or forgotten, the constitution is written. To what purpose are powers limited, and to what purpose is that limitation committed to writing, if these limits may, at any time, be passed by those intended to be restrained? The distinction between a government with limited and unlimited powers is abolished, if those limits do not confine the persons on whom they are imposed, and if acts prohibited and acts allowed, are of equal obligation. It is a proposition too plain to be contested, that the constitution controls any legislative act repugnant to it; or, that the legislature may alter the constitution by an ordinary act.

Between these alternatives, there is no middle ground. The constitution is either a superior paramount law, unchangeable by ordinary means, or it is on a level with ordinary legislative acts, and, like other acts, is alterable when the legislature shall please to alter it. If the former part of the alternative be true, then a legislative act, contrary to the constitution, is not law; if the latter part be true, then written constitutions are absurd attempts, on the part of the people, to limit a power, in its own nature, illimitable.

Certainly, all those who have framed written constitutions contemplate them as forming the fundamental and paramount law of the nation, and consequently, the theory of every such government must be, that an act of the legislature, repugnant to the constitution, is void.

This theory is essentially attached to a written constitution, and is, consequently, to be considered, by this court, as one of the fundamental principles of our society. It is not, therefore, to be lost sight of, in the further consideration of this subject.

If an act of the legislature, repugnant to the constitution, is void, does it, notwithstanding its invalidity, bind the courts, and oblige them to give it effect? Or, in other words, though it be not law, does it constitute a rule as operative as if it was a law? This would be to overthrow, in fact, what was established in theory; and would seem, at first view, an absurdity too gross to be insisted on. It shall, however, receive a more attentive consideration.

It is, emphatically, the province and duty of the judicial department, to say what the law is. Those who apply the rule to particular cases, must of necessity expound and interpret that rule. If two laws conflict with each other, the courts must decide on the operation of each. So, if a law be in opposition to the constitution; if both the law and the constitution apply to a particular case, so that the court must either decide that case, conformably to the law, disregarding the constitution; or conformably to the constitution, disregarding the law; the court must determine which of these conflicting rules governs the case: this is of the very essence of judicial duty. If then, the courts are to regard the constitution, and the constitution is superior to any ordinary act of the legislature, the constitution, and not such ordinary act, must govern the case to which they both apply.

Those, then, who controvert the principle, that the constitution is to be considered, in court, as a paramount law, are reduced to the necessity of maintaining that courts must close their eyes on the constitution, and see only the law. This doctrine would subvert the very foundation of all written constitutions. It would declare that an act which, according to the principles and theory of our government, is entirely void, is yet, in practice, completely obligatory. It would declare, that if the legislature shall do what is expressly forbidden, such act, notwithstanding the express prohibition, is in reality effectual. It would be giving to the legislature a practical and real omnipotence, with the same breath which professes to restrict their powers within narrow limits. It is prescribing limits, and declaring that those limits may be passed at pleasure. That it thus reduces to nothing, what we have deemed the greatest improvement on political institutions, a written constitution, would, of itself, be sufficient, in America, where written constitutions have been viewed with so much reverence, for rejecting the construction. But the peculiar expressions of the constitution of the United States furnish additional arguments in favor of its rejection. The judicial power of the United States is extended to all cases arising under the constitution. Could it be the intention of those who gave this power, to say, that in using it, the constitution should not be looked into? That a case arising under the constitution should be decided, without examining the instrument under which it arises? This is too extravagant to be maintained. In some cases, then, the constitution must be looked into by the judges. And if they can open it at all, what part of it are they forbidden to read or to obey?

There are many other parts of the constitution which serve to illustrate this subject. It is declared, that "no tax or duty shall be laid on articles exported from any state." Suppose, a duty on the export of cotton, of tobacco, or of flour; and a suit instituted to recover it. Ought judgment to be rendered in such a case? Ought the judges to close their eyes on the constitution, and only see the law?

The constitution declares "that no bill of attainder or *ex post facto* law shall be passed." If, however, such a bill should be passed, and a person should be prosecuted under it, must the court condemn to death those victims whom the constitution endeavors to preserve?

"No person," says the constitution, "shall be convicted of treason, unless on the testimony of two witnesses to the same overt act, or on confession in open court." Here, the language of the constitution is addressed especially to the courts. It prescribes, directly for them, a rule of evidence not to be departed from. If the legislature should change that rule, and declare one witness, or a confession out of court, sufficient for conviction, must the constitutional principle yield to the legislative act?

From these, and many other selections which might be made, it is apparent, that the framers of the constitution contemplated that instrument as a rule for the government of courts, as well as of the legislature. Why otherwise does it direct the judges to take an oath to support it? This oath certainly applies, in an especial manner, to their conduct in their official character. How immoral to impose it on them, if they were to be used as the instruments, and the knowing instruments, for violating what they swear to support!

The oath of office, too, imposed by the legislature, is completely demonstrative of the legislative opinion on this subject. It is in these words: "I do solemnly swear, that I will administer justice, without respect to persons, and do equal right to the poor and to the rich; and that I will faithfully and impartially discharge all the duties incumbent on me as—according to the best of my abilities and understanding, agreeable to the constitution and laws of the United States." Why does a judge swear to discharge his duties agreeably to the constitution of the United States, if that constitution forms no rule for his government? If it is closed upon him, and cannot be inspected by him? If such be the real state of things, this is worse than solemn mockery. To prescribe, or to take this oath, becomes equally a crime.

It is also not entirely unworthy of observation, that in declaring what shall be the supreme law of the land, the constitution itself is first mentioned; and not the laws of the United States, generally, but those only which shall be made in pursuance of the constitution, have that rank.

Thus, the particular phraseology of the constitution of the United States confirms and strengthens the principle, supposed to be essential to all written constitutions, that a law repugnant to the constitution is void; and that courts, as well as other departments, are bound by that instrument.

The rule must be discharged.

Eakin v. *Raub*
12 Sergeant & Rawle (Pennsylvania Supreme Court) 330 (1825)

www.routledge.com/9781138227835

The dissenting opinion by Justice John Bannister Gibson of the Pennsylvania Supreme Court in this otherwise unimportant case is generally recognized as the most effective answer to Marshall's argument supporting judicial review. Gibson's opinion, Professor J. B. Thayer observed 68 years later, "is much the ablest discussion of the question [of judicial review] which I have ever seen, not excepting the judgment of Marshall in *Marbury* v. *Madison*, which as I venture to think has been overpraised." Gibson's bold argument was a probable factor in preventing his appointment to the U.S. Supreme Court on the death of Justice Washington in 1830. In 1845 Gibson recanted, because the legislature of Pennsylvania had "sanctioned the pretensions of the courts to deal freely with the acts of the legislature, and from experience of the necessity of the case" (see *Norris* v. *Clymer*, 2 Pa. 281). The former reference was to the state convention which produced the new constitution of 1838 that, by its silence on the subject, seemed to countenance judicial review. Gibson's second reference was to legislative intrusion into judicial matters.

Gibson, J . . . .

I am aware, that a right [in the judiciary] to declare all unconstitutional acts void . . . is generally held as a professional dogma, but, I apprehend, rather as a matter of faith than of reason. I admit that I once embraced the same doctrine, but without examination, and I shall therefore state the arguments that impelled me to abandon it, with great respect for those by whom it is still maintained. But I may premise, that it is not a little remarkable, that although the right in question has all along been claimed by the judiciary, no judge has ventured to discuss it, except Chief Justice Marshall, and if the argument of a jurist so distinguished for the strength of his ratiocinative powers be found inconclusive, it may fairly be set down to the weakness of the position which he attempts to defend. . . .

I begin, then, by observing that in this country, the powers of the judiciary are divisible into those that are POLITICAL and those that are purely civil. Every power by which one organ of the government is enabled to control another, or to exert an influence over its acts, is a political power. . . .

The constitution and the right of the legislature to pass the act, may be in collision. But is that a legitimate subject for judicial determination? If it be, the judiciary must be a peculiar organ, to revise the proceedings of the legislature, and to correct its mistakes; and in what part of the constitution are we to look for this proud pre-eminence? Viewing the matter in the opposite direction, what would be thought of an act of assembly in which it should be declared that the supreme court had, in a particular case, put a wrong construction on the constitution of the United States, and that the judgment should therefore be reversed? It would doubtless be thought a usurpation of judicial power. But it is by no means clear, that to declare a law void which has been enacted according to the forms prescribed in the constitution, is not a usurpation of legislative power. . . . It is the business of the judiciary to interpret the laws, not scan the authority of the lawgiver; and without the latter, it cannot take cognizance of a collision between a law and the constitution. So that to affirm that the judiciary has a right to judge of the existence of such collision, is to take for granted the very thing to be proved.

But it has been said to be emphatically the business of the judiciary, to ascertain and pronounce what the law is; and that this necessarily involves a consideration of the constitution. It does so: but how far? If the judiciary will inquire into anything besides the form of enactment, where shall it stop? . . .

In theory, all the organs of the government are of equal capacity; or, if not equal, each must be supposed to have superior capacity only for those things which peculiarly belong to it; and as legislation peculiarly involves the consideration of those limitations which are put on the law-making power, and the interpretation of the laws when made, involves only the construction of the laws themselves, it follows that the construction of the constitution in this particular belongs to the legislature, which ought therefore to be taken to have superior capacity to judge of the constitutionality of its own acts. . . .

When the entire sovereignty was separated into its elementary parts, and distributed to the appropriate branches, all things incident to the exercise of its powers were committed to each branch exclusively. The negative which each part of the legislature may exercise, in regard to the acts of the other, was thought sufficient to prevent material infractions of the restraints which were put on the power of the whole; for, had it been intended to interpose the judiciary as an additional barrier, the matter would surely not have been left in doubt. The judges would not have been left to stand on the insecure and ever shifting ground of public opinion as to constructive powers; they would have been placed on the impregnable ground of an express grant. They would not have been compelled to resort to debates in the convention, or the opinion that was generally entertained at the time. . . .

The power is said to be restricted to cases that are free from doubt or difficulty. But the abstract existence of a power cannot depend on the clearness or obscurity of the case in which it is to be exercised; for that is a consideration that cannot present itself, before the question of the existence of the power shall have been determined; and, if its existence be conceded, no considerations of policy arising from the obscurity of the particular case, ought to influence the exercise of it. . . . The fault is imputable to the legislature, and on it the responsibility exclusively rests. . . .

To say, therefore, that the power is to be exercised but in perfectly clear cases, is to betray a doubt of the propriety of exercising it at all. Were the same caution used in judging of the existence of the power that is inculcated as to the exercise of it, the profession would perhaps arrive at a different conclusion. The grant of a power so extraordinary ought to appear so plain, that he who should run might read. . . .

What I have in view in this inquiry, is the supposed right of the judiciary to interfere, in cases where the constitution is to be carried into effect through the instrumentality of the legislature, and where that organ must necessarily first decide on the constitutionality of its own act. The oath to support the constitution is not peculiar to the judges, but is taken indiscriminately by every officer of the government, and is designed rather as a test of the political principles of the man, than to bind the officer in the discharge of his duty: otherwise it is difficult to determine what operation it is to have in the case of a recorder of deeds, for instance, who, in the execution of his office, has nothing to do with the constitution. But granting it to relate to the official conduct of the judge, as well as every other officer, and not to his political principles, still it must be understood in reference to supporting the constitution, only as far as that may be involved in his official duty; and, consequently, if his official duty does not comprehend an inquiry into the authority of the legislature, neither does his oath. . . .

But do not the judges do a positive act in violation of the constitution, when they give effect to an unconstitutional law? Not if the law has been passed according to the forms established in the constitution. The fallacy of the question is, in supposing that the judiciary adopts the acts of the legislature as its own . . .

But it has been said, that this construction would deprive the citizen of the advantages which are peculiar to a written constitution, by at once declaring the power of the legislature in practice to be illimitable. . . . But there is no magic or inherent power in parchment and ink, to command respect and protect principles from violation. In the business of government a recurrence to first principles answers the end of an observation at sea with a view to correct the dead reckoning; and for this purpose, a written constitution is an instrument of inestimable value. It is of inestimable value, also, in rendering its first principles familiar to the mass of people; for, after all, there is no effectual guard against legislative usurpation but public opinion, the force of which, in this country is inconceivably great. . . . Once let public opinion be so corrupt as to sanction every misconception of the constitution and abuse of power which the temptation of the moment may dictate, and the party which may happen to be predominant, will laugh at the puny efforts of a dependent power to arrest it in its course.

For these reasons, I am of [the] opinion that it rests with the people, in whom full and absolute sovereign power resides, to correct abuses in legislation, by instructing their representatives to repeal the obnoxious act. . . . It might, perhaps, have been better to vest the power in the judiciary; as it might be expected that its habits of deliberation, and the aid derived from the arguments of counsel, would more frequently lead to accurate conclusions. On the other hand, the judiciary is not infallible; and an error by it would admit of no remedy but a more distinct expression of the public will, through the extraordinary medium of a convention; whereas, an error by the legislature admits of a remedy by an exertion of the same will, in the ordinary exercise of the right of suffrage—a mode better calculated to attain the end, without popular excitement. . . .

But in regard to an act of [a state] assembly, which is found to be in collision with the constitution, laws, or treaties of the United States, I take the duty of the judiciary to be exactly the reverse. By becoming parties to the federal constitution, the states have agreed to several limitations of their individual sovereignty, to enforce which, it was thought to be absolutely necessary to prevent them from giving effect to laws in violation of those limitations, through the instrumentality of their own judges. Accordingly, it is declared in the sixth article and second section of the federal constitution, that, "This constitution, and the laws of the United States which shall be made in pursuance thereof, and all treaties made, or which shall be made under the authority of the United States, shall be the supreme law of the land; and the judges in every state shall be BOUND thereby: anything in the laws or constitution of any state to the contrary notwithstanding." . . .

Scott v. *Sandford*
60 U.S. (19 Howard) 393, 15 L.Ed. 691 (1857)

http://caselaw.findlaw.com/us-supreme-court/60/393.html

In 1834 Dr. John Emerson, an Army surgeon, took his slave Dred Scott from Missouri to Illinois, where slavery was forbidden. In 1836 Emerson took Scott to Fort Snelling in present-day Minnesota, well north of 36° 30′ in the old Louisiana territory, where slavery had been banned by the Missouri Compromise of 1820. In 1838 Emerson returned to Missouri with Scott. After Emerson died, a suit was brought in the Missouri courts against his widow, claiming that Scott's residence in free territory had made him a free person. The lower court held for Scott, but the state supreme court reversed in 1852. Whatever Scott's legal status outside Missouri, he remained a slave under Missouri law. By this time Mrs. Emerson had married Dr. C. C. Chaffee, an abolitionist from Massachusetts. To reopen the case and to shield both his reputation and the friendly nature of the litigation, he transferred ownership of Scott to Mrs. Chaffee's brother, John Sanford, of New York. (In *Howard's Reports*, Sanford's name was incorrectly spelled "Sandford.") In 1853 Chaffee arranged for Roswell Field, an abolitionist attorney in St. Louis, to file suit on Scott's behalf against Sanford in the U.S. Circuit Court in Missouri. On a writ of error from an adverse judgment, Scott appealed to the Supreme Court. The justices twice heard arguments in the case, in February and December 1856. The case came down on March 6, 1857, just two days after James Buchanan's inauguration. Strong pressures from all sides pushed the justices to accomplish judicially what the elected branches had been unable to resolve. Each of the nine justices filed an opinion; Taney's and Curtis's are included here. Majority: Taney, Campbell, Catron, Daniel, Grier, Nelson, Wayne. Dissenting: Curtis, McLean. (Not all members of the majority agreed with Taney's disposition of all points in the case.)

Mr. Chief Justice Taney delivered the opinion of the Court. . . .

The question is simply this: Can a negro, whose ancestors were imported into this country, and sold as slaves, become a member of the political community formed and brought into existence by the Constitution of the United States, and as such become entitled to all the rights, and privileges, and immunities guarantied by that instrument to the citizen? One of which rights is the privilege of suing in a court of the United States in the cases specified in the Constitution.

We think . . . [the people of that race] . . . are not included, and were not intended to be included, under the words "citizens" in the Constitution, and can therefore claim none of the rights and privileges which that instrument provides for and secures to citizens of the United States. On the contrary, they were at that time considered as a subordinate and inferior class of beings, who had been subjugated by the dominant race, and, whether emancipated or not, yet remained subject to their authority, and had no rights or privileges but such as those who held the power and the Government might choose to grant them. . . .

The question then arises, whether the provisions of the Constitution, in relation to the personal rights and privileges to which the citizen of the State should be entitled, embraced the negro African race, at that time in this country, or who might afterwards be imported, who had then or should afterwards be made free in any State; and to put it in the power of a single State to make him a citizen of the United States, and endue him with the full rights of citizenship in every other State without their consent? Does the Constitution of the United States act upon him whenever he shall be made free under the laws of a State, and raised there to the rank of a citizen, and immediately clothe him with all the privileges of a citizen in every other State, and in its own courts?

The court thinks the affirmative of these propositions cannot be maintained. And if it cannot, the plaintiff in error could not be a citizen of the State of Missouri, within the meaning of the Constitution of the United States, and, consequently, was not entitled to sue in its courts. . . .

No one, we presume, supposes that any change in public opinion or feeling, in relation to this unfortunate race, in the civilized nations of Europe or in this country, should induce the court to give to the words of the Constitution a more liberal construction in their favor than they were intended to bear when the instrument was framed and adopted. Such an argument would be altogether inadmissible in any tribunal called on to interpret it. If any of its provisions are deemed unjust, there is a mode prescribed in the instrument itself by which it may be amended; but while it remains unaltered, it must be construed now as it was understood at the time of its adoption. It is not only the same in words, but the same in meaning, and delegates the same powers to the Government, and reserves and secures the same rights and privileges to the citizen; and as long as it continues to exist in its present form, it speaks not only in the same words, but with the same meaning and intent with which it spoke when it came from the hands of its framers, and was voted on and adopted by the people of the United States. Any other rule of construction would abrogate the judicial character of this court, and make it the mere reflex of the popular opinion of the day. . . .

What the construction was at that time, we think can hardly admit of doubt. We have the language of the Declaration of Independence and of the Articles of Confederation, in addition to the plain words of the Constitution itself; we have the legislation of the different States, before, about the time, and since, the Constitution was adopted; we have the legislation of Congress, from the time of its adoption to a recent period; and we have the constant and uniform action of the Executive Department, all concurring together, and leading to the same result. And if anything in relation to the construction of the Constitution can be regarded as settled, it is that which we now give to the word "citizen" and the word "people." . . .

The act of Congress, upon which the plaintiff relies, declares that slavery and involuntary servitude, except as a punishment for crime, shall be forever prohibited in all that part of the territory ceded by France, under the name of Louisiana, which lies north of 36° 30' north latitude, and not included within the limits of Missouri. And the . . . inquiry is whether Congress was authorized to pass this law under any of the powers granted to it by the Constitution; for if the authority is not given by that instrument, it is the duty of this court to declare it void and inoperative, and incapable of conferring freedom upon any one who is held as a slave under the laws of any one of the States.

The counsel for the plaintiff has laid much stress upon that article in the Constitution which confers on Congress the power "to dispose of and make all needful rules and regulations respecting the territory or other property belonging to the United States," but, in the judgment of the court, that provision has no bearing on the present controversy, and the power there given, whatever it may be, is confined, and was intended to be confined, to the territory which at that time belonged to, or was claimed by the United States, and was within their boundaries as settled by the treaty with Great Britain, and can have no influence upon a territory afterwards acquired from a foreign Government. It was a special provision for a known and particular territory, and to meet a present emergency, and nothing more.

. . . The powers of the Government and the rights and privileges of the citizen are regulated and plainly defined by the Constitution itself. And when the Territory becomes a part of the United States, the Federal Government enters into possession in the character impressed upon it by those who created it. It enters upon it with its powers over the citizen strictly defined, and limited by the Constitution, from which it derives its own existence, and by virtue of which alone it continues to exist and act as a Government and sovereignty. It has not power of any kind beyond it; and it cannot, when it enters a Territory of the United States, put off its character and assume discretionary or despotic powers which the Constitution has denied to it. It cannot create for itself a new character separated from the citizens of the United States, and the duties it owes them under the provisions of the Constitution. The Territory being a part of the United States, the Government and the citizen both enter it under the authority of the Constitution, with their respective rights defined and marked out; and the Federal Government can exercise no power over his person or property, beyond what that instrument confers, nor lawfully deny any right which it has reserved. . . .

An Act of Congress which deprives a citizen of the United States of his liberty or property, merely because he came himself or brought his property into a particular Territory of the United States, and who had committed no offense against the laws, could hardly be dignified with the name of due process of law. . . .

And if Congress itself cannot do this—if it is beyond the powers conferred on the Federal Government—it will be admitted . . . that it could not authorize a Territorial Government to exercise them. It could confer no power on any local Government, established by its authority, to violate the provisions of the Constitution. . . .

Upon these considerations, it is the opinion of the court that the act of Congress which prohibited a citizen from holding and owning property of this kind in the territory of the United States north of the line therein mentioned, is not warranted by the Constitution, and is therefore void; and that neither Dred Scott himself, nor any of his family, were made free by being carried into this territory; even if they had been carried there by the owner, with the intention of becoming a permanent resident. . . .

But there is another point in the case which depends on State power and State law. . . . [T]he principle on which it depends was decided in this court . . . in . . . *Strader* v. *Graham* [1851]. . . . In that case, the slaves had been taken from Kentucky to Ohio, with the consent of the owner, and afterwards brought back to Kentucky. And this court held that their status or condition, as free or slave, depended upon the laws of Kentucky, when they were brought back into that State, and not of Ohio; and that this court had no jurisdiction to revise the judgment of a State court upon its own laws. . . .

So in this case. As Scott was a slave when taken into the State of Illinois by his owner, and was there held as such, and brought back in that character, his status, as free or slave, depended on the laws of Missouri, not of Illinois. . . .

[I]t is the judgment of this court, that it appears by the record before us that the plaintiff in error is not a citizen of Missouri, in the sense in which that word is used in the Constitution; and that the Circuit Court . . ., for that reason, had no jurisdiction in the case, and could give no judgment in it. Its judgment for the defendant must, consequently, be reversed, and a mandate issued, directing the suit to be dismissed for want of jurisdiction.

Mr. Justice Curtis, joined by Mr. Justice McLean, dissenting. . . .

To determine whether any free persons, descended from Africans held in slavery, were citizens of the United States under the Confederation, and consequently at the time of the adoption of the Constitution of the United States, it is only necessary to know whether any such persons were citizens of either of the States under the Confederation, at the time of the adoption of the Constitution.

Of this there can be no doubt. At the time of the ratification of the Articles of Confederation, all free native-born inhabitants of the States of New Hampshire, Massachusetts, New York, New Jersey, and North Carolina, though descended from African slaves, were not only citizens of those States, but such of them as had the other necessary qualifications possessed the franchise of electors, on equal terms with other citizens. . . .

Having first decided that they were bound to consider the sufficiency of the plea to the jurisdiction of the Circuit Court, and having decided that this plea showed that the Circuit Court had no jurisdiction, and consequently that this is a case to which the judicial power of the United States does not extend, they have gone on to examine the merits of the case as they appeared on the trial before the court and jury, on the issues joined on the pleas in bar, and so have reached the question of the power of Congress to pass the act of 1820. On so grave a subject as this, I feel obliged to say that, in my opinion, such an exertion of judicial power transcends the limits of the authority of the court, as described by its repeated decisions and, as I understand, acknowledged in this opinion of the majority of the court. . . .

Nor, in my judgment, will the position, that a prohibition to bring slaves into a Territory deprives any one of his property without due process of law, bear examination. . . .

II. EXTERNAL AND INTERNAL CHECKS ON JUDICIAL POWER

Ex parte *McCardle*
74 U.S. (7 Wall.) 506, 19 L.Ed. 264 (1869)

http://caselaw.findlaw.com/us-supreme-court/74/506.html

During Reconstruction after the Civil War, a newspaper editor in Mississippi named William McCardle was jailed by a military commander for trial before a military commission for publishing "incendiary and libelous" articles. McCardle was a civilian and sought release on habeas corpus in the Circuit Court for the Southern District of Mississippi. After hearing his case, the judge remanded McCardle to the custody of the military authorities. McCardle then took an appeal to the Supreme Court authorized by a statute passed by Congress in 1867. Following argument of his case in the Supreme Court and while the justices had it under advisement, Congress overrode President Andrew Johnson's veto and repealed the statute in 1868. The congressional majority apparently feared that the constitutionality of much of its Reconstruction program was at stake in the litigation. Chief Justice Chase noted in his opinion that decision in the case had been delayed by his participation in the president's impeachment trial in the Senate. McCardle should be read in the light of Ex parte *Yerger* (1869) and *United States* v. *Klein* (1872). Majority: Chase, Clifford, Davis, Field, Grier, Miller, Nelson, Swayne.

Mr. Chief Justice Chase delivered the opinion of the Court. . . .

The first question necessarily is that of jurisdiction; for, if the act of March, 1868, takes away the jurisdiction defined by the act of February, 1867, it is useless, if not improper, to enter into any discussion of other questions.

It is quite true, as was argued by the counsel for the petitioner, that the appellate jurisdiction of this court is not derived from acts of Congress. It is, strictly speaking, conferred by the Constitution. But it is conferred "with such exceptions and under such regulations as Congress shall make."

It is unnecessary to consider whether, if Congress had made no exceptions and no regulations, this court might not have exercised general appellate jurisdiction under rules prescribed by itself. For among the earliest acts of the first Congress, at its first session, was the act of September 24th, 1789, to establish the judicial courts of the United States. That act provided for the organization of this court, and prescribed regulations for the exercise of its jurisdiction.

The source of that jurisdiction, and the limitations of it by the Constitution, and by statute, have been on several occasions subjects of consideration here. . . .

The principle that the affirmation of appellate jurisdiction implies the negation of all such jurisdiction not affirmed having been thus established, it was an almost necessary consequence that acts of Congress, providing for the exercise of jurisdiction, should come to be spoken of as acts granting jurisdiction, and not as acts making exceptions to the constitutional grant of it.

The exception to appellate jurisdiction in the case before us, however, is not an inference from the affirmation of other appellate jurisdiction. It is made in terms. The provision of the act of 1867, affirming the appellate jurisdiction of this court in cases of habeas corpus is expressly repealed. It is hardly possible to imagine a plainer instance of positive exception.

We are not at liberty to inquire into the motives of the legislature. We can only examine into its power under the Constitution; and the power to make exceptions to the appellate jurisdiction of this court is given by express words.

What, then, is the effect of the repealing act upon the case before us? We cannot doubt as to this. Without jurisdiction the court cannot proceed at all in any cause. Jurisdiction is power to declare the law, and when it ceases to exist, the only function remaining to the court is that of announcing the fact and dismissing the cause. And this is not less clear upon authority than upon principle. . . .

It is quite clear, therefore, that this court cannot proceed to pronounce judgment in this case, for it has no longer jurisdiction of the appeal; and judicial duty is not less fitly performed by declining ungranted jurisdiction than in exercising firmly that which the Constitution and the laws confer.

Counsel seem to have supposed, if effect be given to the repealing act in question, that the whole appellate power of the court, in cases of habeas corpus, is denied. But this is an error. The act of 1868 does not except from that jurisdiction any cases but appeals from Circuit Courts under the act of 1867. It does not affect the jurisdiction which was previously exercised.

The appeal of the petitioner in this case must be dismissed for want of jurisdiction.

Baker v. *Carr*
369 U.S. 186, 82 S.Ct. 691, 7 L.Ed. 2d 663 (1962)

www.law.cornell.edu/supremecourt/text/369/186#

(This case is reprinted in Chapter Five; see the Table of Contents.)

III. FINALITY OF SUPREME COURT DECISIONS

City of Boerne v. *Flores*
521 U.S. 507, 117 S.Ct. 2157, 138 L.Ed. 2d 624 (1997)

http://caselaw.findlaw.com/us-supreme-court/521/507.html

The Catholic Archbishop of San Antonio applied for a building permit to enlarge a church in Boerne, Texas. When local officials denied the permit under a historic preservation ordinance, the Archbishop challenged the rejection as a violation of the Religious Freedom Restoration Act (RFRA). Congress enacted RFRA in response to the Supreme Court's decision in *Employment Division* v. *Smith* (1990) (see Chapter Twelve). This decision upheld, against a challenge under the free exercise clause, the denial of unemployment benefits to members of the Native American Church who lost their jobs because of the ritual use of peyote in violation of an Oregon statute of general applicability banning the use of certain drugs, including peyote. Preferring the religion-friendly standard from earlier Supreme Court decisions (*Sherbert* v. *Verner*, 1963; and *Wisconsin* v. *Yoder*, 1972) and relying on Section 5 of the Fourteenth Amendment, Congress in RFRA prohibited any local, state, or federal government agency or official from "substantially burden[ing]" a person's exercise of religion even if the burden results from application of a law of general applicability, unless the government can demonstrate that the burden "(1) is in furtherance of a compelling governmental interest; and (2) is the least restrictive means of furthering that . . . interest." The U.S. District Court for the Western District of Texas concluded that by enacting RFRA, Congress exceeded the scope of its enforcement powers under the Fourteenth Amendment, but the Court of Appeals for the Fifth Circuit reversed. Majority: Kennedy, Rehnquist, Stevens, Scalia, Thomas, Ginsburg. Dissenting: O'Connor, Souter, Breyer.

Justice Kennedy delivered the opinion of the Court. . . .

The case calls into question the authority of Congress to enact RFRA. We conclude the statute exceeds Congress' power. . . .

Under our Constitution, the Federal Government is one of enumerated powers. The judicial authority to determine the constitutionality of laws, in cases and controversies, is based on the premise that the "powers of the legislature are defined and limited; and that those limits may not be mistaken, or forgotten, the constitution is written." . . .

The parties disagree over whether RFRA is a proper exercise of Congress' § 5 power to enforce by "appropriate legislation" the constitutional guarantee that no State shall deprive any person of "life, liberty, or property, without due process of law" nor deny any person "equal protection of the laws."

In defense of the Act respondent contends, with support from the United States as amicus, that RFRA is permissible enforcement legislation. Congress, it is said, is only protecting by legislation one of the liberties guaranteed by the Fourteenth Amendment's Due Process Clause, the free exercise of religion, beyond what is necessary under *Smith*. It is said the congressional decision to dispense with proof of deliberate or overt discrimination and instead concentrate on a law's effects accords with the settled understanding that § 5 includes the power to enact legislation designed to prevent as well as remedy constitutional violations. It is further contended that Congress' § 5 power is not limited to remedial or preventive legislation.

All must acknowledge that § 5 is "a positive grant of legislative power" to Congress. . . . Legislation which deters or remedies constitutional violations can fall within the sweep of Congress' enforcement power even if in the process it prohibits conduct which is not itself unconstitutional and intrudes into "legislative spheres of autonomy previously reserved to the States." For example, the Court upheld a suspension of literacy tests and similar voting requirements under Congress' parallel power to enforce the provisions of the Fifteenth Amendment, as a measure to combat racial discrimination in voting, despite the facial constitutionality of the tests under *Lassiter* v. *Northampton County Bd. of Elections* (1959). . . .

It is also true, however, that "[a]s broad as the congressional enforcement power is, it is not unlimited." In assessing the breadth of § 5's enforcement power, we begin with its text. Congress has been given the power "to enforce" the "provisions of this article." We agree with respondent, of course, that Congress can enact legislation under § 5 enforcing the constitutional right to the free exercise of religion. The "provisions of this article," to which § 5 refers, include the Due Process Clause of the Fourteenth Amendment. Congress' power to enforce the Free Exercise Clause follows from our holding in *Cantwell* v. *Connecticut* (1940), that the "fundamental concept of liberty embodied in [the Fourteenth Amendment's Due Process Clause] embraces the liberties guaranteed by the First Amendment." . . .

Congress' power under § 5, however, extends only to "enforc[ing]" the provisions of the Fourteenth Amendment. . . . The design of the Amendment and the text of § 5 are inconsistent with the suggestion that Congress has the power to decree the substance of the Fourteenth Amendment's restrictions on the States. Legislation which alters the meaning of the Free Exercise Clause cannot be said to be enforcing the Clause. Congress does not enforce a constitutional right by changing what the right is. . . . Were it not so, what Congress would be enforcing would no longer be, in any meaningful sense, the "provisions of [the Fourteenth Amendment]."

While the line between measures that remedy or prevent unconstitutional actions and measures that make a substantive change in the governing law is not easy to discern, and

Congress must have wide latitude in determining where it lies, the distinction exists and must be observed. There must be a congruence and proportionality between the injury to be prevented or remedied and the means adopted to that end. . . .

The remedial and preventive nature of Congress' enforcement power, and the limitation inherent in the power, were confirmed in our earliest cases on the Fourteenth Amendment. . . .

Recent cases have continued to revolve around the question of whether § 5 legislation can be considered remedial. . . . In *South Carolina* v. *Katzenbach*, we emphasized that "[t]he constitutional propriety of [legislation adopted under the Enforcement Clause] must be judged with reference to the historical experience . . . it reflects." There we upheld various provisions of the Voting Rights Act of 1965, finding them to be "remedies aimed at areas where voting discrimination has been most flagrant." . . . The new, unprecedented remedies were deemed necessary given the ineffectiveness of the existing voting rights laws and the slow costly character of case-by-case litigation.

Any suggestion that Congress has a substantive, non-remedial power under the Fourteenth Amendment is not supported by our case law. In *Oregon* v. *Mitchell*, a majority of the Court concluded Congress had exceeded its enforcement powers by enacting legislation lowering the minimum age of voters from 21 to 18 in state and local elections. . . .

If Congress could define its own powers by altering the Fourteenth Amendment's meaning, no longer would the Constitution be "superior paramount law, unchangeable by ordinary means." It would be "on a level with ordinary legislative acts, and, like other acts, . . . alterable when the legislature shall please to alter it." Under this approach, it is difficult to conceive of a principle that would limit congressional power. Shifting legislative majorities could change the Constitution and effectively circumvent the difficult and detailed amendment process contained in Article V.

We now turn to consider whether RFRA can be considered enforcement legislation under § 5 of the Fourteenth Amendment.

Respondent contends that RFRA is a proper exercise of Congress' remedial or preventive power. The Act, it is said, is a reasonable means of protecting the free exercise of religion as defined by *Smith*. It prevents and remedies laws which are enacted with the unconstitutional object of targeting religious beliefs and practices. . . . To avoid the difficulty of proving such violations, it is said, Congress can simply invalidate any law which imposes a substantial burden on a religious practice unless it is justified by a compelling interest and is the least restrictive means of accomplishing that interest. If Congress can prohibit laws with discriminatory effects in order to prevent racial discrimination in violation of the Equal Protection Clause, then it can do the same, respondent argues, to promote religious liberty.

While preventive rules are sometimes appropriate remedial measures, there must be a congruence between the means used and the ends to be achieved. . . . Strong measures appropriate to address one harm may be an unwarranted response to another, lesser one.

A comparison between RFRA and the Voting Rights Act is instructive. In contrast to the record which confronted Congress and the judiciary in the voting rights cases, RFRA's legislative record lacks examples of modern instances of generally applicable laws passed because of religious bigotry. The history of persecution in this country detailed in the hearings mentions no episodes occurring in the past 40 years. . . .

Regardless of the state of the legislative record, RFRA cannot be considered remedial, preventive legislation, if those terms are to have any meaning. RFRA is so out of proportion to a supposed remedial or preventive object that it cannot be understood as responsive to, or designed to prevent, unconstitutional behavior. It appears, instead, to attempt a substantive change in constitutional protections. . . .

When the exercise of religion has been burdened in an incidental way by a law of general application, it does not follow that the persons affected have been burdened any more than other citizens, let alone burdened because of their religious beliefs. In addition, the Act imposes in every case a least restrictive means requirement—a requirement that was not used in the pre-*Smith* jurisprudence RFRA purported to codify—which also indicates that the legislation is broader than is appropriate if the goal is to prevent and remedy constitutional violations. . . .

Broad as the power of Congress is under the Enforcement Clause of the Fourteenth Amendment, RFRA contradicts vital principles necessary to maintain separation of powers and the federal balance. The judgment of the Court of Appeals sustaining the Act's constitutionality is reversed.

It is so ordered.

JUSTICE STEVENS, concurring . . . [omitted].

JUSTICE SCALIA, with whom JUSTICE STEVENS joins, concurring in part . . . [omitted].

JUSTICE O'CONNOR, with whom JUSTICE BREYER joins in part, dissenting. . . .

[I]f I agreed with the Court's standard in *Smith*, I would join the opinion. As the Court's careful and thorough historical analysis shows, Congress lacks the "power to decree the substance of the Fourteenth Amendment's restrictions on the States." Rather, its power under § 5 of the Fourteenth Amendment extends only to enforcing the Amendment's provisions. In short, Congress lacks the ability independently to define or expand the scope of constitutional rights by statute . . . This recognition does not, of course, in any way diminish Congress' obligation to draw its own conclusions regarding the Constitution's meaning. Congress, no less than this Court, is called upon to consider the requirements of the Constitution and to act in accordance with its dictates. But when it enacts legislation in furtherance of its delegated powers, Congress must make its judgments consistent with this Court's exposition of the Constitution and with the limits placed on its legislative authority by provisions such as the Fourteenth Amendment.

The Court's analysis of whether RFRA is a constitutional exercise of Congress' § 5 power . . . is premised on the assumption that *Smith* correctly interprets the Free Exercise Clause. This is an assumption that I do not accept. . . . [T]he Free Exercise Clause is not simply an antidiscrimination principle that protects only against those laws that single out religious practice for unfavorable treatment. Rather, the Clause is best understood as an affirmative guarantee of the right to participate in religious practices and conduct without impermissible governmental interference, even when such conduct conflicts with a neutral, generally applicable law. . . .

JUSTICE SOUTER, dissenting . . . [omitted]. JUSTICE BREYER, dissenting . . . [omitted].

Unstaged Debate: Andrew Jackson, Abraham Lincoln, and *Arkansas* v. *The Supreme Court*[3]

When Congress voted to recharter the Bank of the United States in 1832, President Andrew Jackson vetoed the bill in part because he thought it unconstitutional. The Supreme Court in *McCulloch* v. *Maryland* (1819), reprinted in Chapter Four, had upheld the constitutionality of the bank. Jackson's words in the first excerpt were drafted mainly by Roger Brooke Taney, whom Jackson soon appointed to succeed John Marshall as chief justice of the United States. It was the Taney Court's decision in *Scott* v. *Sandford* (1857) that Lincoln had in mind in the second excerpt. A century later *Cooper* v. *Aaron* grew out of official resistance in Little Rock, Arkansas, to the Supreme Court's 1954 school desegregation decision (*Brown* v. *Board of Education*, in Chapter Fourteen). The opinion is unusual in that all nine justices signed it. The quotation from Chief Justice Taney at the end of the opinion comes from *Ableman* v. *Booth*. Note the reliance in *Cooper* on both the supremacy clause and *Marbury* v. *Madison*.

President Jackson Vetoes the Bank Act (1832)

It is maintained by the advocates of the bank that its constitutionality in all its features ought to be considered as settled by precedent and by the decision of the Supreme Court. To this conclusion I can not assent.

If the opinion of the Supreme Court covered the whole ground of this act, it ought not to control the coordinate authorities of this Government. The Congress, the Executive, and the Court must each for itself be guided by its own opinion of the Constitution. Each public officer who takes an oath to support the Constitution swears that he will support it as he understands it, and not as it is understood by others. It is as much the duty of the House of Representatives, of the Senate, and of the President to decide upon the constitutionality of any bill or resolution which may be presented to them for passage or approval as it is of the supreme judges when it may be brought before them for judicial decision. The opinion of the judges has no more authority over Congress than the opinion of Congress has over the judges, and on that point the President is independent of both. The authority of the Supreme Court must not, therefore, be permitted to control the Congress or the Executive when acting in their legislative capacities, but to have only such influence as the force of their reasoning may deserve.

President Lincoln Delivers His First Inaugural Address (1861)

I do not forget the position assumed by some, that constitutional questions are to be decided by the Supreme Court; nor do I deny that such decisions must be binding in any case, upon the parties to a suit, as to the object of that suit, while they are also entitled to a very high respect and consideration, in all parallel cases, by all other departments of government. And while it is obviously possible that such decision may be erroneous in any given case, still the evil effect following it, being limited to that particular case, with the chance that it may be over-ruled, and never become a precedent for other cases, can better be borne than could the evils of a different practice. At the same time the candid citizen must confess that if the policy of the government, upon vital questions, affecting the whole people, is to be irrevocably fixed by decisions of the Supreme Court, the instant they are made, in ordinary litigation between parties, in personal actions, the people will have ceased, to be their own rulers, having to that extent, practically resigned their government, into the hands of that eminent tribunal. Nor is there, in this view, any assault upon the court, or the judges. It is a duty, from which they may not shrink, to decide cases properly brought before them; and it is no fault of theirs, if others seek to turn their decisions to political purposes.

The Supreme Court Decides *Cooper* v. *Aaron* 358 U.S. 1, 78 S.Ct. 1401, 3 L.Ed. 2d 5 (1958)

http://caselaw.findlaw.com/uzs-supreme-court/ 358/1.html

Opinion of the Court by the Chief Justice, Mr. Justice Black, Mr. Justice Frankfurter, Mr. Justice Douglas, Mr. Justice Burton, Mr. Justice Clark, Mr. Justice Harlan, Mr. Justice Brennan, and Mr. Justice Whittaker.

As this case reaches us it raises questions of the highest importance to the maintenance of our federal system of government. It necessarily involves a claim by the Governor and Legislature of a State that there is no duty on state officials to obey federal court orders resting on this Court's considered interpretation of the United States Constitution. Specifically it involves actions by the Governor and Legislature of Arkansas upon the premise that they are not bound by our holding in *Brown* v. *Board of Education*. . . .

What has been said, in the light of the facts developed, is enough to dispose of the case. However, we should answer the premise of the actions of the Governor and Legislature that they are not bound by our holding in the Brown case. It is necessary only to recall some basic constitutional propositions which are settled doctrine.

Article VI of the Constitution makes the Constitution the "supreme Law of the Land." In 1803, Chief Justice Marshall, speaking for a unanimous Court, referring to the Constitution as "the fundamental and paramount law of the nation," declared in the notable case of *Marbury* v. *Madison* . . . that "It is emphatically the province and duty of the judicial department to say what the law is." This decision declared the basic principle that the federal judiciary is supreme in the exposition of the law of the Constitution, and that principle has ever since been respected by this Court and the Country as a permanent and indispensable feature of our constitutional system. It follows that the interpretation of the Fourteenth Amendment enunciated by this Court in the Brown Case is the supreme law of the land, and Art. VI of the Constitution makes it of binding effect on the States "any Thing in the Constitution or Laws of any State to the Contrary notwithstanding." Every state legislator and executive and judicial officer is solemnly committed by oath taken pursuant to Art. VI, cl. 3 "to support this Constitution." Chief Justice Taney, speaking for a unanimous Court in 1859, said that this requirement reflected the framers' "anxiety to preserve it [the Constitution] in full force, in all its powers, and to guard against resistance to or evasion of its authority, on the part of a State. . . ."

No state legislator or executive or judicial officer can war against the Constitution without violating his undertaking to support it. Chief Justice Marshall spoke for a unanimous Court in saying that: "If the legislatures of the several states may, at will, annul the judgments of the courts of the United States, and destroy the rights acquired under those judgments, the constitution itself becomes a solemn mockery . . ." A Governor who asserts a power to nullify a federal court order is similarly restrained. If he had such power, said Chief Justice Hughes, in 1932, also for a unanimous Court, "it is manifest that the fiat of a state Governor, and not the Constitution of the United States, would be the supreme law of the land; that the restrictions of the Federal Constitution upon the exercise of state power would be but impotent phrases. . . ."

Mr. Justice Frankfurter, concurring . . . [omitted].

IV. APPROACHES TO CONSTITUTIONAL INTERPRETATION

Unstaged Debate of 1986: Judge Bork v. Professor Tribe

At the time of this exchange, Robert Bork was a judge on the U.S. Court of Appeals for the District of Columbia Circuit, and Laurence Tribe was Tyler Professor of Constitutional Law at Harvard Law School. In 1987, the Senate rejected President Reagan's nomination of Judge Bork to the Supreme Court. Professor Tribe was one of those who testified at Senate hearings against the nomination.

Robert H. Bork, "Original Intent and the Constitution," *Humanities* 7:1 (Feb. 1986), 22, 26–27

. . . The controversy [over original intent] swirls around the question whether judges, who undertake to strike down laws and executive actions in the name of the Constitution, must do so only in accordance with the intentions of those who wrote, proposed, and ratified the Constitution's various provisions. This philosophy of originalism comports with what most people assume judges are, and should be, doing. But it is not what most academic constitutional specialists want of judges and it is apparently not what some judges conceive their function to be. They have evolved a philosophy of non-originalism according to which judges should create individual rights that supersede democratic decisions. . . .

It is argued by some legal theorists that the Constitution's meaning should evolve and that the course of evolution should be determined by moral and political philosophy. It is not entirely clear why this method of changing the document's meaning, if it is legitimate, should be confined to individual freedoms. . . . It could as well be applied to the interpretation of the powers and structures of government laid out in the first three articles of the Constitution. That is rarely, if ever, proposed, probably because it would make embarrassingly clear that the professors are asking judges to remake our form of government. Yet one form of judicial creativity is no more illegitimate than the other. But the problem with the argument goes deeper. There is no single philosophy or method of philosophic reasoning upon which all Americans agree. . . .

Perhaps recognizing these difficulties, other constitutional theorists would have judges apply not philosophical analysis but something more akin to a sense, almost intuitive, of what "our evolving morality" demands at the moment. This idea rests upon the correct observation that a society's morality does evolve and that the American morality of today differs in a number of respects from the American morality of the late eighteenth century. All quite true, but inadequate to support the conclusion. The Constitution's guarantees—freedom of speech, press, and religion; freedom from unreasonable searches and seizures; freedom from required self-incrimination; and much more—remain highly relevant today. Any free society must respect them. No theorist, to my knowledge, suggests that, if American morality evolves so that these freedoms are disliked, judges should abandon them—yet that is what would seem to be required by this approach. Again, however, the trouble goes deeper. To the degree that the morality that is evolving deserves the name of "our morality," it will be embodied in legislation and executive action. There will be no need for judges to tell the society what the society's morality is. Judges who undertake to apply "our evolving morality" to invalidate democratically enacted law will, in truth, be enforcing their own morality upon the rest of us and calling it the Constitution.

These considerations seem to me to leave only the method of original intent as a legitimate means of applying the Constitution. Only that can give us law that is something other than, and superior to, the judge's will. It is objected that the process of discerning the Framers' intentions can be manipulated and that, in any event, it is impossible to know what the Framers would have done in specific cases. Those things are true and, if they are insuperable objections, the only conclusion left is that the Constitution can never be law and judicial review should be abandoned. The objections are by no means fatal, however.

Any system of argument which is complex and involves questions of degree and of judgment is manipulable. Certainly, it will be easier to detect manipulation of historical materials than of philosophic concepts or subjective estimates of contemporary morality. The only ultimate solution is the selection of intellectually honest judges.

The objection that we can never know what the Framers would have done about specific modern situations is entirely beside the point. The originalist attempts to discern the principles the Framers enacted, the values they sought to protect. All that the philosophy of original intention requires is that the text, structure, and history of the Constitution provide the judge not with a conclusion about a specific case but with a premise from which to begin reasoning about that case. For instance, while the Fourth Amendment, when framed, envisioned protection only against unwarranted searches and seizures by physical invasion, its intended prohibition of unreasonable intrusions by the state against the individual can certainly be applied in the context of electronic surveillance. . . .

Adherence to a philosophy of searching for original intent does not mean that judges will invariably decide cases the way the Framers would have, though many cases will be decided that way. At the very least, the originalist philosophy confines judges to areas the Framers assigned to them and reserves to democratic processes those areas of life the Framers placed there. That much is indispensable if judges are not to usurp the legitimate freedom of the people to govern themselves, and no philosophy other than that of original intent can provide that safeguard.

Laurence H. Tribe, "The Holy Grail of Original Intent," *Humanities* 7:1 (Feb. 1986), 23–25

. . . In today's highly visible and notably politicized constitutional discourse, a particular version of "history"—what some confidently claim to know our country's Founders and our Constitution's Framers "originally intended"—is offered as the only relevant, and indeed the definitive, source of the true meaning of each provision in the constitutional text. But, by standing on its head Santayana's injunction that those who forget the past are condemned to repeat it, these new "originalists" are busily inventing a particular past that might dictate our constitutional future. In doing so, they are claiming for history a decisive authority that is incompatible with the limits of what we can know and false to the nature of the Constitution itself. . . .

To begin with, the very generality of many of the terms the Framers used—such as "liberty," "due process," and "equal protection"—strongly suggests an intent not to confine their meaning to the specific outcomes and contexts that occurred to those who first used them, but to invite the development of meanings in light of the needs and insights of succeeding generations. . . .

The originalists must accordingly persuade us that their own departure from that overarching original intent is justified—and that it may be coherently pursued despite the often conflicting things that the many who wrote, or voted to ratify, the Constitution's provisions had in mind. And they must, in addition, convince us that their program will succeed in its proclaimed objective of placing the interpretive enterprise beyond the reach of personal predilection and subjective judgment.

For my part, I gravely doubt that the program can come even close to succeeding. Consider the justices who wrote in *Dred Scott* that slaves are mere property, the justices who wrote in *Plessy* [v. *Ferguson*, 1896] that racial separation by law need not deny equality, and the justices who wrote in *Lochner* [v. *New York*, 1905] that laws regulating hours and wages invade "freedom of contract." All of them invoked "original intent" with considerable conviction and plausibility . . . If one wants to say—as I do, and as . . . Judge Bork seem[s] to—that those cases were wrongly decided, one must do much better than the originalists have yet done to explain away the awkward facts of history that weighed in on the wrong side of those disputes. Nor can the program of the originalists avoid the charge of subjective and even politically motivated selectivity and manipulation when those who advocate it so readily support the constitutionality of eminently sensible and currently indispensable policies that would certainly have shocked those who framed the Constitution and the Bill of Rights—such as "stop and frisk" practices by police in urban areas, the extraction of coerced testimony in response to promises of immunity, and the authorization of police searches for mere evidence of crime as opposed to contraband. Finally, the originalist project can hardly succeed when even its most ardent proponents counsel that some constitutional decisions, even if originally wrong by their own test of the Framers' intent, have become so deeply rooted that it would be neither prudent nor necessary to roll back the clock. . . .

The major difference between those who insist that they are passively discerning and enforcing the specific intentions of the Framers, and those who concede that they are of necessity doing something more, is likely to come down to this: The originalists seek to deny their own responsibility for the choices they are making and imposing upon the rest of us—whereas their opponents, for better or worse, accept such responsibility as inescapably theirs. . . .

To insist, as I would, that all judicial choices ought to be seriously constrained by constitutional text, structure, and tradition indeed requires one to confess that such choices are never merely the passive products of a single "original intent" existing in history and waiting to be discovered. The danger that judges might wield power in the name of the Constitution but in the service of nothing beyond their personal moral predilections is heightened, not reduced, by the habit of couching judicial determinations in the form of ineluctable readings of a purely external reality. However adorned by scholarly references to history, such claims are far less subject to meaningful dispute, and hence far less constrained by the requirements of persuasion, than are the more modest claims of those who admittedly base their constitutional arguments on a more eclectic, less determinate mix of appeals to language, precedent, and legal philosophy. . . . A candid avowal of the limits of originalism can open the process of constitutional interpretation to the full public debate without which it partakes only of miracle, mystery, and unquestioned authority.

NOTES

1. Published in the *New York Journal and Weekly Register*, Numbers 11 and 15 (1788). Three of the *Brutus* "letters" are reprinted in Edward S. Corwin, *Court over Constitution* (Princeton, NJ: Princeton University Press, 1938), pp. 231–62. It was common practice in the eighteenth and early nineteenth centuries for writers to adopt a signature ("Brutus" for Yates, or "Publius" for the authors of *The Federalist*) as a means to ensure temporary anonymity.
2. Henry Cabot Lodge, ed., *The Federalist* (New York: Putnam, 1904).
3. The Jackson and Lincoln messages appear in James D. Richardson, ed., *A Compilation of the Messages and Papers of the Presidents* (Washington, DC: Bureau of National Literature and Art, 1908), Vol. 2, pp. 581–82, and Vol. 6, p. 9, respectively.

3

Congress and the President

The doctrine of the separation of powers was adopted by the Convention of 1787, not to promote efficiency but to preclude the exercise of arbitrary power. The purpose was, not to avoid friction, but, by means of the inevitable friction incident to the distribution of the governmental powers among three departments, to save the people from autocracy.

—JUSTICE LOUIS D. BRANDEIS (1926)

The principle of separation of powers, propounded by seventeenth and eighteenth century political philosophers Harrington, Locke, and Montesquieu, was a device for limiting government power by taking the ancient lawmaking power from the monarch and vesting it in a legislature. The American development of this doctrine went much further. In place of the traditional division into legislature and executive, the American colonies adopted a threefold division, elevating the judiciary to a coequal position and putting all three under the rule of law established by a written constitution.

SEPARATION OF POWERS

The federal Constitution contains no specific declaration concerning **separation of powers**. The principle is implicit in the organization of the first three articles: (1) "All legislative powers herein granted shall be vested in a Congress of the United States"; (2) "The executive power shall be vested in a President of the United States"; and (3) "The judicial power shall be vested in one Supreme Court and in such inferior courts as the congress shall . . . ordain and establish." From this separation is derived the doctrine that certain functions because of their essential nature may properly be exercised by only a particular branch of the government, that such functions cannot be delegated to any other branch, and that one department may not interfere with another by usurping its powers or by supervising their exercise. Separation of powers was endorsed with virtual unanimity at the Convention of 1787. Inherited from

DOI: 10.4324/9781003164340-4

Montesquieu, the concept is inspired by the conviction that "every man vested with power is apt to abuse it; and carry his authority as far as it will go." One objective of the Constitution, therefore, was to avoid the "accumulation of all powers, legislative, executive, and judiciary, in the same hands, whether of one, a few, or many, and whether hereditary, self-appointed, or elective." Such concentration, declared James Madison in *The Federalist*, No. 47, "may justly be pronounced the very definition of tyranny."

Sharing Within Separation. Separation of powers, however, is a misnomer. No precise line is or could be drawn between the three branches of the national government. The Constitution separates organs of government; it fuses functions and powers. Because of frequently voiced criticism of the blending of executive, legislative, and judiciary in the proposed Constitution, Madison felt compelled to restate the traditional theory. The sharing of powers through the scheme of **checks and balances** was, he explained, a valuable additional restraint on government that complemented the principle of separation of powers. Not only did the blending of powers limit government itself, but it also provided weapons by which each branch could defend its position in the constitutional system. The president's veto, it was urged, protected him against legislative encroachments, and his power of appointment gave him influence against judicial assault. The Court had the power to pass on legislation and was protected by life tenure. The Congress could impeach a president and members of the Court. The national lawmakers controlled the purse on which both the other departments depended, the Senate passed on presidential appointments, and the Congress controlled the appellate jurisdiction of the Supreme Court. The legislature may exercise the executive power of pardon in the form of a grant of amnesty or immunity from prosecution. It may punish contempts and may provide in minute detail the rules of procedure to be followed by the courts. The power of Congress to control the issuance of injunctions by federal courts and to restrict their power to punish disobedience has also been sustained. Although the courts do not legislate in the strict sense of the word, their decisions may be regarded from a realistic point of view as a form of lawmaking. As upheld in ***Morrison* v. *Olson*** (1988), the courts, within limits, may exercise the executive power of appointment, and Congress may confer on them the power to suspend sentence, even though such power is legislative in nature. The president's power over foreign relations is such that the functions of advising and consenting to treaties and of "declaring" war, apparently entrusted by the Constitution to the legislature, have come largely under his control. Executive officers and administrative agencies also exercise functions that belong to other departments. Thus, independent regulatory commissions and the cabinet departments themselves exercise legislative and judicial powers through rulemaking and adjudication.

Two Approaches. In confronting a claim that a policy violates the principle of separation of powers, justices today tend to adopt one of two approaches. The first is tolerant of structural arrangements Congress deems to be in the public interest. It sees relationships among the branches as fluid. Because the Constitution already permits each branch to share some of the functions of the others, the words of the Constitution should not be read literally to preclude useful variations. The second finds within the Constitution a series of structural directives that are not to be transgressed. In this approach, the Constitution purposely commands separate compartments nearly hermetically sealed from each other. Exceptions include only those the Constitution itself allows.

ELEMENTS OF CONGRESSIONAL POWER

Even a quick glance at the Constitution reveals that the framers had more to say about Congress than any other part of the national government. Created nearly full-blown by Article I, Congress—with its twin branches of the House of Representatives and the Senate—is sometimes called "the first branch" or "the people's branch," even though "the people" were not empowered to vote directly for United States Senators until after ratification of the Seventeenth Amendment in 1913.

Lawmaking. Few legislative bodies elsewhere in the world possess greater authority over the lives, property, and happiness of a nation. Yet much of the policy leadership that many of the framers expected from Congress and that Congress exercised during most of the nineteenth century has shifted into the executive branch. Nonetheless, the declaration in the first paragraph of Article I that Congress possesses "[a]ll legislative powers herein granted" is a continuing reminder of this branch's lawmaking function. The vast reach of, and limits on, the lawmaking powers of Congress are largely the subjects of Chapters Six and Seven.

Delegation. In many cases, however, the statutes Congress passes cannot be so detailed as to contain every regulation and form of procedure by which the legislative policies set forth in them are to be carried out. The courts have consequently recognized that administrative officers must be permitted some discretion to determine when a given statute shall become operative and to fill in details through appropriate regulations. This sharing of rule-making authority is called **delegation**. In such situations, Chief Justice Taft explained in *Hampton & Co.* v. *United States* (1928), Congress must "lay down by legislative act an *intelligible principle* to which the person or body authorized to [act] is directed to conform" (emphasis added).

Only twice has the Supreme Court invalidated a statute as an unconstitutional delegation of power to the executive, both times in 1935. A provision of the National Industrial Recovery Act authorizing the president to prohibit the interstate shipment of oil produced or withdrawn in violation of state regulations was struck down in *Panama Refining Co.* v. *Ryan* (Hot Oil Case) because of the absence of guidance for the exercise of discretion. Then *Schechter Poultry Corp.* v. *United States* condemned the same statute's delegation to the president of code-approving authority. The president's discretion, the Court said, was "virtually unfettered," and Cardozo, in a concurring opinion, termed it "delegation run riot." Ordinarily, however, the Court regards even rather vague standards as sufficiently definite. *Whitman* v. *American Trucking Association* (2001), for example, upheld the National Air Quality Standards. The Clean Air Act directed the administrator of the Environmental Protection Agency to set "ambient air quality standards the attainment and maintenance of which . . ., and allowing an adequate margin of safety, are requisite to protect the public health."

Mistretta* v. *United States (1989), which challenged the constitutionality of the Sentencing Reform Act of 1984, illustrates allegations of improper delegation. The statute empowered the U.S. Sentencing Commission (an independent body lodged in the judicial branch) to promulgate binding guidelines for federal judges, including a range of determinate sentences for all categories of federal crimes and defendants. The majority "harbor[ed] no doubt" that the nondelegation principle had not been transgressed. It was "constitutionally sufficient if Congress clearly delineates the general policy, the public agency which is to apply it, and the boundaries of this delegated authority." For dissenting justice Scalia, however, the majority missed the point. The commission was flawed because it existed only to make law, not to make law incidentally to carrying out executive or judicial functions. In short, it was a "junior-varsity Congress."

On Sixth Amendment, not nondelegation, grounds, however, *United States* v. *Booker* (2005) held that the guidelines could continue to function only in an advisory, not a mandatory capacity. In the majority's view, any fact other than a prior conviction that is necessary to support an enhanced sentence must be either admitted by the defendant or found by a jury. Given the more than 76,000 criminal sentences that the federal courts impose each year, *Booker*'s sweep has been broad.

Legislative Veto. The delegation cases point to the fact that much "legislation" today is not enacted by Congress but is promulgated by dozens of administrative agencies. "The rise of administrative bodies probably has been the most significant legal trend of the last century," observed Justice Jackson in 1952. "They have become a veritable fourth branch of the Government. . . ." To control these agencies, Congress wrote nearly 300 "veto" provisions into about 200 statutes between 1932 and 1983, with about half of those enacted after 1970. This **legislative veto** enabled Congress to have its cake and eat it too. Agencies could continue making rules, but Congress could set aside such regulations by a one-house, a two-house, or sometimes even a committee resolution. Of course, such "vetoes" were not subject to presidential vetoes, and here lay the rub. Congress seemed to be making law other than in the constitutionally prescribed fashion, as the Court held in ***Immigration and Naturalization Service* v. *Chadha*** (1983). Although generous in allowing delegated rulemaking, the justices were unwilling to allow this method of controlling it. *Chadha* has frustrated Congress' efforts to keep control of the many agencies to which it has delegated rule-making authority. One response has been the **Congressional Review Act** of 1996 that requires agencies to send their final regulations to Congress for review 60 days before they take effect. A regulation is negated within the review period if Congress passes a joint resolution of disapproval and if the president signs it. The resolution is filibuster-proof but is still subject to presidential veto, which requires a two-thirds vote by both houses to override. As a result, agencies may still craft rules and regulations that could not garner a congressional majority. Through 2016, only one joint resolution of disapproval had been passed. However, in early 2017 and with the expectation of President Trump's support, the House and Senate voted to cancel the accountability rules issued by the Department of Education under the Every Student Succeeds Act, enacted during the Obama administration in 2015. By the end of 2020 an additional 15 rules had been overturned under the CRA.

The Short-Lived Item Veto. When Congress passes a bill, the president must accept or reject the bill in its entirety. American presidents have lacked a power enjoyed by some state governors: the **item veto,** which allows an executive to cross out certain provisions *within* a bill. To be sure, a president could enjoy an item veto by way of constitutional amendment, but could Congress provide something akin to an item veto by statute? In 1996 Congress passed legislation allowing the president to cancel specific items in appropriations and tax bills within five days after signing the bill into law. Congress might reinsert the items by passing a "disapproval bill," but this would be subject to the president's regular veto, which could be overridden only by a two-thirds vote in both houses. Certain senators and representatives who believed the law unwisely strengthened the presidency at Congress' expense challenged the constitutionality of the item veto. In *Raines* v. *Byrd*

(1997), the Supreme Court dismissed the suit because members of Congress had not "alleged a sufficiently concrete injury to have established Article III standing." Asserting an institutional injury as against the executive did not give them standing, for, individually, no member of Congress had been harmed by the law. Within two months of this decision, President Clinton canceled numerous items in bills passed by Congress, including provisions which would have benefited two hospitals in New York City and a potato farmers' cooperative. With demonstrable individual injury, the aggrieved parties renewed the attack. Voting 6–3, the Court held in ***Clinton* v. *City of New York*** (1998) that the item veto act violated the Constitution. "If there is to be a new procedure in which the President will play a different role in determining the final text of what may 'become a law,'" wrote Justice Stevens, "such change must come not by legislation but through the amendment procedures set forth in Article V of the Constitution."

Investigations. A function of Congress vying in importance with lawmaking itself is investigation. Woodrow Wilson rated this "informing function" higher than that of legislation. "[T]he power of inquiry," maintained Justice Van Devanter in *McGrain* v. *Daugherty* (1927), "with process to enforce it—is an essential and appropriate auxiliary to the legislative function." In 1936, Senator Hugo Black, who the next year became a Supreme Court justice, referred to congressional investigations as "among the most useful and fruitful functions of the national legislature." Though derived immediately from the "necessary and proper" clause, the investigatory power is also grounded in the fact that Congress, like Parliament and the early state legislatures, is a deliberative body. Each house, separately or concurrently, may pass resolutions expressing its views on any subject it sees fit. To inform itself on matters likely to become subjects of legislation, Congress establishes committees that may **subpoena** witnesses (i.e., compel their attendance) and take testimony. If witnesses refuse to cooperate, they may be punished for contempt. Such imprisonment, however, may not extend beyond the session of Congress in which the offense was committed, and any investigation must be related to a valid legislative purpose (*Kilbourn* v. *Thompson*, 1881).

During the Cold War, ***Watkins* v. *United States*** (1957) questioned the authority of either house to delve into the private lives of individuals—to "expose for the sake of exposure" or to deny freedom of speech or right of association. The 6–1 majority agreed that the power to conduct investigations "is inherent in the legislative process" but insisted that as a matter of due process of law all witnesses must be informed of the pertinency of the questions put to them. Accordingly, the Court overturned John Watkins's conviction for contempt of Congress after the labor organizer refused to answer questions about the political views of associates. Reaction to the decision both in and out of Congress was hotly critical. Two years later, by construing *Watkins* narrowly, ***Barenblatt* v. *United States*** reached a different result. Five justices affirmed the conviction of a former Vassar College professor for failure to answer questions about past affiliation with the Communist Party.

May Congress require a sitting president to hand over personal financial records? This question reached the Court after Democrats regained control of the U.S. House of Representatives in 2019, as President Trump then became the target of investigations by several House committees. One of these investigations led to his impeachment on two counts in late 2019 and subsequent acquittal on both by the Senate in early 2020. Another committee sought tax and other financial documents belonging to the president and members of his family. In ***Trump* v. *Mazars USA***,

Chief Justice Roberts acknowledged that the case was the first of its kind to receive attention by the justices and admitted reluctance to intervene in a dispute between the executive and legislative branches. Nonetheless, voting 7–2, and giving neither the House nor the president a complete win, the Court settled on a four-part balancing test to guide lower courts in reaching a judgment in this or another similar situation.

Membership and Privilege. On March 1, 1967, the House of Representatives voted to exclude recently reelected Congressman Adam Clayton Powell on the ground that he had misused public funds and was contemptuous of the New York courts and committees of Congress. By a vote of 7–1 (*Powell* v. *McCormack*), the Supreme Court held in 1969 that the House lacked power to exclude from its membership a person duly elected who meets the age, citizenship, and residence requirements specified in the Constitution. **Exclusion**, however, must not be confused with **expulsion**. The first refers to barring representatives from taking their seats; the second is a penalty for members judged by their colleagues to be guilty of extremely serious misconduct. In Chief Justice Warren's last major opinion, the Court reversed the opinion of Appeals Judge Warren E. Burger, the person nominated to succeed him. Invoking separation of powers, Burger had dismissed Powell's suit for reinstatement, contending that courts should not rule on a political issue fraught with possible conflict between Congress and courts. Warren disagreed: "A fundamental principle of our representative democracy is . . . 'that the people should choose whom they please to govern them. . . .' [T]his principle is undermined as much by limiting whom the people can elect as by limiting the franchise itself." *Powell* in turn was the authority for ***U.S. Term Limits, Inc.* v. *Thornton*** (see Chapter Four), when the Court in 1995 struck down state-imposed limits on the number of terms that a member of the U.S. House of Representatives might serve, because such limits altered the qualifications for congressional office already set by the Constitution.

The Court has also declined to allow Congress to be the sole judge of the scope of the privilege enshrined in the **speech or debate clause** of the Constitution. The protection against being "questioned in any other Place" is a pillar of legislative independence. It extends "not only to a member but also to his aides insofar as the conduct of the latter would be a protected legislative act if performed by the member himself" (*Gravel* v. *United States*, 1972). Critical to the scope of the privilege is the definition of a "protected legislative act," by no means an all-inclusive term. Such protection extends to voting and preparing committee reports but not to newsletters and press releases, declared the Court in *Hutchinson* v. *Proxmire* (1979). Senator William Proxmire's "Golden Fleece of the Month Award" had ridiculed a researcher for studies done on animals. In a newsletter the senator claimed that the research had "made a monkey out of the American taxpayer." Without the protection of the speech or debate clause, the Court ruled that Proxmire could be sued for damages.

THE PRESIDENT AND EXECUTIVE POWER

Addressing himself to the executive in *The Federalist*, No. 70, Alexander Hamilton rejected the widely held belief of his day that "a vigorous executive is inconsistent with the genius of republican government." On the contrary, he insisted,

> Energy in the Executive is a leading character in the definition of good government. . . . A feeble executive implies a feeble execution of the government. A feeble execution is

> but another phrase for a bad execution; and a government ill executed, whatever it may be in theory, must be, in practice, a bad government.

Members of the Convention of 1787 who feared that the president inevitably would succumb to an all-powerful legislature have proved to be poor prophets. Of the three branches of government, it is the presidency that has expanded most in power and in the number and variety of its activities. War, economic crisis, and advances in communication have combined to thrust obligations on the executive not contemplated in an earlier age. The sketch of presidential power in the Constitution continues to acquire new dimensions and detail with each new administration. While the swelling of executive authority is hardly unique to America, few if any chief executives of other democratic countries command a more impressive array of powers. "[T]he history of the presidency has been a history of aggrandizement," wrote Professor Edward Corwin in 1941. The president is both head of state and the political head of the government; he is responsible for executing the laws. He exercises the power to pardon, the power to appoint, the veto power, and extensive military and foreign policy powers.

Theories of Presidential Power. Four views purport to describe the nature and scope of presidential power: the *constitutional theory*, the *stewardship theory*, the *unitary executive theory*, and the *prerogative theory*. As William Howard Taft explained in his book *Our Chief Magistrate and His Powers*, three years after leaving the White House, the constitutional theory holds that Article II contains an enumeration of executive powers and that the president must be prepared to justify all his actions on the basis of either enumerated or implied power. Theodore Roosevelt, who preceded Taft in the White House, countered that the president is a "steward of the people" and is therefore under the duty to do "anything that the needs of the nation demanded unless such action was forbidden by the Constitution and the laws." Taft denounced Roosevelt's stewardship theory as calculated to make the president a "universal Providence." As chief justice, however, Taft indicated greater sympathy for it. Going beyond the first Roosevelt's stewardship theory, Franklin D. Roosevelt's concept of his duties conforms essentially to John Locke's description of "prerogative"—"the power to act according to discretion for the public good, without the prescription of the law and sometimes even against it." During his long incumbency, President Roosevelt often sacrificed constitutional and legal restrictions on the altar of "emergency" and a commanding public interest.

Falling just short of prerogative in the extent of its claims is the unitary executive theory whereby the president not only has control over members of the executive branch, but whose authority is restricted only by the Constitution. Congress may hold the president accountable by censure, impeachment, or constitutional amendment but not by legislation that intrudes onto the chief executive's Article II domain. Identified particularly with presidents George W. Bush and Obama, the unitary theory of executive power draws from the "coordinate construction" articulated initially by Thomas Jefferson and echoed by some later presidents, by which all three branches of the federal government, not merely the courts, have the duty to interpret the Constitution and statutes.

Parts of Justice Sutherland's opinion in ***United States* v. *Curtiss-Wright Export Corp.*** (1936) seem to justify "inherent" power, at least in foreign affairs, where the president speaks and acts for the nation. In the domestic sphere, however, this is a highly dubious rationale for presidential action or inaction, even in wartime, as ***Youngstown Sheet & Tube Co.* v. *Sawyer*** (1952) suggests. When the Steel Seizure Case was before the district court, counsel for the United States, asked by the bench to specify the source of President Truman's power to seize the steel mills in peacetime, declared, "We base the President's power on Sections 1, 2, and 3 of Article II of the Constitution, and whatever inherent, implied or residual powers may flow therefrom." "So you contend the Executive has unlimited power in time of an emergency?" the judge inquired. Government counsel replied that the president "has the power to take such action as is necessary to meet the emergency" and indicated that the only limitations on executive power in an emergency are the ballot box and impeachment. In argument before the Supreme Court, however, government counsel stressed that the president's specific powers derived from the duty to execute the laws and as commander in chief. The case also demonstrates that, although the president may not be the subject of judicial orders limiting his actions in executing laws or implementing policy, as *Mississippi* v. *Johnson* (1867) held, subordinate officers in the executive branch may be the objects of injunctive or other forms of relief when they act or threaten to act illegally.

Truman moved against the steel companies through an **executive order**, a legally binding directive issued by the president, acting as the head of the executive branch, to persons or entities in or subject to the administration. While Congress may attempt through legislation to countermand an executive order, any such bill would itself be subject to a presidential veto. Those adversely affected by an executive order may seek to challenge it judicially, as happened in the steel case. Through his one-term presidency President Trump issued some 195 executive orders. By comparison, during their two terms in office, George W. Bush issued 291 and Barack Obama issued 276. Several of President Trump's executive orders restricting access to the United States were challenged on both statutory and constitutional grounds in ***Trump* v. *Hawaii*** (2018).

Executive Privilege. In 1974, ***United States* v. *Nixon*** held that the president himself must respond to a subpoena issued in connection with a pending trial of former government officials. Although expressly acknowledging **executive privilege** for the first time—the right of certain officials in the executive branch to refuse to appear before Congress and the courts and to provide requested documents—the justices ruled that neither the doctrine of separation of powers nor the need for confidentiality of executive communications barred the federal courts from access to White House audiotapes needed as evidence in a criminal case. In constitutional theory and political consequences, the decision remains among the most remarkable in the Court's history. Within days President Nixon complied, and the tapes linked him to a conspiracy to obstruct justice. On August 9, Nixon became the first president to leave office by resignation.

Appointment and Removal of Officers. The Constitution provides that the president "shall nominate and, by and with the advice and consent of the Senate, shall appoint ambassadors . . . judges of the Supreme Court, and all other officers of the United States, whose appointments are not herein otherwise provided for and which shall be established by law. . . ." The Constitution makes no provision for the removal of officers appointed under this clause, but the power of removal is generally regarded as a power derived from the power to appoint. ***Myers* v. *United States*** (1926) strongly suggested that the power of the president to remove officials appointed by him was plenary, free from any limitations by Congress. In that case the Court upheld Woodrow Wilson's removal of a presidentially appointed (and Senate-confirmed) postmaster, even though a statute allowed removal during the postal official's four-year term only with Senate approval. In 1935, however, the Court whittled down the broad rule, holding that the removal of officials from certain independent agencies, such as the Federal Trade Commission, could be limited to causes defined by Congress (***Humphrey's Executor* v. *United States***). The Court distinguished positions in the traditional executive departments, for whose administration the president assumed primary responsibility, from those in agencies established by Congress to carry out legislative policy essentially free from any executive influence other than that resulting from appointment.

Article II also confers on the president authority to make a **recess appointment** "to fill up all Vacancies that may happen during the Recess of the Senate, by granting Commissions which shall expire at the End of their next Session." Acting between *pro forma* sessions the Senate held on January 3 and January 6, 2013, President Obama made three appointments to the National Labor Relations Board (NLRB). In a challenge to a decision by the NLRB, the Court held in *NLRB* v. *Canning* (2014) that the recess appointments clause allowed the president to act on an existing vacancy during any recess of sufficient duration, whether inter- or intra-session, a measure that did not include the three-day adjournment between the two *pro forma* sessions. Because the Senate did not consider itself in session, the appointments were invalid.

Questions of appointment and removal and separation of powers combined in ***Morrison* v. *Olson*** (1988). The politically charged case challenged the provision in the Ethics in Government Act of 1978 for an **independent counsel** to investigate criminal wrongdoing by high officials in the executive branch. Under the terms of the statute, upon receiving information suggesting criminal conduct, the attorney general conducted a preliminary inquiry and then could refer the matter to a division of the Court of Appeals for the District of Columbia Circuit. This division appointed the independent counsel. Once named, the independent counsel could be removed only for cause, and the removal was subject to judicial review. The independent counsel possessed the full investigative and prosecutorial functions of the Department of Justice with respect to the matters within the scope of the referral. In essence, Congress decreed that criminal investigation at the highest levels be done by an attorney not subject to routine control by the attorney general and the president.

Looking back to *Myers* (which recognized broad removal power) and to *Humphrey's Executor* (which narrowed the removal power), eight justices agreed that Congress could place the independent counsel under the terms of the latter. Counsel's independence from the executive branch, Chief Justice Rehnquist explained, did not impermissibly interfere "with the President's exercise of his constitutionally appointed functions." For Justice Scalia in dissent, the majority had effected "a revolution in our constitutional jurisprudence." To take away prosecutorial discretion from the president is "to remove the core of the prosecutorial function"—"a quintessentially executive function."

The statute was allowed to expire in December 1992. Retaining the basic features of the previous version, Congress revived the law in 1994 for a period of five years. In 1999, Republicans and Democrats alike allowed the statute to expire again. The attorney general or designee, acting for the president, may still name a **special prosecutor** in circumstances that, before, might have called for an independent counsel. For example, in May 2017, Robert Mueller was appointed by Deputy Attorney General Rod Rosenstein as special counsel to oversee an investigation into allegations of Russian interference in the 2016 presidential election and related matters. He submitted his report to Attorney General William Barr in March 2019.

Although a special prosecutor, like any other federal prosecutor, serves at the pleasure of the president, removal questions continue to appear on the Supreme Court's docket, as happened in *Seila Law* v. *Consumer Financial Protection Bureau* (2020). In setting up the agency in 2011 to protect consumers in the financial sector, Congress stipulated that its director could be dismissed only for cause—that is, only for "inefficiency, neglect of duty, or malfeasance in office," a restriction on the president's authority that five justices found unacceptable. Chief Justice Roberts explained that the president's authority to remove executive branch officers was subject to only two exceptions: one for multi-member expert agencies that do not wield substantial executive power (as in *Humphrey's Executor*), and the other for inferior officers with limited duties and no policymaking or administrative authority as in *Morrison* v. *Olson*. For the majority, the CFPB fell into neither category.

Immunity. If presidents may have the constitutionality of their policies challenged in court, under what circumstances may a president be subjected to personal lawsuits? In 1982, ***Nixon* v. *Fitzgerald*** bestowed on the president an **absolute immunity** (shared also by federal judges and prosecutors) from private lawsuit that extends to all acts within "the outer perimeter" of his official duties even where, as in this instance, the suit was not commenced until after Nixon resigned. The immunity is a "functionally mandated incident of the President's unique office," declared Justice Powell for a majority of five, "rooted in the constitutional tradition of the separation of powers and supported by the Nation's history." Other checks such as the impeachment remedy, the availability of congressional and public oversight, and concern for one's "place in history" would presumably suffice as guards against presidential wrongdoing. Presidential aides, however, do not enjoy the same unqualified protection. Instead, theirs is a good-faith or **qualified immunity** (also enjoyed by police officers in federal civil rights actions), shielding them from damage suits as long as their conduct does not violate "clearly established" statutory or constitutional rights of which a reasonable person would have known (*Harlow* v. *Fitzgerald*, 1982; *Pearson* v. *Callahan*, 2009).

Fitzgerald's broad declaration of civil immunity, however, does not extend to a White House incumbent sued for actions predating a presidency. In 1997, ***Clinton* v. *Jones*** unanimously rejected President Bill Clinton's request that litigation against him by Paula Jones for sexual harassment be postponed until completion of his second term. The suit grew out of events alleged to have occurred while Clinton was governor of Arkansas. *Jones* turned aside Clinton's argument that allowing the suit to proceed would breach separation of powers by placing the president's schedule in judicial hands. Emphasizing that a trial judge would be expected to be sensitive to competing demands on the president's time, the Court made clear the basis of the immunity recognized in *Fitzgerald*. The latter's immunity exists not because the president is "too busy" but because the threat of personal civil liability might inhibit a president from making crucial decisions. Subsequent proceedings in the Jones suit following the Supreme Court's decision took an ironic turn. They became caught up in an investigation already underway by independent counsel Kenneth Starr, leading eventually to Clinton's impeachment by the House of Representatives in 1998 and his trial and acquittal in the Senate in 1999.

Trump* v. *Vance (2020) posed a somewhat different question for a different occupant of the White House: may a county prosecutor issue a subpoena to a third-party custodian to obtain the financial and tax records of a sitting president in a situation where the president has no claim of executive privilege? Seven justices concluded that the subpoena would not intrude unduly on the president's duties. Moreover, because state law provided adequate avenues to challenge the subpoena as being unduly broad or having been issued in bad faith, the Constitution did not require the prosecutor to show a heightened standard of need for the state grand jury subpoena. In February 2021, after lower courts again ruled against Trump, the Supreme Court, with no noted dissents to a one-sentence order, rejected the former president's efforts to bar prosecutorial access to his tax and other financial records that had been at issue.

FOREIGN POLICY AND NATIONAL SECURITY

Recent presidents have enjoyed considerably more independence in shaping foreign as opposed to domestic policy. When applied abroad, presidential power is limited by Congress only with some difficulty, mainly by congressional control of the purse, approval of trade agreements, and the power to investigate. Even with those restraints, however, the making of foreign and defense policy remains a shared responsibility.

Treaties. Under the Constitution, the executive branch negotiates treaties, but all treaties must receive the consent of two-thirds of the Senate. Once approved, a treaty may then be the basis of implementing legislation that otherwise would not be within the power of Congress. This is the significance of ***Missouri* v. *Holland***. Congress as well may by statute alter or negate the effect of a treaty on domestic law. However, with heavy reliance on the Steel Seizure Case, *Medellin* v. *Texas* (2008) held that a non-self-executing treaty and a decision by the International Court of Justice interpreting it are not binding on American state courts and that, absent implementing congressional legislation, the president lacks authority unilaterally to require state compliance. Nonetheless, the tendency of modern presidents has been to use **executive agreements** in place of treaties, thus freeing them from dependency on the Senate. Under *United States* v. *Belmont* (1937) and *United States* v. *Pink* (1942), such agreements have the same legal effect as treaties. Strengthening the president's hand in foreign policy is the theory of sovereignty set forth in Justice Sutherland's opinion in *Curtiss-Wright* and the great reservoir of inherent power possessed by the president as representative of the United States in dealing with other nations.

An example was President Jimmy Carter's notification in December 1978 to terminate this country's Mutual Defense Treaty with Taiwan on January 1, 1980, without congressional approval. Opponents couched objections in constitutional terms. Even though the treaty provided for termination on a year's notice by either signatory, they argued that the president could not do it without Senate approval. The court of appeals ruled that the Senate's role in ratification did not imply a role in termination. As the nation's agent in foreign affairs, the president had acted within the terms of the treaty. In *Goldwater* v. *Carter* (1979), the Supreme Court, without hearing oral arguments, refused to address the merits of the suit. A treaty may also have a withdrawal provision, as was the case with the Open Skies treaty. Signed in 1992 by some 34 nations, including the United States and Russia, and entered into force in 2002, the agreement permits signatories to carry out unarmed reconnaissance flights over the others' territories. Member nations could withdraw by giving six months' notice, as the Trump administration did in May 2020, with formal withdrawal completed on November 22, 2020. Left unclear was whether Senate approval would be needed should the successor Biden administration seek to rejoin the accord, or whether the president could act unilaterally. Complicating the picture was legislation requiring consultation with Congress four months before any withdrawal.

Military Powers. The power of the federal government over the armed forces of the nation is also divided between the president and Congress. The legislature is given the important powers to "declare war," to raise armies and provide a navy, and to make "rules for the government and regulation" of the armed forces. The president is designated commander in chief of the armed forces. He may issue regulations of his own and may take charge of all military operations in time of peace as well as in war.

The framers thus made war making a joint enterprise. At the urging of James Madison and Elbridge Gerry, the Convention changed the original phrase from "make war" to "declare war." In changing this language, the framers presumably intended to allow the president the authority to repel sudden attacks on the United States, its territories, or its armed forces. The commander-in-chief clause seems to have been designed neither to alter this relationship nor to grant the president additional war-making powers. Rather, the clause established the principle of civilian control over the military. The president was to be, in Hamilton's words, "the first general and admiral." Presidents, however, have used their powers to control the armed forces to manipulate Congress and, to some extent, to preempt the war power itself. Technology has expanded the president's role and correspondingly curtailed the power of Congress. Only since 1970 have legislators attempted to regain their constitutional share of war making or war avoiding. Practice changes the working meaning of the Constitution.

Two contrasting approaches by presidents to the problem of waging war can be found in American history. Under Lincoln, Congress was ignored or asked to ratify executive actions already accomplished or under way. For example, on April 19, 1861, Lincoln ordered a blockade of Confederate ports; on July 13 Congress authorized the president to declare that a state of insurrection existed, and on August 6 voted to ratify retroactively the military decisions that Lincoln had made. Claiming the president had acted unlawfully, owners of four vessels seized before July 13 sued to recover their property. Could the president impose a blockade without congressional authorization? Was an insurrection—the Lincoln administration refused to recognize the Confederacy as a separate country—a "war," to which the rules of prize applied? The Prize Cases (1863) upheld both Lincoln's theory of the war and his authority to act without Congress. The Court, Justice Robert Grier explained for a majority of five, could not be asked "to affect a technical ignorance of the existence of a war, which all the world acknowledges to be the greatest civil war known in the history of the human race." In World Wars I and II, by contrast, Congress passed a large number of general statutes assigning to the president, or to persons designated by him, vast discretionary powers. The broadest of these delegations was upheld in *Bowles* v. *Willingham* (1944).

Vietnam and the War Powers Resolution. In the face of rising public protest against the undeclared Vietnam War, Congress enacted (over President Nixon's veto) the **War Powers Resolution**, designed to curb presidential discretion in committing the armed forces of the nation to combat. The 1973 resolution was a far cry from the Gulf of Tonkin Resolution of 1964, passed early in the Vietnam conflict, which declared "that Congress approves and supports the determination of the President as commander-in-chief, to take all necessary measures to repel any armed attack against the forces of the United States and to prevent further aggression." President Lyndon Johnson viewed the Tonkin Resolution as the functional equivalent of a declaration of war.

In contrast, according to the War Powers Resolution, whenever military action takes place without prior congressional approval, the president is supposed to consult with Congress whenever possible before committing troops, and in any event he is supposed to inform Congress of what he has done within 48 hours. Unless Congress authorizes continued action, use of troops must cease after 60 days. Furthermore, by concurrent resolution (not subject to presidential veto) Congress may order the president to withdraw the troops from combat. *Chadha* casts doubt on the constitutionality of this legislative veto.

Experience since 1973 demonstrates that the War Powers Resolution is not a significant restraint on presidential power. Most presidents have considered the act unconstitutional and have generally failed to "invoke" the act by claiming the law does not apply to military operations they have initiated. They report to Congress "consistent with," not "pursuant to," the terms of the resolution. When presidents do turn to Congress for authorization to use force, it is more often because of the political support the authorization provides than any obligation to the War Powers Resolution itself. Moreover, Congress has yet to display sufficient political will to ensure compliance.

Iraq (I). Iraq's invasion of Kuwait in August 1990 and the American response to it rekindled debate on the president's war powers. After President George H. W. Bush sent 230,000 military personnel to the Persian Gulf region and after the United Nations Security Council imposed a number of economic sanctions and a blockade against Iraq, both houses of Congress in October passed resolutions supporting the action. On November 8, however, Bush ordered a doubling of U.S. military forces to provide an offensive capability. The Security Council then passed Resolution 678 on November 29 authorizing "all necessary means" to force Iraqi troops from Kuwait should they not withdraw by January 15, 1991. All along, the president claimed authority to launch an attack without congressional approval, so initially he did not request it, and Congress offered none. However, on January 8, 1991, Bush formally requested a congressional resolution authorizing the use of force, although he told reporters, "I don't think I need it." On January 12, after vigorous debate, the Senate and the House gave the president the approval he sought. The occasion was historic. It was the first time since World War II that Congress directly debated ahead of time the sending of thousands of American troops into combat. It was also the first request by a president for approval of the use of force since the Gulf of Tonkin Resolution in 1964. Did President Bush blink? In requesting the resolution, was he effectively acknowledging that he lacked constitutional authority to wage war against Iraq unless Congress first approved? Perhaps. Or perhaps Bush had requested only political support, not constitutional authority, recognizing that symbolically the vote placed him in a much stronger position.

The War on Terrorism, Afghanistan, and Iraq (II). The terrorist attacks carried out by **al Qaeda** on the United States on September 11, 2001, have profoundly changed America. Politically, the attacks transformed the presidency of George W. Bush. Constitutionally, they strengthened the executive branch, in the short term at least, because of large-scale military actions, passage of the Patriot Act, and a heightened sense of fear of other attacks that might be far worse than those of September 11. The military initiatives that ensued had a degree of formal congressional support that has been uncommon since the end of the Vietnam War, although to be sure there was skepticism aplenty about the wisdom of the Bush administration's military policy. Yet, among other costs, some civil liberties have been placed at risk. These concerns and the Patriot Act itself are addressed in Chapter Fifteen.

The foundation of the initial military response was laid on September 18, 2001, when Congress approved the **Authorization for Use of Military Force** (AUMF; 115 Stat. 224), which was tantamount to a declaration of war on terrorists. With its words constituting "specific statutory authorization within the meaning of section 5(b) of the War Powers Resolution,"

> the President is authorized to use all necessary and appropriate force against those nations, organizations, or persons he determines planned, authorized, committed, or aided the terrorist attacks that occurred on September 11, 2001, or harbored such organizations or persons, in order to prevent any future acts of international terrorism against the United States by such nations, organizations or persons.

An attack on Afghanistan commenced on October 8, followed by an invasion by American and British forces. The objective was to root out, disrupt, and destroy the al Qaeda terrorist network that was using Afghanistan as one of its bases of operation, to topple the terrorist-friendly Taliban government, and to replace it with an elected one hostile to terrorism.

In the summer of 2002, President Bush and his national security advisers became convinced that Iraq posed an imminent danger not only to the Persian Gulf region but to the United States because it probably possessed biological, chemical, and/or radiological weapons and was prepared to transfer them to terrorists who would then attack the United States. What was needed, Bush concluded, was not merely a disarmed Iraq but a disarmed Iraq without its dictator, Saddam Hussein.

On October 16, Congress gave the president the statutory authority to move ahead. Noting that it constituted "specific statutory authorization within the meaning of section 5 (b) of the War Powers Resolution," House Joint Resolution 114 (116 Stat. 1498) authorized the president to use military force against Iraq.

After lengthy diplomatic efforts failed to obtain the blessing either of the United Nations or of most other major countries for an attack on Iraq at this time, the United States, joined by the United Kingdom and a handful of minor allies, again went to war. Air strikes opened the campaign on March 20, 2003, and were quickly followed by an invasion of ground troops. Three weeks later, U.S. forces were in Baghdad, and the Hussein regime had fallen. By May 1, resistance by organized Iraqi units had ended, and a protracted and dangerous American-directed occupation of Iraq began. The unpopularity of Bush's Iraq policy, among other factors, cost Republicans control of Congress in the midterm elections of 2006 and handed the White House to Democrat Barack Obama in 2009, who promised an end to an American military presence in Iraq, an objective that remained elusive.

Libya, Afghanistan (II), and ISIL. Although highly critical of President Bush's military policies, President Obama deployed American power particularly after 2010. In March 2011, the administration secured passage of Resolution 1973 by the United Nations Security Council authorizing military intervention in Libya against the government of Muammar al-Qaddafi that was attempting to crush opponents of the regime. Air and naval forces of the United States and several other members of

NATO (North Atlantic Treaty Organization) conducted a prolonged series of attacks in support of rebel forces that culminated in Qaddafi's death in October. The Libyan campaign was punctuated in May with the announcement of the killing of Osama bin Laden, mastermind of the attacks of September 11, 2001, by a U.S. Navy SEAL team in Pakistan. Significantly, when congressional leaders pressed President Obama in June that, under the terms of the War Powers Resolution, continued U.S. military action in Libya by that date required approval by Congress, the administration responded that, because of the limited American role, involving as it did no U.S. ground forces, the strictures of the War Powers Resolution did not apply.

In Afghanistan, a resurgent Taliban delayed Obama's plan to withdraw all American forces by the end of 2014. Indeed, by the spring of 2016, at least several hundred additional U.S. troops had been sent to Afghanistan to aid the Afghan National Army. Complicating matters has been the growth of ISIL or ISIS—the militant extremist **Islamic State**—which by 2014 had displaced al Qaeda as a principal sponsor and instigator of terrorism. Attacks in Europe and North America directed or inspired by ISIL have tended less toward spectacular targets in favor of smaller-scale atrocities. Moreover, in contrast to al Qaeda, ISIL acquires territory to support its operations, and was successful in occupying not only key regions of Iraq, but by mid-2016 parts of Syria and Libya as well. In response, Obama approved additional operations in Libya and the dispatch in July of some 4,600 U.S. troops to aid the Iraqi Army. Because Congress had not acted on the president's request in February 2015 for formal authorization of actions in various places against ISIL, the administration continued to rely instead on the original AUMF from the Bush administration in 2001.

The Trump Administration. Part of Donald Trump's campaign for the White House in 2016 was a pledge to stop America's involvement in "endless wars." Yet it was not until the last weeks of his administration, just before Joe Biden's inauguration as president in 2021, that final orders were given for most of the 5,000 American troops remaining in Afghanistan and the 3,000 in Iraq to be withdrawn. This action followed by about a year a drone strike on January 3, 2020 near Baghdad International Airport that killed Qasem Soleimani, a major general in Iran's Revolutionary Guard and perhaps the second most powerful person in that country. American officials justified the Soleimani assassination as necessary to stop an "imminent attack" but later issued a clarification that the action was "in response to an escalating series of attacks."

Nonetheless, the attack alarmed many in Congress that war with Iran was looming, prompting Senator Tim Kaine (Democratic vice presidential nominee in 2016), just hours after the attack, to introduce a resolution (S.J. Res. 68) that directed the president

> to terminate the use of United States armed forces for hostilities against the Islamic Republic of Iran or any part of its government or military, unless explicitly authorized by a declaration of war or specific authorization for use of military force against Iran.

The Republican-controlled Senate approved the resolution 55–45 on February 13, with the Democratic-led House doing likewise 227–186 on March 11. Calling the resolution "very insulting," President Trump vetoed it on May 6, 2020, the third veto of his presidency. As with the previous two, there were insufficient votes in Congress to override. (The nearly two-month gap between the House vote and the president's veto was pandemic-related, in that a delay in the **enrollment process** for the resolution in Congress meant that the president did not receive the measure until May 5.) The first veto override for Trump did not occur until January 1, 2021, after he had rejected the National Defense Authorization Act.

Supreme Court Action. As explained in Chapter Fifteen, the earlier Authorization for Use of Military Force itself has been the subject of litigation in the Supreme Court, most prominently in *Hamdi* v. *Rumsfeld* (2004) and *Hamdan* v. *Rumsfeld* (2006). While *Hamdi* found AUMF an adequate legal basis for the indefinite detention of suspected enemy combatants (including an American citizen), subject to some kind of judicial review, *Hamdan* declared the Bush administration's plan to try such combatants by military commissions wholly lacking legal validity. In 2006, Congress passed the Military Commissions Act (MCA) to correct the deficiencies highlighted in *Hamdan* and to prevent Guantanamo detainees from challenging their confinement in federal court. In ***Boumediene* v. *Bush*** (2008), the Supreme Court struck down the jurisdiction-stripping provision of the MCA.

The power to wage war thus remains constitutionally indeterminate. The president is under a positive obligation "to take care that the laws be faithfully executed." His power must be adapted to changed and changing conditions. But in fulfilling this responsibility, the president must also take into account those principles and provisions of the Constitution that restrict as well as enlarge his powers. Likewise, Congress' share in war making must be adapted to unforeseen developments. Otherwise, technological evolution will vastly alter the constitutional balance. The power of Congress in this sensitive area was not meant to cripple and impede; it was designed to produce a wiser course of action. Sound in 1787, it is no less so today.

KEY TERMS

separation of powers
checks and balances
delegation
legislative veto
Congressional Review Act
item veto
subpoena
exclusion
expulsion
speech or debate clause
constitutional theory
stewardship theory
unitary executive theory
prerogative theory
executive order
executive privilege
independent counsel
special prosecutor
absolute immunity
qualified immunity
executive agreement
War Powers Resolution
al Qaeda
Authorization for Use of Military Force (AUMF)
Islamic State
enrollment process

QUERIES

1. Did the Supreme Court's decisions in *Trump* v. *Mazars* and *Trump* v. *Vance* affect the presidency or only Donald Trump?

2. Plainly, the Supreme Court's decision in *United States* v. *Nixon* was a defeat for President Nixon. Yet was it also at least a partial victory for the presidency?

3. Writing three years after leaving the White House, President Harry Truman argued that "the President . . . must always act in a national emergency . . . [He] must be able to act at all times to meet any sudden threat to the nation's security." Did the majority in the Steel Seizure Case reject this position? What theory of presidential power seems most closely aligned with Truman's comment?

4. What limits does the War Powers Resolution impose on a president's war-making authority? What steps might Congress today take to give legislators a greater voice in influencing a president's use of American military forces?

SELECTED READINGS

Barber, S. A. *The Constitution and the Delegation of Congressional Power*. Chicago: University of Chicago Press, 1975.

Berger, Raoul. *Executive Privilege*. Cambridge, MA: Harvard University Press, 1974.

Calabresi, Steven G., and Christopher S. Yoo. *The Unitary Executive: Presidential Power from Washington to Bush*. New Haven, CT: Yale University Press, 2012.

Collins, Paul M., Jr., and Matthew Eshbaugh-Soha. *The President and the Supreme Court: Going Public on Judicial Decisions from Washington to Trump*. New York: Cambridge University Press, 2019.

Corwin, Edward S. *The President, Office and Powers*, 4th ed. New York: New York University Press, 1957.

Craig, Barbara H. *Chadha*. New York: Oxford University Press, 1988.

Di Paolo, Amanda. *Zones of Twilight: Wartime Presidential Powers and Federal Court Decision Making*. Lanham, MD: Rowman and Littlefield, 2009.

Edelson, Chris. *Emergency Presidential Power: From the Drafting of the Constitution to the War on Terror*. Madison: University of Wisconsin Press, 2013.

Fisher, Louis. *Constitutional Conflicts Between Congress and the President*, 6th ed. Lawrence: University Press of Kansas, 2014a.

Fisher, Louis. *The Law of the Executive Branch: Presidential Power*. New York: Oxford University Press, 2014b.

Fisher, Louis. *President Obama: Constitutional Aspirations and Executive Actions*. Lawrence: University Press of Kansas, 2018.

Gormley, Ken, ed. *Presidents and the Constitution*, 2 vols, rev. ed. New York: New York University Press, 2021.

Marcus, Maeva. *Truman and the Steel Seizure Case*. New York: Columbia University Press, 1977.

Randall, J. G. *Constitutional Problems under Lincoln*, rev. ed. Urbana: University of Illinois Press, 1951.

I. DELEGATION AND LAWMAKING

Mistretta v. *United States*
488 U.S. 361, 109 S.Ct. 647, 102 L.Ed. 2d 714 (1989)

http://caselaw.findlaw.com/us-supreme-court/488/361.html

Because of serious disparities among sentences imposed by federal judges upon similarly situated offenders, Congress passed the Sentencing Reform Act of 1984, which, among other things, established the U.S. Sentencing Commission as an independent body in the judicial branch. The act empowered the commission to promulgate binding sentencing guidelines, including a range of determinate sentences for all categories of federal offenses and defendants according to specific and detailed factors.

On December 10, 1987, John Mistretta was indicted in the U.S. District Court for the Western District of Missouri on three counts centering on a sale of cocaine. He moved to have the promulgated guidelines declared unconstitutional on the grounds that the commission was constituted in violation of the principle of separation of powers and that Congress delegated excessive authority to the commission to create the guidelines. After the district court rejected Mistretta's argument, he pleaded guilty to one count of his indictment. The remaining counts were dropped. Mistretta then filed a notice of appeal to the Court of Appeals for the Eighth Circuit, and both Mistretta and the United States petitioned the U.S. Supreme Court for certiorari before judgment. Mistretta's attack on the commission and the guidelines was only one of many throughout the nation. Prior to the Supreme Court's decision in this case, some 150 district judges had declared the Sentencing Reform Act unconstitutional, and 115 district judges had upheld it. The excerpts that follow are limited to passages dealing with delegation of power. While the Sentencing Commission survived the challenge posed by Mistretta, the guidelines later fell victim to an attack on Sixth Amendment grounds when *United States* v. *Booker* (2005) held that the guidelines could continue to function only in an advisory, not a mandatory capacity. According to *Booker*, any fact other than a prior conviction that is necessary to support an enhanced sentence must be either admitted by the defendant or found by a jury. Majority (in *Mistretta*): Blackmun, Brennan, Kennedy, Marshall, O'Connor, Rehnquist, Stevens, White. Dissenting: Scalia.

Justice Blackmun delivered the opinion of the Court. . . .

Petitioner argues that in delegating the power to promulgate sentencing guidelines for every federal criminal offense to an independent Sentencing Commission, Congress had granted the Commission excessive legislative discretion in violation of the constitutionally based nondelegation doctrine. We do not agree.

The nondelegation doctrine is rooted in the principle of separation of powers that underlies our tripartite system of government. The Constitution provides that "[a]ll legislative Powers herein granted shall be vested in a Congress of the United States," and we long have insisted that "the integrity and maintenance of the system of government ordained by the Constitution," mandate that Congress generally cannot delegate its legislative power to another Branch. . . . So long as Congress "shall lay down by legislative act an intelligible principle to which the person or body authorized to [exercise the delegated authority] is directed to conform, such legislative action is not a forbidden delegation of legislative power."

Applying this "intelligible principle" test to congressional delegations, our jurisprudence has been driven by a practical understanding that in our increasingly complex society, replete with ever changing and more technical problems, Congress simply cannot do its job absent an ability to delegate power under broad general directives. . . . Accordingly, this Court has deemed it "constitutionally sufficient if Congress clearly delineates the general policy, the public agency which is to apply it, and the boundaries of this delegated authority." . . .

In light of our approval of these broad delegations, we harbor no doubt that Congress' delegation of authority to the Sentencing Commission is sufficiently specific and detailed to meet constitutional requirements. . . .

To guide the Commission in its formulation of offense categories, Congress directed it to consider seven factors: the grade of the offense; the aggravating and mitigating circumstances of the crime; the nature and degree of the harm caused by the crime; the community view of the gravity of the offense; the public concern generated by the crime; the deterrent effect that a particular sentence may have on others; and the current incidence of the offense. Congress set forth 11 factors for the Commission to consider in establishing categories of defendants. . . .

We cannot dispute petitioner's contention that the Commission enjoys significant discretion in formulating guidelines. The Commission does have discretionary authority to determine the relative severity of federal crimes and to assess the relative weight of the offender characteristics that Congress listed for the Commission to consider. . . . The Commission also has significant discretion to determine which crimes have been punished too leniently, and which too severely. Congress has called upon the Commission to exercise its judgment about which types of crimes and which types of criminals are to be considered similar for the purposes of sentencing.

But our cases do not at all suggest that delegations of this type may not carry with them the need to exercise judgment on matters of policy. . . . In *Yakus* [v. *U.S.*, 1944], the Court laid down the applicable principle: . . . "Only if we could say that there is an absence of standards for the guidance of the Administrator's action, so that it would be impossible in a proper proceeding to ascertain whether the will of Congress has been obeyed, would we be justified in overriding its choice of means for effecting its declared purpose."

Congress has met that standard here. . . .

Developing proportionate penalties for hundreds of different crimes by a virtually limitless array of offenders is precisely the sort of intricate, labor intensive task for which delegation to an expert body is especially appropriate. Although Congress has delegated significant discretion to the Commission to draw judgments from its analysis of existing sentencing practice and alternative sentencing models, "Congress is not confined to that method of executing its policy which involves the least possible delegation of discretion to administrative officers." We have no doubt that in the hands of the Commission "the criteria which Congress has supplied are wholly adequate for carrying out the general policy and purpose" of the Act. . . .

We conclude that in creating the Sentencing Commission—an unusual hybrid in structure and authority—Congress neither delegated excessive legislative power nor upset the constitutionally mandated balance of powers among the coordinate Branches. The Constitution's structural protections do not . . . prohibit Congress from calling upon the accumulated wisdom and experience of the Judicial Branch in creating policy on a matter uniquely within the ken of judges. Accordingly, we hold that the Act is constitutional.

The judgment of United States District Court for the Western District of Missouri is affirmed.

It is so ordered.

Justice Scalia, dissenting. . . .

Precisely because the scope of delegation is largely uncontrollable by the courts, we must be particularly rigorous in preserving the Constitution's structural restrictions that deter excessive delegation. The major one, it seems to me, is that the power to make law cannot be exercised by anyone other than Congress, except in conjunction with the lawful exercise of executive or judicial power.

The whole theory of *lawful* congressional "delegation" is not that Congress is sometimes too busy or too divided and can therefore assign its responsibility of making law to someone else; but rather that a certain degree of discretion, and thus of lawmaking, *inheres* in most executive or judicial action, and it is up to Congress, by the relative specificity or generality of its statutory commands, to determine—up to a point—how small or how large that degree shall be. . . .

The focus of controversy, in the long line of our so-called excessive delegation cases, has been whether the *degree* of generality contained in the authorization for exercise of executive or judicial powers in a particular field is so unacceptably high as to *amount* to a delegation of legislative powers. I say "so-called excessive delegation" because although that convenient terminology is often used, what is really at issue is whether there has been *any* delegation of legislative power, which occurs (rarely) when Congress authorizes the exercise of executive or judicial power without adequate standards. Strictly speaking, there is *no* acceptable delegation of legislative power. . . . In the present case, however, a pure delegation of legislative power is precisely what we have before us. It is irrelevant whether the standards are adequate, because they are not standards related to the exercise of executive or judicial powers; they are, plainly and simply, standards for further legislation. . . .

By reason of today's decision, I anticipate that Congress will find delegation of its lawmaking powers much more attractive in the future. If rulemaking can be entirely unrelated to the exercise of judicial or executive powers, I foresee all manner of "expert" bodies, insulated from the political process, to which Congress will delegate various portions of its lawmaking responsibility. . . . This is an undemocratic precedent that we set—not because of the scope of the delegated power, but because its recipient is not one of the three Branches of Government. The only governmental power the Commission possesses is the power to make law; and it is not the Congress. . . .

Today's decision follows the regrettable tendency of our recent separation-of-powers jurisprudence to treat the Constitution as though it were no more than a generalized prescription that the functions of the Branches should not be commingled too much—how much is too much to be determined, case-by-case, by this Court. The Constitution is not that. Rather, as its name suggests, it is a prescribed structure, a framework, for the conduct of government. . . .

I think the Court errs . . . because it fails to recognize that this case is . . . about the creation of a new branch altogether, a sort of junior-varsity Congress. It may well be that in some circumstances such a branch would be desirable; perhaps the agency before us here will prove to be so. But there are many desirable dispositions that do not accord with the constitutional structure we live under. . . .

Immigration and Naturalization Service v. *Chadha*
462 U.S. 919, 103 S.Ct. 2764, 77 L.Ed. 2d 317 (1983)

http://caselaw.findlaw.com/us-supreme-court/462/919.html

Section 244(a)(1) of the Immigration and Nationality Act authorized the attorney general at his discretion to suspend the deportation of a deportable alien. Under Section 244(c)(1), the attorney general was required to report such suspension to Congress. Section 244(c)(2) of the act authorized either house of Congress by resolution to invalidate the suspension before the end of the session following the one during which the suspension occurred. The attorney general discharged his responsibilities through the Immigration and Naturalization Service (INS), then part of the Department of Justice.

Jagdish Rai Chadha is an East Indian who was born in Kenya and who was lawfully admitted to the United States in 1966 on a nonimmigrant student visa. He remained in the United States after his visa had expired in 1972 and was soon ordered by the INS to show cause why he should not be deported. Chadha applied for suspension of the deportation order, and in 1974 an immigration judge, acting for the attorney general, ordered the suspension. On December 16, 1975, the House of Representatives exercised the veto authority reserved to it under Section 244(c)(2). Without action by either house of Congress, Chadha's status would have become that of permanent resident alien when Congress adjourned on December 19, 1975.

The immigration judge then reopened the deportation proceedings, but Chadha moved to block further action, arguing that Section 244(c)(2) violated the Constitution. The immigration judge directed that Chadha be deported. Chadha appealed that order to the Board of Immigration Appeals, which upheld the immigration judge. Chadha next asked the Court of Appeals for the Ninth Circuit to review the deportation order. The INS joined Chadha in arguing that Section 244(c)(2) was unconstitutional. At this point, the court of appeals invited both the Senate and the House of Representatives to file briefs amici curiae. This invitation was important because the principal arguments in support of the validity of the legislative veto came from counsel representing the House and Senate. The court of appeals ruled in 1981 that the House of Representatives lacked constitutional authority to order Chadha's deportation. Majority: Burger, Blackmun, Brennan, Marshall, O'Connor, Powell, Stevens. Dissenting: White, Rehnquist.

Chief Justice Burger delivered the opinion of the Court. . . .

Explicit and unambiguous provisions of the Constitution prescribe and define the respective functions of the Congress and of the Executive in the legislative process. Since the precise terms of those familiar provisions are critical to the resolution of this case, we set them out verbatim. Article I provides:

"All legislative Powers herein granted shall be vested in a Congress of the United States, which shall consist of a Senate *and* a House of Representatives." (Emphasis added [by the Chief Justice].)

"Every Bill which shall have passed the House of Representatives and the Senate, *shall*, before it become a Law, be presented to the President of the United States; . . ." (Emphasis added [by the Chief Justice].)

> "*Every* Order, Resolution, or Vote to which the Concurrence of the Senate and House of Representatives may be necessary (except on a question of Adjournment) *shall* be presented to the President of the United States; and before the Same shall take Effect, *shall* be approved by him, or being disapproved by him, shall be repassed by two thirds of the Senate and House of Representatives, according to the Rules and Limitations prescribed in the Case of a Bill." (Emphasis added [by the Chief Justice].)

The records of the Constitutional Convention reveal that the requirement that all legislation be presented to the President before becoming law was uniformly accepted by the Framers. Presentment to the President and the Presidential veto were considered so imperative that the draftsmen took special pains to assure that these requirements could not be circumvented. . . .

The bicameral requirement . . . was of scarcely less concern to the Framers than was the Presidential veto and indeed the two concepts are interdependent. By providing that no law could take effect without the concurrence of the prescribed majority of the Members of both Houses, the Framers reemphasized their belief, already remarked upon in connection with the Presentment Clauses, that legislation should not be enacted unless it has been carefully and fully considered by the Nation's elected officials. . . .

The Constitution sought to divide the delegated powers of the new federal government into three defined categories, legislative, executive and judicial, to assure, as nearly as possible, that each Branch of government would confine itself to its assigned responsibility. The hydraulic pressure inherent within each of the separate Branches to exceed the outer limits of its power, even to accomplish desirable objectives, must be resisted.

Although not "hermetically" sealed from one another, . . . the powers delegated to the three Branches are functionally identifiable. When any Branch acts, it is presumptively exercising the power the Constitution has delegated to it. . . .

Beginning with this presumption, we must nevertheless establish that the challenged action under § 244(c)(2) is of the kind to which the procedural requirements of Article. I, § 7 apply. Not every action taken by either House is subject to the bicameralism and presentment requirements of Article I. . . . Whether actions taken by either House are, in law and fact, an exercise of legislative power depends not on their form but upon "whether they contain matter which is properly to be regarded as legislative in its character and effect." . . .

Examination of the action taken here by one House pursuant to § 244(c)(2) reveals that it was essentially legislative in purpose and effect. In purporting to exercise power . . . to "establish an uniform Rule of Naturalization," the House took action that had the purpose and effect of altering the legal rights, duties and relations of persons, including the Attorney General, Executive Branch officials and Chadha, all outside the legislative branch. . . .

The choices we discern as having been made in the Constitutional Convention impose burdens on governmental processes that often seem clumsy, inefficient, even unworkable, but those hard choices were consciously made by men who had lived under a form of government that permitted arbitrary governmental acts to go unchecked. There is no support in the Constitution or decisions of this Court for the proposition that the cumbersomeness and delays often encountered in complying with explicit Constitutional standards may be avoided, either by the Congress or by the President. . . . With all the obvious flaws of delay, untidiness, and potential for abuse, we have not yet found a better way to preserve freedom than by making the exercise of power subject to the carefully crafted restraints spelled out in the Constitution.

We hold that the Congressional veto provision in § 244(c)(2) is . . . unconstitutional.

Accordingly, the judgment of the Court of Appeals is

Affirmed.

JUSTICE POWELL, concurring . . . [omitted].

JUSTICE WHITE, dissenting. . . .

The prominence of the legislative veto mechanism in our contemporary political system and its importance to Congress can hardly be overstated. It has become a central means by which Congress secures the accountability of executive and independent agencies. Without the legislative veto, Congress is faced with a Hobson's choice: either to refrain from delegating the necessary authority, leaving itself with a hopeless task of writing laws with the requisite specificity to cover endless special circumstances across the entire policy landscape, or in the alternative, to abdicate its lawmaking function to the executive branch and independent agencies. To choose the former leaves major national problems unresolved; to opt for the latter risks unaccountable policymaking by those not elected to fill that role. Accordingly, over the past five decades, the legislative veto has been placed in nearly 200 statutes. The device is known in every field of governmental concern: reorganization, budgets, foreign affairs, war powers, and regulation of trade, safety, energy, the environment and the economy. . . .

The Court's holding today that all legislative-type action must be enacted through the lawmaking process ignores that legislative authority is routinely delegated to the Executive branch, to the independent regulatory agencies, and to private individuals and groups. . . .

If Congress may delegate lawmaking power to independent and executive agencies, it is most difficult to understand Article I as forbidding Congress from also reserving a check on legislative power for itself. Absent the veto, the agencies receiving delegations of legislative or quasi-legislative power may issue regulations having the force of law without bicameral approval and without the President's signature. It is thus not apparent why the reservation of a veto over the exercise of that legislative power must be subject to a more exacting test. . . .

The Court also takes no account of perhaps the most relevant consideration: However resolutions of disapproval under § 244(c)(2) are formally characterized, in reality, a departure from the status quo occurs only upon the concurrence of opinion among the House, Senate, and President. . . .

Section 244(a)(1) authorizes the Attorney General, in his discretion, to suspend the deportation of certain aliens who are otherwise deportable and, upon Congress' approval, to adjust their status to that of aliens lawfully admitted for permanent residence. . . . [T]he suspension proceeding "has two phases: a determination whether the statutory conditions have been met, which generally involves a question of law, and a determination whether relief shall be granted, which [ultimately] . . . is confided to the sound discretion of the Attorney General [and his delegates]." . . .

There is also a third phase to the process. Under § 244(c)(1) the Attorney General must report all such suspensions, with a detailed statement of facts and reasons, to the Congress. Either House may then act, in that session or the next, to block the suspension of deportation by passing a resolution of disapproval § 244(c)(2). Upon Congressional approval of the suspension by its silence—the alien's permanent status is adjusted to that of a lawful resident alien. . . .

At all times, . . . a permanent change in a deportable alien's status could be accomplished only with the agreement of the Attorney General, the House, and the Senate. . . .

JUSTICE REHNQUIST, with whom JUSTICE WHITE joins, dissenting . . . [omitted].

Clinton v. *City of New York*
524 U.S. 417, 118 S.Ct. 2091, 141 L.Ed. 2d 393 (1998)

http://caselaw.findlaw.com/us-supreme-court/524/417.html

In April 1996 Congress passed the Line Item Veto Act, to become effective on January 1, 1997. On January 2, six members of Congress who had voted against the law challenged its constitutionality in a suit filed in the United States District Court for the District of Columbia. The district court held the act unconstitutional, but on appeal the Supreme Court ruled that members of Congress lacked standing to sue because they had not "alleged a sufficiently concrete injury to have established Article III standing" (*Raines* v. *Byrd*, 1997). Within two months of this decision, President Clinton exercised his authority under the law to cancel one provision in the Balanced Budget Act of 1997 and two provisions in the Taxpayer Relief Act of 1997. Adversely affected by the president's actions, the City of New York, a hospital, two hospital associations, two unions representing health care employees, Snake River Potato Growers, Inc., and an individual farmer then challenged the Line Item Veto Act in the same district court. The district court again held the law invalid. Sections of the opinions below dealing with standing have been omitted. (Prior to the Supreme Court's decision in this case, President Clinton wielded his new statutory veto authority 82 times; Congress overrode 38 of the item vetoes early in 1998, and the president withdrew one veto. The remaining 43 vetoes involved $869 million in total spending.) Majority: Stevens, Ginsburg, Kennedy, Rehnquist, Souter, Thomas. Dissenting (with respect to the constitutionality of the act): Scalia, Breyer, O'Connor.

Justice Stevens delivered the opinion of the Court. . . .

The Line Item Veto Act gives the President the power to "cancel in whole" three types of provisions that have been signed into law: "(1) any dollar amount of discretionary budget authority; (2) any item of new direct spending; or (3) any limited tax benefit." It is undisputed that the New York case involves an "item of new direct spending" and that the Snake River case involves a "limited tax benefit" as those terms are defined in the Act. It is also undisputed that each of those provisions had been signed into law pursuant to Article I, § 7, of the Constitution before it was canceled. . . .

A cancellation takes effect upon receipt by Congress of the special message from the President. If, however, a "disapproval bill" pertaining to a special message is enacted into law, the cancellations set forth in that message become "null and void." The Act sets forth a detailed expedited procedure for the consideration of a "disapproval bill," but no such bill was passed for either of the cancellations involved in these cases.

A majority vote of both Houses is sufficient to enact a disapproval bill. The Act does not grant the President the authority to cancel a disapproval bill, but he does, of course, retain his constitutional authority to veto such a bill.

Thus, under the plain text of the statute, the two actions of the President that are challenged in these cases prevented one section of the Balanced Budget Act of 1997 and one section of the Taxpayer Relief Act of 1997 "from having legal force or effect." The remaining provisions of those statutes, with the exception of the second canceled item in the latter, continue to have the same force and effect as they had when signed into law.

In both legal and practical effect, the President has amended two Acts of Congress by repealing a portion of each. . . . There is no provision in the Constitution that authorizes the President to enact, to amend, or to repeal statutes. . . . [A]fter a bill has passed both Houses of Congress, but "before it become[s] a Law," it must be presented to the President. If he approves it, "he shall sign it, but if not he shall return it, with his Objections to that House in which it shall have originated, who shall enter the Objections at large on their Journal, and proceed to reconsider it." His "return" of a bill, which is usually described as a "veto," is subject to being overridden by a two-thirds vote in each House.

There are important differences between the President's "return" of a bill pursuant to Article I, § 7, and the exercise of the President's cancellation authority pursuant to the Line Item Veto Act. The constitutional return takes place before the bill becomes law; the statutory cancellation occurs *after* the bill becomes law. The constitutional return is of the entire bill; the statutory cancellation is of only a part. Although the Constitution expressly authorizes the President to play a role in the process of enacting statutes, it is silent on the subject of unilateral Presidential action that either repeals or amends parts of duly enacted statutes.

There are powerful reasons for construing constitutional silence on this profoundly important issue as equivalent to an express prohibition. The procedures governing the enactment of statutes set forth in the text of Article I were the product of the great debates and compromises that produced the Constitution itself. . . . Our first President understood the text of the Presentment Clause as requiring that he either "approve all the parts of a Bill, or reject it in toto."

What has emerged in these cases from the President's exercise of his statutory cancellation powers, however, are truncated versions of two bills that passed both Houses of Congress. They are not the product of the "finely wrought" procedure that the Framers designed. . . .

The Government advances two related arguments to support its position that despite the unambiguous provisions of the Act, cancellations do not amend or repeal properly enacted statutes in violation of the Presentment Clause. First, . . . the Government contends that the cancellations were merely exercises of discretionary authority granted to the President by the Balanced Budget Act and the Taxpayer Relief Act read in light of the previously enacted Line Item Veto Act. Second, the Government submits that the substance of the authority to cancel tax and spending items "is, in practical effect, no more and no less than the power to 'decline to spend' specified sums of money, or to 'decline to implement' specified tax measures." Neither argument is persuasive. . . .

Neither are we persuaded by the Government's contention that the President's authority to cancel new direct spending and tax benefit items is no greater than his traditional authority to decline to spend appropriated funds. The Government has reviewed in some detail the series of statutes in which Congress has given the Executive broad discretion over the expenditure of appropriated funds. . . . It is argued that the Line Item Veto Act merely confers comparable discretionary authority over the expenditure of appropriated funds. The critical difference between this statute and all of its predecessors, however, is that unlike any of them, this Act gives the President the unilateral power to change the text of duly enacted statutes. None of the Act's predecessors could even arguably have been construed to authorize such a change. . . .

[O]ur decision rests on the narrow ground that the procedures authorized by the Line Item Veto Act are not authorized by the Constitution. The Balanced Budget Act of 1997 is a 500-page document that became "Public Law 105–33" after three procedural steps were taken: (1) a bill containing its exact text was approved by a majority of the Members of the House of Representatives; (2) the Senate approved precisely the same text; and (3) that text was signed into law by the President. The Constitution explicitly requires that each of those three steps be taken before a bill may "become a law." If one paragraph of that text had been omitted at any one of those three stages, Public Law 105–33 would not have been validly enacted. If the Line Item Veto Act were valid, it would authorize the President to create a different law, one whose text was not voted on by either House of Congress or presented to the President for signature. Something that might be known as "Public Law 105–33 as modified by the President" may or may not be desirable, but it is surely not a document that may "become a law" pursuant to the procedures designed by the Framers of Article I, § 7, of the Constitution.

If there is to be a new procedure in which the President will play a different role in determining the final text of what may "become a law," such change must come not by legislation but through the amendment procedures set forth in Article V of the Constitution.

The judgment of the District Court is affirmed.

It is so ordered.

Justice Kennedy, concurring . . . [omitted].

Justice Scalia, with whom Justice O'Connor joins, and with whom Justice Breyer joins in part, concurring in part and dissenting in part . . . [omitted].

Justice Breyer, with whom Justice O'Connor and Justice Scalia join in part, dissenting. . . .

Imagine that the canceled New York health care tax provision at issue here had instead said the following:

Section One. Taxes . . . that were collected by the State of New York from a health care provider before June 1, 1997 and for which a waiver of provisions [requiring payment] have been sought . . . are deemed to be permissible health care related taxes . . . *provided however that the President may prevent the just mentioned provision from having legal force or effect if he determines x, y and z.* (Assume x, y and z to be the same determinations required by the Line Item Veto Act.) Whatever a person might say, or think, about the constitutionality of this imaginary law, there is one thing the English language would prevent one from saying. One could not say that a President who "prevent[s]" the deeming language from "having legal force or effect," has either repealed or amended this particular hypothetical statute. Rather, the President has followed that law to the letter. He has exercised the power it explicitly delegates to him. He has executed the law, not repealed it.

It could make no significant difference to this linguistic point were the italicized proviso to appear, not as part of what I have called Section One, but, instead, at the bottom of the statute page, say referenced by an asterisk, with a statement that it applies to every spending provision in the act next to which a similar asterisk appears. And that being so, it could make no difference if that proviso appeared, instead, in a different, earlier-enacted law, along with legal language that makes it applicable to every future spending provision picked out according to a specified formula. . . .

Because I disagree with the Court's holding of literal violation, I must consider whether the Act nonetheless violates Separation of Powers principles—principles that arise out of the Constitution's vesting of the "executive Power" in "a President," and "[a]ll legislative Powers" in "a Congress." There are three relevant Separation of Powers questions here: (1) Has Congress given the President the wrong kind of power, that is, "non-Executive" power? (2) Has Congress given the President the power to "encroach" upon Congress' own constitutionally reserved territory? (3) Has Congress given the President too much power, violating the doctrine of "nondelegation?" . . . [W]ith respect to this Act, the answer to all these questions is "no."

Viewed conceptually, the power the Act conveys is the right kind of power. It is "executive." As explained above, an exercise of that power "executes" the Act. Conceptually speaking, it closely resembles the kind of delegated authority—to spend or not to spend appropriations, to change or not to change tariff rates—that Congress has frequently granted the President, any differences being differences in degree, not kind. . . .

[O]ne cannot say that the Act "encroaches" upon Congress' power, when Congress retained the power to insert, by simple majority, into any future appropriations bill, into any section of any such bill, or into any phrase of any section, a provision that says the Act will not apply. . . . Where is the encroachment?

Nor can one say the Act's grant of power "aggrandizes" the Presidential office. The grant is limited to the context of the budget. It is limited to the power to spend, or not to spend, particular appropriated items, and the power to permit, or not to permit, specific limited exemptions from generally applicable tax law from taking effect. These powers, as I will explain in detail, resemble those the President has exercised in the past on other occasions. The delegation of those powers to the President may strengthen the Presidency, but any such change in Executive Branch authority seems minute when compared with the changes worked by delegations of other kinds of authority that the Court in the past has upheld. . . .

The "nondelegation" doctrine represents an added constitutional check upon Congress' authority to delegate power to the Executive Branch. And it raises a more serious constitutional obstacle here. The Constitution permits Congress to "see[k] assistance from another branch" of Government, the "extent and character" of that assistance to be fixed "according to commonsense and the inherent necessities of the governmental co-ordination." But there are limits on the way in which Congress can obtain such assistance; it "cannot delegate any part of its legislative power except under the limitation of a prescribed standard." Or, in Chief Justice Taft's more familiar words, the Constitution permits only those delegations where Congress "shall lay down by legislative act an intelligible principle to which the person or body authorized to [act] is directed to conform."

The Act before us seeks to create such a principle in three ways. The first is procedural. The Act tells the President that, in "identifying dollar amounts [or] . . . items . . . for cancellation" (which I take to refer to his selection of the amounts or items he will "prevent from having legal force or effect"), he is to "consider," among other things, "the legislative history, construction, and purposes of the law which contains [those amounts or items, and] . . . any specific sources of information referenced in such law or . . . the best available information. . . ."

The second is purposive. The clear purpose behind the Act, confirmed by its legislative history, is to promote "greater fiscal accountability" and to "eliminate wasteful federal spending and . . . special tax breaks."

The third is substantive. The President must determine that, to "prevent" the item or amount "from having legal force or effect" will "reduce the Federal budget deficit; . . . not impair any essential Government functions; and . . . not harm the national interest."

The resulting standards are broad. But this Court has upheld standards that are equally broad, or broader. . . . To the contrary (a) the broadly phrased limitations in the Act, together with (b) its evident deficit reduction purpose, and (c) a procedure that guarantees Presidential awareness of the reasons for including a particular provision in a budget bill, taken together, guide the President's exercise of his discretionary powers. . . .

In sum, I recognize that the Act before us . . . skirts a constitutional edge. But that edge has to do with means, not ends. The means chosen do not amount literally to the enactment, repeal, or amendment of a law. Nor, for that matter, do they amount literally to the "line item veto" that the Act's title announces. . . . They represent an experiment that may, or may not, help representative government work better. The Constitution, in my view, authorizes Congress and the President to try novel methods in this way. Consequently, with respect, I dissent.

II. CONGRESSIONAL INVESTIGATIONS

Watkins v. *United States*
354 U.S. 178, 77 S.Ct. 1173, 1 L.Ed. 2d 1273 (1957)

http://caselaw.findlaw.com/us-supreme-court/354/178.html

The broad investigating power of Congress was upheld in *McGrain* v. *Daugherty* (1927), where the purpose was to obtain information about alleged wrongdoing by the attorney general and the Department of Justice. After World War II, Congress turned its attention to the activities within the United States of alleged members and officers of the Communist Party. Subpoenaed for a hearing before the House Committee on Un-American Activities in 1954, labor organizer John Watkins refused to answer on the ground that the questions were outside of the proper scope of the committee's activities and not relevant to its work. He was then convicted in U.S. district court under 2 U.S.C. 192, which makes it a misdemeanor for any person summoned as a witness by either house of Congress to refuse to answer any question "pertinent to the question under inquiry." Voting 2–1, the Court of Appeals for the District of Columbia reversed. Upon rehearing en banc, the full bench affirmed the conviction. Majority: Warren, Black, Brennan, Douglas, Frankfurter, Harlan. Dissenting: Clark. Not participating: Burton, Whittaker.

Mr. Chief Justice Warren delivered the opinion of the Court. . . .

We start with several basic premises on which there is general agreement. The power of the Congress to conduct investigations is inherent in the legislative process. That power is broad. . . . But broad as is this power of inquiry, it is not unlimited. There is no general authority to expose the private affairs of individuals without justification in terms of the functions of the Congress. This was freely conceded by the Solicitor General in his argument of this case. . . .

It is unquestionably the duty of all citizens to cooperate with the Congress in its efforts to obtain the facts needed for intelligent legislative action. It is their unremitting obligation to respond to subpoenas, to respect the dignity of the Congress and its committees, and to testify fully with respect to matters within the province of proper investigation. This, of course, assumes that the constitutional rights of witnesses will be respected by the Congress as they are in a court of justice.

In the decade following World War II, there appeared a new kind of congressional inquiry unknown in prior periods of American history. Principally this was the result of the various investigations into the threat of subversion of the United States Government, but other subjects of congressional interest also contributed to the changed scene. This new phase of legislative inquiry involved a broad-scale intrusion into the lives and affairs of private citizens. It brought before the courts novel questions of the appropriate limits of congressional inquiry. Prior cases . . . had defined the scope of investigative power in terms of the inherent limitations of the sources of that power. In the more recent cases, the emphasis shifted to problems of accommodating the interest of the Government with the rights and privileges of individuals. The central theme was the application of the Bill of Rights as a restraint upon the assertion of governmental power in this form.

It was during this period that the Fifth Amendment privilege against self-incrimination was frequently invoked and recognized as a legal limit upon the authority of a committee to require that a witness answer its questions. . . . When the matter reached this Court, the Government did not challenge in any way that the Fifth Amendment protection was available to the witness, and such a challenge could not have prevailed. . . .

A far more difficult task evolved from the claim by witnesses that the committees' interrogations were infringements upon the freedoms of the First Amendment. Clearly, an investigation is subject to the command that the Congress shall make no law abridging freedom of speech or press or assembly. While it is true that there is no statute to be reviewed, and that an investigation is not a law, nevertheless an investigation is part of lawmaking. It is justified solely as an adjunct to the legislative process. The First Amendment may be invoked against infringement of the protected freedoms by law or by lawmaking.

Abuses of the investigative process may imperceptibly lead to abridgement of protected freedoms. The mere summoning of a witness and compelling him to testify, against his will, about his beliefs, expressions or associations is a measure of governmental interference. And when those forced revelations concern matters that are unorthodox, unpopular, or even hateful to the general public, the reaction in the life of the witness may be disastrous. . . .

It is the responsibility of the Congress, in the first instance, to insure that compulsory process is used only in furtherance of a legislative purpose. That requires that the instructions to an investigating committee spell out that group's jurisdiction and purpose with sufficient particularity. Those instructions are embodied in the authorizing resolution. That document is the committee's charter. Broadly drafted and loosely worded, however, such resolutions can leave tremendous latitude to the discretion of investigators. The more vague the committee's charter is, the greater becomes the possibility that the committee's specific actions are not in conformity with the will of the parent House of Congress.

The authorizing resolution of the Un-American Activities Committee was adopted in 1938 when a select committee, under the chairmanship of Representative Dies, was created. Several years later, the Committee was made a standing organ of the House with the same mandate. It defines the Committee's authority as follows:

> The Committee on Un-American Activities, as a whole or by subcommittee, is authorized to make from time to time investigations of (i) the extent, character, and objects of un-American propaganda activities in the United States, (ii) the diffusion within the United States of subversive and un-American propaganda that is instigated from foreign countries or of a domestic origin and attacks the principle of the form of government as guaranteed by our Constitution, and (iii) all other questions in relation thereto that would aid Congress in any necessary remedial legislation. [Rule XI]

It would be difficult to imagine a less explicit authorizing resolution. Who can define the meaning of "un-American?" . . .

Plainly . . . committees are restricted to the missions delegated to them, that is, to acquire certain data to be used by the House or the Senate in coping with a problem that falls within its legislative sphere. No witness can be compelled to make disclosures on matters outside that area. . . . When the definition of jurisdictional pertinency is as uncertain and wavering as in the case of the Un-American Activities Committee, it becomes extremely difficult for the Committee to limit its inquiries to statutory pertinency.

In fulfillment of their obligation under this statute, the courts must accord to the defendants every right which is guaranteed to defendants in all other criminal cases. Among these is the right to have available, through a sufficiently precise statute, information revealing the standard of criminality before the commission of the alleged offense. Applied to persons prosecuted under § 192, this raises a special problem in that the statute defines the crime as refusal to answer "any question pertinent to the question under inquiry." Part of the standard of criminality, therefore, is the pertinency of the questions propounded to the witness.

The problem attains proportion when viewed from the standpoint of the witness who appears before a congressional committee. He must decide at the time the questions are propounded whether or not to answer. . . .

It is obvious that a person compelled to make this choice is entitled to have knowledge of the subject to which the interrogation is deemed pertinent. That knowledge must be available with the same degree of explicitness and clarity that the Due Process Clause requires in the expression of any element of a criminal offense. The "vice of vagueness" must be avoided here as in all other crimes. There are several sources that can outline the "question under inquiry" in such a way that the rules against vagueness are satisfied. The authorizing resolution, the remarks of the chairman or members of the committee, or even the nature of the proceedings themselves might sometimes make the topic clear. This case demonstrates, however, that these sources often leave the matter in grave doubt. . . .

The conclusions which we have reached in this case will not prevent the Congress, through its committees, from obtaining any information it needs for the proper fulfillment of its role in our scheme of government. The legislature is free to determine the kinds of data that should be collected. It is only those investigations that are conducted by use of compulsory process that give rise to a need to protect the rights of individuals against illegal encroachment. . . . That is a small price to pay if it serves to uphold the principles of limited, constitutional government without constricting the power of the Congress to inform itself.

The judgment of the Court of Appeals is reversed, and the case is remanded to the District Court with instructions to dismiss the indictment.

It is so ordered.

MR. JUSTICE FRANKFURTER, concurring . . . [omitted].

MR. JUSTICE CLARK, dissenting . . . [omitted].

Barenblatt v. *United States*
360 U.S. 109, 79 S.Ct. 1081, 3 L.Ed. 2d 1115 (1959)

http://caselaw.findlaw.com/us-supreme-court/360/109.html

In 1954 former college teacher Lloyd Barenblatt was called as a witness before a subcommittee of the House Un-American Activities Committee investigating Communist infiltration in education. Disclaiming any reliance on the Fifth Amendment, he refused to answer questions regarding past affiliation with the Communist Party, contending that the subcommittee had no power to inquire into political beliefs and associations. The Supreme Court vacated his conviction for contempt of Congress and remanded the case for reconsideration in light of the *Watkins* decision. The years 1957–1958 witnessed a flurry of anti-Court legislation introduced in Congress, the most since 1936–1937. Barenblatt's conviction was again upheld by the court of appeals. Majority: Harlan, Clark, Frankfurter, Stewart, Whittaker. Dissenting: Black, Brennan, Douglas, Warren.

Mr. Justice Harlan delivered the opinion of the Court.

Once more the Court is required to resolve the conflicting constitutional claims of congressional power and of an individual's right to resist its exercise. . . .

Broad as it is, the power is not, however, without limitations. Since Congress may only investigate into those areas in which it may potentially legislate or appropriate, it cannot inquire into matters which are within the exclusive province of one of the other branches of the Government. . . . And the Congress, in common with all branches of the Government, must exercise its powers subject to the limitations placed by the Constitution on governmental action, more particularly in the context of this case the relevant limitations of the Bill of Rights. . . .

Rule XI authorized this Subcommittee to compel testimony within the framework of the investigative authority conferred on the Un-American Activities Committee. Petitioner contends that *Watkins* v. *United States* . . . nevertheless held the grant of this power in all circumstances ineffective because of the vagueness of Rule XI in delineating the Committee jurisdiction to which its exercise was to be appurtenant. . . .

The Watkins case cannot properly be read as standing for such a proposition. A principal contention in *Watkins* was that the refusals to answer were justified because the requirement . . . that the questions asked be "pertinent to the question under inquiry" had not been satisfied. . . . This Court reversed the conviction solely on that ground, holding that Watkins had not been adequately apprised of the subject matter of the Subcommittee's investigation or the pertinency thereto of the questions he refused to answer. . . . In so deciding the Court drew upon Rule XI only as one of the facets in the total *mise en scène* in its search for the "question under inquiry" in that particular investigation. . . . In short, while *Watkins* was critical of Rule XI, it did not involve the broad and inflexible holding petitioner now attributes to it. . . .

What we deal with here is whether petitioner was sufficiently apprised of "the topic under inquiry" thus authorized "and the connective reasoning whereby the precise questions asked related to it." . . . In light of this prepared memorandum of constitutional objectives there can be no doubt that this petitioner was well aware of the Subcommittee's authority and purpose to question him as it did. . . . In addition the other sources of this information which we recognized in *Watkins* . . . leave no room for a "pertinency" objection on this record. The subject matter of the inquiry had been identified at the commencement of the investigation as Communist infiltration into the field of education. . . .

The protections of the First Amendment, unlike a proper claim of the privilege against self-incrimination under the Fifth Amendment, do not afford a witness the right to resist inquiry in all circumstances. Where First Amendment rights are asserted to bar governmental interrogation, resolution of the issue always involves a balancing by the courts of the competing private and public interests at stake in the particular circumstances shown. These principles were recognized in the Watkins case. . . .

An investigation of advocacy or of preparation for overthrow certainly embraces the right to identify a witness as a member of the Communist Party . . . and to inquire into various manifestations of the Party's tenets. . . . Nor can it fairly be concluded that this investigation was directed at controlling what is being taught at our universities rather than at overthrow. . . .

Nor can we accept the further contention that this investigation should not be deemed to have been in furtherance of a legislative purpose because the true objective of the Committee and of the Congress was purely "exposure." So long as Congress acts in pursuance of its constitutional power, the Judiciary lacks authority to intervene on the basis of the motives which spurred the exercise of that power. . . .

We conclude that the balance between the individual and the governmental interests here at stake must be struck in favor of the latter, and that therefore the provisions of the First Amendment have not been offended. . . .

Affirmed.

MR. JUSTICE BLACK, with whom the CHIEF JUSTICE and MR. JUSTICE DOUGLAS concur, dissenting . . . [omitted].

MR. JUSTICE BRENNAN, dissenting . . . [omitted].

Trump v. *Mazars USA*
591 U.S. ___, 140 S.Ct. 2019, 207 L.Ed. 2d 951 (2020)

www.supremecourt.gov/opinions/19pdf/19-715_febh.pdf

In 2019, committees of the U.S. House of Representatives issued subpoenas to the accounting firm Mazars USA and to Deutsche Bank seeking information about the finances of President Donald Trump, his children, and affiliated businesses. The president in his personal capacity, along with his children and affiliated businesses, filed two suits in federal court challenging the subpoenas. Adverse rulings by the U.S. District Court for the Southern District of New York and the U.S. District Court for the District of Columbia were then affirmed by the U.S. Courts of Appeals for the Second Circuit and the District of Columbia Circuit, respectively. Majority: Roberts, Breyer, Ginsburg, Gorsuch, Kagan, Kavanaugh, Sotomayor. Dissenting: Alito, Thomas.

CHIEF JUSTICE ROBERTS delivered the opinion of the Court. . . .

We have held that the House has authority under the Constitution to issue subpoenas to assist it in carrying out its legislative responsibilities. The House asserts that the financial information sought here—encompassing a decade's worth of transactions by the President and his family—will help guide legislative reform in areas ranging from money laundering and terrorism to foreign involvement in elections. The President contends that the House lacked a valid legislative aim and instead sought these records to harass him, expose personal matters, and conduct law enforcement activities beyond its authority. The question presented is whether the subpoenas exceed the authority of the House under the Constitution.

We have never addressed a congressional subpoena for the President's information. . . . Here the President's information is sought not by prosecutors or private parties in connection with a particular judicial proceeding, but by committees of Congress that have set forth broad legislative objectives. Congress and the

President—the two political branches established by the Constitution—have an ongoing relationship that the Framers intended to feature both rivalry and reciprocity. That distinctive aspect necessarily informs our analysis of the question before us.

Historically, disputes over congressional demands for presidential documents have not ended up in court. Instead, they have been hashed out in the "hurly-burly, the give-and-take of the political process between the legislative and the executive."

Congress has no enumerated constitutional power to conduct investigations or issue subpoenas, but we have held that each House has power "to secure needed information" in order to legislate. . . . Furthermore, Congress may not issue a subpoena for the purpose of "law enforcement," because "those powers are assigned under our Constitution to the Executive and the Judiciary." Thus Congress may not use subpoenas to "try" someone "before [a] committee for any crime or wrongdoing." Congress has no "'general' power to inquire into private affairs and compel disclosures," and "there is no congressional power to expose for the sake of exposure." "Investigations conducted solely for the personal aggrandizement of the investigators or to 'punish' those investigated are indefensible."

Finally, recipients of legislative subpoenas retain their constitutional rights throughout the course of an investigation. And recipients have long been understood to retain common law and constitutional privileges with respect to certain materials, such as attorney-client communications and governmental communications protected by executive privilege.

The President contends, as does the Solicitor General appearing on behalf of the United States, that the usual rules for congressional subpoenas do not govern here because the President's papers are at issue. They argue for a more demanding standard based in large part on cases involving the Nixon tapes—recordings of conversations between President Nixon and close advisers discussing the break-in at the Democratic National Committee's headquarters at the Watergate complex. The tapes were subpoenaed by a Senate committee and the Special Prosecutor investigating the break-in, prompting President Nixon to invoke executive privilege and leading to two cases addressing the showing necessary to require the President to comply with the subpoenas.

Those cases, the President and the Solicitor General now contend, establish the standard that should govern the House subpoenas here. . . . [T]he President and the Solicitor General argue that the House must show that the financial information is "demonstrably critical" to its legislative purpose.

We disagree that these demanding standards apply here. Unlike the cases before us, [those cases] involved Oval Office communications over which the President asserted executive privilege. That privilege safeguards the public interest in candid, confidential deliberations within the Executive Branch; it is "fundamental to the operation of Government." As a result, information subject to executive privilege deserves "the greatest protection consistent with the fair administration of justice." We decline to transplant that protection root and branch to cases involving non privileged, private information, which by definition does not implicate sensitive Executive Branch deliberations.

The standards proposed by the President and the Solicitor General—if applied outside the context of privileged information—would risk seriously impeding Congress in carrying out its responsibilities. The President and the Solicitor General would apply the same exacting standards to *all* subpoenas for the President's information, without recognizing distinctions between privileged and nonprivileged information, between official and personal information, or between various legislative objectives. Such a categorical approach would represent a significant departure from the longstanding way of doing business between the branches, giving short shrift to Congress's important interests in conducting inquiries to obtain the information it needs to legislate effectively. . . .

The House meanwhile would have us ignore that these suits involve the President. Invoking our precedents concerning investigations that did not target the President's papers, the House urges us to uphold its subpoenas because they "relate[] to a valid legislative purpose" or "concern[] a subject on which legislation could be had." . . . Largely following the House's lead, the courts below treated these cases much like any other, applying precedents that do not involve the President's papers.

The House's approach fails to take adequate account of the significant separation of powers issues raised by congressional subpoenas for the President's information. Congress and the President have an ongoing institutional relationship as the "opposite and rival" political branches established by the Constitution. As a result, congressional subpoenas directed at the President differ markedly from congressional subpoenas we have previously reviewed, and they bear little resemblance to criminal subpoenas issued to the President in the course of a specific investigation.

Far from accounting for separation of powers concerns, the House's approach aggravates them by leaving essentially no limits on the congressional power to subpoena the President's personal records. Any personal paper possessed by a President could potentially "relate to" a conceivable subject of legislation. . . .

In addition, separation of powers concerns are no less palpable here simply because the subpoenas were issued to third parties. Congressional demands for the President's information present an interbranch conflict no matter where the information is held—it is, after all, the President's information.

We therefore conclude that, in assessing whether a subpoena directed at the President's personal information is "related to, and in furtherance of, a legitimate task of the Congress," courts must perform a careful analysis that takes adequate account of the separation of powers principles at stake, including both the significant legislative interests of Congress and the "unique position" of the President. Several special considerations inform this analysis.

First, courts should carefully assess whether the asserted legislative purpose warrants the significant step of involving the President and his papers. . . . Second, to narrow the scope of possible conflict between the branches, courts should insist on a subpoena no broader than reasonably necessary to support Congress's legislative objective. The specificity of the subpoena's request "serves as an important safeguard against unnecessary intrusion into the operation of the Office of the President." Third, courts should be attentive to the nature of the evidence offered by Congress to establish that a subpoena advances a valid legislative purpose. . . .

Fourth, courts should be careful to assess the burdens imposed on the President by a subpoena. We have held that burdens on the President's time and attention stemming from judicial process and litigation, without more, generally do not cross constitutional lines. But burdens imposed by a congressional subpoena should be carefully scrutinized, for they stem from a rival political branch that has an ongoing relationship with the President and incentives to use subpoenas for institutional advantage.

Other considerations may be pertinent as well; one case every two centuries does not afford enough experience for an exhaustive list.

When Congress seeks information "needed for intelligent legislative action," it "unquestionably" remains "the duty of *all* citizens to cooperate." Congressional subpoenas for information from the President, however, implicate special concerns regarding the separation of powers. The courts below did not take adequate account of those concerns. The judgments of the Courts of Appeals for the D. C. Circuit and the Second Circuit are vacated, and the cases are remanded for further proceedings consistent with this opinion.

It is so ordered.

Justice Thomas, dissenting. . . .

Congress' legislative powers do not authorize it to engage in a nationwide inquisition with whatever resources it chooses to appropriate for itself. The majority's solution—a nonexhaustive four-factor test of uncertain origin—is better than nothing. But the power that Congress seeks to exercise here has even less basis in the Constitution than the majority supposes. I would reverse in full because the power to subpoena private, nonofficial documents is not a necessary implication of Congress' legislative powers. If Congress wishes to obtain these documents, it should proceed through the impeachment power. Accordingly, I respectfully dissent.

Justice Alito, dissenting . . . [omitted].

III. PRESIDENTIAL PRIVILEGE AND IMMUNITY

United States v. *Nixon*
418 U.S. 683, 94 S.Ct. 3090, 41 L.Ed. 2d 1039 (1974)

http://caselaw.findlaw.com/us-supreme-court/418/683.html

Following the indictment of seven high-ranking officials—including former presidential assistants H. R. Haldeman and John Ehrlichman and former attorney general John Mitchell—for conspiracy to defraud the U.S. government and obstruction of justice, the special prosecutor obtained a subpoena *duces tecum* directing President Richard M. Nixon to deliver to the trial judge certain tape recordings and memoranda of conversations held in the White House. (A subpoena *duces tecum* is a judicial order requested by a party to a case that compels a person in possession of items relevant to the litigation to produce them in court.) Nixon produced some of the subpoenaed material but withheld other portions, invoking executive privilege, which placed confidential presidential documents beyond judicial reach. The trial judge denied the president's claim, and he appealed to the court of appeals. The special prosecutor asked the Supreme Court to review the case before the court of appeals had passed judgment. The decision, rendered on July 24, led to Nixon's resignation from office on August 9, 1974. Majority: Burger, Blackmun, Brennan, Douglas, Marshall, Powell, Stewart, White. Not participating: Rehnquist.

Mr. Chief Justice Burger delivered the opinion of the Court. . . .

We turn to the claim that the subpoena should be quashed because it demands "confidential conversations between a President and his close advisors that it would be inconsistent with the public interest to produce." . . . The first contention is a broad claim that the separation of powers doctrine precludes judicial review of a President's claim of privilege. The second contention is that if he does not prevail on the claim of absolute privilege, the court should hold as a matter of constitutional law that the privilege prevails over the subpoena *duces tecum*.

In the performance of assigned constitutional duties each branch of the Government must initially interpret the Constitution, and the interpretation of its powers by any branch is due great respect from the others. The President's counsel . . . reads the Constitution as providing an absolute privilege of confidentiality for all presidential communications. Many decisions of this Court, however, have unequivocally reaffirmed the holding of *Marbury* v. *Madison* that "it is emphatically the province and duty of the judicial department to say what the law is." . . .

No holding of the Court has defined the scope of judicial power specifically relating to the enforcement of a subpoena for confidential presidential communications for use in a criminal prosecution, but other exercises of power by the Executive Branch and the Legislative Branch have been found invalid as in conflict with the Constitution. Since this Court has consistently exercised the power to construe and delineate claims arising under express powers, it must follow that the Court has authority to interpret claims with respect to powers alleged to derive from enumerated powers.

In support of his claim of absolute privilege, the President's counsel urges two grounds, one of which is common to all governments and one of which is peculiar to our system of separation of powers. The first ground is the valid need for protection of communications between high government officials and those who advise and assist them in the performance of their manifold duties; the importance of this confidentiality is too plain to require further discussion. . . . Whatever the nature of the privilege of confidentiality of presidential communications in the exercise of Article II powers, the privilege can be said to derive from the supremacy of each branch within its own assigned area of constitutional duties. Certain powers and privileges flow from the nature of enumerated powers; the protection of the confidentiality of presidential communications has similar constitutional underpinnings.

The second ground asserted by the President's counsel in support of the claim of absolute privilege rests on the doctrine of separation of powers. Here it is argued that the independence of the Executive Branch within its own sphere . . . insulates a president from a judicial subpoena in an ongoing criminal prosecution, and thereby protects confidential presidential communications.

However, neither the doctrine of separation of powers, nor the need for confidentiality of high level communications, without more, can sustain an absolute, unqualified presidential privilege of immunity from judicial process under all circumstances. The President's need for complete candor and objectivity from advisers calls for great deference from the courts. However, when the privilege depends solely on the broad, undifferentiated claim of public interest in the confidentiality of such conversations, a confrontation with other values arises. Absent a claim of need to protect military, diplomatic or sensitive national security secrets, we find it difficult to accept the argument that even the very important interest in confidentiality of presidential communications is significantly diminished by production of such material for in camera inspection with all the protection that a district court will be obliged to provide.

The impediment that an absolute, unqualified privilege would place in the way of the primary constitutional duty of the Judicial Branch to do justice in criminal prosecutions would plainly conflict with the function of the courts under Article III. . . .

Since we conclude that the legitimate needs of the judicial process may outweigh presidential privilege, it is necessary to resolve those competing interests in a manner that preserves the essential functions of each branch. . . .

The expectation of a President to the confidentiality of his conversations and correspondence, like the claim of confidentiality of judicial deliberations, for example, has all the values to which we accord deference for the privacy of all citizens and added to those values the necessity for protection of the public interest in candid, objective, and even blunt or harsh opinions in presidential decision-making. . . .

The privilege is fundamental to the operation of government and inextricably rooted in the separation of powers under the Constitution. . . . We agree with Mr. Chief Justice Marshall's observation, therefore, that "in no case of this kind would a court be required to proceed against the President as against an ordinary individual" (*United States* v. *Burr*, 1807).

But this presumptive privilege must be considered in light of our historic commitment to the rule of law. This is nowhere more profoundly manifest than in our view that "the twofold aim of criminal justice is that guilt shall not escape or innocence suffer." The need to develop all relevant facts in the adversary system is both fundamental and comprehensive. . . . To ensure that justice is done, it is imperative to the function of courts that compulsory process be available for the production of evidence needed either by the prosecution or by the defense.

In this case the President challenges a subpoena served on him as a third party requiring the production of materials for use in a criminal prosecution on the claim that he has a privilege against disclosure of confidential communications. He does not place his claim of privilege on the ground they are military or diplomatic secrets. As to these areas of Article II duties, the courts have traditionally shown the utmost deference to presidential responsibilities. . . . No case of the Court . . . has extended this high degree of deference to a President's generalized interest in confidentiality. Nowhere in the Constitution . . . is there any explicit reference to a privilege of confidentiality, yet to the extent this interest relates to the effective discharge of a President's powers, it is constitutionally based.

The right to the production of all evidence at a criminal trial similarly has constitutional dimensions. The Sixth Amendment explicitly confers upon every defendant in a criminal trial the right "to be confronted with the witnesses against him" and "to have compulsory process for obtaining witnesses in his favor." Moreover, the Fifth Amendment also guarantees that no person shall be deprived of liberty without due process of law. It is the manifest duty of the courts to vindicate those guarantees and to accomplish that it is essential that all relevant and admissible evidence be produced. . . .

A President's acknowledged need for confidentiality in the communications of his office is general in nature, whereas the constitutional need for production of relevant evidence in a criminal proceeding is specific and central to the fair adjudication of a particular criminal case in the administration of justice. Without access to specific facts a criminal prosecution may be totally frustrated. . . .

We conclude that when the ground for asserting privilege as to subpoenaed materials sought for use in a criminal trial is based only on the generalized interest in confidentiality, it cannot prevail over the fundamental demands of due process of law in the fair administration of criminal justice. The generalized assertion of privilege must yield to the demonstrated, specific need for evidence in a pending criminal trial. . . .

Affirmed.

Nixon v. *Fitzgerald*
457 U.S. 731, 102 S.Ct. 2690, 73 L.Ed. 2d 349 (1982)

http://caselaw.findlaw.com/us-supreme-court/457/731.html

Ernest Fitzgerald was employed as a civilian analyst by the Air Force. In testimony to Congress in 1968, he revealed anticipated cost overruns of $2 billion, as well as various technical difficulties, in construction of the C-5A transport plane. Hailed as a "whistle-blower" by Congress and the press, Fitzgerald lost his job in 1969, ostensibly in a departmental reorganization. The Civil Service Commission ruled that his dismissal violated government regulations. Fitzgerald filed a suit for damages in the U.S. District Court for the District of Columbia against various persons in the Department of Defense and the White House staff. In January 1973, President Richard Nixon publicly took responsibility for his discharge and in 1978 was named a defendant in the suit, but Nixon claimed an absolute immunity from civil suits stemming from official actions. In its decision, delayed until 1980 (six years after Nixon resigned the presidency) because of several intermediate rulings, the district court rejected Nixon's claim of immunity, and the Court of Appeals for the District of Columbia Circuit dismissed Nixon's appeal. Ironically, had Nixon lost his case in the Supreme Court, Fitzgerald's suit against him for damages would never have gone to trial. After Nixon petitioned the Court for review, he and Fitzgerald agreed to a settlement under the terms of which Nixon paid Fitzgerald $142,000, with an additional $28,000 to be paid in the event Nixon lost in the Supreme Court. Fitzgerald was rehired with back pay by the Air Force in June 1982. Justice Powell's opinion of the Court expressly reserved the question whether Congress might statutorily alter the president's immunity. Majority: Powell, Burger, O'Connor, Rehnquist, Stevens. Dissenting: White, Blackmun, Brennan, Marshall.

Justice Powell delivered the opinion of the Court.

The plaintiff in this lawsuit seeks relief in civil damages from a former President of the United States. The claim rests on actions allegedly taken in the former President's official capacity during his tenure in office. The issue before us is the scope of the immunity possessed by the President of the United States. . . .

This Court consistently has recognized that government officials are entitled to some form of immunity from suits for civil damages. . . . [I]n *Butz* v. *Economou* (1978), . . . we considered for the first time the kind of immunity possessed by *federal* executive officials who are sued for constitutional violations. In *Butz* the Court rejected an argument, based on decisions involving federal officials charged with common-law torts, that all high federal officials have a right to absolute immunity from constitutional damages actions. Concluding that a blanket recognition of absolute immunity would be anomalous in light of the qualified immunity standard applied to state executive officials, we held that federal officials generally have the same qualified immunity possessed by state officials. . . . In so doing we reaffirmed our holdings that some officials, notably judges and prosecutors, "because of the special nature of their responsibilities," "require a full exemption from liability." In *Butz* itself we upheld a claim of absolute immunity for administrative officials engaged in functions analogous to those of judges and prosecutors. We also left open the question whether other federal officials could show that "public policy requires an exemption of that scope."

Here a former President asserts his immunity from civil damages claims of two kinds. He stands named as a defendant in a direct action under the Constitution and in two statutory actions under federal laws of general applicability. In neither case has Congress taken express legislative action to subject the President to civil liability for his official acts.

Applying the principles of our cases to claims of this kind, we hold that petitioner, as a former President of the United States, is entitled to absolute immunity from damages liability predicated on his official acts. We consider this immunity a functionally mandated incident of the President's unique office, rooted in the constitutional tradition of the separation of powers and supported by our history. . . .

In arguing that the President is entitled only to qualified immunity, the respondent relies on cases in which we have recognized immunity of this scope for governors and cabinet officers. We find these cases to be inapposite. The President's unique status under the Constitution distinguishes him from other executive officials.

Because of the singular importance of the President's duties, diversion of his energies by concern with private law suits would raise unique risks to the effective functioning of government. As is the case with prosecutors and judges—for whom absolute immunity now is established—a President must concern himself with matters likely to "arouse the most intense feelings." Yet, as our decisions have recognized, it is in precisely such cases that there exists the greatest public interest in providing an official "the maximum ability to deal fearlessly and impartially with" the duties of his office. This concern is compelling where the officeholder must make the most sensitive and far-reaching decisions entrusted to any official under our constitutional system. Nor can the sheer prominence of the President's office be ignored. In view of the visibility of his office and the effect of his actions on countless people, the President would be an easily identifiable target for suits for civil damages. Cognizance of this personal vulnerability frequently could distract a President from his public duties, to the detriment of not only the President and his office but also the Nation that the Presidency was designed to serve. . . .

Under the Constitution and laws of the United States the President has discretionary responsibility in a broad variety of areas, many of them highly sensitive. In many cases it would be difficult to determine which of the President's innumerable "functions" encompassed a particular action. In this case, for example, respondent argues that he was dismissed in retaliation for his testimony to Congress—a violation of [federal law]. The Air Force, however, has claimed that the underlying reorganization was undertaken to promote efficiency. Assuming that petitioner Nixon ordered the reorganization in which respondent lost his job, an inquiry into the President's motives could not be avoided under the kind of "functional" theory asserted both by respondent and the dissent. Inquiries of this kind could be highly intrusive.

Here respondent argues that petitioner Nixon would have acted outside the outer perimeter of his duties by ordering the discharge of an employee who was lawfully entitled to retain his job in the absence of "'such cause as will promote the efficiency of the service.'" Because Congress has granted this legislative protection, respondent argues, no federal official could, within the outer perimeter of his duties of office, cause Fitzgerald to be dismissed without satisfying this standard in prescribed statutory proceedings.

This construction would subject the President to trial on virtually every allegation that an action was unlawful, or was taken for a forbidden purpose. Adoption of this construction thus would deprive absolute immunity of its intended effect. It clearly is within the President's constitutional and statutory authority to prescribe the manner in which the Secretary will conduct the business of the Air Force. Because this mandate of office must include the authority to prescribe reorganizations and reductions in force, we conclude that petitioner's alleged wrongful acts lay well within the outer perimeter of his authority.

A rule of absolute immunity for the President will not leave the Nation without sufficient protection against misconduct on the part of the Chief Executive. There remains the constitutional remedy of impeachment. In addition, there are formal and informal checks on Presidential action that do not apply with equal force to other executive officials. The President is subjected to constant scrutiny by the press. Vigilant oversight by Congress also may serve to deter Presidential abuses of office, as well as to make credible the threat of impeachment. Other incentives to avoid misconduct may include a desire to earn reelection, the need to maintain prestige as an element of Presidential influence, and a President's traditional concern for his historical stature.

The existence of alternative remedies and deterrents establishes that absolute immunity will not place the President "above the law." For the President, as for judges and prosecutors, absolute immunity merely precludes a particular private remedy for alleged misconduct in order to advance compelling public ends.

For the reasons stated in this opinion, the decision of the Court of Appeals is reversed, and the case is remanded for action consistent with this opinion.

So ordered.

CHIEF JUSTICE BURGER, concurring . . . [omitted].

JUSTICE WHITE, with whom JUSTICE BRENNAN, JUSTICE MARSHALL, and JUSTICE BLACKMUN join, dissenting. . . .

Attaching absolute immunity to the Office of the President, rather than to particular activities that the President might perform, places the President above the law. It is a reversion to the old notion that the King can do no wrong. . . . Now, however, the Court clothes the Office of the President with sovereign immunity, placing it beyond the law. . . .

Unfortunately, the Court now abandons basic principles that have been powerful guides to decision. It is particularly unfortunate since the judgment in this case has few, if any, indicia of a judicial decision; it is almost wholly a policy choice, a choice that is without substantial support and that in all events is ambiguous in its reach and import. . . . The Court casually, but candidly, abandons the functional approach to immunity that has run through all of our decisions. Indeed, the majority turns this rule on its head by declaring that because the functions of the President's office are so varied and diverse and some of them so profoundly important, the office is unique and must be clothed with officewide, absolute immunity. This is policy, not law, and in my view, very poor policy. . . .

JUSTICE BLACKMUN, with whom JUSTICE BRENNAN and JUSTICE MARSHALL join, dissenting . . . [omitted].

Clinton v. *Jones*
520 U.S. 681, 117 S.Ct. 1636, 137 L.Ed. 2d 945 (1997)

http://caselaw.findlaw.com/us-supreme-court/520/681.html

The facts of this case are contained in the opinion below. Majority: Stevens, Rehnquist, O'Connor, Scalia, Kennedy, Souter, Thomas, Ginsburg, Breyer.

JUSTICE STEVENS delivered the opinion of the Court . . .

This case raises a constitutional and a prudential question concerning the Office of the President of the United States. Respondent, a private citizen, seeks to recover damages from the current occupant of that office based on actions allegedly taken before his term began. The President submits that in all but the most exceptional cases the Constitution requires federal courts to defer such litigation until his term ends and that, in any event, respect for the office warrants such a stay. Despite the force of the arguments supporting the President's submissions, we conclude that they must be rejected.

Petitioner, William Jefferson Clinton, was elected to the Presidency in 1992, and re-elected in 1996. His term of office expires on January 20, 2001. In 1991 he was the Governor of the State of Arkansas. Respondent, Paula Corbin Jones, is a resident of California. In 1991 she lived in Arkansas, and was an employee of the Arkansas Industrial Development Commission.

On May 6, 1994, she commenced this action in the United States District Court for the Eastern District of Arkansas by filing a complaint naming petitioner and Danny Ferguson, a former Arkansas State Police officer, as defendants. The complaint alleges two federal claims, and two state law claims over which the federal court has jurisdiction because of the diverse citizenship of the parties. As the case comes to us, we are required to assume the truth of the detailed—but as yet untested—factual allegations in the complaint.

Those allegations principally describe events that are said to have occurred on the afternoon of May 8, 1991, during an official conference held at the Excelsior Hotel in Little Rock, Arkansas. The Governor delivered a speech at the conference; respondent—working as a state employee—staffed the registration desk. She alleges that Ferguson persuaded her to leave her desk and to visit the Governor in a business suite at the hotel, where he made "abhorrent" sexual advances that she vehemently rejected. She further claims that her superiors at work subsequently dealt with her in a hostile and rude manner, and changed her duties to punish her for rejecting those advances. Finally, she alleges that after petitioner was elected President, Ferguson defamed her by making a statement to a reporter that implied she had accepted petitioner's alleged overtures, and that various persons authorized to speak for the President publicly branded her a liar by denying that the incident had occurred. . . .

In response to the complaint, petitioner promptly advised the District Court that he intended to file a motion to dismiss on grounds of Presidential immunity. . . .

The District Judge denied the motion to dismiss on immunity grounds and ruled that discovery in the case could go forward, but ordered any trial stayed until the end of petitioner's Presidency. Although she recognized that a "thin majority" in *Nixon* v. *Fitzgerald* (1982), had held that "the President has absolute immunity from civil damage actions arising out of the execution of official duties of office," she was not convinced that "a President has absolute immunity from civil causes of action arising prior to assuming the office." She was, however, persuaded by some of the reasoning in our opinion in *Fitzgerald* that deferring the trial if one were required would be appropriate. Relying in part on the fact that respondent had failed to bring her complaint until two days before the 3-year period of limitations expired, she concluded that the public interest in avoiding litigation that might hamper the President in conducting the duties of his office outweighed any demonstrated need for an immediate trial.

Both parties appealed. A divided panel of the Court of Appeals affirmed the denial of the motion to dismiss, but because it regarded the order postponing the trial until the President leaves office as the "functional equivalent" of a grant of temporary immunity, it reversed that order. . . .

Petitioner's principal submission—that "in all but the most exceptional cases," the Constitution affords the President temporary immunity from civil damages litigation arising out of events that occurred before he took office—cannot be sustained on the basis of precedent. . . .

The principal rationale for affording certain public servants immunity from suits for money damages arising out of their official acts is inapplicable to unofficial conduct. In cases involving prosecutors, legislators, and judges we have repeatedly explained that the immunity serves the public interest in enabling such officials to perform their designated functions effectively without fear that a particular decision may give rise to personal liability. . . . That rationale provided the principal basis for our holding that a former President of the United States was "entitled to absolute immunity from damages liability predicated on his official acts." Our central concern was to avoid rendering the President "unduly cautious in the discharge of his official duties."

This reasoning provides no support for an immunity for *unofficial* conduct. As we explained in *Fitzgerald*, "the sphere of protected action must be related closely to the immunity's justifying purposes." Because of the President's broad responsibilities, we recognized in that case an immunity from damages claims arising out of official acts extending to the "outer perimeter of his authority." But we have never suggested that the President, or any other official, has an immunity that extends beyond the scope of any action taken in an official capacity. . . .

As our opinions have made clear, immunities are grounded in "the nature of the function performed, not the identity of the actor who performed it." . . .

As a starting premise, petitioner contends that he occupies a unique office with powers and responsibilities so vast and important that the public interest demands that he devote his undivided time and attention to his public duties. He submits that—given the nature of the office—the doctrine of separation of powers places limits on the authority of the Federal Judiciary to interfere with the Executive Branch that would be transgressed by allowing this action to proceed.

We have no dispute with the initial premise of the argument. . . .

It does not follow, however, that separation of powers principles would be violated by allowing this action to proceed. . . .

Rather than arguing that the decision of the case will produce either an aggrandizement of judicial power or a narrowing of executive power, petitioner contends that—as a byproduct of an otherwise traditional exercise of judicial power—burdens will be placed on the President that will hamper the performance of his official duties. We have recognized that "[e]ven when a branch does not arrogate power to itself . . . the separation-of-powers doctrine requires that a branch not impair another in the performance of its constitutional duties." . . . Petitioner's predictive judgment finds little support in either history or the relatively narrow compass of the issues raised in this particular case. As we have already noted, in the more than 200-year history of the Republic, only three sitting Presidents have been subjected to suits for their private actions. If the past is any indicator, it seems unlikely that a deluge of such litigation will ever engulf the Presidency. As for the case at hand, if properly managed by the District Court, it appears to us highly unlikely to occupy any substantial amount of petitioner's time.

Of greater significance, petitioner errs by presuming that interactions between the Judicial Branch and the Executive, even quite burdensome interactions, necessarily rise to the level of constitutionally forbidden impairment of the Executive's ability to perform its constitutionally mandated functions. . . .

First, we have long held that when the President takes official action, the Court has the authority to determine whether he has acted within the law. Perhaps the most dramatic example of such a case is our holding that President Truman exceeded his constitutional authority when he issued an order directing the Secretary of Commerce to take possession of and operate most of the Nation's steel mills in order to avert a national catastrophe. Despite the serious impact of that decision on the ability of the Executive Branch to accomplish its assigned mission, and the substantial time that the President must necessarily have devoted to the matter as a result of judicial involvement, we exercised our Article III jurisdiction to decide whether his official conduct conformed to the law. Our holding was an application of the principle established in *Marbury* v. *Madison*, that "[i]t is emphatically the province and duty of the judicial department to say what the law is."

Second, it is also settled that the President is subject to judicial process in appropriate circumstances. Although Thomas Jefferson apparently thought otherwise, Chief Justice Marshall, when presiding in the treason trial of Aaron

Burr, ruled that a subpoena *duces tecum* could be directed to the President. We unequivocally and emphatically endorsed Marshall's position when we held that President Nixon was obligated to comply with a subpoena commanding him to produce certain tape recordings of his conversations with his aides. . . .

We therefore hold that the doctrine of separation of powers does not require federal courts to stay all private actions against the President until he leaves office.

The reasons for rejecting such a categorical rule apply as well to a rule that would require a stay "in all but the most exceptional cases." Indeed, if the Framers of the Constitution had thought it necessary to protect the President from the burdens of private litigation, we think it far more likely that they would have adopted a categorical rule than a rule that required the President to litigate the question whether a specific case belonged in the "exceptional case" subcategory. In all events, the question whether a specific case should receive exceptional treatment is more appropriately the subject of the exercise of judicial discretion than an interpretation of the Constitution. . . .

Although we have rejected the argument that the potential burdens on the President violate separation-of-powers principles, those burdens are appropriate matters for the District Court to evaluate in its management of the case. The high respect that is owed to the office of the Chief Executive, though not justifying a rule of categorical immunity, is a matter that should inform the conduct of the entire proceeding, including the timing and scope of discovery.

Nevertheless, we are persuaded that it was an abuse of discretion for the District Court to defer the trial until after the President leaves office. Such a lengthy and categorical stay takes no account whatever of the respondent's interest in bringing the case to trial. The complaint was filed within the statutory limitations period—albeit near the end of that period—and delaying trial would increase the danger of prejudice resulting from the loss of evidence, including the inability of witnesses to recall specific facts, or the possible death of a party. . . .

We add a final comment on two matters that are discussed at length in the briefs: the risk that our decision will generate a large volume of politically motivated harassing and frivolous litigation, and the danger that national security concerns might prevent the President from explaining a legitimate need for a continuance.

We are not persuaded that either of these risks is serious. . . . In short, we have confidence in the ability of our federal judges to deal with both of these concerns.

If Congress deems it appropriate to afford the President stronger protection, it may respond with appropriate legislation. . . .

The Federal District Court has jurisdiction to decide this case. Like every other citizen who properly invokes that jurisdiction, respondent has a right to an orderly disposition of her claims. Accordingly, the judgment of the Court of Appeals is affirmed.

It is so ordered.

JUSTICE BREYER, concurring in the judgment . . . [omitted].

Trump v. *Vance*
591 U.S. ___, 140 S.Ct. 2412, 207 L.Ed. 2d 907 (2020)

www.supremecourt.gov/opinions/19pdf/19-635_o7jq.pdf

In 2019, New York County district attorney Cyrus R. Vance, Jr. served a subpoena on Mazars USA, President Donald J. Trump's accounting firm, on behalf of a grand jury, seeking various financial records including tax returns belonging to Trump, who sued in his personal capacity to block the subpoena. The U.S. District Court for the Southern District of New York and the U.S. Court of Appeals for the Second Circuit ruled against Trump. In February 2021, seven months after this case came down and after lower courts again ruled against Trump, the Supreme Court, with no noted dissents to a one-sentence order, rejected the former president's efforts to bar prosecutorial access to his tax and other financial records that had been at issue.

CHIEF JUSTICE ROBERTS delivered the opinion of the Court.

In our judicial system, "the public has a right to everyman's evidence." Since the earliest days of the Republic, "every man" has included the President of the United States. Beginning with Jefferson and carrying on through Clinton, Presidents have uniformly testified or produced documents in criminal proceedings when called upon by federal courts. This case involves—so far as we and the parties can tell—the first *state* criminal subpoena directed to a President. The President contends that the subpoena is unenforceable. We granted certiorari to decide whether Article II and the Supremacy Clause categorically preclude, or require a heightened standard for, the issuance of a state criminal subpoena to a sitting President. . . . [the chief justice's lengthy account of the treason trial of Aaron Burr in 1807 and the ruling by Chief Justice John Marshall, sitting as circuit justice, that a subpoena could issue against a sitting president, is omitted.]

The history surveyed above all involved *federal* criminal proceedings. Here we are confronted for the first time with a subpoena issued to the President by a local grand jury operating under the supervision of a *state* court. In the President's view, that distinction makes all the difference. He argues that the Supremacy Clause gives a sitting President absolute immunity from state criminal subpoenas because compliance with those subpoenas would categorically impair a President's performance of his Article II functions. The Solicitor General, arguing on behalf of the United States, agrees with much of the President's reasoning but does not commit to his bottom line. Instead, the Solicitor General urges us to resolve this case by holding that a state grand jury subpoena for a sitting President's personal records must, at the very least, "satisfy a heightened standard of need," which the Solicitor General contends was not met here. . . .

We begin with the question of absolute immunity. . . . The President's primary contention, which the Solicitor General supports, is that complying with state criminal subpoenas would necessarily divert the Chief Executive from his duties. He grounds that concern in *Nixon* v. *Fitzgerald*, which recognized a President's "absolute immunity from damages liability predicated on his official acts." In explaining the basis for that immunity, this Court observed that the prospect of such liability could "distract a President from his public duties, to the detriment of not only the President and his office but also the Nation that the Presidency was designed to serve." The President contends that the diversion occasioned by a state criminal subpoena imposes an equally intolerable burden on a President's ability to perform his Article II functions.

But *Fitzgerald* did not hold that distraction was sufficient to confer absolute immunity. We instead drew a careful analogy to the common law absolute immunity of judges and prosecutors, concluding that a President, like those officials, must "deal fearlessly and impartially with the duties of his office"—not be made "unduly cautious in the discharge of [those] duties" by the prospect of civil liability for official acts. Indeed, we expressly rejected immunity based on distraction alone 15 years later in *Clinton* v. *Jones* . . . . The same is true of criminal subpoenas. . . .

The President next claims that the stigma of being subpoenaed will undermine his leadership at home and abroad. Notably, the Solicitor General does not endorse this argument . . . But even if a tarnished reputation were a cognizable impairment, there is nothing inherently stigmatizing about a President performing "the citizen's normal duty of . . . furnishing information relevant" to a criminal investigation. . . .

Finally, the President and the Solicitor General warn that subjecting Presidents to state criminal subpoenas will make them "easily identifiable target[s]" for harassment. But we rejected a nearly identical argument in *Clinton*. . . .

Given these safeguards and the Court's precedents, we cannot conclude that absolute immunity is necessary or appropriate under Article II or the Supremacy Clause. Our dissenting colleagues agree. Justice Thomas reaches the same conclusion based on the original understanding of the Constitution. . . . And Justice Alito . . . "agree[s]" that "not all" state criminal subpoenas for a President's records "should be barred." On that point the Court is unanimous.

We next consider whether a state grand jury subpoena seeking a President's private papers must satisfy a heightened need standard. The Solicitor General would require a threshold showing that the evidence sought is "critical" for "specific charging decisions" and that the subpoena is a "last resort," meaning the evidence is "not available from any other source" and is needed "now, rather than at the end of the President's term." . . .

We disagree, for three reasons. First, such a heightened standard would extend protection designed for official documents to the President's private papers. . . . Second, the Solicitor General [has not] established that heightened protection against state subpoenas is necessary for the Executive to fulfill his Article II functions. Beyond the risk of harassment, which we addressed above, the only justification they offer for the heightened standard is protecting Presidents from "unwarranted burdens." . . . Finally, in the absence of a need to protect the Executive, the public interest in fair and effective law enforcement cuts in favor of comprehensive access to evidence. . . .

Rejecting a heightened need standard does not leave Presidents with "no real protection." To start, a President may avail himself of the same protections available to every other citizen. . . . And, as in federal court, "[t]he high respect that is owed to the office of the Chief Executive . . . should inform the conduct of the entire proceeding, including the timing and scope of discovery.". . .

We . . . hold that the President is neither absolutely immune from state criminal subpoenas seeking his private papers nor entitled to a heightened standard of need. . . . The arguments presented here and in the Court of Appeals were limited to absolute immunity and heightened need. The Court of Appeals, however, has directed that the case be returned to the District Court, where the President may raise further arguments as appropriate. We affirm the judgment of the Court of Appeals and remand the case for further proceedings consistent with this opinion.

It is so ordered.

JUSTICE KAVANAUGH with whom JUSTICE GORSUCH joins, concurring in the judgment . . . [omitted].

JUSTICE THOMAS, dissenting . . . [omitted].

JUSTICE ALITO, dissenting.

This case is almost certain to be portrayed as a case about the current President and the current political situation, but the case has a much deeper significance. While the decision will of course have a direct effect on President Trump, what the Court holds today will also affect all future Presidents—which is to say, it will affect the Presidency, and that is a matter of great and lasting importance to the Nation.

The event that precipitated this case is unprecedented. Respondent Vance, an elected state prosecutor, launched a criminal investigation of a sitting President and obtained a grand jury subpoena for his records. The specific question before us—whether the subpoena may be enforced—cannot be answered adequately without considering the broader question that frames it: whether the Constitution imposes restrictions on a State's deployment of its criminal law enforcement powers against a sitting President. If the Constitution sets no such limits, then a local prosecutor may prosecute a sitting President. And if that is allowed, it follows a fortiori that the subpoena at issue can be enforced. On the other hand, if the Constitution does not permit a State to prosecute a sitting President, the next logical question is whether the Constitution restrains any other prosecutorial or investigative weapons.

These are important questions that go to the very structure of the Government created by the Constitution. In evaluating these questions, two important structural features must be taken into account.

The first is the nature and role of the Presidency. . . . The second structural feature is the relationship between the Federal Government and the States. Just as our Constitution balances power against power among the branches of the Federal Government, it also divides power between the Federal Government and the States. The Constitution permitted the States to retain many of the sovereign powers that they previously possessed, but it gave the Federal Government powers that were deemed essential for the Nation's well-being and, indeed, its survival. And it provided for the Federal Government to be independent of and, within its allotted sphere, supreme over the States. Accordingly, a State may not block or interfere with the lawful work of the National Government. This was an enduring lesson of Chief Justice Marshall's landmark opinion for the Court in *McCulloch* v. *Maryland* . . . . After holding that Congress had the authority to establish the bank, Marshall's opinion went on to conclude that the State could not tax it. . . . Marshall thus held, not simply that Maryland was barred from assessing a crushing tax that threatened the bank's ability to operate, but that the State could not tax the bank at all. . . . Building on this principle of federalism, two centuries of case law prohibit the States from taxing, regulating, or otherwise interfering with the lawful work of federal agencies, instrumentalities, and officers. . . .

In *McCulloch*, Maryland's sovereign taxing power had to yield, and in a similar way, a State's sovereign power to enforce its criminal laws must accommodate the indispensable role that the Constitution assigns to the Presidency. This must be the rule with respect to a state prosecution of a sitting President. Both the structure of the Government established by the Constitution and the Constitution's provisions on the impeachment and removal of a President make it clear that the prosecution of a sitting President is out of the question. . . .

In the proceedings below, neither respondent, nor the District Court, nor the Second Circuit was willing to concede the fundamental point that a sitting President may not be prosecuted by a local district attorney. . . . The scenario apparently contemplated by the District Court is striking. If a sitting President were charged in New York County, would he be arrested and fingerprinted? He would presumably be required to appear for arraignment in criminal court, where the judge would set the conditions for his release. Could he be sent to Rikers Island or be required to post bail? Could the judge impose restrictions on his travel? If the President were scheduled to travel abroad—perhaps to attend a G-7 meeting—would he have to get judicial approval? If the President were charged with a complicated offense requiring a long trial, would he have to put his Presidential responsibilities aside for weeks on end while sitting in a Manhattan courtroom? While the trial was in progress, would aides be able to approach him and whisper in his ear about pressing matters? Would he be able to obtain a recess whenever he needed to speak with an aide at greater length or attend to an urgent matter, such as speaking with a foreign leader? Could he effectively carry out all his essential Presidential responsibilities after the trial day ended and at the same time adequately confer with his trial attorneys regarding his defense? Or should he be expected to give up the right to attend his own trial and be tried in absentia? And if he were convicted, could he be imprisoned? Would aides be installed in a nearby cell? This entire imagined scene is farcical. . . .

While the prosecution of a sitting President provides the most dramatic example of a clash between the indispensable work of the Presidency and a State's exercise of its criminal law enforcement powers, other examples are easy to imagine. Suppose state officers obtained and sought to execute a search warrant for a sitting President's private quarters in the White House. Suppose a state court authorized surveillance of a telephone that a sitting President was known to use. Or suppose that a sitting President was subpoenaed to testify before a state grand jury and, as is generally the rule, no Presidential aides, even those carrying the so-called "nuclear football," were permitted to enter the grand jury room. What these examples illustrate is a principle that this Court has recognized: legal proceedings involving a sitting President must take the responsibilities and demands of the office into account. . . .

I now come to the specific investigative weapon at issue in the case before us—a subpoena for a sitting President's records. This weapon is less intrusive in an immediate sense than those mentioned above. Since the records are held by, and the subpoena was issued to, a third party, compliance would not require much work on the President's part. And after all, this is just one subpoena. But we should heed the "great jurist," who rejected a similar argument in *McCulloch*. If we say that a subpoena to a third party is insufficient to undermine a President's performance of his duties, what about a subpoena served on the President himself? . . . And if one subpoena is permitted, what about two? Or three? Or ten? Drawing a line based on such factors would involve the same sort of "perplexing inquiry, so unfit for the judicial department" that Marshall rejected in *McCulloch*. The Court faced a similar issue when it considered whether a President can be sued for an allegedly unlawful act committed in the performance of official duties. We did not ask whether the particular suit before us would have interfered with the carrying out of Presidential duties. (It could not have had that effect because President Nixon had already left office.) Instead, we adopted a rule for all such suits, and we should take a similar approach here. The rule should take into account both the effect of subpoenas on the functioning of the Presidency and the risk that they will be used for harassment.

I turn first to the question of the effect of a state grand jury subpoena for a President's records. . . . We have come to expect our Presidents to shoulder burdens that very few people could bear, but it is unrealistic to think that the prospect of possible criminal prosecution will not interfere with the performance of the duties of the office. . . . As for the potential use of subpoenas to harass, . . . [t]here are more than 2,300 local prosecutors and district attorneys in the country. Many local prosecutors are elected, and many prosecutors have ambitions for higher elected office. . . . If a sitting President is intensely unpopular in a particular district—and that is a common condition—targeting the President may be an alluring and effective electoral strategy. But it is a strategy that would undermine our constitutional structure.

The Framers understood the importance of protecting the Presidency from interference by the States. . . . Two centuries later, the Court's decision in *Clinton* reflected a similar concern. The Court held that a sitting President could be sued in federal court, but the Court took pains to reserve judgment on the question whether "a comparable claim might succeed in a state tribunal."

In light of the above, a subpoena like the one now before us should not be enforced unless it meets a test that takes into account the need to prevent interference with a President's discharge of the responsibilities of the office. I agree with the Court that not all such subpoenas should be barred. There may be situations in which there is an urgent and critical need for the subpoenaed information. . . . But in a case like the one at hand, a subpoena should not be allowed unless a heightened standard is met. . . . Thus, in a case like this one, a prosecutor should be required (1) to provide at least a general description of the possible offenses that are under investigation, (2) to outline how the subpoenaed records relate to those offenses, and (3) to explain why it is important that the records be produced and why it is necessary for production to occur while the President is still in office. . . .

Unlike this rule, which would not undermine any legitimate state interests, the opinion of the Court provides no real protection for the Presidency. . . . For all practical purposes, the Court's decision places a sitting President in the same unenviable position as any other person whose records are subpoenaed by a grand jury. . . .

The lesson we should take from Marshall's jurisprudence is the lesson of *McCulloch*—the importance of preventing a State from undermining the lawful exercise of authority conferred by the Constitution on the Federal Government. There is considerable irony in the Court's invocation of Marshall to defend a decision allowing a State's prosecutorial power to run roughshod over the functioning of a branch of the Federal Government. . . .

I therefore respectfully dissent.

IV. APPOINTMENT AND REMOVAL

Myers v. *United States*
272 U.S. 52, 47 S.Ct. 31, 71 L.Ed. 160 (1926)

http://caselaw.findlaw.com/us-supreme-court/272/52.html

This case was an appeal from the Court of Claims. The facts appear in the opinion of the Court. Majority: Taft, Butler, Sanford, Stone, Sutherland, Van Devanter. Dissenting: Brandeis, Holmes, McReynolds.

Mr. Chief Justice Taft delivered the opinion of the Court.

This case presents the question whether under the Constitution the President has the exclusive power of removing executive officers of the United States whom he has appointed by and with the advice and consent of the Senate. . . .

By the sixth section of the Act of Congress of July 12, 1876 . . . under which Myers was appointed with the advice and consent of the Senate as a first-class postmaster, it is provided that: "Postmasters of the first, second and third classes shall be appointed and may be removed by the President by and with the advice and consent of the Senate, and shall hold their offices for four years unless sooner removed or suspended according to law."

The Senate did not consent to the President's removal of Myers during his term. . . . The government maintains that . . . the President's power of removal of executive officers appointed by him with the advice and consent of the Senate is full and complete without consent of the Senate. . . .

The question where the power of removal of executive officers appointed by the President by and with the advice and consent of the Senate was vested, was presented early in the first session of the First Congress. There is no express provision respecting removals in the Constitution, except as section 4 of Article II provides for removal of office by impeachment. The subject was not discussed in the Constitutional Convention. . . .

The vesting of the executive power in the President was essentially a grant of the power to execute the laws. But the President alone and unaided could not execute the laws. He must execute them by the assistance of subordinates. . . . As he is charged specifically to take care that they be faithfully executed, the reasonable implication, even in the absence of express words, was that as part of his executive power he should select those who were to act for him under his direction in the execution of the laws. The further implication must be, in the absence of any express limitation respecting removals, that as his selection of administrative officers is essential to the execution of the laws by him, so must be his power of removing those for whom he cannot continue to be responsible. . . .

The power to prevent the removal of an officer who has served under the President is different from the authority to consent to or reject his appointment. When a nomination is made, it may be presumed that the Senate is, or may become, as well advised as to the fitness of the nominee as the President, but in the nature of things the defects in ability or intelligence or loyalty in the administration of the laws of one who has served as an officer under the President are facts as to which the President, or his trusted subordinates, must be better informed than the Senate, and the power to remove him may therefore be regarded as confined for very sound and practical reasons, to the governmental authority which has administrative control. The power of removal is incident to the power of appointment, not to the power of advising and consenting to appointment, and when the grant of the executive power is enforced by the express mandate to take care that the laws be faithfully executed, it emphasizes the necessity for including within the executive power as conferred the exclusive power of removal. . . .

A reference of the whole power of removal to general legislation by Congress is quite out of keeping with the plan of government devised by the framers of the Constitution. It could never have been intended to leave to Congress unlimited discretion to vary fundamentally the operation of the great independent executive branch of government and thus most seriously to weaken it. . . .

It is reasonable to suppose also that had it been intended to give to Congress power to regulate or control removals in the manner suggested, it would have been included among the specifically enumerated legislative powers in Article I, or in the specified limitations on the executive power in Article II. . . .

We come now to consider an argument, advanced and strongly pressed on behalf of the complainant, that this case concerns only the removal of a postmaster, that a postmaster is an inferior officer, and that such an office was not included within the legislative decision of 1789, which related only to superior officers to be appointed by the President by and with the advice and consent of the Senate. . . .

The power to remove inferior executive officers, like that to remove superior executive officers, is an incident of the power to appoint them, and is in its nature an executive power. The authority of Congress given by the excepting clause to vest the appointment of such inferior officers in the heads of departments carries with it authority incidentally to invest the heads of departments with power to remove. It has been the practice of Congress to do so and this court has recognized that power. . . . The court also has recognized . . . that Congress, in committing the appointment of such inferior officers to the heads of departments, may prescribe incidental regulations controlling and restricting the latter in the exercise of the power of removal. But the court never has held, nor reasonably could hold, . . . that the excepting clause enables Congress to draw to itself, or to either branch of it, the power to remove or the right to participate in the exercise of that power. To do this would be to go beyond the words and implications of that clause, and to infringe the constitutional principle of the separation of governmental powers.

Assuming, then, the power of Congress to regulate removals as incidental to the exercise of its constitutional power to vest appointments of inferior officers in the heads of departments, certainly so long as Congress does not exercise that power, the power of removal must remain where the Constitution places it, with the President, as part of the executive power. . . .

For the reasons given, we must therefore hold that the provision of the law of 1876 by which the unrestricted power of removal of first-class postmasters is denied to the President is in violation of the Constitution and invalid. . . .

Judgment affirmed.

MR. JUSTICE MCREYNOLDS, dissenting . . . [omitted].

MR. JUSTICE BRANDEIS, dissenting. . . .

The ability to remove a subordinate executive officer, being an essential of effective government, will, in the absence of express constitutional provision to the contrary, be deemed to have been vested in some person or body. But it is not a power inherent in a chief executive. The President's power of removal from statutory civil inferior offices, like the power of appointment to them, comes immediately from Congress. It is true that the exercise of the power of removal is said to be an executive act, and that when the Senate grants or withholds consent to a removal by the President, it participates in an executive act. But the Constitution has confessedly granted to Congress the legislative power to create offices and to prescribe the tenure thereof; and it has not in terms denied to Congress the power to control removals. To prescribe the tenure involves prescribing the conditions under which incumbency shall cease. For the possibility of removal is a condition or qualification of the tenure. When Congress provides that the incumbent shall hold the office for four years unless sooner removed with the consent of the Senate, it prescribes the term of the tenure. . . .

The separation of the powers of government did not make each branch completely autonomous. It left each in some measure, dependent upon the others, as it left to each power to exercise, in some respects, functions in their nature executive, legislative and judicial. . . .

The doctrine of the separation of powers was adopted by the convention of 1787 not to promote efficiency but to preclude the exercise of arbitrary power. The purpose was not to avoid friction, but, by means of the inevitable friction incident to the distribution of the governmental powers among three departments, to save the people from autocracy. In order to prevent arbitrary executive action, the Constitution provided in terms that presidential appointments be made with the consent of the Senate, unless Congress should otherwise provide. . . . Nothing in support of the claim of uncontrollable power can be inferred from the silence of the convention of 1787 on the subject of removal. For the outstanding fact remains that every specific proposal to confer such uncontrollable power upon the President was rejected. In America, as in England, the conviction prevailed then that the people must look to representative assemblies for the protection of their liberties. . . .

MR. JUSTICE HOLMES, dissenting . . . [omitted].

Humphrey's Executor v. *United States* 295 U.S. 602, 55 S.Ct. 869, 79 L.Ed. 1611 (1935)

http://caselaw.findlaw.com/us-supreme-court/295/602.html

In the Federal Trade Commission Act of 1914 Congress provided that the five commissioners appointed by the president with the advice and consent of the Senate for seven-year terms were removable by the president for inefficiency, neglect of duty, or malfeasance in office. In 1933 President Franklin Roosevelt requested the resignation of William Humphrey, a commissioner whose term expired in 1938, in order to replace him with a commissioner whose views harmonized with Roosevelt's. When Humphrey refused to resign, the president removed him. This suit was initiated in the Court of Claims, which certified two questions to the Supreme Court regarding (1) the intent of the statute and (2) the president's removal authority under the Constitution. Majority: Sutherland, Brandeis, Butler, Cardozo, Hughes, McReynolds, Roberts, Stone, Van Devanter.

Mr. Justice Sutherland delivered the opinion of the Court. . . .

The commission is to be nonpartisan; and it must, from the very nature of its duties, act with entire impartiality. It is charged with the enforcement of no policy except the policy of the law. Its duties are neither political nor executive, but predominantly quasi judicial and quasi legislative. Like the Interstate Commerce Commission, its members are called upon to exercise the trained judgment of a body of experts "appointed by law and informed by experience." The legislative reports in both houses of Congress [while the act was under consideration] clearly reflect the view that a fixed term was necessary to the effective and fair administration of the law. . . . The debates in both houses demonstrate that the prevailing view was that the Commission was not to be "subject to anybody in the government but . . . only to the people of the United States;" free from "political domination or control" or the "probability or possibility of such a thing;" to be "separate and apart from any existing department of the government—not subject to the orders of the President." . . .

Thus, the language of the act, the legislative reports, and the general purposes of the legislation as reflected by the debates, all combine to demonstrate the congressional intent to create a body of experts who shall gain experience by length of service; a body which shall be independent of executive authority, *except in its selection*, and free to exercise its judgment without the leave or hindrance of any other official or any department of the government. To the accomplishment of these purposes, it is clear that Congress was of opinion that length and certainty of tenure would vitally contribute. And to hold that, nevertheless, the members of the commission continue in office at the mere will of the President, might be to thwart, in large measure, the very ends which Congress sought to realize by definitely fixing the term of office.

We conclude that the intent of the act is to limit the executive power of removal to the causes enumerated, the existence of none of which is claimed here. . . .

To support its contention that the removal provision, . . . as we have just construed it, is an unconstitutional interference with the executive power of the President, the government's chief reliance is *Myers* v. *United States*. . . .

The office of a postmaster is so essentially unlike the office now involved that the decision in the Myers Case cannot be accepted as controlling our decision here. A postmaster is an executive officer restricted to the performance of executive functions. He is charged with no duty at all related to either the legislative or judicial power. . . .

The Federal Trade Commission is an administrative body created by Congress to carry into effect legislative policies embodied in the statute in accordance with the legislative standard therein prescribed, and to perform other specified duties as a legislative or as a judicial aid. Such a body cannot in any proper sense be characterized as an arm or an eye of the executive. Its duties are performed without executive leave and, in the contemplation of the statute, must be free from executive control. In administering the provisions of the statute in respect of "unfair methods of competition," that is to say, in filling in and administering the details embodied by that general standard, the commission acts in part quasi legislatively and in part quasi-judicially. . . .

If Congress is without authority to prescribe causes for removal of members of the trade commission and limit executive power of removal accordingly, that power at once becomes practically all-inclusive in respect of civil officers with the exception of the judiciary provided for by the Constitution. The Solicitor General, at the bar, apparently recognizing this to be true, with commendable candor, agreed that his view in respect of the removability of members of the Federal Trade Commission necessitated a like view in respect of the Interstate Commerce Commission and the Court of Claims. We are thus confronted with the serious question whether not only the members of these quasi-legislative and quasi-judicial bodies, but the judges of the legislative Court of Claims, exercising judicial power, continue in office only at the pleasure of the President.

We think it plain under the Constitution that illimitable power of removal is not possessed by the President in respect of officers of the character of those just named. The authority of Congress, in creating quasi-legislative or quasi-judicial agencies, to require them to act in discharge of their duties independently of executive control cannot well be doubted; and that authority includes, as an appropriate incident, power to fix the period during which they shall continue, and to forbid their removal except for cause in the meantime. For it is quite evident that one who holds his office only during the pleasure of another cannot be depended upon to maintain an attitude of independence against the latter's will. . . . The sound application of a principle that makes one master in his own house precludes him from imposing his control in the house of another who is master there. . . .

To the extent that, between the decision in the Myers Case, which sustains the unrestrictable power of the President to remove purely executive officers, and our present decision that such power does not extend to an office such as that here involved, there shall remain a field of doubt, we leave such cases as may fall within it for future consideration and determination as they may arise. . . .

Morrison v. *Olson*
487 U.S. 654, 108 S.Ct. 2597, 101 L.Ed. 2d 569 (1988)

http://caselaw.findlaw.com/us-supreme-court/487/654.html

The Ethics in Government Act of 1978 provided for appointment of an independent counsel to investigate and, if appropriate, to prosecute high-ranking officials of the executive branch for violation of federal criminal laws. Once appointed, an independent counsel was removable only for cause. In 1985, after a three-year dispute between Congress and the Reagan administration over the Superfund law and the cleanup of toxic wastes, the House Judiciary Committee issued a report suggesting that Theodore Olson had given false and misleading testimony to the committee and that two others had wrongfully withheld documents from the committee. All three held important positions in the Department of Justice. Under the terms of the act, Attorney General Edwin Meese conducted a preliminary investigation and applied to the Special Division of the Court of Appeals for the District of Columbia Circuit for an independent counsel to investigate Olson alone. The Special Division designated Alexia Morrison as independent counsel. When a grand jury issued subpoenas to Olson and the others, they moved to quash the subpoenas on the grounds that the 1978 act was unconstitutional.

In 1987 the district court upheld the act. A divided court of appeals reversed in 1988, concluding, among other things (1) that the act's restrictions on the attorney general's power to remove an independent counsel infringed the separation of powers and (2) that the act violated the executive's duty to "take care that the Laws be faithfully executed." The excerpts below are limited to the Court's consideration of those two issues. (Four years after this case was decided, the independent counsel law was allowed to expire. Retaining the basic features of the previous version, Congress revived the statute in 1994 for a period of five years, but allowed it to expire again in 1999.) Majority: Rehnquist, Blackmun, Brennan, Marshall, O'Connor, Stevens, White. Dissenting: Scalia. Not participating: Kennedy.

Chief Justice Rehnquist delivered the opinion of the Court.

This case presents us with a challenge to the independent counsel provisions of the Ethics in Government Act of 1978. . . . We hold today that these provisions of the Act do not . . . impermissibly interfere with the President's authority under Article II in violation of the constitutional principle of separation of powers. . . .

Two related issues must be addressed: The first is whether the provision of the Act restricting the Attorney General's power to remove the independent counsel to only those instances in which he can show "good cause," taken by itself, impermissibly interferes with the President's exercise of his constitutionally appointed functions. The second is whether, taken as a whole, the Act violates the separation of powers by reducing the President's ability to control the prosecutorial powers wielded by the independent counsel. . . .

Unlike . . . *Myers*, this case does not involve an attempt by Congress itself to gain a role in the removal of executive officials other than its established powers of impeachment and conviction. . . . In our view, the removal provisions of the Act make this case more analogous to *Humphrey's Executor* v. *United States*. . . .

At the other end of the spectrum from *Myers*, the characterization of the agencies in *Humphrey's Executor* . . . as "quasi-legislative" or "quasi-judicial" in large part reflected our judgment that it was not essential to the President's proper execution of his Article II powers that these agencies be headed up by individuals who were removable at will. . . . [T]he real question is whether the removal restrictions are of such a nature that they impede the President's ability to perform his constitutional duty, and the functions of the officials in question must be analyzed in that light. . . . [T]his case does not involve an attempt by Congress to increase its own powers at the expense of the Executive Branch. . . .

Finally, we do not think that the Act "impermissibly undermine[s]" the powers of the Executive Branch, or "disrupts the proper balance between the coordinate branches [by] prevent[ing] the Executive Branch from accomplishing its constitutionally assigned functions." It is undeniable that the Act reduces the amount of control or supervision that the Attorney General and, through him, the President exercises over the investigation and prosecution of a certain class of alleged criminal activity. The Attorney General is not allowed to appoint the individual of his choice; he does not determine the counsel's jurisdiction; and his power to remove a counsel is limited. Nonetheless, the Act does give the Attorney General several means of supervising or controlling the prosecutorial powers that may be wielded by an independent counsel. Most importantly, the Attorney General retains the power to remove the counsel for "good cause," a power that we have already concluded provides the Executive with substantial ability to ensure that the laws are "faithfully executed" by an independent counsel. No independent counsel may be appointed without a specific request by the Attorney General, and the Attorney General's decision not to request appointment if he finds "no reasonable grounds to believe that further investigation is warranted" is committed to his unreviewable discretion. . . .

In sum, we conclude today that . . . the Act does not violate the separation of powers principle by impermissibly interfering with the functions of the Executive Branch. The decision of the Court of Appeals is therefore

Reversed.

Justice Scalia, dissenting. . . .

The framers of the Federal Constitution . . . viewed the principle of separation of powers as the absolutely central guarantee of a just government. . . .

That is what this suit is about. Power. The allocation of power among Congress, the President and the courts in such fashion as to preserve the equilibrium the Constitution sought to establish—so that "a gradual concentration of the several powers in the same department" can effectively be resisted. Frequently an issue of this sort will come before the Court clad, so to speak, in sheep's clothing: the potential of the asserted principle to effect important change in the equilibrium of power is not immediately evident and must be discerned by a careful and perceptive analysis. But this wolf comes as a wolf. . . .

If to describe this case is not to decide it, the concept of a government of separate and coordinate powers no longer has meaning. . . .

The Court concedes that "[t]here is no real dispute that the functions performed by the independent counsel are 'executive,'" though it qualifies that concession by adding "in the sense that they are 'law enforcement' functions that typically have been undertaken by officials within the Executive Branch." The qualifier adds nothing but atmosphere. In what other sense can one identify "the executive Power" that is supposed to be vested in the President (unless it includes everything the Executive Branch is given to do) except by reference to what has always and everywhere—if conducted by Government at all—been conducted never by the legislature, never by the courts, and always by the executive. There is no possible doubt that the independent counsel's functions fit this description. She is vested with the "full power and independent authority to exercise all investigative and prosecutorial functions and powers of the Department of Justice [and] the Attorney General." Governmental investigation and prosecution of crimes is a quintessentially executive function.

As for the . . . question, whether the statute before us deprives the President of exclusive control over that quintessentially executive activity: The Court does not, and could not possibly, assert that it does not. That is indeed the whole object of the statute. Instead, the Court points out that the President, through his Attorney General, has at least some control. That concession is alone enough to invalidate the statute, but I cannot refrain from pointing out that the Court greatly exaggerates the extent of that "some" presidential control. "Most importan[t]" among these controls, the Court asserts, is the Attorney General's "power to remove the counsel for 'good cause.'" This is somewhat like referring to shackles as an effective means of locomotion. As we recognized in *Humphrey's Executor* . . ., limiting removal power to "good cause" is an impediment to, not an effective grant of, presidential control. . . . What we in *Humphrey's Executor* found to be a means of eliminating presidential control, the Court today considers the "most importan[t]" means of assuring presidential control. Congress, of course, operated under no such illusion when it enacted this statute, describing the "good cause" limitation as "protecting the independent counsel's ability to act independently of the President's direct control" since it permits removal only for "misconduct." . . .

It is not for us to determine, and we have never presumed to determine, how much of the purely executive powers of government must be within the full control of the President. The Constitution prescribes that they all are. . . .

While the separation of powers may prevent us from righting every wrong, it does so in order to ensure that we do not lose liberty. The checks against any Branch's abuse of its exclusive powers are twofold: First, retaliation by one of the other Branch's use of its exclusive powers: Congress, for example, can impeach the Executive who willfully fails to enforce the laws; the Executive can decline to prosecute under unconstitutional statutes; and the courts can dismiss malicious prosecutions. Second, and ultimately, there is the political check that the people will replace those in the political branches . . . who are guilty of abuse. Political pressures produced special prosecutors—for Teapot Dome and for Watergate, for example—long before this statute created the independent counsel. . . .

Since our 1935 decision in *Humphrey's Executor* . . . it has been established that the line of permissible restriction upon removal of principal officers lies at the point at which the powers exercised by those officers are no longer purely executive. . . . By its short-sighted action today, I fear the Court has permanently encumbered the Republic with an institution that will do it great harm.

Worse than what it has done, however, is the manner in which it has done it. . . . Taking all things into account, we conclude that the power taken away from the President here is not really *too* much. . . .

V. FOREIGN POLICY AND NATIONAL SECURITY

Ex parte *Milligan*
71 U.S. (4 Wall.) 2, 18 L.Ed. 281 (1866)

http://caselaw.findlaw.com/us-supreme-court/71/2.html

(This case is reprinted in Chapter Fifteen; see the Table of Contents.)

Missouri v. *Holland*
252 U.S. 416, 40 S.Ct. 382, 64 L.Ed. 641 (1920)

http://caselaw.findlaw.com/us-supreme-court/252/416.html

By a treaty of 1916, the United States and Great Britain undertook the regulation and protection of birds migrating between Canada and various parts of the United States. An act of 1918 gave effect to the treaty by establishing closed seasons and other rules. The state of Missouri sued to prevent a game warden of the United States from enforcing the act and appealed from the district court's dismissal of the case. Majority: Holmes, Brandeis, Clarke, Day, McKenna, McReynolds, White. Dissenting: Pitney, Van Devanter.

Mr. Justice Holmes delivered the opinion of the Court. . . .

The question raised is the general one whether the treaty and statute are void as an interference with the rights reserved to the States.

To answer this question it is not enough to refer to the Tenth Amendment, reserving the powers not delegated to the United States, because by Article II, § 2, the power to make treaties is delegated expressly, and by Article VI treaties made under the authority of the United States, along with the Constitution and laws of the United States made in pursuance thereof, are declared the supreme law of the land. If the treaty is valid there can be no dispute about the validity of the statute under Article I, § 8, as a necessary and proper means to execute the powers of the Government. The language of the Constitution as to the supremacy of treaties being general, the question before us is narrowed to an inquiry into the ground upon which the present supposed exception is placed.

It is said that a treaty cannot be valid if it infringes the Constitution, that there are limits, therefore, to the treaty-making power, and that one such limit is what an act of Congress could not do unaided, in derogation of the powers reserved to the States a treaty cannot do. An earlier act of Congress that attempted by itself and not in pursuance of a treaty to regulate the killing of migratory birds within the States had been held bad in the District Court. Those decisions were supported by arguments that migratory birds were owned by the States in their sovereign capacity for the benefit of their people and that . . . this control was one that Congress had no power to displace. The same argument is supposed to apply now with equal force.

. . . Acts of Congress are the supreme law of the land only when made in pursuance of the Constitution, while treaties are declared to be so when made under the authority of the United States. It is open to question whether the authority of the United States means more than the formal acts prescribed to make the convention. We do not mean to imply that there are no qualifications to the treaty-making power; but they must be ascertained in a different way. It is obvious that there may be matters of the sharpest exigency for the national well-being that an act of Congress could not deal with but that a treaty followed by such an act could, and it is not lightly to be assumed that, in matters requiring national action, "a power which must belong to and somewhere reside in every civilized government" is not to be found. . . . [W]hen we are dealing with words that also are a constituent act, like the Constitution of the United States, we must realize that they have called into life a being the development of which could not have been foreseen completely by the most gifted of its begetters. It was not enough for them to realize or to hope that they had created an organism; it has taken a century and has cost their successors much sweat and blood to prove that they created a nation. The case before us must be considered in the light of our whole experience and not merely in that of what was said a hundred years ago. The treaty in question does not contravene any prohibitory words to be found in the Constitution. The only question is whether it is forbidden by some invisible radiation from the general terms of the Tenth Amendment. We must consider what this country has become in deciding what that Amendment has reserved.

The State as we have intimated founds its claim of exclusive authority upon an assertion of title to migratory birds. . . . To put the claim of the State upon title is to lean upon a slender reed. Wild birds are not in the possession of anyone; and possession is the beginning of ownership. The whole foundation of the State's rights is the presence within their jurisdiction of birds that yesterday had not arrived, tomorrow may be in another State and in a week a thousand miles away. . . .

Here a national interest of very nearly the first magnitude is involved. It can be protected only by national action in concert with that of another power. The subject matter is only transitorily within the State and has no permanent habitat therein. But for the treaty and the statute there soon might be no birds for any powers to deal with. We see nothing in the constitution that compels the Government to sit by while a food supply is cut off and the protectors of our forests and our crops are destroyed. It is not sufficient to rely upon the States. The reliance is vain, and were it otherwise, the question is whether the United States is forbidden to act. We are of opinion that the treaty and statute must be upheld.

Decree affirmed.

MR. JUSTICE VAN DEVANTER and MR. JUSTICE PITNEY dissent [without opinion].

United States v. *Curtiss-Wright Export Corp.* 299 U.S. 304, 57 S.Ct. 216, 81 L.Ed. 255 (1936)

http://caselaw.findlaw.com/us-supreme-court/299/304.html

Congress attempted to limit a war between Bolivia and Paraguay by granting the president authority to prohibit the sale of arms and munitions to the warring nations. The defendant corporation, charged with conspiring to sell 15 machine guns to Bolivia, objected to the indictment on the ground that the delegation of power to the president was invalid. The district court sustained the demurrer. (A demurrer is the formal mode of disputing the sufficiency in law of the pleading of the other side, even if the facts are true.) Majority: Sutherland, Brandeis, Butler, Cardozo, Hughes, Roberts, Van Devanter. Dissenting: McReynolds. Not participating: Stone.

MR. JUSTICE SUTHERLAND delivered the opinion of the Court. . . .

Whether, if the Joint Resolution had related solely to internal affairs, it would be open to the challenge that it constituted an unlawful delegation of legislative power to the Executive, we find it unnecessary to determine. The whole aim of the resolution is to affect a situation entirely external to the United States, and falling within the category of foreign affairs. The determination which we are called to make, therefore, is whether the Joint Resolution . . . is vulnerable to attack under the rule that forbids a delegation of the lawmaking power. In other words, assuming (but not deciding) that the challenged delegation, if it were confined to internal affairs, would be invalid, may it nevertheless be sustained on the ground that its exclusive aim is to afford a remedy for a hurtful condition within foreign territory?

It will contribute to the elucidation of the question if we first consider the differences between the powers of the federal government in respect of foreign or external affairs and those in respect of domestic or internal affairs. . . .

The two classes of powers are different, both in respect of their origin and their nature. The broad statement that the federal government can exercise no powers except those specifically enumerated in the Constitution, and such implied powers as are necessary and proper to carry into effect the enumerated powers, is categorically true only in respect of our internal affairs. In that field, the primary purpose of the Constitution was to carve from the general mass of legislative powers then possessed by the states such portions as it was thought desirable to vest in the federal government leaving those not included in the enumeration still in the states. . . . That this doctrine applies only to powers which the states had is self-evident. And since the states severally never possessed international powers, such powers could not have been carved from the mass of state powers but obviously were transmitted to the United States from some other source. During the Colonial period, those powers were possessed exclusively by and were entirely under the control of the Crown. By the Declaration of Independence, "the Representatives of the United States of America" declared the United (not the several) Colonies to be free and independent states, and as such to have "full Power to levy War, conclude Peace, contract Alliances, establish Commerce and to do all other Acts and Things which Independent States may of right do."

As a result of the separation from Great Britain by the colonies, acting as a unit, the powers of external sovereignty passed from the Crown not to the colonies severally, but to the colonies in their collective and corporate capacity as the United States of America. . . . When, therefore, the external sovereignty of Great Britain in respect of the colonies ceased, it immediately passed to the Union. . . . That fact was given practical application almost at once. The treaty of peace, made on September 3, 1783, was concluded between his Britannic Majesty and the "United States of America." . . .

The Union existed before the Constitution, which was ordained and established among other things to form "a more perfect Union." Prior to that event, it is clear that the Union declared by the Articles of Confederation to be "perpetual," was the sole possessor of external sovereignty, and in the Union it remained without change save in so far as the Constitution in express terms qualified its exercise. The Framers' Convention was called and exerted its powers upon the irrefutable postulate that though the states were several their people in respect of foreign affairs were one. . . .

It results that the investment of the federal government with the powers of external sovereignty did not depend upon the affirmative grants of the Constitution. The powers to declare and wage war, to conclude peace, to make treaties, to maintain diplomatic relations with other sovereignties, if they had never been mentioned in the Constitution, would have vested in the federal government as necessary concomitants of nationality. . . . As a member of the family of nations, the right and power of the United States in that field are equal to the right and power of the other members of the international family. Otherwise, the United States is not completely sovereign. . . .

Not only, as we have shown, is the federal power over external affairs in origin and essential character different from that over internal affairs, but participation in the exercise of the power is significantly limited. In this vast external realm, with its important, complicated, delicate and manifold problems, the President alone has the power to speak or listen as a representative of the nation. He makes treaties with the advice and consent of the Senate; but he alone negotiates. Into the field of negotiation the Senate cannot intrude; and Congress itself is powerless to invade it. . . .

It is important to bear in mind that we are here dealing not alone with an authority vested in the President by an exertion of legislative power, but with such an authority plus the very delicate, plenary and exclusive power of the President as the sole organ of the federal government in the field of international relations—a power which does not require as a basis for its exercise an act of Congress, but which, of course, like every other governmental power, must be exercised in subordination to the applicable provisions of the Constitution. It is quite apparent that if, in the maintenance of our international relations, embarrassment—perhaps serious embarrassment—is to be avoided and success for our aims achieved, congressional legislation which is to be made effective through negotiation and inquiry within the international field must often accord to the President a degree of discretion and freedom from statutory restriction which would not be admissible were domestic affairs alone involved. . . . Indeed, so clearly is this true that the first President refused to accede to a request to lay before the House of Representatives the instructions, correspondence and documents relating to the negotiation of the Jay Treaty—a refusal the wisdom of which was recognized by the House itself and has never been doubted. . . .

[W]e conclude there is sufficient warrant for the broad discretion vested in the President to determine whether the enforcement of the statute will have a beneficial effect upon the reestablishment of peace in the affected countries; whether he shall make proclamation to bring the resolution into operation; whether and when the resolution shall cease to operate and to make proclamation accordingly; and to prescribe limitations and exceptions to which the enforcement of the resolution shall be subject. . . .

Reversed.

Korematsu v. *United States*
323 U.S. 214, 65 S.Ct. 193, 89 L.Ed. 194 (1944)

http://caselaw.findlaw.com/us-supreme-court/323/214.html

(This case is reprinted in Chapter Fifteen; see the Table of Contents.)

Youngstown Sheet & Tube Co. v. *Sawyer* (The Steel Seizure Case)
343 U.S. 579, 72 S.Ct. 863, 96 L.Ed. 1153 (1952)

http://caselaw.findlaw.com/us-supreme-court/343/937.html

Labor unrest in the steel industry that began in 1951 resulted in a 1952 presidential order authorizing the secretary of commerce to seize and operate steel mills. The order was not based on any statute but rather was premised on the national emergency created by the threatened strike in an industry vital to defense production during the Korean War. The steel companies obtained an injunction from a district court restraining Secretary of Commerce Sawyer, and a court of appeals decision stayed the injunction. Majority: Black, Burton, Clark, Douglas, Frankfurter, Jackson. Dissenting: Vinson, Minton, Reed.

MR. JUSTICE BLACK delivered the opinion of the Court.

We are asked to decide whether the President was acting within his constitutional power when he issued an order directing the Secretary of Commerce to take possession of and operate most of the Nation's steel mills. The mill owners argue that the President's order amounts to law making, a legislative function which the Constitution has expressly confided to the Congress and not to the President. The Government's position is that the order was made on findings of the President that his action was necessary to avert a national catastrophe which would inevitably result from a stoppage of steel production, and that in meeting this grave emergency the President was acting within the aggregate of his constitutional powers as the Nation's Chief Executive and the Commander in Chief of the Armed Forces of the United States. . . .

The President's power, if any, to issue the order must stem either from an act of Congress or from the Constitution itself. There is no statute that expressly authorizes the President to take possession of property as he did here. Nor is there any act of Congress to which such a power can fairly be implied. Indeed, we do not understand the Government to rely on statutory authorization for this seizure. . . .

Moreover, the use of the seizure technique to solve labor disputes in order to prevent work stoppages was not only unauthorized by any congressional enactment; prior to this controversy, Congress had refused to adopt that method of settling labor disputes. When the Taft-Hartley Act was under consideration in 1947, Congress rejected an amendment which would have authorized such governmental seizures in case of emergency. . . .

It is clear that if the President had authority to issue the order he did, it must be found in some provision of the Constitution. . . .

The order cannot properly be sustained as an exercise of the President's military power. . . . Even though "theater of war" be an expanding concept, we cannot with faithfulness to our constitutional system hold that the Commander in Chief of the Armed Forces has the ultimate power as such to take possession of private property in order to keep labor disputes from stopping production. This is a job for the Nation's lawmakers, not for its military authorities.

Nor can the seizure order be sustained because of the several constitutional provisions that grant executive power to the President. In the framework of our Constitution, the President's power to see that the laws are faithfully executed refutes the idea that he is to be a lawmaker. The Constitution limits his functions in the lawmaking process to the recommending of laws he thinks wise and the vetoing of laws he thinks bad. And the Constitution is neither silent nor equivocal about who shall make laws which the President is to execute. . . .

The Founders of this Nation entrusted the lawmaking power to the Congress alone in both good and bad times. It would do no good to recall the historical events, the fears of power and the hopes for freedom that lay behind their choice. Such a review would but confirm our holding that this seizure order cannot stand.

The judgment of the District Court is

Affirmed.

MR. JUSTICE FRANKFURTER, concurring. . . .

The Constitution is a framework for government. Therefore the way the framework has consistently operated fairly establishes that it has operated according to its true nature. Deeply embedded traditional ways of conducting government cannot supplant the Constitution or legislation, but they give meaning to the words of a text or supply them. It is an inadmissibly narrow conception of American constitutional law to confine it to the words of the Constitution and to disregard the gloss which life has written upon them. In short, a systematic, unbroken, executive practice, long pursued to the knowledge of the Congress and never before questioned, engaged in by Presidents who have also sworn to uphold the Constitution, making as it were such exercise of power part of the structure of our government, may be treated as a gloss on "executive Power" vested in the President by § 1 of Article II. . . .

Down to the World War II period . . . the record is barren of instances comparable to the one before us. . . . [T]he list of executive assertions of the power of seizure in circumstances comparable to the present reduces to three in the six-month period from June to December of 1941. . . . [I]t suffices to say that these three isolated instances do not add up, either in number, scope, duration or contemporaneous legal justification, to the kind of executive construction of the Constitution [claimed here]. Nor do they come to us sanctioned by long-continued acquiescence of Congress giving decisive weight to a construction by the Executive of its powers.

MR. JUSTICE DOUGLAS, concurring . . . [omitted].

MR. JUSTICE JACKSON, concurring in the judgment and opinion of the Court. . . .

While the Constitution diffuses power the better to secure liberty, it also contemplates that practice will integrate the dispersed powers into a workable government. It enjoins upon its branches separateness but interdependence, autonomy but reciprocity. Presidential powers are not fixed but fluctuate, depending upon their disjunction or conjunction with those of Congress. We may well begin by a somewhat oversimplified grouping of practical situations in which a President may doubt, or others may challenge, his powers. . . .

(1) When the President acts pursuant to an express or implied authorization of Congress his authority is at its maximum, for it includes all that he possesses in his own right plus all that Congress can delegate. In these circumstances, and in these only, may he be said (for what it may be worth) to personify the federal sovereignty. . . . A seizure executed by the President pursuant to an Act of Congress would be supported by the strongest of presumptions and the widest latitude of judicial interpretation, and the burden of persuasion would rest heavily upon any who might attack it.

(2) When the President acts in absence of either a congressional grant or denial of authority, he can only rely upon his own independent powers, but there is a zone of twilight in which he and Congress may have concurrent authority, or in which its distribution is uncertain. Therefore, congressional inertia, indifference or quiescence may sometimes, at least as a practical matter, enable, if not invite, measures on independent presidential responsibility. In this area, any actual test of power is likely to depend on the imperatives of events and contemporary imponderables rather than on abstract theories of law.

(3) When the President takes measures incompatible with the expressed or implied will of Congress, his power is at its lowest ebb, for then he can rely only upon his own constitutional powers minus any constitutional powers of Congress over the matter. Courts can sustain exclusive presidential control in such a case only by disabling the Congress from acting upon the subject. Presidential claim to a power at once so conclusive and preclusive must be scrutinized with caution, for what is at stake is the equilibrium established by our constitutional system.

Into which of these classifications does this executive seizure of the steel industry fit? It is eliminated from the first by admission, for it is conceded that no congressional authorization exists for this seizure. . . .

Can it then be defended under flexible tests available to the second category? It seems clearly eliminated from that class because

Congress has not left seizure of private property an open field but has covered it by three statutory policies inconsistent with this seizure. In cases where the purpose is to supply needs of the Government itself, two courses are provided: one, seizure of a plant which fails to comply with obligatory orders placed by the Government, another, condemnation of facilities, including temporary use under the power of eminent domain. The third is applicable where it is the general economy of the country that is to be protected rather than exclusive governmental interests. None of these were invoked. . . .

The Solicitor General seeks the power of seizure in three clauses of the Executive Article, the first reading, "The executive Power shall be vested in a President of the United States of America." Lest I be thought to exaggerate, I quote the interpretation which his brief puts upon it: "In our view, this clause constitutes a grant of all the executive powers of which the Government is capable." If that be true, it is difficult to see why the forefathers bothered to add several specific items, including some trifling ones.

The example of such unlimited executive power that must have most impressed the forefathers was the prerogative exercised by George III, and the description of its evils in the Declaration of Independence leads me to doubt that they were creating their new Executive in his image. . . . I cannot accept the view that this clause is a grant in bulk of all conceivable executive power but regard it as an allocation to the presidential office of the generic powers thereafter stated.

The clause on which the Government next relies is that "The President shall be Commander in Chief of the Army and Navy of the United States. . . ." These cryptic words have given rise to some of the most persistent controversies in our constitutional history. Of course, they imply something more than an empty title. But just what authority goes with the name has plagued presidential advisers who would not waive or narrow it by nonassertion yet cannot say where it begins or ends. It undoubtedly puts the Nation's armed forces under presidential command. Hence, this loose appellation is sometimes advanced as support for any presidential action, internal or external, involving use of force, the idea being that it vests power to do anything, anywhere, that can be done with an army or navy. . . .

I cannot foresee all that it might entail if the Court should endorse this argument. Nothing in our Constitution is plainer than that declaration of a war is entrusted only to Congress. Of course, a state of war may in fact exist without a formal declaration. But no doctrine that the Court could promulgate would seem to me more sinister and alarming than that a President whose conduct of foreign affairs is so largely uncontrolled, and often even is unknown, can vastly enlarge his mastery over the internal affairs of the country by his own commitment of the Nation's armed forces to some foreign venture. . . .

The third clause in which the Solicitor General finds seizure powers is that "he shall take Care that the Laws be faithfully executed. . . ." That authority must be matched against words of the Fifth Amendment that "No person shall be . . . deprived of life, liberty or property, without due process of law. . . ."

One gives a governmental authority that reaches so far as there is law, the other gives a private right that shall go no farther. These signify about all there is of the principle that ours is a government of laws, not of men, and that we submit ourselves to rulers only if under rules.

The Solicitor General lastly grounds support of the seizure upon nebulous, inherent powers never expressly granted but said to have accrued to the office from the customs and claims of preceding administrations. The plea is for a resulting power to deal with a crisis or an emergency according to the necessities of the case, the unarticulated assumption being that necessity knows no law. . . .

Contemporary foreign experience may be inconclusive as to the wisdom of lodging emergency powers somewhere in a modern government. But it suggests that emergency powers are consistent with free government only when their control is lodged elsewhere than in the Executive who exercises them. That is the safeguard that would be nullified by our adoption of the "inherent powers" formula. . . .

In the practical working of our Government we already have evolved a technique within the framework of the Constitution by which normal executive powers may be considerably expanded to meet an emergency. Congress may and has granted extraordinary authorities which lie dormant in normal times but may be called into play by the Executive in war or upon proclamation of a national emergency. . . .

In view of the ease, expedition and safety with which Congress can grant and has granted large emergency powers, certainly ample to embrace this crisis, I am quite unimpressed with the argument that we should affirm possession of them without statute. Such power either has no beginning or it has no end. If it exists, it need submit to no legal restraint. I am not alarmed that it would plunge us straightaway into dictatorship, but it is at least a step in that wrong direction. . . .

The executive action we have here originates in the individual will of the President and represents an exercise of authority without law. No one, perhaps not even the President, knows the limits of the power he may seek to exert in this instance and the parties affected cannot learn the limit of their rights. We do not know today what powers over labor or property would be claimed to flow from Government possession if we should legalize it, what rights to compensation would be claimed or recognized, or on what contingency it would end. With all its defects, delays and inconveniences, men have discovered no technique for long preserving free government except that the Executive be under the law, and that the law be made by parliamentary deliberations.

Such institutions may be destined to pass away. But it is the duty of the Court to be last, not first, to give them up.

Mr. Justice Burton, concurring . . . [omitted].

Mr. Justice Clark, concurring . . . [omitted].

Mr. Chief Justice Vinson, with whom Mr. Justice Reed and Mr. Justice Minton join, dissenting. . . .

Those who suggest that this is a case involving extraordinary powers should be mindful that these are extraordinary times. A world not yet recovered from the devastation of World War II has been forced to face the threat of another and more terrifying global conflict. . . .

The steel mills were seized for a public use. The power of eminent domain, invoked in this case, is an essential attribute of sovereignty and has long been recognized as a power of the Federal Government. . . .

Admitting that the Government could seize the mills, plaintiffs claim that the implied power of eminent domain can be exercised only under an Act of Congress; under no circumstances, they say, can that power be exercised by the President unless he can point to an express provision in enabling legislation. This was the view adopted by the District Judge when he granted the preliminary injunction. Without an answer, without hearing evidence, he determined the issue on the basis of his "fixed conclusion . . . that defendant's acts are illegal" because the President's only course in the face of an emergency is to present the matter to Congress and await the final passage of legislation which will enable the Government to cope with threatened disaster.

Under this view, the President is left powerless at the very moment when the need for action may be most pressing and when no one, other than he, is immediately capable of action.

Under this view, he is left powerless because a power not expressly given to Congress is nevertheless found to rest exclusively with Congress. . . .

United States v. *United States District Court*
407 U.S. 297, 92 S.Ct. 2125, 32 L.Ed. 2d 752 (1972)

http://caselaw.findlaw.com/us-supreme-court/407/297.html

(This case is reprinted in Chapter Fifteen; see the Table of Contents.)

War Powers Resolution
87 Stat. 555 (1973), 50 U.S.C. ch. 33

www.law.cornell.edu/uscode/text/50/chapter-33#PC33

A peace accord to end American military involvement in Vietnam was signed in January 1973 following several years of domestic discontent over the nation's Indochina policy. After U.S. bombing of Cambodia, Congress passed the War Powers Resolution in the fall of 1973 in an attempt to provide a legal check on the president's authority to commit American forces abroad without congressional approval. President Richard Nixon vetoed the resolution on October 24, calling it both "dangerous" and "unconstitutional." By a vote of 284–135 (four more than the required two-thirds margin) in the House and 75–18 in the Senate, Congress overrode Nixon's veto on November 7.

Resolved by the Senate and House of Representatives of the United States of America in Congress assembled, That: . . .

Sec. 2. (c) The constitutional powers of the President as Commander-in-Chief to introduce United States Armed Forces into hostilities, or into situations where imminent involvement in hostilities is clearly indicated by the circumstances, are exercised only pursuant to (1) a declaration of war; (2) specific statutory authorization; or (3) a national emergency created by attack upon the United States, its territories or possessions, or its armed forces.

Sec. 3. The President in every possible instance shall consult with Congress before introducing United States Armed Forces into hostilities or into situations where imminent involvement in hostilities is clearly indicated by the circumstances, and after every such introduction shall consult regularly with the Congress until United States Armed Forces are no longer engaged in hostilities or have been removed from such situations.

Sec. 4. (a) In the absence of a declaration of war, in any case in which United States Armed Forces are introduced

(1) into hostilities or into situations where imminent involvement in hostilities is clearly indicated by the circumstances; . . .

The President shall submit within 48 hours to the Speaker of the House of Representatives and to the President pro tempore of the Senate a report, in writing, setting forth—

(A) the circumstances necessitating the introduction of United States Armed Forces; . . .

(B) the constitutional and legislative authority under which such introduction took place; and

(C) the estimated scope and duration of the hostilities or involvement. . . .

Sec. 5. (b) Within 60 calendar days after a report is submitted or is required to be submitted pursuant to section 4(a)(1), whichever is earlier, the President shall terminate any use of United States Armed Forces with respect to which such report was submitted (or required to be submitted), unless the Congress (1) has declared war or has enacted a specific authorization for such use of United States Armed Forces; (2) has extended by law such sixty-day period; or (3) is physically unable to meet as a result of an armed attack upon the United States. Such sixty-day period shall be extended for not more than an additional thirty days if the President determines and certifies to the Congress in writing that unavoidable military necessity respecting the safety of United States Armed Forces requires the continued use of such armed forces in the course of bringing about a prompt removal of such forces.

(c) Notwithstanding subsection (b), at any time that United States Armed Forces are engaged in hostilities outside the territory of the United States, its possessions and territories without a declaration of war or specific statutory authorization, such forces shall be removed by the President if the Congress so directs by concurrent resolution. . . .

Boumediene v. *Bush*
553 U.S. 723, 128 S.Ct. 2229, 171 L.Ed. 2d 41 (2008)

www.law.cornell.edu/supct/html/06–1195.ZS.html

(This case is reprinted in Chapter Fifteen; see the Table of Contents.)

Trump v. *Hawaii*
585 U.S. ___, 138 S.Ct. 2392, 201 L.Ed. 2d 775 (2018)

www.supremecourt.gov/opinions/17pdf/17-965_h315.pdf

Against the backdrop of an election campaign in 2016 that emphasized border security and threats of terrorism, President Donald Trump, beginning in January 2017, issued a series of executive orders and proclamations that with specified exceptions barred entry into the United States by foreign nationals from seven countries, a number shortly reduced to six and later raised to eight. The state of Hawaii, the Muslim Association of Hawaii, and individuals with affected family members challenged the orders in federal court, where the district judge issued a nationwide temporary restraining order enjoining enforcement of some of the provisions. The last proclamation was issued on September 24, 2017, and was invalidated by the Court of Appeals for the Ninth Circuit. In the Supreme Court, the case involved three questions: First, did the president's actions violate various provisions of the Immigration and Nationality Act? Second, did the orders and/or proclamations violate the establishment clause of the First Amendment? Third, was the nationwide or global injunction impermissibly broad? The Supreme Court found sufficient statutory authority for the president's actions by executive order and did not decide the question about the scope of the district court's injunction. The excerpts below address the constitutional question. Combined, the several opinions extended across 87 pages. Notably, two opinions referenced the Court's decision in *Korematsu* v. *United States* (1944), dating from World War II and reprinted in Chapter Fifteen. Majority (in this case): Roberts, Alito, Gorsuch, Kennedy, Thomas. Dissenting (in this case): Sotomayor, Breyer, Ginsburg, Kagan.

Chief Justice Roberts delivered the opinion of the Court. . . .

We now turn to plaintiffs' claim that the Proclamation was issued for the unconstitutional purpose of excluding Muslims. . . .

Our cases recognize that "[t]he clearest command of the Establishment Clause is that one religious denomination cannot be officially preferred over another." Plaintiffs believe that the Proclamation violates this prohibition by singling out Muslims for disfavored treatment. The entry suspension, they contend, operates as a "religious gerrymander," in part because most of the countries covered by the Proclamation have Muslim-majority populations. . . . Relying on Establishment Clause precedents concerning laws and policies applied domestically, plaintiffs allege that the primary purpose of the Proclamation was religious animus and that the President's stated concerns about vetting protocols and national security were but pretexts for discriminating against Muslims.

At the heart of plaintiffs' case is a series of statements by the President and his advisers casting doubt on the official objective of the Proclamation. For example, while a candidate on the campaign trail, the President published a "Statement on Preventing Muslim Immigration" that called for a "total and complete shutdown of Muslims entering the United States until our country's representatives can figure out what is going on." That statement remained on his campaign website until May 2017. Then-candidate Trump also stated that "Islam hates us" and asserted that the United States was "having problems with Muslims coming into the country." . . .

Plaintiffs argue that this President's words strike at fundamental standards of respect and tolerance, in violation of our constitutional tradition. But the issue before us is not whether to denounce the statements. It is instead the significance of those statements in reviewing a Presidential directive, neutral on its face, addressing a matter within the core of executive responsibility. In doing so, we must consider not only the statements of a particular President, but also the authority of the Presidency itself. . . .

For more than a century, this Court has recognized that the admission and exclusion of foreign nationals is a "fundamental sovereign attribute exercised by the Government's political departments largely immune from judicial control." . . . Nonetheless, although foreign nationals seeking admission have no constitutional right to entry, this Court has engaged in a circumscribed judicial inquiry when the denial of a visa allegedly burdens the constitutional rights of a U.S. citizen. In *Kleindienst* v. *Mandel*, the Attorney General denied admission to a Belgian journalist and self-described "revolutionary Marxist," Ernest Mandel, who had been invited to speak at a conference at Stanford University. The professors who wished to hear Mandel speak challenged that decision under the First Amendment, and we acknowledged that their constitutional "right to receive information" was implicated. But we limited our review to whether the Executive gave a "facially legitimate and *bonafide*" reason for its action. Given the authority of the political branches over admission, we held that "when the Executive exercises this [delegated] power negatively on the basis of a facially legitimate and bona fide reason, the courts will neither look behind the exercise of that discretion, nor test it by balancing its justification" against the asserted constitutional interests of U.S. citizens. The principal dissent suggests that *Mandel* has no bearing on this case, but our opinions have reaffirmed and applied its deferential standard of review across different contexts and constitutional claims. . . . *Mandel's* narrow standard of review "has particular force" in admission and immigration cases that overlap with "the area of national security."

The upshot of our cases in this context is clear: "Any rule of constitutional law that would inhibit the flexibility" of the President "to respond to changing world conditions should be adopted only with the greatest caution," and our inquiry into matters of entry and national security is highly constrained. We need not define the precise contours of that inquiry in this case. A conventional application of *Mandel*, asking only whether the policy is facially legitimate and *bona fide*, would put an end to our review. But the Government has suggested that it may be appropriate here for the inquiry to extend beyond the facial neutrality of the order. For our purposes today, we assume that we may look behind the face of the Proclamation to the extent of applying rational basis review. That standard of review considers whether the entry policy is plausibly related to the Government's stated objective to protect the country and improve vetting processes. As a result, we may consider plaintiffs' extrinsic evidence, but will uphold the policy so long as it can reasonably be understood to result from a justification independent of unconstitutional grounds.

Given the standard of review, it should come as no surprise that the Court hardly ever strikes down a policy as illegitimate under rational basis scrutiny. On the few occasions where we have done so, a common thread has been that the laws at issue lack any purpose other than a "bare . . . desire to harm a politically unpopular group." . . . The Proclamation does not fit this pattern. It cannot be said that it is impossible to "discern a relationship to legitimate state interests" or that the policy is "inexplicable by anything but animus." Indeed, the dissent can only attempt to argue otherwise by refusing to apply anything resembling rational basis review. . . .

The Proclamation is expressly premised on legitimate purposes: preventing entry of nationals who cannot be adequately vetted and inducing other nations to improve their practices. The text says nothing about religion. Plaintiffs and the dissent nonetheless emphasize that five of the seven nations currently included in the Proclamation have Muslim-majority populations. Yet that fact alone does not support an inference of religious hostility, given that the policy covers just 8% of the world's Muslim population and is limited to countries that were previously designated by Congress or prior administrations as posing national security risks . . . The Proclamation, moreover, reflects the results of a worldwide review process undertaken by multiple Cabinet officials and their agencies. Plaintiffs seek to discredit the findings of the review, pointing to deviations from the review's baseline criteria resulting in the inclusion of Somalia and omission of Iraq. But as the Proclamation explains, in each case the determinations were justified by the distinct conditions in each country. . . .

More fundamentally, plaintiffs and the dissent challenge the entry suspension based on their perception of its effectiveness and wisdom. They suggest that the policy is overbroad and does little to serve national security interests. But we cannot substitute our own assessment for the Executive's predictive judgments on such matters, all of which "are delicate, complex, and involve large elements of prophecy." While we of course "do not defer to the Government's reading of the First Amendment," the Executive's evaluation of the underlying facts is entitled to appropriate weight, particularly in the context of litigation involving "sensitive and weighty interests of national security and foreign affairs." . . .

Finally, the dissent invokes *Korematsu* v. *United States*. Whatever rhetorical advantage the dissent may see in doing so, *Korematsu* has nothing to do with this case. The forcible relocation of U.S. citizens to concentration camps, solely and explicitly on the basis of race, is objectively unlawful and outside the scope of Presidential authority. But it is wholly inapt to liken that morally repugnant order to a facially neutral policy denying certain foreign nationals the privilege of admission. The entry suspension is an act that is well within executive authority and could have been taken by any other President—the only question is evaluating the actions of this particular President in promulgating an otherwise valid Proclamation. The dissent's reference to *Korematsu*, however, affords this Court the opportunity to make express what is already obvious: *Korematsu* was gravely wrong the day it was decided, has been overruled in the court of history, and—to be clear—"has no place in law under the Constitution."

Under these circumstances, the Government has set forth a sufficient national security justification to survive rational basis review. We express no view on the soundness of the policy. We simply hold today that plaintiffs have not demonstrated a likelihood of success on the merits of their constitutional claim. . . .

The judgment of the Court of Appeals is reversed, and the case is remanded for further proceedings consistent with this opinion.

It is so ordered.

JUSTICE KENNEDY, concurring . . . [omitted.]

JUSTICE THOMAS, concurring . . . [omitted].

JUSTICE BREYER, with whom JUSTICE KAGAN joins, dissenting . . . [omitted].

JUSTICE SOTOMAYOR, with whom JUSTICE GINSBURG joins, dissenting. . . .

Plaintiffs challenge the Proclamation on various grounds, both statutory and constitutional. Ordinarily, when a case can be decided on purely statutory grounds, we strive to follow a "prudential rule of avoiding constitutional questions." But that rule of thumb is far from categorical, and it has limited application where, as here, the constitutional question proves far simpler than the statutory one. Whatever the merits of plaintiffs' complex statutory claims, the Proclamation must be enjoined for a more fundamental reason: It runs afoul of the Establishment Clause's guarantee of religious neutrality. . . .

To determine whether plaintiffs have proved an Establishment Clause violation, the Court asks whether a reasonable observer would view the government action as enacted for the purpose of disfavoring a religion. In answering that question, this Court has generally considered the text of the government policy, its operation, and any available evidence regarding "the historical background of the decision under challenge, the specific series of events leading to the enactment or official policy in question, and the legislative or administrative history, including contemporaneous statements made by" the decisionmaker. . . . Although the majority briefly recounts a few of the statements and background events that form the basis of plaintiffs' constitutional challenge, that highly abridged account does not tell even half of the story. The full record paints a far more harrowing picture, from which a reasonable observer would readily conclude that the Proclamation was motivated by hostility and animus toward the Muslim faith.

During his Presidential campaign, then-candidate Donald Trump pledged that, if elected, he would ban Muslims from entering the United States. Specifically, on December 7, 2015, he issued a formal statement "calling for a total and complete shutdown of Muslims entering the United States." . . . While litigation over EO-2 was ongoing, President Trump repeatedly made statements alluding to a desire to keep Muslims out of the country. . . . In September 2017, President Trump tweeted that "[t]he travel ban into the United States should be far larger, tougher and more specific—but stupidly, that would not be politically correct!". . .

Ultimately, what began as a policy explicitly "calling for a total and complete shutdown of Muslims entering the United States" has since morphed into a "Proclamation" putatively based on national-security concerns. But this new window dressing cannot conceal an unassailable fact: the words of the President and his advisers create the strong perception that the Proclamation is contaminated by impermissible discriminatory animus against Islam and its followers.

Rather than defend the President's problematic statements, the Government urges this Court to set them aside and defer to the President on issues related to immigration and national security. The majority accepts that invitation and incorrectly applies a watered-down legal standard in an effort to short circuit plaintiffs' Establishment Clause claim. The majority begins its constitutional analysis by noting that this Court, at times, "has engaged in a circumscribed judicial inquiry when the denial of a visa allegedly burdens the constitutional rights of a U.S. citizen." As the majority notes, *Mandel* held that when the Executive Branch provides "a facially legitimate and *bona fide* reason" for denying a visa, "courts will neither look behind the exercise of that discretion, nor test it by balancing its justification." In his controlling concurrence in *Kerry* v. *Din*, Justice Kennedy applied *Mandel's* holding and elaborated that courts can "'look behind' the Government's exclusion of" a foreign national if there is "an affirmative showing of bad faith on the part of the consular officer who denied [the] visa." The extent to which *Mandel* and *Din* apply at all to this case is unsettled, and there is good reason to think they do not. Indeed, even the Government agreed at oral argument that where the Court confronts a situation involving "all kinds of denigrating comments about" a particular religion and a subsequent policy that is designed with the purpose of disfavoring that religion but that "dot[s] all the i's and . . . cross[es] all the t's," Mandel would not "pu[t] an end to judicial review of that set of facts."

In light of the Government's suggestion "that it may be appropriate here for the inquiry to extend beyond the facial neutrality of the order," the majority rightly declines to apply *Mandel's* "narrow standard of review" and "assume[s] that we may look behind the face of the Proclamation." In doing so, however, the Court, without explanation or precedential support, limits its review of the Proclamation to rational-basis scrutiny. That approach is perplexing, given that in other Establishment Clause cases, including those involving claims of religious animus or discrimination, this Court has applied a more stringent standard of review. . . . But even under rational-basis review, the Proclamation must fall. That is so because the Proclamation is "'divorced from any factual context from which we could discern a relationship to legitimate state interests,' and 'its sheer breadth [is] so discontinuous with the reasons offered for it'" that the policy is "'inexplicable by anything but animus.'" . . .

The majority insists that the Proclamation furthers two interrelated national-security interests: "preventing entry of nationals who cannot be adequately vetted and inducing other nations to improve their practices." But the Court offers insufficient support for its view "that the entry suspension has a legitimate grounding in [those] national security concerns, quite apart from any religious hostility." Indeed, even a cursory review of the Government's asserted national-security rationale reveals that the Proclamation is nothing more than a "'religious gerrymander.'" . . . Today's holding is all the more troubling given the stark parallels between the reasoning of this case and that of *Korematsu* v. *United States*. As here, the Government invoked an ill-defined national-security threat to justify an exclusionary policy of sweeping proportion. As here, the exclusion order was rooted in dangerous stereotypes about, *inter alia*, a particular group's supposed inability to assimilate and desire to harm the United States. As here, the Government was unwilling to reveal its own intelligence agencies' views of the alleged security concerns to the very citizens it purported to protect. . . . And as here, there was strong evidence that impermissible hostility and animus motivated the Government's policy. . . .

Our Constitution demands, and our country deserves, a Judiciary willing to hold the coordinate branches to account when they defy our most sacred legal commitments. Because the Court's decision today has failed in that respect, with profound regret, I dissent.

4

Federalism

Federalism was our Nation's own discovery. The Framers split the atom of sovereignty. It was the genius of their idea that our citizens would have two political capacities, one state and one federal, each protected from incursion by the other. The resulting Constitution created a legal system unprecedented in form and design, establishing two orders of government, each with its own direct relationship, its own privity, its own set of mutual rights and obligations to the people who sustain it and are governed by it.

—JUSTICE ANTHONY M. KENNEDY (1995)

Although many consider judicial review to be America's unique contribution to political science, federalism may continue to be of equal influence on other nations and of unending importance at home. Unfortunately for those who look upon federalism as the key to world or regional order under law, our history—unless one takes the long view—is not reassuring.

A distinguishing characteristic of American government is **federalism—**a dual system in which governmental powers are constitutionally distributed between central (national) and local (state) authorities. The reasons for the adoption of such an arrangement are both historical and rational. During the revolutionary period, the states regarded themselves as independent sovereignties. Under the Articles of Confederation, little of their power over internal affairs was surrendered to the Continental Congress. As Article II of the document declared, "Each state retains its sovereignty, freedom and independence, and every Power, Jurisdiction and right, which is not by this confederation expressly delegated to the United States, in Congress assembled." This meant, Article III explained, that "said states hereby severally enter into a firm league of friendship with each other." Yet, in the face of proved and continuing inability of the Confederation to cope with the problems confronting it, this arrangement, and with it local patriotism, had to yield.

When the Constitutional Convention met, compromise between the advocates of a strong central government and supporters of states' rights was necessary. Federalism fitted into James Madison's basic requirement, reflecting his purpose, as stated

DOI: 10.4324/9781003164340-5

in *The Federalist*, No. 51, to so contrive "the interior structure of the government as that its several constituent parts may, by their mutual relations, be the means of keeping each other in their proper places." Federalism thus complemented separation of powers. Alexander Hamilton, in *The Federalist*, No. 23, listed four chief purposes to be served by union: common defense, public peace, regulation of commerce, and foreign relations. General agreement that these objectives required unified government drew together representatives of small and large states alike.

SOURCES OF CONTENTION

One point on which the nationalists at the Philadelphia Convention remained firm was their determination that no precise line should be drawn dividing national power from state power. The powers of the national government were enumerated but not defined. Alert to possible inroads on the states, Hugh Williamson of North Carolina objected that the effect might be to "restrain the States from regulating their internal affairs." Elbridge Gerry of Massachusetts objected that indefinite power in the central authority might "enslave the States." Alexander Hamilton, Madison, and James Wilson would not budge, contending that a line dividing state and national power would unduly weaken national authority. "When we come near the line," Wilson explained,

> it cannot be found. . . . A discretion must be left on one side or the other. . . . Will it not be most safely lodged on the side of the National Government? . . . What danger is there that the whole will unnecessarily sacrifice a part? But reverse the case, and leave the whole at the mercy of each part, and will not the general interest be continually sacrificed to local interests?

This avowal of national supremacy evoked from opponents of the Constitution a pointed query: "[W]here is the bill of rights which shall check the power of this congress, which shall say, *thus far shall ye come and no farther?* The safety of the people depends on a bill of rights."

Origins of the Tenth Amendment. In the First Congress, Madison and others made good on the assurances they had given during the debates over ratification to make the addition of a bill of rights a priority for the new government. (Documents relating to the development of a bill of rights are reprinted in Chapter Nine.) **Anti-federalists** (those who had opposed ratification in 1787–1788) had conjured up the image of the central government as a colossus, determined to swallow defenseless states. To quiet their fears, Madison included among the amendments submitted on June 8, 1789, the one that became the Tenth: "The powers not delegated to the United States by the Constitution, nor prohibited by it to the States, are reserved to the States respectively, or to the people."

Madison was on record shortly before the Convention as having said that the states should be retained insofar as they could be "subordinately useful." Equally well known was his early aversion to including a bill of rights. "It was obviously and self-evidently the case," he had insisted, "that every thing not granted is reserved." Now with an amendment on the floor, he resisted efforts to convert it into a substantive check on national power. "While I approve of these amendments [the Ninth and Tenth]," Madison tersely stated on August 15, "I should oppose the consideration at this time of such as are likely to change the principles of the government." And when, three days later, Thomas Tucker suggested addition of the word *expressly* to the proposed Tenth Amendment, making it read, "the powers not expressly delegated to the United States by the Constitution," Madison objected. "It was impossible," he explained, "to confine a Government to the exercise of express powers; there must necessarily be admitted powers by implication." Tucker's motion was defeated. Gerry's effort of August 21 to get the word *expressly* inserted suffered the same fate, the vote being 32–17. Had Gerry and Tucker succeeded, the Constitution would have been encumbered with one of the notable defects of the Articles of Confederation, which stipulated that states retained all powers except those *expressly* delegated to the United States, in Congress assembled" (emphasis added).

Madison's position on the floor of Congress about the Tenth Amendment bears out Chief Justice Marshall's later observation in ***McCulloch* v. *Maryland***: it was designed "for the purpose of quieting excessive jealousy which had been excited."

The unavailing struggle to give meaning to the Tenth Amendment underscores the conclusion that for many Antifederalists, states' rights weighed more heavily than their concern for personal rights. This would explain why so many Antifederalists were disappointed with the amendments as they emerged from Congress. To William Grayson, the amendments were "so mutilated and gutted that in fact they are good for nothing. . . ." Richard Henry Lee still saw "the most essential danger" arising from the Constitution's "tendency to a consolidated government, instead of a union of Confederated States. . . ." Instead of "substantial amendments," complained South Carolina's Pierce Butler, here were a "few milk-and-water amendments . . . such as liberty of conscience, a free press, and one or two general things already well secured." Georgia's representative James Jackson agreed: the amendments were not worth "a pinch of salt." Antifederalists had failed to make the Tenth Amendment a limit on national power.

Truism or Independent Check? The distribution of powers agreed on in the Convention and the reassurance given the states by the Tenth Amendment did not preclude conflict. The struggle continued in politics and in the courts, and when prolonged debate and bitter controversy failed to yield a conclusive verdict, the contestants carried this baffling issue of political and constitutional theory to the battlefield in 1861 for settlement by the arbitrament of the sword. Even this holocaust was not conclusive.

The problem of determining the extent of national and state power and of resolving the conflicts between the two centers of authority was ultimately left to the Supreme Court, which has alternated between two ways of thinking about the Tenth Amendment. The one more favorable to national power envisions the Tenth as a "truism," as Justice Stone declared in 1941, meaning that what the states have not surrendered has been retained (*United States* v. *Darby*). Accordingly, states (and those interests dominant in state governments) are to look not to the Constitution but to the political process for protection against Congress. The other regards the amendment as a discrete barrier to national power, in addition to other limits that the Constitution imposes, that is judicially enforceable against Congress on behalf of the states.

NATURE OF NATIONAL AUTHORITY

The authority of the central government in relation to state governments can be classified in several ways.

Dimensions of National Power. Of all the things governments in the United States may do, the powers of the national government are theoretically limited to those assigned to it by the Constitution, expressly or by implication, and are therefore **delegated powers**. This is the premise of the Tenth Amendment. From a national perspective, states therefore possess what remains. These **reserved powers** in turn are a function of state law and may vary from state to state. As a second dimension, the national government may use any and all means to give effect to any power specifically granted. This doctrine of **implied powers** finds its textual basis in Congress' authority to make all laws "necessary and proper" for carrying into execution what are called **express powers**, those powers specifically delegated to it (Art. 1, Sec. 8, Cl. 18). No new or additional powers are granted by the **necessary and proper clause** (also called the "elastic clause"); it merely gives the federal government a choice of means as it operates within the limited sphere of its activity. As an extension of implied powers, **resulting powers** derive from the mass of delegated powers or from a group of them. Such powers include taking of property by eminent domain for a purpose not specified in the Constitution, carrying into effect treaties entered into by the United States, and making paper money legal tender in payment of public and private debts (*Juilliard* v. *Greenman*, 1884). The **supremacy clause** (Art. VI, Para. 2), the keystone of the federal system, supplies a third dimension of national power. It indicates that if the legitimate powers of state and nation conflict, those of the national government shall prevail.

Thus, national power is of three dimensions: (1) the enumeration in which the grant of power is couched; (2) the discretionary choice of means that Congress has for carrying its enumerated powers into execution; and (3) the fact of supremacy. Under this three-dimensional theory of national authority, no subject matter whatever is withdrawn from control or regulation by the United States simply because it also lies within the usual domain of state power.

Concurrent and Exclusive Powers. The powers of the national government may also be classified as **concurrent** or **exclusive**. A concurrent power refers to an authority shared by both state and national governments, such as taxation or operating a court system. States may legislate in such instances, provided they do not conflict with valid national laws or purposes. In contrast, under the following conditions, powers delegated to Congress by the Constitution are exclusive and therefore are denied to the states:

1. Where the right to exercise the power is made exclusive by express provision of the Constitution. Article I, for example, gives Congress exclusive power over the District of Columbia and over property purchased from a state with the consent of its legislature.
2. Where one section of the Constitution grants an express power to Congress and another section prohibits the states from exercising a similar power. For example, Congress is given the power to coin money (Art. I, Sec. 8, Cl. 5), and the states are expressly prohibited from exercising such power (Art. I, Sec. 10, Cl. 1).
3. Where the power granted to Congress, though not in terms exclusive, is such that the exercise of a similar power by the states would be utterly incompatible with national power. In ***Cooley* v. *Board of Wardens*** (1851; see Chapter Six), the Court admitted the existence of a concurrent power to control interstate commerce but limited state power to matters of local concern. Where the subject matter is national in scope and requires uniform legislative treatment, such as the federal government alone can provide, the power of Congress is exclusive. "Exclusive" is here used in a special sense, since the disability of the states arises not from the Constitution but from the nature of

the subject matter to which the power is applied. Such power has been termed "latent concurrent power" since Congress may consent to its exercise by the state.

Preemption. Concurrent powers are fruitful sources of friction between national and state authority. The supremacy clause in Article VI means that state statutes and constitutional provisions must give way when they conflict with the Constitution, treaties, and valid laws of the United States. The latter take precedence over the former. This is **preemption**. What is the outcome when state and national governments choose to legislate on the same topic without enacting conflicting laws? Sometimes, Congress explicitly recognizes a concurrent state interest and so approves complementary state statutes. At other times, Congress explicitly rules out a role for the states. A more difficult issue arises when state policies do not conflict and there is no expressed congressional intent to welcome or to displace action by the states.

In *Pennsylvania* v. *Nelson* (1956), for example, the Court confronted a state statute criminalizing sedition against the United States. In the Smith Act of 1940 (see Chapter Eleven), Congress had prohibited the same thing. In holding that the Smith Act preempted the Pennsylvania law, Chief Justice Warren noted three conditions that suggest supersession: First, the scheme of federal regulation is "so pervasive as to make reasonable the inference that Congress left no room for the states to supplement it. . . ." Second, the national interest is so dominant on a subject that the federal system must "be assumed to preclude enforcement of state laws on the same subject." Third, there is a danger of conflict between state and federal enforcement efforts. The presence of the three conditions in *Nelson* meant that Congress had chosen to "occupy the field."

Judicial Federalism. The fact that much of the Supreme Court's docket each term consists of cases from state courts is another reason why the justices are active players in the game of federalism. Interaction between state and federal courts is called **judicial federalism**. One of its dimensions involves Supreme Court review of state court decisions, which arguably rest on a state, not on the national, constitution.

As explained in Chapter One, the Court may sit in judgment on the decisions of the highest court of each state when federal questions are involved. A case raises a **federal question** when a provision of the U.S. Constitution, a treaty, or a national statute is at issue. Once a federal question is present, the Supreme Court becomes the ultimate arbiter of its resolution. This rule encourages uniformity among the states. In contrast, the absence of a federal question encourages diverse policies because there is no judicial mechanism for imposing uniform rules of law on the states. In such situations resolution of an issue rests with the individual states.

What happens when a state court gives greater protection to a right found in both state and federal constitutions and rests its decision on the former? Noninterference by the Supreme Court in such situations allows states to expand liberties that have parallel protections in both constitutions. The Supreme Court, however, will not accept a state court's interpretation of the federal Constitution at variance with its own, even if the state's decision is more protective of individual liberty.

In *Michigan* v. *Long* (1983), the Supreme Court of Michigan decided that police had infringed Long's rights when making a search of his car. But which rights? Those protected by the Fourth Amendment in the U.S. Constitution, or those in parallel provisions in the Michigan constitution? Prior to this case, the Supreme Court presumed that state court decisions rested on an "adequate and independent state ground" unless the party bringing the case could persuade the justices to the contrary. But in *Long*, the Court changed its mind. According to Justice O'Connor, when

> a state court decision fairly appears to rest primarily on federal law, or to be interwoven with the federal law, and when the adequacy and independence of any possible state law ground is not clear from the face of the opinion, we will accept . . . that the state court decided the case the way it did because it believed that federal law required it to do so.

Accordingly, "[i]f the state court decision indicates clearly and expressly that it is alternatively based on bona fide separate, adequate, and independent grounds, we, of course, will not undertake to review the decision." *Long* means that state courts not only must provide a rationale that disavows reliance on federal law but also must satisfy a majority of the Court that this reliance is "bona fide." Adding "separate" to "adequate" and "independent" makes it much easier for the Court to review any state court decision that makes so much as a passing reference to federal law or the Constitution.

CONCEPTS OF FEDERALISM

As was inevitable, the formal distribution of powers between the national government and the states proved to be a subject of diverse interpretations. The fault line along which supporters and opponents of the Constitution divided in 1787–1788 carried over into debates within the new government over how national authority would be construed. On one side were advocates of national supremacy; on the other were advocates of dual federalism. Echoes of this verbal combat reverberate today.

NATIONAL SUPREMACY: LEGACY OF CHIEF JUSTICE JOHN MARSHALL. As John Adams left the presidency in early 1801, he installed John Marshall, an ardent nationalist and a Virginian, as chief justice. Marshall read into our constitutional law a concept of federalism that magnified national at the expense of state power. Important precedents existed to aid his labors. Besides the House of Representatives debates out of which the Tenth Amendment emerged, there was the 1793 case of ***Chisholm* v. *Georgia*** in which state sovereignty pretensions were denied by a vote of 4–1.

The Court's decision holding the state of Georgia amenable to the jurisdiction of the national judiciary and suable by a citizen of another state in the federal courts was one of the first instances in which the Court gave meaning to the text of the Constitution. However, the ruling provoked speedy and largely unfavorable reaction and prompted immediate steps toward constitutional amendment. On January 8, 1798, three years before Marshall was appointed chief justice, the **Eleventh Amendment** became a part of the Constitution, overturning *Chisholm*. Yet one element of this case should not be overlooked: nearly a decade before Chief Justice Marshall's assertion of judicial review in ***Marbury* v. *Madison*** (reprinted in Chapter Two), the Court's interpretation of the Constitution was apparently equated with the document itself.

Marshall's tenure (1801–1835), covering a period in which his political enemies dominated the political branches of the government, made his fervent nationalism stand out even more dramatically than if he had represented merely the judicial component in a broad nationalist movement. It was not until 1819, however, that the chief justice found himself face-to-face with the dreaded issue of "clashing sovereignties" in ***McCulloch* v. *Maryland***. The state of Maryland levied a tax on the Second Bank of the United States, raising questions not only about the powers of Congress to charter a bank but also about the place of the states in the federal system. For Marshall, the necessary and proper clause gave Congress a discretionary choice of means in implementing granted powers, and the Tenth Amendment in no way limited this freedom of selection. As a result Congress possessed not only those powers expressly granted by the Constitution but an indefinite number of others as well, unless prohibited by the Constitution. Moreover, the breadth that the Constitution allowed in a choice of means was largely a matter for Congress, not the judiciary, to decide. Thus, Marshall established not only the proposition that national powers must be generously construed but also the equally decisive principle that the Tenth Amendment does not create in the states an independent limitation on national authority. In reply to the argument that the taxing power was reserved to the states by the Tenth Amendment and hence could operate even against a legitimate mechanism of national power, Marshall went out of his way to deny state power to tax national instrumentalities. A part of the union could not be allowed to cripple the whole. Anticipating the posture a later bench would assume, the Court thus had a special responsibility to intervene when majoritarian politics undermined the Constitution itself or targeted entities that were themselves politically defenseless.

Two years later, in ***Cohens* v. *Virginia*** (1821), the chief justice refuted the argument that in all cases "arising" in their courts, state judges had final authority to interpret the Constitution and the U.S. laws and treaties made under its authority. Because the people had surrendered portions of state sovereignty to the national government, the supremacy clause and the principle of judicial review required that final decisions on federal constitutional issues in state courts be made only by the Supreme Court. Otherwise a "hydra" in government would result with the Constitution having different meanings from state to state.

Marshall biographer Albert J. Beveridge described the chief justice's opinion in *Cohens* as "one of the strongest and most enduring strands of that mighty cable woven to hold the American people together as a united and imperishable nation." Thomas Jefferson condemned it as indicating judicial determination "to undermine the foundations of our confederated fabric." Denouncing the justices as a "subtle corps of sappers and miners constantly working underground," Jefferson charged that they had transformed the federal system into "a general and supreme one alone."

Marshall's doctrine of **national supremacy** built on the proposition that the central government and states confront each other in the relationship of superior and subordinate. If the exercise of Congress' enumerated powers be legitimate, the fact that their exercise encroaches on the states' traditional authority is of no significance. Moreover, the Court's duty is not to preserve state sovereignty but to protect national power against state encroachments. The Court functions not as an umpire but as an agent of national authority. For Marshall, as for Madison in 1788, the principal danger of the federal system lay in erosive state action. Effective political limitations, such as a Senate then elected by state legislators, existed against national efforts to impinge on state power, but only the Supreme Court could peacefully restrain state action from infringing on the authority of the national government.

Dual Federalism: Legacy of Chief Justice Roger B. Taney. Marshall's doctrine of federalism did not go unchallenged. His successor, Roger B. Taney of Maryland, strove valiantly during his long tenure (1836–1864) to redefine federalism in terms more favorable to state power.

The concept of federalism common to Marshall's critics insisted that the Constitution was a compact of sovereign states, not an ordinance of the people. The national government and the states faced each other as equals across a precise constitutional line defining their respective jurisdictions. This concept of nation-state equality had been the basis of Virginia's anarchical arguments in *Cohens* v. *Virginia*.

Accepting the basic creed of nation-state equality, the Taney Court stripped it of its anarchic implications. Within the powers reserved by the Tenth Amendment, the states were sovereign, but final authority to determine the scope of state powers rested with the national judiciary, an arbitrator standing aloof from the sovereign pretensions of both nation and states. "This judicial power," Taney wrote in *Ableman* v. *Booth* (1859), "was justly regarded as indispensable, not merely to maintain the supremacy of the laws of the United States, but also to guard the states from any encroachment upon their reserved rights by the general government. . . . So long . . . as this Constitution shall endure, this tribunal must exist with it, deciding in the peaceful forum of judicial proceeding the angry and irritating controversies between sovereignties, which in other countries have been determined by the arbitrament of force." For Marshall's concept of national supremacy, the Taney Court substituted a theory of federal equilibrium, later called "dual sovereignty" or **dual federalism**. Yet Marshall and Taney were agreed on one essential point: The Supreme Court provided a forum for keeping conflict within peaceful bounds.

Consequences for Public Policy. Marshall headed the Court for 34 years, Taney for 28, leaving two theories of federalism succeeding justices were free to apply as their inclinations or needs of the time dictated. Particularly in the period from the end of the Civil War to 1937, Taney's dual federalism had considerable impact on national policy. In *Texas* v. *White* (1869), Chief Justice Salmon Chase observed that the Constitution "in all its provisions, looks to an indestructible Union, composed of indestructible states." The sentence was not mere rhetoric. Initially, it was said that the powers of the national government were "enumerated," those of the states "reserved." In the hands of others, Taney's federalism allowed this order of things to change, turning the Tenth Amendment upside down and denying Congress a discretionary choice of means for carrying its enumerated powers into execution. As Chapters Six and Seven will show, the justices ruled on occasion that there were certain subject matters especially regarding economic and social regulation that were "expressly" reserved to the states, and, therefore, beyond national control. Thus, the states enjoyed their own enumerated powers in certain areas, not by the Constitution but by judicial mandate. The effect was to eliminate the second dimension of national power. Since 1937 the Supreme Court has adhered generally to a national supremacy view of federalism. But as explained below, dual federalism has reappeared in a few contexts in recent years.

Taney's passionate concern for states' rights should not, however, obscure the fact that in his day the state **police power** (see Chapter Eight) was the only practical tool at hand to cope with the pressing problems of the day. Taney called it "the power to govern men and things. . . ." It consisted of that mass of regulatory authority that the states had not surrendered to the central government under the Constitution. In a period in which the national government was not yet prepared to deal realistically with economic and social problems, the theory of national supremacy had the effect of posing the unexercised commerce power of Congress or the contract clause as barriers to any government action. Taney's dual federalism in the years before the Civil War enabled states to deal experimentally with problems that the national government would not begin to face for another half century.

Intergovernmental Immunity. In addition to the express limitations and prohibitions on national and state power contained in the Constitution, the Court has developed other limitations stemming from federalism itself. Maintenance of a political system in which two sovereignties must operate side by side led to the adoption of the doctrine that neither government may interfere with the government functions of the other, nor with the agencies and officials through which those functions are executed.

This doctrine of **governmental immunity** had its inception in *McCulloch* v. *Maryland*. On the premise that "the power to tax involves the power to destroy," Chief Justice Marshall declared, "The states have no power, by taxation or otherwise, to retard, impede, burden, or in any manner control the operations of the constitutional laws enacted by Congress to carry into execution the powers vested in the general government." Marshall's immunity doctrine was based on his theory of national supremacy. Regarded in this light, it is consistent with his attitude toward the role of the central government in a federal system. Accordingly, he denied emphatically the proposition that "every argument which would sustain the right of the general government to tax banks chartered by the states will equally sustain the right of the state to tax banks chartered by the general government." "The difference," he explained, "is that which always exists, and always must exist, between the action of the whole on the part, and the part on the whole—between the laws of a government declared to be supreme, and those of a government, which, when in opposition to those laws, is not supreme."

In ***Collector* v. *Day*** (1871), ruling that the salaries of state court judges were immune from a national income tax, the justices established the doctrine of **reciprocal immunity**. Based on the equality of national and state authority, this theory held that if states could not tax the national government, the national government could not tax the states. *Graves* v. *New York* (1939) overruled *Day* so far as it recognized "an implied constitutional immunity from income taxation of salaries of officers or employees of the national or state government or their instrumentalities." The immunity doctrine as to the states had been qualified even earlier in *South Carolina* v. *United States* (1905), which upheld a federal tax on South Carolina's liquor-dispensing business. In *New York* v. *United States* (1946), the Court refused to distinguish South Carolina's traffic in liquor from New York's traffic in mineral water.

The Court made further inroads on the reciprocal immunity doctrine in *South Carolina* v. *Baker* (1988), which expressly overruled *Pollock* v. *Farmers' Loan & Trust Co.* (first hearing, 1895). *Pollock* held that interest earned from municipal bonds was immune from federal taxation. In upholding a 1982 tax which removed the federal income tax exemption from interest earned on bearer (as opposed to registered) municipal bonds, the Court explained in *Baker* that the sources of state and federal immunity were different: "the state immunity arises from the constitutional structure and a concern for protecting state sovereignty, whereas the federal immunity arises from the Supremacy Clause." The states, therefore, "can never tax the United States directly, but can tax any private parties with whom it does business, even though the financial burden falls on the United States, as long as the tax does not discriminate against the United States or those with whom it deals. . . . The rule with respect to state tax immunity is essentially the same . . . except that at least some nondiscriminatory federal taxes can be collected directly from the States even though a parallel state tax could not be collected directly from the Federal Government." So the issue whether a nondiscriminatory federal tax might violate state tax immunity does not even arise today, unless the federal government seeks to collect the tax directly from a state.

Cooperative Federalism. Cooperation—not courtroom combat—more often characterizes the many manifestations of federalism today. Federalism not only shapes American politics but dictates the way many national policies are both developed and implemented. The national government may appropriate funds for such state activities as education, road building, and unemployment relief. It may grant such funds to the states on condition that a like amount or a specified proportion be raised by them for similar purposes, or on condition that the funds be spent in ways specified by federal law. Yet principles of federalism may also impose limits here, as the Court made clear when it ruled on the validity of the Affordable Care Act (Obamacare) in 2012. As seen in Chapter Six, the bench upheld the individual mandate as a proper exercise of Congress' taxing power but ruled that the law's significant expansion of Medicaid was an invalid exercise of Congress' spending power because it would coerce states either to accept the expansion or risk losing existing Medicaid funding (***National Federation of Independent Business* v. *Sebelius***). Changing views on the proper roles of nation and states amply demonstrate that federalism is now, as always, in flux. What presidents, governors, and members of Congress and state legislatures have to say about their respective responsibilities are often as important as judicial decisions in deciding what federalism American-style means.

THE RETURN OF DUAL FEDERALISM

As explained in Chapter Six, the Constitutional Revolution of 1937 reestablished Marshall's doctrine of national supremacy as the guiding principle of American federalism. The view that the Tenth Amendment no longer served as an independent limit on national power marked the end of an era. It also seemed to mark the demise of dual federalism. For several decades the Supreme Court was unimpressed by arguments that an act of Congress could be invalid because it intruded into matters ordinarily of concern to state governments.

However, the federalism wars have resumed in earnest, with several victories for dual federalism since 1992 in two types of cases, usually by votes of 5–4. First, a statute might be found unconstitutional either because Congress exceeded the scope of one of its powers or because the exercise of a legitimate power unduly infringed on matters traditionally belonging to state governments. Second, an act might be unconstitutional because it allowed individuals to sue unconsenting state governments to assert rights that Congress had created. The first involves the Tenth Amendment, and the other involves the Eleventh. With both, some justices believe that political checks alone are inadequate safeguards of federalism and need to be supplemented by judicial checks.

The Tenth Amendment Revived. Led by William Rehnquist, five justices declared in *National League of Cities* v. *Usery* (1976) that Congress could not extend the minimum wage and maximum hours provisions of the Fair Labor Standards Act to employees of states and their political subdivisions. To do so was to regulate "the States as states." The majority recognized

> limits upon the power of Congress to override state sovereignty, even when exercising its otherwise plenary powers to tax or to regulate commerce. . . . [T]here are attributes of sovereignty attaching to every state government which may not be impaired by Congress, not because Congress may lack an affirmative grant of legislative authority to reach the matter, but because the Constitution prohibits it from exercising the authority in that manner.

In a series of cases testing *National League of Cities*, the Court upheld the challenged statute each time. Still, the 1976 decision meant that virtually every congressional statute when applied to states was a candidate for constitutional attack.

Notably, in *Garcia* v. *San Antonio Metropolitan Transit Authority (SAMTA)* (1985), the *National League of Cities* dissenters prevailed. At issue was whether Congress could subject SAMTA to the minimum wage and overtime requirements of the Fair Labor Standards Act. Justice Blackmun, himself a reluctant member of the *National League of Cities* majority, announced for a majority of five that "the attempt to draw the boundaries of state regulatory immunity in terms of 'traditional governmental function' is not only unworkable but is inconsistent with established principles of federalism. . . . That case, accordingly, is overruled." Reaffirmed was a view of the Tenth Amendment in which constitutional limits on Congress are structural, not substantive—that states must find their protection from congressional regulation through the national political process, "not through judicially defined spheres of unregulable state activity."

Accordingly, when faced with the constitutionality of state-imposed limits on the number of terms that a member of the U.S. House of Representatives might serve—that is, a state policy altering the nationally prescribed requirements for public office—the Court voted 5–4 against the state position (***U.S. Term Limits, Inc.* v. *Thornton***, 1995). "[W]e conclude," wrote Justice Stevens, "that the power to add qualifications is not within the 'original powers' of the States by the Tenth Amendment." Moreover, "even if States possessed some original power in this area, . . . the Framers intended the Constitution to be the exclusive source of qualifications for members. . . ." Advocates of term limits would have to resort to constitutional amendment.

Dual federalist thinking reemerged in *Printz* v. *United States* (1997), which struck down, 5–4, a section of the 1993 Brady gun control law that required state officials to conduct background checks of prospective purchasers of handguns. This was an interim arrangement, pending operation of a national database that would allow gun dealers to conduct instant background checks on their own. Although Congress possesses authority under the commerce clause to regulate the firearms trade, the Court reasoned that the Tenth Amendment stands as an independent check on the manner in which that regulation may proceed. With national and state governments existing as coequal sovereigns, state officers could no more be required to administer federal laws than national officers could "be impressed into service for the execution of state laws," maintained Justice Scalia.

If laws challenged in *National League of Cities* and the Brady gun law case were defective because of their impact on state government, the civil remedy provision of the Violence Against Women Act would seem at first glance to have raised few constitutional eyebrows. Enacted by Congress in 1994 with the backing of the attorneys general from 38 states, this law allowed victims of gender-motivated violence to sue their attackers for damages in federal court. When challenged in the Supreme Court, 36 states joined a brief urging that the law be sustained, with only Alabama urging that the law be struck down. But five justices found it constitutionally sustainable neither as an exercise of Congress' power to regulate interstate commerce nor as an exercise of Congress' power to enforce the provisions of the Fourteenth Amendment (***United States* v. *Morrison***, 2000). The "irony of these cases," declared Justice Souter in dissent, is "that the States will be forced to enjoy the new federalism whether they want it or not."

At one level, the decision seemed a replay of ***United States* v. *Lopez*** (1995) (reprinted in Chapter Six), when, for the first time since 1936, the Court invalidated an act of Congress—the Gun-Free School Zones Act—as being beyond the scope of the power to regulate interstate commerce. But there is an important distinction between *Lopez* and *Morrison*. In the former, Congress had not demonstrated a clear nexus between firearms in or near schools and interstate commerce, and the Court majority was unwilling to defer to Congress absent such substantiation. But in *Morrison*, the record contained ample congressional documentation describing the impact of gender-motivated violence on its victims and their families and its effects on interstate commerce. "If accepted," maintained Chief Justice Rehnquist in an attempt to distinguish the national commerce power from a national and nearly boundless police power, "petitioners' reasoning would allow Congress to regulate any crime as long as the nationwide, aggregated impact of that crime has substantial effects on employment, production, transit, or consumption." Because most violence has traditionally been within the jurisdiction of the states, it was the Court's duty to draw the line between what could properly be the subject of national regulation and what could not. "The Constitution requires a distinction between what is truly national and what is truly local."

National power nonetheless prevailed in *Gonzales* v. *Raich* (2005) when the Morrison and Lopez dissenters plus Kennedy and Scalia agreed that the commerce power extended to the local cultivation and personal medicinal use of marijuana even when allowed by state law. Advocates of the medical use of marijuana were advised to look to Congress and not to the courts for relief. For the majority, allowing California's Compassionate Use Act to escape the reach of Congress' Controlled Substances Act would undercut the national effort to restrict the interstate market for this popular recreational drug. Nonetheless, the impact of *Raich* has been largely muted by an increase in the number of states (35 by 2021) allowing medical marijuana, by a partial decriminalization of marijuana use in other locales and by a greatly diminished enforcement effort for this aspect of federal law by the Obama and Trump administrations.

Eleventh Amendment Limitations. "The judicial power of the United States shall not be construed to extend to any suit . . . commenced or prosecuted against one of the United States by Citizens of another State, or by Citizens or Subjects of any Foreign States," declares the Eleventh Amendment. As noted, this amendment was the nation's response to *Chisholm* v. *Georgia* (1793), which allowed a citizen of South Carolina to sue the state of Georgia in federal court. Much interpretation of this amendment deals with technicalities of federal jurisdiction and so lies outside the scope of this book. But some recent rulings illustrate that the amendment has also been a battleground in the federalism wars, partly shielding state governments from congressional authority.

A background summary should demonstrate why the amendment is important in understanding federalism today. In 1890 *Hans* v. *Louisiana* went beyond the actual language of the amendment by barring a suit in federal court by a citizen of Louisiana against the state of Louisiana after the latter failed to pay interest on its bonds. The Court concluded that the principle of **sovereign immunity**—that a state cannot be sued without its consent—was an implied limitation on the jurisdiction of the federal courts outlined in Article III. As a result, the federal courts were off-limits to suits against states by citizens and noncitizens alike. Later cases, however, greatly diminished this immunity. Ex parte *Young* (1908) held that state officials, as distinguished from the state itself, were subject to suits brought in federal court. *Fitzpatrick* v. *Bitzer* (1976) allowed Congress to negate or abrogate a state's Eleventh Amendment immunity in a suit for damages because of Congress' authority under Section 5 of the Fourteenth Amendment (ratified 70 years after the Eleventh Amendment) "to enforce, by appropriate legislation, the provisions of the" amendment. Similarly, *Pennsylvania* v. *Union Gas Co.* (1989) allowed suits against states for monetary damages on the basis of Congress' powers under Article I. Viewing the political process as the primary safeguard of federalism, as in *Garcia*, the Court reasoned that a clear statement in a statute of an intention to abrogate state immunity was an adequate check on congressional overreaching.

This theory was abruptly rejected seven years later in *Seminole Tribe* v. *Florida* (1996). The Court overruled *Union Gas* and denied that Congress could abrogate a state's immunity from suit in federal court under its Article I powers, with or without a clear intention to do so. "The majority's opinion," explained Justice Stevens in dissent, ". . . prevents Congress from providing a federal forum for a broad range of actions against States, from . . . copyright and patent law to those concerning bankruptcy, environmental law, and the regulation of our vast national economy."

Does sovereign immunity apply across state lines? Although *Nevada* v. *Hall* (1979) held that that states have sovereign immunity in each other's courts, *Franchise Tax Board of California* v. *Hyatt* (2019) erased that barrier and overruled *Hall*. This move prompted Justice Breyer to "wonder which cases the Court will overrule next."

The Court's interest in augmenting political safeguards with judicial checks continued in *Alden* v. *Maine* (1999). The Fair Labor Standards Act allowed aggrieved state workers to sue their employer in state court for violating the law's overtime provisions. Because Maine had not consented to the suit, the Court reasoned that Congress could not compel state courts to accept the suit. "[T]he sovereign immunity of the States neither derives from nor is limited by the terms of the Eleventh Amendment," declared Justice Kennedy. Rather, the immunity "is a fundamental aspect of the sovereignty which the States enjoyed before the ratification of the Constitution, and which they retain today . . . except as altered by the plan of the Convention or certain constitutional Amendments." Because the Eleventh Amendment confirmed but did not establish state immunity, "it follows that the scope of the States' immunity from suit is demarcated not by the text of the Amendment alone but by fundamental postulates implicit in the constitutional design." Just as *Seminole Tribe* closed the federal courts to suits against states when Congress acted on its Article I powers, *Alden* blocked them from the courts of unconsenting states.

One term later, the same five justices comprising the majority in *Seminole Tribe* and *Alden* restricted Congress' authority under the Fourteenth Amendment to abrogate state immunity. *Kimel* v. *Florida Board of Regents* held that Congress could not force states to submit to suits for monetary damages in federal courts brought by employees under the Age Discrimination in Employment Act. In reasoning similar to that followed in ***City of Boerne* v. *Flores*** (reprinted in Chapter Two), the Court found that the ADEA was not "appropriate legislation" under section 5 of the amendment because its protections against age discrimination went far beyond what the Court had held the amendment required. Similarly, *Board of Trustees* v. *Garrett* (2001) barred lawsuits against the state by Alabama state employees under Title I of the Americans with Disabilities Act (ADA). When Congress protects a class of people beyond the precise scope of the rights enshrined in section one of the Fourteenth Amendment, there must be both "congruence and proportionality between the injury to be prevented or remedied and the means adopted to that end," a condition Congress failed to satisfy. The ADA's legislative record failed "to show that Congress identified a history and pattern of irrational employment discrimination by the States against the disabled."

Yet, *Tennessee* v. *Lane* (2004) held that Title II of the ADA, which guards against a public entity's denial of benefits or right of access on account of disability—in this instance the physical access of paraplegics to a state's courts—was a valid exercise of Congress' authority to enforce the guarantees of the Fourteenth Amendment.

In holding that state employees may recover money damages in federal court because of a state's failure to comply with the Family and Medical Leave Act (FMLA) of 1993, *Nevada Dept. of Human Resources* v. *Hibbs* (2003) is another exception to this line of recent decisions. Because of evidence of a long history of gender discrimination by the states in their administration of leave benefits, six justices agreed that application of the FMLA to the states was appropriately prophylactic under Section 5, rather than a substantive redefinition by Congress of a state's constitutional obligations. Moreover, according to *United States* v. *Georgia* (2006), Title II of the ADA validly abrogates state sovereign immunity for conduct relating to prison inmates that violates both the ADA and the Fourteenth Amendment, although the Court left unanswered whether states may be sued for conduct that violates only Title II but not the Fourteenth Amendment. The question is important because Title II allows plaintiffs to seek monetary damages, not merely injunctive relief.

Cumulatively, decisions to date re-invoking dual federalism have not tied the hands of the national government to such a degree as to provoke a confrontation between the Congress and the president on one side, and the Court on the other, as happened in 1937. Yet some recent holdings are symbolic warning shots, even if they have been fired by slender majorities. Judicial insistence that Congress be more mindful of the place of the states in the constitutional order may prove to be one of those quiet developments that have long-range effects on American government.

KEY TERMS

federalism
Antifederalists
delegated powers
reserved powers
implied powers
express powers
necessary and proper clause
resulting powers
supremacy clause
concurrent powers
exclusive powers
preemption
judicial federalism
federal question
Eleventh Amendment
national supremacy
dual federalism
police power
governmental immunity
reciprocal immunity
sovereign immunity

QUERIES

1. The Supreme Court's decisions in both *McCulloch* and *Cohens* were highly controversial in their day. Yet in the first, the Court agreed only to accept an institution that Congress had already established; in the second, Virginia actually won on the merits. Why then would certain political groups have found Marshall's opinions in these cases unsettling?

2. "Whatever the judicial role," wrote Justice Kennedy in his concurring opinion in *United States* v. *Lopez*, "it is axiomatic that Congress does have substantial discretion and control over the federal balance. . . . The political branches of the Government must fulfill this grave constitutional obligation if democratic liberty and the federalism that secures it are to endure. At the same time, the absence of structural mechanisms to require those officials to undertake this principled task, and the momentary political convenience often attendant upon their failure to do so, argue against a complete renunciation of the judicial role." Does this passage offer insight into the reasons why some members of the Court believe that political checks to safeguard federalism must be augmented with judicial checks?

3. What is the significance of the Seventeenth Amendment (1913) for the debate over political versus judicial checks on Congress? Does its presence in the Constitution support or undercut Justice Kennedy's statement in query 2?

4. The framers bequeathed a political system heavy on both separation of powers and federalism. To what degree do the two work in consort? For contemporary Americans, is the combination a blessing or curse?

SELECTED READINGS

Beer, Samuel H. *To Make a Nation: The Rediscovery of American Federalism*. Cambridge, MA: Harvard University Press, 1993.

Dichio, Michael A. *The U.S. Supreme Court and the Centralization of National Authority*. Albany: State University of New York Press, 2019.

Ellis, Richard E. *Aggressive Nationalism: McCulloch v. Maryland and the Foundation of Federal Authority in the Young Republic*. New York: Oxford University Press, 2007.

Karch, Andrew, and Shanna Rose. *Responsive States: Federalism and American Public Policy*. New York: Cambridge University Press, 2019.

Killenbeck, Mark R. *M'Culloch v. Maryland*. Lawrence: University Press of Kansas, 2006.

Lofgren, Charles A. "The Origins of the Tenth Amendment." In Ronald K. L. Collins, ed. *Constitutional Government in America*. Durham, NC: Carolina Academic Press, 1980.

Luce, W. Ray. *Cohens v. Virginia (1821)*. New York: Garland, 1990.

Mason, Alpheus T. *The States Rights Debate*. New York: Oxford University Press, 1972.

Mathis, Doyle. "*Chisholm* v. *Georgia*: Background and Settlement." 54 *Journal of American History* 19, 1967.

I. DEFINING THE NATURE OF THE UNION

Chisholm v. *Georgia*
2 U.S. (2 Dall.) 419, 1 L.Ed. 440 (1793)

www.law.cornell.edu/supremecourt/text/2/419

On October 31, 1777, the Executive Council of Georgia authorized state commissioners Thomas Stone and Edward Davies to purchase much-needed supplies from Robert Farquhar, a Charleston, South Carolina, merchant. For his merchandise, Stone and Davies agreed to pay Farquhar $169,613.33 in Continental currency or in indigo at Carolina prices, if currency was not available. Farquhar never received payment. His claims were still unsatisfied when he was hit by the boom of a pilot boat headed for Savannah. A short time after his death, Alexander Chisholm, a Charleston merchant, was qualified as Farquhar's executor and began to press for payment of Farquhar's claim. When Georgia refused to pay, the executor brought suit against the state in the U.S. Circuit Court for the District of Georgia. Alleging its sovereign and independent status under the federal Constitution, Georgia answered that it could not be made a party to any suit by a South Carolina citizen. Judges James Iredell and Nathaniel Pendleton upheld, for different reasons, Georgia's objections.

In 1792, Chisholm filed suit in the Supreme Court, but Georgia failed to respond. When Georgia persisted in its refusal, the case was postponed until February 4, 1793. Again no one appeared, and the justices issued another invitation. Still without a response, the decision came down on February 19. In the face of assurances made by Hamilton, Madison, and Marshall during the ratification debates that a state could not, without its consent, be made a defendant in the federal courts by a citizen of another state, the Court took jurisdiction and decided against the state.

The negative reaction was strong and swift. A House resolution calling for amendment to the Constitution was filed the day of the decision, followed the next day by a supportive Senate resolution. The Eleventh Amendment was proposed by Congress on March 4, 1794, and ratification was completed in 11 months. Official announcement of ratification was not made until January 8, 1798, when President John Adams in a message to Congress declared that it "may now be deemed to be a part of the Constitution." Majority: Wilson, Blair, Cushing, Jay. Dissenting: Iredell.

Wilson, Justice:

This is a case of uncommon magnitude. . . . One of the parties to it is a state; certainly respectable, claiming to be sovereign. The question to be determined is whether this state, so respectable, and whose claim soars so high, is amenable to the jurisdiction of the supreme court of the United States? This question, important in itself, will depend on others, more important still; and, may, perhaps, be ultimately resolved into one, no less radical than this—"do the people of the United States form a nation?" . . .

To the Constitution of the United States the term sovereign is totally unknown. There is but one place where it could have been used with propriety. But, even in that place it would not, perhaps, have comported with the delicacy of those who ordained and established that constitution. They might have announced themselves "sovereign" people of the United States: But serenely conscious of the fact, they avoided the ostentatious declaration. . . .

With the strictest propriety, therefore, classical and political, our national scene opens with the most magnificent object which the nation could present. "The people of the United States" are the first personages introduced. Who were those people? They were the citizens of thirteen states, each of which had a separate constitution and government, and all of which were connected together by articles of confederation. . . .

The question now opens fairly to our view, could the people of those states, among whom were those of Georgia, bind those states, and Georgia, among the others, by the legislative, executive, and judicial power so vested? If the principles on which I have founded myself are just and true, this question must, unavoidably, receive an affirmative answer. . . .

The next question under this head is—Has the constitution done so? Did those people mean to exercise this, their undoubted power? These questions may be resolved, either by fair and conclusive deductions, or by direct and explicit declarations. In order, ultimately, to discover, whether the people of the United States intended to bind those states by the judicial power vested by the national constitution, a previous inquiry will naturally be: Did those people intend to bind those states by the legislative power vested by that constitution? The articles of confederation, it is well known, did not operate upon individual citizens, but operated only upon states. This defect was remedied by the national constitution, which, as all allow, has an operation on individual citizens. But if an opinion, which some seem to entertain, be just; the defect remedied, on one side, was balanced by a defect introduced on the other: for they seem to think, that the present constitution operates only on individual citizens, and not on states. This opinion, however, appears to be altogether unfounded. When certain laws of the states are declared to be "subject to the revision and control of the congress;" it cannot, surely be contended, that the legislative power of the national government was meant to have no operation on the several states. The fact, uncontrovertibly established in one instance, proves the principle in all other instances, to which the facts will be found to apply. We may then infer, that the people of the United States intended to bind the several states, by the legislative power of the national government. . . .

But, in my opinion, this doctrine rests not upon the legitimate result of fair and conclusive deduction from the constitution; it is confirmed, beyond all doubt, by the direct and explicit declaration of the constitution itself. "The judicial power of the United States shall extend to controversies between two States." Two States are supposed to have a controversy between them; this controversy is supposed to be brought before those vested with the judicial power of the United States; can the most consummate degree of professional ingenuity devise a mode by which this "controversy between two States" can be brought before a court of law, and yet neither of those States be a defendant? "The judicial power of the United States shall extend to controversies between a State and citizens of another State." Could the strictest legal language; could even that language which is peculiarly appropriated to an art, deemed by a great master to be one of the most honorable, laudable, and profitable things in our law; could this strict and appropriate language describe with more precise accuracy the cause now pending before the tribunal? Causes, and not parties to causes, are weighed by justice in her equal scales; on the former, solely, her attention is fixed; to the latter she is, as she is painted, blind. . . .

JAY, CHIEF JUSTICE . . . [omitted]

CUSHING, JUSTICE . . . [omitted]

BLAIR, JUSTICE . . . [omitted]

Iredell, Justice: [Dissenting]

A general question of great importance here occurs. What controversy of a civil nature can be maintained against a state by an individual? The framers of the constitution, I presume, must have meant one of two things—Either (1) In the conveyance of that part of the judicial power which did not relate to the execution of the other authorities of the general government . . . to refer to antecedent laws for the construction of the general words they use; or (2) To enable congress in all such cases to pass all such laws as they might deem necessary and proper to carry the purposes of this constitution into full effect, either absolutely at their discretion, or, at least, in cases where prior laws were deficient for such purposes, if any such deficiency existed.

The attorney-general has indeed suggested another construction, a construction, I confess, that I never heard of before, nor can I now consider it grounded on any solid foundation, though it appeared to me to be the basis of the attorney-general's argument. His construction I take to be this: "That the moment a supreme court is formed, it is to exercise all the judicial power vested in it by the constitution, by its own authority, whether the legislature has prescribed methods of doing so, or not." My conception of the constitution is entirely different. I conceive, that all the courts of the United States must receive, not merely their organization as to the number of judges of which they are to consist; but all their authority, as to the manner of their proceeding, from the legislature only. . . .

McCulloch v. *Maryland* 17 U.S. (4 Wheat.) 316, 4 L.Ed. 579 (1819)

www.law.cornell.edu/supremecourt/text/17/316

In 1818 Maryland imposed a tax on banks and bank branches not chartered by the state legislature. James McCulloch, cashier of the Baltimore branch of the Second Bank of the United States, against which the law was directed, failed to pay the $15,000 annual fee or comply with the alternative requirement by affixing tax stamps to the bank notes issued. McCulloch brought a writ of error against the Court of Appeals of Maryland, which had upheld a lower court judgment against him. Majority: Marshall, Duvall, Johnson, Livingston, Story, Todd, Washington.

Marshall, Chief Justice, delivered the opinion of the Court.

In the case now to be determined, the defendant, a sovereign state, denies the obligation of a law enacted by the legislature of the Union; and the plaintiff, on his part, contests the validity of an act which has been passed by the legislature of that state. . . . No tribunal can approach such a question without a deep sense of its importance, and of the awful responsibility involved in its decision. But it must be decided peacefully, or remain a source of hostile legislation, perhaps of hostility of a still more serious nature; and if it is to be so decided, by this tribunal alone can the decision be made. On the supreme court of the United States has the constitution of our country devolved this important duty.

The first question made in the case is, has congress power to incorporate a bank? . . .

In discussing this question, the counsel for the state of Maryland have deemed it of some importance, in the construction of the constitution, to consider that instrument not as emanating from the people, but as the act of sovereign and independent states. The powers of the general government, it has been said, are delegated by the states, who alone are truly sovereign; and must be exercised in subordination to the states, who alone possess supreme dominion. It would be difficult to sustain this proposition. The convention which framed the constitution was, indeed, elected by the state legislatures. But the instrument, when it came from their hands, was a mere proposal, without obligation. . . . It was reported to the then existing congress of the United States, with a request that it might "be submitted to a convention of delegates, chosen in each state by the people thereof, under the recommendation of its legislature, for their assent and ratification." This mode of proceeding was adopted; and by the convention, by congress, and by the state legislatures, the instrument was submitted to the people. They acted upon it, in the only manner in which they can act safely, effectively, and wisely, on such a subject by assembling in convention. It is true, they assembled in their several states; and where else should they have assembled? No political dreamer was ever wild enough to think of breaking down the lines which separate the states, and of compounding the American people into one common mass. Of consequence, when they act, they act in their states. But the measures they adopt do not, on that account, cease to be the measures of the people themselves, or become the measures of the state governments.

From these conventions the constitution derives its whole authority. The government proceeds directly from the people; is "ordained and established" in the name of the people; and is declared to be ordained, "in order to form a more perfect union, establish justice, insure domestic tranquillity, and secure the blessings of liberty, to themselves and to their posterity." The assent of the States, in their sovereign capacity, is implied in calling a convention, and thus submitting that instrument to the people. . . .

This government is acknowledged by all to be one of enumerated powers. . . . [T]hat principle is now universally admitted. But the question respecting the extent of the powers actually granted, is perpetually arising, and will probably continue to arise, as long as our system shall exist. In discussing these questions, the conflicting powers of the general and state governments must be brought into view, and the supremacy of their respective laws, when they are in opposition, must be settled.

If any one proposition could command the universal assent of mankind, we might expect that it would be this—that the government of the Union, though limited in its powers, is supreme within its sphere of action. This would seem to result, necessarily, from its nature. It is the government of all; its powers are delegated by all; it represents all, and acts for all. Though any one state may be willing to control its operations, no state is willing to allow others to control them. The nation, on those subjects on which it can act, must necessarily bind its component parts. But this question is not left to mere reason: the people have, in express terms, decided it, by saying, "this constitution, and the laws of the United States, which shall be made in pursuance thereof," "shall be the supreme law of the land," and by requiring that the members of the state legislatures, and the officers of the executive and judicial departments of the states, shall take the oath of fidelity to it. The government of the United States, then, though limited in its powers, is supreme; and its laws, when made in pursuance of the constitution, form the supreme law of the land, "anything in the constitution or laws of any state, to the contrary notwithstanding."

Among the enumerated powers, we do not find that of establishing a bank or creating a corporation. But there is no phrase in the instrument which, like the articles of confederation, excludes incidental or implied powers;

and which requires that everything granted shall be expressly and minutely described. Even the Tenth Amendment, which was framed for the purpose of quieting the excessive jealousies which had been excited, omits the word "expressly," and declares only that the powers "not delegated to the United States, nor prohibited to the states, are reserved to the states or to the people;" thus leaving the question, whether the particular power which may become the subject of contest, has been delegated to the one government, or prohibited to the other, to depend on a fair construction of the whole instrument. The men who drew and adopted this amendment had experienced the embarrassments resulting from the insertion of this word in the articles of confederation, and probably omitted it, to avoid those embarrassments. A constitution, to contain an accurate detail of all the subdivisions of which its great powers will admit, and of all the means by which they may be carried into execution, would partake of the prolixity of a legal code, and could scarcely be embraced by the human mind. It would, probably, never be understood by the public. Its nature, therefore, requires, that only its great outlines should be marked, its important objects designated, and the minor ingredients which compose those objects, be deduced from the nature of the objects themselves. That this idea was entertained by the framers of the American constitution, is not only to be inferred from the nature of the instrument, but from the language. Why else were some of the limitations, found in the 9th section of the 1st article, introduced? It is also, in some degree, warranted, by their having omitted to use any restrictive term which might prevent its receiving a fair and just interpretation. In considering this question, then, we must never forget, that it is a *constitution* we are expounding.

Although, among the enumerated powers of government, we do not find the word "bank," or "incorporation," we find the great powers, to lay and collect taxes; to borrow money; to regulate commerce; to declare and conduct war; and to raise and support armies and navies. The sword and the purse, all the external relations, and no inconsiderable portion of the industry of the nation, are intrusted to its government. It can never be pretended, that these vast powers draw after them others of inferior importance, merely because they are inferior. Such an idea can never be advanced. But it may with great reason be contended, that a government, intrusted with such ample powers, on the due execution of which the happiness and prosperity of the nation so vitally depends, must also be intrusted with ample means for their execution. The power being given, it is the interest of the nation to facilitate its execution. It can never be their interest, and cannot be presumed to have been their intention, to clog and embarrass its execution, by withholding the most appropriate means. Throughout this vast republic, from the St. Croix to the Gulf of Mexico, from the Atlantic to the Pacific, revenue is to be collected and expended, armies are to be marched and supported. The exigencies of the nation may require, that the treasure raised in the north should be transported to the south, that raised in the east, conveyed to the west, or that this order should be reversed. Is that construction of the constitution to be preferred, which would render these operations difficult, hazardous, and expensive? Can we adopt that construction (unless the words imperiously require it), which would impute to the framers of that instrument, when granting these powers for the public good, the intention of impeding their exercise by withholding a choice of means? . . .

But the constitution of the United States has not left the right of congress to employ the necessary means, for the execution of the powers conferred on the government, to general reasoning. To its enumeration of powers is added, that of making "all laws which shall be necessary and proper, for carrying into execution the foregoing powers, and all other powers vested by this constitution, in the government of the United States, or in any department thereof." . . .

But the argument on which most reliance is placed, is drawn from the peculiar language of this clause. Congress is not empowered by it to make all laws, which may have relation to the powers conferred on the government, but only such as may be "necessary and proper" for carrying them into execution. The word "necessary" is considered as controlling the whole sentence, and as limiting the right to pass laws for the execution of the granted powers, to such as are indispensable, and without which the power would be nugatory. That it excludes the choice of means, and leaves to Congress, in each case, that only which is most direct and simple.

Is it true, that this is the sense in which the word "necessary" is always used? Does it always import an absolute physical necessity, so strong, that one thing, to which another may be termed necessary, cannot exist without that other? We think it does not. If reference be had to its use, in the common affairs of the world, or in approved authors, we find that it frequently imports no more than that one thing is convenient, or useful, or essential to another. To employ the means necessary to an end, is generally understood as employing any means calculated to produce the end, and not as being confined to those single means, without which the end would be entirely unattainable. . . .

This provision is made in a constitution, intended to endure for ages to come, and consequently to be adapted to the various *crises* of human affairs. To have prescribed the means by which government should, in all future times, execute its powers, would have been to change, entirely, the character of the instrument, and give it the properties of a legal code. It would have been an unwise attempt to provide, by immutable rules, for exigencies which, if foreseen at all, must have been seen dimly, and which can be best provided for as they occur. To have declared, that the best means shall not be used, but those alone, without which the power given would be nugatory, would have been to deprive the legislature of the capacity to avail itself of experience, to exercise its reason, and to accommodate its legislation to circumstances. If we apply this principle of construction to any of the powers of the government, we shall find it so pernicious in its operation that we shall be compelled to discard it. . . .

But the argument which most conclusively demonstrates the error of the construction contended for by the counsel for the state of Maryland, is founded on the intention of the convention, as manifested in the whole clause. . . . That this could not be intended is, we should think, had it not been already controverted, too apparent for controversy.

We think so for the following reasons: 1st. The clause is placed among the powers of congress, not among the limitations on those powers. 2d. Its terms purport to enlarge, not to diminish the powers vested in the government. It purports to be an additional power, not a restriction on those already granted. No reason has been, or can be assigned, for thus concealing an intention to narrow the discretion of the national legislature, under words which purport to enlarge it. The framers of the constitution wished its adoption, and well knew that it would be endangered by its strength, not by its weakness. Had they been capable of using language which would convey to the eye one idea, and, after deep reflection, impress on the mind, another, they would rather have disguised the grant of power, than its limitation. If then, their intention had been, by this clause, to restrain the free use of means which might otherwise have been implied, that intention would have been inserted in another place, and would have been expressed in terms resembling these. "In carrying into execution the foregoing powers and all others," &c., "no laws shall be passed but such as are necessary and proper." . . .

We admit, as all must admit, that the powers of the government are limited, and that its limits are not to be transcended. But we think the sound construction of the constitution must allow to the national legislature that discretion, with respect to the means by which the powers it confers are to be carried into execution, which will enable that body to perform the high duties assigned to it, in the manner most beneficial to the people. Let the end be legitimate, let it be within the scope of the constitution, and all means which are appropriate, which are plainly adapted to that end, which are not prohibited, but consistent with the letter and spirit of the constitution, are constitutional. . . .

It being the opinion of the court, that the act incorporating the bank is constitutional; and that the power of establishing a branch in the state of Maryland might be properly exercised by the bank itself, we proceed to inquire—whether the state of Maryland may, without violating the constitution, tax that branch? That the power of taxation is . . . retained by the states; . . . that it is to be concurrently exercised by the two governments are truths which have never been denied. But such is the paramount character of the constitution, that its capacity to withdraw any subject from the action of even this power, is admitted. . . .

On this ground, the counsel for the bank place its claim to be exempted from the power of a state to tax its operations. There is no express provision for the case, but the claim has been sustained on a principle which so entirely pervades the constitution . . . as to be incapable of being separated from it, without rending it into shreds. This great principle is, that the constitution and the laws made in pursuance thereof are supreme; that they control the constitution and laws of the respective states, and cannot be controlled by them. From this, which may be almost termed an axiom, other propositions are deduced as corollaries, on the truth or error of which, and on their application to this case, the cause has been supposed to depend. These are, 1st: That a power to create implies a power to preserve: 2d. That a power to destroy, if wielded by a different hand, is hostile to, and incompatible with, these powers to create and preserve: 3d. That where this repugnancy exists, that authority which is supreme must control, not yield to that over which it is supreme. . . .

The sovereignty of a state extends to everything which exists by its own authority, or is introduced by its permission; but does it extend to those means which are employed by Congress to carry into execution—powers conferred on that body by the people of the United States? We think it demonstrable that it does not. Those powers are not given by the people of a single state. They are given by the people of the United States, to a government whose laws, made in pursuance of the constitution, are declared to be supreme. Consequently, the people of a single state cannot confer a sovereignty which will extend over them.

If we measure the power of taxation residing in a state, by the extent of sovereignty which the people of a single state possess and can confer on its government, we have an intelligible standard, applicable to every case to which the power may be applied. We have a principle which leaves the power of taxing the people and property of a state unimpaired; which leaves to a state the command of all its resources, and which places beyond its reach, all those powers which are conferred by the people of the United States on the government of the Union, and all those means which are given for the purpose of carrying those powers into execution. We have a principle which is safe for the states, and safe for the Union. We are relieved, as we ought to be, from clashing sovereignty; from interfering powers; from a repugnancy between a right in one government to pull down, what there is an acknowledged right in another to build up; from the incompatibility of a right in one government to destroy, what there is an acknowledged right in another to build up; from the incompatibility of a right in one government to destroy, what there is a right in another to preserve. We are not driven to the perplexing inquiry, so unfit for the judicial department, what degree of taxation is a legitimate use, and what degree may amount to the abuse of the power. The attempt to use it on the means employed by the government of the Union, in pursuance of the constitution, is itself an abuse, because it is the usurpation of a power, which the people of a single state cannot give. We find, then, on just theory, a total failure of this original right to tax the means employed by the government of the Union, for the execution of its powers. The right never existed, and the question whether it has been surrendered, cannot arise.

But, waiving this theory for the present, let us resume the inquiry, whether this power can be exercised by the respective states, consistently with a fair construction of the constitution? That the power to tax involves the power to destroy; that the power to destroy may defeat and render useless the power to create; that there is a plain repugnancy in conferring on one government a power to control the constitutional measures of another, which other, with respect to those very measures, is declared to be supreme over that which exerts the control, are propositions not to be denied. But all inconsistencies are to be reconciled by the magic of the word confidence. Taxation, it is said, does not necessarily and unavoidably destroy. To carry it to the excess of destruction, would be an abuse, to presume which, would banish that confidence which is essential to all government. But is this a case of confidence? Would the people of any one state trust those of another with a power to control the most significant operations of their state government? We know they would not. Why, then, should we suppose, that the people of any one state should be willing to trust those of another with a power to control the operations of a government to which they have confided their most important and most valuable interests? In the legislature of the Union alone, all are represented. The legislature of the Union alone, therefore, can be trusted by the people with the power of controlling measures which concern all, in the confidence that it will not be abused.

If we apply the principle for which the state of Maryland contends, to the constitution generally, we shall find it capable of changing totally the character of that instrument. We shall find it capable of arresting all the measures of the government, and of prostrating it at the foot of the states. The American people have declared their constitution and the laws made in pursuance thereof, to be supreme; but this principle would transfer the supremacy, in fact, to the states. If the states may tax one instrument, employed by the government in the execution of its powers, they may tax any and every other instrument. They may tax the mail; they may tax the mint; they may tax patent rights; they may tax the papers of the custom-house; they may tax judicial process; they may tax all the means employed by the government, to an excess which would defeat all the ends of government. This was not intended by the American people. They did not design to make their government dependent on the states. . . .

The question is, in truth, a question of supremacy, and if the right of the states to tax the means employed by the general government be conceded, the declaration that the constitution, and the laws made in pursuance thereof, shall be the supreme law of the land, is empty and unmeaning declamation. . . .

It has also been insisted, that, as the power of taxation in the general and state governments is acknowledged to be concurrent, every argument which would sustain the right of the general government to tax banks chartered by the states, will equally sustain the rights of the states to tax banks chartered by the general government. But the two cases are not the same reason. The people of all the states have created the general government, and have conferred upon it the general power of taxation.

The people of all the states, and the states themselves, are represented in congress, and, by their representatives, exercise this power. When they tax the chartered institutions of the states, they tax their constituents; and these taxes must be uniform. But when a state taxes the operations of the government of the United States, it acts upon institutions created, not by their own constituents, but by people over whom they claim no control. It acts upon the measures of a government created by others as well as themselves, for the benefit of others in common with themselves. The difference is that which always exists, and always must exist, between the action of the whole on a part, and the action of a part on the whole—between the laws of a government declared to be supreme, and those of a government which, when in opposition to those laws, is not supreme. . . . The court has bestowed on this subject its most deliberate consideration. The result is a conviction that the states have no power, by taxation or otherwise, to retard, impede burden, or in any manner control, the operations of the constitutional laws enacted by congress to carry into execution the powers vested in the general government. This is, we think, the unavoidable consequence of that supremacy which the constitution has declared. We are unanimously of opinion, that the law passed by the legislature of Maryland, imposing a tax on the Bank of the United States, is unconstitutional and void. . . .

Cohens v. *Virginia*
19 U.S. (6 Wheat.) 264, 5 L.Ed. 257 (1821)

www.law.cornell.edu/supremecourt/text/19/264

In 1802 Congress authorized the District of Columbia to conduct a lottery. P. J. and M. J. Cohen, agents of the Jacob I. Cohen and Brother Lottery Office of Baltimore, Maryland, sold District lottery tickets in Norfolk, Virginia, but were arrested and convicted under a state law of 1819 that banned the sale of all lottery tickets not approved by the state legislature. Virginia justified the restriction as a means of discouraging the export of capital to finance public improvements elsewhere at a time of financial exigencies at home. The case may have been arranged. The Supreme Court docketed the Cohens' appeal before their case came to trial in Norfolk's borough court, as if the case had already been decided and any possible appeal in the Virginia courts rejected. The portion of the opinion that follows pertains solely to the question of jurisdiction. Majority: Marshall, Duvall, Johnson, Livingston, Story, Todd. Not participating: Washington.

Mr. Chief Justice Marshall delivered the opinion of the Court. . . .

Judgment was rendered against the defendants; and the court in which it was rendered being the highest court of the state in which the cause was cognizable, the record has been brought into this court by a writ of error.

The defendant in error moves to dismiss this writ, for want of jurisdiction.

In support of this motion, three points have been made, and argued with the ability which the importance of the question merits. These points are—

1st. That a state is a defendant.
2nd. That no writ of error lies from this court to a state court. [Point 3 has been omitted.]

The questions presented to the court by the two first points made at the bar are of great magnitude, and may truly be said vitally to affect the Union. They exclude the inquiry whether the constitution and laws of the United States have been violated by the judgment which the plaintiffs in error seek to review; and maintain that, admitting such violation, it is not in the power of the government to apply a corrective. They maintain that the nation does not possess a department capable of restraining, peaceably, and by authority of law, any attempts which may be made, by a part, against the legitimate powers of the whole; and that the government is reduced to the alternative of submitting to such attempts, or of resisting them by force. They maintain that the constitution of the United States has provided no tribunal for the final construction of itself, or of the laws or treaties of the nation; but that this power may be exercised in the last resort by the courts of every state of the Union. That the constitution, laws and treaties may receive as many constructions as there are states; and that this is not a mischief, or, if a mischief is irremediable. . . .

1st. The first question to be considered is, whether the jurisdiction of this court is excluded by the character of the parties, one of them being a state, and the other a citizen of that state? . . .

The American states, as well as the American people . . . have been taught by experience, that this Union cannot exist without a government for the whole; and they have been taught by the same experience that this government would be a mere shadow, that must disappoint all their hopes, unless invested with large portions of that sovereignty which belongs to independent states. Under the influence of this opinion, and thus instructed by experience, the American people, in the conventions of their respective states, adopted the present constitution.

If it could be doubted whether, from its nature, it were not supreme in all cases where it is empowered to act, that doubt would be removed by the declaration that "this constitution, and the laws of the United States which shall be made in pursuance thereof and all treaties made, or which shall be made, under the authority of the United States, shall be the supreme law of the land; and the judges in every state shall be bound thereby, anything in the constitution or laws of any state to the contrary notwithstanding."

This is the authoritative language of the American people; and, if gentlemen please, of the American states. It marks with lines too strong to be mistaken, the characteristic distinction between the government of the Union and those of the states. The general government, though limited as to its objects, is supreme with respect to those objects. This principle is a part of the constitution; and if there be any who deny its necessity, none can deny its authority.

To this supreme government ample powers are confided; and if it were possible to doubt the great purposes for which they were so confided, the people of the United States have declared that they are given "in order to form a more perfect union, establish justice, insure domestic tranquility, provide for the common defense, promote the general welfare, and secure the blessings of liberty to themselves and their posterity."

With the ample powers confided to this supreme government, for these interesting purposes, are connected many express and important limitations on the sovereignty of the states, which are made for the same purposes. The powers of the Union on the great subjects of war, peace, and commerce, and on many others, are in themselves limitations of the sovereignty of the states; but in addition to these, the sovereignty of the states is surrendered in many instances where the surrender can only operate to the benefit of the people, and where, perhaps, no other power is conferred on congress than a conservative power to maintain the principles established in the constitution. The maintenance of these principles in their purity is certainly among the great duties of the government. One of the instruments by which this duty may be peaceably performed is the judicial department. It is authorized to decide all cases, of every description, arising under the constitution or laws of the United States. From this general grant of jurisdiction, no exception is made of those cases in which a state may be a party. When we consider the situation of the government of the Union and of a state, in relation to each other; the nature of our constitution; the subordination of the state governments to that constitution; the great purpose for which jurisdiction over all cases arising under the constitution and laws of the United States, is confided to the judicial department; are we at liberty to insert in this general grant, an exception of those cases in which a state may be a party? Will the spirit of the constitution justify this attempt to control its words? We think it will not. We think a case arising under the constitution or laws of the United States, is cognizable in the courts of the Union, whoever may be the parties of that case. . . .

One of the express objects, then, for which the judicial department was established, is the decision of controversies between states, and between a state and individuals. The mere circumstance, that a state is a party, gives jurisdiction to the court. How, then, can it be contended, that the very same instrument, in the very same section, should be so construed, as that this same circumstance should withdraw a case from the jurisdiction of the court, where the constitution or laws of the United States are supposed to have been violated? . . .

The mischievous consequences of the construction contended for on the part of Virginia, are also entitled to great consideration. It would prostrate, it has been said, the government and its laws at the feet of every state in the Union. And would not this be its effect? What power of the government could be executed by its own means, in any state disposed to resist its execution by a course of legislation? The laws must be executed by individuals acting within the several states. If these individuals may be exposed to penalties, and if the courts of the Union cannot correct the judgments by which these penalties may be enforced, the course of the government may be . . . arrested by the will of one of its members. Each member will possess a veto on the will of the whole. . . .

These collisions may take place in times of no extraordinary commotion. But a constitution is framed for ages to come, and is designed to approach immortality as nearly as human institutions can approach it. Its course cannot always be tranquil. It is exposed to storms and tempests, and its framers must be unwise statesmen indeed, if they have not provided it, as far as its nature will permit, with the means of self-preservation from the perils it may be destined to encounter. No government ought to be so defective in its organization, as not to contain within itself the means of securing the execution of its own laws against other dangers than those which occur every day. Courts of justice are the means most usually employed; and it is reasonable to expect that a government should repose on its own courts, rather than on others. There is certainly nothing in the circumstances under which our constitution was formed; nothing in the history of the times, which would justify the opinion that the confidence reposed in the states was so implicit as to leave in them and their tribunals the power of resisting or defeating, in the form of law, the legitimate measures of the Union. . .

If jurisdiction depended entirely on the character of the parties, and was not given where the parties have not an original right to come into court, that part of the 2d section of the 3d article, which extends the judicial power to all cases arising under the constitution and laws of the United States, would be surplusage. It is to give jurisdiction where the character of the parties would not give it, that this very important part of the clause was inserted. . . .

It is most true, that this court will not take jurisdiction if it should not; but it is equally true, that it must take jurisdiction, if it should.

The judiciary cannot, as the legislature may, avoid a measure, because it approaches the confines of the constitution. We cannot pass it by, because it is doubtful. With whatever doubts, with whatever difficulties, a case may be attended, we must decide it, if it be brought before us. We have no more right to decline the exercise of jurisdiction which is given, than to usurp that which is not given. The one or the other would be treason to the constitution. Questions may occur, which we would gladly avoid; but we cannot avoid them. All we can do is, to exercise our best judgment, and conscientiously to perform our duty. In doing this, on the present occasion, we find this tribunal invested with appellate jurisdiction in all cases arising under the constitution and laws of the United States. We find no exception to this grant, and we cannot insert one. . . .

This leads to a consideration of the 11th amendment. It is in these words: "The judicial power of the United States shall not be construed to extend to any suit in law or equity commenced or prosecuted against one of the United States, by citizens of another state, or by citizens or subjects of any foreign state." It is a part of our history, that, at the adoption of the constitution, all the states were greatly indebted; and the apprehension that these debts might be prosecuted in the federal courts, formed a very serious objection to that instrument. Suits were instituted; and the court maintained its jurisdiction. The alarm was general; and, to quiet the apprehensions that were so extensively entertained, this amendment was proposed in Congress, and adopted by the state legislatures. That its motive was not to maintain the sovereignty of a state from the degradation supposed to attend a compulsory appearance before the tribunal of the nation, may be inferred from the terms of the amendment. It does not comprehend controversies between two or more states, or between a state and a foreign state. The jurisdiction of the court still extends to these cases; and in these a state may still be sued. We must ascribe the amendment, then, to some other cause than the dignity of a state. There is no difficulty in finding this cause. Those who were inhibited from commencing a suit against a state, or from prosecuting one which might be commenced before the adoption of the amendment, were persons who might probably be its creditors. There was not much reason to fear that foreign or sister states would be creditors to any considerable amount, and there was reason to retain the jurisdiction of the court in those cases, because it might be essential to the preservation of peace. The amendment, therefore, extended to suits commenced or prosecuted by individuals, but not to those brought by states. . . .

Under the Judiciary Act, the effect of a writ of error is simply to bring the record into court, and submit the judgment of the inferior tribunal to reexamination. It does not in any manner act upon the parties; it acts only on the record. It removes the record into the supervising tribunal. Where, then, a state obtains a judgment against an individual, and the court rendering such judgment overrules a defense set up under the constitution or laws of the United States, the transfer of this record into the supreme court for the sole purpose of inquiring whether the judgment violates the constitution of the United States, can, with no propriety, we think, be denominated a suit commenced or prosecuted against the state whose judgment is so far reexamined. Nothing is demanded from the state. No claim against it of any description is asserted or prosecuted. The party is not to be restored to the possession of anything. Essentially, it is an appeal on a single point; and the defendant who appeals from a judgment rendered against him, is never said to commence or prosecute a suit against the plaintiff who has obtained the judgment. . . .

It is, then, the opinion of the court, that the defendant who removes a judgment rendered against him by a state court into this court, for the purpose of reexamining the question, whether that judgment be in violation of the constitution or laws of the United States, does not commence or prosecute a suit against the state. . . .

2d. The second objection to the jurisdiction of the court is, that its appellate power cannot be exercised, in any case, over the judgment of a state court. . . .

America has chosen to be, in many respects, and to many purposes, a nation; and for all these purposes, her government is complete; to all these objects it is competent. The people have declared, that in the exercise of all powers given for these objects, it is supreme. It can, then, in effecting these objects, legitimately control all individuals or governments within the American territory. The constitution and laws of a state, so far as they are repugnant to the constitution and laws of the United States, are absolutely void. These states are constituent parts of the United States; they are members of one great empire—for some purposes sovereign, for some purposes subordinate.

In a government so constituted, is it unreasonable, that the judicial power should be competent to give efficacy to the constitutional laws of the legislature? That department can decide on the validity of the constitution or law of a state, if it be repugnant to the constitution or to a law of the United States. Is it unreasonable, that it should also be empowered to decide on the judgment of a state tribunal enforcing such unconstitutional law? . . .

The propriety of entrusting the construction of the constitution, and laws made in pursuance thereof, to the judiciary of the Union has not, we believe, as yet, been drawn into question. It seems to be a corollary from this political axiom, that the federal courts should either possess exclusive jurisdiction in such cases, or a power to revise the judgment rendered in them, by the state tribunals. If the federal and state courts have concurrent jurisdiction in all cases arising under the constitution, laws, and treaties of the United States; and if a case of this description brought in a state court cannot be removed before judgment, nor revised after judgment, then the construction of the constitution, laws, and treaties of the United States is not confided particularly to their judicial department, but is confided equally to that department and to the state courts, however they may be constituted. "Thirteen independent courts," says a very celebrated statesman (and we have now more than twenty such courts), "of final jurisdiction over the same causes, arising upon the same laws, is a hydra in government, from which nothing but contradiction and confusion can proceed."

Dismissing the unpleasant suggestion, that any motives which may not be fairly avowed, or which ought not to exist, can ever influence a state or its courts, the necessity of uniformity, as well as correctness in expounding the constitution and laws of the United States, would itself suggest the propriety of vesting in some single tribunal the power of deciding, in the last resort, all cases in which they are involved.

. . . [T]he words of the constitution . . . give to the supreme court appellate jurisdiction in all cases arising under the constitution, laws, and treaties of the United States. The words are broad enough to comprehend all cases of this description, in whatever court they may be decided. . . .

Let the nature and objects of our Union be considered; let the great fundamental principles, on which the fabric stands, be examined; and we think, the result must be, that there is nothing so extravagantly absurd, in giving to the court of the nation the power of revising the decisions of local tribunals, on questions which affect the nation, as to require the words which import this power should be restricted by a forced construction. . . .

[On the merits of the case, the Supreme Court upheld the convictions, declaring that the federal lottery law afforded no immunity to prosecution outside the District of Columbia.—ED.]

Judgment affirmed.

Collector v. *Day*
78 U.S. (11 Wall.) 113, 20 L.Ed. 122 (1871)

http://caselaw.findlaw.com/us-supreme-court/78/113.html

Various statutes passed by Congress in 1864 imposed a 5 percent tax on all personal incomes over $1,000. J.M. Day, a county probate judge in Massachusetts, paid the tax under protest and then sued in the Circuit Court to recover the amount paid. From a judgment for Day, the United States sought review by a writ of error. Even though the decision reprinted below was overruled by *Graves* v. *New York* (1939), it is included here because Justice Nelson's opinion represents a succinct statement of the doctrine of dual federalism. Majority: Nelson, Chase, Clifford, Davis, Field, Miller, Strong, Swayne. Dissenting: Bradley.

Mr. Justice Nelson delivered the opinion of the court.

The case presents the question whether or not it is competent for Congress, under the Constitution of the United States, to impose a tax upon the salary of a judicial officer of a State? . . .

It is conceded in . . . *McCulloch* v. *Maryland*, that the power of taxation by the States was not abridged by the grant of a similar power to the government of the Union; that it was retained by the States, and that the power is to be concurrently exercised by the two governments; and also that there is no express constitutional prohibition upon the States against taxing the means or instrumentalities of the general government. But, it was held, and, we agree properly held, to be prohibited by necessary implication; otherwise, the States might impose taxation to an extent that would impair, if not wholly defeat, the operations of the Federal authorities when acting in their appropriate sphere. . . . And we shall now proceed to show that, upon the same construction of that instrument, . . . [the general] government is prohibited from taxing the salary of the judicial officer of a State.

It is a familiar rule of construction of the Constitution of the Union, that the sovereign powers vested in the State governments by their respective constitutions, remained unaltered and unimpaired, except so far as they were granted to the government of the United States. . . . The government of the United States, therefore, can claim no powers which are not granted to it by the Constitution, and the powers actually granted must be such as are expressly given, or given by necessary implication.

The general government, and the States, although both exist within the same territorial limits, are separate and distinct sovereignties, acting separately and independently of each other, within their respective spheres. The former in its appropriate sphere is supreme; but the States within the limits of their powers not granted, or, in the language of the tenth amendment, "reserved," are as independent of the general government as that government within its sphere is independent of the States. . . . The Constitution guarantees to the States a republican form of government, and protects each against invasion or domestic violence. . . . [I]t would seem to follow, as a reasonable, if not a necessary consequence, that the means and instrumentalities employed for carrying on the operations of their governments, for preserving their existence, and fulfilling the high and responsible duties assigned to them in the Constitution, should be left free and unimpaired, should not be liable to be crippled, much less defeated by the taxing power of another government, which power acknowledges no limits but the will of the legislative body imposing the tax. And, more especially, those means and instrumentalities which are the creation of their sovereign and reserved rights, one of which is the establishment of the judicial department, and the appointment of officers to administer their laws. Without this power, and the exercise of it, we risk nothing in saying that no one of the States under the form of government guaranteed by the Constitution could long preserve its existence. . . .

The supremacy of the general government, therefore, . . . cannot be maintained. The two governments are upon an equality, and the question is whether the power "to lay and collect taxes" enables the general government to tax the salary of a judicial officer of the State, which officer is a means or instrumentality employed to carry into execution one of its most important functions, the administration of the laws, and which concerns the exercise of a right reserved to the States? . . .

[I]n respect to the reserved powers, the State is as sovereign and independent as the general government. And if the means and instrumentalities employed by that government to carry into operation the powers granted to it are, necessarily, and, for the sake of self-preservation, exempt from taxation by the States, why are not those of the States depending upon their reserved powers, for like reasons, equally exempt from Federal taxation? Their unimpaired existence in the one case is as essential as in the other. It is admitted that there is no express provision in the Constitution that prohibits the general government from taxing the means and instrumentalities of the States, nor is there any prohibiting the States from taxing the means and instrumentalities of that government. In both cases the exemption rests upon necessary implication, and is upheld by the great law of self-preservation; as any government, whose means employed in conducting its operations, if subject to the control of another and distinct government, can exist only at the mercy of that government.

Judgment affirmed.

MR. JUSTICE BRADLEY, dissenting . . . [omitted].

II. NATIONAL SUPREMACY V. DUAL FEDERALISM IN THE MODERN ERA

U.S. Term Limits, Inc. v. *Thornton*
514 U.S. 779, 115 S.Ct. 1842, 131 L.Ed. 2d 881 (1995)

http://caselaw.findlaw.com/us-supreme-court/514/779.html

Joining 21 other states, voters in Arkansas in 1992 amended the state constitution to impose term limits on their legislators. Section 3 of Amendment 73 prohibited the name of an otherwise eligible candidate from appearing on the general election ballot: (1) for the U.S. House of Representatives if the candidate had been elected to the House to three or more terms; and (2) for the U.S. Senate if the candidate had been elected to the Senate to two or more terms. Two legal challenges to the amendment emerged. One involved a national advocacy group and Ray Thornton (by 1995 a six-term member of the U.S. House of Representatives from Arkansas); the other involved Bobbie Hill (past president of the League of Women Voters of Arkansas, on behalf of herself and other voters) and Arkansas attorney general Winston Bryant. In both cases, the state supreme court held that Section 3 violated Article I of the U.S. Constitution. Docketed first at the U.S. Supreme Court, Thornton's case became the name by which this landmark decision is known. While states remain free to impose term limits on state officials, and while candidates and officials at any level of government may informally "term-limit" themselves, the Supreme Court's decision soon squelched the movement to impose term limits on national legislators. The excerpts that follow are greatly compressed; Justice Thomas's dissent alone reached 88 pages. Majority: Stevens, Breyer, Ginsburg, Kennedy, Souter. Dissenting: Thomas, O'Connor, Rehnquist, Scalia.

Justice Stevens delivered the opinion of the Court. . . .

Today's cases present a challenge to an amendment to the Arkansas State Constitution that prohibits the name of an otherwise-eligible candidate for Congress from appearing on the general election ballot if that candidate has already served three terms in the House of Representatives or two terms in the Senate. The Arkansas Supreme Court held that the amendment violates the Federal Constitution. We agree with that holding. Such a state-imposed restriction is contrary to the "fundamental principle of our representative democracy," embodied in the Constitution, that "the people should choose whom they please to govern them." Allowing individual States to adopt their own qualifications for congressional service would be inconsistent with the Framers' vision of a uniform National Legislature representing the people of the United States. If the qualifications set forth in the text of the Constitution are to be changed, that text must be amended. . . .

[T]he constitutionality of Amendment 73 depends critically on the resolution of two distinct issues. The first is whether the Constitution forbids States from adding to or altering the qualifications specifically enumerated in the Constitution. The second is, if the Constitution does so forbid, whether the fact that Amendment 73 is formulated as a ballot access restriction rather than as an outright disqualification is of constitutional significance. Our resolution of these issues draws upon our prior resolution of a related but distinct issue: whether Congress has the power to add to or alter the qualifications of its Members.

Twenty-six years ago, in *Powell* v. *McCormack* (1969), we reviewed the history and text of the Qualifications Clauses in a case involving an attempted exclusion of a duly elected Member of Congress. The principal issue was whether the power granted to each House in Art. I, § 5, to judge the "Qualifications of its own Members" includes the power to impose qualifications other than those set forth in the text of the Constitution. In an opinion by Chief Justice Warren for eight Members of the Court, we held that it does not. . . . [The Court reviews *Powell* at length and reaffirms its holding.]

Petitioners argue that the Constitution contains no express prohibition against state-added qualifications, and that Amendment 73 is therefore an appropriate exercise of a State's reserved power to place additional restrictions on the choices that its own voters may make. We disagree for two independent reasons. First, we conclude that the power to add qualifications is not within the "original powers" of the States, and thus is not reserved to the States by the Tenth Amendment. Second, even if States possessed some original power in this area, we conclude that the Framers intended the Constitution to be the exclusive source of qualifications for members of Congress, and that the Framers thereby "divested" States of any power to add qualifications. . . .

Contrary to petitioners' assertions, the power to add qualifications is not part of the original powers of sovereignty that the Tenth Amendment reserved to the States. Petitioners' Tenth Amendment argument misconceives the nature of the right at issue because that Amendment could only "reserve" that which existed before. . . .

With respect to setting qualifications for service in Congress, no such right existed before the Constitution was ratified. The contrary argument overlooks the revolutionary character of the government that the Framers conceived. Prior to the adoption of the Constitution, the States had joined together under the Articles of Confederation. In that system, "the States retained most of their sovereignty, like independent nations bound together only by treaties." After the Constitutional Convention convened, the Framers were presented with, and eventually adopted a variation of, "a plan not merely to amend the Articles of Confederation but to create an entirely new National Government with a National Executive, National Judiciary, and a National Legislature." In adopting that plan, the Framers envisioned a uniform national system, rejecting the notion that the Nation was a collection of States, and instead creating a direct link between the National Government and the people of the United States. . . . In that National Government, representatives owe primary allegiance not to the people of a State, but to the people of the Nation. . . .

In short, as the Framers recognized, electing representatives to the National Legislature was a new right, arising from the Constitution itself. The Tenth Amendment thus provides no basis for concluding that the States possess reserved power to add qualifications to those that are fixed in the Constitution. Instead, any state power to set the qualifications for membership in Congress must derive not from the reserved powers of state sovereignty, but rather from the delegated powers of national sovereignty. In the absence of any constitutional delegation to the States of power to add qualifications to those enumerated in the Constitution, such a power does not exist.

Even if we believed that States possessed as part of their original powers some control over congressional qualifications, the text and structure of the Constitution, the relevant historical materials, and, most importantly, the "basic principles of our democratic system" all demonstrate that the Qualifications Clauses were intended to preclude the States from exercising any such power and to fix as exclusive the qualifications in the Constitution. . . .

[S]tate-imposed restrictions, unlike the congressionally imposed restrictions at issue in *Powell*, violate a . . . basic principle: that the right to choose representatives belongs not to the States, but to the people. . . . Thus the Framers, in perhaps their most important contribution, conceived of a Federal Government directly responsible to the people, possessed of direct power over the people, and chosen directly, not by States, but by the people. The Framers implemented this ideal most clearly in the provision, extant from the beginning of the Republic, that calls for the Members of the House of Representatives to be "chosen every second Year by the People of the several States." Following the adoption of the 17th Amendment in 1913, this ideal was extended to elections for the Senate. The Congress of the United States, therefore, is not a confederation of nations in which separate sovereigns are represented by appointed delegates, but is instead a body composed of representatives of the people. . . .

The merits of term limits, or "rotation," have been the subject of debate since the formation of our Constitution, when the Framers unanimously rejected a proposal to add such limits to the Constitution. . . . It is not our province to resolve this longstanding debate.

We are, however, firmly convinced that allowing the several States to adopt term limits for congressional service would effect a fundamental change in the constitutional framework. Any such change must come not by legislation adopted either by Congress or by an individual State, but rather—as have other important changes in the electoral process—through the Amendment procedures set forth in Article V. . . .

The judgment is affirmed.

JUSTICE KENNEDY, concurring . . . [omitted].

Justice Thomas, with whom The Chief Justice, Justice O'Connor, and Justice Scalia join, dissenting.

It is ironic that the Court bases today's decision on the right of the people to "choose whom they please to govern them." Under our Constitution, there is only one State whose people have the right to "choose whom they please" to represent Arkansas in Congress. The Court holds, however, that neither the elected legislature of that State nor the people themselves (acting by ballot initiative) may prescribe any qualifications for those representatives. The majority therefore defends the right of the people of Arkansas to "choose whom they please to govern them" by invalidating a provision that won nearly 60 percent of the votes cast in a direct election and that carried every congressional district in the State.

I dissent. Nothing in the Constitution deprives the people of each State of the power to prescribe eligibility requirements for the candidates who seek to represent them in Congress. The Constitution is simply silent on this question. And where the Constitution is silent, it raises no bar to action by the States or the people.

Because the majority fundamentally misunderstands the notion of "reserved" powers, I start with some first principles. Contrary to the majority's suggestion, the people of the States need not point to any affirmative grant of power in the Constitution in order to prescribe qualifications for their representatives in Congress, or to authorize their elected state legislators to do so.

Our system of government rests on one overriding principle: all power stems from the consent of the people. To phrase the principle in this way, however, is to be imprecise about something important to the notion of "reserved" powers. The ultimate source of the Constitution's authority is the consent of the people of each individual State, not the consent of the undifferentiated people of the Nation as a whole. . . .

When they adopted the Federal Constitution, of course, the people of each State surrendered some of their authority to the United States (and hence to entities accountable to the people of other States as well as to themselves). They affirmatively deprived their States of certain powers, and they affirmatively conferred certain powers upon the Federal Government. Because the people of the several States are the only true source of power, however, the Federal Government enjoys no authority beyond what the Constitution confers: the Federal Government's powers are limited and enumerated. . . .

In each State, the remainder of the people's powers . . . are either delegated to the state government or retained by the people. The Federal Constitution does not specify which of these two possibilities obtains; it is up to the various state constitutions to declare which powers the people of each State have delegated to their state government. As far as the Federal Constitution is concerned, then, the States can exercise all powers that the Constitution does not withhold from them. The Federal Government and the States thus face different default rules: where the Constitution is silent about the exercise of a particular power—that is, where the Constitution does not speak either expressly or by necessary implication—the Federal Government lacks that power and the States enjoy it.

These basic principles are enshrined in the Tenth Amendment, which declares that all powers neither delegated to the Federal Government nor prohibited to the States "are reserved to the States respectively, or to the people." With this careful last phrase, the Amendment avoids taking any position on the division of power between the state governments and the people of the States: it is up to the people of each State to determine which "reserved" powers their state government may exercise. But the Amendment does make clear that powers reside at the state level except where the Constitution removes them from that level. All powers that the Constitution neither delegates to the Federal Government nor prohibits to the States are controlled by the people of each State. . . .

The majority's essential logic is that the state governments could not "reserve" any powers that they did not control at the time the Constitution was drafted. But it was not the state governments that were doing the reserving. The Constitution derives its authority instead from the consent of the people of the States. Given the fundamental principle that all governmental powers stem from the people of the States, it would simply be incoherent to assert that the people of the States could not reserve any powers that they had not previously controlled.

The Tenth Amendment's use of the word "reserved" does not help the majority's position. If someone says that the power to use a particular facility is reserved to some group, he is not saying anything about whether that group has previously used the facility. He is merely saying that the people who control the facility have designated that group as the entity with authority to use it. The Tenth Amendment is similar: the people of the States, from whom all governmental powers stem, have specified that all powers not prohibited to the States by the Federal Constitution are reserved "to the States respectively, or to the people." . . .

It is radical enough for the majority to hold that the Constitution implicitly precludes the people of the States from prescribing any eligibility requirements for the congressional candidates who seek their votes. This holding, after all, does not stop with negating the term limits that many States have seen fit to impose on their Senators and Representatives. Today's decision also means that no State may disqualify congressional candidates whom a court has found to be mentally incompetent, who are currently in prison, or who have past vote-fraud convictions. Likewise, after today's decision, the people of each State must leave open the possibility that they will trust someone with their vote in Congress even though they do not trust him with a vote in the election for Congress. . . .

United States v. *Morrison*
529 U.S. 598, 120 S.Ct. 1740, 146 L.Ed. 2d 658 (2000)

http://caselaw.findlaw.com/us-supreme-court/529/598.html

Christy Brzonkala enrolled at Virginia Tech in the fall of 1994 where she met respondents Antonio Morrison and James Crawford, who were also students and members of the varsity football team. In a complaint filed under Virginia Tech's sexual assault policy, Brzonkala alleged that, within 30 minutes of meeting Morrison and Crawford, they assaulted and repeatedly raped her. After a complex series of proceedings on campus failed to result in punishment for Morrison and Crawford, and after learning from a newspaper that Morrison would be returning to campus in the fall of 1995, Brzonkala withdrew from school and filed suit under 42 U.S.C. § 13981 (*Brzonkala* v. *Morrison*). This provision of the Violence Against Women Act of 1994 provided a federal civil remedy for victims of gender-motivated violence, including situations where alleged acts did not result in criminal charges, prosecution, or conviction. The United States District Court for the Western District of Virginia held that Congress lacked authority to enact § 13981 under either the commerce clause or Section 5 of the Fourteenth Amendment. A divided panel of the Court of Appeals for the Fourth Circuit reversed the District Court, but on rehearing en banc, a majority of the appeals court upheld the district court. Majority: Rehnquist, O'Connor, Scalia, Kennedy, Thomas. Dissenting: Souter, Stevens, Ginsburg, Breyer.

CHIEF JUSTICE REHNQUIST delivered the opinion of the Court. . . .

Section 13981 was part of the Violence Against Women Act of 1994. It states that "[a]ll persons within the United States shall have the right to be free from crimes of violence motivated by gender." To enforce that right, subsection (c) declares: "A person . . . who commits a crime of violence motivated by gender and thus deprives another of the right declared in subsection (b) of this section shall be liable to the party injured, in an action for the recovery of compensatory and punitive damages, injunctive and declaratory relief, and such other relief as a court may deem appropriate."

Congress explicitly identified the sources of federal authority on which it relied in enacting § 13981. It said that a "federal civil rights cause of action" is established "[p]ursuant to the affirmative power of Congress . . . under section 5 of the Fourteenth Amendment to the Constitution, as well as under section 8 of Article I of the Constitution." We address Congress' authority to enact this remedy under each of these constitutional provisions in turn. . . .

As we observed in [*United States* v.] *Lopez*, modern Commerce Clause jurisprudence has "identified three broad categories of activity that Congress may regulate under its commerce power." "First, Congress may regulate the use of the channels of interstate commerce." "Second, Congress is empowered to regulate and protect the instrumentalities of interstate commerce, or persons or things in interstate commerce, even though the threat may come only from intrastate activities." "Finally, Congress' commerce authority includes the power to regulate those activities having a substantial relation to interstate commerce, . . . i.e., those activities that substantially affect interstate commerce."

Petitioners do not contend that these cases fall within either of the first two of these categories of Commerce Clause regulation. They seek to sustain § 13981 as a regulation of activity that substantially affects interstate commerce. . . .

Since *Lopez* most recently canvassed and clarified our case law governing this third category of Commerce Clause regulation, it provides the proper framework for conducting the required analysis of § 13981. In *Lopez*, we held that the Gun-Free School Zones Act of 1990, § 922(q), which made it a federal crime to knowingly possess a firearm in a school zone, exceeded Congress' authority under the Commerce Clause. Several significant considerations contributed to our decision.

First, we observed that § 922(q) was "a criminal statute that by its terms has nothing to do with 'commerce' or any sort of economic enterprise, however broadly one might define those terms." . . . [A] fair reading of *Lopez* shows that the noneconomic, criminal nature of the conduct at issue was central to our decision in that case. . . .

The second consideration that we found important in analyzing § 922(q) was that the statute contained "no express jurisdictional element which might limit its reach to a discrete set of firearm possessions that additionally have an explicit connection with or effect on interstate commerce." . . .

Third, we noted that neither § 922(q) "nor its legislative history contain[s] express congressional findings regarding the effects upon interstate commerce of gun possession in a school zone." . . .

Finally, our decision in *Lopez* rested in part on the fact that the link between gun possession and a substantial effect on interstate commerce was attenuated. . . .

With these principles underlying our Commerce Clause jurisprudence as reference points, the proper resolution of the present cases is clear. Gender-motivated crimes of violence are not, in any sense of the phrase, economic activity. While we need not adopt a categorical rule against aggregating the effects of any noneconomic activity in order to decide these cases, thus far in our Nation's history our cases have upheld Commerce Clause regulation of intrastate activity only where that activity is economic in nature.

Like the Gun-Free School Zones Act at issue in *Lopez*, § 13981 contains no jurisdictional element establishing that the federal cause of action is in pursuance of Congress' power to regulate interstate commerce. . . .

In contrast with the lack of congressional findings that we faced in *Lopez*, § 13981 is supported by numerous findings regarding the serious impact that gender-motivated violence has on victims and their families. But the existence of congressional findings is not sufficient, by itself, to sustain the constitutionality of Commerce Clause legislation. . . .

Congress found that gender-motivated violence affects interstate commerce "by deterring potential victims from traveling interstate, from engaging in employment in interstate business, and from transacting with business, and in places involved in interstate commerce; . . . by diminishing national productivity, increasing medical and other costs, and decreasing the supply of and the demand for interstate products." Given these findings and petitioners' arguments, the concern that we expressed in *Lopez* that Congress might use the Commerce Clause to completely obliterate the Constitution's distinction between national and local authority seems well founded. The reasoning that petitioners advance seeks to follow the but-for causal chain from the initial occurrence of violent crime (the suppression of which has always been the prime object of the States' police power) to every attenuated effect upon interstate commerce. If accepted, petitioners' reasoning would allow Congress to regulate any crime as long as the nationwide, aggregated impact of that crime has substantial effects on employment, production, transit, or consumption. . . .

Petitioners' reasoning, moreover, will not limit Congress to regulating violence but may, as we suggested in *Lopez*, be applied equally as well to family law and other areas of traditional state regulation since the aggregate effect of marriage, divorce, and childrearing on the national economy is undoubtedly significant. Congress may have recognized this specter when it expressly precluded § 13981 from being used in the family law context. . . .

We accordingly reject the argument that Congress may regulate noneconomic, violent criminal conduct based solely on that conduct's aggregate effect on interstate commerce. The Constitution requires a distinction between what is truly national and what is truly local. . . .

Because we conclude that the Commerce Clause does not provide Congress with authority to enact § 13981, we address petitioners' alternative argument that the section's civil remedy should be upheld as an exercise of Congress' remedial power under § 5 of the Fourteenth Amendment. . . .

The principles governing an analysis of congressional legislation under § 5 are well settled. Section 5 states that Congress may "'enforce,' by 'appropriate legislation' the constitutional guarantee that no State shall deprive any person of 'life, liberty or property, without due process of law,' nor deny any person 'equal protection of the laws.'" Section 5 is "a positive grant of legislative power" that includes authority to "prohibit conduct which is not itself unconstitutional and [to] intrud[e] into 'legislative spheres of autonomy previously reserved to the States.'" . . .

Petitioners' § 5 argument is founded on an assertion that there is pervasive bias in various state justice systems against victims of gender-motivated violence. This assertion is supported by a voluminous congressional record. Specifically, Congress received evidence that many participants in state justice systems are perpetuating an array of erroneous stereotypes and assumptions. . . . Petitioners contend that this bias denies victims of gender-motivated violence the equal protection of the laws and that Congress therefore acted appropriately in enacting a private civil remedy against the perpetrators of gender-motivated violence to both remedy the States' bias and deter future instances of discrimination in the state courts. . . .

However, the language and purpose of the Fourteenth Amendment place certain limitations on the manner in which Congress may attack discriminatory conduct. These limitations are necessary to prevent the Fourteenth Amendment from obliterating the Framers' carefully crafted balance of power between the States and the National Government. . . . Foremost among these limitations is the time-honored principle that the Fourteenth Amendment, by its very terms, prohibits only state action. . . .

[P]rophylactic legislation under § 5 must have a "congruence and proportionality between the injury to be prevented or remedied and the means adopted to that end." Section 13981 is not aimed at proscribing discrimination by officials which the Fourteenth Amendment might not itself proscribe; it is directed not at any State or state actor, but at individuals who have committed criminal acts motivated by gender bias. . . .

For these reasons, we conclude that Congress' power under § 5 does not extend to the enactment of § 13981.

Petitioner Brzonkala's complaint alleges that she was the victim of a brutal assault. But Congress' effort in § 13981 to provide a federal civil remedy can be sustained neither under the Commerce Clause nor under § 5 of the Fourteenth Amendment. If the allegations here are true, no civilized system of justice could fail to provide her a remedy for the conduct of respondent Morrison. But under our federal system that remedy must be provided by the Commonwealth of Virginia, and not by the United States. The judgment of the Court of Appeals is

Affirmed.

JUSTICE THOMAS, concurring . . . [omitted].

JUSTICE SOUTER, with whom JUSTICES STEVENS, Ginsburg, AND BREYER, join, dissenting. . . .

The business of the courts is to review the congressional assessment, not for soundness but simply for the rationality of concluding that a jurisdictional basis exists in fact. Any explicit findings that Congress chooses to make, though not dispositive of the question of rationality, may advance judicial review by identifying factual authority on which Congress relied. Applying those propositions in these cases can lead to only one conclusion.

One obvious difference from *Lopez* is the mountain of data assembled by Congress, here showing the effects of violence against women on interstate commerce. Passage of the Act in 1994 was preceded by four years of hearings, which included testimony from physicians and law professors; from survivors of rape and domestic violence; and from representatives of state law enforcement and private business. The record includes reports on gender bias from task forces in 21 States, and we have the benefit of specific factual findings in the eight separate Reports issued by Congress and its committees over the long course leading to enactment. . . .

Congress found that "crimes of violence motivated by gender have a substantial adverse effect on interstate commerce, by deterring potential victims from traveling interstate, from engaging in employment in interstate business, and from transacting with business, and in places involved, in interstate commerce . . . [,] by diminishing national productivity, increasing medical and other costs, and decreasing the supply of and the demand for interstate products. . . ." [T]he sufficiency of the evidence before Congress to provide a rational basis for the finding cannot seriously be questioned. . . .

The fact that the Act does not pass muster before the Court today is therefore proof, to a degree that *Lopez* was not, that the Court's nominal adherence to the substantial effects test is merely that. Although a new jurisprudence has not emerged with any distinctness, it is clear that some congressional conclusions about obviously substantial, cumulative effects on commerce are being assigned lesser values than the once-stable doctrine would assign them. . . .

Thus the elusive heart of the majority's analysis in these cases is its statement that Congress' findings of fact are "weakened" by the presence of a disfavored "method of reasoning." This seems to suggest that the "substantial effects" analysis is not a factual enquiry, for Congress in the first instance with subsequent judicial review looking only to the rationality of the congressional conclusion, but one of a rather different sort, dependent upon a uniquely judicial competence.

This new characterization of substantial effects has no support in our cases (the self-fulfilling prophecies of *Lopez* aside), least of all those the majority cites. Perhaps this explains why the majority is not content to rest on its cited precedent but claims a textual justification for moving toward its new system of congressional deference subject to selective discounts. Thus it purports to rely on the sensible and traditional understanding that the listing in the Constitution of some powers implies the exclusion of others unmentioned. . . . It follows, for the majority, not only that there must be some limits to "commerce," but that some particular subjects arguably within the commerce power can be identified in advance as excluded, on the basis of characteristics other than their commercial effects. Such exclusions come into sight when the activity regulated is not itself commercial or when the States have traditionally addressed it in the exercise of the general police power, conferred under the state constitutions but never extended to Congress under the Constitution of the Nation.

The premise that the enumeration of powers implies that other powers are withheld is sound; the conclusion that some particular categories of subject matter are therefore presumptively beyond the reach of the commerce power is, however, a non sequitur. . . .

[F]or significant periods of our history, the Court has defined the commerce power as plenary, unsusceptible to categorical exclusions, and this was the view expressed throughout the latter part of the 20th century in the substantial effects test. These two conceptions of the commerce power, plenary and categorically limited, are in fact old rivals, and today's revival of their competition summons up familiar history. . . . Founders' considered judgment that politics, not judicial review, should mediate between state and national interests as the strength and legislative jurisdiction of the National Government inevitably increased through the expected growth of the national economy. Whereas today's majority takes a leaf from the book of the old judicial economists in saying that the Court should somehow draw the line to keep the federal relationship in a proper balance, Madison, Wilson, and Marshall understood the Constitution very differently. . . .

Since adherence to these formalistically contrived confines of commerce power in large measure provoked the judicial crisis of 1937, one might reasonably have doubted that Members of this Court would ever again toy with a return to the days before *NLRB* v. *Jones & Laughlin Steel Corp.*, which brought the earlier and nearly disastrous experiment to an end. And yet today's decision can only be seen as a step toward recapturing the prior mistakes. . . .

Amendments that alter the balance of power between the National and State Governments, like the Fourteenth, or that change the way the States are represented within the Federal Government, like the Seventeenth, are not rips in the fabric of the Framers' Constitution, inviting judicial repairs. The Seventeenth Amendment may indeed have lessened the enthusiasm of the Senate to represent the States as discrete sovereignties, but the Amendment did not convert the judiciary into an alternate shield against the commerce power. . . .

Why is the majority tempted to reject the lesson so painfully learned in 1937? . . .

[T]he answer is not that the majority fails to see causal connections in an integrated economic world. The answer is that in the minds of the majority there is a new animating theory that makes categorical formalism seem useful again. Just as the old formalism had value in the service of an economic conception, the new one is useful in serving a conception of federalism. It is the instrument by which assertions of national power are to be limited in favor of preserving a supposedly discernible, proper sphere of state autonomy to legislate or refrain from legislating as the individual States see fit. . . .

The facts that cannot be ignored today are the facts of integrated national commerce and a political relationship between States and Nation much affected by their respective treasuries and constitutional modifications adopted by the people. The federalism of some earlier time is no more adequate to account for those facts today than the theory of laissez-faire was able to govern the national economy 70 years ago.

The objection to reviving traditional state spheres of action as a consideration in commerce analysis, however, not only rests on the portent of incoherence, but is compounded by a further defect just as fundamental. The defect, in essence, is the majority's rejection of the Founders' considered judgment that politics, not judicial review, should mediate between state and national interests as the strength and legislative jurisdiction of the National Government inevitably increased through the expected growth of the national economy. Whereas today's majority takes a leaf from the book of the old judicial economists in saying that the Court should somehow draw the line to keep the federal relationship in a proper balance, Madison, Wilson, and Marshall understood the Constitution very differently. . . .

Amendments that alter the balance of power between the National and State Governments, like the Fourteenth, or that change the way the States are represented within the Federal Government, like the Seventeenth, are not rips in the fabric of the Framers' Constitution, inviting judicial repairs. The Seventeenth Amendment may indeed have lessened the enthusiasm of the Senate to represent the States as discrete sovereignties, but the Amendment did not convert the judiciary into an alternate shield against the commerce power. . . .

The facts that cannot be ignored today are the facts of integrated national commerce and a political relationship between States and Nation much affected by their respective treasuries and constitutional modifications adopted by the people. The federalism of some earlier time is no more adequate to account for those facts today than the theory of laissez-faire was able to govern the national economy 70 years ago.

Justice Breyer, with whom Justice Stevens joins and with whom Justices Ginsburg and Breyer join in part, dissenting . . . [omitted].

National Federation of Independent Business v. *Sebelius*
567 U.S. 519, 132 S.Ct. 2566, 183 L.Ed. 2d 450 (2012)

http://caselaw.findlaw.com/us-supreme-court/11-393.html

(This case is reprinted in Chapter Six; see the Table of Contents.)

5

The Electoral Process

The conception of political equality from the Declaration of Independence, to Lincoln's Gettysburg Address, to the Fifteenth, Seventeenth, and Nineteenth Amendments can mean only one thing—one person, one vote.

—JUSTICE WILLIAM O. DOUGLAS (1963)

Preceding chapters illustrate the commonplace observation that the Supreme Court is a political institution. Being political does not mean that the justices routinely campaign for their favorite candidates or run for office themselves, although nineteenth-century American history offers examples of both. Even in the twentieth century, Justice Charles Evans Hughes left the bench to run for president in 1916 (he lost), and Justice William O. Douglas had presidential aspirations in the 1940s and early 1950s. Indeed, justices and other federal judges today are expected to be "above politics" in that they are not supposed to take sides publicly in elections.

But the Court is political in at least four respects. First, as each chapter demonstrates, its decisions shape public policy by deciding what government—national, state, or local—may or may not do. Second, decisions clarify the boundaries of political authority, focusing less on *what* may be done than on *who* may do it or *how* it may be done. As shown in Chapter Three, the Steel Seizure Case of 1952 turned not on whether government could cope with labor disruptions but on whether President Truman had exceeded his authority and intruded into Congress' lawmaking domain. The Legislative Veto case of 1983 did not question government's authority to deport a particular individual but instead challenged the device by which Congress had ordered deportation. Third, the Court itself may become an issue in presidential elections, as has happened at least a dozen times since 1800 because of unpopular decisions. Campaigns in the past four decades would have taken a different shape without the Supreme Court's 1973 abortion decision, for instance. So in these ways, the Court has been political from practically the beginning.

Finally, the justices may affect the electoral process itself, as has happened in cases on voting rights, representation, campaign finance, and certainly in the disputed Florida vote count in the 2000 presidential election and emergency appeals after the 2020

DOI: 10.4324/9781003164340-6

election. This electoral dimension of constitutional law is the subject of this chapter. It is an important part of the Court's work because of the role that political parties and elections play in the life of the nation. It is through the electoral process that "We the people" attempt to control government by choosing those who will govern. Because judges help to determine the ground rules of politics, decisions on the electoral process affect the acquisition and allocation of power in the most fundamental sense.

VOTING

One could write a history of American politics by studying efforts to extend the right to vote, or **franchise**. The Constitution of 1787 left voting qualifications entirely in the hands of the states, with the result that most Americans—women, blacks, native Americans, and some white adult males—were initially kept from the ballot box. By the 1820s, the national trend was to chip away at those restrictions, for whites at least, first with the removal of property qualifications for voting, followed by the Fifteenth, Nineteenth, and Twenty-Sixth Amendments in 1870, 1920, and 1971 that dealt with race, gender, and age, respectively. With race however, many years would pass before the promise of the Fifteenth Amendment was realized.

The White Primary. After the Civil War, national legislation implementing the Fourteenth and Fifteenth Amendments was only occasionally invoked successfully to protect the right of African Americans to vote in congressional elections (Ex parte *Yarbrough*, 1884), as some states employed ingenious means to sidestep the Constitution. In *Guinn* v. *United States* (1915), the Court invalidated one of these racially discriminatory devices called a grandfather clause. It exempted from a literacy test for voting all persons and their lineal descendants who had voted on or before January 1, 1866, a date that excluded virtually every black American. *Guinn* stood in sharp contrast to *Giles* v. *Harris* (1903), in which the Court confessed judicial impotence: remedying an Alabama voter registration system designed to perpetuate white supremacy was beyond the Court's capacity, especially when the discrimination was as widespread as all acknowledged it to be.

Despite a few decisions like *Guinn*, however, some states remained intent on disfranchising blacks, a goal made even easier to reach after the Supreme Court held in *Newberry* v. *United States* (1921) that party primaries were not "elections" in the constitutional sense. Clearly, if blacks could be excluded from primaries in one-party states (and the South by this time had become a largely one-party [Democratic] region), their political influence would evaporate. Nevertheless, the equal protection clause of the Fourteenth Amendment was successfully invoked both against a state law setting up a **white primary** for the Texas Democratic Party (*Nixon* v. *Herndon*, 1927) and against a similar resolution by the Democratic State Executive Committee acting under authority of statute (*Nixon* v. *Condon*, 1932). (The equal protection clause is covered more fully in Chapter Fourteen.) But in *Grovey* v. *Townsend* (1935), a resolution forbidding black participation adopted by the state convention of the Democratic Party was held to be private action and therefore not within the reach of the Constitution. Moreover, along with the white primary, some states had already adopted the **poll tax** (payment of which was required to maintain voter eligibility), as well as literacy tests to prevent blacks (and some whites as well) from voting.

The story was not, however, to end on this note. In 1941, the Court held that the right to vote in a primary election in a one-party state, in this instance Louisiana, where the primary was a step in the election of members of Congress, was a right or privilege secured by the Constitution because the actions at the primary were officially accepted by the state. Hence, the failure of state officials, acting under "color" of state law, to count ballots properly was a violation of the U.S. Criminal Code (*United States* v. *Classic*). Then, *Smith* v. *Allwright* (1944) overruled *Grovey* v. *Townsend* and held that the right to vote guaranteed by the Fifteenth Amendment applied to primaries as well as general elections. Later efforts by Texas to evade the principle of that case by accepting the candidates of the Jaybird Party, a Democratic political organization that conducted an unofficial primary in which blacks could not vote, were similarly deemed invalid (*Terry* v. *Adams*, 1953).

The Voting Rights Act. Courtroom victories over the white primary, however, did little to overcome the more subtle ways in which African Americans could be kept from the polls. Much of the delay in implementing the landmark school integration decision of 1954 (***Brown* v. *Board of Education***), for example, stemmed from the political powerlessness of those who had the most to gain from the ruling (see Chapter Fourteen). As always, effective access to the ballot box was an important condition for equality under the law. Indeed, loss of the vote a half-century earlier had helped to make possible the rigid and pervasive system of legalized segregation attacked in *Brown* and other cases.

Civil rights organizations and their allies realized the hitherto undeveloped potential of the black vote in the South, where in 1961 only one in four eligible persons was registered. Further measures were therefore sought to achieve a dramatic increase in electoral strength. Adoption of the Twenty-Fourth Amendment (1964), which prohibited use of a poll tax in federal elections, was followed by *Harper* v. *Virginia Board of Elections* (1966) which invalidated the poll tax as a voting requirement in state elections. The Court had upheld the tax in *Breedlove* v. *Suttles* (1937).

The **Voting Rights Act** of 1965 remains the most important voter legislation ever enacted by Congress. Its measures (such as a ban on literacy tests) were extreme, but so were the evils it sought to correct. The act, upheld in *South Carolina* v. *Katzenbach* (1966), has had a far-reaching impact. By 1967, black voter registration had doubled in Georgia, nearly tripled in Alabama, and jumped almost 800 percent in Mississippi. In the South today, blacks vote in percentages that almost equal those for whites. In 2006, Congress extended the Voting Rights Act for 25 years.

Three sections of the 1965 act merit attention here. Section 2 repeats the Fifteenth Amendment's prohibition against racial discrimination in voting and applies throughout the United States. An amendment to Section 2 in 1982 expressly prohibits voting regulations that *result* in a denial of the right to vote on account of race. A violation of Section 2 occurs when the "totality of circumstances" reveals that minority voters have less opportunity than others to elect officials "of their choice." Section 4 set up a triggering mechanism for determining which parts of the country are subject to Section 5. Section 5 required that any change in a "standard, practice, or procedure with respect to voting" in those covered jurisdictions could take effect only after being cleared by the attorney general or by the U.S. District Court for the District of Columbia. Locales affected by Section 5 included nine states (most of which were in the South) and parts of seven others, including New York. The Supreme Court has interpreted "standard, practice, or procedure" to include any changes in a locale's electoral system. This preclearance requirement was satisfied only if the jurisdiction proposing the change could demonstrate that the change had neither the purpose nor the effect of "denying or abridging the right to vote on account of race or color." Black voting strength, therefore, could not be weakened or diluted by a change in local election practices.

Thus, **retrogression**—being worse off than before—is ordinarily dispositive for a violation of the Voting Rights Act. However, *Shelby County* v. *Holder* (2013) has significantly reduced the thrust of the Voting Rights Act. While its prohibitions remain, the Court in this decision struck down Section 4 (and therefore effectively made Section 5 inoperable) because it concluded that current conditions no longer justify the unequal treatment among the states that Section 4 embodied.

The Florida Election Case. Florida became a battleground after Election Day 2000 even though all agreed that, nationally, Democratic presidential candidate Al Gore had a lead in the popular vote total of several hundred thousand over Republican candidate George W. Bush. But that national margin made no difference. What mattered was the popular vote *in Florida*, because Florida's 25 electoral votes would decide whether Bush or Gore became the 43rd president.

Some ballots could not be read by the machines because some voters who used punch cards did not completely puncture the card, or, if they did, left a piece of paper (a chad) dangling or left only an impression. The same thing had happened at other times in Florida, but the margins were not as close and the stakes were not as high. Trailing by only 537 votes (out of about 6 million cast), Gore wanted those uncounted ballots read by hand, as allowed by law. Bush feared that any hand count to determine the intention of the voter would inject enough subjectivity into the process to cost him the election.

The U.S. Supreme Court first stopped a hand recount ordered by the Florida Supreme Court and then ruled in ***Bush* v. *Gore*** that hand-counting could not proceed without uniform standards to determine the intent of the voter. With voting by the Electoral College just days away, five justices concluded that no constitutionally acceptable hand-counting was possible. Otherwise, citing the legislative districting cases (discussed below in "Representation"), they reasoned that one person's ballot might be treated differently from another's. The case lent irony to Chief Justice Morrison Waite's 1877 aphorism that "[f]or protection against abuses by legislatures, the people must resort to the polls, not to the courts."

The Electoral College. As *Bush* v. *Gore* reminded Americans, the president and vice president are not chosen directly by the voters but by electors whom the voters (since the mid-nineteenth century) have chosen. Every state (with the partial exceptions of Maine and Nebraska) appoints a slate of electors whose candidate has won the state's popular vote, resulting in a winner-take-all awarding of electoral votes. Most states also compel electors to pledge to support the nominee of the party who gets the most votes in the state. As of 2020, 15 states backed up their pledge laws with some kind of sanction to discourage **faithless electors**. Also called wayward electors, these are electors who vote for a candidate other than the one for whom they have pledged to vote. Moreover, many of these states immediately remove a faithless elector and substitute an alternate whose vote the state reports instead. A few states impose a monetary fine on electors who flout their pledge. ***Chiafalo* v. *Washington*** (2020) unanimously upheld a state's imposition of a $1,000 fine on three electors who disregarded their pledge to vote for Hillary Clinton in the 2016 presidential election. The Court made clear that electors are not independent agents but are chosen to heed the voters' choice. While *Ray* v. *Blair* (1952) had upheld a pledge requirement, it reserved judgment on an enforcement mechanism. Although in most presidential elections a few faithless electors would make no difference in the outcome, in 2000 only four electoral votes separated Bush and Gore. Given that Gore also had a noticeable lead in the national popular vote, Democratic operatives tried unsuccessfully to persuade a handful of Bush electors to switch sides. In 2016, two electors defected from Trump, and five defected from Clinton in a contest where the losing candidate had an even greater popular vote lead than in 2000. There were no faithless electors in 2020, although over the course of American history, there have been a total of 165. *Chiafalo* may lend a push to adoption of the **National Popular Vote Plan**, an agreement among states and the District of Columbia to award all of their electoral votes to the winner of the national popular vote. As of 2021, the plan had been enacted into law by 16 jurisdictions, accounting for 196 electoral votes.

REPRESENTATION

Chief Justice Earl Warren announced his intention to retire in June 1968, and on July 5 in the East Conference Room of the Supreme Court Building, he met with dozens of reporters who asked him to identify his major contribution. The question was potentially difficult because between 1953 and 1969 the Warren Court, with revolutionary effects, had erected landmark decisions across the landscape of American constitutional law. Yet his apparently surprising answer was categorical: the redistricting cases. Why? The right to vote freely and equitably for the candidates of one's choice is the essence of democracy. Untrammeled exercise of this right is essential to the preservation of all others—"the bedrock of our political system," he called it.

Entering the Political Thicket. Chapter Two introduced the **political question doctrine**, which holds that the resolution of certain disputes lies not with the judiciary but with one or both of the "political" branches of government. One of the most important fields in which the Court once invoked this self-imposed limitation is **legislative districting**, the drawing of geographical boundaries within states to determine representation in state legislatures and the U.S. House of Representatives. (**Legislative apportionment** refers generally to the distribution of seats in a legislative body, and specifically to the allocation of U.S. House seats among the states following each decennial census. According to *Dept. of Commerce* v. *U.S. House of Representatives* [1999], this apportionment must be based on an actual count, not sampling techniques.)

In *Colegrove* v. *Green* (1946), Justice Frankfurter considered legislative districting "peculiarly political" and "therefore not meet for judicial determination." Voters seeking relief from Illinois's numerically skewed congressional districts were told to turn to the state legislature or Congress, not to the Court. "Courts ought not to enter this 'political thicket,'" Frankfurter warned. "It is hostile to a democratic system to involve the judiciary in the politics of the people. . . . The remedy for unfairness in districting is to secure state legislatures that will apportion properly, or to invoke the ample powers of Congress." Congress, however, had lately been silent on the subject. Although a statute in 1842 required each state with more than one representative to employ single-member districts "composed of contiguous territory," and statutes in 1901 and 1911 mandated "compact" congressional districts (to rein in rampant gerrymandering), the apportionment act of 1929 left out any requirements for compact, contiguous, or equally populated districts. As the years went by, populations of House districts across the nation grew increasingly imbalanced.

In contrast to *Colegrove*, *Gomillion* v. *Lightfoot* (1960) hinted that a federal judicial remedy might indeed be available. Involved was an Alabama law that redrew the boundaries of Tuskegee from a simple square into a 28-sided monster. The result was to remove from the city all but a handful of black voters, while leaving white voters unaffected. Justice Frankfurter, in spite of his position in *Colegrove* about political questions, declared that the Fifteenth Amendment guarantee against racial discrimination in voting justified judicial action. Left unanswered was the question whether the Fourteenth Amendment's equal protection clause might offer a judicial remedy for nonracial discrimination, based on urban versus suburban or rural residence.

An affirmative answer came in ***Baker* v. *Carr*** (1962). Finding no obstacle in the political question doctrine, Justice Brennan ruled that unequal legislative districts presented a valid question under the equal protection clause and that federal courts were empowered to provide a remedy.

One Person, One Vote. In making belated entrance into this political thicket, *Baker* neglected to lay down guidelines by which a valid districting plan could be distinguished from an invalid plan. That came the next year, in *Gray* v. *Sanders* (1963), in which the Court, applying the **one-person, one-vote** principle, invalidated the Georgia county unit system of primary elections for statewide offices that greatly disfavored urban counties. A candidate could win the popular vote but lose the election. Said Justice Douglas,

> Once the geographical unit for which a representative is to be chosen is designated, all who participate in the election are to have an equal vote—whatever their race, whatever their sex, whatever their occupation, whatever their income, and wherever their home may be in that geographical unit. This is required by the equal protection clause of the Fourteenth Amendment.

In 1964, *Wesberry* v. *Sanders* extended the same principle to congressional districts, holding that the Constitution had the "plain objective of making equal representation for equal numbers of people the fundamental goal for the House of Representatives." "As nearly as practicable," the Court declared, "one man's vote in a congressional election is to be worth as much as another's." The conclusion of the three-round contest, set in motion by *Baker* v. *Carr*, came in ***Reynolds* v. *Sims***. By applying the now-familiar equality principle, the justices challenged the legitimacy of at least 40 state legislatures by mandating numerically equal districts for both legislative chambers. Since 1964, the justices have applied the one-person, one-vote principle in a variety of redistricting cases. Only in certain situations, and then only if congressional districts are not at issue, will the Court make an exception to its rule of numerical equality. For example, *Harris* v. *Arizona Independent Redistricting Commission* (2015) allowed population deviations among state legislative districts of as much as 10 percent in order to achieve compactness and contiguity, to maintain the integrity of political subdivisions and balance among political parties, and perhaps to comply with the Voting Rights Act.

In redistricting, however, what population is to be used as reference: the total number of *people* in an area, or the total number of eligible *voters* in the area? While *Evenwel* v. *Abbott* (2016) left open the question whether a state might draw district lines on the basis of voters rather than people, the Court's opinion strongly hinted a preference for population as the preferred baseline. Moreover, while redistricting in most states is done by the state's legislature (making it politically important which party controls a state legislature in the year following the decennial census), the Supreme Court has made clear that a state may constitutionally assign that function to a body independent of the legislature even for the purpose of drawing congressional districts (*Arizona State Legislature* v. *Arizona Independent Redistricting Commission*, 2015).

Gerrymandering. In 1986, the Court ventured further into the political thicket. In a challenge to a districting plan for the Indiana legislature, the Court concluded in *Davis* v. *Bandemer* that partisan **gerrymandering** (the drawing of district lines to benefit one party at the expense of the other) presented a justiciable issue under the equal protection clause. As Justice Souter later described the practice,

> the spectrum of opportunity runs from cracking a group into impotent fractions, to packing its members into one district for the sake of marginalizing them in another. However equal districts may be in population as a formal matter, the consequence of a vote cast can be minimized or maximized.

Souter's point was that achieving equal numbers among districts is only the beginning, not the end, of examining representation. Yet only two justices found a constitutional defect in the Indiana plan. For future cases, the Court announced a standard much less precise than one-person, one-vote, which made it difficult to show a constitutional violation: "Unconstitutional discrimination occurs only when the electoral system is arranged in a manner that will consistently degrade a voter's or a group of voters' influence on the political process as a whole." Left in doubt was the kind of evidence and the period of time required to prove an unconstitutional gerrymander, particularly in light of the fact that redistricting occurs in every state after each census. Such uncertainties nearly led the Court to overrule *Bandemer* in *Vieth* v. *Jubelirer* (2004), where four justices were prepared to hold that partisan gerrymandering was nonjusticiable for federal courts, a possibility that became reality in 2019 when the Court decided ***Rucho* v. *Common Cause***. The new reality is that the composition of the House of Representatives and state legislatures in many instances will be determined not only by how people vote but by how districts are drawn. Thus, instead of voters chosing their legislators, legislators choose their voters.

Majority–Minority Districts. Legislative districting to enhance the representation of racial minorities has also given rise to constitutional disputes. When states attempt to boost the representation of racial minorities by drawing district lines to create one or more districts where a racial minority is in the majority, white voters have complained that such race-based districting violates the Fourteenth Amendment. Moreover, some political leaders find **majority–minority districts** of dubious value because, in a system of single-member districts, they concentrate minority voters in a few districts, thereby reducing the influence of those voters statewide. In some southern states, for example, majority–minority districts have had the effect of increasing the number of white Republicans elected to Congress, all the while decreasing the number of white Democratic representatives and increasing the number of African American or Latino Democratic representatives.

In the first benign race-conscious districting case to reach the Supreme Court, the justices turned back a challenge to a New York plan that split a Hasidic Jewish community among several state legislative districts in order to increase black representation (*United Jewish Organizations* v. *Carey*, 1977). The case signaled that such steps were not only appropriate under the Voting Rights Act but were permitted by the Constitution.

After the 1990 census, the North Carolina legislature created two black-majority congressional districts, the first and the twelfth, but this time the Court adopted a skeptical posture. District 1 seemed crudely drawn, and critics ridiculed it as resembling a "Rorschach inkblot test." District 12 meandered along Interstate 85 dividing counties and towns en route, its shape also hinting that it was drawn primarily with racial objectives in mind. Without saying outright that either District 12 or 1 violated the equal protection clause, five justices nonetheless declared that the petitioners had a valid "cause of action" and remanded the case so that the district court could determine whether the districts amounted to a racial gerrymander (*Shaw* v. *Reno*, 1993). The district court then concluded that the state's plan was race-based but satisfied strict judicial scrutiny by being narrowly tailored to further a compelling interest in complying with the Voting Rights Act. The Supreme Court reversed definitively with respect to District 12. District 1 had been dropped from the litigation because the white voters who mounted the original challenge had since moved out of the district (*Shaw* v. *Hunt*, 1996). The plan was precluded by ***Miller* v. *Johnson*** (1995), which invalidated a Georgia congressional arrangement that created three majority–minority districts, at least one of which seemed explainable only on the basis of race. (See Figure 5.1.) Left unanswered in *Miller* was (1) how courts in

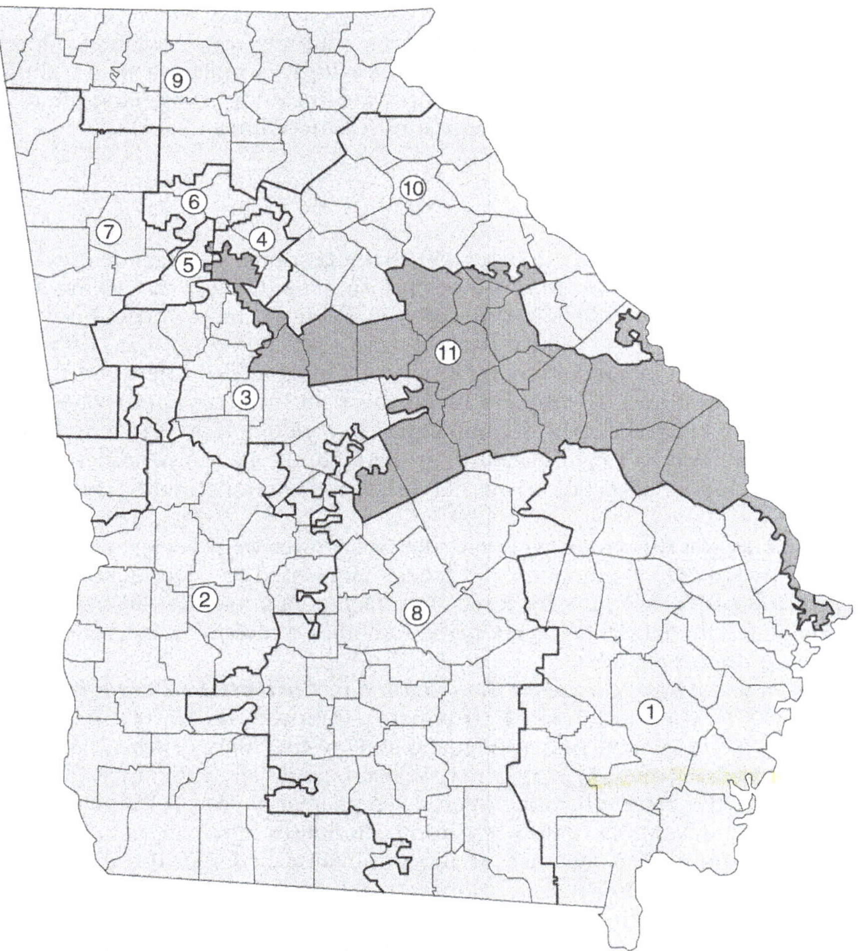

FIGURE 5.1 Georgia Congressional Districting Plan Attacked in *Miller* v. *Johnson*

other situations were to determine the relative weight of factors accounting for a districting plan; (2) whether race-based districting in compliance with Section 5 was sufficiently "compelling" to pass scrutiny under the equal protection clause; and (3) whether nonracial variables might yield a constitutionally acceptable majority–minority district.

The 2000 census had barely been completed when the battle over North Carolina's District 12, launched after the 1990 census, ended in *Hunt [Easley]* v. *Cromartie* (2001), where the Court found the now-reshaped District 12 constitutionally acceptable. Five justices agreed with the district court that the district was created largely for partisan and not racial reasons; therefore, it was judged by the less demanding Fourteenth Amendment standard applied to nonracial gerrymanders.

It remains to be seen whether the Court's razor-thin majority against most race-based districting holds, and if so, whether states seeking to enhance minority representation may meet the inevitable challenges by drawing districts with more conventional shapes. It also remains to be seen whether, because African Americans are among the most reliable Democratic voters, *Cromartie* will now allow *party* to be a proxy for *race* in the effort to increase minority representation. Moreover, *Bethune-Hill* v. *Virginia State Board of Elections* (2017) indicates that compliance with section 5 of the Voting Rights Act is now a sufficiently compelling interest that allows race to be used in drawing a legislative district's lines.

PARTY POLITICS AND CAMPAIGNS

Campaigns and elections are democracy's battlegrounds. Political parties are the organizations created for the purpose of choosing candidates, mobilizing supporters, and conducting campaigns in order to win elections and to enact the values of their coalitions into law. A political party is thus a private group that performs very public functions. Understandably, therefore, conflicts may arise between the party's right to define itself and to carry on its business and the government's interest in how officials are elected and how campaigns are conducted. As explained in Chapter Eleven, at least since 1957 the Court has held that the First Amendment implicitly protects a freedom of association, but like other constitutional rights, this one is not absolute.

Primaries and Elections. As noted, the Court ruled decades ago that the public functions of parties in nominating candidates amounted to "state action," meaning that exclusion of black voters by some state Democratic parties through the white primary violated the Fifteenth Amendment. On other questions, however, party preferences have often prevailed.

This view seemed to explain the outcome in ***California Democratic Party* v. *Jones*** (2000), which invalidated an initiative-imposed system of blanket primaries in place of the closed primaries mandated by the rules of four parties in the state. (In a **blanket primary**, voters may select a candidate from any party for each office.) Against the asserted public interest—presumably served by blanket primaries—in increasing voter turnout by ensuring candidates less extreme, more centrist, and therefore more representative of the population at large, the parties argued successfully that freedom of association allowed them to decide who their nominees (and hence what their messages) would be. Casting doubt on the continued force of *Jones*, however, is *Washington State Grange* v. *Washington State Republican*

Party (2008). Here, seven justices upheld the state's "top two" primary system which allows candidates to self-identify party affiliations on ballots, even if one or another is not the chosen nominee of a party. The two candidates receiving the most votes advance to the general election, even if both have self-identified with the same party. Generally, in applying federal law, the Supreme Court, at least since *Purcell* v. *Gonzalez* in 2006, expects lower federal courts to avoid changing a state's election rules during the time just before an election to avoid confusing both voters and officials charged with administering the election. So in *Republican National Committee* v. *Democratic National Committee* (2020), a bare majority of the justices blocked an injunction issued by a district court that had shifted the deadline by several days until after election day for voters in Wisconsin to return absentee ballots.

Campaign Finance. "There are two things that are important in politics," Republican strategist Mark Hanna is supposed to have said more than a century ago. "The first is money, and I can't remember what the second one is." Restrictions on the source, amount, and use of campaign funds implicate the First Amendment rights of free speech and association because candidates and parties, as well as other political groups, require money to build their organizations and to convey their messages to voters. Money is, in short, a proxy for speech. This view lay at the heart of *Buckley* v. *Valeo* (1976), which reviewed at length the constitutionality of the **Federal Election Campaign Act** (FECA), amended in 1974 to reduce the influence of "big money" in national elections. The objective of FECA was to minimize corruption or the appearance of corruption in federal elections. In a **per curiam** opinion and five separate opinions that consumed 300 pages in the *U.S. Reports*, the Court made an important constitutional distinction between *contributions* and *expenditures*: limitations on the former were deemed less harmful to speech than limitations on the latter. Furthermore, large contributions seemed more easily linked to corruption or to the appearance of corruption. The result was a bench more willing to accept restrictions on contributions than on expenditures. (Per curiam means "by the court" and is a designation the Supreme Court uses for unsigned opinions. A per curiam opinion may indicate that the Court is only applying "settled law" or may be used in situations, as in *Buckley*, where no majority opinion was practical.) Accordingly, the Court disallowed provisions of FECA that put a limit of $50,000 on the use by a presidential candidate of his own or his immediate family's money, as well as a limit on "independent spending" by individuals and groups on behalf of a candidate in a federal election. Endorsed, however, were ceilings on contributions of $1,000 and $5,000 per election from individuals and groups, respectively, to candidates seeking federal office. Also upheld was a conditional scheme of public financing for presidential races (on a matching basis in primaries and caucuses and with full funding in the general election), in return for which candidates agreed to abide by spending limits. However, presidential candidates since 2008 have eschewed the public financing option to avoid its spending restrictions.

Campaign finance issues remain litigious. In 2002, Congress enacted the most sweeping changes to FECA in more than a quarter century. Aside from raising the limit for individual contributions to $2,000 per election (and $25,000 per year to national parties) and indexing those amounts for inflation, the **Bipartisan Campaign Reform Act** (BCRA) bans all "**soft money**" (unregulated) contributions to national party organizations. (In the 2000 elections, for example, Republicans had raised $250 million in soft money and the Democrats $245 million.) Annual contributions to state and local party organizations are capped at $10,000. Moreover, "electioneering communications" that are broadcast or telecast and that refer to a specific candidate were not to be run 30 days before a primary or 60 days before a general election unless they are funded by a party's or a group's "**hard money**" (regulated) contributions.

The Supreme Court upheld almost all provisions of BCRA in ***McConnell* v. *Federal Election Commission*** (2003), including the soft money ban and the restriction on electioneering communications, in a decision that matched *Buckley* in length.

Yet *McConnell* has now been partly superseded by ***Citizens United* v. *Federal Election Commission*** (2010). In this landmark ruling in a case that grew out of the quest for the Democratic presidential nomination in 2008, five justices invalidated BCRA's ban on "electioneering communications" and the federal prohibition on the use of corporate and union treasury funds for express advocacy, while upholding BCRA's disclosure and disclaimer requirements. The decision also overruled *Austin* v. *Michigan Chamber of Commerce* (1990), which upheld against a free speech challenge a state's ban on independent expenditures from corporate treasuries to support or oppose candidates, but allowed such expenditures from the corporation's political action committee (PAC). Dismantling of campaign finance restrictions continued in *McCutcheon* v. *Federal Election Commission* (2014), which invalidated the biennial aggregate limit, previously upheld in *Buckley*, on an individual's contributions to a national political party and candidates for federal office.

Also, surely complicating the work of legislators across the country is *Randall* v. *Sorrell* (2006), the Court's first decision striking down, as too restrictive, a state's limitations on the dollar amount that individuals and parties may contribute to candidates for statewide office. In this instance, Vermont not only had the most restrictive contribution law in the nation but set limits well below anything the Supreme Court had previously upheld. Also judged constitutionally deficient were the state's limitations on a candidate's expenditures. The plurality opinion stressed the negative impact of such limits on speech and volunteer campaign activity, yet no standard emerged from the decision indicating when dollar limits would be *too* low. Yet electioneering continues to consume vast quantities of money, with nearly $14 billion estimated to have been spent in the 2020 elections—about double the amount for 2016, according to several sources.

KEY TERMS

franchise
grandfather clause
white primary
poll tax
Voting Rights Act
retrogression
National Popular Vote Plan
faithless elector
political question doctrine
legislative districting
legislative apportionment
one-person, one-vote
gerrymandering
majority–minority districts
blanket primary
Federal Election Campaign Act (FECA)
per curiam
Bipartisan Campaign Reform Act (BRCA)
soft money
hard money

QUERIES

1. In *Reynolds* v. *Sims* (1964), Justice Stewart agreed with the majority that the badly skewed Alabama legislature violated the Constitution. Yet he refused to accept the majority's automatic application of one-person, one-vote as the constitutionally required standard in all redistricting cases. What did he propose instead?

2. Is there merit to the argument that the single-member district (the most common basis of representation in the United States) unavoidably distorts representation on city councils and in state legislatures and the U.S. House of Representatives?

3. If most agree that partisan gerrymandering is an especially unsavory aspect of American politics, why has the Supreme Court had such difficulty reining it in, especially since it so long ago moved successfully against population disparities among legislative districts?

4. What impact will *Chiafalo* v. *Washington* possibly have on the eventual adoption of the National Popular Vote Plan? This proposal for an interstate compact calls upon each legislature to direct that its electors cast their votes for the presidential ticket that received the most popular votes *nationally* in the presidential election. With a sufficient combination of states as signatories, the plan would mean an end to the current winner-take-all system of awarding electoral votes and that no president would enter the White House without having received at least a plurality of the nationwide popular vote.

SELECTED READINGS

Berman, Ari. *Give Us the Ballot: The Modern Struggle for Voting Rights in America*. New York: Farrar, Straus and Giroux, 2015.

Davidson, Chandler, and Bernard Grofman, eds. *Quiet Revolution in the South: The Impact of the Voting Rights Act, 1965–1990*. Princeton, NJ: Princeton University Press, 1994.

Gillman, Howard. *The Votes That Counted: How the Court Decided the 2000 Election*. Chicago, IL: University of Chicago Press, 2001.

Glenn, Richard A., and Kyle L. Kreider. *Voting Rights in America: A Reference Handbook*. Santa Barbara, CA: ABC-CLIO, 2020.

Hanson, Royce. *The Political Thicket*. Upper Saddle River, NJ: Prentice Hall, 1966.

McGann, Anthony J., et al. *Gerrymandering in America: The House of Representatives, the Supreme Court, and the Future of Popular Sovereignty*. New York: Cambridge University Press, 2016.

Smith, J. Douglas. *On Democracy's Doorstep: The Inside Story of How the Supreme Court Brought "One Person, One Vote" to the United States*. New York: Hill and Wang, 2014.

Stephenson, Donald Grier, Jr. *The Right to Vote*. Santa Barbara, CA: ABC-CLIO, 2004.

Urofsky, Melvin I. *The Campaign Finance Cases*. Lawrence: University Press of Kansas, 2020.

Wroth, L. Kinvin. "Election Contests and the Electoral Vote." 65 *Dickinson Law Review* 321, 1961.

Yarbrough, Tinsley E. *Race and Redistricting: The Shaw-Cromartie Cases*. Lawrence: University Press of Kansas, 2002.

I. VOTING

Bush v. *Gore*
531 U.S. 98, 121 S.Ct. 525, 148 L.Ed. 2d 388 (2000)

www.law.cornell.edu/supct/html/00-949.ZPC.html

This remarkable litigation involving the extended presidential election of 2000 was twice before the U.S. Supreme Court in less than two weeks. At its conclusion, the Court effectively handed the White House to Republican candidate George W. Bush. Some essential facts appear in the per curiam opinion below. The Supreme Court heard oral arguments in *Bush I* on the morning of December 1 and in *Bush II* on the morning of December 11, and in record-setting time rendered its decision on the night of December 12. Twenty-four hours later, Democratic candidate Al Gore conceded the election to Bush. Florida's 25 electoral votes gave Bush a total of 271, one more than the required minimum, to Gore's 267. (The official tally of popular votes set Gore's national plurality at 540,520, of 104 million votes cast.)

In *Bush I*, the petition for certiorari posed three questions. Two dealt with Article II and 3 U.S.C. § 5; the third raised the equal protection issue. In its reply brief, Gore's legal team deflected the third question, and it was excluded from the U.S. Supreme Court's grant of review and the oral argument on December 1. Ironically, with even less time in which to conduct the manual recounts, the equal protection issue resurfaced the following week in *Bush* v. *Gore* (*Bush II*) and proved dispositive. Majority: Rehnquist, O'Connor, Scalia, Kennedy, Thomas. Dissenting: Stevens, Souter, Ginsburg, Breyer.

Per Curiam. . . .

On November 8, 2000, the day following the Presidential election, the Florida Division of Elections reported that petitioner, Governor Bush, had received 2,909,135 votes, and respondent, Vice President Gore, had received 2,907,351 votes, a margin of 1,784 for Governor Bush. Because Governor Bush's margin of victory was less than "one-half of a percent . . . of the votes cast," an automatic machine recount was conducted under § 102.141(4) of the [Florida] election code, the results of which showed Governor Bush still winning the race but by a diminished margin. Vice President Gore then sought manual recounts in Volusia, Palm Beach, Broward, and Miami-Dade Counties, pursuant to Florida's election protest provisions. A dispute arose concerning the deadline for local county canvassing boards to submit their returns to the Secretary of State. The Secretary declined to waive the November 14 deadline imposed by statute. The Florida Supreme Court, however, set the deadline at November 26. We granted certiorari and vacated the Florida Supreme Court's decision, finding considerable uncertainty as to the grounds on which it was based [*Bush* v. *Palm Beach County Canvassing Board* (*Bush I*)]. On December 11, the Florida Supreme Court issued a decision on remand reinstating that date.

On November 26, the Florida Elections Canvassing Commission certified the results of the election and declared Governor Bush the winner of Florida's 25 electoral votes. On November 27, Vice President Gore . . . filed a complaint in Leon County Circuit Court contesting the certification. He sought relief pursuant to § 102.168(3)(c), which provides that "[r]eceipt of a number of illegal votes or rejection of a number of legal votes sufficient to change or place in doubt the result of the election" shall be grounds for a contest. The Circuit Court denied relief, stating that Vice President Gore failed to meet his burden of proof. . . .

Accepting jurisdiction, the Florida Supreme Court . . . held that the Circuit Court had been correct to reject Vice President Gore's challenge to the results certified in Nassau County and his challenge to the Palm Beach County Canvassing Board's determination that 3,300 ballots cast in that county were not, in the statutory phrase, "legal votes." . . .

The Supreme Court held that Vice President Gore had satisfied his burden of proof under § 102.168(3)(c) with respect to his challenge to Miami-Dade County's failure to tabulate, by manual count, 9,000 ballots on which the machines had failed to detect a vote for President ("undervotes"). Noting the closeness of the election, the Court explained that "[o]n this record, there can be no question that there are legal votes within the 9,000 uncounted votes sufficient to place the results of this election in doubt." A "legal vote," as determined by the Supreme Court, is "one in which there is a 'clear indication of the intent of the voter.'" The court therefore ordered a hand recount of the 9,000 ballots in Miami-Dade County. Observing that the contest provisions vest broad discretion in the circuit judge to "provide any relief appropriate under such circumstances," the Supreme Court further held that the Circuit Court could order "the Supervisor of Elections and the Canvassing Boards, as well as the necessary public officials, in all counties that have not conducted a manual recount or tabulation of the undervotes . . . to do so forthwith, said tabulation to take place in the individual counties where the ballots are located." . . .

The petition [in *Bush* v. *Gore* (*Bush II*)] presents the following questions: whether the Florida Supreme Court established new standards for resolving Presidential election contests, thereby violating Art. II, § 1, cl. 2, of the United States Constitution and failing to comply with 3 U.S.C. § 5 and whether the use of standardless manual recounts violates the Equal Protection and Due Process Clauses. With respect to the equal protection question, we find a violation of the Equal Protection Clause. . . .

The individual citizen has no federal constitutional right to vote for electors for the President of the United States unless and until the state legislature chooses a statewide election as the means to implement its power to appoint members of the Electoral College. . . . [I]t may, if it so chooses, select the electors itself, which indeed was the manner used by State legislatures in several States for many years after the Framing of our Constitution. History has now favored the voter, and in each of the several States the citizens themselves vote for Presidential electors. When the state legislature vests the right to vote for President in its people, the right to vote as the legislature has prescribed is fundamental; and one source of its fundamental nature lies in the equal weight accorded to each vote and the equal dignity owed to each voter. . . .

The right to vote is protected in more than the initial allocation of the franchise. Equal protection applies as well to the manner of its exercise. Having once granted the right to vote on equal terms, the State may not, by later arbitrary and disparate treatment, value one person's vote over that of another. . . .

There is no difference between the two sides of the present controversy on these basic propositions. . . . The question before us, however, is whether the recount procedures the Florida Supreme Court has adopted are consistent with its obligation to avoid arbitrary and disparate treatment of the members of its electorate.

Much of the controversy seems to revolve around ballot cards designed to be perforated by a stylus but which, either through error or deliberate omission, have not been perforated with sufficient precision for a machine to count them. In some cases a piece of the card—a chad—is hanging, say by two corners.

In other cases there is no separation at all, just an indentation.

The Florida Supreme Court has ordered that the intent of the voter be discerned from such ballots. For purposes of resolving the equal protection challenge, it is not necessary to decide whether the Florida Supreme Court had the authority under the legislative scheme for resolving election disputes to define what a legal vote is and to mandate a manual recount implementing that definition. The recount mechanisms implemented in response to the decisions of the Florida Supreme Court do not satisfy the minimum requirement for non-arbitrary treatment of voters necessary to secure the fundamental right. Florida's basic command for the count of legally cast votes is to consider the "intent of the voter." This is unobjectionable as an abstract proposition and a starting principle. The problem inheres in the absence of specific standards to ensure its equal application. The formulation of uniform rules to determine intent based on these recurring circumstances is practicable and, we conclude, necessary. . . .

The question before the Court is not whether local entities, in the exercise of their expertise, may develop different systems for implementing elections. Instead, we are presented with a situation where a state court with the power to assure uniformity has ordered a statewide recount with minimal procedural safeguards. . . . Given the Court's assessment that the recount process underway was probably being conducted in an unconstitutional manner, the Court stayed the order directing the recount so it could hear this case and render an expedited decision. The contest provision, as it was mandated by the State Supreme Court, is not well calculated to sustain the confidence that all citizens must have in the outcome of elections. The State has not shown that its procedures include the necessary safeguards. . . .

Upon due consideration of the difficulties identified to this point, it is obvious that the recount cannot be conducted in compliance with the requirements of equal protection and due process without substantial additional work. . . .

The Supreme Court of Florida has said that the legislature intended the State's electors to "participat[e] fully in the federal electoral process," as provided in 3 U.S.C. § 5. That statute, in turn, requires that any controversy or contest that is designed to lead to a conclusive selection of electors be completed by December 12. That date is upon us, and there is no recount procedure in place under the State Supreme Court's order that comports with minimal constitutional standards. Because it is evident that any recount seeking to meet the December 12 date will be unconstitutional for the reasons we have discussed, we reverse the judgment of the Supreme Court of Florida ordering a recount to proceed. . . .

It is so ordered.

Chief Justice Rehnquist, with whom Justice Scalia and Justice Thomas join, concurring. . . .

In *McPherson* v. *Blacker* (1892), we explained that Art. II, § 1, cl. 2, "convey[s] the broadest power of determination" and "leaves it to the legislature exclusively to define the method" of appointment. A significant departure from the legislative scheme for appointing Presidential electors presents a federal constitutional question.

3 U.S.C. § 5 informs our application of Art. II, § 1, cl. 2, to the Florida statutory scheme, which, as the Florida Supreme Court acknowledged, took that statute into account. Section 5 provides that the State's selection of electors "shall be conclusive, and shall govern in the counting of the electoral votes" if the electors are chosen under laws enacted prior to election day, and if the selection process is completed six days prior to the meeting of the electoral college. . . . If we are to respect the legislature's Article II powers, therefore, we must ensure that postelection state-court actions do not frustrate

the legislative desire to attain the "safe harbor" provided by § 5. . . .

The scope and nature of the remedy ordered by the Florida Supreme Court jeopardizes the "legislative wish" to take advantage of the safe harbor provided by 3 U.S.C. § 5. . . . This was done in a search for elusive—perhaps delusive—certainty as to the exact count of 6 million votes. But no one claims that these ballots have not previously been tabulated; they were initially read by voting machines at the time of the election, and thereafter reread by virtue of Florida's automatic recount provision. . . . It significantly departed from the statutory framework in place on November 7, and authorized open-ended further proceedings which could not be completed by December 12, thereby preventing a final determination by that date. . . .

JUSTICE STEVENS, with whom JUSTICE GINSBURG and JUSTICE BREYER join, dissenting . . . [omitted].

JUSTICE GINSBURG, with whom JUSTICE STEVENS joins, and with whom JUSTICE SOUTER and JUSTICE BREYER join in part, dissenting . . . [omitted].

JUSTICE BREYER, with whom JUSTICE STEVENS, JUSTICE SOUTER, and JUSTICE GINSBURG join in part, dissenting. . . .

[T]here is no justification for the majority's remedy, which is simply to reverse the lower court and halt the recount entirely. An appropriate remedy would be, instead, to remand this case with instructions that, even at this late date, would permit the Florida Supreme Court to require recounting all undercounted votes in Florida . . . and to do so in accordance with a single-uniform substandard. The majority justifies stopping the recount entirely on the ground that there is no more time. . . . But the majority reaches this conclusion in the absence of any record evidence that the recount could not have been completed in the time allowed by the Florida Supreme Court. The majority finds facts outside of the record on matters that state courts are in a far better position to address. Of course, it is too late for any such recount to take place by December 12, the date by which election disputes must be decided if a State is to take advantage of the safe harbor provisions of 3 U.S.C. § 5. Whether there is time to conduct a recount prior to December 18, when the electors are scheduled to meet, is a matter for the state courts to determine. And whether, under Florida law, Florida could or could not take further action is obviously a matter for Florida courts, not this Court, to decide. By halting the manual recount, and thus ensuring that the uncounted legal votes will not be counted under any standard, this Court crafts a remedy out of proportion to the asserted harm. . . .

Chiafalo v. *Washington*
591 U.S. ___, 140 S.Ct. 2316, 207 L.Ed. 2d 761 (2020)

www.supremecourt.gov/opinions/19pdf/19-465_i425.pdf

The facts of this case are contained in Justice Kagan's opinion below. Majority: Roberts, Alito, Breyer, Ginsburg, Gorsuch, Kagan, Kavanaugh, Sotomayor, Thomas.

JUSTICE KAGAN delivered the opinion of the Court.

Every four years, millions of Americans cast a ballot for a presidential candidate. Their votes, though, actually go toward selecting members of the Electoral College, whom each State appoints based on the popular returns. Those few "electors" then choose the President.

The States have devised mechanisms to ensure that the electors they appoint vote for the presidential candidate their citizens have preferred. With two partial exceptions, every State appoints a slate of electors selected by the political party whose candidate has won the State's popular vote. Most States also compel electors to pledge in advance to support the nominee of that party. This Court upheld such a pledge requirement decades ago [in Ray v. Blair (1952)], rejecting the argument that the Constitution "demands absolute freedom for the elector to vote his own choice."

Today, we consider whether a State may also penalize an elector for breaking his pledge and voting for someone other than the presidential candidate who won his State's popular vote. We hold that a State may do so.

In the 20th century, many States enacted statutes meant to . . . prohibit so-called faithless voting. Rather than just assume that party-picked electors would vote for their party's winning nominee, those States insist that they do so. As of now, 32 States and the District of Columbia have such statutes on their books. They are typically called pledge laws because most demand that electors take a formal oath or pledge to cast their ballot for their party's presidential (and vice presidential) candidate. Others merely impose that duty by law. Either way, the statutes work to ensure that the electors vote for the candidate who got the most statewide votes in the presidential election. . . . Washington is one of the 15 States with a sanctions-backed pledge law designed to keep the State's electors in line with its voting citizens.

This case involves three Washington electors who violated their pledges in the 2016 presidential election. . . . [T]he State fined the Electors $1,000 apiece for breaking their pledges to support the same candidate its voters had. The Electors challenged their fines in state court, arguing that the Constitution gives members of the Electoral College the right to vote however they please. The Washington Superior Court rejected the Electors' claim in an oral decision, and the State's Supreme Court affirmed that judgment. Ray, however, [had] reserved a question not implicated in the case: Could a State enforce those pledges through legal sanctions? Or would doing so violate an elector's "constitutional freedom" to "vote as he may choose" in the Electoral College? Today, we . . . uphold Washington's penalty-backed pledge law for reasons much like those given in Ray. The Constitution's text and the Nation's history both support allowing a State to enforce an elector's pledge to support his party's nominee—and the state voters' choice—for President.

Article II, § 1's appointments power gives the States far-reaching authority over presidential electors, absent some other constitutional constraint. . . . [In *McPherson* v. *Blacker* (1892)] this Court has described that clause as "conveying the broadest power of determination" over who becomes an elector. And the power to appoint an elector (in any manner) includes power to condition his appointment—that is, to say what the elector must do for the appointment to take effect. A State can require, for example, that an elector live in the State or qualify as a regular voter during the relevant time period. Or more substantively, a State can insist (as Ray allowed) that the elector pledge to cast his Electoral College ballot for his party's presidential nominee, thus tracking the State's popular vote. . . .

And nothing in the Constitution expressly prohibits States from taking away presidential electors' voting discretion as Washington does. The Constitution is barebones about electors. Article II includes only the instruction to each State to appoint, in whatever way it likes, as many electors as it has Senators and Representatives (except that the State may not appoint members of the Federal Government). The Twelfth Amendment then tells electors to meet in their States, to vote for President and Vice President separately, and to transmit lists of all their votes to the President of the United States Senate for counting, and . . . that is all.

The Framers could have done it differently; other constitutional drafters of their time did. In the founding era, two States—Maryland and Kentucky—used electoral bodies selected by voters to choose state senators (and in Kentucky's case, the Governor too). The Constitutions of both States, Maryland's drafted just before and Kentucky's just after the U.S. Constitution, incorporated language that would have made this case look quite different. Both state Constitutions required all electors to take an oath "to elect without favour, affection, partiality, or prejudice, such persons for Senators, as they, in their judgment and conscience, believe best qualified for the office." The emphasis on independent "judgment and conscience" called for the exercise of elector discretion. But although the Framers knew of Maryland's Constitution, no language of that kind made it into the document they drafted. . . .

The Electors argue that three simple words stand in for more explicit language about discretion. Article II, § 1 first names the members of the Electoral College: "electors." The Twelfth Amendment then says that electors shall "vote" and that they shall do so by "ballot." The "plain meaning" of those terms, the Electors say, requires electors to have "freedom of choice." If the States could control their votes, "the electors would not be 'Electors,' and their 'vote by Ballot' would not be a 'vote.'"

But those words need not always connote independent choice. Suppose a person always votes in the way his spouse, or pastor, or union tells him to. We might question his judgment, but we would have no problem saying that he "votes" or fills in a "ballot." In those cases, the choice is in someone else's hands, but the words still apply because they can signify a mechanical act. Or similarly, suppose in a system allowing proxy voting (a common practice in the founding era), the proxy acts on clear instructions from the principal, with no freedom of choice. Still, we might well say that he cast a "ballot" or "voted," though the preference registered was not his own. For that matter, some elections give the voter no real choice because there is only one name on a ballot. . . . Yet if the person in the voting booth goes through the motions, we consider him to have voted. The point of all these examples is to show that although voting and discretion are usually combined, voting is still voting when discretion departs. . . .

The Electors and their amici object that the Framers using those words expected the Electors' votes to reflect their own judgments. . . . Whether by choice or accident, the Framers did not reduce their thoughts about electors' discretion to the printed page. All that they put down about the electors was what we have said: that the States would appoint them, and that they would meet and cast ballots to send to the Capitol. Those sparse instructions took no position on how independent from—or how faithful to—party and popular preferences the electors' votes should be. On that score, the Constitution left much to the future. And the future did not take long in coming. Almost immediately, presidential electors became trusty transmitters of other people's decisions.

The Twelfth Amendment embraced this new reality—both acknowledging and facilitating the Electoral College's emergence as a mechanism not for deliberation but for party-line voting. . . . Courts and commentators throughout the 19th century recognized the electors as merely acting on other people's preferences. Justice Story wrote that "the electors are now chosen wholly with reference to particular candidates," having either "silently" or "publicly pledge[d]" how they will vote. "[N]othing is left to the electors," he continued, "but to register [their] votes, which are already pledged."

State election laws evolved to reinforce that development, ensuring that a State's electors would vote the same way as its citizens. [S]tate legislatures early dropped out of the picture; by the mid-1800s, ordinary voters chose electors. Except that increasingly, they did not do so directly. States listed only presidential candidates on the ballot, on the understanding that electors would do no more than vote for the winner. Usually, the State could ensure that result by appointing electors chosen by the winner's party. But to remove any doubt, States began in the early 1900s to enact statutes requiring electors to pledge that they would squelch any urge to break ranks with voters. Washington's law, penalizing a pledge's breach, is only another in the same vein. It reflects a tradition more than two centuries old. In that practice, electors are not free agents; they are to vote for the candidate whom the State's voters have chosen.

The history going the opposite way is one of anomalies only. The Electors stress that since the founding, electors have cast some 180 faithless votes for either President or Vice President. But that is 180 out of over 23,000. And more than a third of the faithless votes come from 1872, when the Democratic Party's nominee (Horace Greeley) died just after Election Day. Putting those aside, faithless votes represent just one-half of one percent of the total. Still, the Electors counter, Congress has counted all those votes. But because faithless votes have never come close to affecting an outcome, only one has ever been challenged. True enough, that one was counted. But the Electors cannot rest a claim of historical tradition on one counted vote in over 200 years. And anyway, the State appointing that elector had no law requiring a pledge or otherwise barring his use of discretion. Congress's deference to a state decision to tolerate a faithless vote is no ground for rejecting a state decision to penalize one.

The Electors' constitutional claim has neither text nor history on its side. Article II and the Twelfth Amendment give States broad power over electors, and give electors themselves no rights. Early in our history, States decided to tie electors to the presidential choices of others, whether legislatures or citizens. Except that legislatures no longer play a role, that practice has continued for more than 200 years. Among the devices States have long used to achieve their object are pledge laws, designed to impress on electors their role as agents of others. A State follows in the same tradition if, like Washington, it chooses to sanction an elector for breaching his promise. Then too, the State instructs its electors that they have no ground for reversing the vote of millions of its citizens. That direction accords with the Constitution—as well as with the trust of a Nation that here, We the People rule.

The judgment of the Supreme Court of Washington is

Affirmed.

JUSTICE THOMAS, with whom JUSTICE GORSUCH joins in part, concurring in the judgment . . . [omitted].

II. REPRESENTATION

Baker v. *Carr*
369 U.S. 186, 82 S.Ct. 691, 7 L.Ed. 2d 663 (1962)

http://caselaw.findlaw.com/us-supreme-court/369/186.html

Appellants brought suit in U.S. District Court in Tennessee, objecting to a 1901 Tennessee statute that apportioned seats for the state's 95 counties in the General Assembly. They claimed that the legislature's failure subsequently to redistrict the seats to take account of substantial growth and redistribution of the state's population debased their votes and thus denied them equal protection of the laws guaranteed by the Fourteenth Amendment. The facts showed that districts containing 37 percent of Tennessee's population elected 20 of the 33 senators; districts containing 40 percent of the population elected 63 of the 99 representatives. The district court ruled that it lacked jurisdiction of the subject matter. Some scholars believe that tensions within the Court over this case not only precipitated Justice Whittaker's retirement soon after the decision came down on March 26, but may have been a large factor in the massive stroke Justice Frankfurter suffered on April 5 that led to his retirement in August. Majority: Brennan, Black, Clark, Douglas, Stewart, Warren. Dissenting: Frankfurter, Harlan. Not participating: Whittaker.

Mr. Justice Brennan delivered the opinion of the Court. . . .

The complaint alleges that the 1901 statute effects an apportionment that deprives the appellants of the equal protection of the laws in violation of the Fourteenth Amendment. . . .

We hold that the appellants do have standing to maintain this suit. Our decisions plainly support this conclusion. Many of the cases have assumed rather than articulated the premise in deciding the merits of similar claims. And *Colegrove* v. *Green* . . . squarely held that voters who allege facts showing disadvantage to themselves as individuals have standing to sue. [A footnote points out that the concurring opinion of Justice Rutledge and Justice Black's dissenting opinion held there was standing, and expressed doubt whether Justice Frankfurter's opinion intimated lack of it.] . . .

We hold that the claim pleaded here neither rests upon nor implicates the Guaranty Clause and that its justiciability is therefore not foreclosed by our decisions of cases involving that clause. The District Court misinterpreted *Colegrove* and other decisions of this Court on which it relied. Appellants' claim that they are being denied equal protection is justiciable, and if "discrimination is sufficiently shown, the right to relief under the equal protection clause is not diminished by the fact that the discrimination relates to political rights." . . . To show why we reject the argument based on the Guaranty Clause, we must examine the authorities under it. But because there appears to be some uncertainty as to why those cases did present political questions, and specifically as to whether this apportionment case is like those cases, we deem it necessary first to consider the contours of the "political question" doctrine. . . . [The opinion considers foreign relations, "durations of hostilities," validity of enactments of constitutional amendments, and the status of Indian tribes.]

Prominent on the surface of any case held to involve a political question is found a textually demonstrable constitutional commitment of the issue to a coordinate political department; or a lack of judicially discoverable and manageable standards for resolving it; or the impossibility of deciding without an initial policy determination of a kind clearly for nonjudicial discretion; or the impossibility of a court's undertaking independent resolution without expressing lack of the respect due coordinate branches of government; or an unusual need for unquestioning adherence to a political decision already made; or the potentiality of embarrassment from multifarious pronouncements by various departments on one question.

Unless one of these formulations is inextricable from the case at bar, there should be no dismissal for nonjusticiability on the ground of a political question's presence. The doctrine of which we treat is one of "political questions," not one of "political cases." The courts cannot reject as "no lawsuit" a bona fide controversy as to whether some action denominated "political" exceeds constitutional authority. . . .

Several factors were thought by the Court in *Luther* [v. *Borden*] to make the question there "political": the commitment to the other branches of the decision as to which is the lawful state government; the unambiguous action by the President, in recognizing the charter government as the lawful authority; the need for finality in the executive's decision; and the lack of criteria by which a court could determine which form of government was republican.

But the only significance that *Luther* could have for our immediate purposes is in its holding that the Guaranty Clause is not a repository of judicially manageable standards which a court could utilize independently in order to identify a State's lawful government. The Court has since refused to resort to the Guaranty Clause—which alone had been invoked for the purpose—as the source of a constitutional standard for invalidating state action. . . .

We come, finally, to the ultimate inquiry whether our precedents as to what constitutes a nonjusticiable "political question" bring the case before us under the umbrella of that doctrine. A natural beginning is to note whether any of the common characteristics which we have been able to identify and label descriptively are present. We find none: The question here is the consistency of state action with the Federal Constitution. We have no question decided, or to be decided, by a political branch of government coequal with this Court. Nor do we risk embarrassment of our government abroad, or grave disturbance at home if we take issue with Tennessee as to the constitutionality of her action here challenged. Nor need the appellants, in order to succeed in this action, ask the Court to enter upon policy determinations for which judicially manageable standards are lacking. Judicial standards under the Equal Protection Clause are well developed and familiar, and it has been open to courts since the enactment of the Fourteenth Amendment to determine, if on the particular facts they review, that a discrimination reflects no policy, but simply arbitrary and capricious action. . . .

We conclude then that the nonjusticiability of claims resting on the Guaranty Clause which arises from their embodiment of questions that were thought "political," can have no bearing upon the justiciability of the equal protection claim presented in this case. Finally, we emphasize that it is the involvement in Guaranty Clause claims of the elements thought to define "political questions," and no other feature, which could render them nonjusticiable. Specifically, we have said that such claims are not held nonjusticiable because they touch matters of state governmental organization. . . . from injecting itself into the clash of political forces in political settlements. . . .

We conclude that the complaint's allegations of a denial of equal protection present a justiciable constitutional cause of action upon which appellants are entitled to a trial and a decision. The right asserted is within the reach of judicial protection under the Fourteenth Amendment.

The judgment of the District Court is reversed and the cause is remanded for further proceedings consistent with this opinion.

MR. JUSTICE DOUGLAS, concurring . . . [omitted].

MR. JUSTICE CLARK, concurring . . . [omitted].

MR. JUSTICE STEWART, concurring . . . [omitted].

MR. JUSTICE FRANKFURTER, with whom MR. JUSTICE HARLAN joins, dissenting.

The Court today reverses a uniform course of decision established by a dozen cases, including one by which the very claim now sustained was unanimously rejected only five years ago. . . . Such a massive repudiation of the experience of our whole past in asserting destructively novel judicial power demands a detailed analysis of the role of this Court in our constitutional scheme. Disregard of inherent limits in the effective exercise of the Court's "judicial Power" not only presages the futility of judicial intervention in the essentially political conflict of forces by which the relation between population and representation has time out of mind been and now is determined. It may well impair the Court's position as the ultimate organ of "the supreme Law of the Land" in that vast range of legal problems, often strongly entangled in popular feeling, on which this Court must pronounce. The Court's authority—possessed neither of the purse nor the sword—ultimately rests on sustained public confidence in its moral sanction. Such feeling must be nourished by the Court's complete detachment, in fact and in appearance, from political entanglements and by abstention from injecting itself into the clash of political forces in political settlements. . . .

For this Court to direct the District Court to enforce a claim to which the Court has over the years consistently found itself required to deny legal enforcement and at the same time to find it necessary to withhold any guidance to the lower court how to enforce this turnabout, new legal claim, manifests an odd—indeed an esoteric—conception of judicial propriety. . . .

Even assuming the indispensable intellectual disinterestedness on the part of judges in such matters, they do not have accepted legal standards or criteria or even reliable analogies to draw upon for making judicial judgments. To charge courts with the task of accommodating the incommensurable factors of policy that underlie these mathematical puzzles is to attribute, however flatteringly, omnicompetence to judges. . . .

We are soothingly told at the bar of this Court that we need not worry about the kind of remedy a court could effectively fashion once the abstract constitutional right to have courts pass on a statewide system of electoral districting is recognized as a matter of judicial rhetoric, because legislatures would heed the Court's admonition. This is not only an euphoric hope. It implies a sorry confession of judicial impotence in place of a frank acknowledgment that there is not under our Constitution a judicial remedy for every political mischief, for every undesirable exercise of legislative power. The Framers carefully and with deliberate forethought refused so to enthrone the judiciary. In this situation, as in others of like nature, appeal for relief does not belong here. Appeal must be to an informed, civically militant electorate. In a democratic society like ours, relief must come through an aroused popular conscience that sears the conscience of the people's representatives. In any event there is nothing judicially more unseemly nor more self-defeating than for this Court to make in terrorem pronouncements, to indulge in merely empty rhetoric, sounding a word of promise to the ear, sure to be disappointing to the hope. . . .

What, then, is this question of legislative apportionment? Appellants invoke the right to vote and to have their votes counted. But they are permitted to vote and their votes are counted. They go to the polls, they cast their ballots, they send their representatives to the state councils. Their complaint is simply that the representatives are not sufficiently numerous or powerful—in short, that Tennessee has adopted a basis of representation with which they are dissatisfied. Talk of "debasement" or "dilution" is circular talk. One cannot speak of "debasement" or "dilution" of the value of a vote until there is first defined a standard of reference as to what a vote should be worth. What is actually asked of the Court in this case is to choose among competing bases of representation—ultimately, really, among competing theories of political philosophy—in order to establish an appropriate frame of government for the State of Tennessee and thereby for all the States of the Union. . . .

What Tennessee illustrates is an old and still widespread method of representation—representation by local geographical division, only in part respective of population—in preference to others, others, forsooth, more appealing. Appellants contest this choice and seek to make this Court the arbiter of the disagreement. They would make the Equal Protection Clause the charter of adjudication, asserting that the equality which it guarantees comports, if not the assurance of equal weight to every voter's vote, at least the basic conception that representation ought to be proportionate to population, a standard by reference to which the reasonableness of apportionment plans may be judged.

To find such a political conception legally enforceable in the broad and unspecific guarantee of equal protection is to rewrite the Constitution. . . .

Reynolds v. *Sims*
377 U.S. 533, 84 S.Ct. 1362, 12 L.Ed. 2d 506 (1964)

http://caselaw.findlaw.com/us-supreme-court/377/533.html

The climax of a series of cases involving challenges to state districting arrangements came in 1964, when the Court invalidated the legislative apportionments of Alabama, Colorado, Delaware, Maryland, New York, and Virginia. Challenged specifically in Alabama, where the legislature had last been redistricted after the 1900 census, were three distinct apportionment schemes: the existing plan, a proposed plan, and a "stand-by" plan. All contained population variations ranging, at the least, from 31,175 to 634,854 for the 35-member state senate, and from 20,000 to 52,000 for the 106-member house. A three-judge panel of the U.S. District Court for the Middle District of Alabama found each plan constitutionally deficient. The majority opinion in *Reynolds* v. *Sims* (the Alabama case) sets forth the basic principles applied in each of the six cases. Majority: Warren, Black, Brennan, Clark, Douglas, Goldberg, Stewart, White. Dissenting: Harlan. Justice Stewart, joined by Justice Clark, dissented in the New York and Colorado cases, although both were in the majority in *Reynolds*. Stewart's opinion from the New York and Colorado cases is reprinted here following Justice Harlan's dissent.

Mr. Chief Justice Warren delivered the opinion of the Court. . . .

Legislators represent people, not trees or acres. Legislators are elected by voters, not farms or cities or economic interests. As long as ours is a representative form of government, and our legislatures are those instruments of government elected directly by and directly representative of the people, the right to elect legislators in a free and unimpaired fashion is a bedrock of our political system. It could hardly be gainsaid that a constitutional claim had been asserted by an allegation that certain otherwise qualified voters had been entirely prohibited from voting for members of their state legislature. And, if a State should provide that the votes of citizens in one part of the State should be given two times, or five times, or ten times the weight of votes of citizens in another part of the State, it could hardly be contended that the right to vote of those residing in the disfavored areas had not been effectively diluted. It would appear extraordinary to suggest that a state could be constitutionally permitted to enact a law providing that certain of the state's voters could vote two, five, or ten times for their legislative representatives, while voters living elsewhere could vote only once. And it is inconceivable that a state law to the effect that, in counting votes for legislators, the votes of citizens in one part of the State would be multiplied by two, five or ten, while the votes of persons in another area would be counted only at face value, could be constitutionally sustainable. Of course, the effect of state legislative districting schemes which give the same number of representatives to unequal numbers of constituents is identical. . . .

Logically, in a society that is ostensibly grounded on representative government, it would seem reasonable that a majority of the people of the State could elect a majority of that State's legislators. To conclude differently, and to sanction minority control of state legislative bodies, would appear to deny majority rights in a way that far surpasses any possible denial of minority rights that might otherwise be thought to result. Since legislatures are responsible for enacting laws by which all citizens are to be governed, they should be bodies which are collectively responsive to the popular will. And the concept of equal protection has been traditionally viewed as requiring the uniform treatment of persons standing in the same relation to the governmental action questioned or challenged. With respect to the allocation of legislative representation, all voters, as citizens of a State, stand in the same relation regardless of where they live. Any suggested criteria for the differentiation of citizens are insufficient to justify any discrimination, as to the weight of their votes, unless relevant to the permissible purposes of legislative apportionment. Since the achieving of fair and effective representation for all citizens is concededly the basic aim of legislative apportionment, we conclude that the Equal Protection Clause guarantees the opportunity for equal participation by all voters in the election of state legislators. . . .

To the extent that a citizen's right to vote is debased, he is that much less a citizen. The fact that an individual lives here or there is not a legitimate reason for overweighting or diluting the efficacy of his vote. . . .

We hold that, as a basic constitutional standard, the Equal Protection Clause requires that the seats in both houses of a bicameral state legislature must be apportioned on a population basis. Simply stated, an individual's right to vote for state legislators is unconstitutionally impaired when its weight is in a substantial fashion diluted when compared with votes of citizens living in other parts of the State. Since, under neither the existing apportionment provisions nor under either of the proposed plans was either of the houses of the Alabama Legislature apportioned on a population basis, the District Court correctly held that all three of these schemes were constitutionally invalid. . . .

Much has been written since our decision in *Baker* v. *Carr* about the applicability of the so-called federal analogy to state legislative apportionment arrangements. After considering the matter, the court below concluded that no conceivable analogy could be drawn between the federal scheme and the apportionment of seats in the Alabama Legislature under the proposed constitutional amendment. We agree with the District Court and find the federal analogy inapposite and irrelevant to state legislative districting schemes. Attempted reliance on the federal analogy often appears to be little more than an after-the-fact rationalization offered in defense of maladjusted state apportionment arrangements. The original constitutions of 36 of our States provided that representation in both houses of the state legislatures would be based completely, or predominantly, on population. And the Founding Fathers clearly had no intention of establishing a pattern or model for the apportionment of seats in state legislatures when the system of representation in the Federal Congress was adopted. Demonstrative of this is the fact that the Northwest Ordinance, adopted in the same year, 1787, as the Federal Constitution, provided for the apportionment of seats in territorial legislatures solely on the basis of population.

The system of representation in the two Houses of the Federal Congress is one ingrained in our Constitution, as part of the law of the land. It is one conceived out of compromise and concession indispensable to the establishment of our federal republic. Arising from unique historical circumstances, it is based on the consideration that in establishing our type of federalism a group of formerly independent States bound themselves together under one national government. . . .

We do not believe that the concept of bicameralism is rendered anachronistic and meaningless when the predominant basis of representation in the two state legislative bodies is required to be the same—population. A prime reason for bicameralism, modernly considered, is to insure mature and deliberate consideration of, and to prevent precipitate action on, proposed legislative measures. Simply because the controlling criterion for apportioning representation is required to be the same in both houses does not mean that there will be no differences in the composition and complexion of the two bodies. Different constituencies can be represented in the two houses. One body could be composed of single-member districts while the other could have at least some multimember districts. The length of terms of the legislators in the separate bodies could differ. The numerical size of the two bodies could be made to differ, even significantly, and the geographical size of districts from which legislators are elected could also be made to differ. . . . [T]hese and other factors could be, and are presently in many States, utilized to engender differing complexions and collective attitudes in the two bodies of a state legislature, although both are apportioned substantially on a population basis. . . .

[W]e affirm the judgment below and remand the cases for further proceedings consistent with the views stated in this opinion.

It is so ordered.

Mr. Justice Harlan, dissenting. . . .

These decisions also cut deeply into the fabric of our federalism. What must follow from them may eventually appear to be the product of State Legislatures. Nevertheless, no thinking person can fail to recognize that the aftermath of these cases, however desirable it may be thought in itself, will have been achieved at the cost of a radical alteration in the relationship between the States and the Federal Government, more particularly the Federal Judiciary. Only one who has an overbearing impatience with the federal system and its political processes will believe that the cost was not too high or was inevitable.

. . . [T]hese decisions give support to a current mistaken view of the Constitution and the constitutional function of this Court. Amendment, it is not predominantly practiced by the States today." . . . This view, in a nutshell, is that every major social ill in this country can find its cure in some constitutional "principle," and that this Court should "take the lead" in promoting reform when other branches of government fail to act. The Constitution is not a panacea for every blot upon the public welfare, nor should this Court, ordained as a judicial body, be thought of as a general haven for reform movements. The Constitution is an instrument of government, fundamental to which is the premise that in a diffusion of governmental authority lies the greatest promise that this Nation will realize liberty for all its citizens. This Court, limited in function in accordance with that premise, does not serve its high purpose when it exceeds its authority, even to satisfy justified impatience with the slow workings of the political process. For when, in the name of constitutional interpretation, the Court adds something to the Constitution that was deliberately excluded from it, the Court in reality substitutes its view of what should be so for the amending process. . . .

Mr. Justice Stewart, whom Mr. Justice Clark joins, dissenting [in the New York and Colorado cases]. . . .

Simply stated, the question is to what degree, if at all, the Equal Protection Clause of the

Fourteenth Amendment limits each sovereign State's freedom to establish appropriate electoral constituencies from which representatives to the State's bicameral legislative assembly are to be chosen. The Court's answer is a blunt one, and, I think, woefully wrong. The Equal Protection Clause, said the Court, "requires that the seats in both houses of a bicameral state legislature must be apportioned on a population basis." . . .

With all respect, I think that this is not correct, simply as a matter of fact. It has been unanswerably demonstrated before now that this "was not the colonial system, it was not the system chosen for the national government by the Constitution, it was not the system exclusively or even predominantly practiced by the States at the time of adoption of the Fourteenth Amendment, it is not predominantly practiced by the States today. . . .

The Court's draconian pronouncement, which makes unconstitutional the legislatures of most of the 50 States, finds no support in the words of the Constitution, in any prior decision of this Court, or in the 175-year political history of our Federal Union. With all respect, I am convinced these decisions mark a long step backward into that unhappy era when a majority of the members of this Court were thought by many to have convinced themselves and each other that the demands of the Constitution were to be measured not by what it says, but by their own notions of wise political theory. . . .

What the Court has done is to convert a particular political philosophy into a constitutional rule, binding upon each of the 50 States, from Maine to Hawaii, from Alaska to Texas, without regard and without respect for the many individualized and differentiated characteristics stemming from each State's distinct history, distinct geography, distinct distribution of population, and distinct political heritage. My own understanding of the various theories of representative government is that no one theory has ever commanded unanimous assent among political scientists, historians, or others who have considered the problem. But even if it were thought that the rule announced today by the Court is, as a matter of political theory, the most desirable general rule which can be devised as a basis for the make-up of the representative assembly of a typical State, I could not join in the fabrication of a constitutional mandate which imports and forever freezes one theory of political thought into our Constitution, and forever denies to every State any opportunity for enlightened and progressive innovation in the design of its democratic institutions, so as to accommodate within a system of representative government the interests and aspirations of diverse groups of people, without subjecting any group or class to absolute domination by a geographically concentrated or highly organized majority.

Representative government is a process of accommodating group interests through democratic institutional arrangements. Its function is to channel the numerous opinions, interests, and abilities of the people of a State into the making of the State's public policy. Appropriate legislative apportionment, therefore, should ideally be designed to insure effective representation in the State's legislature, in cooperation with other organs of political power, of the various groups and interests making up the electorate. In practice, of course, this ideal is approximated in the particular apportionment system of any State by a realistic accommodation of the diverse and often conflicting political forces operating within the State. . . . the constitutional validity of which the Court does not question, carries with it an acceptance of the idea of legislative representation of regional needs and interests. Yet if geographical residence is irrelevant, as the Court suggests, and the goal is solely that of equally "weighted" votes, I do not understand why the Court's constitutional rule does not require the abolition of districts and the holding of all elections at large. . . .

I think that the Equal Protection Clause demands but two basic attributes of any plan of state legislative apportionment. First, it demands that, in the light of the State's own characteristics and needs, the plan must be a rational one. Second, it demands that the plan must be such as not to permit the systematic frustration of the will of a majority of the electorate of the State. I think it is apparent that any plan of legislative apportionment which could be shown to reflect no policy, but simply arbitrary and capricious action or inaction, and that any plan which could be shown systematically to prevent ultimate effective majority rule, would be invalid under accepted Equal Protection Clause standards. But, beyond this, I think there is nothing in the Federal Constitution to prevent a State from choosing any electoral legislative structure it thinks best suited to the interests, temper, and customs of its people. . . .

The Court today declines to give any recognition to these considerations and countless others, tangible and intangible, in holding unconstitutional the particular systems of legislative apportionment which these States have chosen. Instead, the Court says that the requirements of the Equal Protection Clause can be met in any State only by the uncritical, simplistic, and heavy-handed application of sixth-grade arithmetic. . . .

Rucho v. *Common Cause* and *Lemone* v. *Benisek* 588 U.S. ___, 139 S.Ct. 2484, 207 L.Ed. 2d 931 (2019)

www.supremecourt.gov/opinions/18pdf/18-422_9ol1.pdf

The background of this pair of cases that the Court decided together appears in the chief justice's opinion below. These cases followed *Gill* v. *Whitford* (2018), a partisan gerrymandering case from Wisconsin in which the Court unanimously sidestepped the constitutional issues and instead resolved the case against the plaintiff because of the absence of standing. Majority (in this pair of cases): Roberts, Alito, Gorsuch, Kavanaugh, Thomas. Dissenting: Breyer, Ginsburg, Kagan, Sotomayor.

Chief Justice Roberts delivered the opinion of the Court.

Voters and other plaintiffs in North Carolina and Maryland challenged their States' congressional districting maps as unconstitutional partisan gerrymanders. The North Carolina plaintiffs complained that the State's districting plan discriminated against Democrats; the Maryland plaintiffs complained that their State's plan discriminated against Republicans. The plaintiffs alleged that the gerrymandering violated the First Amendment, the Equal Protection Clause of the Fourteenth Amendment, the Elections Clause, and Article I, § 2, of the Constitution. The District Courts in both cases ruled in favor of the plaintiffs, and the defendants appealed directly to this Court.

These cases require us to consider once again whether claims of excessive partisanship in districting are "justiciable"—that is, properly suited for resolution by the federal courts. This Court has not previously struck down a districting plan as an unconstitutional partisan gerrymander, and has struggled without success over the past several decades to discern judicially manageable standards for deciding such claims. The districting plans at issue here are highly partisan, by any measure. The question is whether the courts below appropriately exercised judicial power when they found them unconstitutional as well. . . .

Chief Justice Marshall famously wrote that it is "the province and duty of the judicial department to say what the law is." Sometimes, however, "the law is that the judicial department has no business entertaining the claim of unlawfulness—because the question is entrusted to one of the political branches or involves no judicially enforceable rights." In such a case the claim is said to present a "political question" and to be nonjusticiable—outside the courts' competence and therefore beyond the courts' jurisdiction. Among the political question cases the Court has identified are those that lack "judicially discoverable and manageable standards for resolving [them].". . .

Partisan gerrymandering is nothing new. Nor is frustration with it. The practice was known in the Colonies prior to Independence, and the Framers were familiar with it at the time of the drafting and ratification of the Constitution. . . . The Framers were aware of electoral districting problems and considered what to do about them. They settled on a characteristic approach, assigning the issue to the state legislatures, expressly checked and balanced by the Federal Congress . . . Courts have nevertheless been called upon to resolve a variety of questions surrounding districting [and] . . . [p]artisan gerrymandering claims have proved far more difficult to adjudicate. . . . The "central problem" is not determining whether a jurisdiction has engaged in partisan gerrymandering. It is "determining when political gerrymandering has gone too far." . . .

Partisan gerrymandering claims rest on an instinct that groups with a certain level of political support should enjoy a commensurate level of political power and influence. Explicitly or implicitly, a districting map is alleged to be unconstitutional because it makes it too difficult for one party to translate statewide support into seats in the legislature. But such a claim is based on a "norm that does not exist" in our electoral system. . . . "Our cases, however, clearly foreclose any claim that the Constitution requires proportional representation or that legislatures in reapportioning must draw district lines to come as near as possible to allocating seats to the contending parties in proportion to what their anticipated statewide vote will be." . . .

The initial difficulty in settling on a "clear, manageable and politically neutral" test for fairness is that it is not even clear what fairness looks like in this context. . . . There are no legal standards discernible in the Constitution for making such judgments, let alone limited and precise standards that are clear, manageable, and politically neutral. . . . And it is only after determining how to define fairness that you can even begin to answer the determinative question: "How much is too much?" At what point does permissible partisanship become unconstitutional?

Appellees contend that if we can adjudicate one-person, one-vote claims, we can also assess partisan gerrymandering claims. But the one-person, one-vote rule is relatively easy to administer as a matter of math. The same cannot be said of partisan gerrymandering claims, because the Constitution supplies no objective measure for assessing whether a districting map treats a political party fairly. It hardly follows from the principle that each person must have an equal say in the election of representatives that a person is entitled to have his political party achieve representation in some way commensurate to its share of statewide support. More fundamentally, "vote dilution" in the one-person, one-vote cases refers to the idea that each vote must carry equal weight. In other words, each representative must be accountable to (approximately) the same number of constituents. That requirement does not extend to political parties. It does not mean that each party must be influential in proportion to its number of supporters. As we stated unanimously in *Gill*, "this Court is not responsible for vindicating generalized partisan preferences.

The Court's constitutionally prescribed role is to vindicate the individual rights of the people appearing before it." . . .

Appellees and the dissent propose a number of "tests" for evaluating partisan gerrymandering claims, but none meets the need for a limited and precise standard that is judicially discernible and manageable. And none provides a solid grounding for judges to take the extraordinary step of reallocating power and influence between political parties. . . .

Even the most sophisticated districting maps cannot reliably account for some of the reasons voters prefer one candidate over another, or why their preferences may change. . . . [A]sking judges to predict how a particular districting map will perform in future elections risks basing constitutional holdings on unstable ground outside judicial expertise. . . .

The District Courts also found partisan gerrymandering claims justiciable under the First Amendment, coalescing around a basic three-part test: proof of intent to burden individuals based on their voting history or party affiliation; an actual burden on political speech or associational rights; and a causal link between the invidious intent and actual burden. Both District Courts concluded that the districting plans at issue violated the plaintiffs' First Amendment right to association. . . .

The plaintiffs' argument is that partisanship in districting should be regarded as simple discrimination against supporters of the opposing party on the basis of political viewpoint. Under that theory, any level of partisanship in districting would constitute an infringement of their First Amendment rights. But as the Court has explained, "[i]t would be idle . . . to contend that any political consideration taken into account in fashioning a reapportionment plan is sufficient to invalidate it." The First Amendment test simply describes the act of districting for partisan advantage. It provides no standard for determining when partisan activity goes too far. . . .

The dissent proposes using a State's own districting criteria as a neutral baseline from which to measure how extreme a partisan gerrymander is. The dissent would have us line up all the possible maps drawn using those criteria according to the partisan distribution they would produce. Distance from the "median" map would indicate whether a particular districting plan harms supporters of one party to an unconstitutional extent. As an initial matter, it does not make sense to use criteria that will vary from State to State and year to year as the baseline for determining whether a gerrymander violates the Federal Constitution. The degree of partisan advantage that the Constitution tolerates should not turn on criteria offered by the gerrymanderers themselves. It is easy to imagine how different criteria could move the median map toward different partisan distributions. As a result, the same map could be constitutional or not depending solely on what the mapmakers said they set out to do. That possibility illustrates that the dissent's proposed constitutional test is indeterminate and arbitrary.

Even if we were to accept the dissent's proposed baseline, it would return us to "the original unanswerable question (How much political motivation and effect is too much?)." Would twenty percent away from the median map be okay? Forty percent? Sixty percent? Why or why not? (We appreciate that the dissent finds all the unanswerable questions annoying, but it seems a useful way to make the point.) The dissent's answer says it all: "This much is too much." That is not even trying to articulate a standard or rule.

Excessive partisanship in districting leads to results that reasonably seem unjust. But the fact that such gerrymandering is "incompatible with democratic principles," does not mean that the solution lies with the federal judiciary. We conclude that partisan gerrymandering claims present political questions beyond the reach of the federal courts. Federal judges have no license to reallocate political power between the two major political parties, with no plausible grant of authority in the Constitution, and no legal standards to limit and direct their decisions. . . .

Our conclusion does not condone excessive partisan gerrymandering. Nor does our conclusion condemn complaints about districting to echo into a void. The States, for example, are actively addressing the issue on a number of fronts. In . . . Provisions in state statutes and state constitutions can provide standards and guidance for state courts to apply. . . . Indeed, numerous other States are restricting partisan considerations in districting through legislation. One way they are doing so is by placing power to draw electoral districts in the hands of independent commissions. . . . As noted, the Framers gave Congress the power to do something about partisan gerrymandering in the Elections Clause. We express no view on any . . . pending proposals. We simply note that the avenue for reform established by the Framers, and used by Congress in the past, remains open. . . .

The judgments of the United States District Court for the Middle District of North Carolina and the United States District Court for the District of Maryland are vacated, and the cases are remanded with instructions to dismiss for lack of jurisdiction.

It is so ordered.

Justice Kagan, with whom Justices Ginsburg, Breyer, and Sotomayor join, dissenting.

For the first time ever, this Court refuses to remedy a constitutional violation because it thinks the task beyond judicial capabilities. And not just any constitutional violation. The partisan gerrymanders in these cases deprived citizens of the most fundamental of their constitutional rights: the rights to participate equally in the political process, to join with others to advance political beliefs, and to choose their political representatives. In so doing, the partisan gerrymanders here debased and dishonored our democracy, turning upside-down the core American idea that all governmental power derives from the people. . . . If left unchecked, gerrymanders like the ones here may irreparably damage our system of government. And checking them is not beyond the courts. . . . Indeed, the majority concedes (really, how could it not?) that gerrymandering is "incompatible with democratic principles." That recognition would seem to demand a response. The majority offers two ideas that might qualify as such. One is that the political process can deal with the problem—a proposition so dubious on its face that I feel secure in delaying my answer for some time. The other is that political gerrymanders have always been with us. . . . The majority's idea instead seems to be that if we have lived with partisan gerrymanders so long, we will survive. . . .

Partisan gerrymandering of the kind before us not only subverts democracy (as if that weren't bad enough). It violates individuals' constitutional rights as well. . . . Partisan gerrymandering operates through vote dilution—the devaluation of one citizen's vote as compared to others. A mapmaker draws district lines to "pack" and "crack" voters likely to support the disfavored party. He packs supermajorities of those voters into a relatively few districts, in numbers far greater than needed for their preferred candidates to prevail. Then he cracks the rest across many more districts, spreading them so thin that their candidates will not be able to win. Whether the person is packed or cracked, his vote carries less weight—has less consequence—than it would under a neutrally drawn (non-partisan) map. In short, the mapmaker has made some votes count for less, because they are likely to go for the other party.

That practice implicates the Fourteenth Amendment's Equal Protection Clause. . . . And partisan gerrymandering implicates the First Amendment too. That Amendment gives its greatest protection to political beliefs, speech, and association. Yet partisan gerrymanders subject certain voters to "disfavored treatment"—again, counting their votes for less—precisely because of "their voting history [and] their expression of political views." And added to that strictly personal harm is an associational one. . . . By diluting the votes of certain citizens, the State frustrates their efforts to translate those affiliations into political effectiveness. . . .

The majority gives two reasons for thinking that the adjudication of partisan gerrymandering claims is beyond judicial capabilities. First and foremost, the majority says, it cannot find a neutral baseline . . . from which to measure injury. . . . And second, the majority argues that even after establishing a baseline, a court would have no way to answer "the determinative question: 'How much is too much?'" No "discernible and manageable" standard is available, the majority claims—and so courts could willy-nilly become embroiled in fixing every districting plan. I'll give the majority this one—and important—thing: It identifies some dangers everyone should want to avoid. Judges should not be apportioning political power based on their own vision of electoral fairness, whether proportional representation or any other. And judges should not be striking down maps left, right, and center, on the view that every smidgen of politics is a smidgen too much. Respect for state legislative processes—and restraint in the exercise of judicial authority—counsels intervention in only egregious cases.

But in throwing up its hands, the majority misses something under its nose: What it says can't be done has been done. Over the past several years, federal courts across the country—including, but not exclusively, in the decisions below—have largely converged on a standard for adjudicating partisan gerrymandering claims (striking down both Democratic and Republican districting plans in the process). And that standard does what the majority says is impossible. The standard does not use any judge-made conception of electoral fairness—either proportional representation or any other; instead, it takes as its baseline a State's own criteria of fairness, apart from partisan gain. And by requiring plaintiffs to make difficult showings relating to both purpose and effects, the standard invalidates the most extreme, but only the most extreme, partisan gerrymanders. . . .

Start with the standard the lower courts used. Both courts focused on the harm of vote dilution, though the North Carolina court mostly grounded its analysis in the Fourteenth Amendment and the Maryland court in the First. And both courts (like others around the country) used basically the same three-part test to decide whether the plaintiffs had made out a vote dilution claim. As many legal standards do, that test has three parts: (1) intent; (2) effects; and (3) causation. First, the plaintiffs challenging a districting plan must prove that state officials' "predominant purpose" in drawing a district's lines was to "entrench [their party] in power" by diluting the votes of citizens favoring its rival. Second, the plaintiffs must establish that the lines drawn in fact have the intended effect by "substantially" diluting their votes. And third, if the plaintiffs make those showings, the State must come up with a legitimate, non-partisan justification to save its map. . . . Turn now to the test's application. First, did the North Carolina and Maryland districters have the predominant purpose of entrenching their own party in power? Here, the two District Courts catalogued the overwhelming direct evidence that they did. . . .

On to the second step of the analysis, where the plaintiffs must prove that the districting plan substantially dilutes their votes. . . . The evidence reveals just how bad the two gerrymanders were (in case you had any doubts). And it shows how the same technologies and data that today facilitate extreme partisan gerrymanders also enable courts to discover them, by exposing just how much they dilute votes. . . .

The majority's broadest claim . . . is that this is a price we must pay because judicial oversight of partisan gerrymandering cannot be "politically neutral" or "manageable." Courts, the majority argues, will have to choose among contested notions of electoral fairness. . . .

The majority's sole response misses the point. According to the majority, "it does not make sense to use" a State's own (non-partisan) districting criteria as the baseline from which to measure partisan gerrymandering because those criteria "will vary from State to State and year to year." But that is a virtue, not a vice—a feature, not a bug. Using the criteria the State itself has chosen at the relevant time prevents any judicial predilections from affecting the analysis—exactly what the majority claims it wants. . . .

The majority's "how much is too much" critique fares no better than its neutrality argument. . . . How much is too much? At the least, any gerrymanders as bad as these.

Of all times to abandon the Court's duty to declare the law, this was not the one. The practices challenged in these cases imperil our system of government. Part of the Court's role in that system is to defend its foundations. None is more important than free and fair elections. With respect but deep sadness, I dissent.

Miller v. *Johnson*
515 U.S. 900, 115 S.Ct. 2475, 132 L.Ed. 2d 762 (1995)

http://caselaw.findlaw.com/us-supreme-court/515/900.html

In 1972, Georgia gained its first African American member of Congress since Reconstruction, and redistricting after the 1980 census created the state's first majority–minority district. Under the 1990 census, Georgia's population (27 percent of which was black) entitled the state to an additional representative in Congress. The state's General Assembly approved a districting plan that contained three majority–minority districts after the Justice Department refused to preclear, under § 5 of the Voting Rights Act, two earlier plans that each contained only two majority-black districts. Elections held in November 1992 resulted in the election of black representatives from all three majority–minority districts. In 1994, white voters in the new Eleventh District challenged the constitutionality of their district on the ground that it was a racial gerrymander in violation of the equal protection clause as interpreted in *Shaw* v. *Reno* (1993). A three-judge panel of the U.S. District Court for the Southern District of Georgia agreed, holding that the state legislature's purpose, as well as the district's irregular borders, showed that race was the overriding and predominant force in the districting determination. The lower court assumed that compliance with the Voting Rights Act would be a compelling interest but found that the plan was not narrowly tailored to meet that interest because the law did not require three majority–minority districts.

After the Supreme Court's decision (reprinted below), the Georgia legislature did not reach agreement on a revised plan by the October 15, 1995, deadline imposed by the district court. The district court then redrew the boundaries of the state's 11 congressional districts, leaving only the one majority–minority district, which roughly corresponded to the district that had been created after the 1980 census. In the November 1996 elections, the black incumbents who had represented the formerly majority–minority districts won reelection to the U.S. House of Representatives, as did the incumbent from the surviving majority–minority district. In 1997, the Supreme Court upheld the districting plan used in the 1996 elections (*Abrams* v. *Johnson*). Majority: Kennedy, Rehnquist, O'Connor, Scalia, Thomas. Dissenting: Stevens, Souter, Ginsburg, Breyer.

JUSTICE KENNEDY delivered the opinion of the Court. . . .

The Equal Protection Clause's . . . central mandate is racial neutrality in governmental decision-making. . . . Laws classifying citizens on the basis of race cannot be upheld unless they are narrowly tailored to achieving a compelling state interest. . . .

In *Shaw* v. *Reno* we recognized that these equal protection principles govern a State's drawing of congressional districts, though, as our cautious approach there discloses, application of these principles to electoral districting is a most delicate task. . . .

This case requires us to apply the principles articulated in *Shaw* to the most recent congressional redistricting plan enacted by the State of Georgia.

In 1965, the Attorney General designated Georgia a covered jurisdiction under § 4(b) of the Voting Rights Act. In consequence, § 5 of the Act requires Georgia to obtain either administrative preclearance by the Attorney General or approval by the United States District Court for the District of Columbia of any change in a "standard, practice, or procedure with respect to voting" made after November 1, 1964. The preclearance mechanism applies to congressional redistricting plans, and requires that the proposed change "not have the purpose and will not have the effect of denying or abridging the right to vote on account of race or color." "[T]he purpose of § 5 has always been to insure that no voting-procedure changes would be made that would lead to a retrogression in the position of racial minorities with respect to their effective exercise of the electoral franchise." . . .

Twice spurned [by the Justice Department], the General Assembly set out to create three majority-minority districts to gain preclearance. Using the A[merican] C[ivil] L[iberties] U[nion]'s "max-black" plan as its benchmark, the General Assembly enacted a plan that "bore all the signs of [the Justice Department's] involvement. . . ." The new plan . . . connect[ed] the black neighborhoods of metropolitan Atlanta and the poor black populace of coastal Chatham County, though 260 miles apart in distance and worlds apart in culture. . . . [T]he social, political and economic makeup of the Eleventh District tells a tale of disparity, not community. . . .

[Appellants] contend that evidence of a legislature's deliberate classification of voters on the basis of race cannot alone suffice to state a claim under *Shaw*. They argue that, regardless of the legislature's purposes, a plaintiff must demonstrate that a district's shape is so bizarre that it is unexplainable other than on the basis of race, and that appellees failed to make that showing here. Appellants' conception of the constitutional violation misapprehends our holding in Shaw. . . .

Our observation in *Shaw* of the consequences of racial stereotyping was not meant to suggest that a district must be bizarre on its face before there is a constitutional violation. . . . Shape is relevant not because bizarreness is . . . the constitutional wrong. . ., but because it may be persuasive circumstantial evidence that race for its own sake, and not other districting principles, was the legislature's dominant and controlling rationale in drawing its district lines. The logical implication, as courts applying *Shaw* have recognized, is that parties may rely on evidence other than bizarreness to establish race-based districting. . . .

In sum, we make clear that parties alleging that a State has assigned voters on the basis of race are neither confined in their proof to evidence regarding the district's geometry and makeup nor required to make a threshold showing of bizarreness. Today's case requires us further to consider the requirements of the proof necessary to sustain this equal protection challenge.

Federal court review of districting legislation represents a serious intrusion on the most vital of local functions. . . . Redistricting legislatures will, for example, almost always be aware of racial demographics; but it does not follow that race predominates in the redistricting process. . . . The distinction between being aware of racial considerations and being motivated by them may be difficult to make. This evidentiary difficulty, together with the sensitive nature of redistricting and the presumption of good faith that must be accorded legislative enactments, requires courts to exercise extraordinary caution in adjudicating claims that a state has drawn district lines on the basis of race. The plaintiff's burden is to show, either through circumstantial evidence of a district's shape and demographics or more direct evidence going to legislative purpose, that race was the predominant factor motivating the legislature's decision to place a significant number of voters within or without a particular district. To make this showing, a plaintiff must prove that the legislature subordinated traditional race-neutral districting principles, including but not limited to compactness, contiguity, respect for political subdivisions or communities defined by actual shared interests, to racial considerations. Where these or other race-neutral considerations are the basis for redistricting legislation, and are not subordinated to race, a state can "defeat a claim that a district has been gerrymandered on racial lines." . . .

In our view, the District Court applied the correct analysis, and its finding that race was the predominant factor motivating the drawing of the Eleventh District was not clearly erroneous. The court found it was "exceedingly obvious" from the shape of the Eleventh District, together with the relevant racial demographics, that the drawing of narrow land bridges to incorporate within the district outlying appendages containing nearly 80 percent of the district's total black population was a deliberate attempt to bring black populations into the district. . . .

As a result, Georgia's congressional redistricting plan cannot be upheld unless it satisfies strict scrutiny, our most rigorous and exacting standard of constitutional review.

To satisfy strict scrutiny, the State must demonstrate that its districting legislation is narrowly tailored to achieve a compelling interest. . . . The State does not argue, however, that it created the Eleventh District to remedy past discrimination, and with good reason: there is little doubt that the State's true interest in designing the Eleventh District was creating a third majority-black district to satisfy the Justice Department's preclearance demands. . . . Whether or not in some cases compliance with the Voting Rights Act, standing alone, can provide a compelling interest independent of any interest in remedying past discrimination, it cannot do so here. . . . The congressional plan challenged here was not required by the Voting Rights Act under a correct reading of the statute. . . .

Georgia's drawing of the Eleventh District was not required under the Act because there was no reasonable basis to believe that Georgia's earlier enacted plans violated § 5. . . . Georgia's first and second proposed plans increased the number of majority-black districts from 1 out of 10 (10 percent) to 2 out of 11 (18.18 percent). These plans were "ameliorative" and could not have violated § 5's nonretrogression principle.

"[T]he purpose of § 5 has always been to insure that no voting-procedure changes would be made that would lead to a retrogression in the position of racial minorities with respect to their effective exercise of the electoral franchise." The Justice Department's maximization policy seems quite far removed from this purpose. We are especially reluctant to conclude that § 5 justifies that policy given the serious constitutional concerns it raises. . . .

The Voting Rights Act, and its grant of authority to the federal courts to uncover official efforts to abridge minorities' right to vote, has been of vital importance in eradicating invidious discrimination from the electoral process and enhancing the legitimacy of our political institutions. Only if our political system and our society cleanse themselves of that discrimination will all members of the polity share an equal opportunity to gain public office regardless of race. . . . It takes a shortsighted and unauthorized view of the Voting Rights Act to invoke that statute, which has played a decisive role in redressing some of our worst forms of discrimination, to demand the very racial stereotyping the Fourteenth Amendment forbids.

The judgment of the District Court is affirmed, and the case is remanded for further proceedings consistent with this decision.

It is so ordered.

JUSTICE O'CONNOR, concurring . . . [omitted].

JUSTICE STEVENS, dissenting . . . [omitted].

JUSTICE GINSBURG, with whom JUSTICES STEVENS and BREYER join, and with whom JUSTICE SOUTER joins in part, dissenting. . . .

[T]he fact that the Georgia General Assembly took account of race in drawing district lines—a fact not in dispute—does not render the State's plan invalid. To offend the Equal Protection Clause, all agree, the legislature had to do more than consider race. How much more, is the issue that divides the Court today. . . .

The record before us does not show that race . . . overwhelmed traditional districting practices in Georgia. Although the Georgia General Assembly prominently considered race in shaping the Eleventh District, race did not crowd out all other factors. . . .

In contrast to the snake-like North Carolina district inspected in *Shaw*, Georgia's Eleventh District is hardly "bizarre," "extremely irregular," or "irrational on its face." . . .

Along with attention to size, shape, and political subdivisions, the Court recognizes as an appropriate districting principle, "respect for . . . communities defined by actual shared interests." The Court finds no community here, however, because a report in the record showed "fractured political, social, and economic interests within the Eleventh District's black population."

But ethnicity itself can tie people together, as volumes of social science literature have documented—even people with divergent economic interests. . . .

To accommodate the reality of ethnic bonds, legislatures have long drawn voting districts along ethnic lines. Our Nation's cities are full of districts identified by their ethnic character—Chinese, Irish, Italian, Jewish, Polish, Russian, for example. . . . The creation of ethnic districts reflecting felt identity is not ordinarily viewed as offensive or demeaning to those included in the delineation. . . .

That ethnicity defines some of these groups is a political reality. Until now, no constitutional infirmity has been seen in districting Irish or Italian voters together, for example, so long as the delineation does not abandon familiar apportionment practices. If Chinese-Americans and Russian-Americans may seek and secure group recognition in the delineation of voting districts, then African-Americans should not be dissimilarly treated. Otherwise, in the name of equal protection, we would shut out "the very minority group whose history in the United States gave birth to the Equal Protection Clause."

Under the Court's approach, judicial review of the same intensity, that is, strict scrutiny, is in order once it is determined that an apportionment is predominantly motivated by race. It matters not at all, in this new regime, whether the apportionment dilutes or enhances minority voting strength. As very recently observed, however, "[t]here is no moral or constitutional equivalence between a policy that is designed to perpetuate a caste system and one that seeks to eradicate racial subordination."

Special circumstances justify vigilant judicial inspection to protect minority voters—circumstances that do not apply to majority voters. . . . The majority, by definition, encounters no such blockage. White voters in Georgia do not lack means to exert strong pressure on their state legislators. The force of their numbers is itself a powerful determiner of what the legislature will do that does not coincide with perceived majority interests. . . .

The Court's disposition renders redistricting perilous work for state legislatures. . . . Only after litigation—under either the Voting Rights Act, the Court's new *Miller* standard, or both—will States now be assured that plans conscious of race are safe. . . . This enlargement of the judicial role is unwarranted. . . . Accordingly, I dissent.

III. PARTY POLITICS AND CAMPAIGNS

California Democratic Party v. *Jones*
530 U.S. 567, 120 S.Ct. 2402, 147 L.Ed. 2d 502 (2000)

http://caselaw.findlaw.com/us-supreme-court/530/567.html

In 1996, voters in California approved Proposition 198 that converted closed party primaries to blanket primaries. Under the closed primary, voters received a ballot limited to candidates of their own party. Democratic voters picked among Democratic candidates, and Republican voters picked among Republican candidates. In the blanket primary, every voter's ballot listed every candidate regardless of party affiliation and allowed voters to choose among them. The candidate of each party who won the greatest number of votes for a particular office became that party's candidate in the ensuing general election. The state Democratic, Republican, Libertarian, and Peace and Freedom parties filed suit against California Secretary of State Bill Jones in the U.S. District Court for the Eastern District of California, asserting that the blanket primary violated their First Amendment freedom of association. Rejecting this claim, the district court concluded that the burden on the parties' right of association was not severe and was justified by the state's interest in "enhanc[ing] the democratic nature of the election process and the representativeness of elected officials." The Court of Appeals for the Ninth Circuit affirmed. Majority: Scalia, Rehnquist, O'Connor, Kennedy, Thomas, Souter, Breyer. Dissenting: Stevens, Ginsburg.

Justice Scalia delivered the opinion of the Court.

This case presents the question whether the State of California may, consistent with the First Amendment to the United States Constitution, use a so-called "blanket" primary to determine a political party's nominee for the general election. . . .

Respondents rest their defense of the blanket primary upon the proposition that primaries play an integral role in citizens' selection of public officials. As a consequence, they contend, primaries are public rather than private proceedings, and the States may and must play a role in ensuring that they serve the public interest. Proposition 198, respondents conclude, is simply a rather pedestrian example of a State's regulating its system of elections.

We have recognized, of course, that States have a major role to play in structuring and monitoring the election process, including primaries. . . .

What we have not held, however, is that the processes by which political parties select their nominees are, as respondents would the party; and once he does so, he is limited to voting for candidates of that party. have it, wholly public affairs that States may regulate freely. . . . In this regard, respondents' reliance on *Smith* v. *Allwright* (1944) and *Terry* v. *Adams* (1953) is misplaced. In *Allwright*, we invalidated the Texas Democratic Party's rule limiting participation in its primary to whites; in *Terry*, we invalidated the same rule promulgated by the Jaybird Democratic Association, a "self-governing voluntary club." These cases held only that, when a State prescribes an election process that gives a special role to political parties, it "endorses, adopts and enforces the discrimination against Negroes," that the parties (or, in the case of the Jaybird Democratic Association, organizations that are "part and parcel" of the parties) bring into the process—so that the parties' discriminatory action becomes state action under the Fifteenth Amendment. . . . They do not stand for the proposition that party affairs are public affairs, free of First Amendment protections—and our later holdings make that entirely clear.

Representative democracy in any populous unit of governance is unimaginable without the ability of citizens to band together in promoting among the electorate candidates who espouse their political views. The formation of national political parties was almost concurrent with the formation of the Republic itself. . . .

In no area is the political association's right to exclude more important than in the process of selecting its nominee. That process often determines the party's positions on the most significant public policy issues of the day, and even when those positions are predetermined it is the nominee who becomes the party's ambassador to the general electorate in winning it over to the party's views. . . .

Proposition 198 forces political parties to associate with—to have their nominees, and hence their positions, determined by—those who, at best, have refused to affiliate with the party, and, at worst, have expressly affiliated with a rival. In this respect, it is qualitatively different from a closed primary. Under that system, even when it is made quite easy for a voter to change his party affiliation the day of the primary, and thus, in some sense, to "cross over," at least he must formally become a member of the party; and once he does so, he is limited to voting for candidates of that party.

The evidence in this case demonstrates that under California's blanket primary system, the prospect of having a party's nominee determined by adherents of an opposing party is far from remote—indeed, it is a clear and present danger. For example, in one 1997 survey of California voters 37 percent of Republicans said that they planned to vote in the 1998 Democratic gubernatorial primary, and 20 percent of Democrats said they planned to vote in the 1998 Republican United States Senate primary. . . .

The record also supports the obvious proposition that these substantial numbers of voters who help select the nominees of parties they have chosen not to join often have policy views that diverge from those of the party faithful. . . .

In any event, the deleterious effects of Proposition 198 are not limited to altering the identity of the nominee. Even when the person favored by a majority of the party members prevails, he will have prevailed by taking somewhat different positions—and, should he be elected, will continue to take somewhat different positions in order to be renominated. As respondents' own expert concluded, "[t]he policy positions of Members of Congress elected from blanket primary states are . . . more moderate, both in an absolute sense and relative to the other party, and so are more reflective of the preferences of the mass of voters at the center of the ideological spectrum." It is unnecessary to cumulate evidence of this phenomenon, since, after all, the whole purpose of Proposition 198 was to favor nominees with "moderate" positions. It encourages candidates—and officeholders who hope to be renominated—to curry favor with persons whose views are more "centrist" than those of the party base. In effect, Proposition 198 has simply moved the general election one step earlier in the process, at the expense of the parties' ability to perform the "basic function" of choosing their own leaders. . . .

In sum, Proposition 198 forces petitioners to adulterate their candidate-selection process—the "basic function of a political party"—by opening it up to persons wholly unaffiliated with the party. Such forced association has the likely outcome—indeed, in this case the intended outcome—of changing the parties' message. We can think of no heavier burden on a political party's associational freedom. Proposition 198 is therefore unconstitutional unless it is narrowly tailored to serve a compelling state interest . . . It is to that question which we now turn.

Respondents proffer seven state interests they claim are compelling. Two of them—producing elected officials who better represent the electorate and expanding candidate debate beyond the scope of partisan concerns—are simply circumlocution for producing nominees and nominee positions other than those the parties would choose if left to their own devices. Indeed, respondents admit as much. . . . And in explaining their desire to increase debate, respondents claim that a blanket primary forces parties to reconsider long standing positions since it "compels [their] candidates to appeal to a larger segment of the electorate." Both of these supposed interests, therefore, reduce to nothing more than a stark repudiation of freedom of political association: Parties should not be free to select their own nominees because those nominees, and the positions taken by those nominees, will not be congenial to the majority.

Respondents' third asserted compelling interest is that the blanket primary is the only way to ensure that disenfranchised persons enjoy the right to an effective vote. By "disenfranchised," respondents do not mean those who cannot vote; they mean simply independents and members of the minority party in "safe" districts. These persons are disenfranchised, according to respondents, because under a closed primary they are unable to participate in what amounts to the determinative election—the majority party's primary; the only way to ensure they have an "effective" vote is to force the party to open its primary to them. . . . We have said, however, that a "nonmember's desire to participate in the party's affairs is overborne by the countervailing and legitimate right of the party to determine its own membership qualifications." . . . Moreover, even if it were accurate to describe the plight of the nonparty-member in a safe district as "disenfranchisement," Proposition 198 is not needed to solve the problem. The voter who feels himself disenfranchised should simply join the party. . . .

Respondents' remaining four asserted state interests—promoting fairness, affording voters greater choice, increasing voter participation, and protecting privacy—are not, like the others, automatically out of the running; but neither are they, in the circumstances of this case, compelling. . . .

Finally, we may observe that even if all these state interests were compelling ones, Proposition 198 is not a narrowly tailored means of furthering them. Respondents could protect them all by resorting to a nonpartisan blanket primary. Generally speaking, under such a system, the State determines what qualifications it requires for a candidate to have a place on the primary ballot—which may include nomination by established parties and voter-petition requirements for independent candidates. Each voter, regardless of party affiliation, may then vote for any candidate, and the top two vote getters (or however many the State prescribes) then move on to the general election. This system has all the characteristics of the partisan blanket primary, save the constitutionally crucial one: Primary voters are not choosing a party's nominee. . . .

The burden Proposition 198 places on petitioners' rights of political association is both severe and unnecessary. The judgment for the Court of Appeals for the Ninth Circuit is reversed.

It is so ordered.

JUSTICE KENNEDY, concurring . . . [omitted].

JUSTICE STEVENS, with whom JUSTICE GINSBURG joins in part, dissenting. . . .

The blanket primary system instituted by Proposition 198 does not abridge "the ability of citizens to band together in promoting among the electorate candidates who espouse their political views." The Court's contrary conclusion rests on the premise that a political party's freedom of expressive association includes a "right not to associate," which in turn includes a right to exclude voters unaffiliated with the party from participating in the selection of that party's nominee in a primary election. In drawing this conclusion, however, the Court blurs two distinctions that are critical: (1) the distinction between a private organization's right to define itself and its messages, on the one hand, and the State's right to define the obligations of citizens and organizations performing public functions, on the other; and (2) the distinction between laws that abridge participation in the political process and those that encourage such participation. associational freedoms is that both the general election and the primary are quintessential forms of state action. It is because the primary is state action that an organization—whether it calls itself a political party or just a "Jaybird" association—may not deny non-Caucasians the right to participate in the selection of its nominees. The Court is quite right in stating that those cases "do not stand for the proposition that party affairs are [wholly] public affairs, free of First Amendment protections." They do, however, stand for the proposition that primary elections, unlike most "party affairs," are state action. The protections that the First Amendment affords to the "internal processes" of a political party do not encompass a right to exclude nonmembers from voting in a state-required, state-financed primary election.

When a political party defines the organization and composition of its governing units, when it decides what candidates to endorse, and when it decides whether and how to communicate those endorsements to the public, it is engaged in the kind of private expressive associational activity that the First Amendment protects. . . .

The so-called "right not to associate" that the Court relies upon, then, is simply inapplicable to participation in a state election. A political party, like any other association, may refuse to allow non-members to participate in the party's decisions when it is conducting its own affairs; California's blanket primary system does not infringe this principle. But an election, unlike a convention or caucus, is a public affair. . . .

[H]owever, the associational rights of political parties are neither absolute nor as comprehensive as the rights enjoyed by wholly private associations. . . . The reason a State may impose this significant restriction on a party's associational freedoms is that both the general election and the primary are quintessential forms of state action. It is because the primary is state action that an organization—whether it calls itself a political party or just a "Jaybird" association—may not deny non-Caucasians the right to participate in the selection of its nominees. The Court is quite right in stating that those cases "do not stand for the proposition that party affairs are [wholly] public affairs, free of First Amendment protections." They do, however, stand for the proposition that primary elections, unlike most "party affairs," are state action. The protections that the First Amendment affords to the "internal processes" of a political party do not encompass a right to exclude nonmembers from voting in a state-required, state-financed primary election.

The so-called "right not to associate" that the Court relies upon, then, is simply inapplicable to participation in a state election. A political party, like any other association, may refuse to allow non-members to participate in the party's decisions when it is conducting its own affairs; California's blanket primary system does not infringe this principle. But an election, unlike a convention or caucus, is a public affair. . . .

McConnell v. *Federal Election Commission* 540 U.S. 93, 124 S.Ct. 619, 157 L.Ed. 2d 491 (2003)

http://caselaw.findlaw.com/us-supreme-court/540/93.html

The Bipartisan Campaign Reform Act of 2002 (BCRA) is the most far-reaching campaign finance legislation passed by Congress since the 1974 amendments to the Federal Election Campaign Act (FECA). BCRA's Title I bans "soft money" contributions to political parties. Title II prohibits certain "issue ads," funded from a corporation's, a union's, or nonprofit corporation's general treasury that appear on a broadcast, cable, or satellite channel within 30 days of a primary or 60 days of an election in which candidates for federal office are on the ballot. Three additional titles impose additional regulations or otherwise make changes in existing law. Soon after the legislation became law, 12 suits challenging the constitutionality of various parts of the act on First Amendment and other grounds were filed in the U.S. District Court for the District of Columbia. On May 1, 2003, a three-judge panel held some parts of BCRA unconstitutional and upheld others. On direct appeal, the Supreme Court heard an extraordinary four hours of oral arguments in a special session on September 8. Its decision on December 10 upheld all but two parts of the act: a requirement in § 213 that political parties choose between coordinating campaign activities with their House and Senate candidates and operating entirely independently of them, and a ban in § 318 on campaign contributions from minors. In addition, the Court construed the limitation on issue ads in § 316 to exclude nonprofit entities that are so-called *MCFL* corporations. [Derived from *FEC* v. *Massachusetts Citizens for Life* (1986), such organizations are formed for the express purpose of promoting political ideas, have no shareholders, and are neither established by a business corporation or labor union nor accept contributions from them.] The excerpts below from the 119-page majority opinion and from Justice Kennedy's 59-page dissent address only Titles I and II. Majority (on the main provisions of Titles I and II): Stevens, O'Connor, Breyer, Ginsburg, Souter. Dissenting: Kennedy, Rehnquist, Scalia, Thomas.

Justice Stevens and Justice O'Connor delivered the opinion of the Court. . . .

Three important developments in the years after our decision in *Buckley* [v. *Valeo*, 1976) persuaded Congress that further legislation was necessary to regulate the role that corporations, unions, and wealthy contributors play in the electoral process. As a preface to our discussion of the specific provisions of BCRA, we comment briefly on the increased importance of "soft money," the proliferation of "issue ads," and the disturbing findings of a Senate investigation into campaign practices related to the 1996 federal elections.

Under FECA, "contributions" must be made with funds that are subject to the Act's disclosure requirements and source and amount limitations. Such funds are known as "federal" or "hard" money. FECA defines the term "contribution," however, to include only the gift or advance of anything of value "made by any person for the purpose of influencing any election for *Federal* office" (emphasis added [by the Court]). Donations made solely for the purpose of influencing state or local elections are therefore unaffected by FECA's requirements and prohibitions. As a result, prior to the enactment of BCRA, federal law permitted corporations and unions, as well as individuals who had already made the maximum permissible contributions to federal candidates, to contribute "nonfederal money"—also known as "soft money"—to political parties for activities intended to influence state or local elections.

Shortly after *Buckley* was decided, questions arose concerning the treatment of contributions intended to influence both federal and state elections. . . . [T]he FEC ruled that political parties could fund mixed-purpose activities—including get-out-the-vote drives and generic party advertising—in part with soft money. In 1995 the FEC concluded that the parties could also use soft money to defray the costs of "legislative advocacy media advertisements," even if the ads mentioned the name of a federal candidate, so long as they did not expressly advocate the candidate's election or defeat.

As the permissible uses of soft money expanded, the amount of soft money raised and spent by the national political parties increased exponentially. . . . The national parties transferred large amounts of their soft money to the state parties, which were allowed to use a larger percentage of soft money to finance mixed-purpose activities under FEC rules. In the year 2000, for example, the national parties diverted $280 million—more than half of their soft money—to state parties. . . .

The solicitation, transfer, and use of soft money thus enabled parties and candidates to circumvent FECA's limitations on the source and amount of contributions in connection with federal elections.

In *Buckley* we construed FECA's disclosure and reporting requirements, as well as its expenditure limitations, "to reach only funds used for communications that expressly advocate the election or defeat of a clearly identified candidate." As a result of that strict reading of the statute, the use or omission of "magic words" such as "Elect John Smith" or "Vote Against Jane Doe" marked a bright statutory line separating "express advocacy" from "issue advocacy." Express advocacy was subject to FECA's limitations and could be financed only using hard money. The political parties, in other words, could not use soft money to sponsor ads that used any magic words, and corporations and unions could not fund such ads out of their general treasuries. So-called issue ads, on the other hand, not only could be financed with soft money, but could be aired without disclosing the identity of, or any other information about, their sponsors.

While the distinction between "issue" and express advocacy seemed neat in theory, the two categories of advertisements proved functionally identical in important respects. . . . Little difference existed, for example, between an ad that urged viewers to "vote against Jane Doe" and one that condemned Jane Doe's record on a particular issue before exhorting viewers to "call Jane Doe and tell her what you think." . . .

[Title I]

Title I is Congress' effort to plug the soft-money loophole. The cornerstone of Title I is new FECA § 323(a), which prohibits national party committees and their agents from soliciting, receiving, directing, or spending any soft money. In short, § 323(a) takes national parties out of the soft-money business. . . .

In *Buckley* and subsequent cases, we have subjected restrictions on campaign expenditures to closer scrutiny than limits on campaign contributions. In these cases we have recognized that contribution limits, unlike limits on expenditures, "entai[l] only a marginal restriction upon the contributor's ability to engage in free communication." . . .

Our treatment of contribution restrictions reflects more than the limited burdens they impose on First Amendment freedoms. It also reflects the importance of the interests that underlie contribution limits—interests in preventing "both the actual corruption threatened by large financial contributions and the eroding of public confidence in the electoral process through the appearance of corruption." . . .

For that reason, when reviewing Congress' decision to enact contribution limits, "there is no place for a strong presumption against constitutionality, of the sort often thought to accompany the words 'strict scrutiny.'" The less rigorous standard of review we have applied to contribution limits (*Buckley*'s "closely drawn" scrutiny) shows proper deference to Congress' ability to weigh competing constitutional interests in an area in which it enjoys particular expertise. It also provides Congress with sufficient room to anticipate and respond to concerns about circumvention of regulations designed to protect the integrity of the political process. . . .

Like the contribution limits we upheld in *Buckley*, § 323's restrictions have only a marginal impact on the ability of contributors, candidates, officeholders, and parties to engage in effective political speech. Complex as its provisions may be, § 323, in the main, . . . merely subjects a greater percentage of contributions to parties and candidates to FECA's source and amount limitations. . . .

The question for present purposes is whether large *soft-money* contributions to national party committees have a corrupting influence or give rise to the appearance of corruption. Both common sense and the ample record in these cases confirm Congress' belief that they do. . . .

Particularly telling is the fact that, in 1996 and 2000, more than half of the top 50 soft-money donors gave substantial sums to *both* major national parties, leaving room for no other conclusion but that these donors were seeking influence, or avoiding retaliation, rather than promoting any particular ideology. . . .

Just as troubling to a functioning democracy as classic *quid pro quo* corruption is the danger that officeholders will decide issues not on the merits or the desires of their constituencies, but according to the wishes of those who have made large financial contributions valued by the officeholder. Even if it occurs only occasionally, the potential for such undue influence is manifest. And unlike straight cash-for-votes transactions, such corruption is neither easily detected nor practical to criminalize. The best means of prevention is to identify and to remove the temptation. . . .

In constructing a coherent scheme of campaign finance regulation, Congress recognized that, given the close ties between federal candidates and state party committees, BCRA's restrictions on national committee activity would rapidly become ineffective if state and local committees remained available as a conduit for soft-money donations. Section 323(b) is designed to foreclose wholesale evasion of § 323(a)'s anticorruption measures by sharply curbing state committees' ability to use large soft-money contributions to influence federal elections. The core of § 323(b) is a straightforward contribution regulation: It prevents donors from contributing nonfederal funds to state and local party committees to help finance "Federal election activity." The term "Federal election activity" encompasses four distinct categories of electioneering: (1) voter registration activity during the 120 days preceding a regularly scheduled federal election; (2) voter identification, get-out-the-vote (GOTV), and generic campaign activity that is "conducted in connection with an election in which a candidate for Federal office appears on the ballot"; (3) any "public communication" that "refers to a clearly identified candidate for Federal office" and "promotes," "supports," "attacks," or "opposes" a candidate for that office; and (4) the services provided by a state committee employee who dedicates more than 25 percent of his or her time to "activities in connection with a Federal election." . . . All activities that fall within the statutory definition must be funded with hard money. . . .

[I]n addressing the problem of soft-money contributions to state committees, Congress both drew a conclusion and made a prediction. Its conclusion, based on the evidence before it, was that the corrupting influence of soft money does not insinuate itself into the political process solely through national party committees. Rather, state committees function as an alternate avenue for precisely the same corrupting forces. . . .

Congress also made a prediction. Having been taught the hard lesson of circumvention by the entire history of campaign finance regulation, Congress knew that soft-money donors would react to § 323(a) by scrambling to find another way to purchase influence. . . .

Finally, plaintiffs argue that Title I violates the equal protection component of the Due Process Clause of the Fifth Amendment because it discriminates against political parties in favor of special interest groups such as the National Rifle Association (NRA), American Civil Liberties Union (ACLU), and Sierra Club. . . . BCRA imposes numerous restrictions on the fundraising abilities of political parties, of which the soft-money ban is only the most prominent. Interest groups, however, remain free to raise soft money to fund voter registration, GOTV activities, mailings, and broadcast advertising (other than electioneering communications). We conclude that this disparate treatment does not offend the Constitution.

As an initial matter, we note that BCRA actually favors political parties in many ways. Most obviously, party committees are entitled to receive individual contributions that substantially exceed FECA's limits on contributions to nonparty political committees; individuals can give $25,000 to political party committees whereas they can give a maximum of $5,000 to nonparty political committees. . . .

More importantly, however, Congress is fully entitled to consider the real-world differences between political parties and interest groups when crafting a system of campaign finance regulation. . . . Political parties have influence and power in the legislature that vastly exceeds that of any interest group. . . . Congress' efforts at campaign finance regulation may account for these salient differences. . . . We therefore reject those arguments. . . .

[Title II]

The first section of Title II, § 201 . . . coins a new term, "electioneering communication," to replace the narrowing construction of FECA's disclosure provisions adopted by this Court in *Buckley*. . . . [T]hat construction limited the coverage of FECA's disclosure requirement to communications expressly advocating the election or defeat of particular candidates. By contrast, the term "electioneering communication" is not so limited, but is defined to encompass any "broadcast, cable, or satellite communication" that

"(I) refers to a clearly identified candidate for Federal office;
"(II) is made within—
"(aa) 60 days before a general, special, or runoff election for the office sought by the candidate; or
"(bb) 30 days before a primary or preference election, or a convention or caucus of a political party that has authority to nominate a candidate, for the office sought by the candidate; and
"(III) in the case of a communication which refers to a candidate other than President or Vice President, is targeted to the relevant electorate."

New FECA § 304(f)(3)(C) further provides that a communication is "targeted to the relevant electorate" if it "can be received by 50,000 or more persons" in the district or State the candidate seeks to represent. . . . ["FECA § 304(f)(3)(B) excludes from the definition of electioneering communications any "communication appearing in a news story, commentary, or editorial distributed through the facilities of any broadcasting station, unless such facilities are owned or controlled by any political party, political committee, or candidate."—Ed.]

The major premise of plaintiffs' challenge to BCRA's use of the term "electioneering communication" is that *Buckley* drew a constitutionally mandated line between express advocacy and so-called issue advocacy, and that speakers possess an inviolable First Amendment right to engage in the latter category of speech. . . .

That position misapprehends our prior decisions. . . .

Nor are we persuaded, independent of our precedents, that the First Amendment erects a rigid barrier between express advocacy and so-called issue advocacy. That notion cannot be squared with our longstanding recognition that the presence or absence of magic words cannot meaningfully distinguish electioneering speech from a true issue ad. . . .

Buckley's express advocacy line, in short, has not aided the legislative effort to combat real or apparent corruption, and Congress enacted BCRA to correct the flaws it found in the existing system.

Finally we observe that new FECA § 304(f)(3)'s definition of "electioneering communication" raises none of the vagueness concerns that drove our analysis in *Buckley*. . . . Thus, the constitutional objection that persuaded the Court in *Buckley* to limit FECA's reach to express advocacy is simply inapposite here. . . .

Thus, under BCRA, corporations and unions may not use their general treasury funds to finance electioneering communications, but they remain free to organize and administer segregated funds, or PACs, for that purpose. Because corporations can still fund electioneering communications with PAC money, it is "simply wrong" to view the provision as a "complete ban" on expression rather than a regulation. . . .

[I]ssue ads broadcast during the 30- and 60-day periods preceding federal primary and general elections are the functional equivalent of express advocacy. The justifications for the regulation of express advocacy apply equally to ads aired during those periods if the ads are intended to influence the voters' decisions and have that effect. . . . [I]n the future corporations and unions may finance genuine issue ads during those time frames by simply avoiding any specific reference to federal candidates, or in doubtful cases by paying for the ad from a segregated fund.

We are therefore not persuaded that plaintiffs have carried their heavy burden of proving that amended FECA § 316(b)(2) is overbroad. . . .

Many years ago we observed that "[t]o say that Congress is without power to pass appropriate legislation to safeguard . . . an election from the improper use of money to influence the result is to deny to the nation in a vital particular the power of self protection." We abide by that conviction in considering Congress' most recent effort to confine the ill effects of aggregated wealth on our political system. We are under no illusion that BCRA will be the last congressional statement on the matter. Money, like water, will always find an outlet. What problems will arise, and how Congress will respond, are concerns for another day. In the main we uphold BCRA's two principal, complementary features: the control of soft money and the regulation of electioneering communications. Accordingly, we affirm in part and reverse in part the District Court's judgment with respect to Titles I and II.

It is so ordered.

The Chief Justice, concurring in part and dissenting in part . . . [omitted].

Justice Kennedy, with whom The Chief Justice joins and with whom Justice Scalia and Justice Thomas join, concurring in part and dissenting in part. . . .

Until today's consolidated cases, the Court has accepted but two principles to use in determining the validity of campaign finance restrictions. First is the anticorruption rationale. The principal concern, of course, is the agreement for a *quid pro quo* between officeholders (or candidates) and those who would seek to influence them. The Court has said the interest in preventing corruption allows limitations on receipt of the *quid* by a candidate or officeholder, regardless of who gives it or of the intent of the donor or officeholder. Second, the Court has analyzed laws that classify on the basis of the speaker's corporate or union identity under the corporate speech rationale. The Court has said that the willing adoption of the entity form by corporations and unions justifies regulating them differently: Their ability to give candidates *quids* may be subject not only to limits but also to outright bans; their electoral speech may likewise be curtailed.

The Court ignores these constitutional bounds and in effect interprets the anticorruption rationale to allow regulation not just of "actual or apparent *quid pro quo* arrangements," but of any conduct that wins goodwill from or influences a Member of Congress. . . . The very aim of *Buckley*'s standard . . . was to define undue influence by reference to the presence of *quid pro quo* involving the officeholder. The Court, in contrast, concludes that access, without more, proves influence is undue. Access, in the Court's view, has the same legal ramifications as actual or apparent corruption of officeholders. This new definition of corruption sweeps away all protections for speech that lie in its path.

Access in itself, however, shows only that in a general sense an officeholder favors someone or that someone has influence on the officeholder. There is no basis, in law or in fact, to say favoritism or influence in general is the same as corrupt favoritism or influence in particular. By equating vague and generic claims of favoritism or influence with actual or apparent corruption, the Court adopts a definition of corruption that dismantles basic First Amendment rules, permits Congress to suppress speech in the absence of a *quid pro quo* threat, and moves beyond the rationale that is *Buckley*'s very foundation.

The generic favoritism or influence theory articulated by the Court is at odds with standard First Amendment analyses because it is unbounded and susceptible to no limiting principle. Any given action might be favored by any given person, so by the Court's reasoning political loyalty of the purest sort can be prohibited. There is no remaining principled method for inquiring whether a campaign finance regulation does in fact regulate corruption in a serious and meaningful way. We are left to defer to a congressional conclusion that certain conduct creates favoritism or influence.

Though the majority cites common sense as the foundation for its definition of corruption, in the context of the real world only a single definition of corruption has been found to identify political corruption successfully and to distinguish good political responsiveness from bad—that is *quid pro quo*. Favoritism and influence are not, as the Government's theory suggests, avoidable in representative politics. It is in the nature of an elected representative to favor certain policies, and, by necessary corollary, to favor the voters and contributors who support those policies. It is well understood that a substantial and legitimate reason, if not the only reason, to cast a vote for, or to make a contribution to, one candidate over another is that the candidate will respond by producing those political outcomes the supporter favors. Democracy is premised on responsiveness. *Quid pro quo* corruption has been, until now, the only agreed upon conduct that represents the bad form of responsiveness and presents a justiciable standard with a relatively clear limiting principle: Bad responsiveness may be demonstrated by pointing to a relationship between an official and a *quid*. . . .

From that it follows that the Court today should not ask, as it does, whether some persons, even Members of Congress, conclusorily assert that the regulated conduct appears corrupt to them. Following *Buckley*, it should instead inquire whether the conduct now prohibited inherently poses a real or substantive *quid pro quo* danger, so that its regulation will stem the appearance of *quid pro quo* corruption. . . .

[I]ndependent party activity, which by definition includes independent receipt and spending of soft money, lacks a possibility for *quid pro quo* corruption of federal officeholders. This must be all the more true of a party's independent receipt and spending of soft money donations neither directed to nor solicited by a candidate. . . .

Few interferences with the speech, association, and free expression of our people are greater than attempts by Congress to say which groups can or cannot advocate a cause, or how they must do it. . . .

The majority permits a new and serious intrusion on speech when it upholds § 203, the key provision in Title II that prohibits corporations and labor unions from using money from their general treasury to fund electioneering communications. . . .

The Government and the majority are right about one thing: The express-advocacy requirement, with its list of magic words, is easy to circumvent. The Government seizes on this observation to defend § 203, arguing it will prevent what it calls "sham issue ads" that are really to the same effect as their more express counterparts. What the Court and the Government call sham, however, are the ads speakers find most effective. . . . It is a measure of the Government's disdain for protected speech that it would label as a sham the mode of communication sophisticated speakers choose because it is the most powerful. . . .

The Government is unwilling to characterize § 203 as a ban, citing the possibility of funding electioneering communications out of a separate segregated fund. This option, though, does not alter the categorical nature of the prohibition on the corporation. . . . What the law allows—permitting the corporation "to serve as the founder and treasurer of a different association of individuals that can endorse or oppose political candidates"—"is not speech by the corporation."

Our cases recognize the practical difficulties corporations face when they are limited to communicating through PACs. . . .

These regulations are more than minor clerical requirements. Rather, they create major disincentives for speech, with the effect falling most heavily on smaller entities that often have the most difficulty bearing the costs of compliance. Even worse, for an organization that has not yet set up a PAC, spontaneous speech that "refers to a clearly identified candidate for Federal office" becomes impossible, even if the group's vital interests are threatened by a piece of legislation pending before Congress on the eve of a federal election. . . .

The majority can articulate no compelling justification for imposing this scheme of compulsory ventriloquism. . . .

[S]uppose a few Senators want to show their constituents in the logging industry how much they care about working families and propose a law, 60 days before the election, that would harm the environment by allowing logging in national forests. Under § 203, a nonprofit environmental group would be unable to run an ad referring to these Senators in their districts. The suggestion that the group could form and fund a PAC in the short time required for effective participation in the political debate is fanciful. For reasons already discussed, moreover, an ad hoc PAC would not be as effective as the environmental group itself in gaining credibility with the public. Never before in our history has the Court upheld a law that suppresses speech to this extent. . . .

The First Amendment commands that Congress "shall make no law . . . abridging the freedom of speech." The command cannot be read to allow Congress to provide for the imprisonment of those who attempt to establish new political parties and alter the civic discourse. Our pluralistic society is filled with voices expressing new and different viewpoints, speaking through modes and mechanisms that must be allowed to change in response to the demands of an interested public. . . . The Court, upholding multiple laws that suppress both spontaneous and concerted speech, leaves us less free than before. Today's decision breaks faith with our tradition of robust and unfettered debate.

For the foregoing reasons, with respect, I dissent from the Court's decision upholding the main features of Titles I and II.

Justice Scalia, concurring in part and dissenting in part . . . [omitted].

Justice Thomas, concurring in part and dissenting in part . . . [omitted].

Citizens United v. *Federal Election Commission* 558 U.S. 310, 130 S.Ct. 876, 175 L.Ed. 2d 753 (2010)

http://caselaw.findlaw.com/us-supreme-court/08-205.html

As amended by § 203 of the Bipartisan Campaign Reform Act of 2002 (BCRA), federal law (§ 441b) prohibits corporations and unions from using their general treasury funds to make independent expenditures for speech that is an "electioneering communication" or for speech that expressly advocates the election or defeat of a candidate prior to a primary or election for federal office. In January 2008, Citizens United, a nonprofit corporation, released a documentary entitled *Hillary* that was critical of Senator Hillary Clinton, then a candidate for the Democratic Party's presidential nomination. Anticipating that it would make *Hillary* available on cable television through video-on-demand within 30 days of primary elections, Citizens United produced television ads to run on broadcast and cable television. Concerned about possible civil and criminal penalties for violating the law, it sought declaratory and injunctive relief in the U.S. District Court for the District of Columbia, arguing that (1) § 441b is unconstitutional as applied to *Hillary* and (2) BCRA's disclaimer, disclosure, and reporting requirements were unconstitutional as applied to *Hillary* and the ads. The district court denied Citizens United a preliminary injunction and granted the Federal Election Commission summary judgment. The opinions filed in the Supreme Court's decision consumed 183 pages. The excerpts that follow are therefore greatly compressed. Majority: Kennedy, Roberts, Alito, Scalia, Thomas: Dissenting: Stevens, Breyer, Ginsburg, Sotomayor.

Justice Kennedy delivered the opinion of the Court.

Federal law prohibits corporations and unions from using their general treasury funds to make independent expenditures for speech defined as an "electioneering communication" or for speech expressly advocating the election or defeat of a candidate. Limits on electioneering communications were upheld in *McConnell* v. *FEC* (2003). The holding of *McConnell* rested to a large extent on an earlier case, *Austin* v. *Michigan Chamber of Commerce* (1990). *Austin* had held that political speech may be banned based on the speaker's corporate identity. In this case we are asked to reconsider *Austin* and, in effect, *McConnell*. . . .

The law before us is an outright ban, backed by criminal sanctions. Section 441b makes it a felony for all corporations—including nonprofit advocacy corporations—either to expressly advocate the election or defeat of candidates or to broadcast electioneering communications within 30 days of a primary election and 60 days of a general election. . . .

Section 441b is a ban on corporate speech notwithstanding the fact that a PAC created by a corporation can still speak. A PAC is a separate association from the corporation. So the PAC exemption from § 441b's expenditure ban, does not allow corporations to speak. . . . PACs are burdensome alternatives; they are expensive to administer and subject to extensive regulations. . . . Section 441b's prohibition on corporate independent expenditures is thus a ban on speech. . . .

Speech is an essential mechanism of democracy, for it is the means to hold officials accountable to the people. . . . For these reasons, political speech must prevail against laws that would suppress it, whether by design or inadvertence. Laws that burden political speech are "subject to strict scrutiny," which requires the Government to prove that the restriction "furthers a compelling interest and is narrowly tailored to achieve that interest." . . .

The Court has recognized that First Amendment protection extends to corporations. . . .

Austin "uph[eld] a direct restriction on the independent expenditure of funds for political speech for the first time in [this Court's] history." There, the Michigan Chamber of Commerce sought to use general treasury funds to run a newspaper ad supporting a specific candidate. Michigan law, however, prohibited corporate independent expenditures that supported or opposed any candidate for state office. A violation of the law was punishable as a felony. The Court sustained the speech prohibition. . . . [T]he Austin Court identified a new governmental interest in limiting political speech: an antidistortion interest. *Austin* found a compelling governmental interest in preventing "the corrosive and distorting effects of immense aggregations of wealth that are accumulated with the help of the corporate form and that have little or no correlation to the public's support for the corporation's political ideas." . . .

If the First Amendment has any force, it prohibits Congress from fining or jailing citizens, or associations of citizens, for simply engaging in political speech. If the antidistortion rationale were to be accepted, however, it would permit Government to ban political speech simply because the speaker is an association that has taken on the corporate form. . . . If *Austin* were correct, the Government could prohibit a corporation from expressing political views in media beyond those presented here, such as by printing books. . . . Thus, under the Government's reasoning, wealthy media corporations could have their voices diminished to put them on par with other media entities. There is no precedent for permitting this under the First Amendment. . . .

The censorship we now confront is vast . . . When Government seeks to use its full power, including the criminal law, to command where a person may get his or her information or what distrusted source he or she may not hear, it uses censorship to control thought. This is unlawful. The First Amendment confirms the freedom to think for ourselves. . . .

[W]e now conclude that independent expenditures, including those made by corporations, do not give rise to corruption or the appearance of corruption. . . . The appearance of influence or access, furthermore, will not cause the electorate to lose faith in our democracy. By definition, an independent expenditure is political speech presented to the electorate that is not coordinated with a candidate. The fact that a corporation, or any other speaker, is willing to spend money to try to persuade voters presupposes that the people have the ultimate influence over elected officials. . . .

When Congress finds that a problem exists, we must give that finding due deference; but Congress may not choose an unconstitutional requirements. The case is remanded for further proceedings consistent with this opinion. remedy. . . . We need not reach the question whether the Government has a compelling interest in preventing foreign individuals or associations from influencing our Nation's political process. Section 441b is not limited to corporations or associations that were created in foreign countries or funded predominately by foreign shareholders. Section 441b therefore would be overbroad even if we assumed, arguendo, that the Government has a compelling interest in limiting foreign influence over our political process. . . .

Rapid changes in technology—and the creative dynamic inherent in the concept of free expression—counsel against upholding a law that restricts political speech in certain media or by certain speakers. Today, 30-second television ads may be the most effective way to convey a political message. Soon, however, it may be that Internet sources, such as blogs and social networking Web sites, will provide citizens with significant information about political candidates and issues. Yet, § 441b would seem to ban a blog post expressly advocating the election or defeat of a candidate if that blog were created with corporate funds. The First Amendment does not permit Congress to make these categorical distinctions based on the corporate identity of the speaker and the content of the political speech. . . .

Austin is overruled. . . . As the Government appears to concede, overruling *Austin* "effectively invalidate[s] not only BCRA Section 203, but also 441b's prohibition on the use of corporate treasury funds for express advocacy." Section 441b's restrictions on corporate independent expenditures are therefore invalid and cannot be applied to *Hillary*. . . .

We find no constitutional impediment to the application of BCRA's disclaimer and disclosure requirements to a movie broadcast via video-on-demand. And there has been no showing that, as applied in this case, these requirements would impose a chill on speech or expression. . . .

The judgment of the District Court is reversed with respect to the constitutionality of 2 U.S.C. § 441b's restrictions on corporate independent expenditures. The judgment is affirmed with respect to BCRA's disclaimer and disclosure

It is so ordered.

Chief Justice Roberts, with whom Justice Alito joins, concurring . . . [omitted].

Justice Scalia, with whom Justice Alito joins, and with whom Justice Thomas joins in part, concurring . . . [omitted].

Justice Stevens, with whom Justice Ginsburg, Justice Breyer, and Justice Sotomayor join, concurring in part and dissenting in part. . . .

The basic premise underlying the Court's ruling is its iteration, and constant reiteration, of the proposition that the First Amendment bars regulatory distinctions based on a speaker's identity, including its "identity" as a corporation. . . . The conceit that corporations must be treated identically to natural persons in the political sphere is not only inaccurate but also inadequate to justify the Court's disposition of this case.

In the context of election to public office, the distinction between corporate and human speakers is significant. . . . They cannot vote or run for office. Because they may be managed and controlled by nonresidents, their interests may conflict in fundamental respects with the interests of eligible voters. The financial resources, legal structure, and instrumental orientation of corporations raise legitimate concerns about their role in the electoral process.

Our lawmakers have a compelling constitutional basis, if not also a democratic duty, to take measures designed to guard against the potentially deleterious effects of corporate spending in local and national races.

The majority's approach to corporate electioneering marks a dramatic break from our past. Congress has placed special limitations on campaign spending by corporations ever since the passage of the Tillman Act in 1907. . . . The Court today rejects a century of history when it treats the distinction between corporate and individual campaign spending as an invidious novelty born of *Austin*. Relying largely on individual dissenting opinions, the majority blazes through our precedents, overruling or disavowing a body of case law. . . . Although I concur in the Court's decision to sustain BCRA's disclosure provisions, I emphatically dissent from its principal holding. . . .

I am not an absolutist when it comes to *stare decisis*, in the campaign finance area or in any other. No one is. But if this principle is to do any meaningful work in supporting the rule of law, it must at least demand a significant justification, beyond the preferences of five Justices, for overturning settled doctrine. . . . In the end, the Court's rejection of *Austin* and *McConnell* comes down to nothing more than its disagreement with their results. Virtually every one of its arguments was made and rejected in those cases, and the majority opinion is essentially an amalgamation of resuscitated dissents. The only relevant thing that has changed since *Austin* and *McConnell* is the composition of this Court. . . .

In many ways, then, § 203 functions as a source restriction or a time, place, and manner restriction. It applies in a viewpoint-neutral fashion to a narrow subset of advocacy messages about clearly identified candidates for federal office, made during discrete time periods through discrete channels. In the case at hand, all Citizens United needed to do to broadcast *Hillary* right before the primary was to abjure business contributions or use the funds in its PAC. . . .

The Court invokes "ancient First Amendment principles" to defend today's ruling, yet it makes only a perfunctory attempt to ground its analysis in the principles or understandings of those who drafted and ratified the Amendment. Perhaps this is because there is not a scintilla of evidence to support the notion that anyone believed it would preclude regulatory distinctions based on the corporate form. To the extent that the Framers' views are discernible and relevant to the disposition of this case, they would appear to cut strongly against the majority's position. . . . The Framers thus took it as a given that corporations could be comprehensively regulated in the service of the public welfare. Unlike our colleagues, they had little trouble distinguishing corporations from human beings, and when they constitutionalized the right to free speech in the First Amendment, it was the free speech of individual Americans that they had in mind. . . .

When the McConnell Court affirmed the judgment of the District Court regarding § 203, we did not rest our holding on a narrow notion of quid pro quo corruption. Instead we relied on the governmental interest in combating the unique forms of corruption threatened by corporations, as recognized in *Austin's* antidistortion and shareholder protection rationales as well as the interest in preventing circumvention of contribution limits . . . The majority's rejection of the Buckley anticorruption rationale on the ground that independent corporate expenditures "do not give rise to [quid pro quo] corruption or the appearance of corruption," is thus unfair as well as unreasonable. . . .

Our colleagues have arrived at the conclusion that *Austin* must be overruled and that § 203 is facially unconstitutional only after mischaracterizing both the reach and rationale of those authorities, and after bypassing or ignoring rules of judicial restraint used to cabin the Court's lawmaking power. Their conclusion that the societal interest in avoiding corruption and the appearance of corruption does not provide an adequate justification for regulating corporate expenditures on candidate elections relies on an incorrect description of that interest, along with a failure to acknowledge the relevance of established facts and the considered judgments of state and federal legislatures over many decades.

In a democratic society, the longstanding consensus on the need to limit corporate campaign spending should outweigh the wooden application of judge-made rules. At bottom, the Court's opinion is thus a rejection of the common sense of the American people, who have recognized a need to prevent corporations from undermining self-government since the founding, and who have fought against the distinctive corrupting potential of corporate electioneering since the days of Theodore Roosevelt. It is a strange time to repudiate that common sense. While American democracy is imperfect, few outside the majority of this Court would have thought its flaws included a dearth of corporate money in politics. I would affirm the judgment of the District Court.

Justice Thomas, concurring in part and dissenting in part . . . [omitted].

6

The Commerce Clause

The desire of the Forefathers to federalize regulation of foreign and interstate commerce stands in sharp contrast to their jealous preservation of the State's power over its internal affairs. No other federal power was so universally assumed to be necessary. No other state power was so readily relinquished.

—Justice Robert H. Jackson (1949)

Section 8 of Article I of the Constitution declares, "The Congress shall have Power. . . . To regulate Commerce with foreign Nations, and among the several States, and with the Indian Tribes. . . ." These 21 words have long been among the most important in the nation's fundamental charter, for both Congress and the states as well. This is because the commerce clause has two dimensions. In its active mode, it empowers Congress; in its dormant or negative mode, it is a self-executing limitation on the states, even in the absence of any legislation by Congress.

As a grant of authority to Congress, the commerce clause did not become a constitutional battleground until the late 1800s, when a truly national economy, tied together by telegraph and railroads, developed. Then, two major questions arose. First, what was the "commerce" that Congress was authorized to regulate? Second, what was the extent of the commerce power? Could the commerce power touch matters and relationships traditionally regarded as local in nature and within the purview of the states? Answers to these questions have greatly affected national policy for well over a century.

Yet, as important as congressional enactments may be, most legislation in the United States comes from state and local governments. These laws are examples of the **police power**—that general, residual, and regulatory authority retained by the states under the Constitution. Is such legislation valid when it also regulates commerce "among the several States" or in some way affects commerce? Such questions engage the commerce clause in its dormant or negative dimension and date from the earliest years of the Republic. "The simple fact," Justice Kennedy has explained, "was that in the early years of the Republic, Congress seldom perceived the necessity to exercise its power in circumstances where its authority would be called into

DOI: 10.4324/9781003164340-7

question. The Court's initial task, therefore, was to elaborate the theories that would permit the States to act where Congress had not done so."

VIEWS OF THE FRAMERS

Removal of trade restrictions imposed by the states was a moving cause of the Convention of 1787. For protection against these burdens, James Madison, as a member of the Continental Congress, had advocated general authority over commerce. Later, he was conspicuous among those who set in motion the sequence of events leading to the successful meeting at Philadelphia.

The Constitutional Convention. There seems to be no doubt that the commerce clause was inserted in the Constitution primarily to prevent the states from interfering with the freedom of commercial intercourse. Yet all the plans offered by the Convention apparently also envisioned a positive power in the national government to regulate commerce, and subsequent developments converted this clause into a significant source of national authority. Was this the intention of those who framed the Constitution? The record of the Convention of 1787 affords no conclusive answer.

On September 15, 1787, Madison commented on the question whether, under Article I, Section 10, a tonnage tax could be levied by the states for purposes of clearing and dredging harbors. "It depends on the extent of the commerce power. These terms—to regulate commerce—are vague but seem to exclude this power of the states. [Madison] was more and more convinced that the regulation of commerce was in its nature indivisible and ought to be wholly under one authority." Immediately following this statement, Roger Sherman of Connecticut observed, "The Power of the United States to regulate trade, being Supreme, can control interferences of the State regulations where such interferences happen; so that there is no danger to be apprehended from a concurrent jurisdiction." Had this issue "been clearly posed and unequivocally settled," Albert S. Abel commented, "it must perhaps have eliminated decades of judicial groping and guessing; on the other hand it might have broken up the convention."

Nonetheless, certain inferences about the nature and scope of the commerce power may be drawn from changes the Convention made in the wording of the commerce clause itself. In the Pinckney Plan, the word *exclusive* was used before *power*. Draft VII of the Committee of Detail used *exclusive*, but in Draft IX it was deleted and reported out in its present form. No evidence has been presented concerning the significance of this deletion. *Exclusive* is used as a description of congressional power only in Clause 17 (laws for the District of Columbia). Even the power of Congress to declare war is not stated to be "exclusive," but Article I, Section 10, explicitly limits state action. The only restriction on states of a commercial nature forbids duty on imports (or exports), except for the amount necessary to meet inspection costs. This seems to suggest freedom of the states to pass other laws regulating or affecting commerce.

Ratification Debates. Because of the motives of the speakers during the heated debates surrounding ratification of the Constitution, contemporary opinion on the meaning of the clause is no sure guide. Those opposed to the new Constitution stressed its centralizing tendencies in lurid colors; supporters, on the other hand, minimized the significance of the commerce power.

The skillful writers of that campaign document *The Federalist* employed their usual tactics. They made clear the dangers of not giving a broad power over commerce to the general government but blurred the precise limits of national power. "The competitions of commerce would be another fruitful source of contention," Alexander Hamilton stated in No. 7. "Each state or separate confederacy would pursue a system of commercial policy peculiar to itself. . . . The infraction of these [state] regulations on one side, the efforts to prevent and repel them on the other, would naturally lead to outrages, and these to reprisals and war." In No. 42, Madison glossed over the nature of the commerce power by discussing it chiefly as a supplement to the power over foreign commerce and by stressing the unfairness of permitting coastal states to levy a toll on states in the interior. In No. 45, Madison again hinted that the commerce power would be exercised chiefly on foreign commerce.

In 1829, after the "Father of the Constitution" had become a proponent of states' rights, Madison wrote to J. C. Cabell that the power to regulate commerce was designed to prevent abuses by the states rather than for positive purposes of the national government: "[I]t is very certain that it . . . was intended as a negative and preventive provision against injustice among the States themselves, rather than as a power to be used for the positive purposes of the General Government, in which alone, however, the remedial power could be lodged."

THE MARSHALL DOCTRINE

The intriguing question of the meaning of the commerce clause was first presented to the Court in 1824. The Marshall Court's experience demonstrated that the commerce clause would be a battleground between believers in state prerogatives and supporters of a strong national presence. Under what circumstances could a state policy be struck down as violative of the national Constitution?

The Steamboat Case. ***Gibbons* v. *Ogden*** involved the steamboat monopoly that the New York legislature had granted to Robert Livingston and Robert Fulton, their heirs, and others, granting them an exclusive right to operate steamboats in the state's waters. Ex-governor Ogden of New Jersey held a license under the monopoly to operate a steam-powered ferry between New York and New Jersey. Gibbons, who possessed a "coasting license" under a congressional statute but no license from the monopoly, operated boats on the same route in competition with Ogden. Chancellor Kent of the New York court upheld the monopoly and maintained that Congress had no direct jurisdiction over internal commerce or waters. Daniel Webster, arguing for Gibbons on appeal to the Supreme Court, asserted that Congress alone could regulate "high branches" of commerce. Counsel for the monopoly claimed that a concurrent power existed whenever such a power was not clearly denied by the Constitution. Webster's prophetic construction of commerce as comprehending "almost all the business and intercourse of life" was countered by the definition of commerce as "the transportation and sale of commodities." Both sides agreed that if an actual collision of state and national power occurred the latter must prevail, but counsel for the monopoly held that state power gave way only to the extent needed to give effect to the federal law. Accordingly, navigation on state waters remained under state control.

Chief Justice Marshall could have resolved the case simply by finding that both state and nation had acted within their powers, but because the state law conflicted with the federal licensing act, it must give way. He chose instead to examine the nature of the commerce power before finding the existence of a conflict. Commerce was more than traffic; "it is intercourse," and comprehended navigation.

He reiterated the point that commerce "among" the states cannot stop at state lines but "may be introduced into the interior." The power to regulate was "complete in itself, may be exercised to its utmost extent, and acknowledges no limitations, other than are prescribed in the Constitution." Though the states retained authority to enact inspection, pilotage, and health laws, even here Congress could enter the field if it chose.

In a separate opinion, Justice William Johnson went beyond Marshall and took an exclusive view of the commerce clause. Even in the absence of the licensing act, the state monopoly must give way. For Johnson, the national commerce power embraced *all* power enjoyed by the states over commerce before the Constitution. It was a grant of the whole power, carrying the whole domain exclusively into the hands of the national government.

With the exception of monopolists and southern slave owners who feared the consequence of a broad definition of national power over commerce, public opinion welcomed the rebuke the decision gave holders of special privilege. Following the decision, the number of steamboats plying in and out of New York harbor increased in one year from 6 to 43.

Defining State Authority. Though Marshall described the subject matter of commerce and national power to regulate it in the most sweeping terms, he did not overlook the tremendous power reserved to the states. But on what authority would state policy rest?

Marshall's view on this question comes out most clearly in *Willson* v. *Black Bird Creek Marsh Co.* (1829). The Delaware legislature had authorized the firm to build a dam across the creek for the purpose of reclaiming marshland. Willson, who owned a sloop licensed under federal authority, broke through the dam and continued to navigate the creek. The company sued for trespass. Upholding the Delaware act, Marshall explained,

> The act of assembly by which the plaintiffs were authorized to construct their dam, shows plainly that this is *one of those many creeks*, passing through a deep, level marsh, adjoining the Delaware, up which the tide flows for some distance. The value of the property on its banks must be enhanced by excluding the water from the marsh, and the *health of the inhabitants probably improved*. Measures calculated to produce these objects, provided they do not come into collision with the powers of the general government, are undoubtedly within those which are reserved to the states. . . .
>
> [C]ounsel . . . insist that it comes in conflict with the power of the United States "to regulate commerce . . . among the several states." If Congress had passed any act which bore upon the case; any act in execution of the power to regulate commerce, the object of which was to control state legislation over *those small navigable creeks* into which the tide flows, and *which abound throughout the lower country of the middle and southern states*, we should feel not much difficulty in saying that a state law coming in conflict with such act would be void. But Congress has passed no such act. . . .
>
> We do not think, that the act empowering the Black Bird Creek Marsh company to place a dam across the creek, can, *under all the circumstances of the case*, be considered as repugnant to the power to regulate commerce in its dormant state, or as being in conflict with any law passed on the subject. [Italics added.]

Marshall was at pains to show the bearing of the dam on land values and the health of the community. As a health measure, enacted under police power, the act was valid until it collided with national authority. He passed over the fact that the sloop in question was federally licensed—the vital consideration in *Gibbons*. Moreover, for the first time Marshall expressly acknowledged the **dormant commerce power**, to refer to the restraint the commerce clause imposes on the states even in the absence of national legislation.

THE DOCTRINE OF THE TANEY COURT

Roger B. Taney became chief justice after Marshall. During his tenure (1836–1864), the Court squarely faced the question Marshall had pointedly sidestepped in *Gibbons*: may the states regulate commerce in the absence of federal regulation? The **concurrent commerce doctrine** would answer that question in the affirmative. The **exclusive commerce doctrine** would dictate otherwise. The importance of the answer cannot be overstressed. Congress was not likely to react positively during this period. Thus invalidation of state laws regulating commerce meant that commerce was likely to be free from all regulation.

The Muddle of Commerce. In *New York* v. *Miln* (1837), the Taney Court issued a confused set of opinions that upheld as a police-power regulation a state act requiring the ship's master on incoming vessels to furnish information concerning the passengers. Justice Thompson, originally assigned the task of writing the opinion, treated the law as a police measure and permissible—in the absence of national action. Because four members of the Court balked at Thompson's analysis, Justice Barbour wrote an opinion holding the state law valid purely as a police measure, but added gratuitous comments that persons were not "subjects of commerce," a pronouncement highly pleasing to the slave states.

In 1847, the even more confused opinions in the License Cases revealed the Court's apparent inability to settle on any one view of the commerce power. Even though the Court unanimously upheld the state laws in question that regulated imported liquor, it was difficult to understand why. Taney and at least three other justices reasoned that Congress' power over commerce was not exclusive. Others insisted that the laws affected only internal commerce and derived from the state police power, and so were not regulations of commerce "among the states."

In the Passenger Cases (1849), argued on three different occasions over a four-year period, litigants challenged state taxes on passengers on incoming vessels. Daniel Webster, who as counsel opposed the laws, feared the absence of a "strong and leading mind" on the Court. Former president Martin Van Buren, arguing for the states, stressed the popular support for the acts and state sovereignty. Webster won a 5–4 decision. Each of the five justices stated his views in such a way, however, that the reporter of decisions could enter as a headnote only that the act was invalid. Three of the four dissenters wrote separate opinions. Taney held that since states could expel undesirable immigrants, they could reject them in the first place, and he cited *New York* v. *Miln* to show that persons were not "subjects of commerce." The majority split—two justices ruling congressional power over foreign commerce to be exclusive, three holding that this was unnecessary for the decision because the state act conflicted with existing national legislation. For those hoping for clarity on the commerce power, disappointment and frustration understandably greeted the decision.

The Cooley Doctrine. The law was in this confusion when President Millard Fillmore appointed Benjamin R. Curtis to the Court in 1851. A brilliant Massachusetts lawyer, Curtis became the mediator between the tenuous coalitions and the effective medium through whom a compromise was reached in ***Cooley* v. *Board of Wardens*** (1851). In this case the Court upheld a state pilotage fee against the charge that it conflicted with the national commerce power. Complicating the situation was a congressional act of 1789 stating that pilots should be regulated in conformity "with such laws as the states may hereafter enact . . . until further legislative provision shall be made by Congress." Combining elements of the "exclusive" and "concurrent" doctrines, Curtis fashioned a new formula of **selective exclusiveness**. His middle ground was this: subjects national in scope required uniform regulation that only Congress could provide, and in the absence of such legislation the states could not act. As to subjects of a local character, not requiring uniform legislation, states could legislate (according to Curtis) until Congress, by acting on the same subject, displaced the state law. Where national and state laws were in conflict, the federal rule would prevail.

The opinions delivered during the Marshall and Taney Courts contained plenty of ammunition for those advocating or opposing commercial regulation by either state or nation. For future courts, substantial difficulties existed, despite the formula fashioned by the Cooley doctrine. How was one to decide whether a subject matter required a national (or uniform) regulation? Was inaction by Congress the same as a declaration that the desired uniformity was no regulation? In the absence of a need for uniform regulation, would any state regulation be acceptable? Answers to these and other questions were left to the future.

STATES AND THE COMMERCE CLAUSE TODAY

As inspired by the Cooley doctrine, the Court's first duty in the absence of congressional legislation has been to determine the nature of the subject matter regulated. Does the state policy disrupt a desired uniformity? If it requires national regulation (or an absence of such regulation), state action is foreclosed. If the subject matter permits local regulation, two questions remain: First, does the state law discriminate against interstate commerce and in favor of local commerce? Second, does the act, although nondiscriminatory, place an unreasonable burden on interstate commerce? Socioeconomic fact and theory, flavored by judicial bias, have entered inevitably into the attempts to answer these questions.

Three Views of State Regulation. More than a half century ago, three basic positions crystallized as the Court attempted to answer these questions. First, then as now, all justices were opposed to **protectionism**: No state could discriminate against interstate commerce merely to gain for itself a commercial advantage over its neighbors. Thus, a law that discriminates against interstate commerce is sustainable only if it serves a legitimate local purpose that could not be served as well by nondiscriminatory means. A few justices believed that was all the commerce clause in its dormant state was meant to prevent. A second group has preferred a balancing-of-interests or cost-benefits rule when faced with state legislation that was not protectionist but that arguably burdened interstate commerce. This is illustrated by ***Southern Pacific Co.* v. *Arizona*** (1945), where the Court had to decide whether a state limit on the length of interstate and intrastate trains could stand. In such situations, the need for the regulation is weighed against its costs to determine whether the burden imposed is undue. Incantation of worthy purposes alone will not suffice to save a state statute from challenge under the commerce clause. A third group has found the first two positions equally objectionable. Neither gave due weight to a danger the commerce clause was designed to avert—**balkanization**—which would permit individual states to raise barriers to commerce. According to this view, even in the absence of congressional legislation, the commerce clause of its own force prohibits states from doing anything to burden, obstruct, hinder, or restrain interstate commerce. Furthermore, it is the duty of the Supreme Court to guard national commerce from such local encroachments.

It has been the second position, sometimes veering toward the third that has most often been reflected in Court decisions in recent decades. As Justice Stewart long ago restated the balancing test,

> Where the statute regulates even-handedly to effectuate a legitimate local public interest, and its effects on interstate commerce are only incidental, it will be upheld unless the burden imposed on such commerce is clearly excessive in relation to the putative local benefits. If a legitimate local purpose is found, then the question becomes one of degree. And the extent of the burden that will be tolerated will of course depend on the nature of the local interest involved, and on whether it could be promoted as well with a lesser impact on interstate activities. (*Pike* v. *Bruce Church, Inc.*, 1970)

This view continues to be reflected in decisions involving the many ways state laws arguably affect commerce. For example, *Granholm* v. *Heald* (2005) invalidated Michigan and New York laws that allowed direct product shipment to residents from in-state wineries but not from out-of-state wineries. For the five-justice majority, the Twenty-First Amendment was insufficient authority for the preferential treatment in-state businesses enjoyed. Moreover, the nondiscrimination principle embodied in the commerce clause was not offset by the states' interests in discouraging both tax evasion and Internet purchases of alcohol by minors, objectives the Court believed could be achieved by even-handed alternatives.

Transportation. Initially, the Court was rather generous in upholding state acts regulating motor transportation, such as the licensing of vehicles (*Buck* v. *Kuykendall*, 1925). In 1938, *South Carolina* v. *Barnwell* approved a statute barring from state roads trucks with loads over 20,000 pounds and widths exceeding 90 inches. In the absence of congressional legislation, it was deemed reasonable to protect roads built and maintained by the state, especially since no discrimination or attempt to burden interstate commerce had been shown. In such situations today, the bench is inclined toward the balancing-of-interests approach reflected in Justice Stone's opinion in the Arizona Train Limit Case, and exhibits less deference to and more skepticism of state restrictions. In truck-length cases, for example, the Court has ruled that state bans on 65-foot double trailers, especially where neighboring states permit them on the highways, violate the commerce clause (*Raymond Motor Transportation, Inc.* v. *Rice*, 1978; *Kassel* v. *Consolidated Freightways Corp.*, 1981). As Justice Powell maintained in *Kassel*, "[T]he incantation of a purpose to promote the public health or safety does not insulate a state law from Commerce Clause attack. Regulations designed for that salutary purpose nevertheless may further the purpose so marginally, and interfere with commerce so substantially, as to be invalid. . . ." The judicial task in these cases is at heart both empirical and political—a weighing of one value against another.

Quality of Life. State and local regulations to protect the environment or to improve the quality of life also meet challenges under the commerce clause. In *Burbank* v. *Lockheed Air Terminal* (1973), the Court struck down an ordinance banning takeoffs and landings by certain jet aircraft at an airport during late-night hours.

Although finding no express preemption by national statutes, Justice Douglas for the Court found an implied one: "If we were to uphold the Burbank ordinance and a significant number of municipalities followed suit, it is obvious that fractionalized control of the timing of takeoffs and landings would severely limit the flexibility of the FAA in controlling air traffic flow. The difficulties of scheduling flights to avoid congestion and the concomitant decrease in safety would be compounded."

Similarly, trash disposal implicates the commerce clause. In 1978, a seven-member majority overturned a New Jersey statute prohibiting the importation of most "solid or liquid waste which originated or was collected outside the territorial limits of the State" (***Philadelphia* v. *New Jersey***). The laudable intent of the law was to prevent the state from becoming a dumping ground for New York and Pennsylvania, and to conserve valuable in-state landfills, but the constitutionally impermissible effect of the law was "to saddle those outside the State with the entire burden of slowing the flow of refuse into New Jersey's remaining landfill sites."

Garbage is commerce not because of its own worth but because of the fact that the one who possesses garbage must pay to get rid of it. There is business in trash. Both the generation of solid waste and the cost of landfill capacity have moved local governments to spend considerable amounts of money on trash control systems and to seek ways to finance them. Thus against arguments based on the New Jersey garbage ruling, *United Haulers* v. *Oneida-Herkimer Solid Waste Authority* (2007) upheld a flow-control ordinance that required private haulers, whether from in or out of state, to deliver collected solid waste to sites operated by a publicly owned entity.

States as Market Participants. That result seems consistent with a distinction the Court has drawn between the state as *market participant* and the state as *market regulator*. The strictures of the dormant commerce clause do not apply to the former in the same way they do to the latter.

Reeves, Inc. v. *Stake* (1980) illustrates the distinction. Here the justices examined the sales policies of a state-owned cement plant where, after a cut in production, the state chose to supply in-state customers first. As a result, an out-of-state concrete business had to reduce its own production by 76 percent. For the majority, Justice Blackmun drew on a novel distinction the Court first employed in *Hughes* v. *Alexandria Scrap Corp.* (1976) between the state as participant or actor in the market and the state as regulator of the market. Admittedly, the state could not have passed a law requiring firms to supply in-state customers at the expense of those out-of-state, but as operator of the plant, it was free to do exactly that. Because the state was acting in the role of the former, there was no violation of the commerce clause even though the state's policy clearly placed out-of-state buyers at a disadvantage.

Taxation. The usual prohibition against laws that discriminate against interstate commerce may not apply to a state policy that taxes income earned by holders of out-of-state bonds but not in-state bonds (*Kentucky Department of Revenue* v. *Davis*, 2008). Viewed alongside *United Haulers*, the Court may now be inclined to invalidate laws that benefit a private local interest but not those that benefit the government itself.

With respect to a different category of taxation, may a state require out-of-state businesses to collect and remit sales tax on merchandise shipped into that state? In *National Bellas Hess* v. *Department of Revenue* (1967) and *Quill Corp.* v. *North Dakota* (1992), the Court allowed such taxation provided the business had a physical presence within the state. Yet in *Direct Marketing Association* v. *Brohl* (2015), Justice Kennedy suggested in a concurring opinion that more recent technological changes called the physical nexus rule into question. Facing a noticeable decline in sales tax revenues brought on by the Internet, the legislature of South Dakota responded with a statute that led to a judicial reverse of course in ***South Dakota v. Wayfair, Inc.*** (2018).

A Continuing Judicial Role. From this chapter thus far, certain conclusions can be drawn. First, the dormant commerce clause has not been used to frustrate state legislation, simply because one might argue that a national rule would be more efficient or desirable. Second, decisions have in fact permitted the erection of what amount to modest trade barriers (motor carrier limitations, taxes, inspection laws, safety laws). Third, Congress for many reasons has not chosen to regulate all subjects that lie within the reach of its commerce power, and so much has been left to the states. Fourth, cases testing state power under the commerce clause unavoidably require the exercise of judicial discretion and remain a staple of the Court's docket.

Throughout, the Supreme Court has undertaken the role of guardian of the national market against efforts to re-erect the type of trade barriers that marked the preconstitutional era. The commerce clause in its twin dimensions has not only been a "prolific source of conflict" between state interests and national prerogatives but, as the remainder of this chapter will show, an equally "prolific source of national power."

THE NATIONAL COMMERCE POWER: COMPETING VISIONS

In the post–Civil War period, state legislatures were under pressure to solve the problems arising from a burgeoning industrialism and an economy that was becoming truly national for the first time. And until the 1880s, regulation—if it was to come at all—would largely be state regulation. However, once Congress began to enact economic legislation of its own, the commerce clause in its active mode became a persistent constitutional issue.

The Wabash and Sugar Trust Cases. It was state regulation of railroads that focused judicial attention on problems that could arise in the absence of congressional action. Initially the Court allowed states to set rates that railroads could charge, even though this regulation had an indirect effect on interstate commerce. However, as state after state adopted its own system of rate regulation, the Court later changed its mind. The facts in the Wabash case (*Wabash, St. Louis & Pacific Ry. Co.* v. *Illinois*, 1886) illustrated the quandary. The railroad charged 15 cents per hundred pounds from Peoria, Illinois, and 25 cents per hundred pounds from Gilman, Illinois, on shipments of similar chattels to New York City. Because Gilman was 86 miles closer to New York, the two rates ran afoul of an Illinois statute banning long–short haul rate discrimination. With most of the distance for each shipment lying outside Illinois, the state was in effect regulating interstate commerce.

The majority in *Wabash* found the state law an invalid intrusion on the national commerce power. "This is commerce of national character," Justice Miller said, "and national regulation is required." *Wabash* was significant in helping to bring about a climate of opinion favorable to national regulation of interstate railroad rates through passage of the Interstate Commerce Act the following year. This 1887 law established the Interstate Commerce Commission, the second permanent federal regulatory agency created by Congress with broad quasi-legislative, executive, and judicial powers.

Three years later, passage of the **Sherman Anti-Trust Act** showed that Congress was prepared to use its commerce power to accomplish purposes far beyond anything hitherto attempted. The rationale of the act was that certain combinations and conspiracies in businesses that had the effect of restraining or monopolizing interstate commerce should be prohibited. Difficult questions arose at the very outset, however, concerning the applicability of the law to industrial and commercial firms, because Congress could outlaw monopolistic practices only in businesses that engaged in commerce "among the states." In ***United States* v. *E. C. Knight Co.*** (the Sugar Trust Case, 1895), the Court held that a monopoly in the production of refined sugar was exempt from the Sherman Act. To Chief Justice Fuller, commerce meant primarily sale and distribution—the physical movement of goods following manufacture. The effect of contracts and combinations to control manufacture, "however inevitable and whatever its extent," would be "indirect," the chief justice believed, and therefore beyond congressional reach. Fuller thus made use of a distinction that would persist for years in the jurisprudence of the commerce clause: **direct versus indirect effects**, with only the former being subject to national regulation. Yet, because he recognized that goods are manufactured *only* because they can be sold and that manufacture and commerce are interrelated, he was much disturbed by the implications of an integrated national economy for federal power. It is no surprise, therefore, that Fuller echoed Justice L.Q.C. Lamar's admonition from *Kidd* v. *Pearson* (1888): "No distinction is more popular to the common mind . . . than that between manufactures and commerce. . . . If it is held that [commerce] includes the regulation of all such manufactures as are intended to be the subject of commercial transactions in the future, . . . Congress would be invested, to the exclusion of the States, with the power to regulate, not only manufacture, but also agriculture, horticulture, stock raising, domestic fisheries, mining—in short, every branch of human industry."

In 1904, however, *Northern Securities Co.* v. *United States* allowed application of the Sherman Act to a scheme by which a holding company had been established to hold the stock of competing interstate railroads, thus eliminating competition between them. In another broad interpretation of the commerce power (*Swift* v. *United States*, 1905), a combination of meat packers was held unlawful under the act, on the ground that their activities, though geographically "local," were important incidents in a "current of commerce." The Sugar Trust Case seemed seriously undermined.

A National Police Power? A series of cases between 1903 and World War I clearly established the principle that the commerce power could also be used as a device for accomplishing purely social goals, apart from regulating commercial activities of large corporations. These decisions meant that Congress in effect possessed a **national police power**, alongside the police power ("the power to govern men and things," Chief Justice Taney once called it) the states had always enjoyed. (See Chapter Eight for a discussion of the development of the state police power.)

In the first case (***Champion* v. *Ames***, 1903), the Court sustained a federal act prohibiting the interstate shipment of lottery tickets. Alongside the majority's frequent references to the evil nature of these tickets, Chief Justice Fuller's dissent insisted that the evil began only with their illegal use at the point of destination. Besides, "[t]o hold that Congress has general police power would be to hold that it may accomplish objects not intrusted to the General Government, and to defeat the operation of the Tenth Amendment." On grounds similar to those in the Lottery Case, the Pure Food and Drug Act withstood attack in 1911 (*Hipolite Egg Co.* v. *United States*). *Hoke*

v. *United States* (1913) approved the Mann Act, making it a felony to transport a woman from one state to another for immoral purposes. In *Houston, E.&W. Texas Ry. Co.* v. *United States* (the Shreveport Case), the Court upheld in 1914 an Interstate Commerce Commission order fixing intrastate railroad rates because of their effect on interstate commerce, echoing Marshall's view that the national commerce power extends to all commerce that "affects more than one state." The inference was that local practices were within the reach of national power if they affected commerce.

The pattern then became confused. ***Hammer* v. *Dagenhart*** (1918) adhered to the Sugar Trust Case by distinguishing between commerce and manufacturing, as the Court invalidated the Keating–Owen Child Labor Act of 1916. Considered a triumph of the Progressive era, it prohibited transportation in interstate commerce of products produced by child labor (age 16 in mines, age 14 in factories, or more than 48 hours a week for the age-group 14–16 years). Justice Day, for the Court, characterized the precedents involving lotteries, food, and prostitution as attempts to regulate where transportation was used to accomplish harmful results; production and its incidents, on the other hand, were (in Day's mind) local matters, and the items produced by child labor were not harmful in themselves. As Chapter Seven explains, Congress then tried an alternate attack on child labor in 1919 relying on the taxing power, but the Court invalidated that law as well, 8–1 (***Bailey* v. *Drexel Furniture Co.***, 1922).

Other cases seemed to indicate once again that the Court might be prepared to accept a broad construction of the commerce power. ***Stafford* v. *Wallace*** (1922) upheld the Packers and Stockyards Act of 1921, which took aim at harmful trade practices in the Chicago meatpacking industry. Chief Justice Taft reasoned that although in a geographic sense the packers were conducting a local business, in an economic sense their activities were only an incident in a continuing interstate market from ranches to dinner tables. Following the same line of reasoning, *Brooks* v. *United States* (1925) sustained the National Motor Theft Act, making it a crime to transport or conceal a stolen automobile that had crossed state lines. These decisions stood in contrast to cases like *Dagenhart* and seemed to portend a return to the broad doctrines of Chief Justice Marshall.

CONSTITUTIONAL CRISIS

Franklin D. Roosevelt was inaugurated president in 1933 in the depths of the Great Depression. His administration achieved rapid passage in Congress of a series of measures designed to aid economic recovery. The first phase of FDR's domestic reform program (called the **New Deal**) involved agricultural and business regulation, price stabilization, public works, and banking and finance regulation. Prominent legislation included the National Industrial Recovery Act (NIRA) and the Agricultural Adjustment Act (AAA), both enacted in 1933. The second phase began in 1935 and emphasized legislation—such as the Social Security Act of 1935 and the Fair Labor Standards Act of 1938—to benefit working people directly and in the long term. What would be the constitutional fate of these bold programs? The Court, after all, had at hand two viable lines of precedent. There were the doctrines established by John Marshall, which had inspired decisions such as *Stafford* v. *Wallace*. Alternatively, there were the restrictive interpretations of the Sugar Trust Case and *Hammer* v. *Dagenhart*.

The New Deal in Court. The first New Deal reform measure reached the Supreme Court for argument in December 1934 under circumstances that did not augur well for the validity of executive orders issued under NIRA. The Panama Refining Company had challenged the act's prohibition against shipment of "hot oil" (that exceeding state allowances) across state lines. Early in the argument government counsel disclosed that criminal penalties attaching to the violation of the relevant code provisions had been inadvertently omitted from the executive order. Judicial curiosity was immediately aroused, and concern deepened when opposing counsel bitterly complained that his client had been arrested, indicted, and held several days in jail for violating this nonexistent "law." With these points against it, the government was at a disadvantage in pressing its argument that Congress could constitutionally empower the president in his discretion to ban hot oil from interstate commerce. Eight justices held Section 9(c) of the NIRA invalid as an unconstitutional delegation of legislative power to the chief executive (*Panama Refining Co.* v. *Ryan*, 1935). Congress, they said, established no "primary standard," thus leaving "the matter to the President without standard or rule, to be dealt with as he pleased."

Before the dust thrown up by the hot oil decision had settled, the Court made headlines in a 5–4 decision scuttling the recently enacted railroad retirement program, which required carriers to subscribe to a pension plan (*Railroad Retirement Board* v. *Alton R. R. Co.*, 1935). Taken together, the Panama Refining and the railroad retirement cases forecast the New Deal's doom. The next blow fell when NIRA (symbolized by the Blue Eagle) was guillotined out of the recovery program (*Schechter Poultry Co.* v. *United States*, 1935). The Schechter brothers, wholesale poultry dealers in Brooklyn, New York, were charged with violating NIRA's Live Poultry Code by ignoring minimum wage and maximum hour requirements, by giving special treatment to preferred customers, and by selling an "unfit chicken" to a butcher. The Court, speaking through Chief Justice Hughes, found the act deficient as an unconstitutional delegation of legislative power. Moreover, government counsel conceded that congressional authority to regulate the Schechter business had to be based on the commerce clause, but the Court held the defendants' business was neither interstate commerce in itself nor closely enough connected with it to "affect" such commerce.

In May of the following year, the justices ruled 6–3 that Congress had exceeded its authority in enacting the Guffey-Snyder Bituminous Coal Conservation Act (***Carter* v. *Carter Coal Co.***, 1936). Through a complex system of wage and price controls administered by a commission, the statute attempted to provide remedies for the notoriously distressed soft coal industry. The situation was so urgent and the benefits of the legislation so evident that President Roosevelt had taken the unusual step of asking the congressional subcommittee, while the coal act was pending, not to "permit doubts as to constitutionality, however reasonable," to block the suggested legislation. The Court, however, was not prepared to set aside such doubts. "[I]t is of vital moment," Justice Sutherland said for the majority, "that, in order to preserve the fixed balance intended by the Constitution, the powers of the general government be not so extended as to embrace any not within the express terms of the several grants or the implications necessary to be drawn therefrom." Sutherland's opinion was clear-cut and unequivocal on the nature of the distinction between direct and indirect effects. "The local character of mining, of manufacturing, and of crop growing is a fact, and remains a fact, whatever may be done with the products," Sutherland said. Going back to Chief Justice Fuller's opinion in the Sugar Trust Case and paraphrasing his words, Sutherland declared, "Such effect as they [working conditions] may have upon commerce, however extensive it may be, is secondary and indirect. An increase in the greatness of the effect adds to its importance. It does not alter its character." Dual federalism (see Chapter Four) remained an independent check on the extent of Congress' power under the commerce clause.

As far as the commerce power was concerned, the Court by 1936 had adopted the view that certain subjects were local in nature and beyond the power of Congress, even though they required national or uniform regulations if they were to be regulated at all. On the other hand, effective state-by-state regulation was clearly impossible; even if it were attempted it might, if any state regulation were found to have a substantial effect on interstate commerce, run afoul of the dormant commerce power. The Court thus had narrowed the commerce doctrines of Marshall by withdrawing from congressional power certain subject matters, such as production, agriculture, and the employer–employee relationship. In effect, the Court had created a category other than those enumerated in the Cooley Case: objects that could not in practice be regulated by either government—a "twilight zone." The situation presented a strong parallel to the Dred Scott decision of 1857 (see Chapter Two) where the Court placed slavery in the territories off limits to both Congress and the territorial legislatures. As Justice Stone wrote to his sister at the end of the Court's term in June 1936, "we seem to have tied Uncle Sam up in a hard knot." Indeed, in the years 1934–1936, the Supreme Court in 12 decisions had declared unconstitutional all or part of 11 New Deal measures,[1] and these decisions were made by a bench without a single Roosevelt appointee. None of the "nine old men" (as some journalists called them) opted to retire during FDR's first term.

The Court-Packing Threat. By the winter of 1936, it looked as if the Court had put the New Deal firmly on the rack of unconstitutionality, rendering government impotent. The entire legislative program overwhelmingly approved by the American people at the polls in 1932, 1934, and 1936 was, as Assistant Attorney General Robert Jackson said, in danger of being lost in "a maze of constitutional metaphors."

President Roosevelt had several options. He and Congress might limit the jurisdiction of the Supreme Court, sponsor constitutional amendments limiting the Court's power or reversing its rulings, or increase the number of judges to override the present majority. Though many members of Congress urged that something be done, they were uncertain what to do, not quite sure whether the trouble was the fault of the Constitution or of judges. The president and his party were uncertain, too, at least on the most feasible remedy politically. The Democratic Party platform in 1936 said, "If these problems [social and economic] cannot be effectively solved by legislation within the Constitution, we shall seek such clarifying amendments as [we] . . . shall find necessary, in order adequately to regulate commerce, protect public health and safety and safeguard economic liberty. Thus we propose to maintain the letter and spirit of the Constitution." Throughout the campaign Democratic orators muted the discord, giving no hint that Roosevelt would, if reelected, wage all-out war on the judiciary.

FDR awaited the propitious moment. With Roosevelt's carrying 46 of the 48 states, the November election had, as one newspaper said, yielded "a roar in which cheers for the Supreme Court were drowned out." Congressional opinion also appeared overtly hostile to the Court. Yet even in the face of his overwhelming electoral triumph, the president could not be sure that the Court would give ground. Did not the traditional theory insist that the justices are and must be immune to election returns? Unwilling to take chances, the president, on February 5, 1937, sent to Congress his message proposing a drastic shake-up in the judiciary. Supreme Court justices past the age of 70 would have six months in which to retire. A justice who failed to retire within the appointed time could continue in office, but the chief executive would appoint an additional justice, up to a maximum bench of 15 justices—presumably younger and better able to carry the heavy load. Because there were six justices in this category, Roosevelt would have been able to make that number of appointments at once. In presenting his proposal, the president gave no hint of wishing to stem the tide of anti–New Deal decisions. He tendered the hemlock cup to the elderly jurists on the elevated ground that they slowed the efficient dispatch of judicial business.

From the very start, the **Court-packing plan**, as it was quickly dubbed, ran into terrific opposition, even though Democrats in the new 75th Congress enjoyed their largest majorities of the twentieth century and Republicans had nearly become an endangered species. Overnight, Supreme Court justices were again pictured as demigods, weighing public policy in the delicate scales of the law. "Constitutionality" was talked about as if it were a tangible fact, undeviating and precise, not merely the current judicial theory of what ought and what ought not to be allowed. The same members of Congress who, before the president's message, had demanded the scalps of reactionary justices were "shocked beyond measure" and turned on Roosevelt in an attitude of anguished surprise. Closing ranks with bar associations, newspapers lined up almost solidly against Court packing. The idea implicit in Roosevelt's scheme, that the Court may change its interpretation in such a way as to sustain legislative power to meet national needs, was called as "false in theory, as it would be ruinous in practice." Throughout the ensuing months, debate waxed furiously. Said Walter Lippmann, "No issue so great or so deep has been raised in America since secession."

Everyone who could read knew that the justices were not the vestal virgins of the Constitution. Yet through the years, and despite increasing evidence that judicial interpretation and not fundamental law shackled the power to govern, the American people had come to regard the Court as the symbol of their freedom. Tarnished though the symbol was, it made, like the English monarchy, for national stability and poise in crisis; moreover, like its English counterpart, the Supreme Court commanded the loyalty of the citizenry, providing perhaps an impregnable barrier against tyrannical government. "The President wants to control the Supreme Court" was hammered home incessantly. If the plan were accepted, the anti–New Deal press averred, nothing would stand between Roosevelt and the absolute dictatorship of the United States.

Quick to sense that his initial approach had been a major blunder, FDR moved closer to the real issue on March 4, when he likened the judiciary to an unruly horse on the government gang plough, unwilling to pull with its teammates, the executive and Congress. As he saw it now, the crucial question was not whether the Court had kept up with its calendar but whether it had kept up with the country. But the president's false assertion that the judges lagged in their work had blurred the issue, diverting public attention so completely that his later effort to face the difficulty squarely never succeeded.

In a nationwide Fireside Chat on March 9, the president threw off the cloak of sophistry and frankly explained, "The Court has been acting not as a judicial body, but as a policymaking body. . . . That is not only my accusation, it is the accusation of most distinguished Justices of the present Supreme Court. . . . In holding the AAA unconstitutional, Justice Stone said of the majority opinion that it was 'a tortured construction of the Constitution' and two other Justices agreed with him. In the case holding the New York Minimum Wage Law unconstitutional [*Morehead* v. *New York* ex rel. *Tipaldo*, 1936], Justice Stone said that the majority were actually reading into the Constitution their own 'personal economic predilections' . . . and two other justices agreed with him."

Counterattack. A vigorous campaign against the president's bill was being waged in the Senate under the leadership of Senator Burton K. Wheeler. White House advisor Tommy Corcoran tried vainly to dissuade the Montana Democrat from making a fight; the president himself told Wheeler of the futility of opposing a measure certain to pass. "A liberal cause," Wheeler explained bluntly, "was never won by stacking a deck of cards, by stuffing a ballot box or packing a Court."

Meanwhile, those able to make the most realistic estimate of the condition of the Court's docket—the justices themselves—maintained a discreet silence. Finally, Senator Wheeler nervously sought an interview with Justice Brandeis who, with Stone and Cardozo, belonged to the trio of justices most inclined to uphold New Deal legislation. Much to his surprise, he found Brandeis cooperative. "Why don't you call on the Chief Justice?" Brandeis suggested. "But I don't know the Chief Justice," the Montana senator hesitated. "Well," said Brandeis, somewhat impatiently, "the Chief Justice knows you and knows what you are doing."

This was late Friday afternoon, March 19, 1937. The next day, Senator Wheeler went to see Chief Justice Hughes. The senator wanted to know from the justices themselves whether the president's oft-repeated allegations about the backlogged docket, lack of efficiency, and so on had any basis in fact. As Brandeis had indicated, the chief justice was not only enlisted but enthusiastic. Though Wheeler had not reached him until Saturday, March 20, Hughes was able somehow to prepare a long and closely reasoned document for the senator's use the following Monday, March 22. "The baby is born," he said with a broad smile, as he put the letter into Wheeler's hand late Sunday afternoon.

Hughes's letter not only scotched the president's charge that the "old men" were not abreast of their docket but also revealed its composer as a canny dialectician. Though carefully refraining from open opposition to the plan, the letter suggested that the president's idea of an enlarged Court and the hearing of cases in divisions might run counter to the constitutional provision for "one Supreme Court." It was extraordinary enough, some of his colleagues thought, for a justice to go out of his way to meet constitutional issues unnecessary for deciding a case; Hughes went further and handed down an advisory opinion on a burning political issue. Hughes also conveyed the erroneous impression that the entire Court had been consulted and endorsed his statement.

The chief justice's letter, combined with the Court's forthcoming about-face, put a fatal crimp in the president's scheme. Then, Justice Van Devanter—one of the New Deal's archenemies—announced his retirement on May 18, ensuring Roosevelt his first opportunity to make an appointment to the Court. (The Supreme Court Retirement Act, signed into law on March 1, 1937, allowed justices to retire at the age of 70 with full salary.) Roosevelt's plan might no longer be needed. "Why run for a train after you've caught it?" asked Senator (and future justice) James Byrnes.

On June 14, the Senate Judiciary Committee voted 10–8 against the president's bill. On July 14, Senator Joseph T. Robinson of Arkansas, the bill's floor leader, died unexpectedly. Ironically, Robinson was thought by many to have been promised Van Devanter's seat, which Roosevelt eventually handed to New Deal stalwart Senator Hugo Black of Alabama. Finally, in an act that was almost anticlimactic, the full

Senate voted 70–20 on July 22 to recommit the bill to committee, thus sealing the plan's fate.

The Court's victory was not, however, unmixed. Roosevelt's plan was defeated, but, as explained below, without the appointment of a single new justice, he extracted from the embattled bench decisions favorable to the New Deal. "In politics the black-robed reactionary Justices had won over the master liberal politician of their day," opined future Justice Robert Jackson. "In law the President defeated the recalcitrant Justices in their own Court." Even as the fight raged about them, the justices had begun destruction of their most recent handiwork.

A Switch in Time. The major issue facing Court and country in the spring of 1937 was posed by the National Labor Relations Act (also known as the Wagner Act). Passed in 1935, the statute was the most encompassing labor legislation ever enacted by Congress. The law established the National Labor Relations Board with authority to oversee all interstate labor affairs. It defined unfair labor practices and gave unions considerable protection against management. Would the justices turn their backs on the Schechter and Carter Coal rulings and permit the national government to substitute law for naked force in labor relations? In the heat of the court fight, industrial peace—or war—seemed to hang in the balance. Then, on April 12, 1937, Chief Justice Hughes put forward a broad and encompassing definition of interstate commerce and conceded to Congress the power to protect the lifelines of the national economy from private industrial warfare (***NLRB* v. *Jones & Laughlin Steel Corp*.**).

Arguments that had proved effective in *Schechter* and *Carter Coal* now availed nothing, even though the Court's membership had not yet changed. "Those cases," the chief justice commented summarily, "are not controlling here." They were not controlling because he now chose to consider the distinction between direct and indirect effects as one of degree rather than kind. Because interstate commerce was now seen as a "practical conception," interference with that commerce "must be appraised by a judgment that does not ignore actual experience." Therefore, it was "idle to say" that interference by strikes or other labor disturbances "would be indirect or remote. It is obvious that it would be immediate and might be catastrophic." "We are asked to shut our eyes to the plainest facts of our national life," the chief justice continued, "and to deal with the question of direct and indirect effects in an intellectual vacuum."

Moreover, the chief justice's sweeping doctrine did not apply solely to large-scale industries, such as steel. On the same day, the Court applied the same doctrine to two smaller concerns, a trailer company and a men's clothing manufacturer (*NLRB* v. *Freuhauf Trailer Co*., *NLRB* v. *Friedman-Harry Marks Clothing Co*.). By a vote of 5–4 each time, this major New Deal enactment was sustained. The **Constitutional Revolution of 1937** was under way. The effects of FDR's assault on the Court, however, went far beyond a string of pro–New Deal rulings. Had there been nothing more than this, the confrontation of 1937 would be important but hardly epochal. Instead, as explained further in Chapter Eight, the event marked a constitutional divide.

THE COMMERCE POWER REBORN

United States v. *Darby* (1941) unanimously upheld the Fair Labor Standards Act (FLSA), which fixed minimum wages and maximum hours for producers of goods shipped in interstate commerce and which banned the interstate shipment of goods manufactured under substandard conditions or by children. In his opinion, Justice Stone included this significant comment: "The motive and purpose of a regulation of interstate commerce are matters for the legislative judgment upon the exercise of which the Constitution places no restriction and over which the Courts are given no control." *Hammer* v. *Dagenhart* was overruled. ***Wickard* v. *Filburn*** (1942) marked just how far the Court had come since 1936 by upholding the marketing provisions of the Agricultural Adjustment Act of 1938 even as applied to wheat grown for home consumption. *Filburn* and *Darby* were light-years removed from *Carter Coal*.

The commerce power had been reborn in three important respects: First, the Court accepted a greatly enlarged definition of "commerce." Second, the Court accepted Congress' judgment as to those conditions that "affected" commerce. Third, the Tenth Amendment (hitherto the guardian of state prerogatives) furnished no independent limitation on Congress, even if the national statute interfered with matters historically within the purview of the states. Was there now any commerce-related activity beyond the reach of congressional power?

Expanded Applications. Decisions sustaining the 1964 Civil Rights Act illustrate the post–New Deal conception of the commerce to which congressional power extends. ***Heart of Atlanta Motel* v. *United States*** and ***Katzenbach* v. *McClung*** (1964) approved the application of Title II of the act barring racial discrimination not only to a private establishment serving interstate travelers (*Atlanta Motel*) but also to Ollie's Barbeque, a restaurant in Birmingham that served mainly a local clientele and purchased all of its supplies in-state (*McClung*). Ollie's was nonetheless deemed part of interstate commerce because half of the food it served had previously "moved" in commerce between the states. "The absence of direct evidence connecting discriminatory restaurant service with the flow of interstate food," observed Justice Clark, "is not . . . a crucial matter." The significance of such deference to Congress became manifest in *Daniel* v. *Paul* (1969), where a recreational facility near Little Rock, Arkansas, was found to be a "public accommodation" affecting commerce and within the reach of the 1964 law. The entire 232-acre establishment, with its golf, swimming, dancing, and other activities, was held to be within the act's provisions because three of the four items sold at the snack bar had originated outside of the state.

Revolution or Counterrevolution? So far as the commerce power is concerned, the Constitutional Revolution of 1937 thus appears as much as a counterrevolution as a revolution. From 1890 to 1936, when the Court began to develop a series of implied limitations on the exercise of the commerce power, it was not doing so in response to any rule of law announced by the Marshall or Taney Court. Marshall, although not denying the power of the states to regulate certain local matters, defined the commerce power broadly and preferred political, not judicial, checks on its exercise. Taney's Court, although more generous to local regulation in the absence of federal legislation, made it clear that Congress' power was broad and to the extent exercised would be upheld, and that the Court would undertake to determine the validity of state acts by measuring the need for uniform regulation in each case. The Court, in other words, would play the difficult role of ascertaining the limits of state power over commerce until Congress should act. In the period 1890–1936, the Court inverted the role of the

Taney Court. At one time, it would use the commerce power to frustrate state acts where they interfered with national commerce, but at other times it would imply limits on the national power to regulate certain aspects of commerce by evolving rules denying to mining, agriculture, and manufacturing any relationship with interstate commerce.

Yet as generous as the Marshall and Taney Courts were in construing Congress' power under the commerce clause, it is also important to remember that Congress made little use of that authority prior to the Civil War. Judicial limitations on the national commerce power emerged after Congress began to make full use of the authority it presumably had.

If one is inclined to protest that the Founders never dreamed of AAA, FLSA, and NLRA, the answer is that of course they did not. This argument, it might be pointed out, could be used to reject the great bulk of modern state and national regulatory acts. But as Marshall said in *McCulloch* v. *Maryland* (1819), "This provision [the necessary and proper clause] is made in a constitution, intended to endure for ages to come, and consequently, to be adapted to the various *crises* of human affairs." In the light of this philosophy, the growth of national power through the commerce clause can be described as the necessary response by government to economic and social change. So when those adversely affected by regulation clamor "back to the Constitution," the question becomes, back to which Constitution—that of 1787, as interpreted by John Marshall, or that of 1890–1936?

A RETURN TO LIMITATIONS

In 1995, for the first time since 1936, the Court struck down an act of Congress on commerce grounds alone. Falling victim in ***United States* v. *Lopez*** was the Gun-Free School Zones Act of 1990, which made it a federal crime to possess a firearm within 1,000 feet of a school. Although the government's brief argued that the presence of guns in or near schools adversely affected education, among other things, and that in turn adversely affected interstate commerce, Congress had not made this link to commerce explicit as part of its "findings" when passing the law. Commentators wondered whether *Lopez* was merely a reprimand to Congress for being legislatively sloppy. For some, it was only a directive to "go back and do it right"—to substantiate connections with commerce. If so, then *Lopez* was no more than a blip. For others, *Lopez* more significantly signaled a more exacting judicial scrutiny. If the Lopez majority believed that firearms possession near a schoolhouse could in no way be sufficiently tied to commerce to bring it within the reach of congressional power, then the statute would be invalid even if Congress had tried to demonstrate a nexus between guns near schools and commerce. Judicial skepticism would take the place of the customary deference to congressional findings.

That the Court had altered its posture toward the commerce clause became plainly evident in 2000 when the same five justices of the Lopez majority struck down a provision of the Violence Against Women Act in ***United States* v. *Morrison*.** Enacted by Congress in 1994, this law allowed victims of gender-motivated violence to sue their attackers for damages in federal court. In contrast to the Gun-Free School Zones Act, the record contained ample congressional documentation describing the impact of gender-motivated violence on its victims and their families and its effects on interstate commerce. But the Court found the law constitutionally unsustainable under the commerce clause. "If accepted," maintained Chief Justice Rehnquist, attempting to prevent the commerce power from transforming itself into a general national police power, "petitioners' reasoning would allow Congress to regulate any crime as long as the nationwide, aggregated impact of that crime has substantial effects on employment, production, transit, or consumption." Because most violence has traditionally been within the jurisdiction of the states, it was the Court's duty to draw the line between what could properly be the subject of national regulation and what could not. "The Constitution requires a distinction between what is truly national and what is truly local," the chief justice declared, echoing Chief Justice Fuller's premise in the Sugar Trust Case.

Yet congressional authority and the persuasiveness of *Wickard* v. *Filburn* combined in *Gonzales* v. *Raich* (2005) to trump the values of state prerogatives. Voting 6–3, the Court upheld application of the Controlled Substances Act to the local cultivation and medicinal use of marijuana, as allowed by California law. In so doing, the majority reversed the Ninth Circuit which had rested its contrary holding on both *Lopez* and *Morrison*. (Because *Morrison* contains prominent federalism as well as commerce themes, its case is reprinted in Chapter Four.)

If FDR deemed the New Deal essential for the nation, passage of the Patient Protection and Affordable Care Act (christened Obamacare) in 2010 was doubtless of equal importance to President Barack Obama and certainly the signature legislative achievement of his first term. While the complex statute embodies several major changes in health care coverage for the nation, perhaps its central and most controversial provision has been the individual mandate that requires individuals without medical care insurance to purchase it, and to pay a penalty if they do not. Against contentions that the mandate violated the Constitution, the administration insisted it had ample authority under the commerce clause not only to regulate the health care market but to force individuals to enter it. In ***National Federation of Independent Business* v. *Sebelius*,** a narrow majority in an opinion by Chief Justice Roberts upheld the mandate but not on commerce clause grounds. Instead, he said the mandate was an acceptable exercise of Congress' taxing power (see Chapter Seven).

With inevitable changes in the Court's membership, the coming years will demonstrate if the commerce clause has truly entered a new era of interpretation. Are rulings like *Lopez* and *Morrison* and the hesitation reflected in the Obamacare ruling merely modest exceptions to an otherwise practically boundless commerce power or an indication that a new regime of limitations is here to stay?

KEY TERMS

police power
dormant commerce power
concurrent commerce doctrine
exclusive commerce doctrine
selective exclusiveness
Cooley doctrine
protectionism
balkanization
Sherman Anti-Trust Act
direct versus indirect effects
national police power
New Deal
Court-packing plan
Constitutional Revolution of 1937

QUERIES

1. What questions left unresolved by *Gibbons* v. *Ogden* did *Cooley* v. *Board of Wardens* attempt to resolve?

2. Concurring in *Bendix Autolite Corp.* v. *Midwesco Enterprises* (1988), Justice Scalia announced that he favored abandoning the "balancing" involved in dormant commerce clause cases, "leav[ing] essentially legislative judgments to Congress. . . . [A] state statute is invalid under the Commerce Clause if, and only if, it accords discriminatory treatment to interstate commerce in a respect not required to achieve a lawful state purpose. When such a validating purpose exists, it is for Congress and not us to determine it is not significant enough to justify the burden on [commerce]."

What would be the probable effect on national commerce were the Court to adopt Scalia's view?

3. In the Court-packing struggle of 1937, both sides won; both sides lost. Explain.

4. If the Affordable Care Act's individual mandate squeaked by on the taxing power, how might it have been justified using the commerce power instead?

SELECTED READINGS

Benson, Paul R., Jr. *The Supreme Court and the Commerce Clause, 1937–1970.* Cambridge, MA: Dunellen, 1970.

Cortner, Richard C. *The Arizona Train Limit Case.* Tucson: University of Arizona Press, 1970a.

Cortner, Richard C. *The Jones & Laughlin Case.* New York: Knopf, 1970b.

Cortner, Richard C. *Civil Rights and Public Accommodations: The Heart of Atlanta and McClung Cases.* Lawrence: University Press of Kansas, 2001.

Corwin, Edward S. *The Commerce Power versus States Rights.* Princeton, NJ: Princeton University Press, 1936.

Cox, Thomas H. *Gibbons v. Ogden: Law and Society in the Early Republic.* Athens: Ohio University Press, 2009.

Farber, Daniel A. "State Regulation and the Dormant Commerce Clause." 3 *Constitutional Commentary* 395, 1986.

Frankfurter, Felix. *The Commerce Clause under Marshall, Taney and Waite.* Chapel Hill: University of North Carolina Press, 1937.

Shesol, Jeff. *Supreme Power: Franklin Roosevelt vs. The Supreme Court.* New York: Norton, 2010.

Simon, James F. *FDR and Chief Justice Hughes: The President, the Supreme Court, and the Epic Battle over the New Deal.* New York: Simon & Schuster, 2012.

White, G. Edward. *The Constitution and the New Deal.* Cambridge, MA: Harvard University Press, 2000.

Wood, Stephen B. *Constitutional Politics in the Progressive Era: Child Labor and the Law.* Chicago, IL: University of Chicago Press, 1968.

I. DEFINING THE COMMERCE POWER

Gibbons v. *Ogden*
22 U.S. (9 Wheat.) 1, 6 L.Ed. 23 (1824)

http://caselaw.findlaw.com/us-supreme-court/22/1.html

In 1811, the state of New York granted the fifth in a series of monopolies to jurist and diplomat Robert Livingston and steamboat pioneer Robert Fulton to operate steamboats on the waterways of New York. The monopoly required all persons navigating by steam in New York to obtain a license from Livingston and Fulton, their heirs or assigns. Any unlicensed vessel, "together with the engine, tackle and apparel thereof," would be forfeited to them. Ex-governor Aaron Ogden of New Jersey operated a licensed steam-powered ferry between New York and New Jersey. In 1818, his former associate Thomas Gibbons, who held a "coasting license" under a 1793 act of Congress but no license under the New York monopoly, began to run boats along the same route in competition with Ogden. Ogden brought action in the New York Court of Chancery in 1819 to stop his rival. Chancellor James Kent ruled for Ogden, holding that the congressional statute was not in conflict with the New York monopoly and conferred no right on Gibbons to navigate on New York waters. The New York Court of Errors affirmed in 1820, and Gibbons appealed. This dispute gave rise to the first important case in the Supreme Court concerning the meaning of the commerce clause. Writing a century after the decision, Albert J. Beveridge found that Marshall's opinion "has done more to knit the American people into an indivisible Nation than any other one force in our history, excepting only war." Majority: Marshall, Duvall, Johnson, Story, Todd, Washington. Not participating: Thompson.

Chief Justice Marshall delivered the opinion of the court. . . .

This instrument [the Constitution] contains an enumeration of powers expressly granted by the people to their government. It has been said, that these powers ought to be construed strictly. But why ought they to be so construed? Is there one sentence in the constitution which gives countenance to this rule? In the last of the enumerated powers, that which grants, expressly, the means for carrying all others into execution, congress is authorized "to make all laws which shall be necessary and proper" for the purpose. But this limitation on the means which may be used, is not extended to the powers which are conferred; nor is there one sentence in the constitution, which has been pointed out by the gentlemen of the bar, or which we have been able to discern, that prescribes this rule. We do not, therefore, think ourselves justified in adopting it. What do gentlemen mean, by a strict construction? If they contend only against that enlarged construction, which would extend words beyond their natural and obvious import, we might question the application of the term, but should not controvert the principle. If they contend for that narrow construction which, in support of some theory not to be found in the constitution, would deny to the government those powers which the words of the grant, as usually understood, import, and which are consistent with the general views and objects of the instrument—for that narrow construction, which would cripple the government, and render it unequal to the objects for which it is declared to be instituted, and to which the powers given, as fairly understood, render it competent—then we cannot perceive the propriety of this strict construction, nor adopt it as the rule by which the constitution is to be expounded. As men whose intentions require no concealment, generally employ the words which most directly and aptly express the ideas they intend to convey, the enlightened patriots who framed our constitution, and the people who adopted it, must be understood to have employed words in their natural sense, and to have intended what they have said. . . .

The words are: "Congress shall have power to regulate commerce with foreign nations, and among the several states, and with the Indian tribes." The subject to be regulated is commerce; and our constitution being, as was aptly said at the bar, one of enumeration, and not of definition, to ascertain the extent of the power, it becomes necessary to settle the meaning of the word. The counsel for the appellee would limit it to traffic, to buying and selling, or the interchange of commodities, and do not admit that it comprehends navigation. This would restrict a general term, applicable to many objects, to one of its significations. Commerce, undoubtedly, is traffic, but it is something more—it is intercourse. It describes the commercial intercourse between nations, and parts of nations, in all its branches, and is regulated by prescribing rules for carrying on that intercourse. The mind can scarcely conceive a system for regulating commerce between nations which shall exclude all laws concerning navigation, which shall be silent on the admission of the vessels of the one nation into the ports of the other, and confined to prescribing rules for the conduct of individuals, in the actual employment of buying and selling or of barter. If commerce does not include navigation, the government of the Union has no direct power over that subject, and can make no law prescribing what shall constitute American vessels, or requiring that they shall be navigated by American seamen. Yet this power has been exercised from the commencement of the government, has been exercised with the consent of all, and has been understood by all to be a commercial regulation. All America understands, and has uniformly understood, the word "commerce," to comprehend navigation. It was so understood, and must have been so understood, when the constitution was framed. The power over commerce, including navigation, was one of the primary objects for which the people of America adopted their government, and must have been contemplated in forming it. The convention must have used the word in that sense, because all have understood it in that sense; and the attempt to restrict it comes too late. If the opinion that "commerce," as the word is used in the constitution, comprehends navigation also, requires any additional confirmation, that additional confirmation is, we think, furnished by the words of the instrument itself. It is a rule of construction, acknowledged by all, that the exceptions from a power mark its extent: for it would be absurd, as well as useless, to except from a granted power, that which was not granted—that which the words of the grant could not comprehend. If, then, there are in the constitution plain exceptions from the power over navigation, plain inhibitions to the exercise of that power in a particular way, it is a proof that those who made these exceptions, and prescribed these inhibitions, understood the power to which they applied as being granted. The 9th section of the last article declares, that "no preference shall be given, by any regulation of commerce or revenue, to the ports of one state over those of another." This clause cannot be understood as applicable to those laws only which are passed for the purposes of revenue, because it is expressly applied to commercial regulations; and the most obvious preference which can be given to one port over another, in regulating commerce, relates to navigation. But the subsequent part of the sentence is still more explicit. It is, "nor shall vessels bound to or from one state, be obliged to enter, clear or pay duties in another." These words have a direct reference to navigation. . . .

The word used in the constitution, then, comprehends, and has been always understood to comprehend, navigation within its meaning; and a power to regulate navigation, is as expressly granted, as if that term had been added to the word "commerce." To what commerce does this power extend? The constitution informs us, to commerce "with foreign nations, and among the several states, and with the Indian tribes." It has, we believe, been universally admitted, that these words comprehend every species of commercial intercourse between the United States and foreign nations. No sort of trade can be carried on between this country and any other, to which this power does not extend. It has been truly said, that commerce, as the word is used in the constitution, is a unit, every part of which is indicated by the term. . . .

But, in regulating commerce with foreign nations, the power of congress does not stop at the jurisdictional lines of the several states. It would be a very useless power, if it could not pass those lines. The commerce of the United States with foreign nations is that of the whole United States; every district has a right to participate in it. The deep streams which penetrate our country in every direction pass through the interior of almost every state in the Union, and furnish the means of exercising this right. If congress has the power to regulate it, that power must be exercised whenever the subject exists. If it exists within the states, if a foreign voyage may commence or terminate at a port within a state, then the power of congress may be exercised within a state.

This principle is, if possible, still more clear, when applied to commerce "among the several states." They either join each other, in which case they are separated by a mathematical line, or they are remote from each other, in which case other states lie between them. What is commerce "among" them; and how is it to be conducted? Can a trading expedition between two adjoining states, commence and terminate outside of each? And if the trading intercourse be between two states remote from each other, must it not commence in one, terminate in the other, and probably pass through a third? Commerce among the states must of necessity, be commerce with the states. In the regulation of trade with the Indian tribes, the action of the law, especially, when the constitution was made, was chiefly within a state. The power of congress, then, whatever it may be, must be exercised within the territorial jurisdiction of the several states. The sense of the nation on this subject, is unequivocally manifested by the provisions made in the laws for transporting goods, by land, between Baltimore and Providence, between New York and Philadelphia, and between Philadelphia and Baltimore.

We are now arrived at the inquiry—what is this power? It is the power to regulate; that is, to prescribe the rule by which commerce is to be governed. This power, like all others vested in congress, is complete in itself, may be exercised to its utmost extent, and acknowledges no limitations, other than are prescribed in the constitution. . . . If, as has always been understood, the sovereignty of congress, though limited to specified objects, is plenary as to those objects, the power over commerce with foreign nations, and among the several states, is vested in congress as absolutely as it would be in a single government, having in its constitution the same restrictions on the exercise of the power as are found in the constitution of the United States. The wisdom and the discretion of congress, their identity with the people, and the influence which their constituents possess at elections, are, in this, as in many other instances, as that, for example, of declaring war, the sole restraints on which they have relied, to secure them from its abuse. They are the restraints on which the people must often rely solely, in all representative governments. . . .

But it has been urged, with great earnestness, that although the power of congress to regulate commerce with foreign nations, and among the several states, be co-extensive with the subject itself, and have no other limits than are prescribed in the constitution, yet the states may severally exercise the same power within their respective jurisdictions. In support of this argument, it is said that they possessed it as an inseparable attribute of sovereignty before the formation of the constitution, and still retain it, except so far as they have surrendered it by that instrument; that this principle results from the nature of the government, and is secured by the tenth amendment; that an affirmative grant of power is not exclusive, unless in its own nature it be such that the continued exercise of it by the former possessor is inconsistent with the grant, and that this is not of that description. The appellant conceding these postulates, except the last, contends that full power to regulate a particular subject implies the whole power, and leaves no residuum; that a grant of the whole is incompatible with the existence of a right in another to any part of it. . . .

The grant of the power to lay and collect taxes is, like the power to regulate commerce, made in general terms, and has never been understood to interfere with the exercise of the same power by the states; and hence has been drawn an argument which has been applied to the question under consideration. But the two grants are not, it is conceived, similar in their terms or their nature. Although many of the powers formerly exercised by the states are transferred to the government of the Union, yet the state governments remain, and constitute a most important part of our system. The power of taxation is indispensable to their existence, and is a power which, in its own nature, is capable of residing in, and being exercised by, different authorities at the same time. We are accustomed to see it placed, for different purposes, in different hands. . . . When, then, each government exercises the power of taxation, neither is exercising the power of the other. But when a state proceeds to regulate commerce with foreign nations, or among the several states, it is exercising the very power that is granted to congress, and is doing the very thing which congress is authorized to do. There is no analogy then, between the power of taxation and the power of regulating commerce. . . .

But the inspection laws are said to be regulations of commerce, and are certainly recognized in the constitution as being passed in the exercise of a power remaining with the states.

That inspection laws may have a remote and considerable influence on commerce, will not be denied; but that a power to regulate commerce is the source from which the right to pass them is derived, cannot be admitted. The object of inspection laws, is to improve the quality of articles produced by the labor of a country; to fit them for exportation; or it may be, for domestic use. They act upon the subject, before it becomes an article of foreign commerce, or of commerce among the states, and prepare it for that purpose. They form a portion of that immense mass of legislation, which embraces everything within the territory of a state, not surrendered to a general government; all of which can be most advantageously exercised by the states themselves. Inspection laws, quarantine laws, health laws of every description, as well as laws for regulating the internal commerce of a state, and those which respect turnpike roads, ferries, etc., are component parts of this mass.

No direct general power over these objects is granted to congress, and, consequently, they remain subject to state legislation. If the legislative power of the Union can reach them, it must be, where the power is expressly given for a special purpose, or is clearly incidental to some power which is expressly given. It is obvious, that the government of the Union, in the exercise of its express powers, that, for example, of regulating commerce with foreign nations and among the states, may use means that may also be employed by a state, in the exercise of its acknowledged powers; that, for example, of regulating commerce within the state. If congress licenses vessels to sail from one port to another, in the same state, the act is supposed to be, necessarily, incidental to the power expressly granted to congress, and implies no claim of a direct power to regulate the purely internal commerce of a state, or to act directly on its system of police. So, if a state, in passing laws on subjects acknowledged to be within its control, and with a view to those subjects, shall adopt a measure of the same character with one which congress may adopt, it does not derive its authority from the particular power which has been granted, but from some other which remains with the state. . . .

Since, however, in exercising the power of regulating their own purely internal affairs, whether of trading or police, the states may sometimes enact laws, the validity of which depends on their [not] interfering with, and being contrary to, an act of congress passed in pursuance of the constitution, the court will enter upon the inquiry whether the laws of New York, as expounded by the highest tribunal of that state, have, in their application to this case, come into collision with an act of congress, and deprived a citizen of a right to which that act entitles him. Should this collision exist, it will be immaterial whether those laws were passed in virtue of a concurrent power "to regulate commerce with foreign nations and among the several States," or, in virtue of a power to regulate their domestic trade and police. In one case and the other, the acts of New York must yield to the law of congress, and the decision sustaining the privilege they confer, against a right given by a law of the Union, must be erroneous. . . .

In argument, however, it has been contended, that if a law passed by a state, in the exercise of its acknowledged sovereignty comes into conflict with a law passed by congress in pursuance of the constitution, they affect the subject, and each other, like equal opposing powers.

But the framers of our constitution foresaw this state of things, and provided for it, by declaring the supremacy not only of itself, but of the laws made in pursuance of it. The nullity of any act, inconsistent with the constitution, is produced by the declaration, that the constitution is the supreme law. . . . In every such case, the act of congress, or the treaty, is supreme; and the law of the state, though enacted in the exercise of powers not controverted, must yield to it. . . .

Powerful and ingenious minds, taking, as postulates, that the powers expressly granted to the government of the Union are to be contracted, by construction, into the narrowest possible compass, and that the original powers of the States are retained, if any possible construction will retain them, may, by a course of well digested, but refined and metaphysical reasoning, founded on these premises, explain away the constitution of our country, and leave it a magnificent structure indeed, to look at, but totally unfit for use. They may so entangle and perplex the understanding, as to obscure principles which were before thought quite plain, and induce doubts where, if the mind were to pursue its own course, none would be perceived. In such a case, it is peculiarly necessary to recur to safe and fundamental principles to sustain those principles, and, when sustained, to make them the tests of the arguments to be examined.

Mr. Justice Johnson . . .

Power to regulate foreign commerce, is given in the same words, and in the same breath, as it were, with that over the commerce of the states and with the Indian tribes. But the power to regulate foreign commerce is necessarily exclusive.

If there was any one object riding over every other in the adoption of the constitution, it was to keep the commercial intercourse among the states free from all invidious and partial restraints. And I cannot overcome the conviction, that if the licensing act was repealed tomorrow, the rights of the appellant to a reversal of the decision complained of, would be as strong as it is under this license. . . .

Cooley v. *Board of Wardens* 53 U.S. (12 How.) 299, 13 L.Ed. 996 (1851)

http://caselaw.findlaw.com/us-supreme-court/53/299.html

A Pennsylvania pilotage law of 1803 required vessels leaving the port of Philadelphia to pay one-half of the standard pilotage fee for use of the Society for the Relief of Distressed and Decayed Pilots, their Widows and Children, if a local pilot were not hired. An act of the United States of 1789 declared that existing state pilotage acts should continue in effect. Cooley, the consignee of two vessels outward-bound from Philadelphia, refused to pay the fee. From adverse judgments in the state courts, he brought writs of error. Majority: Curtis, Catron, Daniel, Grier, Nelson, Taney. Dissenting: McLean, Wayne. Not participating: McKinley.

Mr. Justice Curtis delivered the opinion of the Court. . . .

It remains to consider the objection that it [the state act] is repugnant to the third clause of the eighth section of the first article. "The Congress shall have power to regulate commerce with foreign nations and among the several states, and with the Indian tribes."

That the power to regulate commerce includes the regulation of navigation, we consider settled. . . .

The act of 1789 . . . already referred to, contains a clear legislative exposition of the Constitution by the first Congress, to the effect that the power to regulate pilots was conferred on Congress by the Constitution. . . . And a majority of the court are of opinion that a regulation of pilots is a regulation of commerce, within the grant to Congress of the commercial power, contained in the third clause of the eighth section of the first article of the Constitution.

It becomes necessary, therefore, to consider whether this law of Pennsylvania, being a regulation of commerce, is valid.

The act of Congress of the 7th of August, 1789, sec. 4, is as follows:

> That all pilots in the bays, inlets, rivers, harbors, and ports of the United States shall continue to be regulated in conformity with the existing laws of the states, respectively wherein such pilots may be, or with such laws as the states may respectively hereafter enact for the purpose, until further legislative provision shall be made by Congress.

If the law of Pennsylvania, now in question, had been in existence at the date of this act of Congress, we might hold it to have been adopted by Congress, and thus made a law of the United States, and so valid. Because this act does, in effect, give the force of an act of Congress, to the then existing state laws on this subject, so long as they should continue unrepealed by the state which enacted them.

But the law on which these actions are founded was not enacted till 1803. What effect then can be attributed to so much of the act of 1789, as declares, that pilots shall continue to be regulated in conformity "with such laws as the states may respectively hereafter enact for the purpose, until further legislative provision shall be made by Congress?"

If the states were divested of the power to legislate on this subject by the grant of the commercial power to Congress, it is plain this act could not confer upon them power thus to legislate. If the Constitution excluded the states from making any law regulating commerce, certainly Congress cannot regrant, or in any manner reconvey to the states that power. And yet this act of 1789 gives its sanction only to laws enacted by the States. This necessarily implies a constitutional power to legislate; for only a rule created by the sovereign power of a state acting in its legislative capacity, can be deemed a law enacted by a state; and if the state has so limited its sovereign power that it no longer extends to a particular subject, manifestly it cannot, in any proper sense, be said to enact law thereon. Entertaining these views, we are brought directly and unavoidably to the consideration of the question, whether the grant of the commercial power to Congress, did per se deprive the states of all power to regulate pilots. This question has never been decided by this court, nor, in our judgment, has any case depending upon all the considerations which must govern this one, come before this court. The grant of commercial power to Congress does not contain any terms which expressly exclude the states from exercising an authority over its subject matter. If they are excluded, it must be because the nature of the power, thus granted to Congress, requires that a similar authority should not exist in the states. . . .

Now the power to regulate commerce embraces a vast field, containing not only many, but exceedingly various subjects, quite unlike in their nature; some imperatively demanding a single uniform rule, operating equally on the commerce of the United States in every port; and some, like the subject now in question, as imperatively demanding that diversity which alone can meet the local necessities of navigation.

Either absolutely to affirm, or deny that the nature of this power requires exclusive legislation by Congress, is to lose sight of the nature of the subjects of this power, and to assert concerning all of them, what is really applicable but to a part. Whatever subjects of this power are in their nature national, or admit only of one uniform system, or plan of regulation, may justly be said to be of such a nature as to require exclusive legislation by Congress. That this cannot be affirmed of laws for the regulation of pilots and pilotage is plain. The act of 1789 contains a clear and authoritative declaration by the first Congress that the nature of this subject is such that until Congress should find it necessary to exert its power, it should be left to the legislation of the states; that it is local and not national; that it is likely to be the best provided for, not by one system, or plan or regulation but by as many as the legislative discretion of the several states should deem applicable to the local peculiarities of the ports within their limits.

Viewed in this light, so much of this act of 1789 as declares that pilots shall continue to be regulated "by such laws as the states may respectively hereafter enact for that purpose," . . . manifests the understanding of Congress, at the outset of the government, that the nature of this subject is not such as to require its exclusive legislation. . . .

It is the opinion of a majority of the court that the mere grant to Congress of the power to regulate commerce did not deprive the states of power to regulate pilots, and that although Congress has legislated on this subject, its legislation manifests an intention, with a single exception not to regulate this subject, but to leave its regulation to the several states. To these precise questions, which are all we are called on to decide, this opinion must be understood to be confined. It does not extend to the question what other subjects, under the commercial power, are within the exclusive control of Congress, or may be regulated by the states in the absence of all congressional legislation; nor to the general question, how far any regulation of a subject by Congress, may be deemed to operate as an exclusion of all legislation by the states upon the same subject. . . . We go no further. . . .

We are of opinion that this state law was enacted by virtue of a power, residing in the state to legislate; that it is not in conflict with any law of Congress; that it does not interfere with any system which Congress has established by making regulations, or by intentionally leaving individuals to their own unrestricted action: that this law is therefore valid, and the judgment of the Supreme Court of Pennsylvania in each case must be affirmed.

MR. JUSTICE DANIEL, concurring in the judgment . . . [omitted].

MR. JUSTICE MCLEAN, dissenting . . . [omitted].

MR. JUSTICE WAYNE dissented [without opinion].

II. STATES AND THE COMMERCE POWER

Southern Pacific Co. v. *Arizona* 325 U.S. 761, 65 S.Ct. 1515, 89 L.Ed. 1915 (1945)

http://caselaw.findlaw.com/us-supreme-court/325/761.html

The Arizona Train Limit Law of 1912 made it unlawful to operate within the state a railroad train of more than 14 passenger or 70 freight cars. In 1940, when the state sought to collect penalties for violations of the act, the appellant company objected, claiming that the act was unconstitutional. The Supreme Court of Arizona upheld the constitutionality of the law, and the company appealed. Majority: Stone, Frankfurter, Jackson, Murphy, Reed, Roberts, Rutledge. Dissenting: Black, Douglas.

MR. CHIEF JUSTICE STONE delivered the opinion of the Court. . . .

We are . . . brought to appellant's contention, that the state statute contravenes the commerce clause of the Federal Constitution.

Although the commerce clause conferred on the national government power to regulate commerce, its possession of the power does not exclude all state power of regulation. . . . [I]n the absence of conflicting legislation by Congress, there is a residuum of power in the state to make laws governing matters of local concern which nevertheless in some measure affect interstate commerce or even, to some extent, regulate it. . . . Thus the states may regulate matters which, because of their number and diversity, may never be adequately dealt with by Congress. . . . When the regulation of matters of local concern is local in character and effect, and its impact on the national commerce does not seriously interfere with its operation, and the consequent incentive to deal with them nationally is slight, such regulation has been generally held to be within state authority. . . .

But . . . the states have not been deemed to have authority to impede substantially the free flow of commerce from state to state, or to regulate those phases of the national commerce which, because of the need of national uniformity, demand that their regulation, if any, be prescribed by a single authority. . . .

For a hundred years it has been accepted constitutional doctrine that the commerce clause, without the aid of Congressional legislation, thus affords some protection from state legislation inimical to the national commerce, and that in such cases, where Congress has not acted, this Court, and not the state legislature, is under the commerce clause the final arbiter of the competing demands of state and national interests. . . .

Congress has undoubted power to redefine the distribution of power over interstate commerce. It may either permit the states to regulate the commerce in a manner which would otherwise not be permissible . . . or exclude state regulation even of matters of peculiarly local concern which nevertheless affect interstate commerce. . . .

But in general Congress has left it to the courts to formulate the rules thus interpreting the commerce clause in its application, doubtless because it has appreciated the destructive consequences to the commerce of the nation if their protection were withdrawn and has been aware that in their application state laws will not be invalidated without the support of relevant factual material which will "afford a sure basis" for an informed judgment. . . . Hence the matters for ultimate determination here are the nature and extent of the burden which the state regulation of interstate trains, adopted as a safety measure, imposes on interstate commerce, and whether the relative weights of the state and national interests involved are such as to make inapplicable the rule, generally observed, that the free flow of interstate commerce and its freedom from local restraints in matters requiring uniformity of regulation are interests safeguarded by the commerce clause from state interference. . . .

The findings show that the operation of long trains, that is trains of more than fourteen passenger and more than seventy freight cars, is standard practice over the main lines of the railroads of the United States, and that, if the length of trains is to be regulated at all, national uniformity in the regulation adopted, such as only Congress can prescribe, is practically indispensable to the operation of an efficient and economical national railway system. . . .

The unchallenged findings leave no doubt that the Arizona Train Limit Law imposes a serious burden on the interstate commerce conducted by appellant. It materially impedes the movement of appellant's interstate trains through that state and interposes a substantial obstruction to the national policy proclaimed by Congress, to promote adequate, economical and efficient railway transportation service. . . . Enforcement of the law in Arizona, while train lengths remain unregulated or are regulated by varying standards in other states, must inevitably result in an impairment of uniformity of efficient railroad operation because the railroads are subjected to regulation which is not uniform in its application. Compliance with a state statute limiting train lengths requires interstate trains of a length lawful in other states to be broken up and reconstituted as they enter each state according as it may impose varying limitations upon train lengths. The alternative is for the carrier to conform to the lowest train limit restriction of any of the states through which its trains pass, whose laws thus control the carriers' operations both within and without the regulating state. . . .

The trial court found that the Arizona law had no reasonable relation to safety, and made train operation more dangerous. Examination of the evidence and the detailed findings makes it clear that this conclusion was rested on facts found which indicate that such increased danger of accident and personal injury as may result from the greater length of trains is more than offset by the increase in the number of accidents resulting from the larger number of trains when train lengths are reduced. In considering the effect of the statute as a safety measure, therefore, the factor of controlling significance for present purposes is not whether there is basis for the conclusion of the Arizona Supreme Court that the increase in length of trains beyond the statutory maximum has an adverse effect upon safety of operation. The decisive question is whether in the circumstances the total effect of the law as a safety measure in reducing accidents and casualties is so slight or problematical as not to outweigh the national interest in keeping interstate commerce free from interferences which seriously impede it and subject it to local regulation which does not have a uniform effect on the interstate train journey which it interrupts. . . .

We think, as the trial court found, that the Arizona Train Limit Law, viewed as a safety measure, affords at most slight and dubious advantage, if any, over unregulated train lengths, because it results in an increase in the number of trains and train operations and the consequent increase in train accidents of a character generally more severe than those due to slack action. Its undoubted effect on the commerce is the regulation, without securing uniformity, of the length of trains operated in interstate commerce, which lack is itself a primary cause of preventing the free flow of commerce by delaying it and by substantially increasing its cost and impairing its efficiency. In these respects the case differs from those where a state, by regulatory measures affecting the commerce, has removed or reduced safety hazards without substantial interference with the interstate movement of trains. . . .

Appellees especially rely on the full train crew cases, . . . and also on *South Carolina v. Barnwell Bros.*, as supporting the state's authority to regulate the length of interstate trains. While the full train crew laws undoubtedly placed an added financial burden on the railroads in order to serve a local interest, they did not obstruct interstate transportation or seriously impede it. . . .

Barnwell Bros. was concerned with the power of the state to regulate the weight and width of motor cars passing interstate over its highways, a legislative field over which the state has a far more extensive control than over interstate railroads. In that case . . . we were at pains to point out that there are few subjects of state regulation affecting interstate commerce which are so peculiarly of local concern as is the use of the state's highways. Unlike the railroads local highways are built, owned and maintained by the state or its municipal subdivisions. The state is responsible for their safe and economical administration. . . . Their regulation is akin to quarantine measures, game laws, and like local regulations of rivers, harbors, piers, and docks, with respect to which the state has exceptional scope for the exercise of its regulatory power, and which, Congress not acting, have been sustained even though they materially interfere with interstate commerce. . . .

Here examination of all the relevant factors makes it plain that the state interest is outweighed by the interest of the Nation in an adequate, economical and efficient railway transportation service, which must prevail.

Reversed.

Mr. Justice Rutledge concurs in the result.

Mr. Justice Black, dissenting.

I think that legislatures, to the exclusion of courts, have the constitutional power to enact laws limiting train lengths, for the purpose of reducing injuries brought about by "slack movements." Their power is not less because a requirement of short trains might increase grade crossing accidents. This latter fact raises an entirely different element of danger which is itself subject to legislative regulation. For legislatures may, if necessary, require railroads to take appropriate steps to reduce the likelihood of injuries at grade crossings. . . . And the fact that grade-crossing improvements may be expensive is no sufficient reason to say that an unconstitutional "burden" is put upon a railroad even though it be an interstate road. . . .

This record in its entirety leaves me with no doubt whatever that many employees have been seriously injured and killed in the past, and that many more are likely to be so in the future, because of "slack movement" in trains. Everyday knowledge as well as direct evidence presented at the various hearings, substantiates the report of the Senate Committee that danger from slack movement is greater in long trains than in short trains. It may be that offsetting dangers are possible in the operation of short trains. The balancing of these probabilities, however, is not in my judgment a matter for judicial determination, but one which calls for legislative consideration. Representatives elected by the people to make their laws, rather than judges appointed to interpret those laws, can best determine the policies which govern the people. That at least is the basic principle on which our democratic society rests. I would affirm the judgment of the Supreme Court of Arizona.

Philadelphia v. *New Jersey*
437 U.S. 617, 98 S.Ct. 2531, 57 L.Ed. 2d 475 (1978)

http://caselaw.findlaw.com/us-supreme-court/437/617.html

A 1974 New Jersey law (referred to below as "chapter 363") provided, "No person shall bring into this State any solid or liquid waste which originated or was collected outside the territorial limits of the State, except garbage to be fed to swine in the State . . . until the commissioner [of the state Department of Environmental Protection] shall determine that such action can be permitted without endangering the public health, safety and welfare and has promulgated regulations permitting and regulating the treatment and disposal of such waste in this State." As authorized, the commissioner issued regulations permitting four categories of waste to enter the state, mainly for recycling and reprocessing. The city of Philadelphia, other out-of-state cities, and private landfills—all affected by the statute—challenged the law on commerce clause grounds. Majority: Stewart, Blackmun, Brennan, Marshall, Powell, Stevens, White. Dissenting: Rehnquist, Burger.

Mr. Justice Stewart delivered the opinion of the Court.

The crucial inquiry . . . must be directed to determining whether ch. 363 is basically a protectionist measure, or whether it can fairly be viewed as a law directed to legitimate local concerns, with effects upon interstate commerce that are only incidental.

The purpose of ch. 363 is set out in the statute itself as follows:

> The Legislature finds and determines that . . . the volume of solid and liquid waste continues to rapidly increase, that the treatment and disposal of these wastes continues to pose an even greater threat to the quality of the environment of New Jersey, that the available and appropriate landfill sites within the State are being diminished, that the environment continues to be threatened by the treatment and disposal of waste which originated or was collected outside the State and that the public health, safety and welfare require that the treatment and disposal within this State of all wastes generated outside of the State be prohibited.

The New Jersey Supreme Court accepted this statement of the state legislature's purpose. The state court additionally found that New Jersey's existing landfill sites will be exhausted within a few years; that to go on using these sites or to develop new ones will take a heavy environmental toll, both from pollution and from loss of scarce open lands; that new techniques to divert waste from landfills to other methods of disposal and resource recovery processes are under development, but that these changes will require time; and finally, that "the extension of the lifespan of existing landfills, resulting from the exclusion of out-of-state waste, may be of crucial importance in preventing further virgin wetlands or other undeveloped lands from being devoted to landfill purposes." Based on these findings, the court concluded that ch. 363 was designed to protect not the State's economy, but its environment, and that its substantial benefits outweigh its "slight" burden on interstate commerce.

The appellants strenuously contend that ch. 363, "while outwardly cloaked 'in the currently fashionable garb of environmental protection' . . . is actually no more than a legislative effort to suppress competition and stabilize the cost of solid waste disposal for New Jersey residents. . . ."

This dispute about ultimate legislative purpose need not be resolved, because its resolution would not be relevant to the constitutional issue to be decided in this case. Contrary to the evident assumption of the state court and the parties, the evil of protectionism can reside in legislative means as well as legislative ends. Thus, it does not matter whether the ultimate aim of ch. 363 is to reduce the waste disposal costs of New Jersey residents or to save remaining open lands from pollution, for we assume New Jersey has every right to protect its residents' pocketbooks as well as their environment. And it may be assumed as well that New Jersey may pursue those ends by slowing the flow of all waste into the State's remaining landfills, even though interstate commerce may incidentally be affected. But whatever New Jersey's ultimate purpose, it may not be accomplished by discriminating against articles of commerce coming from outside the State unless there is some reason, apart from their origin, to treat them differently. Both on its face and in its plain effect, ch. 363 violates this principle of nondiscrimination. . . .

The New Jersey law at issue in this case falls squarely within the area that the Commerce Clause puts off-limits to state regulation. On its face, it imposes on out-of-state commercial interests the full burden of conserving the State's remaining landfill space. It is true that in our previous cases the scarce natural resource was itself the article of commerce, whereas here the scarce resource and the article of commerce are distinct. But that difference is without consequence. In both instances, the State has overtly moved to slow or freeze the flow of commerce for protectionist reasons. It does not matter that the State has shut the article of commerce inside the State in one case and outside the State in the other. What is crucial is the attempt by one State to isolate itself from a problem common to many by erecting a barrier against the movement of interstate trade. . . .

It is true that certain quarantine laws have not been considered forbidden protectionist measures, even though they were directed against out-of-state commerce. . . . But those quarantine laws banned the importation of articles such as diseased livestock that required destruction as soon as possible because their very movement risked contagion and other evils. Those laws thus did not discriminate against interstate commerce as such, but simply prevented traffic in noxious articles, whatever their origin.

The New Jersey statute is not such a quarantine law. There has been no claim here that the very movement of waste into or through New Jersey endangers health, or that waste must be disposed of as soon and as close to its point of generation as possible. The harms caused by waste are said to arise after its disposal in landfill sites, and at that point, as New Jersey concedes, there is no basis to distinguish out-of-state waste from domestic waste. If one is inherently harmful, so is the other. Yet New Jersey has banned the former while leaving its landfill sites open to the latter. The New Jersey law blocks the importation of waste in an obvious effort to saddle those outside the State with the entire burden of slowing the flow of refuse into New Jersey's remaining landfill sites. That legislative effort is clearly impermissible under the Commerce Clause of the Constitution. . . .

The judgment is reversed.

Mr. Justice Rehnquist, with whom The Chief Justice joins, dissenting. . . .

The Court recognizes that States can prohibit the importation of items "which, on account of their existing condition, would bring in and spread disease, pestilence, and death, such as rags or other substances infected with the germs of yellow fever or the virus of smallpox, or cattle or meat or other provisions that are diseased or decayed, or otherwise, from their condition and quality, unfit for human use or consumption." . . .

The Court's effort to distinguish these prior cases is unconvincing. It first asserts that the quarantine laws which have previously been upheld "ban the importation of articles such as diseased livestock that required destruction as soon as possible because their very movement risked contagion and other evils." According to the Court, the New Jersey law is distinguishable from these other laws, and invalid, because the concern of New Jersey is not with the movement of solid waste but of the present inability to safely dispose of it once it reaches its destination. But I think it far from clear that the State's law has as limited a focus as the Court imputes to it: Solid waste which is a health hazard when it reaches its destination may in all likelihood be an equally great health hazard in transit. . . .

Second, the Court implies that the challenged laws must be invalidated because New Jersey has left its landfills open to domestic waste. But, as the Court notes, this Court has repeatedly upheld quarantine laws "even though they appear to single out interstate commerce for special treatment." The fact that New Jersey has left its landfill sites open for domestic waste does not, of course, mean that solid waste is not innately harmful. Nor does it mean that New Jersey prohibits importation of solid waste for reasons other than the health and safety of its population. New Jersey must out of sheer necessity treat and dispose of its solid waste in some fashion, just as it must treat New Jersey cattle suffering from hoof-and-mouth disease. It does not follow that New Jersey must, under the Commerce Clause, accept solid waste or diseased cattle from outside its borders and thereby exacerbate its problems. . . .

South Dakota v. *Wayfair, Inc.*
585 U.S. ___, 138 S.Ct. 2080, 201 L.Ed. 2d 403 (2018)

www.supremecourt.gov/opinions/17pdf/17-494_j4el.pdf

The facts of this case appear in Justice Kennedy's opinion below. Majority: Kennedy, Alito, Ginsburg, Gorsuch, Thomas. Dissenting: Roberts, Breyer, Kagan, Sotomayor.

Justice Kennedy delivered the opinion of the Court.

When a consumer purchases goods or services, the consumer's State often imposes a sales tax. This case requires the Court to determine when an out-of-state seller can be required to collect and remit that tax. All concede that taxing the sales in question here is lawful. The question is whether the out-of-state seller can be held responsible for its payment, and this turns on a proper interpretation of the Commerce Clause.

In two earlier cases [*National Bellas Hess, Inc.* v. *Department of Revenue of Illinois* (1967) and *Quill Corp.* v. *North Dakota* (1992)] the Court held that an out-of-state seller's liability to collect and remit the tax to the consumer's State depended on whether the seller had a physical presence in that State, but that mere shipment of goods into the consumer's State, following an order from a catalog, did not satisfy the physical presence requirement. The Court granted certiorari here to reconsider the scope and validity of the physical presence rule mandated by those cases. . . .

In 2016, South Dakota confronted the serious inequity *Quill* imposes by enacting S. 106. . . . [T]he Act requires out-of-state sellers to collect and remit sales tax "as if the seller had a physical presence in the state." . . . Respondents are merchants with no employees or real estate in South Dakota. . . . Each of these three companies ships its goods directly to purchasers throughout the United States, including South Dakota. Each easily meets the minimum sales or transactions requirement of the Act, but none collects South Dakota sales tax. Pursuant to the Act's provisions for expeditious judicial review, South Dakota filed a declaratory judgment action against respondents in state court, seeking a declaration that the requirements of the Act are valid and applicable to respondents and an injunction requiring respondents to register for licenses to collect and remit sales tax. Respondents moved for summary judgment, arguing that the Act is unconstitutional. . . . The trial court granted summary judgment to respondents. The South Dakota Supreme Court affirmed. . . .

Although the Commerce Clause is written as an affirmative grant of authority to Congress, this Court has long held that in some instances it imposes limitations on the States absent congressional action. Of course, when Congress exercises its power to regulate commerce by enacting legislation, the legislation controls. But this Court has observed that "in general Congress has left it to the courts to formulate the rules" to preserve "the free flow of interstate commerce." . . .

Modern precedents rest upon two primary principles that mark the boundaries of a State's authority to regulate interstate commerce. First, state regulations may not discriminate against interstate commerce; and second, States may not impose undue burdens on interstate commerce. State laws that discriminate against interstate commerce face "a virtually per se rule of invalidity." State laws that "regulat[e] evenhandedly to effectuate a legitimate local public interest . . . will be upheld unless the burden imposed on such commerce is clearly excessive in relation to the putative local benefits." Although subject to exceptions and variations, these two principles guide the courts in adjudicating cases challenging state laws under the Commerce Clause.

These principles also animate the Court's Commerce Clause precedents addressing the validity of state taxes. . . . The Court will sustain a tax so long as it (1) applies to an activity with a substantial nexus with the taxing State, (2) is fairly apportioned, (3) does not discriminate against interstate commerce, and (4) is fairly related to the services the State provides. . . .

The physical presence rule has "been the target of criticism over many years from many quarters." *Quill*, it has been said, was "premised on assumptions that are unfounded" and "riddled with internal inconsistencies." . . . Each year, the physical presence rule becomes further removed from economic reality and results in significant revenue losses to the States. These critiques underscore that the physical presence rule, both as first formulated and as applied today, is an incorrect interpretation of the Commerce Clause.

Quill is flawed on its own terms. First, the physical presence rule is not a necessary interpretation of the requirement that a state tax must be "applied to an activity with a substantial nexus with the taxing State.". Second, *Quill* creates rather than resolves market distortions. And third, *Quill* imposes the sort of arbitrary, formalistic distinction that the Court's modern Commerce Clause precedents disavow. . . .

Worse still, the rule produces an incentive to avoid physical presence in multiple States. Distortions caused by the desire of businesses to avoid tax collection mean that the market may currently lack storefronts, distribution points, and employment centers that otherwise would be efficient or desirable. The Commerce Clause must not prefer interstate commerce only to the point where a merchant physically crosses state borders. Rejecting the physical presence rule is necessary to ensure that artificial competitive advantages are not created by this Court's precedents. This Court should not prevent States from collecting lawful taxes through a physical presence rule that can be satisfied only if there is an employee or a building in the State.

The Quill Court itself acknowledged that the physical presence rule is "artificial at its edges." That was an understatement when *Quill* was decided; and when the day-to-day functions of marketing and distribution in the modern economy are considered, it is all the more evident that the physical presence rule is artificial in its entirety. Modern e-commerce does not align analytically with a test that relies on the sort of physical presence defined in *Quill*.

The physical presence rule as defined and enforced in *Bellas Hess* and *Quill* is not just a technical legal problem—it is an extraordinary imposition by the Judiciary on States' authority to collect taxes and perform critical public functions. Forty-one States, two Territories, and the District of Columbia now ask this Court to reject the test formulated in *Quill*. *Quill's* physical presence rule intrudes on States' reasonable choices in enacting their tax systems. And that it allows remote sellers to escape an obligation to remit a lawful state tax is unfair and unjust. It is unfair and unjust to those competitors, both local and out of State, who must remit the tax; to the consumers who pay the tax; and to the States that seek fair enforcement of the sales tax, a tax many States for many years have considered an indispensable source for raising revenue. In essence, respondents ask this Court to retain a rule that allows their customers to escape payment of sales taxes—taxes that are essential to create and secure the active market they supply with goods and services. . . .

"Although we approach the reconsideration of our decisions with the utmost caution, *stare decisis* is not an inexorable command." Here, *stare decisis* can no longer support the Court's prohibition of a valid exercise of the States' sovereign power. If it becomes apparent that the Court's Commerce Clause decisions prohibit the States from exercising their lawful sovereign powers in our federal system, the Court should be vigilant in correcting the error. While it can be conceded that Congress has the authority to change the physical presence rule, Congress cannot change the constitutional default rule. It is inconsistent with the Court's proper role to ask Congress to address a false constitutional premise of this Court's own creation. Courts have acted as the front line of review in this limited sphere; and hence it is important that their principles be accurate and logical, whether or not Congress can or will act in response. It is currently the Court, and not Congress, that is limiting the lawful prerogatives of the States. . . .

The Quill Court did not have before it the present realities of the interstate marketplace. In 1992, less than 2 percent of Americans had Internet access. Today that number is about 89 percent. When it decided *Quill*, the Court could not have envisioned a world in which the world's largest retailer would be a remote seller. The Internet's prevalence and power have changed the dynamics of the national economy. In 1992, mail-order sales in the United States totaled $180 billion. Last year, e-commerce retail sales alone were estimated at $453.5 billion. . . .

This expansion has also increased the revenue shortfall faced by States seeking to collect their sales and use taxes. In 1992, it was estimated that the States were losing between $694 million and $3 billion per year in sales tax revenues as a result of the physical presence rule. Now estimates range from $8 to $33 billion. . . .

For these reasons, the Court concludes that the physical presence rule of *Quill* is unsound and incorrect. The Court's decisions in *Quill Corp.* v. *North Dakota*, and *National Bellas Hess*, v. *Department of Revenue* should be, and now are, overruled. . . .

The judgment of the Supreme Court of South Dakota is vacated, and the case is remanded for further proceedings not inconsistent with this opinion.

It is so ordered.

JUSTICE THOMAS, concurring, . . . [omitted].

JUSTICE GORSUCH, concurring, . . . [omitted].

Chief Justice Roberts, with whom Justice Breyer, Justice Sotomayor, and Justice Kagan join, dissenting. . . .

I agree that *Bellas Hess* was wrongly decided, for many of the reasons given by the Court. The Court argues in favor of overturning that decision because the "Internet's prevalence and power have changed the dynamics of the national economy." But that is the very reason I oppose discarding the physical-presence rule. E-commerce has grown into a significant and vibrant part of our national economy against the backdrop of established rules, including the physical-presence rule. Any alteration to those rules with the potential to disrupt the development of such a critical segment of the economy should be undertaken by Congress. The Court should not act on this important question of current economic policy, solely to expiate a mistake it made over 50 years ago.

This Court "does not overturn its precedents lightly." Departing from the doctrine of *stare decisis* is an "exceptional action" demanding "special justification." The bar is even higher in fields in which Congress "exercises primary authority" and can, if it wishes, override this Court's decisions with contrary legislation. . . . That is so "even where the error is a matter of serious concern, provided correction can be had by legislation."

We have applied this heightened form of *stare decisis* in the dormant Commerce Clause context. Under our dormant Commerce Clause precedents, when Congress has not yet legislated on a matter of interstate commerce, it is the province of "the courts to formulate the rules." But because Congress "has plenary power to regulate commerce among the States," it may at any time replace such judicial rules with legislation of its own.

In *Quill*, this Court emphasized that the decision to hew to the physical-presence rule on *stare decisis* grounds was "made easier by the fact that the underlying issue is not only one that Congress may be better qualified to resolve, but also one that Congress has the ultimate power to resolve." Even assuming we had gone astray in *Bellas Hess*, the "very fact" of Congress's superior authority in this realm "g[a] ve us pause and counsel[ed] withholding our hand." Quill . . . The Court thus left it to Congress "to decide whether, when, and to what extent the States may burden interstate mail-order concerns with a duty to collect use taxes."

This is neither the first, nor the second, but the third time this Court has been asked whether a State may obligate sellers with no physical presence within its borders to collect tax on sales to residents. Whatever salience the adage "third time's a charm" has in daily life, it is a poor guide to Supreme Court decisionmaking. If stare decisis applied with special force in *Quill*, it should be an even greater impediment to overruling precedent now, particularly since this Court in *Quill* "tossed [the ball] into Congress's court, for acceptance or not as that branch elects."

Congress has in fact been considering whether to alter the rule established in *Bellas Hess* for some time. . . . Nothing in today's decision precludes Congress from continuing to seek a legislative solution. But by suddenly changing the ground rules, the Court may have waylaid Congress's consideration of the issue. . . . The Court proceeds with an inexplicable sense of urgency. It asserts that the passage of time is only increasing the need to take the extraordinary step of overruling *Bellas Hess* and *Quill*: . . . The Court, for example, breezily disregards the costs that its decision will impose on retailers. Correctly calculating and remitting sales taxes on all e-commerce sales will likely prove baffling for many retailers. . . .

The burden will fall disproportionately on small businesses. One vitalizing effect of the Internet has been connecting small, even "micro" businesses to potential buyers across the Nation. People starting a business selling their embroidered pillowcases or carved decoys can offer their wares throughout the country—but probably not if they have to figure out the tax due on every sale. . . . And the software said to facilitate compliance is still in its infancy, and its capabilities and expense are subject to debate. The Court's decision today will surely have the effect of dampening opportunities for commerce in a broad range of new markets. A good reason to leave these matters to Congress is that legislators may more directly consider the competing interests at stake. Unlike this Court, Congress has the flexibility to address these questions in a wide variety of ways. . . .

An erroneous decision from this Court may well have been an unintended factor contributing to the growth of e-commerce. The Court is of course correct that the Nation's economy has changed dramatically since the time that *Bellas Hess* and *Quill* roamed the earth. I fear the Court today is compounding its past error by trying to fix it in a totally different era. The Constitution gives Congress the power "[t]o regulate Commerce . . . among the several States." I would let Congress decide whether to depart from the physical-presence rule that has governed this area for half a century. I respectfully dissent.

III. COMPETING VISIONS OF CONGRESS' COMMERCE POWER

United States v. *E. C. Knight Co.* 156 U.S. 1, 15 S.Ct. 249, 39 L.Ed. 325 (1895)

http://caselaw.findlaw.com/us-supreme-court/156/1.html

The American Sugar Refining Company, which controlled the bulk of sugar-refining capacity in the United States, attempted to attain an almost complete monopoly by purchasing control of the E. C. Knight Company and three other companies, which together produced about one-third of the national output. Alleging that the defendant companies (American Sugar, E. C. Knight, and three others) had entered into contracts that constituted combinations in restraint of trade, and that these companies had conspired to restrain trade, both contrary to the Sherman Anti-Trust Act of 1890, the government sought to obtain a court order canceling the various agreements. The lower federal courts refused to grant this relief on the ground that the combination or conspiracy involved in this case pertained to manufacturing and not to interstate commerce. Majority: Fuller, Brewer, Brown, Field, Gray, Jackson, Shiras, White. Dissenting: Harlan.

Mr. Chief Justice Fuller . . . delivered the opinion of the Court.

The fundamental question is, whether conceding that the existence of a monopoly in manufacture is established by the evidence, that monopoly can be directly suppressed under the act of Congress in the mode attempted by this bill.

It cannot be denied that the power of a state to protect the lives, health, and property of its citizens, and to preserve good order and the public morals, "the power to govern men and things within the limits of its dominion," is a power originally and always belonging to the States, not surrendered by them to the general government, nor directly restrained by the Constitution of the United States, and essentially exclusive. The relief of the citizens of each State from the burden of monopoly and the evils resulting from the restraint of trade among such citizens was left with the States to deal with, and this court has recognized their possession of that power even to the extent of holding that an employment or business carried on by private individuals, when it becomes a matter of such public interest and importance as to create a common charge or burden upon the citizen; in other words, when it becomes a practical monopoly, to which the citizen is compelled to resort and by means of which a tribute can be exacted from the community, is subject to regulation by state legislative power. On the other hand, the power of Congress to regulate commerce among the several States is also exclusive. The Constitution does not provide that interstate commerce shall be free, but, by the grant of this exclusive power to regulate it, it was left free except as Congress might impose restraints. . . . That which belongs to commerce is within the jurisdiction of the United States, but that which does not belong to commerce is within the jurisdiction of the police power of the State. . . .

The argument is that the power to control the manufacture of refined sugar is a monopoly over a necessary of life, to the enjoyment of which by a large part of the population of the United States interstate commerce is indispensable, and that, therefore, the general government in the exercise of the power to regulate commerce may repress such monopoly directly and set aside the instruments which have created it. But this argument cannot be confined to necessaries of life merely, and must include all articles of general consumption. Doubtless the power to control the manufacture of a given thing involves in a certain sense the control of its disposition, but this is a secondary and not the primary sense; and although the exercise of that power may result in bringing the operation of commerce into play, it does not control it, and affects it only incidentally and indirectly. Commerce succeeds to manufacture, and is not a part of it. The power to regulate commerce is the power to prescribe the rule by which commerce shall be governed, and is a power independent of the power to suppress monopoly. But it may operate in repression of monopoly whenever that comes within the rules by which commerce is governed or whenever the transaction is itself a monopoly of commerce. . . .

It is vital that the independence of the commercial power and of the police power, and the delimitation between them, however sometimes perplexing, should always be recognized and observed, for while the one furnishes the strongest bond of union, the other is essential to the preservation of the autonomy of the States as required by our dual form of government; and acknowledged evils, however grave and urgent they may appear to be, had better be borne, than the risk be run, in the effort to suppress them, of more serious consequences by resort to expedients of even doubtful constitutionality. . . .

Slight reflection will show that if the national power extends to all contracts and combinations in manufacture, agriculture, mining, and other productive industries, whose ultimate result may affect external commerce, comparatively little of business operations and affairs would be left for state control.

It was in the light of well-settled principles that the act of July 2, 1890, was framed. Congress did not attempt thereby to assert the power to deal with monopoly directly as such. . . . [W]hat the law struck at was combinations, contracts, and conspiracies to monopolize trade and commerce among the several States or with foreign nations; but the contracts and acts of the defendants related exclusively to the acquisition of the Philadelphia refineries and the business of sugar refining in Pennsylvania, and bore no direct relation to commerce between the States or with foreign nations. . . .

Decree affirmed.

Mr. Justice Harlan, dissenting.

If this combination, so far as its operations necessarily or directly affect interstate commerce, cannot be restrained or suppressed under some power granted to Congress, it will be cause for regret that the patriotic statesmen who framed the Constitution did not foresee the necessity of investing the national government with power to deal with gigantic monopolies holding in their grasp, and injuriously controlling in their own interest, the entire trade among the States in food products that are essential to the comfort of every household in the land. . . .

The power of Congress covers and protects the absolute freedom of such intercourse and trade among the States as may or must succeed manufacture and precede transportation from the place of purchase. This would seem to be conceded; for, the court in the present case expressly declares that "contracts to buy, sell, or exchange goods to be transported among the several States, the transportation and its instrumentalities, and articles bought, sold, or exchanged for the purpose of such transit among the States, or put in the way of transit, may be regulated, but this is because they form part of interstate trade or commerce." Here is a direct admission—one which the settled doctrines of this court justify—that contracts to buy and the purchasing of goods to be transported from one State to another, and transportation, with its instrumentalities, are all parts of interstate trade or commerce. Each part of such trade is then under the protection of Congress. And yet, by the opinion and judgment in this case, if I do not misapprehend them, Congress is without power to protect the commercial intercourse that such purchasing necessarily involves against the restraints and burdens arising from the existence of combinations that meet purchasers, from whatever State they come, with the threat—for it is nothing more or less than a threat—that they shall not purchase what they desire to purchase, except at the prices fixed by such combinations. . . .

The common government of all the people is the only one that can adequately deal with a matter which directly and injuriously affects the entire commerce of the country, which concerns equally all the people of the Union, and which, it must be confessed, cannot be adequately controlled by any one State. Its authority should not be so weakened by construction that it cannot reach and eradicate evils that, beyond all question, tend to defeat an object which that government is entitled, by the Constitution, to accomplish. . . .

Champion v. *Ames* (The Lottery Case)
188 U.S. 321, 23 S.Ct. 321, 47 L.Ed. 492 (1903)

http://caselaw.findlaw.com/us-supreme-court/188/321.html

> An act of Congress in 1895 made it an offense to send or conspire to send lottery tickets in interstate commerce. The defendants, who were convicted under the statute, appealed from a circuit court order dismissing a writ of habeas corpus. Majority: Harlan, Brown, Holmes, McKenna, White. Dissenting: Fuller, Brewer, Peckham, Shiras.

Mr. Justice Harlan . . . delivered the opinion of the Court.

The appellant insists that the carrying of lottery tickets from one State to another State by an express company engaged in carrying freight and packages, from State to State, although such tickets may be contained in a box or package, does not constitute, and cannot by any act of Congress be legally made to constitute, commerce among the states within the meaning of the . . . Constitution of the United States. . . ; consequently, that Congress cannot make it an offense to cause such tickets to be carried from one State to another. . . .

What is the import of the word "commerce" as used in the Constitution? It is not defined by that instrument. Undoubtedly, the carrying from one State to another by independent carriers of things or commodities that are ordinary subjects of traffic, and which have in themselves a recognized value in money, constitutes interstate commerce. But does not commerce among the several States include something more? Does not the carrying from one State to another, by independent carriers, of lottery tickets that entitle the holder to the payment of a certain amount of money therein specified, also constitute commerce among the States? . . .

The cases cited . . . show that commerce among the States embraces navigation, intercourse, communication, traffic, the transit of persons, and the transmission of messages by telegraph. They also show that the power to regulate commerce among the several States is vested in Congress as absolutely as it would be in a single government, having in its constitution the same restrictions on the exercise of the power as are found in the Constitution of the United States; that such power is plenary, complete in itself, and may be exerted by Congress to its utmost extent, subject only to such limitations as the Constitution imposes upon the exercise of the powers granted by it; and that in determining the character of the regulations to be adopted Congress has a large discretion which is not to be controlled by the courts, simply because, in their opinion, such regulations may not be the best or most effective that could be employed.

We come then to inquire whether there is any solid foundation upon which to rest the contention that Congress may not regulate the carrying of lottery tickets from one State to another, at least by corporations or companies whose business it is, for hire, to carry tangible property from one State to another. . . .

We are of opinion that lottery tickets are subjects of traffic, and therefore are subjects of commerce, and the regulation of the carriage of such tickets from State to State, at least by independent carriers, is a regulation of commerce among the several States.

But it is said that the statute in question does not regulate the carrying of lottery tickets from State to State, but by punishing those who cause them to be so carried Congress in effect prohibits such carrying; that in respect of the carrying from one State to another of articles or things that are, in fact, or according to usage in business, the subjects of commerce, the authority given Congress was not to *prohibit*, but only to *regulate*. . . .

If a State, when considering legislation for the suppression of lotteries within its own limits, may properly take into view the evils that inhere in the raising of money, in that mode, why may not Congress, invested with the power to regulate commerce among the several States, provide that such commerce shall not be polluted by the carrying of lottery tickets from one State to another? In this connection it must not be forgotten that the power of Congress to regulate commerce among the States is plenary, is complete in itself, and is subject to no limitations except such as may be found in the Constitution. What provision in that instrument can be regarded as limiting the exercise of the power granted? . . .

If it be said that the act of 1895 is inconsistent with the Tenth Amendment, reserving to the States respectively, or to the people, the powers not delegated to the United States, the answer is that the power to regulate commerce among the States has been expressly delegated to Congress. . . .

We should hesitate long before adjudging that an evil of such appalling character, carried on through interstate commerce, cannot be met and crushed by the only power competent to that end. . . .

It is said, however, that if, in order to suppress lotteries carried on through interstate commerce, Congress may exclude lottery tickets from such commerce, that principle leads necessarily to the conclusion that Congress may arbitrarily exclude from commerce among the States any article, commodity, or thing, of whatever kind or nature, or however useful or valuable, which it may choose, no matter with what motive, to declare shall not be carried from one State to another. It will be time enough to consider the constitutionality of such legislation when we must do so. The present case does not require the court to declare the full extent of the power that Congress may exercise in the regulation of commerce among the States. We may, however, repeat, in this connection, what the court has heretofore said, that the power of Congress to regulate commerce among the States, although plenary, cannot be deemed arbitrary, since it is subject to such limitations or restrictions as are prescribed by the Constitution. . . .

Affirmed.

Mr. Chief Justice Fuller dissenting. . .

The power of the State to impose restraints and burdens on persons and property in conservation and promotion of the public health, good order, and prosperity is a power originally and always belonging to the States, not surrendered by them to the general government, nor directly restrained by the Constitution of the United States, and essentially exclusive, and the suppression of lotteries as a harmful business falls within this power, commonly called, of police. . . .

It is urged, however, that because Congress is empowered to regulate commerce between the several States, it, therefore, may suppress lotteries by prohibiting the carriage of lottery matter. Congress may, indeed, make all laws necessary and proper for carrying the powers granted to it into execution, and doubtless an act prohibiting the carriage of lottery matter would be necessary and proper to the execution of a power to suppress lotteries; but that power belongs to the States and not to Congress. To hold that Congress has general police power would be to hold that it may accomplish objects not intrusted to the General Government, and to defeat the operation of the Tenth Amendment. . . .

To say that the mere carrying of an article which is not an article of commerce in and of itself nevertheless becomes such the moment it is to be transported from one State to another, is to transform a non-commercial article into one simply because it is transported. I cannot conceive that any such result can properly follow. . . .

This in effect breaks down all the differences between that which is, and that which is not, an article of commerce, and the necessary consequence is to take from the States all jurisdiction over the subject so far as interstate communication is concerned. It is a long step in the direction of wiping out all traces of state lines, and the creation of a centralized Government. . . .

The power to prohibit the transportation of diseased animals and infected goods over railroads or on steamboats is an entirely different thing, for they would be in themselves injurious to the transaction of interstate commerce, and, moreover, are essentially commercial in their nature. And the exclusion of diseased persons rests on different ground, for nobody would pretend that persons could be kept off the trains because they were going from one state to another to engage in the lottery business. However enticing that business may be, we do not understand how these pieces of paper themselves can communicate bad principles by contact. . . .

I regard this decision as inconsistent with the views of the framers of the Constitution, and of Marshall, its great expounder. Our form of government may remain notwithstanding legislation or decision, but, as long ago observed, it is with governments, as with religions, the form may survive the substance of the faith.

In my opinion the act in question in the particular under consideration is invalid, and the judgments below ought to be reversed, and my brothers Brewer, Shiras and Peckham concur in this dissent.

Hammer v. *Dagenhart*
247 U.S. 251, 38 S.Ct. 529, 62 L.Ed. 1101 (1918)

http://caselaw.findlaw.com/us-supreme-court/247/251.html

The Keating-Owen Child Labor Act of 1916 forbade the shipment in interstate commerce of products of child labor. A father of two minor children who worked in a cotton mill in Charlotte, North Carolina, obtained an injunction from the U.S. District Court for the Western District of North Carolina against enforcement of the act, on the ground that it was unconstitutional. Majority: Day, McReynolds, Pitney, Van Devanter, White. Dissenting: Holmes, Brandeis, Clarke, McKenna.

Mr. Justice Day delivered the opinion of the Court. . . .

The controlling question for decision is: Is it within the authority of Congress in regulating commerce among the States to prohibit the transportation in interstate commerce of manufactured goods, the product of a factory in which, within 30 days prior to their removal therefrom, children under the age of 14 have been employed or permitted to work, or children between the ages of 14 and 16 years have been employed or permitted to work more than eight hours in any day, or more than six days in any week, or after the hour of 7 o'clock p.m. or before the hour of 6 o'clock a.m.?

The power essential to the passage of this act, the Government contends, is found in the commerce clause of the Constitution which authorizes Congress to regulate commerce with foreign nations and among the States. . . .

[I]t is insisted that adjudged cases in this court establish the doctrine that the power to regulate given to Congress incidentally includes the authority to prohibit the movement of ordinary commodities and therefore that the subject is not open for discussion. The cases demonstrate the contrary. They rest upon the character of the particular subjects dealt with and the fact that the scope of governmental authority, state or national, possessed over them is such that the authority to prohibit is as to them but the exertion of the power to regulate. . . .

In each of these instances the use of interstate transportation was necessary to the accomplishment of harmful results. In other words, although the power over interstate transportation was to regulate, that could only be accomplished by prohibiting the use of the facilities of interstate commerce to effect the evil intended.

This element is wanting in the present case. The thing intended to be accomplished by this statute is the denial of the facilities of interstate commerce to those manufacturers in the States who employ children within the prohibited ages. The act in its effect does not regulate transportation among the States, but aims to standardize the ages at which children may be employed in mining and manufacturing within the States. The goods shipped are of themselves harmless. The act permits them to be freely shipped after 30 days from the time of their removal from the factory. When offered for shipment, and before transportation begins, the labor of their production is over, and the mere fact that they were intended for interstate commerce transportation does not make their production subject to federal control under the commerce power. . . .

That there should be limitations upon the right to employ children in mines and factories in the interest of their own and the public welfare, all will admit. That such employment is generally deemed to require regulation is shown by the fact that the brief of counsel states that every State in the Union has a law upon the subject, limiting the right to thus employ children. In North Carolina, the State wherein is located the factory in which the employment was had in the present case, no child under 12 years of age is permitted to work.

It may be desirable that such laws be uniform, but our Federal Government is one of enumerated powers. . . .

In interpreting the Constitution it must never be forgotten that the nation is made up of States to which are entrusted the powers of local government. And to them and to the people the powers not expressly [*sic*] delegated to the national government are reserved. . . . Thus the act in a twofold sense is repugnant to the Constitution. It not only transcends the authority delegated to Congress over commerce but also exerts a power as to a purely local matter to which the federal authority does not extend. The far-reaching result of upholding the act cannot be more plainly indicated than by pointing out that if Congress can thus regulate matters entrusted to local authority by prohibition of the movement of commodities in interstate commerce, all freedom of commerce will be at an end, and the power of the states over local matters may be eliminated, and thus our system of government be practically destroyed.

For these reasons we hold that this law exceeds the constitutional authority of Congress. It follows that the decree of the District Court must be

Affirmed.

Mr. Justice Holmes, dissenting.

[T]he statute in question is within the power expressly given to Congress if considered only as to its immediate effects and that if invalid it is so only upon some collateral ground. The statute confines itself to prohibiting the carriage of certain goods in interstate or foreign commerce. Congress is given power to regulate such commerce in unqualified terms. . . . I cannot doubt that the regulation may prohibit any part of such commerce that Congress sees fit to forbid. At all events it is established by the Lottery Case and others that have followed it that a law is not beyond the regulative power of Congress merely because it prohibits certain transportation out and out. . . .

The question then is narrowed to whether the exercise of its otherwise constitutional power by Congress can be pronounced unconstitutional because of its possible reaction upon the conduct of the States in a matter upon which I have admitted that they are free from direct control. I should have thought that that matter had been disposed of so fully as to leave no room for doubt. I should have thought that the most conspicuous decisions of this Court had made it clear that the power to regulate commerce and other constitutional powers could not be cut down or qualified by the fact that it might interfere with the carrying out of the domestic policy of any State. . . .

[I]f there is any matter upon which civilized countries have agreed—far more unanimously than they have with regard to intoxicants and some other matters over which this country is now emotionally aroused—it is the evil of premature and excessive child labor. I should have thought that if we were to introduce our own moral conceptions where in my opinion they do not belong, this was preeminently a case for upholding the exercise of all its powers by the United States.

But I had thought that the propriety of the exercise of a power admitted to exist in some cases was for the consideration of Congress alone and that this Court always had disavowed the right to intrude its judgment upon questions of policy or morals. It is not for this Court to pronounce when prohibition is necessary to regulation if it ever may be necessary—to say that it is permissible as against strong drink but not as against the product of ruined lives.

The act does not meddle with anything belonging to the States. They may regulate their internal affairs and their domestic commerce as they like. But when they seek to send their products across the state line they are no longer within their rights. If there were no Constitution and no Congress their power to cross the line would depend upon their neighbors. Under the Constitution such commerce belongs not to the States but to Congress to regulate. . . .

MR. JUSTICE MCKENNA, MR. JUSTICE BRANDEIS and MR. JUSTICE CLARKE concur in this opinion.

Stafford v. *Wallace* 258 U.S. 495, 42 S.Ct. 397, 66 L.Ed. 735 (1922)

http://caselaw.findlaw.com/us-supreme-court/258/495.html

The Packers and Stockyards Act of 1921 imposed regulations on stockyard sales of livestock and other practices involving meat products that took place between the two legs of an interstate journey. Stafford unsuccessfully sought an injunction against enforcement of the act. Majority: Taft, Brandeis, Clarke, Holmes, McKenna, Pitney, Van Devanter. Dissenting: McReynolds. Not participating: Day.

MR. CHIEF JUSTICE TAFT . . . delivered the opinion of the Court.

The Packers and Stockyards Act of 1921 seeks to regulate the business of the packers done in interstate commerce and forbids them to engage in unfair, discriminatory or deceptive practices in such commerce, or to subject any person to unreasonable prejudice therein, or to do any of a number of acts to control prices or establish a monopoly in the business. . . .

The object to be secured by the act is the free and unburdened flow of live stock from the ranges and farms of the West and the Southwest through the great stockyards and slaughtering centers on the borders of that region, and thence in the form of meat products to the consuming cities of the country in the Middle West and East, or, still as live stock, to the feeding places and fattening farms in the Middle West or East for further preparation for the market.

The chief evil feared is the monopoly of the packers, enabling them unduly and arbitrarily to lower prices to the shipper who sells, and unduly and arbitrarily to increase the price to the consumer who buys. Congress thought that the power to maintain this monopoly was aided by control of the stockyards. Another evil which it sought to provide against by the act, was exorbitant charges, duplication of commissions, deceptive practices in respect of prices, in the passage of the live stock through the stockyards, all made possible by collusion between the stockyards management and the commission men, on the one hand, and the packers and dealers on the other.

The stockyards are not a place of rest or final destination. Thousands of head of live stock arrive daily by carload and trainload lots, and must be promptly sold and disposed of and moved out to give place to the constantly flowing traffic that presses behind. The stockyards are but a throat through which the current flows, and the transactions which occur therein are only incident to this current from the West to the East, and from one State to another. Such transactions cannot be separated from the movement to which they contribute and necessarily take on its character. . . . The stockyards and the sales are necessary factors in the middle of this current of commerce.

The act, therefore, treats the various stockyards of the country as great national public utilities to promote the flow of commerce from the ranges and farms of the West to the consumers in the East. It assumes that they conduct a business affected by a public use of a national character and subject to national regulation. That it is a business within the power of regulation by legislative action needs no discussion. That has been settled since the case of *Munn* v. *Illinois*. . . . Nor is there any doubt that in the receipt of live stock by rail and in their delivery by rail the stockyards are an interstate commerce agency. . . . The only question here is whether the business done in the stockyards between the receipt of the live stock in the yards and the shipment of them therefrom is a part of interstate commerce, or is so associated with it as to bring it within the power of national regulation. A similar question has been before this court and had great consideration in *Swift & Co.* v. *United States*. The judgment in that case gives a clear and comprehensive exposition which leaves to us in this case little but the obvious application of the principles there declared. . . .

The application of the commerce clause of the Constitution in the Swift Case was the result of the natural development of interstate commerce under modern conditions. It was the inevitable recognition of the great central fact that such streams of commerce from one part of the country to another which are ever flowing are in their very essence the commerce among the States and with foreign nations which historically it was one of the chief purposes of the Constitution to bring under national protection and control. This court declined to defeat this purpose in respect of such a stream and take it out of complete national regulation by a nice and technical inquiry into the non-interstate character of some of its necessary incidents and facilities when considered alone and without reference to their association with the movement of which they were an essential but subordinate part. . . .

If Congress could provide for punishment or restraint of such conspiracies after their formation through the Anti-Trust Law as in the Swift Case, certainly it may provide regulation to prevent their formation. . . . Whatever amounts to more or less constant practice, and threatens to obstruct or unduly to burden the freedom of interstate commerce is within the regulatory power of Congress under the commerce clause, and it is primarily for Congress to consider and decide the fact of danger and meet it. This court will certainly not substitute its judgment for that of Congress in such a matter unless the relation of the subject to interstate commerce and its effect upon it are clearly nonexistent. . . .

The orders of the District Court refusing the interlocutory injunctions are

Affirmed.

MR. JUSTICE MCREYNOLDS dissents [without opinion].

IV. THE NEW DEAL IN COURT

Carter v. *Carter Coal Co.* 298 U.S. 238, 56 S.Ct. 855, 80 L.Ed. 1160 (1936)

http://caselaw.findlaw.com/us-supreme-court/298/238.html

In the Bituminous Coal Conservation Act of 1935, Congress attempted to stabilize the production and marketing of coal. The law provided for a National Bituminous Coal Commission with general supervisory powers over the industry through a Bituminous Coal Code. In each of 23 districts, boards were to be given the power to fix minimum coal prices. National hours of labor and district minimum-wage agreements were to be effective when the producers of two-thirds of the annual tonnage and representatives of more than one-half of the employed workers agreed to terms. A labor board in the Department of Labor was given the duty of protecting the collective bargaining process and adjudicating labor disputes. Producers were to be induced to accept these codes by a tax provision that allowed 90 percent of a tax of 15 percent on sales at the mines to be refunded to those producers who accepted the code provisions. Four cases involving suits to bar payment of the tax and acceptance of the code were consolidated on certiorari from circuit courts of appeals and from district courts. A majority of the Supreme Court held the delegation of code-drafting power to a part of the producers and workers to be invalid. The following excerpts from the opinion deal with whether federal regulation of mining activities was permissible under the commerce clause. Majority: Sutherland, Butler, Hughes, McReynolds, Roberts, Van Devanter. Dissenting: Cardozo, Brandeis, Stone.

Mr. Justice Sutherland delivered the opinion of the Court. . . .

The general rule with regard to the respective powers of the national and the state governments under the Constitution is not in doubt. The States were before the Constitution; and, consequently, their legislative powers antedated the Constitution. Those who framed and those who adopted that instrument meant to carve from the general mass of legislative powers, then possessed by the States, only such portions as it was thought wise to confer upon the federal government; and in order that there should be no uncertainty in respect of what was taken and what was left, the national powers of legislation were not aggregated but enumerated—with the result that what was not embraced by the enumeration remained vested in the States without change or impairment. . . . While the States are not sovereign in the true sense of that term, but only quasi-sovereign, yet in respect of all powers reserved to them they are supreme—"as independent of the general government as that government within its sphere is independent of the States." And since every addition to the national legislative power to some extent detracts from or invades the power of the States, it is of vital moment that, in order to preserve the fixed balance intended by the Constitution, the powers of the general government be not so extended as to embrace any not within the express terms of the several grants or implications necessarily to be drawn therefrom. It is no longer open to question that the general government, unlike the States . . . possesses no inherent power in respect of the internal affairs of the States; and emphatically not with regard to legislation. . . .

Every journey to a forbidden end begins with the first step; and the danger of such a step by the federal government in the direction of taking over the powers of the states is that the end of the journey may find the states so despoiled of their powers, or—what may amount to the same thing—so relieved of the responsibilities which possession of the powers necessarily enjoins, as to reduce them to little more than geographical subdivisions of the national domain. It is safe to say that if, when the Constitution was under consideration, it had been thought that any such danger lurked behind its plain words, it would never have been ratified. . . .

Since the validity of the act depends upon whether it is a regulation of interstate commerce, the nature and extent of the power conferred upon Congress by the commerce clause becomes the determinative question in this branch of the case. . . . We first inquire, then—What is commerce? The term, as this court many times has said, is one of extensive import. No all-embracing definition has ever been formulated. The question is to be approached both affirmatively and negatively—that is to say, from the points of view as to what it includes and what it excludes. . . .

That commodities produced or manufactured within a State are intended to be sold or transported outside the State does not render their production or manufacture subject to federal regulation under the commerce clause. . . .

We have seen that the word "commerce" is the equivalent of the phrase "intercourse for the purposes of trade." Plainly, the incidents leading up to and culminating in the mining of coal do not constitute such intercourse. The employment of men, the fixing of their wages, hours of labor, and working conditions, the bargaining in respect of these things—whether carried on separately or collectively—each and all constitute intercourse for the purposes of production, not of trade. The latter is a thing apart from the relation of employer and employee, which in all producing occupations is purely local in character. Extraction of coal from the mine is the aim and the completed result of local activities. Commerce in the coal mined is not brought into being by force of these activities, but by negotiations, agreements and circumstances entirely apart from production. Mining brings the subject matter of commerce into existence. Commerce disposes of it.

A consideration of the foregoing . . . renders inescapable the conclusion that the effect of the labor provisions of the act, including those in respect of minimum wages, wage agreements, collective bargaining, and the Labor Board and its powers, primarily falls upon production and not upon commerce; and confirms the further resulting conclusion that production is a purely local activity. It follows that none of these essential antecedents of production constitutes a transaction in or forms any part of interstate commerce. . . .

That the production of every commodity intended for interstate sale and transportation has some effect upon interstate commerce may be, if it has not already been, freely granted: and we are brought to the final and decisive inquiry, whether here that effect is direct, as the "preamble" recites, or indirect. The distinction is not formal, but substantial in the highest degree as we pointed out in the Schechter case. . . . "If the commerce clause were construed," we there said, "to reach all enterprises and transactions which could be said to have an indirect effect upon interstate commerce, the federal authority would embrace practically all the activities of the people and the authority of the State over its domestic concerns would exist only by sufferance of the federal government. Indeed, on such a theory, even the development of the State's commercial facilities would be subject to federal control." It was also pointed out. . . "that the distinction between direct and indirect effects of intrastate transactions upon interstate commerce must be recognized as a fundamental one, essential to the maintenance of our constitutional system."

Whether the effect of a given activity or condition is direct or indirect is not always easy to determine. The word "direct" implies that the activity or condition invoked or blamed shall operate proximately—not mediately, remotely, or collaterally—to produce the effect. It connotes the absence of an efficient intervening agency or condition. And the extent of the effect bears no logical relation to its character. The distinction between a direct and an indirect effect turns, not upon the magnitude of either the cause or the effect, but entirely upon the manner in which the effect has been brought about. If the production by one man of a single ton of coal intended for interstate sale and shipment, and actually so sold and shipped, affects interstate commerce indirectly, the effect does not become direct by multiplying the tonnage, or increasing the number of men employed, or adding to the expense or complexities of the business, or by all combined. It is quite true that rules of law are sometimes qualified by considerations of degree, as the government argues. But the matter of degree has no bearing upon the question here, since that question is not—What is the extent of the local activity or condition, or the extent of the effect produced upon interstate commerce? but—What is the relation between the activity or condition and the effect?

Much stress is put upon the evils which come from the struggle between employers and employees over the matter of wages, working conditions, the right of collective bargaining, etc., and the resulting strikes, curtailment, and irregularity of production and effect on prices; and it is insisted that interstate commerce is greatly affected thereby. But, in addition to what has just been said, the conclusive answer is that the evils are all local evils over which the federal government has no legislative control. The relation of employer and employee is a local relation. . . . Such effect as they may have upon commerce, however extensive it may be, is secondary and indirect. An increase in the greatness of the effect adds to its importance. It does not alter its character. . . . [T]he want of power on the part of the federal government is the same whether the wages, hours of service, and working conditions, and the bargaining about them, are related to production before interstate commerce has begun, or to sale and distribution after it has ended. . . .

It is so ordered.

MR. JUSTICE CARDOZO, dissenting. . . .

I am satisfied that the Act is within the power of the central government in so far as it provides for minimum and maximum prices upon sales of bituminous coal in the transactions of interstate commerce and in those of intrastate commerce where interstate commerce is directly or intimately affected. . . .

[S]o far as the Act is directed to interstate transactions, . . . sales made in such conditions constitute interstate commerce, and do not merely "affect" it. . . . To regulate the price for such transactions is to regulate commerce itself, and not alone its antecedent conditions or its ultimate consequences. The very act of sale is limited and governed. Prices in interstate transactions may not be regulated by the States. They must therefore be subject to the power of the nation unless they are to be withdrawn altogether from governmental supervision. . . . If such a vacuum were permitted, many a public evil incidental to interstate transactions would be left without a remedy. . . .

Regulation of prices being an exercise of the commerce power in respect of interstate transactions, the question remains whether it comes within that power as applied to intrastate sales where interstate prices are directly or intimately affected. Mining and agriculture and manufacture are not interstate commerce considered by themselves, yet their relation to that commerce may be such that for the protection of the one there is need to regulate the other. . . . Sometimes it is said that the relation must be "direct" to bring that power into play. In many circumstances such a description will be sufficiently precise to meet the needs of the occasion. But a great principle of constitutional law is not susceptible of comprehensive statement in an adjective. The underlying thought is merely this, that "the law is not indifferent to considerations of degree."

. . . It cannot be indifferent to them without an expansion of the commerce clause that would absorb or imperil the reserved powers of the States. At times, as in the case cited, the waves of causation will have radiated so far that their undulatory motion, if discernible at all, will be too faint or obscure, too broken by crosscurrents, to be heeded by the law. In such circumstances the holding is not directed at prices or wages considered in the abstract, but at prices or wages in particular conditions. The relation may be tenuous or the opposite according to the facts. Always the setting of the facts is to be viewed if one would know the closeness of the tie. Perhaps, if one group of adjectives is to be chosen in preference to another, "intimate" and "remote" will be found to be as good as any. At all events, "direct" and "indirect," even if accepted as sufficient, must not be read too narrowly. . . . A survey of the cases shows that the words have been interpreted with suppleness of adaptation and flexibility of meaning. The power is as broad as the need that evokes it. . . .

I am authorized to state that MR. JUSTICE BRANDEIS and MR. JUSTICE STONE join in this opinion.

National Labor Relations Board v. *Jones & Laughlin Steel Corporation* 301 U.S. 1, 57 S.Ct. 615, 81 L.Ed. 893 (1937)

http://caselaw.findlaw.com/us-supreme-court/301/1.html

The National Labor Relations Act of 1935 protects the right of workers to organize and to encourage collective bargaining procedures. In this case, the National Labor Relations Board ordered the steel company to cease and desist from certain "unfair labor practices." When the corporation failed to comply, the NLRB unsuccessfully petitioned the circuit court of appeals (as provided in the act) to enforce the board's order. Majority: Hughes, Brandeis, Cardozo, Roberts, Stone. Dissenting: McReynolds, Butler, Sutherland, Van Devanter.

MR. CHIEF JUSTICE HUGHES delivered the opinion of the Court. . . .

The Act is challenged in its entirety as an attempt to regulate all industry, thus invading the reserved powers of the States over their local concerns. . . .

If this conception of terms, intent and consequent inseparability were sound, the Act would necessarily fall by reason of the limitation upon the federal power which inheres in the constitutional grant, as well as because of the explicit reservation of the Tenth Amendment. . . . The authority of the federal government may not be pushed to such an extreme as to destroy the distinction, which the commerce clause itself establishes, between commerce "among the several States" and the internal concerns of a State. That distinction between what is national and what is local in the activities of commerce is vital to the maintenance of our federal system. . . .

We think it clear that the National Labor Relations Act may be construed so as to operate within the sphere of constitutional authority. The jurisdiction conferred upon the Board, and invoked in this instance, is found in § 10(a), which provides: "Sec. 10(a). The Board is empowered, as hereinafter provided, to prevent any person from engaging in any unfair labor practice (listed in § 8) affecting commerce." . . .

There can be no question that the commerce thus contemplated by the Act (aside from that within a Territory or the District of Columbia) is interstate and foreign commerce in the constitutional sense. The Act also defines the term "affecting commerce" (§ 2(6)):

"The term 'affecting commerce' means in commerce, or burdening or obstructing commerce or the free flow of commerce, or having led or tending to lead to a labor dispute burdening or obstructing commerce or the free flow of commerce."

This definition is one of exclusion as well as inclusion. The grant of authority to the Board does not purport to extend to the relationship between all industrial employees and employers. Its terms do not impose collective bargaining upon all industry regardless of effects upon interstate or foreign commerce. It purports to reach only what may be deemed to burden or obstruct that commerce and, thus qualified, it must be construed as contemplating the exercise of control within constitutional bounds. . . .

Respondent says that whatever may be said of employees engaged in interstate commerce, the industrial relations and activities in the manufacturing department of respondent's enterprise are not subject to federal regulation. The argument rests upon the proposition that manufacturing in itself is not commerce. . . .

The congressional authority to protect interstate commerce from burdens and obstructions is not limited to transactions which can be deemed to be an essential part of a "flow" of interstate or foreign commerce. Burdens and obstructions may be due to injurious action springing from other sources. The fundamental principle is that the power to regulate commerce is the power to enact "all appropriate legislation" for "its protection and advancement." . . . That power is plenary and may be exerted to protect interstate commerce "no matter what the source of the dangers which threaten it." . . . Although activities may be intrastate in character when separately considered, if they have such a close and substantial relation to interstate commerce that their control is essential or appropriate to protect that commerce from burdens and obstructions, Congress cannot be denied the power to exercise that control. . . . Undoubtedly the scope of this power must be considered in the light of our dual system of government and may not be extended so as to embrace effects upon interstate commerce so indirect and remote that to embrace them, in view of our complex society, would effectually obliterate the distinction between what is national and what is local and create a completely centralized government. . . . The question is necessarily one of degree. . . .

It is thus apparent that the fact that the employees here concerned were engaged in production is not determinative. The question remains as to the effect upon interstate commerce of the labor practice involved. In the Schechter case, we found that the effect there was so remote as to be beyond the federal power. To find "immediacy or directness" there was to find it "almost everywhere," a result inconsistent with the maintenance of our federal system. In the Carter case, the Court was of the opinion that the provisions of the statute relating to production were invalid upon several grounds—that there was improper delegation of legislative power, and that the requirements not only went beyond any sustainable measure of protection of interstate commerce but were also inconsistent with due process. These cases are not controlling here.

Giving full weight to respondent's contention with respect to a break in the complete continuity of the "stream of commerce" by reason of respondent's manufacturing operations, the fact remains that the stoppage of those operations by industrial strife would have a most serious effect upon interstate commerce. In view of respondent's far-flung activities, it is idle to say that the effect would be indirect or remote. It is obvious that it would be immediate and might be catastrophic. We are asked to shut our eyes to the plainest facts of our national life and to deal with the question of direct and indirect effects in an intellectual vacuum. . . . When industries organize themselves on a national scale, making their relation to interstate commerce the dominant factor in their activities, how can it be maintained that their industrial labor relations constitute a forbidden field into which Congress may not enter when it is necessary to protect interstate commerce from the paralyzing consequences of industrial war? We have often said that interstate commerce itself is a practical conception. It is equally true that interferences with that commerce must be appraised by a judgment that does not ignore actual experience. . . .

Our conclusion is that the order of the Board was within its competency and that the Act is valid as here applied. The judgment of the Circuit Court of Appeals is reversed and the case is remanded for further proceedings in conformity with this opinion.

Reversed.

Mr. Justice McReynolds, dissenting.

Mr. Justice Van Devanter, Mr. Justice Sutherland, Mr. Justice Butler and I are unable to agree with the decisions just announced. . . .

Every consideration brought forward to uphold the Act before us was applicable to support the Acts held unconstitutional in cases decided within two years. And the lower courts rightly deemed them controlling. . . .

Any effect on interstate commerce by the discharge of employees shown here, would be indirect and remote in the highest degree, as consideration of the facts will show. In No. 419 (*NLRB* v. *Jones & Laughlin*) ten men out of ten thousand were discharged; in the other cases only a few. The immediate effect in the factory may be to create discontent among all those employed and a strike may follow, which, in turn, may result in reducing production, which ultimately may reduce the volume of goods moving in interstate commerce. By this chain of indirect and progressively remote events we finally reach the evil with which it is said the legislation under consideration undertakes to deal. A more remote and indirect interference with interstate commerce or a more definite invasion of the powers reserved to the States is difficult, if not impossible, to imagine. The constitution still recognizes the existence of States with indestructible powers; the Tenth Amendment was supposed to put them beyond controversy.

V. CONTEMPORARY VIEWS OF THE COMMERCE POWER

Wickard v. *Filburn*
317 U.S. 111, 63 S.Ct. 82, 87 L.Ed. 122 (1942)

http://caselaw.findlaw.com/us-supreme-court/317/111.html

The Agricultural Adjustment Act of 1938 was passed by Congress in an effort to stabilize agricultural production. The basic scheme as applied to wheat involved an annual proclamation by the secretary of agriculture of a national acreage allotment, which was then apportioned to states and eventually passed on in the form of quotas to individual farmers. Penalties were imposed for production in excess of an agreed-upon quota. Ohio farmer Roscoe Filburn planted wheat each year to feed his livestock and poultry. He accepted an allotment of 11.1 acres, but actually planted 23 acres and grew 239 bushels in excess of his quota. Filburn resisted payment of the penalty and obtained an injunction in the U.S. District Court for the Southern District of Ohio against Secretary of Agriculture Claude R. Wickard and other officials. Majority: Jackson, Black, Douglas, Frankfurter, Murphy, Reed, Roberts, Stone.

MR. JUSTICE JACKSON delivered the opinion of the Court.

It is argued that under the Commerce Clause . . . Congress does not possess the power it has in this instance sought to exercise. The question would merit little consideration . . . except for the fact that this Act extends federal regulation to production not intended in any part for commerce but wholly for consumption on the farm.

Appellee says that this is a regulation of production and consumption of wheat. Such activities are, he urges, beyond the reach of Congressional power under the Commerce Clause, since they are local in character, and their effects upon interstate commerce are at most "indirect." In answer the Government argues that the statute regulates neither production nor consumption, but only marketing; and, in the alternative, that if the Act does go beyond the regulation of marketing it is sustainable as a "necessary and proper" implementation of the power of Congress over interstate commerce. . . .

We believe that a review of the course of decision under the Commerce Clause will make plain that questions of the power of Congress are not to be decided by reference to any formula which would give controlling force to nomenclature such as "production" and "indirect" and foreclose consideration of the actual effects of the activity in question upon interstate commerce. . . .

The Court's recognition of the relevance of the economic effects in the application of the Commerce Clause . . . has made the mechanical application of legal formulas no longer feasible. Once an economic measure of the reach of the power granted to Congress in the Commerce Clause is accepted, questions of federal power cannot be decided simply by finding the activity in question to be "production" nor can consideration of its economic effects be foreclosed by calling them "indirect." . . .

Whether the subject of the regulation in question was "production," "consumption," or "marketing" is, therefore, not material for purposes of deciding the question of federal power before us. That an activity is of local character may help in a doubtful case to determine whether Congress intended to reach it. The same consideration might help in determining whether in the absence of Congressional action it would be permissible for the state to exert its power on the subject matter, even though in so doing it to some degree affected interstate commerce. But even if appellant's activity be local and though it may not be regarded as commerce, it may still, whatever its nature, be reached by Congress if it exerts a substantial economic effect on interstate commerce and this irrespective of whether such effect is what might at some earlier time have been defined as "direct" or "indirect." . . .

The effect of consumption of home-grown wheat on interstate commerce is due to the fact that it constitutes the most variable factor in the disappearance of the wheat crop. Consumption on the farm where grown appears to vary in an amount greater than 10 percent of average production. The total amount of wheat consumed as food varies but relatively little, and use as seed is relatively constant. . . .

It is well established by decisions of this Court that the power to regulate commerce includes the power to regulate the prices at which commodities in that commerce are dealt in and practices affecting such prices. One of the primary purposes of the Act in question was to increase the market price of wheat and to that end to limit the volume thereof that could affect the market. It can hardly be denied that a factor of such volume and variability as home-consumed wheat would have a substantial influence on price and market conditions. This may arise because being in marketable condition such home-grown wheat overhangs the market and if induced by rising prices tends to flow into the market and check price increases. But if we assume that it is never marketed, it supplies a need of the man who grew it which would otherwise be reflected by purchases in the open market. Home-grown wheat in this sense competes with wheat in commerce. The stimulation of commerce is a use of a regulatory function quite as definitely as prohibitions or restrictions thereon. This record leaves us in no doubt that Congress may properly have considered that wheat consumed on the farm where grown if wholly outside the scheme of regulation would have a substantial effect in defeating and obstructing its purpose to stimulate trade therein at increased prices.

It is said, however, that this Act, forcing some farmers into the market to buy what they could provide for themselves, is an unfair promotion of the markets and prices of specializing wheat growers. It is of the essence of regulation that it lays a restraining hand on the self-interest of the regulated and that advantages from the regulation commonly fall to others. The conflicts of economic interest between the regulated and those who advantage by it are wisely left under our system to resolution by the Congress under its more flexible and responsible legislative process. Such conflicts rarely lend themselves to judicial determination. And with the wisdom, workability, or fairness, of the plan of regulation we have nothing to do. . . .

Reversed.

Heart of Atlanta Motel v. *United States*
379 U.S. 241, 85 S.Ct. 348, 13 L.Ed. 2d 258 (1964)

http://caselaw.findlaw.com/us-supreme-court/379/241.html

Katzenbach v. *McClung*
379 U.S. 294, 85 S.Ct. 377, 13 L.Ed. 2d 290 (1964)

http://caselaw.findlaw.com/us-supreme-court/379/294.html

In the Civil Rights Act of 1964, Congress sought, among other purposes, to eliminate racial discrimination in hotels, motels, restaurants, and similar places of public accommodation, basing its action on the commerce clause as well as on the equal protection clause and Section 5 of the Fourteenth Amendment. In *Atlanta Motel*, the act was applied to a business where 75 percent of the guests were from out of state. In contrast, *McClung* began not at the federal government's initiative but as an action against the attorney general by the owner of Ollie's Barbeque in Birmingham, Alabama, who wanted to avoid being lumped with national restaurant and motel chains. Ollie McClung challenged the provision banning discrimination in any restaurant that "serves or offers to serve interstate travelers or a substantial portion of the food which it serves . . . has moved in commerce." Even though Ollie's was a homespun eatery, well removed from major highways and the airport, approximately half the food served, though purchased within Alabama, had "moved" in commerce. The motel appealed from a district court injunction against its refusal to accept black lodgers, and the attorney general appealed in *McClung* from a district court holding that the act could not be applied to the restaurant. Although Justices Douglas and Goldberg would have upheld the act under the Fourteenth Amendment as well as the commerce clause, the majority rested its decision on the commerce clause. An excerpt from Justice Clark's opinion for the Court in *Atlanta Motel* is followed by an extract from his opinion in *McClung*. Majority: Clark, Black, Brennan, Douglas, Goldberg, Harlan, Stewart, Warren, White.

Mr. Justice Clark delivered the opinion of the Court. . . . (*Atlanta Motel*)

It is admitted that the operation of the motel brings it within the provisions of § 201(a) of the Act and that appellant refused to provide lodging for transient Negroes because of their race or color and that it intends to continue that policy unless restrained. . . .

The determinative test of the exercise of power by the Congress under the Commerce Clause is simply whether the activity sought to be regulated is "commerce which concerns more than one state" and has a real and substantial relation to the national interest. . . .

It is said that the operation of the motel here is of a purely local character. But, assuming this to be true, "if it is interstate commerce that feels the pinch, it does not matter how local the operation that applies the squeeze." . . .

The power of Congress to promote interstate commerce also includes the power to regulate the local incidents thereof, including local activities in both the States of origin and destination, which might have a substantial and harmful effect upon that commerce. One need only examine the evidence which we have discussed above to see that Congress may—as it has—prohibit racial discrimination by motels serving travelers, however "local" their operations may appear. . . .

Affirmed.

Mr. Justice Clark delivered the opinion of the Court. . . . (*McClung*)

The activities that are beyond the reach of Congress are "those which are completely within a particular State, which do not affect other States, and with which it is not necessary to interfere, for the purpose of executing some of the general powers of the government." . . . This rule is as good today as it was when Chief Justice Marshall laid it down almost a century and a half ago.

This Court has held time and again that this power extends to activities of retail establishments, including restaurants, which directly or indirectly burden or obstruct interstate commerce. . . .

Here, as there, Congress has determined for itself that refusals of service to Negroes have imposed burdens both upon the interstate flow of food and upon the movement of products generally. Of course, the mere fact that Congress has said when particular activity shall be deemed to affect commerce does not preclude further examination by this Court. But where we find that the legislators, in light of the facts and testimony before them, have a rational basis for finding a chosen regulatory scheme necessary to the protection of commerce, our investigation is at an end. . . .

Confronted as we are with the facts laid before Congress, we must conclude that it had a rational basis for finding that racial discrimination in restaurants had a direct and adverse effect on the free flow of interstate commerce. . . .

The absence of direct evidence connecting discriminatory restaurant service with the flow of interstate food, a factor on which the appellees place much reliance, is not, given the evidence as to the effect of such practices on other aspects of commerce, a crucial matter.

The power of Congress in this field is broad and sweeping; where it keeps within its sphere and violates no express constitutional limitation it has been the rule of this Court, going back almost to the founding days of the Republic, not to interfere. The Civil Rights Act of 1964, as here applied, we find to be plainly appropriate in the resolution of what the Congress found to be a national commercial problem of the first magnitude. We find it in no violation of any express limitations of the Constitution and we therefore declare it valid.

The judgment is therefore

Reversed.

Mr. Justice Black, concurring . . . [omitted].
Mr. Justice Douglas, concurring . . . [omitted].
Mr. Justice Goldberg, concurring . . . [omitted].

United States v. *Lopez*
514 U.S. 549, 115 S.Ct. 1624, 131 L.Ed. 2d 626 (1995)

http://caselaw.findlaw.com/us-supreme-court/514/549.html

In the Gun-Free School Zones Act of 1990, referred to below as § 922(q), Congress made it a federal crime "for any individual knowingly to possess a firearm at a . . . public, parochial or private school" or "within a distance of 1,000 feet from the grounds of a . . . school." On March 12, 1992, Alfonso Lopez, Jr., was found carrying a concealed 0.38 caliber handgun and five bullets at Edison High School in San Antonio, Texas, where he was a senior. He was arrested under a Texas law that banned possession of a firearm on school premises. On March 13, the state dismissed charges after federal agents charged Lopez with violation of the Gun-Free School Zones Act. Over an objection that the federal statute violated the Constitution, the U.S. District Court for the Western District of Texas found Lopez guilty at a bench trial and sentenced him to six months' imprisonment and two years' supervised release. The Court of Appeals for the Fifth Circuit reversed, holding that § 922(q) was "invalid as beyond the power of Congress under the Commerce Clause." Majority: Rehnquist, Kennedy, O'Connor, Scalia, Thomas. Dissenting: Breyer, Ginsburg, Souter, Stevens.

CHIEF JUSTICE REHNQUIST delivered the opinion of the Court. . . .

We start with first principles. The Constitution creates a Federal Government of enumerated powers. . . .

[*NLRB* v.] *Jones & Laughlin Steel*, [*United States* v.] *Darby*, and *Wickard* [v. *Filburn*] ushered in an era of Commerce Clause jurisprudence that greatly expanded the previously defined authority of Congress under that Clause. In part, this was a recognition of the great changes that had occurred in the way business was carried on in this country. Enterprises that had once been local or at most regional in nature had become national in scope. But the doctrinal change also reflected a view that earlier Commerce Clause cases artificially had constrained the authority of Congress to regulate interstate commerce.

But even these modern-era precedents which have expanded congressional power under the Commerce Clause confirm that this power is subject to outer limits. . . .

Consistent with this structure, we have identified three broad categories of activity that Congress may regulate under its commerce power. First, Congress may regulate the use of the channels of interstate commerce. . . . Second, Congress is empowered to regulate and protect the instrumentalities of interstate commerce, or persons or things in interstate commerce, even though the threat may come only from intrastate activities. . . . Finally, Congress' commerce authority includes the power to regulate those activities having a substantial relation to interstate commerce, that is, those activities that substantially affect interstate commerce.

Within this final category, admittedly, our case law has not been clear whether an activity must "affect" or "substantially affect" interstate commerce in order to be within Congress' power to regulate it under the Commerce Clause. . . . We conclude, consistent with the great weight of our case law, that the proper test requires an analysis of whether the regulated activity "substantially affects" interstate commerce.

We now turn to consider the power of Congress, in the light of this framework, to enact § 922(q). The first two categories of authority may be quickly disposed of: § 922(q) is not a regulation of the use of the channels of interstate commerce, nor is it an attempt to prohibit the interstate transportation of a commodity through the channels of commerce; nor can § 922(q) be justified as a regulation by which Congress has sought to protect an instrumentality of interstate commerce or a thing in interstate commerce. Thus, if § 922(q) is to be sustained, it must be under the third category as a regulation of an activity that substantially affects interstate commerce. . . .

Section 922(q) is a criminal statute that by its terms has nothing to do with "commerce" or any sort of economic enterprise, however broadly one might define those terms. Section 922(q) is not an essential part of a larger regulation of economic activity, in which the regulatory scheme could be undercut unless the intrastate activity were regulated. It cannot, therefore, be sustained under our cases upholding regulations of activities that arise out of or are connected with a commercial transaction, which viewed in the aggregate, substantially affects interstate commerce.

Second, § 922(q) contains no jurisdictional element which would ensure, through case-by-case inquiry, that the firearm possession in question affects interstate commerce. . . .

Although as part of our independent evaluation of constitutionality under the Commerce Clause we of course consider legislative findings, and indeed even congressional committee findings, regarding effect on interstate commerce, the Government concedes that "[n]either the statute nor its legislative history contain[s] express congressional findings regarding the effects upon interstate commerce of gun possession in a school zone." We agree with the Government that Congress normally is not required to make formal findings as to the substantial burdens that an activity has on interstate commerce. . . . But to the extent that congressional findings would enable us to evaluate the legislative judgment that the activity in question substantially affected interstate commerce, even though no such substantial effect was visible to the naked eye, they are lacking here. . . .

The Government's essential contention, in fine, is that we may determine here that § 922(q) is valid because possession of a firearm in a local school zone does indeed substantially affect interstate commerce. The Government argues that possession of a firearm in a school zone may result in violent crime and that violent crime can be expected to affect the functioning of the national economy in two ways. First, the costs of violent crime are substantial, and, through the mechanism of insurance, those costs are spread throughout the population. Second, violent crime reduces the willingness of individuals to travel to areas within the country that are perceived to be unsafe. The Government also argues that the presence of guns in schools poses a substantial threat to the educational process by threatening the learning environment. A handicapped educational process, in turn, will result in a less productive citizenry. That, in turn, would have an adverse effect on the Nation's economic well-being. As a result, the Government argues that Congress could rationally have concluded that § 922(q) substantially affects interstate commerce.

We pause to consider the implications of the Government's arguments. The Government admits, under its "costs of crime" reasoning, that Congress could regulate not only all violent crime, but all activities that might lead to violent crime, regardless of how tenuously they relate to interstate commerce. Similarly, under the Government's "national productivity" reasoning, Congress could regulate any activity that it found was related to the economic productivity of individual citizens: family law (including marriage, divorce, and child custody), for example. Under the theories that the Government presents in support of § 922(q), it is difficult to perceive any limitation on federal power, even in areas such as criminal law enforcement or education where States historically have been sovereign. Thus, if we were to accept the Government's arguments, we are hard-pressed to posit any activity by an individual that Congress is without power to regulate.

Although Justice Breyer argues that acceptance of the Government's rationales would not authorize a general federal police power, he is unable to identify any activity that the States may regulate but Congress may not. . . .

Justice Breyer focuses, for the most part, on the threat that firearm possession in and near schools poses to the educational process and the potential economic consequences flowing from that threat. Specifically, the dissent reasons that (1) gun-related violence is a serious problem; (2) that problem, in turn, has an adverse effect on classroom learning; and (3) that adverse effect on classroom learning, in turn, represents a substantial threat to trade and commerce. This analysis would be equally applicable, if not more so, to subjects such as family law and direct regulation of education. . . .

To uphold the Government's contentions here, we would have to pile inference upon inference in a manner that would bid fair to convert congressional authority under the Commerce Clause to a general police power of the sort retained by the States. Admittedly, some of our prior cases have taken long steps down that road, giving great deference to congressional action. The broad language in these opinions has suggested the possibility of additional expansion, but we decline here to proceed any further. To do so would require us to conclude that the Constitution's enumeration of powers does not presuppose something not enumerated, and that there never will be a distinction between what is truly national and what is truly local. This we are unwilling to do.

For the foregoing reasons the judgment of the Court of Appeals is

Affirmed.

Justice Kennedy, with whom Justice O'Connor joins, concurring . . . [omitted].

Justice Thomas, concurring . . . [omitted]. Justice Stevens, dissenting . . . [omitted].

Justice Souter, dissenting . . . [omitted].

Justice Breyer, with whom Justice Stevens, Justice Souter, and Justice Ginsburg join, dissenting.

In my view, the statute falls well within the scope of the commerce power as this Court has understood that power over the last half-century.

In reaching this conclusion, I apply three basic principles of Commerce Clause interpretation. First, the power to "regulate Commerce . . . among the several States" encompasses the power to regulate local activities insofar as they significantly affect interstate commerce. . . .

Second, in determining whether a local activity will likely have a significant effect upon interstate commerce, a court must consider, not the effect of an individual act (a single instance of gun possession), but rather the cumulative effect of all similar instances (that is, the effect of all guns possessed in or near schools). . . .

Third, the Constitution requires us to judge the connection between a regulated activity and interstate commerce, not directly, but at one remove. Courts must give Congress a degree of leeway in determining the existence of a significant factual connection between the regulated activity and interstate commerce—both because the Constitution delegates the commerce power directly to Congress and because the determination requires an empirical judgment of a kind that a legislature is more likely than a court to make with accuracy. The traditional words "rational basis" capture this leeway. Thus, the specific question before us, as the Court recognizes, is not whether the "regulated activity sufficiently affected interstate commerce," but, rather, whether Congress could have had "a rational basis" for so concluding. . . .

Applying these principles to the case at hand, we must ask whether Congress could have . . . found that "violent crime in school zones," through its effect on the "quality of education," significantly (or substantially) affects "interstate" or "foreign commerce?" As long as one views the commerce connection, . . . as "a practical one," the answer to this question must be yes. Numerous reports and studies—generated both inside and outside government—make clear that Congress could reasonably have found the empirical connection that its law, implicitly or explicitly, asserts. . . .

Having found that guns in schools significantly undermine the quality of education in our Nation's classrooms, Congress could also have found, given the effect of education upon interstate and foreign commerce, that gun-related violence in and around schools is a commercial, as well as a human, problem. Education, although far more than a matter of economics, has long been inextricably intertwined with the Nation's economy. . . .

The economic links I have just sketched seem fairly obvious. . . . That is to say, guns in the hands of six percent of inner-city high school students and gun-related violence throughout a city's schools must threaten the trade and commerce that those schools support. The only question, then, is whether the latter threat is (to use the majority's terminology) "substantial." And, the evidence of (1) the extent of the gun-related violence problem; (2) the extent of the resulting negative effect on classroom learning; and (3) the extent of the consequent negative commercial effects, when taken together, indicate a threat to trade and commerce that is "substantial." At the very least, Congress could rationally have concluded that the links are "substantial." . . .

In sum, a holding that the particular statute before us falls within the commerce power would not expand the scope of that Clause. Rather, it simply would apply pre-existing law to changing economic circumstances. . . .

United States v. *Morrison*
529 U.S. 598, 120 S.Ct. 1740, 146 L.Ed. 2d 658 (2000)

http://caselaw.findlaw.com/us-supreme-court/529/598.html

(This case is reprinted in Chapter Four; see the Table of Contents.)

National Federation of Independent Business v. *Sebelius*
567 U.S. 519, 132 S.Ct. 2566, 183 L.Ed. 2d 450 (2012)

In 2010 President Obama signed into law the Patient Protection and Affordable Care Act. Challenges arose immediately to the constitutional validity of two key provisions of the legislation: the individual mandate, which requires individuals to purchase a health insurance policy providing a minimum level of coverage; and the Medicaid expansion, which would give funds to the states on the condition that they provide specified health care to all citizens whose income falls below a certain threshold. The United States Court of Appeals for the Eleventh Circuit struck down the mandate but left the other provision of the law intact. The excerpts below concern mainly those two provisions. Reflecting the complexity of the statute, the Court scheduled oral argument on three days: March 26, 27, and 28, 2012. At a press conference in April, President Obama, presumably intending to nudge the Court to support his signature legislation, commented, "I'm confident that the Supreme Court will not take what would be an unprecedented, extraordinary step of overturning a law that was passed by a strong majority of a democratically elected Congress." The Court's decision in this case came down on June 28. Mandate majority: Roberts, Breyer, Ginsburg, Kagan, Sotomayor; Dissenting: Alito, Kennedy, Scalia, Thomas. Medicaid majority: Roberts, Alito, Breyer, Kagan, Kennedy, Scalia, Thomas. Dissenting: Ginsburg, Sotomayor.

Chief Justice Roberts announced the judgment of the Court and delivered the opinion of the Court with respect to Parts I, II, and III–C, an opinion with respect to Part IV, in which Justice Breyer and Justice Kagan join, and an opinion with respect to Parts III–A, III–B, and III–D.

Today we resolve constitutional challenges to two provisions of the Patient Protection and Affordable Care Act of 2010: the individual mandate, which requires individuals to purchase a health insurance policy providing a minimum level of coverage; and the Medicaid expansion, which gives funds to the States on the condition that they provide specified health care to all citizens whose income falls below a certain threshold. We do not consider whether the Act embodies sound policies. That judgment is entrusted to the Nation's elected leaders. We ask only whether Congress has the power under the Constitution to enact the challenged provisions. . . .

The Federal Government "is acknowledged by all to be one of enumerated powers." . . . If no enumerated power authorizes Congress to pass a certain law, that law may not be enacted, even if it would not violate any of the express prohibitions in the Bill of Rights or elsewhere in the Constitution. . . .

The same does not apply to the States, because the Constitution is not the source of their power. The Constitution may restrict state governments. . . . But where such prohibitions do not apply, state governments do not need constitutional authorization to act. The States thus can and do perform many of the vital functions of modern government . . . even though the Constitution's text does not authorize any government to do so. Our cases refer to this general power of governing, possessed by the States but not by the Federal Government, as the "police power." . . .

This case concerns two powers that the Constitution does grant the Federal Government, but which must be read carefully to avoid creating a general federal authority akin to the police power. The Constitution authorizes Congress to "regulate Commerce with foreign Nations, and among the several States, and with the Indian Tribes." Our precedents read that to mean that Congress may regulate "the channels of interstate commerce," "persons or things in interstate commerce," and "those activities that substantially affect interstate commerce." The power over activities that substantially affect interstate commerce can be expansive. . . .

Congress may also "lay and collect Taxes, Duties, Imposts and Excises, to pay the Debts and provide for the common Defence and general Welfare of the United States." Put simply, Congress may tax and spend. This grant gives the Federal Government considerable influence even in areas where it cannot directly regulate. The Federal Government may enact a tax on an activity that it cannot authorize, forbid, or otherwise control. And in exercising its spending power, Congress may offer funds to the States, and may condition those offers on compliance with specified conditions. These offers may well induce the States to adopt policies that the Federal Government itself could not impose. . . .

The reach of the Federal Government's enumerated powers is broader still because the Constitution authorizes Congress to "make all Laws which shall be necessary and proper for carrying into Execution the foregoing Powers." We have long read this provision to give Congress great latitude in exercising its powers. . . .

Those decisions are entrusted to our Nation's elected leaders, who can be thrown out of office if the people disagree with them. It is not our job to protect the people from the consequences of their political choices. . . .

I. [Omitted]

II. Before turning to the merits, we need to be sure we have the authority to do so. The Anti-Injunction Act provides that "no suit for the purpose of restraining the assessment or collection of any tax shall be maintained in any court by any person, whether or not such person is the person against whom such tax was assessed." . . . This statute protects the Government's ability to collect a consistent stream of revenue, by barring litigation to enjoin or otherwise obstruct the collection of taxes. Because of the Anti-Injunction Act, taxes can ordinarily be challenged only after they are paid, by suing for a refund. [The Chief Justice concludes that the mandate is a penalty, not a tax, so the Anti-Injunction Act does not apply.]

III. The Government advances two theories for the proposition that Congress had constitutional authority to enact the individual mandate. First, the Government argues that Congress had the power to enact the mandate under the Commerce Clause. Under that theory, Congress may order individuals to buy health insurance because the failure to do so affects interstate commerce, and could undercut the Affordable Care Act's other reforms. Second, the Government argues that if the commerce power does not support the mandate, we should nonetheless uphold it as an exercise of Congress's power to tax. According to the Government, even if Congress lacks the power to direct individuals to buy insurance, the only effect of the individual mandate is to raise taxes on those who do not do so, and thus the law may be upheld as a tax.

The Government's first argument is that the individual mandate is a valid exercise of Congress's power under the Commerce Clause and the Necessary and Proper Clause. According to the Government, the health care market is characterized by a significant cost-shifting problem. Everyone will eventually need health care at a time and to an extent they cannot predict, but if they do not have insurance, they often will not be able to pay for it. Because state and federal laws nonetheless require hospitals to provide a certain degree of care to individuals without regard to their ability to pay, hospitals end up receiving compensation for only a portion of the services they provide. To recoup the losses, hospitals pass on the cost to insurers through higher rates, and insurers, in turn, pass on the cost to policy holders in the form of higher premiums. . . .

By requiring that individuals purchase health insurance, the mandate prevents cost-shifting by those who would otherwise go without it. In addition, the mandate forces into the insurance risk pool more healthy individuals, whose premiums on average will be higher than their health care expenses. This allows insurers to subsidize the costs of covering the unhealthy individuals the reforms require them to accept. The Government claims that Congress has power under the Commerce and Necessary and Proper Clauses to enact this solution.

The Government contends that the individual mandate is within Congress's power because the failure to purchase insurance "has a substantial and deleterious effect on interstate commerce" by creating the cost-shifting problem. . . .

As expansive as our cases construing the scope of the commerce power have been, they all have one thing in common: They uniformly describe the power as reaching "activity." . . .

The individual mandate, however, does not regulate existing commercial activity. It instead compels individuals to become active in commerce by purchasing a product, on the ground that their failure to do so affects interstate commerce. Construing the Commerce Clause to permit Congress to regulate individuals precisely because they are doing nothing would open a new and potentially vast domain to congressional authority. Every day individuals do not do an infinite number of things. In some cases they decide not to do something; in others they simply fail to do it. Allowing Congress to justify federal regulation by pointing to the effect of inaction on commerce would bring countless decisions an individual could potentially make within the scope of federal regulation, and—under the Government's theory—empower Congress to make those decisions for him.

Applying the Government's logic to the familiar case of *Wickard* v. *Filburn* shows how far that logic would carry us from the notion of a government of limited powers. In *Wickard*, the Court famously upheld a federal penalty imposed on a farmer for growing wheat for consumption on his own farm. That amount of wheat caused the farmer to exceed his quota under a program designed to support the price of wheat by limiting supply. The Court rejected the farmer's argument that growing wheat for home consumption was beyond the reach of the commerce power. It did so on the ground that the farmer's decision to grow wheat for his own use allowed him to avoid purchasing wheat in the market. That decision, when considered in the aggregate along with similar decisions of others, would have had a substantial effect on the interstate market for wheat.

Wickard has long been regarded as "perhaps the most far reaching example of Commerce Clause authority over intrastate activity," but the Government's theory in this case would go much further. Under *Wickard* it is within Congress's power to regulate the market for wheat by supporting its price. But price can be supported by increasing demand as well as by decreasing supply. The aggregated decisions of some consumers not to purchase wheat have a substantial effect on the price of wheat, just as decisions not to purchase health insurance have on the price of insurance. Congress can therefore command that those not buying wheat do so, just as it argues here that it may command that those not buying health insurance do so. The farmer in *Wickard* was at least actively engaged in the production of wheat, and the Government could regulate that activity because of its effect on commerce. The Government's theory here would effectively override that limitation, by establishing that individuals may be regulated under the Commerce Clause whenever enough of them are not doing something the Government would have them do.

Indeed, the Government's logic would justify a mandatory purchase to solve almost any problem. . . . To consider a different example in the health care market, many Americans do not eat a balanced diet. That group makes up a larger percentage of the total population than those without health insurance. The failure of that group to have a healthy diet increases health care costs, to a greater extent than the failure of the uninsured to purchase insurance. . . . Under the Government's theory, Congress could address the diet problem by ordering everyone to buy vegetables. . . . That is not the country the Framers of our Constitution envisioned. . . .

The Government regards it as sufficient to trigger Congress's authority that almost all those who are uninsured will, at some unknown point in the future, engage in a health care transaction. Asserting that "[t]here is no temporal limitation in the Commerce Clause," the Government argues that because "[e]veryone subject to this regulation is in or will be in the health care market," they can be "regulated in advance."

The proposition that Congress may dictate the conduct of an individual today because of prophesied future activity finds no support in our precedent. We have said that Congress can anticipate the effects on commerce of an economic activity. . . . But we have never permitted Congress to anticipate that activity itself in order to regulate individuals not currently engaged in commerce. . . . The Commerce Clause is not a general license to regulate an individual from cradle to grave, simply because he will predictably engage in particular transactions. Any police power to regulate individuals as such, as opposed to their activities, remains vested in the States. . . .

The Government next contends that Congress has the power under the Necessary and Proper Clause to enact the individual mandate because the mandate is an "integral part of a comprehensive scheme of economic regulation"—the guaranteed-issue and community-rating insurance reforms. Under this argument, it is not necessary to consider the effect that an individual's inactivity may have on interstate commerce; it is enough that Congress regulate commercial activity in a way that requires regulation of inactivity to be effective. . . .

Applying these principles, the individual mandate cannot be sustained under the Necessary and Proper Clause as an essential component of the insurance reforms. . . .

Even if the individual mandate is "necessary" to the Act's insurance reforms, such an expansion of federal power is not a "proper" means for making those reforms effective. . . .

That is not the end of the matter. Because the Commerce Clause does not support the individual mandate, it is necessary to turn to the Government's second argument: that the mandate may be upheld as within Congress's enumerated power to "lay and collect Taxes." . . .

The most straightforward reading of the mandate is that it commands individuals to purchase insurance. . . . Under the mandate, if an individual does not maintain health insurance, the only consequence is that he must make an additional payment to the IRS when he pays his taxes. That, according to the Government, means the mandate can be regarded as establishing a condition—not owning health insurance—that triggers a tax—the required payment to the IRS. Under that theory, the mandate is not a legal command to buy insurance. Rather, it makes going without insurance just another thing the Government taxes, like buying gasoline or earning income. And if the mandate is in effect just a tax hike on certain taxpayers who do not have health insurance, it may be within Congress's constitutional power to tax. . . . Granting the Act the full measure of deference owed to federal statutes, it can be so read. . . .

The exaction the Affordable Care Act imposes on those without health insurance looks like a tax in many respects. . . .

It is of course true that the Act describes the payment as a "penalty," not a "tax." But while that label is fatal to the application of the Anti-Injunction Act, it does not determine whether the payment may be viewed as an exercise of Congress's taxing power. It is up to Congress whether to apply the Anti-Injunction Act to any particular statute, so it makes sense to be guided by Congress's choice of label on that question. That choice does not, however, control whether an exaction is within Congress's constitutional power to tax. . . .

We have similarly held that exactions not labeled taxes nonetheless were authorized by Congress's power to tax. . . . Our cases confirm this functional approach. . . .

IV. The States also contend that the Medicaid expansion exceeds Congress's authority under the Spending Clause. They claim that Congress is coercing the States to adopt the changes it wants by threatening to withhold all of a State's Medicaid grants, unless the State accepts the new expanded funding and complies with the conditions that come with it. This, they argue, violates the basic principle that the "Federal Government may not compel the States to enact or administer a federal regulatory program."

The Spending Clause grants Congress the power "to pay the Debts and provide for the . . . general Welfare of the United States. We have long recognized that Congress may use this power to grant federal funds to the States, and may condition such a grant upon the States' "taking certain actions that Congress could not require them to take." . . .

At the same time, our cases have recognized limits on Congress's power under the Spending Clause to secure state compliance with federal objectives. . . . Respecting this limitation is critical to ensuring that Spending Clause legislation does not undermine the status of the States as independent sovereigns in our federal system. . . . Permitting the Federal Government to force the States to implement a federal program would threaten the political accountability key to our federal system. . . .

Congress may attach appropriate conditions to federal taxing and spending programs to preserve its control over the use of federal funds. In the typical case we look to the States to defend their prerogatives by adopting "the simple expedient of not yielding" to federal blandishments when they do not want to embrace the federal policies as their own. The States are separate and independent sovereigns. Sometimes they have to act like it.

The States, however, argue that the Medicaid expansion is far from the typical case. They object that Congress has "crossed the line distinguishing encouragement from coercion," in the way it has structured the funding: Instead of simply refusing to grant the new funds to States that will not accept the new conditions, Congress has also threatened to withhold those States' existing Medicaid funds. The States claim that this threat serves no purpose other than to force unwilling States to sign up for the dramatic expansion in health care coverage effected by the Act.

Given the nature of the threat and the programs at issue here, we must agree.

The Affordable Care Act is constitutional in part and unconstitutional in part. The individual mandate cannot be upheld as an exercise of Congress's power under the Commerce Clause. That Clause authorizes Congress to regulate interstate commerce, not to order individuals to engage in it. In this case, however, it is reasonable to construe what Congress has done as increasing taxes on those who have a certain amount of income, but choose to go without health insurance. Such legislation is within Congress's power to tax.

As for the Medicaid expansion, that portion of the Affordable Care Act violates the Constitution by threatening existing Medicaid funding. Congress has no authority to order the States to regulate according to its instructions. Congress may offer the States grants and require the States to comply with accompanying conditions, but the States must have a genuine choice whether to accept the offer. The States are given no such choice in this case: They must either accept a basic change in the nature of Medicaid, or risk losing all Medicaid funding. The remedy for that constitutional violation is to preclude the Federal Government from imposing such a sanction. That remedy does not require striking down other portions of the Affordable Care Act.

The Framers created a Federal Government of limited powers, and assigned to this Court the duty of enforcing those limits. The Court does so today. But the Court does not express any opinion on the wisdom of the Affordable Care Act. Under the Constitution, that judgment is reserved to the people.

The judgment of the Court of Appeals for the Eleventh Circuit is affirmed in part and reversed in part.

It is so ordered.

Justice Scalia, Justice Kennedy, Justice Thomas, and Justice Alito, dissenting. . . .

This case is in one respect difficult: it presents two questions of first impression. The first of those is whether failure to engage in economic activity (the purchase of health insurance) is subject to regulation under the Commerce Clause. . . . The second question is whether the congressional power to tax and spend permits the conditioning of a State's continued receipt of all funds under a massive state-administered federal welfare program upon its acceptance of an expansion to that program. . . . Those questions are difficult.

The case is easy and straightforward, however, in another respect. What is absolutely clear, affirmed by the text of the 1789 Constitution, by the Tenth Amendment ratified in 1791, and by innumerable cases of ours in the 220 years since, is that there are structural limits upon federal power—upon what it can prescribe with respect to private conduct, and upon what it can impose upon the sovereign States. Whatever may be the conceptual limits upon the Commerce Clause and upon the power to tax and spend, they cannot be such as will enable the Federal Government to regulate all private conduct and to compel the States to function as administrators of federal programs.

That clear principle carries the day here. The striking case of *Wickard* v. *Filburn*, which held that the economic activity of growing wheat, even for one's own consumption, affected commerce sufficiently that it could be regulated, always has been regarded as *the ne plus ultra* of expansive Commerce Clause jurisprudence. To go beyond that, and to say the failure to grow wheat (which is not an economic activity, or any activity at all) nonetheless affects commerce and therefore can be federally regulated, is to make mere breathing in and out the basis for federal prescription and to extend federal power to virtually all human activity.

As for the constitutional power to tax and spend for the general welfare: The Court has long since expanded that beyond (what Madison thought it meant) taxing and spending for those aspects of the general welfare that were within the Federal Government's enumerated powers. Thus, we now have sizable federal Departments devoted to subjects not mentioned among Congress' enumerated powers, and only marginally related to commerce. . . .

The principal practical obstacle that prevents Congress from using the tax-and-spend power to assume all the general-welfare responsibilities traditionally exercised by the States is the sheer impossibility of managing a Federal Government large enough to administer such a system. That obstacle can be overcome by granting funds to the States, allowing them to administer the program. That is fair and constitutional enough when the States freely agree to have their powers employed and their employees enlisted in the federal scheme. But it is a blatant violation of the constitutional structure when the States have no choice.

The Act before us here exceeds federal power both in mandating the purchase of health insurance and in denying nonconsenting States all Medicaid funding. These parts of the Act are central to its design and operation, and all the Act's other provisions would not have been enacted without them. In our view it must follow that the entire statute is inoperative. . . .

The Court today decides to save a statute Congress did not write. It rules that what the statute declares to be a requirement with a penalty is instead an option subject to a tax. And it changes the intentionally coercive sanction of a total cut-off of Medicaid funds to a supposedly noncoercive cut-off of only the incremental funds that the Act makes available.

The Court regards its strained statutory interpretation as judicial modesty. It is not. It amounts instead to a vast judicial overreaching. . . .

The Constitution, though it dates from the founding of the Republic, has powerful meaning and vital relevance to our own times. The constitutional protections that this case involves are protections of structure. Structural protections—notably, the restraints imposed by federalism and separation of powers—are less romantic and have less obvious a connection to personal freedom than the provisions of the Bill of Rights or the Civil War Amendments. Hence they tend to be undervalued or even forgotten by our citizens. It should be the responsibility of the Court to teach otherwise, to remind our people that the Framers considered structural protections of freedom the most important ones, for which reason they alone were embodied in the original Constitution and not left to later amendment. The fragmentation of power produced by the structure of our Government is central to liberty, and when we destroy it, we place liberty at peril. Today's decision should have vindicated, should have taught, this truth; instead, our judgment today has disregarded it.

For the reasons here stated, we would find the Act invalid in its entirety. We respectfully dissent.

JUSTICE GINSBURG, with whom JUSTICE SOTOMAYOR joins, and with whom JUSTICE BREYER and JUSTICE KAGAN join in part, concurring in the judgment in part, and dissenting in part. . . .

Consistent with the Framers' intent, we have repeatedly emphasized that Congress' authority under the Commerce Clause is dependent upon "practical" considerations, including "actual experience." . . . Until today, this Court's pragmatic approach to judging whether Congress validly exercised its commerce power was guided by two familiar principles. First, Congress has the power to regulate economic activities "that substantially affect interstate commerce." This capacious power extends even to local activities that, viewed in the aggregate, have a substantial impact on interstate commerce. . . .

Second, we owe a large measure of respect to Congress when it frames and enacts economic and social legislation. . . . When appraising such legislation, we ask only (1) whether Congress had a "rational basis" for concluding that the regulated activity substantially affects interstate commerce, and (2) whether there is a "reasonable connection between the regulatory means selected and the asserted ends." In answering these questions, we presume the statute under review is constitutional and may strike it down only on a "plain showing" that Congress acted irrationally.

Straightforward application of these principles would require the Court to hold that the minimum coverage provision is proper Commerce Clause legislation. Beyond dispute, Congress had a rational basis for concluding that the uninsured, as a class, substantially affect interstate commerce. Those without insurance consume billions of dollars of health-care products and services each year. Those goods are produced, sold, and delivered largely by national and regional companies who routinely transact business across state lines. The uninsured also cross state lines to receive care. Some have medical emergencies while away from home. Others, when sick, go to a neighboring State that provides better care for those who have not prepaid for care. . . .

In the early 20th century, this Court regularly struck down economic regulation enacted by the peoples' representatives in both the States and the Federal Government. The Chief Justice's Commerce Clause opinion, and even more so the joint dissenters' reasoning, bear a disquieting resemblance to those long-overruled decisions.

This Court, time and again, has respected Congress' prescription of spending conditions, and has required States to abide by them. . . .

At bottom, my colleagues' position is that the States' reliance on federal funds limits Congress' authority to alter its spending programs. This gets things backwards: Congress, not the States, is tasked with spending federal money in service of the general welfare. And each successive Congress is empowered to appropriate funds as it sees fit. . . . I disagree that any such withholding would violate the Spending Clause. Accordingly, I would affirm the decision of the Court of Appeals for the Eleventh Circuit in this regard. . . .

JUSTICE THOMAS, dissenting . . . [omitted].

NOTE

1. Economy Act of 1933 in *Lynch* v. *United States* (1934); Agricultural Adjustment Act of 1933 in *United States* v. *Butler* (1936); Joint Resolution of June 5, 1933, in *Perry* v. *United States* (1935); National Industrial Recovery Act of 1933 in *Schechter Poultry Corp.* v. *United States* (1935) and *Panama Refining Co.* v. *Ryan* (1935); Independent

Offices Appropriation Act of 1933 in *Booth* v. *United States* (1934); 1933 Amendments to Home Owners' Loan Act in *Hopkins Savings Assn.* v. *Cleary* (1935); 1934 Amendments to Bankruptcy Act of 1898 in *Ashton* v. *Cameron County Dist.* (1936); Railroad Retirement Act of 1934 in *Railroad Retirement Board* v. *Alton R. Co.* (1935); Frazier-Lemke Act of 1934 in *Louisville Bank* v. *Radford* (1935); AAA Amendments of 1935 in *Rickert Rice Mills* v. *Fontenot* (1936); Bituminous Coal Conservation Act in *Carter* v. *Carter Coal Co.* (1936).

7

National Taxing and Spending Power

Taxes are what we pay for civilized society. . . .

—Justice Oliver Wendell Holmes (1927)

Government, like individual citizens, must have regular income to pay bills and maintain credit. Government programs cost money, whether in building aircraft carriers, sponsoring cancer research, or maintaining national parks. Moreover, government must have coercive power to collect taxes. No government can carry on effectively if it has to depend, as did the Congress under the **Articles of Confederation**, on what amounted to voluntary contributions. Indeed, the principal weakness of the central government under the Articles was absence of power to levy taxes. National expenditures were defrayed out of a common treasury supplied by the states in proportion to the occupied land in each state, and upon requisition by Congress. The states reserved the right to levy taxes for this purpose and were usually delinquent in making payments.

Therefore, it is not surprising that, although members of the federal Convention were sharply divided on many issues, they were almost unanimous in their insistence that Congress should have broad power to tax and spend. Heading the list of enumerated powers in Article I, Section 8, stands the provision that Congress shall have power "to lay and collect taxes, duties, imposts and excises, to pay the debts and provide for the common defense and general welfare of the United States."

It would be difficult to fashion more sweeping language. In the exercise of its taxing and spending power, the national government acts directly on individual citizens and their property as though there were no states. Nor are there any limits (apart from those imposed on Congress at the ballot box) on the amount Congress may attempt to collect through taxation. The only limitations on the taxing power are those that the Supreme Court has established and those that the Constitution specifically provides in Article I. Section 9 specifically bars a preference to one state's ports over another's and forbids a tax on exports (a concession made in 1787 to southern exporters). These provisions have occasioned no difficulties. Yet the

DOI: 10.4324/9781003164340-8

Court's interpretation of the stipulation on direct taxes in the same section led to a constitutional amendment.

DIRECT AND INDIRECT TAXES

The Constitution declares that taxes are of two kinds and sets forth briefly the rules by which Congress may use each. Article I, Section 9, declares that **direct taxes** shall be levied according to the rule of apportionment among the several states on the basis of census enumeration or population. **Indirect taxes** shall be levied according to the rule of uniformity, which means geographical uniformity, as *Knowlton* v. *Moore* (1900) made clear. That is, a tax must be laid at the same rate and on the same basis in all parts of the United States. The meaning of indirect taxes, which include all excises and duties, has rarely concerned the Court, but the definition of direct taxes has proved troublesome.

Views of the Framers. James Madison's notes from the federal Convention throw no light on the mystery of what is a direct tax. The single entry on this question runs, "Mr. Davie of North Carolina rose to ask the meaning of the direct taxes. Mr. King said he did not know." Like so many other terms in the Constitution, the meaning of direct taxes had to be spelled out by judicial construction.

The Court first addressed the subject in 1796 in ***Hylton* v. *United States***, where a federal tax on carriages was held to be an indirect tax and therefore not subject to apportionment. The Court's ruling was based first on the nature of the carriage tax, which it considered a levy on the privilege of using carriages and, second, on the impossibility of fairly apportioning a tax of this kind because the ratio of carriages to population was obviously not the same in each state. The justices agreed that the only direct taxes were capitation and land taxes, and these categories remained frozen for a century.

The Income Tax Case. Believing that the Court would adhere to this definition, Congress first levied an income tax during the Civil War. It was challenged unsuccessfully in *Springer* v. *United States* (1881), a precedent that stood until the 1890s, when Congress enacted another income tax, levied, as the Civil War tax had been, as if it were indirect. This time, in ***Pollock* v. *Farmers' Loan & Trust Co.***, the Court changed its mind, boldly rewriting the definition of direct taxes given in *Hylton*, thus correcting, by a margin of one vote, "a century of error." In his brief attacking the validity of the income tax (on the theory that it was direct and had to be apportioned), Joseph H. Choate, one of the leaders of the American bar, referred to the tax in caustic terms—he called it "communism," "socialism," and "populism." Adopting Choate's sulphurous language, Justice Field in a concurring opinion warned, "The present assault upon capital is but the beginning . . . the stepping stone to others . . . till our political contests will become a war of the poor against the rich." He insisted that this kind of class struggle had to be stopped. The dissenting judges decried in equally fervent language what they deemed a disastrous blow to congressional power and an unwarranted expansion of judicial review.

The immediate effect of this decision was to add income taxes to the category of direct taxes, and because it was not feasible to apportion income taxes, Congress was deprived of this fruitful source of revenue for nearly 20 years. To correct this situation, Congress and the states resorted finally to the cumbersome formal amending process, which in 1913 resulted in the Sixteenth Amendment: "The Congress shall have power to lay and collect taxes on incomes, from whatever source derived, without apportionment among the several states, and without regard to any census or enumeration."

Even this seemingly comprehensive language, however, was not allowed to mean all that it seemed to say. By judicial construction, the amendment was held to mean only that income taxes need not be apportioned and was not interpreted as authorizing taxes on all incomes. Thus, salaries of federal judges, the Court ruled in *Evans* v. *Gore* (1920), were still exempt from the income tax. However, without any revision of the Sixteenth Amendment, *Evans* was overruled in 1939 by *O'Malley* v. *Woodrough*. As Justice Frankfurter observed, "To suggest that it [a nondiscriminatory income tax] makes inroads upon the independence of judges . . . by making them bear their aliquot share of the cost of maintaining the government is to trivialize the great historic experience on which the framers based the safeguards of Article 3, Section 1."

REGULATION THROUGH TAXATION

In addition to express limitations, the Supreme Court developed two others through interpretation. The first is the doctrine of reciprocal immunity of the state and national governments from taxation by the other (a subject covered in Chapter Four). The second is the **independent constitutional bar** (or external check) that the Court has constructed when Congress has arguably used its taxing or spending power to accomplish an objective forbidden by the Constitution. This second limitation typically arises in the context of **regulatory taxation**. As a check on national power, both today are mere shadows of their former selves.

While the most obvious and normal purpose of taxation is the raising of revenue, this is not taxation's only legitimate purpose. A protective tariff, for example, exists not to enrich the federal treasury but to shield an industry or a commodity from foreign competition. Taxes on tobacco products enrich the treasury but are also designed to discourage their use, especially among younger smokers, by making cigarettes expensive. Whether a tax is primarily for revenue or regulation is frequently a matter of degree, for strictly speaking, no tax is or can be solely a revenue measure.

Enumerated and Unenumerated Powers. One aspect of this question has been definitely settled. Congress may use its taxing power primarily for purposes of regulation, or even destruction, when the tax serves to aid Congress in exercising one of its other **enumerated**, or delegated, **powers**, such as regulating interstate commerce, controlling the currency, or maintaining a postal service. An illustrative case is *Veazie Bank* v. *Fenno* (1869), involving an act of Congress that placed a 10 percent tax on state bank notes to protect the notes of the new national banks from the state banks' competition. The tax was of course destructive, as it was intended to be, yet the Court upheld it on the ground that Congress could have achieved the same end by absolute prohibition of state bank notes under the currency power.

A more controversial question remains: May Congress use a tax primarily as a regulatory device, that is, to enforce some social or economic policy, when no enumerated power of Congress can be invoked in justification? For a long period, the Court's answers to this question wavered between a clear yes and an equally clear no.

An important affirmative case is ***McCray* v. *United States*** (1904), which concerned the validity of a **destructive tax** on oleomargarine artificially colored to resemble butter. That the primary purpose of the tax was regulation and not revenue was clear from the much higher tax on colored oleomargarine (10 cents per pound), as compared to the uncolored product (3 cents per pound). Yet the Court held that because Congress had virtually unlimited discretion in the selection of the objects of taxation, it was not part of the judicial function to explore congressional motives. Under this judicial hands-off policy, Congress proceeded to regulate by taxation the manufacture of phosphorus matches and narcotics and the retail sale of certain firearms. The McCray doctrine came close to making the question of the validity of destructive and regulatory taxation a political question.

In due course, the Court evolved a more effective technique for imposing limitations on the destructive use of the federal taxing power for social and economic regulation. The change came in 1922 in ***Bailey* v. *Drexel Furniture Co.***, which involved the constitutionality of a 10 percent federal tax on the net income of any employer of child labor, regardless of the number of children employed. In addition, the act set up an elaborate code for regulating each employer's conduct, a matter over which Congress admittedly had no direct control. Speaking through Chief Justice Taft, an all but unanimous Court condemned the act primarily because it was a "penalty" and not a tax, and secondarily because by regulating production the act invaded the reserved powers of the states. (Four years earlier in ***Hammer* v. *Dagenhart*** [see Chapter Six], the Court invalidated a child labor law Congress had passed under its commerce power.)

Taxing, Spending, and the General Welfare. In 1935–1936, when taxation provisions of President Franklin Roosevelt's New Deal programs were tested, two lines of precedents were thus available. If the Court chose to sustain a measure under the taxing power, it could employ the generous principle of *McCray*. If, on the other hand, the Court chose to set aside the legislation, it could look on the tax—as Chief Justice Taft did in *Drexel Furniture*—as a "penalty," a form of "regulation," an invasion of domain reserved to the states.

One of FDR's campaign promises in 1932 was restoration of agricultural prosperity. The Agricultural Adjustment Act of 1933 levied a processing tax on basic commodities such as wheat, corn, and cotton. From the funds thus accumulated, money was paid out to farmers as "inducement" to reduce acreage. Popular with both farmers and their suppliers, it was a self-financing scheme to subsidize farmers as the protective tariff had long subsidized industry. And it was effective, transferring millions of dollars from the nonagricultural sector of the economy into farming.

Despite high expectations, the program became shrouded in doubt when the Supreme Court considered a challenge to the law in ***United States* v. *Butler***. Attacking the act's constitutionality at oral argument in the newly finished Supreme Court Building was Philadelphia's most eminent lawyer, George Wharton Pepper. Perfectly cast for the role, Pepper observed,

> I have tried very hard to argue this case calmly and dispassionately, because it seems to me that this is the best way in which an advocate can discharge his duty to this Court. But I do not want Your Honors to think my feelings are not involved and that my emotions are not deeply stirred. Indeed, may it please Your Honors, I believe I am standing here today to plead the cause of the America I have loved; and I pray Almighty God that not in my time may "the land of the regimented" be accepted as a worthy substitute for "the land of the free."

For Pepper, economic dogma, no less than congressional taxing power, was at stake.

The former senator's prayer was soon answered. Within a month, the Court announced its decision. According to Justice Owen J. Roberts, Pepper's former student at the University of Pennsylvania Law School, the processing tax could not be upheld as a tax. "The word has never been thought to connote the expropriation of money from one group for the benefit of another." If valid, the exaction could be supported only as an exercise of the disputed power to tax and spend for the general welfare. The Court was thus face to face with an unresolved issue dating from George Washington's first term.

Was the authorization in Section 8 of Article I to tax and spend in providing for the general welfare a substantive, independent power, as Alexander Hamilton maintained at the founding? Or was it no power at all, but rather an appendage of Congress' other enumerated powers, as Madison contended? Through many administrations, regardless of party, appropriations of money had been made to accomplish purposes not identified with those that Congress is authorized to promote under its other powers. Hamilton had upheld this view in his famous *Report on Manufactures* (1791), and Justice Roberts emphatically embraced it. Yet having just adopted the **Hamiltonian theory**, Roberts amazingly then proceeded to enforce, for all practical purposes, the narrow **Madisonian theory** he had just repudiated. Congress might appropriate money for an objective designated as the general welfare, but it could attach no terms or conditions to the use of funds so appropriated unless such terms or conditions were themselves authorized by another specific congressional grant. Federal money might be spent for the broad purposes outlined by Hamilton, but Congress could control the expenditure only if the objectives were within the narrow scope Madison gave the general welfare clause.

Probing congressional motives, Justice Roberts discovered that this was not a tax at all but payment of benefits to farmers to induce (or coerce) them into curtailing agricultural production. Congress, he said, had no power to regulate production. The tax was thus in effect an ingeniously disguised regulation, an invalid invasion of the reserved domain of the states. "It is an established principle," he concluded, "that the attainment of a prohibited end may not be accomplished under the pretext of the exertion of powers which are granted."

Having chosen to adopt a narrow construction of the taxing power in *Butler*, the Court reverted to the more generous rule of *McCray* two years later, when *Steward Machine Co.* v. *Davis* (1937) upheld the unemployment compensation component of the landmark Social Security Act of 1935. On the same day, seven justices upheld the payroll tax dedicated to funding benefits for the elderly against a challenge, among others, that it also contravened the Tenth Amendment. The discretion to define the general welfare, Cardozo wrote, "is not confided to the courts. The discretion belongs to Congress, unless the choice is clearly wrong, a display of arbitrary power, not an exercise of judgment" (*Helvering* v. *Davis*). Reflecting the "revolution" of 1937 discussed in Chapter Six, both opinions represented a significant shift in constitutional interpretation and in the Court's view of the federal system. The Court today is also prepared to uphold retroactive taxation as suggested by a low-threshold two-part test that emerged from *Carlton* v. *United States* (1994). The legislation must have (1) a rational legislative purpose and not be arbitrary and (2) a nonexcessive period of retroactivity. As the Court noted, "[t]ax legislation is not a promise, and a taxpayer has no vested right in the Internal Revenue Code."

REGULATION THROUGH SPENDING

In the years since the New Deal legislation of the 1930s, Congress has employed its spending power to achieve various policy objectives by allocating billions of dollars in grants to state and local governments, private organizations, and even individuals. These grants routinely come with a variety of conditions attached. Constitutional questions arise when Congress attempts through such **conditional spending** to accomplish indirectly what the Constitution might not allow it to do directly.

Alcohol. The 1980s witnessed efforts by Congress to cope with alcohol-related traffic accidents by imposing indirectly a national drinking age through conditional spending. The National Minimum Drinking Age Amendment of 1982 directed the secretary of transportation to withhold 5 percent of allotted federal highway funds from states with a legal drinking age under 21. Justice Roberts in *Butler* had relied on the Tenth Amendment to block indirect federal regulation of agriculture. Now South Dakota contended that the Twenty-First Amendment, which not only ended Prohibition but affirmed state control over the sale and use of alcoholic beverages, limited this new use of the spending power. ***South Dakota* v. *Dole*** (1987) rejected the state's claim. Although seven justices left open the question whether Congress could legislate a national drinking age directly, they had little doubt about its authority to do so by way of disbursement of funds. In her dissent, Justice O'Connor paid special attention to Roberts's reasoning in *Butler*. "The immense size and power of the Government of the United States ought not obscure its fundamental character. It remains a Government of enumerated powers."

In 2000, the drinking age decision was authority for congressional legislation directing each state to set a 0.08 percent blood-alcohol level to combat drunken driving. (At the time, 31 states used the less stringent limit of 0.1 percent.) States not complying by 2007 would lose 8 percent of their federal highway trust funds. By 2010, all states and the District of Columbia had adopted the 0.08 percent level.

Civil Liberties. What happens when conditional spending appears to collide with a protection in the Bill of Rights or the Fourteenth Amendment? An act of Congress declares that no federal funds can be spent in programs where abortion is part of family planning. In 1988, the Department of Health and Human Services issued regulations under the statute barring employees at clinics receiving federal funds from counseling pregnant women about the availability of abortion. *Rust* v. *Sullivan* (1991) upheld the gag rule against an attack on privacy and First Amendment free speech grounds.

National Endowment for the Arts v. *Finley* (1998) posed perhaps an equally difficult question. At issue were congressionally mandated standards for the National Endowment for the Arts in awarding grants. Aside from judging applicants by criteria of "artistic excellence and artistic merit," Congress directed the NEA to "tak[e] into consideration general standards of decency and respect for the diverse beliefs and values of the American public." The language on decency and beliefs had been added after public outcry over several NEA-funded exhibits. In a free speech challenge to the new standard, all members of the Court agreed that no one could be criminally punished for displaying "indecent" art, but in upholding the statute eight justices were less demanding when government acted not as regulator but as a patron, subsidizer, or consumer of art. Similarly, *Rumsfeld* v. *Forum for Academic and Institutional Rights, Inc.* (2006) sustained Congress' stipulation in the **Solomon Amendment** barring federal funds to institutions of higher education that denied equal access to military recruiters. The decision rejected a concerted action on First

Amendment grounds by an association of law schools that objected to Defense Department policy, later abolished in 2011, that discriminated against gays.

Congress' broad powers to spend continue to raise questions under the Constitution. For example, **Medicaid**, set up in 1965, is a health care program for people with low incomes that is jointly funded by the state and federal governments and administered by the states. In ***National Federation of Independent Business* v. *Sebelius*** (2012), discussed and reprinted in Chapter Six, a majority upheld the individual mandate component of the Affordable Care Act but invalidated the same statute's expansion of Medicaid as an improper use of the spending power because it coerced the states into an expansion of Medicaid at the risk of losing federal Medicaid funding entirely.

KEY TERMS

Articles of Confederation
direct taxes
indirect taxes
independent constitutional bar
regulatory taxation
enumerated powers
destructive tax
Hamiltonian theory
Madisonian theory
conditional spending
Solomon Amendment
Medicaid

QUERIES

1. In what way does *Hylton* v. *United States* anticipate Chapter Two's *Marbury* v. *Madison?*

2. Review the materials in Chapter Four discussing the revival of dual federalism in some recent Supreme Court decisions. In what way was dual federalism a factor in Justice Roberts's opinion in *United States* v. *Butler*?

3. How do you explain the Court's willingness to apply a judicial check to Congress' spending power in *National Federation of Independent Business* v. *Sebelius* but not in *South Dakota* v. *Dole*?

4. In evaluating Congress' powers under the spending clause, what difference does it make whether the Court prefers the Hamiltonian or Madisonian theory?

SELECTED READINGS

Corwin, Edward S. "The Spending Power of Congress." 36 *Harvard Law Review* 548, 1923.

Cummings, Jasper L., Jr. *The Supreme Court, Federal Taxation, and the Constitution*. Washington, DC: American Bar Association Section of Taxation, 2013.

Epstein, Richard A. "Foreword: Unconstitutional Conditions, State Power, and the Limits of Consent." 102 *Harvard Law Review* 4, 1988.

Lawson, James F. *The General Welfare Clause*. Washington, DC: J. F. Lawson, 1926.

McCoy, Thomas R., and Barry Friedman. "Conditional Spending: Federalism's Trojan Horse." 1988 *Supreme Court Review* 85, 1988.

Stanley, Robert. *Dimensions of Law in the Service of Order: Origins of the Federal Income Tax, 1861–1913*. New York: Oxford University Press, 1993.

I. DIRECT AND INDIRECT TAXES

Hylton v. *United States*
3 U.S. (3 Dall.) 171, 1 L.Ed. 556 (1796)

http://caselaw.findlaw.com/us-supreme-court/3/171.html

Daniel Hylton claimed that a congressional act of 1794 levying a tax of $16 on each carriage was a direct tax and must be laid in proportion to the census. With an ownership of 125 carriages, Hylton obtained review of an adverse judgment in the U.S. circuit court in Virginia. Majority: Chase, Iredell, Paterson, Wilson. Not participating: Ellsworth, Cushing.

CHASE, JUSTICE.

By the case stated, only one question is submitted to the opinion of this court—whether the law of Congress of the 5th of June 1794, entitled, "An act to lay duties upon carriages for the conveyance of persons," is unconstitutional and void?

The principles laid down, to prove the above law void, are these: that a tax on carriages is a direct tax, and, therefore, by the constitution, must be laid according to the census, directed by the constitution to be taken, to ascertain the number of representatives from each state. And that the tax in question on carriages is not laid by that rule of apportionment, but by the rule of uniformity, prescribed by the constitution in the case of duties, imposts and excises; and a tax on carriages is not within either of those descriptions. . . .

I think, an annual tax on carriages, for the conveyance of persons, may be considered as within the power granted to congress to lay duties. . . .

I am inclined to think but of this I do not give a judicial opinion, that the direct taxes contemplated by the constitution, are only two, to wit, a capitation or poll tax, simply, without regard to property, profession or any other circumstance; and a tax on land. I doubt, whether a tax, by a general assessment of personal property, within the United States, is included within the term direct tax. . . .

PATERSON, JUSTICE. . . .

I never entertained a doubt that the principal, I will not say, the only, objects, that the framers of the constitution contemplated, as falling within the rules of apportionment, were a capitation tax and a tax on land. Local considerations, and the particular circumstances, and relative situation of the states, naturally lead to this view of the subject. The provision was made in favor of the southern states; they possessed a large number of slaves; they had extensive tracts of territory, thinly settled, and not very productive. A majority of the states had but few slaves, and several of them a limited territory, well settled, and in a high state of cultivation. The southern states, if no provision had been introduced in the constitution, would have been wholly at the mercy of the other states. Congress in such case, might tax slaves, at discretion or arbitrarily, and land in every part of the Union, after the same rate or measure: so much a head in the first instance, and so much an acre, in the second. To guard them against imposition, in these particulars, was the reason of introducing the clause in the constitution, which directs that representatives and direct taxes shall be apportioned among the states, according to their respective numbers. . . .

IREDELL, JUSTICE. . . .

As all direct taxes must be apportioned, it is evident, that the constitution contemplated none as direct, but such as could be apportioned. If this cannot be apportioned, it is, therefore, not a direct tax in the sense of the constitution.

That this tax cannot be apportioned, is evident. Suppose, ten dollars contemplated as a tax on each chariot, or post chaise, in the United States, and the number of both in all the United States be computed at 105, the number of representatives in congress.

This would produce in the whole. . . . $1,050.00
The share of Virginia being 19/105 parts, would be. 190.00
The share of Connecticut being 7/105 parts, would be. 70.00
Then suppose Virginia had 50 carriages, Connecticut 2, The share of Virginia being $190, this must, of course, be collected from the owners of carriages, and there would, therefore, be collected from each carriage. 3.80
The share of Connecticut being $70, each carriage would pay. 35.00

If any state had no carriages, there could be no apportionment at all. This mode is too manifestly absurd to be supported, and has not even been attempted in debate. . . .

WILSON, JUSTICE. — . . . [omitted].

BY THE COURT. —Let the judgment of the circuit court be affirmed.

Pollock v. *Farmers' Loan & Trust Company* 158 U.S. 601, 15 S.Ct. 673, 39 L.Ed. 1108 (1895) (Rehearing)

http://caselaw.findlaw.com/us-supreme-court/158/601.html

In 1894, Congress imposed a tax of 2 percent on income above $4,000 derived from various classes of property, as well as that resulting from personal services. In the first decision (April 1895) involving the act, the Court, with Justice Howell Jackson absent, declared the act invalid insofar as it was applied to the income from real estate and the interest on municipal bonds. The Court was evenly divided on other questions presented. In May 1895, the Court decided the remaining questions on a rehearing after the terminally ill Jackson made a special trip to Washington. Jackson's vote to uphold the tax meant that one of the other justices changed sides. Majority: Fuller, Brewer, Field, Gray, Shiras. Dissenting: Harlan, Brown, Jackson, White.

MR. CHIEF JUSTICE FULLER delivered the opinion of the Court. . .

The Constitution divided Federal taxation into two great classes, the class of direct taxes and the class of duties, imposts, and excises, and prescribed two rules which qualified the grant of power as to each class.

The power to lay direct taxes, apportioned among the several States in proportion to their representation in the popular branch of Congress, a representation based on population as ascertained by the census, was plenary and absolute, but to lay direct taxes without apportionment was forbidden. The power to lay duties, imposts, and excises was subject to the qualification that the imposition must be uniform throughout the United States.

Our previous decision was confined to the consideration of the validity of the tax on the income from real estate, and on the income from municipal bonds. . . .

We are now permitted to broaden the field of inquiry, and determine to which of the two great classes a tax upon a person's entire income, whether derived from rents, or products, or otherwise, of real estate, or from bonds, stocks or other forms of personal property, belongs; and we are unable to conclude that the enforced subtraction from the yield of all the owner's real or personal property, in the manner prescribed, is so different from a tax upon the property itself, that it is not a direct, but an indirect tax. . . .

We know of no reason for holding otherwise than that the words "direct taxes" on the one hand, and "duties, imposts, and excises" on the other, were used in the Constitution in their natural and obvious sense, nor, in arriving at what those terms embrace, do we perceive any ground for enlarging them beyond, or narrowing them within, their natural and obvious import at the time the Constitution was framed and ratified. . . .

The reasons for the clauses of the Constitution in respect of direct taxation are not far to seek. The States, respectively, possessed plenary powers of taxation. . . . They retained the power of direct taxation, and to that they looked as their chief resource; but even in respect of that, they granted the concurrent power, and if the tax were placed by both governments on the same subject, the claim of the United States had preference. Therefore, they did not grant the power of direct taxation without regard to their own condition and resources as States; but they granted the power of apportioned direct taxation, a power just as efficacious to serve the needs of the general government, but securing to the States the opportunity to pay the amount apportioned, and to recoup from their own citizens in the most feasible way, and in harmony with their systems of local self-government. . . .

It is said that a tax on the whole income of property is not a direct tax in the meaning of the Constitution, but a duty, and, as a duty, leviable without apportionment, whether direct or indirect. We do not think so. Direct taxation was not restricted in one breath, and the restriction blown to the winds in another. . . .

Whatever the speculative views of political economists or revenue reformers may be, can it be properly held that the Constitution, taken in its plain and obvious sense, and with due regard to the circumstances attending the formation of the government, authorizes a general unapportioned tax on the products of the farm and the rents of real estate, although imposed merely because of ownership and with no possible means of escape from payment, as belonging to a totally different class from that which includes the property from which the income proceeds?

There can be only one answer, unless the constitutional restriction is to be treated as utterly illusory and futile, and the object of its framers defeated. We find it impossible to hold that a fundamental requisition, deemed so important as to be enforced by two provisions, one affirmative and one negative, can be refined away by forced distinctions between that which gives value to property and the property itself.

Nor can we perceive any ground why the same reasoning does not apply to capital in personalty held for the purpose of income or ordinarily yielding income, and to the income therefrom. All the real estate of the country, and all its invested personal property, are open to the direct operation of the taxing power if an apportionment be made according to the Constitution. The Constitution does not say that no direct tax shall be laid by apportionment on any other property than land; on the contrary, it forbids all unapportioned direct taxes; and we know of no warrant for excepting personal property from the exercise of the power, or any reason why an apportioned direct tax cannot be laid and assessed. . . .

We have considered the act only in respect of the tax on income derived from real estate, and from invested personal property, and have not commented on so much of it as bears on gains or profits from business, privileges, or employments, in view of the instances in which taxation on business, privileges, or employments has assumed the guise of an excise tax and been sustained as such.

Being of opinion that so much of the sections of this law as lays a tax on income from real and personal property is invalid, we are brought to the question of the effect of that conclusion upon these sections as a whole.

It is elementary that the same statute may be in part constitutional and in part unconstitutional, and if the parts are wholly independent of each other, that which is constitutional may stand while that which is unconstitutional will be rejected. And in the case before us there is no question as to validity of this act, except sections 27–37 inclusive, which relate to the subject which has been under discussion; and as to them we think that . . . if the different parts "are so mutually connected with and dependent on each other, as conditions, considerations or compensations for each other, as to warrant the belief that the legislature intended them as a whole, and that, if all could not be carried into effect, the legislature would not pass the residue independently, and some parts are unconstitutional, all the provisions which are thus dependent, conditional or connected, must fall with them." . . .

Our conclusions may, therefore, be summed up as follows:

First. We adhere to the opinion already announced, that, taxes on real estate being indisputably direct taxes, taxes on the rents or incomes of real estate are equally direct taxes.

Second. We are of opinion that taxes on personal property, or on the income of personal property, are likewise direct taxes.

Third. The tax imposed by sections 27–37, inclusive, of the act of 1894, so far as it falls on the income of real estate and of personal property, being a direct tax within the meaning of the Constitution, and, therefore, unconstitutional and void because not apportioned according to representation, all those sections, constituting one entire scheme of taxation, are necessarily invalid.

Mr. Justice Harlan dissenting. . . .

In my judgment—to say nothing of the disregard of the former adjudications of this court, and of the settled practice of the government this decision may well excite the gravest apprehensions. It strikes at the very foundations of national authority, in that it denies to the general government a power which is, or may become, vital to the very existence and preservation of the Union in a national emergency, such as that of war with a great commercial nation, during which the collection of all duties upon imports will cease or be materially diminished. It tends to reestablish that condition of helplessness in which Congress found itself during the period of the Articles of Confederation, when it was without authority by laws operating directly upon individuals, to lay and collect, through its own agents, taxes sufficient to pay the debts and defray the expenses of government, but was dependent, in all such matters, upon the good will of the States, and their promptness in meeting requisitions made upon them by Congress.

Why do I say that the decision just rendered impairs or menaces the national authority? The reason is so apparent that it need only be stated. In its practical operation this decision withdraws from national taxation not only all incomes derived from real estate, but tangible personal property, *invested* personal property, bonds, stocks, investments of all kinds, and the income that may be derived from such property. This results from the fact that by the decision of the court, all such personal property and all incomes from real estate and personal property are placed beyond national taxation otherwise than by *apportionment* among the States *on the basis* simply *of population*. No such apportionment can possibly be made without doing gross injustice to the many for the benefit of the favored few in particular States. Any attempt upon the part of Congress to apportion among the States, upon the basis simply of their population, taxation of personal property or of incomes, would tend to arouse such indignation among the freemen of America that it would never be repeated. When therefore, this court adjudges, as it does now adjudge, that Congress cannot impose a duty or tax upon personal property, or upon income arising either from rents of real estate or from personal property, including invested personal property, bonds, stocks, and investments of all kinds, except by apportioning the sum to be so raised among the States according to population, it *practically* decides that, *without an amendment of the Constitution* . . . such property and incomes can never be made to contribute to the support of the national government. . . .

MR. JUSTICE BROWN, dissenting . . . [omitted].

MR. JUSTICE JACKSON, dissenting . . . [omitted].

MR. JUSTICE WHITE dissenting. . . .

[The decision] takes invested wealth and reads it into the Constitution as a favored and protected class of property, which cannot be taxed without apportionment, whilst it leaves the occupation of the minister, the doctor, the professor, the lawyer, . . . the merchant, the mechanic, and all other forms of industry upon which the prosperity of a people must depend, subject to taxation without that condition. A rule which works out this result, which . . . stultifies the Constitution by making it an instrument of the most grievous wrong, should not be adopted, especially when, in order to do so, the decisions of this court, the opinions of the law writers and publicists, tradition, practice, and the settled policy of the government must be overthrown. . . .

II. REGULATION THROUGH TAXATION

McCray v. *United States*
195 U.S. 27, 24 S.Ct. 769, 49 L.Ed. 78 (1904)

http://caselaw.findlaw.com/us-supreme-court/195/27.html

The Oleomargarine Act, passed by Congress in 1886 and amended in 1902, levied a tax of one-quarter cent per pound on uncolored oleomargarine and ten cents per pound on oleomargarine colored yellow. (The tax was not removed until 1950.) McCray, a licensed dealer, failed to pay the higher tax in making sales of the colored product and was fined. Majority: White, Brewer, Day, Harlan, Holmes, McKenna. Dissenting: Fuller, Brown, Peckham.

MR. JUSTICE WHITE . . . delivered the opinion of the court. . . .

That the acts in question on their face impose excise taxes which Congress had the power to levy is so completely established as to require only statement. . . .

It is, however, argued if a lawful power may be exerted for an unlawful purpose, and thus by abusing the power it may be made to accomplish a result not intended by the Constitution, all limitations of power must disappear, and the grave function lodged in the judiciary, to confine all the departments within the authority conferred by the Constitution, will be of no avail. This, when reduced to its last analysis, comes to this, that, because a particular department of the government may exert its lawful powers with the object or motive of reaching an end not justified, therefore it becomes the duty of the judiciary to restrain the exercise of a lawful power wherever it seems to the judicial mind that such lawful power has been abused. But this reduces itself to the contention that, under our constitutional system, the abuse by one department of the government of its lawful powers is to be corrected by the abuse of its powers by another department. . . .

It is, of course, true, as suggested, that if there be no authority in the judiciary to restrain a lawful exercise of power by another department of the government, where a wrong motive or purpose has impelled to the exertion of the power, that abuses of a power conferred may be temporarily effectual. The remedy for this, however, lies, not in the abuse by the judicial authority of its functions, but in the people, upon whom, after all, under our institutions, reliance must be placed for the correction of abuses committed in the exercise of a lawful power. . . .

It being thus demonstrated that the motive or purpose of Congress in adopting the acts in question may not be inquired into, we are brought to consider the contentions relied upon to show that the acts assailed were beyond the power of Congress, putting entirely out of view all considerations based upon purpose or motive. . . .

Since . . . the taxing power conferred by the Constitution knows no limits except those expressly stated in that instrument, it must follow, if a tax be within the lawful power, the exertion of that power may not be judicially restrained because of the results to arise from its exercise. . . .

Whilst undoubtedly both the Fifth and Tenth Amendments qualify, insofar as they are applicable, all the provisions of the Constitution, nothing in those amendments operates to take away the grant of power to tax conferred by the Constitution upon Congress. The contention on this subject rests upon the theory that the purpose and motive of Congress in exercising its undoubted powers may be inquired into by the courts, and the proposition is therefore disposed of by what has been said on that subject.

The right of Congress to tax within its delegated powers being unrestrained, except as limited by the Constitution, it was within the authority conferred on Congress to select the objects upon which an excise should be laid. It therefore follows that, in exerting its power, no want of due process of law could possibly result, because that body chose to impose an excise on artificially colored oleomargarine and not upon natural butter artificially colored. The judicial power may not usurp the functions of the legislative in order to control that branch of the government in the performance of its lawful duties. . . .

Let us concede that if a case was presented where the abuse of the taxing power was so extreme as to be beyond the principles which we have previously stated, and where it was plain to the judicial mind that the power had been called into play not for revenue but solely for the purpose of destroying rights which could not be rightfully destroyed consistently with the principles of freedom and justice upon which the Constitution rests, that it would be the duty of the courts to say that such an arbitrary act was not merely an abuse of a delegated power, but was the exercise of an authority not conferred. This concession, however, like the one previously made, must be without influence upon the decision of this case for the reasons previously stated: that is, that the manufacture of artificially colored oleomargarine may be prohibited by a free government without a violation of fundamental rights.

Affirmed.

The Chief Justice, Mr. Justice Brown, and Mr. Justice Peckham dissent [without opinion].

Bailey v. *Drexel Furniture Co.* (Child Labor Tax Case) 259 U.S. 20, 42 S.Ct. 449, 66 L.Ed. 817 (1922)

http://caselaw.findlaw.com/us-supreme-court/259/20.html

In the Revenue Act of 1919, Congress imposed a tax on mine and quarry employers of children under 16, and factory employers of children under 14, or who permitted children between 14 and 16 to work more than an eight-hour day and a six-day week. Drexel Furniture Co. which had employed a boy under 14, paid the tax under protest and sued to recover the amount paid. The U.S. District Court for the Western District of North Carolina sustained the company, and J. W. Bailey, collector of internal revenue appealed. Majority: Taft, Brandeis, Butler, Holmes, McKenna, McReynolds, Pitney, Van Devanter. Dissenting: Clarke.

Mr. Chief Justice Taft delivered the opinion of the Court.

This case presents the question of the constitutional validity of the Child Labor Tax Law. . . .

The law is attacked on the ground that it is a regulation of the employment of child labor in the states—an exclusively state function under the federal Constitution and within the reservations of the Tenth Amendment. It is defended on the ground that it is a mere excise tax levied by the Congress of the United States under its broad power of taxation conferred by section 8, article 1, of the federal Constitution. . . . Does this law impose a tax with only that incidental restraint and regulation which a tax must inevitably involve? Or does it regulate by the use of the so-called tax as a penalty? If a tax, it is clearly an excise. If it were an excise on a commodity or other thing of value, we might not be permitted under previous decisions of this court to infer solely from its heavy burden that the act intends a prohibition instead of a tax. But this act is more. It provides a heavy exaction for a departure from a detailed and specified course of conduct in business. . . . If an employer departs from this prescribed course of business, he is to pay to the government one-tenth of his entire net income in the business for a full year. . . . In the light of these features of the act, a court must be blind not to see that the so-called tax is imposed to stop the employment of children within the age limits prescribed. Its prohibitory and regulatory effect and purpose are palpable. All others can see and understand this. How can we properly shut our minds to it? . . .

The good sought in unconstitutional legislation is an insidious feature, because it leads citizens and legislators of good purpose to promote it, without thought of the serious breach it will make in the ark of our covenant, or the harm which will come from breaking down recognized standards. In the maintenance of local self-government, on the one hand, and the national power, on the other, our country has been able to endure and prosper for near a century and a half.

Out of a proper respect for the acts of a coordinate branch of the government, this court has gone far to sustain taxing acts as such, even though there has been ground for suspecting, from the weight of the tax, it was intended to destroy its subject. But in the act before us the presumption of validity cannot prevail, because the proof of the contrary is found on the very face of its provisions. Grant the validity of this law, and all that Congress would need to do, hereafter, in seeking to take over to its control any one of the great number of subjects of public interest, jurisdiction of which the states have never parted with, and which are reserved to them by the Tenth Amendment, would be to enact a detailed measure of complete regulation of the subject and enforce it by a so-called tax upon departures from it. To give such magic to the word "tax" would be to break down all constitutional limitation of the powers of Congress and completely wipe out the sovereignty of the states.

The difference between a tax and a penalty is sometimes difficult to define, and yet the consequences of the distinction in the required method of their collection often are important. Where the sovereign enacting the law has power to impose both tax and penalty, the difference between revenue production and mere regulation may be immaterial, but not so when one sovereign can impose a tax only, and the power of regulation rests in another. Taxes are occasionally imposed in the discretion of the Legislature on proper subjects with the primary motive of obtaining revenue from them and with the incidental motive of discouraging them by making their continuance onerous. They do not lose their character as taxes because of the incidental motive. But there comes a time in the extension of the penalizing features of the so-called tax when it loses its character as such and becomes a mere penalty, with the characteristics of regulation and punishment. Such is the case in the law before us. Although Congress does not invalidate the contract of employment or expressly declare that the employment within the mentioned ages is illegal, it does exhibit its intent practically to achieve the latter result by adopting the criteria of wrongdoing and imposing its principal consequence on those who transgress its standard. The case before us cannot be distinguished from that of *Hammer* v. *Dagenhart*. Congress there enacted a law to prohibit transportation in interstate commerce of goods made at a factory in which there was employment of children within the same ages and for the same number of hours a day and days in a week as are penalized by the act in this case. . . .

In the case at the bar, Congress in the name of a tax which on the face of the act is penalty seeks to do the same thing, and the effort must be equally futile. . . .

But it is pressed upon us that this court has gone so far in sustaining taxing measures the effect and tendency of which was to accomplish purposes not directly within congressional power that we are bound by authority to maintain this law. . . .

In [none] of these cases did the law objected to show on its face as does the law before us the detailed specifications of a regulation of a state concern and business with a heavy exaction to promote the efficacy of such regulation. . . . For the reasons given, we must hold the Child Labor Tax Law invalid and the judgment of the District Court is

Affirmed.

MR. JUSTICE CLARKE dissents [without opinion].

III. REGULATION THROUGH SPENDING

United States v. *Butler*
297 U.S. 1, 56 S.Ct. 312, 80 L.Ed. 477 (1936)

http://caselaw.findlaw.com/us-supreme-court/297/1.html

As part of President Roosevelt's New Deal, Congress enacted the Agricultural Adjustment Act in 1933 to benefit farm producers by raising commodity prices and assuring farmers purchasing power comparable to their position in 1909–1914.

In order to bring supply in line with demand, the government made payments to farmers in return for their promise to reduce crop acreage. To finance the program, a processing tax was levied on the first processor of the commodity involved. In the first year of the program, more than 40 million acres were taken out of cultivation, and payments to farmers totaled several hundred million dollars. Butler, the receiver for a processor, refused to pay the tax. The district court ordered it paid, but the court of appeals reversed. With *Carter* v. *Carter Coal Co.*, decided two months later, this decision helped to precipitate the Court-packing fight of 1937 (see Chapter Six). Majority: Roberts, Butler, Hughes, McReynolds, Sutherland, Van Devanter. Dissenting: Stone, Brandeis, Cardozo.

Mr. Justice Roberts delivered the opinion of the Court. . . .

There should be no misunderstanding as to the function of this court in such a case. It is sometimes said that the court assumes a power to overrule or control the action of the people's representatives. This is a misconception. . . . When an act of Congress is appropriately challenged in the courts as not conforming to the constitutional mandate, the judicial branch of the Government has only one duty—to lay the article of the Constitution which is invoked beside the statute which is challenged and to decide whether the latter squares with the former. All the court does, or can do, is to announce its considered judgment upon the question. The only power it has, if such it may be called, is the power of judgment. This court neither approves nor condemns any legislative policy. Its delicate and difficult office is to ascertain and declare whether the legislation is in accordance with, or in contravention of, the provisions of the Constitution; and having done that, its duty ends. . . .

The clause thought to authorize the legislation . . . confers upon the Congress power "to lay and collect Taxes, Duties, Imposts and Excises, to pay the Debts and provide for the common Defense and general Welfare of the United States. . . ." It is not contended that this provision grants power to regulate agricultural production upon the theory that such legislation would promote the general welfare. The government concedes that the phrase "to provide for the general welfare" qualifies the power "to lay and collect taxes." The view that the clause grants power to provide for the general welfare, independently of the taxing power, has never been authoritatively accepted. Mr. Justice Story points out that, if it were adopted, "it is obvious that under color of the generality of the words, to 'provide for the common defence and general welfare,' the government of the United States is, in reality, a government of general and unlimited powers, notwithstanding the subsequent enumeration of specific powers." The true construction undoubtedly is that the only thing granted is the power to tax for the purpose of providing funds for payment for the nation's debts and making provision for the general welfare.

Nevertheless, the Government asserts that warrant is found in this clause for the adoption of the Agricultural Adjustment Act. The argument is that Congress may appropriate and authorize the spending of moneys for the "general welfare"; that the phrase should be liberally construed to cover anything conducive to national welfare; that decision as to what will promote such welfare rests with Congress alone, and the courts may not review its determination; and, finally, that the appropriation under attack was in fact for the general welfare of the United States.

The Congress is expressly empowered to lay taxes to provide for the general welfare. . . .

Since the foundation of the nation, sharp differences of opinion have persisted as to the true interpretation of the phrase. Madison asserted it amounted to no more than a reference to the other powers enumerated in the subsequent clauses of the same section; that, as the United States is a government of limited and enumerated powers, the grant of power to tax and spend for the general national welfare must be confined to the enumerated legislative fields committed to the Congress. In this view the phrase is mere tautology, for taxation and appropriation are or may be necessary incidents of the exercise of any of the enumerated legislative powers. Hamilton, on the other hand, maintained the clause confers a power separate and distinct from those later enumerated, is not restricted in meaning by the grant of them, and Congress consequently has a substantive power to tax and to appropriate, limited only by the requirement that it shall be exercised to provide for the general welfare of the United States. Each contention has had the support of those whose views are entitled to weight. This court has noticed the question, but has never found it necessary to decide which is the true construction. Mr. Justice Story, in his Commentaries, espouses the Hamiltonian position. We shall not review the writings of public men and commentators or discuss the legislative practice. Study of all these leads us to conclude that the reading advocated by Mr. Justice Story is the correct one. While, therefore, the power to tax is not unlimited, its confines are set in the clause which confers it and not in those of Section 8 which bestow and define the legislative powers of the Congress. It results that the power of Congress to authorize expenditure of public moneys for public purposes is not limited by the direct grants of legislative power found in the Constitution.

But the adoption of the broader construction leaves the power to spend subject to limitations. . . .

Story says that if the tax be not proposed for the common defence or general welfare, but for other objects wholly extraneous, it would be wholly indefensible upon constitutional principles. And he makes it clear that the powers of taxation and appropriation extend only to matters of national, as distinguished from local welfare. . . .

We are not now required to ascertain the scope of the phrase "general welfare of the United States" or to determine whether an appropriation in aid of agriculture falls within it. Wholly apart from that question, another principle embedded in our Constitution prohibits the enforcement of the Agricultural Adjustment Act. The act invades the reserved rights of the states. It is a statutory plan to regulate and control agricultural production, a matter beyond the powers delegated to the federal government. The tax, the appropriation of the funds raised, and the direction for their disbursement, are but parts of the plan. They are but means to an unconstitutional end.

From the accepted doctrine that the United States is a government of delegated powers, it follows that those not expressly granted, or reasonably to be implied from such as are conferred, are reserved to the states or to the people. To forestall any suggestion to the contrary, the Tenth Amendment was adopted. The same proposition, otherwise stated, is that powers not granted are prohibited. None to regulate agricultural production is given, and therefore legislation by Congress for that purpose is forbidden. . . .

If the act before us is a proper exercise of the federal taxing power, evidently the regulation of all industry throughout the United States may be accomplished by similar exercises of the same power. . . .

Until recently no suggestion of the existence of any such power in the federal government has been advanced. The expressions of the framers of the Constitution, the decisions of this court interpreting that instrument and the writings of great commentators will be searched in vain for any suggestion that there exists in the clause under discussion or elsewhere in the Constitution, the authority whereby every provision and every fair implication from that instrument may be subverted, the independence of the individual states obliterated, and the United States converted into a central government exercising uncontrolled police power in every state of the Union, superseding all local control or regulation of the affairs or concerns of the states. . . .

Affirmed.

MR. JUSTICE STONE, dissenting. . . .

The power of courts to declare a statute unconstitutional is subject to two guiding principles of decision which ought never to be absent from judicial consciousness. One is that courts are concerned only with the power to enact statutes, not with their wisdom. The other is that while unconstitutional exercise of power by the executive and legislative branches of the government is subject to judicial restraint, the only check upon our own exercise of power is our own sense of self-restraint. For the removal of unwise laws from the statute books appeal lies not to the courts but to the ballot and to the processes of democratic government. . . .

The spending power of Congress is in addition to the legislative power and not subordinate to it. This independent grant of the power of the purse, and its very nature, involving in its exercise the duty to insure expenditure within the granted power presuppose freedom of selection among diverse ends and aims, and the capacity to impose such conditions as will render the choice effective. It is a contradiction in terms to say that there is power to spend for the national welfare, while rejecting any power to impose conditions reasonably adapted to the attainment of the end which alone would justify the expenditure.

The limitation now sanctioned must lead to absurd consequences. The government may give seeds to farmers, but may not condition the gift upon their being planted in places where they are most needed or even planted at all. . . . It may give money to sufferers from earthquake, fire, tornado, pestilence or flood, but may not impose conditions—health precautions designed to prevent the spread of disease, or induce the movement of population to safer or more sanitary areas. All that, because it is purchased regulation infringing state powers, must be left for the states, who are unable or unwilling to supply the necessary relief. . . .

A tortured construction of the Constitution is not to be justified by recourse to extreme examples of reckless congressional spending which might occur if courts could not prevent expenditures which, even if they could be thought to effect any national purpose, would be possible only by action of a legislature lost to all sense of public responsibility. Such suppositions are addressed to the mind accustomed to believe that it is the business of courts to sit in judgment on the wisdom of legislative action. Courts are not the only agency of government that must be assumed to have capacity to govern.

MR. JUSTICE BRANDEIS and MR. JUSTICE CARDOZO joined in this opinion.

South Dakota v. *Dole*
483 U.S. 203, 107 S.Ct. 2793, 97 L.Ed. 2d 171 (1987)

http://caselaw.findlaw.com/us-supreme-court/483/203.html

In 1984, Congress enacted the National Minimum Drinking Age Amendment, referred to in the following opinions as § 158. It directed the Department of Transportation to withhold 5 percent of federal highway funds from states "in which the purchase or public possession of any alcoholic beverage by a person who is less than twenty-one years of age is lawful." At the time South Dakota permitted persons 19 years of age or older to purchase beer containing 3.2 percent alcohol. The state sued Transportation Secretary Elizabeth Dole in U.S. district court, asserting that the law exceeded Congress' spending power and that it violated the Twenty-First Amendment. The district court rejected South Dakota's claims, and the Court of Appeals for the Eighth Circuit affirmed. Majority: Rehnquist, Blackmun, Marshall, Powell, Scalia, Stevens, White. Dissenting: Brennan, O'Connor.

Chief Justice Rehnquist delivered the opinion of the Court. . . .

Despite the extended treatment of the question by the parties . . . we need not decide in this case whether [the Twenty-first] Amendment would prohibit an attempt by Congress to legislate directly a national minimum drinking age. Here, Congress has acted indirectly under its spending power to encourage uniformity in the States' drinking ages. As we explain below, we find this legislative effort within constitutional bounds even if Congress may not regulate drinking ages directly. . . .

The spending power is of course not unlimited, but is instead subject to several general restrictions articulated in our cases. The first of these limitations is derived from the language of the Constitution itself: the exercise of the spending power must be in pursuit of "the general welfare." In considering whether a particular expenditure is intended to serve general public purposes, courts should defer substantially to the judgment of Congress. Second, we have required that if Congress desires to condition the States' receipt of federal funds, it "must do so unambiguously . . . enabl[ing] the States to exercise their choice knowingly, cognizant of the consequences of their participation." Third, our cases have suggested (without significant elaboration) that conditions on federal grants might be illegitimate if they are unrelated "to the federal interest in particular national projects or programs." . . . Finally, we have noted that other constitutional provisions may provide an independent bar to the conditional grant of federal funds. . . .

South Dakota does not seriously claim that § 158 is inconsistent with any of the first three restrictions mentioned above.

[T]he basic point of disagreement between the parties—is whether the Twenty-first Amendment constitutes an "independent constitutional bar" to the conditional grant of federal funds. Petitioner, relying on its view that the Twenty-first Amendment prohibits direct regulation of drinking ages by Congress, asserts that "Congress may not use the spending power to regulate that which it is prohibited from regulating directly under the Twenty-first Amendment." But our cases show that this "independent constitutional bar" limitation on the spending power is not of the kind petitioner suggests. *United States* v. *Butler*, for example, established that the constitutional limitations on Congress when exercising its spending power are less exacting than those on its authority to regulate directly.

We have also held that a perceived Tenth Amendment limitation on congressional regulation of state affairs did not concomitantly limit the range of conditions legitimately placed on federal grants. . . .

These cases establish that the "independent constitutional bar" limitation on the spending power is not, as petitioner suggests, a prohibition on the indirect achievement of objectives which Congress is not empowered to achieve directly. Instead, we think that the language in our earlier opinions stands for the unexceptionable proposition that the power may not be used to induce the States to engage in activities that would themselves be unconstitutional. . . . But no such claim can be or is made here. Were

South Dakota to succumb to the blandishments offered by Congress and raise its drinking age to 21, the State's action in so doing would not violate the constitutional rights of anyone.

Our decisions have recognized that in some circumstances the financial inducement offered by Congress might be so coercive as to pass the point at which "pressure turns into compulsion." Here, however, Congress has directed only that a State desiring to establish a minimum drinking age lower than 21 lose a relatively small percentage of certain federal highway funds. Petitioner contends that the coercive nature of this program is evident from the degree of success it has achieved. We cannot conclude, however, that a conditional grant of federal money of this sort is unconstitutional simply by reason of its success in achieving the congressional objective.

When we consider, for a moment, that all South Dakota would lose if she adheres to her chosen course as to a suitable minimum drinking age is 5 percent of the funds otherwise obtainable under specified highway grant programs, the argument as to coercion is shown to be more rhetoric than fact. . . .

Accordingly, the judgment of the Court of Appeals is

Affirmed.

JUSTICE BRENNAN, dissenting . . . [omitted].

JUSTICE O'CONNOR, dissenting. . . .

[T]he Court's application of the requirement that the condition imposed be reasonably related to the purpose for which the funds are expended, is cursory and unconvincing. We have repeatedly said that Congress may condition grants under the Spending Power only in ways reasonably related to the purpose of the federal program. . . .

[T]he Court asserts the reasonableness of the relationship between the supposed purpose of the expenditure—"safe interstate travel"—and the drinking age condition. The Court reasons that Congress wishes that the roads it builds may be used safely, that drunk drivers threaten highway safety, and that young people are more likely to drive while under the influence of alcohol under existing law than would be the case if there were a uniform national drinking age of 21. It hardly needs saying, however, that if the purpose of § 158 is to deter drunken driving, it is far too over- and under-inclusive. It is over-inclusive because it stops teenagers from drinking even when they are not about to drive on interstate highways. It is under-inclusive because teenagers pose only a small part of the drunken driving problem in this Nation. . . .

There is a clear place at which the Court can draw the line between permissible and impermissible conditions on federal grants. It is the line identified in the Brief for the National Conference of State Legislatures as *Amici Curiae:*

> Congress has the power to *spend* for the general welfare, it has the power to *legislate* only for delegated purposes. . . .
>
> The appropriate inquiry, then, is whether the spending requirement or prohibition is a condition on a grant or whether it is regulation. The difference turns on whether the requirement specifies in some way how the money should be spent, so that Congress' intent in making the grant will be effectuated. Congress has no power under the Spending Clause to impose requirements on a grant that go beyond specifying how the money should be spent. A requirement that is not such a specification is not a condition, but a regulation, which is valid only if it falls within one of Congress' delegated regulatory powers.

This approach harks back to *United States* v. *Butler*, the last case in which this Court struck down an Act of Congress as beyond the authority granted by the Spending Clause. There the Court wrote that "[t]here is an obvious difference between a statute stating the conditions upon which moneys shall be expended and one effective only upon assumption of a contractual obligation to submit to a regulation which otherwise could not be enforced." The Butler Court saw the Agricultural Adjustment Act for what it was—an exercise of regulatory, not spending, power. The error in *Butler* was not the Court's conclusion that the Act was essentially regulatory, but rather its crabbed view of the extent of Congress' regulatory power under the Commerce Clause. . . .

While *Butler's* authority is questionable insofar as it assumes that Congress has no regulatory power over farm production, its discussion of the Spending Power and its description of both the power's breadth and its limitations remains sound. The Court's decision in *Butler* also properly recognizes the gravity of the task of appropriately limiting the Spending Power. If the Spending Power is to be limited only by Congress' notion of the general welfare, the reality, given the vast financial resources of the Federal Government, is that the Spending Clause gives "power to the Congress to tear down the barriers, to invade the states' jurisdiction, and to become a parliament of the whole people, subject to no restrictions save such as are self-imposed." This, of course, as *Butler* held, was not the Framers' plan and it is not the meaning of the Spending Clause. . . .

The immense size and power of the Government of the United States ought not obscure its fundamental character. It remains a Government of enumerated powers. . . .

National Federation of Independent Business v. *Sebelius* 567 U.S. 519, 132 S.Ct. 2566, 183 L.Ed. 2d 450 (2012)

http://caselaw.findlaw.com/us-supreme-court/11-393.html

(This case is reprinted in Chapter Six; see the Table of Contents.)

8

Property Rights and the Development of Due Process

That government can scarcely be deemed to be free where the rights of property are left solely dependent upon the will of a legislative body without any restraint. The fundamental maxims of a free government seem to require that the rights of personal liberty and private property should be sacred.

—Justice Joseph Story (1829)

Chapters Six and Seven were concerned partly with national power—the power of Congress to regulate commerce and to tax and spend. Out of the Court's interpretation of national power emerged one of the first great antinomies of constitutional law—national supremacy versus dual federalism. By 1937, the Court had largely resolved that conflict in favor of national power.

This chapter features another major **antinomy**, or conflict between doctrines—**vested rights** versus state **police power**. The first emphasizes the sanctity of private property and demands that legislation not unduly or unreasonably restrict rights of ownership. The second includes the authority states retain to promote health, safety, and the general welfare. In *Brown* v. *Maryland* (1827), Chief Justice Marshall spoke of the police power as *residual*, comprising what remained of a state's authority beyond the other great prerogatives of eminent domain and taxation. Insistence on vested rights at the expense of the police power eventually pushed the Court in the 1930s to a radical restatement of its role. The chapter concludes with a review of that shift, Fifth Amendment "takings," and the "new property."

Prominent throughout is the ongoing debate about the proper adjustment of competing claims involving the police power, individual rights, and the constitutional limitations on that power. As much as in any other area of constitutional law, this debate reflects not just opposing views on what the proper adjustment should be but opposing views on the Court's place in the political system. So, the chapter displays a debate over judicial review itself, anticipating the later controversy over abortion and the Court's development of a constitutional right of privacy (see Chapter Thirteen).

DOI: 10.4324/9781003164340-9

THE DOCTRINE OF VESTED RIGHTS

The struggle between vested rights and police power is a variant of the earlier conflict between theories of natural rights, on the one hand, and the principle of legislative supremacy, on the other. On this side of the Atlantic, these two doctrines represent the reaction on each other of the prerevolutionary contest between the natural rights of the colonists and parliamentary supremacy. The same phenomenon was manifest after 1776 in the efforts by state legislative majorities to regulate the property and contract rights of individual citizens.

Of the two doctrines, that of vested rights is of earlier origin, being rooted in the notion that property is the basic social institution—the guardian of every other right. The term connotes a way of thinking that emphasizes protection of a person's property from interference by other individuals or even by the government except under specified conditions. Antedating civil society itself, property fixes the limits within which even supreme legislative authority may properly operate. Indeed, the main function of government, its raison d'être, is to protect property. "The right of acquiring and possessing property and having it protected," Justice Paterson wrote in an early circuit court opinion, "is one of the natural inherent and unalienable rights of man. Men have a sense of property: Property is necessary to their subsistence, and correspondent to their natural wants and desires; its security was one of the objects that induced them to unite in society. No man would become a member of a community in which he could not enjoy the fruits of his honest labor and industry. The preservation of property, then, is a primary object of the social compact" (*Vanhorne's Lessee* v. *Dorrance*, 1795).

At the Convention. Among the major causes of the federal Convention of 1787 was the claimed injustice of state laws concerning property, calling into question a fundamental principle of republican government: That the majority could be trusted to safeguard both the public good and private rights. That point was illustrated by the colloquy that occurred in the early days of the Philadelphia Convention between Roger Sherman of Connecticut and James Madison of Virginia. Sherman enumerated the objects of the Convention as defense against foreign danger and internal disputes and the need for a central authority to make treaties with foreign nations and to regulate foreign commerce. Madison agreed that these objects were important but insisted on combining with them "the necessity of providing more effectually for the security of private rights and the steady dispensation of justice within the states." "Interferences with these," Madison added, "were evils which had, more perhaps than anything else, produced this convention."

What Madison had in mind was state legislation on behalf of the debt-burdened but politically dominant small-farmer class, led by such rabble-rousers as Daniel Shays in Massachusetts. They sought special legislation to alter the legal rights of designated parties; intervention by state legislatures in private controversies pending in or already decided by the courts; and legislation setting aside judgments, granting new hearings, voiding valid wills, or validating void wills. Those who wished to see the menace of special legislation and state legislative supremacy abated and those who felt the need for outside protection of the rights of property and of contract naturally supported the movement afoot for a constitutional convention.

But how were the framers to secure such protection? Various measures were proposed, but every motion looking to the imposition of a property qualification for suffrage or office holding failed. The suggestion that the Senate be organized to shield property was also defeated. Even the difficult and delicate matter of suffrage was ultimately left to the states. As the Constitution came from the hands of the framers, it contained only one brief clause that might afford vested rights protection against state legislative majorities—Article I, Section 10: "No State shall . . . pass any . . . ex post facto law or laws impairing the obligation of contracts. . . ."

The Court's Response. When it was construed in ***Calder* v. *Bull***, even this clause was given a very narrow construction. Confining the application of **ex post facto laws** to retroactive penal legislation, the Court held that it was not "inserted to secure the citizen in his private rights of either property or contracts," thus creating a wide breach in the constitutional protection afforded civil rights. Justice Chase seemed nearly apologetic, suggesting that legislation adversely affecting vested rights might be set aside as violation of natural law. "There are certain vital principles," Chase observed, "in our free republican governments which will determine and overrule an apparent and flagrant abuse of legislative power. An act of the legislature (for I cannot call it a law) contrary to the great principles of the social compact cannot be considered a rightful exercise of the legislative authority."

But Justice Iredell questioned whether natural law could be judicially applied to limit legislative power. He characterized such talk as the plaything of "some speculative jurists" and said that if the Constitution itself imposed no checks on legislative power, "whatever the legislature chose to enact would be lawfully enacted, and the judicial power could never interpose to pronounce it void."

Which of these views on the scope of judicial power has prevailed? In appearance Iredell's, but a century later, Chase's views were for all practical purposes triumphant. By 1890, the Court achieved, under the due process clause of the Fourteenth Amendment, the very power to supervise and control legislative action in relation to abstract principles of justice against which Iredell had so strongly protested.

EXPANSION OF THE CONTRACT CLAUSE

The Marshall Court had its first opportunity to examine the contract clause in *Fletcher* v. *Peck* (1810). "Marshall," Edward Corwin observed, found here "a task of restoration awaiting him in that great field of Constitutional Law which defines state power in relation to private rights." Alexander Hamilton had laid solid foundations for an effective national government; no such preliminary work had been done in the task now confronting the chief justice. Indeed, *Calder* v. *Bull* presented a well-nigh insuperable barrier.

The Yazoo Land Case. *Fletcher* v. *Peck* illustrates the speculative spirit rife in America at the close of the 1700s. Land companies found Georgia an especially inviting field. Between 1789 and 1795, speculators badgered the Georgia legislators without success. Finally, however, on January 7, 1795, the governor of Georgia signed a bill granting the greater part of what is now Alabama and Mississippi to four groups of purchasers, known as the Yazoo Land Companies, at 1½ cents per acre. The "purchasers" included men of national reputation and local politicians (all but one member of the Georgia legislature who voted for the act held shares in one or more of the companies). Indignation ran high, and in 1796 a new legislature repealed the land-grab act. By the time of repeal, some of the lands had passed into the hands of purchasers, mostly Boston capitalists, who in turn sold extensively to investors in New England and the Middle Atlantic states.

Contending that the repeal act of 1796 could not constitutionally divest them of their titles, these innocent purchasers decided to test their rights in federal court.

The case, an "arranged" suit, first came before the Supreme Court in the 1809 term; it was reargued the next year, and a decision was rendered on March 16, 1810. Sustaining the contention of the Yazoo claimants in the first decision by the Court invalidating a state statute on constitutional grounds, Chief Justice Marshall held that the 1796 repeal act was an unconstitutional impairment of the obligation of a contract. At the outset, Marshall suggested that the rescinding act of the Georgia legislature was void as a violation of vested rights and hence contrary to the underlying principles of society and government. But apparently realizing that a decision based on such flimsy ground would be less secure than one grounded in the Constitution, he turned to the **contract clause**. In doing this, he was confronted with two difficulties: First, the sort of contract the framers had in mind must have been executory—a contract in which the obligation of performance is still to be discharged. Marshall got around this by saying that every grant is attended by an implied contract on the part of the grantor not to reassert his or her right to the thing granted. Therefore, the clause covered executed contracts in which performance has been fulfilled as well as executory contracts.

The greater difficulty was that the contract before the Court was public, not private. In private contracts, it is easy enough to distinguish the contract as an agreement between the parties from the obligation that comes from the law and holds the parties to their agreement. Who, in this case, was to hold Georgia to its engagement? Certainly neither Georgia, which had passed the rescinding act, nor the Georgia state court. Marshall escaped the dilemma by ruling that Georgia's obligation was moral and that this moral injunction had been elevated to legal status by Article I, Section 10—"a Bill of Rights for the people of each State," Marshall called it. But the chief justice was uncertain at the very end. The last paragraph of his opinion states that Georgia was restrained from passing the rescinding act "either by general principles that are common to our free institutions, or by particular provisions of the Constitution."

Filling the Breach. Relying as it did on the contract clause, *Fletcher* went a long way toward bridging the gap opened by *Calder* v. *Bull* in the constitutional protection of private rights. But since Marshall's ruling was somewhat ambiguous, there remained the question of whether the clause safeguarded corporate charters as well as public grants against legislative interference. In 1819, by his opinion in ***Dartmouth College* v. *Woodward***, Marshall filled in the breach *Calder* v. *Bull* had created in the constitutional protection of vested rights.

The college's original charter was granted by the King of England. Parliament could have destroyed it at any time before 1776, and before 1788 the state of New Hampshire could have wiped it out. After that year, Marshall held that it must continue in perpetuity. His opinion adds up to these propositions: the college was not public, but a "private eleemosynary institution"; its charter was the outgrowth of a contract between the original donors and the Crown; the trustees represented the interest of the donors; the Constitution protects this representative interest. Marshall agonized at only one point: the requirement of the contract clause was admittedly designed to protect those having a vested beneficial interest. No one then living, not even the trustees, had any such interest in Dartmouth College. But Marshall held that the case came within the spirit, if not the words, of the Constitution.

The nub of Marshall's decision is the proposition that any ambiguity in a charter must be construed in favor of the adventurers and against the state. With perpetuity thus implied, the college charter was placed beyond the reach of the legislature. By that same token, the charters of profit-seeking corporations were also beyond the control of legislative majorities. In short, the doctrine of vested rights, heretofore having no safeguard except the principles of natural law, now enjoyed the solid protection of a specific provision of the Constitution—the contract clause.

In a separate opinion in the same case, Marshall's scholarly colleague Joseph Story (who had been elected to Harvard's board of overseers a year earlier) suggested the means by which states might in the future avoid the restrictive effect of Marshall's holding. Speaking of the state's power over corporations, Story observed that there was "no other control, than what is expressly or implicitly reserved by the charter itself." Indeed, as early as 1805, Virginia had used a **reservation clause** (reserving to the state the power to alter, amend, or repeal a charter) in special incorporation acts. In 1827, following the Dartmouth decision, New York enacted a general law making all charters "hereafter granted . . . subject to alteration, suspension and repeal, in the discretion of the legislature." All states now have such a provision in their constitutions, in general acts, or in both.

By 1830, the doctrine of vested rights was nevertheless accepted in a majority of the states and by leading lawyers and judges as a limit on legislative power. This meant that property rights fixed the contours within which the legislature exercised its powers. These were America's "preferred freedoms"—values so generally recognized and accepted that no such phrase was needed to describe them.

TWILIGHT OF THE CONTRACT CLAUSE

Meanwhile, political forces of great significance for the development of constitutional law were taking shape. The year 1828 saw the election as president of the democratically inclined Andrew Jackson, an election in which Chief Justice Marshall told friends he would vote for the first time in 24 years (and there remains little doubt that his vote was *against* Jackson). In the same decade, Massachusetts, New York, and Virginia called conventions to remove certain state constitutional safeguards for economic privilege and to broaden the suffrage. Out of all this emerged the doctrine of **popular sovereignty**, the notion that the will of the people is to be discovered at the ballot box, not merely in a document framed in 1787, and that the people's will should at all times prevail. The juristic expression of popular sovereignty is the doctrine of the police power, which was given classic expression and interpretation by Jackson's appointee and Marshall's successor, Roger Brooke Taney.

In the License Cases of 1847, Taney gave the state police power succinct definition: "The power to govern men and things within the limits of its own dominion." A concept of incalculable potential, "police power" came to not only mean legislative authority to remove government-created privilege, but also sanction for state legislation having broad social purpose. Taney's doctrine of the police power did in fact stimulate considerable legislative activity.

The two cases of *Dartmouth College* and ***Charles River Bridge* v. *Warren Bridge*** (1837) illustrate two alternate approaches to the police power and to progress. Chief Justice Marshall's thoughts in the first case turned toward security of property and contract rights against government encroachment. Without losing sight of these values, Chief Justice Taney argued in the second case that the community also has rights and it is the object and end of government to promote the prosperity and happiness of all. In holding against the Charles River Bridge Co., Taney maintained that disputes over implied grants of monopolistic privilege should be resolved in favor of the public, not the investors.

After *Charles River Bridge*, which rejected constitutional protection for such **implied contracts**, the contract clause never regained its earlier stature as a barrier against legislative encroachment on property rights. Indeed, in 1934, in one of the first cases foreshadowing the ultimately favorable constitutional fate of the New Deal (***Home Building & Loan Association* v. *Blaisdell***), the justices, voting 5–4, refused to hold that the contract clause had been breached by a state statute changing the terms of mortgage agreements. The legislation seemed to fly in the face of Article I, Section 10. Distinguishing between the obligation of the contract and the remedy, Chief Justice Hughes tried to demonstrate that the moratorium placed on mortgage foreclosures did not impair the obligation; the statute merely modified the remedy. Justices Cardozo and Stone read the chief justice's first draft with misgivings so serious that each considered writing a concurring opinion. The former actually prepared a draft (reprinted in this chapter) that advocated a contract clause that would adapt with the times.

In *El Paso* v. *Simmons* (1965), this flexible interpretation of the clause won well-nigh unanimous support when eight justices held that not every modification of a contractual promise, even one embodied in a state statute, impairs the obligation of contract. Yet, the flexible approach goes only so far. Twelve years after *El Paso*, the Court invalidated the repeal in 1974 during a national energy crisis of a covenant accepted in 1962 by the Port Authority of New York and New Jersey, limiting subsidization of rail passenger transportation. The repeal amounted to an impairment of the Authority's contract with the bondholders (*United States Trust Co.* v. *New Jersey*, 1977).

ORIGINS OF DUE PROCESS

No sooner had the contract clause been weakened than a new judicial formula was found for defeating government action under the police power. The 1830s had seen the establishment of public schools; the 1840s witnessed the first steps toward primitive factory legislation and regulation of the liquor traffic. The character and volume of social legislation created the need for a new constitutional weapon. Special credit for the invention of that weapon must go to the New York Court of Appeals—and to the leading case of *Wynehamer* v. *New York* (1856).

The defendant, Wynehamer, was indicted and convicted by a jury in the Court of Sessions of Erie County for selling liquor in small quantities contrary to the act, passed April 9, 1855, "for the prevention of intemperance, pauperism and crime." It was admitted that the defendant owned the liquors in question before and at the time the law took effect. But on appeal, Wynehamer's counsel insisted that he was entitled to an acquittal on the ground, among others, that the statute was unconstitutional and void. The court agreed.

Judge Comstock, who spoke for New York's high court, noted that although "the legislative power" is vested in the legislature, it is subject to special limitations in the state constitution, "which are of very great interest and importance" in that they prohibit the deprivation of life, liberty, and property without due process of law. He thus introduced a constitutional injunction of tremendous possibilities—**due process**. What does it mean? To the lay mind this phrase suggests procedural limitations—that is, if it limits legislative power at all, it does so in terms not of *what* can be done but of *how* something must be done. Comstock and the concurring justices made clear that they had something more sweeping in mind. Because the legislature has only limited powers, it cannot encroach, Comstock contended, on the rights of any species of property, even where the action would be of "absolute benefit" to the people of the state. To allow the legislature such a power, even in the public interest, would "subvert the fundamental idea of property." "In a government like ours," he observed, "theories of public good or public necessity may be so plausible, or even so truthful, as to command popular majorities. But whether truthful or plausible merely, and by whatever numbers they are assented to, there are some absolute private rights beyond their reach, and among these the constitution places the right of property." In short, due process placed substantive as well as procedural restraints on legislative power.

Thus, by mid-nineteenth century two great forces were meeting head on: the doctrine of vested rights and the doctrine of the police power. Professor Corwin suggested that on the eve of the Civil War, courts and country were faced with a reincarnation of the old conundrum: What happens when an irresistible force—the doctrine of the police power—meets an immovable object—the doctrine of vested rights? What, moreover, was to be the role of the courts in this situation?

Confronted with cases such as that of *Charles River Bridge*, judges might have done one of two things: surrender the view that rights of property and of contract set absolute barriers against the exercise of public power, or cast about for a new constitutional formula to protect vested rights against regulatory legislative power. Would the phrase *due process* serve this purpose? Could a term suggesting procedural limitations only be fashioned into a limitation on the substance of lawmaking? The significance of *Wynehamer* is that by 1856 an answer was at hand.

JUDICIAL RESTRAINT AND THE FOURTEENTH AMENDMENT

Before the Civil War, except for the Taney Court's disastrous decision in *Dred Scott* (see Chapter Two), the due process clause in the Fifth Amendment had created no serious limitation on the substance of national legislation. Indeed, in the same year the New York court decided *Wynehamer*, Justice Benjamin Curtis and the U.S. Supreme Court gave due process its traditional meaning as embodying "settled usages and modes of proceeding" (*Murray's Lessee* v. *Hoboken Land and Improvement Co.*, 1856). But the clause was no sooner inserted in the Fourteenth Amendment than it became a rallying point for those who resisted the effort of government to regulate the expanding industrial economy. The amendment seemed to add a weapon of untold potentialities to the judicial arsenal; henceforth, the battles to protect property rights against state regulation were destined to revolve around due process. Accordion-like in its contour, it was broad enough to embrace the concept of natural rights.

Testing the New Amendment. Nonetheless, the Supreme Court was at first reluctant to exploit this new source of authority. In the **Slaughterhouse Cases** (1873), Justice Miller and four colleagues were altogether unreceptive to constitutional objections raised by New Orleans butchers against a Louisiana law that required all slaughtering in the city to be done in a single facility. In Miller's view, the privileges and immunities clause in Section 1 of the amendment did not break down the distinction between state and national citizenship. The Fourteenth Amendment conferred on the national government the duty of protecting rights adhering in or deriving from national, not state, citizenship. Rights of national citizenship included such matters as coming to the seat of the government and protection on the high seas. By contrast, state citizenship, predating the Constitution, encompassed the fundamental right to acquire and possess property, among other rights. Because the rights allegedly infringed by the Louisiana statute derived from state, not national, citizenship, the butchers could not look beyond the state for protection.

Miller was equally cool to application of the equal protection and due process clauses, also part of Section 1. As for equal protection, he doubted its relevance except in cases involving the rights of the recently freed slaves. As for due process, under no interpretation he had seen could the challenged statute be held lacking in due process. Why did Miller take such a narrow view of judicial power? Essentially it grew out of his conception of the Union—"the structure and spirit of our institutions." The Fourteenth Amendment did not change "the whole theory of the relations of the State and Federal governments to each other and of both these governments to the people." "A ruling for the butchers," Miller said, "would constitute this Court a perpetual censor upon all legislation of the states on the civil rights of their own citizens, with authority to nullify such as it did not approve." The Court felt duty-bound to curb any effort to change the federal balance, even by the amending process.

A Public Interest. Judicial hands-off was maintained four years later in ***Munn* v. *Illinois***, which upheld a statute fixing rates for grain warehouses. Harking back to principles of common law, Chief Justice Waite reasoned that when people devote their property to a use in which the public has an interest, the property ceases to be private; it becomes "affected with a public interest" and hence subject to a greater degree of regulation. The legislature, not the Court, was to determine how much regulation was permissible, whether it was arbitrary, and whether the business was so affected.

The implications of *Munn* were far-reaching. "Our boasted security in property rights falls away for the lack of a constitutional guaranty against this sovereign power thus discovered in our legislatures," observed commentator George C. Marshall in 1890. "It is apparent that against the whim of a temporary majority, inflamed with class prejudice, envy or revenge, the property of no man is safe. And the danger is even greater in an age teeming with shifting theories of social reform and economic science, which seem to have but one common principle—the subjection of private property to governmental control for the good—or alleged good—of the public." He advised, however, that *Munn* was as sound in constitutional law as it was objectionable in its result. The defect, therefore, could be remedied only by an amendment to the Constitution.

The insecurity revealed by *Munn* was destined to be corrected. But this would be done by interpretation and not by formal amendment, just as a similar breach had been bridged by Chief Justice Marshall years before, when he expanded the scope of the contract clause to overcome *Calder* v. *Bull*. Various forces and factors joined in this movement.

JUDICIAL ACTIVISM AND THE FOURTEENTH AMENDMENT

In 1878, one year after *Munn*, the American Bar Association was organized. By 1881, it was embarked on a deliberate and persistent campaign of education designed to reverse the Court's broad conception of legislative power. The association stood with John Stuart Mill for individualism, agreed with Charles Darwin's view of the inevitability of the human struggle, and accepted Herbert Spencer's evolutionary theories of politics. Extracts from addresses and papers reveal such thoughts as "The great curse of the world is too much government" and "Forces which make for growth should be left absolutely free to all."[1]

Judicial Revolution. A shift from the view that the Court had espoused in *Munn* came swiftly. *Santa Clara Co.* v. *Southern Pacific R. R.* (1886) acknowledged that corporations were "persons" under the due process clause. "It does not at all follow that every statute enacted ostensibly for the promotion of these ends [morals and welfare] is to be accepted as a legitimate exertion of the police powers of the state," commented Justice Harlan for the Court in *Mugler* v. *Kansas* (1887). Legitimacy was to be determined by the Court. "The courts are not bound by mere forms, nor are they to be misled by mere pretenses. They are at liberty—indeed, are under a solemn duty—to look at the substance of things."

At least two factors had been at work to effect this change—the bar association's campaign and powerful dissenting opinions. By the late 1880s, a third element was added—change in judicial personnel. Between 1877 and 1890, seven justices who had participated in the Slaughterhouse and Munn cases retired or died. Field, who had dissented in both, lived on and in 1888 was joined by his nephew David J. Brewer and Chief Justice Melville W. Fuller.

With new justices came a repudiation of *Munn's* hands-off approach. In *Chicago, Milwaukee & St. Paul R. R. Co.* v. *Minnesota* (1890), six justices decided that the question of the reasonableness of rates could not be left by the legislature to a state commission but must be subject to judicial review. This decision completed a judicial revolution. The Court became what Justice Miller had feared in the Slaughterhouse Cases—a "perpetual censor" of state legislation.

The new view was reflected in remarks Justice Brewer made to the New York Bar Association in 1893. Taking account of the state of affairs and of popular and professional protest against the expansion of judicial power, Brewer advocated judicial activism—"strengthening the judiciary." Brewer believed with Judge John F. Dillon that the Supreme Court was "the only breakwater against the haste and the passions of the people—against the tumultuous ocean of democracy."

The most reasoned response to Brewer's advocacy of judicial activism came from Harvard law professor James Bradley Thayer, who proclaimed a standard of judicial self-restraint. Justice Frankfurter later rated Thayer's article of 1893 "the most important single essay in constitutional law, . . . the great guide for judges, and the great guide for understanding by nonjudges." Excerpts from both Brewer and Thayer appear as an "unstaged debate" in this chapter.

The Bake Shop Case. Until the Court's about-face in 1937 (see Chapter Six), Thayer's sober counsel was to no avail. The Court played a role it had earlier spurned. Virtually a superlegislature, it proceeded to discharge the delicate responsibility of mediating between public power and private rights. Due process was a poor measuring instrument because it varied according to the user. But its very uncertainty as a test of what a legislature might do was useful for judges who wanted to be able to say no, and yet plead inability to say what might be done in the future or precisely what was wrong with that which had been done in the past. It would seem, then, that Justice Iredell's scorn of natural law as a limitation on state legislative power in *Calder* v. *Bull* might be applied equally well to due process. Because this concept provided no "fixed standard," all that the Court could properly say in raising it as a constitutional bar was that the legislature had passed an act that, in the opinion of the judges, was inconsistent with abstract principles of justice.

Once the Court abandoned its previous attitude of judicial self-restraint, how could the justices avoid reading their own predilections into the Constitution? The problem was squarely presented in 1905 in the famous Bake Shop Case, ***Lochner* v. *New York***. The Court had previously held in an insurance case that **liberty of contract** was implicit in the due process that the Fourteenth Amendment shielded from state interference (*Allgeyer* v. *Louisiana*, 1897). And in 1898, because of the dangerous work involved, it upheld a Utah statute fixing an eight-hour day for miners as a reasonable restriction on liberty of contract (*Holden* v. *Hardy*). Now a bakery owner claimed that New York's maximum hours law for bakers impermissibly intruded into the right of employer and employee to agree on the terms of labor. Justice Rufus Peckham's measure of "due process" in delivering the Court's opinion contrasts sharply with Chief Justice Waite's in *Munn*. "To common understanding," wrote Peckham, "the trade of a baker has never been regarded as an unhealthy one." The statute was unconstitutional because five justices thought it unnecessary.

The Brandeis Brief. After *Lochner*, reformers realized that saving social legislation from judicial veto called for a different approach. In 1907, the National Consumers League, learning that the Oregon 10-hour law for women was soon to be contested in the Supreme Court, began a search for outstanding counsel to defend the statute. Joseph H. Choate, one of the most distinguished lawyers of his time, the man who had blocked the "march of Communism" in the Income Tax Case of 1895 (see Chapter Seven), refused a retainer, saying that he saw no reason why "a big husky Irish woman should not work more than ten hours in a laundry if she and her employers so desired." The day after Choate's refusal, attorney Louis D. Brandeis of Boston accepted the retainer and began work on his now famous factual brief in *Muller* v. *Oregon* (1908).

"In our judgment," Peckham had said in *Lochner*, "it is not possible *in fact* to discover the connection between the number of hours a baker must work in a bakery and the healthful quality of the bread made by the workman" (emphasis added). Peckham's assumption had been that the bake shop law was not health-based but class (labor) legislation instead and therefore an unacceptable use of the police power. Accepting this challenge, Brandeis took a bold and unprecedented step: He furnished the Court with the requisite social and economic statistics to demonstrate a relationship between working hours and public health and safety. Heretofore lawyers had lacked confidence in their ability to make the judges see a "reasonable" relation, grounded in facts, between the ends and the means. Brandeis had confidence in both himself and the judges.

Instead of the usual array of legal precedents, Brandeis produced facts and statistics on women's health to show that the legislation was within the legal principles already enumerated by the Court. He brought to a bench disposed to make economic and social judgments a method for performing its task more intelligently and more fairly. The **Brandeis brief** contained two pages of conventional legal arguments and over 100 pages of data drawn from reports of government bureaus, legislative committees, commissions on hygiene, and factory inspections—all proving that long hours are, *as a matter of fact*, dangerous to women's health and safety, and that short hours result in general social and economic benefits.

The Court approved Oregon's 10-hour law, and a more tolerant judicial attitude soon became apparent. In 1917, the Court upheld a 10-hour-day law with an overtime provision for men (*Bunting* v. *Oregon*). But such progressivism was short-lived. Brandeis himself was appointed to the bench in 1916, but his appointment did little more than balance President Woodrow Wilson's earlier elevation of his attorney general, James C. McReynolds, to associate justice. Within a few years, Warren G. Harding succeeded Wilson and named William Howard Taft chief justice and George Sutherland associate justice. So skepticism continued to mark the Court's attitudes toward facts. For example, Justice Sutherland, confronted in 1923 with a mass of sociological data in support of a District of Columbia act regulating women's wages, brushed all such extralegal matter aside as "interesting, but only mildly persuasive" (*Adkins* v. *Children's Hospital*). "Freedom of contract is the general rule," Sutherland commented in setting aside the wage law, "restraint the exception."

By contrast, Justice Brandeis considered the Court's function circumscribed whether he approved or disapproved of a particular economic policy. In 1925, the Oklahoma legislature provided that no one could engage in the manufacture of ice for sale without obtaining a license. If a state commission found that the community was adequately served, it might turn down the bid of a would-be competitor, and in this way, perhaps, advance monopoly. On its face, this legislation encouraged precisely the trend Brandeis had tried to prevent as an attorney. "The control here asserted," the Court ruled in a 6–2 opinion setting aside the act, "does not protect against monopoly, but tends to foster it." Yet Brandeis dissented. "Our function," he wrote, echoing Thayer, "is only to determine the reasonableness of the legislature's belief in the existence of evils and in the effectiveness of the remedy. . . ." Viewing the states as social laboratories, Brandeis believed that government should have power "to remould, through experimentation, our economic practices and institutions to meet changing social and economic needs. . . . This Court has the power to prevent an experiment. We may strike down the statute which embodies it on the ground that, in our opinion, the measure is arbitrary, capricious, or unreasonable. . . . But in the exercise of this high power, we must be ever on guard, lest we erect our prejudices into legal principles" (*New State Ice Co.* v. *Liebmann*, 1932).

The Decline of Due Process Protection of Property Rights. In 1934, five justices hinted a return to judicial restraint as ***Nebbia* v. *New York*** sustained a New York statute fixing minimum and maximum milk prices. "With the wisdom of the policy adopted," declared Justice Owen J. Roberts, "the Courts are both incompetent and unauthorized to deal." Yet in 1936 (*Morehead* v. *New York* ex rel. *Tipaldo*), the justices returned to *Adkins* in striking down the state's minimum wage law for women and children, also 5–4. Nevertheless, it was soon evident that *Nebbia* had marked the beginning of the end of due process as a substantive limitation on legislation affecting economic rights. The death blow came in 1937 when ***West Coast Hotel Co.* v. *Parrish*** expressly overruled *Adkins*, just as the Court was also relaxing commerce clause constraints on Congress, as described in Chapter Six. Upholding Washington State's minimum wage for women, Chief Justice Hughes declared, "[T]he liberty safeguarded is liberty in a social organization which requires the protection of law against the evils which menace the health, safety, morals and welfare of the people." Liberty could be infringed by forces other than government, and infringement by those forces required the affirmative action of government for its protection.

The Court relinquished a self-acquired guardianship. Due process would no longer serve as a shield against the substance of commercial regulations. Within a year, without a single change in judicial personnel, self-restraint became the order of the day. Only President Roosevelt's Court-packing threat, reviewed in Chapter Six, had intervened.

It would be extreme to say that the Court has completely abandoned its supervisory role over state economic regulation, but decisions since 1937 reveal a greatly diminished judicial role. As Justice Black emphasized in 1963 (***Ferguson***

v. *Skrupa*), "The doctrine that prevailed in *Lochner* . . . and like cases—that due process authorizes courts to hold laws unconstitutional when they believe the legislature has acted unwisely—has long since been discarded. We have returned to the original constitutional proposition that courts do not substitute their social and economic beliefs for the judgment of legislative bodies, who are elected to pass laws."

***Lochner's* Legacy**. For Progressive-era and, later, New Deal and post–New Deal reformers, *Lochner* and its progeny stand out as abuses of judicial review. The Court was trying to write laissez-faire economic theory into the Constitution and to protect the entrenched "malefactors of great wealth," as President Theodore Roosevelt had labeled them in 1907. Recently others, while conceding that the *Lochner* majority was misguided, see the decision as opposition to class legislation and as a reflection of ideas of limited government dating from the era of Jacksonian democracy before the Civil War. Regardless, *Lochner* did not pose an insurmountable barrier to all social legislation. During the three decades after *Lochner*, the Court sustained many more reform laws than it struck down. Nonetheless, advocates of social reform had real grounds for concern: The Court had the last word. Any new measure had to jump through the judicial hoops of due process, liberty of contract, and the police power.

While the Supreme Court had abandoned stringent protection of property rights by 1937, *Lochner* nonetheless stands as a harbinger of some of the modern Court's decisions in other contexts in at least four ways: First, it rested on a right—liberty of contract—neither mentioned in the Fourteenth Amendment nor probably intended by those who drafted it. Second, it attributed substantive, not merely procedural, content to the concept of due process of law. Third, it was defense of a right the Court considered fundamental. Fourth, it was the antithesis of judicial deference to lawmaking bodies. For Peckham, the judicial task was essentially legislative: independently to evaluate the need for the regulation, presumably the same task in which the legislature had engaged.

SEARCH FOR A ROLE: FOOTNOTE FOUR

At the very moment the Court relaxed its supervisory control over social and economic policy, Justice Harlan Stone outlined an affirmative thrust for judicial review. In contrast to his expression of judicial tolerance for regulation of property, he suggested that certain other freedoms deserved heightened constitutional protection. In reviewing state or national action affecting speech, press, or religion, for instance, the Court might employ assumptions and presumptions that differed from those relied on in other cases where the question of constitutionality was raised. The Court began to have a vision of a new hierarchy of constitutionally protected values, with the First Amendment at the apex and property rights placed much further down. The challenge facing the justices was what Alexander M. Bickel later called the **countermajoritarian difficulty**: The apparent contradiction presented when *unelected* judges use the power of judicial review to nullify the actions of *elected* legislators or executives.

In the otherwise obscure case of *United States* v. *Carolene Products Co.* (1938), Stone offered a tentative solution. In the body of his opinion upholding a congressional ban on the shipment of "filled milk" (a milk product in which palm oil had been substituted for butterfat) against a challenge on due process grounds, he wrote, "Regulatory legislation affecting ordinary commercial transactions is not to be pronounced unconstitutional unless in the light of the facts made known or generally assumed it is of such a character as to preclude the assumption that it rests upon some rational basis within the knowledge and experience of the legislators." He would not go so far as to say that no economic legislation would ever violate constitutional restraints, but he did suggest strictly confining the Court's role. Attached to this proposition was **Footnote Four**:

> There may be narrower scope for operation of the presumption of constitutionality when legislation appears on its face to be within a specific prohibition of the Constitution, such as those of the first ten amendments, which are deemed equally specific when held to be embraced within the Fourteenth. . . .
>
> It is unnecessary to consider now whether legislation which restricts those political processes which can ordinarily be expected to bring about repeal of undesirable legislation, is to be subjected to more exacting judicial scrutiny under the general prohibitions of the Fourteenth Amendment than are most other types of legislation. . . .
>
> Nor need we enquire whether similar considerations enter into the review of statutes directed at particular religious . . . or national . . . or racial minorities . . . whether prejudice against discrete and insular minorities may be a special condition, which tends seriously to curtail the operation of those political processes ordinarily to be relied upon to protect minorities, and which may call for a correspondingly more searching judicial inquiry. . . .

The three paragraphs of this footnote, which Justice Lewis Powell later called "the most celebrated footnote in constitutional law," contain a corresponding number of ideas. The first suggests that when legislation, on its face, contravenes the specific constitutional negatives set out in the Bill of Rights, the Court's usual presumption of constitutionality may be curtailed or even waived. The second paragraph indicates that the judiciary has a special responsibility to defend those liberties essential to the effective functioning of the political process. The Court thus becomes the ultimate guardian against abuses that would poison what Madison called the "primary control" on government, "dependence on the people"—the ballot box. As the Court polices the channels of political change, it must protect those liberties on which the effectiveness of political action depends. The third paragraph suggests a special judicial role as protector of minorities and unpopular groups particularly helpless at the polls in the face of discriminatory or repressive policies, as may happen when majoritarianism runs amuck.

In short, Justice Stone attempted to lay out a justification for judicial review—the situations which would allow an unelected Court to intervene and set aside policies made by the elected representative of the people. Under what was claimed to be a new banner of self-restraint, the justices would leave protection of property to the political process. Judicial activism old-style was dead; judicial activism new-style was just around the corner. Judicial supervision would continue to be an important part of the political system, but new concerns would replace the old. These concerns are largely the topics covered in Chapters Nine through Fifteen.

TAKINGS, LAND USE, AND THE FIFTH AMENDMENT

With the decline of the due process clause as a barrier to commercial regulation, the **takings clause** of the Fifth Amendment has become a battleground for those who oppose public restrictions on property—especially laws governing land use. The clause states, "nor shall property be taken for public use, without just compensation." As explained in Chapter Nine, the takings clause was the first provision of the Bill of Rights to be applied to the states through the due process clause of the Fourteenth Amendment (*Chicago, B. & Q. R. Co.* v. *Chicago*, 1897).

In its plainest sense, the takings clause restricts the power of **eminent domain—**government's authority to acquire control of private property. When that is done, "just compensation" must be paid. The takings clause thus disperses the costs of public policy. A taking without compensation places the burden squarely on the property owner. A taking with compensation distributes the burden or costs among the taxpaying public.

The clause gives rise to at least three questions: First, what constitutes a "taking"? Second, what is "public use"? And finally, what compensation is "just"?

Takings. "[Q]uite simply," confessed Justice Brennan in *Penn Central Transportation Co.* v. *New York City* (1978), the Supreme Court "has been unable to develop any 'set formula' for determining when justice and fairness require that economic injuries caused by public action be compensated by the government. . . ." Whether a Fifth Amendment "taking" has occurred depends instead on the circumstances of individual cases. Several factors seem significant: the economic impact of the regulation, the extent to which the regulation adversely affects "investment-backed" expectations, the effect of the regulation on the property "as a whole," and the public interest the regulation serves. In the Court's eyes, most zoning laws and other regulations of property are not takings. Neither are taxes, even though they can negatively affect economic values.

Generally, land use regulations do not effect a taking if they promote a legitimate state interest without denying all economically viable use of the land. Moreover, government's power to ban certain uses of land to advance a legitimate interest includes the power to condition such use on some concession by the owner. This relationship between the interest and the concession was apparently crucial to the outcome of *Nollan* v. *California Coastal Commission* (1987). Five justices invalidated a state regulation that beachfront property owners had to allow public access across their beach as a condition for obtaining a permit to replace a house with a larger one. Absent in this case, according to the majority, was a close nexus between the restriction and the public interest it was supposed to serve.

Public Use. A taking must be for public, not private, use. Although this stipulation has not been nearly so troublesome as the definition of a taking, it has become clear that the Court does not confine **public use** to property maintained by a government agency and accessible to the general public. For example, *Hawaii Housing Authority* v. *Midkiff* (1984) presented a situation in which the state required large landowners to sell their property to others. Against the charge that the law took private property for private use, all eight participating justices decided that Hawaii's plan served a public purpose. "Where the legislature's purpose is legitimate and its means are not irrational," declared Justice O'Connor, "our cases make clear that empirical debates over the wisdom of takings—no less than debates over the wisdom of other kinds of socioeconomic legislation—are not to be carried out in the federal courts." Midkiff's hands-off approach may explain ***Kelo* v. *New London*** (2005), where five justices determined that the Connecticut city's resort to eminent domain for economic revitalization comported with the public use requirement even though the planned redevelopment took the homes of several long-term residents. *Kelo* has proven to be one of the Court's most controversial decisions of recent years. Since the case came down, some 43 states have enacted a variety of measures designed to limit or forestall *Kelo*-style applications of eminent domain.

Just Compensation. If a property owner is not satisfied with the price a government agency is willing to pay, courts ultimately settle the dispute. Owners are "entitled to receive what a willing buyer would pay in cash to a willing seller at the time of the taking," the Court announced in *United States* v. *564.54 Acres of Land* (1979). **Just compensation** is the fair market value of the property taken, not apparently the cost of replacement facilities. Exceptions include situations "where market value has been too difficult to find, or when . . . injustice to owner or public [would result]."

"NEW PROPERTY" AND DUE PROCESS OF LAW

Expanded economic and social roles for government at all levels are a hallmark of America today. Government has increasingly become a provider, not merely the regulator. As a result, substantial numbers of people are dependent on the government for income support, employment, or services essential to economic wellbeing. These interests have been labeled the **new property**. To what degree are such government benefits (**entitlements**) constitutionally protected? Put another way, although government may not be constitutionally required to license drivers or to hire college teachers, for example, what constitutional standards, if any, apply when a state suspends a license or fires an instructor? Constitutional protection means that the entitlement, once extended, may not be withdrawn without due process of law.

New property questions differ, therefore, from other issues in this chapter. With *Lochner* v. *New York* or *Ferguson* v. *Skrupa*, the substance of the regulation was at stake. Could a state constitutionally limit the hours of work in a bakery or restrict debt adjustment to lawyers? Raising procedural concerns, new property cases assume the legitimacy of the entitlement or regulatory policy. At issue is procedure—the manner in which entitlements are curtailed and property is restricted.

A Protected Interest. Having a constitutionally protected entitlement depends on whether the benefit involves a "liberty" or "property" interest within the meaning given the due process clauses of the Fifth and Fourteenth Amendments. In *Goldberg* v. *Kelly* (1970), the Supreme Court concluded that welfare benefits are more "like property than a 'gratuity.'" "Much of the existing wealth in this country," wrote Justice Brennan, "takes the form of rights that do not fall within traditional common law concepts of property." Thus a state could not stop public assistance payments without affording the recipient "the opportunity for an evidentiary hearing prior to termination."

Public employment may also be "property" if government specifies that a person can be discharged only "for cause" or if an understanding to that effect exists. In *Perry* v. *Sindermann* (1972), the Court held that a fourth-year instructor may have been entitled to a hearing before a junior college decided not to renew his contract. Even without explicit tenure rules, "there may be an unwritten 'common law' . . . that certain employees shall have the equivalent of tenure." But the majority found no such property interest in *Board of Regents* v. *Roth* (1972), where an instructor was let go after a single year of teaching. According to state law, the "decision whether to rehire a nontenured teacher for another year" was left "to the unfettered discretion of university officials." Unlike *Perry*, there was no other basis such as past practice on which to base the property interest.

Government action implicates a protected "liberty" when a person's good name, reputation, honor, or integrity is at stake. *Goss* v. *Lopez* (1975), for instance, held that the due process clause protected students from suspension from a public school in Columbus, Ohio. A state statute permitting up to a 10-day suspension with neither notice nor a hearing was found constitutionally defective because it infringed on both liberty and property interests.

What Process is Due? If a court decides that the due process clause applies, it must then determine the process that is due. At one extreme, criminal prosecutions (discussed in Chapter Ten) demand formal proceedings guided by a host of rules designed to ensure fairness. At the other extreme are brief, informal exchanges, which usually occur before a decision is made. In *Goss*, although the majority concluded that the due process clause applied to school suspensions, only the barest process would have sufficed: (1) oral or written notice of the charge against a student, and (2) an opportunity for a student to present his or her side of the story. There need be no delay between the moment of "notice" and the "hearing." The latter could amount to little more than "an informal give-and-take between student and disciplinarian, preferably prior to the suspension. . . ."

Mathews v. *Elridge* (1976) attempted to establish guidelines for the process various situations require. At issue was termination of disability insurance payments under the Social Security program. Existing procedures allowed the recipient to submit additional information by mail prior to termination and, within six months of the cutoff, to seek reconsideration in a hearing. Elridge demanded an evidentiary hearing prior to termination. Speaking for the majority, Justice Powell explained that a decision rested on several factors:

> First, the private interest that will be affected by the official action; second, the risk of an erroneous deprivation of such interest through the procedures used, and the probable value, if any, of additional or substitute procedural safeguards; and finally, the Government's interest, including the function involved and the fiscal and administrative burdens that the additional or substitute procedural requirement would entail.

Measured by this formulation, existing procedure satisfied the Constitution. "[T]he prescribed procedures not only provide the claimant with an effective process for asserting his claim prior to any administrative action, but also assure a right to an evidentiary hearing, as well as to subsequent judicial review, before the denial of his claim becomes final."

Mathews makes explicit the balancing of interests involved, not in deciding whether a constitutionally protected interest is threatened, but in deciding the process by which it may be withdrawn. The thinking in *Mathews* is economic—the weighing of benefits of added procedure (which would minimize the risks of error) against its costs (which might come out of the resources available for social welfare programs). *Mathews* also leans in favor of a presumption of the adequacy of existing procedure and away from a heightened judicial scrutiny of what the state has offered.

New Property and the Privileges and Immunities Clause. In the Slaughterhouse Cases, discussed earlier in this chapter, the justices all but wrote the privileges and immunities clause out of the Fourteenth Amendment. Between 1873 and 1999, the Court relied on the clause but once (*Colgate* v. *Harvey*, 1935), only to overrule that decision five years later (*Madden* v. *Kentucky*, 1940). In *Saenz* v. *Roe* (1999), however, the Court breathed new life into this provision when it invalidated California's residency requirement (and indirectly the congressional act allowing it) for welfare benefits. Otherwise, eligible welfare recipients had to reside in the state for a year in order to receive benefits paid to other eligible Californians; until then, they received an amount equal to what their previous state of residence had paid. Coupling the right to travel with the privileges and immunities clause, seven justices concluded that California's rule denied newer citizens a right of citizenship in their new state of residence. Previously the Court had examined such discriminations under the equal protection clause of the same amendment, as in ***Shapiro v. Thompson*** (1969), reprinted in Chapter Fourteen. *Saenz* may threaten other state policies that treat people differentially and hints that the once moribund privileges and immunities clause may someday become a repository of new constitutional rights.

Punitive Damages. The award of punitive or exemplary damages in even a single civil suit may amount to millions of dollars. Long a favorite of the tort bar, **punitive damages** further a state's interest in punishing and deterring unlawful conduct. (Punitive damages are in addition to **compensatory damages,** the latter consisting of the concrete loss sustained and nothing more.) Government compels the transfer of money (property) from the defendant (the **tortfeasor** or wrongdoer) to the plaintiff (the one who has been wronged). To what extent does the Constitution set limits on this time-honored practice? The Court confronted this question for the first time in *Pacific Mutual Life Insurance Co.* v. *Haslip* (1991). While agreeing that the Fourteenth Amendment imposed at least some procedural and substantive limits on a state's authority to impose punitive damage awards, *Haslip* left unsaid what those limits were. Not until *BMW* v. *Gore* (1996) did the Court overturn a punitive award because it was "grossly excessive." In this case, an Alabama jury awarded $4 million (a sum subsequently cut in half by the state supreme court) to the purchaser of a new automobile that, unknown to the purchaser, had been repainted because of damage in transit. The repainting reduced the value of the new car by 10 percent ($4,000). The decision effectively established a substantive due process right against grossly excessive judgments; moreover, the Court attempted to mark the limits of acceptability. Reviewing courts were instructed to consider: (1) the degree of reprehensibility of the defendant's misconduct; (2) the disparity between the actual and potential harm suffered by the plaintiff and the punitive award; and (3) the difference between the punitive award and civil penalties that might be imposed for similar conduct. *State Farm Mutual* v. *Campbell* (2003) reemphasized those points from *Gore*, as it set aside a $145 million punitive award where the actual damages were only $1 million. While refusing to set a "bright-line ratio which a punitive damages award cannot exceed," Justice Kennedy admonished "that, in practice, few awards exceeding a single-digit ratio between punitive and compensatory damages, to a significant degree, will satisfy due process." That standard may explain *Exxon Shipping* v. *Baker* (2008) which perhaps ends nearly 19 years of litigation following the gigantic oil spill from the *Exxon Valdez* into Alaska's Prince William Sound. When a tortfeasor does not benefit from the tort and does not act maliciously, punitive damages ($2.5 billion in this instance) may not exceed an amount equal to total compensatory damages ($287 million here).

The procedural standards accorded liberty and property interests make these subjects some of the most encompassing in all constitutional law. Few if any constitutional safeguards touch more citizens directly and on a day-to-day basis. Perhaps in no other subset are more Americans likely at some time in their lives to experience infringement of what may be their constitutionally protected liberty or property.

KEY TERMS

antinomy
vested rights
police power
ex post facto laws
contract clause
reservation clause
popular sovereignty
implied contracts
due process
liberty of contract
Brandeis brief
countermajoritarian difficulty
Footnote Four
takings clause
eminent domain
public use
just compensation
new property
entitlements
punitive damages
compensatory damages
tortfeasor

QUERIES

1. The decisions in *Dartmouth College* v. *Woodward* and *Charles River Bridge* v. *Warren Bridge* reflect contrasting views on the rigors of the contract clause. Does each also represent contrasting views on the nature of property?

2. Use of the due process clause to protect property may have represented an effort to amend the Constitution judicially, to add to the document protections that the framers failed to include. Is there evidence to support this statement in the Slaughterhouse Cases, *Munn* v. *Illinois*, and *Lochner* v. *New York*?

3. In 1893, Justice David J. Brewer and Professor James Bradley Thayer spoke out on judicial activism versus judicial restraint. What did they recommend concerning the Court's role?

4. Justices on the modern Court have made clear that they reject the judicial philosophy reflected in *Lochner* v. *New York*. Yet, they have by no means turned their backs on intervention in other realms of public policy. Precisely what was wrong with *Lochner*? Does it deserve its bad reputation?

SELECTED READINGS

Ely, James W., Jr. *The Guardian of Every Other Right: A Constitutional History of Property Rights*. New York: Oxford University Press, 1992.

Ely, James W., Jr. *The Contract Clause: A Constitutional History*. Lawrence: University Press of Kansas, 2016.

Fishel, William A. *Regulatory Takings*. Cambridge, MA: Harvard University Press, 1995.

Hobson, Charles F. *The Great Yazoo Land Sales: The Case of Fletcher v. Peck*. Lawrence: University Press of Kansas, 2016.

Kens, Paul. *Judicial Power and Reform Politics: The Anatomy of Lochner v. New York*. Lawrence: University Press of Kansas, 1990.

Kutler, Stanley I. *Privilege and Creative Destruction: The Charles River Bridge Case*. Philadelphia: Lippincott, 1972.

Labbé, Ronald M., and Jonathan Lurie. *The Slaughterhouse Cases: Regulation, Reconstruction, and the Fourteenth Amendment*. Lawrence: University Press of Kansas, 2003.

Price, Polly J. *Property Rights*. Santa Barbara, CA: ABC-CLIO, 2003.

Somin, Ilya. *The Grasping Hand: Kelo v. City of New London and the Limits of Eminent Domain*. Chicago: University of Chicago Press, 2016.

I. VESTED RIGHTS AND THE EX POST FACTO CLAUSE

Calder v. *Bull*
3 U.S. (3 Dall.) 386, 1 L.Ed. 648 (1798)

http://caselaw.findlaw.com/us-supreme-court/3/386.html

The legislature of Connecticut passed a law granting a new hearing to Caleb and Abigail Bull, after their right to appeal a probate court decree had expired. At the second hearing, the Bulls were successful, and John and Jennet Calder the other claimants, after appealing unsuccessfully to the highest Connecticut court, brought their case to the Supreme Court on a writ of error. The opinions of Justices Chase and Iredell are important, not only for their definition of ex post facto laws but also for the views expressed about natural law and judicial review. Majority: Chase, Cushing, Iredell, Paterson. Not participating: Ellsworth, Wilson.

Chase, Justice . . .

The counsel for the plaintiffs in error contend, that the . . . law of the legislature of Connecticut, granting a new hearing, in the above case, is an *ex post facto law*, prohibited by the constitution of the United States; that any law of the federal government, or of any of the state governments, contrary to the constitution of the United States, is void; and that this court possess the power to declare such law void. . . .

Whether the legislature of any of the states can revise and correct by law, a decision of any of its courts of justice, although not prohibited by the constitution of the state, is a question of very great importance, and not necessary now to be determined; because the resolution or law in question does not go so far. I cannot subscribe to the omnipotence of a state legislature, or that it is absolute and without control; although its authority should not be expressly restrained by the constitution, or fundamental law of the state. . . . There are acts which the federal or state legislature cannot do, without exceeding their authority. There are certain vital principles in our free republican governments which will determine and overrule an apparent and flagrant abuse of legislative power; as to authorize manifest injustice by positive law; or to take away that security for personal liberty, or private property, for the protection whereof the government was established. An act of the legislature (for I cannot call it a law), contrary to the great first principles of the social compact, cannot be considered a rightful exercise of legislative authority. The obligation of a law in governments established on express compact, and on republican principles, must be determined by the nature of the power on which it is founded.

A few instances will suffice to explain what I mean. A law that punished a citizen for an innocent action, or, in other words, for an act which, when done, was in violation of no existing law; a law that destroys, or impairs, the lawful private contracts of citizens; a law that makes a man a judge in his own cause; or a law that takes property from A, and gives it to B. It is against all reason and justice for a people to intrust a legislature with such powers; and, therefore, it cannot be presumed that they have done it. The genius, the nature, and the spirit of such acts of legislation; and the general principles of law and reason forbid them. The legislature may enjoin, permit, forbid and punish; they may declare new crimes, and establish rules of conduct for all its citizens in future cases; they may command what is right, and prohibit what is wrong; but they cannot change innocence into guilt, or punish innocence as a crime; or violate the right of an antecedent lawful private contract; or the right of private property. To maintain that our federal or state legislature possesses such powers, if they had not been expressly restrained, would, in my opinion, be a political heresy altogether inadmissible in our free republican governments. . . .

I will state what laws I consider *ex post facto* laws, within the words and the intent of the prohibition. 1st. Every law that makes an action done before the passing of the law, and which was innocent when done, criminal; and punishes such action. 2d. Every law that aggravates a crime, or makes it greater than it was, when committed. 3d. Every law that changes the punishment, and inflicts a greater punishment, than the law annexed to the crime, when committed. 4th. Every law that alters the legal rules of evidence, and receives less, or different testimony, than the law required at the time of the commission of the offense, in order to convict the offender. All these, and similar laws, are manifestly unjust and oppressive. In my opinion, the true distinction is between *ex post facto* laws, and retrospective laws. Every *ex post facto* law must necessarily be retrospective; but every retrospective law is not an *ex post facto* law; the former only are prohibited. Every law that takes away or impairs rights vested, agreeably to existing laws, is retrospective, and is generally unjust, and may be oppressive; and it is a good general rule, that a law should have no retrospect; but there are cases in which laws may justly, and for the benefit of the community, and also of individuals, relate to a time antecedent to their commencement; as statutes of oblivion or of pardon. They are certainly retrospective, and literally both concerning and after the facts committed. But I do not consider any law *ex post facto*, within the prohibition, that mollifies the rigor of the criminal law; but only those that create or aggravate the crime; or increase the punishment, or change the rules of evidence, for the purpose of conviction. Every law that is to have an operation before the making thereof, as to commence at an antecedent time; or to save time from the statute of limitations; or to excuse acts which were unlawful, and before committed, and the like, is retrospective. But such laws may be proper or necessary, as the case may be. There is a great and apparent difference between making an unlawful act lawful; and the making an innocent action criminal, and punishing it as a crime. . . .

The restraint against making any *ex post facto* laws was not considered, by the framers of the constitution, as extending to prohibit the depriving a citizen even of a vested right to property; or the provision, "that private property should not be taken for public use, without just compensation," was unnecessary.

It seems to me that the right of property, in its origin, could only arise from compact express or implied, and I think it the better opinion, that the right, as well as the mode or manner of acquiring property, and of alienating or transferring, inheriting or transmitting it, is conferred by society, is regulated by civil institution, and is always subject to the rules prescribed by positive law. When I say that a right is vested in a citizen, I mean, that he has the power to do certain actions, or to possess certain things, according to the law of the land. . . .

PATERSON, JUSTICE . . . [omitted].

IREDELL, JUSTICE . . .

It is true, that some speculative jurists have held, that a legislative act against natural justice must, in itself, be void; but I cannot think that, under such a government any court of justice would possess a power to declare it so. . . . [I]t has been the policy of all the American states, which have, individually, framed their state constitutions, since the revolution, and of the people of the United States, when they framed the federal constitution, to define with precision the objects of legislative power, and to restrain its exercise within marked and settled boundaries. If any act of congress, or of the legislature of the state, violates those constitutional provisions, it is unquestionably void; though, I admit, that as the authority to declare it void is of a delicate and awful nature, the court will never resort to that authority, but in a clear and urgent case. If, on the other hand, the legislature of the Union, or the legislature of any member of the Union, shall pass a law, within the general scope of their constitutional power, the court cannot pronounce it to be void, merely because it is, in their judgment, contrary to the principles of natural justice. The ideas of natural justice are regulated by no fixed standards: the ablest and the purest men have differed upon the subject; and all that the court could properly say, in such an event, would be, that the legislature (possessed of an equal right of opinion) had passed an act which, in the opinion of the judges, was inconsistent with the abstract principles of natural justice. . . .

Still, however, in the present instance, the act or resolution of the legislature of Connecticut, cannot be regarded as an *ex post facto* law; for the true construction of the prohibition extends to criminal, not to civil issues. . . .

The policy, the reason and humanity of the prohibition, do not . . . extend to civil cases, to cases that merely affect the private property of citizens. Some of the most necessary and important acts of legislation are, on the contrary, founded upon the principle, that private rights must yield to public exigencies. . . . Without the possession of this power, the operations of government would often be obstructed, and society itself would be endangered. It is not sufficient to urge, that the power may be abused, for such is the nature of all power—such is the tendency of every human institution. . . . We must be content to limit power, where we can, and where we cannot, consistently with its use, we must be content to repose a salutary confidence. It is our consolation, that there never existed a government, in ancient or modern times, more free from danger in this respect, than the governments of America. . . .

CUSHING, JUSTICE . . . [omitted].

Judgment affirmed.

II. THE CONTRACT CLAUSE

Dartmouth College v. *Woodward*
17 U.S. (4 Wheat.) 518, 4 L.Ed. 629 (1819)

http://caselaw.findlaw.com/us-supreme-court/17/518.html

This case involved rival claimants to the records, the seal, and other objects signifying control of Dartmouth College. The college trustees (mainly Federalist in their politics) based their claim on a charter granted in 1769 by King George III and sought to regain control from a mainly Republican group whose authority had been created by three New Hampshire legislative acts in 1816. These amended the original charter by increasing the number of trustees and vesting the future power of appointment of trustees in the governor and his council. The state Superior Court of Judicature upheld Woodward and the new control group. In 1885, Sir Henry Maine characterized the Marshall Court's decision as "the bulwark of American individualism against democratic impatience and socialistic fantasy." Majority: Marshall, Johnson, Livingston, Story, Washington. Dissenting: Duvall. Not participating: Todd.

The opinion of the Court was delivered by MARSHALL, CH. J. . . .

It can require no argument to prove, that the circumstances of this case constitute a contract. An application is made to the crown for a charter to incorporate a religious and literary institution. In the application, it is stated, that large contributions have been made for the object, which will be conferred on the corporation, as soon as it shall be created. The charter is granted, and on its faith the property is conveyed. Surely, in this transaction every ingredient of a complete and legitimate contract is to be found. The points for consideration are; (1) Is this contract protected by the constitution of the United States? (2) Is it impaired by the acts under which the defendant holds? . . .

1. . . . If the act of incorporation be a grant of political power, if it creates a civil institution, to be employed in the administration of the government, or if the funds of the college be public property, or if the state of New Hampshire, as a government, be alone interested in its transactions, the subject is one in which the legislature of the state may act according to its judgment, unrestrained by any limitation of its power imposed by the constitution of the United States.

But if this be a private eleemosynary institution, endowed with a capacity to take property, for objects unconnected with government, whose funds are bestowed by individuals, on the faith of the charter; if the donors have stipulated for the future disposition and management of those funds, in the manner prescribed by themselves; there may be more difficulty in the case, although neither the persons who have made these stipulations, nor those for whose benefit they were made, should be parties to the cause. . . .

A corporation is an artificial being, invisible, intangible, and existing only in contemplation of law. Being the mere creature of law, it possesses only those properties which the charter of its creation confers upon it, either expressly or as incidental to its very existence. These are such as are supposed best calculated to effect the object for which it was created. Among the most important are immortality, and, if the expression may be allowed, individuality; properties by which a perpetual succession of many persons are considered as the same, and may act as a single individual. . . . It is no more a state instrument than a natural person exercising the same powers would be. If, then, a natural person, employed by individuals in the education of youth, or for the government of a seminary in which youth is educated, would not become a public officer, or be considered as a member of the civil government, how is it that this artificial being, created by law for the purpose of being employed by the same individuals for the same purposes, should become a part of the civil government of the country? . . .

. . . Dartmouth College is an eleemosynary institution, incorporated for the purpose of perpetuating the application of the bounty of the donors to the specified objects of the bounty; that its trustees or governors were originally named by the founder, and invested with the power of perpetuating themselves; that they are not public officers, nor is it a civil institution, participating in the administration of government; but a charity school, or a seminary of education, incorporated for the preservation of its property, and the perpetual application of that property to the objects of its creation. Yet a question remains to be considered of more real difficulty, on which more doubt has been entertained than on all that have been discussed. The founders of the college, at least those whose contributions were in money, have parted with the property bestowed upon it, and their representatives have no interest in that property. The donors of land are equally without interest so long as the corporation shall exist. Could they be found, they are unaffected by any alteration in its constitution, and probably regardless of its form or even of its existence. The students are fluctuating, and no individual among our youth has a vested interest in the institution which can be asserted in a court of justice. Neither the founders of the college, nor the youth for whose benefit it was founded, complain of the alteration made in its charter, or think themselves injured by it. The trustees alone complain, and the trustees have no beneficial interest to be protected. Can this be such a contract as the constitution intended to withdraw from the power of state legislation? Contracts, the parties to which have a vested beneficial interest, and those only, it has been said, are the objects about which the constitution is solicitous, and to which its protection is extended.

The court has bestowed on this argument the most deliberate consideration, and the result will be stated. Dr. Wheelock, acting for himself and for those who, at his solicitation, had made contributions to his school, applied for this charter, as the instrument which should enable him and them to perpetuate their beneficent intention. It was granted. An artificial, immortal being was created by the crown, capable of receiving and distributing forever, according to the will of the donors, the donations which should be made to it. On this being, the contributions which had been collected were immediately bestowed. These gifts were made, not indeed to make a profit for the donors or their posterity, but for something, in their opinion, of inestimable value; for something which they deemed a full equivalent for the money with which it was purchased. The consideration for which they stipulated, is the perpetual application of the fund to its objects, in the mode prescribed by themselves. Their descendants may take no interest in the preservation of this consideration. But in this respect their descendants are not their representatives. They are represented by the corporation. The corporation is the assignee of their rights, stands in their place, and distributes their bounty, as they would themselves have distributed it had they been immortal. So with respect to the students who are to derive learning from this source. The corporation is a trustee for them also. Their potential rights, which, taken distributively, are imperceptible, amount collectively to a most important interest. These are, in the aggregate, to be exercised, asserted, and protected by the corporation. They were as completely out of the donors, at the instant of their being vested in the corporation, and as incapable of being asserted by the students, as at present. . . .

This is plainly a contract to which the donors, the trustees, and the crown (to whose rights and obligations New Hampshire succeeds) were the original parties. It is a contract made on a valuable consideration. It is a contract for the security and disposition of property. It is a contract on the faith of which real and personal estate has been conveyed to the corporation. It is then a contract within the letter of the constitution, and within its spirit also, unless the fact that the property is invested by the donors in trustees, for the promotion of religion and education, for the benefit of persons who are perpetually changing, though the objects remain the same, shall create a particular exception, taking this case out of the prohibition contained in the constitution. . . .

On what safe and intelligible ground can this exception stand? There is no expression in the constitution, no sentiment delivered by its contemporaneous expounders, which would justify us in making it. . . .

. . . These eleemosynary institutions do not fill the place, which would otherwise be occupied by government, but that which would otherwise remain vacant. They are complete acquisitions to literature. They are donations to education; donations, which any government must be disposed rather to encourage than to discountenance. It requires no very critical examination of the human mind, to enable us to determine, that one great inducement to these gifts is the conviction felt by the giver, that the disposition he makes of them is immutable. . . . All such gifts are made in the pleasing, perhaps delusive hope, that the charity will flow forever in the channel which the givers have marked out for it. If every man finds in his own bosom strong evidence of the universality of this sentiment, there can be but little reason to imagine, that the framers of our constitution were strangers to it, and that, feeling the necessity and policy of giving permanence and security to contracts, of withdrawing them from the influence of legislative bodies, whose fluctuating policy, and repeated interferences, produced the most perplexing and injurious embarrassments, they still deemed it necessary to leave these contracts subject to those interferences. The motives for such an exception must be very powerful, to justify the construction which makes it. . . .

2. We next proceed to the inquiry, whether its obligation has been impaired by those acts of the legislature of New Hampshire, to which the special verdict refers? . . .

It has been already stated, that the act "to amend the charter, and enlarge and improve the corporation of Dartmouth College," increases the number of trustees to 21, gives the appointment of the additional members to the executive of the state, and creates a board of overseers, to consist of 25 persons, of whom twenty-one are also appointed by the executive of New Hampshire, who have power to inspect and control the most important acts of the trustees. . . .

The whole power of governing the college is transferred from trustees appointed according to the will of the founder, expressed in the charter, to the executive of New Hampshire. The management and application of the funds of this eleemosynary institution, which are placed by the donors in the hands of trustees named in the charter, and empowered to perpetuate themselves, are placed by this act under the control of the government of the state. The will of the state is substituted for the will of the donors, in every essential operation of the college. This is not an immaterial change. . . .

It results from this opinion, that the acts of the legislature of New Hampshire, which are stated in the special verdict found in this cause, are repugnant to the constitution of the United States; and that the judgment on this special verdict ought to have been for the plaintiffs. The judgment of the State Court must, therefore, be reversed.

MR. JUSTICE WASHINGTON, concurring . . . [omitted].

MR. JUSTICE STORY, concurring . . . [omitted].

MR. JUSTICE DUVALL dissented [without opinion].

Charles River Bridge v. *Warren Bridge* 36 U.S. (11 Pet.) 420, 9 L.Ed. 773 (1837)

http://caselaw.findlaw.com/us-supreme-court/36/420.html

In 1785, the Massachusetts legislature granted to the Charles River Bridge Co. the right to construct a bridge between Charlestown and Boston, with the power to collect tolls for 40 years (later extended to 70 years). This franchise replaced an exclusive ferry right formerly possessed by Harvard College, but which the college yielded in return for annual payments during the life of the bridge charter. In 1828, some Charlestown merchants received a legislative charter for construction of the Warren Bridge, with the power to collect tolls until they had been reimbursed. At that point, title to the Warren Bridge would pass to the state, and passage would become free. Proprietors of the Charles River Bridge, who would be deprived of their anticipated tolls because the new bridge was to be built close to the old one, unsuccessfully sought an injunction and other relief in state court. The case was first argued in the Supreme Court in 1831, while Marshall was chief justice, but absenteeism and a sharp division among the justices delayed decision. The case was reargued in 1837 after Taney succeeded Marshall. A very short excerpt from Justice Story's 65-page dissenting opinion follows Taney's opinion for the Court. Majority: Taney, Baldwin, Barbour, Wayne. Dissenting: McLean, Story, Thompson.

Mr. Chief Justice Taney delivered the opinion of the Court. . . .

This brings us to the act of the legislature of Massachusetts, of 1785, by which the plaintiffs were incorporated by the name of "The Proprietors of the Charles River Bridge"; and it is here, and in the law of 1792, prolonging their charter, that we must look for the extent and nature of the franchise conferred upon the plaintiffs.

Much has been said in the argument of the principles of construction by which this law is to be expounded, and what undertakings, on the part of the state, may be implied. The court thinks there can be no serious difficulty on that head. It is the grant of certain franchises by the public to a private corporation, and in a matter where the public interest is concerned. The rule of construction in such cases is well settled, both in England and by the decisions of our own tribunals. . . . "This, like many other cases, is a bargain between a company of adventurers and the public, the terms of which are expressed in the statute; and the rule of construction, in all such cases, is now fully established to be this; that any ambiguity in the terms of the contract must operate against the adventurers, and in favor of the public, and the plaintiffs can claim nothing that is not clearly given them by the act." And the doctrine thus laid down is abundantly sustained by the authorities referred to in this decision. . . .

The argument in favor of the proprietors of the Charles River bridge, is . . . that the power claimed by the state, if it exists, may be so used as to destroy the value of the franchise they have granted to the corporation. . . . The existence of the power does not, and cannot depend upon the circumstance of its having been exercised or not. . . .

The object and end of all government is to promote the happiness and prosperity of the community by which it is established, and it can never be assumed, that the government intended to diminish its powers of accomplishing the end for which it was created. And in a country like ours, free, active, and enterprising, continually advancing in numbers and wealth, new channels of communication are daily found necessary, both for travel and trade; and are essential to the comfort, convenience, and prosperity of the people. A state ought never to be presumed to surrender this power, because, like the taxing power, the whole community has an interest in preserving it undiminished. And when a corporation alleges, that a state has surrendered, for 70 years, its power of improvement and public accommodation, in a great and important line of travel, along which a vast number of its citizens must daily pass, the community has a right to insist, in the language of this court above quoted, "that its abandonment ought not to be presumed in a case in which the deliberate purpose of the state to abandon it does not appear." The continued existence of a government would be of no great value, if by implications and presumptions it was disarmed by the powers necessary to accomplish the ends of its creation; and the functions it was designed to perform, transferred to the hands of privileged corporations. . . . While the rights of private property are sacredly guarded, we must not forget that the community also has rights, and that the happiness and well-being of every citizen depends on their faithful preservation.

Adopting the rule of construction above stated as the settled one, we proceed to apply it to the charter of 1785, to the proprietors of the Charles River bridge. This act of incorporation is in the usual form, and the privileges such as are commonly given to corporations of that kind. It confers on them the ordinary faculties of a corporation, for the purpose of building the bridge; and establishes certain rates of toll, which the company is authorized to take: this is the whole grant. There is no exclusive privilege given to them over the water of Charles River, above or below their bridge; no right to erect another bridge themselves, nor to prevent other persons from erecting one, no engagement from the state, that another shall not be erected; and no undertaking not to sanction competition, not to make improvements that may diminish the amount of its income. Upon all these subjects, the charter is silent; and nothing is said in it about a line of travel, so much insisted on in the argument, in which they are to have exclusive privileges. . . .

In short, all the franchises and rights of property, enumerated in the charter, and there mentioned to have been granted to it, remain unimpaired. But its income is destroyed by the Warren bridge; which, being free, draws off the passengers and property which would have gone over it, and renders their franchise of no value. This is the gist of the complaint. For it is not pretended, that the erection of the Warren bridge would have done them any injury, or in any degree affected their right of property, if it had not diminished the amount of their tolls. In order, then, to entitle themselves to relief, it is necessary to show, that the legislature contracted not to do the act of which they complain; and that they impaired, or in other words, violated, that contract by the erection of the Warren bridge.

The inquiry, then, is, does the charter contain such a contract on the part of the state? Is there any such stipulation to be found in that instrument? It must be admitted on all hands, that there is none; no words that even relate to another bridge, or to the diminution of their tolls, or to the line of travel. If a contract on that subject can be gathered from the charter, it must be by implication; and cannot be found in the words used. Can such an agreement be implied? The rule of construction before stated is an answer to the question; in charters of this description, no rights are taken from the public, or given to the corporation, beyond those which the words of the charter, by their natural and proper construction, purport to convey. There are no words which import such a contract as the plaintiffs in error contend for, and none can be implied. . . .

Indeed, the practice and usage of almost every state in the Union, old enough to have commenced the work of internal improvement, is opposed to the doctrine contended for on the part of the plaintiffs in error. Turnpike roads have been made in succession, on the same line of travel; the later ones interfering materially with the profits of the first. These corporations have, in some instances, been utterly ruined by the introduction of newer and better modes of transportation and traveling. In some cases, railroads have rendered the turnpike roads on the same line of travel so entirely useless, that the franchise of the turnpike corporation is not worth preserving. Yet in none of these cases have the corporations supposed that their privileges were invaded, or any contract violated on the part of the state. . . .

And what would be the fruits of this doctrine of implied contracts, on the part of the states, and of property in a line of travel by a corporation, if it should now be sanctioned by this court? To what results would it lead us? . . . Let it once be understood, that such charters carry with them these implied contracts, and give this unknown and undefined property in a line of traveling; and you will soon find the old turnpike corporations awakening from their sleep and calling upon this court to put down the improvements which have taken their place. The millions of property which have been invested in railroads and canals, upon lines of travel which had been before occupied by turnpike corporations, will be put in jeopardy. We shall be thrown back to the improvements of the last century, and obliged to stand still, until the claims of the old turnpike corporations shall be satisfied; and they shall consent to permit these states to avail themselves of the lights of modern science, and to partake of the benefit of those improvements which are now adding to the wealth and prosperity, and the convenience and comfort, of every other part of the civilized world. . . . This court is not prepared to sanction principles which must lead to such results. . . .

The judgment of the supreme judicial court of the commonwealth of Massachusetts, dismissing the plaintiff's bill, must therefore, be affirmed with costs.

MR. JUSTICE Baldwin, concurring . . . [omitted].
MR. JUSTICE MCLEAN, dissenting . . . [omitted].

MR. JUSTICE STORY, dissenting. . . .

I admit, that where the terms of a grant are to impose burdens upon the public, or to create a restraint injurious to the public interests, there is sound reason for interpreting the terms, if ambiguous, in favor of the public. But at the same time, I insist, that there is not the slightest reason for saying, even in such a case, that the grant is not to be construed favorably to the grantee, so as to secure him in the enjoyment of what is actually granted. . . .

For my own part, I can conceive of no surer plan to arrest all public improvements, founded on private capital and enterprise, than to make the outlay of that capital uncertain, and questionable both as to security, and as to productiveness. No man will hazard his capital in any enterprise, in which, if there be a loss, it must be borne exclusively by himself; and if there be success, he has not the slightest security of enjoying the rewards of that success for a single moment. . . .

MR. JUSTICE THOMPSON, dissenting . . . [omitted].

Home Building & Loan Association v. *Blaisdell* 290 U.S. 398, 54 S.Ct. 231, 78 L.Ed. 413 (1934)

http://caselaw.findlaw.com/us-supreme-court/290/398.html

The Minnesota Mortgage Moratorium Law of 1933 was designed to prevent the foreclosure of mortgages during the Depression by extending the redemption period of mortgages under conditions set by a court. The act was to remain in effect "only during the continuance of the emergency and in no event beyond May 1, 1935." Blaisdell had mortgaged a house and lot to the appellant company; when Blaisdell failed to make timely payments, the company foreclosed, and Blaisdell sought an extension. A state court extended the redemption period on condition that certain monthly payments be made, and the Supreme Court of Minnesota affirmed. Majority: Hughes, Brandeis, Cardozo, Roberts, Stone. Dissenting: Sutherland, Butler, McReynolds, Van Devanter.

Mr. Chief Justice Hughes delivered the opinion of the Court. . . .

The statute does not impair the integrity of the mortgage indebtedness. . . . Aside from the extension of time, the other conditions of redemption are unaltered. . . .

In determining whether the provision for this temporary and conditional relief exceeds the power of the state by reason of the clause in the Federal Constitution prohibiting impairment of the obligations of contracts, we must consider the relation of emergency to constitutional power, the historical setting of the contract clause, the development of the jurisprudence of this Court in the construction of that clause, and the principles of construction which we may consider to be established.

Emergency does not create power. Emergency does not increase granted power or remove or diminish the restrictions imposed upon power granted or reserved. . . .

While emergency does not create power, emergency may furnish the occasion for the exercise of power. . . . The constitutional question presented in the light of an emergency is whether the power possessed embraces the particular exercise of it in response to particular conditions. Thus, the war power of the federal government is not created by the emergency of war, but it is a power given to meet that emergency. It is a power to wage war successfully, and thus it permits the harnessing of the entire energies of the people in a supreme cooperative effort to preserve the nation. But even the war power does not remove constitutional limitations safeguarding essential liberties. When the provisions of the Constitution, in grant or restriction, are specific, so particularized as not to admit of construction, no question is presented. . . . But, where constitutional grants and limitations of power are set forth in general clauses, which afford a broad outline, the process of construction is essential to fill in the details. That is true of the contract clause. . . .

In the construction of the contract clause, the debates in the Constitutional Convention are of little aid. But the reasons which led to the adoption of that clause, and of the other prohibitions of Section 10 of Article I, are not left in doubt, and have frequently been described with eloquent emphasis. The widespread distress following the revolutionary period, and the plight of debtors had called forth in the states an ignoble array of legislative schemes for the defeat of creditors and the invasion of contractual obligations. Legislative interferences had been so numerous and extreme that the confidence essential to prosperous trade had been undermined and the utter destruction of credit was threatened. . . .

It is manifest . . . that there has been a growing appreciation of public needs and of the necessity of finding ground for a rational compromise between individual rights and public welfare. . . .

It is no answer to say that this public need was not apprehended a century ago, or to insist that what the provision of the Constitution meant to the vision of that day it must mean to the vision of our time. If by the statement that what the Constitution meant at the time of its adoption it means today, it is intended to say that the great clauses of the Constitution must be confined to the interpretation which the framers, with the conditions and outlook of their time, would have placed upon them, the statement carries its own refutation. It was to guard against such a narrow conception that Chief Justice Marshall uttered the memorable warning: "We must never forget, that it is a *constitution* we are expounding"; "a constitution intended to endure for ages to come, and consequently, to be adapted to the various crises of human affairs." . . .

With a growing recognition of public needs and the relation of individual right to public security, the Court has sought to prevent the perversion of the clause through its use as an instrument to throttle the capacity of the states to protect their fundamental interests. . . .

We are of the opinion that the Minnesota statute as here applied does not violate the contract clause of the Federal Constitution. Whether the legislation is wise or unwise as a matter of policy is a question with which we are not concerned. . . .

The judgment of the Supreme Court of Minnesota is affirmed.

Judgment affirmed.

Mr. Justice Sutherland, dissenting. . . .

A provision of the Constitution, it is hardly necessary to say, does not admit of two distinctly opposite interpretations. It does not mean one thing at one time and an entirely different thing at another time. If the contract impairment clause, when framed and adopted, meant that the term of a contract for the payment of money could not be altered *in invitum* [against one not assenting] by a state statute enacted for the relief of hardly pressed debtors to the end and with the effect of postponing payment or enforcement during and because of an economic or financial emergency, it is but to state the obvious to say that it means the same now. . . .

The provisions of the Federal Constitution, undoubtedly, are pliable in the sense that in appropriate cases they have the capacity of bringing within their grasp every new condition which falls within their meaning. But, their *meaning* is changeless; it is only their *application* which is extensible. . . .

A candid consideration of the history and circumstances which led up to and accompanied the framing and adoption of this clause will demonstrate conclusively that it was framed and adopted with the specific and studied purpose of preventing legislation designed to relieve debtors *especially* in time of financial distress. Indeed, it is not probable that any other purpose was definitely in the minds of those who composed the framers' convention or the ratifying state conventions which followed, although the restriction has been given a wider application upon principles clearly stated by Chief Justice Marshall in the Dartmouth College Case. . . .

The defense of the Minnesota law is made upon grounds which were discountenanced by the makers of the Constitution and have many times been rejected by this court. . . . With due regard for the process of logical thinking, it legitimately cannot be urged that conditions which produced the rule may now be invoked to destroy it.

. . . The opinion concedes that emergency does not create power, or increase granted power, or remove or diminish restrictions upon power granted or reserved. It then proceeds to say, however, that while emergency does not create power, it may furnish the occasion for the exercise of power. I can only interpret what is said on that subject as meaning that while an emergency does not diminish a restriction upon power it furnishes an occasion for diminishing it; and this, as it seems to me, is merely to say the same thing by the use of another set of words, with the effect of affirming that which has just been denied. . . .

I am authorized to say that Mr. Justice Van Devanter, Mr. Justice McReynolds and Mr. Justice Butler concur in this opinion.

Mr. Justice Cardozo, concurring in an *unpublished* opinion.[2] . . .

The economic and social changes wrought by the industrial revolution and by the growth of population have made it necessary for government at this day to [do] a thousand things that were beyond the experience or the thought of a century ago. With the growing recognition of this need, courts have awakened to the truth that the contract clause is perverted from its proper meaning when it throttles the capacity of the states to exert their governmental power in response to crying needs. . . . The early cases dealt with the problem as one affecting the conflicting rights and interests of individuals and classes. This was the attitude of the courts up to the Fourteenth Amendment; and the tendency to some extent persisted even later. . . . The rights and interests of the state itself were involved, as it seemed, only indirectly and remotely, if they were thought to be involved at all. We know better in these days, with the passing of the frontier and of the unpeopled spaces of the west. With these and other changes, the welfare of the social organism in any of its parts is bound up more inseparably than ever with the welfare of the whole. . . . The state when it acts today by statutes like the one before us is not furthering the selfish good of individuals or classes as ends of ultimate validity. It is furthering its own good by maintaining the economic structure on which the good of all depends. Such at least is its endeavor, however much it miss the mark. The attainment of that end, so august and impersonal, will not be barred and thwarted by the obstruction of a contract set up along the way.

Looking back over the century, one perceives a process of evolution too strong to be set back. . . . [T]he court in its interpretation of the contract clause has been feeling its way toward a rational compromise between private rights and public welfare. From the beginning it was seen that something must be subtracted from the words of the Constitution in all their literal and stark significance. . . . Contracts were still to be preserved. . . . But a promise exchanged between individuals was not to paralyze the state in its endeavor in times of direful crisis to keep its life-blood flowing.

To hold this may be inconsistent with things that men said in 1787 when expounding to compatriots the newly written constitution. They did not see the changes in the relation between states and nation or in the play of social forces that lay hidden in the womb of time. It may be inconsistent with things that they believed or took for granted. Their beliefs to be significant must be adjusted to the world they knew. It is not in my judgment inconsistent with what they would say today, nor with what today they would believe, if they were called upon to interpret "in the light of our whole experience" the constitution that they framed for the needs of an expanding future.

III. PROPERTY RIGHTS AND THE FOURTEENTH AMENDMENT

Slaughterhouse Cases (*Butchers' Benevolent Association* v. *Crescent City Livestock Landing & Slaughter-House Co.*) 83 U.S. (16 Wall.) 36, 21 L.Ed. 394 (1873)

http://caselaw.findlaw.com/us-supreme-court/83/36.html

In 1869, the Louisiana legislature granted a monopoly to a slaughterhouse company for the sheltering and butchering of animals within three parishes, including the city of New Orleans. All other butchers were required to use the slaughterhouse company's facilities, upon payment of a fee. By one account, more than a thousand butchers and their employees were adversely affected by the law. Various butchers then unsuccessfully sought an injunction against the monopoly in the state courts. The three cases which went to the U.S. Supreme Court are collectively known as the Slaughterhouse Cases. The lead suit was brought by the Butchers' Benevolent Association with former justice John A. Campbell as counsel. Majority: Miller, Clifford, Davis, Hunt, Strong. Dissenting: Field, Bradley, Chase, Swayne.

Mr. Justice Miller . . . delivered the opinion of the Court. . . .

The statute is denounced not only as creating a monopoly and conferring odious and exclusive privileges upon a small number of persons at the expense of the great body of the community of New Orleans, but it is asserted that it deprives a large and meritorious class of citizens—the whole of the butchers of the city—of the right to exercise their trade, the business to which they have been trained and on which they depend for the support of themselves and their families; and that the unrestricted exercise of the business of butchering is necessary to the daily subsistence of the population of the city. . . .

The wisdom of the monopoly granted by the legislature may be open to question, but it is difficult to see a justification for the assertion that the butchers are deprived of the right to labor in their occupation, or the people of their daily service in preparing food, or how this statute, with the duties and guards imposed upon the company, can be said to destroy the business of the butcher, or seriously interfere with its pursuit. . . .

The plaintiffs in error . . . allege that the statute is a violation of the Constitution of the United States in these several particulars:

That it creates an involuntary servitude forbidden by the thirteenth article of amendment;

That it abridges the privileges and immunities of citizens of the United States;

That it denies to the plaintiffs the equal protection of the laws; and,

That it deprives them of their property without due process of law; contrary to the provisions of the first section of the fourteenth article of amendment.

This court is thus called upon for the first time to give construction to these articles. . . . On the most casual examination of the language of these amendments [the Thirteenth, Fourteenth, and Fifteenth], no one can fail to be impressed with the one pervading purpose found in them all, lying at the foundation of each, and without which none of them would have even been suggested; we mean the freedom of the slave race, the security and firm establishment of that freedom, and the protection of the newly-made freeman and citizen from the oppressions of those who had formerly exercised unlimited dominion over him. It is true that only the fifteenth amendment, in terms, mentions the negro by speaking of his color and his slavery. But it is just as true that each of the other articles was addressed to the grievances of that race, and designed to remedy them as the fifteenth.

We do not say that no one else but the negro can share in this protection. . . . But what we do say, and what we wish to be understood is, that in any fair and just construction of any section or phrase of these amendments, it is necessary to look to the purpose which we have said was the pervading spirit of them all, the evil which they were designed to remedy, and the process of continued addition to the Constitution, until that purpose was supposed to be accomplished as far as constitutional law can accomplish it. . . .

The next observation is more important in view of the arguments of counsel in the present case. It is, that the distinction between citizenship of the United States and citizenship of a State is clearly recognized and established. Not only may a man be a citizen of the United States without being a citizen of a State, but an important element is necessary to convert the former into the latter. He must reside within the State to make him a citizen of it, but it is only necessary that he should be born or naturalized in the United States to be a citizen of the Union.

It is quite clear, then, that there is a citizenship of the United States, and a citizenship of a State, which are distinct from each other, and which depend upon different characteristics or circumstances in the individual.

We think this distinction and its explicit recognition in this amendment of great weight in this argument, because the next paragraph of this same section, which is the one mainly relied on by the plaintiffs in error, speaks only of privileges and immunities of citizens of the United States, and does not speak of those of citizens of the several States. The argument, however, in favor of the plaintiffs rests wholly on the assumption that the citizenship is the same, and the privileges and immunities guaranteed by the clause are the same.

The language is, "No State shall make or enforce any law which shall abridge the privileges or immunities of citizens *of the United States*." It is a little remarkable, if this clause was intended as a protection to the citizen of a State against the legislative power of his own State, that the word citizen of the State should be left out when it is so carefully used, and used in contradistinction to citizens of the United States, in the very sentence which precedes it. It is too clear for argument that the change in phraseology was adopted understandingly and with a purpose.

Of the privileges and immunities of the citizen of the United States, and of the privileges and immunities of the citizen of the State, and what they respectively are, we will presently consider; but we wish to state here that it is only the former which are placed by this clause under the protection of the Federal Constitution, and that the latter, whatever they may be, are not intended to have any additional protection by this paragraph of the amendment.

If, then, there is a difference between the privileges and immunities belonging to a citizen of the United States as such, and those belonging to the citizen of the State as such, the latter must rest for their security and protection where they have heretofore rested; for they are not embraced by this paragraph of the amendment. . . .

Fortunately we are not without judicial construction of this clause of the Constitution. The first and the leading case on the subject is that of *Corfield* v. *Coryell* decided by Mr. Justice Washington in the Circuit Court for the District of Pennsylvania in 1823.

"The inquiry," he says, "is, what are the privileges and immunities of citizens of the several States? We feel no hesitation in confining these expressions to those privileges and immunities which are fundamental; which belong of right to the citizens of all free governments, and which have at all times been enjoyed by citizens of the several States which compose this Union, from the time of their becoming free, independent, and sovereign. What these fundamental principles are, it would be more tedious than difficult to enumerate. They may all, however, be comprehended under the following general heads: protection by the government, with the right to acquire and possess property of every kind, and to pursue and obtain happiness and safety, subject, nevertheless, to such restraints as the government may prescribe for the general good of the whole." . . .

It would be the vainest show of learning to attempt to prove by citations of authority, that up to the adoption of the recent amendments, no claim or pretense was set up that those rights depended on the Federal government for their existence or protection, beyond the very few express limitations which the Federal Constitution imposed upon the States—such, for instance, as the prohibition against ex post facto laws, bills of attainder, and laws impairing the obligation of contracts. But with the exception of these and a few other restrictions, the entire domain of the privileges and immunities of the citizens of the States, as above defined, lay within the constitutional and legislative power of the States, and without that of the Federal government. Was it the purpose of the Fourteenth Amendment, by the simple declaration that no State should make or enforce any law which shall abridge the privileges and immunities of citizens of the United States, to transfer the security and protection of all the civil rights which we have mentioned, from the States to the Federal government? And where it is declared that Congress shall have the power to enforce that article, was it intended to bring within the power of Congress the entire domain of civil rights heretofore belonging exclusively to the States?

All this and more must follow, if the proposition of the plaintiffs in error be sound. For not only are these rights subject to the control of Congress whenever in its discretion any of them are supposed to be abridged by State legislation, but that body may also pass laws in advance, limiting and restricting the exercise of legislative power by the States, in their most ordinary and usual functions, as in its judgment it may think proper on all such subjects. And still further, such a construction followed by the reversal of the judgments of the Supreme Court of Louisiana in these cases, would constitute this court a perpetual censor upon all legislation of the States, on the civil rights of their own citizens, with authority to nullify such as it did not approve as consistent with those rights, as they existed at the time of the adoption of this amendment. The argument we admit is not always the most conclusive which is drawn from the consequences urged against the adoption of a particular construction of an instrument. But when, as in the case before us, these consequences are so serious, so far-reaching and pervading, so great a departure from the structure and spirit of our institutions; when the effect is to fetter and degrade the State governments by subjecting them to the control of Congress, in the exercise of powers heretofore universally conceded to them of the most ordinary and fundamental character; when in fact it radically changes the whole theory of the relations of the State and Federal governments to each other and of both these governments to the people; the argument has a force that is irresistible, in the absence of language which expresses such a purpose too clearly to admit of doubt.

We are convinced that no such results were intended by the Congress which proposed these amendments, nor by the legislatures of the States which ratified them. . . .

[W]e may hold ourselves excused from defining the privileges and immunities of citizens of the United States which no State can abridge, until some case involving those privileges may make it necessary to do so.

But lest it should be said that no such privileges and immunities are to be found if those we have been considering are excluded, we venture to suggest some which owe their existence to the Federal government, its National character, its Constitution, or its laws.

One of these . . . described in . . . *Crandall* v. *Nevada* . . . is the right of the citizen of this country, protected by implied guarantees of its Constitution, "to come to the seat of government to assert any claim he may have upon that government, to transact any business he may have with it, to seek its protection, to share its offices, to engage in administering its functions. He has the right of free access to its seaports, through which all operations of foreign commerce are conducted, to the sub-treasuries, land offices, and courts of justice in the several states." . . .

Another privilege of a citizen of the United States is to demand the care and protection of the Federal government over his life, liberty, and property when on the high seas or within the jurisdiction of a foreign government. Of this there can be no doubt, nor that the right depends upon his character as a citizen of the United States. The right to peaceably assemble and petition for redress of grievances, the privilege of the writ of habeas corpus, are rights of the citizen guaranteed by the Federal Constitution. The right to use the navigable waters of the United States, however they may penetrate the territory of the several States, all rights secured to our citizens by treaties with foreign nations, are dependent upon citizenship of the United States, and not citizenship of a State. . . .

But it is useless to pursue this branch of the inquiry, since we are of opinion that the rights claimed by these plaintiffs in error, if they have any existence, are not privileges and immunities of citizens of the United States within the meaning of the clause of the fourteenth amendment under consideration. . . .

The argument has not been much pressed in these cases that the defendant's charter deprives the plaintiffs of their property without due process of law, or that it denies to them the equal protection of the law. The first of these paragraphs has been in the Constitution since the adoption of the fifth amendment, as a restraint upon the Federal power. . . .

We are not without judicial interpretation, therefore, both State and National, of the meaning of this clause. And it is sufficient to say that under no construction of that provision that we have ever seen, or any that we deem admissible, can the restraint imposed by the State of Louisiana upon the exercise of their trade by the butchers of New Orleans be held to be a deprivation of property within the meaning of that provision.

"Nor shall any State deny to any person within its jurisdiction the equal protection of the laws."

In the light of the history of these amendments, and the pervading purpose of them, which we have already discussed, it is not difficult to give a meaning to this clause. The existence of laws in the States where the newly emancipated negroes resided, which discriminated with gross injustice and hardship against them as a class, was the evil to be remedied by this clause, and by it such laws are forbidden. . . .

We doubt very much whether any action of a State not directed by way of discrimination against the negroes as a class, or on account of their race, will ever be held to come within the purview of this provision. It is so clearly a provision for that race and that emergency, that a strong case would be necessary for its application to any others. . . .

The judgments of the Supreme Court of Louisiana in these cases are

Affirmed.

Mr. Justice Field, dissenting. . . .

The question presented is . . . is nothing less than the question whether the recent amendments to the Federal Constitution protect the citizens of the United States against the deprivation of their common rights by legislation. In my judgment the fourteenth amendment does afford such protection, and was so intended by the Congress which framed and the States which adopted it.

The amendment does not attempt to confer any new privileges or immunities upon citizens, or to enumerate or define those already existing. It assumes that there are such privileges and immunities which belong of right to citizens as such, and ordains that they shall not be abridged by State legislation. If this inhibition has no reference to privileges and immunities of this character, but only refers, as held by the majority of the court in their opinion, to such privileges and immunities as were before its adoption specially designated in the Constitution or necessarily implied as belonging to citizens of the United States, it was a vain and idle enactment, which accomplished nothing, and most unnecessarily excited Congress and the people on its passage. With privileges and immunities thus designated or implied no State could ever have interfered by its laws and no new constitutional provision was required to inhibit such interference. The supremacy of the Constitution and the laws of the United States always controlled any State legislation of that character. But if the amendment refers to the natural and inalienable rights which belong to all citizens, the inhibition has a profound significance and consequence.

What, then, are the privileges and immunities which are secured against abridgment by State legislation? . . .

The terms, "privileges and immunities" are not new in the Amendment; they were in the Constitution before the Amendment was adopted. They are found in the 2d section of the 4th article, which declares that "the citizens of each State shall be entitled to all privileges and immunities of citizens in the several States," and they have been the subject of frequent consideration in judicial decisions. In *Corfield* v. *Coryell* . . . Mr. Justice Washington said he had "no hesitation in confining these expressions to those privileges and immunities which were, in their nature, fundamental; which belong of right to citizens of all free governments, and which have at all times been enjoyed by the citizens of the several States which compose the Union, from the time of their becoming free, independent, and sovereign"; and in considering what those fundamental privileges were, he said that perhaps it would be more tedious than difficult to enumerate them, but that they might be "all comprehended under the following general heads: protection by the government; the enjoyment of life and liberty, with the right to acquire and possess property of every kind, and to pursue and obtain happiness and safety, subject, nevertheless to such restraints as the government may justly prescribe for the general good of the whole." This appears to me to be a sound construction of the clause in question. The privileges and immunities designated are those *which of right belong to the citizens of all free governments.* Clearly among these must be placed the right to pursue a lawful employment in a lawful manner, without other restraint than such as equally affects all persons. . . .

This equality of right, with exemption from all disparaging and partial enactments, in the lawful pursuits of life, throughout the whole country, is the distinguishing privilege of citizens of the United States. To them, everywhere, all pursuits, all professions, all avocations are open without other restrictions than such as are imposed equally upon all others of the same age, sex, and condition. The State may prescribe such regulations for every pursuit and calling of life as will promote the public health, secure the good order and advance the general prosperity of society, but when once prescribed the pursuit or calling must be free to be followed by every citizen who is within the conditions designated, and will conform to the regulations. This is the fundamental idea upon which our institutions rest, and unless adhered to in the legislation of the country our government will be a republic only in name. . . .

I am authorized by the Chief Justice [Chase], Mr. Justice Swayne, and Mr. Justice Bradley, to state that they concur with me in this dissenting opinion.

Mr. Justice Bradley, dissenting . . . [omitted].
Mr. Justice Swayne, dissenting . . . [omitted].

Munn v. *Illinois*
94 U.S. 113, 24 L.Ed. 77 (1877)

http://caselaw.findlaw.com/us-supreme-court/94/113.html

Article XIII of the Constitution of Illinois, adopted in 1870, declared grain warehouses to be "public warehouses" and gave to the General Assembly the power of passing laws relating to the storage of grain. An act of 1871 fixed the rates warehouse owners might charge, required licenses, and made other regulations governing the conduct of warehouse owners. Munn and his partner Scott were convicted of operating a warehouse without a license and other unlawful practices, and sought review from an adverse judgment in the Illinois Supreme Court. That part of the chief justice's opinion dealing with the commerce clause is omitted. *Munn* and several railroad rate cases also decided on March 1, 1877, are collectively known as the Granger Cases. These cases came down just as the Electoral Commission was completing its task of trying to resolve the disputed presidential election of 1876. That commission consisted of Waite Court justices

Clifford, Field, Bradley, Miller, and Strong, plus five members of the House of Representatives and five senators. Majority: Waite, Bradley, Clifford, Davis, Hunt, Miller, Swayne. Dissenting: Field, Strong.

Mr. Chief Justice Waite delivered the opinion of the Court.

The question to be determined in this case is whether the general assembly of Illinois can, under the limitations upon the legislative powers of the States imposed by the Constitution of the United States, fix by law the maximum of charges for the storage of grain in warehouses at Chicago and other places in the State having not less than one hundred thousand inhabitants, "in which grain is stored in bulk, and in which the grain of different owners is mixed together, or in which grain is stored in such a manner that the identity of different lots or parcels cannot be accurately preserved." . . .

When one becomes a member of society, he necessarily parts with some rights or privileges which, as an individual not affected by his relations to others, he might retain. "A body politic," as aptly defined in the preamble of the Constitution of Massachusetts, "is a social compact by which the whole people covenants with each citizen, and each citizen with the whole people, that all shall be governed by certain laws for the common good." This does not confer power upon the whole people to control rights which are purely and exclusively private . . . but it does authorize the establishment of laws requiring each citizen to so conduct himself, and so use his own property, as not unnecessarily to injure another. This is the very essence of government, and has found expression in the maxim, *sic utere tuo ut alienum non laedas.* [So use your own as not to injure others.] From this source come the police powers, which, as was said by Mr. Chief Justice Taney in the License Cases, "are nothing more or less than the powers of government inherent in every sovereignty . . . that is to say . . . the power to govern men and things." Under these powers the government regulates the conduct of its citizens one towards another, and the manner in which each shall use his own property, when such regulation becomes necessary for the public good. In their exercise it has been customary in England from time immemorial, and in this country from its first colonization, to regulate ferries, common carriers, hackmen, bakers, millers, wharfingers, innkeepers, &c., and in so doing to fix a maximum of charge to be made for services rendered, accommodations furnished, and articles sold. To this day, statutes are to be found in many of the States upon some or all these subjects; and we think it has never yet been successfully contended that such legislation came within any of the constitutional prohibitions against interference with private property. With the Fifth Amendment in force, Congress in 1820 conferred power upon the city of Washington "to regulate . . . the rates of wharfage at private wharves . . . the sweeping of chimneys, and to fix the rates of fees therefor . . . and the weight and quality of bread" . . . and, in 1848, "to make all necessary regulations respecting hackney carriages and the rates of fare of the same, and the rates of hauling by cartmen, wagoners, carmen, and draymen, and the rates of commission of auctioneers." . . .

From this it is apparent that, down to the time of the adoption of the Fourteenth Amendment, it was not supposed that statutes regulating the use, or even the price of the use, of private property necessarily deprived an owner of his property without due process of law. Under some circumstances they may, but not under all. The amendment does not change the law in this particular: it simply prevents the States from doing that which will operate as such a deprivation.

This brings us to inquire as to the principles upon which this power of regulation rests, in order that we may determine what is within and what is without its operative effect. Looking, then, to the common law, from whence came the right which the Constitution protects, we find that when private property is "affected with a public interest, it ceases to be *juris privati* [of private right] only." This was said by Lord Chief Justice Hale more than 200 years ago, in his treatise *De Portibus Maris* . . . and has been accepted without objection as an essential element in the law of property ever since. Property does become clothed with a public interest, when used in a manner to make it of public consequence, and affect the community at large. When, therefore, one devotes his property to a use in which the public has an interest, he, in effect, grants to the public an interest in that use, and must submit to be controlled by the public for the common good, to the extent of the interest he has thus created. He may withdraw his grant by discontinuing the use; but, so long as he maintains the use, he must submit to the control. . . .

It is difficult to see why, if the common carrier, or the miller, or the ferryman, or the innkeeper, or the wharfinger, or the baker, or the cartman, or the hackney-coachman, pursues a public employment and exercises "a sort of public office," these plaintiffs in error do not. They stand, to use again the language of their counsel, in the very "gateway of commerce," and take toll from all who pass. . . . Certainly, if any business can be clothed "with a public interest and cease to be *juris privati* only," this has been. It may not be made so by the operation of the Constitution of Illinois or this statute, but it is by the facts.

. . . For our purposes we must assume that, if a state of facts could exist that would justify such legislation, it actually did exist when the statute now under consideration was passed. For us the question is one of power, not of expediency. If no state of circumstances could exist to justify such a statute, then we may declare this one void, because in excess of the legislative power of the State. But if it could, we must presume it did. Of the propriety of legislative interference within the scope of legislative power, the legislature is the exclusive judge. . . .

It is insisted, however, that the owner of property is entitled to a reasonable compensation for its use, even though it be clothed with a public interest, and that what is reasonable is a judicial and not a legislative question. As has already been shown, the practice had been otherwise. . . .

We know that this is a power which may be abused; but that is no argument against its existence. For protection against abuses by legislatures the people must resort to the polls, not to the courts. . . .

Judgment affirmed.

Mr. Justice Field, dissenting. . . .

The declaration of the Constitution of 1870, that private buildings used for private purposes shall be deemed public institutions, does not make them so. The receipt and storage of grain in a building erected by private means for that purpose does not constitute the building a public warehouse. There is no magic in the language, though used by a constitutional convention, which can change a private business into a public one, or alter the character of the building in which the business is transacted. A tailor's or a shoemaker's shop would still retain its private character, even though the assembled wisdom of the State should declare, by organic act or legislative ordinance, that such a place was a public workshop, and that the workmen were public tailors or public shoemakers. One might as well attempt to change the nature of colors, by giving them a new designation. . . .

The doctrine declared is that property "becomes clothed with a public interest when used in a manner to make it of public consequence, and affect the community at large"; and from such clothing the right of the legislature is deduced to control the use of the property, and to determine the compensation which the owner may receive for it. When Sir Matthew Hale, and the sages of the law in his day, spoke of property as affected by a public interest, and ceasing from that cause to be *juris privati* solely, that is ceasing to be held merely in private right, they referred to property dedicated by the owner to public uses, or to property the use of which was granted by the government, or in connection with which special privileges were conferred. Unless the property was thus dedicated or some right bestowed by the government was held with the property, either by specific grant or by prescription of so long a time as to imply a grant originally, the property was not affected by any public interest so as to be taken out of the category of property held in private right. But it is not in any such sense that the terms "clothing property with a public interest" are used in this case. From the nature of the business under consideration—the storage of grain—which, in any sense in which the words can be used, is a private business, in which the public are interested only as they are interested in the storage of other products of the soil, or in articles of manufacture, it is clear that the court intended to declare that, whenever one devotes his property to a business which is useful to the public—"affects the community at large"—the legislature can regulate the compensation which the owner may receive for its use, and for his own services in connection with it. . . .

If this be sound law, if there be no protection, either in the principles upon which our republican government is founded, or in the prohibitions of the Constitution against such invasion of private rights, all property and all business in the State are held at the mercy of a majority of its legislature.

There is nothing in the character of the business of the defendants as warehousemen which called for the interference complained of in this case. . . . The legislation in question is nothing less than a bold assertion of absolute power by the state to control at its discretion the property and business of the citizen, and fix the compensation he shall receive. . . .

I deny the power of any legislature under our government to fix the price which one shall receive for his property of any kind. If the power can be exercised as to one article, it may as to all articles, and the prices of every thing, from a calico gown to a city mansion, may be the subject of legislative direction. . . .

MR. JUSTICE STRONG, dissenting . . . [omitted].

UNSTAGED DEBATE OF 1893: JUSTICE BREWER V. PROFESSOR THAYER

DAVID J. BREWER, "The Movement of Coercion," an Address Before the New York State Bar Association, January 17, 1893

. . . It is the unvarying law, that the wealth of a community will be in the hands of a few; and the greater the general wealth, the greater the individual accumulations. The large majority of men are unwilling to endure that long self-denial and saving which makes accumulation possible; they have not the business tact and sagacity which bring about large combinations and great financial results; and hence it always has been, and until human nature is remodeled always will be true, that the wealth of a nation is in the hands of a few, while the many subsist upon the proceeds of their daily toil. But security is the chief end of government; and other things being equal, the government is best which protects to the fullest extent each individual, rich or poor, high or low, in the possession of his property and the pursuit of his business. It was the boast of our ancestors in the old country, that they were able to wrest from the power of the king so much security for life, liberty and property. . . .

Here there is no monarch threatening trespass upon the individual. The danger is from the multitudes—the majority, with whom is the power. . . .

This movement expresses itself in two ways: First, in the improper use of labor organizations to destroy the freedom of the laborer, and control the uses of capital. . . .

The other form of this movement assumes the guise of a regulation of the charges for the use of property subjected, or supposed to be, to a public use. This acts in two directions: One by extending the list of those things, charges for whose use the government may prescribe; until now we hear it affirmed that whenever property is devoted to a use in which the public has an interest, charges for that use may be fixed by law. And if there be any property in the use of which the public or some portion of it has no interest, I hardly know what it is or where to find it. And second, in so reducing charges for the use of property, which in fact is subjected to a public use, that no compensation or income is received by those who have so invested their property. By the one it subjects all property and its uses to the will of the majority; by the other it robs property of its value. Statutes and decisions both disclose that this movement, with just these results, has a present and alarming existence. . . .

It may be said that that majority will not be so foolish, selfish and cruel as to strip that property of its earning capacity. I say that so long as constitutional guarantees lift on American soil their buttresses and bulwarks against wrong, and so long as the American judiciary breathes the free air of courage, it cannot. . . .

As might be expected, they who wish to push this movement to the extreme, who would brook no restraint on aught that seems to make for their gain, are unanimous in crying out against judicial interference, and are constantly seeking to minimize the power of the courts. . . . The argument is that judges are not adapted by their education and training to settle such matters as these; that they lack acquaintance with affairs and are tied to precedents; that the procedure in the courts is too slow and that no action could be had therein until long after the need of action has passed. It would be folly to assert that this argument is barren of force. . . . But the great body of judges are as well versed in the affairs of life as any, and they who unravel all the mysteries of accounting between partners, settle the business of the largest corporations and extract all the truth from the mass of scholastic verbiage that falls from the lips of expert witnesses in patent cases, will have no difficulty in determining what is right and wrong between employer and employees, and whether proposed rates of freight and fare are reasonable as between the public and the owners; while as for speed, is there anything quicker than a writ of injunction? . . .

The mischief-makers in this movement ever strive to get away from courts and judges, and to place the power of decision in the hands of those who will the more readily and freely yield to the pressure of numbers, that so-called demand of the majority. . . .

And so it is, that because of the growth of this movement, . . . arises the urgent need of giving to the judiciary the utmost vigor and efficiency. Now, if ever in the history of this country, must there be somewhere and somehow a controlling force which speaks for justice, and for justice only. . . .

What, then, ought to be done? My reply is, strengthen the judiciary. . . .

It may be said that this is practically substituting government by the judges for government by the people, and thus turning back the currents of history. . . . But this involves a total misunderstanding of the relations of judges to government. There is nothing in this power of the judiciary detracting in the least from the idea of government of and by the people. The courts hold neither purse nor sword; they cannot corrupt nor arbitrarily control. They make no laws, they establish no policy, they never enter into the domain of popular action. They do not govern. Their functions in relation to the State are limited to seeing that popular action does not trespass upon right and justice as it exists in written constitutions and natural law. . . .

I am firmly persuaded that the salvation of the Nation, the permanence of government of and by the people, rests upon the independence and vigor of the judiciary. To stay the waves of popular feeling, to restrain the greedy hand of the many from filching from the few that which they have honestly acquired, and to protect in every man's possession and enjoyment, be he rich or poor, that which he hath, demands a tribunal as strong as is consistent with the freedom of human action, and as free from all influences and suggestions other than is compassed in the thought of justice, as can be created out of the infirmities of human nature. To that end the courts exist. . . .

JAMES BRADLEY THAYER, "The Origin and Scope of the American Doctrine of Constitutional Law," 7 *Harvard Law Review* 129 (1893)

How did our American doctrine, which allows to the judiciary the power to declare legislative Acts unconstitutional, and to treat them as null, come about, and what is the true scope of it? . . .

The court's duty, we are told, is the mere and simple office of construing two writings and comparing one with another, as two contracts or two statutes are construed and compared when they are said to conflict; of declaring the true meaning of each, and, if they are opposed to each other, of carrying into effect the constitution as being of superior obligation—an ordinary and humble judicial duty, as the courts sometimes describe it. This way of putting it easily results in the wrong kind of disregard of legislative considerations; not merely in refusing to let them directly operate as grounds of judgment, but in refusing to consider them at all. Instead of taking them into account and allowing for them as furnishing possible grounds of legislative action, there takes place a pedantic and academic treatment of the texts of the constitution and the laws. And so we miss that combination of a lawyer's rigor with a statesman's breadth of view which should be found in dealing with this class of questions in constitutional law. . . .

The courts have perceived with more or less distinctness that this exercise of the judicial function does in truth go far beyond the simple business which judges sometimes describe. If their duty were in truth merely and nakedly to ascertain the meaning of the text of the constitution and of the impeached Act of the legislature, and to determine, as an academic question, whether in the court's judgment the two were in conflict, it would, to be sure, be an elevated and important office, one dealing with great matters, involving large public considerations, but yet a function far simpler than it really is. Having ascertained all this, yet there remains a question—the really momentous question—whether, after all, the court can disregard the Act. It cannot do this as a mere matter of course—merely because it is concluded that upon a just and true construction the law is unconstitutional. That is precisely the significance of the rule of administration that the courts lay down. It can only disregard the Act when those who have the right to make laws have not merely made a mistake, but have made a very clear one—so clear that it is not open to rational question. That is the standard of duty to which the courts bring legislative Acts; that is the test which they apply—not merely their own judgment as to constitutionality, but their conclusion as to what judgment is permissible to another department which the constitution has charged with the duty of making it. This rule recognizes that, having regard to the great, complex, ever-unfolding exigencies of government, much which will seem unconstitutional to one man, or body of men, may reasonably not seem so to another; that the constitution often admits of different interpretations; that there is often a range of choice and judgment; that in such cases the constitution does not impose upon the legislature any one specific opinion, but leaves open this range of choice; and that whatever choice is rational is constitutional. . . . [A legislator] may vote against a measure as being, in his judgment, unconstitutional; and, being subsequently placed on the bench, when this measure, having been passed by the legislature in spite of his opposition, comes before him judicially, may there find it his duty, although he has in no degree changed his opinion, to declare it constitutional. . . .

The legislature in determining what shall be done, what it is reasonable to do, does not divide its duty with the judges, nor must it conform to their conception of what is prudent or reasonable legislation. The judicial function is merely that of fixing the outside border of reasonable legislative action, the boundary beyond which the taxing power, the power of eminent domain, police power, and legislative power in general, cannot go without violating the prohibitions of the constitution or crossing the line of its grants. . . . *[T]he ultimate question is not what is the true meaning of the constitution, but whether legislation is sustainable or not.* . . .

What really took place in adopting our theory of constitutional law was this: we introduced for the first time into the conduct of government through its great departments a judicial sanction, as among these departments, not full and complete, but partial. The judges were allowed, indirectly and in a degree, the power to revise the action of other departments and to pronounce it null. In simple truth, while this is a mere judicial function, it involves, owing to the subject matter with which it deals, taking a part, a secondary part, in the political conduct of government. If that be so, then the judges must apply methods and principles that befit their task. In such a work there can be no permanent or fitting *modus vivendi* [arrangement] between the different departments unless each is sure of the full cooperation of the others, as long as its own action conforms to any reasonable and fairly permissible view of its constitutional power. The ultimate arbiter of what is rational and permissible is indeed always the courts, so far as litigated cases bring the question before them. This leaves to our courts a great and stately jurisdiction. It will only imperil the whole of it if it is sought to give them more. They must not step into the shoes of the lawmaker. . . .

I am not stating a new doctrine, but attempting to restate more exactly and truly an admitted one. If what I have said be sound, it is greatly to be desired that it should be more emphasized by our courts, in its full significance. It has been often remarked that private rights are more respected by the legislatures of some countries which have no written constitution, than by ours. No doubt our doctrine of constitutional law has had a tendency to drive out questions of justice and right, and to fill the mind of legislators with thoughts of mere legality, of what the constitution allows. And, moreover, even in the matter of legality, they have felt little responsibility; if we are wrong, they say, the courts will correct it. If what I have been saying is true, the safe and permanent road towards reform is that of impressing upon our people a far stronger sense than they have of the great range of possible harm and evil that our system leaves open, and must leave open, to the legislatures, and of the clear limits of judicial powers; so that responsibility may be brought sharply home where it belongs. . . . Under no system can the power of courts go far to save a people from ruin; our chief protection lies elsewhere. . . .

Lochner v. *New York*
198 U.S. 45, 25 S.Ct. 539, 49 L.Ed. 937 (1905)

http://caselaw.findlaw.com/us-supreme-court/198/45.html

Joseph Lochner, a bakery owner in Utica, New York, was convicted of violating a state law that limited the hours of employment in bakeries and confectionery establishments to 10 hours a day and 60 hours a week. The New York appellate courts sustained the conviction. A little-known aspect of the litigation concerns Henry Weismann, formerly a baker who was active in the labor movement in New York. In 1895, as editor of *The Baker's Journal*, he led the drive that resulted in passage of the statute challenged in this case. He later became a master baker, studied law, was admitted to the bar, and came to believe that the law for which he had labored was a mistake. In 1904, he was engaged by the State Association of Master Bakers to advance Lochner's case from the New York Court of Appeals to the U.S. Supreme Court. The bench of 1905 included one justice (McKenna) who had been reared in a baker's home. Majority: Peckham, Brewer, Brown, Fuller, McKenna. Dissenting: Harlan, Day, Holmes, White.

MR. JUSTICE PECKHAM . . . delivered the opinion of the Court. . . .

The statute necessarily interferes with the right of contract between the employer and employees, concerning the number of hours in which the latter may labor in the bakery of the employer. The general right to make a contract in relation to his business is part of the liberty of the individual protected by the Fourteenth Amendment of the federal constitution. . . . The right to purchase or to sell labor is part of the liberty protected by this amendment, unless there are circumstances which exclude the right. There are, however, certain powers, existing in the sovereignty of each state in the Union, somewhat vaguely termed police powers, the exact description and limitation of which have not been attempted by the courts. Those powers, broadly stated, and without, at present, any attempt at a more specific limitation, relate to the safety, health, morals and general welfare of the public. Both property and liberty are held on such reasonable conditions as may be imposed by the governing power of the state in the exercise of those powers, and with such conditions the Fourteenth Amendment was not designed to interfere.

It must, of course, be conceded that there is a limit to the valid exercise of the police power by the state. . . . Otherwise the Fourteenth Amendment would have no efficacy and the legislatures of the states would have unbounded power, and it would be enough to say that any piece of legislation was enacted to conserve the morals, the health, or the safety of the people; such legislation would be valid, no matter how absolutely without foundation the claim might be. The claim of the police power would be a mere pretext—become another and delusive name for the supreme sovereignty of the state to be exercised free from constitutional restraint. . . . In every case that comes before this court, therefore, where legislation of this character is concerned, and where the protection of the federal Constitution is sought, the question necessarily arises: Is this a fair, reasonable, and appropriate exercise of the police power of the state, or is it an unreasonable, unnecessary, and arbitrary interference with the right of the individual to his personal liberty, or to enter into those contracts in relation to labor which may seem to him appropriate or necessary for the support of himself and his family? Of course the liberty of contract relating to labor includes both parties to it. The one has as much right to purchase as the other to sell labor.

This is not a question of substituting the judgment of the court for that of the legislature. If the act be within the power of the state it is valid, although the judgment of the court might be totally opposed to the enactment of such a law. But the question would still remain: Is it within the police power of the state? and that question must be answered by the court.

The question whether this act is valid as a labor law, pure and simple, may be dismissed in a few words. There is no reasonable ground for interfering with the liberty of person or the right of free contract, by determining the hours of labor, in the occupation of a baker. There is no contention that bakers as a class are not equal in intelligence and capacity to men in other trades or manual occupations, or that they are not able to assert their rights and care for themselves without the protecting arm of the state, interfering with their independence of judgment and of action. They are in no sense wards of the state. Viewed in the light of a purely labor law, with no reference whatever to the question of health, we think that a law like the one before us involves neither the safety, the morals, nor the welfare, of the public, and that the interest of the public is not in the slightest degree affected by such an act. The law must be upheld, if at all, as a law pertaining to the health of the individual engaged in the occupation of a baker. It does not affect any other portion of the public than those who are engaged in that occupation. Clean and wholesome bread does not depend upon whether the baker works but 10 hours per day or only 60 hours a week. The limitation of the hours of labor does not come within the police power on that ground. . . .

We think that there can be no fair doubt that the trade of a baker, in and of itself, is not an unhealthy one to that degree which would authorize the legislature to interfere with the right to labor, and with the right of free contract on the part of the individual, either as employer or employee. In looking through statistics regarding all trades and occupations, it may be true that the trade of a baker does not appear to be as healthy as some other trades, and is also vastly more healthy than still others. To the common understanding the trade of a baker has never been regarded as an unhealthy one. Very likely physicians would not recommend the exercise of that or of any other trade as a remedy for ill health. Some occupations are more healthy than others, but we think there are none which might not come under the power of the legislature to supervise and control the hours of working therein, if the mere fact that the occupation is not absolutely and perfectly healthy is to confer that right upon the legislative department of the government. It might be safely affirmed that almost all occupations more or less affect the health. . . . But are we all, on that account, at the mercy of legislative majorities? . . .

We do not believe in the soundness of the views which uphold this law. . . . The act is not, within any fair meaning of the term, a health law, but is an illegal interference with the rights of individuals, both employers and employees, to make contracts regarding labor upon such terms as they may think best, or which they may agree upon with the other parties to such contracts. . . .

Reversed.

Mr. Justice Harlan, with whom Mr. Justice White and Mr. Justice Day concurred, dissenting. . . .

It is plain that this statute was enacted in order to protect the physical well-being of those who work in bakery and confectionery establishments. . . . [T]he question of the number of hours during which a workman should continuously labor has been . . . a subject of serious consideration among civilized peoples, and by those having special knowledge of the laws of health. . . .

I do not stop to consider whether any particular view of this economic question presents the sounder theory. What the precise facts are it may be difficult to say. It is enough for the determination of this case . . . that the question is one about which there is room for debate and for an honest difference of opinion. There are many reasons . . . in support of the theory that, all things considered, more than 10 hours' steady work each day, from week to week, in a bakery or confectionery establishment, may endanger the health and shorten the lives of the workmen. . . .

If some reasons exist that ought to be the end of this case. . . .

Mr. Justice Holmes, dissenting. . . .

This case is decided upon an economic theory which a large part of the country does not entertain. If it were a question whether I agree with that theory, I should desire to study it further and long before making up my mind. But I do not conceive that to be my duty, because I strongly believe that my agreement or disagreement has nothing to do with the right of a majority to embody their opinions in law. It is settled by various decisions of this court that state Constitutions and state laws may regulate life in many ways which we as legislators might think as injudicious, or if you like as tyrannical as this, and which, equally with this, interfere with the liberty to contract. Sunday laws and usury laws are ancient examples. A more modern one is the prohibition of lotteries. The liberty of the citizen to do as he likes so long as he does not interfere with the liberty of others to do the same, which has been a shibboleth for some well-known writers, is interfered with by school laws, by the post office, by every state or municipal institution which takes his money for purposes thought desirable, whether he likes it or not. The Fourteenth Amendment does not enact Mr. Herbert Spencer's Social Statics. . . . [A] constitution is not intended to embody a particular economic theory, whether of paternalism and the organic relation of the citizen to the state or of *laissez faire*. It is made for people of fundamentally differing views, and the accident of our finding certain opinions natural and familiar, or novel, and even shocking, ought not to conclude our judgment upon the question whether statutes embodying them conflict with the Constitution of the United States.

General propositions do not decide concrete cases. The decisions will depend on a judgment or intuition more subtle than any articulate major premise. But I think that the proposition just stated, if it is accepted, will carry us far toward the end. Every opinion tends to become a law. I think that the word "liberty," in the Fourteenth Amendment, is perverted when it is held to prevent the natural outcome of a dominant opinion, unless it can be said that a rational and fair man necessarily would admit that the statute proposed would infringe fundamental principles as they have been understood by the traditions of our people and our law. It does not need research to show that no such sweeping condemnation can be passed upon the statute before us. . . .

Nebbia v. *New York*
291 U.S. 502, 54 S.Ct. 505, 78 L.Ed. 940 (1934)

http://caselaw.findlaw.com/us-supreme-court/291/502.html

To combat some of the effects of economic depression on the milk industry, the legislature of New York in 1933 adopted a milk control law under which minimum prices could be set. The board established by the law set a minimum price for the retail sale of milk, which Leo Nebbia, a grocer in Rochester, violated. The New York Court of Appeals affirmed his conviction. Many commentators saw the Court's decision in this case, especially the proposition that "the power to promote the general welfare is inherent in government," as indicating judicial approval of the New Deal. Majority: Roberts, Brandeis, Cardozo, Hughes, Stone. Dissenting: McReynolds, Butler, Sutherland, Van Devanter.

Mr. Justice Roberts delivered the opinion of the Court. . . .

Under our form of government the use of property and the making of contracts are normally matters of private and not of public concern. The general rule is that both shall be free of governmental interference. But neither property rights nor contract rights are absolute; for government cannot exist if the citizen may at will use his property to the detriment of his fellows, or exercise his freedom of contract to work them harm. Equally fundamental with the private right is that of the public to regulate it in the common interest. . . .

These correlative rights, that of the citizen to exercise exclusive dominion over property and freely to contract about his affairs, and that of the state to regulate the use of property and the conduct of business, are always in collision. No exercise of the private right can be imagined which will not in some respect, however slight, affect the public; no exercise of the legislative prerogative to regulate the conduct of the citizen which will not to some extent abridge his liberty or affect his property. But subject only to constitutional restraint the private right must yield to the public need.

The Fifth Amendment, in the field of federal activity, and the Fourteenth, as respects state action, do not prohibit governmental regulation for the public welfare. They merely condition the exertion of the admitted power, by securing that the end shall be accomplished by methods consistent with due process. And the guarantee of due process, as has often been held, demands only that the law shall not be unreasonable, arbitrary, or capricious, and that the means selected shall have a real and substantial relation to the object sought to be attained. . . . [T]he reasonableness of each regulation depends upon the relevant facts. . . .

But we are told that because the law essays to control prices it denies due process. . . . The argument runs that the public control of rates or prices is per se unreasonable and unconstitutional, save as applied to businesses affected with a public interest; that a business so affected is one in which property is devoted to an enterprise of a sort which the public itself might appropriately undertake, or one whose owner relies on a public grant or franchise for the right to conduct the business, or in which he is bound to serve all who apply; in short, such as is commonly called a public utility; or a business in its nature a monopoly. The milk industry, it is said, possesses none of these characteristics, and, therefore, not being affected with a public interest, its charges may not be controlled by the state. Upon the soundness of this contention the appellant's case against the statute depends.

We may as well say at once that the dairy industry is not, in the accepted sense of the phrase, a public utility. . . . But if, as must be conceded, the industry is subject to regulation in the public interest, what constitutional principle bars the state from correcting existing maladjustments by legislation touching prices? We think there is no such principle. The due process clause makes no mention of sales or prices any more than it speaks of business or contracts or buildings or other incidents of property. The thought seems nevertheless to have persisted that there is something peculiarly sacrosanct about the price one may charge for what he makes or sells, and that, however able to regulate other elements of manufacture or trade, with incidental effect upon price, the state is incapable of directly controlling the price itself. This view was negatived many years ago. . . .

The phrase "affected with a public interest" can, in the nature of things, mean no more than that an industry, for adequate reason, is subject to control for the public good. . . .

So far as the requirement of due process is concerned, and in the absence of other constitutional restriction, a state is free to adopt whatever economic policy may reasonably be deemed to promote public welfare, and to enforce that policy by legislation adapted to its purpose. The courts are without authority either to declare such policy, or, when it is declared by the legislative arm, to override it. If the laws passed are seen to have a reasonable relation to a proper legislative purpose and are neither arbitrary nor discriminatory, the requirements of due process are satisfied. . . . With the wisdom of the policy adopted, with the adequacy or practicability of the law enacted to forward it, the courts are both incompetent and unauthorized to deal. . . .

Tested by these considerations we find no basis in the due process clause of the Fourteenth Amendment for condemning the provision of the Agriculture and Markets Law here drawn into question.

The judgment is

Affirmed.

Separate opinion of Mr. Justice McReynolds. . . .

If . . . liberty or property may be struck down because of difficult circumstances, we must expect that hereafter every right must yield to the voice of an impatient majority when stirred by distressful exigency. . . . Certain fundamentals have been set beyond experimentation; the Constitution has released them from control by the state. . . .

The exigency is of a kind which inevitably arises when one set of men continue to produce more than all others can buy. The distressing result of the producer followed his ill-advised but voluntary effort. . . .

Of the assailed statute the Court of Appeals says. . . "With the wisdom of the legislation we have naught to do. . . ."

But plainly, I think, this Court must have regard to the wisdom of the enactment.

The Legislature cannot lawfully destroy guaranteed rights of one man with the prime purpose of enriching another, even if for the moment, this may seem advantageous to the public. And the adoption of any "concept of jurisprudence" which permits facile disregard of the Constitution as long interpreted and respected will inevitably lead to its destruction. Then, all rights will be subject to the caprice of the hour; government by stable laws will pass. . . .

Grave concern for embarrassed farmers is everywhere; but this should neither obscure the rights of others nor obstruct judicial appraisement of measures proposed for relief. The ultimate welfare of the producer, like that of every other class, requires dominance of the Constitution. And zealously to uphold this in all its parts is the highest duty intrusted to the courts.

The judgment of the court below should be reversed.

Mr. Justice Van Devanter, Mr. Justice Sutherland, and Mr. Justice Butler authorize me to say that they concur in this opinion.

West Coast Hotel Co. v. *Parrish*
300 U.S. 379, 57 S.Ct. 578, 81 L.Ed. 703 (1937)

http://caselaw.findlaw.com/us-supreme-court/300/379.html

A Washington State act of 1913 authorized the fixing of minimum wages for women and minors by an administrative board. The West Coast Hotel Co. argued unsuccessfully in state court that the statute was invalid on due process grounds because of its similarity to the laws set aside in *Adkins* v. *Children's Hospital* (1923) and in *Morehead* v. *New York* ex rel. *Tipaldo* (1936). *Adkins* in turn had rested on *Lochner* v. *New York*. The decision in *West Coast Hotel*, handed down by the same Supreme Court personnel that had decided the Morehead case in 1936, marked the first stage of the "constitutional revolution" of 1937 (see Chapter Six). Majority: Hughes, Brandeis, Cardozo, Roberts, Stone. Dissenting: Sutherland, Butler, McReynolds, Van Devanter.

MR. CHIEF JUSTICE HUGHES delivered the opinion of the Court.

This case presents the question of the constitutional validity of the minimum wage law of the state of Washington. . . .

The principle which must control our decision is not in doubt. The constitutional provision invoked is the due process clause of the Fourteenth Amendment governing the states, as the due process clause invoked in the Adkins case governed Congress. In each case the violation alleged by those attacking minimum wage regulation for women is deprivation of freedom of contract. What is this freedom? The Constitution does not speak of freedom of contract. It speaks of liberty and prohibits the deprivation of liberty without due process of law. In prohibiting that deprivation the Constitution does not recognize an absolute and uncontrollable liberty. Liberty in each of its phases has its history and connotation. But the liberty safeguarded is liberty in a social organization which requires the protection of law against the evils which menace the health, safety, morals, and welfare of the people. Liberty under the Constitution is thus necessarily subject to the restraints of due process, and regulation which is reasonable in relation to its subject and is adopted in the interests of the community is due process. . . .

The minimum wage to be paid under the Washington statute is fixed after full consideration by representatives of employers, employees and the public. It may be assumed that the minimum wage is fixed in consideration of the services that are performed in the particular occupations under normal conditions. . . .

We think that the decision in the Adkins case was a departure from the true application of the principles governing the regulation by the state of the relation of employer and employed. . . .

The legislature of the state was clearly entitled to consider the situation of women in employment, the fact that they are in the class receiving the least pay, that their bargaining power is relatively weak, and that they are the ready victims of those who would take advantage of their necessitous circumstances. . . . Legislative response to that conviction cannot be regarded as arbitrary or capricious and that is all we have to decide. Even if the wisdom of the policy be regarded as debatable and its effects uncertain, still the legislature is entitled to its judgment. . . .

We may take judicial notice of the unparalleled demands for relief which arose during the recent period of depression and still continue to an alarming extent despite the degree of economic recovery which has been achieved. It is unnecessary to cite official statistics to establish what is of common knowledge through the length and breadth of the land. . . . The community is not bound to provide what is in effect a subsidy for unconscionable employers. The community may direct its law-making power to correct the abuse which springs from their selfish disregard of the public interest. . . .

Our conclusion is that the case of *Adkins* v. *Children's Hospital* should be, and it is, overruled. The judgment of the Supreme Court of the State of Washington is

Affirmed.

MR. JUSTICE SUTHERLAND, dissenting.

MR. JUSTICE VAN DEVANTER, MR. JUSTICE MCREYNOLDS, MR. JUSTICE BUTLER and I think the judgment of the court below should be reversed. . . .

The suggestion that the only check upon the exercise of the judicial power, when properly invoked, to declare a constitutional right superior to an unconstitutional statute is the judge's own faculty of self-restraint,[3] is both ill considered and mischievous. Self-restraint belongs in the domain of will and not of judgment. The check upon the judge is that imposed by his oath of office, by the Constitution and by his own conscientious and informed convictions; and since he has the duty to make up his own mind and adjudge accordingly, it is hard to see how there could be any other restraint. . . .

It is urged that the question involved should now receive fresh consideration, among other reasons, because of "the economic conditions which have supervened"; but the meaning of the Constitution does not change with the ebb and flow of economic events. We frequently are told in more general words that the Constitution must be construed in the light of the present. If by that it is meant that the Constitution is made up of living words that apply to every new condition which they include, the statement is quite true. But to say, if that be intended, that the words of the Constitution mean today what they did not mean when written—that is, that they do not apply to a situation now to which they would have applied then—is to rob that instrument of the essential element which continues it in force as the people have made it until they, and not their official agents, have made it otherwise. . . .

The judicial function is that of interpretation; it does not include the power of amendment under the guise of interpretation. To miss the point of difference between the two is to miss all that the phrase "supreme law of the land" stands for and to convert what was intended as inescapable and enduring mandates into mere moral reflections.

If the Constitution, intelligently and reasonably construed in the light of these principles, stands in the way of desirable legislation, the blame must rest upon that instrument, and not upon the court for enforcing it according to its terms. The remedy in that situation—and the only true remedy—is to amend the Constitution. . . .

Ferguson v. *Skrupa*
372 U.S. 726, 83 S.Ct. 1028, 10 L.Ed. 2d 93 (1963)

http://caselaw.findlaw.com/us-supreme-court/372/726.html

The relevant facts are included in the opinion. Majority: Black, Brennan, Clark, Douglas, Goldberg, Harlan, Stewart, Warren, White.

Mr. Justice Black delivered the opinion of the Court.

In this case, . . . we are asked to review the judgment of a three-judge District Court enjoining, as being in violation of the Due Process Clause of the Fourteenth Amendment, a Kansas statute making it a misdemeanor for any person to engage "in the business of debt adjusting" except as an incident to "the lawful practice of law in this state." The statute defines "debt adjusting" as "the making of a contract, express, or implied with a particular debtor whereby the debtor agrees to pay a certain amount of money periodically to the person engaged in the debt adjusting business who shall for a consideration distribute the same among certain specified creditors in accordance with a plan agreed upon." . . .

The three-judge court heard evidence by Skrupa tending to show the usefulness and desirability of his business and evidence by the state officials tending to show that "debt adjusting" lends itself to grave abuses against distressed debtors, particularly in the lower income brackets, and that these abuses are of such gravity that a number of States have strictly regulated "debt adjusting" or prohibited it altogether. The court found that Skrupa's business did fall within the Act's proscription and concluded, one judge dissenting, that the Act was prohibitory, not regulatory, but that even if construed in part as regulatory it was an unreasonable regulation of a "lawful business," which the court held amounted to a violation of the Due Process Clause of the Fourteenth Amendment. . . .

Under the system of government created by our Constitution, it is up to legislatures, not courts, to decide on the wisdom and utility of legislation. There was a time when the Due Process Clause was used by this Court to strike down laws which were thought unreasonable, that is, unwise or incompatible with some particular economic or social philosophy. . . .

We have returned to the original constitutional proposition that courts do not substitute their social and economic beliefs for the judgment of legislative bodies, who are elected to pass laws. . . .

We conclude that the Kansas Legislature was free to decide for itself that legislation was needed to deal with the business of debt adjusting. Unquestionably, there are arguments showing that the business of debt adjusting has social utility, but such arguments are properly addressed to the legislature, not to us. We refuse to sit as a "superlegislature to weigh the wisdom of legislation," and we emphatically refuse to go back to the time when courts used the Due Process Clause "to strike down state laws, regulatory of business and industrial conditions, because they may be unwise, improvident, or out of harmony with a particular school of thought." . . . Whether the legislature takes for its textbook Adam Smith, Herbert Spencer, Lord Keynes, or some other is no concern of ours. The Kansas debt adjusting statute may be wise or unwise. But relief, if any be needed, lies not with us but with the body constituted to pass laws for the State of Kansas. . . .

Reversed.

Mr. Justice Harlan concurs in the judgment on the ground that this state measure bears a rational relationship to a constitutionally permissible objective.

IV. FIFTH AMENDMENT TAKINGS AND LAND USE

Kelo v. *City of New London*
545 U.S. 469, 125 S.Ct. 2655, 162 L.Ed. 2d 439 (2005)

http://caselaw.findlaw.com/us-supreme-court/545/469.html

The facts of the case appear in Justice Stevens's opinion below. Majority: Stevens, Breyer, Ginsburg, Kennedy, Souter. Dissenting: O'Connor, Rehnquist, Scalia, Thomas.

Justice Stevens delivered the opinion of the Court.

In 2000, the city of New London approved a development plan that, in the words of the Supreme Court of Connecticut, was "projected to create in excess of 1,000 jobs, to increase tax and other revenues, and to revitalize an economically distressed city, including its downtown and waterfront areas." In assembling the land needed for this project, the city's development agent has purchased property from willing sellers and proposes to use the power of eminent domain to acquire the remainder of the property from unwilling owners in exchange for just compensation. The question presented is whether the city's proposed disposition of this property qualifies as a "public use" within the meaning of the Takings Clause of the Fifth Amendment to the Constitution. . . .

Petitioner Susette Kelo has lived in the Fort Trumbull area since 1997. She has made extensive improvements to her house, which she prizes for its water view. Petitioner Wilhelmina Dery was born in her Fort Trumbull house in 1918 and has lived there her entire life. . . . In all, the nine petitioners own 15 properties in Fort Trumbull. . . . Ten of the parcels are occupied by the owner or a family member; the other five are held as investment properties. There is no allegation that any of these properties is blighted or otherwise in poor condition; rather, they were condemned only because they happen to be located in the development area.

In December 2000, petitioners brought this action in the New London Superior Court. They claimed, among other things, that the taking of their properties would violate the "public use" restriction in the Fifth Amendment. . . . After the Superior Court ruled, both sides took appeals to the Supreme Court of Connecticut. That court held, over a dissent, that all of the City's proposed takings were valid. . . . [R]elying on cases such as *Hawaii Housing Authority* v. *Midkiff* (1984), and *Berman* v. *Parker* (1954), the court held that such economic development qualified as a valid public use under both the Federal and State Constitutions. . . .

Two polar propositions are perfectly clear. On the one hand, it has long been accepted that the sovereign may not take the property of A for the sole purpose of transferring it to another private party B, even though A is paid just compensation. On the other hand, it is equally clear that a State may transfer property from one private party to another if future "use by the public" is the purpose of the taking. . . . Neither of these propositions, however, determines the disposition of this case.

As for the first proposition, the City would no doubt be forbidden from taking petitioners' land for the purpose of conferring a private benefit on a particular private party. . . . The takings before us, however, would be executed pursuant to a "carefully considered" development plan. . . .

On the other hand, this is not a case in which the City is planning to open the condemned land—at least not in its entirety—to use by the general public. Nor will the private lessees of the land in any sense be required to operate like common carriers, making their services available to all comers. But although such a projected use would be sufficient to satisfy the public use requirement, this "Court long ago rejected any literal requirement that condemned property be put into use for the general public." Indeed, while many state courts in the mid-19th century endorsed "use by the public" as the proper definition of public use, that narrow view steadily eroded over time. Not only was the "use by the public" test difficult to administer (*e.g.*, what proportion of the public need have access to the property? at what price?), but it proved to be impractical given the diverse and always evolving needs of society. Accordingly, when this Court began applying the Fifth Amendment to the States at the close of the 19th century, it embraced the broader and more natural interpretation of public use as "public purpose." . . . We have repeatedly and consistently rejected that narrow test ever since.

The disposition of this case therefore turns on the question whether the City's development plan serves a "public purpose." Without exception, our cases have defined that concept broadly, reflecting our longstanding policy of deference to legislative judgments in this field.

In *Berman*, this Court upheld a redevelopment plan targeting a blighted area of Washington, D.C., in which most of the housing for the area's 5,000 inhabitants was beyond repair. Under the plan, the area would be condemned and part of it utilized for the construction of streets, schools, and other public facilities. The remainder of the land would be leased or sold to private parties for the purpose of redevelopment, including the construction of low-cost housing. . . .

In *Midkiff*, the Court considered a Hawaii statute whereby fee title was taken from lessors and transferred to lessees (for just compensation) in order to reduce the concentration of land ownership. We unanimously upheld the statute and rejected the Ninth Circuit's view that it was "a naked attempt on the part of the state of Hawaii to take the property of A and transfer it to B solely for B's private use and benefit." Reaffirming *Berman's* deferential approach to legislative judgments in this field, we concluded that the State's purpose of eliminating the "social and economic evils of a land oligopoly" qualified as a valid public use. . . .

Viewed as a whole, our jurisprudence has recognized that the needs of society have varied between different parts of the Nation, just as they have evolved over time in response to changed circumstances. . . . For more than a century, our public use jurisprudence has wisely eschewed rigid formulas and intrusive scrutiny in favor of affording legislatures broad latitude in determining what public needs justify the use of the takings power.

Those who govern the City were not confronted with the need to remove blight in the Fort Trumbull area, but their determination that the area was sufficiently distressed to justify a program of economic rejuvenation is entitled to our deference. The City has carefully formulated an economic development plan that it believes will provide appreciable benefits to the community, including—but by no means limited to—new jobs and increased tax revenue. As with other exercises in urban planning and development, the City is endeavoring to coordinate a variety of commercial, residential, and recreational uses of land, with the hope that they will form a whole greater than the sum of its parts. . . . Because that plan unquestionably serves a public purpose, the takings challenged here satisfy the public use requirement of the Fifth Amendment.

To avoid this result, petitioners urge us to adopt a new bright-line rule that economic development does not qualify as a public use. . . . [N]either precedent nor logic supports petitioners' proposal. Promoting economic development is a traditional and long accepted function of government. There is, moreover, no principled way of distinguishing economic development from the other public purposes that we have recognized. . . .

It is further argued that without a bright-line rule nothing would stop a city from transferring citizen A's property to citizen B for the sole reason that citizen B will put the property to a more productive use and thus pay more taxes. Such a one-to-one transfer of property, executed outside the confines of an integrated development plan, is not presented in this case. While such an unusual exercise of government power would certainly raise a suspicion that a private purpose was afoot, the hypothetical cases posited by petitioners can be confronted if and when they arise. . . .

In affirming the City's authority to take petitioners' properties, we do not minimize the hardship that condemnations may entail, notwithstanding the payment of just compensation. We emphasize that nothing in our opinion precludes any State from placing further restrictions on its exercise of the takings power. . . . This Court's authority, however, extends only to determining whether the City's proposed condemnations are for a "public use" within the meaning of the Fifth Amendment to the Federal Constitution. Because over a century of our case law interpreting that provision dictates an affirmative answer to that question, we may not grant petitioners the relief that they seek.

The judgment of the Supreme Court of Connecticut is affirmed.

It is so ordered.

Justice Kennedy, concurring . . . [omitted].

JUSTICE O'CONNOR, with whom THE CHIEF JUSTICE, JUSTICE SCALIA, and JUSTICE THOMAS join, dissenting. . . .

To reason, as the Court does, that the incidental public benefits resulting from the subsequent ordinary use of private property render economic development takings "for public use" is to wash out any distinction between private and public use of property—and thereby effectively to delete the words "for public use" from the Takings Clause of the Fifth Amendment. Accordingly I respectfully dissent. . . .

When interpreting the Constitution, we begin with the unremarkable presumption that every word in the document has independent meaning, "that no word was unnecessarily used, or needlessly added." In keeping with that presumption, we have read the Fifth Amendment's language to impose two distinct conditions on the exercise of eminent domain: "the taking must be for a 'public use' and 'just compensation' must be paid to the owner." . . . Together they ensure stable property ownership by providing safeguards against excessive, unpredictable, or unfair use of the government's eminent domain power—particularly against those owners who, for whatever reasons, may be unable to protect themselves in the political process against the majority's will.

While the Takings Clause presupposes that government can take private property without the owner's consent, the just compensation requirement spreads the cost of condemnations and thus "prevents the public from loading upon one individual more than his just share of the burdens of government." The public use requirement, in turn, imposes a more basic limitation, circumscribing the very scope of the eminent domain power: Government may compel an individual to forfeit her property for the public's use, but not for the benefit of another private person. This requirement promotes fairness as well as security.

Where is the line between "public" and "private" property use? We give considerable deference to legislatures' determinations about what governmental activities will advantage the public. But were the political branches the sole arbiters of the public—private distinction, the Public Use Clause would amount to little more than hortatory fluff. An external, judicial check on how the public use requirement is interpreted, however limited, is necessary if this constraint on government power is to retain any meaning. . . .

Our cases have generally identified three categories of takings that comply with the public use requirement, though it is in the nature of things that the boundaries between these categories are not always firm. Two are relatively straightforward and uncontroversial. First, the sovereign may transfer private property to public ownership—such as for a road, a hospital, or a military base. Second, the sovereign may transfer private property to private parties, often common carriers, who make the property available for the public's use—such as with a railroad, a public utility, or a stadium. But "public ownership" and "use-by-the-public" are sometimes too constricting and impractical ways to define the scope of the Public Use Clause. Thus we have allowed that, in certain circumstances and to meet certain exigencies, takings that serve a public purpose also satisfy the Constitution even if the property is destined for subsequent private use.

This case returns us for the first time in over 20 years to the hard question of when a purportedly "public purpose" taking meets the public use requirement. It presents an issue of first impression: Are economic development takings constitutional? I would hold that they are not. We are guided by two precedents about the taking of real property by eminent domain. In *Berman*, we upheld takings within a blighted neighborhood of Washington, D.C. . . .

In *Midkiff*, we upheld a land condemnation scheme in Hawaii whereby title in real property was taken from lessors and transferred to lessees. . . .

In those decisions, we emphasized the importance of deferring to legislative judgments about public purpose. . . .

Yet for all the emphasis on deference, *Berman* and *Midkiff* hewed to a bedrock principle without which our public use jurisprudence would collapse: "A purely private taking could not withstand the scrutiny of the public use requirement; it would serve no legitimate purpose of government and would thus be void." . . .

The Court's holdings in *Berman* and *Midkiff* were true to the principle underlying the Public Use Clause. In both those cases, the extraordinary, precondemnation use of the targeted property inflicted affirmative harm on society—in *Berman* through blight resulting from extreme poverty and in *Midkiff* through oligopoly resulting from extreme wealth. . . . Thus a public purpose was realized when the harmful use was eliminated. Because each taking directly achieved a public benefit, it did not matter that the property was turned over to private use. Here, in contrast, New London does not claim that Susette Kelo's and Wilhelmina Dery's well-maintained homes are the source of any social harm. . . .

In moving away from our decisions sanctioning the condemnation of harmful property use, the Court today significantly expands the meaning of public use. It holds that the sovereign may take private property currently put to ordinary private use, and give it over for new, ordinary private use, so long as the new use is predicted to generate some secondary benefit for the public—such as increased tax revenue, more jobs, maybe even aesthetic pleasure. But nearly any lawful use of real private property can be said to generate some incidental benefit to the public. Thus, if predicted (or even guaranteed) positive side-effects are enough to render transfer from one private party to another constitutional, then the words "for public use" do not realistically exclude any takings, and thus do not exert any constraint on the eminent domain power. . . . Today nearly all real property is susceptible to condemnation on the Court's theory. . . .

Any property may now be taken for the benefit of another private party, but the fallout from this decision will not be random. The beneficiaries are likely to be those citizens with disproportionate influence and power in the political process, including large corporations and development firms. As for the victims, the government now has license to transfer property from those with fewer resources to those with more. The Founders cannot have intended this perverse result. "[T]hat alone is a just government," wrote James Madison, "which impartially secures to every man, whatever is his own." . . .

Justice Thomas, dissenting . . . [omitted].

NOTES

1. Along with William Graham Sumner, English philosopher Herbert Spencer had a profound impact in the late nineteenth century on American social and economic thought with his emphasis on a minimalist state. The historian Richard Hofstadter credited Spencer with having coined the phrase "survival of the fittest," usually attributed to Charles Darwin.
2. This is part of a draft of an unpublished concurring opinion that Justice Cardozo wrote and sent to Chief Justice Hughes, who incorporated some of Cardozo's ideas into his own majority opinion. Harlan Fiske Stone Papers, Library of Congress.—Ed.
3. Justice Sutherland refers to the statement by Justice Stone, dissenting in *United States* v. *Butler* (1936), reprinted in Chapter Seven.—Ed.

9

The Bill of Rights and the Second Amendment

The very purpose of a Bill of Rights was to withdraw certain subjects from the vicissitudes of political controversy, to place them beyond the reach of majorities and officials and to establish them as legal principles to be applied by the courts. . . . [F]undamental rights may not be submitted to vote; they depend on the outcome of no election.

—Justice Robert H. Jackson (1943)

Preceding chapters have shown that the Supreme Court's regard for certain strictures in the Constitution dates from the earliest years of the Republic. Aside from property interests, however, judicial attention to the Bill of Rights, though it has been part of the Constitution since 1791, is of more recent origin. Almost all cases that have shaped the meaning of constitutionally protected expression (the First Amendment) and that have defined personal liberty and the rights of persons accused of crimes (the Fourth, Fifth, Sixth, and Eighth Amendments) have been decided since 1920. As late as the 1935–1936 term, only two of the Court's 160 decisions concerned a nonproperty-related **civil liberty** (a guaranty in law against unwarranted governmental intrusion into one's life) or **civil right** (a legally protected freedom to participate in society and in the political system on an equal footing with others). In 1960–1961, the number increased to 54 of the 120 cases decided by full opinion. Disproportionate judicial concern for these matters continues. In 2005–2006, cases involving the Bill of Rights and related provisions accounted for 34 of the term's 87 decisions, and in 2019–2020, 29 of that term's 53 decisions. The data reflect not only an enhanced interest in the Bill of Rights but also the Court's application of the Bill of Rights to the states, a process that has involved due process of law.

PATHS OF DUE PROCESS OF LAW

The phrase "due process of law" first appeared in an English statute during the reign of King Edward III (1327–1377): "No man of what state or condition he be, shall be

DOI: 10.4324/9781003164340-10

put out of his lands or tenements, nor taken, nor imprisoned, nor disinherited, nor put to death, without he be brought to answer by due process of law." The phrase in turn derived from the "law of the land" clause in Magna Carta of 1215. Early American state constitutions carried over parts of both and expanded on them, as illustrated by the Massachusetts Constitution of 1780: "No subject shall be arrested, imprisoned, despoiled, or deprived of his property, immunities, or privileges, put out of the protection of the law, exiled, or deprived of his life, liberty, or estate, but by the judgment of his peers or the law of the land." The thrust across those centuries was procedural. As it acted on the people, government was supposed to follow custom or pre-established rules. Otherwise individual liberty would be imperiled. So it was hardly surprising that the framers of the Fifth and Fourteenth Amendments included provisions forbidding the national and state governments, respectively, from depriving any person of "life, liberty, or property without due process of law."

Chapter Eight chronicled the Supreme Court's transformation of **due process of law** from a procedural limitation on government into a substantive one too. The concept moved beyond being solely a restriction on the manner in which government proceeded against its citizens (*how* something could be done) to a restriction on policy choices themselves (*what* could be done). Between the 1890s and 1937, the Court sat in judgment on economic and social legislation enacted by Congress and state legislatures. Only those regulations the justices deemed "reasonable" passed the constitutional test of due process of law. Even though that use of due process has long since passed into history, due process of law remains very much a lively part of American constitutional law.

At heart, due process is a safeguard against arbitrary government. When government today attempts to deprive a person of life, liberty, or property, officials must follow certain standards that judges view as fair and appropriate. Relaxed and informal procedures might suffice for disciplinary actions in a public school, while far stricter and formal procedures are required in law enforcement when someone is accused of a crime. Generally, as the degree of potential harm that government might do to an individual increases, so does the Court's expectation of what process is due. This would explain the heightened attention to procedure that the Court demands in death penalty cases, as shown in Chapter Ten. Embodying notions of basic fairness, due process can thus be a bulwark of personal freedom in addition to other more specific guaranties of liberty that the Constitution contains. Thus, principles of due process may require a judge's **recusal**: the voluntary withdrawal by a judge of herself from a case where there is a serious risk of actual bias. For example, as the Court held in *Williams* v. *Pennsylvania* (2016), there is an impermissible risk of bias and therefore a violation of due process when a judge (in this instance the chief justice of the Pennsylvania Supreme Court) was previously involved in a case as prosecutor and then declined to recuse himself when the conviction was before his court on appeal.

Due process is also intimately connected in a substantive way with the right of privacy that is explored in Chapter Thirteen. Although ***Griswold* v. *Connecticut*** (1965) found the right of privacy implied by several provisions of the Bill of Rights, the Court's ruling in 2015 on same-sex marriage (***Obergefell* v. *Hodges***) relied mainly on due process of law. Even more important in terms of its impact on American government, due process has been the vehicle by which the Court has applied the Bill of Rights to the states. Yet, ironically the national Bill of Rights was "an almost forgotten appendage."

CREATION OF THE BILL OF RIGHTS

Unlike almost all the first state constitutions adopted in 1776–1777, the Constitution as it came from the hands of the framers in 1787 lacked a declaration of rights. Alongside a few prohibitions on national authority, the powers of the national government were enumerated but not defined. Without specification or definition, other powers were reserved to the states or to the people. While the states pondered ratification, Thomas Jefferson urged specific restraints on national authority. Arguing that "a bill of rights is what the people are entitled to against every government on earth," he insisted that natural rights should not be left to "rest on inference."

Alexander Hamilton and James Wilson countered that a bill of rights was not needed. Why make exceptions to power not granted? "In a government of enumerated powers," Wilson declared, "such a measure would not only be unnecessary, but preposterous and dangerous." A list of rights implied that those not included remained unprotected. For Hamilton, bills of rights "would sound much better in a treatise on ethics than in a constitution of government."

Thanks to Jefferson, these arguments did not prevail. Insisting on curbs over and beyond the ballot box and structural checks, he advocated "binding up the several branches of the government by certain laws, which when they transgress their acts become nullities." This would "render unnecessary an appeal to the people, or in other words a rebellion on every infraction of their rights." When a reluctant James Madison yielded to Jefferson's plea for a bill of rights and deduced supporting reasons, Jefferson singled out the argument of "great weight" for him—the legal check it would put in the hands of the judiciary. In presenting bill-of-rights amendments to the first Congress in 1789, Madison made Jefferson's argument his own. With a bill of rights, "independent tribunals of justice" would be "an impenetrable bulwark against every assumption of power in the legislative or executive." The **Jefferson–Madison correspondence** is reprinted in this chapter.

As a member of the First Congress elected under the new Constitution, Madison drew up 17 amendments. By 1791, 10 were ratified, the first 8 of which constitute the Bill of Rights. Urged but not ratified on Madison's list was number 14: "No *state* shall infringe the right of trial by jury in criminal cases, nor the right of conscience, nor the freedom of speech or press" (emphasis added). Believing that there was more danger of abuse of power by state governments than by the national government, Madison conceived number 14 to be "the most valuable amendment in the whole list. If there were any reason to restrain the Government of the United States from infringing these essential rights, it was equally necessary that they should be secured against the State governments."

Madison's concern was prophetic. It anticipated the adoption of the Fourteenth Amendment 79 years later. It foreshadowed the drive to apply the specific provisions of the Bill of Rights to state action by way of the Fourteenth Amendment. Without application of the Bill of Rights to the states, the full impact of Justice Stone's *Carolene Products* Footnote Four, discussed in Chapter Eight, could not be felt.

The idea of a bill of rights was hardly unique to Americans, however. Bills of rights in the state constitutions and the federal Bill of Rights were themselves offshoots of English constitutional documents such as the Petition of Right of 1628 and the Bill of Rights of 1689. But the onset of democratic government—government by the consent of the governed—changed the nature of bills of rights. Initially, a bill of rights was a device to protect the majority ("the people") from the minority (the Crown), the many from the few. Now, with political power lodged in the hands of a majority of those admitted to the political community, bills of rights came to be devices to protect the few from the many. In Madison's words, "Wherever the real power in a Government lies, there is the danger of oppression."

Fundamental rights gained no greater moral sanctity by being written into the Constitution, but individuals could thereafter resort to courts for protection. Rights formerly natural became civil. Moreover, "'tho' written constitutions may be violated in moments of passion or delusion," Jefferson declared, "they furnish a text to which those who are watchful may again rally and recall the people; they fix too for the people principles for their political creed."

APPLYING THE BILL OF RIGHTS TO THE STATES

It was not until 1833 that the Supreme Court answered the question whether the first eight amendments limited state as well as national action. To Chief Justice John Marshall, this was a question "of great importance, but not of much difficulty" (*Barron* v. *Baltimore*). The city of Baltimore, under acts of the Maryland legislature, had diverted the flow of several streams. As a result of the changes, silt was deposited around John Barron's wharf, making it unfit for shipping and, Barron claimed, depriving him of property without just compensation. Denying the Supreme Court's jurisdiction to declare the state acts repugnant to the Constitution, Marshall observed, "We are of the opinion, that the provision in the Fifth Amendment to the Constitution, declaring that private property shall not be taken for public use without just compensation is intended solely as a limitation of the power of the United States, and is not applicable to the legislation of the states." That was an understandable conclusion. As he explained, "In almost every convention by which the constitution was adopted, amendments to guard against the abuse of power were recommended. These amendments demanded security against the apprehended encroachments of the general [federal] government, not against those of the local [state] governments."

A contrary ruling would have had immense consequences for the jurisdiction of the Court. As a result of *Barron*, most legal disputes between a state government and one of its citizens remained outside the federal judicial system, unless the commerce or contract clause was at issue. This is important to remember, because until recent decades, government action and government policy largely meant the action and policy of state and local governments.

Beginnings. Shortly after the end of the Civil War, the question of the applicability of the Bill of Rights to the states reappeared. This time there was a difference. The Fourteenth Amendment had become part of the Constitution in 1868. Did its ratification result in **incorporation**—application of the Bill of Rights to the states—either through the privileges and immunities clause or by virtue of the due process clause? This was a natural question for some people to ask because in June 1866, when Congress sent the Fourteenth Amendment to the states for ratification, many thought that applying the Bill of Rights to the states was one of the amendment's principal objectives. Yet, after the Slaughterhouse Cases, reprinted in Chapter Eight, emasculated the privileges and immunities clause in 1873, only due process remained as a possible medium to make that expectation a reality.

The Court gave its first serious attention to this issue in *Hurtado* v. *California* (1884). (Recall from the previous chapter that it was in this same period that litigants were trying to persuade the bench that the due process clause also put limits on the power of states to enact social and economic legislation.) *Hurtado* posed the question whether the due process clause of the Fourteenth Amendment prevented a state from substituting a prosecutor's written accusation for grand jury indictment. The Fifth Amendment called for a grand jury indictment in federal criminal cases, as did most state constitutions for state trials. Did the Fourteenth Amendment mandate the use of grand jury indictments in the states? For the majority, Justice Matthews said no. He rejected the view that "any proceeding . . . not . . . sanctioned by usage, or which supersedes and displaces one that is, cannot be regarded as due process of law. . . . [T]o hold that such a characteristic is essential to due process of law, would be to deny every quality of the law but its age, and to render it incapable of progress or improvement. It would be to stamp upon our jurisprudence the unchangeableness attributed to the laws of the Medes and Persians." Besides, the fact that the Fifth Amendment already contained a due process clause meant that "due process" was not intended to include that particular safeguard of the Bill of Rights. If the Fourteenth Amendment required use of grand jury indictments, "it would have embodied, as did the Fifth Amendment, express declarations to that effect."

What, therefore, did "due process" allow? "[A]ny legal proceeding . . . whether sanctioned by age and custom, or newly devised . . . in furtherance of the general public good, which regards and preserves these principles of liberty and justice, must be held to be due process of law." Thus, if a procedure was traditional, that would ordinarily be sufficient ground for finding it compatible with due process. If a procedure was new, that fact alone would be insufficient to invalidate it under the due process clause. The tilt of the opinion was clearly toward welcoming procedural innovation. Nonetheless, the Court placed itself in the position of being the final judge concerning "those fundamental principles of liberty and justice which lie at the base of all our civil and political institutions. . . ." Thus, it was in *Hurtado* that the Court first squarely blended the idea of fundamental fairness into the concept of due process.

Thirteen years later in *Chicago, B. & Q. R. Co.* v. *Chicago* (1897), the Court cast doubt on the *Hurtado* doctrine by ruling that the Fourteenth Amendment's due process clause limited the taking of property for public use without just compensation. The Fifth Amendment contained the same safeguard. Then, *Twining* v. *New Jersey* (1908) took another step beyond *Hurtado*. While rejecting the argument that due process encompassed the Fifth Amendment's protection against self-incrimination, the Court expressly laid to rest the view that the inclusion of a right in the Bill of Rights necessarily excluded that right from the protection offered by the due process clause of the Fourteenth Amendment. "[I]t is possible," acknowledged Justice Moody, "that some of the personal rights safeguarded by the first eight Amendments against national action may also be safeguarded against state action. . . . If this is so, it is not because those rights are enumerated in the first eight Amendments, but because they are of such a nature that they are included in the conception of due process of law." Thus, he asked, did the claim involve "a fundamental principle of liberty and justice which inheres in the very idea of free government and is the inalienable right of a citizen of such a government? If it is, and if it is of a nature that pertains to process of law, this court has declared it to be essential to due process of law."

Ordered Liberty. In the 1920s and 1930s, the Supreme Court agreed that the "liberty" protected by the due process clause included some First Amendment freedoms. For example, ***Gitlow* v. *New York*** (1925) (see Chapter Eleven) "assume[d] that freedom of speech and of the press . . . are among the fundamental personal rights and 'liberties' protected by the due process clause . . . from impairment by the states." Six years later, in *Near* v. *Minnesota*, Chief Justice Hughes insisted that it was "no longer open to doubt that the liberty of the press . . . is within the liberty safeguarded by the due process clause . . . from invasion by state action." And Justice Sutherland in ***Powell* v. *Alabama*** (1932) (see Chapter Ten) reasoned that the Sixth Amendment's guaranty of right to counsel was a "necessary requisite of due process of law" and so required states to provide counsel for indigent defendants, at least in capital cases.

Yet because most other provisions of the Bill of Rights had not been absorbed by the Fourteenth Amendment, why were some rights "in" while others remained "out"? Justice Cardozo attempted to answer this question in ***Palko* v. *Connecticut*** (1937), which presented the Court with yet another procedural claim—this time, the Fifth Amendment's ban on double jeopardy. Reaffirming the Court's long-held view that the entire Bill of Rights was not incorporated into the Fourteenth Amendment, Cardozo built on *Twining* to spell out and justify a selective process. Due process encompassed those provisions of the Bill of Rights that were essential to a "scheme of **ordered liberty**."

> There emerges the perception of a rationalizing principle which gives to discrete instances a proper order and coherence. The right to trial by jury and the immunity from prosecution except as a result of an indictment may have value and importance. Even so, they are not of the very essence of *a scheme of ordered liberty*. To abolish them is not to violate a "principle of justice so rooted in the traditions and conscience of our people as to be ranked as fundamental. . . ."
>
> We reach a different plane of social and moral values when we pass to the privileges and immunities that have been taken over from the earlier articles of the Federal Bill of Rights and brought within the Fourteenth Amendment by a process of absorption. These in their origin were effective against the federal government. If the Fourteenth Amendment has absorbed them, the process of absorption has had its source in the belief that neither liberty nor justice would exist if they were sacrificed [emphasis added].

For Cardozo, the provisions in the Bill of Rights were not of equal value.

Yet this ordered liberty method of hand-picking rights did not go unchallenged. Consider Justice Black's advocacy of **total incorporation** in ***Adamson* v. *California*** (1947):

> My study of the historical events that culminated in the Fourteenth Amendment, and the expressions of those who sponsored and favored, as well as those who opposed its submission and passage, persuades me that one of the chief objects that the provisions of the Amendment's first section, separately, and as a whole were intended to accomplish, was to make the Bill of Rights applicable to the states.

Black's theory never attracted the votes of more than three other justices at any one time, but it pointed in the direction that the Court was moving.

Triumph of Selective Incorporation. As shown in Table 9.1, especially almost all of the provisions of the Bill of Rights have now been applied to the states on a case-by-case basis. The pace of this incorporation accelerated during the 1960s, suggesting that the Court had abandoned or at least substantially modified the ordered liberty test from *Palko*.

Justice White's opinion in ***Duncan* v. *Louisiana*** (1968) reveals what had taken place. The Court was both rethinking the importance of the specific guaranties

Table 9.1 Nationalization of the Bill of Rights

Amendment	Rights Applicable to States	Case Applying Right to States	Rights Not Applicable to the States
I	Establishment of religion	*Everson* v. *Board of Education* (1947)	
	Free exercise of religion	*Cantwell* v. *Connecticut* (1940)	
	Speech	*Gitlow* v. *New York* (1925)	
	Press	*Near* v. *Minnesota* (1931)	
	Peaceable assembly	*De Jonge* v. *Oregon* (1937)	
	Petition	*De Jonge* v. *Oregon* (1937)	
II	To keep and bear arms	*McDonald* v. *City of Chicago* (2010)	
III			No quartering of soldiers in homes
IV	Protection against unreasonable searches and seizures	*Wolf* v. *Colorado* (1949)	
	(With the exclusionary rule)	*Mapp* v. *Ohio* (1961)	
V	Protection against double jeopardy	*Benton* v. *Maryland* (1969)	Indictment by grand jury
	Protection against compelled self-incrimination	*Malloy* v. *Hogan* (1964)	
	Just compensation for public seizure of private property	*Chicago, B. & Q. R. Co.* v. *Chicago* (1897)	
VI	Speedy trial	*Klopfer* v. *North Carolina* (1967)	Trial in state and district of offense
	Public trial	In *re Oliver* (1948)	
	Impartial jury	*Parker* v. *Gladden* (1966)	
	Trial by jury in nonpetty criminal case	*Duncan* v. *Louisiana* (1968)	
	Nature and cause of accusation	*Cole* v. *Arkansas* (1948)	
	Confrontation of accusers	*Pointer* v. *Texas* (1965)	
	Compulsory process for appearance of witnesses	*Washington* v. *Texas* (1967)	
	Assistance of counsel	*Powell* v. *Alabama* (1932)	
		Gideon v. *Wainwright* (1963)	
		Argersinger v. *Hamlin* (1972)	
		Scott v. *Illinois* (1979)	
		Strickland v. *Washington* (1984)	
VII			Jury trial in specific civil cases
VIII	Cruel and unusual punishment	*Robinson* v. *California* (1962)	
	Ban on excessive bail and fines	*Schilb* v. *Kuebel* (1971)	
		Timbs v. *Indiana* (2019)	

in the Bill of Rights and recasting the Palko standard. Rather than asking in the abstract whether a particular right was essential for a political system that valued liberty and justice, the Court asked whether a particular right "is fundamental . . . to an Anglo-American regime of ordered liberty."

By 1968, the Court had accomplished almost as much selectively as Black would have done instantly in *Adamson*. The most recent step in this constitutional march occurred in 2019 with ***Timbs v. Indiana***, in which the Court applied to the states the Eighth Amendment's protection against excessive fines. Moreover, it took this step in a case involving a civil forfeiture, yet refrained from laying out a test that would consider a defendant's ability to pay, leaving that aspect of excessiveness for lower tribunals to develop. Beyond the incorporation process itself today are the protections enshrined in due process beyond those strictly enumerated in the Bill of Rights. It is here that Justice Black's total incorporation approach (this much, and no more) stops, and a variation on Justice Cardozo's ordered liberty doctrine begins. If the Fourteenth Amendment's due process clause is not bound to the meaning of the Bill of Rights, it remains a source of inspiration for those who wish to enlarge the list of constitutionally protected liberties.

Today, no one would accept Sir Henry Maine's nineteenth-century characterization of the Bill of Rights as a "certain number of amendments on comparatively unimportant points."

Due Process Revolution. The nationalization of almost all parts of the Bill of Rights has had immense consequences for federalism, personal freedom, and judicial power. Until incorporation became a reality, Americans remained subject to a **double standard** of justice under the Constitution. For a defendant standing trial, the federal constitutional rights one enjoyed depended on whether the trial was in state or federal court. Supreme Court review was far more demanding of the latter than the former. As *Palko* demonstrated, Connecticut was allowed under the Fourteenth Amendment's due process clause to employ a procedure that the Fifth Amendment flatly barred the U.S. government from using. As long as the totality of circumstances indicated that the defendant had been given a fair trial in state court, the demands of due process were satisfied. This was the **fair trial rule**. "If due process of law requires only fundamental fairness," explained Justice Harlan in his Duncan dissent, "then the inquiry in each case must be whether a state trial process was a fair one."

As Table 9.1 suggests, the Supreme Court devoted more and more time to criminal cases, both state and national, beginning in the 1960s. The result was the **due process revolution**. Never before had an American court brought such rapid and extensive change to virtually all stages of criminal justice. This revolution had at least three elements. The first was the near complete incorporation of the Bill of Rights into the Fourteenth Amendment. By the end of the Warren Court in 1969, there had ceased to be any significant difference under the U.S. Constitution between rights applicable in federal courts and in state courts. The venerable double standard had vanished. Criminal cases from state courts now crowded the High Court's docket. Second, decisions reflected a deep appreciation of the liberties enshrined in the Bill of Rights. As explained in detail in Chapter Ten, judicial bombshells demolished or recast many of the old ways of fighting crime, state and federal. Third, and as a result of the first two, this restructuring made the Court for the first time the constitutional overseer of almost every aspect of local law enforcement in each of the 50 states.

THE NEW JUDICIAL FEDERALISM: A NEW DOUBLE STANDARD

During the Warren Court (1953–1969), the bench often found itself pushing state criminal justice systems to provide a longer list of rights for the accused. With less enthusiasm on the Burger (1969–1986), Rehnquist (1986–2005), and Roberts (2005–) Courts for some rights of criminal defendants, many state courts have maintained or enlarged these rights as a matter of *state* constitutional law. This phenomenon is sometimes called the **new judicial federalism** and the result has been the rise of a **new double standard**.

The opportunity for expanded state protection is present because virtually all the states have bills of rights similar to, or even more lengthy than, the federal Bill of Rights. Protection of individual liberties by state courts interpreting state constitutions presents no federal constitutional difficulties, provided the minimum standards of the latter are met. (See the section on judicial federalism in Chapter Four.) Federalism allows a state to grant more (but not less) freedom under its own constitution than its citizens are granted by the national Constitution.

THE SECOND AMENDMENT

This new judicial federalism will be affected by the Supreme Court's recent interest in the **Second Amendment**: "A well regulated Militia, being necessary to the security of a free State, the right of the people to keep and bear Arms, shall not be infringed." This component of the Bill of Rights grew from two interconnected beliefs that took root during the American colonial experience: (1) mistrust of a standing army that, as an organization apart from the citizenry, might be used as an instrument of government to oppress the people, and (2) preference for locally organized and controlled militias that seemed consistent with the new democratic spirit. Accordingly, public policy in the colonial and early national years typically required most adult white males to possess arms and to bear them when called to duty. Ratification of the Constitution in 1789 impinged on these convictions in two important ways. The new national government possessed the authority both to create and maintain a professional standing army and to control the state-run militias when pressed into service for the Union. Against this backdrop, the Second Amendment thus reflects the concerns of **Antifederalists** that brought forth the rest of the Bill of Rights: Fear of an overreaching national power that might threaten liberty and displace the states.

As the tragedies of mass shootings have sparked calls for increased firearms regulations, the Second Amendment has become one of the most politically charged parts of the Constitution. Opponents of such legislation look to the amendment as a declaration of a constitutionally protected individual right of gun ownership for sporting purposes and self-defense. On the other side, advocates of gun control view the amendment not as protecting an individual right against interference by government but as merely a guaranty of a collective right of the people of the states to organize for mutual self-defense. From this second perspective, the amendment is little more than an artifact from the late eighteenth century that has little bearing in an age of professional police forces and modern warfare when state militias survive today only as the National Guard.

Despite its high political profile, the Second Amendment ironically has generated little litigation for the Supreme Court. Thanks to *Barron* v. *Baltimore*, discussed earlier in this chapter, the amendment, along with other parts of the Bill of Rights, was long seen as a restraint only on Congress and so did not embrace state laws and local ordinances, a position the Court reaffirmed in its Reconstruction-era decision in *United States* v. *Cruikshank* (1876) and then again a decade later in *Presser* v. *Illinois* (1886). Indeed, it was only after Congress enacted significant firearms regulation in the twentieth century that the Court rendered an important decision on the Second Amendment. *United States* v. *Miller* (1939) involved a challenge to the National Firearms Act of 1934. Passed at the end of Prohibition, the statute governed the interstate transportation of various weapons. In this case, two individuals challenged their conviction for illegally transporting an unregistered 12-gauge sawed-off shotgun across state lines. Through an opinion by Justice McReynolds, a unanimous bench rejected the claim that the statute violated the Second Amendment, holding that the amendment did not encompass the sawed-off shotgun in question.

Miller figured prominently in ***District of Columbia* v. *Heller*** (2008), when the Court forthrightly ruled on the protection afforded by the Second Amendment. In dispute was the validity of an ordinance in the District of Columbia that effectively banned the possession of handguns and required that rifles in the home be disassembled or disabled by trigger locks. Speaking for five justices in striking down the ordinance, Justice Scalia explained that "on the basis of both text and history . . . the Second Amendment conferred an individual right to keep and bear arms." *Heller* is highly significant because it declared for the first time the existence of a personal constitutional right of firearm possession, particularly in the context of self-defense.

In so doing, however, *Heller* has hardly ended the firearms debate. In acknowledging that the Second Amendment right is not "unlimited," the Court left open the possibility of constitutionally acceptable firearm regulation, as opposed to outright prohibition. Validity would thus presumably turn on reasonableness, although the contours of such regulatory reasonableness must still be determined. Moreover, would the right recognized by *Heller* apply to state regulation of firearms? This question was crucial because most firearms regulation in the United States is the product not of Congress but of state and local governments.

An answer was forthcoming in ***McDonald* v. *City of Chicago*** (2010), which for the first time applied the Second Amendment to the states. Given the developments in *Heller* and *McDonald*, the prospects seem strong that the Second Amendment will remain politically and legally significant.

KEY TERMS

civil liberty
civil right
due process of law
recusal
incorporation
ordered liberty
total incorporation
double standard
fair trial rule
due process revolution
new judicial federalism
new double standard
Second Amendment
Antifederalists

QUERIES

1. Reread the statement by Justice Jackson on the Bill of Rights at the very beginning of this chapter. Should it be qualified in any way?

2. In his dissent in *McDonald* v. *City of Chicago*, to what extent does Justice Stevens attempt to change the debate over Fourteenth Amendment incorporation?

3. If the Supreme Court did not begin to decide substantial numbers of cases involving the Bill of Rights until the 1940s, how were rights and liberties protected prior to that time?

4. Compare Justice Thomas's concurring opinion in *Timbs* v. *Indiana* with Justice Field's dissent in the Slaughterhouse Cases from Chapter Eight. What similarities do you find?

SELECTED READINGS

Abraham, Henry J., and Barbara A. Perry. *Freedom and the Court*, 8th ed. Lawrence: University Press of Kansas, 2003.

Brennan, William J., Jr. "The Bill of Rights and the States: The Revival of State Constitutions as Guardians of Individual Rights." 61 *New York University Law Review* 535, 1986.

Fairman, Charles. "Does the Fourteenth Amendment Incorporate the Bill of Rights? The Original Understanding." 2 *Stanford Law Review* 5, 1949.

Frankfurter, Felix. "Memorandum on 'Incorporation' of the Bill of Rights into the Due Process Clause of the Fourteenth Amendment." 78 *Harvard Law Review* 746, 1965.

Levinson, Sanford. "The Embarrassing Second Amendment." 99 *Yale Law Journal* 637, 1989.

Mason, Alpheus T. "The Bill of Rights: An Almost Forgotten Appendage." In Stephen C. Halpern, ed. *The Future of Our Liberties*. Westport, CT: Greenwood, 1982.

Spitzer, Robert J. *The Right to Bear Arms*. Santa Barbara, CA: ABC-CLIO, 2001.

Spitzer, Robert J. *The Politics of Gun Control*, 7th ed. New York: Routledge, 2017.

I. DRIVE FOR A BILL OF RIGHTS

Jefferson–Madison Correspondence, 1787–1789

The principal author of the Declaration of Independence, Thomas Jefferson was abroad as minister to France during the time the Constitution was written, debated, and ratified. He thus had no direct hand in shaping its contents. From late 1787 into 1789, James Madison, who was a chief mover at the Constitutional Convention, and Jefferson exchanged a series of letters on the Constitution. Recall that trans-Atlantic mail in that day traveled on slow-sailing ships and so letters took weeks to reach their destination. Upon receiving a copy of the Constitution from Madison, one of Jefferson's major concerns was the absence of a bill of rights, an omission he found striking, given the threats to liberty posed by the French monarchy, which he observed daily. (Jefferson's diplomatic service in France concluded just as the French Revolution began.) Less fearful than others of the tyranny of the majority, Jefferson thought the most important objective of constitutional limitations was to "guard the people against the federal government, as they are already guarded against their state governments in most instances."

THOMAS JEFFERSON TO JAMES MADISON, 20 DECEMBER 1787

I like much the general idea of framing a government which should go on of itself peaceably, without needing continual recurrence to the state legislatures. . . .

There are other good things of less moment. I will now add what I do not like. First the omission of a bill of rights providing clearly and without the aid of sophisms for freedom of religion, freedom of the press, protection against standing armies, restriction against monopolies, the eternal and unremitting force of the habeas corpus laws, and trials by jury in all matters of fact triable by the laws of the land and not by the law of Nations. To say, as Mr. [James] Wilson does, that a bill of rights was not necessary because all is reserved in the case of the general government which is not given, while in the particular ones all is given which is not reserved might do for the Audience to whom it was addressed, but is surely *gratis dictum* [a mere assertion], opposed by strong inferences from the body of the instrument, as well as from the omission of the clause of our present confederation which had declared that in express terms. It was a hard conclusion to say because there has been no uniformity among the states as to the cases triable by jury, because some have been so incautious as to abandon this mode of trial, therefore the more prudent states shall be reduced to the same level of calamity. It would have been much more just and wise to have concluded the other way that as most of the states had judiciously preserved this palladium, those who had wandered should be brought back to it, and to have established general right instead of general wrong. Let me add that a bill of rights is what the people are entitled to against every government on earth, general or particular, and what no just government should refuse, or rest on inference. . . .

JAMES MADISON TO THOMAS JEFFERSON, 17 OCTOBER 1788

Experience proves the inefficacy of a bill of rights on those occasions when its control is most needed. Repeated violations of these parchment barriers have been committed by overbearing majorities in every State. . . . Wherever the real power in a Government lies, there is the danger of oppression. In our Government, the real power lies in the majority of the Community, and the invasion of private rights is *chiefly* to be apprehended, not from acts of government contrary to the sense of its constituents, but from acts in which the Government is the mere instrument of the major number of the Constituents. This is a truth of great importance, but not yet sufficiently attended to; and is probably more strongly impressed on my mind by facts, and reflections suggested by them, than on yours which has contemplated abuses of power issuing from a very different quarter. Wherever there is an interest and power to do wrong, wrong will generally be done, and not less readily by a powerful & interested party than by a powerful and interested prince. . . .

What use then it may be asked can a bill of rights serve in popular Governments? I answer the two following which, though less essential than in other Governments, sufficiently recommend the precaution: 1. The political truths declared in that solemn manner acquire by degrees the character of fundamental maxims of free Governments, and as they become incorporated with the national sentiment, counteract the impulses of interest and passion. 2. Altho, it be generally true as above stated that the danger of oppression lies in the interested majorities of the people rather than in usurped acts of the Government, yet there may be occasions on which the evil may spring from the latter source; and on such, a bill of rights will be a good ground for an appeal to the sense of the community. . . . It is a melancholy reflection that liberty should be equally exposed to danger whether the Government have too much or too little power, and that the line which divides these extremes should be so inaccurately defined by experience. . . .

THOMAS JEFFERSON TO JAMES MADISON, 15 MARCH 1789

. . . In the arguments in favor of a declaration of rights, you omit one which has great weight with me, the legal check which it puts into the hands of the judiciary. This is a body, which if rendered independent, and kept strictly to their own department merits great confidence for their learning and integrity. . . .

Experience proves the inefficacy of a bill of rights. True. But tho it is not absolutely efficacious under all circumstances, it is of great potency always, and rarely inefficacious. A brace the more will often keep up the building which would have fallen with that brace the less. There is a remarkable difference between the characters of the inconveniences which attend a Declaration of rights, and those which attend the want of it. The inconveniences of the Declaration are that it may cramp government in its useful exertions. But the evil of this is short-lived, moderate and reparable. The inconveniences of the want of a Declaration are permanent, afflicting and irreparable: they are in constant progression from bad to worse. The executive in our government is not the sole, it is scarcely the principal object of my jealousy. The tyranny of the legislatures is the most formidable dread at present, and will be for long years. That of the executive will come in its turn, but it will be at a remote period. . . .

JAMES MADISON, SPEECH PLACING THE PROPOSED BILL OF RIGHTS AMENDMENTS BEFORE THE HOUSE OF REPRESENTATIVES, 8 JUNE 1789

Mr. Madison rose, and reminded the House that this was the day that he had heretofore named for bringing forward amendments to the constitution, as contemplated in the fifth article of the constitution. . . .

The first of these amendments relates to what may be called a bill of rights. . . .

It has been said, that it is unnecessary to load the constitution with this provision, because it was not found effectual in the constitution of the particular States. It is true, there are a few particular States in which some of the most valuable articles have not, at one time or other, been violated; but it does not follow but they may have, to a certain degree, a salutary effect against the abuse of power. If they are incorporated into the constitution, independent tribunals of justice will consider themselves in a peculiar manner the guardians of those rights; they will be an impenetrable bulwark against every assumption of power in the legislative or executive; they will be naturally led to resist every encroachment upon rights expressly stipulated for in the constitution by the declaration of rights. Besides this security, there is a great probability that such a declaration in the federal system would be enforced; because the State Legislatures will jealously and closely watch the operations of this Government, and be able to resist with more effect every assumption of power, than any other power on earth can do; and the greatest opponents to a Federal Government admit the State Legislatures to be sure guardians of the people's liberty. I conclude, from this view of the subject, that it will be proper in itself, and highly politic, for the tranquility of the public mind, and the stability of the Government, that we should offer something, in the form I have proposed, to be incorporated in the system of Government, as a declaration of the rights of the people.

I wish also, in revising the constitution, we may throw into that section, which interdicts the abuse of certain powers in the State Legislatures, some other provisions of equal, if not greater importance than those already made. The words, "No State shall pass any bill of attainder, ex post facto law," &c. were wise and proper restrictions in the constitution. I think there is more danger of those powers being abused by the State Governments than by the Government of the United States. The same may be said of other powers which they possess, if not controlled by the general principle, that laws are unconstitutional which infringe the rights of the community. I should therefore wish to extend this interdiction, and add that no State shall violate the equal right of conscience, freedom of the press, or trial by jury in criminal cases; because it is proper that every Government should be disarmed of powers which trench upon those particular rights. I know, in some of the State constitutions, the power of the Government is controlled by such a declaration; but others are not. I cannot see any reason against obtaining even a double security on those points; and nothing can give a more sincere proof of the attachment of those who opposed this constitution to these great and important rights, than to see them join in obtaining the security I have now proposed: because it must be admitted, on all hands, that the State Governments are as liable to attack these invaluable privileges as the General Government is, and therefore ought to be as cautiously guarded against. . . .

[An amendment providing for safeguards against the states was proposed, but it failed of adoption.—Ed.]

II. THE BILL OF RIGHTS AND THE STATES

Palko v. *Connecticut*
302 U.S. 319, 58 S.Ct. 149, 82 L.Ed. 288 (1937)

http://caselaw.findlaw.com/us-supreme-court/302/319.html

By statute, Connecticut permitted the state to appeal from rulings and decisions in its criminal courts on points of law. Convicted of murder in the second degree and given a life sentence, Palko was retried after a successful state appeal. His second trial, held in spite of his objection that he was being twice placed in jeopardy, resulted in a conviction for first-degree murder and a death sentence. Majority: Cardozo, Black, Brandeis, Hughes, Roberts, Sutherland, Stone, Van Devanter. Dissenting: Butler.

Mr. Justice Cardozo delivered the opinion of the Court. . . .

The argument for appellant is that whatever is forbidden by the Fifth Amendment is forbidden by the Fourteenth Amendment also. . . .

[The] thesis is even broader. Whatever would be a violation of the original bill of rights (Amendments I to VIII) if done by the federal government is now equally unlawful by force of the Fourteenth Amendment if done by a state. There is no such general rule.

The Fifth Amendment provides, among other things, that no person shall be held to answer for a capital or otherwise infamous crime unless on presentment or indictment of a grand jury. This court has held that, in prosecutions by a state, presentment or indictment by a grand jury may give way to informations at the instance of a public officer. . . . The Fifth Amendment provides also that no person shall be compelled in any criminal case to be a witness against himself. This court has said that, in prosecutions by a state, the exemption will fail if the state elects to end it. . . . The Sixth Amendment calls for a jury trial in criminal cases and the Seventh for a jury trial in civil cases of common law where the value in controversy shall exceed twenty dollars. This court has ruled that consistently with those amendments trial by jury may be modified by a state or abolished altogether. . . .

On the other hand, the due process clause of the Fourteenth Amendment may make it unlawful for a state to abridge by its statutes the freedom of speech which the First Amendment safeguards against encroachment by the Congress . . . or the like freedom of the press . . . or the right of peaceable assembly, without which speech would be unduly trammeled. . . .

The line of division may seem to be wavering and broken if there is a hasty catalogue of the cases on the one side and the other. Reflection and analysis will induce a different view. There emerges the perception of a rationalizing principle which gives to discrete instances a proper order and coherence. The right to trial by jury and the immunity from prosecution except as the result of an indictment may have value and importance. Even so, they are not of the very essence of a scheme of ordered liberty. To abolish them is not to violate a "principle of justice so rooted in the traditions and conscience of our people as to be ranked as fundamental." . . . Few would be so narrow or provincial as to maintain that a fair and enlightened system of justice would be impossible without them. What is true of jury trials and indictments is true also, as the cases show, of the immunity from compulsory self-incrimination. . . . This too might be lost, and justice still be done. . . .

We reach a different plane of social and moral values when we pass to the privileges and immunities that have been taken over from the earlier articles of the Federal Bill of Rights and brought within the Fourteenth Amendment by a process of absorption. These in their origin were effective against the federal government alone. If the Fourteenth Amendment has absorbed them, the process of absorption has had its source in the belief that neither liberty nor justice would exist if they were sacrificed. . . . This is true, for illustration, of freedom of thought and speech. Of that freedom one may say that it is the matrix, the indispensable condition, of nearly every other form of freedom. . . .

Our survey of the cases serves, we think, to justify the statement that the dividing line between them, if not unfaltering throughout its course, has been true for the most part to a unifying principle. On which side of the line the case made out by the appellant has appropriate location must be the next inquiry and the final one. Is that kind of double jeopardy to which the statute has subjected him a hardship so acute and shocking that our polity will not endure it? Does it violate those "fundamental principles of liberty and justice which lie at the base of all our civil and political institutions?" . . . The answer surely must be "no." What the answer would have to be if the state were permitted after a trial free from error to try the accused over again or to bring another case against him, we have no occasion to consider. We deal with the statute before us and no other. The state is not attempting to wear the accused out by a multitude of cases with accumulated trials. It asks no more than this, that the case against him shall go on until there shall be a trial free from the corrosion of substantial legal error. . . .

The judgment is

Affirmed.

MR. JUSTICE BUTLER dissents [without opinion].

Adamson v. *California*
332 U.S. 46, 67 S.Ct. 1672, 91 L.Ed. 1903 (1947)

http://caselaw.findlaw.com/us-supreme-court/332/46.html

Adamson appealed from a judgment of the Supreme Court of California affirming his conviction of murder. The basis of his appeal was the alleged invalidity of a California code provision that permitted the prosecution and the court to comment on the failure of a defendant to take the witness stand to explain or deny evidence against him. In his trial Adamson, who had a record of three previous felony convictions, chose not to take the stand, thus causing adverse comments by the district attorney and court. However, if he had chosen to testify, the district attorney could then have revealed his record of previous convictions to impeach his testimony. It should be noted that in 1947 a majority of state jurisdictions and the federal courts did not permit comment on a defendant's failure to testify. Majority: Reed, Burton, Frankfurter, Jackson, Vinson. Dissenting: Black, Douglas, Murphy, Rutledge.

MR. JUSTICE REED delivered the opinion of the Court. . . .

A right to a fair trial is a right admittedly protected by the due process clause of the Fourteenth Amendment. Therefore, appellant argues, the due process clause of the Fourteenth Amendment protects his privilege against self-incrimination. The due process clause of the Fourteenth Amendment, however, does not draw all the rights of the federal Bill of Rights under its protection. That contention was made and rejected in *Palko* v. *Connecticut*. . . .

Specifically, the due process clause does not protect, by virtue of its mere existence, the accused's freedom from giving testimony by compulsion in state trials that is secured to him against federal interference by the Fifth Amendment. . . . For a state to require testimony from an accused is not necessarily a breach of a state's obligation to give a fair trial. . . .

California . . . is one of a few states that permit limited comment upon a defendant's failure to testify. . . . It seems quite natural that when a defendant has opportunity to deny or explain facts and determines not to do so, the prosecution should bring out the strength of the evidence by commenting upon defendant's failure to explain or deny it. The prosecution evidence may be of facts that may be beyond the knowledge of the accused. If so, his failure to testify would have little if any weight. But the facts may be such as are necessarily in the knowledge of the accused. In that case a failure to explain would point to an inability to explain. . . .

It is true that if comment were forbidden, an accused in this situation could remain silent and avoid evidence of former crimes and comment upon his failure to testify. We are of the view, however, that a state may control such a situation in accordance with its own ideas of the most efficient administration of criminal justice. The purpose of due process is not to protect an accused against a proper conviction but against an unfair conviction.

Affirmed.

Mr. Justice Frankfurter, concurring. . . .

Between the incorporation of the Fourteenth Amendment into the Constitution and the beginning of the present membership of the Court—a period of seventy years—the scope of that Amendment was passed upon by forty-three judges. Of all these judges, only one [the first Justice Harlan], who may respectfully be called an eccentric exception, ever indicated the belief that the . . . Amendment was a shorthand summary of the first eight Amendments. . . . And so they did not find that the Fourteenth Amendment, concerned as it was with matters fundamental to the pursuit of justice, fastened upon the States procedural arrangements which, in the language of Mr. Justice Cardozo, only those who are "narrow and provincial" would deem essential to "a fair and enlightened system of justice." To suggest that it is inconsistent with a truly free society to begin prosecutions without an indictment, to try petty civil cases without the paraphernalia of a common law jury, to take into consideration that one who has full opportunity to make a defense remains silent is, in de Tocqueville's phrase, to confound the familiar with the necessary. . . .

The Amendment neither comprehends the specific provisions by which the founders deemed it appropriate to restrict the federal government nor is it confined to them. The Due Process Clause . . . has an independent potency. . . .

It seems pretty late in the day to suggest that a phrase so laden with historic meaning should be given an improvised content consisting of some but not all of the provisions of the first eight Amendments, selected on an undefined basis. . . .

And so, when . . . a conviction in a State court is here for review under a claim that a right protected by the Due Process Clause . . . has been denied, the issue is not whether an infraction of one of the specific provisions of the first eight Amendments is disclosed by the record. The relevant question is whether the criminal proceedings which resulted in conviction deprived the accused of the due process of law to which the United States Constitution entitled him. Judicial review of that guaranty . . . inescapably imposes on this Court an exercise of judgment upon the whole course of the proceedings in order to ascertain whether they offend those canons of decency and fairness which express the notions of justice of English-speaking peoples. . . . These standards of justice are not authoritatively formulated anywhere as though they were prescriptions in a pharmacopoeia. But neither does the application of the Due Process Clause imply that judges are wholly at large. The judicial judgment . . . must move within the limits of accepted notions of justice and is not to be based upon the idiosyncrasies of a merely personal judgment. The fact that judges among themselves may differ whether in a particular case a trial offends accepted notions of justice is not disproof that general rather than idiosyncratic standards are applied. . . .

Mr. Justice Black, with whom Mr. Justice Douglas concurs, dissenting. . . .

This decision reasserts a constitutional theory spelled out in *Twining* v. *New Jersey* . . . that this Court is endowed by the Constitution with boundless power under "natural law" periodically to expand and contract constitutional standards to conform to the Court's conception of what at a particular time constitutes "civilized decency" and "fundamental liberty and justice." Invoking this *Twining* rule, the Court concludes that although comment upon testimony in a federal court would violate the Fifth Amendment, identical comment in a state court does not violate today's fashion in civilized decency and fundamentals and is therefore not prohibited by the Federal Constitution as amended. . . .

My study of the historical events that culminated in the Fourteenth Amendment, and the expressions of those who sponsored and favored, as well as those who opposed its submission and passage, persuades me that one of the chief objects that the provisions of the Amendment's first section, separately, and as a whole, were intended to accomplish was to make the Bill of Rights applicable to the states. With full knowledge of the import of the Barron decision, the framers and backers of the Fourteenth Amendment proclaimed its purpose to be to overturn the constitutional rule that case had announced. . . .

I fear to see the consequences of the Court's practice of substituting its own concepts of decency and fundamental justice for the language of the Bill of Rights as its point of departure in interpreting and enforcing that Bill of Rights. . . . I would follow what I believe was the original purpose of the Fourteenth Amendment—to extend to all the people of the nation the complete protection of the Bill of Rights. To hold that this Court can determine what, if any, provisions of the Bill of Rights will be enforced, and if so to what degree, is to frustrate the great design of a written Constitution. . . .

Mr. Justice Murphy, with whom Mr. Justice Rutledge concurs, dissenting . . . [omitted].

Duncan v. *Louisiana*
391 U.S. 145, 88 S.Ct. 1444, 20 L.Ed. 2d 491 (1968)

http://caselaw.findlaw.com/us-supreme-court/391/145.html

Gary Duncan was convicted of simple battery, a misdemeanor punishable under Louisiana law by two years' imprisonment and a $300 fine. His request for trial by jury was denied because the state constitution restricted trial by jury to capital offenses and those punishable by hard labor. The Louisiana Supreme Court denied his claim that his right to jury trial under the Sixth and Fourteenth Amendments had been violated. The lengthy footnote in Justice White's opinion is important because it summarizes the changes that transpired in the Court's thinking about the Fourteenth Amendment after *Adamson*. Majority: White, Black, Brennan, Douglas, Fortas, Marshall, Warren. Dissenting: Harlan, Stewart.

Mr. Justice White delivered the opinion of the Court. . . .

The test for determining whether a right extended by the Fifth and Sixth Amendments with respect to federal criminal proceedings is also protected against state action by the Fourteenth Amendment has been phrased in a variety of ways in the opinions of this Court. The question has been asked whether a right is among those "fundamental principles of liberty and justice which lie at the base of all our civil and political institutions," whether it is "basic in our system of jurisprudence," and whether it is "a fundamental right, essential to a fair trial." The claim before us is that the right to trial by jury guaranteed by the Sixth Amendment meets these tests. The position of Louisiana, on the other hand, is that the Constitution imposes upon the States no duty to give a jury trial in any criminal case, regardless of the seriousness of the crime or the size of the punishment which may be imposed. Because we believe that trial by jury in criminal cases is fundamental to the American scheme of justice, we hold that the Fourteenth Amendment guarantees a right of jury trial in all criminal cases which—were they to be tried in a federal court—would come within the Sixth Amendment's guarantee.[1] Since we consider the appeal before us to be such a case, we hold that the Constitution was violated when appellant's demand for jury trial was refused. . . . The judgment below is reversed and the case is remanded for proceedings not inconsistent with this opinion.

Mr. Justice Black, with whom Mr. Justice Douglas joins, concurring. . . .

While I do not wish at this time to discuss at length my disagreement with Brother Harlan's forthright and frank restatement of the now discredited Twining doctrine, I do want to point out what appears to me to be the basic difference between us. His view, as was indeed the view of *Twining*, is that "due process is an evolving concept" and therefore that it entails a "gradual process of judicial inclusion and exclusion" to ascertain those "immutable principles of free government which no member of the Union may disregard." Thus the Due Process Clause is treated as prescribing no specific and clearly ascertainable constitutional command that judges must obey in interpreting the Constitution, but rather as leaving judges free to decide at any particular time whether a particular rule or judicial formulation embodies an "immutable principle of free government" or "is implicit in the concept of ordered liberty," or whether certain conduct "shocks the judge's conscience" or runs counter to some other similar, undefined and undefinable standard. Thus due process, according to my Brother Harlan, is to be a word with no permanent meaning, but one which is found to shift from time to time in accordance with judges' predilections and understandings of what is best for the country. If due process means this, the Fourteenth Amendment, in my opinion, might as well have been written that "no person shall be deprived of life, liberty or property except by laws that the judges of the United States Supreme Court shall find to be consistent with the immutable principles of free government." It is impossible for me to believe that such unconfined power is given to judges in our Constitution that is a written one in order to limit governmental power. . . .

Mr. Justice Fortas, concurring . . . [omitted].

Mr. Justice Harlan, [with] whom Mr. Justice Stewart joins, dissenting. . . .

The Court's approach to this case is an uneasy and illogical compromise among the views of various Justices on how the Due Process Clause should be interpreted. The Court does not say that those who framed the Fourteenth Amendment intended to make the Sixth Amendment applicable to the States. And the Court concedes that it finds nothing unfair about the procedure by which the present appellant was tried. Nevertheless, the Court reverses his conviction: it holds, for some reason not apparent to me, that the Due Process Clause incorporates the particular clause of the Sixth Amendment that requires trial by jury in federal criminal cases—including, as I read its opinion, the sometimes trivial accompanying baggage of judicial interpretation in federal contexts. . . . With all respect, the Court's approach and its reading of history are altogether topsy-turvy. . . .

Apart from the approach taken by the absolute incorporationists, I can see only one method of analysis that has any internal logic. That is to start with the words "liberty" and "due process of law" and attempt to define them in a way that accords with American traditions and our system of government. This approach, involving a much more discriminating process of adjudication than does "incorporation," is, albeit difficult, the one that was followed throughout the nineteenth and most of the present century. It entails a "gradual process of judicial inclusion and exclusion," seeking, . . . to ascertain those "immutable principles of free government which no member of the Union may disregard." . . .

The relationship of the Bill of Rights to this "gradual process" seems to me to be twofold. In the first place it has long been clear that the Due Process Clause imposes some restrictions on state action that parallel Bill of Rights restrictions on federal action. Second, and more important than this accidental overlap, is the fact that the Bill of Rights is evidence, at various points, of the content Americans find in the term "liberty" and of American standards of fundamental fairness. . . .

The argument that jury trial is not a requisite of due process is quite simple. The central proposition of *Palko* . . . a proposition to which I would adhere, is that "due process of law" requires only that criminal trials be fundamentally fair. . . . I do not see what else "due process of law" can intelligibly be thought to mean. If due process of law requires only fundamental fairness, then the inquiry in each case must be whether a state trial process was a fair one. The Court has held, properly I think, that in an adversary process it is a requisite of fairness, for which there is no adequate substitute, that a criminal defendant be afforded a right to counsel and to cross-examine opposing witnesses. But it simply has not been demonstrated, nor, I think, can it be demonstrated, that trial by jury is the only fair means of resolving issues of fact. . . .

Timbs v. *Indiana*
586 U.S. ___, 139 S.Ct. 682, 230 L.Ed. 2d 11 (2019)

www.supremecourt.gov/opinions/18pdf/17-1091_5536.pdf

The facts of this case appear in Justice Ginsburg's opinion below. Majority: Ginsburg, Alito, Breyer, Gorsuch, Kagan, Kavanaugh, Roberts, Sotomayor, Thomas.

Justice Ginsburg delivered the opinion of the Court.

Tyson Timbs pleaded guilty in Indiana state court to dealing in a controlled substance and conspiracy to commit theft. The trial court sentenced him to one year of home detention and five years of probation, which included a court-supervised addiction-treatment program. The sentence also required Timbs to pay fees and costs totaling $1,203. At the time of Timbs's arrest, the police seized his vehicle, a Land Rover SUV Timbs had purchased for about $42,000. . . .

The State engaged a private law firm to bring a civil suit for forfeiture of Timbs's Land Rover, charging that the vehicle had been used to transport heroin. After Timbs's guilty plea in the criminal case, the trial court held a hearing on the forfeiture demand. Although finding that Timbs's vehicle had been used to facilitate violation of a criminal statute, the court denied the requested forfeiture, observing that Timbs had recently purchased the vehicle for $42,000, more than four times the maximum $10,000 monetary fine assessable against him for his drug conviction. Forfeiture of the Land Rover, the court determined, would be grossly disproportionate to the gravity of Timbs's offense, hence unconstitutional under the Eighth Amendment's Excessive Fines Clause. The Court of Appeals of Indiana affirmed that determination, but the Indiana Supreme Court reversed. The Indiana Supreme Court did not decide whether the forfeiture would be excessive. Instead, it held that the Excessive Fines Clause constrains only federal action and is inapplicable to state impositions. . . .

The question presented: Is the Eighth Amendment's Excessive Fines Clause an "incorporated" protection applicable to the States under the Fourteenth Amendment's Due Process Clause? Like the Eighth Amendment's proscriptions of "cruel and unusual punishment" and "[e]xcessive bail," the protection against excessive fines guards against abuses of government's punitive or criminal law-enforcement authority. This safeguard, we hold, is "fundamental to our scheme of ordered liberty," with "dee[p] root[s] in [our] history and tradition." The Excessive Fines Clause is therefore incorporated by the Due Process Clause of the Fourteenth Amendment. . . . Taken together, these Clauses place "parallel limitations" on "the power of those entrusted with the criminal-law function of government." . . .

The Excessive Fines Clause traces its venerable lineage back to at least 1215, when Magna Carta guaranteed that "[a] Free-man shall not be amerced for a small fault, but after the manner of the fault; and for a great fault after the greatness thereof, saving to him his contenement. . . ." As relevant here, Magna Carta required that economic sanctions "be proportioned to the wrong" and "not be so large as to deprive [an offender] of his livelihood." . . . When James II was overthrown in the Glorious Revolution, the attendant English Bill of Rights reaffirmed Magna Carta's guarantee by providing that "excessive Bail ought not to be required, nor excessive Fines imposed; nor cruel and unusual Punishments inflicted." . . .

Adoption of the Excessive Fines Clause was in tune not only with English law; the Clause resonated as well with similar colonial-era provisions. An even broader consensus obtained in 1868 upon ratification of the Fourteenth Amendment. By then, the constitutions of 35 of the 37 States—accounting for over 90% of the U.S. population—expressly prohibited excessive fines. Notwithstanding the States' apparent agreement that the right guaranteed by the Excessive Fines Clause was fundamental, abuses continued. Following the Civil War, Southern States enacted Black Codes to subjugate newly freed slaves and maintain the prewar racial hierarchy. Among these laws' provisions were draconian fines for violating broad proscriptions on "vagrancy" and other dubious offenses. When newly freed slaves were unable to pay imposed fines, States often demanded involuntary labor instead. . . .

Today, acknowledgment of the right's fundamental nature remains widespread. As Indiana itself reports, all 50 States have a constitutional provision prohibiting the imposition of excessive fines either directly or by requiring proportionality. Indeed, Indiana explains that its own Supreme Court has held that the Indiana Constitution should be interpreted to impose the same restrictions as the Eighth Amendment.

For good reason, the protection against excessive fines has been a constant shield throughout Anglo-American history: Exorbitant tolls undermine other constitutional liberties. Excessive fines can be used, for example, to retaliate against or chill the speech of political enemies, as the Stuarts' critics learned several centuries ago. Even absent a political motive, fines may be employed "in a measure out of accord with the penal goals of retribution and deterrence," for "fines are a source of revenue," while other forms of punishment "cost a State money."

In short, the historical and logical case for concluding that the Fourteenth Amendment incorporates the Excessive Fines Clause is overwhelming. Protection against excessive punitive economic sanctions secured by the Clause is, to repeat, both "fundamental to our scheme of ordered liberty" and "deeply rooted in this Nation's history and tradition."

The State of Indiana does not meaningfully challenge the case for incorporating the Excessive Fines Clause as a general matter. Instead, the State argues that the Clause does not apply to its use of civil *in rem* forfeitures because, the State says, the Clause's specific application to such forfeitures is neither fundamental nor deeply rooted. In *Austin* v. *United States* (1993), however, this Court held that civil *in rem* forfeitures fall within the Clause's protection when they are at least partially punitive. *Austin* arose in the federal context. But when a Bill of Rights protection is incorporated, the protection applies "identically to both the Federal Government and the States." Accordingly, to prevail, Indiana must persuade us either to overrule our decision in *Austin* or to hold that, in light of *Austin*, the Excessive Fines Clause is not incorporated because the Clause's application to civil *in rem* forfeitures is neither fundamental nor deeply rooted. The first argument is not properly before us, and the second misapprehends the nature of our incorporation inquiry. . . .

As a fallback, Indiana argues that the Excessive Fines Clause cannot be incorporated if it applies to civil *in rem* forfeitures. We disagree. In considering whether the Fourteenth Amendment incorporates a protection contained in the Bill of Rights, we ask whether the right guaranteed—not each and every particular application of that right—is fundamental or deeply rooted. Indiana's suggestion to the contrary is inconsistent with the approach we have taken in cases concerning novel applications of rights already deemed incorporated. For example, in *Packingham* v. *North Carolina* (2017), we held that a North Carolina statute prohibiting registered sex offenders from accessing certain commonplace social media websites violated the First Amendment right to freedom of speech. In reaching this conclusion, we noted that the First Amendment's Free Speech Clause was "applicable to the States under the Due Process Clause of the Fourteenth Amendment." We did not, however, inquire whether the Free Speech Clause's application specifically to social media websites was fundamental or deeply rooted. . . . Similarly here, regardless of whether application of the Excessive Fines Clause to civil *in rem* forfeitures is itself fundamental or deeply rooted, our conclusion that the Clause is incorporated remains unchanged. For the reasons stated, the judgment of the Indiana Supreme Court is vacated, and the case is remanded for further proceedings not inconsistent with this opinion.

It is so ordered.

Justice Gorsuch, concurring . . . [omitted].

Justice Thomas, concurring in the judgment.

I agree with the Court that the Fourteenth Amendment makes the Eighth Amendment's prohibition on excessive fines fully applicable to the States. But I cannot agree with the route the Court takes to reach this conclusion. Instead of reading the Fourteenth Amendment's Due Process Clause to encompass a substantive right that has nothing to do with "process," I would hold that the right to be free from excessive fines is one of the "privileges or immunities of citizens of the United States" protected by the Fourteenth Amendment. . . . "On its face, this appears to grant . . . United States citizens a certain collection of rights—i.e., privileges or immunities—attributable to that status." But as I have previously explained, this Court "marginaliz[ed]" the Privileges or Immunities Clause in the late 19th century by defining the collection of rights covered by the Clause "quite narrowly." Litigants seeking federal protection of substantive rights against the States thus needed "an alternative fount of such rights," and this Court "found one in a most curious place"—the Fourteenth Amendment's Due Process Clause. . . .

Because this Clause speaks only to "process," the Court has "long struggled to define" what substantive rights it protects. The Court ordinarily says, as it does today, that the Clause protects rights that are "fundamental." Sometimes that means rights that are "'deeply rooted in this Nation's history and tradition.'" Other times, when that formulation proves too restrictive, the Court defines the universe of "fundamental" rights so broadly as to border on meaningless. . . . Because the oxymoronic "substantive" "due process" doctrine has no basis in the Constitution, it is unsurprising that the Court has been unable to adhere to any "guiding principle to distinguish 'fundamental' rights that warrant protection from nonfundamental rights that do not." And because the Court's substantive due process precedents allow the Court to fashion fundamental rights without any textual constraints, it is equally unsurprising that among these precedents are some of the Court's most notoriously incorrect decisions. *E.g., Roe* v. *Wade* (1973); *Dred Scott* v. *Sandford* (1857).

The present case illustrates the incongruity of the Court's due process approach to incorporating fundamental rights against the States. Petitioner argues that the forfeiture of his vehicle is an excessive punishment. He does not argue that the Indiana courts failed to "'proceed according to the "law of the land"—that is, according to written constitutional and statutory provisions,'" or that the State failed to provide "some baseline procedures." His claim has nothing to do with any "process" "due" him. I therefore decline to apply the "legal fiction" of substantive due process.

When the Fourteenth Amendment was ratified, "the terms 'privileges' and 'immunities' had an established meaning as synonyms for 'rights.'" Those "rights" were the "inalienable rights" of citizens that had been "long recognized," and "the ratifying public understood the Privileges or Immunities Clause to protect constitutionally enumerated rights" against interference by the States. . . . The question here is whether the Eighth Amendment's prohibition on excessive fines was considered such a right. The historical record overwhelmingly demonstrates that it was. . . . In sum, at the time of the founding, the prohibition on excessive fines was a longstanding right of Englishmen. . . .

The prohibition on excessive fines remained fundamental at the time of the Fourteenth Amendment. In 1868, 35 of 37 state constitutions "expressly prohibited excessive fines." These and other examples of excessive fines from the historical record informed the Nation's consideration of the Fourteenth Amendment. . . . As a constitutionally enumerated right understood to be a privilege of American citizenship, the Eighth Amendment's prohibition on excessive fines applies in full to the States.

III. THE SECOND AMENDMENT

District of Columbia v. *Heller*
554 U.S. 570, 128 S.Ct. 2783, 171 L.Ed. 2d 637 (2008)

http://caselaw.findlaw.com/us-supreme-court/554/570.html

A 1976 ordinance in the District of Columbia effectively banned the possession of handguns and required that rifles in the home be disassembled or disabled by trigger locks. Dick Heller is a special police officer authorized to carry a handgun while on duty at the Federal Judicial Center. He applied for a registration certificate for a handgun that he wished to keep at his home in the District, but was refused. He then filed suit in the U.S. District Court for the District of Columbia seeking, on Second Amendment grounds, to enjoin the city from enforcing the ordinance. The district court dismissed Heller's complaint, but the Court of Appeals for the District of Columbia Circuit reversed, holding that the Second Amendment protects an individual right to possess firearms and that the city's total ban on handguns, as well as its requirement that firearms in the home be kept nonfunctional even when necessary for self-defense, violated that right. In remarks to a Harvard Club luncheon in 2009, Justice Ginsburg said that the dissents in this case were crafted with an eye to helping a "future, wiser" Court overturn *Heller*. Majority: Scalia, Alito, Kennedy, Roberts, Thomas. Dissenting: Stevens, Breyer, Ginsburg, Souter.

Justice Scalia delivered the opinion of the Court. . . .

The two sides in this case have set out very different interpretations of the Amendment. Petitioners and today's dissenting Justices believe that it protects only the right to possess and carry a firearm in connection with militia service. Respondent argues that it protects an individual right to possess a firearm unconnected with service in a militia, and to use that arm for traditionally lawful purposes, such as self-defense within the home.

The Second Amendment is naturally divided into two parts: its prefatory clause and its operative clause. The former does not limit the latter grammatically, but rather announces a purpose. The Amendment could be rephrased, "Because a well regulated Militia is necessary to the security of a free State, the right of the people to keep and bear Arms shall not be infringed." . . .

The first salient feature of the operative clause is that it codifies a "right of the people." Nowhere else in the Constitution does a "right" attributed to "the people" refer to anything other than an individual right. . . .

This contrasts markedly with the phrase "the militia" in the prefatory clause. As we will describe below, the "militia" in colonial America consisted of a subset of "the people"—those who were male, able bodied, and within a certain age range. Reading the Second Amendment as protecting only the right to "keep and bear Arms" in an organized militia therefore fits poorly with the operative clause's description of the holder of that right as "the people." We start therefore with a strong presumption that the Second Amendment right is exercised individually and belongs to all Americans. . . .

We move now from the holder of the right—"the people"—to the substance of the right: "to keep and bear Arms."

Before addressing the verbs "keep" and "bear," we interpret their object: "Arms." The 18th-century meaning is no different from the meaning today. . . . The term was applied, then as now, to weapons that were not specifically designed for military use and were not employed in a military capacity. . . .

We turn to the phrases "keep arms" and "bear arms." . . . [T]he most natural reading of "keep Arms" in the Second Amendment is to "have weapons." . . .

[P]etitioners and Justice Stevens . . . manufacture a hybrid definition, whereby "bear arms" connotes the actual carrying of arms . . . but only in the service of an organized militia. No dictionary has ever adopted that definition, and we have been apprised of no source that indicates that it carried that meaning at the time of the founding. . . .

Putting all of these textual elements together, we find that [the words of the amendment] guarantee the individual right to possess and carry weapons in case of confrontation. This meaning is strongly confirmed by the historical background of the Second Amendment. We look to this because it has always been widely understood that the Second Amendment, like the First and Fourth Amendments, codified a pre-existing right. The very text of the Second Amendment implicitly recognizes the pre-existence of the right and declares only that it "shall not be infringed." . . .

Of course the right was not unlimited. . . . Before turning to limitations upon the individual right, however, we must determine whether the prefatory clause of the Second Amendment comports with our interpretation of the operative clause. . . .

It fits perfectly, once one knows the history that the founding generation knew and that we have described above. That history showed that the way tyrants had eliminated a militia consisting of all the able-bodied men was not by banning the militia but simply by taking away the people's arms, enabling a select militia or standing army to suppress political opponents. This is what had occurred in England that prompted codification of the right to have arms in the English Bill of Rights. . . .

The prefatory clause does not suggest that preserving the militia was the only reason Americans valued the ancient right; most undoubtedly thought it even more important for self-defense and hunting. But the threat that the new Federal Government would destroy the citizens' militia by taking away their arms was the reason that right—unlike some other English rights—was codified in a written Constitution. . . .

We now ask whether any of our precedents forecloses the conclusions we have reached about the meaning of the Second Amendment. . . .

Justice Stevens places overwhelming reliance upon this Court's decision in *United States* v. *Miller* (1939). . . . And what is, according to Justice Stevens, the holding of *Miller* that demands such obeisance? That the Second Amendment "protects the right to keep and bear arms for certain military purposes, but that it does not curtail the legislature's power to regulate the nonmilitary use and ownership of weapons."

Nothing so clearly demonstrates the weakness of Justice Stevens' case. *Miller* did not hold that and cannot possibly be read to have held that. The judgment in the case upheld against a Second Amendment challenge two men's federal convictions for transporting an unregistered short-barreled shotgun in interstate commerce, in violation of the National Firearms Act. It is entirely clear that the Court's basis for saying that the Second Amendment did not apply was not that the defendants were "bear[ing] arms" not "for . . . military purposes" but for "nonmilitary use." Rather, it was that the type of weapon at issue was not eligible for Second Amendment protection: "In the absence of any evidence tending to show that the possession or use of a [short-barreled shotgun] at this time has some reasonable relationship to the preservation or efficiency of a well regulated militia, we cannot say that the Second Amendment guarantees the right to keep and bear *such an instrument*." [Emphasis added by Justice Scalia.] "Certainly," the Court continued, "it is not within judicial notice that this weapon is any part of the ordinary military equipment or that its use could contribute to the common defense." Beyond that, the opinion provided no explanation of the content of the right.

This holding is not only consistent with, but positively suggests, that the Second Amendment confers an individual right to keep and bear arms (though only arms that "have some reasonable relationship to the preservation or efficiency of a well regulated militia"). Had the Court believed that the Second Amendment protects only those serving in the militia, it would have been odd to examine the character of the weapon rather than simply note that the two crooks were not militiamen. Justice Stevens can say again and again that *Miller* did "not turn on the difference between muskets and sawed-off shotguns, it turned, rather, on the basic difference between the military and nonmilitary use and possession of guns," but the words of the opinion prove otherwise. The most Justice Stevens can plausibly claim for *Miller* is that it declined to decide the nature of the Second Amendment right, despite the Solicitor General's argument (made in the alternative) that the right was collective. *Miller* stands only for the proposition that the Second Amendment right, whatever its nature, extends only to certain types of weapons. It is particularly wrongheaded to read *Miller* for more than what it said, because the case did not even purport to be a thorough examination of the Second Amendment. . . .

We may as well consider at this point (for we will have to consider eventually) what types of weapons *Miller* permits. Read in isolation, *Miller's* phrase "part of ordinary military equipment" could mean that only those weapons useful in warfare are protected. That would be a startling reading of the opinion, since it would mean that the National Firearms Act's restrictions on machineguns (not challenged in *Miller*) might be unconstitutional, machineguns being useful in warfare in 1939. We think that *Miller's* "ordinary military equipment" language must be read in tandem with what comes after: "[O]rdinarily when called for [militia] service [able-bodied] men were expected to appear bearing arms supplied by themselves and of the kind in common use at the time." The traditional militia was formed from a pool of men bringing arms "in common use at the time" for lawful purposes like self-defense. "In the colonial and revolutionary war era, [small-arms] weapons used by militiamen and weapons used in defense of person and home were one and the same." Indeed, that is precisely the way in which the Second Amendment's operative clause furthers the purpose announced in its preface. We therefore read *Miller* to say only that the Second Amendment does not protect those weapons not typically possessed by law-abiding citizens for lawful purposes, such as short-barreled shotguns. . . .

[N]othing in our opinion should be taken to cast doubt on longstanding prohibitions on the possession of firearms by felons and the mentally ill, or laws forbidding the carrying of firearms in sensitive places such as schools and government buildings, or laws imposing conditions and qualifications on the commercial sale of arms[.]

We also recognize another important limitation on the right to keep and carry arms. *Miller* said, as we have explained, that the sorts of weapons protected were those "in common use at the time." We think that limitation is fairly supported by the historical tradition of prohibiting the carrying of "dangerous and unusual weapons."

It may be objected that if weapons that are most useful in military service—M-16 rifles and the like—may be banned, then the Second Amendment right is completely detached from the prefatory clause. But . . . the conception of the militia at the time of the Second Amendment's ratification was the body of all citizens capable of military service, who would bring the sorts of lawful weapons that they possessed at home to militia duty. It may well be true today that a militia, to be as effective as militias in the 18th century, would require sophisticated arms that are highly unusual in society at large. Indeed, it may be true that no amount of small arms could be useful against modern-day bombers and tanks. But the fact that modern developments have limited the degree of fit between the prefatory clause and the protected right cannot change our interpretation of the right.

We turn finally to the law at issue here. As we have said, the law totally bans handgun possession in the home. It also requires that any lawful firearm in the home be disassembled or bound by a trigger lock at all times, rendering it inoperable. . . . [T]he inherent right of self-defense has been central to the Second Amendment right. The handgun ban amounts to a prohibition of an entire class of "arms" that is overwhelmingly chosen by American society for that lawful purpose. The prohibition extends, moreover, to the home, where the need for defense of self, family, and property is most acute. Under any of the standards of scrutiny that we have applied to enumerated constitutional rights, banning from the home "the most preferred firearm in the nation to 'keep' and use for protection of one's home and family," would fail constitutional muster. . . .

We must also address the District's requirement (as applied to respondent's handgun) that firearms in the home be rendered and kept inoperable at all times. This makes it impossible for citizens to use them for the core lawful purpose of self-defense and is hence unconstitutional. . . .

Assuming that Heller is not disqualified from the exercise of Second Amendment rights, the District must permit him to register his handgun and must issue him a license to carry it in the home.

We are aware of the problem of handgun violence in this country. . . . But the enshrinement of constitutional rights necessarily takes certain policy choices off the table. These include the absolute prohibition of handguns held and used for self-defense in the home. [W]hat is not debatable is that it is not the role of this Court to pronounce the Second Amendment extinct. We affirm the judgment of the Court of Appeals.

It is so ordered.

Justice Stevens, with whom Justice Souter, Justice Ginsburg, and Justice Breyer join, dissenting. . . .

Neither the text of the Amendment nor the arguments advanced by its proponents evidenced the slightest interest in limiting any legislature's authority to regulate private civilian uses of firearms. Specifically, there is no indication that the Framers of the Amendment intended to enshrine the common-law right of self-defense in the Constitution. . . .

The view of the Amendment we took in *Miller*—that it protects the right to keep and bear arms for certain military purposes, but that it does not curtail the Legislature's power to regulate the nonmilitary use and ownership of weapons—is both the most natural reading of the Amendment's text and the interpretation most faithful to the history of its adoption. . . .

When each word in the text is given full effect, the Amendment is most naturally read to secure to the people a right to use and possess arms in conjunction with service in a well-regulated militia. So far as appears, no more than that was contemplated by its drafters or is encompassed within its terms. . . .

Thus, for most of our history, the invalidity of Second-Amendment-based objections to firearms regulations has been well settled and uncontroversial. . . . After reviewing many of the same sources that are discussed at greater length by the Court today, the Miller Court unanimously concluded that the Second Amendment did not apply to the possession of a firearm that did not have "some reasonable relationship to the preservation or efficiency of a well regulated militia." The key to that decision did not, as the Court belatedly suggests, turn on the difference between muskets and sawed-off shotguns; it turned, rather, on the basic difference between the military and nonmilitary use and possession of guns. Indeed, if the Second Amendment were not limited in its coverage to military uses of weapons, why should the Court in *Miller* have suggested that some weapons but not others were eligible for Second Amendment protection? If use for self-defense were the relevant standard, why did the Court not inquire into the suitability of a particular weapon for self-defense purposes? . . .

Until today, it has been understood that legislatures may regulate the civilian use and misuse of firearms so long as they do not interfere with the preservation of a well-regulated militia. . . . Today judicial craftsmen have confidently asserted that a policy choice that denies a "law-abiding, responsible citize[n]" the right to keep and use weapons in the home for self-defense is "off the table." Given the presumption that most citizens are law abiding, and the reality that the need to defend oneself may suddenly arise in a host of locations outside the home, I fear that the District's policy choice may well be just the first of an unknown number of dominoes to be knocked off the table. . . . Absent compelling evidence that is nowhere to be found in the Court's opinion, I could not possibly conclude that the Framers made such a choice. For these reasons, I respectfully dissent.

JUSTICE BREYER, with whom JUSTICE STEVENS, JUSTICE SOUTER, and JUSTICE GINSBURG join, dissenting . . . [omitted].

McDonald v. *City of Chicago* 561 U.S. 742, 130 S.Ct. 3020, 177 L.Ed. 2d 894 (2010)

http://caselaw.findlaw.com/us-supreme-court/08–1521.html

Soon after the Supreme Court's decision in *District of Columbia* v. *Heller* (2008), Otis McDonald, the National Rifle Association, and other parties filed suit in the U.S. District Court for the Northern District of Illinois challenging the validity under the Second and Fourteenth Amendments of ordinances respectively of the City of Chicago and the Village of Oak Park, Illinois, that effectively ban the private possession of handguns. The district court rejected plaintiffs' contention, and the U.S. Court of Appeals for the Seventh Circuit affirmed. Majority: Alito, Kennedy, Roberts, Scalia, Thomas. Dissenting: Stevens, Breyer, Ginsburg, Sotomayor.

JUSTICE ALITO announced the judgment of the Court and delivered the opinion of the Court with respect to most parts of which the CHIEF JUSTICE, JUSTICE SCALIA, JUSTICE KENNEDY, and JUSTICE THOMAS joined. . . .

We have previously held that most of the provisions of the Bill of Rights apply with full force to both the Federal Government and the States. Applying the standard that is well established in our case law, we hold that the Second Amendment right is fully applicable to the States. . . .

Petitioners argue that the Chicago and Oak Park laws violate the right to keep and bear arms for two reasons. Petitioners' primary submission is that this right is among the "privileges or immunities of citizens of the United States" and that the narrow interpretation of the Privileges or Immunities Clause adopted in the *Slaughter-House Cases* should now be rejected. As a secondary argument, petitioners contend that the Fourteenth Amendment's Due Process Clause "incorporates" the Second Amendment right. . . . For many decades, the question of the rights protected by the Fourteenth Amendment against state infringement has been analyzed under the Due Process Clause of that Amendment and not under the Privileges or Immunities Clause. We therefore decline to disturb the *Slaughter-House* holding. . . .

In the late 19th century, the Court began to consider whether the Due Process Clause prohibits the States from infringing rights set out in the Bill of Rights. . . .

[E]ven when a right set out in the Bill of Rights was held to fall within the conception of due process, the protection or remedies afforded against state infringement sometimes differed from the protection or remedies provided against abridgment by the Federal Government. . . .

[T]he Court eventually [initiated] what has been called a process of "selective incorporation," i.e., the Court . . . made it clear that the governing standard is not whether any "civilized system [can] be imagined that would not accord the particular protection." Instead, the Court inquired whether a particular Bill of Rights guarantee is fundamental to *our* scheme of ordered liberty and system of justice. . . . The Court eventually incorporated almost all of the provisions of the Bill of Rights. Only a handful of the Bill of Rights protections remain unincorporated.

Finally, the Court abandoned "the notion that the Fourteenth Amendment applies to the States only a watered-down, subjective version of the individual guarantees of the Bill of Rights. . . ." Instead, the Court decisively held that incorporated Bill of Rights protections "are all to be enforced against the States under the Fourteenth Amendment according to the same standards that protect those personal rights against federal encroachment." . . .

[W]e now turn directly to the question whether the Second Amendment right to keep and bear arms is incorporated in the concept of due process. In answering that question . . . we must decide whether the right to keep and bear arms is fundamental to our scheme of ordered liberty, or as we have said in a related context, whether this right is "deeply rooted" in this Nation's history and tradition.

Our decision in *Heller* points unmistakably to the answer. Self-defense is a basic right, recognized by many legal systems from ancient times to the present day, and in *Heller*, we held that individual self-defense is "the central component" of the Second Amendment right. Explaining that "the need for defense of self, family, and property is most acute" in the home, we found that this right applies to handguns because they are "the most preferred firearm in the nation to 'keep' and use for protection of one's home and family." . . .

In debating the Fourteenth Amendment, the 39th Congress referred to the right to keep and bear arms as a fundamental right deserving of protection. . . .

The right to keep and bear arms was also widely protected by state constitutions at the time when the Fourteenth Amendment was ratified. In sum, it is clear that the Framers and ratifiers of the Fourteenth Amendment counted the right to keep and bear arms among those fundamental rights necessary to our system of ordered liberty. . . . Municipal respondents maintain that the Second Amendment differs from all of the other provisions of the Bill of Rights because it concerns the right to possess a deadly implement and thus has implications for public safety. The right to keep and bear arms, however, is not the only constitutional right that has controversial public safety implications. All of the constitutional provisions that impose restrictions on law enforcement and on the prosecution of crimes fall into the same category. . . .

We likewise reject municipal respondents' argument that we should depart from our established incorporation methodology on the ground that making the Second Amendment binding on the States and their subdivisions is inconsistent with principles of federalism and will stifle experimentation. . . . There is nothing new in the argument that, in order to respect federalism and allow useful state experimentation, a federal constitutional right should not be fully binding on the States. This argument was made repeatedly and eloquently by Members of this Court who rejected the concept of incorporation and urged retention of the two-track approach to incorporation. . . .

Time and again, however, those pleas failed. . . .

As evidence that the Fourteenth Amendment has not historically been understood to restrict the authority of the States to regulate firearms, municipal respondents and supporting amici cite a variety of state and local firearms laws that courts have upheld. But what is most striking about their research is the paucity of precedent sustaining bans comparable to those at issue here and in *Heller*. . . . We made it clear in *Heller* that our holding did not cast doubt on such longstanding regulatory measures as "prohibitions on the possession of firearms by felons and the mentally ill," "laws forbidding the carrying of firearms in sensitive places such as schools and government buildings, or laws imposing conditions and qualifications on the commercial sale of arms." We repeat those assurances here. Despite municipal respondents' dooms day proclamations, incorporation does not imperil every law regulating firearms. . . .

[T]he Second Amendment protects the right to possess a handgun in the home for the purpose of self-defense. . . . We therefore hold that the Due Process Clause of the Fourteenth Amendment incorporates the Second Amendment right recognized in *Heller*. The judgment of the Court of Appeals is reversed, and the case is remanded for further proceedings.

It is so ordered.

Justice Scalia, concurring . . . [omitted]. Justice Thomas, concurring . . . [omitted].

Justice Stevens, dissenting. . . .

The rights protected against state infringement by the Fourteenth Amendment's Due Process Clause need not be identical in shape or scope to the rights protected against Federal Government infringement by the various provisions of the Bill of Rights. . . . Elementary considerations of constitutional text and structure suggest there may be legitimate reasons to hold state governments to different standards than the Federal Government in certain areas. . . .

It is true . . . that during the 1960's the Court decided a number of cases involving procedural rights in which it treated the Due Process Clause as if it transplanted language from the Bill of Rights into the Fourteenth Amendment. . . . In my judgment, this line of cases is best understood as having concluded that, to ensure a criminal trial satisfies essential standards of fairness, some procedures should be the same in state and federal courts: The need for certainty and uniformity is more pressing, and the margin for error slimmer, when criminal justice is at issue. That principle has little relevance to the question whether a non procedural rule set forth in the Bill of Rights qualifies as an aspect of the liberty protected by the Fourteenth Amendment. . . .

[W]hen the Court has used the Due Process Clause to recognize rights distinct from the trial context—rights relating to the primary conduct of free individuals—Justice Cardozo's test has been our guide. The right to free speech, for instance, has been safeguarded from state infringement not because the States have always honored it, but because it is "essential to free government" and "to the maintenance of democratic institutions"—that is, because the right to free speech is implicit in the concept of ordered liberty. . . .

The question in this case, then, is not whether the Second Amendment right to keep and bear arms (whatever that right's precise contours) applies to the States because the Amendment has been incorporated into the Fourteenth Amendment. It has not been. The question, rather, is whether the particular right asserted by petitioners applies to the States because of the Fourteenth Amendment itself, standing on its own bottom. . . . It is likewise possible for the Court to find in this case that some part of the *Heller* right applies to the States, and then to find in later cases that other parts of the right also apply, or apply on different terms. . . . Having unleashed in *Heller* a tsunami of legal uncertainty, and thus litigation, and now on the cusp of imposing a national rule on the States in this area for the first time in United States history, the Court could at least moderate the confusion, upheaval, and burden on the States by adopting a rule that is clearly and tightly bounded in scope. . . .

I am ultimately persuaded that a better reading of our case law supports the city of Chicago.

First, firearms have a fundamentally ambivalent relationship to liberty. Just as they can help homeowners defend their families and property from intruders, they can help thugs and insurrectionists murder innocent victims. . . .

Second, the right to possess a firearm of one's choosing is different in kind from the liberty interests we have recognized under the Due Process Clause. . . .

Third, the experience of other advanced democracies, including those that share our British heritage, undercuts the notion that an expansive right to keep and bear arms is intrinsic to ordered liberty. . . .

Fourth, the Second Amendment differs in kind from the Amendments that surround it, with the consequence that its inclusion in the Bill of Rights is not merely unhelpful but positively harmful to petitioners' claim. . . .

From the early days of the Republic. . ., States and municipalities have placed extensive licensing requirements on firearm acquisition, restricted the public carriage of weapons, and banned altogether the possession of especially dangerous weapons, including handguns. . . .

I would proceed more cautiously. . . . Accordingly, I respectfully dissent.

JUSTICE BREYER with whom Justices GINSBURG and SOTOMAYOR join, dissenting . . . [omitted].

NOTE

1. In one sense recent cases applying provisions of the first eight Amendments to the States represent a new approach to the "incorporation" debate. Earlier the Court can be seen as having asked, when inquiring into whether some particular procedural safeguard was required of a state, if a civilized system could be imagined that would not accord the particular protection. . . . The recent cases, on the other hand, have proceeded upon the valid assumption that state criminal processes are not imaginary and theoretical schemes but actual systems bearing virtually every characteristic of the common-law system that has been developing contemporaneously in England and in this country. The question thus is whether given this kind of system a particular procedure is fundamental—whether, that is, a procedure is necessary to an Anglo-American regime of ordered liberty. . . . Of each of these determinations that a constitutional provision originally written to bind the Federal Government should bind the States as well it might be said that the limitation in question is not necessarily fundamental to fairness in every criminal system that might be imagined but is fundamental in the context of the criminal processes maintained by the American States.

   When the inquiry is approached in this way the question whether the States can impose criminal punishment without granting a jury trial appears quite different from the way it appeared in the older cases opining that States might abolish jury trial. A criminal process which was fair and equitable but used no juries is easy to imagine. It would make use of alternative guarantees and protections which would serve the purposes that the jury serves in the English and American systems. Yet no American State has undertaken to construct such a system. Instead, every American State, including Louisiana, uses the jury extensively, and imposes very serious punishments only after a trial at which the defendant has a right to a jury's verdict. . . .

10

Criminal Justice

The history of American freedom is in no small measure the history of procedure.
—JUSTICE FELIX FRANKFURTER (1945)

Thanks to Fourteenth Amendment incorporation, as the previous chapter explained, almost all the strictures in the Bill of Rights now apply with equal force to the states, as well as to the national government. Because most of the provisions of the Bill of Rights involve criminal procedure, this fact has had enormous consequences for law enforcement at all levels. While some 92,678 criminal cases were filed in U.S. district courts in 2020, criminal cases involving serious offenses filed in state courts now number in the millions. And in one way or another, every one of these cases intersected the Bill of Rights.

The cases in this chapter illustrate a struggle between two cherished and not necessarily antithetical values. The conflict is between the public's interest in safety and the public's interest in the protection of individual liberty. It is misleading to view the clash as a contest between the safety of law-abiding people and the protection of criminals. Constitutional safeguards belong to everyone, law-abiding and law-breaking alike. The judicial task is one of determining how much protection can be accorded each individual without unduly hampering the effort of government to maintain order, without which there can be no freedom. Small wonder the framers of our national and state constitutions gave special attention to procedural rights. Far from demonstrating fondness for technicalities, this emphasis highlights the belief that without limits to authority, America would be a far different place in which to live. The framers knew firsthand the dangers that the government-as-prosecutor could pose to freedom. Even today, authoritarian regimes in other lands routinely use the tools of law enforcement—arrests, searches, detentions, as well as prosecutions—to squelch political opposition. Limits in the Bill of Rights on government's crime-fighting powers thus help safeguard democracy.

What follows is a brief survey of some of the topics in criminal procedure and a review of the major cases. The field is too vast to include them all. Cases on

DOI: 10.4324/9781003164340-11

criminal justice are as myriad as the variety of citizen-police-courtroom encounters themselves.

SEARCHES AND SEIZURES

"The right of the people," the **Fourth Amendment** grandly declares, "to be secure in their persons, houses, papers, and effects, against unreasonable searches and seizures, shall not be violated, and no Warrants shall issue, but upon probable cause, supported by Oath or affirmation, and particularly describing the place to be searched, and the persons or things to be seized." This amendment differs in at least two important ways from some of the other parts of the Bill of Rights.

First, it has no direct antecedent in English constitutional documents such as Magna Carta of 1215, the Petition of Right of 1628, and the Bill of Rights of 1689. Rather, its origins lie in Great Britain's attempt to collect duties in the American colonies after 1767 on imports such as glass, lead, paint, and tea. To combat smuggling, customs officials were handed **writs of assistance**. These were general search warrants, valid for the life of the sovereign, which allowed virtually unlimited searches of anyone or any place at any time for any reason or for no reason at all. The framers of the Bill of Rights learned a lesson from that experience: When government encroaches on personal liberty, it usually has very good reasons for doing so. The grim experience with writs of assistance also explains the wording of the Fourth Amendment. The emphasis throughout is on *particularity*, not generality. There must be a documented reason—the amendment calls it **probable cause**—to search a particular place or to seize a particular person. The **warrant,** the official authorization for the search or the arrest, must also be particular in describing what is to be searched and what is expected to be found. In addition, an assumption of the amendment is that the warrant is to be issued by a judge. This is the principle of separation of powers at work in law enforcement. Before the executive branch, acting through a police officer, may invade a person's physical privacy, the judicial branch must be convinced of the need for *this* search of *this* place before giving its approval.

Second, excepting only the First Amendment, more Americans continually benefit from the protections of the Fourth Amendment than any other part of the Bill of Rights. Provisions of the Fifth, Sixth, and Eighth Amendments, while important, do not normally come into play for an individual until after a criminal investigation has made some headway or until the person has been charged with an offense or has been found guilty. By prohibiting "unreasonable searches and seizures," the Fourth Amendment seeks to guard the physical security of all even in a digital age.

The wording of the Fourth Amendment lends itself generally to two interpretations by the Court. Each involves conclusions about the clauses in the amendment that ban "unreasonable searches and seizures" and specify the conditions for issuance of a warrant. The first approach views the two clauses as inseparably linked. A reasonable and therefore a permissible search is one conducted with a warrant. Accordingly, a warrantless search is unreasonable and impermissible, unless it falls into a handful of exceptions. The second approach, more friendly to law enforcement, sees the two clauses as standing alone. From this perspective, searches must be "reasonable" to be lawful, but a warrant is not an essential element of reasonableness. In operation, this reading of the amendment allows police more flexibility, in the absence of a warrant, to make stops and to conduct searches.

Whose Rights? To say that all Americans benefit from the protection of the Fourth Amendment, however, does not mean that the amendment applies to everyone in all situations. That reality lay at the heart of ***Minnesota* v. *Carter*** (1998). Police arrested two men after an officer, having been tipped by an informer, peeked through an apartment window and observed them and the lessee of the apartment bagging cocaine. The Court sidestepped the intriguing question whether the peek was a search, concluding instead that the men could assert no Fourth Amendment rights in that situation because they were merely short-term guests of the woman who had allowed them to use her apartment for business purposes.

Defining a Search. The question that the Court never reached in *Carter* is ordinarily an essential threshold issue in every Fourth Amendment case: Has a "search" or "seizure" actually occurred? If it has not, the constraints of the amendment, such as probable cause and a warrant, do not apply. For example, consider ***United States* v. *Jones*** (2012), where the Court ruled that installation by police of a GPS tracking device on an automobile amounted to a search. Similarly, a narrow majority held the following year that use of a trained drug-sniffing dog on the front porch of a residence was itself a search. Therefore the warrant that had been obtained on the basis of the pooch's positive signal was constitutionally defective (*Florida* v. *Jardines*).

Probable Cause. With a few exceptions discussed later in this chapter, lawful searches must be predicated upon probable cause. The term suggests more than a hunch that someone is engaged in illegal activity, but less than the degree of certainty a prosecutor needs at trial to establish guilt beyond a reasonable doubt. Justice Wiley Rutledge once characterized the standard in this manner:

> In dealing with probable cause . . . we deal with probabilities. These are not technical; they are the factual and practical considerations of everyday life on which reasonable and prudent men, not legal technicians, act. . . . Probable cause exists where the facts and circumstances within [the officers'] knowledge, and of which they had reasonably trustworthy information, [are] sufficient in themselves to warrant a man of reasonable caution in the belief that an offense has been or is being committed.

Probable cause, Rutledge said, seeks "to safeguard citizens from rash and unreasonable interferences with privacy and from unfounded charges of crime. [It also seeks] to give fair leeway for enforcing the law in the community's protection." For the Court to require "more would unduly hamper law enforcement. To allow less would be to leave law-abiding citizens at the mercy of the officers' whim or caprice" (*Brinegar* v. *United States*, 1949). Later, the Court emphasized that the standard "is to be applied, not according to a fixed and rigid formula, but rather in the light of the 'totality of the circumstances' made known to the magistrate" who issues the warrant. "[T]he task of a reviewing court," in overseeing the Fourth Amendment, "is not to conduct a de novo determination of probable cause, but only to determine whether there is substantial evidence in the record supporting the magistrate's decision to issue the warrant" (*Massachusetts* v. *Upton*, 1984).

A factor complicating judicial oversight of police practices is the use of anonymous informers in establishing probable cause. Many of the affidavits signed by police officers to establish probable cause recite certain details they learned secondhand from such people, anonymous even to the magistrate issuing the warrant. The constitutional objection to the use of informers on the ground that suspects could not confront their accusers was overcome in *McCray* v. *Illinois* (1967). Key to preventing anonymity from becoming a shield for fictitiousness is the requirement that the officer demonstrate the informant's reliability to the magistrate. Since *Illinois* v. *Gates* (1983), the Court has relied on a totality-of-circumstances approach. Accordingly, the magistrate must make a practical, "commonsense" decision whether, given all the information the officer provides both from and about the informer, a fair probability exists that evidence of a crime will be found in a particular place.

The Exclusionary Rule. If the Fourth Amendment sets standards for a lawful search, what happens when evidence is seized in violation of the amendment? In English common law, material and relevant evidence has always been held admissible at a trial even though officials may have obtained it through an improper search. Moreover, in the twenty-first century, unlawfully obtained evidence is admissible in the courts of nearly every country in the world. In *Weeks* v. *United States* (1914), however, the Supreme Court fashioned a broad **exclusionary rule** that barred the use at federal trials of evidence obtained illegally by federal agents. In 1949, *Wolf* v. *Colorado* made the Fourth Amendment guaranty against unreasonable search and seizure applicable to the states but refrained from imposing the federal exclusionary rule, asserting with more confidence than accuracy that other remedies were available to state victims of illegal searches and seizures. By 1961, nearly half the states still admitted unlawfully seized evidence in state trials. By then, the Supreme Court had learned what others had long known: civil tort remedies against offending police officers, criminal prosecution, or public outcry had all failed to stop abuses. ***Mapp* v. *Ohio*** did what *Wolf* had failed to do and applied the exclusionary rule to the states. Justice Clark's opinion emphasized the twin pillars for suppressing illegally seized evidence: deterrence of unlawful police conduct and the maintenance of judicial integrity. *Mapp* marked the beginning of the Supreme Court's heightened concern with the realities of criminal justice at the state level. As much as any other single decision, *Mapp* has put the Court in charge of standards for day-to-day police work.

Mapp remains the linchpin for much of the due process revolution set loose by the Warren Court and discussed in Chapter Nine. Most citizen encounters with law enforcement authorities are with state and local police. Court decisions specifying proper police procedure for stops, searches, and arrests thus have real impact on the criminal justice system when coupled with the exclusionary rule. No wonder Supreme Court decisions interpreting the Fourth Amendment attract such widespread attention, for they define constitutionally correct conduct for all law enforcement officers in the land. *Mapp* gave those rules teeth because a violation of the Fourth Amendment meant a loss of otherwise useful, reliable, and probative evidence. Under *Mapp*, admissibility of evidence depends upon the lawfulness of the search, not on what the search uncovers.

Yet because of the social costs of the rule—a person does not benefit directly from its operation unless incriminating evidence is found—it has long been a center of controversy. Justices antagonistic to the exclusionary rule got results in 1984, as ***United States* v. *Leon*** modified the exclusionary rule to permit a limited "good-faith" or "reasonable mistake" exception. Because the ruling applies only to searches with warrants, not warrantless searches, *Leon* does not affect all Fourth Amendment cases. However, *Leon*'s reasoning allowed the use of the fruits of an unlawful search that occurred because of an error in a police department's database, where an officer arrested and searched an individual mistakenly believed to be wanted in an adjacent county (*Herring* v. *United States*, 2009). Even more generously, in *Utah* v. *Strieff* (2016), the Court admitted evidence after an admittedly illegal stop in connection with the routine investigation of a suspected drug house revealed an outstanding warrant. Justice Thomas's opinion for the majority reasoned that, unless there was egregious police conduct, existence of the valid (and untainted) warrant was sufficiently attenuated or removed from the initial (and invalid) stop so as not to have tainted the methamphetamine and drug pipe that the officer found when he arrested Strieff once he learned of the warrant. Justice Sotomayor's dissent noted in particular the impact the decision could have in broadening police authority.

> This case allows the police to stop you on the street, demand your identification, and check it for outstanding traffic warrants—even if you are doing nothing wrong. . . . The Court today holds that the discovery of a warrant for an unpaid parking ticket will forgive a police officer's violation of your Fourth Amendment rights. . . . [T]his case tells everyone, white and black, guilty and innocent, that an officer can verify your legal status at any time. It says that your body is subject to invasion while courts excuse the violation of your rights. It implies that you are not a citizen of a democracy but the subject of a carceral state, just waiting to be cataloged.

Warrantless Searches. The Court has usually shown a preference for searches authorized by warrants, as opposed to warrantless intrusions. There are times, however, when the requirement for a warrant is so impractical as to pose a serious hindrance to law enforcement.

(1) *Search Incident to a Lawful Arrest.* One of these situations arises at the time of the arrest itself, as illustrated by the Strieff case discussed above. No warrant is needed to search places under the control of the arrestee so that police can avoid the danger of concealed weapons and prevent destruction of evidence. The permissible extent of this kind of warrantless search, however, has been subject to different interpretations. In *United States* v. *Rabinowitz* (1950), for example, federal agents thoroughly searched an entire office incident to a lawful arrest, and the Court approved the admission at trial of forged stamps discovered during the search. In contrast, the 1969 decision in ***Chimel* v. *California*** sharply curtailed the area subject to a warrantless search and, consequently, induced greater use of search warrants.

Under *Chimel*, police making a lawful arrest may search the person and the area within the arrestee's control or reach. The basis of the exception to the warrant requirement is thus the safety of the police and the protection of evidence. Moreover, according to *Maryland* v. *Buie* (1990), where police making an arrest have reason to believe that someone may be present in another part of the house who might pose a threat to them, they may conduct a "protective sweep" for their own safety, even though they have no search warrant. Contraband or other evidence that they see lying about in "plain view" may then be lawfully seized. In situations where there is probable cause to believe that contraband is present in a building, *Illinois* v. *McArthur* (2001) allows police to prevent a suspect from entering his home unaccompanied—in this case for two hours—while a warrant is being procured.

Chimel was the basis of *United States* v. *Robinson* (1973), which admitted heroin from the search of a crumpled cigarette package found in Robinson's coat pocket after he had been arrested for driving without a valid license. Yet the Court unanimously stopped short of equating Robinson's crumpled pack of smokes with a cell phone, as seen in ***Riley* v. *California*** and ***United States* v. *Wurie*** (2014). Moreover, in *Carpenter* v. *United States* (2018) a narrow majority blocked the government's warrantless use of cell-site records to track a suspect's movements and locations, weighing a person's "reasonable expectation of privacy" (a concept discussed later in connection with ***Katz*** v. ***United States*** [1967] more heavily than the fact that users of cell phones voluntarily turn over such data to third parties [the cell phone carriers]).

(2) *The Automobile Exception*. The automobile has long been an exception to the general rule that warrants are needed in advance of searches. *Carroll* v. *United States* (1925) allowed the warrantless search of a car when there was probable cause to believe it was carrying illegal liquor or was being used to violate the law. Motor vehicles are not only mobile, and so might quickly depart the jurisdiction while an officer attempted to obtain a warrant, but are already highly regulated by government. Moreover, some justices also see them as involving lesser expectations of privacy than, say, someone's home. Nonetheless, a unanimous bench held in *Byrd* v. *United States* (2018) that the Fourth Amendment's protection extends to the driver of a rental car whose name is not listed on the rental agreement but is driving with the permission of the renter of the vehicle. However, eight justices in *Collins* v. *Virginia* (2018) declined to stretch the automobile exception to validate a warrantless search with probable cause of a vehicle (in this instance a motorcycle) parked in the driveway a few feet from a house. The Court viewed the driveway as part of the curtilage of the house, an area deemed as constitutionally protected as the house itself.

If the automobile itself may be searched without a warrant, what about containers police find in the automobile that may contain contraband? Police who have reason to search a car may coincidentally come across a container, just as police who have reason to search a container may coincidentally find it in a car. The Court has given conflicting answers in such situations. *Arkansas* v. *Sanders* (1979), for example, disallowed the warrantless search of a suitcase—itself the target of the investigation—after police removed it from the trunk of a taxi in which it had just been placed by the suspects. *Robbins* v. *California* (1981) reversed a drug conviction based on a warrantless opening of opaque wrapped bricks of marijuana, which police discovered in the tire well of a station wagon during an otherwise lawful search. *United States* v. *Ross* (1982) overturned *Robbins* by holding that the warrantless search of an automobile based on probable cause justified "the search of every part of the vehicle and its contents that may conceal the object of the search."

Yet *Ross* also expressly reaffirmed the result in *Sanders*, thus creating what some called the "Ross anomaly." That is, where probable cause existed to search only a container which happened to be in an automobile (as in *Sanders*), a warrant was necessary to open the container. Yet no warrant would be needed to open a container police discovered during a warrantless search of an entire vehicle, provided the vehicle itself was the object of the search.

California* v. *Acevedo (1991) resolved the Ross anomaly in favor of law enforcement interests. In so doing, however, it may have created its own anomaly: A container located in a motor vehicle may now be subject to a warrantless search; the same container carried by a suspect walking along the sidewalk ordinarily is not.

Does arrest alone justify search of an automobile? According to *Arizona* v. *Gant* (2009), a police officer needs a warrant before searching a car after arrest of the car's occupant, unless at the time of the search (1) the person is unsecured and within reaching distance of the passenger compartment of the vehicle, or (2) police officers have reason to believe that the evidence for the crime for which the person is being arrested will be found in the vehicle.

(3) *Consent.* A warrant is not required when an individual consents to a search. However, the situation becomes complicated when one co-occupant of a residence objects to a warrantless search, while the other occupant consents. In *Georgia* v. *Randolph* (2006), for example, the Court held on the particular facts of the case that the Fourth Amendment rights of a physically present and objecting occupant overrode the co-occupant's consent. Accordingly, any evidence uncovered in the course of the partly unconsented search was inadmissible. *Fernandez* v. *California* (2014) declined to extend Randolph to a situation where the objecting cotenant is no longer on the premises to object—in this instance because he had been arrested and removed from the scene shortly before police entered the apartment with the other tenant's consent.

(4) *Community Caretaking. Cady* v. *Dombrowski* (1973) recognized an exception to the warrant requirement when police assist persons in distress. However, in *Caniglia* v. *Strom* (2021), a unanimous bench refused to extend that exception to the home. Thus, the home remains the most sacred space under the Fourth Amendment in that without a warrant, exigency, or consent, governmental search or seizure within it is unconstitutional.

Yet police are not required to inform suspects that they have a right to refuse consent. Rather, reviewing courts are to conclude from the circumstances of a particular situation whether a "reasonable person" would understand that she or he is free to refuse to submit to a search. Consider the facts in *United States* v. *Drayton* (2002) that involved suspicionless searches of two passengers on a bus in Florida. One of three police officers who boarded the bus asked the two to identify their luggage, and they consented to a search of their bag. When the officer asked, "Do you mind if I check your person?" the first consented and opened his jacket and positioned himself in a manner that would facilitate the search. Packets of the kind used to transport cocaine were found, and the first passenger was led from the bus. Then the officer asked the second passenger, "Mind if I check you?" He also consented, and similar packets were found. For six justices, both searches were reasonable under the Fourth Amendment.

Arrests, Other Detentions, and Frisks. Police may make felony arrests in public places without warrants where probable cause exists (*United States* v. *Watson*, 1976), but arrest warrants are required when police make felony arrests in a private residence (*Payton* v. *New York*, 1980) in the absence of exigent circumstances. Moreover, in serving an arrest or search warrant, the Fourth Amendment incorporates the common-law requirement that police knock on a dwelling's door and announce their identity and purpose before attempting a forced entry (*Wilson* v. *Arkansas*, 1995). This rule gives way only when the totality of circumstances suggests that there is a threat of physical violence or that evidence will probably be destroyed if advance notice is given (*United States* v. *Banks*, 2003). For less serious crimes such as misdemeanors and summary offenses, police ordinarily may arrest without a warrant only when the criminal behavior occurs in their presence. Even then, the Fourth Amendment gives police wide latitude in deciding whether to take an offender into custody, as ***Atwater* v. *City of Lago Vista*** (2001) illustrates. Nonetheless, *Brendin* v. *California* (2007) makes clear that in a traffic stop a passenger, and not merely the driver of the detained vehicle, has been "seized" for Fourth Amendment purposes.

For many years, police stopped persons behaving suspiciously and, to protect themselves, patted down (frisked) those who might be armed. Civil libertarians criticized the **frisk** because police normally lacked probable cause for an arrest; the law simply had no provision for a detention less restrictive than arrest. Critics also claimed that stopping, questioning, and frisking for weapons was a police tactic too often directed toward minority groups. ***Terry* v. *Ohio*** (1968) presented the Court with a situation in which a police officer confronted suspicious persons and, while frisking one of them, found a weapon. This of course was no search incident to arrest, because no one had been arrested before the frisk. Had the officer acted in accord with the Fourth Amendment? Admitting that probable cause was absent, the Court upheld the search based on a lesser degree of certainty called **reasonable suspicion**.

Not surprisingly, it remains uncertain what combination of facts will satisfy the Court that a legitimate stop and limited search under *Terry* have occurred. For example, the Court ruled admissible the fruits of a frisk that occurred after officers observed an individual in a high-crime area who fled from them without apparent provocation (*Illinois* v. *Wardlow*, 2000). In the same term, however, the Court disallowed evidence seized in a frisk after police received a tip from an anonymous caller that a young black male standing at a particular bus stop and wearing a plaid shirt was carrying a gun. When police arrived at the bus stop, they saw three black males, one of whom was wearing a plaid shirt. Apart from the tip, the officers had no reason to suspect any of the three of illegal conduct. One of the officers frisked the young man in the plaid shirt and seized a gun from his pocket (*Florida* v. *J.L.*, 2000). In the Court's view, the tip failed to provide the reasonable suspicion dictated by *Terry*. However, *Navarette* v. *California* (2014) allowed an investigative stop and the search of the vehicle that followed based solely on an anonymous and uncorroborated tip about drunk driving.

Terry-type encounters affect large numbers of people. For example, data released for 2019 revealed that police in New York City made 13,459 such stops, with some 59 percent involving African Americans, 29 percent Latinx, and 9 percent whites, with 66 percent resulting in no arrest. The data reflect the outcome of litigation in federal court in 2013 (*Floyd* v. *City of New York*) that had successfully challenged police tactics which as late as 2012, had led to 532,911 stops in New York City for an average of 1,460 stops per day. The racially disparate impact of police practices in many locales have led to numerous protests by Black Lives Matter and other groups. The actions in question have come under especially strong scrutiny following killings by police of people of color, such as that of George Floyd in Minneapolis in 2020, among many others.

Police may make some stops even when there is no suspicion at all. *Michigan Department of State Police* v. *Sitz* (1990) approved the use of sobriety checkpoints along highways at which police stop and briefly detain all motorists to look for signs of intoxication. However, vehicle checkpoints operated by police who deployed a narcotics-detection dog to sniff the exterior of stopped vehicles violate the Fourth Amendment (*Indianapolis* v. *Edmond*, 2000). In the Court's view, the sobriety checkpoints upheld in 1990 were closely related to roadway safety, but the narcotics checkpoints were designed primarily to detect evidence of ordinary criminal activity. The latter would require an individualized suspicion that was absent. However, *Illinois* v. *Caballes* (2005), declaring any private interest in contraband as illegitimate, upheld the use of canine detection during a routine traffic stop even where there were no facts to suggest drug activity.

When driving under the influence of alcohol is suspected, police may require the driver to undergo a Breathalyzer test, but the Fourth Amendment does not permit a state to criminalize refusal to submit to a blood test in the absence of a warrant (*Birchfield* v. *North Dakota*, 2016). In *Mitchell* v. *Wisconsin* (2019), Justice Alito summarized the Court's position with respect to a warrantless blood alcohol concentration (BAC) test for a motorist who appears to have been driving under the influence of alcohol. "First, an officer may conduct a BAC test if the facts of a particular case bring it within the exigent-circumstances exception to the Fourth Amendment's general requirement of a warrant. Second, if an officer has probable cause to arrest a motorist for drunk driving, the officer may conduct a breath test (but not a blood test) under the rule allowing warrantless searches of a person incident to arrest." In a situation where the driver is unconscious and therefore cannot be given a breath test, he added, "the exigent circumstances rule almost always permits a blood test." For the Court, a breath test, unlike a BAC, involves minimal physical intrusion to obtain and is something that is routinely exposed to the public. Similar reasoning allowed police to administer a warrantless DNA swab as part of routine arrest procedure (*Maryland* v. *King*, 2013).

Electronic Surveillance. Electronic means of surveillance have presented the Court with new questions concerning possible violations of the Fourth Amendment. In ***Olmstead* v. *United States*** (1928), a sharply divided Court held that wiretapping did not violate the Fourth Amendment guaranty against unreasonable searches and seizures because there was no physical search: no seizure of papers, tangible material effects, or actual invasion of the house. Electronic surveillance by police at all levels of government continued for nearly 40 years without close federal judicial supervision. Only on the infrequent occasions when defense counsel learned of an official physical trespass on the property subject to the wiretap or eavesdrop was the Court prepared to find a Fourth Amendment violation (*Silverman* v. *United States*, 1961).

For different reasons, both civil libertarians and law enforcement agents welcomed ***Katz* v. *United States*** (1967), which expressly overruled *Olmstead*. The Court's emphasis now was not on whether a physical trespass had occurred (there was none in *Katz*) but whether the surveillance invaded one's "expectation of privacy." The "Fourth Amendment protects people, not places," declared Justice Stewart. Yet the individual's expectation must also be one society is prepared to acknowledge as reasonable. Moreover, for the first time the majority made it plain that Congress could establish constitutionally correct standards governing electronic surveillance with a warrant. The Court was willing to exchange legitimacy for controls. A year after *Katz*, Congress accepted this invitation in the Omnibus Crime Control and Safe Streets Act.

Electronic surveillance law today features a three-tiered system that tries to balance law enforcement needs and confidentiality. For some serious offenses, Title III of the 1968 statute established an elaborate warrant process for electronic surveillance. (As explained further in Chapter Fifteen, the **Patriot Act** of 2001, which was reauthorized in 2010 and then renewed in 2015 as the **Freedom Act**, added terrorism and some computer crimes to Title III's list of predicate offenses.) For covered offenses, and no others, a Title III warrant, or its state counterpart, may authorize eavesdropping on telephone conversations, face-to-face conversations, or computer and other forms of electronic communication. This is the most stringent level of protection. On a lower tier, with respect to *any* criminal offense, federal law allows warrant-based access to telephone records, email held in third-party storage, and stored voice mail. Still more relaxed procedures apply to the government's use of trap-and-trace devices and pen registers that capture the source and destination of telephone calls (but not their contents). Those can be put in place on the government's certification alone, rather than the probable cause finding of a court, that the information will be relevant to a criminal investigation. As the Court held in *Smith v. Maryland* (1979), persons making a call voluntarily convey the number being called to a third party (the telecom company) and so have no expectation of privacy in that number. Because no "search" within the meaning of the Fourth Amendment has occurred, no warrant is necessary. Yet when the Freedom Act expired in 2020 without being reauthorized, some key investigatory tools became unavailable, as explained in Chapter Fifteen.

The 1968 act, however, presented its own constitutional questions from the outset. One provision of the law arguably exempted national security electronic surveillance from the warrant requirement, when done on the authority of the president. In a highly significant interpretation of the act in 1972 that involved domestic threats, ***United States v. United States District Court*** rejected that construction of the law.

The 1968 statute continues to play an important role in crime fighting, especially narcotics and racketeering offenses. By 2019 (the most recent year for which full data are available), 44 states (seven more than in 1993), the Virgin Islands, Puerto Rico, and the District of Columbia, in addition to the federal government, had legislatively authorized electronic surveillance. During 2019 judges issued 1,417 federal and 1,808 state orders—the totals being respectively 3 and 10 percent greater than reported for 2018—approving various kinds of electronic surveillance: wire, oral or otherwise. In 28 states, a total of 147 separate local jurisdictions (including counties, cities, and judicial districts) reported wiretap applications for 2019. Applications concentrated in six states (New York, California, Nevada, Colorado, North Carolina, and Pennsylvania) accounted for 79 percent of all state wiretap applications. Applications in California and New York alone constituted 50 percent of all applications approved by state judges. Moreover, intercepts typically cast big nets, with the typical intercept involving dozens of individuals and hundreds or even thousands of conversations or messages. For example, the federal wiretap with the most intercepts occurred during a conspiracy investigation in California and resulted in the interception of 3,113,551 messages over 149 days. The state wiretap with the most intercepts was a 484-day wiretap for a narcotics investigation in New York, which resulted in the interception of 365,934 cell phone conversations and messages. The most common method reported was wire surveillance that used a telephone (landline, cellular, cordless, or mobile), with telephone wiretaps accounting for 53 percent of the intercepts installed in 2019, the majority of which involving cellular telephones. Nonetheless, the greater limitation on the use of electronic surveillance may be fiscal, not legal. The average cost of an intercept in 2019 was $75,160, up 13 percent from the average cost in 2018. The most expensive state wiretap was in Georgia, where costs for a 178-day intercept conducted to investigate a narcotics offense that resulted in 17 arrests and one conviction totaled $1,920,777. For federal wiretaps the average cost was $94,872, a 40 percent increase from 2018. The most expensive federal wiretap completed during 2019 occurred in Maryland, where costs for a 120-day wiretap in a narcotics investigation that resulted in five arrests and no convictions totaled $2,511,137.[1]

Congressional action to legitimize electronic surveillance in national security matters came in the **Foreign Intelligence Surveillance Act** of 1978 (FISA).

The statute established two special courts. The **Foreign Intelligence Surveillance Court** (FISC) consists (since 2001) of 11 sitting U.S. district judges from seven circuits (at least three of whom must live within 20 miles of the District of Columbia) who are chosen for the FISC by the chief justice. It hears requests by the executive branch for warrants to conduct secret physical searches and electronic surveillance of "U.S. persons" believed to be working on behalf of a "foreign power" or an "agent of a foreign power." During 2019 (the most recent year for which data are available) the FISC denied 20 applications in full and 38 applications in part. The court modified the orders sought in an additional 264 applications and granted the orders sought without modifications for 688 applications.[2]

The second special court is the **Foreign Intelligence Court of Review**, which consists of three sitting U.S. district or appeals judges who are also appointed by the chief justice. It hears appeals from decisions by the FISC. Whether on the FISC or the Court of Review, each judge serves for a maximum of seven years and is ineligible for redesignation.

Nonetheless, even with these apparent safeguards, extensive warrantless electronic surveillance by the National Security Agency of telephone calls and email to and from the United States began in the fall of 2001—all outside the rubric of FISA. Responding to critics after this terrorist surveillance program became public in late 2005, President George W. Bush insisted that the executive branch possessed inherent authority to conduct such warrantless surveillance of hostile groups and their agents. However, in 2007, the Justice Department announced that any further such surveillance would be subject to the approval of the FISC. Moreover, in 2008 Congress enacted amendments to FISA that protect telecommunications companies from lawsuits in situations where they have cooperated with federal authorities, and require FISA court permission to wiretap Americans who are overseas. The Freedom Act signed by President Obama in 2015 is supposed to have ended bulk collection of telephone data by the National Security Agency. Instead, telephone companies retain the data which can be accessed by NSA through a judicial order. As of 2020, the terrorist surveillance program had not been the subject of a Supreme Court decision.

Electronic surveillance of a different kind lay at the center of ***United States* v. *Jones*** (2012), where the Court examined use by law enforcement of a GPS tracking device. Oddly, Justice Scalia's opinion for the majority reverted to the trespass concept that the Court had presumably abandoned in *Katz*, at least for technology-laden cases. In contrast was Justice Alito's reliance in his concurring opinion on one's legitimate expectation of privacy that reflected Justice Brandeis's dissent in the *Olmstead* wiretap case.

Administrative Searches. Searches by public officials for reasons other than enforcing the criminal law, usually termed **administrative searches**, benefit from a relaxed Fourth Amendment standard. Health and safety inspections of homes and most businesses, for example, require an administrative warrant if the occupant refuses entry, not a criminal warrant. The former does not have to have the particularity of the latter, nor does there need to be evidence of a violation. Rather, a reasonable plan of enforcement authorized by statute suffices so long as the state's objective is some **special need** other than enforcement of the criminal law (*Camara* v. *Municipal Court*, 1967). Especially where the risk to public safety is substantial, even blanket suspicionless searches, such as those that routinely occur in airports and at the entrances of public buildings, may be deemed equally "reasonable."

Such reasoning led the Court to uphold, against Fourth Amendment challenges, tests of blood and urine samples to detect use of illegal drugs among certain classes of employees on the railroads and in the Customs Service (*Skinner* v. *Railway Labor Executives' Association* and *Treasury Employees Union* v. *Von Raab*, 1989). In neither scheme was the testing necessarily triggered by particularized or individualized suspicion, which is normally the requisite for any valid search of the person, even for a frisk. The "special need" served in the first case was public safety; the need served in the second was promotion of public confidence in a drug-free workforce. The vote in the railroad case was 7–2 and in the customs case 5–4, suggesting that widespread legally mandated drug testing might not be approved.

Nonetheless, six justices approved a school district policy in 1995 that subjected interscholastic athletes to random, suspicionless drug testing. "[S]pecial needs beyond the normal need for law enforcement," noted Justice Scalia, "make the warrant and probable cause requirement impracticable." Along with the addictive effects of drugs among young people generally, drug use by athletes poses a higher risk of harm to the user, and student athletes are frequently "role models" for their peers. Besides, school students have a reduced expectation of privacy, he observed, with student athletes having even less. "School sports are not for the bashful." There is "an element of 'communal undress' inherent in athletic participation" (*Vernonia School District* v. *Acton*). Presumably important in *Acton* were the facts that the school district faced rampant drug use among its students and that drug use by athletes posed health risks to themselves and to others.

That emphasis might explain *Chandler* v. *Miller* two years later, when an all but unanimous bench declared that what was acceptable for student athletes and railroad and customs workers was unacceptable for political candidates. Georgia violated the Fourth Amendment when it stipulated that candidates for designated state offices (including judgeships) test negative for various illegal drugs after submitting to urinalysis. Absent was convincing evidence of a "special need," explained Justice Ginsburg. "However well-meant, the . . . test . . . diminishes personal privacy for a symbol's sake." *Chandler* appears to reject the "symbolism" or "public image" rationale as sole justification for warrantless, suspicionless drug testing. Yet the Court still seems tolerant of suspicionless drug testing in public schools. ***Board of Education* v. *Earls*** (2002) upheld random drug testing even when those eligible for testing included participants in *any* competitive extracurricular activity, athletic or not, and in a school district without a serious drug problem. The Court's general acceptance of administrative searches, however, did not extend to a strip search of a middle school student by school officials who found her in possession of prescription-strength ibuprofen pills in violation of school rules. For the majority, the scope of the search must be justified by its circumstances (*Safford School District* v. *Redding*, 2009).

RIGHT TO COUNSEL

Legal representation may well be "a right by which virtually all other rights are protected in practice." As William M. Beaney explained, "whenever the judicial process unfolds, whether against the unlicensed orator in a public park, the protagonist of unpopular religious beliefs, or the citizen accused of assault or murder, the trial and its result give us in practice whatever meaning the rule of law possesses." That reality explains the assurance in the **Sixth Amendment** that in "all criminal prosecutions, the accused shall enjoy the right . . . to have the Assistance of Counsel for his defence."

Historically, the Sixth Amendment meant that the government could not deny a person the opportunity to retain counsel. But was there also a constitutional obligation to provide counsel for an accused person who could not afford a lawyer? ***Powell* v. *Alabama*** (1932) partially answered that question in the affirmative: Where indigent, young, inexperienced, and illiterate defendants were on trial for their lives, states were constitutionally required to furnish counsel for them. Six years later, *Johnson* v. *Zerbst* construed the Sixth Amendment so that *every* defendant in federal criminal trials was to be offered counsel, at the government's expense if necessary. Yet the same rule was not mandated for defendants in state courts. In an example of the double standard at work (see Chapter Nine), *Betts* v. *Brady* (1942) dictated appointment of counsel in state courts only where the totality of circumstances made it necessary for a fair trial.

This rule, which resulted in a requirement of counsel in some, but not most, state noncapital cases, was overturned by ***Gideon* v. *Wainwright*** (1963), which imposed the prevailing federal rule on state procedures. Accordingly, indigents were entitled to government-provided counsel in all felony prosecutions. Justice Black's opinion sought to give the impression that *Betts* had broken with its own precedents. To one who reexamines *Powell* v. *Alabama* and subsequent decisions, however, Black's reasoning may seem contrived. Yet Black was correct in stating, "The right of one charged with crime to counsel may not be deemed fundamental and essential to fair trials in some countries, but it is in ours."

For counsel at trial, the Burger Court broadened the Gideon rule to include petty offenses when confinement for any period is part of the sentence. The trial judge's decision to appoint counsel thus affects the sentence imposed later if the defendant is found guilty (*Scott* v. *Illinois*, 1979, clarifying *Argersinger* v. *Hamlin*, 1972). This extension of *Gideon* was significant: In the early 1970s, one study found that 75 percent of people accused of these less serious crimes were legally unrepresented. Nevertheless, a defendant has a constitutional right to refuse counsel if the choice is made voluntarily and intelligently (*Faretta* v. *California*, 1975).

Right to counsel is now pervasive throughout the criminal justice process beginning as early as the **arraignment**—the judicial proceeding at which defendants are formally charged and at which they plead guilty or not guilty (*Hamilton* v. *Alabama*, 1961). Counsel must also be provided for indigents:

- On an appeal by right, not where the appeal is discretionary (*Douglas* v. *California*, 1963; *Pennsylvania* v. *Finley*, 1987).
- While in custody (A defendant's damaging statements overheard by a paid informer are inadmissible at trial [*Massiah* v. *United States*, 1964] but may be used for impeachment purposes [*Kansas* v. *Ventris*, 2009]. Also inadmissible are statements coached by police outside the lawyer's presence [*Brewer* v. *Williams*, 1977]). However, when a court appoints counsel for an indigent defendant in the absence of any request on his part, there is no basis for a presumption that any subsequent waiver of the right to counsel will be involuntary (*Montejo* v. *Louisiana*, 2009). Moreover, the general prohibition against interrogation of a suspect who initially invoked the right to counsel becomes inapplicable when there is a break in custody or a substantial lapse in time of more than two weeks before interrogation resumes (*Maryland* v. *Shatzer*, 2010).

- At police lineups, to avoid faulty identification (*United States* v. *Wade*, 1967), but not including informal identification that occurs prior to initiation of criminal prosecution (*Kirby* v. *Illinois*, 1972).
- At some probation revocation proceedings (*Gagnon* v. *Scarpelli*, 1973).
- Under sentence of death when they seek federal habeas corpus relief (*McFarland* v. *Scott*, 1994).

Work of defense counsel was significantly aided by *Brady* v. *Maryland* (1963), in which the Court held that the prosecution is obliged to share exculpatory evidence when counsel requests. With enactment of the Due Process Protection Act in 2020, Congress directed federal trial judges to ensure that prosecutors comply with what has become known as the **Brady Rule**.

Both at trial and on direct appeal, the Court has clarified the Sixth Amendment to require *effective* assistance of counsel (*Strickland* v. *Washington*, 1984). The justices have concluded that a right to assistance of counsel means little if that right does not include effective assistance. But showing ineffective assistance is not easy. What is mandated is not an error-free defense. Rather, one must demonstrate that, but for counsel's mistakes, the result of the proceeding would have been different and that the overall fairness and reliability of the trial were deficient (*Lockhart* v. *Fretwell*, 1993).

The Confrontation Clause. Aside from protecting the right to counsel, the Sixth Amendment through the **confrontation clause** assures the right of the accused person "to be confronted with the witnesses against him." Ordinarily the provision excludes **hearsay** (secondhand) testimony and so bars admission of testimonial statements of witnesses who did not appear at trial, unless the witness was unable to appear, *and* if the defense had a prior opportunity to cross-examine the witness (*Crawford* v. *Washington*, 2004). In decisions that significantly affect domestic violence cases where the victim is often afraid or otherwise reluctant to testify, *Davis* v. *Washington* and *Hammon* v. *Indiana* (2006) held that statements are nontestimonial, and therefore admissible, "when made in the course of police interrogation under circumstances objectively indicating that the primary purpose of the interrogation is to enable police assistance to an ongoing emergency." They are testimonial, and therefore inadmissible, "when the circumstances objectively indicate that there is no such ongoing emergency, and that the primary purpose of the interrogation is to establish or prove past events potentially relevant to later criminal prosecution." Thus, in this pair of cases, introduction at trial of a 911 call, where the person placing the call was not present at trial, was not deemed a violation of the confrontation clause. In contrast, introduction of statements by a police officer relating comments by a crime-scene victim, who was absent from trial, did constitute a violation. Or as *Michigan* v. *Bryant* (2011) elaborated, a testimonial statement is one where the primary purpose of the conversation is to create an out-of-court substitute for trial testimony. Accordingly, *Ohio* v. *Clark* (2015) allowed statements made by a minor child to a child care worker to be used at trial because they were made solely in the context of dealing with possible child abuse and so were nontestimonial. In contrast, forensic lab reports are considered testimonial and are covered by the confrontation clause according to *Melendez-Diaz* v. *Massachusetts* (2009). They may be introduced without cross-examination only after waiver of the defendant's Sixth Amendment right.

SELF-INCRIMINATION

Assurance in the **Fifth Amendment** that "no person . . . shall be compelled in any criminal case to be a witness against himself" is a right "hard-earned by our forefathers," said Chief Justice Warren. The reasons "for its inclusion in the Constitution—and the necessities for its preservation—are to be found in the lessons of history." The right is a central feature of a system of criminal justice that presumes innocence—that is, which places the burden of proof on the prosecution to establish guilt. No one accused of a crime should have to assist the state in proving its case. Along with other provisions in the Bill of Rights, the protection against self-incrimination stands for the proposition that determining guilt and innocence by fair procedures is as important as punishing the guilty.

The extent of this safeguard has nonetheless presented the Supreme Court with hard questions. How far should the needs of law enforcement be accommodated, and how much freedom should be accorded the individual?

Immunity. One may claim Fifth Amendment protection in refusing to testify before a grand jury, trial jury, or legislative committee or in being compelled to produce papers or other evidence (*Counselman* v. *Hitchcock*, 1892; *Quinn* v. *United States*, 1955). Yet the Court has allowed Congress to grant immunity from prosecution to extract testimony from reluctant witnesses, an especially useful technique in investigations of organized crime. "Immunity displaces the danger. Once the reason for the privilege ceases, the privilege ceases," reasoned Justice Frankfurter in *Ullman* v. *United States* (1956). The Immunity Act of 1954 challenged in *Ullman* provided for complete (or "transactional") immunity from both state and federal prosecution in exchange for testimony about various criminal activities. But the Organized Crime Control Act of 1970 permits a federal court, agency, or congressional committee to offer "use and derivative use," as opposed to **transactional immunity** in exchange for compelled testimony. The former is less generous to the witness than the latter because under **use immunity** the witness can still be prosecuted for crimes about which the witness has testified. The limitation on the government is that the prosecutor may not later use this testimony against the witness. Five justices found even this arrangement harmonious with the Fifth Amendment in *Kastigar* v. *United States* (1972).

Interrogations. Police interrogation of suspects raises obvious due process and Fifth Amendment questions. For decades, the rule in federal trials was that only voluntary confessions were admissible. The presumption "that one who is innocent will not imperil his safety . . . by an untrue statement," reasoned the first Justice Harlan well over a century ago, ended when hopes or threats deprived the accused "of that freedom of will or self-control essential to make his confessional voluntary" (*Hopt* v. *Utah*, 1884). Moreover, beginning with *Brown* v. *Mississippi* (1936), the Court applied a similar standard against the use of coerced confessions in state courts. In that case, a unanimous bench reversed three murder convictions marked by what Chief Justice Hughes called "compulsion by torture to extort a confession. . . . It would be difficult to conceive of methods more revolting to the sense of justice than those taken to procure the confessions of these petitioners, and the use of the confessions thus obtained as the basis for conviction and sentence was a clear denial of due process."

Some justices later wondered whether interrogations could be anything but threatening and intimidating, even in the absence of threats or use of force, if the accused was denied the right to have a lawyer present. Thus, in *Escobedo* v. *Illinois*

(1964), the Court condemned the police practice of preventing a suspect from consulting with a lawyer until the interrogation had ended. This and numerous other cases over the previous three decades had made the Court aware of a variety of law enforcement practices that seemed unfair to accused persons, many of whom were young, uneducated, and members of minority groups. The Court inched toward what Herbert Packer termed the due process model of criminal justice (which stressed fairness and the rights of the accused), in contrast to the older crime control model (which stressed the powers of the prosecution). In ***Miranda* v. *Arizona*** (1966), the Court held 5–4 that federal and state officials must give suspects specified warnings or equivalent advice before beginning to interrogate them about alleged crimes. Many police departments have printed the now familiar ***Miranda* warnings** on cards from which the arresting and/or interrogating officer reads:

> You have the right to remain silent and refuse to answer any questions.
>
> Anything you say may be used against you in a court of law.
>
> As we discuss this matter, you have a right to stop answering my questions at any time you desire.
>
> You have a right to a lawyer before speaking to me, to remain silent until you can talk to him/her, and to have him/her present when you are being questioned.
>
> If you want a lawyer but cannot afford one, one will be provided to you at no cost.
>
> Do you understand each of these rights I have explained to you?
>
> Now that I have advised you of your rights, are you willing to answer my questions without an attorney present?

Without such warnings, statements made are inadmissible at trial. The Warren Court's view was that the privilege against self-incrimination could be secured in no other way. Joined were the Sixth Amendment's provisions for right to counsel and the Fifth Amendment's guard against self-incrimination. The belief was that events occurring in the station house greatly influence the outcome of events in the courthouse.

For law enforcement, *Miranda* at first seemed a disaster. But statements made by suspects outside the presence of an attorney may still be introduced as evidence, provided they waived their right to silence "voluntarily, knowingly, and intelligently." Legal challenges to such statements typically turn on whether (1) the suspect has validly waived the *Miranda* rights, thus agreeing to answer questions, or (2) a *Miranda*-type "interrogation" has occurred.

Miranda-related questions alone accounted for more than 60 decisions in the Supreme Court between 1966 and 2003. Generally the justices have been hesitant to extend the ruling, and several cases have restricted its scope. For instance:

- Statements, inadmissible as direct testimony because of a *Miranda* violation, may be used to attack credibility of statements the accused makes on the witness stand (*Harris* v. *New York*, 1971).
- Questioning that occurs before arrest for a traffic offense does not amount to "custodial interrogation" within *Miranda*'s reach (*Berkemer* v. *McCarty*, 1984).

- Offhand comment by one police offer to another in the presence of a thrice-warned suspect, who had asked to speak to an attorney, which prompts an incriminating statement is not an interrogation (*Rhode Island* v. *Innis*, 1980).
- Public safety allows police to ask a suspect the whereabouts of a gun before administering a *Miranda* warning (*New York* v. *Quarles*, 1984).
- Incriminating, but unwarned, statements do not necessarily taint later incriminating, and warned, statements (*Oregon* v. *Elstad*, 1985).
- Rights under *Miranda* must be explicitly invoked but may be implicitly waived (*Berghuis* v. *Thompkins*, 2010).

Miranda* Revisited**. In 2000, delayed application of a provision in a 32-year-old law reopened matters the Court had presumably settled in *Miranda*. Section 3501 in the Omnibus Crime Control and Safe Streets Act of 1968 attempted to overrule *Miranda* by substituting the pre-*Miranda* standard of voluntariness in place of *Miranda*'s specific warnings. In federal prosecutions, confessions that the trial judge deemed voluntary on the basis of the totality of circumstances would be admissible, even if the *Miranda* warnings had not been administered. At the insistence of a succession of U.S. attorneys general, Section 3501 lay lifeless until 1997, when the Court of Appeals for the Fourth Circuit held that incriminating but unwarned statements by Charles Dickerson in a bank robbery investigation were admissible because they had been voluntarily rendered. If, as the Fourth Circuit held, the *Miranda* rules were merely judicially crafted rules of evidence, then Congress, as lawmaker in chief, was free to change them. On the other hand, if the *Miranda* rules were constitutionally grounded, as both Dickerson and the U.S. solicitor general insisted, then Congress was without authority to set aside by statute a regimen that the Constitution required. Even in the latter instance, the Court could decide that *Miranda* had been wrongly decided—that adherence to the litany of warnings was not constitutionally mandated. If so, the pre-*Miranda* voluntariness standard would be constitutionally sufficient. The outcome in ***Dickerson* v. *United States was ironic. Not only did *Miranda* survive (and Section 3501 succumb) by a 7–2 vote (thus exceeding *Miranda*'s original majority of five), but it was reaffirmed by a bench more ideologically conservative than the bench that had decided *Miranda* in 1966. Moreover, the majority opinion in *Dickerson* was authored by Chief Justice Rehnquist, initially named to the Court in 1971 by President Richard Nixon, who fashioned his campaign for the White House in 1968 in part by attacking *Miranda*.

PUNISHMENT

"Excessive bail shall not be required, nor excessive fines imposed, nor cruel and unusual punishments inflicted," declares the **Eighth Amendment**. Similar to language in the English Bill of Rights of 1689, these three clauses are the only express limitations in the Constitution on the severity of punishments in criminal cases, and of these, it has been the ban on "cruel and unusual punishments" that has generated the most litigation in the Supreme Court.

Capital Punishment. In *Furman* v. *Georgia* (1972), the Supreme Court imposed a moratorium on executions in the United States when it ruled 5–4 that the death penalty as then administered was cruel and unusual in violation of the Eighth Amendment. Too much discretion in the hands of trial judges and juries made application of the death sentence capricious. Thirty-five states and Congress promptly reinstated capital punishment with more carefully drawn statutes to meet the Court's objections. In ***Gregg* v. *Georgia*** (1976), a majority of the bench concluded that the death penalty was not inherently cruel and unusual and upheld a two-step sentencing scheme designed to set strict standards for trial courts. A jury would first decide the question of guilt and then in a separate proceeding impose punishment. Executions could resume, and they did.

As of early 2021, more than 2,660 convicted felons were under sentence of death (a number that has been in decline in recent years). Since 1976, 1,532 persons have been executed (more than a third of them in Texas alone) in the 25 states that have the death penalty and by the U.S. government.[3] (The U.S. military may also impose the death penalty for crimes committed by persons in the armed forces.) One reason for the large difference between the number of prisoners on death row and the number of executions is that the Court, although approving capital punishment in principle, has raised substantial obstacles to carrying it out. Some of the conditions that have led to an invalidation of a death sentence include:

- Complete removal of trial court discretion by making capital punishment mandatory (*Woodson* v. *North Carolina*, 1976).
- Failure to allow the introduction of any mitigating circumstances (*Roberts* v. *Louisiana*, 1977).
- Death penalty imposed for rape (*Coker* v. *Georgia*, 1977).
- The presence of jurors who would vote for the death penalty regardless of any evidence in mitigation (*Morgan* v. *Illinois*, 1992). This decision mirrors *Witherspoon* v. *Illinois* (1968), which bars imposition of the death penalty by a jury from which persons with scruples against capital punishment are excluded.
- Failure to inform the jury that a life sentence carried no possibility of parole (*Shafer* v. *South Carolina*, 2001).
- A convicted murderer who is mentally retarded (*Atkins* v. *Virginia*, 2002).
- Someone under 18 when murder was committed (*Roper* v. *Simmons*, 2005).
- Death penalty imposed for child rape (*Kennedy* v. *Louisiana*, 2008).
- Where the law requires a judge, not the jury, to assess the factors that result in a death sentence, following a conviction for murder (*Ring* v. *Arizona*, 2002).
- Where a fixed IQ score serves as conclusive evidence of a defendant's intellectual capacity (*Hall* v. *Florida*, 2014).

Since *Gregg*, a consensus has emerged on the Court that capital sentencing must be both individualized and predictable. This means leaving controlled discretion in the sentencer's hand. Too much discretion opens the door to caprice and discrimination that so worried the Court in *Furman*; too little discretion denies fairness to the defendant by closing off consideration of mitigating factors. The Court would like to believe that the procedures it has approved rationally distinguish between those murderers who should receive life sentences and those who should be put to death. Neither the value of fairness nor the value of rationality, however, can be fully realized without danger to the other, and the justices do not always agree among themselves how the balance between the two should be struck in particular cases. For example, *Kansas* v. *Marsh* (2006) allowed a capital sentence to be imposed when aggravating and mitigating factors were equally balanced.

The most common method of execution today is by lethal injection and in *Glossip* v. *Gross* (2015), the Court refused to block an execution on the claim that the three-drug concoction in use led to botched executions and induced a painful death.

It was in this case that Justice Breyer in a dissent joined by Justice Ginsburg stated, "I believe it highly likely that the death penalty violates the Eighth Amendment. At the very least, the Court should call for full briefing on the basic question."

In contrast to procedural attacks on death sentences that the Court faces every term, ***McCleskey* v. *Kemp*** (1987) remains the only significant frontal assault on capital punishment since *Gregg*. It also continues to illustrate the persistent presence of race in sentencing, especially with respect to capital sentencing, where as of early 2021 persons of color accounted for 53 percent of the death row population. At the heart of McCleskey's case was a statistical study by David Baldus and others which showed that in Georgia, during the 1970s, killers of whites were 4.3 times more likely to receive the death penalty than killers of blacks. Although statistics had been sufficient to establish discrimination in jury selection and employment, five justices were unpersuaded by the numbers in this context. The study did not prove that race had been a factor in McCleskey's particular case, they reasoned. Because each capital jury is unique, explained Justice Powell, and because "discretion is essential to the criminal justice process, we would demand exceptionally clear proof before we would infer that the discretion has been abused."

Looking beyond the role of race in capital sentencing, a study directed by James S. Liebman at Columbia University Law School in 2000 depicted a death penalty system that appears to be replete with error at the trial level. Examining nearly 5,500 judicial decisions between 1973 and 1995, the study made some startling findings: (1) Reversals occurred in 68 percent of capital cases whose appeals were completed during the specified time period. (2) Of those whose death sentences were overturned, 82 percent were given a sentence less than death after the errors were corrected on retrial; 7 percent were found not guilty. (3) High error rates occurred across the country, with 90 percent of states that meted out death sentences having overall error rates of 52 percent or higher.

Federal Habeas Corpus. Federal courts may review death sentences (as well as convictions for noncapital crimes) imposed by state courts through a congressionally authorized procedure called **habeas corpus** (Latin for "you have the body"). These proceedings ordinarily begin once a prisoner's sentence becomes final—that is, once prisoners have exhausted their direct appeals in state courts and perhaps have been denied review by the U.S. Supreme Court. Under the standard the Court announced in 1963, these collateral attacks on convictions could encompass not only issues already considered by the state courts but "new" issues as well, unless the defendant had "deliberately bypassed" them on direct appeal (*Fay* v. *Noia*). The result has been to keep some cases in the courts for years, not by enlarging the scope of a defendant's constitutional rights but by increasing the defendant's opportunities to convince a judge that a constitutional violation had occurred. Not surprisingly, prisoners on death row have relied heavily on habeas corpus; indeed, as many as two-thirds of all death sentences since 1976 have been set aside in this way.

In the Antiterrorism and Effective Death Penalty Act of 1996, Congress made it more difficult for federal courts to entertain claims from state courts on collateral review. Upheld by the Supreme Court only two months after its enactment (*Felker* v. *Turpin*), the statute erects special hurdles for a state prisoner seeking relief through a second or successive (a claim already rebuffed by one federal court and raised again) petition for habeas corpus in federal court. First, the act directs dismissal of any claim raised in a prior petition by the same petitioner. Second, a claim presented for the first time in a second petition must be dismissed unless the petitioner meets one of two conditions: (a) that the claim relies on a new rule of constitutional law that the Supreme

Court has made retroactive to cases on collateral review; or (b) that the factual basis for the claim could not have been discovered previously and that, with the newly acquired information, no reasonable fact finder would have found the petitioner guilty. Third, before seeking relief in a district court, the petitioner must request permission to do so from the proper court of appeals. This court authorizes the petition only if it meets the standards set out above. Finally, the law provides that the appeals court's determination "shall not be the subject of . . . a writ of certiorari" to the Supreme Court.

Noncapital Sentencing. Only recently has the Court appeared willing to scrutinize noncapital sentences that might violate the Eighth Amendment because they are excessive. True, the Court in 1910 (*Weems* v. *United States*) struck down as excessive a sentence of a Philippine court which entailed, among other penalties, 12 years of imprisonment at hard labor, while chained day and night at the wrists and ankles. And in 1962 (*Robinson* v. *California*), the Court found "excessive" a 90-day jail term for the crime of being "addicted to the use of narcotics." But a bare majority in *Rummel* v. *Estelle* (1980) refused to become involved in proportionality review of various lengths of prison terms. At issue was application of the Texas recidivist statute under which Rummel was sentenced to life imprisonment after conviction for his third felony for defrauding others. The total amount in question from Rummel's three run-ins with the law was about $230.

In 1983, an equally bare majority in *Solem* v. *Helm* "distinguished" *Rummel*. While stressing that successful challenges to the proportionality of particular sentences would be rare, Justice Powell declared,

> [W]e hold as a matter of principle that a criminal sentence must be proportionate to the crime for which the defendant has been convicted. . . . [N]o penalty is per se constitutional. . . . [A] court's proportionality analysis under the Eighth Amendment should be guided by objective criteria, including (i) the gravity of the offense and the harshness of the penalty; (ii) the sentences imposed on other criminals in the same jurisdiction; and (iii) the sentences imposed for commission of the same crime in other jurisdictions.

Successful challenges will be rare indeed. In *Harmelin* v. *Michigan* (1991), five justices rejected a *Solem*-based attack on the state's drug sentencing statute (the toughest in the nation), which mandated life imprisonment, without possibility of parole, for possession of more than 650 grams of a substance containing cocaine. The law allowed for no mitigating circumstances (such as the potency of the substance or being a first offender), nor did it take drug purity into account. Harmelin had been caught with 672 grams (1½ pounds) during a routine arrest after he ran a red light. The case demonstrates how disagreement flows from the level of generality employed. Some justices asked whether life in prison without parole is cruel and unusual. The dissenters posed a different question: Is life in prison without parole cruel and unusual punishment in *this* case? A similar outcome followed in *Ewing* v. *California* (2003), where five justices found no constitutional objection to a sentence of 25 years to life, under the state's "three strikes" law, for felony theft of three golf clubs valued at $399 each. Yet, *Graham* v. *Florida* (2010) barred a sentence of life without parole for juveniles convicted of nonhomicide crimes.

Thus, in the Court's view the Eighth Amendment imposes a far greater restraint in capital, in contrast to noncapital, cases. For the latter category and short of the macabre, the Court has handed legislators nearly boundless discretion, except perhaps with respect to fines, as indicated by ***Timbs v. Indiana*** (2019), reprinted in Chapter Nine. Nonetheless, whether in capital or noncapital cases, *Ramos* v. *Louisiana* (2020) makes clear that the Sixth Amendment permits only unanimous jury verdicts. The question whether *Ramos* would apply retroactively was answered in *Edwards* v. *Vannoy* (2021) when a six-justice bench held broadly that "new procedural rules would not apply retroactively on federal collateral review."

KEY TERMS

Fourth Amendment
writs of assistance
probable cause
warrant
exclusionary rule
Patriot Act
Freedom Act
Foreign Intelligence Surveillance Act
Foreign Intelligence Surveillance Court
Foreign Intelligence Court of Review
frisk
reasonable suspicion
administrative searches
special need
Sixth Amendment
arraignment
Brady Rule
confrontation clause
hearsay
Fifth Amendment
transactional immunity
use immunity
Miranda warnings
Eighth Amendment
habeas corpus

QUERIES

1. Why did *Mapp* v. *Ohio* result in a greatly increased number of Fourth Amendment cases on the Supreme Court's docket?

2. Why should the police have to abide by special strict rules while criminals are acting like thugs?

3. What constitutional questions arise from increased use of drones by law enforcement?

4. What questions about the role of race in capital sentencing are raised by *McCleskey* v. *Kemp*?

SELECTED READINGS

Breyer, Stephen G., and John Bessler. *Against the Death Penalty*. Washington, DC: Brookings Institution Press, 2016.

Helmholz, R. H., Charles M. Gray, John H. Langbein, Eben Moglen, Henry E. Smith, and Albert W. Alschuler. *The Privilege against Self-Incrimination: Its Origins and Development*. Chicago, IL: University of Chicago Press, 1997.

Lewis, Anthony. *Gideon's Trumpet*. New York: Random House, 1964.

Liebman, James, J. Fagan, V. West, and J. Lloyd. "Capital Attrition: Error Rates in Capital Cases, 1973–1995." 78 *Texas Law Review* 1839, 2000.

Maclin, Tracey. *The Supreme Court and the Fourth Amendment's Exclusionary Rule*. New York: Oxford University Press, 2013.

Melusky, Joseph A., and Keith A. Pesto. *Cruel and Unusual Punishment*. Santa Barbara, CA: ABC-CLIO, 2003.

Pizzi, William T. *The Supreme Court's Role in Mass Incarceration*. New York: Routledge, 2020.

Stephens, Otis H., and Richard A. Glenn. *Unreasonable Searches and Seizures*. Santa Barbara, CA: ABC-CLIO, 2006.

Stuart, Gary L. *Miranda*. Tucson: University of Arizona Press, 2004.

Taylor, John B. *Right to Counsel and Privilege against Self-Incrimination*. Santa Barbara, CA: ABC-CLIO, 2004.

I. SEARCHES AND SEIZURES

A. Whose Rights?

Minnesota v. *Carter*
525 U.S. 83, 119 S.Ct. 469, 142 L.Ed. 2d 373 (1998)

http://caselaw.findlaw.com/us-supreme-court/525/83.html

After receiving a tip from an informer, a police officer in Eagan, Minnesota, looked in a ground-level apartment window through a gap in the closed blind and observed Wayne Carter and Melvin Johns bagging cocaine with Kimberly Thompson, the lessee of the apartment. Carter and Johns were arrested after they left the apartment. At trial, they moved to suppress the evidence, arguing that the officer's initial observation was an unreasonable search in violation of the Fourth Amendment. The trial court held that since they were not overnight social guests, they were not entitled to Fourth Amendment protection, and that the officer's observation was not a "search." The state court of appeals held that Carter did not have standing to object to the officer's actions because he used the apartment for a business purpose—to package drugs—and, separately, affirmed Johns's conviction without addressing the standing issue. In reversing, the state supreme court held that (1) Carter and Johns could claim Fourth Amendment protection because they had a legitimate expectation of privacy in the invaded place, and (2) the officer's warrantless observation constituted an unreasonable search. (Thompson was not a party to this appeal.) Majority: Rehnquist, O'Connor, Scalia, Kennedy, Thomas, Breyer. Dissenting: Ginsburg, Stevens, Souter.

Chief Justice Rehnquist delivered the opinion of the Court. . . .

The [Fourth] Amendment protects persons against unreasonable searches of "their persons [and] houses" and thus indicates that [it] is a personal right that must be invoked by an individual. . . . But the extent to which the Fourth Amendment protects people may depend upon where those people are. We have held that "capacity to claim the protection of the Fourth Amendment depends . . . upon whether the person who claims the protection of the Amendment has a legitimate expectation of privacy in the invaded place."

The text of the Amendment suggests that its protections extend only to people in "their" houses. But we have held that in some circumstances a person may have a legitimate expectation of privacy in the house of someone else. In *Minnesota* v. *Olson* (1990), for example, we decided that an overnight guest in a house had the sort of expectation of privacy that the Fourth Amendment protects.

In *Jones* v. *United States* (1960), the defendant seeking to exclude evidence resulting from a search of an apartment had been given the use of the apartment by a friend. He had clothing in the apartment, had slept there "maybe a night," and at the time was the sole occupant of the apartment. But while the holding of *Jones*—that a search of the apartment violated the defendant's Fourth Amendment rights—is still valid, its statement that "anyone legitimately on the premises where a search occurs may challenge its legality," was expressly repudiated in *Rakas* v. *Illinois* (1978). Thus an overnight guest in a home may claim the protection of the Fourth Amendment, but one who is merely present with the consent of the householder may not.

Respondents here were obviously not overnight guests, but were essentially present for a business transaction and were only in the home a matter of hours. There is no suggestion that they had a previous relationship with Thompson, or that there was any other purpose to their visit. Nor was there anything similar to the overnight guest relationship in *Olson* to suggest a degree of acceptance into the household. While the apartment was a dwelling place for Thompson, it was for these respondents simply a place to do business. . . .

If we regard the overnight guest in *Olson* as typifying those who may claim the protection of the Fourth Amendment in the home of another, and one merely "legitimately on the premises" as typifying those who may not do so, the present case is obviously somewhere in between. But the purely commercial nature of the transaction engaged in here, the relatively short period of time on the premises, and the lack of any previous connection between respondents and the householder, all lead us to conclude that respondents' situation is closer to that of one simply permitted on the premises. We therefore hold that any search which may have occurred did not violate their Fourth Amendment rights.

Because we conclude that respondents had no legitimate expectation of privacy in the apartment, we need not decide whether the police officer's observation constituted a "search." The judgment of the Supreme Court of Minnesota is accordingly reversed, and the cause is remanded for proceedings not inconsistent with this opinion.

It is so ordered.

JUSTICE SCALIA, with whom JUSTICE THOMAS joins, concurring . . . [omitted].

JUSTICE KENNEDY, concurring . . . [omitted].

JUSTICE BREYER, concurring in the judgment . . . [omitted].

JUSTICE GINSBURG, with whom JUSTICE STEVENS and JUSTICE SOUTER join, dissenting.

The Court's decision undermines not only the security of short-term guests, but also the security of the home resident herself. In my view, when a homeowner or lessor personally invites a guest into her home to share in a common endeavor, whether it be for conversation, to engage in leisure activities, or for business purposes licit or illicit, that guest should share his host's shelter against unreasonable searches and seizures. . . .

A home dweller places her own privacy at risk, the Court's approach indicates, when she opens her home to others, uncertain whether the duration of their stay, their purpose, and their "acceptance into the household" will earn protection. It remains textbook law that "[s] earches and seizures inside a home without a warrant are presumptively unreasonable absent exigent circumstances." The law in practice is less secure. Human frailty suggests that today's decision will tempt police to pry into private dwellings without warrant, to find evidence incriminating guests who do not rest there through the night. . . . As I see it, people are not genuinely "secure in their . . . houses . . . against unreasonable searches and seizures," if their invitations to others increase the risk of unwarranted governmental peering and prying into their dwelling places.

Through the host's invitation, the guest gains a reasonable expectation of privacy in the home. *Minnesota* v. *Olson* so held with respect to an overnight guest. The logic of that decision extends to shorter term guests as well. . . .

Our leading decision in *Katz [v. United States]* is key to my view of this case. There, we ruled that the Government violated the petitioner's Fourth Amendment rights when it electronically recorded him transmitting wagering information while he was inside a public telephone booth. We were mindful that "the Fourth Amendment protects people, not places," and held that this electronic monitoring of a business call "violated the privacy upon which [the caller] justifiably relied while using the telephone booth." Our obligation to produce coherent results in this often visited area of the law requires us to inform our current expositions by benchmarks already established. . . .

The Court's decision in this case veers sharply from the path marked in *Katz*. I do not agree that we have a more reasonable expectation of privacy when we place a business call to a person's home from a public telephone booth on the side of the street, than when we actually enter that person's premises to engage in a common endeavor. . . .

B. The Exclusionary Rule

Mapp v. *Ohio*
367 U.S. 643, 81 S.Ct. 1684, 6 L.Ed. 2d 1081 (1961)

http://caselaw.findlaw.com/us-supreme-court/367/643.html

Cleveland police officers, acting on information that a bombing-case suspect and betting equipment might be found in Dollree Mapp's house, forced their way in after being refused admission and, without a search warrant, subjected the house and its contents to a thorough search. In a basement trunk, they found literature that provided the basis for her conviction for possessing obscene materials. The Ohio Supreme Court upheld the conviction. The brief filed on behalf of Ms. Mapp in the U.S. Supreme Court argued that the statute criminalizing possession of obscene materials was unconstitutionally vague and that the high-handed behavior by the police amounted to a violation of due process of law but did not ask that the exclusionary rule be applied to state criminal proceedings. That point was raised, seemingly as an afterthought, by the American Civil Liberties Union in its *amicus* brief when it requested the Court to reexamine *Wolf* v. *Colorado* (1949). Ms. Mapp, who has been called the "Rosa Parks of the Fourth Amendment," died in 2014 in Conyers, Georgia, at the age of 91. Majority: Clark, Black, Brennan, Douglas, Stewart, Warren. Dissenting: Harlan, Frankfurter, Whittaker.

Mr. Justice Clark delivered the opinion of the Court. . . .

Today we once again examine *Wolf's* constitutional documentation of the right to privacy free from unreasonable state intrusion, and, after its dozen years on our books, are led by it to close the only courtroom door remaining open to evidence secured by official lawlessness in flagrant abuse of that basic right, reserved to all persons as a specific guarantee against that very same unlawful conduct. We hold that all evidence obtained by searches and seizures in violation of the Constitution is, by that same authority, inadmissible in a state court.

Since the Fourth Amendment's right of privacy has been declared enforceable against the States through the Due Process Clause of the Fourteenth, it is enforceable against them by the same sanction of exclusion as is used against the Federal Government. . . . [T]he admission of the new constitutional right by *Wolf* could not consistently tolerate denial of its most important constitutional privilege, namely, the exclusion of the evidence which an accused had been forced to give by reason of the unlawful seizure. To hold otherwise is to grant the right but in reality to withhold its privilege and enjoyment. . . .

Indeed, we are aware of no restraint, similar to that rejected today, conditioning the enforcement of any other basic constitutional right. The right to privacy, no less important than any other right carefully and particularly reserved to the people, would stand in marked contrast to all other rights declared as "basic to a free society."

This Court has not hesitated to enforce as strictly against the States as it does against the Federal Government the rights of free speech and of a free press, the rights to notice and to a fair, public trial, including, as it does, the right not to be convicted by use of a coerced confession, however logically relevant it be, and without regard to its reliability. . . . And nothing could be more certain than that when a coerced confession is involved, "the relevant rules of evidence" are overridden without regard to "the incidence of such conduct by the police," slight or frequent. Why should not the same rule apply to what is tantamount to coerced testimony by way of unconstitutional seizure of goods, papers, effects, documents, etc.? . . .

The ignoble shortcut to conviction left open to the State tends to destroy the entire system of constitutional restraints on which the liberties of the people rest. Having once recognized that the right to privacy embodied in the Fourth Amendment is enforceable against the States and that the right to be secure against rude invasions of privacy by state officers is, therefore, constitutional in origin, we can no longer permit that right to remain an empty promise. Because it is enforceable in the same manner and to like effect as other basic rights secured by the Due Process Clause, we can no longer permit it to be revocable at the whim of any police officer who, in the name of law enforcement itself, chooses to suspend its enjoyment. Our decision, founded on reason and truth, gives to the individual no more than that which the Constitution guarantees him, to the police officer no less than that to which honest law enforcement is entitled, and, to the courts, that judicial integrity so necessary in the true administration of justice. . . .

Reversed and remanded.

MR. JUSTICE BLACK, concurring . . . [omitted].
MR. JUSTICE DOUGLAS, concurring . . . [omitted].
MR. JUSTICE STEWART, concurring . . . [omitted].

MR. JUSTICE HARLAN, whom MR. JUSTICE FRANKFURTER and MR. JUSTICE WHITTAKER join, dissenting. . . .

At the heart of the majority's opinion in this case is the following syllogism: (1) the rule excluding in federal criminal trials evidence which is the product of an illegal search and seizure is a "part and parcel" of the Fourth Amendment; (2) *Wolf* held that the "privacy" assured against federal action by the Fourth Amendment is also protected against state action by the Fourteenth Amendment; and (3) it is therefore "logically and constitutionally necessary" that the Weeks exclusionary rule should also be enforced against the States.

This reasoning ultimately rests on the unsound premise that because *Wolf* carried into the States, as part of "the concept of ordered liberty" embodied in the Fourteenth Amendment, the principle of "privacy" underlying the Fourth Amendment, it must follow that whatever configurations of the Fourth Amendment have been developed in the particularizing federal precedents are likewise to be deemed a part of "ordered liberty," and as such are enforceable against the States. For me, this does not follow at all. . . .

United States v. Leon
468 U.S. 897, 104 S.Ct. 3405, 82 L.Ed. 2d 677 (1984)

http://caselaw.findlaw.com/us-supreme-court/468/897.html

With information from a confidential informant, police officers in Burbank, California, undertook surveillance of Alberto Leon and others for suspected drug-trafficking activities. Based on an affidavit summarizing police observations, Officer Rombach prepared a warrant application to search three residences and the automobiles of the individuals who lived there. Several deputy district attorneys reviewed Rombach's application, and a state judge issued the warrant. The searches that followed turned up large quantities of illegal drugs and other evidence. Leon and his cohorts were indicted for violating federal drug laws, but the district court suppressed some of the evidence seized in the searches because the affidavit contained insufficient information to establish probable cause to search all of the residences. The Court of Appeals for the Ninth Circuit affirmed. The government's petition for certiorari did not claim that probable cause was present but raised only the question of whether a good-faith exception to the exclusionary rule should be recognized under the Fourth Amendment. Majority: White, Blackmun, Burger, O'Connor, Powell, Rehnquist. Dissenting: Brennan, Marshall, Stevens.

Justice White delivered the opinion of the Court.

This case presents the question whether the Fourth Amendment exclusionary rule should be modified so as not to bar the use in the prosecution's case-in-chief of evidence obtained by officers acting in reasonable reliance on a search warrant issued by a detached and neutral magistrate but ultimately found to be unsupported by probable cause. To resolve this question, we must consider once again the tension between the sometimes competing goals of, on the one hand, deterring official misconduct and removing inducements to unreasonable invasions of privacy and, on the other, establishing procedures under which criminal defendants are "acquitted or convicted on the basis of all the evidence which exposes the truth." . . .

The Fourth Amendment contains no provision expressly precluding the use of evidence obtained in violation of its commands, and an examination of its origin and purposes makes clear that the use of fruits of a past unlawful search or seizure "work[s] no new Fourth Amendment wrong." . . . The wrong condemned by the Amendment is "fully accomplished" by the unlawful search or seizure itself . . . and the exclusionary rule is neither intended nor able to "cure the invasion of the defendant's rights which he has already suffered." . . . The rule thus operates as "a judicially created remedy designed to safeguard Fourth Amendment rights generally through its deterrent effect, rather than a personal constitutional right of the person aggrieved." . . .

Whether the exclusionary sanction is appropriately imposed in a particular case, our decisions make clear, is "an issue separate from the question whether the Fourth Amendment rights of the party seeking to invoke the rule were violated by police conduct." . . . Only the former question is currently before us, and it must be resolved by weighing the costs and benefits of preventing the use in the prosecution's case-in-chief of inherently trustworthy tangible evidence obtained in reliance on a search warrant issued by a detached and neutral magistrate that ultimately is found to be defective.

The substantial social costs exacted by the exclusionary rule for the vindication of Fourth Amendment rights have long been a source of concern. . . .

Particularly when law enforcement officers have acted in objective good faith or their transgressions have been minor, the magnitude of the benefit conferred on such guilty defendants offends basic concepts of the criminal justice system. . . .

To the extent that proponents of exclusion rely on its behavioral effects on judges and magistrates in these areas, their reliance is misplaced. First, the exclusionary rule is designed to deter police misconduct rather than to punish the errors of judges and magistrates. Second, there exists no evidence suggesting that judges and magistrates are inclined to ignore or subvert the Fourth Amendment or that lawlessness among these actors requires application of the extreme sanction of exclusion.

Third, and most important, we discern no basis, and are offered none, for believing that exclusion of evidence seized pursuant to a warrant will have a significant deterrent effect on the issuing judge or magistrate. . . . The threat of exclusion thus cannot be expected significantly to deter them. Imposition of the exclusionary sanction is not necessary meaningfully to inform judicial officers of their errors, and we cannot conclude that admitting evidence obtained pursuant to a warrant while at the same time declaring that the warrant was somehow defective will in any way reduce judicial officers' professional incentives to comply with the Fourth Amendment, encourage them to repeat their mistakes, or lead to the granting of all colorable warrant requests.

If exclusion of evidence obtained pursuant to a subsequently invalidated warrant is to have any deterrent effect, therefore, it must alter the behavior of individual law enforcement officers or the policies of their departments. . . .

[E]ven assuming that the rule effectively deters some police misconduct and provides incentives for the law enforcement profession as a whole to conduct itself in accordance with the Fourth Amendment, it cannot be expected, and should not be applied, to deter objectively reasonable law enforcement activity. . . .

This is particularly true, we believe, when an officer acting with objective good faith has obtained a search warrant from a judge or magistrate and acted within its scope. In most such cases, there is no police illegality and thus nothing to deter. It is the magistrate's responsibility to determine whether the officer's allegations establish probable cause and, if so, to issue a warrant comporting in form with the requirements of the Fourth Amendment. In the ordinary case, an officer cannot be expected to question the magistrate's probable-cause determination or his judgment that the form of the warrant is technically sufficient. . . . Penalizing the officer for the magistrate's error, rather than his own, cannot logically contribute to the deterrence of Fourth Amendment violations.

We conclude that the marginal or nonexistent benefits produced by suppressing evidence obtained in objectively reasonable reliance on a subsequently invalidated search warrant cannot justify the substantial costs of exclusion. We do not suggest, however, that exclusion is always inappropriate in cases where an officer has obtained a warrant and abided by its terms. . . .

Suppression therefore remains an appropriate remedy if the magistrate or judge in issuing a warrant was misled by information in an affidavit that the affiant knew was false or would have known was false except for his reckless disregard of the truth. . . .

When the principles we have enunciated today are applied to the facts of this case, it is apparent that the judgment of the Court of Appeals cannot stand. . . .

Accordingly, the judgment of the Court of Appeals is

Reversed.

Justice Blackmun, concurring . . . [omitted].

Justice Brennan, with whom Justice Marshall joins, dissenting. . . .

The majority ignores the fundamental constitutional importance of what is at stake here. While the machinery of law enforcement and indeed the nature of crime itself have changed dramatically since the Fourth Amendment became part of the Nation's fundamental law in 1791, what the Framers understood then remains true today—that the task of combatting crime and convicting the guilty will in every era seem of such critical and pressing concern that we may be lured by the temptations of expediency into forsaking our commitment to protecting individual liberty and privacy. It was for that very reason that the Framers of the Bill of Rights insisted that law enforcement efforts be permanently and unambiguously restricted in order to preserve personal freedoms. In the constitutional scheme they ordained, the sometimes unpopular task of ensuring that the government's enforcement efforts remain within the strict boundaries fixed by the Fourth Amendment was entrusted to the courts. . . .

At the outset, the Court suggests that society has been asked to pay a high price—in terms either of setting guilty persons free or of impeding the proper functioning of trials—as a result of excluding relevant physical evidence in cases where the police, in conducting searches and seizing evidence, have made only an "objectively reasonable" mistake concerning the constitutionality of their actions. . . . But what evidence is there to support such a claim?

Significantly, the Court points to none, and, indeed, as the Court acknowledges, . . . recent studies have demonstrated that the "costs" of the exclusionary rule—calculated in terms of dropped prosecutions and lost convictions are quite low. Contrary to the claims of the rule's critics that exclusion leads to "the release of countless guilty criminals" . . . these studies have demonstrated that federal and state prosecutors very rarely drop cases because of potential search and seizure problems. . . .

When such faulty scales are used, it is little wonder that the balance tips in favor of restricting the application of the rule.

What then supports the Court's insistence that this evidence be admitted? Apparently, the Court's only answer is that even though the costs of exclusion are not very substantial, the potential deterrent effect in these circumstances is so marginal that exclusion cannot be justified. The key to the Court's conclusion in this respect is its belief that the prospective deterrent effect of the exclusionary rule operates only in those situations in which police officers, when deciding whether to go forward with some particular search, have reason to know that their planned conduct will violate the requirements of the Fourth Amendment. . . .

The flaw in the Court's argument, however, is that its logic captures only one comparatively minor element of the generally acknowledged deterrent purposes of the exclusionary rule. To be sure, the rule operates to some extent to deter future misconduct by individual officers who have had evidence suppressed in their own cases. But what the Court overlooks is that the deterrence rationale for the rule is not designed to be, nor should it be thought of as, a form of "punishment" of individual police officers for their failures to obey the restraints imposed by the Fourth Amendment. . . . Instead, the chief deterrent function of the rule is its tendency to promote institutional compliance with Fourth Amendment requirements on the part of law enforcement agencies generally. . . .

After today's decision, however, that institutional incentive will be lost. Indeed, the Court's "reasonable mistake" exception to the exclusionary rule will tend to put a premium on police ignorance of the law. Armed with the assurance provided by today's decision that evidence will always be admissible whenever an officer has "reasonably" relied upon a warrant, police departments will be encouraged to train officers that if a warrant has simply been signed, it is reasonable, without more, to rely on it. . . .

Although the Court brushes these concerns aside, a host of grave consequences can be expected to result from its decision to carve this new exception out of the exclusionary rule. A chief consequence of today's decision will be to convey a clear and unambiguous message to magistrates that their decisions to issue warrants are now insulated from subsequent judicial review. Creation of this new exception for good faith reliance upon a warrant implicitly tells magistrates that they need not take much care in reviewing warrant applications, since their mistakes will from now on have virtually no consequence: If their decision to issue a warrant was correct, the evidence will be admitted; if their decision was incorrect but the police relied in good faith on the warrant, the evidence will also be admitted. Inevitably, the care and attention devoted to such an inconsequential chore will dwindle. . . .

JUSTICE STEVENS dissenting . . . [omitted].

C. SEARCH INCIDENT TO ARREST

Chimel v. *California* 395 U.S. 752, 89 S.Ct. 2034, 23 L.Ed. 2d 685 (1969)

http://caselaw.findlaw.com/us-supreme-court/395/752.html

Possessing an arrest warrant but no search warrant, police arrested Ted Chimel in his home for burglary of a coin shop. They conducted a search of his entire three-bedroom house, including the attic, the garage, a small workshop, and various drawers. Certain items found through the search were admitted into evidence against him and he was convicted. Both the California Court of Appeal and the California Supreme Court affirmed the conviction, holding that although the officers had no search warrant, the search of the defendant's house had been justified on the ground that it had been incident to a valid arrest. Majority: Stewart, Brennan, Douglas, Fortas, Harlan, Marshall, Warren. Dissenting: White, Black.

MR. JUSTICE STEWART delivered the opinion of the Court.

This case raises basic questions concerning the permissible scope under the Fourth Amendment of a search incident to a lawful arrest. . . .

When an arrest is made, it is reasonable for the arresting officer to search the person arrested in order to remove any weapons that the latter might seek to use in order to resist or effect his escape. Otherwise, the officer's safety might well be endangered, and the arrest itself frustrated. In addition, it is entirely reasonable for the arresting officer to search for and seize any evidence on the arrestee's person in order to prevent its concealment or destruction. And the area into which an arrestee might reach in order to grab a weapon or evidentiary items must, of course, be governed by a like rule. A gun on a table or in a drawer in front of one who is arrested can be as dangerous to the arresting officer as one concealed in the clothing of the person arrested. There is ample justification, therefore, for a search of the arrestee's person and the area "within his immediate control"—construing that phrase to mean the area from within which he might gain possession of a weapon or destructible evidence.

There is no comparable justification, however, for routinely searching through all the desk drawers or other closed or concealed areas in that room itself. Such searches, in the absence of well recognized exceptions, may be made only under the authority of a search warrant. The "adherence to judicial processes" mandated by the Fourth Amendment requires no less. . . .

It is argued in the present case that it is "reasonable" to search a man's house when he is arrested in it. But that argument is founded on little more than a subjective view regarding the acceptability of certain sorts of police conduct, and not on considerations relevant to Fourth Amendment interests. Under such an unconfined analysis, Fourth Amendment protection in this area would approach the evaporation point. It is not easy to explain why, for instance, it is less subjectively "reasonable" to search a man's house when he is arrested on his front lawn—or just down the street—than it is when he happens to be in the house at the time of arrest. . . .

Application of sound Fourth Amendment principles to the facts of this case produces a clear result. The search here went far beyond the petitioner's person and the area from within which he might have obtained either a weapon or something that could have been used as evidence against him. There was no constitutional justification, in the absence of a search warrant, for extending the search beyond that area. The scope of the search was, therefore, "unreasonable" under the Fourth and Fourteenth Amendments, and the petitioner's conviction cannot stand.

Reversed.

MR. JUSTICE HARLAN, concurring . . . [omitted].

MR. JUSTICE WHITE, with whom MR. JUSTICE BLACK joins, dissenting. . . .

The case provides a good illustration of my point that it is unreasonable to require police to leave the scene of an arrest in order to obtain a search warrant when they already have probable cause to search and there is a clear danger that the items for which they may reasonably search will be removed before they return with a warrant. Petitioner was arrested in his home after an arrest whose validity will be explored below, but which I will now assume was valid. There was doubtless probable cause not only to arrest petitioner, but also to search his house. He had obliquely admitted, both to a neighbor and to the owner of the burglarized store, that he had committed the burglary. In light of this, and the fact that the neighbor had seen other admittedly stolen property in petitioner's house, there was surely probable cause on which a warrant could have [been] issued to search the house for the stolen coins. Moreover, had the police simply arrested petitioner, taken him off to the station house, and later returned with a warrant, it seems very likely that petitioner's wife, who in view of petitioner's generally garrulous nature must have known of the robbery, would have removed the coins. For the police to search the house while the evidence they had probable cause to search out and seize was still there cannot be considered unreasonable. . . .

If circumstances so often require the warrantless arrest that the law generally permits it, the typical situation will find the arresting officers lawfully on the premises without arrest or search warrant. Like the majority, I would permit the police to search the person of a suspect and the area under his immediate control either to assure the safety of the officers or to prevent the destruction of evidence. And like the majority, I see nothing in the arrest alone furnishing probable cause for a search of any broader scope. However, whereas here the existence of probable cause is independently established and would justify a warrant for a broader search for evidence, I would follow past cases and permit such a search to be carried out without a warrant, since the fact of arrest supplies an exigent circumstance justifying police action before the evidence can be removed, and also alerts the suspect to the fact of the search so that he can immediately seek judicial determination of probable cause in an adversary proceeding, and appropriate redress. . . .

Riley v. *California* and *United States* v. *Wurie* 573 U.S. 782, 134 S.Ct. 999, 187 L.Ed. 2d 847 (2014)

http://caselaw.findlaw.com/us-supreme-court/13-132-nr1.html

In the first case, David Riley was stopped in San Diego for driving with expired registration tags. Pursuant to department policy after also learning that his driver's license had been suspended, police impounded his vehicle and conducted an inventory during which concealed and loaded firearms were found. In a search of Riley incident to arrest police found a smartphone as well as evidence linking him to a street gang. Noticing what seemed to be other gang-related indications in the phone's contents, the officer gave the phone to another officer who specialized in gang activity. Information discovered on the phone then tied Riley to a shooting for which he was ultimately convicted and sentenced to 15 years to life imprisonment. Over a claim that the warrantless search of his phone violated the Fourth Amendment, the California Court of Appeal affirmed the conviction and the Supreme Court of California denied review.

In the second case, Brima Wurie was arrested after police in Boston observed him participate in an apparent drug sale. At the police station, the officers seized a flip cell phone from Wurie's person and noticed that the phone was receiving multiple calls from a source identified as "my house" on its external screen. The officers opened the phone, accessed its call log, identified the number associated with the "my house" label, and traced that number to what they suspected was Wurie's apartment. They secured a search warrant for the apartment and found drugs, a firearm and ammunition, and cash. Wurie was then charged with drug and firearm offenses. He moved to suppress the evidence obtained from the search of the apartment. The U.S. District Court for Massachusetts denied the motion, and Wurie was convicted and sentenced to 262 months in prison. The U.S. Court of Appeals for the First Circuit reversed the denial of the motion to suppress and vacated the relevant convictions. Majority: Roberts, Alito, Breyer, Ginsburg, Kagan, Kennedy, Scalia, Sotomayor, Thomas.

Chief Justice Roberts delivered the opinion of the Court.

These two cases raise a common question: whether the police may, without a warrant, search digital information on a cell phone seized from an individual who has been arrested. . . .

The two cases before us concern the reasonableness of a warrantless search incident to a lawful arrest. In 1914, this Court first acknowledged in dictum "the right on the part of the Government, always recognized under English and American law, to search the person of the accused when legally arrested to discover and seize the fruits or evidences of crime." Since that time, it has been well accepted that such a search constitutes an exception to the warrant requirement. Indeed, the label "exception" is something of a misnomer in this context, as warrantless searches incident to arrest occur with far greater frequency than searches conducted pursuant to a warrant. . . .

Three related precedents set forth the rules governing such searches:

The first, *Chimel* v. *California*, laid the groundwork for most of the existing search incident to arrest doctrine. . . . The Court crafted the following rule for assessing the reasonableness of a search incident to arrest: "When an arrest is made, it is reasonable for the arresting officer to search the person arrested in order to remove any weapons that the latter might seek to use in order to resist arrest or effect his escape. Otherwise, the officer's safety might well be endangered, and the arrest itself frustrated. In addition, it is entirely reasonable for the arresting officer to search for and seize any evidence on the arrestee's person in order to prevent its concealment or destruction." . . .

Four years later, in *United States* v. *Robinson*, the Court applied the Chimel analysis in the context of a search of the arrestee's person. A police officer had arrested Robinson for driving with a revoked license. The officer conducted a patdown search and felt an object that he could not identify in Robinson's coat pocket. He removed the object, which turned out to be a crumpled cigarette package, and opened it. Inside were 14 capsules of heroin.

The Court of Appeals concluded that the search was unreasonable because Robinson was unlikely to have evidence of the crime of arrest on his person, and because it believed that extracting the cigarette package and opening it could not be justified as part of a protective search for weapons. This Court reversed, rejecting the notion that "case-by-case adjudication" was required to determine "whether or not there was present one of the reasons supporting the authority for a search of the person incident to a lawful arrest." As the Court explained, ". . . a custodial arrest of a suspect based on probable cause is a reasonable intrusion under the Fourth Amendment; that intrusion being lawful, a search incident to the arrest requires no additional justification."

The Court thus concluded that the search of Robinson was reasonable even though there was no concern about the loss of evidence, and the arresting officer had no specific concern that Robinson might be armed. In doing so, the Court did not draw a line between a search of Robinson's person and a further examination of the cigarette pack found during that search. . . .

The search incident to arrest trilogy concludes with [*Arizona* v.] *Gant*, which analyzed searches of an arrestee's vehicle. *Gant*, like *Robinson*, recognized that the Chimel concerns for officer safety and evidence preservation underlie the search incident to arrest exception. As a result, the Court concluded that *Chimel* could authorize police to search a vehicle "only when the arrestee is unsecured and within reaching distance of the passenger compartment at the time of the search." *Gant* added, however, an independent exception for a warrantless search of a vehicle's passenger compartment "when it is 'reasonable to believe evidence relevant to the crime of arrest might be found in the vehicle.'" That exception stems not from *Chimel*, the Court explained, but from "circumstances unique to the vehicle context."

These cases require us to decide how the search incident to arrest doctrine applies to modern cell phones, which are now such a pervasive and insistent part of daily life that the proverbial visitor from Mars might conclude they were an important feature of human anatomy. A smart phone of the sort taken from Riley was unheard of ten years ago; a significant majority of American adults now own such phones. Even less sophisticated phones like Wurie's, which have already faded in popularity since Wurie was arrested in 2007, have been around for less than 15 years. Both phones are based on technology nearly inconceivable just a few decades ago, when *Chimel* and *Robinson* were decided.

Absent more precise guidance from the founding era, we generally determine whether to exempt a given type of search from the warrant requirement "by assessing, on the one hand, the degree to which it intrudes upon an individual's privacy and, on the other, the degree to which it is needed for the promotion of legitimate governmental interests." Such a balancing of interests supported the search incident to arrest exception in *Robinson*, and a mechanical application of *Robinson* might well support the warrantless searches at issue here.

But while *Robinson's* categorical rule strikes the appropriate balance in the context of physical objects, neither of its rationales has much force with respect to digital content on cell phones. On the government interest side, *Robinson* concluded that the two risks identified in Chimel—harm to officers and destruction of evidence—are present in all custodial arrests. There are no comparable risks when the search is of digital data. In addition, *Robinson* regarded any privacy interests retained by an individual after arrest as significantly diminished by the fact of the arrest itself. Cell phones, however, place vast quantities of personal information literally in the hands of individuals. A search of the information on a cell phone bears little resemblance to the type of brief physical search considered in *Robinson*.

We therefore decline to extend *Robinson* to searches of data on cell phones, and hold instead that officers must generally secure a warrant before conducting such a search.

We first consider each *Chimel* concern in turn. . . . Rather than requiring the "case-by-case adjudication" that *Robinson* rejected, we ask instead whether application of the search incident to arrest doctrine to this particular category of effects would "untether the rule from the justifications underlying the *Chimel* exception."

Digital data stored on a cell phone cannot itself be used as a weapon to harm an arresting officer or to effectuate the arrestee's escape. Law enforcement officers remain free to examine the physical aspects of a phone to ensure that it will not be used as a weapon. . . . Perhaps the same might have been said of the cigarette pack seized from Robinson's pocket. Once an officer gained control of the pack, it was unlikely that Robinson could have accessed the pack's contents. But unknown physical objects may always pose risks, no matter how slight, during the tense atmosphere of a custodial arrest. . . . No such unknowns exist with respect to digital data.

The United States and California both suggest that a search of cell phone data might help ensure officer safety in more indirect ways, for example by alerting officers that confederates of the arrestee are headed to the scene. There is undoubtedly a strong government interest in warning officers about such possibilities, but neither the United States nor California offers evidence to suggest that their concerns are based on actual experience. . . .

The United States and California focus primarily on the second *Chimel* rationale: preventing the destruction of evidence. Both *Riley* and *Wurie* concede that officers could have seized and secured their cell phones to prevent destruction of evidence while seeking a warrant. And once law enforcement officers have secured a cell phone, there is no longer any risk that the arrestee himself will be able to delete incriminating data from the phone. The United States and California argue that information on a cell phone may nevertheless be vulnerable to two types of evidence destruction unique to digital data—remote wiping and data encryption. . . . This can happen when a third party sends a remote signal or when a phone is preprogrammed to delete data upon entering or leaving certain geographic areas. . . .

We have also been given little reason to believe that either problem is prevalent. . . . In any event, as to remote wiping, law enforcement is not without specific means to address the threat. . . .

The search incident to arrest exception rests not only on the heightened government interests at stake in a volatile arrest situation, but also on an arrestee's reduced privacy interests upon being taken into police custody. *Robinson* focused primarily on the first of those rationales. . . . Put simply, a patdown of Robinson's clothing and an inspection of the cigarette pack found in his pocket constituted only minor additional intrusions compared to the substantial government authority exercised in taking Robinson into custody. . . .

Robinson is the only decision from this Court applying *Chimel* to a search of the contents of an item found on an arrestee's person. . . . The United States asserts that a search of all data stored on a cell phone is "materially indistinguishable" from searches of these sorts of physical items. That is like saying a ride on horseback is materially indistinguishable from a flight to the moon. Both are ways of getting from point A to point B, but little else justifies lumping them together. Modern cell phones, as a category, implicate privacy concerns far beyond those implicated by the search of a cigarette pack, a wallet, or a purse. A conclusion that inspecting the contents of an arrestee's pockets works no substantial additional intrusion on privacy beyond the arrest itself may make sense as applied to physical items, but any extension of that reasoning to digital data has to rest on its own bottom.

Cell phones differ in both a quantitative and a qualitative sense from other objects that might be kept on an arrestee's person. The term "cell phone" is itself misleading shorthand; many of these devices are in fact minicomputers that also happen to have the capacity to be used as a telephone. They could just as easily be called cameras, video players, rolodexes, calendars, tape recorders, libraries, diaries, albums, televisions, maps, or newspapers.

One of the most notable distinguishing features of modern cell phones is their immense storage capacity. Before cell phones, a search of a person was limited by physical realities and tended as a general matter to constitute only a narrow intrusion on privacy. Most people cannot lug around every piece of mail they have received for the past several months, every picture they have taken, or every book or article they have read—nor would they have any reason to attempt to do so. But the possible intrusion on privacy is not physically limited in the same way when it comes to cell phones. . . .

The storage capacity of cell phones has several interrelated consequences for privacy. First, a cell phone collects in one place many distinct types of information—an address, a note, a prescription, a bank statement, a video—that reveal much more in combination than any isolated record. Second, a cell phone's capacity allows even just one type of information to convey far more than previously possible. The sum of an individual's private life can be reconstructed through a thousand photographs labeled with dates, locations, and descriptions; the same cannot be said of a photograph or two of loved ones tucked into a wallet. Third, the data on a phone can date back to the purchase of the phone, or even earlier. A person might carry in his pocket a slip of paper reminding him to call Mr. Jones; he would not carry a record of all his communications with Mr. Jones for the past several months, as would routinely be kept on a phone. Finally, there is an element of pervasiveness that characterizes cell phones but not physical records. Prior to the digital age, people did not typically carry a cache of sensitive personal information with them as they went about their day. Now it is the person who is not carrying a cell phone, with all that it contains, who is the exception. . . . A decade ago police officers searching an arrestee might have occasionally stumbled across a highly personal item such as a diary. But those discoveries were likely to be few and far between. Today, by contrast, it is no exaggeration to say that many of the more than 90% of American adults who own a cell phone keep on their person a digital record of nearly every aspect of their lives—from the mundane to the intimate. Allowing the police to scrutinize such records on a routine basis is quite different from allowing them to search a personal item or two in the occasional case.

Although the data stored on a cell phone is distinguished from physical records by quantity alone, certain types of data are also qualitatively different. An Internet search and browsing history, for example, can be found on an Internet-enabled phone and could reveal an individual's private interests or concerns . . . Data on a cell phone can also reveal where a person has been. Historic location information is a standard feature on many smart phones and can reconstruct someone's specific movements down to the minute, not only around town but also within a particular building. . . .

To further complicate the scope of the privacy interests at stake, the data a user views on many modern cell phones may not in fact be stored on the device itself. Treating a cell phone as a container whose contents may be searched incident to an arrest is a bit strained as an initial matter. . . . But the analogy crumbles entirely when a cell phone is used to access data located elsewhere, at the tap of a screen. That is what cell phones, with increasing frequency, are designed to do by taking advantage of "cloud computing." . . .

We cannot deny that our decision today will have an impact on the ability of law enforcement to combat crime. Cell phones have become important tools in facilitating coordination and communication among members of criminal enterprises, and can provide valuable incriminating information about dangerous criminals. Privacy comes at a cost.

Our holding, of course, is not that the information on a cell phone is immune from search; it is instead that a warrant is generally required before such a search, even when a cell phone is seized incident to arrest. . . . Moreover, even though the search incident to arrest exception does not apply to cell phones, other case-specific exceptions may still justify a warrantless search of a particular phone. "One well-recognized exception applies when 'the exigencies of the situation' make the needs of law enforcement so compelling that [a] warrantless search is objectively reasonable under the Fourth Amendment." Such exigencies could include the need to prevent the imminent destruction of evidence in individual cases, to pursue a fleeing suspect, and to assist persons who are seriously injured or are threatened with imminent injury. . . .

Modern cell phones are not just another technological convenience. With all they contain and all they may reveal, they hold for many Americans "the privacies of life." The fact that technology now allows an individual to carry such information in his hand does not make the information any less worthy of the protection for which the Founders fought. Our answer to the question of what police must do before searching a cell phone seized incident to an arrest is accordingly simple—get a warrant.

We reverse the judgment of the California Court of Appeal . . . and remand the case for further proceedings not inconsistent with this opinion. We affirm the judgment of the First Circuit. . . .

It is so ordered.

JUSTICE ALITO, concurring . . . [omitted].

D. Automobile Searches

California v. *Acevedo*
500 U.S. 565, 111 S.Ct. 1982, 114 L.Ed. 2d 619 (1991)

http://caselaw.findlaw.com/us-supreme-court/500/565.html

Police in Santa Ana, California, observed Charles Steven Acevedo leave an apartment carrying a brown paper bag. The bag was the size of one of several wrapped marijuana packages which they knew had been delivered to the apartment earlier in the day. Acevedo placed the bag in the trunk of his car. As he drove away, police stopped the car, opened the trunk and the bag, and found marijuana. Acevedo pleaded guilty to possession of marijuana for sale after his motion to suppress the evidence was denied. However, the California Court of Appeal for the Fourth Appellate District reversed, holding that while police had probable cause to believe the bag contained marijuana, they lacked probable cause to suspect the car itself. Consequently, a warrant was necessary before police could lawfully open the bag. The Supreme Court of California denied review. Majority: Blackmun, Rehnquist, O'Connor, Scalia, Kennedy, Souter. Dissenting: White, Stevens, Marshall.

Justice Blackmun delivered the opinion of the Court.

This case requires us once again to consider the so-called "automobile exception" to the warrant requirement of the Fourth Amendment and its application to the search of a closed container in the trunk of a car. . . .

In *Carroll [v. United States* (1925)*]*, this Court established an exception to the warrant requirement for moving vehicles, for it recognized

> a necessary difference between a search of a store, dwelling house or other structure in respect of which a proper official warrant readily may be obtained, and a search of a ship, motor boat, wagon or automobile, for contraband goods, where it is not practicable to secure a warrant because the vehicle can be quickly moved out of the locality or jurisdiction in which the warrant must be sought.

It therefore held that a warrantless search of an automobile based upon probable cause to believe that the vehicle contained evidence of crime in the light of an exigency arising out of the likely disappearance of the vehicle did not contravene the Warrant Clause of the Fourth Amendment. . . .

In *United States* v. *Ross*, decided in 1982, we held that a warrantless search of an automobile under the Carroll doctrine could include a search of a container or package found inside the car when such a search was supported by probable cause. The warrantless search of Ross' car occurred after an informant told the police that he had seen Ross complete a drug transaction using drugs stored in the trunk of his car. The police stopped the car, searched it, and discovered in the trunk a brown paper bag containing drugs. We decided that the search of Ross's car was not unreasonable under the Fourth Amendment: "The scope of a warrantless search based on probable cause is no narrower—and no broader—than the scope of a search authorized by a warrant supported by probable cause." . . .

In addition to this clarification, *Ross* distinguished the Carroll doctrine from the separate rule that governed the search of closed containers. The Court had announced this separate rule, unique to luggage and other closed packages, bags, and containers, in *United States* v. *Chadwick* (1977). In *Chadwick*, federal narcotics agents had probable cause to believe that a 200-pound double-locked footlocker contained marijuana. The agents tracked the locker as the defendants removed it from a train and carried it through the station to a waiting car. As soon as the defendants lifted the locker into the trunk of the car, the agents arrested them, seized the locker, and searched it. In this Court, the United States did not contend that the locker's brief contact with the automobile's trunk sufficed to make the Carroll doctrine applicable. Rather, the United States urged that the search of movable luggage could be considered analogous to the search of an automobile.

The Court rejected this argument because, it reasoned, a person expects more privacy in his luggage and personal effects than he does in his automobile. Moreover, it concluded that as "may often not be the case when automobiles are seized," secure storage facilities are usually available when the police seize luggage.

In *Arkansas* v. *Sanders* (1979), the Court extended *Chadwick's* rule to apply to a suitcase actually being transported in the trunk of a car. . . .

In *Ross*, the Court endeavored to distinguish between *Carroll*, which governed the Ross automobile search, and *Chadwick*, which governed the Sanders automobile search. It held that the Carroll doctrine covered searches of automobiles when the police had probable cause to search an entire vehicle but that the Chadwick doctrine governed searches of luggage when the officers had probable cause to search only a container within the vehicle. Thus, in a Ross situation, the police could conduct a reasonable search under the Fourth Amendment without obtaining a warrant, whereas in a Sanders situation, the police had to obtain a warrant before they searched. . . . *Ross* took the critical step of saying that closed containers in cars could be searched without a warrant because of their presence within the automobile. Despite the protection that *Sanders* purported to extend to closed containers, the privacy interest in those closed containers yielded to the broad scope of an automobile search. . . .

We now agree that a container found after a general search of the automobile and a container found in a car after a limited search for the container are equally easy for the police to store and for the suspect to hide or destroy. In fact, we see no principled distinction in terms of either the privacy expectation or the exigent circumstances between the paper bag found by the police in *Ross* and the paper bag found by the police here. Furthermore, by attempting to distinguish between a container for which the police are specifically searching and a container which they come across in a car, we have provided only minimal protection for privacy and have impeded effective law enforcement. . . .

At the moment when officers stop an automobile, it may be less than clear whether they suspect with a high degree of certainty that the vehicle contains drugs in a bag or simply contains drugs. If the police know that they may open a bag only if they are actually searching the entire car, they may search more extensively than they otherwise would in order to establish the general probable cause required by *Ross*. . . .

To the extent that the Chadwick-Sanders rule protects privacy, its protection is minimal. Law enforcement officers may seize a container and hold it until they obtain a search warrant. . . . And the police often will be able to search containers without a warrant, despite the Chadwick-Sanders rule, as a search incident to a lawful arrest.

Finally, the search of a paper bag intrudes far less on individual privacy than does the incursion sanctioned long ago in *Carroll*. In that case, prohibition agents slashed the upholstery of the automobile. This Court nonetheless found their search to be reasonable under the Fourth Amendment. If destroying the interior of an automobile is not unreasonable, we cannot conclude that looking inside a closed container is. In light of the minimal protection to privacy afforded by the Chadwick-Sanders rule, and our serious doubt whether that rule substantially serves privacy interests, we now hold that the Fourth Amendment does not compel separate treatment for an automobile search that extends only to a container within the vehicle. . . .

Until today, this Court has drawn a curious line between the search of an automobile that coincidentally turns up a container and the search of a container that coincidentally turns up in an automobile. The protections of the Fourth Amendment must not turn on such coincidences. We therefore interpret *Carroll* as providing one rule to govern all automobile searches. The police may search an automobile and the containers within it where they have probable cause to believe contraband or evidence is contained.

The judgment of the California Court of Appeal is reversed and the case is remanded to that court for further proceedings not inconsistent with this opinion.

It is so ordered.

JUSTICE SCALIA, concurring . . . [omitted].

JUSTICE WHITE, dissenting . . . [omitted].

JUSTICE STEVENS, with whom JUSTICE MARSHALL joins, dissenting. . . .

We held in *Ross* that "the scope of the warrantless search authorized by [the automobile] exception is no broader and no narrower than a magistrate could legitimately authorize by warrant." The inherent mobility of the vehicle justified the immediate search without a warrant, but did not affect the scope of the search. Thus, the search could encompass containers, which might or might not conceal the object of the search, as well as the remainder of the vehicle. . . .

We explained that, in such instances, "prohibiting police from opening immediately a container in which the object of the search is most likely to be found and instead forcing them first to comb the entire vehicle would actually exacerbate the intrusion on privacy interests." . . .

These concerns that justified our holding in *Ross* are not implicated in cases like *Chadwick* and *Sanders* in which the police have probable cause to search a particular container rather than the entire vehicle. . . . *Chadwick* and *Sanders* had not created a special rule for container searches, but rather had merely applied the cardinal principle that warrantless searches are per se unreasonable unless justified by an exception to the general rule. *Ross* dealt with the scope of the automobile exception; *Chadwick* and *Sanders* were cases in which the exception simply did not apply. . . .

To the extent there was any "anomaly" in our prior jurisprudence, the Court has "cured" it at the expense of creating a more serious paradox. For, surely it is anomalous to prohibit a search of a briefcase while the owner is carrying it exposed on a public street yet to permit a search once the owner has placed the briefcase in the locked trunk of his car. . . .

Under the Court's holding today, the privacy interest that protects the contents of a suitcase or a briefcase from a warrantless search when it is in public view simply vanishes when its owner climbs into a taxicab. Unquestionably the rejection of the Sanders line of cases by today's decision will result in a significant loss of individual privacy. . . .

Even if the warrant requirement does inconvenience the police to some extent, that fact does not distinguish this constitutional requirement from any other procedural protection secured by the Bill of Rights. It is merely a part of the price that our society must pay in order to preserve its freedom. . . .

E. ELECTRONIC SURVEILLANCE

Olmstead v. *United States*
277 U.S. 438, 48 S.Ct. 564, 72 L.Ed. 944 (1928)

http://caselaw.findlaw.com/us-supreme-court/277/438.html

Roy Olmstead and others were charged and convicted of conspiring to violate the national Prohibition Act. Evidence proving the conspiracy had been obtained by four federal agents who tapped the telephone lines of several of the defendants, without, however, committing any trespass on their property. A statute of the state of Washington made it a misdemeanor to "intercept, read or in any way interrupt or delay the sending of a message over any telegraph or telephone line. . . ." Majority: Taft, McReynolds, Sanford, Sutherland, Van Devanter. Dissenting: Brandeis, Butler, Holmes, Stone.

Mr. Chief Justice Taft delivered the opinion of the Court. . . .

The well-known historical importance of the Fourth Amendment, directed against general warrants and writs of assistance, was to prevent the use of governmental force to search a man's house, his person, his papers and his effects, and to prevent their seizure against his will. . . .

The amendment itself shows that the search is to be of material things—the person, the house, his papers, or his effects. The description of the warrant necessary to make the proceeding lawful is that it must specify the place to be searched and the person or things to be seized. . . . The language of the amendment cannot be extended and expanded to include telephone wires, reaching to the whole world from the defendant's house or office. The intervening wires are not part of his house or office, any more than are the highways along which they are stretched. . . .

Congress may, of course, protect the secrecy of telephone messages by making them, when intercepted, inadmissible in evidence in federal criminal trials, by direct legislation, and thus depart from the common law of evidence. But the courts may not adopt such a policy by attributing an enlarged and unusual meaning to the Fourth Amendment. The reasonable view is that one who installs in his house a telephone instrument with connecting wires intends to project his voice to those quite outside, and that the wires beyond his house, and messages while passing over them, are not within the protection of the Fourth Amendment. Here those who intercepted the projected voices were not in the house of either party to the conversation.

Neither the cases we have cited nor any of the many federal decisions brought to our attention hold the Fourth Amendment to have been violated as against a defendant, unless there has been an official search and seizure of his person or such a seizure of his papers or his tangible material effects or an actual physical invasion of his house "or curtilage" for the purpose of making a seizure.

We think, therefore, that the wire tapping here disclosed did not amount to a search or seizure within the meaning of the Fourth Amendment. . . .

Our general experience shows that much evidence has always been receivable, although not obtained by conformity to the highest ethics. The history of criminal trials shows numerous cases of prosecutions of oath bound conspiracies for murder, robbery, and other crimes, where officers of the law have disguised themselves and joined the organizations, taken the oaths, and given themselves every appearance of active members engaged in the promotion of crime for the purpose of securing evidence. Evidence secured by such means has always been received.

A standard which would forbid the reception of evidence, if obtained by other than nice ethical conduct by government officials, would make society suffer and give criminals greater immunity than has been known heretofore. In the absence of controlling legislation by Congress, those who realize the difficulties in bringing offenders to justice may well deem it wise that the exclusion of evidence should be confined to cases where rights under the Constitution would be violated by admitting it. . . .

Affirmed.

Mr. Justice Holmes, dissenting . . . [omitted].

Mr. Justice Brandeis, dissenting. . . .

"We must never forget," said Mr. Chief Justice Marshall in *McCulloch* v. *Maryland*, "that it is a *constitution* we are expounding." Since then, this Court has repeatedly sustained the exercise of power by Congress, under various clauses of that instrument, over objects of which the Fathers could not have dreamed. . . . We have likewise held that general limitations on the powers of Government, like those embodied in the due process clauses of the Fifth and Fourteenth Amendments, do not forbid the United States or the States from meeting modern conditions by regulations which "a century ago, or even half a century ago, probably would have been rejected as arbitrary and oppressive." . . . Clauses guaranteeing to the individual protection against specific abuses of power, must have a similar capacity of adaptation to a changing world. . . .

When the Fourth and Fifth Amendments were adopted, . . . [f]orce and violence were then the only means known to man by which a Government could directly effect self-incrimination. It could compel the individual to testify—a compulsion effected, if need be, by torture. It could secure possession of his papers and other articles incident to his private life—a seizure effected, if need be, by breaking and entry. Protection against such invasion of "the sanctities of a man's home and the privacies of life" was provided in the Fourth and Fifth Amendments, by specific language. But "time works changes, brings into existence new conditions and purposes." Subtler and more far-reaching means of invading privacy have become available to the government. Discovery and invention have made it possible for the government, by means far more effective than stretching upon the rack, to obtain disclosure in court of what is whispered in the closet.

Moreover, "in the application of a constitution, our contemplation cannot be only of what has been, but of what may be." The progress of science in furnishing the government with means of espionage is not likely to stop with wire-tapping. Ways may some day be developed by which the government, without removing papers from secret drawers, can reproduce them in court, and by which it will be enabled to expose to a jury the most intimate occurrences of the home. Advances in the psychic and related sciences may bring means of exploring unexpressed beliefs, thoughts and emotions.

. . . [C]an it be that the Constitution affords no protection against such invasions of individual security? . . .

The makers of our Constitution undertook to secure conditions favorable to the pursuit of happiness. They recognized the significance of man's spiritual nature, of his feelings and of his intellect. They knew that only a part of the pain, pleasure and satisfactions of life are to be found in material things. They sought to protect Americans in their beliefs, their thoughts, their emotions and their sensations. They conferred, as against the Government, the right to be let alone—the most comprehensive of rights and the right most valued by civilized men. To protect that right, every unjustifiable intrusion by the Government upon the privacy of the individual, whatever the means employed, must be deemed a violation of the Fourth Amendment. And the use, as evidence in a criminal proceeding, of facts ascertained by such intrusion must be deemed a violation of the Fifth.

Applying to the Fourth and Fifth Amendments the established rule of construction, the defendant's objections to the evidence obtained by a wire-tapping must, in my opinion, be sustained. It is, of course, immaterial where the physical connection with the telephone wires leading into the defendants' premises was made. And it is also immaterial that the intrusion was in aid of law enforcement. Experience should teach us to be most on our guard to protect liberty when the government's purposes are beneficent. Men born to freedom are naturally alert to repel invasion of their liberty by evil-minded rulers. The greatest dangers to liberty lurk in insidious encroachment by men of zeal, well-meaning, but without understanding. . . .

MR. JUSTICE BUTLER, dissenting . . . [omitted].
MR. JUSTICE STONE, dissenting . . . [omitted].

Katz v. *United States*
389 U.S. 347, 88 S.Ct. 507, 19 L.Ed. 2d 576 (1967)

http://caselaw.findlaw.com/us-supreme-court/389/347.html

Charles Katz was convicted of transmitting wagering information by telephone from Los Angeles to Miami and Boston in violation of a federal statute. At the trial, the government was permitted to introduce evidence gathered from attaching an electronic listening device to the outside of a public telephone booth from which he placed his calls. The Supreme Court granted certiorari to determine if the recordings had been obtained in violation of the Fourth Amendment. Pay particular attention to the exchange between Justices Douglas and White that anticipates the issue in *U.S. v. U.S. District Court* (1972), reprinted in Chapter Fifteen. Majority: Stewart, Brennan, Douglas, Fortas, Harlan, Warren, White. Dissenting: Black. Not participating: Marshall.

MR. JUSTICE STEWART delivered the opinion of the Court. . . .

The petitioner has strenuously argued that the booth was a "constitutionally protected area." The Government has maintained with equal vigor that it was not. But this effort to decide whether or not a given "area," viewed in the abstract, is "constitutionally protected" deflects attention from the problem presented by this case. For the Fourth Amendment protects people, not places. What a person knowingly exposes to the public, even in his own home or office, is not a subject of Fourth Amendment protection. . . . But what he seeks to preserve as private, even in an area accessible to the public, may be constitutionally protected. . . .

The Government stresses the fact that the telephone booth from which the petitioner made his calls was constructed partly of glass, so that he was as visible after he entered it as he would have been if he had remained outside. But what he sought to exclude when he entered the booth was not the intruding eye—it was the uninvited ear. He did not shed his right to do so simply because he made his calls from a place where he might be seen. No less than an individual in a business office, in a friend's apartment, or in a taxicab, a person in a telephone booth may rely upon the protection of the Fourth Amendment. One who occupies it, shuts the door behind him, and pays the toll that permits him to place a call, is surely entitled to assume that the words he utters into the mouthpiece will not be broadcast to the world. To read the Constitution more narrowly is to ignore the vital role that the public telephone has come to play in private communication.

The Government contends, however, that the activities of its agents in this case should not be tested by Fourth Amendment requirements, for the surveillance technique they employed involved no physical penetration of the telephone booth from which the petitioner placed his calls. It is true that the absence of such penetration was at one time thought to foreclose further Fourth Amendment inquiry. . . . Thus, although a closely divided Court supposed in *Olmstead* that surveillance without any trespass and without the seizure of any material object fell outside the ambit of the Constitution, we have since departed from the narrow view on which that decision rested. . . . Once this much is acknowledged, and once it is recognized that the Fourth Amendment protects people—and not simply "areas"—against unreasonable searches and seizures, it becomes clear that the reach of that Amendment cannot turn upon the presence or absence of a physical intrusion into any given enclosure.

. . . We conclude that the underpinnings of *Olmstead* . . . have been so eroded by our subsequent decisions that the "trespass" doctrine there enunciated can no longer be regarded as controlling. The Government's activities in electronically listening to and recording the petitioner's words violated the privacy upon which he justifiably relied while using the telephone booth and thus constituted a "search and seizure" within the meaning of the Fourth Amendment. The fact that the electronic device employed to achieve that end did not happen to penetrate the wall of the booth can have no constitutional significance.

The question remaining for decision, then, is whether the search and seizure conducted in this case complied with constitutional standards. In that regard, the Government's position is that its agents acted in an entirely defensible manner: They did not begin their electronic surveillance until investigation of the petitioner's activities had established a strong probability that he was using the telephone in question to transmit gambling information to persons in other States, in violation of federal law. Moreover, the surveillance was limited, both in scope and in duration, to the specific purpose of establishing the contents of the petitioner's unlawful telephonic communications. The agents confined their surveillance to the brief periods during which he used the telephone booth, and they took great care to overhear only the conversations of the petitioner himself.

Accepting this account of the Government's actions as accurate, it is clear that this surveillance was so narrowly circumscribed that a duly authorized magistrate, properly notified of the need for such investigation, specifically informed of the basis on which it was to proceed, and clearly apprised of the precise intrusion it would entail, could constitutionally have authorized, with appropriate safeguards, the very limited search and seizure that the Government asserts in fact took place. . . .

It is apparent that the agents in this case acted with restraint. Yet the inescapable fact is that this restraint was imposed by the agents themselves, not by a judicial officer. They were not required, before commencing the search, to present their estimate of probable cause for detached scrutiny by a neutral magistrate. They were not compelled, during the conduct of the search itself, to observe precise limits established in advance by a specific court order. Nor were they directed, after the search had been completed, to notify the authorizing magistrate in detail of all that had been seized. In the absence of such safeguards, this Court has never sustained a search upon the sole ground that officers reasonably expected to find evidence of a particular crime and voluntarily confined their activities to the least intrusive means consistent with that end. Searches conducted without warrants have been held unlawful "notwithstanding facts unquestionably showing probable cause," . . . for the Constitution requires "that the deliberate, impartial judgment of a judicial officer . . . be interposed between the citizen and the police. . . ." . . . [S]earches conducted outside the judicial process, without prior approval by judge or magistrate, are per se unreasonable under the Fourth Amendment—subject only to a few specifically established and well-delineated exceptions. . . .

The Government . . . argues that surveillance of a telephone booth should be exempted from the usual requirement of advance authorization by a magistrate upon a showing of probable cause. We cannot agree. Omission of such authorization "bypasses the safeguards provided by an objective predetermination of probable cause, and substitutes instead the far less reliable procedure of an after-the-event justification for the . . . search, too likely to be subtly influenced by the familiar shortcomings of hindsight judgment." . . .

And bypassing a neutral predetermination of the scope of a search leaves individuals secure from Fourth Amendment violations "only in the discretion of the police." . . .

The government agents here ignored "the procedure of antecedent justification . . . that is central to the Fourth Amendment," a procedure that we hold to be a constitutional precondition of the kind of electronic surveillance involved in this case. Because the surveillance here failed to meet that condition, and because it led to the petitioner's conviction, the judgment must be reversed.

It is so ordered.

Mr. Justice Douglas, with whom Mr. Justice Brennan joins, concurring.

While I join the opinion of the Court, I feel compelled to reply to the separate concurring opinion of my Brother White, which I view as a wholly unwarranted green light for the Executive Branch to resort to electronic eavesdropping without a warrant in cases which the Executive Branch itself labels "national security" matters.

Neither the President nor the Attorney General is a magistrate. In matters where they believe national security may be involved they are not detached, disinterested, and neutral as a court or magistrate must be. Under the separation of powers created by the Constitution, the Executive Branch is not supposed to be neutral and disinterested. Rather it should vigorously investigate and prevent breaches of national security and prosecute those who violate the pertinent federal laws. The President and Attorney General are properly interested parties, cast in the role of adversary, in national security cases. They may even be the intended victims of subversive action. Since spies and saboteurs are as entitled to the protection of the Fourth Amendment as suspected gamblers like petitioner, I cannot agree that where spies and saboteurs are involved adequate protection of Fourth Amendment rights is assured when the President and Attorney General assume both the position of adversary-and-prosecutor and disinterested, neutral magistrate. . . .

Mr. Justice Harlan, concurring. . . .

As the Court's opinion states, "the Fourth Amendment protects people, not places." The question, however, is what protection it affords to those people. Generally, as here, the answer to that question requires reference to a "place." My understanding of the rule that has emerged from prior decisions is that there is a twofold requirement, first that a person have exhibited an actual (subjective) expectation of privacy and, second, that the expectation be one that society is prepared to recognize as "reasonable." Thus a man's home is, for most purposes, a place where he expects privacy, but objects, activities, or statements that he exposes to the "plain view" of outsiders are not "protected" because no intention to keep them to himself has been exhibited. On the other hand, conversations in the open would not be protected against being overheard, for the expectation of privacy under the circumstances would be unreasonable.

Mr. Justice White, concurring.

In joining the Court's opinion, I note the Court's acknowledgment that there are circumstances in which it is reasonable to search without a warrant. In this connection . . . the Court points out that today's decision does not reach national security cases. Wiretapping to protect the security of the Nation has been authorized by successive Presidents. The present Administration would apparently save national security cases from restrictions against wiretapping. . . . We should not require the warrant procedure and the magistrate's judgment if the President of the United States or his chief legal officer, the Attorney General, had considered the requirements of national security and authorized electronic surveillance as reasonable.

Mr. Justice Black, dissenting. . . .

My basic objection is twofold: (1) I do not believe that the words of the Amendment will bear the meaning given them by today's decision, and (2) I do not believe that it is the proper role of this Court to rewrite the Amendment in order "to bring it into harmony with the times" and thus reach a result that many people believe to be desirable. . . .

The first clause protects "persons, houses, papers, and effects, against unreasonable searches and seizures. . . ." These words connote the idea of tangible things with size, form, and weight, things capable of being searched, seized, or both. The second clause of the Amendment still further establishes its Framers' purpose to limit its protection to tangible things by providing that no warrants shall issue but those "particularly describing the place to be searched and the person or things to be seized." A conversation overheard by eavesdropping whether by plain snooping or wiretapping, is not tangible and, under the normally accepted meanings of the words, can neither be searched nor seized. In addition the language of the second clause indicates that the Amendment refers to something not only tangible so it can be seized but to something already in existence so it can be described. Yet the Court's interpretation would have the Amendment apply to overhearing future conversations which by their very nature are nonexistent until they take place. . . . Rather than using language in a completely artificial way, I must conclude that the Fourth Amendment simply does not apply to eavesdropping.

Tapping telephone wires, of course, was an unknown possibility at the time the Fourth Amendment was adopted. . . . "In those days the eavesdropper listened by naked ear under the eaves of houses or their windows, or beyond their walls seeking out private discourse." . . . There can be no doubt that the Framers were aware of this practice, and if they had desired to outlaw or restrict the use of evidence obtained by eavesdropping, I believe that they would have used the appropriate language to do so in the Fourth Amendment. They certainly would not have left such a task to the ingenuity of language-stretching judges. . . . It was never meant for this Court to have such power, which in effect would make us a continuously functioning constitutional convention. . . .

United States v. *United States District Court*
407 U.S. 297, 92 S.Ct. 2125, 32 L.Ed. 2d 752 (1972)

http://caselaw.findlaw.com/us-supreme-court/407/297.html

(This case is reprinted in Chapter Fifteen; see the Table of Contents.)

United States v. *Jones*
565 U.S. 400, 132 S.Ct. 945, 181 L.Ed. 2d 911 (2012)

http://caselaw.findlaw.com/us-supreme-court/10-1259.html

In 2005, government agents obtained a search warrant permitting installation of a Global Positioning System (GPS) tracking device on a vehicle registered to Antoine Jones's spouse. The warrant authorized installation in the District of Columbia within 10 days, but agents installed the device on the 11th day and in Maryland. The government then tracked the vehicle's movements for 28 days. Searches based on the GPS data led to an indictment of Jones and others on drug trafficking charges. The U.S. District Court for the District of Columbia suppressed the GPS data obtained while the vehicle was parked at Jones's residence, but held the remaining data admissible because Jones had no reasonable expectation of privacy when the vehicle was on public streets. In 2010 the Court of Appeals for the District of Columbia Circuit reversed Jones's conviction, concluding that admission of the evidence obtained by warrantless use of the GPS device violated the Fourth Amendment. Majority: Scalia, Alito, Breyer, Ginsburg, Kennedy, Kagan, Roberts, Sotomayor, Thomas.

Justice Scalia delivered the opinion of the Court.

We decide whether the attachment of a Global-Positioning-System (GPS) tracking device to an individual's vehicle, and subsequent use of that device to monitor the vehicle's movements on public streets, constitutes a search or seizure within the meaning of the Fourth Amendment. . . .

It is beyond dispute that a vehicle is an "effect" as that term is used in the [Fourth] Amendment. We hold that the Government's installation of a GPS device on a target's vehicle, and its use of that device to monitor the vehicle's movements, constitutes a "search."

It is important to be clear about what occurred in this case: The Government physically occupied private property for the purpose of obtaining information. . . .

[O]ur Fourth Amendment jurisprudence was tied to common-law trespass, at least until the latter half of the 20th century.

Our later cases, of course, have deviated from that exclusively property-based approach. . . . [They] have applied the analysis of Justice Harlan's concurrence in [*Katz* v. *United States*], which said that a violation occurs when government officers violate a person's "reasonable expectation of privacy."

The Government contends that the Harlan standard shows that no search occurred here, since Jones had no "reasonable expectation of privacy" in the area of the Jeep accessed by Government agents (its underbody) and in the locations of the Jeep on the public roads, which were visible to all. But we need not address the Government's contentions, because Jones's Fourth Amendment rights do not rise or fall with the *Katz* formulation. At bottom, we must "assur[e] preservation of that degree of privacy against government that existed when the Fourth Amendment was adopted."

The Government contends that several of our post-*Katz* cases foreclose the conclusion that what occurred here constituted a search. It relies principally on two cases in which we rejected Fourth Amendment challenges to "beepers," electronic tracking devices that represent another form of electronic monitoring. The first case, *Knotts* [v. *United States*], upheld against Fourth Amendment challenge the use of a "beeper" that had been placed in a container of chloroform, allowing law enforcement to monitor the location of the container. We said that there had been no infringement of Knotts' reasonable expectation of privacy since the information obtained—the location of the automobile carrying the container on public roads, and the location of the off-loaded container in open fields near Knotts' cabin—had been voluntarily conveyed to the public. But as we have discussed, the *Katz* reasonable-expectation-of-privacy test has been added to, not substituted for, the common-law trespassory test. The holding in *Knotts* addressed only the former, since the latter was not at issue. The beeper had been placed in the container before it came into Knotts' possession, with the consent of the then-owner. Knotts did not challenge that installation, and we specifically declined to consider its effect on the Fourth Amendment analysis.

The second "beeper" case, *United States* v. *Karo*, does not suggest a different conclusion. There we addressed the question left open by *Knotts*, whether the installation of a beeper in a container amounted to a search or seizure. As in *Knotts*, at the time the beeper was installed the container belonged to a third party, and it did not come into possession of the defendant until later. Thus, the specific question we considered was whether the installation "with the consent of the original owner constitute[d] a search or seizure . . . when the container is delivered to a buyer having no knowledge of the presence of the beeper." We held not. The Government, we said, came into physical contact with the container only before it belonged to the defendant Karo; and the transfer of the container with the unmonitored beeper inside did not convey any information and thus did not invade Karo's privacy. That conclusion is perfectly consistent with the one we reach here. Karo accepted the container as it came to him, beeper and all, and was therefore not entitled to object to the beeper's presence, even though it was used to monitor the container's location. Jones, who possessed the Jeep at the time the Government trespassorily inserted the information-gathering device, is on much different footing. . . .

The concurrence faults our approach for "present[ing] particularly vexing problems" in cases that do not involve physical contact, such as those that involve the transmission of electronic signals. We entirely fail to understand that point. For unlike the concurrence, which would make *Katz* the exclusive test, we do not make trespass the exclusive test. Situations involving merely the transmission of electronic signals without trespass would remain subject to *Katz* analysis. . . .

The judgment of the Court of Appeals for the D.C. Circuit is affirmed.

It is so ordered.

JUSTICE ALITO, with whom JUSTICE GINSBURG, JUSTICE BREYER, and JUSTICE KAGAN join, concurring in the judgment.

This case requires us to apply the Fourth Amendment's prohibition of unreasonable searches and seizures to a 21st-century surveillance technique, the use of a Global Positioning System (GPS) device to monitor a vehicle's movements for an extended period of time. Ironically, the Court has chosen to decide this case based on 18th-century tort law. By attaching a small GPS device to the underside of the vehicle that respondent drove, the law enforcement officers in this case engaged in conduct that might have provided grounds in 1791 for a suit for trespass to chattels. And for this reason, the Court concludes, the installation and use of the GPS device constituted a search.

This holding, in my judgment, is unwise. It strains the language of the Fourth Amendment; it has little if any support in current Fourth Amendment case law; and it is highly artificial.

I would analyze the question presented in this case by asking whether respondent's reasonable expectations of privacy were violated by the long-term monitoring of the movements of the vehicle he drove.

The Fourth Amendment prohibits "unreasonable searches and seizures," and the Court makes very little effort to explain how the attachment or use of the GPS device fits within these terms. The Court does not contend that there was a seizure. . . . Indeed, the success of the surveillance technique that the officers employed was dependent on the fact that the GPS did not interfere in any way with the operation of the vehicle, for if any such interference had been detected, the device might have been discovered.

The Court does claim that the installation and use of the GPS constituted a search, but this conclusion is dependent on the questionable proposition that these two procedures cannot be separated for purposes of Fourth Amendment analysis. If these two procedures are analyzed separately, it is not at all clear from the Court's opinion why either should be regarded as a search. It is clear that the attachment of the GPS device was not itself a search; if the device had not functioned or if the officers had not used it, no information would have been obtained. And the Court does not contend that the use of the device constituted a search either. On the contrary, the Court accepts the holding in *United States* v. *Knotts*, that the use of a surreptitiously planted electronic device to monitor a vehicle's movements on public roads did not amount to a search. . . .

The Court's reasoning in this case is very similar to that in the Court's early decisions involving wiretapping and electronic eavesdropping, namely, that a technical trespass followed by the gathering of evidence constitutes a search. By contrast, in cases in which there was no trespass, it was held that there was no search. . . .

Katz finally did away with the old approach, holding that a trespass was not required for a Fourth Amendment violation. What mattered, the Court now held, was whether the conduct at issue "violated the privacy upon which [the defendant] justifiably relied. . . ." Under this approach, as the Court later put it when addressing the relevance of a technical trespass, "an actual trespass is neither necessary nor sufficient to establish a constitutional violation." . . . In sum, the majority is hard pressed to find support in post-*Katz* cases for its trespass-based theory.

Disharmony with a substantial body of existing case law is only one of the problems with the Court's approach in this case.

I will briefly note four others. First, the Court's reasoning largely disregards what is really important (the use of a GPS for the purpose of long-term tracking) and instead attaches great significance to something that most would view as relatively minor (attaching to the bottom of a car a small, light object that does not interfere in any way with the car's operation). . . .

Second, the Court's approach leads to incongruous results. If the police attach a GPS device to a car and use the device to follow the car for even a brief time, under the Court's theory, the Fourth Amendment applies. But if the police follow the same car for a much longer period using unmarked cars and aerial assistance, this tracking is not subject to any Fourth Amendment constraints.

In the present case, the Fourth Amendment applies, the Court concludes, because the officers installed the GPS device after respondent's wife, to whom the car was registered, turned it over to respondent for his exclusive use. But if the GPS had been attached prior to that time, the Court's theory would lead to a different result. . . .

Third, under the Court's theory, the coverage of the Fourth Amendment may vary from State to State. If the events at issue here had occurred in a community property State or a State that has adopted the Uniform Marital Property Act, respondent would likely be an owner of the vehicle, and it would not matter whether the GPS was installed before or after his wife turned over the keys. In non-community-property States, on the other hand, the registration of the vehicle in the name of respondent's wife would generally be regarded as presumptive evidence that she was the sole owner.

Fourth, the Court's reliance on the law of trespass will present particularly vexing problems in cases involving surveillance that is carried out by making electronic, as opposed to physical, contact with the item to be tracked. For example, suppose that the officers in the present case had followed respondent by surreptitiously activating a stolen vehicle detection system that came with the car when it was purchased. Would the sending of a radio signal to activate this system constitute a trespass to chattels? Trespass to chattels has traditionally required a physical touching of the property. . . .

The *Katz* expectation-of-privacy test avoids the problems and complications noted above, but it is not without its own difficulties. It involves a degree of circularity, and judges are apt to confuse their own expectations of privacy with those of the hypothetical reasonable person to which the *Katz* test looks. In addition, the *Katz* test rests on the assumption that this hypothetical reasonable person has a well-developed and stable set of privacy expectations. But technology can change those expectations. Dramatic technological change may lead to periods in which popular expectations are in flux and may ultimately produce significant changes in popular attitudes. New technology may provide increased convenience or security at the expense of privacy, and many people may find the tradeoff worthwhile. And even if the public does not welcome the diminution of privacy that new technology entails, they may eventually reconcile themselves to this development as inevitable.

On the other hand, concern about new intrusions on privacy may spur the enactment of legislation to protect against these intrusions. This is what ultimately happened with respect to wiretapping. . . ., and since that time, the regulation of wiretapping has been governed primarily by statute and not by case law. In an ironic sense, although *Katz* overruled *Olmstead*, Chief Justice Taft's suggestion in the latter case that the regulation of wiretapping was a matter better left for Congress, has been borne out.

Recent years have seen the emergence of many new devices that permit the monitoring of a person's movements. Perhaps most significant, cell phones and other wireless devices now permit wireless carriers to track and record the location of users—and as of June 2011, it has been reported, there were more than 322 million wireless devices in use in the United States. . . . Similarly, phone-location-tracking services are offered as "social" tools, allowing consumers to find (or to avoid) others who enroll in these services. The availability and use of these and other new devices will continue to shape the average person's expectations about the privacy of his or her daily movements.

In the pre-computer age, the greatest protections of privacy were neither constitutional nor statutory, but practical. Traditional surveillance for any extended period of time was difficult and costly and therefore rarely undertaken. The surveillance at issue in this case—constant monitoring of the location of a vehicle for four weeks—would have required a large team of agents, multiple vehicles, and perhaps aerial assistance. Only an investigation of unusual importance could have justified such an expenditure of law enforcement resources. Devices like the one used in the present case, however, make long-term monitoring relatively easy and cheap.

In circumstances involving dramatic technological change, the best solution to privacy concerns may be legislative. A legislative body is well situated to gauge changing public attitudes, to draw detailed lines, and to balance privacy and public safety in a comprehensive way. To date, however, Congress and most States have not enacted statutes regulating the use of GPS tracking technology for law enforcement purposes. The best that we can do in this case is to apply existing Fourth Amendment doctrine and to ask whether the use of GPS tracking in a particular case involved a degree of intrusion that a reasonable person would not have anticipated.

Under this approach, relatively short-term monitoring of a person's movements on public streets accords with expectations of privacy that our society has recognized as reasonable. But the use of longer term GPS monitoring in investigations of most offenses impinges on expectations of privacy. For such offenses, society's expectation has been that law enforcement agents and others would not—and indeed, in the main, simply could not—secretly monitor and catalogue every single movement of an individual's car for a very long period. In this case, for four weeks, law enforcement agents tracked every movement that respondent made in the vehicle he was driving. We need not identify with precision the point at which the tracking of this vehicle became a search, for the line was surely crossed before the 4-week mark. Other cases may present more difficult questions. But where uncertainty exists with respect to whether a certain period of GPS surveillance is long enough to constitute a Fourth Amendment search, the police may always seek a warrant. . . .

For these reasons, I conclude that the lengthy monitoring that occurred in this case constituted a search under the Fourth Amendment. I therefore agree with the majority that the decision of the Court of Appeals must be affirmed.

Justice Sotomayor, concurring . . . [omitted].

F. Arrests, Detentions, and Frisks

Atwater v. *City of Lago Vista*
532 U.S. 318, 121 S.Ct. 6, 149 L.Ed. 2d 549 (2001)

http://caselaw.findlaw.com/us-supreme-court/532/318.html

Texas law makes it a misdemeanor, punishable only by fine, either for a front-seat passenger in a car equipped with safety belts not to wear one or for the driver to fail to secure any small child riding in front. State law also expressly authorizes the warrantless arrest of anyone violating these provisions, but police, at their discretion, may issue citations in place of arrest. Bart Turek, a police officer in Lago Vista, observed Gail Atwater driving her truck with her small children riding unrestrained in the front seat. Turek pulled Atwater over, berated and handcuffed her, placed her in his squad car, and drove her to the local police station, where she was made to remove her shoes, jewelry, and eyeglasses, and empty her pockets. Officers took her "mug shot" and placed her in a jail cell for an hour, after which she was taken before a magistrate and released on bond. She pleaded no contest to the seatbelt misdemeanors and paid a $50 fine. She and her husband then filed suit alleging that the city had violated her Fourth Amendment right to be free from unreasonable seizure. The U.S. District Court for the Western District of Texas found the Fourth Amendment claim meritless. A panel of the Court of Appeals for the Fifth Circuit reversed, but, sitting en banc, the appeals court affirmed. Majority: Souter, Kennedy, Rehnquist, Scalia, Thomas. Dissenting: O'Connor, Breyer, Ginsburg, Stevens.

Justice Souter delivered the opinion of the Court.

The question is whether the Fourth Amendment forbids a warrantless arrest for a minor criminal offense, such as a misdemeanor seatbelt violation punishable only by a fine. We hold that it does not. . . .

In reading the Amendment, we are guided by "the traditional protections against unreasonable searches and seizures afforded by the common law at the time of the framing," since "[a]n examination of the common-law understanding of an officer's authority to arrest sheds light on the obviously relevant, if not entirely dispositive, consideration of what the Framers of the Amendment might have thought to be reasonable." Thus, the first step here is to assess Atwater's claim that peace officers' authority to make warrantless arrests for misdemeanors was restricted at common law (whether "common law" is understood strictly as law judicially derived or, instead, as the whole body of law extant at the time of the framing). Atwater's specific contention is that "founding-era common-law rules" forbade peace officers to make warrantless misdemeanor arrests except in cases of "breach of the peace," a category she claims was then understood narrowly as covering only those non-felony offenses "involving or tending toward violence." Although her historical argument is by no means insubstantial, it ultimately fails. . . . Neither the history of the framing era nor subsequent legal development indicates that the Fourth Amendment was originally understood, or has traditionally been read, to embrace Atwater's position. . . .

What we have here, then, is just the opposite of what we had in *Wilson* v. *Arkansas*. There, we emphasized that during the founding era a number of States had "enacted statutes specifically embracing" the common-law knock-and-announce rule; here, by contrast, those very same States passed laws extending warrantless arrest authority to a host of nonviolent misdemeanors, and in so doing acted very much inconsistently with Atwater's claims about the Fourth Amendment's object. Of course, the Fourth Amendment did not originally apply to the States, but that does not make state practice irrelevant in unearthing the Amendment's original meaning. A number of state constitutional search-and-seizure provisions served as models for the Fourth Amendment, and the fact that many of the original States with such constitutional limitations continued to grant their own peace officers broad warrantless misdemeanor arrest authority undermines Atwater's contention that the founding generation meant to bar federal law enforcement officers from exercising the same authority. . . .

The story, on the contrary, is of two centuries of uninterrupted (and largely unchallenged) state and federal practice permitting warrantless arrests for misdemeanors not amounting to or involving breach of the peace. . . .

Small wonder, then, that today statutes in all 50 States and the District of Columbia permit warrantless misdemeanor arrests by at least some (if not all) peace officers without requiring any breach of the peace, as do a host of congressional enactments. . . .

While it is true here that history, if not unequivocal, has expressed a decided, majority view that the police need not obtain an arrest warrant merely because a misdemeanor stopped short of violence or a threat of it, Atwater does not wager all on history. Instead, she asks us to mint a new rule of constitutional law on the understanding that when historical practice fails to speak conclusively to a claim grounded on the Fourth Amendment, courts are left to strike a current balance between individual and societal interests by subjecting particular contemporary circumstances to traditional standards of reasonableness. Atwater accordingly argues for a modern arrest rule, one not necessarily requiring violent breach of the peace, but nonetheless forbidding custodial arrest, even upon probable cause, when conviction could not ultimately carry any jail time and when the government shows no compelling need for immediate detention.

If we were to derive a rule exclusively to address the uncontested facts of this case, Atwater might well prevail. She was a known and established resident of Lago Vista with no place to hide and no incentive to flee, and common sense says she would almost certainly have buckled up as a condition of driving off with a citation. In her case, the physical incidents of arrest were merely gratuitous humiliations imposed by a police officer who was (at best) exercising extremely poor judgment. Atwater's claim to live free of pointless indignity and confinement clearly outweighs anything the City can raise against it specific to her case. But we have traditionally recognized that a responsible Fourth Amendment balance is not well served by standards requiring sensitive, case-by-case determinations of government need, lest every discretionary judgment in the field be converted into an occasion for constitutional review. Often enough, the Fourth Amendment has to be applied on the spur (and in the heat) of the moment, and the object in implementing its command of reasonableness is to draw standards sufficiently clear and simple to be applied with a fair prospect of surviving judicial second-guessing months and years after an arrest or search is made. Courts attempting to strike a reasonable Fourth Amendment balance thus credit the government's side with an essential interest in readily administrable rules. . . .

At first glance, Atwater's argument may seem to respect the values of clarity and simplicity, so far as she claims that the Fourth Amendment generally forbids warrantless arrests for minor crimes not accompanied by violence or some demonstrable threat of it (whether "minor crime" be defined as a fine-only traffic offense, a fine-only offense more generally, or a misdemeanor). But the claim is not ultimately so simple, nor could it be, for complications arise the moment we begin to think about the possible applications of the several criteria Atwater proposes for drawing a line between minor crimes with limited arrest authority and others not so restricted.

One line, she suggests, might be between "jail-able" and "fine-only" offenses, between those for which conviction could result in commitment and those for which it could not. The trouble with this distinction, of course, is that an officer on the street might not be able to tell. It is not merely that we cannot expect every police officer to know the details of frequently complex penalty schemes, . . . but that penalties for ostensibly identical conduct can vary on account of facts difficult (if not impossible) to know at the scene of an arrest. Is this the first offense or is the suspect a repeat offender? Is the weight of the marijuana a gram above or a gram below the fine-only line? Where conduct could implicate more than one criminal prohibition, which one will the district attorney ultimately decide to charge? And so on.

But Atwater's refinements would not end there. She represents that if the line were drawn at nonjailable traffic offenses, her proposed limitation should be qualified by a proviso authorizing warrantless arrests where "necessary for enforcement of the traffic laws or when [an] offense would otherwise continue and pose a danger to others on the road." . . . The proviso only compounds the difficulties. Would, for instance, either exception apply to speeding? At oral argument, Atwater's counsel said that "it would not be reasonable to arrest a driver for speeding unless the speeding rose to the level of reckless driving." But is it not fair to expect that the chronic speeder will speed again despite a citation in his pocket, and should that not qualify as showing that the "offense would . . . continue" under Atwater's rule? And why, as a constitutional matter, should we assume that only reckless driving will "pose a danger to others on the road" while speeding will not? . . .

Just how easily the costs could outweigh the benefits may be shown by asking, as one Member of this Court did at oral argument, "how bad the problem is out there." The very fact that the law has never jelled the way Atwater would have it leads one to wonder whether warrantless misdemeanor arrests need constitutional attention, and there is cause to think the answer is no. . . .

The upshot of all these influences, combined with the good sense (and, failing that, the political accountability) of most local lawmakers and law-enforcement officials, is a dearth of horribles demanding redress. . . .

Accordingly, we confirm today what our prior cases have intimated: the standard of probable cause "applie[s] to all arrests, without the need to 'balance' the interests and circumstances involved in particular situations." If an officer has probable cause to believe that an individual has committed even a very minor criminal offense in his presence, he may, without violating the Fourth Amendment, arrest the offender. . . .

The Court of Appeals's en banc judgment is affirmed.

It is so ordered.

JUSTICE O'CONNOR, with whom JUSTICE STEVENS, JUSTICE GINSBURG, and JUSTICE BREYER join, dissenting. . . .

A custodial arrest exacts an obvious toll on an individual's liberty and privacy, even when the period of custody is relatively brief. The arrestee is subject to a full search of her person and confiscation of her possessions. If the arrestee is the occupant of a car, the entire passenger compartment of the car, including packages therein, is subject to search as well. The arrestee may be detained for up to 48 hours without having a magistrate determine whether there in fact was probable cause for the arrest. Because people arrested for all types of violent and nonviolent offenses may be housed together awaiting such review, this detention period is potentially dangerous. And once the period of custody is over, the fact of the arrest is a permanent part of the public record. . . .

Because a full custodial arrest is such a severe intrusion on an individual's liberty, its reasonableness hinges on "the degree to which it is needed for the promotion of legitimate governmental interests." In light of the availability of citations to promote a State's interests when a fine-only offense has been committed, I cannot concur in a rule which deems a full custodial arrest to be reasonable in every circumstance. Giving police officers constitutional carte blanche to effect an arrest whenever there is probable cause to believe a fine-only misdemeanor has been committed is irreconcilable with the Fourth Amendment's command that seizures be reasonable. Instead, I would require that when there is probable cause to believe that a fine-only offense has been committed, the police officer should issue a citation unless the officer is "able to point to specific and articulable facts which, taken together with rational inferences from those facts, reasonably warrant [the additional] intrusion" of a full custodial arrest.

The majority insists that a bright-line rule focused on probable cause is necessary to vindicate the State's interest in easily administrable law enforcement rules. . . .

While clarity is certainly a value worthy of consideration in our Fourth Amendment jurisprudence, it by no means trumps the values of liberty and privacy at the heart of the Amendment's protections. . . .

Such unbounded discretion carries with it grave potential for abuse. The majority takes comfort in the lack of evidence of "an epidemic of unnecessary minor-offense arrests." But the relatively small number of published cases dealing with such arrests proves little and should provide little solace. Indeed, as the recent debate over racial profiling demonstrates all too clearly, a relatively minor traffic infraction may often serve as an excuse for stopping and harassing an individual. After today, the arsenal available to any officer extends to a full arrest and the searches permissible concomitant to that arrest. An officer's subjective motivations for making a traffic stop are not relevant considerations in determining the reasonableness of the stop. But it is precisely because these motivations are beyond our purview that we must vigilantly ensure that officers' post-stop actions—which are properly within our reach—comport with the Fourth Amendment's guarantee of reasonableness.

The Court neglects the Fourth Amendment's express command in the name of administrative ease. In so doing, it cloaks the pointless indignity that Gail Atwater suffered with the mantle of reasonableness. . . .

Terry v. *Ohio*
392 U.S. 1, 88 S.Ct. 1868, 20 L.Ed. 2d 889 (1968)

http://caselaw.findlaw.com/us-supreme-court/392/1.html

This case examined the constitutionality of the "stop and frisk" by police and presented the Warren Court with a Fourth Amendment dilemma. Was the situation Officer Martin McFadden observed sufficient to establish probable cause for arrest? If so, what would such a ruling do to the limits imposed on police behavior by the Constitution? If the Court found McFadden's actions constitutionally unacceptable, could the justices reasonably expect police officers in the future not to do precisely what McFadden had done? The reader should pay particular attention to Chief Justice Warren's emphasis on the facts. The decision came down after several years of increasingly violent street crime. In the courts below, the convictions of John Terry and his companion Richard Chilton for carrying concealed weapons had been upheld. Majority: Warren, Black, Brennan, Fortas, Harlan, Marshall, Stewart, White. Dissenting: Douglas.

Mr. Chief Justice Warren delivered the opinion of the Court. . . .

Petitioner Terry was convicted of carrying a concealed weapon and sentenced to the statutorily prescribed term of one to three years in the penitentiary. Following the denial of a pretrial motion to suppress, the prosecution introduced in evidence two revolvers and a number of bullets seized from Terry and a codefendant, Richard Chilton, by Cleveland Police Detective Martin McFadden. At the hearing on the motion to suppress this evidence, Officer McFadden testified that while he was patrolling in plain clothes in downtown Cleveland at approximately 2:30 in the afternoon of October 31, 1963, his attention was attracted by two men, Chilton and Terry, standing on the corner of Huron Road and Euclid Avenue. He had never seen the two men before, and he was unable to say precisely what first drew his eye to them. However, he testified that he had been a policeman for 39 years and a detective for 35 and that he had been assigned to patrol this vicinity of downtown Cleveland for shoplifters and pickpockets for 30 years. . . .

His interest aroused, Officer McFadden took up a post of observation in the entrance to a store 300 to 400 feet away from the two men. . . . He saw one of the men leave the other one and walk southwest on Huron Road, past some stores. The man paused for a moment and looked in a store window, then walked on a short distance, turned around and walked back toward the corner, pausing once again to look in the same store window. He rejoined his companion at the corner, and the two conferred briefly. Then the second man went through the same series of motions, strolling down Huron Road, looking in the same window, walking on a short distance, turning back, peering in the store window again, and returning to confer with the first man at the corner. The two men repeated this ritual alternately between five and six times apiece—in all, roughly a dozen trips. At one point, while the two were standing together on the corner, a third man approached them and engaged them briefly in conversation. This man then left the two others and walked west on Euclid Avenue. Chilton and Terry resumed their measured pacing, peering, and conferring. After this had gone on for 10 to 12 minutes, the two men walked off together, heading west on Euclid Avenue, following the path taken earlier by the third man.

By this time Officer McFadden had become thoroughly suspicious. He testified that after observing their elaborately casual and oftrepeated reconnaissance of the store window on Huron Road, he suspected the two men of "casing a job, a stick-up," and that he considered it his duty as a police officer to investigate further. He added that he feared "they may have a gun." Thus, Officer McFadden followed Chilton and Terry and saw them stop in front of Zucker's store to talk to the same man who had conferred with them earlier on the street corner. Deciding that the situation was ripe for direct action, Officer McFadden approached the three men, identified himself as a police officer and asked for their names. At this point his knowledge was confined to what he had observed. He was not acquainted with any of the three men by name or by sight, and he had received no information concerning them from any other source. When the men "mumbled something" in response to his inquiries, Officer McFadden grabbed petitioner Terry, spun him around so that they were facing the other two, with Terry between McFadden and the others, and patted down the outside of his clothing. In the left breast pocket of Terry's overcoat Officer McFadden felt a pistol. He reached inside the overcoat pocket, but was unable to remove the gun. At this point, keeping Terry between himself and the others, the officer ordered all three men to enter Zucker's store. As they went in, he removed Terry's overcoat completely, removed a .38-caliber revolver from the pocket and ordered all three men to face the wall with their hands raised. Officer McFadden proceeded to pat down the outer clothing of Chilton and the third man, Katz. He discovered another revolver in the outer pocket of Chilton's overcoat, but no weapons were found on Katz. . . .

Our first task is to establish at what point in this encounter the Fourth Amendment becomes relevant. That is, we must decide whether and when Officer McFadden "seized" Terry and whether and when he conducted a "search." . . . It is quite plain that the Fourth Amendment governs "seizures" of the person which do not eventuate in a trip to the station house and prosecution for a crime—"arrests" in traditional terminology. It must be recognized that whenever a police officer accosts an individual and restrains his freedom to walk away, he has "seized" that person. And it is nothing less than sheer torture of the English language to suggest that a careful exploration of the outer surfaces of a person's clothing all over his or her body in an attempt to find weapons is not a "search." . . .

The danger in the logic which proceeds upon distinctions between a "stop" and an "arrest," or "seizure" of the person, and between a "frisk" and a "search" is twofold. It seeks to isolate from constitutional scrutiny the initial stages of the contact between the policeman and the citizen. And by suggesting a rigid all-or-nothing model of justification and regulation under the Amendment, it obscures the utility of limitations upon the scope, as well as the initiation, of police action as a means of constitutional regulation. . . .

We therefore reject the notions that the Fourth Amendment does not come into play at all as a limitation upon police conduct if the officers stop short of something called a "technical arrest" or a "full-blown search." . . .

[W]e cannot blind ourselves to the need for law enforcement officers to protect themselves and other prospective victims of violence in situations where they may lack probable cause for an arrest. When an officer is justified in believing that the individual whose suspicious behavior he is investigating at close range is armed and presently dangerous to the officer or to others, it would appear to be clearly unreasonable to deny the officer the power to take necessary measures to determine whether the person is in fact carrying a weapon and to neutralize the threat of physical harm. . . .

We conclude that the revolver seized from Terry was properly admitted in evidence against him. . . . Each case of this sort will, of course, have to be decided on its own facts. We merely hold today that where a police officer observes unusual conduct which leads him reasonably to conclude in light of his experience that criminal activity may be afoot and that the persons with whom he is dealing maybe armed and presently dangerous, where in the course of investigating this behavior he identifies himself as a policeman and makes reasonable inquiries, and where nothing in the initial stages of the encounter serves to dispel his reasonable fear for his own or others' safety, he is entitled for the protection of himself and others in the area to conduct a carefully limited search of the outer clothing of such persons in an attempt to discover weapons which might be used to assault him.

Such a search is a reasonable search under the Fourth Amendment, and any weapons seized may properly be introduced in evidence against the person from whom they were taken.

Affirmed.

MR. JUSTICE HARLAN, concurring . . . [omitted].
MR. JUSTICE WHITE, concurring . . . [omitted].

MR. JUSTICE DOUGLAS, dissenting. . . .

[I]t is a mystery how that "search" and that "seizure" can be constitutional by Fourth Amendment standards, unless there was "probable cause" to believe that (1) a crime had been committed or (2) a crime was in the process of being committed or (3) a crime was about to be committed. . . .

G. ADMINISTRATIVE SEARCHES

Board of Education of Pottawatomie County v. *Earls* 536 U.S. 822, 122 S.Ct. 2559, 153 L.Ed. 2d 735 (2002)

http://caselaw.findlaw.com/us-supreme-court/536/822.html

The Pottawatomie County School Board in the rural community of Tecumseh, Oklahoma, adopted the Student Activities Drug Testing Policy that requires all middle and high school students to consent to urinalysis testing for drugs in order to participate in any extracurricular activity. In practice, the policy has been applied only to competitive extracurricular activities sanctioned by the Oklahoma Secondary Schools Activities Association. Lindsay Earls, a high school student, was a member of the show choir, the marching band, the Academic Team, and the National Honor Society. Daniel James, another student, hoped to participate on the Academic Team. They and their parents challenged the policy as a violation of the Fourth Amendment. Applying *Vernonia School District* v. *Acton* (1995), the U.S. District Court for the Western District of Oklahoma granted the school district summary judgment. The U.S. Court of Appeals for the Tenth Circuit reversed, concluding that the school board had failed to demonstrate (1) the existence of a drug problem among those tested, and (2) the efficacy of the policy in addressing whatever drug problem might exist. Majority: Thomas, Breyer, Kennedy, Rehnquist, Scalia. Dissenting: Ginsburg, O'Connor, Souter, Stevens.

Justice Thomas delivered the opinion of the Court.

The Student Activities Drug Testing Policy implemented by the Board of Education of Independent School District No. 92 of Pottawatomie County requires all students who participate in competitive extracurricular activities to submit to drug testing. Because this Policy reasonably serves the School District's important interest in detecting and preventing drug use among its students, we hold that it is constitutional. . . .

Searches by public school officials, such as the collection of urine samples, implicate Fourth Amendment interests. We must therefore review the School District's Policy for "reasonableness," which is the touchstone of the constitutionality of a governmental search. . . .

Given that the School District's Policy is not in any way related to the conduct of criminal investigations, respondents do not contend that the School District requires probable cause before testing students for drug use. Respondents instead argue that drug testing must be based at least on some level of individualized suspicion. . . . But we have long held that "the Fourth Amendment imposes no irreducible requirement of [individualized] suspicion." "[I]n certain limited circumstances, the Government's need to discover such latent or hidden conditions, or to prevent their development, is sufficiently compelling to justify the intrusion on privacy entailed by conducting such searches without any measure of individualized suspicion." Therefore, in the context of safety and administrative regulations, a search unsupported by probable cause may be reasonable "when 'special needs, beyond the normal need for law enforcement, make the warrant and probable-cause requirement impracticable.'" . . .

In *Vernonia*, this Court held that the suspicionless drug testing of athletes was constitutional. The Court, however, did not simply authorize all school drug testing, but rather conducted a fact-specific balancing of the intrusion on the children's Fourth Amendment rights against the promotion of legitimate governmental interests. Applying the principles of *Vernonia* to the somewhat different facts of this case, we conclude that Tecumseh's Policy is also constitutional.

We first consider the nature of the privacy interest allegedly compromised by the drug testing. . . .

A student's privacy interest is limited in a public school environment where the State is responsible for maintaining discipline, health, and safety. Schoolchildren are routinely required to submit to physical examinations and vaccinations against disease. Securing order in the school environment sometimes requires that students be subjected to greater controls than those appropriate for adults.

Respondents argue that because children participating in nonathletic extracurricular activities are not subject to regular physicals and communal undress, they have a stronger expectation of privacy than the athletes tested in *Vernonia*. This distinction, however, was not essential to our decision in *Vernonia*, which depended primarily upon the school's custodial responsibility and authority.

In any event, students who participate in competitive extracurricular activities voluntarily subject themselves to many of the same intrusions on their privacy as do athletes. Some of these clubs and activities require occasional off-campus travel and communal undress. All of them have their own rules and requirements for participating students that do not apply to the student body as a whole. . . . We therefore conclude that the students affected by this Policy have a limited expectation of privacy.

Next, we consider the character of the intrusion imposed by the Policy. Urination is "an excretory function traditionally shielded by great privacy." But the "degree of intrusion" on one's privacy caused by collecting a urine sample "depends upon the manner in which production of the urine sample is monitored."

Under the Policy, a faculty monitor waits outside the closed restroom stall for the student to produce a sample and must "listen for the normal sounds of urination in order to guard against tampered specimens and to insure an accurate chain of custody." The monitor then pours the sample into two bottles that are sealed and placed into a mailing pouch along with a consent form signed by the student. This procedure is virtually identical to that reviewed in *Vernonia*, except that it additionally protects privacy by allowing male students to produce their samples behind a closed stall. Given that we considered the method of collection in *Vernonia* a "negligible" intrusion, the method here is even less problematic.

Moreover, the test results are not turned over to any law enforcement authority. Nor do the test results here lead to the imposition of discipline or have any academic consequences. Rather, the only consequence of a failed drug test is to limit the student's privilege of participating in extracurricular activities. Indeed, a student may test positive for drugs twice and still be allowed to participate in extracurricular activities. . . .

Given the minimally intrusive nature of the sample collection and the limited uses to which the test results are put, we conclude that the invasion of students' privacy is not significant.

Finally, this Court must consider the nature and immediacy of the government's concerns and the efficacy of the Policy in meeting them. This Court has already articulated in detail the importance of the governmental concern in preventing drug use by schoolchildren. . . .

Additionally, the School District in this case has presented specific evidence of drug use at Tecumseh schools. Teachers testified that they had seen students who appeared to be under the influence of drugs and that they had heard students speaking openly about using drugs. . . .

Respondents consider the proffered evidence insufficient and argue that there is no "real and immediate interest" to justify a policy of drug testing nonathletes. We have recognized, however, that "[a] demonstrated problem of drug abuse . . . [is] not in all cases necessary to the validity of a testing regime," but that some showing does "shore up an assertion of special need for a suspicionless general search program." The School District has provided sufficient evidence to shore up the need for its drug testing program.

Furthermore, this Court has not required a particularized or pervasive drug problem before allowing the government to conduct suspicionless drug testing. For instance, in *[Treasury Employees Union* v.*] Von Raab* the Court upheld the drug testing of customs officials on a purely preventive basis, without any documented history of drug use by such officials. . . . Likewise, the need to prevent and deter the substantial harm of childhood drug use provides the necessary immediacy for a school testing policy. Indeed, it would make little sense to require a school district to wait for a substantial portion of its students to begin using drugs before it was allowed to institute a drug testing program designed to deter drug use.

Given the nationwide epidemic of drug use, and the evidence of increased drug use in Tecumseh schools, it was entirely reasonable for the School District to enact this particular drug testing policy. We reject the Court of Appeals' novel test that "any district seeking to impose a random suspicionless drug testing policy as a condition to participation in a school activity must demonstrate that there is some identifiable drug abuse problem among a sufficient number of those subject to the testing, such that testing that group of students will actually redress its drug problem." . . .

We also reject respondents' argument that drug testing must presumptively be based upon an individualized reasonable suspicion of wrongdoing because such a testing regime would be less intrusive. . . . Moreover, we question whether testing based on individualized suspicion in fact would be less intrusive. Such a regime would place an additional burden on public school teachers who are already tasked with the difficult job of maintaining order and discipline. A program of individualized suspicion might unfairly target members of unpopular groups. The fear of lawsuits resulting from such targeted searches may chill enforcement of the program, rendering it ineffective in combating drug use. . . .

Finally, we find that testing students who participate in extracurricular activities is a reasonably effective means of addressing the School District's legitimate concerns in preventing, deterring, and detecting drug use. . . .

Within the limits of the Fourth Amendment, local school boards must assess the desirability of drug testing schoolchildren. In upholding the constitutionality of the Policy, we express no opinion as to its wisdom. Rather, we hold only that Tecumseh's Policy is a reasonable means of furthering the School District's important interest in preventing and deterring drug use among its schoolchildren. Accordingly, we reverse the judgment of the Court of Appeals.

It is so ordered.

JUSTICE BREYER, concurring . . . [omitted].

JUSTICE O'CONNOR, with whom JUSTICE SOUTER joins, dissenting . . . [omitted].

JUSTICE GINSBURG, with whom JUSTICE STEVENS, JUSTICE O'CONNOR, and JUSTICE SOUTER join, dissenting. . . .

The particular testing program upheld today is not reasonable, it is capricious, even perverse: Petitioners' policy targets for testing a student population least likely to be at risk from illicit drugs and their damaging effects. I therefore dissent. . . .

This case presents circumstances dispositively different from those of *Vernonia*. True, as the Court stresses, Tecumseh students participating in competitive extracurricular activities other than athletics share two relevant characteristics with the athletes of *Vernonia*. First, both groups attend public schools. Concern for student health and safety is basic to the school's caretaking, and it is undeniable that "drug use carries a variety of health risks for children, including death from overdose."

Those risks, however, are present for *all* schoolchildren. *Vernonia* cannot be read to endorse invasive and suspicionless drug testing of all students upon any evidence of drug use, solely because drugs jeopardize the life and health of those who use them. . . . If a student has a reasonable subjective expectation of privacy in the personal items she brings to school, surely she has a similar expectation regarding the chemical composition of her urine. Had the *Vernonia* Court agreed that public school attendance, in and of itself, permitted the State to test each student's blood or urine for drugs, the opinion in *Vernonia* could have saved many words. interscholastic athletics and other competitive extracurricular activities. . . .

The comparison is enlightening. While extracurricular activities are "voluntary" in the sense that they are not required for graduation, they are part of the school's educational program; for that reason, the petitioner (hereinafter School District) is justified in expending public resources to make them available. Participation in such activities is a key component of school life, essential in reality for students applying to college, and, for all participants, a significant contributor to the breadth and quality of the educational experience. Students "volunteer" for extracurricular pursuits in the same way they might volunteer for honors classes: They subject themselves to additional requirements, but they do so in order to take full advantage of the education offered them. . . .

Voluntary participation in athletics has a distinctly different dimension: Schools regulate student athletes discretely because competitive school sports by their nature require communal undress and, more important, expose students to physical risks that schools have a duty to mitigate. For the very reason that schools cannot offer a program of competitive athletics without intimately affecting the privacy of students, *Vernonia* reasonably analogized school athletes to "adults who choose to participate in a closely regulated industry." . . . Interscholastic athletics similarly require close safety and health regulation; a school's choir, band, and academic team do not. . . .

Vernonia initially considered "the nature of the privacy interest upon which the search [there] at issue intrude[d]." The Court emphasized that student athletes' expectations of privacy are necessarily attenuated. . . .

Competitive extracurricular activities other than athletics, however, serve students of all manner: the modest and shy along with the bold and uninhibited. Activities of the kind plaintiff-respondent Lindsay Earls pursued—choir, show choir, marching band, and academic team—[are] situations [that] are hardly equivalent to the routine communal undress associated with athletics. . . .

The second commonality to which the Court points is the voluntary character of both interscholastic athletics and other competitive extracurricular activities. . . .

The comparison is enlightening. While extracurricular activities are "voluntary" in the sense that they are not required for graduation, they are part of the school's educational program; for that reason, the petitioner (hereinafter School District) is justified in expending public resources to make them available. Participation in such activities is a key component of school life, essential in reality for students applying to college, and, for all participants, a significant contributor to the breadth and quality of the educational experience. Students "volunteer" for extracurricular pursuits in the same way they might volunteer for honors classes: They subject themselves to additional requirements, but they do so in order to take full advantage of the education offered them. . . .

Voluntary participation in athletics has a distinctly different dimension: Schools regulate student athletes discretely because competitive school sports by their nature require communal undress and, more important, expose students to physical risks that schools have a duty to mitigate. For the very reason that schools cannot offer a program of competitive athletics without intimately affecting the privacy of students, *Vernonia* reasonably analogized school athletes to "adults who choose to participate in a closely regulated industry." . . . Interscholastic athletics similarly require close safety and health regulation; a school's choir, band, and academic team do not. . . .

Vernonia initially considered "the nature of the privacy interest upon which the search [there] at issue intrude[d]." The Court emphasized that student athletes' expectations of privacy are necessarily attenuated. . . .

Competitive extracurricular activities other than athletics, however, serve students of all manner: the modest and shy along with the bold and uninhibited. Activities of the kind plaintiff-respondent Lindsay Earls pursued—choir, show choir, marching band, and academic team—[are] situations [that] are hardly equivalent to the routine communal undress associated with athletics. . . .

Finally, the "nature and immediacy of the governmental concern" faced by the Vernonia School District dwarfed that confronting Tecumseh administrators. . . .

Not only did the Vernonia and Tecumseh districts confront drug problems of distinctly different magnitudes, they also chose different solutions: Vernonia limited its policy to athletes; Tecumseh indiscriminately subjected to testing all participants in competitive extracurricular activities. Urging that "the safety interest furthered by drug testing is undoubtedly substantial for all children, athletes and nonathletes alike," the Court cuts out an element essential to the *Vernonia* judgment. Citing medical literature on the effects of combining illicit drug use with physical exertion, the *Vernonia* Court emphasized that "the particular drugs screened by [Vernonia's] Policy have been demonstrated to pose substantial physical risks to athletes." . . . Notwithstanding nightmarish images of out-of-control flatware, livestock run amok, and colliding tubas disturbing the peace and quiet of Tecumseh, the great majority of students the School District seeks to test in truth are engaged in activities that are not safety sensitive to an unusual degree. . . .

The Vernonia district, in sum, had two good reasons for testing athletes: Sports team members faced special health risks and they "were the leaders of the drug culture." No similar reason, and no other tenable justification, explains Tecumseh's decision to target for testing all participants in every competitive extracurricular activity. . . .

II. RIGHT TO COUNSEL

Powell v. *Alabama*
287 U.S. 45, 53 S.Ct. 55, 77 L.Ed. 158 (1932)

http://caselaw.findlaw.com/us-supreme-court/287/45.html

The 1931 conviction in Scottsboro, Alabama, of seven black men charged with the rape of two white women resulted in a series of legal challenges in the Supreme Court of the United States, of which this case was the first. The chief justice of the Alabama Supreme Court had dissented from that court's affirmance of the convictions, chiefly because of the hostile atmosphere that surrounded the trial and the speed and casualness with which the trial judge had dealt with the question of counsel for the defendants. After the ruling by the Alabama Supreme Court, the Communist-dominated International Labor Defense (ILD) wrested control of the case from the National Association for the Advancement of Colored People (NAACP), which was the first outside group to offer assistance of counsel after the defendants' convictions. The ILD then used the case in a worldwide campaign of mass meetings and picketing of American embassies while it pressed the appeals in the U.S. Supreme Court. Majority: Sutherland, Brandeis, Cardozo, Hughes, Roberts, Stone, Van Devanter. Dissenting: Butler, McReynolds.

MR. JUSTICE SUTHERLAND delivered the opinion of the Court. . . .

The record shows that immediately upon the return of the indictment defendants were arraigned and pleaded not guilty. Apparently they were not asked whether they had, or were able to employ, counsel, or wished to have counsel appointed; or whether they had friends or relatives who might assist in that regard if communicated with. That it would not have been an idle ceremony to have given the defendants reasonable opportunity to communicate with their families and endeavor to obtain counsel is demonstrated by the fact that very soon after conviction, able counsel appeared in their behalf. . . .

It is hardly necessary to say that the right to counsel being conceded, a defendant should be afforded a fair opportunity to secure counsel of his own choice. Not only was that not done here, but such designation of counsel as was attempted was either so indefinite or so close upon the trial as to amount to a denial of effective and substantial aid in that regard. This will be amply demonstrated by a brief review of the record.

April 6, six days after indictment, the trials began. When the first case was called, the court inquired whether the parties were ready for trial. The state's attorney replied that he was ready to proceed. No one answered for the defendants or appeared to represent or defend them.

Mr. Roddy, a Tennessee lawyer not a member of the local bar, addressed the court, saying that he had not been employed, but that people who were interested had spoken to him about the case. He was asked by the court whether he intended to appear for the defendants, and answered that he would like to appear along with counsel that the court might appoint. . . .

And in this casual fashion the matter of counsel in a capital case was disposed of.

It thus will be seen that until the very morning of the trial no lawyer had been named or definitely designated to represent the defendants. . . .

[D]uring perhaps the most critical period of the proceedings against these defendants, that is to say, from the time of their arraignment until the beginning of their trial, when consultation, thorough-going investigation and preparation were vitally important, the defendants did not have the aid of counsel in any real sense, although they were as much entitled to such aid during that period as at the trial itself.

The Constitution of Alabama provides that in all criminal prosecutions the accused shall enjoy the right to have the assistance of counsel; and a state statute requires the court in a capital case, where the defendant is unable to employ counsel, to appoint counsel for him. The state Supreme Court held that these provisions had not been infringed, and with that holding we are powerless to interfere. The question, however, which it is our duty, and within our power, to decide, is whether the denial of the assistance of counsel contravenes the due process clause of the Fourteenth Amendment to the Federal Constitution. . . .

An affirmation of the right to the aid of counsel in petty offenses, and its denial in the case of crimes of the gravest character, where such aid is most needed, is so outrageous and so obviously a perversion of all sense of proportion that the rule was constantly, vigorously and sometimes passionately assailed by English statesmen and lawyers. . . .

The rule was rejected by the colonies. . . .

The Sixth Amendment, in terms, provides that in all criminal prosecutions the accused shall enjoy the right "to have the Assistance of Counsel for his defence." In the face of the reasoning of the Hurtado case, if it stood alone, it would be difficult to justify the conclusion that the right to counsel, being thus specifically granted by the Sixth Amendment, was also within the intendment of the due process of law clause. But the Hurtado case does not stand alone. In the later case of *Chicago, Burlington & Q. R. Co.* v. *Chicago*, this court held that a judgment of a state court, even though authorized by statute, by which private property was taken for public use without just compensation, was in violation of the due process of law required by the Fourteenth Amendment, notwithstanding that the Fifth Amendment explicitly declares that private property shall not be taken for public use without just compensation. . . .

The fact that the right involved is of such a character that it cannot be denied without violating those "fundamental principles of liberty and justice which lie at the base of all our civil and political institutions" is obviously one of those compelling considerations which must prevail in determining whether it is embraced within the due process clause of the Fourteenth Amendment, although it be specifically dealt with in another part of the Federal Constitution. . . . While the question has never been categorically determined by this court, a consideration of the nature of the right and a review of the expressions of this and other courts makes it clear that the right to the aid of counsel is of this fundamental character. . . .

What, then, does a hearing include? Historically and in practice, in our own country at least, it has always included the right to the aid of counsel when desired and provided by the party asserting the right. The right to be heard would be, in many cases, of little avail if it did not comprehend the right to be heard by counsel. Even the intelligent and educated layman has small and sometimes no skill in the science of law. If charged with crime, he is incapable, generally, of determining for himself whether the indictment is good or bad. He is unfamiliar with the rules of evidence. Left without the aid of counsel he may be put on trial without a proper charge, and convicted upon incompetent evidence, or evidence irrelevant to the issue or otherwise inadmissible. He lacks both the skill and knowledge adequately to prepare his defense, even though he have a perfect one. He requires the guiding hand of counsel at every step in the proceedings against him. Without it, though he be not guilty, he faces the danger of conviction because he does not know how to establish his innocence. If that be true of men of intelligence, how much more true is it of the ignorant and illiterate, or those of feeble intellect. If in any case, civil or criminal, a state or federal court were arbitrarily to refuse to hear a party by counsel, employed by and appearing for him, it reasonably may not be doubted that such a refusal would be a denial of a hearing, and, therefore, of due process in the constitutional sense. . . .

In the light of the facts outlined in the forepart of this opinion—the ignorance and illiteracy of the defendants, their youth, the circumstances of public hostility, the imprisonment and the close surveillance of the defendants by the military forces, the fact that their friends and families were all in other states and communication with them necessarily difficult, and above all that they stood in deadly peril of their lives—we think the failure of the trial court to give them reasonable time and opportunity to secure counsel was a clear denial of due process.

But passing that, and assuming their inability, even if opportunity had been given, to employ counsel, as the trial court evidently did assume, we are of opinion that, under the circumstances just stated, the necessity of counsel was so vital and imperative that the failure of the trial court to make an effective appointment of counsel was likewise a denial of due process within the meaning of the Fourteenth Amendment. Whether this would be so in other criminal prosecutions, or under other circumstances, we need not determine. All that it is necessary now to decide, as we do decide, is that in a capital case, where the defendant is unable to employ counsel, and is incapable adequately of making his own defense because of ignorance, feeblemindedness, illiteracy, or the like, it is the duty of the court, whether requested or not, to assign counsel for him as a necessary requisite of due process of law; and that duty is not discharged by an assignment at such a time or under such circumstances as to preclude the giving of effective aid in the preparation and trial of the case. . . .

Judgments reversed.

MR. JUSTICE BUTLER, with whom MR. JUSTICE MCREYNOLDS concurs, dissenting . . . [omitted].

Gideon v. *Wainwright*
372 U.S. 335, 83 S.Ct. 792, 9 L.Ed. 2d 799 (1963)

http://caselaw.findlaw.com/us-supreme-court/372/335.html

Clarence Gideon was charged in a Florida state court with breaking and entering a poolroom with the intent to commit a crime. This was a felony under Florida law. He appeared in court without a lawyer, and when he requested that the trial court appoint one for him because he could not afford retained counsel, the judge refused. Florida law at the time provided appointed counsel for indigents only in capital cases. Following conviction, Gideon filed a petition for habeas corpus in the Florida Supreme Court, which denied relief without opinion. Majority: Black, Brennan, Clark, Douglas, Goldberg, Harlan, Stewart, Warren, White.

Mr. Justice Black delivered the opinion of the Court. . . .

Since 1942, when *Betts* v. *Brady* . . . was decided by a divided Court, the problem of a defendant's federal constitutional right to counsel in a state court has been a continuing source of controversy and litigation in both state and federal courts. . . .

The facts upon which Betts claimed that he had been unconstitutionally denied the right to have counsel appointed to assist him are strikingly like the facts upon which Gideon here bases his federal constitutional claim. Betts was indicted for robbery in a Maryland state court. On arraignment, he told the trial judge of his lack of funds to hire a lawyer and asked the court to appoint one for him. Betts was advised that it was not the practice in that county to appoint counsel for indigent defendants except in murder and rape cases. He then pleaded not guilty, had witnesses summoned, crossexamined the State's witnesses, examined his own, and chose not to testify himself. He was found guilty by the judge, sitting without a jury, and sentenced to eight years in prison.

Like Gideon, Betts sought release by habeas corpus, alleging that he had been denied the right to assistance of counsel in violation of the Fourteenth Amendment. Betts was denied any relief, and on review this Court affirmed. It was held that a refusal to appoint counsel for an indigent defendant charged with a felony did not necessarily violate the Due Process Clause of the Fourteenth Amendment, which for reasons given the Court deemed to be the only applicable federal constitutional provision. The Court said,

> Asserted denial [of due process] is to be tested by an appraisal of the totality of facts in a given case. That which may, in one setting, constitute a denial of fundamental fairness, shocking to the universal sense of justice, may, in other circumstances, and in the light of other considerations, fall short of such denial. . . .

Treating due process as "a concept less rigid and more fluid than those envisaged in other specific and particular provisions of the Bill of Rights," the Court held that refusal to appoint counsel under the particular facts and circumstances in the Betts case was not so "offensive to the common and fundamental ideas of fairness" as to amount to a denial of due process. . . .

We accept *Betts* v. *Brady's* assumption, based as it was on our prior cases, that a provision of the Bill of Rights which is "fundamental and essential to a fair trial" is made obligatory upon the States by the Fourteenth Amendment. We think the Court in *Betts* was wrong, however, in concluding that the Sixth Amendment's guarantee of counsel is not one of these fundamental rights. Ten years before *Betts*, this Court, after full consideration of all the historical data examined in *Betts*, had unequivocally declared that "the right to the aid of counsel is of this fundamental character." While the Court at the close of its Powell opinion did by its language, as this Court frequently does, limit its holding to the particular facts and circumstances of that case, its conclusions about the fundamental nature of the right to counsel are unmistakable. . . .

The fact is that in deciding as it did—that "appointment of counsel is not a fundamental right, essential to a fair trial"—the Court in *Betts* . . . made an abrupt break with its own well-considered precedents. In returning to these old precedents, sounder we believe than the new, we but restore constitutional principles established to achieve a fair system of justice. Not only these precedents but also reason and reflection require us to recognize that in our adversary system of criminal justice, any person haled into court, who is too poor to hire a lawyer, cannot be assured a fair trial unless counsel is provided for him. This seems to us to be an obvious truth. Governments, both state and federal, quite properly spend vast sums of money to establish machinery to try defendants accused of crime. Lawyers to prosecute are everywhere deemed essential to protect the public's interest in an orderly society. Similarly, there are few defendants charged with crime, few indeed, who fail to hire the best lawyers they can get to prepare and present their defenses. That government hires lawyers to prosecute and defendants who have the money hire lawyers to defend are the strongest indications of the widespread belief that lawyers in criminal courts are necessities, not luxuries. The right of one charged with crime to counsel may not be deemed fundamental and essential to fair trials in some countries, but it is in ours. From the very beginning, our state and national constitutions and laws have laid great emphasis on procedural and substantive safeguards designed to assure fair trials before impartial tribunals in which every defendant stands equal before the law. This noble ideal cannot be realized if the poor man charged with crime has to face his accusers without a lawyer to assist him.

The Court in *Betts* . . . departed from the sound wisdom upon which the Court's holding in *Powell* v. *Alabama* rested. Florida, supported by two other States, has asked that *Betts* . . . be left intact. Twenty-two States, as friends of the Court, argue that *Betts* was "an anachronism when handed down" and that it should now be overruled. We agree.

The judgment is reversed and the cause is remanded to the Supreme Court of Florida for further action not inconsistent with this opinion.

Reversed.

MR. JUSTICE DOUGLAS, concurring . . . [omitted].
MR. JUSTICE CLARK, concurring . . . [omitted].

MR. JUSTICE HARLAN, concurring. . . .

In noncapital cases, the "special circumstances" rule has continued to exist in form while its substance has been substantially and steadily eroded. In the first decade after *Betts*, there were cases in which the Court found special circumstances to be lacking, but usually by a sharply divided vote. However, no such decision has been cited to us, and I have found none, after *Quicksall* v. *Michigan* . . . decided in 1950. . . . The Court has come to recognize, in other words, that the mere existence of a serious criminal charge constituted in itself special circumstances requiring the services of counsel at trial. In truth the *Betts* . . . rule is no longer a reality.

This evolution, however, appears not to have been fully recognized by many state courts, in this instance charged with the frontline responsibility for the enforcement of constitutional rights. To continue a rule which is honored by this Court only with lip service is not a healthy thing and in the long run will do disservice to the federal system. . . .

III. SELF-INCRIMINATION

Miranda v. *Arizona*
384 U.S. 436, 86 S.Ct. 1602, 16 L.Ed. 2d 694 (1966)

http://caselaw.findlaw.com/us-supreme-court/384/436.html

In *Escobedo* v. *Illinois* (1964), five justices overturned a conviction after police interrogated the defendant without first advising him of a right to remain silent and to consult with counsel in circumstances where police also denied his request to consult with counsel waiting outside the interrogation room. Two years later, the Court reviewed four cases that plainly raised the question whether police had an affirmative obligation to advise suspects of certain rights before interrogating them, if the fruits of the interrogation were to be admissible at trial. Although the interrogations in the four cases took place for varying lengths of time, none of the cases contained an allegation of violence or threat of violence to coerce the confession.

In one case, police in Phoenix, Arizona, arrested Ernesto Miranda in 1963 on rape and kidnapping charges. The complaining witness identified him at the police station. Without advising him of a right to have an attorney present, two officers then questioned Miranda for two hours and obtained a signed confession from him. At the top of the statement was a typed paragraph explaining that the confession was made voluntarily, without threats or promises of immunity, and "with full knowledge of my legal rights, understanding any statement I make may be used against me." One of the officers later explained that he read this paragraph to Miranda, but apparently only after Miranda had confessed orally. The prosecution introduced the signed confession at trial, and Miranda was convicted of rape and kidnapping. The Supreme Court of Arizona affirmed. Majority: Warren, Black, Brennan, Douglas, Fortas. Dissenting: Harlan, Clark, Stewart, White.

Mr. Chief Justice Warren delivered the opinion of the Court. . . .

Our holding . . . briefly stated . . . is this: the prosecution may not use statements, whether exculpatory or inculpatory, stemming from custodial interrogation of the defendant unless it demonstrates the use of procedural safeguards effective to secure the privilege against self-incrimination. By custodial interrogation, we mean questioning initiated by law enforcement officers after a person has been taken into custody or otherwise deprived of his freedom of action in any significant way. As for the procedural safeguards to be employed, unless other fully effective means are devised to inform accused persons of their right of silence and to assure a continuous opportunity to exercise it, the following measures are required. Prior to any questioning, the person must be warned that he has a right to remain silent, that any statement he does make may be used as evidence against him, and that he has a right to the presence of an attorney, either retained or appointed. The defendant may waive effectuation of these rights, provided the waiver is made voluntarily, knowingly and intelligently. If, however, he indicates in any manner and at any stage of the process that he wishes to consult with an attorney before speaking there can be no questioning. Likewise, if the individual is alone and indicates in any manner that he does not wish to be interrogated, the police may not question him. The mere fact that he may have answered some questions or volunteered some statements on his own does not deprive him of the right to refrain from answering any further inquiries until he has consulted with an attorney and thereafter consents to be questioned.

The constitutional issue we decide in each of these cases is the admissibility of statements obtained from a defendant questioned while in custody and deprived of his freedom of action. In each, the defendant was questioned by police officers, detectives, or a prosecuting attorney in a room in which he was cut off from the outside world. In none of these cases was the defendant given a full and effective warning of his rights at the outset of the interrogation process. In all the cases, the questioning elicited oral admissions, and in three of them, signed statements as well which were admitted at their trials. They all thus share salient features—incommunicado interrogation of individuals in a police-dominated atmosphere, resulting in self-incriminating statements without full warnings of constitutional rights.

An understanding of the nature and setting of this in-custody interrogation is essential to our decisions today. . . .

[T]he modern practice of in-custody interrogation is psychologically rather than physically oriented. . . . Interrogation still takes place in privacy. Privacy results in secrecy and this in turn results in a gap in our knowledge as to what in fact goes on in the interrogation rooms. A valuable source of information about present police practices, however, may be found in various police manuals and texts which document procedures employed with success in the past, and which recommend various other effective tactics. [The opinion surveys manuals and texts.]

From these representative samples of interrogation techniques, the setting prescribed by the manuals and observed in practice becomes clear. In essence, it is this: To be alone with the subject is essential to prevent distraction and to deprive him of any outside support. The aura of confidence in his guilt undermines his will to resist. He merely confirms the preconceived story the police seek to have him describe. Patience and persistence, at times relentless questioning, are employed. To obtain a confession, the interrogator must "patiently maneuver himself or his quarry into a position from which the desired object may be obtained." When normal procedures fail to produce the needed result, the police may resort to deceptive stratagems such as giving false legal advice. It is important to keep the subject off balance, for example, by trading on his insecurity about himself or his surroundings. The police then persuade, trick, or cajole him out of exercising his constitutional rights.

Even without employing brutality, the "third degree" or the specific stratagems described above, the very fact of custodial interrogation exacts a heavy toll on individual liberty and trades on the weakness of individuals.

In these cases, we might not find the defendants' statements to have been involuntary in traditional terms. Our concern for adequate safeguards to protect precious Fifth Amendment rights is, of course, not lessened in the slightest. To be sure, the records do not evince overt physical coercion or patented psychological ploys. The fact remains that in none of these cases did the officers undertake to afford appropriate safeguards at the outset of the interrogation to insure that the statements were truly the product of free choice. . . .

The circumstances surrounding in-custody interrogation can operate very quickly to overbear the will of one merely made aware of his privilege by his interrogators. Therefore, the right to have counsel present at the interrogation is indispensable to the protection of the Fifth Amendment privilege under the system we delineate today. Our aim is to assure that the individual's right to choose between silence and speech remains unfettered throughout the interrogation process. . . .

Our decision is not intended to hamper the traditional function of police officers in investigating crime. . . . General on-the-scene questioning as to facts surrounding a crime or other general questioning of citizens in the fact-finding process is not affected by our holding. It is an act of responsible citizenship for individuals to give whatever information they may have to aid in law enforcement. In such situations the compelling atmosphere inherent in the process of in-custody interrogation is not necessarily present.

In dealing with statements obtained through interrogation, we do not purport to find all confessions inadmissible. Confessions remain a proper element in law enforcement. Any statement given freely and voluntarily without any compelling influences is, of course, admissible in evidence. The fundamental import of the privilege while an individual is in custody is not whether he is allowed to talk to the police without the benefit of warnings and counsel, but whether he can be interrogated. There is no requirement that police stop a person who enters a police station and states that he wishes to confess to a crime, or a person who calls the police to offer a confession or any other statement he desires to make. Volunteered statements of any kind are not barred by the Fifth Amendment and their admissibility is not affected by our holding today. . . .

It is so ordered.

Mr. Justice Clark, dissenting . . . [omitted].

Mr. Justice Harlan, whom Mr. Justice Stewart and Mr. Justice White join, dissenting. . . .

I believe the decision of the Court represents poor constitutional law and entails harmful consequences for the country at large. How serious these consequences may prove to be only time can tell. . . . The new rules are not designed to guard against police brutality or other unmistakably banned forms of coercion. Those who use third-degree tactics and deny them in court are equally able and destined to lie as skillfully about warnings and waivers. Rather, the thrust of the new rules is to negate all pressures, to reinforce the nervous or ignorant suspect, and ultimately to discourage any confession at all. The aim in short is toward "voluntariness" in a utopian sense, or to view it from a different angle, voluntariness with a vengeance.

To incorporate this notion into the Constitution requires a strained reading of history and precedent and a disregard of the very pragmatic concerns that alone may on occasion justify such strains. I believe that reasoned examination will show that the Due Process Clause provides an adequate tool for coping with confessions and that, even if the Fifth Amendment privilege against self-incrimination be invoked, its precedents taken as a whole do not sustain the present rules. . . .

The more important premise is that pressure on the suspect must be eliminated though it be only the subtle influence of the atmosphere and surroundings. The Fifth Amendment, however, has never been thought to forbid all pressure to incriminate oneself in the situations covered by it. . . . However, the Court's unspoken assumption that any pressure violates the privilege is not supported by the precedents and it has failed to show why the Fifth Amendment prohibits that relatively mild pressure the Due Process Clause permits. . . .

Examined as an expression of public policy, the Court's new regime proves so dubious that there can be no due compensation for its weakness in constitutional law. . . . [T]he Court has not and cannot make the powerful showing that its new rules are plainly desirable in the context of our society, something which is surely demanded before those rules are engrafted onto the Constitution and imposed on every State and county in the land. . . .

Until today, the role of the constitution has been only to sift out undue pressure, not to assure spontaneous confessions.

Mr. Justice White, with whom Mr. Justice Harlan and Mr. Justice Stewart join, dissenting. . . .

[E]ven if one assumed that there was an adequate factual basis for the conclusion that all confessions obtained during in-custody interrogation are the product of compulsion, the rule propounded by the Court would still be irrational, for, apparently, it is only if the accused is also warned of his right to counsel and waives both that right and the right against self-incrimination that the inherent compulsiveness of interrogation disappears. But if the defendant may not answer without a warning a question such as "Where were you last night?" without having his answer be a compelled one, how can the Court ever accept his negative answer to the question of whether he wants to consult his retained counsel or counsel whom the court will appoint? And why if counsel is present and the accused nevertheless confesses, or counsel tells the accused to tell the truth, and that is what the accused does, is the situation any less coercive insofar as the accused is concerned? The Court apparently realizes its dilemma of foreclosing questioning without the necessary warnings but at the same time permitting the accused, sitting in the same chair in front of the same policemen, to waive his right to consult an attorney. It expects, however, that the accused will not often waive the right; and if it is claimed that he has, the State faces a severe, if not impossible burden of proof. . . .

Dickerson v. *United States*
530 U.S. 428, 120 S.Ct. 2326, 147 L.Ed. 2d 405 (2000)

http://caselaw.findlaw.com/us-supreme-court/530/428.html

Two years after the Court decided *Miranda* v. *Arizona*, Congress passed the Omnibus Crime Control and Safe Streets Act. Section 3501 attempted to sidestep *Miranda* by allowing use in federal courts of confessions voluntarily given, even if they were not preceded by the precise *Miranda* warnings. Between 1968 and 1997, a succession of attorneys general made no use of § 3501. In January 1997, Charles Dickerson confessed to an FBI agent and a detective that he had been involved in robbing as many as seven banks in Maryland and Virginia. Following his indictment on federal bank robbery charges, the U.S. District Court for the Northern District of Virginia suppressed the confession because Dickerson had made it before receiving the *Miranda* warnings. The U.S. attorney asked the district court to reconsider its ruling. Even if the confession ran afoul of *Miranda*, the government contended, it was nonetheless admissible under § 3501 because, by the district court's own holding, the confession was "voluntary." Attorney General Janet Reno's office intervened, directing the U.S. attorney to abandon reliance on § 3501. Accordingly, the government's appeal to the U.S. Court of Appeals for the Fourth Circuit Court maintained, among other things, that Dickerson had confessed only after the *Miranda* warnings had been administered. In a 2–1 ruling in 1999, the Fourth Circuit agreed with the district court that Dickerson's confession was unwarned (and so was at odds with *Miranda*) but that, because of § 3501, the confession was admissible. In the appeals court's view, *Miranda*'s required warnings were judicially created rules of evidence to guard against involuntary (and hence unconstitutional) confessions. As rules of evidence, not dictates of the Constitution, they were subject to modification by Congress. When the case reached the Supreme Court, both counsel for Dickerson and U.S. solicitor general Seth Waxman argued against the validity of § 3501. At invitation of the Court, Professor Paul G. Cassell appeared as amicus curiae in support of the statute. Majority: Rehnquist, Stevens, O'Connor, Kennedy, Souter, Ginsburg, Breyer. Dissenting: Scalia, Thomas.

Chief Justice Rehnquist delivered the opinion of the Court. . . .

We hold that *Miranda*, being a constitutional decision of this Court, may not be in effect overruled by an Act of Congress, and we decline to overrule *Miranda* ourselves. We therefore hold that *Miranda* and its progeny in this Court govern the admissibility of statements made during custodial interrogation in both state and federal courts. . . .

Prior to *Miranda*, we evaluated the admissibility of a suspect's confession under a voluntariness test. The roots of this test developed in the common law, as the courts of England and then the United States recognized that coerced confessions are inherently untrustworthy. . . . Over time, our cases recognized two constitutional bases for the requirement that a confession be voluntary to be admitted into evidence: the Fifth Amendment right against self-incrimination and the Due Process Clause of the Fourteenth Amendment. . . .

[F]or the middle third of the 20th century our cases based the rule against admitting coerced confessions primarily, if not exclusively, on notions of due process. We applied the due process voluntariness test in "some 30 different cases decided during the era that intervened between *Brown* [v. *Mississippi* (1936)] and *Escobedo* v. *Illinois* (1964)." Those cases refined the test into an inquiry that examines "whether a defendant's will was overborne" by the circumstances surrounding the giving of a confession. The due process test takes into consideration "the totality of all the surrounding circumstances—both the characteristics of the accused and the details of the interrogation." . . .

We have never abandoned this due process jurisprudence, and thus continue to exclude confessions that were obtained involuntarily. But our decisions in *Malloy* v. *Hogan* (1964) and *Miranda* changed the focus of much of the inquiry in determining the admissibility of suspects' incriminating statements. In *Malloy*, we held that the Fifth Amendment's Self-Incrimination Clause is incorporated in the Due Process Clause of the Fourteenth Amendment and thus applies to the States. We decided *Miranda* on the heels of *Malloy*.

In *Miranda*, we noted that the advent of modern custodial police interrogation brought with it an increased concern about confessions obtained by coercion. . . . We concluded that the coercion inherent in custodial interrogation blurs the line between voluntary and involuntary statements, and thus heightens the risk that an individual will not be "accorded his privilege under the Fifth Amendment . . . not to be compelled to incriminate himself." Accordingly, we laid down "concrete constitutional guidelines for law enforcement agencies and courts to follow. Those guidelines established that the admissibility in evidence of any statement given during custodial interrogation of a suspect would depend on whether the police provided the suspect with four warnings." . . .

Two years after *Miranda* was decided, Congress enacted § 3501. That section provides, in relevant part:

> a. In any criminal prosecution brought by the United States or by the District of Columbia, a confession . . . shall be admissible in evidence if it is voluntarily given. . . .
> b. The trial judge in determining the issue of voluntariness shall take into consideration all the circumstances surrounding the giving of the confession, including (1) the time elapsing between arrest and arraignment of the defendant making the confession, if it was made after arrest and before arraignment, (2) whether such defendant knew the nature of the offense with which he was charged or of which he was suspected at the time of making the confession, (3) whether or not such defendant was advised or knew that he was not required to make any statement and that any such statement could be used against him, (4) whether or not such defendant had been advised prior to questioning of his right to the assistance of counsel; and (5) whether or not such defendant was without the assistance of counsel when questioned and when giving such confession. . . .

Given § 3501's express designation of voluntariness as the touchstone of admissibility, its omission of any warning requirement, and the instruction for trial courts to consider a nonexclusive list of factors relevant to the circumstances of a confession, we agree with the Court of Appeals that Congress intended by its enactment to overrule *Miranda*. . . . Because of the obvious conflict between our decision in *Miranda* and § 3501, we must address whether Congress has constitutional authority to thus supersede *Miranda*. If Congress has such authority, § 3501's totality-of-the-circumstances approach must prevail over *Miranda's* requirement of warnings; if not, that section must yield to *Miranda's* more specific requirements.

The law in this area is clear. This Court has supervisory authority over the federal courts, and we may use that authority to prescribe rules of evidence and procedure that are binding in those tribunals. However, the power to judicially create and enforce nonconstitutional "rules of procedure and evidence for the federal courts exists only in the absence of a relevant Act of Congress." Congress retains the ultimate authority to modify or set aside any judicially created rules of evidence and procedure that are not required by the Constitution.

But Congress may not legislatively supersede our decisions interpreting and applying the Constitution. This case therefore turns on whether the Miranda Court announced a constitutional rule or merely exercised its supervisory authority to regulate evidence in the absence of congressional direction. Recognizing this point, the Court of Appeals surveyed *Miranda* and its progeny to determine the constitutional status of the Miranda decision. . . . [T]he Court of Appeals concluded that the protections announced in *Miranda* are not constitutionally required.

We disagree with the Court of Appeals' conclusion, although we concede that there is language in some of our opinions that supports the view taken by that court. But first and foremost of the factors on the other side—that *Miranda* is a constitutional decision—is that both *Miranda* and two of its companion cases applied the rule to proceedings in state courts. . . .

In fact, the majority opinion is replete with statements indicating that the majority thought it was announcing a constitutional rule. . . .

Whether or not we would agree with *Miranda's* reasoning and its resulting rule, were we addressing the issue in the first instance, the principles of stare decisis weigh heavily against overruling it now. . . .

In sum, we conclude that *Miranda* announced a constitutional rule that Congress may not supersede legislatively. Following the rule of stare decisis, we decline to overrule *Miranda* ourselves. The judgment of the Court of Appeals is therefore

Reversed.

JUSTICE SCALIA, with whom JUSTICE THOMAS joins, dissenting. . . .

One will search today's opinion in vain . . . for a statement (surely simple enough to make) that what 18 U.S.C. § 3501 prescribes—the use at trial of a voluntary confession, even when a Miranda warning or its equivalent has failed to be given—violates the Constitution. The reason the statement does not appear is not only (and perhaps not so much) that it would be absurd, inasmuch as § 3501 excludes from trial precisely what the Constitution excludes from trial, viz., compelled confessions; but also that Justices whose votes are needed to compose today's majority are on record as believing that a violation of *Miranda* is not a violation of the Constitution. . . .

It was once possible to characterize the so-called Miranda rule as resting (however implausibly) upon the proposition that what the statute here before us permits—the admission at trial of un-Mirandized confessions—violates the Constitution. That is the fairest reading of the Miranda case itself. The Court began by announcing that the Fifth Amendment privilege against self-incrimination applied in the context of extrajudicial custodial interrogation—itself a doubtful proposition as a matter both of history and precedent. . . . Having extended the privilege into the confines of the station house, the Court liberally sprinkled throughout its sprawling 60-page opinion suggestions that, because of the compulsion inherent in custodial interrogation, the privilege was violated by any statement thus obtained that did not conform to the rules set forth in *Miranda*, or some functional equivalent. . . .

So understood, *Miranda* was objectionable for innumerable reasons, not least the fact that cases spanning more than 70 years had rejected its core premise that, absent the warnings and an effective waiver of the right to remain silent and of the (hitherto unknown) right to have an attorney present, a statement obtained pursuant to custodial interrogation was necessarily the product of compulsion. . . . Moreover, history and precedent aside, the decision in *Miranda*, if read as an explication of what the Constitution requires, is preposterous. There is, for example, simply no basis in reason for concluding that a response to the very first question asked, by a suspect who already knows all of the rights described in the Miranda warning, is anything other than a volitional act. . . . And even if one assumes that the elimination of compulsion absolutely requires informing even the most knowledgeable suspect of his right to remain silent, it cannot conceivably require the right to have counsel present. There is a world of difference, which the Court recognized under the traditional voluntariness test but ignored in *Miranda*, between compelling a suspect to incriminate himself and preventing him from foolishly doing so of his own accord. Only the latter (which is not required by the Constitution) could explain the Court's inclusion of a right to counsel and the requirement that it, too, be knowingly and intelligently waived. Counsel's presence is not required to tell the suspect that he need not speak; the interrogators can do that. The only good reason for having counsel there is that he can be counted on to advise the suspect that he should not speak. . . .

As the Court today acknowledges, since *Miranda* we have explicitly, and repeatedly, interpreted that decision as having announced, not the circumstances in which custodial interrogation runs afoul of the Fifth or Fourteenth Amendment, but rather only "prophylactic" rules that go beyond the right against compelled self-incrimination. Of course the seeds of this "prophylactic" interpretation of *Miranda* were present in the decision itself. . . . In subsequent cases, the seeds have sprouted and borne fruit: The Court has squarely concluded that it is possible—indeed not uncommon—for the police to violate *Miranda* without also violating the Constitution. . . . [Justice Scalia discusses *Michigan* v. *Tucker* (1974), *Oregon* v. *Hass* (1975), *New York* v. *Quarles* (1984), and *Oregon* v. *Elstad* (1985).]

In light of these cases, . . . it is simply no longer possible for the Court to conclude, even if it wanted to, that a violation of Miranda's rules is a violation of the Constitution. . . .

These decisions illustrate the principle—not that *Miranda* is not a constitutional rule—but that no constitutional rule is immutable. No court laying down a general rule can possibly foresee the various circumstances in which counsel will seek to apply it, and the sort of modifications represented by these cases are as much a normal part of constitutional law as the original decision.

The issue, however, is not whether court rules are "mutable"; they assuredly are. It is not whether, in the light of "various circumstances," they can be "modifi[ed]"; they assuredly can. The issue is whether, as mutated and modified, they must make sense. The requirement that they do so is the only thing that prevents this Court from being some sort of nine-headed Caesar, giving thumbs-up or thumbs-down to whatever outcome, case by case, suits or offends its collective fancy. And if confessions procured in violation of *Miranda* are confessions "compelled" in violation of the Constitution, the post-*Miranda* decisions I have discussed do not make sense. The only reasoned basis for their outcome was that a violation of *Miranda* is not a violation of the Constitution. . . .

Finally, the Court asserts that *Miranda* must be a "constitutional decision" announcing a "constitutional rule," and thus immune to congressional modification, because we have since its inception applied it to the States. . . . [T]hough it is true that our cases applying *Miranda* against the States must be reconsidered if *Miranda* is not required by the Constitution, it is likewise true that our cases (discussed above) based on the principle that *Miranda* is not required by the Constitution will have to be reconsidered if it is. So the stare decisis argument is a wash. If, on the other hand, the argument is meant as an appeal to logic rather than stare decisis, it is a classic example of begging the question: Congress' attempt to set aside *Miranda*, since it represents an assertion that violation of *Miranda* is not a violation of the Constitution, also represents an assertion that the Court has no power to impose *Miranda* on the States. To answer this assertion—not by showing why violation of *Miranda* is a violation of the Constitution—but by asserting that *Miranda* does apply against the States, is to assume precisely the point at issue. In my view, our continued application of the Miranda code to the States despite our consistent statements that running afoul of its dictates does not necessarily—or even usually—result in an actual constitutional violation, represents not the source of *Miranda's* salvation but rather evidence of its ultimate illegitimacy. . . .

IV. CAPITAL PUNISHMENT

Gregg v. *Georgia*
428 U.S. 153, 96 S.Ct. 2909, 49 L.Ed. 2d 859 (1976)

http://caselaw.findlaw.com/us-supreme-court/428/153.html

Furman v. *Georgia* (1972) held that, as then administered, capital punishment was "cruel and unusual punishment" in violation of the Eighth and Fourteenth Amendments. Of the five-justice majority, only Brennan and Marshall found the death penalty fundamentally at odds with the Constitution. The remaining three justices (Douglas, Stewart, and White) concluded that capital punishment, as then administered, was invalid: Too much discretion in the hands of juries and too few standards for judges made the death sentence capricious and unpredictable. In addition, Douglas stated that the extreme selectivity of the death penalty created an inequality because those executed were "poor, young, and ignorant." Stewart disallowed retribution alone as a constitutionally acceptable objective of punishment. For White, the death penalty was pointless as well: "The threat of execution is too attenuated to be of substantial service to criminal justice." The positions of Stewart and White were unexpected because they had been part of a six-justice majority in *McGautha* v. *California* (1971), which upheld a death sentence for first-degree murder against arguments similar to those they found persuasive in *Furman*. The four dissenting justices in *Furman* (Burger, Blackmun, Powell, and Rehnquist) were willing to allow the states ample freedom in administration of capital punishment. *Furman* halted executions not only in Georgia but in the 38 other states that allowed the death penalty in 1972.

To meet the Court's objections, the Georgia legislature then enacted a new death penalty law, under which Gregg was sentenced. The new statute provided a bifurcated trial: Only after rendering a verdict of guilty would the jury determine the sentence. A death sentence required a finding beyond a reasonable doubt that at least one of ten specified "aggravating circumstances" was present, as well as consideration of "mitigating circumstances" such as the offender's youth, cooperation with police, and emotional state when committing the crime. When the U.S. Supreme Court decided *Gregg*, Douglas had been replaced by Stevens. The justices were unable to agree on a majority opinion, but seven justices concluded that the state's new sentencing scheme was constitutional under the Eighth and Fourteenth Amendments. Majority: Stewart, Blackmun, Burger, Powell, Rehnquist, Stevens, White. Dissenting: Brennan, Marshall.

Judgment of the Court, and opinion of Mr. Justice Stewart, Mr. Justice Powell, and Mr. Justice Stevens, announced by Mr. Justice Stewart. . . .

We address initially the basic contention that the punishment of death for the crime of murder is, under all circumstances, "cruel and unusual" in violation of the Eighth and Fourteenth Amendments of the Constitution. . . .

Although this issue was presented and addressed in *Furman*, it was not resolved by the Court. Four Justices would have held that capital punishment is not unconstitutional per se; two Justices would have reached the opposite conclusion; and three Justices, while agreeing that the statutes then before the Court were invalid as applied, left open the question whether such punishment may ever be imposed. We now hold that the punishment of death does not invariably violate the Constitution. . . .

It is from the foregoing precedents that the Eighth Amendment has not been regarded as a static concept. As Chief Justice Warren said, in an oft-quoted phrase, "[the] amendment must draw its meaning from the evolving standards of decency that mark the progress of a maturing society." . . . Thus, an assessment of contemporary values concerning the infliction of a challenged sanction is relevant to the application of the Eighth Amendment. As we develop below more fully, this assessment does not call for a subjective judgment. It requires, rather, that we look to objective indicia that reflect the public attitude toward a given sanction. . . .

But our cases also make clear that public perceptions of standards of decency with respect to criminal sanctions are not conclusive. A penalty also must accord with "the dignity of man," which is the "basic concept underlying the Eighth Amendment." . . . This means, at least, that the punishment not be "excessive." When a form of punishment in the abstract (in this case, whether capital punishment may ever be imposed as a sanction for murder) rather than in the particular (the propriety of death as a penalty to be applied to a specific defendant for a specific crime) is under consideration, the inquiry into "excessiveness" has two aspects. First, the punishment must not involve the unnecessary and wanton infliction of pain. Second, the punishment must not be grossly out of proportion to the severity of the crime. . . .

The petitioners in the capital case before the Court today renew the "standards of decency" argument, but developments during the four years since *Furman* have undercut substantially the assumptions upon which their argument rested. Despite the continuing debate, dating back to the 19th century, over the morality and utility of capital punishment, it is now evident that a large proportion of American society continues to regard it as an appropriate and necessary sanction.

The most marked indication of society's endorsement of the death penalty for murder is the legislative response to *Furman*. The legislatures of at least 35 states have enacted new statutes that provide for the death penalty for at least some crimes that result in the death of another person. And the Congress of the United States, in 1974, enacted a statute providing the death penalty for aircraft piracy that results in death. . . .

We now consider specifically whether the sentence of death for the crime of murder is a per se violation of the Eighth and Fourteenth Amendments to the Constitution. . . . We note first that history and precedent strongly support a negative answer to this question. . . .

It is apparent from the text of the Constitution itself that the existence of capital punishment was accepted by the framers. At the time the Eighth Amendment was ratified, capital punishment was a common sanction in every state. Indeed, the first Congress of the United States enacted legislation providing death as the penalty for specified crimes. . . .

For nearly two centuries, this Court, repeatedly and often expressly, has recognized that capital punishment is not invalid per se. . . .

Four years ago, the petitioners in *Furman* and its companion cases predicated their argument primarily upon the asserted proposition that standards of decency had evolved to the point where capital punishment no longer could be tolerated. The petitioners in those cases said, in effect, that the evolutionary process had come to an end, and that standards of decency required that the Eighth Amendment be construed finally as prohibiting capital punishment for any crime regardless of its depravity and impact on society. . . .

Although some of the studies suggest that the death penalty may not function as a significantly greater deterrent than lesser penalties, there is no convincing empirical evidence either supporting or refuting this view. We may nevertheless assume safely that there are murderers, such as those who act in passion, for whom the threat of death has little or no deterrent effect. But for many others, the death penalty undoubtedly is a significant deterrent. . . .

In sum, we cannot say that the judgment of the Georgia Legislature that capital punishment may be necessary in some cases is clearly wrong. Considerations of federalism, as well as respect for the ability of a legislature to evaluate, in terms of its particular state the moral consensus concerning the death penalty and its social utility as a sanction, require us to conclude, in the absence of more convincing evidence, that the infliction of death as a punishment for murder is not without justification and thus is not unconstitutionally severe.

Finally, we must consider whether the punishment of death is disproportionate in relation to the crime for which it is imposed. There is no question that death as a punishment is unique in its severity and irrevocability. . . . When a defendant's life is at stake, the Court has been particularly sensitive to insure that every safeguard is observed. . . .

But we are concerned here only with the imposition of capital punishment for the crime of murder, and when a life has been taken deliberately by the offender, we cannot say that the punishment is invariably disproportionate to the crime. It is an extreme sanction, suitable to the most extreme of crimes. . . .

We now consider whether Georgia may impose the death penalty on the petitioner. . . .

The basic concern of *Furman* centered on those defendants who were being condemned to death capriciously and arbitrarily. Under the procedures before the Court in that case, sentencing authorities were not directed to give attention to the nature or circumstances of the crime committed or to the character or record of the defendant. Left unguided, juries imposed the death sentence in a way that could only be called freakish. The new Georgia sentencing procedures, by contrast, focus the jury's attention on the particularized nature of the crime and the particularized characteristics of the individual defendant. While the jury is permitted to consider any aggravating or mitigating circumstances, it must find and identify at least one statutory aggravating factor before it may impose a penalty of death. In this way the jury's discretion is channeled. No longer can a jury wantonly and freakishly impose the death sentence; it is always circumscribed by the legislative guidelines. . . .

For the reasons expressed in this opinion, we hold that the statutory system under which Gregg was sentenced to death does not violate the Constitution. Accordingly, the judgment of the Georgia Supreme Court is affirmed.

It is so ordered.

Mr. Chief Justice Burger, with whom Mr. Justice Rehnquist joins, concurring . . . [omitted].

Mr. Justice White, with whom Mr. Chief Justice Burger and Mr. Justice Rehnquist join, concurring . . . [omitted].

Mr. Justice Blackmun, concurring . . . [omitted]. Mr. Justice Brennan, dissenting. . . . [omitted].

Mr. Justice Marshall, dissenting. . . .

Since the decision in *Furman*, the legislatures of 35 states have enacted new statutes authorizing the imposition of the death sentence for certain crimes, and Congress has enacted a law providing the death penalty for air piracy resulting in death. I would be less than candid if I did not acknowledge that these developments have a significant bearing on a realistic assessment of the moral acceptability of the death penalty to the American people. But if the constitutionality of the death penalty turns, as I have urged, on the opinion of an informed citizenry, then even the enactment of new death statutes cannot be viewed as conclusive. In *Furman*, I observed that the American people are largely unaware of the information critical to a judgment on the morality of the death penalty, and concluded that if they were better informed they would consider it shocking, unjust, and unacceptable. . . .

There remains for consideration, however, what might be termed the purely retributive justification for the death penalty—that the death penalty is appropriate, not because of its beneficial effect on society, but because the taking of the murderer's life is itself morally good. Some of the language of the plurality's opinion appears positively to embrace this notion of retribution for its own sake as a justification for capital punishment. . . .

To be sustained under the Eighth Amendment, the death penalty must "[comport] with the basic concept of human dignity at the core of the amendment"; the objective in imposing it must be "[consistent] with our respect for the dignity of other men." Under these standards, the taking of life "because the wrongdoer deserves it" surely must fall, for such a punishment has as its very basis the total denial of the wrongdoer's dignity and worth. . . .

McCleskey v. *Kemp*
481 U.S. 279, 107 S.Ct. 1756, 95 L.Ed. 2d 262 (1987)

http://laws.findlaw.com/us/481/279.html

In 1978 Warren McCleskey, a black man, was convicted of murder and sentenced to death in Superior Court of Fulton County, Georgia. He had been charged with the killing of a white police officer during the robbery of a furniture store. On appeal, the Georgia Supreme Court affirmed, and the United States Supreme Court denied certiorari. McCleskey then filed a petition for a writ of habeas corpus in state court. Relief was denied, the state supreme court affirmed, and again the U.S. Supreme Court denied certiorari. McCleskey next filed a petition for a writ of habeas corpus in U.S. district court. Among his claims was that the capital sentencing process in Georgia was administered in a racially discriminatory manner in violation of the Eighth and Fourteenth Amendments. In support, counsel put forth a statistical study by David C. Baldus, George Woodworth, and Charles Pulanski ("Comparative Review of Death Sentences: An Empirical Study of the Georgia Experience," 74

Journal of Criminal Law and Criminology 661 [1983]). The study examined more than 2,000 murder cases in Georgia in the 1970s. Dividing the cases according to the combination of the race of the defendant and the race of the victim, the authors found that the death penalty was imposed in 22 percent of the cases involving a black defendant and a white victim, 8 percent of the cases with a white defendant and a white victim, 1 percent of the cases with a black defendant and a black victim, and 3 percent of the cases with a white defendant and a black victim. In further analysis, taking account of 39 nonracial variables, the authors showed that defendants charged with killing whites were 4.3 times as likely to receive the death sentence as those charged with killing blacks. McCleskey's counsel contended that black defendants who kill white victims have the greatest likelihood of receiving the death penalty.

In 1984 the district court questioned the study's methodology and concluded that the "statistics do not demonstrate a *prima facie* case in support of the contention that the death penalty was imposed upon him because of his race, because of the race of the victim, or because of any Eighth Amendment concern." In 1985 the Court of Appeals for the Eleventh Circuit, sitting en banc, assumed the validity of the study but found it "insufficient to demonstrate discriminatory intent or unconstitutional discrimination . . . [and] insufficient to show irrationality, arbitrariness and capriciousness under any kind of Eighth Amendment analysis."

McCleskey failed again in the High Court in 1991 when it refused to consider a Sixth Amendment issue because he had not raised it previously (*McCleskey* v. *Zant*). Georgia authorities executed McCleskey on September 25, 1991. According to John C. Jeffries, Jr., Justice Powell's biographer, Powell changed his mind about his position in the McCleskey case after retiring from the Court in 1987. "I would vote the other way in any capital case.. . . I have come to think that capital punishment should be abolished." ["A Change of Mind That Came Too Late," *New York Times*, June 23, 1994, p. A23.] Majority: Powell, O'Connor, Rehnquist, Scalia, White. Dissenting: Brennan, Blackmun, Marshall, Stevens.

Justice Powell delivered the opinion of the Court.

This case presents the question whether a complex statistical study that indicates a risk that racial considerations enter into capital sentencing determinations proves that petitioner McCleskey's capital sentence is unconstitutional under the Eighth or Fourteenth Amendment. . . .

Our analysis begins with the basic principle that a defendant who alleges an equal protection violation has the burden of proving "the existence of purposeful discrimination." A corollary to this principle is that a criminal defendant must prove that the purposeful discrimination "had a discriminatory effect" on him.. . . Thus, to prevail under the Equal Protection Clause, McCleskey must prove that the decisionmakers in his case acted with discriminatory purpose. He offers no evidence specific to his own case that would support an inference that racial considerations played a part in his sentence. Instead, he relies solely on the Baldus study. McCleskey argues that the Baldus study compels an inference that his sentence rests on purposeful discrimination. McCleskey's claim that these statistics are sufficient proof of discrimination, without regard to the facts of a particular case, would extend to all capital cases in Georgia, at least where the victim was white and the defendant is black.. . .

Finally, McCleskey's statistical proffer must be viewed in the context of his challenge. McCleskey challenges decisions at the heart of the State's criminal justice system. "[O]ne of society's most basic tasks is that of protecting the lives of its citizens and one of the most basic ways in which it achieves the task is through criminal laws against murder." Implementation of these laws necessarily requires discretionary judgments. Because discretion is essential to the criminal justice process, we would demand exceptionally clear proof before we would infer that the discretion has been abused. The unique nature of the decisions at issue in this case also counsel against adopting such an inference from the disparities indicated by the Baldus study. Accordingly, we hold that the Baldus study is clearly insufficient to support an inference that any of the decisionmakers in McCleskey's case acted with discriminatory purpose.. . .

McCleskey also suggests that the Baldus study proves that the State as a whole has acted with a discriminatory purpose. He appears to argue that the State has violated the Equal Protection Clause by adopting the capital punishment statute and allowing it to remain in force despite its allegedly discriminatory application.. . .

As legislatures necessarily have wide discretion in the choice of criminal laws and penalties, and as there were legitimate reasons for the Georgia Legislature to adopt and maintain capital punishment . . . we will not infer a discriminatory purpose on the part of the State of Georgia. Accordingly, we reject McCleskey's equal protection claims.

McCleskey also argues that the Baldus study demonstrates that the Georgia capital sentencing system violates the Eighth Amendment. We begin our analysis of this claim by reviewing the restrictions on death sentences established by our prior decisions under that Amendment.. . .

In sum, our decisions since Furman have identified a constitutionally permissible range of discretion in imposing the death penalty. First, there is a required threshold below which the death penalty cannot be imposed. In this context, the State must establish rational criteria that narrow the decisionmaker's judgment as to whether the circumstances of a particular defendant's case meet the threshold. Moreover, a societal consensus that the death penalty is disproportionate to a particular offense prevents a State from imposing the death penalty for that offense. Second, States cannot limit the sentencer's consideration of any relevant circumstance that could cause it to decline to impose the penalty. In this respect, the State cannot channel the sentencer's discretion, but must allow it to consider any relevant information offered by the defendant.. . .

Because McCleskey's sentence was imposed under Georgia sentencing procedures that focus discretion "on the particularized nature of the crime and the particularized characteristics of the individual defendant," we lawfully may presume that McCleskey's death sentence was not "wantonly and freakishly" imposed, and thus that the sentence is not disproportionate within any recognized meaning under the Eighth Amendment.

Although our decision in Gregg as to the facial validity of the Georgia capital punishment statute appears to foreclose McCleskey's disproportionality argument, he further contends that the Georgia capital punishment system is arbitrary and capricious in application, and therefore his sentence is excessive, because racial considerations may influence capital sentencing decisions in Georgia. We now address this claim.

To evaluate McCleskey's challenge, we must examine exactly what the Baldus study may show. Even Professor Baldus does not contend that his statistics prove that race enters into any capital sentencing decisions or that race was a factor in McCleskey's particular case. Statistics at most may show only a likelihood that a particular factor entered into some decisions. There is, of course, some risk of racial prejudice influencing a jury's decision in a criminal case. There are similar risks that other kinds of prejudice will influence other criminal trials. The question "is at what point that risk becomes constitutionally unacceptable." McCleskey asks us to accept the likelihood allegedly shown by the Baldus study as the constitutional measure of an unacceptable risk of racial prejudice influencing capital sentencing decisions. This we decline to do.. . .

At most, the Baldus study indicates a discrepancy that appears to correlate with race. Apparent disparities in sentencing are an inevitable part of our criminal justice system.. . .

Where the discretion that is fundamental to our criminal process is involved, we decline to assume that what is unexplained is invidious. In light of the safeguards designed to minimize racial bias in the process, the fundamental value of jury trial in our criminal justice system, and the benefits that discretion provides to criminal defendants, we hold that the Baldus study does not demonstrate a constitutionally significant risk of racial bias affecting the Georgia capital-sentencing process.. . .

Two additional concerns inform our decision in this case. First, McCleskey's claim, taken to its logical conclusion, throws into serious question the principles that underlie our entire criminal justice system. The Eighth Amendment is not limited in application to capital punishment, but applies to all penalties. Thus, if we accepted McCleskey's claim that racial bias has impermissibly tainted the capital sentencing decision, we could soon be faced with similar claims as to other types of penalty.. . .

Second, McCleskey's arguments are best presented to the legislative bodies. It is not the responsibility—or indeed even the right—of this Court to determine the appropriate punishment for particular crimes. It is the legislatures, the elected representatives of the people, that are "constituted to respond to the will and consequently the moral values of the people.". . . Capital punishment is now the law in more than two thirds of our States. It is the ultimate duty of courts to determine on a case-by-case basis whether these laws are applied consistently with the Constitution. Despite McCleskey's wide ranging arguments that basically challenge the validity of capital punishment in our multi-racial society, the only question before us is whether in his case, the law of Georgia was properly applied. We agree with the District Court and the Court of Appeals for the Eleventh Circuit that this was carefully and correctly done in this case.

Accordingly, we affirm the judgment of the Court of Appeals for the Eleventh Circuit.

It is so ordered.

Justice Brennan, with whom Justice Marshall joins, and with whom Justice Blackmun and Justice Stevens join in part, dissenting.. . .

It is important to emphasize at the outset that the Court's observation that McCleskey cannot prove the influence of race on any particular sentencing decision is irrelevant in evaluating his Eighth Amendment claim. Since *Furman* v. *Georgia*, the Court has been concerned with the risk of the imposition of an arbitrary sentence, rather than the proven fact of one.. . .

Defendants challenging their death sentences thus never have had to prove that impermissible considerations have actually infected sentencing decisions. We have required instead that they establish that the system under which they were sentenced posed a significant risk of such an occurrence. McCleskey's claim does differ, however, in one respect from these earlier cases: it is the first to base a challenge not on speculation about how a system might operate, but on empirical documentation of how it does operate.. . .

McCleskey's statistics have particular force because most of them are the product of sophisticated multiple-regression analysis. Such analysis is designed precisely to identify patterns in the aggregate, even though we may not be able to reconstitute with certainty any individual decision that goes to make up that pattern. Multiple-regression analysis is particularly well-suited to identify the influence of impermissible considerations in sentencing, since it is able to control for permissible factors that may explain an apparent arbitrary pattern.. . .

The Court cites four reasons for shrinking from the implications of McCleskey's evidence: the desirability of discretion for actors in the criminal-justice system, the existence of statutory safeguards against abuse of that discretion, the potential consequences for broader challenges to criminal sentencing, and an understanding of the contours of the judicial role. While these concerns underscore the need for sober deliberation, they do not justify rejecting evidence as convincing as McCleskey has presented.

The Court maintains that petitioner's claim "is antithetical to the fundamental role of discretion in our criminal justice system." It states that "[w]here the discretion that is fundamental to our criminal process is involved, we decline to assume that what is unexplained is invidious."

Reliance on race in imposing capital punishment, however, is antithetical to the very rationale for granting sentencing discretion. Discretion is a means, not an end. It is bestowed in order to permit the sentencer to "trea[t] each defendant in a capital case with that degree of respect due the uniqueness of the individual.". . .

The Court also declines to find McCleskey's evidence sufficient in view of "the safeguards designed to minimize racial bias in the [capital sentencing] process.". . .

It has now been over 13 years since Georgia adopted the provisions upheld in *Gregg*. Professor Baldus and his colleagues have compiled data on almost 2500 homicides committed during the period 1973–1979. They have taken into account the influence of 230 nonracial variables, using a multitude of data from the State itself, and have produced striking evidence that the odds of being sentenced to death are significantly greater than average if a defendant is black or his or her victim is white. The challenge to the Georgia system is not speculative or theoretical; it is empirical.. . .

The Court next states that its unwillingness to regard the petitioner's evidence as sufficient is based in part on the fear that recognition of McCleskey's claim would open the door to widespread challenges to all aspects of criminal sentencing. Taken on its face, such a statement seems to suggest a fear of too much justice.. . .

Those whom we would banish from society or from the human community itself often speak in too faint a voice to be heard above society's demand for punishment. It is the particular role of courts to hear these voices, for the Constitution declares that the majoritarian chorus may not alone dictate the conditions of social life. The Court thus fulfills, rather than disrupts, the scheme of separation of powers by closely scrutinizing the imposition of the death penalty, for no decision of a society is more deserving of the "sober second thought."

Justice Blackmun, with whom Justice Marshall and Justice Stevens join, and with whom Justice Brennan joins in part, dissenting . . . [omitted].

Justice Stevens, with whom Justice Blackmun joins, dissenting . . . [omitted].

NOTES

1. Administrative Office of U.S. Courts, *Wiretap Report* (2019).
2. *Report of the Director of the Administrative Office of U.S. Courts on the Activities of the Foreign Intelligence Surveillance Court* (2019).
3. Bureau of Justice Statistics, U.S. Department of Justice.

11

Freedom of Expression

The greater the importance of safeguarding the community from incitements to the overthrow of our institutions by force and violence, the more imperative is the need to preserve inviolate the constitutional rights of free speech, free press and free assembly in order to maintain the opportunity for free political discussion, to the end that government may be responsive to the will of the people and that changes, if desired, may be obtained by peaceful means. Therein lies the security of the Republic, the very foundation of constitutional government.

—Chief Justice Charles Evans Hughes (1937)

The American political tradition has always opposed unlimited government power. In particular, protections of the First Amendment—free speech, free press, and the rights of peaceable assembly and petition—make possible a continuing debate on issues large and small, without which the electoral process becomes an empty ritual and self-expression and the search for truth are stifled. (The religion clauses of the First Amendment are treated separately in the next chapter.)

First Amendment freedoms confront the Court with a difficult task, one that is not present in all cases of judicial review. Where enumerated powers of Congress or the president are subject to interpretation, for example, the Court's function is at an end when the action taken is found to be within the limits of constitutionally granted power. In reaching such a conclusion, the Court is aided by the well-established presumption of constitutionality that accompanies review of most legislative and executive actions.

In cases involving freedom of speech, however, the Court must interpret and apply a grant of power—frequently the "reserved" police power of the states—while, at the same time, it must interpret and apply a constitutional limitation on government power. Such cases thus involve a clash of important objectives: The need for both order and freedom. Government must have authority to "insure domestic Tranquility," just as it must have military power to resist attacks from abroad. Yet, excessive emphasis on order negates the freedom the political system is designed to protect. Thus, the easy path to constitutional decision by way of presumption of

DOI: 10.4324/9781003164340-12

constitutionality of legislative or administrative action is not readily available in this field.

TESTS OF FREEDOM

Free-speech cases have been a fixture on the Supreme Court's docket for barely a century. During this time, the justices have developed no single theoretical perspective or framework for resolving them. Instead, when confronted with clashes over free speech, the Court has formulated a series of tests or analytical approaches of varying sophistication. Generally these fall into at least four categories. Whatever measures are used, the Court's answers depend ultimately on the justices' view of correct social policy and their conception of the role of the judiciary in achieving balance between freedom and order.

The first category considers free-speech cases in terms of the threat that the speaker poses. As discussed in the following section, by 1925, two such tests had emerged: the **clear-and-present-danger test**, which promised greater judicial protection for speech, and the **bad tendency test**, which was deferential to legislative action. Each emerged from post–World War I cases involving wartime national security legislation. Much later, the clear-and-present-danger test evolved into the **incitement test**, as illustrated by ***Brandenburg* v. *Ohio*** (1969). More permissive for expression than the clear-and-present-danger test, it emphasizes the immediacy of lawless action. A majority has never preferred a fourth and extremely permissive approach advocated by a few justices such as Hugo Black. From this **absolute approach**, once expression is deemed to fall within the purview of the First Amendment (a significant qualification), all government restrictions on what is said are forbidden. The threat posed by the speaker is irrelevant.

The second category looks at free-speech cases not so much from the perspective of the danger the speaker poses but the danger that a law poses to those engaged in legitimate speech. For instance, the **overbreadth doctrine** may be applicable when a law sweeps too broadly, reaching not only speech or speech-related behavior that might constitutionally be proscribed but protected speech as well. Such laws may also be struck down because they have a **chilling effect**: At the margin they may deter people from engaging in expression that the Constitution allows. For similar reasons, the Court may declare a law **void for vagueness**. Due process requires that individuals have fair warning of prohibited conduct. A vague statute blurs the line between legal and illegal behavior and therefore may discourage speech by causing people to censor themselves.

The third category focuses on how a regulation affects speech. Initially, the Court will determine whether government has restricted the *substance* of a speaker's message—that is, whether a regulation discriminates against a certain point of view. If so, the Court applies **strict scrutiny**, its most demanding standard of review. For the statute to survive, government must demonstrate a compelling and legitimate interest in what the restriction is designed to accomplish and demonstrate that the objective can be achieved in no other way. *Ward* v. *Rock Against Racism* (1989), which challenged a New York City regulation mandating use of the city's sound system and technicians as a means to control volume at the bandstand in Central Park, offered a three-part test to determine whether a regulation is in fact viewpoint-neutral. First, the regulation must concern where or how something is said, not what is said. Second, its adoption must not have been based on disagreement with any particular message. Third, government's interests in having the regulation must be unrelated to the viewpoint of any speaker.

If a law passes the viewpoint-neutrality test, it may nonetheless adversely affect the flow and distribution of a message—the *how*—even though the law is not aimed at a particular message—the *what*. In such situations, the Court applies a lower standard of review, balancing the impact on speech against the importance of the regulation. "[A] regulation of the time, place, or manner of protected speech," wrote Justice Kennedy in *Ward*, "must be narrowly tailored to serve the government's legitimate content-neutral interests but . . . it need not be the least-restrictive or least-intrusive means of doing so." The standard "is satisfied 'so long as [the] regulation promotes a substantial government interest that would be achieved less effectively absent the regulation.'" Such regulations are more easily upheld when there are "ample alternative channels of communication" left open to the speaker.

In contrast to the third category's focus on *viewpoint* discrimination, a fourth (and still evolving) interpretive approach examines *content* discrimination: situations in which government may proscribe certain types of speech but not others within a *class* of expression. For example, the federal government may criminalize threats of violence that are directed to the president of the United States without necessarily being required to criminalize threats of violence that are directed to all other federal officials. "[T]he reasons why threats of violence are outside the First Amendment . . . have a special force when applied to the person of the President." When the content discrimination in question rests entirely on "the very reason the entire domain of speech at issue is proscribable, no significant danger of idea or viewpoint discrimination exists" (*R. A. V.* v. *City of St. Paul*, 1995). So, a law criminalizing threats of violence directed to the president is permissible content discrimination, while a law criminalizing such threats made only by Democrats or only by Republicans would be impermissible viewpoint discrimination. (A cautionary note on word usage is in order: Supreme Court opinions occasionally create their own internal confusion by using the terms *content* and *viewpoint* interchangeably. And to complicate matters, there is not always agreement on the bench whether a particular discrimination is content or viewpoint in nature.)

INTERNAL SECURITY

At the end of the first decade of government under the Constitution, the Federalists curbed the speech of their political opponents. With the ink barely dry on the First Amendment, the **Sedition Act of 1798** criminalized in sweeping terms publication of

> any false, scandalous and malicious writing or writings against the government of the United States, or either House of the Congress of the United States, or the President of the United States, with intent to defame the said government, or either House of the said Congress, or the said President, or to bring them, or either of them, into contempt or disrepute; or to excite against them, or either or any of them, the hatred of the good people of the United States.

Before the law expired by its own terms on March 3, 1801, the government obtained indictments against 14 persons and convictions of 10. Considered unconstitutional by many at the time, the law was never tested because Thomas Jefferson and the Democratic-Republicans, against whom the law was aimed, feared that the Federalist Supreme Court would uphold the law, thus establishing an unfortunate precedent, and because the Court's appellate jurisdiction at that time did not encompass criminal cases. It is noteworthy that proponents of the Sedition Act, many of whom had played leading roles in the dramatic formulation of the Constitution, used an argument that has become a familiar defense of limitations on speech. Threats to national security, they argued, made restrictions inevitable; preservation of the Constitution was more important than protection of any one right it guaranteed. Obviously, this logic could be used to justify destruction of all constitutional rights.

Clear-and-Present-Danger Test. Except for President Abraham Lincoln's unofficial suppression of northern critics of his policies during the Civil War, there was no further significant national government action raising free-speech issues until World War I, when Congress passed two laws that focused public attention on basic issues of freedom of speech in wartime. The first, the Espionage Act of 1917, prohibited interferences with recruitment or acts adversely affecting military morale. It was in ***Schenck* v. *United States*** (1919) that Justice Holmes, in upholding the act as applied to antidraft leaflets, first announced the clear-and-present-danger test: "The question in every case is whether the words used are used in such circumstances and are of such a nature as to create a clear and present danger that they will bring about the substantive evils that Congress has a right to prevent." Holmes's test invited more questions than it answered. Enmeshed with highly complex issues of proximity, degree, and content, it nevertheless displayed a preference for a wide latitude of speech.

The second, the Sedition Act of 1918, went far beyond the 1917 law, making punishable speech that now would be deemed mere political comment. It singled out for punishment any "disloyal, profane, scurrilous, or abusive language about the form of government, the Constitution, soldiers and sailors, flag or uniform of the armed forces," and in addition made unlawful any "word or act [favoring] the cause of the German Empire . . . or [opposing] the cause of the United States." This law was upheld in *Abrams* v. *United States* (1919), in which pamphlets opposing the Allied intervention in Russia after the revolution were held to be within its terms. It was in his dissent in *Abrams* that Justice Holmes began to develop the idea he had introduced in *Schenck*:

> Persecution for the expression of opinions seems to me perfectly logical. If you have no doubt of your premises or your power, and want a certain result with all your heart, you naturally express your wishes in law, and sweep away all opposition. To allow opposition by speech seems to indicate that you think the speech impotent, as when a man says that he has squared the circle, or that you do not care wholeheartedly for the result, or that you doubt either your power or your premises. But when men have realized that time has upset many fighting faiths, they may come to believe even more than they believe the very foundations of their own conduct that the ultimate good desired is better reached by free trade in ideas—that the best test of truth is the power of the thought to get itself accepted in the competition of the market, and that truth is the only ground upon which their wishes safely can be carried out. That, at any rate, is the theory of our Constitution. It is an experiment, as all life is an experiment. Every year, if not every day, we have to wager our salvation upon some prophecy based upon imperfect knowledge. While that experiment is part of our system, I think that we should be eternally vigilant against attempts to check the expression of opinions that we loathe and believe to be fraught with death, unless they so imminently threaten immediate

> interference with the lawful and pressing purposes of the law that an immediate check is required to save the country.

Holmes's language was so bold that several of the other justices visited him at his residence in an effort to persuade him to withdraw or otherwise sharply modify the draft dissent that he had circulated among "the brethren." Once this flurry of litigation subsided, cases involving federal action under the First Amendment virtually disappeared until after World War II.

Bad Tendency Test. In the period between the two world wars, the states were more active in seeking curbs against radical action, principally through efforts to outlaw **criminal syndicalism** and anarchy. Such laws, aimed at left-wing groups, forbade the advocacy of violence to accomplish social reform. This was the basis for Benjamin Gitlow's conviction after he circulated pamphlets urging workers to revolutionary mass action and "dictatorship of the proletariat" (***Gitlow* v. *New York***, 1925). Application of the bad tendency test in *Gitlow* meant that states had as much authority to stamp out noxious ideas as they did to destroy adulterated meat. Nonetheless, the case did declare that the free-speech clause of the First Amendment was applicable to the states through the Fourteenth Amendment. Similar reasoning prevailed in ***Whitney* v. *California*** (1927), when the Court ruled that even brief membership in the Communist Labor Party and participation in its convention constituted a violation of the state's criminal syndicalism statute. Of lasting interest from *Whitney* is Brandeis's concurring opinion in which he refashioned the merits and justification of the clear-and-present-danger test. Brandeis concurred in the result because he believed that Whitney's counsel should have raised Holmes's test as a defense, in an effort to distinguish mere membership from the threat of dangerous action.

By World War II, "clear and present danger" had become the accepted test of potential harm. Applied to both state and federal laws, it became the measure of the criminality of unpopular beliefs and potentially dangerous action.

Cold War Cases. The heightened tension between the United States and the Soviet Union after World War II, with the accompanying fear of Communist subversives, presented new free-speech problems. Intended initially to target Nazis, Section 1 of the **Smith Act** of 1940 made it a felony to advocate the violent overthrow of the government of the United States or to conspire to organize a group advocating such violence. In upholding the law as applied to 11 leaders of the American Communist Party, ***Dennis* v. *United States*** (1951) discarded the clear-and-present-danger test in these circumstances and selected instead a test Judge Learned Hand crafted in his opinion when *Dennis* was before the Second Circuit Court of Appeals: "In each case Courts must ask whether the gravity of the 'evil,' discounted by its improbability, justifies such invasion of free speech as is necessary to avoid the danger." In the Supreme Court's view, the clear-and-present-danger test, although applicable to the isolated speech of individuals or small groups, was inappropriate for testing words associated with a large-scale conspiratorial movement. Instead, the majority approved Judge Harold Medina's holding at trial that as a matter of law, defendants' alleged activities presented "a sufficient danger of a substantive evil" to justify the application of the statute under the First Amendment. Judge Hand's formula in its application seemed more closely to resemble the bad tendency test.

Dennis posed the dilemma every democracy faces sooner or later: What to do about antidemocratic forces, which, if they come to power, would surely destroy democratic institutions and processes as one of the first orders of business? Should the government wait until subversive elements have committed particular criminal acts (as Justices Black and Douglas advocated in their Dennis dissents), or should the government take steps to protect the nation and its constitutional processes only on the basis of the noxious ideas suspected subversives preach? If the latter option is chosen, how can the nation make the content of speech a crime, given the wording of the First Amendment? Moreover, if the government moves against those who wish the nation ill, how do law enforcement agencies cast the net without placing lawful dissent in danger?

In *Yates* v. *United States* (1957), the Court was again called on to examine the scope of the Smith Act. Its decision took a stricter view of the proof necessary to convict by requiring evidence of the advocacy of *action* and not merely the advocacy of *doctrine* and consequently made it difficult for the government to maintain successful prosecutions. In light of *Yates*, many thought that the membership provisions of the Smith Act would be held invalid. But in *Scales* v. *United States* (1961), the Court rescued the challenged clause by insisting that only active and knowing membership was within the act's coverage. *Scales* and *Yates* thus had the effect of requiring the government to prove more to sustain a conviction under the Smith Act. In exchange for sustaining the constitutionality of the legislation, the justices diminished the circle of people against whom the law could realistically be expected to apply.

Dennis turned out to be the high-water mark of judicial tolerance of various state and federal devices to punish subversive speech. In a succession of cases lasting over a decade, the Court sometimes declared such policies unconstitutional or approved them in principle but required such exacting procedures that implementation of the various policies became more difficult. The justices seemed to be saying that the First Amendment does not prevent the nation from defending itself from internal threats but that, in doing so, the nation must be careful not to tread too heavily on First Amendment values.

Incitement Test. The prevailing view on the Court today is set firmly against virtually all **viewpoint-based restrictions,** as ***Brandenburg* v. *Ohio*** illustrates. This case involved yet another state criminal syndicalism law, but the defendant this time was no leftist but a member of the Ku Klux Klan. Ohio banned "advocating . . . the duty, necessity, or propriety of crime, sabotage, violence or unlawful methods of terrorism as a means of accomplishing industrial or political reform." Clarence Brandenburg notified a Cincinnati reporter of a scheduled Ku Klux Klan rally, and film clips of Brandenburg's remarks were telecast on a local station and on a national network. Recorded for posterity was his speech decrying government repression of the Caucasian race and references to the possibility of revenge. Some people in the crowd carried weapons. With this as evidence, an Ohio court fined him $1,000 and sentenced him to 10 years in prison. The Supreme Court reversed, saying that a state may not proscribe "advocacy of the use of force or of law violations except when it is directed to inciting or producing imminent lawless action and is likely to incite or produce such action." *Brandenburg* sets a tough standard for government restrictions aimed at dissident groups. It means that the First Amendment bars practically any conviction based on someone's point of view. Moreover, in striking down the Stolen Valor Act 43 years later, the Court made clear that government may not criminalize the making of false statements of fact in situations where their utterance is unlikely to cause harm (*United States* v. *Alvarez*, 2012).

PUBLIC FORUM

Closely related to regulation of what is said is regulation of where it may be said. This is the problem illustrated by the **public forum**—publicly owned property where people may express their views. A trichotomy has evolved through a series of decisions: The traditional (or open) public forum, the designated (or limited) public forum, and the nonpublic forum. As explained in *Perry Education Association* v. *Perry Local Educators' Association* (1983), the first includes areas such as streets and parks that have long been opened to speech and debate and has the highest free-speech protection.

> For the state to enforce a content-based exclusion it must show that its regulation is necessary to serve a compelling state interest and that it is narrowly drawn to achieve that end. The state may also enforce regulations of the time, place, and manner of expression which are content-neutral, are narrowly tailored to serve a significant government interest, and leave open ample alternative channels of communication.

One such time-place-manner regulation lay at the heart of *Clark* v. *Community for Creative Non-Violence* (1984), where a divided Court upheld against challenge by protestors a policy of the National Park Service that prohibited camping and sleeping on the National Mall in Washington.

The second category includes places that the government has chosen to open to expressive activity for limited purposes, either for use by certain groups (such as student organizations with access to facilities at a state university) or for discussion of certain subjects (such as a school board meeting for discussion of educational policy). Within those limits, however, government may impose viewpoint-based restrictions only if its regulation meets the rigorous standards of the traditional public forum. Thus, the Court ruled that the University of Virginia violated the First Amendment when it denied funding for the printing of a student-edited Christian journal (*Wide Awake*) while funding other student publications. This was viewpoint discrimination in a designated or limited public forum, five justices declared. The case was complicated by the university's insistence, which the Court found unpersuasive, that to fund the journal would amount to a violation of the same amendment's ban on laws "respecting an establishment of religion" (*Rosenberger* v. *Rector*, 1995). The Virginia case in turn was authority for ***Good News Club v. Milford Central School*** (2001) that upheld a Christian group's free-speech right of access to public school facilities that had been open for certain uses by the public after school hours.

The third category—the nonpublic forum—includes public property not by tradition or designation considered an arena for the free exchange of ideas. In addition to time, place, and manner regulations, government may reserve the space for its intended use, communicative or otherwise, so long as the regulation is reasonable and not based on opposition to a speaker's point of view. Thus, no visitor to the U.S. Capitol has a right to make a speech in the gallery of the House of Representatives. Likewise, military bases and grounds around a prison ordinarily may be closed to certain communicative activities entirely (*Adderley* v. *Florida*, 1966; *Greer* v. *Spock*, 1976). Indeed, there are places often designated as public forums where the doctrine does not apply. Thus, without resolving the embedded establishment clause issue the case presented, *Pleasant Grove* v. *Sum-mum* (2009) rejected a religious group's claim that it had a free-speech right to erect a monument inscribed with the main principles of its teachings in a public park that contained several privately donated monuments including one inscribed with the Ten Commandments. In the Court's view, the monuments present in the park represented **government speech** and so the usual First Amendment strictures did not apply. Otherwise, bizarre and contradictory displays might follow. Speech by government thus complicates traditional public forum analysis, as *Walker* v. *Sons of Confederate Veterans* (2015) illustrates. Here the Court rejected a claim of viewpoint discrimination in upholding a state's decision to bar a particular license plate design.

The Court has also tenuously defined the public forum based on a distinction between proprietary and regulatory functions of government (*International Society for Krishna Consciousness* v. *Lee*, 1992). Where government acts as manager of a site's internal operations, such as at a municipally owned airport, no traditional public forum exists. Accordingly, bans on solicitation, for instance, "will not be subject to the heightened review to which [government's] actions as lawmaker may be subject." Regulations of expression are therefore permissible so long as they are reasonable and viewpoint-neutral. This distinction may be easier to state than to apply, however. In the very same case that articulated the distinction, a majority voted to uphold a ban on repetitive solicitation of funds inside New York City area airports but struck down a prohibition on distribution of literature in the same terminals.

PROTEST AND SYMBOLIC SPEECH

The public forum is frequently the setting for the variety of ways in which Americans express their opinions to other citizens, businesses and organizations, and the government. Those expressions can be subdued or raucous, crude or clever, thoughtful or hate-filled, temperate or vituperative. All implicate the First Amendment.

Fighting Words. Insults and other abusive language present their own First Amendment problem. *Chaplinsky* v. *New Hampshire* (1942) unanimously upheld the conviction of a Jehovah's Witness who in a dispute with a police officer called him a "God damned racketeer" and "a damned Fascist." The Court recognized Chaplinsky's words as "likely to provoke the average person to retaliation." Certain utterances, of which **fighting words** are a part, "are no essential part of any exposition of ideas and are of such slight social value as a step to truth that any benefit that may be derived from them is clearly outweighed by the social interest in order and morality." However, in light of *Brandenburg* and increased societal tolerance of coarse language, it seems unlikely that much force remains in the fighting words doctrine.

Especially here, context is important. *Cohen* v. *California* (1971) reversed the conviction of a young man who, as a method of protest, emblazoned the words "Fuck the draft" on his jacket. He was arrested in a courthouse corridor and charged with "disturbing the peace." "No individual actually or likely to be present could reasonably have regarded the words . . . as a direct personal insult," wrote patrician Justice Harlan. "Nor do we have here an instance of the exercise of the State's police power to prevent a speaker from intentionally provoking a given group to hostile reaction. . . . [W]hile the particular four-letter word being litigated here is perhaps more distasteful than most others of its genre, it is nevertheless often true that one man's vulgarity is another's lyric. Indeed . . . because government officials cannot make principled distinctions in this area . . . the Constitution leaves matters of taste and style so largely to the individual."

Symbolic Speech. Frequently those protesting government policy resort to tactics that go beyond conventional speech as a way to dramatize a cause and attract media attention. There are also other activities that are obviously expressive even though the feelings and attitudes conveyed are not "political." **Symbolic speech** thus refers to expressive activity—action (or inaction) designed to communicate a message. A constitutional question arises when the actions, stripped of any message, are themselves illegal. Are otherwise illegal actions protected by the First Amendment when they have speech content? In the Court's view, to be considered "speech" at all, there must be intent to convey a particular message and a reasonable likelihood that the message will be understood by an audience. Second, as with parades, the justices agree that speech symbolized by conduct is subject to reasonable time, place, and manner rules. Third, symbolic speech may be prohibited or regulated if the conduct itself can constitutionally be regulated. Fourth, the regulation must be narrowly written and must further "a substantial governmental interest." Fifth, that interest must be unrelated to suppressing free speech. Consider how these criteria were applied in ***United States* v. *O'Brien*** (1968) where the Court sustained a protestor's conviction for destroying his draft card in violation of federal law.

May a state or the national government protect the flag of the United States from defacement or destruction? In ***Texas* v. *Johnson*** (1989), the Court overturned a conviction for burning the American flag in violation of Texas law. In a demonstration at the Dallas City Hall during the Republican National Convention in 1984, protesters chanted, "America, the red, white, and blue, we spit on you," doused the flag with kerosene, and set it ablaze. Short of a protest that sparks a breach of the peace or causes some other kind of serious harm, five justices concluded that government may not criminalize the symbolic act of flag burning. The reasoning is that a flag-protection law is viewpoint-based: Government protects the physical integrity of the flag because the flag is the symbol of the nation. Just as people may verbally speak out against what they believe the nation "stands for," they may also express the same thought by defacing or destroying a national symbol. But the right does not extend to destroying flags or other symbols that are government property.

Johnson was not the first time the Court had confronted flag-desecration laws, but it was the first time a majority had spoken forthrightly on their constitutionality under the First Amendment. Johnson's case was also not the last. In the wake of widespread criticism of the Court's ruling, the administration asked Congress for a constitutional amendment to give the states and the national government authority to protect the physical integrity of the American flag. Congress failed to approve the amendment but instead passed the Flag Protection Act, which President George H. W. Bush allowed to become law without his signature. Protestors promptly burned the flag in several cities in defiance of the new law. In *United States* v. *Eichman* the following year, the Court held that the First Amendment also barred Congress from criminalizing flag burning, a decision that sparked a drive, thus far unsuccessful, to add a flag protection amendment to the Constitution. At one time or another, the legislatures of all states but Vermont have passed resolutions favoring such an amendment.

Hate Speech and Hate Crimes. First Amendment questions also arise when government seeks to protect certain groups or classes of people from offensive or hurtful speech or displays. In two important cases, the Supreme Court has signaled the corrective measures it is prepared to reject and accept.

In *R. A. V.* v. *City of St. Paul* (1992), all nine justices voted to invalidate a city ordinance that criminalized the placing of a symbol or graffiti "on public or private property . . . including, but not limited to, a burning cross or Nazi swastika, which one knows or has reasonable grounds to know arouses anger, alarm or resentment in others on the basis of race, color, creed, religion or gender. . . ." Led by Scalia, five justices concluded that the ordinance was viewpoint-based and therefore defective because it banned invectives ("fighting words") aimed only at certain groups, not all. While admitting that government had compelling reason to protect groups that historically have been the target of discrimination, content-neutral alternatives were available to achieve that end. Scalia distinguished decisions that allowed proscription of classes of expression such as libel and obscenity. Those categories could be banned "because of their constitutionally proscribable content." But within a category, government could not ban only libel against the government, for example. For Justice White and three others, Scalia's reasoning was faulty. His approach required a ban on a wider category of speech to reach a smaller category of troublesome speech. Instead, White argued that the ordinance was defective on grounds of over-breadth: Along with expression that could constitutionally be punished, it also criminalized protected expression, such as symbols that merely caused resentment.

Eleven years later, ***Virginia* v. *Black*** struck down Virginia's cross-burning statute. Six justices indicated, however, that they would accept a law that criminalized cross-burning, and perhaps similar acts as well, that were intended to intimidate. The deficiency in the Virginia law was not that it banned cross-burning but that it contained a provision allowing jurors to infer intent from the act of cross-burning itself. Presumably the statute would have escaped censure had the burden been on the prosecution to demonstrate that the act was a threat and not merely symbolic expression.

Picketing. In 1940, peaceful picketing was brought under the protection of freedom of speech (*Thornhill* v. *Alabama*). However, picketing is a special kind of symbolic expression that involves problems of the proper forum as well as the rights of those who are picketed. Picketers convey messages as much through their sheer physical presence as through their placards and spoken words. Nowhere is this clash of rights any more obvious than in the picketing of abortion clinics by anti-abortion activists. On the one hand are the speech interests of abortion opponents. On the other are interests in protecting access to medical services, including termination of a pregnancy, in minimizing the potential for trauma to patients, in assuring public order, and in ensuring the free flow of traffic. Accordingly, *Madsen* v. *Women's Health Center, Inc*. (1994) held that the usual time-place-manner standard commonly used in picketing cases was not sufficiently rigorous to protect speech interests. Instead, the Court announced that the test in such situations was "whether the challenged provisions of the injunction burden no more speech than necessary to serve a significant government interest." In this case, the Court upheld a 36-foot buffer zone around a clinic as well as limits on noise. Bans on posting observable images, approaching patients without their consent within 200 feet of the clinic, and picketing within 300 feet of staff residences, however, went beyond what was deemed necessary to prevent intimidation and to ensure access. In 2014, however, the Court unanimously invalidated a Massachusetts statute that set up a 35-foot buffer zone because in its particulars the law was not narrowly tailored to preserve the rights of protestors (*McCullen* v. *Coakley*). Clearly controversies over protest restrictions remain a murky part of First Amendment law.

Public Schools. As the school strip search case noted in Chapter Ten illustrates, young Americans do not relinquish all constitutional rights when they walk through the schoolhouse door. A 1969 decision voided a school rule that barred the wearing of black armbands to protest the war in Vietnam (*Tinker* v. *Des Moines Community School District*). Only if expression interfered with "appropriate discipline" could the rule be sustained. Yet, *Hazelwood School District* v. *Kuhlmeier* (1988) upheld a principal's censorship of a high school newspaper. "[T]he standard articulated in *Tinker* for determining when a school may punish student expression," Justice White concluded, "need not also be the standard for determining when a school may refuse to lend its name and resources to the dissemination of student expression. Instead, we hold that educators do not offend the First Amendment by exercising editorial control over the style and content of student speech in school-sponsored expressive activities so long as their actions are reasonably related to legitimate pedagogical concerns." Such activities would include not merely publications but theatrical productions and, presumably, art exhibitions as well. *Kuhlmeier* thus erected a taxonomy of school censorship, with *Tinker* applicable to student expression that happens to take place on school premises but not to expression in the context of school-sponsored events.

FREEDOM OF ASSOCIATION

Organizations have long populated American culture. If Americans "want to proclaim a truth or propagate some feeling. . . ," observed Alexis de Tocqueville in the 1830s, "they form an association. In every case, at the head of any new undertaking, . . . you are sure to find an association." Free speech would certainly be less valuable were people unable to act collectively to achieve common objectives. As Chapter Five illustrated with respect to political parties and electoral politics, life in the United States would be vastly different without associations and interest groups of nearly every variety.

NAACP v. *Alabama* (1958) first formally recognized a First Amendment right of association as a derivative of the speech and assembly clauses. In that case a unanimous bench barred the state's order that a civil rights organization disclose its membership lists as a condition for continuing to do business in the state. Because of the hostile environment over civil rights at that time, the justices believed that the directive would threaten the organization's existence and "chill" constitutionally protected liberties. But like other First Amendment freedoms, that of association is not absolute.

Some state and local governments have restricted the right of association for the purpose of eliminating various forms of discrimination in clubs and other private organizations. (Discrimination by most clubs is forbidden by neither the Constitution nor, at present, federal law.) The view is that such discrimination denies women and racial minorities full participation in the business and professional life of a community. Although continuing to recognize the importance of associational rights staked out in *NAACP*, the Court has nonetheless upheld three state and local antidiscrimination measures aimed at private organizations (*Roberts* v. *Jaycees*, 1984; *Rotary International* v. *Rotary Club of Duarte*, 1987; and *New York State Club Association* v. *New York City*, 1988). In each, the Court found that banning gender discrimination, especially in large membership groups, did not significantly restrict the groups' **expressive association,** that is, speech that was synonymous with the organization itself. For associational rights to prevail over an antidiscrimination law, there would have to be a nexus between a group's message and its exclusion of women.

This qualification probably explains the outcome in *Hurley* v. *Irish-American Gay, Lesbian and Bisexual Group* (1995). Here, the Court held unanimously that Massachusetts could not apply its public accommodations statute to force a private association of veterans' groups—sponsors of Boston's St. Patrick's Day parade—to include among the marchers a gay rights group whose message the sponsors did not wish their parade to convey. A contrary result would have violated a "fundamental rule" of the First Amendment, "that a speaker has the autonomy to choose the content of his own message."

Are the Boy Scouts more analogous to the parade sponsors in *Hurley* or to the New York City clubs, the Jaycees, and the Rotarians? The answer to that question determined whether James Dale would continue as an assistant scoutmaster in New Jersey. The Scouts' Monmouth Council revoked Dale's adult membership, and with it his right to be a scout leader, because of his sexual orientation. The state supreme court held that New Jersey's law banning such discrimination by a "public accommodation" applied to the Scouts and so the revocation was illegal. The U.S. Supreme Court reversed, finding a sufficient link—which the four dissenting justices chided as practically nonexistent—between the organization's principles and objectives and its membership policy regarding openly gay people (***Boy Scouts of America and Monmouth Council* v. *Dale***, 2000). "Dale's presence in the Boy Scouts would, at the very least," wrote Chief Justice Rehnquist, "force the organization to send a message, both to youth members and the world, that the Boy Scouts accepts homosexual conduct as a legitimate form of behavior." (While the Boy Scouts changed its policy in 2015 and now allows openly gay adult leaders to serve, local sponsoring organizations such as churches have the option to use sexual orientation as a guideline in selecting leaders.) Yet, the claim of expressive association that was dispositive for the Scouts in *Dale* proved insufficient for an association of law schools in *Rumsfeld* v. *Forum for Academic and Institutional Rights* (2006), reprinted in Chapter Seven. There, the Solomon Amendment, which bars recipients of federal aid from denying equal access to military recruiters, easily prevailed over a policy of many law schools to exclude recruiters representing employers, such as the U.S. military, that then practiced discrimination based on sexual orientation.

Constitutional questions may also arise from a worker's membership in a union, as illustrated by ***Janus* v. *American Federation of State, County, and Municipal Employees*** (AFSCME) (2018) that overruled *Abood* v. *Detroit Board of Education* (1977). In *Abood* the Court upheld a state law requiring non-union employees to pay an agency or "fair share" fee to the union to cover costs associated with the collective bargaining which benefitted union members and non-members alike. Without such fees, unions insisted that members would have an incentive to become "free-riders," benefiting from collective bargaining but not contributing to its costs. *Janus* is instructive not only because of the issue in the case but because of the exchange between Justices Alito and Kagan about *stare decisis* (Latin for "to stand by what is decided") and the circumstances that justify overruling a prior decision of the Court.

PRINT AND ELECTRONIC MEDIA

"A free press," declared Justice Frankfurter, "is indispensable to the workings of our democratic society." Whether through newspaper, magazine, radio, film, Internet, or television, journalism is an industry that "serves one of the most vital of all general interests," surmised Judge Learned Hand—"the dissemination of news from as many different sources, and with as many different facets and colors as is possible." Right conclusions "are more likely to be gathered out of a multitude of tongues, than through any kind of authoritative selection. To many this is, and always will be, folly; but we have staked upon it our all." The First Amendment lays down a claim for a free press, but the involvement of the press with "the workings of our democratic society" guarantees conflict between journalists and public officials.

Prior Restraints. At the very least, the First Amendment was designed to prevent "all such previous restraints upon publications as had been practised by other governments," noted Justice Holmes over a century ago (*Patterson* v. *Colorado*, 1907). A **prior restraint**—legal action that blocks further publication—is still regarded as the most onerous kind of abridgement of press freedom and is the restriction that the Court is most reluctant to approve.

In the landmark 1931 decision of *Near* v. *Minnesota*, the Court held unconstitutional a Minnesota statute that gave the state power to shut down any "malicious, scandalous and defamatory newspaper, magazine or periodical." Truth published with good motives was available as a defense. Jay Near published the *Saturday Press*, which devoted several issues to virulent attacks on various public officials accusing them of being in cahoots with gangsters. The attacks were anti-Semitic in tone and thoroughly tasteless, and the county attorney succeeded in having the law applied to Near. "This is . . . the essence of censorship," concluded Chief Justice Hughes, by a margin of one vote. Five years later, the Court went beyond *Near*'s invalidation of outright censorship, when *Grosjean* v. *American Press Co.* struck down tax legislation in Louisiana crafted to apply only to the state's 13 daily newspapers, all but one of which strongly opposed Governor Huey P. (the "Kingfish") Long. Facially, the tax scheme was not censorial, but the justices considered it be "a deliberate and calculated device . . . to limit the circulation of information."

Near itself went on trial in June 1971, when the United States sought to enjoin first the *New York Times* and then the *Washington Post* from publishing the contents of a classified study the *Times* had obtained, titled "History of U.S. Decision-Making Process on Vietnam Policy" (***New York Times Company* v. *United States***—the "Pentagon Papers" case). Unlike *Near*, there was no statute giving courts power to block continued publication of a newspaper, even to protect national security. With no time for anyone to write a majority opinion, the Court simply issued a brief per curiam order stating that the government had not met the necessary burden of "showing justification for the enforcement of such a restraint," followed by six concurring and three dissenting opinions. Such prior restraints on publication remain the hobgoblin of American constitutional interpretation. Indeed, anyone contemplating a prior restraint today must take into account the Internet and all it has done to transform information technology. Short of unplugging the entire international telecommunications system, the physical demands of a prior restraint that works are mind-boggling.

Libel. Although American judges historically have looked warily on prior restraints, the press has been on notice that it must take responsibility for what it publishes. The press may not be restrained in advance, but it may be punished for what it prints. **Libel** (written defamation of a person's reputation) is one of these subsequent punishments and has long been regarded as an exception to the press freedom protected by the First Amendment. In 1964, however, ***New York Times Co.* v. *Sullivan*** virtually abolished the right of public officials to collect damages for libel. Under this decision, the press and perhaps anyone else has the right to publish libelous statements about public officials. "Actual malice" must be shown by a plaintiff under the Sullivan rule. The Court's rationale has been summed up this way: "What is added to the field of libel is taken from the arena of debate, and democracy calls for robust, wide-open debate about public issues. Libel, then, that deals with public affairs is not evil; it serves a socially useful function." *Curtis Publishing Co.* v. *Butts* in 1967 extended the Sullivan rule to prominent people outside government. Even parodies that are plainly false and intended to cause emotional distress are protected, the Court held in *Hustler Magazine* v. *Falwell* (1988). Here, a magazine had published a supposed interview with a television evangelist in which he revealed that his "first time" was an intoxicated tryst with his mother in an outhouse.

Sullivan has not ended libel suits by public officials and figures. Decisions have allowed more cases to go to trial by making the issue of malice one for the jury to decide. By preserving the possibility of a successful libel action, libel law understandably makes journalists wary. Even if unsuccessful, a suit is costly because of the amount of time a defense requires. A major television network may be able to absorb the costs, but a small newspaper or station would not and therefore might forgo controversial investigative reporting that might spark a libel suit.

Pornography. State and national governments alike continue to be involved in the less dramatic function of protecting the welfare of their citizens. Where these policies attempt to curtail sexually explicit materials, First Amendment problems arise.

Roth v. *United States* (1957) was the Court's first formal acceptance under the First Amendment of state and federal action directed against pornography. Justice Brennan wrote for the majority that "obscenity is utterly without redeeming social importance." Therefore, it "is not within the area of constitutionally protected speech or press." The key of course was to define the obscene, and the constitutional standard became "whether to the average person, applying contemporary community standards, the dominant theme of the material taken as a whole appeals to prurient interest."

Roth raised as many questions as it answered and only began the Court's long struggle with what Justice Harlan later called "the intractable obscenity problem." In effect, the justices became the censorship board for the nation. With unusual candor, Justice Stewart confessed that his colleagues were trying to define the indefinable. "[U]nder the First and Fourteenth Amendments criminal laws in this area are constitutionally limited to hard-core pornography. I shall not today attempt further to define the kinds of material I understand to be embraced within that shorthand description; and perhaps I could never succeed in intelligibly doing so. But I know it when I see it . . ." (*Jacobellis* v. *Ohio*, 1964).

In 1966, in *Memoirs of a Woman of Pleasure* v. *Massachusetts*, the justices tightened the Roth test and made it more difficult for government to maintain a successful obscenity prosecution. Although formally endorsed only by a plurality, the elements of proof now included a demonstration that the material in question be "patently offensive" and "utterly without redeeming social value." Definitional problems abounded, and as a result so did the number of obscenity cases on the Court's docket. Some of the justices found themselves with no choice but to look at the material in question. The staff then obligingly set up a special viewing room on the ground level of the Supreme Court Building. Harlan dutifully attended the video sessions despite cataracts that badly obscured his vision. Justice Stewart sat next to him and described the activity taking place on the screen. As radio journalist Nina

Totenberg reported, "And about once every five minutes Harlan would exclaim in his proper way: 'By George, extraordinary.'"

In 1969, *Stanley* v. *Georgia* gave the strong hint that all obscenity laws were living on borrowed time, as the Court held that mere private possession of obscene materials was protected by the First Amendment. But the majority pulled back from the logical implications of *Stanley* in *Miller* v. *California* (1973) and announced new standards. Most significantly, the prosecution now had to show that the material in question lacked only "serious value," not that it was "utterly without" value. Ironically, just as the Court relaxed constitutional protection for sexually explicit matter, society was generally becoming more tolerant of it, especially as the Internet was making it both easily accessible and less expensive. The result has been a sharp decline in obscenity prosecutions involving material depicting adults.

Instead, prosecutorial emphasis in recent years has been on child pornography. According to *Ferber* v. *New York* (1982), government may proscribe materials that photographically portray sexual acts or lewd exhibitions of genitalia by children even when the materials are not obscene under *Miller*. The Court's rationale was that such laws were needed to stop sexual exploitation of minors. Yet, the battle against child pornography has been complicated by computer technology, allowing the creation of "virtual child pornography." Congress addressed the problem in the Child Pornography Prevention Act of 1996, but its key provisions fell victim to the overbreadth doctrine in ***Ashcroft* v. *Free Speech Coalition*** (2002). Similar concerns led the Court to invalidate a 1999 act of Congress that criminalized the production of and trafficking in video recordings (so-called crush videos) of "conduct in which a living animal is intentionally maimed, mutilated, tortured, wounded or killed." The First Amendment, explained Chief Justice Roberts, "means that government has no power to restrict expression because of its message, its ideas, its subject matter or its content." Acknowledging that some kinds of speech—including obscenity, defamation, fraud, incitement, and speech integral to criminal conduct—have historically been granted no constitutional protection, he insisted that the Court had no "freewheeling authority to declare new categories of speech outside the scope of the First Amendment." Child pornography was a "special case" because the market for it is "intrinsically related to the underlying abuse" (*United States* v. *Stevens*, 2010). Particularly for laws intended to protect minors, any restriction needs to be narrowly tailored and to avoid overbreadth. That principle was a key point in *Packingham v. North Carolina* (2017), in which the Court struck down a state law making it a felony for a registered sex offender "to access a commercial social networking Web site where the sex offender knows that the site permits minor children to become members or to create or maintain personal Web pages." Justice Kennedy's plurality opinion noted that the case "is one of the first this Court has taken to address the relationship between the First Amendment and the modern Internet," but warned that the court should "exercise extreme caution before suggesting that the First Amendment provides scant protection for access" to ubiquitous social networking sites like Facebook and Twitter. Concurring in the judgment, Justice Alito warned against any notion that cyberspace is "the 21st century equivalent of public streets and parks." Equating the Internet with a public forum would leave states with "little ability to restrict the sites that may be visited by even the most dangerous sex offenders," given that "there are important differences between cyberspace and the physical world."

Commercial Speech. Regulations on advertisements and other commercial messages present a special problem. Not until *Virginia State Board of Pharmacy*

v. *Virginia Consumer Council* (1976) did the justices include **commercial speech** under the shield of the First Amendment, when the Court set aside a law that barred price advertising of prescription drugs. Later cases have extended the freedom to advertise to lawyers (*Bates* v. *State Bar of Arizona*, 1977) and the freedom to solicit in person and by telephone to accountants, but not yet to attorneys (*Edenfield* v. *Fane*, 1993). Nonetheless, governments still have greater latitude in regulating commercial as compared with other kinds of speech. *Central Hudson Gas & Electric Corp.* v. *Public Service Commission of New York* (1980) laid down a four-part analysis that the Court continues to use.

> At the outset, we must determine whether the expression is protected by the First Amendment. For commercial speech to come within that provision, it at least must concern lawful activity and not be misleading. Next, we ask whether the asserted governmental interest is substantial. If both inquiries yield positive answers, we must determine whether the regulation directly advances the governmental interest asserted, and whether it is not more extensive than is necessary to serve that interest.

Even a brand name can raise a constitutional issue, as happened in *Matel* v. *Tam* (2017). In this case, the Court struck down as impermissible viewpoint discrimination the disparagement clause of the Lanham Act of 1946, which barred trademarks containing "immoral, deceptive, or scandalous matter; or matter which may disparage or falsely suggest a connection with persons, living or dead, institutions, beliefs, or national symbols, or bring them into contempt, or disrepute." The dispute arose after a rock band applied for federal trademark registration of its name, "The Slants." The word is a derogatory term for persons of Asian descent, but members of the band are Asian-Americans who believed that by taking that slur as the name of their group, they would help to "reclaim" the term and drain its denigrating force. The Patent and Trademark Office in the Department of Commerce disagreed, but the Court sided with the band. In Justice Alito's words, the clause "offends a bedrock First Amendment principle: Speech may not be banned on the ground that it expresses ideas that offend."

Radio, Television, and the Internet. Print and broadcast media do not stand as equals under the First Amendment. While the gap has narrowed in recent years, newspapers and magazines—like the orators and pamphleteers also known to the framers—have been accorded more freedom than radio and television. Perhaps nowhere else has Justice Holmes's observation been more apt: "a page of history is worth a volume of logic."

As commercial radio and television evolved in the 1920s and 1940s, respectively, some regulation by the federal government was deemed essential. With a finite broadcast spectrum, chaos would reign on the airwaves without allocation of frequencies and limitations on transmitting locations and power. Coupled with the necessity of licensing, oversight, and license renewal was the premise that access to the broadcast spectrum should be conditional. Stipulations (such as operating "in the public interest," affording "equal time" to political candidates, and telecasting educational programs for children) were imposed that would be constitutionally unacceptable if applied to newspapers. Moreover, because of the pervasiveness of radio and television, the likelihood that listeners and viewers could be exposed to undesirable programming without warning, and the ease with which children could come in contact with such programming, courts may accept carefully drawn regulations to keep offensive material off the air, at least during certain hours of the day. Such regulations typically do not apply to subscription satellite radio services.

Advances in technology seem largely to have undercut the "scarcity" rationale for regulation. Frequencies may remain finite, but almost every home has greater access to radio and television than to newspapers. Commercial and educational stations outnumber daily newspapers by more than seven to one. Thanks to cable and satellite companies that convey outlets (such as ESPN and CNBC) in addition to those from traditional broadcast stations, most households now receive dozens of video channels, and many receive hundreds. Yet, enlarged capacity in the hands of cable monopolies at the community level has itself become a basis for regulation. Against a challenge on First Amendment grounds, *Turner Broadcasting System, Inc.* v. *FCC* (1997) approved a federal "must carry" statute, requiring local cable systems to relay nearby commercial and public broadcast stations even if the cable system preferred to substitute out-of-area stations or cable channels in their place.

The Internet demonstrates that technology continues to generate constitutional questions. An outgrowth of a military program called ARPANET (Advanced Research Project Agency Network), created in 1969 to enable computers operated by the military, defense contractors, and universities to communicate with one another on redundant circuits in wartime, the Internet has become both an international network of interconnected computers and a wholly new medium of communication. For a user, the Internet is comparable to a vast library of readily available and indexed publications, a vast source of entertainment, and a mall offering goods and services. For the operator of a website, the Internet is a platform through which to reach a worldwide audience of readers, voters, researchers, and customers.

In 1996, Congress passed the Communications Decency Act to protect minors from obscene and indecent materials on the Internet. One section criminalized the knowing transmission of "obscene or indecent" messages to any recipient under 18 years of age. Another section made unlawful knowingly sending or displaying to someone under 18 any message that "in context depicts or describes, in terms patently offensive as measured by contemporary community standards, sexual or excretory activities or organs." Several groups immediately challenged the legislation as a violation of freedom of speech. With a history of contrasting approaches in regulating different media, was the Internet to be treated for regulatory purposes like a newspaper or a television station? The Internet, after all, incorporated elements of each. A nearly unanimous answer came in *Reno* v. *American Civil Liberties Union* (1997), the first application of the Constitution to cyberspace, where the Court sharply curtailed government's authority to censor content on the Internet. "We are persuaded that the CDA lacks the precision that the First Amendment requires when a statute regulates the content of speech," explained Justice Stevens. "In order to deny minors access to potentially harmful speech, the CDA effectively suppresses a large amount of speech that adults have a constitutional right to receive and to address to one another. . . . [T]he Government may not 'reduc[e] the adult population . . . to . . . only what is fit for children.'"

POSTSCRIPT

If speech in recent decades has typically prevailed over competing interests, does this mean that the First Amendment is in a favored or preferred position? Justice Stone's Footnote Four in the *Carolene Products* case, discussed in Chapter Eight, suggests precisely that. In response, Justice Scalia contended that "the First Amendment is not everything." Regardless, constitutional rights are not rights against government so much as rights against the dominant majority represented by government. It would be difficult to label a political system as "democratic" if individuals with points of view in the minority could not freely campaign to become the majority. The Bill of Rights expresses the judgment of the Founders that the majority is neither always right nor likely to be tolerant. "The very purpose of a Bill of Rights," Justice Jackson declared in 1943, "was to withdraw certain subjects from the vicissitudes of political controversy, to place them beyond the reach of majorities." Thus, the irony of the First Amendment: A guarantee of free speech presupposes a population capable of rational thought and considered judgment; it also assumes a population sometimes eager to squelch unpopular ideas.

KEY TERMS

clear-and-present-danger test
bad tendency test
incitement test
absolute approach
overbreadth doctrine
chilling effect
void for vagueness
strict scrutiny
Sedition Act of 1798
criminal syndicalism
Smith Act
viewpoint-based restrictions
public forum
government speech
fighting words
symbolic speech
expressive association
stare decisis
prior restraint
libel
commercial speech

QUERIES

1. Why should freedom of speech be extended to persons who, were they to acquire political power, would deny that freedom to others?

2. In a dissenting opinion in *Tah* v. *Global Witness Publishing, Inc.*, 991 F. 3d 231 (2021), decided by the U.S. Court of Appeals for the District of Columbia Circuit, Judge Laurence Silberman called for discarding the broad rule the Supreme Court announced in *New York Times* v. *Sullivan*.

> After observing my colleagues' efforts to stretch the actual malice rule like a rubber band, I am prompted to urge the overruling of *New York Times* v. *Sullivan*. Justice Thomas has already persuasively demonstrated that *New York Times* was a policy-driven decision masquerading as constitutional law. See *McKee* v. *Cosby*, 139 S. Ct. 675 (2019). The holding has no relation to the text, history, or structure of the Constitution, and it baldly constitutionalized an area of law refined over centuries of common law adjudication. As with the rest of the opinion, the actual malice requirement was simply cut from whole cloth. *New York Times* should be overruled on these grounds alone. Nevertheless, I recognize how difficult it will be to persuade the Supreme Court to overrule such a "landmark" decision. After all, doing so would incur the wrath of press and media. But new considerations have arisen over the last 50 years that make the *New York Times* decision . . . a threat to American Democracy. It must go. . . . Our court was once concerned about the institutional consolidation of the press leading to a "bland and homogenous" marketplace of ideas. It turns out that ideological consolidation of the press (helped along by economic consolidation) is the far greater threat. . . .

What are Judge Silberman's reasons for abandoning the Sullivan rule? Do they have merit? What would be the effects of his position on freedom of the press were the Court to accept Silberman's suggestion?

3. Could a flag-protection law have been written that would have satisfied the majority in *Texas* v. *Johnson?* Consider the language of Congress' Flag Protection Act of 1989, which the Court found unacceptable in *United States* v. *Eichman:* "Whoever knowingly mutilates, defaces, physically defiles, burns, maintains on the floor or ground, or tramples upon any flag of the United States shall be fined . . . or imprisoned. . . ." Is it possible to separate protection of the flag from protection of the values it symbolizes? In his dissenting opinion in *Johnson*, what rationale does Justice Stevens offer for flag protection?

4. In *Beauharnais* v. *Illinois* (1952), the Supreme Court, voting 5–4, upheld the application to a white supremacist of a group libel law that prohibited publications that portrayed "depravity, criminality, unchastity, or lack of virtue of a class of citizens, of any race, color, creed or religion, [or which] exposes the citizens of any race, color, creed or religion to contempt, derision, or obloquy, or which is productive of breach of the peace or riots." Does *Beauharnais* have relevance to the debate today about efforts to control hate speech? Has *Beauharnais* been eroded by later decisions?

SELECTED READINGS

Chafee, Zechariah, Jr. *Free Speech in the United States*. Cambridge, MA: Harvard University Press, 1942.

Ellis, Richard. *Judging the BSA: Gay Rights, Freedom of Association, and the Dale Case*. Lawrence: University Press of Kansas, 2014.

Healy, Thomas. *The Great Dissent: How Oliver Wendell Holmes Changed His Mind—and Changed the History of Free Speech in America*. New York: Metropolitan Books/ Henry Holt, 2013.

Kersch, Ken I. *Freedom of Speech*. Santa Barbara, CA: ABC-CLIO, 2003.

Levy, Leonard W. *Emergence of a Free Press*. New York: Oxford University Press, 1985.

Pozen, David E., ed. *The Perilous Public Square: Structural Threats to Free Expression Today*. New York: Columbia University Press, 2020.

Rudenstine, David. *The Day the Presses Stopped: A History of the Pentagon Papers Case*. Berkeley: University of California Press, 1996.

Stone, Geoffrey R. *Perilous Times: Free Speech in Wartime from the Sedition Act of 1798 to the War on Terrorism*. New York: Norton, 2004.

Strum, Philippa. *Speaking Freely: Whitney v. California and American Free Speech Law*. Lawrence: University Press of Kansas, 2015.

Whittington, Keith. *Speak Freely: Why Universities Must Defend Free Speech*. Princeton: Princeton University Press, 2018.

I. INTERNAL SECURITY

Schenck v. *United States*
249 U.S. 47, 39 S.Ct. 247, 63 L.Ed. 470 (1919)

http://caselaw.findlaw.com/us-supreme-court/249/47.html

Charles Schenck and others were convicted of conspiracy to obstruct the draft and other violations of the Espionage Act of 1917. Their specific offense was printing and distributing leaflets that opposed the war effort generally and conscription specifically. Majority: Holmes, Brandeis, Clarke, Day, McKenna, McReynolds, Pitney, Van Devanter, White.

Mr. Justice Holmes delivered the opinion of the court. . . .

The document in question upon its first printed side recited the first section of the Thirteenth Amendment, said that the idea embodied in it was violated by the Conscription Act, and that a conscript is little better than a convict. In impassioned language it intimated that conscription was despotism in its worst form and a monstrous wrong against humanity in the interest of Wall Street's chosen few. It said, "Do not submit to intimidation," but in form at least confined itself to peaceful measures such as a petition for the repeal of the act. The other and later printed side of the sheet was headed "Assert Your Rights." It stated reasons for alleging that any one violated the Constitution when he refused to recognize "your right to assert your opposition to the draft," and went on "If you do not assert and support your rights, you are helping to deny or disparage rights which it is the solemn duty of all citizens and residents of the United States to retain." It described the arguments on the other side as coming from cunning politicians and a mercenary capitalist press, and even silent consent to the conscription law as helping to support an infamous conspiracy. It denied the power to send our citizens away to foreign shores to shoot up the people of other lands, and added that words could not express the condemnation such cold-blooded ruthlessness deserves, & c., winding up "You must do your share to maintain, support and uphold the rights of the people of this country." Of course the document would not have been sent unless it had been intended to have some effect, and we do not see what effect it could be expected to have upon persons subject to the draft except to influence them to obstruct the carrying out of it. The defendants do not deny that the jury might find against them on this point.

But it is said, suppose that that was the tendency of this circular, it is protected by the First Amendment to the Constitution. Two of the strongest expressions are said to be quoted respectively from well-known public men. It well may be that the prohibition of laws abridging the freedom of speech is not confined to previous restraints, although to prevent them may have been the main purpose. . . . We admit that in many places and in ordinary times the defendants in saying all that was said in the circular would have been within their constitutional rights. But the character of every act depends upon the circumstances in which it is done. . . . The most stringent protection of free speech would not protect a man in falsely shouting fire in a theatre and causing a panic. It does not even protect a man from an injunction against uttering words that may have all the effect of force. . . . The question in every case is whether the words are used in such circumstances and are of such a nature as to create a clear and present danger that they will bring about the substantive evils that Congress has a right to prevent. It is a question of proximity and degree. When a nation is at war many things that might be said in time of peace are such a hindrance to its effort that their utterance will not be endured so long as men fight and that no Court could regard them as protected by any constitutional right. It seems to be admitted that if an actual obstruction of the recruiting service were proved, liability for words that produced that effect might be enforced. The statute of 1917 in § 4 punishes conspiracies to obstruct as well as actual obstruction. If the act (speaking, or circulating a paper), its tendency and the intent with which it is done are the same, we perceive no ground for saying that success alone warrants making the act a crime.

Judgments affirmed.

Gitlow v. *New York*
268 U.S. 652, 45 S.Ct. 625, 69 L.Ed. 1138 (1925)

http://caselaw.findlaw.com/us-supreme-court/268/652.html

Benjamin Gitlow, a member of the left-wing section of the Socialist Party, was convicted of the New York crime of criminal anarchy. Majority: Sanford, Butler, McReynolds, Sutherland, Taft, Van Devanter. Dissenting: Holmes, Brandeis. Not participating: Stone.

Mr. Justice Sanford delivered the opinion of the Court. . . .

The indictment was in two counts. The first charged that the defendant had advocated, advised and taught the duty, necessity and propriety of overthrowing and overturning organized government by force, violence and unlawful means, by certain writings therein set forth entitled "The Left Wing Manifesto"; the second that he had printed, published and knowingly circulated and distributed a certain paper called "The Revolutionary Age," containing the writings set forth in the first count, advocating, advising and teaching the doctrine that organized government should be overthrown by force, violence and unlawful means. . . .

The precise question presented, and the only question which we can consider under this writ of error, then is, whether the statute, as construed and applied in this case by the state courts, deprived the defendant of his liberty of expression in violation of the due process clause of the Fourteenth Amendment.

The statute does not penalize the utterance or publication of abstract "doctrine" or academic discussion having no quality of incitement to any concrete action. . . . What it prohibits is language advocating, advising or teaching the overthrow of organized government by unlawful means. . . .

The Manifesto, plainly, is neither the statement of abstract doctrine nor, as suggested by counsel, mere prediction that industrial disturbances and revolutionary mass strikes will result spontaneously in an inevitable process of evolution in the economic system. It advocates and urges in fervent language mass action which shall progressively foment industrial disturbances and through political mass strikes and revolutionary mass action overthrow and destroy organized parliamentary government. It concludes with a call to action in these words: "The proletariat revolution and the Communist reconstruction of society—the struggle for these—is now indispensable. . . . The Communist International calls the proletariat of the world to the final struggle!" This is not the expression of philosophical abstractions, the mere prediction of future events; it is the language of direct incitement. . . . it has enkindled the flame or blazed into the conflagration. . . .

For present purposes we may add and do assume that freedom of speech and of the press—which are protected by the First Amendment from abridgment by Congress—are among the fundamental personal rights and "liberties" protected by the due process clause of the Fourteenth Amendment from impairment by the states. . . .

That a State in the exercise of its police power may punish those who abuse this freedom by utterances inimical to the public welfare, tending to corrupt public morals, incite to crime, or disturb the public peace, is not open to question. . . .

By enacting the present statute the State has determined, through its legislative body, that utterances advocating the overthrow of organized government by force, violence and unlawful means, are so inimical to the general welfare and involve such danger of substantive evil that they may be penalized in the exercise of its police power. That determination must be given great weight. Every presumption is to be indulged in favor of the validity of the statute. . . . That utterances inciting to the overthrow of organized government by unlawful means, present a sufficient danger of substantive evil to bring their punishment within the range of legislative discretion, is clear. Such utterances, by their very nature, involve danger to the public peace and to the security of the State. They threaten breaches of the peace and ultimate revolution. And the immediate danger is none the less real and substantial, because the effect of a given utterance cannot be accurately foreseen. The State cannot reasonably be required to measure the danger from every such utterance in the nice balance of a jeweler's scale. A single revolutionary spark may kindle a fire that, smouldering for a time, may burst into a sweeping and destructive conflagration. It cannot be said that the State is acting arbitrarily or unreasonably when in the exercise of its judgment as to the measures necessary to protect the public peace and safety, it seeks to extinguish the spark without waiting until it has enkindled the flame or blazed into the conflagration. . . .

We cannot hold that the present statute is an arbitrary or unreasonable exercise of the police power of the State unwarrantably infringing the freedom of speech or press; and we must and do sustain its constitutionality. . . .

Affirmed.

Mr. Justice Holmes, dissenting.

Mr. Justice Brandeis and I are of opinion that this judgment should be reversed. . . . I think that the criterion sanctioned by the full court in *Schenck* v. *United States* . . . applies. It is manifest that there was no present danger of an attempt to overthrow the government by force on the part of the admittedly small minority who shared the defendant's views. It is said that this manifesto was more than a theory, that it was an incitement. Every idea is an incitement. It offers itself for belief and if believed it is acted on unless some other belief outweighs it or some failure of energy stifles the movement at its birth. The only difference between the expression of an opinion and an incitement in the narrower sense is the speaker's enthusiasm for the result. Eloquence may set fire to reason. But whatever may be thought of the redundant discourse before us it had no chance of starting a present conflagration. If in the long run the beliefs expressed in proletarian dictatorship are destined to be accepted by the dominant forces of the community, the only meaning of free speech is that they should be given their chance and have their way.

If the publication of this document had been laid out as an attempt to induce an uprising against government at once and not at some indefinite time in the future it would have presented a different question.

The object would have been one with which the law might deal, subject to the doubt whether there was any danger that the publication could produce any result, or in other words, whether it was not futile and too remote from possible consequences. But the indictment alleges the publication and nothing more.

Whitney v. *California* 274 U.S. 357, 47 S.Ct. 641, 71 L.Ed. 1095 (1927)

http://caselaw.findlaw.com/us-supreme-court/274/357.html

Charlotte Anita Whitney—prominent suffragist, Socialist, and niece of former Justice Stephen Field—was convicted of violating California's criminal syndicalism act of 1919 for having participated in a convention of the Communist Labor Party of California, which was affiliated with the Communist International of Moscow. Evidence showed that she had personally proposed a resolution advocating a strictly political role for the party, which the convention had rejected in favor of a national program advocating various revolutionary measures including national strikes. She remained until the end of the convention and did not withdraw from the party. The case remains significant because of Justice Brandeis's concurring opinion, which soon led the Court to apply the clear-and-present-danger test in many free speech cases. However, given the strong defense of freedom of speech offered by Brandeis, why is his opinion, which Justice Holmes joined, entered as a concurrence and not a dissent? The answer to that obvious question comes at the end of his opinion and is an insight into an older Court with older procedural expectations. While *Whitney* was not formally overruled until *Brandenburg* v. *Ohio* in 1969, Philippa Strum has written that Brandeis's opinion has become "a canon of American law, and the basis of the uniquely permissive American approach to speech" across a broad range of decisions. As indicative of its influence, she reports that as of 2015, the case, and Brandeis's opinion in particular, had been referred to by the Supreme Court in "close to 100 cases and by state and lower federal courts in over 250." Majority: Sanford, Butler, Brandeis, Holmes, McReynolds, Stone, Sutherland, Taft, Van Devanter.

MR. JUSTICE SANFORD delivered the opinion of the Court. . . .

By enacting the provisions of the Syndicalism Act the State has declared, through its legislative body, that to knowingly be or become a member of or assist in organizing an association to advocate, teach or aid and abet the commission of crimes or unlawful acts of force, violence or terrorism as a means of accomplishing industrial or political changes, involves such danger to the public peace and the security of the State, that these acts should be penalized in the exercise of its police power. That determination must be given great weight. Every presumption is to be indulged in favor of the validity of the statute . . . and it may not be declared unconstitutional unless it is an arbitrary or unreasonable attempt to exercise the authority vested in the State in the public interest. . . .

Affirmed.

MR. JUSTICE BRANDEIS, concurring. . . .

Despite arguments to the contrary which had seemed to me persuasive, it is settled that the due process clause of the Fourteenth Amendment applies to matters of substantive law as well as to matters of procedure. Thus all fundamental rights comprised within the term *liberty* are protected by the Federal Constitution from invasion by the states. . . . But, although the rights of free speech and assembly are fundamental, they are not in their nature absolute. Their exercise is subject to restriction, if the particular restriction proposed is required in order to protect the state from destruction or from serious injury, political, economic or moral. That the necessity which is essential to a valid restriction does not exist unless speech would produce, or is intended to produce, a clear and imminent danger of some substantive evil which the state constitutionally may seek to prevent has been settled. . . .

This court has not yet fixed the standard by which to determine when a danger shall be deemed clear; how remote the danger may be and yet be deemed present; and what degree of evil shall be deemed sufficiently substantial to justify resort to abridgment of free speech and assembly as the means of protection. To reach sound conclusions on these matters, we must bear in mind why a state is, ordinarily, denied the power to prohibit dissemination of social, economic and political doctrine which a vast majority of its citizens believes to be false and fraught with evil consequence.

Those who won our independence believed that the final end of the state was to make men free to develop their faculties, and that in its government the deliberative forces should prevail over the arbitrary. They valued liberty both as an end and as a means. They believed liberty to be the secret of happiness and courage to be the secret of liberty. They believed that freedom to think as you will and to speak as you think are means indispensable to the discovery and spread of political truth; that without free speech and assembly discussion would be futile; that with them, discussion affords ordinarily adequate protection against the dissemination of noxious doctrine; that the greatest menace to freedom is an inert people; that public discussion is a political duty; and that this should be a fundamental principle of the American government. They recognized the risks to which all human institutions are subject. But they knew that order cannot be secured merely through fear of punishment for its infraction; that it is hazardous to discourage thought, hope and imagination; that fear breeds repression; that repression breeds hate; that hate menaces stable government; that the path of safety lies in the opportunity to discuss freely supposed grievances and proposed remedies; and that the fitting remedy for evil counsels is good ones. Believing in the power of reason as applied through public discussion, they eschewed silence coerced by law—the argument of force in its worst form. Recognizing the occasional tyrannies of governing majorities, they amended the Constitution so that free speech and assembly should be guaranteed.

Fear of serious injury cannot alone justify suppression of free speech and assembly. Men feared witches and burnt women. It is the function of speech to free men from the bondage of irrational fears. To justify suppression of free speech there must be reasonable ground to fear that serious evil will result if free speech is practiced. There must be reasonable ground to believe that the danger apprehended is imminent. There must be reasonable ground to believe that the evil to be prevented is a serious one. . . . The wide difference between advocacy and incitement, between preparation and attempt, between assembling and conspiracy, must be borne in mind. In order to support a finding of clear and present danger it must be shown either that immediate serious violence was to be expected or was advocated, or that the past conduct furnished reason to believe that such advocacy was then contemplated.

Those who won our independence by revolution were not cowards. They did not fear political change. They did not exalt order at the cost of liberty. To courageous, self-reliant men, with confidence in the power of free and fearless reasoning applied through the process of popular government, no danger flowing from speech can be deemed clear and present, unless the incidence of the evil apprehended is so imminent that it may befall before there is opportunity for full discussion. If there be time to expose through discussion the falsehood and fallacies, to avert the evil by the processes of education, the remedy to be applied is more speech, not enforced silence. Only an emergency can justify repression. Such must be the rule if authority is to be reconciled with freedom. Such, in my opinion, is the command of the Constitution. It is therefore always open to Americans to challenge a law abridging free speech and assembly by showing that there was no emergency justifying it.

Moreover, even imminent danger cannot justify resort to prohibition of these functions essential to effective democracy, unless the evil apprehended is relatively serious. Prohibition of free speech and assembly is a measure so stringent that it would be inappropriate as the means for averting a relatively trivial harm to society. A police measure may be unconstitutional merely because the remedy, although effective as means of protection, is unduly harsh or oppressive. . . . The fact that speech is likely to result in some violence or in destruction of property is not enough to justify its suppression. There must be the probability of serious injury to the State. Among free men, the deterrents ordinarily to be applied to prevent crime are education and punishment for violations of the law, not abridgment of the rights of free speech and assembly.

Whether in 1919, when Miss Whitney did the things complained of, there was in California such clear and present danger of serious evil, might have been made the important issue in this case. She might have required that the issue be determined either by the court or by the jury. She claimed below that the statute as applied to her violated the federal Constitution; but she did not claim that it was void because there was no clear and present danger of serious evil, nor did she request that the existence of these conditions of a valid measure thus restricting the rights of free speech and assembly be passed upon by the court or a jury. On the other hand, there was evidence on which the court or jury might have found that such danger existed. . . . Our power of review in this case is limited not only to the question whether a right guaranteed by the federal Constitution was denied but to the particular claims duly made below, and denied. We lack here the power occasionally exercised on review of judgments of lower federal courts to correct in criminal cases vital errors, although the objection was not taken in the trial court. This is a writ of error to a state court. Because we may not inquire into the errors now alleged I concur in affirming the judgment of the state court.

MR. JUSTICE HOLMES joins in this opinion.

Dennis v. *United States*
341 U.S. 494, 71 S.Ct. 857, 95 L.Ed. 1137 (1951)

http://caselaw.findlaw.com/us-supreme-court/341/494.html

This case represents the last stage of the 1949 trial of the 11 leaders of the Communist Party of the United States for violations of the Smith Act of 1940. The Supreme Court's grant of certiorari to the Second Circuit Court of Appeals was limited to a review of whether Sections 2 or 3 of the Smith Act, inherently or as construed and applied, violated the First or Fifth Amendment. Majority: Vinson, Burton, Frankfurter, Jackson, Minton, Reed. Dissenting: Black, Douglas. Not participating: Clark.

Mr. Chief Justice Vinson announced the judgment of the court and an opinion in which Mr. Justice Reed, Mr. Justice Burton, and Mr. Justice Minton join. . . .

Sections 2 and 3 of the Smith Act, provide as follows:

> Sec. 2
> (a) It shall be unlawful for any person—
> (1) to knowingly or willfully advocate, abet, advise, or teach the duty, necessity, desirability, or propriety of overthrowing or destroying any government in the United States by force or violence, or by the assassination of any officer of such government;
> (2) with the intent to cause the overthrow or destruction of any government in the United States, to print, publish, edit, issue, circulate, sell, distribute, or publicly display any written or printed matter advocating, advising, or teaching the duty, necessity, desirability, or propriety of overthrowing or destroying any government in the United States by force or violence;
> (3) to organize or help to organize any society, group, or assembly of persons who teach, advocate, or encourage the overthrow or destruction of any government in the United States by force or violence; or to be or become a member of, or affiliate with, any such society, group, or assembly of persons, knowing the purposes thereof. . . .
> Sec. 3. It shall be unlawful for any person to attempt to commit, or to conspire to commit, any of the acts prohibited by the provisions of . . . this title. . . .

The obvious purpose of the statute is to protect existing Government, not from change by peaceable, lawful and constitutional means, but from change by violence, revolution and terrorism. . . . No one could conceive that it is not within the power of Congress to prohibit acts intended to overthrow the Government by force and violence. The question with which we are concerned here is not whether Congress has such power, but whether the *means* which it has employed conflict with the First and Fifth Amendments to the Constitution.

One of the bases for the contention that the means which Congress has employed are invalid takes the form of an attack on the face of the statute on the grounds that by its terms it prohibits academic discussion of the merits of Marxism-Leninism, that it stifles ideas and is contrary to all concepts of a free speech and a free press. . . .

The very language of the Smith Act negates the interpretation which petitioners would have us impose on that Act. It is directed at advocacy, not discussion. Thus, the trial judge properly charged the jury that they could not convict if they found that petitioners did "no more than pursue peaceful studies and discussions or teaching and advocacy in the realm of ideas." He further charged that it was not unlawful "to conduct in an American college or university a course explaining the philosophical theories set forth in the books which have been placed in evidence." Such a charge is in strict accord with the statutory language, and illustrates the meaning to be placed on those words. Congress did not intend to eradicate the free discussion of political theories, to destroy the traditional rights of Americans to discuss and evaluate ideas without fear of governmental sanction. Rather Congress was concerned with the very kind of activity in which the evidence showed these petitioners engaged. . . .

The basis of the First Amendment is the hypothesis that speech can rebut speech, propaganda will answer propaganda, free debate of ideas will result in the wisest governmental policies. It is for this reason that this Court has recognized the inherent value of free discourse. An analysis of the leading cases in this Court which have involved direct limitations on speech, however, will demonstrate that both the majority of the Court and dissenters in particular cases have recognized that this is not an unlimited, unqualified right, but that the societal value of speech must, on occasion, be subordinated to other values and considerations. . . .

The rule we deduce from [past] cases is that where an offense is specified by a statute in nonspeech or nonpress terms, a conviction relying upon speech or press as evidence of violation may be sustained only when the speech or publication created a "clear and present danger" of attempting or accomplishing the prohibited crime, for example, interference with enlistment. The dissents, we repeat, in emphasizing the value of speech, were addressed to the argument of the sufficiency of the evidence. . . .

Although no case subsequent to *Whitney* and *Gitlow* has expressly overruled the majority opinions in those cases, there is little doubt that subsequent opinions have inclined toward the Holmes-Brandeis rationale. . . . In this case we are squarely presented with the application of the "clear and present danger" test, and must decide what that phrase imports. . . .

Obviously, the words cannot mean that before the Government may act, it must wait until the putsch is about to be executed, the plans have been laid and the signal is awaited. . . . In the instant case the trial judge charged the jury that they could not convict unless they found that petitioners intended to overthrow the Government "as speedily as circumstances would permit." This does not mean, and could not properly mean, that they would not strike until there was certainty of success. What was meant was that the revolutionists would strike when they thought the time was ripe. We must therefore reject the contention that success or probability of success is the criterion.

The situation with which Justices Holmes and Brandeis were concerned in *Gitlow* was a comparatively isolated event, bearing little relation in their minds to any substantial threat to the safety of the community. . . . They were not confronted with any situation comparable to the instant one—the development of an apparatus designed and dedicated to the overthrow of the Government, in the context of world crisis after crisis.

Chief Judge Learned Hand, writing for the majority below, interpreted the phrase as follows: "In each case [courts] must ask whether the gravity of the 'evil,' discounted by its improbability, justifies such invasion of free speech as is necessary to avoid the danger." . . . We adopt this statement of the rule. As articulated by Chief Judge Hand, it is as succinct and inclusive as any other we might devise at this time. It takes into consideration those factors which we deem relevant, and relates their significances. More we cannot expect from words.

Likewise, we are in accord with the court below, which affirmed the trial court's finding that the requisite danger existed. The mere fact that from the period 1945 to 1948 petitioners' activities did not result in an attempt to overthrow the Government by force and violence is of course no answer to the fact that there was a group that was ready to make the attempt. The formation by petitioners of such a highly organized conspiracy, with rigidly disciplined members subject to call when the leaders, these petitioners, felt that the time had come for action, coupled with the inflammable nature of world conditions, similar uprisings in other countries, and the touch-and-go nature of our relations with countries with whom petitioners were in the very least ideologically attuned, convince us that their convictions were justified on this score. And this analysis disposes of the contention that a conspiracy to advocate, as distinguished from the advocacy itself, cannot be constitutionally restrained, because it comprises only the preparation. It is the existence of the conspiracy which creates the danger. . . . If the ingredients of the reaction are present, we cannot bind the government to wait until the catalyst is added. . . .

Affirmed.

MR. JUSTICE FRANKFURTER, concurring in affirmance of the judgment. . . .

The demands of free speech in a democratic society as well as the interest in national security are better served by candid and informed weighing of the competing interests, within the confines of the judicial process, than by announcing dogmas too inflexible for the non-Euclidian problems to be solved.

But how are competing interests to be assessed? Since they are not subject to quantitative ascertainment, the issue necessarily resolves itself into asking, who is to make the adjustment?—who is to balance the relevant factors and ascertain which interest is in the circumstances to prevail? Full responsibility for the choice cannot be given to the courts. Courts are not representative bodies. They are not designed to be a good reflex of a democratic society. . . .

Primary responsibility for adjusting the interests which compete in the situation before us of necessity belongs to the Congress. The nature of the power to be exercised by this Court has been delineated in decisions not charged with the emotional appeal of situations such as that now before us. . . .

It is not for us to decide how we would adjust the clash of interests which this case presents were the primary responsibility for reconciling it ours. Congress has determined that the danger created by advocacy of overthrow justifies the ensuing restriction on freedom of speech. The determination was made after due deliberation, and the seriousness of the congressional purpose is attested by the volume of legislation passed to effectuate the same ends.

Can we then say that the judgment Congress exercised was denied it by the Constitution? . . . Can we hold that the First Amendment deprives Congress of what it deemed necessary for the Government's protection?

To make validity of legislation depend on judicial reading of events still in the womb of time—a forecast, that is, of the outcome of forces at best appreciated only with knowledge of the topmost secrets of nations—is to charge the judiciary with duties beyond its equipment. . . . It is as absurd to be confident that we can measure the present clash of forces and their outcome as to ask us to read history still enveloped in clouds of controversy. . . .

Civil liberties draw at best only limited strength from legal guaranties. Preoccupation by our people with the constitutionality, instead of with the wisdom of legislation or of executive action, is preoccupation with a false value. . . . Focusing attention on constitutionality tends to make constitutionality synonymous with wisdom. When legislation touches freedom of thought and freedom of speech, such a tendency is a formidable enemy of the free spirit. Much that should be rejected as illiberal, because repressive and envenoming, may well be not unconstitutional. The ultimate reliance for the deepest needs of civilization must be found outside their vindication in courts of law; apart from all else, judges, howsoever they may conscientiously seek to discipline themselves against it, unconsciously are too apt to be moved by the deep undercurrents of public feeling. A persistent, positive translation of the liberating faith into the feelings and thoughts and actions of men and women is the real protection against attempts to straitjacket the human mind. . . . Without open minds there can be no open society. And if society be not open the spirit of man is mutilated and becomes enslaved. . . .

MR. JUSTICE JACKSON, concurring . . . [omitted].

MR. JUSTICE BLACK, dissenting. . . .

I want to emphasize what the crime involved in this case is, and what it is not. These petitioners were not charged with an attempt to overthrow the Government. They were not charged with overt acts of any kind designed to overthrow the Government. They were not even charged with saying anything or writing anything designed to overthrow the Government. The charge was that they agreed to assemble and to talk and publish certain ideas at a later date: The indictment is that they conspired to organize the Communist Party and to use speech or newspapers and other publications in the future to teach and advocate the forcible overthrow of the Government. No matter how it is worded, this is a virulent form of prior censorship of speech and press, which I believe the First Amendment forbids. I would hold § 3 of the Smith Act authorizing this prior restraint unconstitutional on its face and as applied. . . .

Mr. Justice Douglas, dissenting. . . .

[F]ree speech is the rule, not the exception. The restraint to be constitutional must be based on more than fear, on more than passionate opposition against the speech, on more than a revolted dislike for its contents. There must be some immediate injury to society that is likely if speech is allowed. . . .

How it can be said that there is a clear and present danger that this advocacy will succeed is, therefore, a mystery. Some nations less resilient than the United States, where illiteracy is high and where democratic traditions are only budding, might have to take drastic steps and jail these men for merely speaking their creed. But in America they are miserable merchants of unwanted ideas; their wares remain unsold. The fact that their ideas are abhorrent does not make them powerful. . . . Our faith should be that our people will never give support to these advocates of revolution, so long as we remain loyal to the purposes for which our Nation was founded.

Brandenburg v. *Ohio*
395 U.S. 444, 89 S.Ct. 1827, 23 L.Ed. 2d 430 (1969)

http://caselaw.findlaw.com/us-supreme-court/395/444.html

This case tested the constitutionality of the Ohio criminal syndicalism statute of 1919. The facts are contained in the per curiam opinion that follows. Resort to the per curiam form here may be partly explained by the resignation of Justice Fortas on May 14, three weeks before the case came down. According to Tinsley Yarbrough's *John Marshall Harlan* (1992), the Court's opinion was originally Fortas's. Majority: Warren, Black, Brennan, Douglas, Harlan, Marshall, Stewart, White.

Per Curiam.

The appellant [Clarence Brandenburg], a leader of a Ku Klux Klan group, was convicted under the Ohio Criminal Syndicalism statute of "advocat[ing] . . . the duty, necessity, or propriety of crime, sabotage, violence, or unlawful methods of terrorism as a means of accomplishing industrial or political reform" and of "voluntarily assembl[ing] with any society, group or assemblage of persons formed to teach or advocate the doctrines of criminal syndicalism." . . . He was fined $1,000 and sentenced to one to 10 years' imprisonment. The appellant challenged the constitutionality of the criminal syndicalism statute under the First and Fourteenth Amendments to the United States Constitution, but the intermediate appellate court of Ohio affirmed his conviction without opinion. The Supreme Court of Ohio dismissed his appeal "for the reason that no substantial constitutional question exists herein." It did not file an opinion or explain its conclusions. Appeal was taken to this Court, and we noted probable jurisdiction. . . . We reverse.

The record shows that a man, identified at trial as the appellant, telephoned an announcer-reporter on the staff of a Cincinnati television station and invited him to come to a Ku Klux Klan "rally" to be held at a farm in Hamilton County. With the cooperation of the organizers, the reporter and a cameraman attended the meeting and filmed the events. Portions of the films were later broadcast on the local station and on a national network.

The prosecution's case rested on the films and on testimony identifying the appellant as the person who communicated with the reporter and who spoke at the rally. . . .

One film showed 12 hooded figures, some of whom carried firearms. They were gathered around a large wooden cross, which they burned. No one was present other than the participants and the newsmen who made the film. Most of the words uttered during the scene were incomprehensible when the film was projected, but scattered phrases could be understood that were derogatory of Negroes and, in one instance, of Jews.[1] Another scene on the same film showed the appellant, in Klan regalia, making a speech. The speech, in full, was as follows:

> This is an organizers' meeting. We have had quite a few members here today which are—we have hundreds, hundreds of members throughout the State of Ohio. I can quote from a newspaper clipping from the Columbus Ohio Dispatch, five weeks ago Sunday morning. The Klan has more members in the State of Ohio than does any other organization. We're not a revengent organization, but if our President, our Congress, our Supreme Court, continues to suppress the white, Caucasian race, it's possible that there might have to be some revengence taken.
>
> We are marching on Congress July the Fourth, four hundred thousand strong. From there we are dividing into two groups, one group to march on St. Augustine, Florida, the other group to march into Mississippi. Thank you.

The second film showed six hooded figures one of whom, later identified as the appellant, repeated a speech very similar to that recorded on the first film. The reference to the possibility of "revengence" was omitted, and one sentence was added: "Personally, I believe the nigger should be returned to Africa, the Jew returned to Israel." Though some of the figures in the films carried weapons, the speaker did not.

The Ohio Criminal Syndicalism Statute was enacted in 1919. From 1917 to 1920, identical or quite similar laws were adopted by 20 States and two territories. . . . In 1927, this Court sustained the constitutionality of California's Criminal Syndicalism Act . . . the text of which is quite similar to that of . . . Ohio. . . . The Court upheld the statute on the ground that, without more, "advocating" violent means to effect political and economic change involves such danger to the security of the State that the State may outlaw it. . . . But *Whitney* has been thoroughly discredited by later decisions. . . . These later decisions have fashioned the principle that the constitutional guarantees of free speech and free press do not permit a State to forbid or proscribe advocacy of the use of force or of law violation except where such advocacy is directed to inciting or producing imminent lawless action and is likely to incite or produce such action. . . . "[T]he mere abstract teaching . . . of the moral propriety or even moral necessity for a resort to force and violence, is not the same as preparing a group for violent action and steeling it to such action." . . . A statute which fails to draw this distinction impermissibly intrudes upon the freedoms guaranteed by the First and Fourteenth Amendments. It sweeps within its condemnation speech which our Constitution has immunized from governmental control. . . .

Measured by this test, Ohio's Criminal Syndicalism Act cannot be sustained. . . . Neither the indictment nor the trial judge's instructions to the jury in any way refined the statute's bald definition of the crime in terms of mere advocacy not distinguished from incitement to imminent lawless action.

Accordingly, we are here confronted with a statute which, by its own words and as applied, purports to punish mere advocacy and to forbid, on pain of criminal punishment, assembly with others merely to advocate the described type of action. Such a statute falls within the condemnation of the First and Fourteenth Amendments. The contrary teaching of *Whitney* v. *California* . . . cannot be supported, and that decision is therefore overruled.

Reversed.

MR. JUSTICE BLACK, concurring . . . [omitted].
MR. JUSTICE DOUGLAS, concurring . . . [omitted].

II. PUBLIC FORUM

Good News Club v. *Milford Central School* 533 U.S. 98, 121 S.Ct. 2093, 150 L.Ed. 2d 151 (2001)

http://caselaw.findlaw.com/us-supreme-court/533/98.html

Under New York law, Milford Central School enacted a policy authorizing district residents to use its building after school for, among other things: (1) instruction in education, learning, or the arts; and (2) social, civic, recreational, and entertainment uses pertaining to the community welfare. In 1996 Stephen and Darleen Fournier, sponsors of the Good News Club (a Christian organization for children ages 6–12), asked school officials for permission to hold the Club's weekly afterschool meetings in the school. They denied the request in 1997 on the ground that the proposed use—to sing songs, hear Bible lessons, memorize scripture, and pray—was the equivalent of religious worship prohibited by the community use policy. The Club filed suit in the U.S. District Court for the Northern District of New York, alleging that denial of the Club's application violated its free speech rights. Both sides in the litigation agreed that the school policy had established a limited public forum. In 1998 the District Court found the Club's subject matter to be religious in nature, not merely a discussion of secular matters from a religious perspective that was otherwise permitted, and granted the school summary judgment. In 2000 the U.S. Court of Appeals for the Second Circuit affirmed. In its view the policy was constitutionally acceptable subject-matter (content) discrimination, not unconstitutional viewpoint discrimination. Majority: Thomas, Breyer, Kennedy, O'Connor, Rehnquist, Scalia. Dissenting: Stevens, Souter, Ginsburg.

JUSTICE THOMAS delivered the opinion of the Court. . . .

When the State establishes a limited public forum, the State is not required to and does not allow persons to engage in every type of speech. The State may be justified "in reserving [its forum] for certain groups or for the discussion of certain topics." The State's power to restrict speech, however, is not without limits. The restriction must not discriminate against speech on the basis of viewpoint, and the restriction must be "reasonable in light of the purpose served by the forum."

Applying this test, we first address whether the exclusion constituted viewpoint discrimination. We are guided in our analysis by two of our prior opinions, *Lamb's Chapel* [v. *Center Moriches School District* (1993)] and *Rosenberger* [v. *Rector* (1995)]. In *Lamb's Chapel*, we held that a school district violated the Free Speech Clause of the First Amendment when it excluded a private group from presenting films at the school based solely on the films' discussions of family values from a religious perspective. Likewise, in *Rosenberger*, we held that a university's refusal to fund a student publication because the publication addressed issues from a religious perspective violated the Free Speech Clause. Concluding that Milford's exclusion of the Good News Club based on its religious nature is indistinguishable from the exclusions in these cases, we hold that the exclusion constitutes viewpoint discrimination. Because the restriction is viewpoint discriminatory, we need not decide whether it is unreasonable in light of the purposes served by the forum.

Milford has opened its limited public forum to activities that serve a variety of purposes, including events "pertaining to the welfare of the community." Milford interprets its policy to permit discussions of subjects such as child rearing, and of "the development of character and morals from a religious perspective." For example, this policy would allow someone to use Aesop's Fables to teach children moral values. Additionally, a group could sponsor a debate on whether there should be a constitutional amendment to permit prayer in public schools, and the Boy Scouts could meet "to influence a boy's character, development and spiritual growth." In short, any group that "promote[s] the moral and character development of children" is eligible to use the school building.

Just as there is no question that teaching morals and character development to children is a permissible purpose under Milford's policy, it is clear that the Club teaches morals and character development to children . . . Nonetheless, because Milford found the Club's activities to be religious in nature—"the equivalent of religious instruction itself"—it excluded the Club from use of its facilities.

Applying *Lamb's Chapel*, we find it quite clear that Milford engaged in viewpoint discrimination when it excluded the Club from the afterschool forum. In *Lamb's Chapel*, the local New York school district similarly had adopted § 414's "social, civic or recreational use" category as a permitted use in its limited public forum. The district also prohibited use "by any group for religious purposes." Citing this prohibition, the school district excluded a church that wanted to present films teaching family values from a Christian perspective. . . .

Like the church in *Lamb's Chapel*, the Club seeks to address a subject otherwise permitted under the rule, the teaching of morals and character, from a religious standpoint. . . . The only apparent difference between the activity of Lamb's Chapel and the activities of the Good News Club is that the Club chooses to teach moral lessons from a Christian perspective through live storytelling and prayer, whereas Lamb's Chapel taught lessons through films. This distinction is inconsequential. . . . Thus, the exclusion of the Good News Club's activities, like the exclusion of Lamb's Chapel's films, constitutes unconstitutional viewpoint discrimination.

Our opinion in *Rosenberger* also is dispositive. In *Rosenberger*, a student organization at the University of Virginia was denied funding for printing expenses because its publication, *Wide Awake*, offered a Christian viewpoint. . . . *Wide Awake* "challenge[d] Christians to live, in word and deed, according to the faith they proclaim and . . . encourage[d] students to consider what a personal relationship with Jesus Christ means." Because the university "select[ed] for disfavored treatment those student journalistic efforts with religious editorial viewpoints," we held that the denial of funding was unconstitutional. . . . Given the obvious religious content of *Wide Awake*, we cannot say that the Club's activities are any more "religious" or deserve any less First Amendment protection than did the publication of *Wide Awake* in *Rosenberger*.

Despite our holdings in *Lamb's Chapel* and *Rosenberger*, the Court of Appeals, like Milford, believed that its characterization of the Club's activities as religious in nature warranted treating the Club's activities as different in kind from the other activities permitted by the school. . . . The "Christian viewpoint" is unique, according to the court, because it contains an "additional layer" that other kinds of viewpoints do not. That is, the Club "is focused on teaching children how to cultivate their relationship with God through Jesus Christ," which it characterized as "quintessentially religious." . . .

We disagree that something that is "quintessentially religious" or "decidedly religious in nature" cannot also be characterized properly as the teaching of morals and character development from a particular viewpoint. . . . What matters for purposes of the Free Speech Clause is that we can see no logical difference in kind between the invocation of Christianity by the Club and the invocation of teamwork, loyalty, or patriotism by other associations to provide a foundation for their lessons. . . . According to the Court of Appeals, reliance on Christian principles taints moral and character instruction in a way that other foundations for thought or viewpoints do not. We, however, have never reached such a conclusion. Instead, we reaffirm our holdings in *Lamb's Chapel* and *Rosenberger* that speech discussing otherwise permissible subjects cannot be excluded from a limited public forum on the ground that the subject is discussed from a religious viewpoint. Thus, we conclude that Milford's exclusion of the Club from use of the school, pursuant to its community use policy, constitutes impermissible viewpoint discrimination. . . .

[In the last section of his opinion, Justice Thomas concludes "that permitting the Club to meet on the school's premises would not have violated the Establishment Clause. . . . Because Milford has not raised a valid Establishment Clause claim, we do not address the question whether such a claim could excuse Milford's viewpoint discrimination."]

The judgment of the Court of Appeals is reversed, and the case is remanded for further proceedings consistent with this opinion.

It is so ordered.

Justice Scalia, concurring . . . [omitted].

Justice Breyer, concurring in part . . . [omitted].

Justice Stevens, dissenting. . . .

Speech for "religious purposes" may reasonably be understood to encompass three different categories. First, there is religious speech that is simply speech about a particular topic from a religious point of view. . . . Second, there is religious speech that amounts to worship, or its equivalent. . . . Third, there is an intermediate category that is aimed principally at proselytizing or inculcating belief in a particular religious faith.

A public entity may not generally exclude even religious worship from an open public forum. Similarly, a public entity that creates a limited public forum for the discussion of certain specified topics may not exclude a speaker simply because she approaches those topics from a religious point of view. . . .

The novel question that this case presents . . . is whether a school can, consistently with the First Amendment, create a limited public forum that admits the first type of religious speech without allowing the other two.

Distinguishing speech from a religious viewpoint, on the one hand, from religious proselytizing, on the other, is comparable to distinguishing meetings to discuss political issues from meetings whose principal purpose is to recruit new members to join a political organization. If a school decides to authorize after school discussions of current events in its classrooms, it may not exclude people from expressing their views simply because it dislikes their particular political opinions. But must it therefore allow organized political groups—for example, the Democratic Party, the Libertarian Party, or the Ku Klux Klan—to hold meetings, the principal purpose of which is not to discuss the current-events topic from their own unique point of view but rather to recruit others to join their respective groups? I think not. Such recruiting meetings may introduce divisiveness and tend to separate young children into cliques that undermine the school's educational mission. . . .

It is clear that, by "religious purposes," the school district did not intend to exclude all speech from a religious point of view. . . . Instead, it sought only to exclude religious speech whose principal goal is to "promote the gospel." . . . As long as this is done in an evenhanded manner, I see no constitutional violation in such an effort. The line between the various categories of religious speech may be difficult to draw, but I think that the distinctions are valid, and that a school, particularly an elementary school, must be permitted to draw them. . . .

JUSTICE SOUTER, dissenting . . . [omitted].

III. PROTEST AND SYMBOLIC SPEECH

United States v. *O'Brien*
391 U.S. 367, 88 S.Ct. 1673, 20 L.Ed. 2d 672 (1968)

http://caselaw.findlaw.com/us-supreme-court/391/367.html

As a protest against the war in Vietnam, David O'Brien and three companions burned their draft cards on the steps of the South Boston Courthouse in front of an angry crowd on March 31, 1966. FBI agents arrested O'Brien for violating the 1965 amendment to the Universal Military Training and Service Act (UMTSA) of 1948, which provided criminal penalties for anyone who "knowingly destroys [or] knowingly mutilates" a draft card. Following his conviction in the U.S. District Court for the District of Massachusetts, the Court of Appeals for the First Circuit reversed, declaring that the 1965 amendment violated the First Amendment. The Appeals Court nonetheless held that O'Brien could be sentenced because his action violated a regulation of the Selective Service System against nonpossession of one's draft card. Under the UMTSA, violation of a Selective Service regulation was a criminal offense.

According to Bernard Schwartz's *Super Chief* (1983), Chief Justice Warren's first draft of the Court's opinion simply declared O'Brien's act to be nonverbal communication outside the protection of the First Amendment. Harlan and Brennan, however, were sharply critical. Brennan stressed that the conduct did fall under the First Amendment, but that the government's interest in regulating it was "compelling." Warren's revised opinion generally followed Brennan's approach, except that the former rested the outcome on the government's "important or substantial" interest. Majority: Warren, Black, Harlan, Brennan, Stewart, White, Fortas. Dissenting: Douglas. Not participating: Marshall.

MR. CHIEF JUSTICE WARREN delivered the opinion of the Court. . . .

O'Brien first argues that the 1965 Amendment is unconstitutional as applied to him because his act of burning his registration certificate was protected "symbolic speech" within the First Amendment. . . .

. . . This Court has held that when "speech" and "nonspeech" elements are combined in the same course of conduct, a sufficiently important governmental interest in regulating the nonspeech element can justify incidental limitations on First Amendment freedoms. To characterize the quality of the governmental interest which must appear, the Court has employed a variety of descriptive terms: compelling; substantial; subordinating; paramount; cogent; strong. Whatever imprecision inheres in these terms, we think it clear that a government regulation is sufficiently justified if it is within the constitutional power of the Government; if it furthers an important or substantial governmental interest; if the governmental interest is unrelated to the suppression of free expression; and if the incidental restriction on alleged First Amendment freedoms is no greater than is essential to the furtherance of that interest. We find that the 1965 Amendment to § 12(b)(3) of the Universal Military Training and Service Act meets all of these requirements, and consequently that O'Brien can be constitutionally convicted for violating it.

The constitutional power of Congress to raise and support armies and to make all laws necessary and proper to that end is broad and sweeping. The power of Congress to classify and conscript manpower for military service is "beyond question." Pursuant to this power, Congress may establish a system of registration for individuals liable for training and service, and may require such individuals within reason to cooperate in the registration system. The issuance of certificates indicating the registration and eligibility classification of individuals is a legitimate and substantial administrative aid in the functioning of this system. And legislation to insure the continuing availability of issued certificates serves a legitimate and substantial purpose in the system's administration.

O'Brien's argument to the contrary is necessarily premised upon his unrealistic characterization of Selective Service certificates. He essentially adopts the position that such certificates are so many pieces of paper designed to notify registrants of their registration or classification, to be retained or tossed in the wastebasket according to the convenience or taste of the registrant. . . . We agree that the registration certificate contains much information of which the registrant needs no notification. This circumstance, however, does not lead to the conclusion that the certificate serves no purposes but that, like the classification certificate, it serves purposes in addition to initial notification. Many of these purposes would be defeated by the certificates' destruction or mutilation. Among these are:

1. The registration certificate serves as proof that the individual described thereon has registered for the draft. The classification certificate shows the eligibility classification of a named but undescribed individual. Voluntarily displaying the two certificates is an easy and painless way for a young man to dispel a question as to whether he might be delinquent in his Selective Service obligations. . . .
2. The information supplied on the certificates facilitates communication between registrants and local boards, simplifying the system and benefiting all concerned. . . .
3. Both certificates carry continual reminders that the registrant must notify his local board of any change of address, and other specified changes in his status. . . .
4. The regulatory scheme involving Selective Service certificates includes clearly valid prohibitions against the alteration, forgery, or similar deceptive misuse of certificates. The destruction or

> mutilation of certificates obviously increases the difficulty of detecting and tracing abuses such as these. Further, a mutilated certificate might itself be used for deceptive purposes. . . .

We think it apparent that the continuing availability to each registrant of his Selective Service certificates substantially furthers the smooth and proper functioning of the system that Congress has established to raise armies. . . . We perceive no alternative means that would more precisely and narrowly assure the continuing availability of issued Selective Service certificates than a law which prohibits their wilful mutilation or destruction. When O'Brien deliberately rendered unavailable his registration certificate, he wilfully frustrated this governmental interest. For this non-communicative impact of his conduct, and for nothing else, he was convicted. . . .

O'Brien finally argues that the 1965 Amendment is unconstitutional as enacted because what he calls the "purpose" of Congress was "to suppress freedom of speech." We reject this argument because under settled principles the purpose of Congress, as O'Brien uses that term, is not a basis for declaring this legislation unconstitutional.

It is a familiar principle of constitutional law that this Court will not strike down an otherwise constitutional statute on the basis of an alleged illicit legislative motive. . . .

Inquiries into congressional motives or purposes are a hazardous matter. When the issue is simply the interpretation of legislation, the Court will look to statements by legislators for guidance as to the purpose of the legislature, because the benefit to sound decision-making in this circumstance is thought sufficient to risk the possibility of misreading Congress' purpose. It is entirely a different matter when we are asked to void a statute that is, under well-settled criteria, constitutional on its face, on the basis of what fewer than a handful of Congressmen said about it. What motivates one legislator to make a speech about a statute is not necessarily what motivates scores of others to enact it, and the stakes are sufficiently high for us to eschew guesswork. . . .

Since the 1965 Amendment to § 12(b)(3) of the Universal Military Training and Service Act is constitutional as enacted and as applied, the Court of Appeals should have affirmed the judgment of conviction entered by the District Court. Accordingly, we vacate the judgment of the Court of Appeals, and reinstate the judgment and sentence of the District Court. . . .

It is so ordered.

MR. JUSTICE HARLAN, concurring . . . [omitted].

MR. JUSTICE DOUGLAS, dissenting . . . [omitted].

Texas v. *Johnson*
491 U.S. 397, 109 S.Ct. 2533, 105 L.Ed. 2d 342 (1989)

http://caselaw.findlaw.com/us-supreme-court/491/397.html

Under Texas law, "A person commits an offense if he intentionally or knowingly desecrates: (1) a public monument; (2) a place of worship or burial; or (3) a state or national flag. . . . '[D]esecrate' means deface, damage, or otherwise physically mistreat in a way the actor knows will seriously offend one or more persons likely to observe or discover his action." Gregory Lee Johnson was convicted for violating this statute after an American flag was burned at a demonstration in Dallas during the time of the Republican National Convention in August 1984. A description of the event follows in Justice Brennan's opinion below. The state Court of Appeals for the Fifth District affirmed, but the Texas Court of Criminal Appeals reversed, concluding that Johnson's conduct was protected speech. Majority: Brennan, Marshall, Blackmun, Scalia, Kennedy. Dissenting: Rehnquist, White, Stevens, O'Connor.

JUSTICE BRENNAN delivered the opinion of the Court. . . .

Johnson was convicted of flag desecration for burning the flag rather than for uttering insulting words. This fact somewhat complicates our consideration of his conviction under the First Amendment. We must first determine whether Johnson's burning of the flag constituted expressive conduct, permitting him to invoke the First Amendment in challenging his conviction. If his conduct was expressive, we next decide whether the State's regulation is related to the suppression of free expression. If the State's regulation is not related to expression, then the less stringent standard we announced in *O'Brien* for regulations of noncommunicative conduct controls. If it is, then we are outside of *O'Brien's* test, and we must ask whether this interest justifies Johnson's conviction under a more demanding standard. A third possibility is that the State's asserted interest is simply not implicated on these facts, and in that event the interest drops out of the picture. . . .

The State of Texas conceded for purposes of its oral argument in this case that Johnson's conduct was expressive conduct. . . .

In order to decide whether *O'Brien's* test applies here . . . we must decide whether Texas has asserted an interest in support of Johnson's conviction that is unrelated to the suppression of expression. . . . The State offers two separate interests to justify this conviction: preventing breaches of the peace, and preserving the flag as a symbol of nationhood and national unity. We hold that the first interest is not implicated on this record and that the second is related to the suppression of expression.

Texas claims that its interest in preventing breaches of the peace justifies Johnson's conviction for flag desecration. However, no disturbance of the peace actually occurred or threatened to occur because of Johnson's burning of the flag. . . . The only evidence offered by the State at trial to show the reaction to Johnson's actions was the testimony of several persons who had been seriously offended by the flag-burning.

The State's position, therefore, amounts to a claim that an audience that takes serious offense at particular expression is necessarily likely to disturb the peace and that the expression may be prohibited on this basis. . . . [W]e have not permitted the Government to assume that every expression of a provocative idea will incite a riot, but have instead required careful consideration of the actual circumstances surrounding such expression, asking whether the expression "is directed to inciting or producing imminent lawless action and is likely to incite or produce such action." To accept Texas' arguments that it need only demonstrate "the potential for a breach of the peace," and that every flag-burning necessarily possesses that potential, would be to eviscerate our holding in *Brandenburg*. This we decline to do.

Nor does Johnson's expressive conduct fall within that small class of "fighting words" that are "likely to provoke the average person to retaliation, and thereby cause a breach of the peace." No reasonable onlooker would have regarded Johnson's generalized expression of dissatisfaction with the policies of the Federal Government as a direct personal insult or an invitation to exchange fisticuffs.

We thus conclude that the State's interest in maintaining order is not implicated on these facts. . . .

The State also asserts an interest in preserving the flag as a symbol of nationhood and national unity. . . . The State, apparently, is concerned that such conduct will lead people to believe either that the flag does not stand for nationhood and national unity, but instead reflects other, less positive concepts, or that the concepts reflected in the flag do not in fact exist, that is, we do not enjoy unity as a Nation. These concerns blossom only when a person's treatment of the flag communicates some message, and thus are related "to the suppression of free expression" within the meaning of *O'Brien*. We are thus outside of *O'Brien'* s test altogether. . . .

Johnson's political expression was restricted because of the content of the message he conveyed. We must therefore subject the State's asserted interest in preserving the special symbolic character of the flag to "the most exacting scrutiny."

According to Texas, if one physically treats the flag in a way that would tend to cast doubt on either the idea that nationhood and national unity are the flag's referents or that national unity actually exists, the message conveyed thereby is a harmful one and therefore may be prohibited.

If there is a bedrock principle underlying the First Amendment, it is that the Government may not prohibit the expression of an idea simply because society finds the idea itself offensive or disagreeable. We have not recognized an exception to this principle even where our flag has been involved. . . . We never before have held that the Government may ensure that a symbol be used to express only one view of that symbol or its referents. . . .

To conclude that the Government may permit designated symbols to be used to communicate only a limited set of messages would be to enter territory having no discernible or defensible boundaries. Could the Government, on this theory, prohibit the burning of state flags? Of copies of the Presidential seal? Of the Constitution? In evaluating these choices under the First Amendment, how would we decide which symbols were sufficiently special to warrant this unique status? To do so, we would be forced to consult our own political preferences, and impose them on the citizenry, in the very way that the First Amendment forbids us to do.

There is, moreover, no indication—either in the text of the Constitution or in our cases interpreting it—that a separate juridical category exists for the American flag alone. Indeed, we would not be surprised to learn that the persons who framed our Constitution and wrote the Amendment that we now construe were not known for their reverence for the Union Jack. The First Amendment does not guarantee that other concepts virtually sacred to our Nation as a whole—such as the principle that discrimination on the basis of race is odious and destructive—will go unquestioned in the marketplace of ideas. We decline, therefore, to create for the flag an exception to the joust of principles protected by the First Amendment.

It is not the State's ends, but its means, to which we object. . . .

The way to preserve the flag's special role is not to punish those who feel differently about these matters. It is to persuade them that they are wrong. . . . We can imagine no more appropriate response to burning a flag than waving one's own, no better way to counter a flag-burner's message than by saluting the flag that burns, no surer means of preserving the dignity even of the flag that burned than by—as one witness here did—according its remains a respectful burial. We do not consecrate the flag by punishing its desecration, for in doing so we dilute the freedom that this cherished emblem represents. . . .

The judgment of the Texas Court of Criminal Appeals is therefore

Affirmed.

Chief Justice Rehnquist, with whom Justice White and Justice O'Connor join, dissenting . . . [omitted].

Justice Stevens, dissenting. . . .

The value of the flag as a symbol cannot be measured. Even so, I have no doubt that the interest in preserving that value for the future is both significant and legitimate. Conceivably that value will be enhanced by the Court's conclusion that our national commitment to free expression is so strong that even the United States as ultimate guarantor of that freedom is without power to prohibit the desecration of its unique symbol. But I am unpersuaded. The creation of a federal right to post bulletin boards and graffiti on the Washington Monument might enlarge the market for free expression, but at a cost I would not pay. Similarly, in my considered judgment, sanctioning the public desecration of the flag will tarnish its value—both for those who cherish the ideas for which it waves and for those who desire to don the robes of martyrdom by burning it. That tarnish is not justified by the trivial burden on free expression—occasioned by requiring that an available, alternative mode of expression including uttering words critical of the flag,—be employed.

The Court is therefore quite wrong in blandly asserting that respondent "was prosecuted for his expression of dissatisfaction with the policies of this country, expression situated at the core of our First Amendment values." Respondent was prosecuted because of the method he chose to express his dissatisfaction with those policies. Had he chosen to spray-paint—or perhaps convey with a motion picture projector—his message of dissatisfaction on the I of the Lincoln Memorial, there would be no question about the power of the Government to prohibit his means of expression. The prohibition would be supported by the legitimate interest in preserving the quality of an important national asset. Though the asset at stake in this case is intangible, given its unique value, the same interest supports a prohibition on the desecration of the American flag.

The ideas of liberty and equality have been an irresistible force in motivating leaders like Patrick Henry, Susan B. Anthony, and Abraham Lincoln, schoolteachers like Nathan Hale and Booker T. Washington, the Philippine Scouts who fought at Bataan, and the soldiers who scaled the bluff at Omaha Beach. If those ideas are worth fighting for—and our history demonstrates that they are—it cannot be true that the flag that uniquely symbolizes their power is not itself worthy of protection from unnecessary desecration.

Virginia v. *Black*
538 U.S. 343, 123 S.Ct. 1536, 155 L.Ed. 2d 535 (2003)

http://caselaw.findlaw.com/us-supreme-court/538/343.html

With permission of the owner, Barry Black organized a Ku Klux Klan rally in a field in Carroll County, Virginia, in 1998. As part of the concluding ritual Klan members set fire to a 25-foot cross that was also visible to nearby residents. In May of the same year, Richard Elliott and Jonathan O'Mara attempted to burn a cross in the yard of James Jubilee, an African American and Elliott's next-door neighbor in Virginia Beach, Virginia, although Jubilee did not notice the partly burned cross until the next morning. Neither Elliott nor O'Mara belonged to the Klan. They apparently wanted to get even with Jubilee for complaining after Elliott used his backyard as a firing range. In separate proceedings the three men were convicted of violating Virginia's cross-burning statute: "It shall be unlawful for any person or persons, with the intent of intimidating any person or group of persons, to burn, or cause to be burned, a cross on the property of another, a highway or other public place. . . . Any such burning of a cross shall be prima facie evidence of an intent to intimidate a person or group of persons." Against challenges on First Amendment grounds, the state court of appeals affirmed the convictions, but the Supreme Court of Virginia reversed. In the U.S. Supreme Court, the voting alignment was complex. Six justices held that a properly drafted cross-burning statute *could be* constitutional, while seven justices deemed *this* statute unconstitutional. Majority (on the first point): O'Connor, Breyer, Rehnquist, Scalia, Stevens, Thomas. Dissenting: Souter, Ginsburg, Kennedy. Majority (on the second point): O'Connor, Breyer, Ginsburg, Kennedy, Rehnquist, Souter, Stevens. Dissenting: Scalia, Thomas.

JUSTICE O'CONNOR announced the judgment of the Court and delivered the opinion of the Court with respect to Parts I, II, and III, and an opinion with respect to Parts IV and V, in which THE CHIEF JUSTICE, JUSTICE STEVENS, and JUSTICE BREYER joined.

In this case we consider whether the Commonwealth of Virginia's statute banning cross burning with "an intent to intimidate a person or group of persons" violates the First Amendment. We conclude that while a State, consistent with the First Amendment, may ban cross burning carried out with the intent to intimidate, the provision in the Virginia statute treating any cross burning as prima facie evidence of intent to intimidate renders the statute unconstitutional in its current form.

I [omitted]

II

. . . Burning a cross in the United States is inextricably intertwined with the history of the Ku Klux Klan. . . .

Often, the Klan used cross burnings as a tool of intimidation and a threat of impending violence. . . . These cross burnings embodied threats to people whom the Klan deemed antithetical to its goals. And these threats had special force given the long history of Klan violence. . . .

And after a cross burning in Suffolk, Virginia, during the late 1940s, the Virginia Governor stated that he would "not allow any of our people of any race to be subjected to terrorism or intimidation in any form by the Klan or any other organization." These incidents of cross burning, among others, helped prompt Virginia to enact its first version of the cross-burning statute in 1950. . . .

To this day, regardless of whether the message is a political one or whether the message is also meant to intimidate, the burning of a cross is a "symbol of hate." . . .

In sum, while a burning cross does not inevitably convey a message of intimidation, often the cross burner intends that the recipients of the message fear for their lives. And when a cross burning is used to intimidate, few if any messages are more powerful.

III

. . . The hallmark of the protection of free speech is to allow "free trade in ideas"—even ideas that the overwhelming majority of people might find distasteful or discomforting. . . . The First Amendment affords protection to symbolic or expressive conduct as well as to actual speech.

The protections afforded by the First Amendment, however, are not absolute, and we have long recognized that the government may regulate certain categories of expression consistent with the Constitution. . . . The First Amendment permits "restrictions upon the content of speech in a few limited areas, which are 'of such slight social value as a step to truth that any benefit that may be derived from them is clearly outweighed by the social interest in order and morality.'"

Thus, for example, a State may punish those words "which by their very utterance inflict injury or tend to incite an immediate breach of the peace." . . . We have consequently held that fighting words—"those personally abusive epithets which, when addressed to the ordinary citizen, are, as a matter of common knowledge, inherently likely to provoke violent reaction"—are generally proscribable under the

First Amendment. . . . And the First Amendment also permits a State to ban a "true threat."

"True threats" encompass those statements where the speaker means to communicate a serious expression of an intent to commit an act of unlawful violence to a particular individual or group of individuals. . . . The speaker need not actually intend to carry out the threat. Rather, a prohibition on true threats "protect[s] individuals from the fear of violence" and "from the disruption that fear engenders," in addition to protecting people "from the possibility that the threatened violence will occur." Intimidation in the constitutionally proscribable sense of the word is a type of true threat, where a speaker directs a threat to a person or group of persons with the intent of placing the victim in fear of bodily harm or death. . . .

The Supreme Court of Virginia ruled that in light of *R. A. V.* v. *City of St. Paul*, even if it is constitutional to ban cross burning in a content-neutral manner, the Virginia cross-burning statute is unconstitutional because it discriminates on the basis of content and viewpoint. . . .

In *R. A. V.*, we held that a local ordinance that banned certain symbolic conduct, including cross burning, when done with the knowledge that such conduct would "arouse anger, alarm or resentment in others on the basis of race, color, creed, religion or gender" was unconstitutional. We held that the ordinance did not pass constitutional muster because it discriminated on the basis of content by targeting only those individuals who "provoke violence" on a basis specified in the law. The ordinance did not cover "[t]hose who wish to use 'fighting words' in connection with other ideas—to express hostility, for example, on the basis of political affiliation, union membership, or homosexuality." This content-based discrimination was unconstitutional because it allowed the city "to impose special prohibitions on those speakers who express views on disfavored subjects."

We did not hold in *R. A. V.* that the First Amendment prohibits all forms of content-based discrimination within a proscribable area of speech. Rather, we specifically stated that some types of content discrimination did not violate the First Amendment.

"When the basis for the content discrimination consists entirely of the very reason the entire class of speech at issue is proscribable, no significant danger of idea or viewpoint discrimination exists. Such a reason, having been adjudged neutral enough to support exclusion of the entire class of speech from First Amendment protection, is also neutral enough to form the basis of distinction within the class."

Indeed, we noted that it would be constitutional to ban only a particular type of threat: "[T]he Federal Government can criminalize only those threats of violence that are directed against the President . . . since the reasons why threats of violence are outside the First Amendment . . . have special force when applied to the person of the President." And a State may "choose to prohibit only that obscenity which is the most patently offensive in its prurience—that is, that which involves the most lascivious displays of sexual activity." Consequently, while the holding of *R. A. V.* does not permit a State to ban only obscenity based on "offensive political messages," or "only those threats against the President that mention his policy on aid to inner cities," the First Amendment permits content discrimination "based on the very reasons why the particular class of speech at issue . . . is proscribable."

Similarly, Virginia's statute does not run afoul of the First Amendment insofar as it bans cross burning with intent to intimidate. Unlike the statute at issue in *R. A. V.*, the Virginia statute does not single out for opprobrium only that speech directed toward "one of the specified disfavored topics." It does not matter whether an individual burns a cross with intent to intimidate because of the victim's race, gender, or religion, or because of the victim's "political affiliation, union membership, or homosexuality." Moreover, as a factual matter it is not true that cross burners direct their intimidating conduct solely to racial or religious minorities. . . .

Indeed, in the case of Elliott and O'Mara, it is at least unclear whether the respondents burned a cross due to racial animus. . . .

The First Amendment permits Virginia to outlaw cross burnings done with the intent to intimidate because burning a cross is a particularly virulent form of intimidation. Instead of prohibiting all intimidating messages, Virginia may choose to regulate this subset of intimidating messages in light of cross burning's long and pernicious history as a signal of impending violence. . . . A ban on cross burning carried out with the intent to intimidate is fully consistent with our holding in *R. A. V.* and is proscribable under the First Amendment.

IV

. . . The jury in the case of Richard Elliott did not receive any instruction on the prima facie evidence provision, and the provision was not an issue in the case of Jonathan O'Mara because he pleaded guilty. The court in Barry Black's case, however, instructed the jury that the provision means: "The burning of a cross, by itself, is sufficient evidence from which you may infer the required intent." . . .

The prima facie evidence provision, as interpreted by the jury instruction, renders the statute unconstitutional. . . .

As the history of cross burning indicates, a burning cross is not always intended to intimidate. Rather, sometimes the cross burning is a statement of ideology, a symbol of group solidarity. . . . Indeed, occasionally a person who burns a cross does not intend to express either a statement of ideology or intimidation. Cross burnings have appeared in movies such as *Mississippi Burning*, and in plays such as the stage adaptation of Sir Walter Scott's *The Lady of the Lake*.

The prima facie provision makes no effort to distinguish among these different types of cross burnings. . . .

It may be true that a cross burning, even at a political rally, arouses a sense of anger or hatred among the vast majority of citizens who see a burning cross. But this sense of anger or hatred is not sufficient to ban all cross burnings. . . . The prima facie evidence provision in this case ignores all of the contextual factors that are necessary to decide whether a particular cross burning is intended to intimidate. The First Amendment does not permit such a shortcut.

For these reasons, the prima facie evidence provision, as interpreted through the jury instruction and as applied in Barry Black's case, is unconstitutional on its face. . . .

V

With respect to Barry Black, we agree with the Supreme Court of Virginia that his conviction cannot stand, and we affirm the judgment of the Supreme Court of Virginia. With respect to Elliott and O'Mara, we vacate the judgment of the Supreme Court of Virginia, and remand the case for further proceedings.

It is so ordered.

Justice Stevens, concurring . . . [omitted].

Justice Scalia, with whom Justice Thomas joins in part, concurring in part, concurring in the judgment in part, and dissenting in part . . . [omitted].

Justice Souter, with whom Justice Kennedy and Justice Ginsburg join, concurring in the judgment in part and dissenting in part.

I agree with the majority that the Virginia statute makes a content-based distinction within the category of punishable intimidating or threatening expression, the very type of distinction we considered in *R. A. V.* I disagree that any exception should save Virginia's law from unconstitutionality under the holding in *R. A. V.* or any acceptable variation of it.

The issue is whether the statutory prohibition restricted to this symbol falls within one of the exceptions to *R. A. V.* 's general condemnation of limited content-based proscription within a broader category of expression proscribable generally. Because of the burning cross's extraordinary force as a method of intimidation, the *R. A. V.* exception most likely to cover the statute is the first of the three mentioned there, which the *R. A. V.* opinion called an exception for content discrimination on a basis that "consists entirely of the very reason the entire class of speech at issue is proscribable." This is the exception the majority speaks of here as covering statutes prohibiting "particularly virulent" proscribable expression.

I do not think that the Virginia statute qualifies for this virulence exception as *R. A. V.* explained it . . ., the most obvious hurdle being the statute's prima facie evidence provision. That provision is essential to understanding why the statute's tendency to suppress a message disqualifies it from any rescue by exception from *R. A. V.* 's general rule.

R. A. V. defines the special virulence exception to the rule barring content-based subclasses of categorically proscribable expression this way: prohibition by subcategory is nonetheless constitutional if it is made "entirely" on the "basis" of "the very reason" that "the entire class of speech at issue is proscribable" at all. The Court explained that when the subcategory is confined to the most obviously proscribable instances, "no significant danger of idea or viewpoint discrimination exists," and the explanation was rounded out with some illustrative examples. None of them, however, resembles the case before us. . . .

I thus read *R. A. V.* 's examples of the particular virulence exception as covering prohibitions that are not clearly associated with a particular viewpoint, and that are consequently different from the Virginia statute. . . .

[N]o content-based statute should survive even under a pragmatic recasting of *R. A. V.* without a high probability that no "official suppression of ideas is afoot." I believe the prima facie evidence provision stands in the way of any finding of such a high probability here. . . .

As I see the likely significance of the evidence provision, its primary effect is to skew jury deliberations toward conviction in cases where the evidence of intent to intimidate is relatively weak and arguably consistent with a solely ideological reason for burning. . . .

To the extent the prima facie evidence provision skews prosecutions, then, it skews the statute toward suppressing ideas. Thus, the appropriate way to consider the statute's prima facie evidence term, in my view, is not as if it were an overbroad statutory definition amenable to severance or a narrowing construction. The question here is not the permissible scope of an arguably overbroad statute, but the claim of a clearly content-based statute to an exception from the general prohibition of content-based proscriptions, an exception that is not warranted if the statute's terms show that suppression of ideas may be afoot. Accordingly, the way to look at the prima facie evidence provision is to consider it for any indication of what is afoot. And if we look at the provision for this purpose, it has a very obvious significance as a mechanism for bringing within the statute's prohibition some expression that is doubtfully threatening though certainly distasteful. . . .

I conclude that the statute under which all three of the respondents were prosecuted violates the First Amendment, since the statute's content-based distinction was invalid at the time of the charged activities, regardless of whether the prima facie evidence provision was given any effect in any respondent's individual case. . . .

Justice Thomas, dissenting. . . .

Although I agree with the majority's conclusion that it is constitutionally permissible to "ban . . . cross burning carried out with intent to intimidate," I believe that the majority errs in imputing an expressive component to the activity in question. . . .

It strains credulity to suggest that a state legislature that adopted a litany of segregationist laws self-contradictorily intended to squelch the segregationist message [in the 1950s]. Even for segregationists, violent and terroristic conduct, the Siamese twin of cross burning, was intolerable. The ban on cross burning with intent to intimidate demonstrates that even segregationists understood the difference between intimidating and terroristic conduct and racist expression. It is simply beyond belief that, in passing the statute now under review, the Virginia legislature was concerned with anything but penalizing conduct it must have viewed as particularly vicious. Accordingly, this statute prohibits only conduct, not expression. . . .

IV. FREEDOM OF ASSOCIATION

Boy Scouts of America and Monmouth Council v. *Dale* 530 U.S. 640, 120 S.Ct. 2446, 147 L.Ed. 2d 554 (2000)

http://caselaw.findlaw.com/us-supreme-court/530/640.html

James Dale became a Boy Scout in New Jersey in 1981 and achieved the rank of Eagle Scout in 1988. In 1989 he applied for adult membership in the Boy Scouts and was named assistant scoutmaster of Troop 73. At about the same time he entered Rutgers University, where he first acknowledged publicly that he was gay and where he became active in the Lesbian/Gay Alliance. In July 1990 a newspaper published his photograph and an interview with him about his advocacy of teenagers' need for gay role models. Shortly, the Monmouth Executive Council of the Boy Scouts revoked Dale's adult membership on the grounds that the organization "specifically forbid[s] membership to homosexuals." Dale filed a complaint against the Boy Scouts in New Jersey Superior Court, claiming the Boy Scouts had violated the state's public accommodation law by revoking his membership because of his sexual orientation. The court ruled that the statute was inapplicable to the Boy Scouts, but the appellate division concluded in 1998 that the law applied to the Boy Scouts, that the Boy Scouts had violated it, and that no federal constitutional rights of the Boy Scouts had been abridged. In 1999, the New Jersey Supreme Court affirmed. (The Boy Scouts changed its policy in 2015 and now allows openly gay adult leaders to serve, but local sponsoring organizations such as churches retain the option to use sexual orientation as a guideline in selecting leaders.) Majority: Rehnquist, O'Connor, Scalia, Kennedy, Thomas. Dissenting: Stevens, Souter, Ginsburg, Breyer.

Chief Justice Rehnquist delivered the opinion of the Court. . . .

We granted the Boy Scouts' petition for certiorari to determine whether the application of New Jersey's public accommodations law violated the First Amendment. . . .

The forced inclusion of an unwanted person in a group infringes the group's freedom of expressive association if the presence of that person affects in a significant way the group's ability to advocate public or private viewpoints. But the freedom of expressive association, like many freedoms, is not absolute. We have held that the freedom could be overridden "by regulations adopted to serve compelling state interests, unrelated to the suppression of ideas, that cannot be achieved through means significantly less restrictive of associational freedoms."

To determine whether a group is protected by the First Amendment's expressive associational right, we must determine whether the group engages in "expressive association." The First Amendment's protection of expressive association is not reserved for advocacy groups. But to come within its ambit, a group must engage in some form of expression, whether it be public or private. . . .

[T]he general mission of the Boy Scouts is clear: "[T]o instill values in young people." . . . During the time spent with the youth members, the scoutmasters and assistant scoutmasters inculcate them with the Boy Scouts' values—both expressly and by example. It seems indisputable that an association that seeks to transmit such a system of values engages in expressive activity. . . .

Given that the Boy Scouts engages in expressive activity, we must determine whether the forced inclusion of Dale as an assistant scoutmaster would significantly affect the Boy Scouts' ability to advocate public or private viewpoints. This inquiry necessarily requires us first to explore, to a limited extent, the nature of the Boy Scouts' view of homosexuality. . . . not to propound a point of view contrary to its beliefs. . . .

The Boy Scouts explains that the Scout Oath and Law provide "a positive moral code for living; they are a list of 'do's' rather than 'don'ts.'" The Boy Scouts asserts that homosexual conduct is inconsistent with the values embodied in the Scout Oath and Law, particularly with the values represented by the terms "morally straight" and "clean."

Obviously, the Scout Oath and Law do not expressly mention sexuality or sexual orientation. And the terms "morally straight" and "clean" are by no means self-defining. Different people would attribute to those terms very different meanings. . . .

The Boy Scouts asserts that it "teach[es] that homosexual conduct is not morally straight," and that it does "not want to promote homosexual conduct as a legitimate form of behavior." We accept the Boy Scouts' assertion. . . .

We must then determine whether Dale's presence as an assistant scoutmaster would significantly burden the Boy Scouts' desire to not "promote homosexual conduct as a legitimate form of behavior." As we give deference to an association's assertions regarding the nature of its expression, we must also give deference to an association's view of what would impair its expression. . . .

Hurley [v. *Irish-American GLIB*, 1995] is illustrative on this point. There we considered whether the application of Massachusetts' public accommodations law to require the organizers of a private St. Patrick's Day parade to include among the marchers an Irish-American gay, lesbian, and bisexual group, GLIB, violated the parade organizers' First Amendment rights. We noted that the parade organizers did not wish to exclude the GLIB members because of their sexual orientations, but because they wanted to march behind a GLIB banner. . . .

As the presence of GLIB in Boston's St. Patrick's Day parade would have interfered with the parade organizers' choice not to propound a particular point of view, the presence of Dale as an assistant scoutmaster would just as surely interfere with the Boy Scout's choice not to propound a point of view contrary to its beliefs. . . .

Having determined that the Boy Scouts is an expressive association and that the forced inclusion of Dale would significantly affect its expression, we inquire whether the application of New Jersey's public accommodations law to require that the Boy Scouts accept Dale as an assistant scoutmaster runs afoul of the Scouts' freedom of expressive association. We conclude that it does. . . .

We recognized in cases such as *Roberts* [v. *Jaycees* (1984)] and [*Rotary Int'l.* v. *Rotary Club of*] *Duarte* (1987) that States have a compelling interest in eliminating discrimination against women in public accommodations. But in each of these cases we went on to conclude that the enforcement of these statutes would not materially interfere with the ideas that the organization sought to express. . . .

So in these cases, the associational interest in freedom of expression has been set on one side of the scale, and the State's interest on the other. . . .

We have already concluded that a state requirement that the Boy Scouts retain Dale as an assistant scoutmaster would significantly burden the organization's right to oppose or disfavor homosexual conduct. The state interests embodied in New Jersey's public accommodations law do not justify such a severe intrusion on the Boy Scouts' rights to freedom of expressive association. That being the case, we hold that the First Amendment prohibits the State from imposing such a requirement through the application of its public accommodations law. . . .

The judgment of the New Jersey Supreme Court is reversed, and the cause remanded for further proceedings not inconsistent with this opinion.

It is so ordered.

JUSTICE STEVENS, with whom JUSTICE SOUTER, JUSTICE GINSBURG and JUSTICE BREYER join, dissenting. . . .

BSA's claim finds no support in our cases. . . . In fact, until today, we have never once found a claimed right to associate in the selection of members to prevail in the face of a State's antidiscrimination law. To the contrary, we have squarely held that a State's antidiscrimination law does not violate a group's right to associate simply because the law conflicts with that group's exclusionary membership policy. . . .

Several principles are made perfectly clear by *Jaycees* and *Rotary Club*. First, to prevail on a claim of expressive association in the face of a State's antidiscrimination law, it is not enough simply to engage in some kind of expressive activity. Both the Jaycees and the Rotary Club engaged in expressive activity protected by the First Amendment, yet that fact was not dispositive. Second, it is not enough to adopt an openly avowed exclusionary membership policy. Both the Jaycees and the Rotary Club did that as well. Third, it is not sufficient merely to articulate some connection between the group's expressive activities and its exclusionary policy. . . .

The evidence before this Court makes it exceptionally clear that BSA has, at most, simply adopted an exclusionary membership policy and has no shared goal of disapproving of homosexuality. BSA's mission statement and federal charter say nothing on the matter; its official membership policy is silent; its Scout Oath and Law—and accompanying definitions—are devoid of any view on the topic; its guidance for Scouts and Scoutmasters on sexuality declare that such matters are "not construed to be Scouting's proper area," but are the province of a Scout's parents and pastor; and BSA's posture respecting religion tolerates a wide variety of views on the issue of homosexuality. Moreover, there is simply no evidence that BSA otherwise teaches anything in this area, or that it instructs Scouts on matters involving homosexuality in ways not conveyed in the Boy Scout or Scoutmaster Handbooks. In short, Boy Scouts of America is simply silent on homosexuality. There is no shared goal or collective effort to foster a belief about homosexuality at all—let alone one that is significantly burdened by admitting homosexuals.

As in *Jaycees*, there is "no basis in the record for concluding that admission of [homosexuals] will impede the [Boy Scouts'] ability to engage in [its] protected activities or to disseminate its preferred views" and New Jersey's law "requires no change in [BSA's] creed." And like *Rotary Club*, New Jersey's law "does not require [BSA] to abandon or alter any of" its activities. The evidence relied on by the Court is not to the contrary. . .

Though *Hurley* has a superficial similarity to the present case, a close inspection reveals a wide gulf between that case and the one before us today. . . .

First, it was critical to our analysis that GLIB was actually conveying a message by participating in the parade—otherwise, the parade organizers could hardly claim that they were being forced to include any unwanted message at all. . . .

Second, we found it relevant that GLIB's message "would likely be perceived" as the parade organizers' own speech. . . .

Dale's inclusion in the Boy Scouts is nothing like the case in *Hurley*. His participation sends no cognizable message to the Scouts or to the world. . . . Though participating in the Scouts could itself conceivably send a message on some level, it is not the kind of act that we have recognized as speech. . . .

Justice Souter, with whom Justice Ginsburg and Justice Breyer join, dissenting . . . [omitted].

Janus v. *American Federation of State, County, and Municipal Employees, Council 31*
585 U.S. ___, 138 S.Ct. 2448, 201 L.Ed. 2d 924 (2018)

www.supremecourt.gov/opinions/17pdf/16-1466_2b3j.pdf

The background of this case appears in Justice Alito's opinion for the Court. After the petitioner filed suit in U.S. District Court for the Northern District of Illinois, that court granted the respondents' motion to dismiss, and the U.S. Court of Appeals for the Seventh Circuit affirmed. [The section of the Court's opinion dealing with jurisdiction is omitted.] Majority: Alito, Gorsuch, Kennedy, Roberts, Thomas. Dissenting: Breyer, Ginsburg, Kagan, Sotomayor.

Justice Alito delivered the opinion of the Court.

Under Illinois law, public employees are forced to subsidize a union, even if they choose not to join and strongly object to the positions the union takes in collective bargaining and related activities. We conclude that this arrangement violates the free speech rights of nonmembers by compelling them to subsidize private speech on matters of substantial public concern.

We upheld a similar law in *Abood* v. *Detroit Board of Education* (1977), and we recognize the importance of following precedent unless there are strong reasons for not doing so. But there are very strong reasons in this case. Fundamental free speech rights are at stake. *Abood* was poorly reasoned. It has led to practical problems and abuse. It is inconsistent with other First Amendment cases and has been undermined by more recent decisions. Developments since *Abood* was handed down have shed new light on the issue of agency fees, and no reliance interests on the part of public-sector unions are sufficient to justify the perpetuation of the free speech violations that *Abood* has countenanced for the past 41 years. *Abood* is therefore overruled. . . .

Petitioner Mark Janus is employed by the Illinois Department of Healthcare and Family Services as a child support specialist. The employees in his unit are among the 35,000 public employees in Illinois who are represented by respondent American Federation of State, County, and Municipal Employees, Council 31 (Union). Janus refused to join the Union because he opposes "many of the public policy positions that [it] advocates," including the positions it takes in collective bargaining. Janus believes that the Union's "behavior in bargaining does not appreciate the current fiscal crises in Illinois and does not reflect his best interests or the interests of Illinois citizens." Therefore, if he had the choice, he "would not pay any fees or otherwise subsidize [the Union]." Under his unit's collective-bargaining agreement, however, he was required to pay an agency fee of $44.58 per month—which would amount to about $535 per year. . . .

The First Amendment, made applicable to the States by the Fourteenth Amendment, forbids abridgment of the freedom of speech. We have held time and again that freedom of speech "includes both the right to speak freely and the right to refrain from speaking at all."

The right to eschew association for expressive purposes is likewise protected. . . . Compelling individuals to mouth support for views they find objectionable violates that cardinal constitutional command, and in most contexts, any such effort would be universally condemned. . . . When speech is compelled, however, additional damage is done. In that situation, individuals are coerced into betraying their convictions. Forcing free and independent individuals to endorse ideas they find objectionable is always demeaning, and for this reason, one of our landmark free speech cases said that a law commanding "involuntary affirmation" of objected-to beliefs would require "even more immediate and urgent grounds" than a law demanding silence. Compelling a person to subsidize the speech of other private speakers raises similar First Amendment concerns. We have therefore recognized that a "'significant impingement on First Amendment rights'" occurs when public employees are required to provide financial support for a union that "takes many positions during collective bargaining that have powerful political and civic consequences." Because the compelled subsidization of private speech seriously impinges on First Amendment rights, it cannot be casually allowed. . . .

In *Abood*, the main defense of the agency-fee arrangement was that it served the State's interest in "labor peace," By "labor peace," the Abood Court meant avoidance of the conflict and disruption that it envisioned would occur if the employees in a unit were represented by more than one union. In such a situation, the Court predicted, "inter-union rivalries" would foster "dissension within the work force," and the employer could face "conflicting demands from different unions." . . . We assume that "labor peace," in this sense of the term, is a compelling state interest, but *Abood* cited no evidence that the pandemonium it imagined would result if agency fees were not allowed, and it is now clear that *Abood's* fears were unfounded. The Abood Court assumed that designation of a union as the exclusive representative of all the employees in a unit and the exaction of agency fees are inextricably linked, but that is simply not true. The federal employment experience is illustrative. . . .

In addition to the promotion of "labor peace," *Abood* cited "the risk of 'free riders'" as justification for agency fees. Respondents and some of their amici endorse this reasoning, contending that agency fees are needed to prevent nonmembers from enjoying the benefits of union representation without shouldering the costs. Petitioner strenuously objects to this free-rider label. He argues that he is not a free rider on a bus headed for a destination that he wishes to reach but is more like a person shanghaied for an unwanted voyage. Whichever description fits the majority of public employees who would not subsidize a union if given the option, avoiding free riders is not a compelling interest. . . . In simple terms, the First Amendment does not permit the government to compel a person to pay for another party's speech just because the government thinks that the speech furthers the interests of the person who does not want to pay. . . . In sum, we do not see any reason to treat the free-rider interest any differently in the agency-fee context than in any other First Amendment context. . . .

For the reasons given above, we conclude that public-sector agency-shop arrangements violate the First Amendment, and *Abood* erred in concluding otherwise. There remains the question whether *stare decisis* nonetheless counsels against overruling *Abood*. It does not.

"*Stare decisis* is the preferred course because it promotes the evenhanded, predictable, and consistent development of legal principles, fosters reliance on judicial decisions, and contributes to the actual and perceived integrity of the judicial process." We will not overturn a past decision unless there are strong grounds for doing so. . . .

The doctrine "is at its weakest when we interpret the Constitution because our interpretation can be altered only by constitutional amendment or by overruling our prior decisions." And *stare decisis* applies with perhaps least force of all to decisions that wrongly denied First Amendment rights. . . . Our cases identify factors that should be taken into account in deciding whether to overrule a past decision. Five of these are most important here: the quality of *Abood's* reasoning, the workability of the rule it established, its consistency with other related decisions, developments since the decision was handed down, and reliance on the decision. After analyzing these factors, we conclude that *stare decisis* does not require us to retain *Abood*.

An important factor in determining whether a precedent should be overruled is the quality of its reasoning. . . . *Abood* judged the constitutionality of public-sector agency fees under a deferential standard that finds no support in our free speech cases. (As noted, today's dissent makes the same fundamental mistake.) *Abood* did not independently evaluate the strength of the government interests that were said to support the challenged agency-fee provision; nor did it ask how well that provision actually promoted those interests or whether they could have been adequately served without impinging so heavily on the free speech rights of nonmembers. . . . Such deference to legislative judgments is inappropriate in deciding free speech issues. . . .

Another relevant consideration in the *stare decisis* calculus is the workability of the precedent in question, and that factor also weighs against *Abood*. *Abood's* line between chargeable and nonchargeable union expenditures has proved to be impossible to draw with precision. . . .

In some cases, reliance provides a strong reason for adhering to established law, and this is the factor that is stressed most strongly by respondents, their amici, and the dissent. They contend that collective-bargaining agreements now in effect were negotiated with agency fees in mind and that unions may have given up other benefits in exchange for provisions granting them such fees. In this case, however, reliance does not carry decisive weight. For one thing, it would be unconscionable to permit free speech rights to be abridged in perpetuity in order to preserve contract provisions that will expire on their own in a few years' time. . . . For another, *Abood* does not provide "a clear or easily applicable standard, so arguments for reliance based on its clarity are misplaced." This is especially so because public-sector unions have been on notice for years regarding this Court's misgivings about *Abood* . . . . In short, the uncertain status of *Abood*, the lack of clarity it provides, the short-term nature of collective-bargaining agreements, and the ability of unions to protect themselves if an agency-fee provision was crucial to its bargaining all work to undermine the force of reliance as a factor supporting *Abood*.

We recognize that the loss of payments from nonmembers may cause unions to experience unpleasant transition costs in the short term, and may require unions to make adjustments in order to attract and retain members. But we must weigh these disadvantages against the considerable windfall that unions have received under *Abood* for the past 41 years. It is hard to estimate how many billions of dollars have been taken from nonmembers and transferred to public-sector unions in violation of the First Amendment. Those unconstitutional exactions cannot be allowed to continue indefinitely. . . .

For these reasons, States and public-sector unions may no longer extract agency fees from nonconsenting employees. Under Illinois law, if a public-sector collective-bargaining agreement includes an agency-fee provision and the union certifies to the employer the amount of the fee, that amount is automatically deducted from the nonmember's wages. No form of employee consent is required. This procedure violates the First Amendment and cannot continue. Neither an agency fee nor any other payment to the union may be deducted from a nonmember's wages, nor may any other attempt be made to collect such a payment, unless the employee affirmatively consents to pay. By agreeing to pay, nonmembers are waiving their First Amendment rights, and such a waiver cannot be presumed. Rather, to be effective, the waiver must be freely given and shown by "clear and compelling" evidence. . . .

Abood was wrongly decided and is now overruled. The judgment of the United States Court of Appeals for the Seventh Circuit is reversed, and the case is remanded for further proceedings consistent with this opinion.

It is so ordered.

JUSTICE SOTOMAYOR, dissenting, . . . [omitted].

JUSTICE KAGAN, with whom JUSTICE GINSBURG, JUSTICE BREYER, and JUSTICE SOTOMAYOR join, dissenting.

For over 40 years, *Abood* struck a stable balance between public employees' First Amendment rights and government entities' interests in running their workforces as they thought proper. Under that decision, a government entity could require public employees to pay a fair share of the cost that a union incurs when negotiating on their behalf over terms of employment. But no part of that fair-share payment could go to any of the union's political or ideological activities.

That holding fit comfortably with this Court's general framework for evaluating claims that a condition of public employment violates the First Amendment. The Court's decisions have long made plain that government entities have substantial latitude to regulate their employees' speech—especially about terms of employment—in the interest of operating their workplaces effectively. *Abood* allowed governments to do just that. While protecting public employees' expression about non-workplace matters, the decision enabled a government to advance important managerial interests—by ensuring the presence of an exclusive employee representative to bargain with. Far from an "anomaly," the *Abood* regime was a paradigmatic example of how the government can regulate speech in its capacity as an employer.

Not any longer. Today, the Court succeeds in its 6-year campaign to reverse *Abood*. Its decision will have large-scale consequences. Public employee unions will lose a secure source of financial support. State and local governments that thought fair-share provisions furthered their interests will need to find new ways of managing their workforces. Across the country, the relationships of public employees and employers will alter in both predictable and wholly unexpected ways.

Rarely if ever has the Court overruled a decision—let alone one of this import—with so little regard for the usual principles of *stare decisis*. There are no special justifications for reversing *Abood*. It has proved workable. No recent developments have eroded its underpinnings. And it is deeply entrenched, in both the law and the real world. More than 20 States have statutory schemes built on the decision. Those laws underpin thousands of ongoing contracts involving millions of employees. Reliance interests do not come any stronger than those surrounding *Abood*. And likewise, judicial disruption does not get any greater than what the Court does today. I respectfully dissent. . . .

Unlike the majority, I see nothing "questionable" about *Abood*'s analysis. The decision's account of why some government entities have a strong interest in agency fees (now often called fair-share fees) is fundamentally sound. And the balance *Abood* struck between public employers' interests and public employees' expression is right at home in First Amendment doctrine. . . . In many cases over many decades, this Court has addressed how the First Amendment applies when the government, acting not as sovereign but as employer, limits its workers' speech. Those decisions have granted substantial latitude to the government, in recognition of its significant interests in managing its workforce so as to best serve the public. *Abood* fit neatly with that caselaw, in both reasoning and result. Indeed, its reversal today creates a significant anomaly—an exception, applying to union fees alone, from the usual rules governing public employees' speech. *Abood* thus dovetailed with the Court's usual attitude in First Amendment cases toward the regulation of public employees' speech. That attitude is one of respect—even solicitude—for the government's prerogatives as an employer. So long as the government is acting as an employer—rather than exploiting the employment relationship for other ends—it has a wide berth, comparable to that of a private employer. And when the regulated expression concerns the terms and conditions of employment—the very stuff of the employment relationship—the government really cannot lose. There, managerial interests are obvious and strong. And so government employees are . . . just employees, even though they work for the government. Except that today the government does lose, in a first for the law. Now, the government can constitutionally adopt all policies regulating core workplace speech in pursuit of managerial goals—save this single one. . . .

And *Abood* is not just any precedent: It is embedded in the law . . . in a way not many decisions are. Over four decades, this Court has cited *Abood* favorably many times, and has affirmed and applied its central distinction between the costs of collective bargaining (which the government can charge to all employees) and those of political activities (which it cannot) . . . .

The majority is likewise wrong to invoke "workability" as a reason for overruling *Abood*. Does *Abood* require drawing a line? Yes, between a union's collective-bargaining activities and its political activities. Is that line perfectly and pristinely "precis[e]," as the majority demands? Well, not quite that—but as exercises of constitutional line drawing go, *Abood* stands well above average. In the 40 years since *Abood*, this Court has had to resolve only a handful of cases raising questions about the distinction. . . .

And in any event, one *stare decisis* factor—reliance—dominates all others here and demands keeping *Abood*. *Stare decisis*, this Court has held, "has added force when the legislature, in the public sphere, and citizens, in the private realm, have acted in reliance on a previous decision." That is because overruling a decision would then "require an extensive legislative response" or "dislodge settled rights and expectations." Both will happen here: The Court today wreaks havoc on entrenched legislative and contractual arrangements. . . .

The majority has overruled *Abood* for no exceptional or special reason, but because it never liked the decision. It has overruled *Abood* because it wanted to. Because, that is, it wanted to pick the winning side in what should be—and until now, has been—an energetic policy debate. Some state and local governments (and the constituents they serve) think that stable unions promote healthy labor relations and thereby improve the provision of services to the public. Other state and local governments (and their constituents) think, to the contrary, that strong unions impose excessive costs and impair those services. Americans have debated the pros and cons for many decades—in large part, by deciding whether to use fair-share arrangements. . . . Today, that healthy—that democratic—debate ends. The majority has adjudged who should prevail. And maybe most alarming, the majority has chosen the winners by turning the First Amendment into a sword, and using it against workaday economic and regulatory policy. Today is not the first time the Court has wielded the First Amendment in such an aggressive way. And it threatens not to be the last. Speech is everywhere—a part of every human activity. . . . For that reason, almost all economic and regulatory policy affects or touches speech. So the majority's road runs long. And at every stop are black-robed rulers overriding citizens' choices. The First Amendment was meant for better things. It was meant not to undermine but to protect democratic governance—including over the role of public-sector unions.

V. PRINT AND ELECTRONIC MEDIA

New York Times Co. v. *Sullivan*
376 U.S. 254, 84 S.Ct. 710, 11 L.Ed. 2d 686 (1964)

http://caselaw.findlaw.com/us-supreme-court/376/254.html

L. B. Sullivan, an elected city commissioner in Montgomery, Alabama—whose duties included supervision of the police department—brought an action for libel in the Circuit Court of Montgomery County against the *New York Times*. At issue was a paid advertisement that the *Times* had published which described maltreatment in Montgomery of black students protesting racial segregation. Sullivan's suit also named as defendants four individuals whose names, among others, appeared in the advertisement. The jury awarded plaintiff damages of $500,000 against each defendant, and the judgment on the verdict was affirmed by the Supreme Court of Alabama on the grounds that the statements in the advertisement were libelous per se, false, and not privileged, and that the evidence showed malice on the part of the newspaper. The state court rejected the defendants' constitutional objections on the ground that the First Amendment does not protect libelous publications. Majority: Brennan, Black, Clark, Douglas, Goldberg, Harlan, Stewart, Warren, White.

Mr. Justice Brennan delivered the opinion of the Court.

We are required for the first time in this case to determine the extent to which the constitutional protections for speech and press limit a State's power to award damages in a libel action brought by a public official against critics of his official conduct. . . .

Respondent's complaint alleged that he had been libeled by statements in a full-page advertisement that was carried in the *New York Times* on March 29, 1960. Entitled "Heed Their Rising Voices," the advertisement began by stating that "As the whole world knows by now, thousands of Southern Negro students are engaged in widespread non-violent demonstrations in positive affirmation of the right to live in human dignity as guaranteed by the U.S. Constitution and the Bill of Rights." It went on to charge that "in their efforts to uphold these guarantees, they are being met by an unprecedented wave of terror by those who would deny and negate that document which the whole world looks upon as setting the pattern for modern freedom. . . ."

Of the 10 paragraphs of text in the advertisement, the third and a portion of the sixth were the basis of respondent's claim of libel. . . .

Although neither of these statements mentions respondent by name, he contended that the word "police" in the third paragraph referred to him as the Montgomery Commissioner who supervised the Police Department, so that he was being accused of "ringing" the campus with police. He further claimed that the paragraph would be read as imputing to the police, and hence to him, the padlocking of the dining hall in order to starve the students into submission. As to the sixth paragraph, he contended that since arrests are ordinarily made by the police, the statement "They have arrested [Dr. Martin Luther King] seven times" would be read as referring to him; he further contended that the "they" who did the arresting would be equated with the "they" who committed the other described acts and with the "Southern violators." . . .

We hold that the rule of law applied by the Alabama courts is constitutionally deficient for failure to provide the safeguards for freedom of speech and of the press that are required by the First and Fourteenth Amendments in a libel action brought by a public official against critics of his official conduct. We further hold that under the proper safeguards the evidence presented in this case is constitutionally insufficient to support the judgment for respondent. . . .

Respondent relies heavily, as did the Alabama courts, on statements of this Court to the effect that the Constitution does not protect libelous publications. Those statements do not foreclose our inquiry here. None of the cases sustained the use of libel laws to impose sanctions upon expression critical of the official conduct of public officials. . . . In the only previous case that did present the question of constitutional limitations upon the power to award damages for libel of a public official, the Court was equally divided and the question was not decided. . . .

The general proposition that freedom of expression upon public questions is secured by the First Amendment has long been settled by our decisions. . . .

Thus we consider this case against the background of a profound national commitment to the principle that debate on public issues should be uninhibited, robust, and wide-open, and that it may well include vehement, caustic, and sometimes unpleasantly sharp attacks on government and public officials. . . . The present advertisement, as an expression of grievance and protest on one of the major public issues of our time, would seem clearly to qualify for the constitutional protection. The question is whether it forfeits that protection by the falsity of some of its factual statements and by its alleged defamation of respondent. . . .

Authoritative interpretations of the First Amendment guarantees have consistently refused to recognize an exception for any test of truth, whether administered by judges, juries, or administrative officials—and especially not one that puts the burden of proving truth on the speaker. . . . The constitutional protection does not turn upon "the truth, popularity, or social utility of the ideas and beliefs which are offered." . . . As Madison said, "Some degree of abuse is inseparable from the proper use of every thing; and in no instance is this more true than in that of the press."

[E]rroneous statement is inevitable in free debate. . . .

Injury to official reputation affords no more warrant for repressing speech that would otherwise be free than does factual error. Where judicial officers are involved, this Court has held that concern for the dignity and reputation of the courts does not justify the punishment as criminal contempt of criticism of the judge or his decision. . . . If judges are to be treated as "men of fortitude, able to thrive in a hardy climate," surely the same must be true of other government officials, such as elected city commissioners. Criticism of their official conduct does not lose its constitutional protection merely because it is effective criticism and hence diminishes their official reputations.

If neither factual error nor defamatory content suffices to remove the constitutional shield from criticism of official conduct, the combination of the two elements is no less inadequate. This is the lesson to be drawn from the great controversy over the Sedition Act of 1798, which first crystallized a national awareness of the central meaning of the First Amendment. . . .

Although the Sedition Act was never tested in this Court, the attack upon its validity has carried the day in the court of history. Fines levied in its prosecution were repaid by Act of Congress on the ground that it was unconstitutional. . . . The invalidity of the Act has also been assumed by Justices of this Court. . . . These views reflect a broad consensus that the Act, because of the restraint it imposed upon criticism of government and public officials, was inconsistent with the First Amendment. . . .

A rule compelling the critic of official conduct to guarantee the truth of all his factual assertions—and to do so on pain of libel judgments virtually unlimited in amount—leads to a comparable "self-censorship." Allowance of the defense of truth, with the burden of proving it on the defendant, does not mean that only false speech will be deterred. Even courts accepting this defense as an adequate safeguard have recognized the difficulties of adducing legal proofs that the alleged libel was true in all its factual particulars. . . .

Applying these standards, we consider that the proof presented to show actual malice lacks the convincing clarity which the constitutional standard demands, and hence that it would not constitutionally sustain the judgment for respondent under the proper rule of law. The case of the individual petitioners requires little discussion. Even assuming that they could constitutionally be found to have authorized the use of their names on the advertisement, there was no evidence whatever that they were aware of any erroneous statements or were in any way reckless in that regard. The judgment against them is thus without constitutional support.

Under such a rule would-be critics of official conduct may be deterred from voicing their criticism, even though it is believed to be true and even though it is in fact true, because of doubt whether it can be proved in court or fear of the expense of having to do so. They tend to make only statements which "steer far wider of the unlawful zone." . . . The rule thus dampens the vigor and limits the variety of public debate. . . .

As to the *Times*, we similarly conclude that the facts do not support a finding of actual malice. . . . We think the evidence against the *Times* supports at most a finding of negligence in failing to discover the misstatements, and is constitutionally insufficient to show the recklessness that is required for a finding of actual malice. . . .

The constitutional guarantees require, we think, a federal rule that prohibits a public official from recovering damages for a defamatory falsehood relating to his official conduct unless he proves that the statement was made with "actual malice"—that is, with knowledge that it was false or with reckless disregard of whether it was false or not. . . .

Reversed and remanded.

Mr. Justice Black, with whom Mr. Justice Douglas joins, concurring . . . [omitted].

Mr. Justice Goldberg, with whom Mr. Justice Douglas joins, concurring in the result . . . [omitted].

New York Times Co. v. *United States*
403 U.S. 713, 91 S.Ct. 2140, 29 L.Ed. 2d 822 (1971)

http://caselaw.findlaw.com/us-supreme-court/403/713.html

This testing of the limits of prior restraint produced one of the fastest start-to-finish bouts of litigation in Supreme Court history. The *New York Times* and the

Washington Post acquired copies of a 7,000-page classified study (popularized as the "Pentagon Papers") prepared for the Department of Defense on the evolution of U.S. Vietnam policy. On June 13, 1971, the *Times* published the first of what would be several installments, which *Times* editors had secretly condensed from the longer study. Serialization began in the *Post* on June 18. On June 15, the Nixon administration went into U.S. District Court in New York, and later in the District of Columbia, to obtain injunctions blocking further publication. The move against the *Post* proved unsuccessful, but the Second Circuit Court of Appeals enjoined further publication in the *Times* pending the outcome of the government's case. On June 25, the Supreme Court granted expedited review, with oral arguments scheduled the next day. The Court rendered its decision four days later on June 30. The format of opinions was unusual—per curiam, with each justice delivering a separate opinion. Opinions by four justices are reprinted here. The opinions of Justices Black and Harlan were their last. Majority: Black, Brennan, Douglas, Marshall, Stewart, White. Dissenting: Burger, Blackmun, Harlan.

Per Curiam . . .

"Any system of prior restraints of expression comes to this Court bearing a heavy presumption against its constitutional validity." . . . The Government "thus carries a heavy burden of showing justification for the enforcement of such a restraint." . . . The District Court for the Southern District of New York in the *New York Times* case and the District Court for the District of Columbia and the Court of Appeals for the District of Columbia Circuit in the *Washington Post* case held that the Government had not met that burden. We agree. . . .

Mr. Justice Black, with whom Mr. Justice Douglas joins, concurring.

I adhere to the view that the Government's case against the *Washington Post* should have been dismissed and that the injunction against the *New York Times* should have been vacated without oral argument when the cases were first presented to this Court. I believe that every moment's continuance of the injunctions against these newspapers amounts to a flagrant, indefensible, and continuing violation of the First Amendment. . . . In my view it is unfortunate that some of my Brethren are apparently willing to hold that the publication of news may sometimes be enjoined. Such a holding would make a shambles of the First Amendment.

Our Government was launched in 1789 with the adoption of the Constitution. The Bill of Rights, including the First Amendment, followed in 1791. Now, for the first time in the 182 years since the founding of the Republic, the federal courts are asked to hold that the First Amendment does not mean what it says, but rather means that Government can halt the publication of current news of vital importance to the people of this country.

In seeking injunctions against these newspapers and in its presentation to the Court, the Executive Branch seems to have forgotten the essential purpose and history of the First Amendment. When the Constitution was adopted, many people strongly opposed it because the document contained no Bill of Rights to safeguard certain basic freedoms. They especially feared that the new powers granted to a central Government might be interpreted to permit the Government to curtail freedom of religion, press, assembly, and speech. In response to an overwhelming public clamor, James Madison offered a series of amendments to satisfy citizens that these great liberties would remain safe and beyond the power of government to abridge. . . . The amendments were offered to curtail and restrict the general powers granted to the Executive, Legislative, and Judicial Branches two years before in the original Constitution. The Bill of Rights changed the original Constitution into a new charter under which no branch of government could abridge the people's freedoms of press, speech, religion, and assembly. Yet the Solicitor General argues and some members of the Court appear to agree that the general powers of the Government adopted in the original Constitution should be interpreted to limit and restrict the specific and emphatic guarantees of the Bill of Rights adopted later. I can imagine no greater perversion of history. . . .

In the First Amendment the Founding Fathers gave the free press the protection it must have to fulfill its essential role in our democracy. The press was to serve the governed, not the governors. The Government's power to censor the press was abolished so that the press would remain forever free to censure the Government. The press was protected so that it could bare the secrets of government and inform the people. Only a free and unrestrained press can effectively expose deception in government. And paramount among the responsibilities of a free press is the duty to prevent any part of the government from deceiving the people and sending them off to distant lands to die of foreign fevers and foreign shot and shell. In my view, far from deserving condemnation for their courageous reporting, the *New York Times*, the *Washington Post*, and other newspapers should be commended for serving the purpose that the Founding Fathers saw so clearly. In revealing the workings of government that led to the Vietnam war, the newspapers nobly did precisely that which the Founders hoped and trusted they would do. . . .

[W]e are asked to hold that despite the First Amendment's emphatic command, the Executive Branch, the Congress, and the Judiciary can make laws enjoining publication of current news and abridging freedom of the press in the name of "national security." The Government does not even attempt to rely on any act of Congress. Instead it makes the bold and dangerously far-reaching contention that the courts should take it upon themselves to "make" a law abridging freedom of the press in the name of equity, presidential power and national security, even when the representatives of the people in Congress have adhered to the command of the First Amendment and refused to make such a law. . . .

The word "security" is a broad, vague generality whose contours should not be invoked to abrogate the fundamental law embodied in the First Amendment. The guarding of military and diplomatic secrets at the expense of informed representative government provides no real security for our Republic. The Framers of the First Amendment, fully aware of both the need to defend a new nation and the abuses of the English and Colonial governments, sought to give this new society strength and security by providing that freedom of speech, press, religion, and assembly should not be abridged. . . .

MR. JUSTICE DOUGLAS, with whom MR. JUSTICE BLACK joins, concurring . . . [omitted].

MR. JUSTICE BRENNAN, concurring . . . [omitted].

MR. JUSTICE STEWART, with whom MR. JUSTICE WHITE joins, concurring.

In the governmental structure created by our Constitution, the Executive is endowed with enormous power in the two related areas of national defense and international relations. This power, largely unchecked by the Legislative and Judicial branches, has been pressed to the very hilt since the advent of the nuclear missile age. For better or for worse, the simple fact is that a President of the United States possesses vastly greater constitutional independence in these two vital areas of power than does, say, a prime minister of a country with a parliamentary form of government.

In the absence of the governmental checks and balances present in other areas of our national life, the only effective restraint upon executive policy and power in the areas of national defense and international affairs may lie in an enlightened citizenry—in an informed and critical public opinion which alone can here protect the values of democratic government. For this reason, it is perhaps here that a press that is alert, aware, and free most vitally serves the basic purpose of the First Amendment. For without an informed and free press there cannot be an enlightened people.

Yet it is elementary that the successful conduct of international diplomacy and the maintenance of an effective national defense require both confidentiality and secrecy. Other nations can hardly deal with this Nation in an atmosphere of mutual trust unless they can be assured that their confidences will be kept. And within our own executive departments, the development of considered and intelligent international policies would be impossible if those charged with their formulation could not communicate with each other freely, frankly, and in confidence. In the area of basic national defense the frequent need for absolute secrecy is, of course, self-evident.

I think there can be but one answer to this dilemma, if dilemma it be. The responsibility must be where the power is. If the Constitution gives the Executive a large degree of unshared power in the conduct of foreign affairs and the maintenance of our national defense, then under the Constitution the Executive must have the largely unshared duty to determine and preserve the degree of internal security necessary to exercise that power successfully. . . . [I]t is clear to me that it is the constitutional duty of the Executive—as a matter of sovereign prerogative and not as a matter of law as the courts know law—through the promulgation and enforcement of executive regulations, to protect the confidentiality necessary to carry out its responsibilities in the fields of international relations and national defense.

This is not to say that Congress and the courts have no role to play. Undoubtedly Congress has the power to enact specific and appropriate criminal laws to protect government property and preserve government secrets. Congress has passed such laws, and several of them are of very colorable relevance to the apparent circumstances of these cases. And if a criminal prosecution is instituted, it will be the responsibility of the courts to decide the applicability of the criminal law under which the charge is brought. Moreover, if Congress should pass a specific law authorizing civil proceedings in this field, the courts would likewise have the duty to decide the constitutionality of such a law as well as its applicability to the facts proved.

But in the cases before us we are asked neither to construe specific regulations nor to apply specific laws. We are asked, instead, to perform a function that the Constitution gave to the Executive, not the Judiciary. We are asked, quite simply, to prevent the publication by two newspapers of material that the Executive Branch insists should not, in the national interest, be published. I am convinced that the Executive is correct with respect to some of the documents involved. But I cannot say that disclosure of any of them will surely result in direct, immediate, and irreparable damage to our Nation or its people. That being so, there can under the First Amendment be but one judicial resolution of the issues before us. I join the judgments of the Court.

Mr. Justice White, with whom Mr. Justice Stewart joins, concurring . . . [omitted].

Mr. Justice Marshall, concurring . . . [omitted].

Mr. Chief Justice Burger, dissenting. . . .

The newspapers make a derivative claim under the First Amendment; they denominate this right as the public "right-to-know"; by implication, the *Times* asserts a sole trusteeship of that right by virtue of its journalistic "scoop." The right is asserted as an absolute. Of course, the First Amendment right itself is not an absolute, as Justice Holmes so long ago pointed out in his aphorism concerning the right to shout fire in a crowded theatre. . . . There are no doubt other exceptions no one has had occasion to describe or discuss. Conceivably such exceptions may be lurking in these cases and would have been flushed had they been properly considered in the trial courts, free from unwarranted deadlines and frenetic pressures. A great issue of this kind should be tried in a judicial atmosphere conducive to thoughtful, reflective deliberation, especially when haste, in terms of hours, is unwarranted in light of the long period the *Times*, by its own choice, deferred publication.

It is not disputed that the *Times* has had unauthorized possession of the documents for 3–4 months, during which it has had its expert analysts studying them, presumably digesting them and preparing the material for publication. During all of this time, the *Times*, presumably in its capacity as trustee of the public's "right to know," has held up publication for purposes it considered proper and thus public knowledge was delayed. No doubt this was for a good reason; the analysis of 7,000 pages of complex material drawn from a vastly greater volume of material would inevitably take time and the writing of good news stories takes time. But why should the United States Government, from whom this information was illegally acquired by someone, along with all the counsel, trial judges, and appellate judges be placed under needless pressure? . . .

We all crave speedier judicial processes but when judges are pressured as in these cases the result is a parody of the judicial process.

Mr. Justice Harlan, with whom The Chief Justice and Mr. Justice Blackmun join, dissenting. . . .

With all respect, I consider that the Court has been almost irresponsibly feverish in dealing with these cases. . . .

Forced as I am to reach the merits of these cases, I dissent from the opinion and judgments of the Court. . . .

It is plain to me that the scope of the judicial function in passing upon the activities of the Executive Branch of the Government in the field of foreign affairs is very narrowly restricted. This view is, I think, dictated by the concept of separation of powers upon which our constitutional system rests. . . .

The power to evaluate the "pernicious influence" of premature disclosure is not, however, lodged in the Executive alone. I agree that, in performance of its duty to protect the values of the First Amendment against political pressures, the judiciary must review the initial Executive determination to the point of satisfying itself that the subject matter of the dispute does lie within the proper compass of the President's foreign relations power. Constitutional considerations forbid "a complete abandonment of judicial control." . . . Moreover, the judiciary may properly insist that the determination that disclosure of the subject matter would irreparably impair the national security be made by the head of the Executive Department concerned here the Secretary of State or the Secretary of Defense—after actual personal consideration by that officer. This safeguard is required in the analogous area of executive claims of privilege for secrets of state. . . .

Even if there is some room for the judiciary to override the executive determination, it is plain that the scope of review must be exceedingly narrow. I can see no indication in the opinions of either the District Court or the Court of Appeals, in the *Post* litigation that the conclusions of the Executive were given even the deference owing to an administrative agency, much less that owing to a coequal branch of the Government operating within the field of its constitutional prerogative. . . .

Mr. Justice Blackmun, concurring . . . [omitted].

Ashcroft v. *Free Speech Coalition* 535 U.S. 234, 122 S.Ct. 1389, 152 L.Ed. 2d 403 (2002)

http://caselaw.findlaw.com/us-supreme-court/535/234.html

The Child Pornography Prevention Act of 1996 (CPPA) expanded the federal prohibition on child pornography to include not only pornographic images made using actual children, but also [in section 2258(8)(B)] "any visual depiction, including any photograph, film, video, picture, or computer or computer-generated image or picture" that "is, or appears to be, of a minor engaging in sexually explicit conduct," and [in section 2256(8)(D)] any sexually explicit image that is "advertised, promoted, presented, described, or distributed in such a manner that conveys the impression" it depicts "a minor engaging in sexually explicit conduct." Fearing that the CPPA threatened their activities, an adult-entertainment trade association and others organized as the Free Speech Coalition filed suit alleging that the "appears to be" and "conveys the impression" provisions were overbroad and vague, chilling production of works protected by the First Amendment. The U.S. District Court for the Northern District of California granted the government summary judgment. In 1999 the U.S. Court of Appeals for the Ninth Circuit reversed. Majority: Kennedy, Breyer, Ginsburg, Souter, Stevens, Thomas. Dissenting (on most points): Rehnquist, O'Connor, Scalia.

Justice Kennedy delivered the opinion of the Court. . . .

By prohibiting child pornography that does not depict an actual child, the statute goes beyond *Ferber v. New York* (1982), which distinguished child pornography from other sexually explicit speech because of the State's interest in protecting the children exploited by the production process. As a general rule, pornography can be banned only if obscene, but under *Ferber*, pornography showing minors can be proscribed whether or not the images are obscene under the definition set forth in *Miller* v. *California* (1973). *Ferber* recognized that "[t]he *Miller* standard, like all general definitions of what may be banned as obscene, does not reflect the State's particular and more compelling interest in prosecuting those who promote the sexual exploitation of children." . . .

Like the law in *Ferber*, the CPPA seeks to reach beyond obscenity, and it makes no attempt to conform to the *Miller* standard. For instance, the statute would reach visual depictions, such as movies, even if they have redeeming social value.

The principal question to be resolved, then, is whether the CPPA is constitutional where it proscribes a significant universe of speech that is neither obscene under *Miller* nor child pornography under *Ferber*.

Before 1996, Congress defined child pornography as the type of depictions at issue in *Ferber*, images made using actual minors. The CPPA retains that prohibition and adds three other prohibited categories of speech, of which the first, § 2256(8)(B), and the third, § 2256(8)(D), are at issue in this case. . . .

These images do not involve, let alone harm, any children in the production process; but Congress decided the materials threaten children in other, less direct, ways. Pedophiles might use the materials to encourage children to participate in sexual activity. . . . Furthermore, pedophiles might "whet their own sexual appetites" with the pornographic images, "thereby increasing the creation and distribution of child pornography and the sexual abuse and exploitation of actual children." Under these rationales, harm flows from the content of the images, not from the means of their production. In addition, Congress identified another problem created by computer-generated images: Their existence can make it harder to prosecute pornographers who do use real minors. As imaging technology improves, Congress found, it becomes more difficult to prove that a particular picture was produced using actual children. To ensure that defendants possessing child pornography using real minors cannot evade prosecution, Congress extended the ban to virtual child pornography. . . .

As a general principle, the First Amendment bars the government from dictating what we see or read or speak or hear. The freedom of speech has its limits; it does not embrace certain categories of speech, including defamation, incitement, obscenity, and pornography produced with real children. While these categories may be prohibited without violating the First Amendment, none of them includes the speech prohibited by the CPPA. In his dissent from the opinion of the Court of Appeals, Judge Ferguson recognized this to be the law and proposed that virtual child pornography should be regarded as an additional category of unprotected speech. It would be necessary for us to take this step to uphold the statute.

As we have noted, the CPPA is much more than a supplement to the existing federal prohibition on obscenity. Under *Miller* v. *California*, the Government must prove that the work, taken as a whole, appeals to the prurient interest, is patently offensive in light of community standards, and lacks serious literary, artistic, political, or scientific value. The CPPA, however, extends to images that appear to depict a minor engaging in sexually explicit activity without regard to the *Miller* requirements. The materials need not appeal to the prurient interest. Any depiction of sexually explicit activity, no matter how it is presented, is proscribed. The CPPA applies to a picture in a psychology manual, as well as a movie depicting the horrors of sexual abuse. It is not necessary, moreover, that the image be patently offensive. Pictures of what appear to be 17-year-olds engaging in sexually explicit activity do not in every case contravene community standards.

The CPPA prohibits speech despite its serious literary, artistic, political, or scientific value. The statute proscribes the visual depiction of an idea—that of teenagers engaging in sexual activity—that is a fact of modern society and has been a theme in art and literature throughout the ages. Under the CPPA, images are prohibited so long as the persons appear to be under 18 years of age. . . . It is, of course, undeniable that some youths engage in sexual activity before the legal age, either on their own inclination or because they are victims of sexual abuse.

Both themes—teenage sexual activity and the sexual abuse of children—have inspired countless literary works. William Shakespeare created the most famous pair of teenage lovers, one of whom is just 13 years of age. . . . Shakespeare may not have written sexually explicit scenes for the Elizabethean audience, but were modern directors to adopt a less conventional approach, that fact alone would not compel the conclusion that the work was obscene.

Contemporary movies pursue similar themes. Last year's Academy Awards featured the movie, "Traffic," which was nominated for Best Picture. The film portrays a teenager, identified as a 16-year-old, who becomes addicted to drugs. The viewer sees the degradation of her addiction, which in the end leads her to a filthy room to trade sex for drugs. The year before, "American Beauty" won the Academy Award for Best Picture. In the course of the movie, a teenage girl engages in sexual relations with her teenage boyfriend, and another yields herself to the gratification of a middle-aged man. The film also contains a scene where, although the movie audience understands the act is not taking place, one character believes he is watching a teenage boy performing a sexual act on an older man. . . .

Whether or not the films we mention violate the CPPA, they explore themes within the wide sweep of the statute's prohibitions. If these films, or hundreds of others of lesser note that explore those subjects, contain a single graphic depiction of sexual activity within the statutory definition, the possessor of the film would be subject to severe punishment without inquiry into the work's redeeming value. This is inconsistent with an essential First Amendment rule: The artistic merit of a work does not depend on the presence of a single explicit scene. . . .

The Government . . . argues that the CPPA is necessary because pedophiles may use virtual child pornography to seduce children. There are many things innocent in themselves, however, such as cartoons, video games, and candy, that might be used for immoral purposes, yet we would not expect those to be prohibited because they can be misused. . . . The objective is to prohibit illegal conduct, but this restriction goes well beyond that interest by restricting the speech available to law-abiding adults.

The Government submits further that virtual child pornography whets the appetites of pedophiles and encourages them to engage in illegal conduct. This rationale cannot sustain the provision in question. The mere tendency of speech to encourage unlawful acts is not a sufficient reason for banning it. . . . The right to think is the beginning of freedom, and speech must be protected from the government because speech is the beginning of thought. . . .

The Government next argues that its objective of eliminating the market for pornography produced using real children necessitates a prohibition on virtual images as well. Virtual images, the Government contends, are indistinguishable from real ones; they are part of the same market and are often exchanged. In this way, it is said, virtual images promote the trafficking in works produced through the exploitation of real children. The hypothesis is somewhat implausible. If virtual images were identical to illegal child pornography, the illegal images would be driven from the market by the indistinguishable substitutes. Few pornographers would risk prosecution by abusing real children if fictional, computerized images would suffice. . . .

Finally, the Government says that the possibility of producing images by using computer imaging makes it very difficult for it to prosecute those who produce pornography by using real children. Experts, we are told, may have difficulty in saying whether the pictures were made by using real children or by using computer imaging. The necessary solution, the argument runs, is to prohibit both kinds of images. The argument, in essence, is that protected speech may be banned as a means to ban unprotected speech. This analysis turns the First Amendment upside down. . . .

In sum, § 2256(8)(B) covers materials beyond the categories recognized in *Ferber* and *Miller*, and the reasons the Government offers in support of limiting the freedom of speech have no justification in our precedents or in the law of the First Amendment. The provision abridges the freedom to engage in a substantial amount of lawful speech. For this reason, it is overbroad and unconstitutional.

The First Amendment requires a more precise restriction. . . .

The judgment of the Court of Appeals is affirmed.

It is so ordered.

Justice Thomas, concurring in the judgment . . . [omitted].

Chief Justice Rehnquist, with whom Justice Scalia joins in part, dissenting. . . .

We normally do not strike down a statute on First Amendment grounds "when a limiting instruction has been or could be placed on the challenged statute." . . . This case should be treated no differently.

Other than computer generated images that are virtually indistinguishable from real children engaged in sexually explicitly conduct, the CPPA can be limited so as not to reach any material that was not already unprotected before the CPPA. The CPPA's definition of "sexually explicit conduct" is quite explicit in this regard. It makes clear that the statute only reaches "visual depictions" of: "[A]ctual or simulated . . . sexual intercourse, including genital-genital, oral-genital, anal-genital, or oral-anal, whether between persons of the same or opposite sex; . . . bestiality; . . . masturbation; . . . sadistic or masochistic abuse; . . . or lascivious exhibition of the genitals or pubic area of any person."

The Court and Justice O'Connor suggest that this very graphic definition reaches the depiction of youthful looking adult actors engaged in suggestive sexual activity, presumably because the definition extends to "simulated" intercourse. Read as a whole, however, I think the definition reaches only the sort of "hard core of child pornography" that we found without protection in *Ferber*. So construed, the CPPA bans visual depictions of youthful looking adult actors engaged in *actual* sexual activity; mere *suggestions* of sexual activity, such as youthful looking adult actors squirming under a blanket, are more akin to written descriptions than visual depictions, and thus fall outside the purview of the statute.

The reference to "simulated" has been part of the definition of "sexually explicit conduct" since the statute was first passed. But the inclusion of "simulated" conduct, alongside "actual" conduct, does not change the "hard core" nature of the image banned. The reference to "simulated" conduct simply brings within the statute's reach depictions of hard core pornography that are "made to look genuine," including the main target of the CPPA, computer-generated images virtually indistinguishable from real children engaged in sexually explicit conduct. Neither actual conduct nor simulated conduct, however, is properly construed to reach depictions such as those in a film portrayal of *Romeo and Juliet*, which are far removed from the hard core pornographic depictions that Congress intended to reach. . . .

This narrow reading of "sexually explicit conduct" not only accords with the text of the CPPA and the intentions of Congress; it is exactly how the phrase was understood prior to the broadening gloss the Court gives it today. Indeed, had "sexually explicit conduct" been thought to reach the sort of material the Court says it does, then films such as "Traffic" and "American Beauty" would not have been made the way they were. . . . "Traffic" won its Academy Award in 2001. "American Beauty" won its Academy Award in 2000. But the CPPA has been on the books, and has been enforced, since 1996. The chill felt by the Court has apparently never been felt by those who actually make movies. . . .

The aim of ensuring the enforceability of our Nation's child pornography laws is a compelling one. The CPPA is targeted to this aim by extending the definition of child pornography to reach computer-generated images that are virtually indistinguishable from real children engaged in sexually explicit conduct. The statute need not be read to do any more than precisely this, which is not offensive to the First Amendment. . . .

Justice O'Connor, with whom The Chief Justice and Justice Scalia join in part, concurring in the judgment in part and dissenting in part . . . [omitted].

NOTE

1. The significant phrases that could be understood were:

   "How far is the nigger going to—yeah"
   "This is what we are going to do to the niggers"
   "A dirty nigger"
   "Send the Jews back to Israel"
   "Let's give them back to the dark garden"
   "Save America"
   "Let's go back to constitutional betterment"
   "Bury the niggers"
   "We intend to do our part"
   "Give us our state rights"
   "Freedom for the whites"
   "Nigger will have to fight for every inch he gets from now on."

12

Religious Liberty

Believing . . . that religion is a matter which lies solely between man and his God, that he owes account to none other for his faith or his worship, that the legislative powers of government reach actions only, and not opinions, I contemplate with sovereign reverence that act of the whole American people which declared that their legislature should "make no law respecting an establishment of religion, or prohibiting the free exercise thereof," thus building a wall of separation between church and state.

—THOMAS JEFFERSON (1802)

Congress shall "make no law respecting an establishment of religion, or prohibiting the free exercise thereof," begins the First Amendment. The **establishment** and **free exercise clauses** embody the American solution to one of the dilemmas of the modern world—the proper relation of state and religion, and of individuals to their God and their government. These clauses are central to the protection of religious beliefs and to the maintenance of civil peace in a religiously diverse culture.

COMPETING VISIONS

By the time the Bill of Rights became part of the Constitution in 1791, two competing visions had developed that shaped laws affecting religious liberty: accommodation and separation. Even today, debates about the meaning of the religion clauses in the Constitution are often defined in terms of which of these visions is to prevail.

Accommodation is the older of the two visions and stresses freedom *of* religion. Alongside protection for religious practice, it seeks government acknowledgment of and sometimes support for religion (Protestant Christianity, in particular, in the eighteenth and nineteenth centuries). Accommodationists believe that government best serves its own purposes when it encourages religion and recognizes religion's contributions to society while tolerating different faiths. Government is not to meddle in the affairs of particular denominations, but laws should respect, and reflect, dominant religious values. This seems to have been

DOI: 10.4324/9781003164340-13

the prevailing view in most of the American states in the late 1700s and for a long time afterward. For example, the Pennsylvania Constitution of 1776 required state legislators, as part of their oath, to affirm belief in the divine inspiration of both the Old and New Testaments in the Bible. Practically on the eve of the Constitutional Convention of 1787, Virginia came close to reinstating a general taxpayer assessment in support of religious congregations. In 1824, the Supreme Court of Pennsylvania affirmed that Christianity was part of the common law of the Commonwealth. Blasphemy was punishable as a crime in many states. Until 1961, Maryland required officeholders to declare belief in the existence of God. As public education took hold in the nineteenth century, religious instruction was part of the curriculum in many states. Brief religious exercises in public schools were widespread as late as the 1960s and remain a subject of contention. People over 70 remember "blue laws" that kept many businesses closed on Sunday, the holy day of rest for most Christians.

A second, more secular, vision that took shape in the United States was closely identified two centuries ago with leaders such as Thomas Jefferson and James Madison. It stresses **separation—**freedom *from* religion. It seeks greater distance between religion and government in a nation that is not only one of the most religious but also one of the most religiously diverse countries on earth. For separationists, both political and religious institutions are more likely to prosper if each involves itself as little as possible in the affairs of the other.

Symbolic of the separationist vision are passages in the national Constitution. In the original text of the Constitution, there is a single but nonetheless significant reference to religion. Article VI declares: "no religious Test shall ever be required as a Qualification to any Office or public Trust under the United States." At the outset, by barring **religious tests—**a religious belief requirement—the Constitution disallowed a policy for the nation that was followed by most of the American states and virtually every other country at that time. In its leadership, the federal government could not be sectarian. In the Bill of Rights, the twin provisions of nonestablishment and free exercise have complementary objectives—preserving liberty and order. The free exercise clause preserves a sphere of religious practice free of interference by the government. Most Americans of two centuries ago probably did not crave toleration for beliefs other than their own. Given the presence of so many faiths, however, they had no choice. The violent alternative—as demonstrated in some places in the world today—was unacceptable.

Even though a few states still maintained some kind of officially supported or designated church in 1791, the establishment clause declared that the nation could not have one. Nonestablishment was thus part of the price of union. The First Amendment sets the government off limits as a prize in a nation of competing faiths. The establishment clause thus protects free exercise by disabling all groups so that none can employ public resources to advance itself and to threaten the others.

The presence of these provisions in the First Amendment, however, raises a question. Why would the states have demanded, and then ratified, a Bill of Rights that in its clauses on religion seemed to contrast sharply with laws and practices in most of the states at that time? In their own eyes, local leaders were being neither foolish nor inconsistent. If religion was to be addressed by government at all, it was a subject for state, not national control. Ironically, the incorporation of the religion clauses into the Fourteenth Amendment in the 1940s—depicted in Table 9.1 in Chapter Nine—meant that the rules that tied the hands of the national government with respect to religion eventually bound the states as well.

Religion's special place in the Constitution also raises an obvious but perplexing problem in interpretation. What is a religion? What is a religious belief? The Supreme Court has given no definitive answer. Indeed, none may be completely acceptable. Generally, the approach in recent decades has been to broaden the meaning of religion to include more than theistic beliefs (*United States* v. *Seeger*, 1965). Religion is usually defined from the believer's perspective (*Thomas* v. *Review Board*, 1981), and while courts may validly inquire into the sincerity of one's beliefs, they may not test their validity (*United States* v. *Ballard*, 1944). Still, "religion" presumably does not encompass every strongly held belief; otherwise, its separate enumeration in the First Amendment would be pointless.

THE ESTABLISHMENT CLAUSE

The establishment clause limits government support of religious endeavors and, more important, bars it from becoming the tool of one faith against others. Like most other constitutional limitations, however, this one is not self-defining. At the very least, the establishment clause would prohibit a "Church of the United States." But given the many ways in which government may interact with religious institutions, how does one know when a policy "respect[s] an establishment of religion?"

The Modern Era. It was not until 1947 and *Everson* v. *Board of Education* that laws began receiving regular scrutiny under the establishment clause. Applying this part of the First Amendment to the states through the Fourteenth Amendment, the Court allowed a state to pay the costs of bus transportation of children attending sectarian as well as public and nonsectarian private schools. Nonetheless, drawing on Thomas Jefferson's reply to the Danbury Baptist Association of Connecticut in 1802, the decision set forth the principle that the religious clauses of the Constitution erected a "wall of separation" between church and state. Dissenting in *Everson*, Justice Rutledge issued a prophetic warning:

> Two great drives are constantly in motion to abridge, in the name of education, the complete division of religion and civil authority which our forefathers made. One is to introduce religious education and observances into the public schools. The other, to obtain public funds for the aid and support of various private religious schools. . . .
>
> In my opinion both avenues were closed by the Constitution. Neither should be opened by this Court. The matter is not one of quantity, to be measured by the amount of money expended. Now as in Madison's day it is one of principle, to keep separate the separate spheres as the First Amendment drew them; to prevent the first experiment upon our liberties; and to keep the question from becoming entangled in corrosive precedents. We should not be less strict to keep strong and untarnished the one side of the shield of religious freedom than we have been of the other.

Everson remains significant for several reasons. First, nationalization of the establishment clause has meant that individual state governments no longer have the final say on church–state matters within their borders. Second, because of the many ways in which state governments may interact with religion, *Everson* was an unmistakable invitation for further litigation. Because the Court upheld the New Jersey law challenged in that case, a reasonable conclusion was that not every policy that arguably supported religion ran afoul of the establishment clause. Later cases would have to discern constitutional limits. Third, the reach of the establishment clause remains broad because, according to *Everson*, it prohibits programs that "aid all religions," not merely those that "aid one religion" or "prefer one over the other."

Testing Establishment. In subsequent cases, the justices have devised various "tests" or criteria by which to determine when a government has violated the establishment clause.

1. **Lemon test**. So named because of its use in ***Lemon* v. *Kurtzman*** (1971), this test consists of three elements or "prongs." To pass scrutiny, (a) a policy must have a "secular purpose," (b) its primary effect must be "neutral" (i.e., neither advancing nor hindering religion), and (c) it must not promote an "excessive entanglement" between government and religion.
2. **Endorsement test**. A violation of the establishment clause occurs when government sends a signal that religion is favored or preferred, thus making some people feel as "outsiders" and others as "insiders."
3. **Agostini test**. So named because of ***Agostini* v. *Felton*** (1997), which modified the Lemon test, it is an elaboration of the endorsement test. A challenged policy must have both a secular purpose and a neutral effect. A policy has the impermissible effect of advancing religion if it (a) results in indoctrination of religion by government; (b) defines its recipients or beneficiaries according to religion; *or* (c) creates an excessive entanglement between government and religion.
4. **Coercion test**. This test allows government to acknowledge or accommodate religion but bars any policy that coerces anyone to support or to participate in any religion or religious exercise.
5. **Child-benefit theory**. Sometimes employed in cases involving state aid to religious schools, this approach focuses on the primary beneficiaries of the challenged plan—the children, rather than the schools themselves—where the aid is a result of decisions made by families about where their children should enroll, and not a result of government decisions to aid religious schools directly.

The fact that the Court has applied different tests to a variety of factual situations at different times has generated uncertainty and sometimes exasperation. One reason may be that no one of the tests appropriately fits all or even most of the establishment clause cases that reach the Court. The result is that one case resorts to *Lemon* (or another test), and the next one might not. Sometimes the Court relies on none of the tests by name.

Religion in Public Schools. Of all the establishment clause issues that the Court has faced, those dealing with religious expression in public schools have generated the most controversy and yielded the least inconsistency. In the first of these in 1948, the Court struck down a **released-time** program for religious instruction in Champaign, Illinois (*McCollum* v. *Board of Education*). Students had the option of attending religion classes on site during the school day. Yet factual distinctions only four years later in *Zorach* v. *Clauson* led to the Court's approval of a program in New York, where similar instruction in the school day occurred off school premises. "We are a religious people whose institutions presuppose a Supreme Being," declared Justice Douglas for the majority. "When the state encourages religious instruction or cooperates with religious authorities by adjusting the schedule of public events to sectarian needs, it follows the best of our traditions." The contrast in outcomes prompted Justice Jackson to note in dissent that *Zorach* would "be more interesting to students of psychology and of the judicial processes than to students of constitutional law."

The first of Justice Rutledge's "great drives," however, continued to heat in the crucible of litigation. Any satisfaction to proponents of religion in public schools brought by *Zorach* was short-lived. Prayers and Bible reading in schools next came under fire. *Engel* v. *Vitale* (1962) invalidated the use in New York's public schools of a short prayer, approved by the Board of Regents, to be recited during opening exercises of each school day. In 1963, eight justices went further, declaring in *School District of Abington Township* v. *Schempp* that Bible reading and recitation of the Lord's Prayer in Pennsylvania classrooms were also invalid. In deciding whether the "wall of separation" had been breached, Justice Clark explained, "[T]o withstand the strictures of the Establishment Clause, there must be a secular legislative purpose and a primary effect that neither advances nor inhibits religion."

Engel and *Schempp* hardly ended the school prayer controversy. Some school districts plainly ignored the decisions. In the early 1980s, President Ronald Reagan campaigned for the restoration of prayer in the schools and advocated amending the Constitution to make that possible. "God never should have been expelled from America's classrooms," he declared in his 1983 State of the Union address. So it was not surprising that the justices continued to face the prayer issue. In 1985, *Wallace* v. *Jaffree* tested Alabama's requirement of a minute of silence "for meditation or voluntary prayer" in the public schools. More than two dozen states had enacted similar laws. Even Justice Brennan's concurring opinion in *Schempp* had suggested that moments of silence might not be unconstitutional. But six justices thought the Alabama law was defective. "[T]he State intends to characterize prayer as a favored practice," announced Justice Stevens. "Such an end is not consistent with the established principle that the Government must pursue a course of complete neutrality toward religion." The Court's decision, with its flurry of separate opinions, seemed Solomonic. Strongly hinted was the constitutionality of a law setting aside a moment of silence "for meditation" where it was not obvious from the record that the state's purpose was one of making an "end run" around *Engel* and *Schempp*.

By only a bare margin, however, did the Court maintain its opposition to public school prayer in 1992. In *Lee* v. *Weisman*, a family contested the brief invocation and benediction to be delivered at the principal's invitation by a rabbi at a public middle school commencement ceremony in Providence, Rhode Island. Although inclusive and sensitive to different religious traditions, the prayers were nonetheless addressed to God, asking for blessings and giving thanks. "It is beyond dispute that, at a minimum, the Constitution guarantees that government may not coerce anyone to support or participate in religion or its exercise," declared Justice Kennedy.

Eight years later, the Court confronted another dispute over prayer that varied from *Lee* in several respects (*Santa Fe Independent School District* v. *Doe*, 2000). Under attack was prayer at a high school football game. Moreover, students and not school officials—through two elections—decided whether invocations should be delivered at games, and, if so, selected the person who would pray. Nonetheless, the Court maintained its stance against any official religious expression on school premises, regardless of its source or setting. "The District," wrote Justice Stevens, "asks us to pretend that we do not recognize what every Santa Fe High School student understands clearly—that this policy is about prayer. . . . We refuse to turn a blind eye to the context in which this policy arose, and that context quells any doubt that this policy was implemented with the purpose of endorsing school prayer." *Santa Fe* was significant for another reason as well: Six justices (not five, as in *Lee*) found the policy constitutionally deficient.

Religion in Other Official Settings. Perhaps because of the impressionable nature of schoolchildren and the unique role public schools have long had in the life of the nation, the justices have been quicker to strike down religious influences in the classroom than in other official places. Outside the schoolroom, the Court's responses have been decidedly mixed. In *Marsh* v. *Chambers* (1983), for example, a majority of the Court found no constitutional objection to the Nebraska practice of having a chaplain for the state legislature paid out of public funds. Nor was a majority prepared to say that the First Amendment banned city officials in Pawtucket, Rhode Island, from annually erecting a municipally owned Christmas display, including a crèche, in a private park (*Lynch* v. *Donnelly*, 1984). In contrast, five justices found unacceptable the display of a privately owned crèche in the county courthouse in Pittsburgh, Pennsylvania, which was adorned by a banner proclaiming "Gloria in excelsis Deo" (*County of Allegheny* v. *American Civil Liberties Union*, 1989). Yet in the same case six justices had no constitutional objection to a display on the steps of the nearby City-County Building, which combined an 18-foot menorah and a 45-foot tree decorated with holiday ornaments. These holdings suggest that publicly sponsored religious displays are permissible only if they have become secularized. Government may "recognize" but not "endorse" religion. That distinction combined with its holding in *Marsh* may account for the outcome in ***Town of Greece* v. *Galloway*** (2014), where a sharply divided bench found no constitutional objection to the practice of opening town meetings with prayer even though most of the prayers had been offered by Christian clergy.

The line between recognition and endorsement is apparently thin indeed, particularly in light of *McCreary County* v. *A.C.L.U. of Kentucky* (2005), which upheld a lower court's invalidation of a courthouse display which included the Ten Commandments intermingled with various secular documents. On the same day that the display case came down, *Van Orden* v. *Perry* found no constitutional violation in the presence of a large monument on which the Ten Commandments had been inscribed that was sited on the Texas state capitol grounds. The monolith in question was one of 16 monuments and 21 historical markers located nearby that were supposed to commemorate people, ideals, and events that comprise Texan identity.

Constitutional line-drawing became even more complex in ***American Legion* v. *American Humanist Association*** (2019). This case involved a 40-foot-tall cross, which had been erected in 1925 as a memorial to fallen soldiers in World War I and was situated on a traffic island at a three-way junction of Bladensburg Road, Baltimore Avenue, and Annapolis Road in Bladensburg, Maryland. Even though the cross is unquestionably a Christian symbol, seven justices found no violation of the establishment clause, even with public ownership and upkeep. Justice Alito's plurality opinion floated what might be called the historical practices test or the passive-religious-display-with-a-long-pedigree test, or maybe the passage-of-time test. Passing years will reveal if one or another sticks. Yet with no opinion attracting the votes of more than four justices, the Bladensburg Cross Case may prove of limited precedential value.

State Aid to Religious Schools. Litigation involving state assistance to religious schools—the second of Justice Rutledge's "great drives"—has been a fixture on the Court's docket since the 1960s when state legislatures began to devise various ways to support financially pinched private schools, most of which were operated by the Roman Catholic Church. Some plans made private schools and their students eligible for certain benefits already enjoyed by public schools. Other plans singled out private schools for special assistance. *Lemon* v. *Kurtzman* (1971) marked the Court's first decision against such programs.

Lemon challenged Pennsylvania and Rhode Island laws that, among other things, provided funds for partial support of the salaries of teachers of secular subjects in private schools, including religious schools. In the Court's view, such funding would be acceptable only if the state could demonstrate that the plan had (1) a "secular purpose," (2) a primary effect that was "neutral" (these elements came from *Schempp*), and (3) an absence of "excessive entanglement" between government and religion. This third element of the Lemon test first appeared in *Walz* v. *Tax Commission* in 1970, which upheld state tax exemptions for real property owned by religious and other charitable institutions, even when the property was used for religious purposes. (The Court's reasoning in Walz was that tax exemptions created only "minimal and remote involvement between church and state and far less than taxation of churches.")

Judged against *Lemon*'s prongs, the Pennsylvania and Rhode Island statutes were constitutionally defective. Although both states could demonstrate a purpose that was secular (supporting education), the plans were snared on a "Catch-22" combination of the second and third prongs. Although the requirement that government and religion not be excessively entangled had been used to save the tax exemption in *Walz*, that same standard proved fatal in *Lemon*. Efforts by the state to ensure a neutral effect were bound to create excessive entanglement. Absent such entanglement, the state could not assure a neutral effect.

The Court's rulings in state-aid cases since *Lemon*, however, have not been a model of consistency. A series of decisions demonstrate the complexities. In *Grand Rapids School District* v. *Ball* and *Aguilar* v. *Felton*, decided together in 1985, the Court, voting 5–4, barred the use of state and federal funds, respectively, for **shared-time** programs providing enrichment and remedial instruction by public school teachers on religious school premises. Even though no money changed hands between government and religious schools, the programs were deemed constitutionally defective for at least two reasons: First, public employees might succumb to their surroundings and inject religion into the instruction; second, the program fostered a symbolic union of church and state. As Justice Brennan explained in *Ball*, "Teachers in [a religious] atmosphere may well subtly (or overtly) conform their instruction to the environment in which they teach, while students will perceive the instruction in the context of the dominantly religious message of the institution." Moreover, government "promotes religion as effectively when it fosters a close identification of its powers with those of any—or all—religious denominations as when it attempts to inculcate specific religious doctrines." The result of *Ball* and *Aguilar* was that such programs could continue only by moving instruction into publicly owned and maintained trailers parked off-site.

In 1993, an equally narrow majority in *Zobrest* v. *Catalina Foothills School District* moved away from the 1985 rulings in one major respect. James Zobrest, who is deaf, enrolled in a Roman Catholic high school in Tucson, Arizona. He and his parents asked the local school district to provide a sign-language interpreter to attend classes with him. Under the Individuals with Disabilities Education Act and its Arizona counterpart, an interpreter would have been provided had James attended either public school or a nonsectarian private school. Because James attended a church-operated school, however, the school board declined his request. In the board's view, providing an interpreter at public expense for James would violate the establishment clause. The Supreme Court disagreed. Rather than aiding the sectarian school, the district would be assisting only the child. James merely wanted to take advantage of a government program designed to benefit a broad class of disabled persons. As the dissenters were quick to note, for the first time the Court approved a policy that paid a public employee to perform an official function in a sectarian classroom. *Zobrest* seemed to follow *Witters* v. *Washington Department of Service for the Blind*, a decision by a unanimous bench in 1986 that allowed a state to fund an individual's ministerial education through a vocational rehabilitation program.

Building on *Zobrest* and *Witters*, ***Agostini* v. *Felton*** (1997) revisited the precise question addressed, and presumably settled, in *Ball* and *Aguilar*. Again voting 5–4, the Court concluded that, with respect to on-site instruction, the 1985 rulings were wrong: The establishment clause tolerates both enrichment and remediation by public employees in sectarian schools—instruction of the sort already provided in the public schools. Dissenters wondered how far the ruling might extend. If enrichment and remediation were acceptable, what about ordinary instruction in between?

Agostini made two important modifications in the *Lemon–Ball–Aguilar* analysis: First, once a secular purpose has been demonstrated, *Lemon*'s concern over entanglement is now but one of three independent elements used to assure a neutral effect. A policy does not meet the neutrality criterion if it (1) results in indoctrination of religion by government; (2) defines its recipients or beneficiaries according to religion; *or* (3) creates an excessive entanglement. Second, unlike *Ball* and *Aguilar, Agostini* does not presume that indoctrination or a symbolic union will result from the absence of excessively entangling oversight. Thus *Agostini* removes the Catch-22 that had so often been fatal to school-aid programs.

Mitchell v. *Helms* (2000) demonstrates the extent of the changes *Agostini* brought to the establishment clause. The five justices in the *Agostini* majority plus Justice Breyer upheld the inclusion of religious schools under a provision of the Education Consolidation and Improvement Act of 1981 that provides federal funds to local educational agencies that in turn lend instructional materials and equipment (including library materials and computer hardware and software) to public and private schools for use in "secular, neutral, and nonideological" programs. Just as *Agostini* did not presume that indoctrination would result from the instruction in question, *Mitchell* did not presume "diversion"—that is, the use of publicly funded equipment for religious purposes.

The Court's school voucher decision in ***Zelman* v. *Simmons-Harris*** (2002) yielded the most lenient construction to date of the establishment clause, both in terms of the dollar amount and the number of sectarian schools involved. For the majority, the outcome was consistent with religion-friendly decisions like *Zobrest*. For the dissenters, approval of vouchers represented a "dramatic departure from basic Establishment Clause principle."

These cases provide strikingly different ways of thinking about aid to religious schools. One might as well have two sets of eyeglasses through which to view the problem. Through one pair, students in church-related schools are merely the beneficiaries of government programs that extend benefits to a broad class of people without reference to religion. Through the other pair, government is an active participant in and underwriter of educational programs in religious schools, providing materials and services that the schools otherwise would have to purchase themselves, or do without.

When government distributes a benefit, may religion be a factor in determining eligible recipients? In *Locke* v. *Davey* (2004), a 7–2 majority allowed administrators of Washington State's college scholarship program to exclude tuition grants for ministerial education because of a provision in the state's constitution against expenditures of public funds for religious purposes. Against an establishment clause challenge, *Witters* in 1986 had allowed public funds to be used for such purposes. However, *Trinity Lutheran Church of Columbia* v. *Comer* (2017) pointed in a different direction when seven justices held that a church-operated preschool and day care center could not be denied a grant for pulverized scrap tires to use in resurfacing its playground solely because it was a religious institution. With links to both *Davey* and *Trinity Lutheran*, ***Espinoza* v. *Montana Department of Revenue*** intersects with the free exercise clause, a topic addressed in the section below. In *Espinoza*, the Court not only overturned the state supreme court's decision that barred a religious school from a scholarship program but implicitly reinstated the program. *Davey, Trinity Lutheran*, and *Espinoza* each involved application of a provision in the respective state constitution commonly known as a **Blaine amendment**.

Blaine amendments refer to restrictions in some state constitutions on the use of public funds at religious schools or for religious purposes. They are named for James G. Blaine of Maine, who proposed such an amendment to the U.S. Constitution while he was speaker of the U.S. House of Representatives in 1875. Blaine's amendment passed overwhelmingly (180–7) in the U.S. House of Representatives but failed by four votes in the Senate to get the required two-thirds majority, and so it was never submitted to the states for ratification. However, copycat versions were later attached to constitutions in about three dozen states, Montana among them. Some historians consider the campaign for the Blaine amendment an outgrowth of the rampant anti-Catholicism and nativism that emerged in this country during the mid- to late nineteenth century, in response to waves of Roman Catholic immigrants who had arrived on American shores. Blaine would have thought that such an amendment to the U.S. Constitution was needed because at the time the First Amendment's establishment clause did not apply to the states, and would not until *Everson* was decided in 1947.

THE FREE EXERCISE CLAUSE

Cases under the establishment clause typically test public policies that arguably *aid* religion. In contrast, cases under the free exercise clause challenge public policies that seem to *burden* religion.

Religious persecution—that is, penalizing people *because of* their religious beliefs—was undoubtedly the most obvious evil the free exercise clause was intended to prevent. Debate about this part of the First Amendment today, however, usually involves laws of general application that are religiously neutral in their content but in their application work a hardship on members of one faith or another. A law might forbid believers from doing what their faith requires, or it might require them to do something their faith forbids. Does the free exercise clause entitle them to a **faith-based exemption** from an otherwise valid law? The answer given to that question largely follows from how judges perceive the free exercise clause itself. Does it embody merely a nondiscrimination principle that protects believers from hostile legislation, or does it also elevate religious practice to a preferred status? Of course, chaos would result if everyone received an exemption from a law just because it ran counter to the tenets of one's faith. Still, the free exercise clause suggests that the government should not always prevail when the commands of the state and the dictates of faith pull in opposite directions.

This conflict lay at the heart of the first major decision under the free exercise clause. *Reynolds* v. *United States* (1879) upheld application of a law criminalizing polygamy in federal territories to a Mormon whose religion included the practice of polygamy. Chief Justice Waite emphasized the sovereignty of the individual over religious belief but the sovereignty of the state over conduct, a distinction that prevailed for over eight decades. "Congress was deprived of all legislative power over mere opinion," he wrote, "but was left free to reach actions which were in violation of social duties, or subversive of good order."

The Flag-Salute Cases. In one of the first applications of the free exercise clause to the states, the Court sustained a policy requiring all schoolchildren, over the religious objection of Jehovah's Witnesses, to salute the American flag (***Minersville School District* v. *Gobitis***). Justice Frankfurter's opinion even garnered support from liberal Justices Black, Douglas, and Murphy. Only Justice Stone dissented. In an effort to win Stone's support, Frankfurter wrote his colleague at length in a letter reprinted in this chapter, arguing that the case be decided "in the particular setting of our time and circumstances." "It is relevant," he pleaded, "to make the adjustment we have to make within the framework of present circumstances and those that are clearly ahead of us." The year was 1940, soon after Hitler unleashed his diabolical blitzkrieg in Europe and as British forces were being evacuated from the beaches at Dunkirk.

Two years later, Black, Douglas, and Murphy, in a remarkable about-face, recanted:

> Since we joined in the opinion in the Gobitis case, we think this is an appropriate occasion to state that we now believe that it was also wrongly decided. Certainly our democratic form of government functioning under the historical Bill of Rights has a high responsibility to accommodate itself to the religious views of minorities however unpopular and unorthodox those views may be. The First Amendment does not put the right freely to exercise religion in a subordinate position. We fear, however, that the opinion in these and the Gobitis case do exactly that.
>
> (*Jones* v. *Opelika*, 1942)

Encouraged by the *Opelika* dissent and the appointment of Justices Jackson and Rutledge, Walter Barnette and several other Jehovah's Witnesses brought suit to enjoin enforcement of the flag salute against their children. Voting 6–3 (***West Virginia State Board of Education* v. *Barnette***), the Court reversed itself in 1943, holding that First Amendment freedoms may be restricted "only to prevent grave and immediate dangers." There are few instances in the Court's history in which the change of views and of judicial personnel were so quickly reflected in judicial decisions. However, *Barnette* turned on the free-speech clause, not the free exercise clause. The flag-salute rule was unconstitutional as applied to anyone, regardless of whether the objection was religiously based, so the *Reynolds* rule remained in force.

The Checkered Career of Religiously Based Exemptions. The first occasion in which the Supreme Court, resting its decision squarely on the free exercise clause, ordered a faith-based exemption to an otherwise valid policy came in ***Sherbert* v. *Verner*** (1963). (Earlier decisions in addition to *Barnette* had invalidated application of state laws to religiously inspired conduct, but the Court treated these as free-speech cases.) South Carolina law denied unemployment compensation to someone available for work who refused to accept a job. Adell Sherbert, a Seventh-Day Adventist, refused to work on Saturday and lost her job because of her refusal but was otherwise available for work. No one claimed that South Carolina intended to persecute members of this particular church, but as applied to her, the policy required her to choose between a job and religious disobedience on the one hand, and no compensation and religious obedience on the other. A majority of the justices found the law unconstitutional *as applied to Adell Sherbert*, because it unduly burdened her faith. The state had not convinced the justices that it had compelling reasons for denying the unemployment benefits. Faith trumped law.

This decision encouraged adjudication of other free exercise claims. For example, *Sherbert* was authority for *Wisconsin* v. *Yoder* (1972), which exempted Old Order Amish from a state law requiring parents to send their children to school until the age of 16. An all-but-unanimous bench concluded that the rule compelled the Amish, who are a separatist sect and who do not provide formal education beyond the eighth grade, "to perform acts undeniably at odds with fundamental tenets of their religious beliefs. . . . [C]ompulsory school attendance . . . carries with it a very real threat of undermining the Amish community and religious practice as they exist today; they must either abandon belief and be assimilated into society at large, or be forced to migrate to some other and more tolerant region. . . ." Balanced was the threat to the faith posed by the law against the state's interest in uniform minimum school attendance for all.

Neither *Sherbert* nor *Yoder*, however, should suggest that all free exercise claims during this period prevailed over government regulations. Especially when federal law was challenged, the Court appeared reluctant to apply the free exercise clause with full force, as was seen in *United States* v. *Lee* (1982), which denied Amish an exemption from certain Social Security taxes. In 1988, the Court refused to block a road-building project by the U.S. Forest Service despite the Service's own finding that the road "would cause serious and irreparable damage to the sacred areas which are an integral and necessary part of the belief systems and lifeway of Northwest California Indian peoples" (*Lyng* v. *Northwest Indian Cemetery Protective Association*). Significantly, the claim by the Native American group went beyond most claims based on the free exercise clause. They did not ask for an exemption from application of a law but for the cancellation of the government's project.

Then in 1990, five justices not only refrained from expanding the *Sherbert* principle but took a step that confined *Sherbert* to its facts. ***Employment Division* v. *Smith*** ruled against two drug counselors who were fired from their jobs after they ingested peyote (a hallucinogen) as part of a religious ritual of the Native American Church. Oregon officials had denied them unemployment compensation because their loss of employment resulted from "misconduct." Under state law, peyote was a controlled substance, and its use was forbidden, even for religious purposes. The two ex-counselors cited scientific and anthropological evidence that the sacramental use of peyote was an ancient practice and was not harmful. The Supreme Court, however, concluded that when action based on religious belief runs afoul of a valid law of general application (even when, as in this case, the litigants had not been criminally charged), the latter prevails. Law trumped faith. *Smith* left *Sherbert* dangling by a hair.

Smith was widely criticized by religious organizations and civil liberties groups, and Congress responded. Believing that the Court in *Smith* made it too easy for government to infringe on religious liberty, Congress in 1993 passed the **Religious Freedom Restoration Act** (RFRA). Resting on Congress' enforcement powers under Section 5 of the Fourteenth Amendment, RFRA sought to reverse *Smith* and to restore *Sherbert* v. *Verner* fully in situations where laws of general application conflicted with religious liberty. A test of RFRA did not take long to materialize. A Catholic church in Boerne, Texas, wanted to enlarge its building. Because of a historic preservation ordinance, however, the city refused to issue a permit. Under RFRA, Archbishop Flores argued, the city would need compelling justification to block construction; otherwise the church could proceed, even if a Walmart or a Walgreens could not. In ***City of Boerne* v. *Flores*** (1997), the Court ruled that Congress' noble intentions exceeded its authority. *Smith* embodied the meaning of the free exercise clause, and according to it the church could claim no faith-based exception under the preservation ordinance. Because RFRA altered that meaning, the act was unconstitutional, at least as applied to *state* laws and policies. Excerpts from *City of Boerne* are reprinted in Chapter Two.

As noted in Chapter Two, however, the Court remains willing to apply RFRA to *congressional* policies, as *Burwell* v. *Hobby Lobby Stores, Inc.* (2014) demonstrates. Concluding that RFRA applies not only to individuals but to closely held for-profit corporations, five justices allowed a religiously based exemption from the contraception mandate for employers under the Affordable Care Act. Moreover, in 2000, Congress passed a partial substitute for RFRA. The **Religious Land Use and Institutionalized Persons Act** declares that no "government shall impose or implement a land use regulation in a manner that imposes a substantial burden on the religious exercise of a person, including a religious assembly or institution, unless the government demonstrates that imposition of the burden on that person, assembly, or institution (a) is in furtherance of a compelling governmental interest; and (b) is the least restrictive means of furthering that compelling governmental interest." The law applies "even if the burden results from a rule of general applicability" and includes regulations by entities receiving federal funds and regulations that affect interstate commerce. Accordingly, *Holt* v. *Hobbs* (2015) upheld the religiously based claim of Abdul Maalik Muhammad, an Arkansas prison inmate and a practicing Salafi Muslim, who objected to the grooming policy that allowed trimmed mustaches and quarter-inch beards for diagnosed dermatological problems but otherwise no facial hair. RFRA also allows lawsuits for damages against federal officials in their personal capacity, as the Court unanimously held in *Tanzin* v. *Tanvir* (2020), after FBI agents placed several Muslim men on the no-fly list allegedly because they refused to become informants.

Thus, despite *Smith*, the Court has hardly declared open season on religious practice. The free exercise clause still guards against government hostility to religion that is covert as well as overt, as illustrated by *Church of Lukumi Babalu Aye, Inc.* v. *Hialeah* (1993). Here the city council of this Florida city had passed a series of ordinances banning animal sacrifice, a central element of worship in Santeria, an Afro-Cuban religion. The ordinances prohibited nothing *except* religious practice and so amounted, in Justice Kennedy's words, to a "religious gerrymander." Because they were hardly religiously neutral, the Court judged them alongside the "compelling interest" test that the Court had applied in *Sherbert*. This was a standard the city could not meet.

Religious liberty values also prevailed in ***Masterpiece Cakeshop* v. *Colorado Civil Rights Commission*** (2018), a case that pitted religious freedom against a state law banning discrimination based on sexual orientation. In this instance, the Court ruled 7–2 for the owners of a cakeshop who refused on religious grounds to bake a wedding cake for a same-sex couple. However, the precedential value of the decision is questionable because of emphasis the majority placed on the overtly hostile treatment the cakeshop's owners received from members of the state's civil rights commission who had also appeared not to have taken the owners' religious objections seriously.

Among threats to religious liberty, surely the most recent for many have arisen from responses by state and local governments to the COVID-19 pandemic. As explained in Chapter Fifteen, various lockdown orders not only brought about economic hardship but in some instances severely impacted houses of worship, as illustrated by ***Roman Catholic Diocese of Brooklyn* v. *Cuomo*** (2020). Voting 5–4, the Court provided injunctive relief after petitioners argued that a governor's edict treated religious institutions more harshly than secular businesses.

VALUES IN TENSION

Even though the religion clauses work together to guard religious freedom, they focus on different threats and so at times may be in tension. Rigorous insistence on separationist values may infringe free exercise. Rigorous application of free exercise values may create an establishment of religion. In granting the exemption that Adell Sherbert wanted, for example, the Court not only recognized the religious basis of her claim but aided religion as well. This is no isolated conflict. Consider property tax exemptions for nonprofit organizations, including religious institutions, which the Court upheld in *Walz*. No one can deny that such exemptions amount annually to an enormous public subsidy; yet, excluding religious institutions from the list of tax-exempt organizations would penalize groups because of their religious nature.

The conflict also arises in public education. Most public schools allow student clubs to meet in the school building during the school day or during a special activity period before or after classes. Because of the Supreme Court's interpretation of the establishment clause banning school-sponsored religious exercises, however, administrators in some schools have not extended the same opportunity to student religious clubs. But denying members of religious clubs a privilege that all other student organizations enjoy is arguably a violation of the free exercise as well as the free-speech clauses of the First Amendment. If the Chess Club and the Scuba Diving Club may meet, why not the Bible Club? Congress addressed this issue in 1984 when it passed the Equal Access Act that directs schools receiving federal financial assistance to follow a nondiscriminatory policy. In a case challenging nonrecognition of religious clubs at a high school in Omaha, Nebraska, the Court sided with the students and upheld the act (*Westside Community Schools* v. *Mergens*, 1990). A similar result followed in ***Good News Club* v. *Milford Central School*** (2001), reprinted in Chapter Eleven. Clearly, neither decision could satisfy fully the values of both the establishment and free exercise clauses. Or, recall the tension reflected in *Espinoza* v. *Montana Department of Revenue* that presented both a free exercise puzzle and the establishment clause dilemma.

In the coming years, these and other controversies will continue to probe the fuzzy boundaries of the establishment and free exercise clauses. The framers bequeathed certain values by way of a written Constitution and left it to later generations to apply those values to situations the Founders could not foresee. The establishment clause calls for separation, while the free exercise clause leaves Americans free to work for objectives dictated by their faiths. Together, they guarantee that the division mandated by the one will forever be tested because of the freedom ensured by the other.

KEY TERMS

establishment clause
free exercise clause
accommodation
separation
religious test
Lemon test
endorsement test
Agostini test
coercion test
child-benefit theory
released-time
shared-time
Blaine amendment
faith-based exemption
Religious Freedom Restoration Act
Religious Land Use and Institutionalized Persons Act

QUERIES

1. The First Amendment's free-speech clause protects expression of opinions and beliefs, including religious ones. Should the free exercise clause provide special protection for religious practice?

2. Consider *Town of Greece* v. *Galloway* alongside the Court's six decades of insistence that there be no officially sponsored prayer in public schools. Is there justification for approving prayer in one setting but not the other?

3. What legitimate role remains for religious expression in public life? Consider that question in light of *Newdow* v. *U.S. Congress* (2002), where the U.S. Court of Appeals for the Ninth Circuit held unconstitutional both a 1954 statute that added "under God" to the Pledge of Allegiance to the Flag and a California school district's policy that included a voluntary recitation of the pledge as part of the school day. In the appeals court's view, the 1954 act of Congress was invalid under the endorsement test and first prong of the Lemon test; the state policy was invalid under the coercion test and the second prong of the Lemon test. In *Elk Grove School District* v. *Newdow* (2004), the Supreme Court dodged the substantive question and reversed because Newdow lacked standing. If a case like Newdow's reached the Court today with proper standing, what would be the probable decision?

4. Is the free exercise clause implicated by a state law regulating pharmacies that, with respect to the dispensing of certain contraceptives, bars a denial of service that is based on "conscience"?

SELECTED READINGS

Chemerinsky, Erwin, and Howard Gillman. *The Religion Clauses: The Case for Separating Church and State*. New York: Oxford University Press, 2020.

Drakeman, Donald L. *Church, State and Original Intent*. New York: Cambridge University Press, 2010.

Greenawalt, Kent. *When Free Exercise and Nonestablishment Conflict*. Cambridge: Harvard University Press, 2017.

Locke, John. *A Letter Concerning Toleration*. Indianapolis, IN: Bobbs-Merrill, 1979; originally published in 1689.

Madison, James. "Memorial and Remonstrance against Religious Assessments." 1785; reprinted as an appendix to *Everson v. Board of Education*, 330 U.S. 1, 63, 1947.

Muñoz, Vincent Phillip. "James Madison's Principle of Religious Liberty." 97 *American Political Science Review* 17, 2003.

Peters, Shawn Francis. *Judging Jehovah's Witnesses*. Lawrence: University Press of Kansas, 2000.

Solomon, Steven D. *Ellery's Protest: How One Young Man Defied Tradition and Sparked the Battle over School Prayer*. Ann Arbor: University of Michigan Press, 2007.

Urofsky, Melvin I. *Religious Freedom*. Santa Barbara, CA: ABC-CLIO, 2002.

Waltman, Jerold. *Congress, The Supreme Court, and Religious Liberty: The Case of City of Boerne v. Flores*. New York, NY: Palgrave Macmillan, 2013.

I. RELIGION IN OFFICIAL SETTINGS

Town of Greece v. *Galloway*
572 U.S. 565, 134 S.Ct. 1811, 188 L.Ed. 2d 835 (2014)

http://caselaw.findlaw.com/us-supreme-court/12–696.html

Since 1999, the monthly town board meetings in Greece, New York, have opened with a roll call, recitation of the Pledge of Allegiance, and a prayer given by clergy selected from congregations listed in a local directory. While the prayer program has been open to all faiths, nearly all of the local congregations are Christian; thus, nearly all of the participating prayer givers have been Christian as well. Some citizens who attend the meetings filed suit, alleging that the town violated the First Amendment's establishment clause by preferring Christians over other prayer givers and by sponsoring sectarian prayers. They sought to limit the town to "inclusive and ecumenical" prayers that referred only to a "generic God." The U.S. District Court for the Western District of New York upheld the prayer practice on summary judgment, but the U.S. Court of Appeals for the Second Circuit reversed, ruling that some aspects of the prayer program, viewed in their totality by a reasonable observer, conveyed the message that the town was endorsing Christianity. Majority: Kennedy, Alito Roberts, Scalia, Thomas. Dissenting: Kagan, Breyer, Ginsburg, Sotomayor.

Justice Kennedy delivered the opinion of the Court.

The Court must decide whether the town of Greece, New York, imposes an impermissible establishment of religion by opening its monthly board meetings with a prayer. It must be concluded, consistent with the Court's opinion in *Marsh* v. *Chambers* (1983) that no violation of the Constitution has been shown.

In *Marsh* the Court found no First Amendment violation in the Nebraska Legislature's practice of opening its sessions with a prayer delivered by a chaplain paid from state funds. The decision concluded that legislative prayer, while religious in nature, has long been understood as compatible with the Establishment Clause. As practiced by Congress since the framing of the Constitution, legislative prayer lends gravity to public business, reminds lawmakers to transcend petty differences in pursuit of a higher purpose, and expresses a common aspiration to a just and peaceful society. The Court has considered this symbolic expression to be a "tolerable acknowledgement of beliefs widely held," rather than a first, treacherous step towards establishment of a state church. . . .

Yet *Marsh* must not be understood as permitting a practice that would amount to a constitutional violation if not for its historical foundation. The case teaches instead that the Establishment Clause must be interpreted "by reference to historical practices and understandings. That the First Congress provided for the appointment of chaplains only days after approving language for the First Amendment demonstrates that the Framers considered legislative prayer a benign acknowledgment of religion's role in society. In the 1850's, the judiciary committees in both the House and Senate reevaluated the practice of official chaplaincies after receiving petitions to abolish the office. The committees concluded that the office posed no threat of an establishment because lawmakers were not compelled to attend the daily prayer, no faith was excluded by law, nor any favored; and the cost of the chaplain's salary imposed a vanishingly small burden on taxpayers. *Marsh* stands for the proposition that it is not necessary to define the precise boundary of the Establishment Clause where history shows that the specific practice is permitted. . . .

Respondents assert that the town's prayer exercise falls outside that tradition and transgresses the Establishment Clause for two independent but mutually reinforcing reasons. First, they argue that *Marsh* did not approve prayers containing sectarian language or themes, such as the prayers offered in Greece that referred to the "death, resurrection, and ascension of the Savior Jesus Christ," and the "saving sacrifice of Jesus Christ on the cross." Second, they argue that the setting and conduct of the town board meetings create social pressures that force nonadherents to remain in the room or even feign participation in order to avoid offending the representatives who sponsor the prayer and will vote on matters citizens bring before the board. The sectarian content of the prayers compounds the subtle coercive pressures, they argue, because the nonbeliever who might tolerate ecumenical prayer is forced to do the same for prayer that might be inimical to his or her beliefs. . . .

An insistence on nonsectarian or ecumenical prayer as a single, fixed standard is not consistent with the tradition of legislative prayer outlined in the Court's cases. The Court found the prayers in *Marsh* consistent with the First Amendment not because they espoused only a generic theism but because our history and tradition have shown that prayer in this limited context could "coexis[t] with the principles of disestablishment and religious freedom." . . .

The contention that legislative prayer must be generic or nonsectarian derives from dictum in *County of Allegheny* v. *American Civil Liberties Union* (1989) that was disputed when written and has been repudiated by later cases. There the Court held that a crèche placed on the steps of a county courthouse to celebrate the Christmas season violated the Establishment Clause because it had "the effect of endorsing a patently Christian message." Four dissenting Justices disputed that endorsement could be the proper test, as it likely would condemn a host of traditional practices that recognize the role religion plays in our society, among them legislative prayer and the "forthrightly religious" Thanksgiving proclamations issued by nearly every President since Washington. The Court sought to counter this criticism by recasting *Marsh* to permit only prayer that contained no overtly Christian references. . . .

Marsh nowhere suggested that the constitutionality of legislative prayer turns on the neutrality of its content. The opinion noted that Nebraska's chaplain . . . modulated the "explicitly Christian" nature of his prayer and "removed all references to Christ" after a Jewish law-maker complained. With this footnote, the Court did no more than observe the practical demands placed on a minister who holds a permanent, appointed position in a legislature and chooses to write his or her prayers to appeal to more members, or at least to give less offense to those who object. *Marsh* did not suggest that Nebraska's prayer practice would have failed had the chaplain not acceded to the legislator's request. Nor did the Court imply the rule that prayer violates the Establishment Clause any time it is given in the name of a figure deified by only one faith or creed. . . .

To hold that invocations must be nonsectarian would force the legislatures that sponsor prayers and the courts that are asked to decide these cases to act as supervisors and censors of religious speech, a rule that would involve government in religious matters to a far greater degree than is the case under the town's current practice of neither editing or approving prayers in advance nor criticizing their content after the fact. . . . Once it invites prayer into the public sphere, government must permit a prayer giver to address his or her own God or gods as conscience dictates, unfettered by what an administrator or judge considers to be nonsectarian.

That a prayer is given in the name of Jesus, Allah, or Jehovah, or that it makes passing reference to religious doctrines, does not remove it from that tradition. . . . Our tradition assumes that adult citizens, firm in their own beliefs, can tolerate and perhaps appreciate a ceremonial prayer delivered by a person of a different faith. . . .

Finally, the Court disagrees with the view taken by the Court of Appeals that the town of Greece contravened the Establishment Clause by inviting a predominantly Christian set of ministers to lead the prayer. The town made reasonable efforts to identify all of the congregations located within its borders and represented that it would welcome a prayer by any minister or layman who wished to give one. That nearly all of the congregations in town turned out to be Christian does not reflect an aversion or bias on the part of town leaders against minority faiths. So long as the town maintains a policy of nondiscrimination, the Constitution does not require it to search beyond its borders for non-Christian prayer givers in an effort to achieve religious balancing. The quest to promote "a 'diversity' of religious views" would require the town "to make wholly inappropriate judgments about the number of religions [it] should sponsor and the relative frequency with which it should sponsor each," a form of government entanglement with religion that is far more troublesome than the current approach.

Respondents further seek to distinguish the town's prayer practice from the tradition upheld in *Marsh* on the ground that it coerces participation by nonadherents. . . . Respondents argue that the public may feel subtle pressure to participate in prayers that violate their beliefs in order to please the board members from whom they are about to seek a favorable ruling. . . . On the record in this case the Court is not persuaded that the town of Greece, through the act of offering a brief, solemn, and respectful prayer to open its monthly meetings, compelled its citizens to engage in a religious observance. . . .

The principal audience for these invocations is not, indeed, the public but lawmakers themselves, who may find that a moment of prayer or quiet reflection sets the mind to a higher purpose and thereby eases the task of governing. . . .

The analysis would be different if town board members directed the public to participate in the prayers, singled out dissidents for opprobrium, or indicated that their decisions might be influenced by a person's acquiescence in the prayer opportunity. No such thing occurred in the town of Greece. Although board members themselves stood, bowed their heads, or made the sign of the cross during the prayer, they at no point solicited similar gestures by the public. [The preceding three paragraphs were not joined by Justices Scalia and Thomas.—Ed.]

The judgment of the U.S. Court of Appeals for the Second Circuit is reversed.

It is so ordered.

Justice Thomas, with whom Justice Scalia joins, concurring in part and concurring in the judgment . . . [omitted.]

Justice Alito, with whom Justice Scalia joins, concurring . . . [omitted].

Justice Kagan, with whom Justice Ginsburg, Justice Breyer, and Justice Sotomayor join, dissenting. . . .

For centuries now, people have come to this country from every corner of the world to share in the blessing of religious freedom. Our Constitution promises that they may worship in their own way, without fear of penalty or danger, and that in itself is a momentous offering. Yet our Constitution makes a commitment still more remarkable—that however those individuals worship, they will count as full and equal American citizens. . . .

I respectfully dissent from the Court's opinion because I think the Town of Greece's prayer practices violate that norm of religious equality—the breathtakingly generous constitutional idea that our public institutions belong no less to the Buddhist or Hindu than to the Methodist or Episcopalian. I do not contend that principle translates here into a bright separationist line. To the contrary, I agree with the Court's decision in *Marsh*. . . . And I believe that pluralism and inclusion in a town hall can satisfy the constitutional requirement of neutrality; such a forum need not become a religion-free zone. But still, the Town of Greece should lose this case. The practice at issue here differs from the one sustained in *Marsh* because Greece's town meetings involve participation by ordinary citizens, and the invocations given—directly to those citizens—were predominantly sectarian in content. Still more, Greece's Board did nothing to recognize religious diversity: In arranging for clergy members to open each meeting, the Town never sought (except briefly when this suit was filed) to involve, accommodate, or in any way reach out to adherents of non-Christian religions. . . .

Relying on that "unbroken" national tradition, *Marsh* upheld (I think correctly) the Nebraska Legislature's practice of opening each day with a chaplain's prayer as "a tolerable acknowledgment of beliefs widely held among the people of this country." And so I agree with the majority that the issue here is "whether the prayer practice in the Town of Greece fits within the tradition long followed in Congress and the state legislatures."

Where I depart from the majority is in my reply to that question. The town hall here is a kind of hybrid. Greece's Board indeed has legislative functions, as Congress and state assemblies do—and that means some opening prayers are allowed there. But . . . the Board's meetings are also occasions for ordinary citizens to engage with and petition their government, often on highly individualized matters. That feature calls for Board members to exercise special care to ensure that the prayers offered are inclusive—that they respect each and every member of the community as an equal citizen. But the Board, and the clergy members it selected, made no such effort. Instead, the prayers given in Greece, addressed directly to the Town's citizenry, were more sectarian, and less inclusive, than anything this Court sustained in *Marsh*. For those reasons, the prayer in Greece departs from the legislative tradition that the majority takes as its benchmark.

Start by comparing two pictures, drawn precisely from reality. The first is of Nebraska's (unicameral) Legislature, as this Court and the state senators themselves described it. The second is of town council meetings in Greece, as revealed in this case's record. . . .

Let's count the ways in which these pictures diverge. First, the governmental proceedings at which the prayers occur differ significantly in nature and purpose. The Nebraska Legislature's floor sessions—like those of the U.S. Congress and other state assemblies—are of, by, and for elected lawmakers. Members of the public take no part in those proceedings; any few who attend are spectators only, watching from a high-up visitors' gallery. (In that respect, note that neither the Nebraska Legislature nor the Congress calls for prayer when citizens themselves participate in a hearing—say, by giving testimony relevant to a bill or nomination.) Greece's town meetings, by contrast, revolve around ordinary members of the community. . . . So the meetings, both by design and in operation, allow citizens to actively participate in the Town's governance—sharing concerns, airing grievances, and both shaping the community's policies and seeking their benefits.

Second (and following from what I just said), the prayers in these two settings have different audiences. In the Nebraska Legislature, the chaplain spoke to, and only to, the elected representatives. . . . The very opposite is true in Greece: Contrary to the majority's characterization, the prayers there are directed squarely at the citizens. Remember that the chaplain of the month stands with his back to the Town Board; his real audience is the group he is facing—the 10 or so members of the public, perhaps including children. . . . In essence, the chaplain leads, as the first part of a town meeting, a highly intimate (albeit relatively brief) prayer service, with the public serving as his congregation.

And third, the prayers themselves differ in their content and character. *Marsh* characterized the prayers in the Nebraska Legislature as "in the Judeo-Christian tradition," and stated, as a relevant (even if not dispositive) part of its analysis, that the chaplain had removed all explicitly Christian references at a senator's request. And as the majority acknowledges, *Marsh* hinged on the view that "that the prayer opportunity ha[d] [not] been exploited to proselytize or advance any one . . . faith or belief"; had it been otherwise, the Court would have reached a different decision. . . .

Those three differences, taken together, remove this case from the protective ambit of *Marsh* and the history on which it relied. . . .

How, then, does the majority go so far astray, allowing the Town of Greece to turn its assemblies for citizens into a forum for Christian prayer? The answer does not lie in first principles: I have no doubt that every member of this Court believes as firmly as I that our institutions of government belong equally to all, regardless of faith. Rather, the error reflects two kinds of blindness. First, the majority misapprehends the facts of this case, as distinct from those characterizing traditional legislative prayer. And second, the majority misjudges the essential meaning of the religious worship in Greece's town hall, along with its capacity to exclude and divide. . . .

But just for that reason, the not-so-implicit message of the majority's opinion—"What's the big deal, anyway?"—is mistaken. The content of Greece's prayers is a big deal, to Christians and non-Christians alike. A person's response to the doctrine, language, and imagery contained in those invocations reveals a core aspect of identity—who that person is and how she faces the world. And the responses of different individuals, in Greece and across this country, of course vary. Contrary to the majority's apparent view, such sectarian prayers are not "part of our expressive idiom" or "part of our heritage and tradition," assuming the word "our" refers to all Americans. They express beliefs that are fundamental to some, foreign to others—and because that is so they carry the ever-present potential to both exclude and divide. . . . I would treat more seriously the multiplicity of Americans' religious commitments, along with the challenge they can pose to the project—the distinctively American project—of creating one from the many, and governing all as united. . . .

JUSTICE BREYER, dissenting . . . [omitted].

American Legion v. *American Humanist Association*
588 U.S. ___, 139 S.Ct. 2067, 204 L.Ed. 2d 452 (2019)

www.supremecourt.gov/opinions/18pdf/17-1717_4f14.pdf

The facts of this case appear in Justice Alito's opinion below. Majority: Alito, Breyer, Gorsuch, Kagan, Kavanaugh, Roberts, Thomas. Dissenting: Ginsburg, Sotomayor.

JUSTICE ALITO announced the judgment of the Court and delivered an opinion which THE CHIEF JUSTICE, JUSTICE BREYER, and JUSTICE KAVANAUGH join in part.

Since 1925, the Bladensburg [Maryland] Peace Cross (Cross) has stood as a tribute to 49 area soldiers who gave their lives in the First World War. Eighty-nine years after the dedication of the Cross, respondents filed this lawsuit, claiming that they are offended by the sight of the memorial on public land and that its presence there and the expenditure of public funds to maintain it violate the Establishment Clause of the First Amendment. To remedy this violation, they asked a federal court to order the relocation or demolition of the Cross or at least the removal of its arms. The Court of Appeals for the Fourth Circuit agreed that the memorial is unconstitutional and remanded [to the U.S. District Court for the District of Maryland] for a determination of the proper remedy. We now reverse. . . .

The Religion Clauses of the Constitution aim to foster a society in which people of all beliefs can live together harmoniously, and the presence of the Bladensburg Cross on the land where it has stood for so many years is fully consistent with that aim. The cross came into widespread use as a symbol of Christianity by the fourth century, and it retains that meaning today. But there are many contexts in which the symbol has also taken on a secular meaning. Indeed, there are instances in which its message is now almost entirely secular. . . .

The Establishment Clause of the First Amendment provides that "Congress shall make no law respecting an establishment of religion." While the concept of a formally established church is straightforward, pinning down the meaning of a "law respecting an establishment of religion" has proved to be a vexing problem. . . . After grappling with such cases for more than 20 years, *Lemon* [v. *Kurtzman* (1971)] ambitiously attempted to distill from the Court's existing case law a test that would bring order and predictability to Establishment Clause decisionmaking. That test, as noted, called on courts to examine the purposes and effects of a challenged government action, as well as any entanglement with religion that it might entail. The Court later elaborated that the "effect[s]" of a challenged action should be assessed by asking whether a "reasonable observer" would conclude that the action constituted an "endorsement" of religion.

If the Lemon Court thought that its test would provide a framework for all future Establishment Clause decisions, its expectation has not been met. In many cases, this Court has either expressly declined to apply the test or has simply ignored it. . . . This pattern is a testament to the Lemon test's short-comings. As Establishment Clause cases involving a great array of laws and practices came to the Court, it became more and more apparent that the Lemon test could not resolve them. It could not "explain the Establishment Clause's tolerance, for example, of the prayers that open legislative meetings, . . . certain references to, and invocations of, the Deity in the public words of public officials; the public references to God on coins, decrees, and buildings; or the attention paid to the religious objectives of certain holidays, including Thanksgiving." The test has been harshly criticized by Members of this Court, lamented by lower court judges, and questioned by a diverse roster of scholars.

For at least four reasons, the Lemon test presents particularly daunting problems in cases, including the one now before us, that involve the use, for ceremonial, celebratory, or commemorative purposes, of words or symbols with religious associations. Together, these considerations counsel against efforts to evaluate such cases under *Lemon* and toward application of a presumption of constitutionality for longstanding monuments, symbols, and practices.

First, these cases often concern monuments, symbols, or practices that were first established long ago, and in such cases, identifying their original purpose or purposes may be especially difficult. . . . Second, as time goes by, the purposes associated with an established monument, symbol, or practice often multiply. Take the example of Ten Commandments monuments . . . For believing Jews and Christians, the Ten Commandments are the word of God handed down to Moses on Mount Sinai, but the image of the Ten Commandments has also been used to convey other meanings. They have historical significance as one of the foundations of our legal system, and for largely that reason, they are depicted in the marble frieze in our courtroom and in other prominent public buildings in our Nation's capital. . . .

Third, just as the purpose for maintaining a monument, symbol, or practice may evolve, "[t]he 'message' conveyed . . . may change over time." Consider, for example, the message of the Statue of Liberty, which began as a monument to the solidarity and friendship between France and the United States and only decades later came to be seen "as a beacon welcoming immigrants to a land of freedom." With sufficient time, religiously expressive monuments, symbols, and practices can become embedded features of a community's landscape and identity. The community may come to value them without necessarily embracing their religious roots. . . .

In the same way, consider the many cities and towns across the United States that bear religious names. Religion undoubtedly motivated those who named Bethlehem, Pennsylvania; Las Cruces, New Mexico; Providence, Rhode Island; Corpus Christi, Texas; Nephi, Utah, and the countless other places in our country with names that are rooted in religion. Yet few would argue that this history requires that these names be erased from the map. . . .

Fourth, when time's passage imbues a religiously expressive monument, symbol, or practice with this kind of familiarity and historical significance, removing it may no longer appear neutral, especially to the local community for which it has taken on particular meaning. A government that roams the land, tearing down monuments with religious symbolism and scrubbing away any reference to the divine will strike many as aggressively hostile to religion. Militantly secular regimes have carried out such projects in the past, and for those with a knowledge of history, the image of monuments being taken down will be evocative, disturbing, and divisive. . . . These four considerations show that retaining established, religiously expressive monuments, symbols, and practices is quite different from erecting or adopting new ones. The passage of time gives rise to a strong presumption of constitutionality.

The role of the cross in World War I memorials is illustrative of each of the four preceding considerations. . . . This is not to say that the cross's association with the war was the sole or dominant motivation for the inclusion of the symbol in every World War I memorial that features it. But today, it is all but impossible to tell whether that was so. . . . Similar reasoning applies to other memorials and monuments honoring important figures in our Nation's history.

While the Lemon Court ambitiously attempted to find a grand unified theory of the Establishment Clause, in later cases, we have taken a more modest approach that focuses on the particular issue at hand and looks to history for guidance. Our cases involving prayer before a legislative session are an example. . . . We reached these results even though it was clear, as stressed by the *Marsh* [v. *Chambers* (1983)] dissent, that prayer is by definition religious. As the Court put it in *Town of Greece* [v. *Galloway* (2014]: "*Marsh* must not be understood as permitting a practice that would amount to a constitutional violation if not for its historical foundation." "The case teaches instead that the Establishment Clause must be interpreted 'by reference to historical practices and understandings.'" . . . Applying these principles, we conclude that the Bladensburg Cross does not violate the Establishment Clause. . . .

The cross is undoubtedly a Christian symbol, but that fact should not blind us to everything else that the Bladensburg Cross has come to represent. For some, that monument is a symbolic resting place for ancestors who never returned home. For others, it is a place for the community to gather and honor all veterans and their sacrifices for our Nation. For others still, it is a historical landmark. For many of these people, destroying or defacing the Cross that has stood undisturbed for nearly a century would not be neutral and would not further the ideals of respect and tolerance embodied in the First Amendment. For all these reasons, the Cross does not offend the Constitution. We reverse the judgment of the Court of Appeals for the Fourth Circuit and remand the cases for further proceedings.

It is so ordered.

JUSTICE BREYER, with whom JUSTICE KAGAN joins, concurring . . . [omitted].

JUSTICE KAVANAUGH, concurring . . . [omitted].

JUSTICE KAGAN, concurring in part . . . [omitted].

JUSTICE THOMAS, concurring in the judgment . . . [omitted].

JUSTICE GORSUCH, with whom JUSTICE THOMAS joins, concurring in the judgment.

With *Lemon* now shelved, little excuse will remain for the anomaly of offended observer standing, and the gaping hole it tore in standing doctrine in the courts of appeals should now begin to close. Nor does this development mean colorable Establishment Clause violations will lack for proper plaintiffs. . . . Abandoning offended observer standing will mean only a return to the usual demands of Article III, requiring a real controversy with real impact on real persons to make a federal case out of it. Along the way, this will bring with it the welcome side effect of rescuing the federal judiciary from the sordid business of having to pass aesthetic judgment, one by one, on every public display in this country for its perceived capacity to give offense. It's a business that has consumed volumes of the federal reports, invited erratic results, frustrated generations of judges, and fomented "the very kind of religiously based divisiveness that the Establishment Clause seeks to avoid." No one can predict the rulings—but one thing is certain: Between the challenged practices and the judicial decisions, just about everyone will wind up offended. Nor have we yet come close to exhausting the potential sources of offense and federal litigation *Lemon* invited. . . .

JUSTICE GINSBURG, with whom JUSTICE SOTOMAYOR joins, dissenting. . . .

Decades ago, this Court recognized that the Establishment Clause of the First Amendment to the Constitution demands governmental neutrality among religious faiths, and between religion and nonreligion. . . . Today the Court erodes that neutrality commitment, diminishing precedent designed to preserve individual liberty and civic harmony in favor of a "presumption of constitutionality for longstanding monuments, symbols, and practices."

The Latin cross is the foremost symbol of the Christian faith, embodying the "central theological claim of Christianity: that the son of God died on the cross, that he rose from the dead, and that his death and resurrection offer the possibility of eternal life." Precisely because the cross symbolizes these sectarian beliefs, it is a common marker for the graves of Christian soldiers. For the same reason, using the cross as a war memorial does not transform it into a secular symbol . . . By maintaining the Peace Cross on a public highway, the [Maryland-National Capital Park and Planning] Commission elevates Christianity over other faiths, and religion over nonreligion. . . .

In cases challenging the government's display of a religious symbol, the Court has tested fidelity to the principle of neutrality by asking whether the display has the "effect of 'endorsing' religion." As I see it, when a cross is displayed on public property, the government may be presumed to endorse its religious content. The venue is surely associated with the State; the symbol and its meaning are just as surely associated exclusively with Christianity. . . .

The Commission urges in defense of its monument that the Latin cross "is not merely a reaffirmation of Christian beliefs"; rather, "when used in the context of a war memorial," the cross becomes "a universal symbol of the sacrifices of those who fought and died." The Commission's "[a]ttempts to secularize what is unquestionably a sacred [symbol] defy credibility and disserve people of faith." . . . Every Court of Appeals to confront the question has held that "[m]aking a . . . Latin cross a war memorial does not make the cross secular," it "makes the war memorial sectarian."

Trump v. *Hawaii*
585 U.S. ___, 138 S.Ct. 2392, 201 L.Ed. 2d 775 (2018)

www.supremecourt.gov/opinions/17pdf/17-965_h315.pdf

(This case is reprinted in Chapter Three; see the Table of Contents.)

II. STATE AID TO RELIGIOUS SCHOOLS

Lemon v. *Kurtzman*
403 U.S. 602, 91 S.Ct. 2105, 29 L.Ed. 2d 745 (1971)

http://caselaw.findlaw.com/us-supreme-court/403/602.html

This case marked the first time the Supreme Court ruled on the constitutionality of direct state financial support for sectarian schools. Pennsylvania's Nonpublic Elementary and Secondary Education Act of 1968 allowed the state to reimburse private schools directly for costs of teachers' salaries, textbooks, and instructional materials in specified secular subjects. Annual expenses under the law were $5 million, divided among some 1,181 nonpublic schools with an enrollment of 535,000 (more than 20 percent of the total number of students in the state). More than 96 percent of these students attended sectarian schools, most of which were operated by the Roman Catholic Church. The Court combined this case with a challenge to a Rhode Island law enacted in 1969, which authorized state officials to supplement the salaries of teachers of secular subjects in private schools by an amount not exceeding 15 percent of the teachers' annual salary. Rhode Island's nonpublic schools accommodated about 25 percent of the students in the state, of which about 95 percent attended Catholic schools. Some 250 teachers (all from Catholic schools) applied for benefits under the Rhode Island program. In a suit brought in the U.S. District Court for the District of Rhode Island, a three-judge court struck down the salary supplement plan as a violation of the establishment clause. In an action on similar grounds in the U.S. District Court for the Eastern District of Pennsylvania, a three-judge panel upheld the Pennsylvania plan. Majority (in the Pennsylvania case): Burger, Douglas, Black, Brennan, Harlan, Stewart, White, Blackmun. Not participating: Marshall. Majority (in the Rhode Island case): Burger, Douglas, Black, Brennan, Harlan, Stewart, Marshall, Blackmun. Dissenting: White. (Justice White sided with the majority in the Pennsylvania case only because he believed the case should be remanded. However, he rejected the majority's conclusion that the law was unconstitutional on its face.)

Mr. Chief Justice Burger delivered the opinion of the Court. . . .

The language of the Religion Clauses of the First Amendment is at best opaque, particularly when compared with other portions of the Amendment. Its authors did not simply prohibit the establishment of a state church or a state religion, an area history shows they regarded as very important and fraught with great dangers. Instead they commanded that there should be "no law respecting an establishment of religion." . . . A given law might not establish a state religion but nevertheless be one "respecting" that end in the sense of being a step that could lead to such establishment and hence offend the First Amendment.

Every analysis in this area must begin with consideration of the cumulative criteria developed by the Court over many years. Three such tests may be gleaned from our cases. First, the statute must have a secular legislative purpose; second, its principal or primary effect must be one that neither advances nor inhibits religion . . . ; finally, the statute must not foster "an excessive government entanglement with religion." . . .

Inquiry into the legislative purposes of the Pennsylvania and Rhode Island statutes affords no basis for a conclusion that the legislative intent was to advance religion.

The two legislatures, however, have . . . recognized that church-related elementary and secondary schools have a significant religious mission and that a substantial portion of their activities is religiously oriented. They have therefore sought to create statutory restrictions designed to guarantee the separation between secular and religious educational functions and to ensure that State financial aid supports only the former. . . . We need not decide whether these legislative precautions restrict the principal or primary effect of the programs to the point where they do not offend the Religion Clauses, for we conclude that the cumulative impact of the entire relationship arising under the statutes in each State involves excessive entanglement between government and religion. . . .

In *Walz* v. *Tax Commission*, the Court upheld state tax exemptions for real property owned by religious organizations and used for religious worship. That holding, however, tended to confine rather than enlarge the area of permissible state involvement with religious institutions by calling for close scrutiny of the degree of entanglement involved in the relationship. The objective is to prevent, as far as possible, the intrusion of either into the precincts of the other.

Our prior holdings do not call for total separation between church and state; total separation is not possible in an absolute sense. Some relationship between government and religious organizations is inevitable. Fire inspections, building and zoning regulations, and state requirements under compulsory school-attendance laws are examples of necessary and permissible contacts. Indeed, under the statutory exemption before us in *Walz*, the State had a continuing burden to ascertain that the exempt property was in fact being used for religious worship. Judicial caveats against entanglement must recognize that the line of separation, far from being a "wall," is a blurred, indistinct, and variable barrier depending on all the circumstances of a particular relationship. . . .

In order to determine whether the government entanglement with religion is excessive, we must examine the character and purposes of the institutions that are benefited, the nature of the aid that the State provides, and the resulting relationship between the government and the religious authority. . . .

The church schools involved in the program [in the Rhode Island case] are located close to parish churches. This understandably permits convenient access for religious exercises since instruction in faith and morals is part of the total educational process. The school buildings contain identifying religious symbols such as crosses on the exterior and crucifixes, and religious paintings and statues either in the classrooms or hallways. Although only approximately 30 minutes a day are devoted to direct religious instruction, there are religiously oriented extracurricular activities. Approximately two-thirds of the teachers in these schools are nuns of various religious orders. Their dedicated efforts provide an atmosphere in which religious instruction and religious vocations are natural and proper parts of life in such schools.

On the basis of these findings the District Court concluded that the parochial schools constituted "an integral part of the religious mission of the Catholic Church." The dangers and corresponding entanglements are enhanced by the particular form of aid that the Rhode Island Act provides. . . .

To ensure that no trespass occurs, the State has therefore carefully conditioned its aid with pervasive restrictions. An eligible recipient must teach only those courses that are offered in the public schools and use only those texts and materials that are found in the public schools. In addition the teacher must not engage in teaching any course in religion.

A comprehensive, discriminating, and continuing state surveillance will inevitably be required to ensure that these restrictions are obeyed and the First Amendment otherwise respected. Unlike a book, a teacher cannot be inspected once so as to determine the extent and intent of his or her personal beliefs and subjective acceptance of the limitations imposed by the First Amendment. These prophylactic contacts will involve excessive and enduring entanglement between state and church. . . .

There is another area of entanglement in the Rhode Island program that gives concern. The statute excludes teachers employed by nonpublic schools whose average per-pupil expenditures on secular education equal or exceed the comparable figures for public schools. In the event that the total expenditures of an otherwise eligible school exceed this norm, the program requires the government to examine the school's records in order to determine how much of the total expenditures is attributable to secular education and how much to religious activity. This kind of state inspection and evaluation of the religious content of a religious organization is fraught with the sort of entanglement that the Constitution forbids. It is a relationship pregnant with dangers of excessive government direction of church schools and hence of churches. . . .

The complaint [in the Pennsylvania case] describes an educational system that is very similar to the one existing in Rhode Island. . . . [T]he very restrictions and surveillance necessary to ensure that teachers play a strictly nonideological role give rise to entanglements between church and state. The Pennsylvania statute, like that of Rhode Island, fosters this kind of relationship. . . .

The Pennsylvania statute, moreover, has the further defect of providing state financial aid directly to the church-related school. . . . The history of government grants of a continuing cash subsidy indicates that such programs have almost always been accompanied by varying measures of control and surveillance. The government cash grants before us now provide no basis for predicting that comprehensive measures of surveillance and controls will not follow. In particular the government's post-audit power to inspect and evaluate a church-related school's financial records and to determine which expenditures are religious and which are secular creates an intimate and continuing relationship between church and state. . . .

A broader base of entanglement of yet a different character is presented by the divisive political potential of these state programs. In a community where such a large number of pupils are served by church-related schools, it can be assumed that state assistance will entail considerable political activity. Partisans of parochial schools, understandably concerned with rising costs and sincerely dedicated to both the religious and secular educational mission of their schools, will inevitably champion this cause and promote political action to achieve their goals. Those who oppose state aid, whether for constitutional, religious, or fiscal reasons, will inevitably respond and employ all of the usual political campaign techniques to prevail. Candidates will be forced to declare and voters to choose. It would be unrealistic to ignore the fact that many people confronted with issues of this kind will find their votes aligned with their faith.

Ordinarily political debate and division, however vigorous or even partisan, are normal and healthy manifestations of our democratic system of government, but political division along religious lines was one of the principal evils against which the First Amendment was intended to protect. . . . The potential divisiveness of such conflict is a threat to the normal political process. . . .

The potential for political divisiveness related to religious belief and practice is aggravated in these two statutory programs by the need for continuing annual appropriations and the likelihood of larger and larger demands as costs and populations grow. . . .

The judgment of the Rhode Island District Court . . . is affirmed. The judgment of the Pennsylvania District Court . . . is reversed, and the case is remanded for further proceedings consistent with this opinion.

Mr. Justice Douglas, whom Mr. Justice Black joins, concurring . . . [omitted].

Mr. Justice Brennan, concurring . . . [omitted].

Mr. Justice White, dissenting. . . .

The Court strikes down the Rhode Island statute on its face. No fault is found with the secular purpose of the program; there is no suggestion that the purpose of the program was aid to religion disguised in secular attire. Nor does the Court find that the primary effect of the program is to aid religion rather than to implement secular goals. The Court nevertheless finds that impermissible "entanglement" will result from administration of the program.

The Court thus creates an insoluble paradox for the State and the parochial schools. The State cannot finance secular instruction if it permits religion to be taught in the same classroom; but if it exacts a promise that religion not be so taught—a promise the school and its teachers are quite willing and on this record able to give—and enforces it, it is then entangled in the "no entanglement" aspect of the Court's Establishment Clause jurisprudence. . . .

With respect to Pennsylvania, the Court, accepting as true the factual allegations of the complaint, as it must for purpose of a motion to dismiss, would reverse the dismissal of the complaint and invalidate the legislation. The critical allegations, as paraphrased by the Court, are that "the church-related elementary and secondary schools are controlled by religious organizations, have the purpose of propagating and promoting a particular religious faith, and conduct their operations to fulfill that purpose." . . . From these allegations the Court concludes that forbidden entanglements would follow from enforcing compliance with the secular purpose for which the state money is being paid.

I disagree. There is no specific allegation in the complaint that sectarian teaching does or would invade secular classes supported by state funds. That the schools are operated to promote a particular religion is quite consistent with the view that secular teaching devoid of religious instruction can successfully be maintained. . . .

I do agree, however, that the complaint should not have been dismissed for failure to state a cause of action. . . . Hence, I would reverse the judgment of the District Court and remand the case for trial, thereby holding the Pennsylvania legislation valid on its face but leaving open the question of its validity as applied to the particular facts of this case. . . .

Agostini v. *Felton*
521 U.S. 203, 117 S.Ct. 1997, 138 L.Ed. 2d 391 (1997)

http://caselaw.findlaw.com/us-supreme-court/521/203.html

In *Aguilar* v. *Felton* (1985) the Supreme Court, with Chief Justice Burger and Justices White, Rehnquist, and O'Connor dissenting, held that New York City's program that sent public school teachers into parochial schools to provide remedial education to disadvantaged children pursuant to Title I of the Elementary and Secondary Education Act of 1965 violated the First Amendment's establishment clause. The U.S. District Court for the Eastern District of New York then entered a permanent injunction reflecting that ruling. As a result Title I services were provided to parochial school students in mobile units parked off-site. Some ten years later, petitioners—the parties bound by the injunction—filed motions in the same court seeking relief from the injunction, arguing that *Aguilar* could not be squared with the Court's intervening establishment clause decisions. The District Court denied the motion on the merits, declaring that *Aguilar's* demise had "not yet occurred." The Second Circuit Court of Appeals affirmed. When the case reached the Supreme Court, the solicitor general asked that *Aguilar* be overruled on a limited basis. This case is unusual not particularly because the Supreme Court changed its mind but because the Court did so on a reconsideration of the original case itself. Majority: O'Connor, Rehnquist, Scalia, Kennedy, Thomas. Dissenting: Stevens, Souter, Ginsburg, Breyer.

Justice O'Connor delivered the opinion of the Court. . . .

In order to evaluate whether *Aguilar* has been eroded by our subsequent Establishment Clause cases, it is necessary to understand the rationale upon which *Aguilar*, as well as its companion case, *School Dist. of Grand Rapids* v. *Ball* (1985), rested.

In *Ball*, the Court evaluated two programs implemented by the School District of Grand Rapids, Michigan. The district's Shared Time program, the one most analogous to Title I, provided remedial and "enrichment" classes, at public expense, to students attending nonpublic schools. The classes were taught during regular school hours by publicly employed teachers, using materials purchased with public funds, on the premises of nonpublic schools. The Shared Time courses were in subjects designed to supplement the "core curriculum" of the nonpublic schools. Of the 41 nonpublic schools eligible for the program, 40 were "pervasively sectarian" in character—that is, "the purpos[e] of [those] schools [was] to advance their particular religions."

The Court conducted its analysis by applying the three-part test set forth in *Lemon* v. *Kurtzman* (1971). . . . The Court acknowledged that the Shared Time program served a purely secular purpose, thereby satisfying the first part of the so-called Lemon test. Nevertheless, it ultimately concluded that the program had the impermissible effect of advancing religion.

The Court found that the program violated the Establishment Clause's prohibition against "government-financed or government-sponsored indoctrination into the beliefs of a particular religious faith" in at least three ways. First, drawing upon the analysis in *Meek* v. *Pittenger* (1975), the Court observed that "the teachers participating in the programs may become involved in intentionally or inadvertently inculcating particular religious tenets or beliefs." *Meek* invalidated a Pennsylvania program in which full-time public employees provided supplemental "auxiliary services"—remedial and accelerated instruction, guidance counseling and testing, and speech and hearing services—to nonpublic school children at their schools. Although the auxiliary services themselves were secular, they were mostly dispensed on the premises of parochial schools, where "an atmosphere dedicated to the advancement of religious belief [was] constantly maintained." Instruction in that atmosphere was sufficient to create "[t]he potential for impermissible fostering of religion." . . .

The Court concluded that Grand Rapids' program shared these defects. As in *Meek*, classes were conducted on the premises of religious schools. Accordingly, a majority found a "substantial risk" that teachers—even those who were not employed by the private schools—might "subtly (or overtly) conform their instruction to the [pervasively sectarian] environment in which they [taught]." The danger of "state-sponsored indoctrination" was only exacerbated by the school district's failure to monitor the courses for religious content. Notably, the Court disregarded the lack of evidence of any specific incidents of religious indoctrination as largely irrelevant, reasoning that potential witnesses to any indoctrination—the parochial school students, their parents, or parochial school officials—might be unable to detect or have little incentive to report the incidents.

The presence of public teachers on parochial school grounds had a second, related impermissible effect: It created a "graphic symbol of the 'concert or union or dependency' of church and state," especially when perceived by "children in their formative years." The Court feared that this perception of a symbolic union between church and state would "conve[y] a message of government endorsement . . . of religion" and thereby violate a "core purpose" of the Establishment Clause.

Third, the Court found that the Shared Time program impermissibly financed religious indoctrination by subsidizing "the primary religious mission of the institutions affected." The Court separated its prior decisions evaluating programs that aided the secular activities of religious institutions into two categories: those in which it concluded that the aid resulted in an effect that was "indirect, remote, or incidental" (and upheld the aid); and those in which it concluded that the aid resulted in "a direct and substantial advancement of the sectarian enterprise" (and invalidated the aid). . . .

The New York City Title I program challenged in *Aguilar* closely resembled the Shared Time program struck down in *Ball*, but the Court found fault with an aspect of the Title I program not present in *Ball:* The Board had "adopted a system for monitoring the religious content of publicly funded Title I classes in the religious schools." Even though this monitoring system might prevent the Title I program from being used to inculcate religion, the Court concluded, as it had in *Lemon* and *Meek*, that the level of monitoring necessary to be "certain" that the program had an exclusively secular effect would "inevitably resul[t] in the excessive entanglement of church and state," thereby running afoul of *Lemon*'s third prong. . . .

Distilled to essentials, the Court's conclusion that the Shared Time program in *Ball* had the impermissible effect of advancing religion rested on three assumptions: (i) any public employee who works on the premises of a religious school is presumed to inculcate religion in her work; (ii) the presence of public employees on private school premises creates a symbolic union between church and state; and (iii) any and all public aid that directly aids the educational function of religious schools impermissibly finances religious indoctrination, even if the aid reaches such schools as a consequence of private decision-making. Additionally, in *Aguilar* there was a fourth assumption: that New York City's Title I program necessitated an excessive government entanglement with religion because public employees who teach on the premises of religious schools must be closely monitored to ensure that they do not inculcate religion.

Our more recent cases have undermined the assumptions upon which *Ball* and *Aguilar* relied. To be sure, the general principles we use to evaluate whether government aid violates the Establishment Clause have not changed since *Aguilar* was decided. For example, we continue to ask whether the government acted with the purpose of advancing or inhibiting religion, and the nature of that inquiry has remained largely unchanged. . . . Likewise, we continue to explore whether the aid has the "effect" of advancing or inhibiting religion. What has changed since we decided *Ball* and *Aguilar* is our understanding of the criteria used to assess whether aid to religion has an impermissible effect.

As we have repeatedly recognized, government inculcation of religious beliefs has the impermissible effect of advancing religion. Our cases subsequent to *Aguilar* have, however, modified in two significant respects the approach we use to assess indoctrination. First, we have abandoned the presumption erected in *Meek* and *Ball* that the placement of public employees on parochial school grounds inevitably results in the impermissible effect of state-sponsored indoctrination or constitutes a symbolic union between government and religion. In *Zobrest* v. *Catalina Foothills School Dist.* (1993), we examined whether the IDEA [Individuals with Disabilities Education Act] was constitutional as applied to a deaf student who sought to bring his state-employed sign-language interpreter with him to his Roman Catholic high school. We held that this was permissible, expressly disavowing the notion that "the Establishment Clause [laid] down [an] absolute bar to the placing of a public employee in a sectarian school." . . . Because the only government aid in *Zobrest* was the interpreter, who was herself not inculcating any religious messages, no government indoctrination took place and we were able to conclude that "the provision of such assistance [was] not barred by the Establishment Clause." *Zobrest* therefore expressly rejected the notion—relied on in *Ball* and *Aguilar*—that, solely because of her presence on private school property, a public employee will be presumed to inculcate religion in the students. *Zobrest* also implicitly repudiated another assumption on which *Ball* and *Aguilar* turned: that the presence of a public employee on private school property creates an impermissible "symbolic link" between government and religion. . . .

Second, we have departed from the rule relied on in *Ball* that all government aid that directly aids the educational function of religious schools is invalid. In *Witters* v. *Washington Dept. of Servs. for Blind* (1986), we held that the Establishment Clause did not bar a State from issuing a vocational tuition grant to a blind person who wished to use the grant to attend a Christian college and become a pastor, missionary, or youth director. Even though the grant recipient clearly would use the money to obtain religious education, we observed that the tuition grants were "made available generally without regard to the sectarian-nonsectarian, or public-nonpublic nature of the institution benefited." The grants were disbursed directly to students, who then used the money to pay for tuition at the educational institution of their choice. In our view, this transaction was no different from a State's issuing a paycheck to one of its employees, knowing that the employee would donate part or all of the check to a religious institution. In both situations, any money that ultimately went to religious institutions did so "only as a result of the genuinely independent and private choices of" individuals. . . .

Zobrest and *Witters* make clear that, under current law, the Shared Time program in *Ball* and New York City's Title I program in *Aguilar* will not, as a matter of law, be deemed to have the effect of advancing religion through indoctrination. Indeed, each of the premises upon which we relied in *Ball* to reach a contrary conclusion is no longer valid. First, there is no reason to presume that, simply because she enters a parochial school classroom, a full-time public employee such as a Title I teacher will depart from her assigned duties and instructions and embark on religious indoctrination, any more than there was a reason in *Zobrest* to think an interpreter would inculcate religion by altering her translation of classroom lectures. Certainly, no evidence has ever shown that any New York City Title I instructor teaching on parochial school premises attempted to inculcate religion in students. . . .

As discussed above, *Zobrest* also repudiates *Ball*'s assumption that the presence of Title I teachers in parochial school classrooms will, without more, create the impression of a "symbolic union" between church and state. . . .

What is most fatal to the argument that New York City's Title I program directly subsidizes religion is that it applies with equal force when those services are provided off-campus, and *Aguilar* implied that providing the services off-campus is entirely consistent with the Establishment Clause. . . .

We turn now to *Aguilar*'s conclusion that New York City's Title I program resulted in an excessive entanglement between church and state. Whether a government aid program results in such an entanglement has consistently been an aspect of our Establishment Clause analysis. . . .

Not all entanglements, of course, have the effect of advancing or inhibiting religion. Interaction between church and state is inevitable, and we have always tolerated some level of involvement between the two. Entanglement must be "excessive" before it runs afoul of the Establishment Clause. . . . The pre-*Aguilar* Title I program does not result in an "excessive" entanglement that advances or inhibits religion. As discussed previously, the Court's finding of "excessive" entanglement in *Aguilar* rested on three grounds: (i) the program would require "pervasive monitoring by public authorities" to ensure that Title I employees did not inculcate religion; (ii) the program required "administrative cooperation" between the Board and parochial schools; and (iii) the program might increase the dangers of "political divisiveness." Under our current understanding of the Establishment Clause, the last two considerations are insufficient by themselves to create an "excessive" entanglement. They are present no matter where Title I services are offered, and no court has held that Title I services cannot be offered off-campus. Further, the assumption underlying the first consideration has been undermined. In *Aguilar*, the Court presumed that full-time public employees on parochial school grounds would be tempted to inculcate religion, despite the ethical standards they were required to uphold. Because of this risk pervasive monitoring would be required. But after *Zobrest* we no longer presume that public employees will inculcate religion simply because they happen to be in a sectarian environment. . . .

To summarize, New York City's Title I program does not run afoul of any of three primary criteria we currently use to evaluate whether government aid has the effect of advancing religion: it does not result in governmental indoctrination; define its recipients by reference to religion; or create an excessive entanglement. We therefore hold that a federally funded program providing supplemental, remedial instruction to disadvantaged children on a neutral basis is not invalid under the Establishment Clause when such instruction is given on the premises of sectarian schools by government employees pursuant to a program containing safeguards such as those present here. The same considerations that justify this holding require us to conclude that this carefully constrained program also cannot reasonably be viewed as an endorsement of religion. . . . Accordingly, we must acknowledge that *Aguilar*, as well as the portion of *Ball* addressing Grand Rapids' Shared Time program, are no longer good law. . . .

For these reasons, we reverse the judgment of the Court of Appeals and remand to the District Court with instructions to vacate its September 26, 1985, order.

It is so ordered.

JUSTICE SOUTER, with whom JUSTICE STEVENS and JUSTICE GINSBURG join, and with whom JUSTICE BREYER joins in part, dissenting. . . .

[T]he flat ban on subsidization . . . expresses the hard lesson learned over and over again in the American past and in the experiences of the countries from which we have come, that religions supported by governments are compromised just as surely as the religious freedom of dissenters is burdened when the government supports religion. . . . The human tendency, of course, is to forget the hard lessons, and to overlook the history of governmental partnership with religion when a cause is worthy, and bureaucrats have programs. That tendency to forget is the reason for having the Establishment Clause (along with the Constitution's other structural and libertarian guarantees), in the hope of stopping the corrosion before it starts.

These principles were violated by the programs at issue in *Aguilar* and *Ball*. . . .

What, therefore, was significant . . . about the placement of state-paid teachers into the physical and social settings of the religious schools was not only the consequent temptation of some of those teachers to reflect the schools' religious missions in the rhetoric of their instruction, with a resulting need for monitoring and the certainty of entanglement. . . . What was so remarkable was that the schemes in issue assumed a teaching responsibility indistinguishable from the responsibility of the schools themselves. The obligation of primary and secondary schools to teach reading necessarily extends to teaching those who are having a hard time at it, and the same is true of math. Calling some classes remedial does not distinguish their subjects from the schools' basic subjects, however inadequately the schools may have been addressing them. . . .

There is simply no line that can be drawn between the instruction paid for at taxpayers' expense and the instruction in any subject that is not identified as formally religious. If a State may constitutionally enter the schools to teach in the manner in question, it must in constitutional principle be free to assume, or assume payment for, the entire cost of instruction provided in any ostensibly secular subject in any religious school. . . .

It is accordingly puzzling to find the Court insisting that the aid scheme administered under Title I and considered in *Aguilar* was comparable to the programs in *Witters* and *Zobrest*. Instead of aiding isolated individuals within a school system, New York City's Title I program before *Aguilar* served about 22,000 private school students, all but 52 of whom attended religious schools. . . .

Finally, instead of aid that comes to the religious school indirectly in the sense that its distribution results from private decision-making, a public educational agency distributes Title I aid in the form of programs and services directly to the religious schools. . . .

In sum, nothing since *Ball* and *Aguilar* and before this case has eroded the distinction between "direct and substantial" and "indirect and incidental." That principled line is being breached only here and now. . . .

JUSTICE GINSBURG, with whom JUSTICE STEVENS, JUSTICE SOUTER, and JUSTICE BREYER join, dissenting . . . [omitted].

Zelman v. *Simmons-Harris*
536 U.S. 639, 122 S.Ct. 2460, 153 L.Ed. 2d 604 (2002)

http://caselaw.findlaw.com/us-supreme-court/536/639.html

Ohio's Pilot Project Scholarship Program provides tuition aid for certain students in the Cleveland City School District, the only qualifying district at the time of this litigation, to attend participating public or private schools of their parent's choosing and tutorial aid for students who choose to remain enrolled in public school. Both religious and nonreligious schools in the district may participate, as may public schools in adjacent school districts. Tuition aid is distributed to parents according to financial need, and where the aid is spent depends solely upon where parents choose to enroll their children. The number of tutorial assistance grants provided to students remaining in public school must equal the number of tuition aid scholarships. In the 1999–2000 school year, 82 percent of the participating private schools had a religious affiliation, none of the adjacent public schools participated, and 96 percent of the students participating in the scholarship program were enrolled in religiously affiliated schools. Cleveland school-children also have the option of enrolling in community schools, which are funded under state law but run by their own school boards and receive twice the per-student funding as participating private schools, or magnet schools, which are public schools emphasizing a particular subject area, teaching method, or service, and for which the school district receives the same amount per student as it does for a student enrolled at a traditional public school. Simmons-Harris and other Ohio taxpayers sought to enjoin the program on the ground that it violated the establishment clause. In 1999 the U.S. District Court for the Northern District of Ohio granted them summary judgment, and the U.S. Court of Appeals for the Sixth Circuit affirmed in 2000. Majority: Rehnquist, Kennedy, O'Connor, Scalia, Thomas. Dissenting: Souter, Breyer, Ginsburg, Stevens.

Chief Justice Rehnquist delivered the opinion of the Court. . . .

The question presented is whether [the Ohio] program offends the Establishment Clause of the United States Constitution. We hold that it does not.

There are more than 75,000 children enrolled in the Cleveland City School District. The majority of these children are from low-income and minority families. Few of these families enjoy the means to send their children to any school other than an inner-city public school. For more than a generation, however, Cleveland's public schools have been among the worst performing public schools in the Nation. . . .

It is against this backdrop that Ohio enacted, among other initiatives, its Pilot Project Scholarship Program. . . .

The Establishment Clause of the First Amendment, applied to the States through the Fourteenth Amendment, prevents a State from enacting laws that have the "purpose" or "effect" of advancing or inhibiting religion. . . . There is no dispute that the program challenged here was enacted for the valid secular purpose of providing educational assistance to poor children in a demonstrably failing public school system. Thus, the question presented is whether the Ohio program nonetheless has the forbidden "effect" of advancing or inhibiting religion.

To answer that question, our decisions have drawn a consistent distinction between government programs that provide aid directly to religious schools, . . . and programs of true private choice, in which government aid reaches religious schools only as a result of the genuine and independent choices of private individuals. . . . While our jurisprudence with respect to the constitutionality of direct aid programs has "changed significantly" over the past two decades, our jurisprudence with respect to true private choice programs has remained consistent and unbroken. Three times we have confronted Establishment Clause challenges to neutral government programs that provide aid directly to a broad class of individuals, who, in turn, direct the aid to religious schools or institutions of their own choosing. Three times we have rejected such challenges.

In *Mueller* [v. *Allen*], we rejected an Establishment Clause challenge to a Minnesota program authorizing tax deductions for various educational expenses, including private school tuition costs, even though the great majority of the program's beneficiaries (96 percent) were parents of children in religious schools. . . .

In *Witters* [v. *Washington*], we used identical reasoning to reject an Establishment Clause challenge to a vocational scholarship program that provided tuition aid to a student studying at a religious institution to become a pastor. Looking at the program as a whole, we observed that "[a]ny aid . . . that ultimately flows to religious institutions does so only as a result of the genuinely independent and private choices of aid recipients." . . .

Finally, in *Zobrest* [v. *Catalina Foothills School District*], we applied *Mueller* and *Witters* to reject an Establishment Clause challenge to a federal program that permitted sign-language interpreters to assist deaf children enrolled in religious schools. Reviewing our earlier decisions, we stated that "government programs that neutrally provide benefits to a broad class of citizens defined without reference to religion are not readily subject to an Establishment Clause challenge." . . . Its "primary beneficiaries," we said, were "disabled children, not sectarian schools." . . .

Mueller, Witters, and *Zobrest* thus make clear that where a government aid program is neutral with respect to religion, and provides assistance directly to a broad class of citizens who, in turn, direct government aid to religious schools wholly as a result of their own genuine and independent private choice, the program is not readily subject to challenge under the Establishment Clause. A program that shares these features permits government aid to reach religious institutions only by way of the deliberate choices of numerous individual recipients. The incidental advancement of a religious mission, or the perceived endorsement of a religious message, is reasonably attributable to the individual recipient, not to the government, whose role ends with the disbursement of benefits. . . .

We believe that the program challenged here is a program of true private choice, consistent with *Mueller, Witters*, and *Zobrest*, and thus constitutional. As was true in those cases, the Ohio program is neutral in all respects toward religion. It is part of a general and multifaceted undertaking by the State of Ohio to provide educational opportunities to the children of a failed school district. It confers educational assistance directly to a broad class of individuals defined without reference to religion, that is, any parent of a school-age child who resides in the Cleveland City School District. The program permits the participation of *all* schools within the district, religious or nonreligious. . . .

Respondents suggest that even without a financial incentive for parents to choose a religious school, the program creates a "public perception that the State is endorsing religious practices and beliefs." But . . . [a]ny objective observer familiar with the full history and context of the Ohio program would reasonably view it as one aspect of a broader undertaking to assist poor children in failed schools, not as an endorsement of religious schooling in general.

There also is no evidence that the program fails to provide genuine opportunities for Cleveland parents to select secular educational options for their school-age children. Cleveland schoolchildren enjoy a range of educational choices. . . . That 46 of the 56 private schools now participating in the program are religious schools does not condemn it as a violation of the Establishment Clause. The Establishment Clause question is whether Ohio is coercing parents into sending their children to religious schools, and that question must be answered by evaluating *all* options Ohio provides Cleveland schoolchildren, only one of which is to obtain a program scholarship and then choose a religious school.

. . . Cleveland's preponderance of religiously affiliated private schools certainly did not arise as a result of the program; it is a phenomenon common to many American cities. Indeed, by all accounts the program has captured a remarkable cross-section of private schools, religious and nonreligious. It is true that 82 percent of Cleveland's participating private schools are religious schools, but it is also true that 81 percent of private schools in Ohio are religious schools. To attribute constitutional significance to this figure, moreover, would lead to the absurd result that a neutral school-choice program might be permissible in some parts of Ohio, such as Columbus, where a lower percentage of private schools are religious schools, but not in inner-city Cleveland, where Ohio has deemed such programs most sorely needed, but where the preponderance of religious schools happens to be greater. . . .

The constitutionality of a neutral educational aid program simply does not turn on whether and why, in a particular area, at a particular time, most private schools are run by religious organizations, or most recipients choose to use the aid at a religious school. . . .

This point is aptly illustrated here. The 96 percent figure upon which respondents and Justice Souter rely discounts entirely (1) the more than 1,900 Cleveland children enrolled in alternative community schools; (2) the more than 13,000 children enrolled in alternative magnet schools; and (3) the more than 1,400 children enrolled in traditional public schools with tutorial assistance. Including some or all of these children in the denominator of children enrolled in nontraditional schools during the 1999–2000 school year drops the percentage enrolled in religious schools from 96 percent to under 20 percent. . . .

In sum, the Ohio program is entirely neutral with respect to religion. It provides benefits directly to a wide spectrum of individuals, defined only by financial need and residence in a particular school district. It permits such individuals to exercise genuine choice among options public and private, secular and religious. The program is therefore a program of true private choice. In keeping with an unbroken line of decisions rejecting challenges to similar programs, we hold that the program does not offend the Establishment Clause.

The judgment of the Court of Appeals is reversed.

It is so ordered.

JUSTICE O'CONNOR, concurring . . . [omitted].
JUSTICE THOMAS, concurring . . . [omitted].
JUSTICE STEVENS, dissenting . . . [omitted].

JUSTICE SOUTER, with whom JUSTICE STEVENS, JUSTICE GINSBURG, and JUSTICE BREYER join, dissenting. . . .

If there were an excuse for giving short shrift to the Establishment Clause, it would probably apply here. But there is no excuse. Constitutional limitations are placed on government to preserve constitutional values in hard cases, like these. . . .

The applicability of the Establishment Clause to public funding of benefits to religious schools was settled in *Everson* v. *Board of Ed. of Ewing* (1947), which inaugurated the modern era of establishment doctrine. The Court stated the principle in words from which there was no dissent: "No tax in any amount, large or small, can be levied to support any religious activities or institutions, whatever they may be called, or whatever form they may adopt to teach or practice religion." . . .

How can a Court consistently leave *Everson* on the books and approve the Ohio vouchers? The answer is that it cannot. It is only by ignoring *Everson* that the majority can claim to rest on traditional law in its invocation of neutral aid provisions and private choice to sanction the Ohio law. It is, moreover, only by ignoring the meaning of neutrality and private choice themselves that the majority can even pretend to rest today's decision on those criteria. . . .

Viewed with the necessary generality, [Establishment Clause] cases can be categorized in three groups. In the period from 1947 to 1968, the basic principle of no aid to religion through school benefits was unquestioned. Thereafter for some 15 years, the Court termed its efforts as attempts to draw a line against aid that would be divertible to support the religious, as distinct from the secular, activity of an institutional beneficiary. Then, starting in 1983, concern with divertibility was gradually lost in favor of approving aid in amounts unlikely to afford substantial benefits to religious schools, when offered evenhandedly without regard to a recipient's religious character, and when channeled to a religious institution only by the genuinely free choice of some private individual. Now, the three stages are succeeded by a fourth, in which the substantial character of government aid is held to have no constitutional significance, and the espoused criteria of neutrality in offering aid, and private choice in directing it, are shown to be nothing but examples of verbal formalism. . . .

Consider first the criterion of neutrality. . . .

In order to apply the neutrality test, then, it makes sense to focus on a category of aid that may be directed to religious as well as secular schools, and ask whether the scheme favors a religious direction. Here, one would ask whether the voucher provisions, allowing for as much as $2,250 toward private school tuition (or a grant to a public school in an adjacent district), were written in a way that skewed the scheme toward benefiting religious schools.

This, however, is not what the majority asks. The majority looks not to the provisions for tuition vouchers, but to every provision for educational opportunity. . . . The majority then finds confirmation that "participation of *all* schools" satisfies neutrality by noting that the better part of total state educational expenditure goes to public schools, thus showing there is no favor of religion.

The illogic is patent. If regular, public schools (which can get no voucher payments) "participate" in a voucher scheme with schools that can, and public expenditure is still predominantly on public schools, then the majority's reasoning would find neutrality in a scheme of vouchers available for private tuition in districts with no secular private schools at all. "Neutrality" as the majority employs the term is, literally, verbal and nothing more. . . . [P]ublic tutors may receive from the State no more than $324 per child to support extra tutoring (that is, the State's 90 percent of a total amount of $360), whereas the tuition voucher schools (which turn out to be mostly religious) can receive up to $2,250. . . .

The majority addresses the issue of choice the same way it addresses neutrality, by asking whether recipients or potential recipients of voucher aid have a choice of public schools among secular alternatives to religious schools. Again, however, the majority asks the wrong question and misapplies the criterion. The majority has confused choice in spending scholarships with choice from the entire menu of possible educational placements, most of them open to anyone willing to attend a public school. . . . The majority's view that all educational choices are comparable for purposes of choice thus ignores the whole point of the choice test: It is a criterion for deciding whether indirect aid to a religious school is legitimate because it passes through private hands that can spend or use the aid in a secular school. The question is whether the private hand is genuinely free to send the money in either a secular direction or a religious one. The majority now has transformed this question about private choice in channeling aid into a question about selecting from examples of state spending (on education) including direct spending on magnet and community public schools that goes through no private hands and could never reach a religious school under any circumstance. When the choice test is transformed from where to spend the money to where to go to school, it is cut loose from its very purpose. . . .

The scale of the aid to religious schools approved today is unprecedented, both in the number of dollars and in the proportion of systemic school expenditure supported.

When government aid goes up, so does reliance on it; the only thing likely to go down is independence. . . . A day will come when religious schools will learn what political leverage can do, just as Ohio's politicians are now getting a lesson in the leverage exercised by religion.

Increased voucher spending is not, however, the sole portent of growing regulation of religious practice in the school, for state mandates to moderate religious teaching may well be the most obvious response to the third concern behind the ban on establishment, its inextricable link with social conflict. . . .

[T]he intensity of the expectable friction can be gauged by realizing that the scramble for money will energize not only contending sectarians, but taxpayers who take their liberty of conscience seriously. Religious teaching at taxpayer expense simply cannot be cordoned from taxpayer politics, and every major religion currently espouses social positions that provoke intense opposition. Not all taxpaying Protestant citizens, for example, will be content to underwrite the teaching of the Roman Catholic Church condemning the death penalty. Nor will all of America's Muslims acquiesce in paying for the endorsement of the religious Zionism taught in many religious Jewish schools, which combines "a nationalistic sentiment" in support of Israel with a "deeply religious" element. . . . Views like these, and innumerable others, have been safe in the sectarian pulpits and classrooms of this Nation not only because the Free Exercise Clause protects them directly, but because the ban on supporting religious establishment has protected free exercise, by keeping it relatively private. With the arrival of vouchers in religious schools, that privacy will go, and along with it will go confidence that religious disagreement will stay moderate. . . .

Everson's statement is still the touchstone of sound law, even though the reality is that in the matter of educational aid the Establishment Clause has largely been read away. True, the majority has not approved vouchers for religious schools alone, or aid earmarked for religious instruction. But no scheme so clumsy will ever get before us, and in the cases that we may see, like these, the Establishment Clause is largely silenced. I . . . hope that a future Court will reconsider today's dramatic departure from basic Establishment Clause principle.

Justice Breyer, with whom Justice Stevens and Justice Souter join, dissenting . . . [omitted].

Espinoza v. *Montana Department of Revenue* 591 U.S. ___, 140 S.Ct. 2246, 207 L.Ed. 2d 679 (2020)

www.supremecourt.gov/opinions/19pdf/18-1195_g314.pdf

The facts of this case appear in the chief justice's opinion below. Majority: Roberts, Alito, Gorsuch, Kavanaugh, Thomas. Dissenting: Breyer, Ginsburg, Kagan, Sotomayor.

Chief Justice Roberts delivered the opinion of the Court.

The Montana Legislature established a program to provide tuition assistance to parents who send their children to private schools. The program grants a tax credit [of up to $150] to anyone who donates to certain organizations that in turn award scholarships to selected students attending such schools. When petitioners sought to use the scholarships at a religious school, the Montana Supreme Court struck down the program. The Court relied on the "no-aid" provision of the State Constitution, which prohibits any aid to a school controlled by a "church, sect, or denomination.". . .

We have recognized a "'play in the joints' between what the Establishment Clause permits and the Free Exercise Clause compels." Here, the parties do not dispute that the scholarship program is permissible under the Establishment Clause. Nor could they. We have repeatedly held that the Establishment Clause is not offended when religious observers and organizations benefit from neutral government programs. Any Establishment Clause objection to the scholarship program here is particularly unavailing because the government support makes its way to religious schools only as a result of Montanans independently choosing to spend their scholarships at such schools. The Montana Supreme Court, however, held as a matter of state law that even such indirect government support qualified as "aid" prohibited under the Montana Constitution.

The question for this Court is whether the Free Exercise Clause precluded the Montana Supreme Court from applying Montana's no-aid provision to bar religious schools from the scholarship program. For purposes of answering that question, we accept the Montana Supreme Court's interpretation of state law—including its determination that the scholarship program provided impermissible "aid" within the meaning of the Montana Constitution—and we assess whether excluding religious schools and affected families from that program was consistent with the Federal Constitution.

The Free Exercise Clause, which applies to the States under the Fourteenth Amendment, "protects religious observers against unequal treatment" and against "laws that impose special disabilities on the basis of religious status." . . . Most recently, *Trinity Lutheran* [v. *Comer* (2017)] distilled these and other decisions to the same effect into the "unremarkable" conclusion that disqualifying otherwise eligible recipients from a public benefit "solely because of their religious character" imposes "a penalty on the free exercise of religion that triggers the most exacting scrutiny." In *Trinity Lutheran*, Missouri provided grants to help nonprofit organizations pay for playground resurfacing, but a state policy disqualified any organization "owned or controlled by a church, sect, or other religious entity." Because of that policy, an otherwise eligible church-owned preschool was denied a grant to resurface its playground. Missouri's policy discriminated against the Church "simply because of what it is—a church," and so the policy was subject to the "strictest scrutiny," which it failed. . . .

Here too Montana's no-aid provision bars religious schools from public benefits solely because of the religious character of the schools. The provision also bars parents who wish to send their children to a religious school from those same benefits, again solely because of the religious character of the school. This is apparent from the plain text. The provision bars aid to any school "controlled in whole or in part by any church, sect, or denomination."

The Department [of Revenue] counters that *Trinity Lutheran* does not govern here because the no-aid provision applies not because of the religious character of the recipients, but because of how the funds would be used—for "religious education." In *Trinity Lutheran*, a majority of the Court concluded that the Missouri policy violated the Free Exercise Clause because it discriminated on the basis of religious status. A plurality declined to address discrimination with respect to "religious uses of funding or other forms of discrimination." The plurality saw no need to consider such concerns because Missouri had expressly discriminated "based on religious identity," which was enough to invalidate the state policy without addressing how government funds were used.

This case also turns expressly on religious status and not religious use. . . . The Department points to some language in the decision below indicating that the no-aid provision has the goal or effect of ensuring that government aid does not end up being used for "sectarian education" or "religious education." The Department also contrasts what it characterizes as the "completely non-religious" benefit of playground resurfacing in *Trinity Lutheran* with the unrestricted tuition aid at issue here. General school aid, the Department stresses, could be used for religious ends by some recipients, particularly schools that believe faith should "permeate[]" everything they do. Regardless, those considerations were not the Montana Supreme Court's basis for applying the no-aid provision to exclude religious schools; that hinged solely on religious status. Status-based discrimination remains status based even if one of its goals or effects is preventing religious organizations from putting aid to religious uses.

Undeterred by Trinity *Lutheran*, the Montana Supreme Court applied the no-aid provision to hold that religious schools could not benefit from the scholarship program . . . To be eligible for government aid under the Montana Constitution, a school must divorce itself from any religious control or affiliation. Placing such a condition on benefits or privileges "inevitably deters or discourages the exercise of First Amendment rights." . . . It is enough in this case to conclude that strict scrutiny applies under *Trinity Lutheran* because Montana's no-aid provision discriminates based on religious status.

Seeking to avoid *Trinity Lutheran*, the Department contends that this case is instead governed by *Locke* v. Davey (2004). *Locke* also involved a scholarship program. The State of Washington provided scholarships paid out of the State's general fund to help students pursuing postsecondary education. The scholarships could be used at accredited religious and nonreligious schools alike, but Washington prohibited students from using the scholarships to pursue devotional theology degrees, which prepared students for a calling as clergy. This prohibition prevented Davey from using his scholarship to obtain a degree that would have enabled him to become a pastor. We held that Washington had not violated the Free Exercise Clause.

Locke differs from this case in two critical ways. First, *Locke* explained that Washington had "merely chosen not to fund a distinct category of instruction": the "essentially religious endeavor" of training a minister "to lead a congregation." Thus, Davey "was denied a scholarship because of what he proposed to do—use the funds to prepare for the ministry." Apart from that narrow restriction, Washington's program allowed scholarships to be used at "pervasively religious schools" that incorporated religious instruction throughout their classes. By contrast, Montana's Constitution does not zero in on any particular "essentially religious" course of instruction at a religious school. Rather, . . . the no-aid provision bars all aid to a religious school "simply because of what it is," putting the school to a choice between being religious or receiving government benefits. At the same time, the provision puts families to a choice between sending their children to a religious school or receiving such benefits.

Second, *Locke* invoked a "historic and substantial" state interest in not funding the training of clergy, explaining that "opposition to . . . funding 'to support church leaders' lay at the historic core of the Religion Clauses." But no comparable "historic and substantial" tradition supports Montana's decision to disqualify religious schools from government aid. In the founding era and the early 19th century, governments provided financial support to private schools, including denominational ones. . . . After the Civil War, Congresses pent large sums on education for emancipated freedmen, often by supporting denominational schools in the South through the Freedmen's Bureau.

The Department argues that a tradition against state support for religious schools arose in the second half of the 19th century, as more than 30 States—including Montana—adopted no-aid provisions. . . . [M]any of the no-aid provisions belong to a more checkered tradition shared with the Blaine Amendment of the 1870s. That proposal—which Congress nearly passed—would have added to the Federal Constitution a provision similar to the state no-aid provisions, prohibiting States from aiding "sectarian" schools. "[I]t was an open secret that 'sectarian' was code for 'Catholic.'" The Blaine Amendment was "born of bigotry" and "arose at a time of pervasive hostility to the Catholic Church and to Catholics in general"; many of its state counterparts have a similarly "shameful pedigree." The no-aid provisions of the 19th century hardly evince a tradition that should inform our understanding of the Free Exercise Clause. . . .

Because the Montana Supreme Court applied the no-aid provision to discriminate against schools and parents based on the religious character of the school, the "strictest scrutiny" is required. . . . To satisfy it, government action "must advance 'interests of the highest order' and must be narrowly tailored in pursuit of those interests." The Montana Supreme Court asserted that the no-aid provision serves Montana's interest in separating church and State "more fiercely" than the Federal Constitution. . . . An infringement of First Amendment rights, however, cannot be justified by a State's alternative view that the infringement advances religious liberty. Our federal system prizes state experimentation, but not "state experimentation in the suppression of free speech," and the same goes for the free exercise of religion.

Furthermore, we do not see how the no-aid provision promotes religious freedom. . . . Montana's . . . prohibition is far more sweeping than the policy in *Trinity Lutheran*, which barred churches from one narrow program for playground resurfacing . . . And the prohibition before us today burdens not only religious schools but also the families whose children attend or hope to attend them. A State need not subsidize private education. But once a State decides to do so, it cannot disqualify some private schools solely because they are religious.

The Department argues that, at the end of the day, there is no free exercise violation here because the Montana Supreme Court ultimately eliminated the scholarship program altogether. According to the Department, now that there is no program, religious schools and adherents cannot complain that they are excluded from any generally available benefit. . . .

The descriptions are not accurate. The Montana Legislature created the scholarship program; the Legislature never chose to end it, for policy or other reasons. The program was eliminated by a court, and not based on some innocuous principle of state law. Rather, the Montana Supreme Court invalidated the program pursuant to a state law provision that expressly discriminates on the basis of religious status. The Court applied that provision to hold that religious schools were barred from participating in the program. Then, seeing no other "mechanism" to make absolutely sure that religious schools received no aid, the court chose to invalidate the entire program.

The final step in this line of reasoning eliminated the program, to the detriment of religious and non-religious schools alike. But the Court's error of federal law occurred at the beginning. When the Court was called upon to apply a state law no-aid provision to exclude religious schools from the program, it was obligated by the Federal Constitution to reject the invitation. Had the Court recognized that this was, indeed, "one of those cases" in which application of the no-aid provision "would violate the Free Exercise Clause," the Court would not have proceeded to find a violation of that provision. And, in the absence of such a state law violation, the Court would have had no basis for terminating the program. Because the elimination of the program flowed directly from the Montana Supreme Court's failure to follow the dictates of federal law, it cannot be defended as a neutral policy decision, or as resting on adequate and independent state law grounds. . . .

Given the conflict between the Free Exercise Clause and the application of the no-aid provision here, the Montana Supreme Court should have "disregard[ed]" the no-aid provision and decided this case "conformably to the [C]onstitution" of the United States. That "supreme law of the land" condemns discrimination against religious schools and the families whose children attend them. . . .

The judgment of the Montana Supreme Court is reversed, and the case is remanded for further proceedings not inconsistent with this opinion.

It is so ordered.

JUSTICE THOMAS, with whom Justice Gorsuch joins, concurring . . . [omitted].

JUSTICE ALITO, concurring . . . [omitted].

Justice Gorsuch, concurring . . . [omitted].

JUSTICE GINSBURG, with whom JUSTICE KAGAN joins, dissenting . . . [omitted].

JUSTICE SOTOMAYOR, dissenting.

The majority holds that a Montana scholarship program unlawfully discriminated against religious schools by excluding them from a tax benefit. The threshold problem, however, is that such tax benefits no longer exist for anyone in the State. The Montana Supreme Court invalidated the program on state-law grounds, thereby foreclosing the as-applied challenge petitioners raise here. . . . The Court nevertheless reframes the case and appears to ask whether a longstanding Montana constitutional provision is facially invalid under the Free Exercise Clause, even though petitioners disavowed bringing such a claim. But by resolving a constitutional question not presented, the Court fails to heed Article III principles older than the Religion Clause it expounds. Not only is the Court wrong to decide this case at all, it decides it wrongly. . . .

To be sure, petitioners may want to apply for scholarships and would prefer that Montana subsidize their children's religious education. But this Court had never before held unconstitutional government action that merely failed to benefit religious exercise. "The crucial word in the constitutional text is 'prohibit': 'For the Free Exercise Clause is written in terms of what the government cannot do to the individual, not in terms of what the individual can exact from the government.'" Put another way, the Constitution does not compel Montana to create or maintain a tax subsidy. . . .

Today's decision replaces a remedy chosen by representatives of Montanans and designed to honor the will of the electorate with one that the Court prefers instead. In sum, the decision below neither upheld a program that "disqualif[ies] some private schools solely because they are religious," nor otherwise decided the case on federal grounds. The Court's opinion thus turns on a counterfactual hypothetical it is powerless (and unwise) to decide.

Even on its own terms, the Court's answer to its hypothetical question is incorrect. The Court relies principally on *Trinity Lutheran*, which found that disqualifying an entity from a public benefit "solely because of [the entity's] religious character" could impose "a penalty on the free exercise of religion." *Trinity Lutheran* held that ineligibility for a government benefit impermissibly burdened a church's religious exercise by "put[ting it] to the choice between being a church and receiving a government benefit." Invoking that precedent, the Court concludes that Montana must subsidize religious education if it also subsidizes nonreligious education. The Court's analysis of Montana's defunct tax program reprises the error in *Trinity Lutheran* . . . .

Until *Trinity Lutheran*, the right to exercise one's religion did not include a right to have the State pay for that religious practice. . . . The relevant question had always been not whether a State singles out religious entities, but why it did so. . . . Properly understood, this case is no different from *Locke* because petitioners seek to procure what the plaintiffs in *Locke* could not: taxpayer funds to support religious schooling. . . .

Today's ruling is perverse. Without any need or power to do so, the Court appears to require a State to reinstate a tax-credit program that the Constitution did not demand in the first place. We once recognized that "[w]hile the Free Exercise Clause clearly prohibits the use of state action to deny the rights of free exercise to anyone, it has never meant that a majority could use the machinery of the State to practice its beliefs." Today's Court, by contrast, rejects the Religion Clauses' balanced values in favor of a new theory of free exercise, and it does so only by setting aside well-established judicial constraints. I respectfully dissent.

III. FREE EXERCISE OF RELIGION

The Flag-Salute Cases
Minersville School District v. *Gobitis*
310 U.S. 586, 60 S.Ct. 1010, 84 L.Ed. 1375 (1940)

http://caselaw.findlaw.com/us-supreme-court/310/586.html

West Virginia State Board of Education v. *Barnette*
319 U.S. 624, 63 S.Ct. 1178, 87 L.Ed. 1628 (1943)

http://caselaw.findlaw.com/us-supreme-court/319/624.html

One of the most dramatic reversals of a Court decision occurred in 1943 when a precedent of only three years' standing was overruled. Both cases presented the same issue: Could schoolchildren, members of the sect known as Jehovah's Witnesses, be required to salute the flag, a practice forbidden by their religious tenets? In the earlier case, the Court in an 8–1 decision reversed the district court and upheld the action of a Pennsylvania school board expelling two pupils, but in the later case, the Court held a similar action unconstitutional. It should be noted that this about-face was the result partly of personnel changes (which brought Justices Jackson and Rutledge to the bench) and partly of the change of viewpoint of Justices Black, Douglas, and Murphy. Court records misspelled the Gobitas and Barnett family names, hence the landmark decisions continue the error. In both cases, U.S. district courts ruled in favor of the Jehovah's Witnesses. In his *Judging Jehovah's Witnesses*, Shawn Francis Peters calls the majority opinion in *Gobitis* "Felix's Fall-of-France Opinion." Majority in *Gobitis:* Frankfurter, Black, Douglas, Hughes, McReynolds, Murphy, Reed, Roberts. Dissenting: Stone. Majority in *Barnette:* Jackson, Black, Douglas, Murphy, Rutledge, Stone. Dissenting: Frankfurter, Reed, Roberts.

Minersville School District v. *Gobitis* (1940)

MR. JUSTICE FRANKFURTER delivered the opinion of the court. . . .

Lillian Gobitis, aged 12, and her brother William, aged ten, were expelled from the public schools of Minersville, Pennsylvania, for refusing to salute the national flag as part of a daily school exercise. . . .

The Gobitis children were of an age for which Pennsylvania makes school attendance compulsory. Thus they were denied a free education, and their parents had to put them into private schools. To be relieved of the financial burden thereby entailed, their father, on behalf of the children and in his own behalf, brought this suit. He sought to enjoin the authorities from continuing to exact participation in the flag-salute ceremony as a condition of his children's attendance at the Minersville School. . . .

We must decide whether the requirement of participation in such a ceremony, exacted from a child who refuses upon sincere religious grounds, infringes without due process of law the liberty guaranteed by the Fourteenth Amendment.

Centuries of strife over the erection of particular dogmas as exclusive or all-comprehending faiths led to the inclusion of a guarantee for religious freedom in the Bill of Rights. The First Amendment, and the Fourteenth through its absorption of the First, sought to guard against repetition of those bitter religious struggles by prohibiting the establishment of a state religion and by securing to every sect the free exercise of its faith. So pervasive is the acceptance of this precious right that its scope is brought into question, as here, only when the conscience of individuals collides with the felt necessities of society.

Certainly the affirmative pursuit of one's convictions about the ultimate mystery of the universe and man's relation to it is placed beyond the reach of law. Government may not interfere with organized or individual expression of belief or disbelief. Propagation of belief—or even of disbelief in the super-natural—is protected, whether in church or chapel, mosque or synagogue, tabernacle or meetinghouse. . . .

But the manifold character of man's relations may bring his conception of religious duty into conflict with the secular interests of his fellowmen. When does the constitutional guarantee compel exemption from doing what society thinks necessary for the promotion of some great common end, or from a penalty for conduct which appears dangerous to the general good? To state the problem is to recall the truth that no single principle can answer all of life's complexities. The right to freedom of religious belief, however dissident and however obnoxious to the cherished beliefs of others—even of a majority—is itself the denial of an absolute. But to affirm that the freedom to follow conscience has itself no limits in the life of a society would deny that very plurality of principles which, as a matter of history, underlies protection of religious toleration. . . . Our present task then, as so often the case with courts, is to reconcile two rights in order to prevent either from destroying the other. . . .

The religious liberty which the Constitution protects has never excluded legislation of general scope not directed against doctrinal loyalties of particular sects. Judicial nullification of legislation cannot be justified by attributing to the framers of the Bill of Rights views for which there is no historic warrant. Conscientious scruples have not, in the course of the long struggle for religious toleration, relieved the individual from obedience to a general law not aimed at the promotion or restriction of religious beliefs. The mere possession of religious convictions which contradict the relevant concerns of a political society does not relieve the citizen from the discharge of political responsibilities. The necessity for this adjustment has again and again been recognized.

. . . [T]he question remains whether school children, like the Gobitis children, must be excused from conduct required of all the other children in the promotion of national cohesion. We are dealing with an interest inferior to none in the hierarchy of legal values. National unity is the basis of national security. . . .

Situations like the present are phases of the profoundest problems confronting a democracy—the problem which Lincoln cast in memorable dilemma: "Must a government of necessity be too strong for the liberties of its people, or too weak to maintain its own existence?" No mere textual reading or logical talisman can solve the dilemma. And when the issue demands judicial determination, it is not the personal notion of judges of what wise adjustment requires which must prevail.

. . . [T]he case before us is not concerned with an exertion of legislative power for the promotion of some specific need or interest of secular society. . . . The ultimate foundation of a free society is the binding ties of cohesive sentiment. Such a sentiment is fostered by all those agencies of the mind and spirit which may serve to gather up the traditions of a people, transmit them from generation to generation, and thereby create that continuity of a treasured common life which constitutes a civilization. "We live by symbols." The flag is the symbol of our national unity, transcending all internal differences, however large, within the framework of the Constitution. . . .

The precise issue, then, for us to decide is whether the legislatures of the various states and the authorities in a thousand counties and school districts of this country are barred from determining the appropriateness of various means to evoke that unifying sentiment without which there can ultimately be no liberties, civil or religious. To stigmatize legislative judgment in providing for this universal gesture of respect for the symbol of our national life in the setting of the common school as a lawless inroad on that freedom of conscience which the Constitution protects, would amount to no less than the pronouncement of pedagogical and psychological dogma in a field where courts possess no marked and certainly no controlling competence. The influences which help toward a common feeling for the common country are manifold. . . . Surely, however, the end is legitimate. And the effective means for its attainment are still so uncertain and so unauthenticated by science as to preclude us from putting the widely prevalent belief in flag-saluting beyond the pale of legislative power. It mocks reason and denies our whole history to find in the allowance of a requirement to salute our flag on fitting occasions the seeds of sanction for obeisance to a leader.

The wisdom of training children in patriotic impulses by those compulsions which necessarily pervade so much of the educational process is not for our independent judgment. Even were we convinced of the folly of such a measure, such belief would be no proof of its unconstitutionality. . . . Perhaps it is best, even from the standpoint of those interests which ordinances like the one under review seek to promote, to give to the least popular sect leave from conformities like those here in issue. But the courtroom is not the arena for debating issues of educational policy. It is not our province to choose among competing considerations in the subtle process of securing effective loyalty to the traditional ideals of democracy, while respecting at the same time individual idiosyncracies among a people so diversified in racial origins and religious allegiances. So to hold would in effect make us the school board for the country. That authority has not been given to this Court, nor should we assume it. . . .

Judicial review, itself a limitation on popular government, is a fundamental part of our constitutional scheme. But to the legislature no less than to courts is committed the guardianship of deeply cherished liberties. . . . Where all the effective means of inducing political changes are left free from interference, education in the abandonment of foolish legislation is itself a training in liberty. To fight out the wise use of legislative authority in the forum of public opinion and before legislative assemblies rather than to transfer such a contest to the judicial arena, serves to vindicate the self-confidence of a free people.

Reversed.

MR. JUSTICE MCREYNOLDS concurs in the result.

MR. JUSTICE STONE, dissenting. . . .

The guaranties of civil liberty are but guaranties of freedom of the human mind and spirit and of reasonable freedom and opportunity to express them. They presuppose the right of the individual to hold such opinions as he will and to give them reasonably free expression, and his freedom, and that of the state as well, to teach and persuade others by the communication of ideas. The very essence of the liberty which they guarantee is the freedom of the individual from compulsion as to what he shall think and what he shall say, at least where the compulsion is to bear false witness to his religion. If these guaranties are to have any meaning they must, I think, be deemed to withhold from the state any authority to compel belief or the expression of it where that expression violates religious convictions, whatever may be the legislative view of the desirability of such compulsion.

History teaches us that there have been but few infringements of personal liberty by the state which have not been justified, as they are here, in the name of righteousness and the public good, and few which have not been directed, as they are now, at politically helpless minorities. . . . The Constitution may well elicit expressions of loyalty to it and to the government which it created, but it does not command such expressions or otherwise give any indication that compulsory expressions of loyalty play any such part in our scheme of government as to override the constitutional protection of freedom of speech and religion. And while such expressions of loyalty, when voluntarily given, may promote national unity, it is quite another matter to say that their compulsory expression by children in violation of their own and their parents' religious convictions can be regarded as playing so important a part in our national unity as to leave school boards free to exact it despite the constitutional guarantee of freedom of religion. The very terms of the Bill of Rights preclude, it seems to me, any reconciliation of such compulsions with the constitutional guaranties by a legislative declaration that they are more important to the public welfare than the Bill of Rights.

But even if this view be rejected and it is considered that there is some scope for the determination by legislatures whether the citizen shall be compelled to give public expression of such sentiments contrary to his religion, I am not persuaded that we should refrain from passing upon the legislative judgment "as long as the remedial channels of the democratic process remain open and unobstructed." This seems to me no more than the surrender of the constitutional protection of the liberty of small minorities to the popular will. We have previously pointed to the importance of a searching judicial inquiry into the legislative judgment in situations where prejudice against discrete and insular minorities may tend to curtail the operation of those political processes ordinarily to be relied on to protect minorities. See *United States* v. *Carolene Products Co.*, note 4 [reprinted in the essay for Chapter Eight]. And until now we have not hesitated similarly to scrutinize legislation restricting the civil liberty of racial and religious minorities although no political process was affected. . . .

Here we have such a small minority entertaining in good faith a religious belief, which is such a departure from the usual course of human conduct, that most persons are disposed to regard it with little toleration or concern. In such circumstances careful scrutiny of legislative efforts to secure conformity of belief and opinion by a compulsory affirmation of the desired belief, is especially needful if civil rights are to receive any protection. Tested by this standard, I am not prepared to say that the right of this small and helpless minority, including children having a strong religious conviction, whether they understand its nature or not, to refrain from an expression obnoxious to their religion, is to be overborne by the interest of the state in maintaining discipline in the schools.

The Constitution expresses more than the conviction of the people that democratic processes must be preserved at all costs. It is also an expression of faith and a command that freedom of mind and spirit must be preserved, which government must obey, if it is to adhere to that justice and moderation without which no free government can exist. For this reason it would seem that legislation which operates to repress the religious freedom of small minorities, which is admittedly within the scope of the protection of the Bill of Rights, must at least be subject to the same judicial scrutiny as legislation which we have recently held to infringe the constitutional liberty of religious and racial minorities. . . .

Justice Frankfurter to Justice Stone, May 27, 1940: A *Qualified* Plea for Judicial Self-Restraint

Students of constitutional interpretation have long wondered why it took Black and Douglas, two of the sharpest minds on the Court, both of them ardent liberals, so long to discover their error in joining Frankfurter's well-nigh unanimous opinion in the first Flag-Salute Case. A clue may be found in the letter Frankfurter wrote Stone in trying to win his vote. Hitler's armies were then on the march, threatening to envelop Europe. In this struggle America could not escape involvement.

SUPREME COURT OF THE UNITED STATES
WASHINGTON, D.C.

CHAMBERS
OF JUSTICE FELIX FRANKFURTER

MAY 27, 1940

DEAR STONE:

Were No. 690 an ordinary case, I should let the opinion speak for itself. But that you should entertain doubts has naturally stirred me to an anxious reexamination of my own views, even though I can assure you that nothing has weighed as much on my conscience, since I have come on this Court, as has this case. Your doubts have stirred me to a reconsideration of the whole matter, because I am not happy that you should entertain doubts that I cannot share or meet in a domain where constitutional power is on one side and my private notions of liberty and toleration and good sense are on the other. After all, the vulgar intrusion of law in the domain of conscience is for me a very sensitive area. For various reasons . . . a good part of my mature life has thrown whatever weight it has had against foolish and harsh manifestations of coercion and for the amplest expression of dissident views, however absurd or offensive these may have been to my own notions of rationality and decency. I say this merely to indicate that all my bias and predisposition are in favor in giving the fullest elbow room to every variety of religious, political, and economic view.

But no one has more clearly in his mind than you, that even when it comes to these ultimate civil liberties, insofar as they are protected by the Constitution, we are not in the domain of absolutes. Here, also, we have an illustration of what the Greeks thousands of years ago recognized as a tragic issue, namely, the clash of rights, not the clash of wrongs. For resolving such clash we have no calculus. But there is for me, and I know also for you, a great makeweight for dealing with this problem, namely, that we are not the primary resolvers of the clash. We are not exercising an independent judgment; we are sitting in judgment upon the judgment of the legislature. I am aware of the important distinction which you so skillfully adumbrated in your footnote 4 (particularly the second paragraph of it) in the Carolene Products Co. case. I agree with that distinction; I regard it as basic. I have taken over that distinction in its central aspect, however inadequately, in the present opinion by insisting on the importance of keeping open all those channels of free expression by which undesirable legislation may be removed, and keeping unobstructed all forms of protest against what are deemed invasions of conscience, however much the invasion may be justified on the score of the deepest interests of national well-being.

What weighs with me strongly in this case is my anxiety that, while we lean in the direction of the libertarian aspect, we do not exercise our judicial power unduly, and as though we ourselves were legislators by holding with too tight a rein the organs of popular government. In other words, I want to avoid the mistake comparable to that made by those whom we criticized when dealing with the control of property. . . . I cannot rid myself of the notion that it is not fantastic, although I think foolish and perhaps worse, for school authorities to believe—as the record in this case explicitly shows the school authorities to have believed—that to allow exemption to some of the children goes far towards disrupting the whole patriotic exercise. And since certainly we must admit the general right of the school authorities to have such flag-saluting exercises, it seems to me that we do not trench on an undebatable territory of libertarian immunity to permit the school authorities a judgment as to the effect of this exemption in the particular setting of our time and circumstances.

For time and circumstances are surely not irrelevant considerations in resolving the conflicts that we do have to resolve in this particular case. . . . [C]ertainly it is relevant to make the adjustment that we have to make within the framework of present circumstances and those that are clearly ahead of us. . . . After all, despite some of the jurisprudential "realists," a decision decides not merely the particular case. . . . [S]o this case would have a tail of implications as to legislative power that is certainly debatable and might easily be invoked far beyond the size of the immediate kite, were it to deny the very minimum exaction, however foolish as to the Gobitis children, of an expression of faith in the heritage and purposes of our country.

For my intention—and I hope my execution did not lag too far behind—was to use this opinion as a vehicle for preaching the true democratic faith of not relying on the Court for the impossible task of assuring a vigorous, mature, self-protecting and tolerant democracy by bringing the responsibility for a combination of firmness and toleration directly home where it belongs—to the people and their representatives themselves. . . .

The duty of compulsion being as minimal as it is for an act, the normal legislative authorization of which certainly cannot be denied, and all channels of affirmative free expression being open to both children and parents, I cannot resist the conviction that we ought to let the legislative judgment stand and put the responsibility for its exercise where it belongs. In any event, I hope you will be good enough to give me the benefit of what you think should be omitted or added to the opinion.

Faithfully yours,
s/Felix Frankfurter

West Virginia State Board of Education v. *Barnette* (1943)

MR. JUSTICE JACKSON delivered the opinion of the Court. . . .

This case calls upon us to reconsider a precedent decision, as the Court throughout its history often has been required to do. Before turning to the Gobitis case, however, it is desirable to notice certain characteristics by which this controversy is distinguished. . . .

There is no doubt that, in connection with the pledges, the flag salute is a form of utterance. Symbolism is a primitive but effective way of communicating ideas. . . .

It is also to be noted that the compulsory flag salute and pledge requires [*sic*] affirmation of a belief and an attitude of mind. . . . To sustain the compulsory flag salute we are required to say that a Bill of Rights which guards the individual's right to speak his own mind, left it open to public authorities to compel him to utter what is not in his mind. . . .

The Gobitis decision, however, *assumed*, as did the argument in that case and in this, that power exists in the State to impose the flag salute discipline upon school children in general. The Court only examined and rejected a claim based on religious beliefs of immunity from an unquestioned general rule. The question which underlies the flag salute controversy is whether such a ceremony so touching matters of opinion and political attitude may be imposed upon the individual by official authority under powers committed to any political organization under our Constitution. . . .

The very purpose of a Bill of Rights was to withdraw certain subjects from the vicissitudes of political controversy, to place them beyond the reach of majorities and officials and to establish them as legal principles to be applied by the courts. One's right to life, liberty, and property, to free speech, a free press, freedom of worship and assembly, and other fundamental rights may not be submitted to vote; they depend on the outcome of no elections.

In weighing arguments of the parties it is important to distinguish between the due process clause of the Fourteenth Amendment as an instrument for transmitting the principles of the First Amendment and those cases in which it is applied for its own sake. The test of legislation which collides with the Fourteenth Amendment because it also collides with the principles of the First, is much more definite than the test when only the Fourteenth is involved. Much of the vagueness of the due process clause disappears when the specific prohibitions of the First become its standard. The right of a State to regulate, for example, a public utility may well include, so far as the due process test is concerned, power to impose all of the restrictions which a legislature may have a "rational basis" for adopting. But freedoms of speech and of press, of assembly, and of worship may not be infringed on such slender grounds. They are susceptible of restriction only to prevent grave and immediate danger to interests which the State may lawfully protect. It is important to note that while it is the Fourteenth Amendment which bears directly upon the State it is the more specific limiting principles of the First Amendment that finally govern this case.

Nor does our duty to apply the Bill of Rights to assertions of official authority depend upon our possession of marked competence in the field where the invasion of rights occurs. True, the task of translating the majestic generalities of the Bill of Rights, conceived as part of the pattern of liberal government in the eighteenth century, into concrete restraints on officials dealing with the problems of the twentieth century, is one to disturb self-confidence. . . . But we act in these matters not by authority of our competence but by force of our commissions. We cannot, because of modest estimates of our competence in such specialties as public education, withhold the judgment that history authenticates as the function of this Court when liberty is infringed. . . .

The case is made difficult not because the principles of its decision are obscure but because the flag involved is our own. Nevertheless, we apply the limitations of the Constitution with no fear that freedom to be intellectually and spiritually diverse or even contrary will disintegrate the social organization. To believe that patriotism will not flourish if patriotic ceremonies are voluntary and spontaneous instead of a compulsory routine is to make an unflattering estimate of the appeal of our institutions to free minds. We can have intellectual individualism and the rich cultural diversities that we owe to exceptional minds only at the price of occasional eccentricity and abnormal attitudes. When they are so harmless to others or to the State as those we deal with here, the price is not too great. But freedom to differ is not limited to things that do not matter much. That would be a mere shadow of freedom. The test of its substance is the right to differ as to things that touch the heart of the existing order.

If there is any fixed star in our constitutional constellation, it is that no official, high or petty, can prescribe what shall be orthodox in politics, nationalism, religion, or other matters of opinion or force citizens to confess by word or act their faith therein. If there are any circumstances which permit an exception, they do not now occur to us. . . .

The decision of this Court in *Minersville School District* v. *Gobitis* . . . [is] overruled, and the judgment enjoining enforcement of the West Virginia Regulation is affirmed.

MR. JUSTICE BLACK, with whom MR. JUSTICE DOUGLAS joins, concurring . . . [omitted].

MR. JUSTICE MURPHY, concurring . . . [omitted].

MR. JUSTICE ROBERTS, with whom MR. JUSTICE REED joins, dissenting . . . [omitted].

MR. JUSTICE FRANKFURTER, dissenting.

One who belongs to the most vilified and persecuted minority in history is not likely to be insensible to the freedoms guaranteed by our Constitution. Were my purely personal attitude relevant I should wholeheartedly associate myself with the general libertarian views in the Court's opinion, representing as they do the thought and action of a lifetime. But as judges we are neither Jew nor Gentile, neither Catholic nor agnostic. We owe equal attachment to the Constitution and are equally bound by our judicial obligations whether we derive our citizenship from the earliest or the latest immigrants to these shores. As a member of this Court I am not justified in writing my private notions of policy into the Constitution, no matter how deeply I may cherish them or how mischievous I may deem their disregard. . . . It can never be emphasized too much that one's own opinion about the wisdom or evil of a law should be excluded altogether when one is doing one's duty on the bench. . . .

There is no warrant in the constitutional basis of this Court's authority for attributing different roles to it depending upon the nature of the challenge to the legislation. Our power does not vary according to the particular provision of the Bill of Rights which is invoked. The right not to have property taken without just compensation has, so far as the scope of judicial power is concerned, the same constitutional dignity as the right to be protected against unreasonable searches and seizures, and the latter has no less claim than freedom of the press or freedom of speech or religious freedom. In no instance is this Court the primary protector of the particular liberty that is invoked. . . .

Of course patriotism cannot be enforced by the flag salute. But neither can the liberal spirit be enforced by judicial invalidation of illiberal legislation. Our constant preoccupation with the constitutionality of legislation rather than with its wisdom tends to preoccupation of the American mind with a false value. The tendency of focusing attention on constitutionality is to make constitutionality synonymous with wisdom, to regard a law as all right if it is constitutional. Such an attitude is a great enemy of liberalism. Particularly in legislation affecting freedom of thought and freedom of speech much which should offend a free-spirited society is constitutional. Reliance for the most precious interests of civilization, therefore, must be found outside of their vindication in courts of law. Only a persistent positive translation of the faith of a free society into the convictions and habits and actions of a community is the ultimate reliance against unabated temptations to fetter the human spirit.

Sherbert v. *Verner*
374 U.S. 398, 83 S.Ct. 1790, 10 L.Ed. 2d 965 (1963)

http://caselaw.findlaw.com/us-supreme-court/374/398.html

Adell Sherbert was a member of the Seventh-Day Adventist Church who lost her job in South Carolina because she would not work on Saturday, the Sabbath of her religion. After looking for other work and finding none because of her strictures against Saturday work, she filed a claim for unemployment compensation under South Carolina law. Her claim was denied because she failed to accept "suitable work when offered . . . by the employment office or the employer. . . ." This ruling of the Employment Security Commission was sustained by the Court of Common Pleas of Spartanburg County. The South Carolina Supreme Court affirmed. Majority: Brennan, Black, Clark, Douglas, Goldberg, Stewart, Warren. Dissenting: Harlan, White.

Mr. Justice Brennan delivered the opinion of the Court. . . .

We turn first to the question whether the disqualification for benefits imposes any burden on the free exercise of appellant's religion. We think it is clear that it does. In a sense the consequences of such a disqualification to religious principles and practices may be only an indirect result of welfare legislation within the State's general competence to enact; it is true that no criminal sanctions directly compel appellant to work a six-day week. But this is only the beginning, not the end, of our inquiry. For "[i]f the purpose or effect of a law is to impede the observance of one or all religions or is to discriminate invidiously between religions, that law is constitutionally invalid even though the burden may be characterized as being only indirect." Here not only is it apparent that appellant's declared ineligibility for benefits derives solely from the practice of her religion, but the pressure upon her to forgo that practice is unmistakable. The ruling forces her to choose between following the precepts of her religion and forfeiting benefits, on the one hand, and abandoning one of the precepts of her religion in order to accept work, on the other hand. Governmental imposition of such a choice puts the same kind of burden upon the free exercise of religion as would a fine imposed against appellant for her Saturday worship. . . .

We must next consider whether some compelling state interest enforced in the eligibility provisions of the South Carolina statute justifies the substantial infringement of appellant's First Amendment right. . . . No such abuse or danger has been advanced in the present case. The appellees suggest no more than a possibility that the filing of fraudulent claims by unscrupulous claimants feigning religious objections to Saturday work might not only dilute the unemployment compensation fund but also hinder the scheduling by employers of necessary Saturday work. . . . But . . . there is no proof whatever to warrant such fears of malingering or deceit as those which the respondents now advance. . . .

In holding as we do, plainly we are not fostering the "establishment" of the Seventh-day Adventist religion in South Carolina, for the extension of unemployment benefits to Sabbatarians in common with Sunday worshipers reflects nothing more than the governmental obligation of neutrality in the face of religious differences, and does not represent that involvement of religious with secular institutions which it is the object of the Establishment Clause to forestall. . . .

The judgment of the South Carolina Supreme Court is reversed and the case is remanded for further proceedings not inconsistent with this opinion.

It is so ordered.

MR. JUSTICE DOUGLAS, concurring . . . [omitted].

MR. JUSTICE STEWART concurring in the result. . . .

I think that the Court's approach to the Establishment Clause has on occasion . . . accorded to the Establishment Clause a meaning which neither the words, the history, nor the intention of the authors of that specific constitutional provision even remotely suggests.

. . . And the result is that there are many situations where legitimate claims under the Free Exercise Clause will run into head-on collision with the Court's insensitive and sterile construction of the Establishment Clause. The controversy now before us is clearly such a case.

Because the appellant refuses to accept available jobs which would require her to work on Saturdays, South Carolina has declined to pay unemployment compensation benefits to her. Her refusal to work on Saturdays is based on the tenets of her religious faith. The Court says that South Carolina cannot under these circumstances declare her to be not "available for work" within the meaning of its statute because to do so would violate her constitutional right to the free exercise of her religion.

Yet what this Court has said about the Establishment Clause must inevitably lead to a diametrically opposite result. If the appellant's refusal to work on Saturdays were based on indolence, or on a compulsive desire to watch the Saturday television programs, no one would say that South Carolina could not hold that she was not "available for work" within the meaning of its statute. That being so, the Establishment Clause as construed by this Court not only permits but affirmatively requires South Carolina equally to deny the appellant's claim for unemployment compensation when her refusal to work on Saturdays is based upon her religious creed. . . .

MR. JUSTICE HARLAN, whom MR. JUSTICE WHITE joins, dissenting. . . .

The South Carolina Supreme Court has uniformly applied this law in conformity with its clearly expressed purpose. It has consistently held that one is not "available for work" if his unemployment has resulted not from the inability of industry to provide a job but rather from personal circumstances, no matter how compelling. . . .

Thus in no proper sense can it be said that the State discriminated against the appellant on the basis of her religious beliefs or that she was denied benefits because she was a Seventh-day Adventist. She was denied benefits just as any other claimant would be denied benefits who was not "available for work" for personal reasons. . . .

With this background, this Court's decision comes into clearer focus. What the Court is holding is that if the State chooses to condition unemployment compensation on the applicant's availability for work, it is constitutionally compelled to carve out an exception—and to provide benefits—for those whose unavailability is due to their religious convictions. . . .

My own view is that at least under the circumstances of this case it would be a permissible accommodation of religion for the State, if it chose to do so, to create an exception to its eligibility requirements for persons like the appellant. . . .

Employment Division v. Smith
494 U.S. 872, 110 S.Ct. 1595, 108 L.Ed. 2d 876 (1990)

http://caselaw.findlaw.com/us-supreme-court/494/872.html

In its controlled substance law, Oregon prohibits the knowing possession of a variety of drugs, including peyote, a cactus containing the hallucinogen mescaline. Alfred Smith and Galen Black were fired from their jobs with a private drug rehabilitation clinic because they ingested peyote as part of a ritual of the Native American Church. When they applied for unemployment compensation, the Employment Division of Oregon's Department of Human Resources ruled them ineligible because they had been dismissed for work-related misconduct. The state Court of Appeals reversed, holding that the denial of benefits violated their rights under the free exercise clause of the First Amendment. In 1986 the Supreme Court of Oregon affirmed. The U.S. Supreme Court remanded the case in 1988 for a determination whether the religious use of peyote was a violation of state law. The Oregon Supreme Court ruled that the statute provided no exception for religious use and held that under the free exercise clause the state could not deny unemployment benefits to those who engaged in the practice for religious reasons. Majority: Scalia, Rehnquist, White, Stevens, Kennedy, O'Connor. Dissenting: Blackmun, Brennan, Marshall.

Justice Scalia delivered the opinion of the Court.

This case requires us to decide whether the Free Exercise Clause of the First Amendment permits the State of Oregon to include religiously inspired peyote use within the reach of its general criminal prohibition on use of that drug, and thus permits the State to deny unemployment benefits to persons dismissed from their jobs because of such religiously inspired use. . . .

The free exercise of religion means, first and foremost, the right to believe and profess whatever religious doctrine one desires. Thus, the First Amendment obviously excludes all "governmental regulation of religious beliefs as such." The government may not compel affirmation of religious belief, punish the expression of religious doctrines it believes to be false, impose special disabilities on the basis of religious views or religious status, or lend its power to one or the other side in controversies over religious authority or dogma. . . .

Respondents in the present case, however, seek to carry the meaning of "prohibiting the free exercise [of religion]" one large step further. They contend that their religious motivation for using peyote places them beyond the reach of a criminal law that is not specifically directed at their religious practice, and that is concededly constitutional as applied to those who use the drug for other reasons. They assert, in other words, that "prohibiting the free exercise [of religion]" includes requiring any individual to observe a generally applicable law that requires (or forbids) the performance of an act that his religious belief forbids (or requires). As a textual matter, we do not think the words must be given that meaning. It is no more necessary to regard the collection of a general tax, for example, as "prohibiting the free exercise [of religion]" by those citizens who believe support of organized government to be sinful, than it is to regard the same tax as "abridging the freedom . . . of the press" of those publishing companies that must pay the tax as a condition of staying in business. It is a permissible reading of the text, in the one case as in the other, to say that if prohibiting the exercise of religion (or burdening the activity of printing) is not the object of the tax but merely the incidental effect of a generally applicable and otherwise valid provision, the First Amendment has not been offended. . . .

Our decisions reveal that the latter reading is the correct one. We have never held that an individual's religious beliefs excuse him from compliance with an otherwise valid law prohibiting conduct that the State is free to regulate. . . .

The only decisions in which we have held that the First Amendment bars application of a neutral, generally applicable law to religiously motivated action have involved not the Free Exercise Clause alone, but the Free Exercise Clause in conjunction with other constitutional protections, such as freedom of speech and of the press. . . .

The present case does not present such a hybrid situation, but a free exercise claim unconnected with any communicative activity or parental right. Respondents urge us to hold, quite simply, that when otherwise prohibitable conduct is accompanied by religious convictions, not only the convictions but the conduct itself must be free from governmental regulation. We have never held that, and decline to do so now. . . .

Respondents argue that even though exemption from generally applicable criminal laws need not automatically be extended to religiously motivated actors, at least the claim for a religious exemption must be evaluated under the balancing test set forth in *Sherbert* v. *Verner*. Under the Sherbert test, governmental actions that substantially burden a religious practice must be justified by a compelling governmental interest. Applying that test we have, on three occasions, invalidated state unemployment compensation rules that conditioned the availability of benefits upon an applicant's willingness to work under conditions forbidden by his religion. We have never invalidated any governmental action on the basis of the Sherbert test except the denial of unemployment compensation. Although we have sometimes purported to apply the Sherbert test in contexts other than that, we have always found the test satisfied. In recent years we have abstained from applying the Sherbert test (outside the unemployment compensation field) at all. . . .

Even if we were inclined to breathe into *Sherbert* some life beyond the unemployment compensation field, we would not apply it to require exemptions from a generally applicable criminal law. . . .

. . . We conclude today that the sounder approach, and the approach in accord with the vast majority of our precedents, is to hold the test inapplicable to such challenges. . . .

Nor is it possible to limit the impact of respondent's proposal by requiring a "compelling state interest" only when the conduct prohibited is "central" to the individual's religion. It is no more appropriate for judges to determine the "centrality" of religious beliefs before applying a "compelling interest" test in the free exercise field, than it would be for them to determine the "importance" of ideas before applying the "compelling interest" test in the free speech field. What principle of law or logic can be brought to bear to contradict a believer's assertion that a particular act is "central" to his personal faith? Judging the centrality of different religious practices is akin to the unacceptable "business of evaluating the relative merits of differing religious claims." . . .

If the "compelling interest" test is to be applied at all, then, it must be applied across the board, to all actions thought to be religiously commanded. Moreover, if "compelling interest" really means what it says (and watering it down here would subvert its rigor in the other fields where it is applied), many laws will not meet the test. Any society adopting such a system would be courting anarchy, but that danger increases in direct proportion to the society's diversity of religious beliefs, and its determination to coerce or suppress none of them. Precisely because "we are a cosmopolitan nation made up of people of almost every conceivable religious preference," and precisely because we value and protect that religious divergence, we cannot afford the luxury of deeming presumptively invalid, as applied to the religious objector, every regulation of conduct that does not protect an interest of the highest order. The rule respondents favor would open the prospect of constitutionally required religious exemptions from civic obligations of almost every conceivable kind. . . .

Values that are protected against government interference through enshrinement in the Bill of Rights are not thereby banished from the political process. Just as a society that believes in the negative protection accorded to the press by the First Amendment is likely to enact laws that affirmatively foster the dissemination of the printed word, so also a society that believes in the negative protection accorded to religious belief can be expected to be solicitous of that value in its legislation as well. It is therefore not surprising that a number of States have made an exception to their drug laws for sacramental peyote use. But to say that a nondiscriminatory religious-practice exemption is permitted, or even that it is desirable, is not to say that it is constitutionally required, and that the appropriate occasions for its creation can be discerned by the courts. It may fairly be said that leaving accommodation to the political process will place at a relative disadvantage those religious practices that are not widely engaged in; but that unavoidable consequence of democratic government must be preferred to a system in which each conscience is a law unto itself or in which judges weigh the social importance of all laws against the centrality of all religious beliefs.

Because respondents' ingestion of peyote was prohibited under Oregon law, and because that prohibition is constitutional, Oregon may, consistent with the Free Exercise Clause, deny respondents unemployment compensation when their dismissal results from use of the drug. The decision of the Oregon Supreme Court is accordingly reversed.

It is so ordered.

JUSTICE O'CONNOR concurring in the judgment. . . . [She rejected the majority's reasoning, believing instead that the same result could be reached using the traditional analysis preferred by the dissenters.]

JUSTICE BLACKMUN, with whom JUSTICE BRENNAN and JUSTICE MARSHALL join, dissenting.

This Court over the years painstakingly has developed a consistent and exacting standard to test the constitutionality of a state statute that burdens the free exercise of religion. Such a statute may stand only if the law in general, and the State's refusal to allow a religious exemption in particular, are justified by a compelling interest that cannot be served by less restrictive means.

Until today, I thought this was a settled and inviolate principle of this Court's First Amendment jurisprudence. The majority, however, perfunctorily dismisses it as a "constitutional anomaly." . . .

Oregon has never sought to prosecute respondents, and does not claim that it has made significant enforcement efforts against other religious users of peyote. The State's asserted interest thus amounts only to the symbolic preservation of an unenforced prohibition. . . .

The State proclaims an interest in protecting the health and safety of its citizens from the dangers of unlawful drugs. It offers, however, no evidence that the religious use of peyote has ever harmed anyone. . . .

The Federal Government, which created the classifications of unlawful drugs from which Oregon's drug laws are derived, apparently does not find peyote so dangerous as to preclude an exemption for religious use. . . .

Finally, the State argues that granting an exception for religious peyote use would erode its interest in the uniform, fair, and certain enforcement of its drug laws. The State fears that, if it grants an exemption for religious peyote use, a flood of other claims to religious exemptions will follow. . . .

The State's apprehension of a flood of other religious claims is purely speculative. Almost half the States, and the Federal Government, have maintained an exemption for religious peyote use for many years, and apparently have not found themselves overwhelmed by claims to other religious exemptions. Allowing an exemption for religious peyote use would not necessarily oblige the State to grant a similar exemption to other religious groups. . . . That the State might grant an exemption for religious peyote use, but deny other religious claims arising in different circumstances, would not violate the Establishment Clause. . . .

Finally, although I agree . . . that courts should refrain from delving into questions of whether, as a matter of religious doctrine, a particular practice is "central" to the religion, I do not think this means that the courts must turn a blind eye to the severe impact of a State's restrictions on the adherents of a minority religion. . . .

Respondents believe, and their sincerity has never been at issue, that the peyote plant embodies their deity, and eating it is an act of worship and communion. Without peyote, they could not enact the essential ritual of their religion. . . .

For these reasons, I conclude that Oregon's interest in enforcing its drug laws against religious use of peyote is not sufficiently compelling to outweigh respondents' right to the free exercise of their religion. Since the State could not constitutionally enforce its criminal prohibition against respondents, the interests underlying the State's drug laws cannot justify its denial of unemployment benefits. . . .

City of Boerne v. *Flores*
521 U.S. 507, 117 S.Ct. 2157, 138 L.Ed. 2d 624 (1997)

http://caselaw.findlaw.com/us-supreme-court/521/507.html

(This case is reprinted in Chapter Two; see the Table of Contents.)

Masterpiece Cakeshop v. Colorado Civil Rights Commission 584 U.S. ___, 138 S.Ct. 1719, 201 L.Ed. 2d 35 (2018)

www.supremecourt.gov/opinions/17pdf/16-111_j4el.pdf

The facts of this case appear in Justice Kennedy's opinion below. Majority: Kennedy, Alito, Breyer, Gorsuch, Kagan, Roberts, Thomas. Dissenting: Ginsburg, Sotomayor.

Justice Kennedy delivered the opinion of the Court.

In 2012 a same-sex couple [Charlie Craig and Dave Mullins] visited Masterpiece Cakeshop, a bakery in [Lakewood] Colorado, to make inquiries about ordering a cake for their wedding reception. The shop's owner [Jack Phillips] told the couple that [while he would sell them other baked goods] he would not create a cake for their wedding because of his religious opposition to same-sex marriages—marriages the State of Colorado itself did not recognize at that time. The couple filed a charge with the Colorado Civil Rights Commission alleging discrimination on the basis of sexual orientation in violation of the Colorado Anti-Discrimination Act. The Commission determined that the shop's actions violated the Act and ruled in the couple's favor. The Colorado state courts affirmed the ruling and its enforcement order, and this Court now must decide whether the Commission's order violated the Constitution.

The case presents difficult questions as to the proper reconciliation of at least two principles. The first is the authority of a State and its governmental entities to protect the rights and dignity of gay persons who are, or wish to be, married but who face discrimination when they seek goods or services. The second is the right of all persons to exercise fundamental freedoms under the First Amendment, as applied to the States through the Fourteenth Amendment.

The freedoms asserted here are both the freedom of speech and the free exercise of religion. The free speech aspect of this case is difficult, for few persons who have seen a beautiful wedding cake might have thought of its creation as an exercise of protected speech. This is an instructive example, however, of the proposition that the application of constitutional freedoms in new contexts can deepen our understanding of their meaning. . . .

Whatever the confluence of speech and free exercise principles might be in some cases, the Colorado Civil Rights Commission's consideration of this case was inconsistent with the State's obligation of religious neutrality. The reason and motive for the baker's refusal were based on his sincere religious beliefs and convictions. The Court's precedents make clear that the baker, in his capacity as the owner of a business serving the public, might have his right to the free exercise of religion limited by generally applicable laws. Still, the delicate question of when the free exercise of his religion must yield to an otherwise valid exercise of state power needed to be determined in an adjudication in which religious hostility on the part of the State itself would not be a factor in the balance the State sought to reach. That requirement, however, was not met here. When the Colorado Civil Rights Commission considered this case, it did not do so with the religious neutrality that the Constitution requires. Given all these considerations, it is proper to hold that whatever the outcome of some future controversy involving facts similar to these, the Commission's actions here violated the Free Exercise Clause; and its order must be set aside.

Our society has come to the recognition that gay persons and gay couples cannot be treated as social outcasts or as inferior in dignity and worth. For that reason the laws and the Constitution can, and in some instances must, protect them in the exercise of their civil rights. The exercise of their freedom on terms equal to others must be given great weight and respect by the courts. At the same time, the religious and philosophical objections to gay marriage are protected views and in some instances protected forms of expression. As this Court observed in *Obergefell* v. *Hodges*, "[t]he First Amendment ensures that religious organizations and persons are given proper protection as they seek to teach the principles that are so fulfilling and so central to their lives and faiths." Nevertheless, while those religious and philosophical objections are protected, it is a general rule that such objections do not allow business owners and other actors in the economy and in society to deny protected persons equal access to goods and services under a neutral and generally applicable public accommodations law. . . .

When it comes to weddings, it can be assumed that a member of the clergy who objects to gay marriage on moral and religious grounds could not be compelled to perform the ceremony without denial of his or her right to the free exercise of religion. This refusal would be well understood in our constitutional order as an exercise of religion, an exercise that gay persons could recognize and accept without serious diminishment to their own dignity and worth. Yet if that exception were not confined, then a long list of persons who provide goods and services for marriages and weddings might refuse to do so for gay persons, thus resulting in a community-wide stigma inconsistent with the history and dynamics of civil rights laws that ensure equal access to goods, services, and public accommodations.

It is unexceptional that Colorado law can protect gay persons, just as it can protect other classes of individuals, in acquiring whatever products and services they choose on the same terms and conditions as are offered to other members of the public. And there are no doubt innumerable goods and services that no one could argue implicate the First Amendment. Petitioners conceded, moreover, that if a baker refused to sell any goods or any cakes for gay weddings, that would be a different matter and the State would have a strong case under this Court's precedents that this would be a denial of goods and services that went beyond any protected rights of a baker who offers goods and services to the general public and is subject to a neutrally applied and generally applicable public accommodations law.

Phillips claims, however, that a narrower issue is presented. He argues that he had to use his artistic skills to make an expressive statement, a wedding endorsement in his own voice and of his own creation. As Phillips would see the case, this contention has a significant First Amendment speech component and implicates his deep and sincere religious beliefs. In this context the baker likely found it difficult to find a line where the customers' rights to goods and services became a demand for him to exercise the right of his own personal expression for their message, a message he could not express in a way consistent with his religious beliefs. . . .

The neutral and respectful consideration to which Phillips was entitled was compromised here, however. The Civil Rights Commission's treatment of his case has some elements of a clear and impermissible hostility toward the sincere religious beliefs that motivated his objection. That hostility surfaced at the Commission's formal, public hearings, as shown by the record. . . . To describe a man's faith as "one of the most despicable pieces of rhetoric that people can use" is to disparage his religion in at least two distinct ways: by describing it as despicable, and also by characterizing it as merely rhetorical—something insubstantial and even insincere. The commissioner even went so far as to compare Phillips' invocation of his sincerely held religious beliefs to defenses of slavery and the Holocaust. This sentiment is inappropriate for a Commission charged with the solemn responsibility of fair and neutral enforcement of Colorado's anti-discrimination law—a law that protects discrimination on the basis of religion as well as sexual orientation. The record shows no objection to these comments from other commissioners. . . . Nor were the comments by the commissioners disavowed in the briefs filed in this Court. For these reasons, the Court cannot avoid the conclusion that these statements cast doubt on the fairness and impartiality of the Commission's adjudication of Phillips' case. . . .

For the reasons just described, the Commission's treatment of Phillips' case violated the State's duty under the First Amendment not to base laws or regulations on hostility to a religion or religious viewpoint. . . . The Free Exercise Clause bars even "subtle departures from neutrality" on matters of religion. Here, that means the Commission was obliged under the Free Exercise Clause to proceed in a manner neutral toward and tolerant of Phillips' religious beliefs. . . .

While the issues here are difficult to resolve, it must be concluded that the State's interest could have been weighed against Phillips' sincere religious objections in a way consistent with the requisite religious neutrality that must be strictly observed. The official expressions of hostility to religion in some of the commissioners' comments—comments that were not disavowed at the Commission or by the State at any point in the proceedings that led to affirmance of the order—were inconsistent with what the Free Exercise Clause requires. . . . For these reasons, the order must be set aside. . . . The outcome of cases like this in other circumstances must await further elaboration in the courts, all in the context of recognizing that these disputes must be resolved with tolerance, without undue disrespect to sincere religious beliefs, and without subjecting gay persons to indignities when they seek goods and services in an open market. The judgment of the Colorado Court of Appeals is reversed.

It is so ordered.

JUSTICE KAGAN, with whom JUSTICE BREYER joins, concurring . . . [omitted].

JUSTICE GORSUCH, with whom JUSTICE ALITO joins, concurring . . . [omitted].

JUSTICE THOMAS, with whom JUSTICE GORSUCH joins, concurring in part and concurring in the judgment . . . [omitted].

JUSTICE GINSBURG, with whom JUSTICE SOTOMAYOR joins, dissenting.

As Justice Thomas observes, the Court does not hold that wedding cakes are speech or expression entitled to First Amendment protection. Nor could it, consistent with our First Amendment precedents. . . . [F]or conduct to constitute protected expression, the conduct must be reasonably understood by an observer to be communicative. . . .

Statements made at the Commission's public hearings on Phillips' case provide no firmer support for the Court's holding today. Whatever one may think of the statements in historical context, I see no reason why the comments of one or two Commissioners should be taken to overcome Phillips' refusal to sell a wedding cake to Craig and Mullins. The proceedings involved several layers of independent decisionmaking, of which the Commission was but one. First, the Division had to find probable cause that Phillips violated CADA. Second, the [administrative law judge] entertained the parties' cross-motions for summary judgment. Third, the Commission heard Phillips' appeal. Fourth, after the Commission's ruling, the Colorado Court of Appeals considered the case de novo. What prejudice infected the determinations of the adjudicators in the case before and after the Commission? The Court does not say. Phillips' case is thus far removed from the only precedent upon which the Court relies, *Church of Lukumi Babalu Aye, Inc.* v. *Hialeah* (1993), where the government action that violated a principle of religious neutrality implicated a sole decisionmaking body, the city council.

For the reasons stated, sensible application of CADA to a refusal to sell any wedding cake to a gay couple should occasion affirmance of the Colorado Court of Appeals' judgment. I would so rule.

Roman Catholic Diocese of Brooklyn* v. *Cuomo
592 U.S. ___, 141 S.Ct. 63, 208 L.Ed. 2d 206 (2020)

(This case is reprinted in Chapter Fifteen; see the Table of Contents.)

13

Privacy

The makers of our Constitution . . . conferred, as against the government, the right to be let alone—the most comprehensive of rights and the right most valued by civilized men.

—JUSTICE LOUIS D. BRANDEIS (1928)

The word *privacy* appears not once in the Constitution, yet some aspects of privacy or individual autonomy were recognized by the framers of the Constitution as fundamental—as essential elements of liberty. Today, protection of certain privacy interests is integral to American constitutional law. Privacy is also an idea with few apparent limits. Paul Freund once called it a "greedy legal concept." What is privacy? How do questions of privacy involve the Constitution? How are judges supposed to decide what privacy encompasses?

DIMENSIONS OF PRIVACY

Privacy denotes different things. For some it is a broad right "to be let alone." So put, **privacy** is almost synonymous with freedom. Accordingly, individuals should be allowed to make decisions about their lives without undue interference from others. Carried to an extreme, however, privacy would make organized society impossible. Every day, laws impinge on the liberty of individuals in numerous ways. Being in society means that people are by no means "let alone" to go their own direction entirely in their own way.

More narrowly conceived, privacy may mean physical separation from others. People enter their homes, close the door, and pull the shades for the express purpose of keeping themselves, their activities, and their belongings hidden from public view. Such ordinary actions make it plain that people intend to shield the interior from the prying eyes of neighbors, as well as those of government.

Protecting one's reputation from defamatory comment is another dimension of privacy. As Chapter Eleven explained, courts must reconcile the privacy interest,

DOI: 10.4324/9781003164340-14

recognized by the law of libel, with a competing interest—a free press—recognized by the First Amendment. A third and related dimension is control over information about oneself. Medical records, academic transcripts, bank and credit card statements, and tax returns all contain information that the persons about whom the information is compiled probably intend not to become public. **Informational privacy** fosters a dual concern: accuracy and access. Are the data correct, and who is allowed to see and use them? These are questions made more urgent in the age of computers and the Internet where identity theft has become a constant danger.

Privacy may also denote security from intrusion on the intimacies of life, a dimension that is the focus of this chapter. Certain decisions regarding companionship, marriage, and child rearing may not be entirely free of government restrictions, but they should preserve a core of freedom from outside restraint. This suggests a zone of autonomy, which the government may not penetrate without justification.

PRIVATE LAW AND PUBLIC LAW BEGINNINGS

Not all dimensions of privacy involve the Constitution. Some are regulated by statute alone. From the beginning, American law has offered redress from physical trespass and intrusion, and libel actions have allowed damages when one's reputation has been besmirched. (Both are examples of **private law** at work: legal rules governing relations among individuals. **Public law** involves regulations overseeing the operations of government as well as relations between individuals and their governments. Constitutional law, for example, is a field of public law.) "At common law," Chief Justice Rehnquist said, "even the touching of one person by another without consent and without legal justification was a battery." As the Supreme Court declared in *Union Pacific R. Co.* v. *Botsford* (1891), "No right is held more sacred, or is more carefully guarded, by the common law, than the right of every individual to the possession and control of his own person, free from all restraint or interference of others, unless by clear and unquestionable authority of law."

Threats to privacy or autonomy are the focus of several provisions of the Constitution. By banning religious tests for public office, Article VI protects the sanctity of personal religious beliefs, and the First Amendment guards rights of individual expression, religious and otherwise. The Third Amendment virtually proscribes the quartering of troops in homes. The Fourth Amendment proclaims "the right of the people to be secure in their persons, houses, papers and effects" and prohibits "unreasonable searches and seizures." The Fifth Amendment protects the integrity of the individual by curtailing the state's power to force people to be witnesses against themselves in criminal proceedings. The Fifth and the Fourteenth Amendments remove government's power to take away a person's "life, liberty, or property without due process of law." Spiritual and bodily integrity are important as well in the ban on "cruel and unusual punishments" in the Eighth Amendment. In its own way, each of these provisions addresses some dimension of personhood or autonomy.

Yet it was not until after 1890 that "privacy" began to take on life as a subject of its own. In that year, Boston attorneys Samuel Warren and Louis Brandeis published a seminal article called "The Right to Privacy." Their immediate concern was nondefamatory but nonetheless offensive gossip in the newspapers. Although existing law provided redress for libel and slander, Warren and Brandeis believed that persons should be able to sue for damages when certain kinds of unwanted, unpleasant information appeared about them in the press. Their goal was law to guard "an inviolate personality," to enforce "the right of the individual to be left alone." The article was partly successful in stemming some of the abuses that troubled its authors. But its more lasting impact lay in stimulating thinking about the concept of privacy generally.

Privacy was at least a peripheral concern in several decisions by the U.S. Supreme Court before 1965. In *Meyer* v. *Nebraska* (1923), eight justices overturned a state statute that both prohibited the teaching of subjects in any language other than English and forbade the teaching of foreign languages to any pupil who had not passed the eighth grade. According to Justice McReynolds, liberty "denotes not merely freedom from bodily restraint but also the right of any individual to contract, to engage in any of the common occupations of life, to acquire useful knowledge, to marry, establish a home and bring up children . . . and generally to enjoy those privileges long recognized at common law as essential to the orderly pursuit of happiness by free men." Similarly, *Pierce* v. *Society of Sisters* (1925) invalidated an Oregon law forbidding parents from sending their children to private schools. The "liberty" of the Fourteenth Amendment was construed to include the right of the parents to direct the upbringing of their children.

In *Skinner* v. *Oklahoma* (1942), the Court struck down a compulsory sterilization scheme mandated by Oklahoma for certain classes of habitual criminals. Although the decision rested mainly on equal protection grounds (see Chapter Fourteen), Justice Douglas's majority opinion suggested a broader basis: "the Oklahoma legislation . . . involves one of the basic civil rights of man. Marriage and procreation are fundamental to the very existence and survival of the race." The foreign language and private school decisions had arguably been related to the First Amendment, although the Court construed them in traditional terms of "calling" and property. Yet in *Skinner*, the right infringed was tied neither to the First Amendment nor to any other express constitutional provision, for that matter. Barely half a decade after discrediting judicial creation of substantive rights in the wake of President Roosevelt's Court-packing plan (see Chapter Six), the justices created another.

Justice Douglas was persistent. When a divided Court in *Public Utilities Commission* v. *Pollack* (1952) refused to recognize a right not to be disturbed by piped-in music in public conveyances, his dissent reflected Brandeis's influence: "Liberty in the constitutional sense must mean more than freedom from unlawful governmental restraint; it must include privacy as well, if it is to be a repository of freedom. The right to be left alone is indeed the beginning of all freedom."

The 1961 decision in ***Mapp* v. *Ohio*** (see Chapter Ten), in which the Court applied the exclusionary rule to the states as a way of putting "teeth" into the Fourth Amendment, was also proclaimed in the context of protecting privacy. Without the suppression of illegally acquired evidence, said Justice Clark, "the freedom from state invasions of privacy would be so ephemeral and so neatly severed from its conceptual nexus with the freedom from all brutish means of coercing evidence as not to merit this Court's high regard as a freedom "implicit in the concept of ordered liberty." The same term witnessed an unsuccessful challenge in *Poe* v. *Ullman* to Connecticut's law banning the use of birth control devices. Dissenting, Justice Harlan drew an analogy between the Connecticut law and the protections of the Fourth Amendment:

> Certainly the safeguarding of the home does not follow merely from the sanctity of property rights. The home derives its preeminence as the seat of family life. And the integrity of that life is something so fundamental that it has been found to draw to its

> protection the principles of more than one explicitly granted Constitutional right. . . . Of this whole "private realm of family life" it is difficult to imagine what is more private or more intimate than a husband and wife's marital relations. . . . [T]he intimacy of husband and wife is necessarily an essential and accepted feature of the institution of marriage, an institution which the State not only must allow, but which always and in every age it has fostered and protected. It is one thing when the State exerts its power either to forbid extra-marital sexuality altogether, or to say who may marry, but it is quite another when, having acknowledged a marriage and the intimacies inherent in it, it undertakes to regulate by means of the criminal law the details of that intimacy. . . .

Thus, by 1961, thinking about privacy had evolved well beyond Warren and Brandeis's article of 1890. The rudiments of a new constitutional right were at hand.

INVIGORATING A RIGHT OF PRIVACY

The Connecticut anticontraceptive statute came before the Court again in 1965 in ***Griswold* v. *Connecticut***. "Any person who uses any drug, medicinal article or instrument for the purpose of preventing conception," declared the act, "shall be fined not less than fifty dollars or imprisoned not less than sixty days nor more than one year or be both fined and imprisoned." The law had been on the books since 1879, but this was apparently only the second time anyone had been charged. Arrested and convicted were the state director of Planned Parenthood and a medical professor at Yale. Both had given instruction and advice to married persons.

Though it violated no express provision in the Constitution, the ban foundered on the right of privacy implicit in the Constitution. For the majority, Justice Douglas announced that no fewer than eight amendments (he named the First, Third, Fourth, Fifth, Sixth, Eighth, Ninth, and Fourteenth) "have penumbras, formed by emanations from those guarantees that give them life and substance." In other words, the specific guarantees in the Constitution implied others, equally important though unenumerated. By impinging on "an intimate relation of husband and wife . . ." the statute violated "a right of privacy older than the Bill of Rights. . . ." (An astronomical term, **penumbra** is the partial shadow surrounding a complete shadow in an eclipse.)

If privacy is a penumbral right, how far does it extend? Two years later in ***Loving* v. *Virginia***, the Court struck down Virginia's law banning interracial marriages. Relying mainly on the equal protection clause, Chief Justice Warren also drew authority from the constitutionally protected "freedom to marry"—"one of the vital personal rights essential to the orderly pursuit of happiness by free men." (*Loving* is reprinted in Chapter Fourteen.) Then a 1968 decision, *Stanley* v. *Georgia*, invalidated a state law forbidding private possession of obscene material. Combining privacy as well as First Amendment interests, Justice Marshall reasoned, "Whatever may be the justifications for other statutes regulating obscenity, we do not think they reach into the privacy of one's home."

Griswold formed the basis of *Eisenstadt* v. *Baird*, a 1972 challenge to a Massachusetts statute that confined distribution of contraceptive devices to married people. According to Justice Brennan:

> If under *Griswold* the distribution of contraceptives to married persons cannot be prohibited, a ban on distribution to unmarried persons would be equally impermissible. . . . If the right of privacy means anything, it is the right of the individual, married or single,

> to be free from unwarranted governmental intrusion into matters so fundamentally affecting a person as the decision whether to bear or beget a child.

ABORTION

Abortion laws also affected the decision to bear a child. If a state could not proscribe birth control devices, could it nonetheless ban most abortions?

Nationalizing a Right to Abortion. The landmark 7–2 decision in ***Roe* v. *Wade*** (1973) provided an answer to that question. Stoking the flames of a political conflagration, Justice Blackmun's majority opinion acknowledged abortion as an aspect of the constitutionally protected right of privacy. "[W]hether it be founded in the Fourteenth Amendment's concept of personal liberty and restrictions upon state action, as we feel it is, or . . . in the Ninth Amendment's reservation of rights to the people, [it] is broad enough to encompass a woman's decision whether or not to terminate her pregnancy." Yet the right to abortion was not absolute. According to Blackmun,

> [A] state may properly assert important interests in safeguarding health, in maintaining medical standards, and in protecting potential life. At some point in pregnancy, these respective interests become sufficiently compelling to sustain regulation of the factors that govern the abortion decision. The privacy right involved, therefore, cannot be . . . absolute. . . . These interests are separate and distinct. Each grows in substantiality as the woman approaches term and, at a point during pregnancy, each becomes "compelling."

Roe called into question the abortion laws of almost every state. In 1973, 21 states had highly restrictive laws similar to the one from Texas invalidated in *Roe* that permitted only those abortions necessary to preserve the woman's life. Typically, these laws dated from the nineteenth century. An additional 25 states also allowed some forms of therapeutic abortions: When continuation of the pregnancy would seriously impair the woman's health, when the fetus would probably be born with a grave and irremediable mental or physical defect, or when the pregnancy resulted from incest or rape. (These less restrictive statutes embodied some or all of the recommendations of the American Law Institute's Model Penal Code of 1962.) The remaining four states (Alaska, Hawaii, New York, and Washington) had repealed all criminal penalties for both elective and therapeutic abortions performed early in the pregnancy. Under *Roe*, no outright ban in any state would be allowed before the 25th week of pregnancy. According to Blackmun, even then, a need to protect a woman's life or health would always supersede a ban on later-term abortions.

Furthermore, by finding a protection for abortion in the Constitution, the Court nationalized the abortion debate. No longer would a state's abortion laws be the product of clashing interests within its own legislature. After 1973, much of the battle between those who believed *Roe* was right and those who believed it was wrong shifted to Congress, presidential campaigns, and the courts. Moreover, *Roe* reinvigorated debate over the proper role of the Supreme Court as expositor of the Constitution.

Testing the Limits of *Roe*. Those who opposed the new abortion right began almost at once to press for regulations limiting the availability of abortion and discouraging its use.

Bellotti v. *Baird* (1979) invalidated a Massachusetts parental consent requirement for minors seeking an abortion. The decision was based on the lack of an adequate alternative or "bypass" procedure under which an abortion could be performed without parental consent. The Court's position was essentially a compromise: Neither parents nor minor would necessarily have the final word. Under *Bellotti*, a bypass must meet four criteria. First, the minor must be allowed to demonstrate to a third party (such as a judge) that she possesses the maturity to make the decision. Second, even if she is unable to demonstrate maturity, the minor must be allowed to show that the abortion would be in her best interest. Third, the minor's anonymity must be protected. Fourth, the bypass must be conducted speedily. Additionally, as the Court later suggested in *Ayotte* v. *Planned Parenthood* (2006), judges may enjoin application of that part of a notification statute that lacks an emergency health exception, without necessarily invalidating the entire law. Indeed, as of 2021, 38 states (five fewer than in 2016) had parental notification statutes of some sort.

Litigation has also centered on government's discretion to fund some abortions but not others. *Maher* v. *Roe* (1977) upheld Connecticut's policy of granting Medicaid support for therapeutic abortions but not for elective ones. Against the state's argument that it could constitutionally discourage abortions in this fashion because of its rational interest in promoting childbirth, opponents charged that paying for childbirth but not for elective abortions burdened the exercise of a constitutional right, financially forcing poor women to carry a pregnancy full term.

The Court extended the *Maher* reasoning to Congress in *Harris* v. *McRae* (1980). The **Hyde Amendment** (so named because of its sponsor, Representative Henry Hyde of Illinois) went a step beyond Connecticut's restriction and barred federal Medicaid funds from being spent even on some medically necessary abortions. Only abortions necessary to save the life of the woman or those where the pregnancy results from rape or incest qualify. A majority of five concluded that a state was not required to pay for those Medicaid abortions for which federal reimbursement under the Hyde Amendment was unavailable. Neither was the Hyde Amendment itself unconstitutional. It placed no government obstacle, concluded the majority, in the way of an abortion. A poor woman was no worse off than if no Medicaid funds were available for any medical needs.

Thornburgh v. *American College of Obstetricians and Gynecologists* (1986) marked the last time that the Court struck down a comprehensive scheme of abortion regulations. At stake was a Pennsylvania statute governing consent, information, record keeping, determination of viability, care of the fetus, and the need for a second physician in postviability abortions. None of the challenged provisions survived.

Impact of a Changing Court. The 7–2 majority for *Roe* in 1973 had shrunk to 5–4 by 1986. Retiring immediately after *Thornburgh*, Chief Justice Burger had already let it be known that he thought *Roe* was wrongly decided. The division on the bench in 1987 therefore made Justice Powell's retirement and the designation of a successor all the more critical. More than anything else, the widely held conviction that Judge Robert Bork would undermine the 1973 abortion decision led to his rejection by the Senate when President Reagan nominated him to take Powell's seat. (Bork's confirmation battle is reviewed in the Introduction.) Pro-choice and pro-life activists alike awaited the views of Justice Anthony Kennedy.

His views became partly known in *Webster* v. *Reproductive Health Services* (1989). In dispute was a Missouri statute, which (1) declared in its preamble that life begins at conception, (2) prohibited abortions performed in public facilities or by public employees, (3) prohibited public funding of abortion counseling, and (4) required viability testing prior to an abortion in a pregnancy of 20 weeks or more. Kennedy and four other justices voted to uphold the act. According to Chief Justice Rehnquist's opinion of the Court, the preamble merely expressed a point of view, and the restrictions on use of funds were valid under the Court's own prior decisions. The viability testing provision (the primary focus of both the majority and dissenting opinions) was constitutional because it "permissibly furthers the State's interest in protecting human life." Yet there were not five votes to overturn *Roe* v. *Wade* outright. Writing separately, Justice Scalia would have made that move. Chief Justice Rehnquist and Justice White, both dissenters in *Roe*, might have been expected to agree. Justice O'Connor, however, was not prepared to go that far, preferring instead to accept the statute as not "impos[ing] an *undue burden* on a woman's abortion decision" (emphasis added).

Nonetheless, *Roe* did not survive unscathed. In addition to upholding a statute which the *Thornburgh* majority of 1986 surely would have struck down, the Court went out of its way to lay aside *Roe*'s trimester analysis which had rested on a balancing of the woman's decision to abort, the state's interest in her health, and the state's interest in prenatal life. Moreover, recall that *Roe* had declared the abortion right to be "fundamental," meaning that limits on the right would be approved only for "compelling" reasons. After *Webster*, at least in the view of Rehnquist, White, Kennedy, and Scalia, limits on abortion were now in the category with restrictions on many other forms of behavior and would be constitutional as long as they were "reasonable." For O'Connor, regulations were permissible unless they imposed an "**undue burden**" on the woman. As a result, the abortion right, practically speaking, occupied a lower category in the ranking of constitutionally protected liberties.

The Remnants of *Roe*. The retirements of Brennan in 1990 and Marshall in 1991 meant that the views of replacement Justices Souter and Thomas would be decisive. With the number of *Roe*'s stalwart defenders reduced to two, both pro-life and pro-choice camps awaited the outcome of ***Planned Parenthood* v. *Casey*** (1992). Under review was a Pennsylvania law that imposed several conditions for obtaining an abortion, including informed consent, a 24-hour waiting period, parental consent for minors, spousal notification, and record-keeping requirements for medical personnel. The decision surprised both sides in the abortion controversy. It was neither the complete victory pro-life groups had sought nor the broad defeat pro-choice forces had feared. While the Court upheld all elements of the statute except the spousal notification provision, the fifth vote to overturn *Roe* v. *Wade* again failed to materialize. Confessing "reservations" about the correctness of *Roe* in 1973, Justices Souter, Kennedy, and O'Connor nonetheless reaffirmed what they termed *the central holding* of *Roe*, that abortion involved a constitutionally protected liberty that states were forbidden to burden unduly. Coupled with *Roe*'s avowed champions Blackmun and Stevens, the alignment left *Roe*'s avowed adversaries (White, Rehnquist, Scalia, and Thomas) in the minority.

Stenberg v. *Carhart* (2000) raised a different issue. As had 30 other states, Nebraska banned a specific late-term medical procedure which it called "partial birth" abortion. But five justices held that "the woman's right to choose" overrode the state's interests in protecting the unborn and "the partially-born," preserving the integrity of the medical profession, and "erecting a barrier to infanticide." Nebraska's law fell for two reasons: First, its wording was vague and thus imposed an undue burden by effectively prohibiting legal abortions as well. Second, the statute lacked the health exception as mandated by *Roe* and *Casey*.

In 2003, President Bush signed into law the first national ban on the same late-term abortion procedure that Nebraska had attempted to prohibit. Like Nebraska's, the **Partial Birth Abortion Ban Act** contains no exception for a woman's health. In sustaining the statute, *Gonzales* v. *Carhart* (2007) became the Court's first decision upholding the prohibition of a specific abortion procedure, as well as its first approval of an abortion regulation with no health exception. Led by *Stenberg* dissenter Kennedy, a majority of five deemed the law sufficiently specific and, more importantly, deferred to Congress' finding that the procedure was never medically necessary. Accordingly, absence of a health exception did not impose an undue burden on a woman's right to terminate her pregnancy. With Justice Alito voting to uphold a law that Justice O'Connor probably would have found invalid, *Carhart* was another reminder that presidential elections have constitutional consequences.

Combined, *Casey* and *Carhart* point to several conclusions about the constitutional status of abortion. First, abortion no longer has status as a fundamental right but has intermediate constitutional protection. Second, and as a consequence of the first, total or near-total bans on previability abortions are almost certainly unconstitutional. Third, the Court will accept restrictions on abortions that would have been quickly rejected two decades ago. However, just how numerous and how burdensome such restrictions may be, beyond the terms of the 2003 statute, remains the true focus of debate—and litigation, as *Whole Woman's Health* v. *Hellerstedt* (2016) illustrated.

Whole Woman's Health tested the validity of two restrictions that Texas imposed: An admitting privileges requirement for abortion physicians and a surgical center requirement for abortion facilities. The Court found both stipulations constitutionally deficient in what was the most significant abortion ruling in a decade. First, the decision marked the first time that Justice Kennedy had voted to strike down an abortion law in its entirety. Second, and more important, Justice Breyer's opinion made clear that the undue burden standard from *Casey* in 1992 required reviewing courts to examine not only a regulation's impact on access to abortion but the degree to which a regulation purporting to protect the health of women undergoing abortions was medically justified.

Chief Justice Roberts was among the three dissenters in *Whole Women's Health*, yet when a Louisiana law nearly identical to the Texas law came before the Court in ***June Medical Services* v. *Russo*** (2020), he was in the majority that found it unconstitutional as well. Left in doubt as a result of *June Medical* was the Court's true fealty to the test from *Planned Parenthood* v. *Casey*. Thus, as much as at any time since 1973, a woman's freedom to terminate a pregnancy now depends heavily on what degree of regulation judges at all levels are prepared to allow.

A DEVELOPING CONCEPT

As the previous sections demonstrate, a right once acknowledged invites application to new situations. The joint opinion in *Casey* recognized as much: "At the heart of liberty is the right to define one's own concept of existence, of meaning, of the universe, and of the mystery of human life." And as the Court has addressed personal autonomy in other contexts, the justices have tended to ground it more on the substantive "liberty" that derives from the due process clause, rather than, strictly speaking, on a right of privacy itself.

The Right to Die. Another aspect of autonomy concerns the refusal of medical treatment and, more recently, the choice of the manner and timing of one's death. Each is made more complex because medical technology can now sustain life well past the point where natural forces would have once brought death. The complexity is only heightened when a patient is comatose.

The seminal decision is *In re Quinlan* (1976), in which the New Jersey Supreme Court held that the father of Karen Quinlan could approve the removal of the respirator from his daughter, who had suffered severe brain damage in an accident. In the state court's view, Karen Quinlan's right of privacy under the U.S. Constitution included the right to terminate treatment. The court dismissed her previous statements on the subject because they were both casual and equivocal. Instead, it allowed her family (subject to approval by an ethics committee) to make the decision for her. The "only practical way to prevent destruction of the right is to permit the guardian and family of Karen to render their best judgment . . . as to whether she would exercise it in these circumstances."

The general liberty of the Fourteenth Amendment formed the basis of the U.S. Supreme Court's first consideration of the question. In *Cruzan* v. *Director* (1990), the Missouri Supreme Court had turned back the efforts of the parents of Nancy Cruzan to terminate artificial nutrition and hydration for their daughter, who was living in a vegetative condition following an automobile accident. Without nutrition and hydration, Nancy Cruzan would of course die. In the state court's view, because Nancy Cruzan had not complied with Missouri's "living will" statutes and because there was no "clear and convincing, inherently reliable evidence" of the patient's wishes not to continue life under such circumstances, treatment would continue. In other words, short of persuasive evidence that the patient would reject treatment if she could, the presumption was that she would choose treatment. (**Living wills** set the terms for the withdrawal or withholding of life-sustaining treatment for patients with incurable conditions when the patients are incapable of making decisions regarding their medical treatment.)

On appeal, five justices of the U.S. Supreme Court found the state's standard constitutionally acceptable. According to Chief Justice Rehnquist, a state may require "clear and convincing evidence" (as opposed to the less demanding standard of "preponderance of the evidence") of an incompetent patient's wishes to refuse medical treatment. For the four dissenting justices who regarded the liberty interest at stake as "fundamental," Missouri's requirement of heightened proof was unconstitutionally intrusive into the patient's right to refuse treatment. *Cruzan* was partly responsible for passage of the **Patient Self-Determination Act** in 1991. Under this federal law, hospital employees must ask all patients if they want to plan for their death by making a living will or by designating a health care proxy, to make decisions should they become incapacitated. (In December 1990, Nancy Cruzan died in a Missouri hospital 12 days after a feeding tube was removed under a court order requested by her parents. Following the U.S. Supreme Court's decision, the trial court concluded that the record revealed "clear and convincing evidence" of her wishes not to sustain her life artificially under the circumstances.)

As is sometimes true with a "first step" in constitutional law, *Cruzan* raised as many questions as it answered. Read narrowly, the decision at most acknowledged the right of a conscious and competent person to refuse medical treatment. The Court divided, after all, on the standard of proof that the state could require with respect to the wishes of a comatose patient. Read broadly, the right to refuse medical treatment was an aspect of something far more encompassing: The right to determine the timing of one's own death.

Not surprisingly, terminally ill patients and their doctors challenged laws banning assisted suicide. The courtroom debate thus shifted from the circumstances under which government could require the administration of life-sustaining nutrition and hydration (i.e., forcing a person to remain alive) to the state's authority to deny the administration of life-ending medication (i.e., forbidding the active intervention of one person in ending another's life). In *Compassion in Dying* v. *Washington*, the Ninth Circuit Court of Appeals ruled in 1995 that Washington State's ban on assisted suicide, at least with respect to physicians and terminally ill patients, violated the liberty protected by the due process clause of the Fourteenth Amendment. While falling short of a "fundamental" liberty, the Ninth Circuit deemed the liberty interest nonetheless "significant," overriding the state's interest in preserving life. In *Quill* v. *Vacco* (1996), the Second Circuit decreed the same fate for a similar statute in New York but did so on different grounds. That court saw no valid difference between competent persons who refuse treatment (thus ending their lives) and competent persons who seek treatment to end their lives. Thus, the state lacked legitimate reasons, as required by the equal protection clause of the Fourteenth Amendment, for treating similarly circumstanced or situated people differently.

In *Washington* v. *Glucksberg* and *Vacco* v. *Quill* (1997), the Supreme Court reversed both appeals courts. Denying the existence of any constitutional right to commit suicide or to seek the assistance of another in doing so, the High Court preferred to leave the difficult moral and social choices in this area to state legislatures and state courts. Nonetheless, concurring opinions indicated that as many as five justices would reject any state's attempt to block access to pain-relieving medication where its administration would hasten a patient's death.

Sexual Orientation and Marriage Equality. A person's sexual orientation and practice also involve a dimension of autonomy, an issue the Supreme Court squarely confronted in 1986 in *Bowers* v. *Hardwick*. Five justices upheld the constitutionality of Georgia's sodomy statute, which made criminal certain combinations of private parts. The law applied to heterosexual as well as homosexual behavior, but Justice White's opinion of the Court regarded the act as if it made only the latter criminal.

The 5–4 split revealed that no consensus existed on the Court concerning what privacy encompassed. Since *Griswold*, privacy's "scorecard" in the Supreme Court had been good. Many observers were surprised that five balked at an extension. Close reading of Justice White's majority opinion and the principal dissent by Justice Blackmun provides insight. To discover what rights, though not expressly mentioned, are constitutionally protected, White looked to two sources: Those "implicit in the concept of ordered liberty" and those "deeply rooted in the nation's history and tradition." Framing the investigation in this way, White concluded "that neither of these formulations would extend a fundamental right to homosexuals to engage in acts of consensual sodomy." For Blackmun, the majority asked the wrong question. The case was not "about 'a fundamental right to engage in homosexual sodomy.' . . . Rather, this case is about 'the most comprehensive of rights . . . the right to be let alone.' [W]hat the Court really has refused to recognize is the fundamental interest all individuals have in controlling the nature of their intimate associations with others." White scanned a category of rights. Blackmun focused on a constitutionally protected realm of intimate association.

The Court revisited sexual intimacy in ***Lawrence* v. *Texas*** (2003), which not only invalidated a statute that criminalized same-sex sodomy but went out of its way to impugn the intellectual integrity of White's opinion in *Bowers*.

As suggested by *Lawrence* and Scalia's fierce dissent in that case, the Supreme Court next confronted laws defining marriage as a union only between a woman and a man. In 1999, the Vermont Supreme Court had held that the common benefits clause in the state constitution entitled same-sex couples to the legal benefits and protections offered married couples in Vermont (*Baker* v. *State*, 1999). The decision led the state legislature to authorize same-sex "civil unions" that amounted to ordinary marriages in everything but name. Other states then recognized similar unions. Relying on its state constitution, the Supreme Judicial Court of Massachusetts moved further, ruling that same-sex couples have a legal right to marry (*Goodridge* v. *Dept. of Public Health*, 2003). Yet in 1996 President Clinton had signed into law the **Defense of Marriage Act** which provided that no "State, territory, or possession of the United States, or Indian tribe, shall be required to give effect to any public act, record, or judicial proceeding of any other State, territory, possession, or tribe respecting a relationship between persons of the same sex that is treated as a marriage under the laws of such other State, territory, possession, or tribe, or a right or claim arising from such relationship." Moreover, for purposes of federal law, the statute defined "marriage" to mean "only a legal union between one man and one woman as husband and wife" and the word "*spouse*" to refer "only to a person of the opposite sex who is a husband or a wife." Many states then enacted similar definitions of marriage either in statutes or their constitutions. However, a remarkable, perhaps unprecedented, tide of change both in law and public opinion was clearly already underway. In 2016, the Supreme Court invalidated the Clinton-era Defense of Marriage Act in *United States* v. *Windsor* using the equal protection component of the Fifth Amendment that is explained in the following chapter. Indeed, by 2015, same-sex marriage had been allowed (either by lower courts or the political process) in 37 states and the District of Columbia: Alabama, Alaska, Arizona, California, Colorado, Connecticut, Delaware, Florida, Hawaii, Idaho, Illinois, Indiana, Iowa, Kansas, Maine, Maryland, Massachusetts, Minnesota, Montana, Nevada, New Hampshire, New Jersey, New Mexico, New York, North Carolina, Oklahoma, Oregon, Pennsylvania, Rhode Island, South Carolina, Utah, Vermont, Virginia, Washington, West Virginia, Wisconsin, and Wyoming. Thus, the High Court's ruling in ***Obergefell* v. *Hodges*** (2015), making same-sex marriage allowable throughout the United States, was hardly a surprise. Justice Kennedy's majority opinion grounded the decision on both the Fourteenth Amendment's due process clause and the same amendment's equal protection clause. Moreover, the ruling directed states to recognize a marriage between two people of the same sex that was legally licensed and performed in another state.

Questions of marriage and sexual practice, like other privacy issues, will continue to arise particularly as they intersect with religious freedom. Heightened sensitivity throughout the United States to issues of individual privacy virtually guarantees a continued involvement by judges in demarcating the dimensions of the constitutional right "to be let alone."

KEY TERMS

privacy
informational privacy
private law
public law
penumbra
Hyde Amendment
undue burden
Partial Birth Abortion Ban Act
living wills
Patient Self-Determination Act
Defense of Marriage Act (DOMA)

QUERIES

1. In his opinion in *Griswold* v. *Connecticut*, why would Justice Douglas have relied on "penumbras" from the Bill of Rights rather than the Fourteenth Amendment's due process clause?

2. Chapter Two posed the question, what is "the Constitution" that justices interpret? What answers to that question are suggested by the several opinions filed in *Griswold* v. *Connecticut*?

3. Consider Chief Justice Roberts's concurring opinion in *June Medical Services* v. *Russo* alongside his dissent in *South Dakota* v. *Wayfair, Inc.*, a case reprinted in Chapter Six. From them, what do you glean about his views on *stare decisis*? How might the chief justice react were the Court squarely to confront a case testing the continuing viability of *Roe* v. *Wade*?

4. In the wake of *Obergefell* v. *Hodges*, some states have enacted measures described as "religious freedom laws" that seek to protect individuals, businesses and organizations from legal action if they deny services to lesbian, gay, bisexual and transgender people when the refusal is based on sincerely held religious beliefs or convictions. What constitutional questions do such laws present? Consider this question in light of *Masterpiece Cakeshop* v. *Colorado Civil Rights Commission* (2018), reprinted in Chapter Twelve.

SELECTED READINGS

Beaney, William M. "The Constitutional Right to Privacy in the Supreme Court." *Supreme Court Review* 212, 1962.

Carpenter, Dale. *Flagrant Conduct: The Story of Lawrence v. Texas*. New York: Norton, 2013.

Craig, Barbara, and David O'Brien. *Abortion and American Politics*. Chatham, NJ: Chatham House, 1993.

Garrow, David J. *Liberty and Sexuality: The Right to Privacy and the Making of Roe v. Wade*. New York: Macmillan, 1994.

Glenn, Richard A. *The Right to Privacy*. Santa Barbara, CA: ABC-CLIO, 2003.

Hull, N. E. H., and Peter Charles Hoffer. *Roe v. Wade: The Abortion Rights Controversy in American History*, 3rd ed. Lawrence: University Press of Kansas, 2021.

Mezey, Susan Gluck. *Queers in Court: Gay Rights Law and Public Policy*. Lanham, MD: Rowman & Littlefield, 2007.

Warren, Samuel, and Louis D. Brandeis. "The Right to Privacy." *4 Harvard Law Review 220*, 1890.

Wilson, Joshua. *The New States of Abortion Politics*. Redwood City, CA: Stanford University Press, 2016.

I. INVIGORATING A RIGHT OF PRIVACY

Griswold v. *Connecticut*
381 U.S. 479, 85 S.Ct. 1678, 14 L.Ed. 2d 510 (1965)

http://caselaw.findlaw.com/us-supreme-court/381/479.html

A Connecticut statute of 1879 made the use of contraceptives a criminal offense. Estelle Griswold, executive director of the Planned Parenthood League of Connecticut, was convicted on a charge of having violated the statute as an accessory by giving information, instruction, and advice to married persons as a means of preventing conception. A professor at the Yale Medical School, serving as medical director for the league, was a codefendant. The Appellate Division of the Circuit Court and the Supreme Court of Errors of Connecticut affirmed the conviction. Majority: Douglas, Brennan, Clark, Goldberg, Harlan, Warren, White. Dissenting: Black, Stewart.

Mr. Justice Douglas delivered the opinion of the Court. . . .

Coming to the merits, we are met with a wide range of questions that implicate the Due Process Clause of the Fourteenth Amendment. Overtones of some arguments suggest that *Lochner* v. *New York* . . . should be our guide. But we decline that invitation. . . . We do not sit as a super-legislature to determine the wisdom, need, and propriety of laws that touch economic problems, business affairs, or social conditions. This law, however, operates directly on an intimate relation of husband and wife and their physician's role in one aspect of that relation. . . .

[S]pecific guarantees in the Bill of Rights have penumbras, formed by emanations from those guarantees that help give them life and substance. . . . Various guarantees create zones of privacy. The right of association contained in the penumbra of the First Amendment is one. . . . The Third Amendment in its prohibition against the quartering of soldiers "in any house" in time of peace without the consent of the owner is another facet of that privacy. The Fourth Amendment explicitly affirms the "right of the people to be secure in their persons, houses, papers, and effects against unreasonable searches and seizures." The Fifth Amendment in its Self-Incrimination Clause enables the citizen to create a zone of privacy which government may not force him to surrender to his detriment. The Ninth Amendment provides: "The enumeration in the Constitution, of certain rights, shall not be construed to deny or disparage others retained by the people." . . .

The present case, then, concerns a relationship lying within the zone of privacy created by several fundamental constitutional guarantees. And it concerns a law which, in forbidding the use of contraceptives rather than regulating their manufacture or sale, seeks to achieve its goals by means having a maximum destructive impact upon that relationship. Such a law cannot stand in light of the familiar principle, so often applied by this Court, that a "governmental purpose to control or prevent activities constitutionally subject to state regulation may not be achieved by means which sweep unnecessarily broadly and thereby invade the area of protected freedom." Would we allow the police to search the sacred precincts of marital bedrooms for telltale signs of the use of contraceptives? The very idea is repulsive to the notions of privacy surrounding the marriage relationship.

We deal with a right of privacy older than the Bill of Rights—older than our political parties, older than our school system. Marriage is a coming together for better or for worse, hopefully enduring, and intimate to the degree of being sacred. It is an association that promotes a way of life, not causes; a harmony in living, not political faiths; a bilateral loyalty, not commercial or social projects. Yet it is an association for as noble a purpose as any involved in our prior decisions.

Reversed.

MR. JUSTICE GOLDBERG, whom THE CHIEF JUSTICE and MR. JUSTICE BRENNAN join, concurring. . . .

The Ninth Amendment to the Constitution may be regarded by some as a recent discovery and may be forgotten by others, but since 1791 it has been a basic part of the Constitution which we are sworn to uphold. To hold that a right so basic and fundamental and so deep-rooted in our society as the right of privacy in marriage may be infringed because that right is not guaranteed in so many words by the first eight amendments to the Constitution is to ignore the Ninth Amendment and to give it no effect whatsoever. . . .

Nor am I turning somersaults with history in arguing that the Ninth Amendment is relevant in a case dealing with a State's infringement of a fundamental right. While the Ninth Amendment—and indeed the entire Bill of Rights—originally concerned restrictions upon federal power, the subsequently enacted Fourteenth Amendment prohibits the States as well from abridging fundamental personal liberties. And, the Ninth Amendment, in indicating that not all such liberties are specifically mentioned in the first eight amendments, is surely relevant in showing the existence of other fundamental personal rights, now protected from state, as well as federal, infringement. In sum, the Ninth Amendment simply lends strong support to the view that the "liberty" protected by the Fifth and Fourteenth Amendments from infringement by the Federal Government or the States is not restricted to rights specifically mentioned in the first eight amendments. . . .

MR. JUSTICE HARLAN, concurring in the judgment. . . .

In my view, the proper constitutional inquiry in this case is whether this . . . statute infringes the Due Process Clause of the Fourteenth Amendment because the enactment violates basic values "implicit in the concept of ordered liberty." For reasons stated at length in my dissenting opinion in *Poe* v. *Ullman*, I believe that it does. While the relevant inquiry may be aided by resort to one or more of the provisions of the Bill of Rights, it is not dependent on them or any of their radiations. The Due Process Clause . . . stands . . . on its own bottom. . . .

MR. JUSTICE WHITE, concurring . . . [omitted].

MR. JUSTICE BLACK, with whom MR. JUSTICE STEWART joins, dissenting. . . .

The Court talks about a constitutional "right of privacy" as though there is some constitutional provision or provisions forbidding any law ever to be passed which might abridge the "privacy" of individuals. But there is not. . . .

. . . I like my privacy as well as the next one, but I am nevertheless compelled to admit that government has a right to invade it unless prohibited by some specific constitutional provision. For these reasons I cannot agree with the Court's judgment and the reasons it gives for holding this Connecticut law unconstitutional. . . .

I think that if properly construed neither the Due Process Clause nor the Ninth Amendment, nor both together, could under any circumstances be a proper basis for invalidating the Connecticut law. I discuss the due process and Ninth Amendment arguments together because on analysis they turn out to be the same thing—merely using different words to claim for this Court and the federal judiciary power to invalidate any legislative act which the judges find irrational, unreasonable or offensive.

The due process argument . . . is based . . . on the premise that this Court is vested with power to invalidate all state laws that it considers to be arbitrary, capricious, unreasonable, or oppressive, or because of this Court's belief that a particular state law under scrutiny has no "rational or justifying purpose," or is offensive to a "sense of fairness and justice." If these formulas based on "natural justice," or others which mean the same thing, are to prevail, they require judges to determine what is or is not constitutional on the basis of their own appraisal of what laws are unwise or unnecessary. The power to make such decisions is of course that of a legislative body. Surely it has to be admitted that no provision of the Constitution specifically gives such blanket power to courts to exercise such a supervisory veto over the wisdom and value of legislative policies and to hold unconstitutional those laws which they believe unwise or dangerous. I readily admit that no legislative body, state or national, should pass laws that can justly be given any of the invidious labels invoked as constitutional excuses to strike down state laws. But perhaps it is not too much to say that no legislative body ever does pass laws without believing that they will accomplish a sane, rational, wise and justifiable purpose. . . . I do not believe that we are granted power by the Due Process Clause or any other constitutional provision or provisions to measure constitutionality by our belief that legislation is arbitrary, capricious or unreasonable, or accomplishes no justifiable purpose, or is offensive to our own notions of "civilized standards of conduct." Such an appraisal of the wisdom of legislation is an attribute of the power to make laws, not of the power to interpret them. The use by federal courts of such a formula or doctrine or whatnot to veto federal or state laws simply takes away from Congress and States the power to make laws based on their own judgment of fairness and wisdom and transfers that power to this Court for ultimate determination—a power which was specifically denied to federal courts by the convention that framed the Constitution. . . .

If any broad, unlimited power to hold laws unconstitutional because they offend what this Court conceives to be "the collective conscience of our people" is vested in this Court by the Ninth Amendment, or any other provision of the Constitution, it was not given by the Framers, but rather has been bestowed on the Court by the Court. . . .

MR. JUSTICE STEWART, with whom MR. JUSTICE BLACK joins, dissenting. . . .

[T]his is an uncommonly silly law. . . .

At the oral argument . . . we were told that the Connecticut law does not "conform to current community standards." But it is not the function of this Court to decide cases on the basis of community standards. . . . If, as I should surely hope, the law before us does not reflect the standards of the people of Connecticut, the people of Connecticut can freely exercise their true Ninth and Tenth Amendment rights to persuade their elected representatives to repeal it. That is the constitutional way to take this law off the books.

II. ABORTION

Roe v. *Wade*
410 U.S. 113, 93 S.Ct. 705, 35 L.Ed. 2d 147 (1973)

http://caselaw.findlaw.com/us-supreme-court/410/113.html

In 1970, Norma McCorvey of Dallas, Texas, wished to terminate her pregnancy. Because Texas law prohibited abortions except those performed by a physician for the purpose of saving the life of the woman (an exception that did not apply to her), she filed suit against Henry Wade, District Attorney of Dallas County, in the U.S. District Court for the Northern District of Texas, claiming that the Texas law was unconstitutional and seeking an injunction against its enforcement. To protect her anonymity, she used the pseudonym of Jane Roe throughout the litigation. The district court held that the state statute was void on its face because it was unconstitutionally vague and overbroad and violated rights protected by the Ninth Amendment, but declined to enjoin further enforcement of the statute. (An attorney helped to arrange for the newborn's adoption later in 1970.) The Supreme Court twice heard oral arguments in the case—in December of 1971 and October of 1972. Majority: Blackmun, Brennan, Burger, Douglas, Marshall, Powell, Stewart. Dissenting: Rehnquist, White.

Mr. Justice Blackmun delivered the opinion of the Court. . . .

The principal thrust of the appellant's attack on the Texas statutes is that they improperly invade a right, said to be possessed by the pregnant woman, to choose to terminate her pregnancy. Appellant would discover this right in the concept of personal "liberty" embodied in the Fourteenth Amendment's Due Process Clause; or in personal, marital, familial, and sexual privacy said to be protected by the Bill of Rights or its penumbras. . . . Before addressing this claim, we feel it desirable briefly to survey, in several aspects, the history of abortion, for such insight as that history may afford us, and then to examine the state purposes and interests behind the criminal abortion laws.

It perhaps is not generally appreciated that the restrictive criminal abortion laws in effect in a majority of States today derive from statutory changes effected, for the most part, in the latter half of the 19th century. . . .

Three reasons have been advanced to explain historically the enactment of criminal abortion laws in the 19th century and to justify their continued existence.

It has been argued occasionally that these laws were the product of a Victorian social concern to discourage illicit sexual conduct. Texas, however, does not advance this justification in the present case, and it appears that no court or commentator has taken the argument seriously. . . .

A second reason is concerned with abortion as a medical procedure. When most criminal abortion laws were first enacted, the procedure was a hazardous one for the woman. This was particularly true prior to the development of antisepsis. . . . Abortion mortality was high. . . .

Modern medical techniques have altered this situation. . . . Mortality rates for women undergoing early abortions, where the procedure is legal, appear to be as low or lower than the rates for normal childbirth. . . . Of course, important state interests in the area of health and medical standards do remain. The State has a legitimate interest in seeing to it that abortion, like any other medical procedure, is performed under circumstances that insure maximum safety for the patient. . . . Moreover, the risk to the woman increases as her pregnancy continues. Thus the State retains a definite interest in protecting the woman's own health and safety when an abortion is proposed at a late stage of pregnancy.

The third reason is the State's interest—some phrase it in terms of duty—in protecting prenatal life. Some of the argument for this justification rests on the theory that a new human life is present from the moment of conception. The State's interest and general obligation to protect life then extends, it is argued, to prenatal life. Only when the life of the pregnant mother herself is at stake, balanced against the life she carries within her, should the interests of the embryo or fetus not prevail. Logically, of course, a legitimate state interest in this area need not stand or fall on acceptance of the belief that life begins at conception or at some other point prior to live birth. In assessing the State's interest, recognition may be given to the less rigid claim that as long as at least potential life is involved, the State may assert interests beyond the protection of the pregnant woman alone. . . .

It is with these interests, and the weight to be attached to them, that this case is concerned.

The Constitution does not explicitly mention any right of privacy. In a line of decisions, however, going back perhaps as far as *Union Pacific R. Co.* v. *Botsford* (1891), the Court has recognized that a right of personal privacy, or a guarantee of certain areas or zones of privacy, does exist under the Constitution. In varying contexts the Court or individual Justices have indeed found at least the roots of that right in the First Amendment . . . in the Fourth and Fifth Amendments . . . in the penumbras of the Bill of Rights . . . in the Ninth Amendment . . . or in the concept of liberty guaranteed by the first section of the Fourteenth Amendment. . . . These decisions make it clear that only personal rights that can be deemed "fundamental" or "implicit in the concept of ordered liberty" . . . are included in this guarantee of personal privacy. They also make it clear that the right has some extension to activities relating to marriage . . . procreation, contraception, family relationships, and child rearing and education. . . .

We therefore conclude that the right of personal privacy includes the abortion decision, but that this right is not unqualified and must be considered against important state interests in regulation. . . . [A]t some point the state interests as to protection of health, medical standards, and prenatal life, become dominant. . . .

Where certain "fundamental rights" are involved, the Court has held that regulation limiting these rights may be justified only by a "compelling state interest," and that legislative enactments must be narrowly drawn to express only the legitimate state interests at stake. . . .

The appellee and certain amici argue that the fetus is a "person" within the language and meaning of the Fourteenth Amendment. . . .

The Constitution does not define "person" in so many words. Section 1 of the Fourteenth Amendment contains three references to "person." The first, in defining "citizens," speaks of "persons born or naturalized in the United States." The word also appears both in the Due Process Clause and in the Equal Protection Clause. "Person" is used in other places in the Constitution. . . . But in nearly all these instances, the use of the word is such that it has application only postnatally. None indicates, with any assurance, that it has any possible prenatal application. . . .

Texas urges that, apart from the Fourteenth Amendment, life begins at conception and is present throughout pregnancy, and that, therefore, the State has a compelling interest in protecting that life from and after conception. We need not resolve the difficult question of when life begins. When those trained in the respective disciplines of medicine, philosophy, and theology are unable to arrive at any consensus, the judiciary, at this point in the development of man's knowledge, is not in a position to speculate as to the answer. . . .

We do not agree that, by adopting one theory of life, Texas may override the rights of the pregnant woman that are at stake. We repeat, however, that the State does have an important and legitimate interest in preserving and protecting the health of the pregnant woman, whether she be a resident of the State or a nonresident who seeks medical consultation and treatment there, and that it has still another important and legitimate interest in protecting the potentiality of human life. These interests are separate and distinct. Each grows in substantiality as the woman approaches term and, at a point during pregnancy, each becomes "compelling."

With respect to the State's important and legitimate interest in the health of the mother, the "compelling" point, in the light of present medical knowledge, is at approximately the end of the first trimester. This is so because of the now established medical fact . . . that until the end of the first trimester mortality in abortion is less than mortality in normal childbirth. It follows that, from and after this point, a State may regulate the abortion procedure to the extent that the regulation reasonably relates to the preservation and protection of maternal health. Examples of permissible state regulation in this area are requirements as to the qualifications of the person who is to perform the abortion; as to the licensure of that person; as to the facility in which the procedure is to be performed, that is, whether it must be a hospital or may be a clinic or some other place of less-than-hospital status; as to the licensing of the facility; and the like.

This means, on the other hand, that, for the period of pregnancy prior to this "compelling" point, the attending physician, in consultation with his patient, is free to determine, without regulation by the State, that in his medical judgment the patient pregnancy should be terminated. If that decision is reached, the judgment may be effectuated by an abortion free of interference by the State. . . .

With respect to the State's important and legitimate interest in potential life, the "compelling" point is at viability. This is so because the fetus then presumably has the capability of meaningful life outside the mother's womb. State regulation protective of fetal life after viability thus has both logical and biological justifications. If the State is interested in protecting fetal life after viability, it may go so far as to proscribe abortion during that period except when it is necessary to preserve the life or health of the mother.

Measured against these standards . . . [t]he statute, therefore, cannot survive the constitutional attack made upon it here. . . .

To summarize and to repeat: A state criminal abortion statute of the current Texas type, that excepts from criminality only a life-saving procedure on behalf of the mother, without regard to pregnancy stage and without recognition of the other interests involved, is violative of the Due Process Clause of the Fourteenth Amendment.

a) For the stage prior to approximately the end of the first trimester, the abortion decision and its effectuation must be left to the medical judgment of the pregnant woman's attending physician.
b) For the stage subsequent to approximately the end of the first trimester, the State, in promoting its interest in the health of the mother, may, if it chooses, regulate the abortion procedure in ways that are reasonably related to maternal health.
c) For the stage subsequent to viability, the State in promoting its interest in the potentiality of human life may, if it chooses, regulate, and even proscribe, abortion except where it is necessary, in appropriate medical judgment, for the preservation of the life or health of the mother. . . .

The judgment of the District Court . . . is affirmed. . . .

It is so ordered.

MR. CHIEF JUSTICE BURGER, concurring . . . [omitted].

MR. JUSTICE DOUGLAS, concurring . . . [omitted].

MR. JUSTICE STEWART, concurring . . . [omitted].

MR. JUSTICE WHITE, with whom MR. JUSTICE REHNQUIST joins, dissenting . . . [omitted].

MR. JUSTICE REHNQUIST, dissenting. . . .

I agree with the statement of Mr. Justice Stewart in his concurring opinion that the "liberty," against deprivation of which without due process the Fourteenth Amendment protects, embraces more than the rights found in the Bill of Rights. But that liberty is not guaranteed absolutely against deprivation, but only against deprivation without due process of law. The test traditionally applied in the area of social and economic legislation is whether or not a law such as that challenged has a rational relation to a valid state objective. . . . But the Court's sweeping invalidation of any restrictions on abortion during the first trimester is impossible to justify under that standard, and the conscious weighing of competing factors which the Court's opinion apparently substitutes for the established test is far more appropriate to a legislative judgment than to a judicial one. . . .

While the Court's opinion quotes from the dissent of Mr. Justice Holmes in *Lochner* v. *New York* . . . the result it reaches is more closely attuned to the majority opinion of Mr. Justice Peckham in that case. As in *Lochner* and similar cases applying substantive due process standards to economic and social welfare legislation, the adoption of the compelling state interest standard will inevitably require this Court to examine the legislative policies and pass on the wisdom of these policies in the very process of deciding whether a particular state interest put forward may or may not be "compelling." The decision here to break the term of pregnancy into three distinct terms and to outline the permissible restrictions the State may impose in each one, for example, partakes more of judicial legislation than it does of a determination of the intent of the drafters of the Fourteenth Amendment.

The fact that a majority of the States, reflecting after all the majority sentiment in those States, have had restrictions on abortions for at least a century seems to me as strong an indication there is that the asserted right to an abortion is not "so rooted in the traditions and conscience of our people as to be ranked as fundamental." . . . Even today, when society's views on abortion are changing, the very existence of the debate is evidence that the "right" to an abortion is not so universally accepted as the appellants would have us believe.

To reach its result the Court necessarily has had to find within the scope of the Fourteenth Amendment a right that was apparently completely unknown to the drafters of the Amendment. As early as 1821, the first state law dealing directly with abortion was enacted by the Connecticut legislature. . . . By the time of the adoption of the Fourteenth Amendment in 1868 there were at least 36 laws enacted by state or territorial legislatures limiting abortion. While many States have amended or updated their laws, 21 of the laws on the books in 1868 remain in effect today. . . .

The only conclusion possible from this history is that the drafters did not intend to have the Fourteenth Amendment withdraw from the States the power to legislate with respect to this matter. . . .

Planned Parenthood of Southeastern Pennsylvania v. *Casey*
505 U.S. 833, 112 S.Ct. 2791, 120 L.Ed. 2d 674 (1992)

http://caselaw.findlaw.com/us-supreme-court/505/833.html

Amendments in 1988 and 1989 to Pennsylvania's Abortion Control Act mandated "informed consent" counseling, a 24-hour waiting period, consent of one parent (with a judicial bypass procedure) for minors, and spousal notification; furthermore, the act defined a "medical emergency" that would excuse compliance with these requirements, and imposed certain reporting requirements on facilities providing abortions. The U.S. District Court for the Eastern District of Pennsylvania enjoined enforcement of all the amendments. A panel of the Court of Appeals for the Third Circuit that included future Justice Samuel Alito reversed except for the spousal notification requirement. (Judge Alito dissented from that part of the appeals court's holding.) In deciding the case, the Supreme Court produced five opinions totaling over 125 pages. The voting alignment was complex. Justices White, Scalia, Thomas, and Chief Justice Rehnquist would have upheld all the requirements; Justices O'Connor, Kennedy, and Souter found unconstitutional only the spousal notification requirement; Justice Stevens voted to strike down all but the informed-consent provision; and Justice Blackmun found all the provisions constitutionally deficient. The Court divided 5–4 in support of the position that the Constitution protected, at least to some degree, a woman's decision to abort her pregnancy. Majority: O'Connor, Blackmun, Stevens, Kennedy, Souter. Dissenting: Rehnquist, White, Scalia, Thomas.

Justice O'Connor, Justice Kennedy, and Justice Souter announced the judgment of the Court and delivered an opinion which Justice Blackmun and Justice Stevens joined in part.

Liberty finds no refuge in a jurisprudence of doubt. Yet 19 years after our holding that the Constitution protects a woman's right to terminate her pregnancy in its early stages, that definition of liberty is still questioned. Joining the respondents as amicus curiae, the United States, as it has done in five other cases in the last decade, again asks us to overrule *Roe*. . . .

After considering the fundamental constitutional questions resolved by *Roe*, principles of institutional integrity, and the rule of stare decisis, we are led to conclude this: the essential holding of *Roe* v. *Wade* should be retained and once again reaffirmed. . . .

Our law affords constitutional protection to personal decisions relating to marriage, procreation, contraception, family relationships, child rearing, and education. . . . These matters, involving the most intimate and personal choices a person may make in a lifetime, choices central to personal dignity and autonomy, are central to the liberty protected by the Fourteenth Amendment. At the heart of liberty is the right to define one's own concept of existence, of meaning, of the universe, and of the mystery of human life. Beliefs about these matters could not define the attributes of personhood were they formed under compulsion of the State. . . .

Abortion is a unique act. It is an act fraught with consequences for others; for the woman who must live with the implications of her decision; for the persons who perform and assist in the procedure; for the spouse, family, and society which must confront the knowledge that these procedures exist, procedures some deem nothing short of an act of violence against innocent human life; and, depending on one's beliefs, for the life or potential life that is aborted. Though abortion is conduct, it does not follow that the State is entitled to proscribe it in all instances. That is because the liberty of the woman is at stake in a sense unique to the human condition and so unique to the law. The mother who carries a child to full term is subject to anxieties, to physical constraints, to pain that only she must bear. That these sacrifices have from the beginning of the human race been endured by woman with a pride that ennobles her in the eyes of others and gives to the infant a bond of love cannot alone be grounds for the State to insist she make the sacrifice. Her suffering is too intimate and personal for the State to insist, without more, upon its own vision of the woman's role, however dominant that vision has been in the course of our history and our culture. The destiny of the woman must be shaped to a large extent on her own conception of her spiritual imperatives and her place in society. . . .

It was this dimension of personal liberty that *Roe* sought to protect. . . .

While we appreciate the weight of the arguments made on behalf of the State in the case before us, arguments which in their ultimate formulation conclude that *Roe* should be overruled, the reservations any of us have in reaffirming the central holding of *Roe* are outweighed by the explication of individual liberty we have given combined with the force of stare decisis. . . .

The sum of the . . . inquiry to this point shows *Roe*'s underpinnings unweakened in any way affecting its central holding. While it has engendered disapproval, it has not been unworkable. An entire generation has come of age free to assume *Roe*'s concept of liberty in defining the capacity of women to act in society, and to make reproductive decisions; no erosion of principle going to liberty or personal autonomy has left *Roe*'s central holding a doctrinal remnant; *Roe* portends no developments at odds with other precedent for the analysis of personal liberty; and no changes of fact have rendered viability more or less appropriate as the point at which the balance of interests tips. Within the bounds of normal stare decisis analysis, then, and subject to the considerations on which it customarily turns, the stronger argument is for affirming *Roe*'s central holding, with whatever degree of personal reluctance any of us may have, not for overruling it. . . .

Our analysis would not be complete, however, without explaining why overruling *Roe*'s central holding would not only reach an unjustifiable result under principles of stare decisis, but would seriously weaken the Court's capacity to exercise the judicial power and to function as the Supreme Court of a Nation dedicated to the rule of law. To understand why this would be so it is necessary to understand the source of this Court's authority, the conditions necessary for its preservation, and its relationship to the country's understanding of itself as a constitutional Republic.

The root of American governmental power is revealed most clearly in the instance of the power conferred by the Constitution upon the Judiciary of the United States and specifically upon this Court. As Americans of each succeeding generation are rightly told, the Court cannot buy support for its decisions by spending money and, except to a minor degree, it cannot independently coerce obedience to its decrees. The Court's power lies, rather, in its legitimacy, a product of substance and perception that shows itself in the people's acceptance of the Judiciary as fit to determine what the Nation's law means and to declare what it demands.

The underlying substance of this legitimacy is of course the warrant for the Court's decisions in the Constitution and the lesser source of legal principle on which the Court draws. That substance is expressed in the Court's opinions, and our contemporary understanding is such that a decision without principled justification would be no judicial act at all. But even when justification is furnished by apposite legal principle, something more is required. Because not every conscientious claim of principled justification will be accepted as such, the justification claimed must be beyond dispute. The Court must take care to speak and act in ways that allow people to accept its decisions on the terms the Court claims for them, as grounded truly in principle, not as compromises with social and political pressures having, as such, no bearing on the principled choices that the Court is obliged to make. Thus, the Court's legitimacy depends on making legally principled decisions under circumstances in which their principled character is sufficiently plausible to be accepted by the Nation. . . .

In two circumstances, however, the Court would almost certainly fail to receive the benefit of the doubt in overruling prior cases. There is, first, a point beyond which frequent overruling would overtax the country's belief in the Court's good faith. . . .

That first circumstance can be described as hypothetical; the second is to the point here and now. Where, in the performance of its judicial duties, the Court decides a case in such a way as to resolve the sort of intensely divisive controversy reflected in *Roe* and those rare, comparable cases, its decision has a dimension that the resolution of the normal case does not carry. It is the dimension present whenever the Court's interpretation of the Constitution calls the contending sides of a national controversy to end their national division by accepting a common mandate rooted in the Constitution.

The Court is not asked to do this very often. . . . But when the Court does act in this way, its decision requires an equally rare precedential force to counter the inevitable efforts to overturn it and to thwart its implementation. Some of those efforts may be mere unprincipled emotional reactions; others may proceed from principles worthy of profound respect. But whatever the premises of opposition may be, only the most convincing justification under accepted standards of precedent could suffice to demonstrate that a later decision overruling the first was anything but a surrender to political pressure, and an unjustified repudiation of the principle on which the Court staked its authority in the first instance. So to overrule under fire in the absence of the most compelling reason to reexamine a watershed decision would subvert the Court's legitimacy beyond any serious question. . . .

The Court's duty in the present case is clear. In 1973, it confronted the already-divisive issue of governmental power to limit personal choice to undergo abortion, for which it provided a new resolution based on the due process guaranteed by the Fourteenth Amendment. Whether or not a new social consensus is developing on that issue, its divisiveness is no less today than in 1973, and pressure to overrule the decision, like pressure to retain it, has grown only more intense. A decision to overrule *Roe*'s essential holding under the existing circumstances would address error, if error there was, at the cost of both profound and unnecessary damage to the Court's legitimacy, and to the Nation's commitment to the rule of law. It is therefore imperative to adhere to the essence of *Roe*'s original decision, and we do so today. . . .

The woman's liberty is not so unlimited, however, that from the outset the State cannot show its concern for the life of the unborn, and at a later point in fetal development the State's interest in life has sufficient force so that the right of the woman to terminate the pregnancy can be restricted. . . .

We conclude the line should be drawn at viability, so that before that time the woman has a right to choose to terminate her pregnancy. . . .

We give this summary:

a) To protect the central right recognized by *Roe* v. *Wade* while at the same time accommodating the State's profound interest in potential life, we will employ the undue burden analysis as explained in this opinion. An undue burden exists, and therefore a provision of law is invalid, if its purpose or effect is to place a substantial obstacle in the path of a woman seeking an abortion before the fetus attains viability.
b) We reject the rigid trimester framework of *Roe* v. *Wade*. To promote the State's profound interest in potential life, throughout pregnancy the State may take measures to ensure that the woman's choice is informed, and measures designed to advance this interest will not be invalidated as long as their purpose is to persuade the woman to choose childbirth over abortion. These measures must not be an undue burden on the right.
c) As with any medical procedure, the State may enact regulations to further the health or safety of a woman seeking an abortion. Unnecessary health regulations that have the purpose or effect of presenting a substantial obstacle to a woman seeking an abortion impose an undue burden on the right.
d) Our adoption of the undue burden analysis does not disturb the central holding of *Roe* v. *Wade*, and we reaffirm that holding. Regardless of whether exceptions are made for particular circumstances, a State may not prohibit any woman from making the ultimate decision to terminate her pregnancy before viability.
e) We also reaffirm *Roe*'s holding that "subsequent to viability, the State in promoting its interest in the potentiality of human life may, if it chooses, regulate, and even proscribe, abortion except where it is necessary, in appropriate medical judgment, for the preservation of the life or health of the mother."

These principles control our assessment of the Pennsylvania statute, and we now turn to the issue of the validity of its challenged provisions. [The plurality concludes that only the spousal notification rule violates the "undue burden" test.]

[T]he case is remanded for proceedings consistent with this opinion. . . .

It is so ordered.

Justice Stevens, concurring in part and dissenting in part . . . [omitted].

Justice Blackmun, concurring in part and dissenting in part . . . [omitted].

The Chief Justice, with whom Justice White, Justice Scalia, and Justice Thomas join, concurring in the judgment in part and dissenting in part.

The joint opinion, following its newly minted variation on stare decisis, retains the outer shell of *Roe* v. *Wade*, but beats a wholesale retreat from the substance of that case. We believe that *Roe* was wrongly decided, and that it can and should be overruled consistently with our traditional approach to stare decisis in constitutional cases. We would adopt the approach of the plurality in *Webster* v. *Reproductive Health Services*, and uphold the challenged provisions of the Pennsylvania statute in their entirety. . . .

The joint opinion . . . cannot bring itself to say that *Roe* was correct as an original matter, but the authors are of the view that "the immediate question is not the soundness of *Roe*'s resolution of the issue, but the precedential force that must be accorded to its holding." Instead of claiming that *Roe* was correct as a matter of original constitutional interpretation, the opinion therefore contains an elaborate discussion of stare decisis. This discussion of the principle of stare decisis appears to be almost entirely dicta, because the joint opinion does not apply that principle in dealing with *Roe*. *Roe* decided that a woman had a fundamental right to an abortion. The joint opinion rejects that view. *Roe* decided that abortion regulations were to be subjected to "strict scrutiny" and could be justified only in the light of "compelling state interests." The joint opinion rejects that view. *Roe* analyzed abortion regulation under a rigid trimester framework, a framework which has guided this Court's decision-making for 19 years. The joint opinion rejects that framework. . . .

We have stated above our belief that the Constitution does not subject state abortion regulations to heightened scrutiny. . . . A woman's interest in having an abortion is a form of liberty protected by the Due Process Clause, but States may regulate abortion procedures in ways rationally related to a legitimate state interest. With this rule in mind, we examine each of the challenged provisions. [Chief Justice Rehnquist concludes that each provision of the Pennsylvania statute is rationally related to a legitimate state interest.]

Justice Scalia, with whom The Chief Justice, Justice White, and Justice Thomas join, concurring in the judgment in part and dissenting in part. . . .

The States may, if they wish, permit abortion on demand, but the Constitution does not require them to do so. The permissibility of abortion, and the limitations upon it, are to be resolved like most important questions in our democracy: by citizens trying to persuade one another and then voting. As the Court acknowledges, "where reasonable people disagree the government can adopt one position or the other." The Court is correct in adding the qualification that this "assumes a state of affairs in which the choice does not intrude upon a protected liberty,"—but the crucial part of that qualification is the penultimate word. A State's choice between two positions on which reasonable people can disagree is constitutional even when (as is often the case) it intrudes upon a "liberty" in the absolute sense. Laws against bigamy, for example—which entire societies of reasonable people disagree with—intrude upon men and women's liberty to marry and live with one another. But bigamy happens not to be a liberty specially "protected" by the Constitution.

That is, quite simply, the issue in this case: not whether the power of a woman to abort her unborn child is a "liberty" in the absolute sense; or even whether it is a liberty of great importance to many women. Of course it is both. The issue is whether it is a liberty protected by the Constitution of the United States. I am sure it is not. I reach that conclusion not because of anything so exalted as my views concerning the "concept of existence, of meaning, of the universe, and of the mystery of human life." Rather, I reach it for the same reason I reach the conclusion that bigamy is not constitutionally protected—because of two simple facts: (1) the Constitution says absolutely nothing about it, and (2) the longstanding traditions of American society have permitted it to be legally proscribed. . . .

I am as distressed as the Court . . . about the "political pressure" directed to the Court. . . .

What makes all this relevant to the bothersome application of "political pressure" against the Court are the twin facts that the American people love democracy and the American people are not fools. As long as this Court thought (and the people thought) that we Justices were doing essentially lawyers' work up here—reading text and discerning our society's traditional understanding of that text—the public pretty much left us alone. Texts and traditions are facts to study, not convictions to demonstrate about. But if in reality our process of constitutional adjudication consists primarily of making value judgments, . . . then a free and intelligent people's attitude towards us can be expected to be (ought to be) quite different. The people know that their value judgments are quite as good as those taught in any law school—maybe better. If, indeed, the "liberties" protected by the Constitution are, as the Court says, undefined and unbounded, then the people should demonstrate, to protest that we do not implement their values instead of ours. Not only that, but confirmation hearings for new Justices should deteriorate into question-and-answer sessions in which Senators go through a list of their constituents' most favored and most disfavored alleged constitutional rights, and seek the nominee's commitment to support or oppose them. Value judgments, after all, should be voted on, not dictated. . . .

June Medical Services v. *Russo*
591 U.S. ___, 140 S.Ct. 2103, 207 L.Ed. 2d 566 (2020)

www.supremecourt.gov/opinions/19pdf/18-1323_c07d.pdf

The facts of this case follow in Justice Breyer's opinion below. The section of his opinion dealing with standing is omitted. In 2016 when the Court decided *Whole Woman's Health* v. *Hellerstedt*, Justice Breyer wrote the opinion of the Court that was joined by Justices Ginsburg, Kagan, Kennedy, and Sotomayor. Chief Justice Roberts and Justices Alito and Thomas dissented. Majority in this case: Breyer, Ginsburg, Kagan, Roberts, Sotomayor. Dissenting: Alito, Gorsuch, Kavanaugh, Thomas.

Justice Breyer announced the judgment of the Court and delivered an opinion, in which Justices Ginsburg, Sotomayor, and Kagan join.

In *Whole Woman's Health* v. *Hellerstedt*, we held that "'[u]nnecessary health regulations that have the purpose or effect of presenting a substantial obstacle to a woman seeking an abortion impose an undue burden on the right'" and are therefore "constitutionally invalid." We explained that this standard requires courts independently to review the legislative findings upon which an abortion-related statute rests and to weigh the law's "asserted benefits against the burdens" it imposes on abortion access. The Texas statute at issue in *Whole Woman's Health* required abortion providers to hold "'active admitting privileges at a hospital'" within 30 miles of the place where they perform abortions. Reviewing the record for ourselves, we found ample evidence to support the District Court's finding that the statute did not further the State's asserted interest in protecting women's health. The evidence showed, moreover, that conditions on admitting privileges that served no "relevant credentialing function," "help[ed] to explain" the closure of half of Texas' abortion clinics. Those closures placed a substantial obstacle in the path of Texas women seeking an abortion. And that obstacle, "when viewed in light of the virtual absence of any health benefit," imposed an "undue burden" on abortion access in violation of the Federal Constitution.

In this case, we consider the constitutionality of a Louisiana statute, Act 620, that is almost word-for-word identical to Texas' admitting-privileges law. As in *Whole Woman's Health*, the District Court found that the statute offers no significant health benefit. It found that conditions on admitting privileges common to hospitals throughout the State have made and will continue to make it impossible for abortion providers to obtain conforming privileges for reasons that have nothing to do with the State's asserted interests in promoting women's health and safety. And it found that this inability places a substantial obstacle in the path of women seeking an abortion. As in *Whole Woman's Health*, the substantial obstacle the Act imposes, and the absence of any health-related benefit, led the District Court to conclude that the law imposes an undue burden and is therefore unconstitutional.

The Court of Appeals [for the Fifth Circuit] agreed with the District Court's interpretation of the standards we have said apply to regulations on abortion. It thought, however, that the District Court [for the Middle District of Louisiana] was mistaken on the facts. We disagree. We have examined the extensive record carefully and conclude that it supports the District Court's findings of fact. Those findings mirror those made in *Whole Woman's Health* in every relevant respect and require the same result. We consequently hold that the Louisiana statute is unconstitutional.

As was true in Texas, Louisiana law already required abortion providers either to possess local hospital admitting privileges or to have a patient "transfer" arrangement with a physician who had such privileges. The new law eliminated that flexibility. Act 620 requires any doctor who performs abortions to hold "active admitting privileges at a hospital that is located not further than thirty miles from the location at which the abortion is performed or induced and that provides obstetrical or gynecological health care services." . . . Act 620 does not advance Louisiana's legitimate interest in protecting the health of women seeking abortions. Instead, Act 620 would increase the risk of harm to women's health by dramatically reducing the availability of safe abortion in Louisiana. . . .

[W]e apply the constitutional standards set forth in our earlier abortion-related cases, and in particular in *Casey* and *Whole Woman's Health*. At the risk of repetition, we remind the reader of the standards we described above. In *Whole Woman's Health*, we quoted *Casey* in explaining that "'a statute which, while furthering [a] valid state interest has the effect of placing a substantial obstacle in the path of a woman's choice cannot be considered a permissible means of serving its legitimate ends.'" We added that "'[u]nnecessary health regulations'" impose an unconstitutional "'undue burden'" if they have "'the purpose or effect of presenting a substantial obstacle to a woman seeking an abortion.'"

We went on to explain that, in applying these standards, courts must "consider the burdens a law imposes on abortion access together with the benefits those laws confer." We cautioned that courts "must review legislative 'factfinding under a deferential standard.'" But they "must not 'place dispositive weight' on those 'findings,'" for the courts "'retai[n] an independent constitutional duty to review factual findings where constitutional rights are at stake.'". . .

. . . The Court of Appeals disagreed with the District Court, not so much in respect to the legal standards that we have just set forth, but because it did not agree with the factual findings on which the District Court relied in assessing both the burdens that Act 620 imposes and the health-related benefits it might bring. We have consequently reviewed the record in detail ourselves. In doing so, we . . . find that the testimony and other evidence contained in the extensive record developed over the 6-day trial support the District Court's ultimate conclusion that, "[e]ven if Act 620 could be said to further women's health to some marginal degree, the burdens it imposes far outweigh any such benefit, and thus the Act imposes an unconstitutional undue burden.

The District Court found that enforcing the admitting-privileges requirement would "result in a drastic reduction in the number and geographic distribution of abortion providers." In light of demographic, economic, and other evidence, the court concluded that this reduction would make it impossible for "many women seeking a safe, legal abortion in Louisiana . . . to obtain one" and that it would impose "substantial obstacles" on those who could. . . .

We turn finally to the law's asserted benefits. The District Court found that there was "'no significant health-related problem that the new law helped to cure.'" . . . First, the District Court found that the admitting-privileges requirement serves no "relevant credentialing function." As we have seen, hospitals can, and do, deny admitting privileges for reasons unrelated to a doctor's ability safely to perform abortions. And Act 620's requirement that physicians obtain privileges at a hospital within 30 miles of the place where they perform abortions further constrains providers for reasons that bear no relationship to competence. . . .

Second, the District Court found that the admitting-privileges requirement "does not conform to prevailing medical standards and will not improve the safety of abortion in Louisiana." . . . As in *Whole Woman's Health*, the State introduced no evidence "showing that patients have better outcomes when their physicians have admitting privileges" or "of any instance in which an admitting privileges requirement would have helped even one woman obtain better treatment."

We conclude, in light of the record, that the District Court's significant factual findings—both as to burdens and as to benefits—have ample evidentiary support. None is "clearly erroneous." . . . We also agree with its ultimate legal conclusion that, in light of these findings and our precedents, Act 620 violates the Constitution . . . The Court of Appeals' judgment is erroneous. It is

Reversed.

Chief Justice Roberts, concurring in the judgment. . . .

I joined the dissent in *Whole Woman's Health* and continue to believe that the case was wrongly decided. The question today however is not whether *Whole Woman's Health* was right or wrong, but whether to adhere to it in deciding the present case. . . . The legal doctrine of *stare decisis* requires us, absent special circumstances, to treat like cases alike. The Louisiana law imposes a burden on access to abortion just as severe as that imposed by the Texas law, for the same reasons. Therefore Louisiana's law cannot stand under our precedents. . . .

Under *Casey*, the State may not impose an undue burden on the woman's ability to obtain an abortion. "A finding of an undue burden is a shorthand for the conclusion that a state regulation has the purpose or effect of placing a substantial obstacle in the path of a woman seeking an abortion of a nonviable fetus." Laws that do not pose a substantial obstacle to abortion access are permissible, so long as they are "reasonably related" to a legitimate state interest. After faithfully reciting this standard, the Court in Whole *Woman's Health* added the following observation: "The rule announced in *Casey* . . . requires that courts consider the burdens a law imposes on abortion access together with the benefits those laws confer." The plurality repeats today that the undue burden standard requires courts "to weigh the law's asserted benefits against the burdens it imposes on abortion access."

Read in isolation from *Casey*, such an inquiry could invite a grand "balancing test in which unweighted factors mysteriously are weighed." . . . *Casey* instead focuses on the existence of a substantial obstacle, the sort of inquiry familiar to judges across a variety of contexts. . . .

We should respect the statement in *Whole Woman's Health* that it was applying the undue burden standard of Casey. . . . Here the plurality expressly acknowledges that we are not considering how to analyze an abortion regulation that does not present a substantial obstacle. "That," the plurality explains, "is not this case." In this case, *Casey's* requirement of finding a substantial obstacle before invalidating an abortion regulation is therefore a sufficient basis for the decision, as it was in *Whole Woman's Health*. In neither case, nor in *Casey* itself, was there call for consideration of a regulation's benefits, and nothing in *Casey* commands such consideration. Under principles of *stare decisis*, I agree with the plurality that the determination in *Whole Woman's Health* that Texas's law imposed a substantial obstacle requires the same determination about Louisiana's law. Under those same principles, I would adhere to the holding of *Casey*, requiring a substantial obstacle before striking down an abortion regulation. Because Louisiana's admitting privileges requirement would restrict women's access to abortion to the same degree as Texas's law, it also cannot stand under our precedent. . . .

JUSTICE THOMAS, dissenting . . . [omitted].

JUSTICE ALITO, with whom JUSTICES THOMAS, GORSUCH, and KAVANAUGH join in part, dissenting.

The majority bills today's decision as a facsimile of *Whole Woman's Health*, and it's true they have something in common. In both, the abortion right recognized in this Court's decisions is used like a bulldozer to flatten legal rules that stand in the way. . . . Even . . . *Casey* was altered . . . The divided majority cannot agree on what the abortion right requires, but it nevertheless strikes down a Louisiana law, Act 620, that the legislature enacted for the asserted purpose of protecting women's health. . . .

The plurality eschews the constitutional test set out in *Casey* and instead employs the balancing test adopted in *Whole Woman's Health*. The plurality concludes that the Louisiana law does nothing to protect the health of women, but that is disproved by substantial evidence in the record. And the plurality upholds the District Court's finding that the Louisiana law would cause a drastic reduction in the number of abortion providers in the State even though this finding was based on an erroneous legal standard and a thoroughly inadequate factual inquiry. . . .

Both the plurality and the Chief Justice hold that abortion providers can invoke a woman's abortion right when they attack state laws that are enacted to protect a woman's health. Neither waiver nor *stare decisis* can justify this holding, which clashes with our general rule on third-party standing. And the idea that a regulated party can invoke the right of a third party for the purpose of attacking legislation enacted to protect the third party is stunning. Given the apparent conflict of interest, that concept would be rejected out of hand in a case not involving abortion. . . .

Under our precedent, the critical question in this case is whether the challenged Louisiana law places a "substantial obstacle in the path of a woman seeking an abortion of a nonviable fetus." If a law like that at issue here does not have that effect, it is constitutional. The petitioners urge us to adopt a rule that is more favorable to abortion providers. At oral argument, their attorney maintained that a law that has no effect on women's access to abortion is nevertheless unconstitutional if it is not needed to protect women's health.

Casey . . . rules out the balancing test adopted in *Whole Woman's Health*. *Whole Woman's Health* simply misinterpreted *Casey*, and I agree that *Whole Woman's Health* should be overruled insofar as it changed the *Casey* test. Unless *Casey* is reexamined—and Louisiana has not asked us to do that—the test it adopted should remain the governing standard. . . .

In sum, contrary to the plurality's assertion, there is ample evidence in the record showing that requiring admitting privileges has health and safety benefits. There is certainly room for debate about the need for this requirement, but under our case law, this Court's task is not to ascertain whether a law "adds significantly" to the existing regulatory framework. Instead, when confronted with a genuine dispute about a law's benefits, we have afforded legislatures "wide discretion" in assessing whether a regulation serves a legitimate medical need and is medically reasonable even in the face of medical and scientific uncertainty. For these reasons, both the plurality and the Chief Justice err in concluding that the admitting-privileges requirement serves no valid purpose. . . .

The Court should remand this case for a new trial under the correct legal standards. The District Court should apply *Casey's* "substantial obstacle" test, not the *Whole Woman's Health* balancing test. . . . The decision in this case, like that in *Whole Woman's Health*, twists the law, and I therefore respectfully dissent.

JUSTICE GORSUCH, dissenting . . . [omitted].

JUSTICE KAVANAUGH, dissenting . . . [omitted].

III. SEXUAL ORIENTATION AND MARRIAGE EQUALITY

Lawrence v. *Texas*
539 U.S. 558, 123 S.Ct. 2472, 156 L.Ed. 2d 508 (2003)

http://caselaw.findlaw.com/us-supreme-court/539/558.html

Because of a reported weapons disturbance, police in Houston, Texas, entered the apartment of John Lawrence where they observed Lawrence and Tyron Garner, both adults, engaging in consensual anal intercourse. Both Lawrence and Garner were arrested and convicted under a Texas law that criminalized "deviate sexual intercourse with another individual of the same sex." Deviate sexual intercourse was in turn defined as: "(a) any contact between any part of the genitals of one person and the mouth or anus of another person; or (b) the penetration of the genitals or the anus of another person with an object." Against objections that the statute violated the due process and equal protection clauses of the Fourteenth Amendment, the Texas Court of Appeals for the Fourteenth District in 2001 affirmed their convictions, citing the U.S. Supreme Court's decision in *Bowers* v. *Hardwick* (1986) as dispositive of their due process claim. Justice Kennedy's opinion of the Court is noteworthy because it was the first to cite a decision by the European Court of Human Rights. Majority: Kennedy, Breyer, Ginsburg, O'Connor, Souter, Stevens. Dissenting: Scalia, Rehnquist, Thomas.

Justice Kennedy delivered the opinion of the Court. . . .

Liberty presumes an autonomy of self that includes freedom of thought, belief, expression, and certain intimate conduct. . . .

The question before the Court is the validity of a Texas statute making it a crime for two persons of the same sex to engage in certain intimate sexual conduct. . . .

We conclude the case should be resolved by determining whether the petitioners were free as adults to engage in the private conduct in the exercise of their liberty under the Due Process Clause of the Fourteenth Amendment to the Constitution. For this inquiry we deem it necessary to reconsider the Court's holding in *Bowers*. . . .

The facts in *Bowers* had some similarities to the instant case. A police officer, whose right to enter seems not to have been in question, observed Hardwick, in his own bedroom, engaging in intimate sexual conduct with another adult male. The conduct was in violation of a Georgia statute making it a criminal offense to engage in sodomy. One difference between the two cases is that the Georgia statute prohibited the conduct whether or not the participants were of the same sex, while the Texas statute, as we have seen, applies only to participants of the same sex. Hard-wick was not prosecuted, but he brought an action in federal court to declare the state statute invalid. He alleged he was a practicing homosexual and that the criminal prohibition violated rights guaranteed to him by the Constitution. The Court, in an opinion by Justice White, sustained the Georgia law. . . . Four Justices dissented.

The Court began its substantive discussion in *Bowers* as follows: "The issue presented is whether the Federal Constitution confers a fundamental right upon homosexuals to engage in sodomy and hence invalidates the laws of the many States that still make such conduct illegal and have done so for a very long time." That statement, we now conclude, discloses the Court's own failure to appreciate the extent of the liberty at stake. To say that the issue in *Bowers* was simply the right to engage in certain sexual conduct demeans the claim the individual put forward, just as it would demean a married couple were it to be said marriage is simply about the right to have sexual intercourse. The laws involved in *Bowers* and here are, to be sure, statutes that purport to do no more than prohibit a particular sexual act. Their penalties and purposes, though, have more far-reaching consequences, touching upon the most private human conduct, sexual behavior, and in the most private of places, the home. The statutes do seek to control a personal relationship that, whether or not entitled to formal recognition in the law, is within the liberty of persons to choose without being punished as criminals.

This, as a general rule, should counsel against attempts by the State, or a court, to define the meaning of the relationship or to set its boundaries absent injury to a person or abuse of an institution the law protects. It suffices for us to acknowledge that adults may choose to enter upon this relationship in the confines of their homes and their own private lives and still retain their dignity as free persons. When sexuality finds overt expression in intimate conduct with another person, the conduct can be but one element in a personal bond that is more enduring. The liberty protected by the Constitution allows homosexual persons the right to make this choice.

Having misapprehended the claim of liberty there presented to it, and thus stating the claim to be whether there is a fundamental right to engage in consensual sodomy, the Bowers Court said: "Proscriptions against that conduct have ancient roots." In academic writings, and in many of the scholarly amicus briefs filed to assist the Court in this case, there are fundamental criticisms of the historical premises relied upon by the majority and concurring opinions in *Bowers*. We need not enter this debate in the attempt to reach a definitive historical judgment, but the following considerations counsel against adopting the definitive conclusions upon which *Bowers* placed such reliance. . . .

[E]arly American sodomy laws were not directed at homosexuals as such but instead sought to prohibit nonprocreative sexual activity more generally. This does not suggest approval of homosexual conduct. It does tend to show that this particular form of conduct was not thought of as a separate category from like conduct between heterosexual persons.

Laws prohibiting sodomy do not seem to have been enforced against consenting adults acting in private. . . .

It was not until the 1970's that any State singled out same-sex relations for criminal prosecution, and only nine States have done so. . . .

It must be acknowledged, of course, that the Court in *Bowers* was making the broader point that for centuries there have been powerful voices to condemn homosexual conduct as immoral. . . . For many persons these are not trivial concerns but profound and deep convictions accepted as ethical and moral principles to which they aspire and which thus determine the course of their lives. These considerations do not answer the question before us, however. The issue is whether the majority may use the power of the State to enforce these views on the whole society through operation of the criminal law. . . .

In all events we think that our laws and traditions in the past half century are of most relevance here. These references show an emerging awareness that liberty gives substantial protection to adult persons in deciding how to conduct their private lives in matters pertaining to sex. "[H]istory and tradition are the starting point but not in all cases the ending point of the substantive due process inquiry."

This emerging recognition should have been apparent when *Bowers* was decided. In 1955 the American Law Institute promulgated the Model Penal Code and made clear that it did not recommend or provide for "criminal penalties for consensual sexual relations conducted in private." . . .

[A]lmost five years before *Bowers* was decided the European Court of Human Rights considered a case with parallels to *Bowers* and to today's case. An adult male resident in Northern Ireland alleged he was a practicing homosexual who desired to engage in consensual homosexual conduct. The laws of Northern Ireland forbade him that right. He alleged that he had been questioned, his home had been searched, and he feared criminal prosecution. The court held that the laws proscribing the conduct were invalid under the European Convention on Human Rights. Authoritative in all countries that are members of the Council of Europe (21 nations then, 45 nations now), the decision is at odds with the premise in *Bowers* that the claim put forward was insubstantial in our Western civilization.

In our own constitutional system the deficiencies in *Bowers* became even more apparent in the years following its announcement. The 25 States with laws prohibiting the relevant conduct referenced in the Bowers decision are reduced now to 13, of which 4 enforce their laws only against homosexual conduct. In those States where sodomy is still proscribed, whether for same-sex or heterosexual conduct, there is a pattern of nonenforcement with respect to consenting adults acting in private. . . .

Bowers was not correct when it was decided, and it is not correct today. It ought not to remain binding precedent. *Bowers* v. *Hardwick* should be and now is overruled.

The present case does not involve minors. It does not involve persons who might be injured or coerced or who are situated in relationships where consent might not easily be refused. It does not involve public conduct or prostitution. It does not involve whether the government must give formal recognition to any relationship that homosexual persons seek to enter. The case does involve two adults who, with full and mutual consent from each other, engaged in sexual practices common to a homosexual lifestyle. The petitioners are entitled to respect for their private lives. The State cannot demean their existence or control their destiny by making their private sexual conduct a crime. Their right to liberty under the Due Process Clause gives them the full right to engage in their conduct without intervention of the government. The Texas statute furthers no legitimate state interest which can justify its intrusion into the personal and private life of the individual.

Had those who drew and ratified the Due Process Clauses of the Fifth Amendment or the Fourteenth Amendment known the components of liberty in its manifold possibilities, they might have been more specific. They did not presume to have this insight. They knew times can blind us to certain truths and later generations can see that laws once thought necessary and proper in fact serve only to oppress. As the Constitution endures, persons in every generation can invoke its principles in their own search for greater freedom.

The judgment of the Court of Appeals for the Texas Fourteenth District is reversed, and the case is remanded for further proceedings not inconsistent with this opinion.

It is so ordered.

Justice O'Connor, concurring in the judgment.

I joined *Bowers*, and do not join the Court in overruling it. Nevertheless, I agree with the Court that Texas' statute banning same sex sodomy is unconstitutional. Rather than relying on the substantive component of the Fourteenth Amendment's Due Process Clause, as the Court does, I base my conclusion on the Fourteenth Amendment's Equal Protection Clause. . . .

Justice Scalia, with whom The Chief Justice and Justice Thomas join, dissenting.

"Liberty finds no refuge in a jurisprudence of doubt." That was the Court's sententious response [in *Planned Parenthood* v. *Casey*], barely more than a decade ago, to those seeking to overrule *Roe* v. *Wade*. The Court's response today, to those who have engaged in a 17-year crusade to overrule *Bowers* v. *Hardwick* is very different. The need for stability and certainty presents no barrier. . . .

Our opinions applying the doctrine known as "substantive due process" hold that the Due Process Clause prohibits States from infringing fundamental liberty interests, unless the infringement is narrowly tailored to serve a compelling state interest. . . . All other liberty interests may be abridged or abrogated pursuant to a validly enacted state law if that law is rationally related to a legitimate state interest.

Bowers held, first, that criminal prohibitions of homosexual sodomy are not subject to heightened scrutiny because they do not implicate a "fundamental right" under the Due Process Clause. . . .

The Court today does not overrule this holding. Not once does it describe homosexual sodomy as a "fundamental right" or a "fundamental liberty interest," nor does it subject the Texas statute to strict scrutiny. Instead, having failed to establish that the right to homosexual sodomy is "deeply rooted in this Nation's history and tradition," the Court concludes that the application of Texas's statute to petitioners' conduct fails the rational-basis test, and overrules *Bowers*' holding to the contrary. . . .

I shall address that rational-basis holding presently. First, however, I address some aspersions that the Court casts upon *Bowers'* conclusion that homosexual sodomy is not a "fundamental right"—even though, as I have said, the Court does not have the boldness to reverse that conclusion. . . .

It is (as *Bowers* recognized) entirely irrelevant whether the laws in our long national tradition criminalizing homosexual sodomy were "directed at homosexual conduct as a distinct matter." Whether homosexual sodomy was prohibited by a law targeted at same-sex sexual relations or by a more general law prohibiting both homosexual and heterosexual sodomy, the only relevant point is that it was criminalized—which suffices to establish that homosexual sodomy is not a right "deeply rooted in our Nation's history and tradition." The Court today agrees that homosexual sodomy was criminalized and thus does not dispute the facts on which *Bowers* actually relied.

Next the Court makes the claim, again unsupported by any citations, that "[l]aws prohibiting sodomy do not seem to have been enforced against consenting adults acting in private." The key qualifier here is "acting in private"—since the Court admits that sodomy laws were enforced against consenting adults (although the Court contends that prosecutions were "infrequent"). I do not know what "acting in private" means; surely consensual sodomy, like heterosexual intercourse, is rarely performed on stage. If all the Court means by "acting in private" is "on private premises, with the doors closed and windows covered," it is entirely unsurprising that evidence of enforcement would be hard to come by. (Imagine the circumstances that would enable a search warrant to be obtained for a residence on the ground that there was probable cause to believe that consensual sodomy was then and there occurring.) . . . There are 203 prosecutions for consensual, adult homosexual sodomy reported in the West Reporting system and official state reporters from the years 1880–1995. . . . *Bowers'* conclusion that homosexual sodomy is not a fundamental right "deeply rooted in this Nation's history and tradition" is utterly unassailable.

Realizing that fact, the Court instead says: "[W]e think that our laws and traditions in the past half century are of most relevance here. These references show an emerging awareness that liberty gives substantial protection to adult persons in deciding how to conduct their private lives in matters pertaining to sex." Apart from the fact that such an "emerging awareness" does not establish a "fundamental right," the statement is factually false. States continue to prosecute all sorts of crimes by adults "in matters pertaining to sex": prostitution, adult incest, adultery, obscenity, and child pornography. . . .

Constitutional entitlements do not spring into existence because some States choose to lessen or eliminate criminal sanctions on certain behavior. Much less do they spring into existence, as the Court seems to believe, because foreign nations decriminalize conduct. . . . The Court's discussion of these foreign views (ignoring, of course, the many countries that have retained criminal prohibitions on sodomy) is therefore meaningless dicta. Dangerous dicta, however, since "this Court . . . should not impose foreign moods, fads, or fashions on Americans."

I turn now to the ground on which the Court squarely rests its holding: the contention that there is no rational basis for the law here under attack. This proposition is so out of accord with our jurisprudence—indeed, with the jurisprudence of any society we know—that it requires little discussion.

The Texas statute undeniably seeks to further the belief of its citizens that certain forms of sexual behavior are "immoral and unacceptable"—the same interest furthered by criminal laws against fornication, bigamy, adultery, adult incest, bestiality, and obscenity. *Bowers* held that this was a legitimate state interest. The Court today reaches the opposite conclusion. The Texas statute, it says, "furthers no legitimate state interest which can justify its intrusion into the personal and private life of the individual." The Court embraces instead Justice Stevens' declaration in his *Bowers* dissent, that "the fact that the governing majority in a State has traditionally viewed a particular practice as immoral is not a sufficient reason for upholding a law prohibiting the practice." This effectively decrees the end of all morals legislation. If, as the Court asserts, the promotion of majoritarian sexual morality is not even a legitimate state interest, none of the above-mentioned laws can survive rational-basis review. . . .

Let me be clear that I have nothing against homosexuals, or any other group, promoting their agenda through normal democratic means.

Social perceptions of sexual and other morality change over time, and every group has the right to persuade its fellow citizens that its view of such matters is the best. That homosexuals have achieved some success in that enterprise is attested to by the fact that Texas is one of the few remaining States that criminalize private, consensual homosexual acts. . . . It is . . . the premise of our system that those judgments are to be made by the people, and not imposed by a governing caste that knows best.

One of the benefits of leaving regulation of this matter to the people rather than to the courts is that the people, unlike judges, need not carry things to their logical conclusion. The people may feel that their disapprobation of homosexual conduct is strong enough to disallow homosexual marriage, but not strong enough to criminalize private homosexual acts—and may legislate accordingly. The Court today pretends that it possesses a similar freedom of action, so that we need not fear judicial imposition of homosexual marriage, as has recently occurred in Canada. . . . At the end of its opinion—after having laid waste the foundations of our rational-basis jurisprudence—the Court says that the present case "does not involve whether the government must give formal recognition to any relationship that homosexual persons seek to enter." Do not believe it. More illuminating than this bald, unreasoned disclaimer is the progression of thought displayed by an earlier passage in the Court's opinion, which notes the constitutional protections afforded to "personal decisions relating to marriage, procreation, contraception, family relationships, child rearing, and education," and then declares that "[p]ersons in a homosexual relationship may seek autonomy for these purposes, just as heterosexual persons do." Today's opinion dismantles the structure of constitutional law that has permitted a distinction to be made between heterosexual and homosexual unions, insofar as formal recognition in marriage is concerned. If moral disapprobation of homosexual conduct is "no legitimate state interest" for purposes of proscribing that conduct, . . . what justification could there possibly be for denying the benefits of marriage to homosexual couples exercising "[t]he liberty protected by the Constitution?" Surely not the encouragement of procreation, since the sterile and the elderly are allowed to marry. This case "does not involve" the issue of homosexual marriage only if one entertains the belief that principle and logic have nothing to do with the decisions of this Court. Many will hope that, as the Court comfortingly assures us, this is so. . . .

Justice Thomas, dissenting . . . [omitted].

Obergefell v. *Hodges*
576 U.S. 644, 135 S.Ct. 2584, 192 L.Ed. 2d 609 (2015)

http://caselaw.findlaw.com/us-supreme-court/14–556.html

Along with many states, Michigan, Kentucky, Ohio, and Tennessee defined marriage as a union between one man and one woman. The petitioners, 14 same-sex couples and two men whose same-sex partners were deceased, filed suits in U.S. district courts in their home states, claiming that respondent state officials violated the Fourteenth Amendment by denying them the right to marry or to have marriages lawfully performed in another state given full recognition. Each district court ruled in petitioners' favor, but the U.S. Court of Appeals for the Sixth Circuit consolidated the cases and reversed. The Supreme Court granted certiorari limited to two questions. The first, presented by the cases from Michigan and Kentucky, is whether the Fourteenth Amendment requires a state to license a marriage between two people of the same sex. The second, presented by the cases from Ohio, Tennessee, and, again, Kentucky, is whether the Fourteenth Amendment requires a state to recognize a same-sex marriage licensed and performed in a state which does grant that right. Majority: Kennedy, Breyer, Ginsburg, Kagan, Sotomayor. Dissenting: Alito, Roberts, Scalia, Thomas.

Justice Kennedy delivered the opinion of the Court. . . .

The fundamental liberties protected by [the Due Process] Clause include most of the rights enumerated in the Bill of Rights. In addition these liberties extend to certain personal choices central to individual dignity and autonomy, including intimate choices that define personal identity and beliefs.

The identification and protection of fundamental rights is an enduring part of the judicial duty to interpret the Constitution. That responsibility, however, "has not been reduced to any formula." Rather, it requires courts to exercise reasoned judgment in identifying interests of the person so fundamental that the State must accord them its respect. That process is guided by many of the same considerations relevant to analysis of other constitutional provisions that set forth broad principles rather than specific requirements. History and tradition guide and discipline this inquiry but do not set its outer boundaries. That method respects our history and learns from it without allowing the past alone to rule the present.

The nature of injustice is that we may not always see it in our own times. The generations that wrote and ratified the Bill of Rights and the Fourteenth Amendment did not presume to know the extent of freedom in all of its dimensions, and so they entrusted to future generations a charter protecting the right of all persons to enjoy liberty as we learn its meaning. When new insight reveals discord between the Constitution's central protections and a received legal stricture, a claim to liberty must be addressed.

Applying these established tenets, the Court has long held the right to marry is protected by the Constitution. . . . It cannot be denied that this Court's cases describing the right to marry presumed a relationship involving opposite-sex partners. The Court, like many institutions, has made assumptions defined by the world and time of which it is a part. . . . This Court's cases . . . have identified essential attributes of that right based in history, tradition, and other constitutional liberties inherent in this intimate bond. . . .

This analysis compels the conclusion that same-sex couples may exercise the right to marry. The four principles and traditions to be discussed demonstrate that the reasons marriage is fundamental under the Constitution apply with equal force to same-sex couples.

A first premise of the Court's relevant precedents is that the right to personal choice regarding marriage is inherent in the concept of individual autonomy. . . . Like choices concerning contraception, family relationships, procreation, and childrearing, all of which are protected by the Constitution, decisions concerning marriage are among the most intimate that an individual can make. . . .

A second principle in this Court's jurisprudence is that the right to marry is fundamental because it supports a two-person union unlike any other in its importance to the committed individuals. This point was central to *Griswold v. Connecticut*. . . .

A third basis for protecting the right to marry is that it safeguards children and families and thus draws meaning from related rights of childrearing, procreation, and education. . . . Excluding same-sex couples from marriage thus conflicts with a central premise of the right to marry. Without the recognition, stability, and predictability marriage offers, their children suffer the stigma of knowing their families are somehow lesser. They also suffer the significant material costs of being raised by unmarried parents, relegated through no fault of their own to a more difficult and uncertain family life. . . .

Fourth and finally, this Court's cases and the Nation's traditions make clear that marriage is a keystone of our social order. . . . For that reason, just as a couple vows to support each other, so does society pledge to support the couple, offering symbolic recognition and material benefits to protect and nourish the union. . . .

The right of same-sex couples to marry that is part of the liberty promised by the Fourteenth Amendment is derived, too, from that Amendment's guarantee of the equal protection of the laws. The Due Process Clause and the Equal Protection Clause are connected in a profound way, though they set forth independent principles. Rights implicit in liberty and rights secured by equal protection may rest on different precepts and are not always co-extensive, yet in some instances each may be instructive as to the meaning and reach of the other. In any particular case one Clause may be thought to capture the essence of the right in a more accurate and comprehensive way, even as the two Clauses may converge in the identification and definition of the right. This interrelation of the two principles furthers our understanding of what freedom is and must become. . . .

Finally, it must be emphasized that religions, and those who adhere to religious doctrines, may continue to advocate with utmost, sincere conviction that, by divine precepts, same-sex marriage should not be condoned. The First Amendment ensures that religious organizations and persons are given proper protection as they seek to teach the principles that are so fulfilling and so central to their lives and faiths, and to their own deep aspirations to continue the family structure they have long revered. The same is true of those who oppose same-sex marriage for other reasons. In turn, those who believe allowing same-sex marriage is proper or indeed essential, whether as a matter of religious conviction or secular belief, may engage those who disagree with their view in an open and searching debate. . . .

These cases also present the question whether the Constitution requires States to recognize same-sex marriages validly performed out of State. . . . Leaving the current state of affairs in place would maintain and promote instability and uncertainty. . . .

The Court, in this decision, holds same-sex couples may exercise the fundamental right to marry in all States. It follows that the Court also must hold—and it now does hold—that there is no lawful basis for a State to refuse to recognize a lawful same-sex marriage performed in another State on the ground of its same-sex character. . . .

The judgment of the Court of Appeals for the Sixth Circuit is reversed.

It is so ordered.

Chief Justice Roberts, with whom Justice Scalia and Justice Thomas join, dissenting. . . .

The majority's decision is an act of will, not legal judgment. The right it announces has no basis in the Constitution or this Court's precedent. The majority expressly disclaims judicial "caution" and omits even a pretense of humility, openly relying on its desire to remake society according to its own "new insight" into the "nature of injustice." As a result, the Court invalidates the marriage laws of more than half the States and orders the transformation of a social institution that has formed the basis of human society for millennia, for the Kalahari Bushmen and the Han Chinese, the Carthaginians and the Aztecs. Just who do we think we are? . . .

Petitioners and their amici base their arguments on the "right to marry" and the imperative of "marriage equality." There is no serious dispute that, under our precedents, the Constitution protects a right to marry and requires States to apply their marriage laws equally. The real question in these cases is what constitutes "marriage," or—more precisely—who decides what constitutes "marriage"? . . .

The Constitution itself says nothing about marriage, and the Framers thereby entrusted the States with "[t]he whole subject of the domestic relations of husband and wife." There is no dispute that every State at the founding—and every State throughout our history until a dozen years ago—defined marriage in the traditional, biologically rooted way. . . .

Shortly after this Court struck down racial restrictions on marriage in *Loving* [v. *Virginia*], a gay couple in Minnesota sought a marriage license. They argued that the Constitution required States to allow marriage between people of the same sex for the same reasons that it requires States to allow marriage between people of different races. The Minnesota Supreme Court rejected their analogy to *Loving*, and this Court summarily dismissed an appeal [in] *Baker* v. *Nelson* (1972).

In the decades after *Baker*, greater numbers of gays and lesbians began living openly, and many expressed a desire to have their relationships recognized as marriages. Over time, more people came to see marriage in a way that could be extended to such couples. Until recently, this new view of marriage remained a minority position. After the Massachusetts Supreme Judicial Court in 2003 interpreted its State Constitution to require recognition of same-sex marriage, many States—including the four at issue here—enacted constitutional amendments formally adopting the longstanding definition of marriage.

Over the last few years, public opinion on marriage has shifted rapidly. In 2009, the legislatures of Vermont, New Hampshire, and the District of Columbia became the first in the Nation to enact laws that revised the definition of marriage to include same-sex couples, while also providing accommodations for religious believers. In 2011, the New York Legislature enacted a similar law. In 2012, voters in Maine did the same, reversing the result of a referendum just three years earlier in which they had upheld the traditional definition of marriage. In all, voters and legislators in eleven States and the District of Columbia have changed their definitions of marriage to include same-sex couples. The highest courts of five States have decreed that same result under their own Constitutions. The remainder of the States retain the traditional definition of marriage. . . .

Petitioners first contend that the marriage laws of their States violate the Due Process Clause. The Solicitor General of the United States, appearing in support of petitioners, expressly disowned that position before this Court. The majority nevertheless resolves these cases for petitioners based almost entirely on the Due Process Clause.

The majority purports to identify four "principles and traditions" in this Court's due process precedents that support a fundamental right for same-sex couples to marry. In reality, however, the majority's approach has no basis in principle or tradition, except for the unprincipled tradition of judicial policymaking that characterized discredited decisions such as *Lochner* v. *New York*. Stripped of its shiny rhetorical gloss, the majority's argument is that the Due Process Clause gives same-sex couples a fundamental right to marry because it will be good for them and for society. If I were a legislator, I would certainly consider that view as a matter of social policy. But as a judge, I find the majority's position indefensible as a matter of constitutional law. . . .

This Court has interpreted the Due Process Clause to include a "substantive" component that protects certain liberty interests against state deprivation "no matter what process is provided." The theory is that some liberties are "so rooted in the traditions and conscience of our people as to be ranked as fundamental," and therefore cannot be deprived without compelling justification.

Allowing unelected federal judges to select which unenumerated rights rank as "fundamental"—and to strike down state laws on the basis of that determination—raises obvious concerns about the judicial role. Our precedents have accordingly insisted that judges "exercise the utmost care" in identifying implied fundamental rights, "lest the liberty protected by the Due Process Clause be subtly transformed into the policy preferences of the Members of this Court." . . . The need for restraint in administering the strong medicine of substantive due process is a lesson this Court has learned the hard way. The Court first applied substantive due process to strike down a statute in *Dred Scott* v. *Sandford* (1857). . . .

Perhaps recognizing how little support it can derive from precedent, the majority goes out of its way to jettison the "careful" approach to implied fundamental rights taken by this Court in [*Washington* v.] *Glucksberg*. . . . Ultimately, only one precedent offers any support for the majority's methodology: *Lochner* v. *New York* . . . ."

One immediate question invited by the majority's position is whether States may retain the definition of marriage as a union of two people. Although the majority randomly inserts the adjective "two" in various places, it offers no reason at all why the two-person element of the core definition of marriage may be preserved while the man-woman element may not. Indeed, from the standpoint of history and tradition, a leap from opposite-sex marriage to same-sex marriage is much greater than one from a two-person union to plural unions, which have deep roots in some cultures around the world. If the majority is willing to take the big leap, it is hard to see how it can say no to the shorter one. . . . When asked about a plural marital union at oral argument, petitioners asserted that a State "doesn't have such an institution." But that is exactly the point: the States at issue here do not have an institution of same-sex marriage, either. . . .

The majority's understanding of due process lays out a tantalizing vision of the future for Members of this Court: If an unvarying social institution enduring over all of recorded history cannot inhibit judicial policymaking, what can? But this approach is dangerous for the rule of law. The purpose of insisting that implied fundamental rights have roots in the history and tradition of our people is to ensure that when unelected judges strike down democratically enacted laws, they do so based on something more than their own beliefs. The Court today not only overlooks our country's entire history and tradition but actively repudiates it, preferring to live only in the heady days of the here and now. . . .

In addition to their due process argument, petitioners contend that the Equal Protection Clause requires their States to license and recognize same-sex marriages. The majority does not seriously engage with this claim. Its discussion is, quite frankly, difficult to follow. The central point seems to be that there is a "synergy between" the Equal Protection Clause and the Due Process Clause, and that some precedents relying on one Clause have also relied on the other. Absent from this portion of the opinion, however, is anything resembling our usual framework for deciding equal protection cases. . . .

Yet the majority fails to provide even a single sentence explaining how the Equal Protection Clause supplies independent weight for its position, nor does it attempt to justify its gratuitous violation of the canon against unnecessarily resolving constitutional questions. . . . In any event, the marriage laws at issue here do not violate the Equal Protection Clause, because distinguishing between opposite-sex and same-sex couples is rationally related to the States' "legitimate state interest" in "preserving the traditional institution of marriage." . . .

When decisions are reached through democratic means, some people will inevitably be disappointed with the results. But those whose views do not prevail at least know that they have had their say, and accordingly are—in the tradition of our political culture—reconciled to the result of a fair and honest debate. In addition, they can gear up to raise the issue later, hoping to persuade enough on the winning side to think again. . . . But today the Court puts a stop to all that. By deciding this question under the Constitution, the Court removes it from the realm of democratic decision. There will be consequences to shutting down the political process on an issue of such profound public significance. Closing debate tends to close minds. People denied a voice are less likely to accept the ruling of a court on an issue that does not seem to be the sort of thing courts usually decide. As a thoughtful commentator observed about another issue, "The political process was moving. . ., not swiftly enough for advocates of quick, complete change, but majoritarian institutions were listening and acting. Heavy-handed judicial intervention was difficult to justify and appears to have provoked, not resolved, conflict." Indeed, however heartened the proponents of same-sex marriage might be on this day, it is worth acknowledging what they have lost, and lost forever: the opportunity to win the true acceptance that comes from persuading their fellow citizens of the justice of their cause. And they lose this just when the winds of change were freshening at their backs. . . .

In the face of all this, a much different view of the Court's role is possible. That view is more modest and restrained. It is more skeptical that the legal abilities of judges also reflect insight into moral and philosophical issues. It is more sensitive to the fact that judges are unelected and unaccountable, and that the legitimacy of their power depends on confining it to the exercise of legal judgment. It is more attuned to the lessons of history, and what it has meant for the country and Court when Justices have exceeded their proper bounds. And it is less pretentious than to suppose that while people around the world have viewed an institution in a particular way for thousands of years, the present generation and the present Court are the ones chosen to burst the bonds of that history and tradition. . . .

If you are among the many Americans—of whatever sexual orientation—who favor expanding same-sex marriage, by all means celebrate today's decision. . . . But do not celebrate the Constitution. It had nothing to do with it.

I respectfully dissent.

Justice Scalia, with whom Justice Thomas joins, dissenting.

I join the Chief Justice's opinion in full. I write separately to call attention to this Court's threat to American democracy.

The substance of today's decree is not of immense personal importance to me. . . . It is of overwhelming importance, however, who it is that rules me. Today's decree says that my Ruler, and the Ruler of 320 million Americans coast-to-coast, is a majority of the nine lawyers on the Supreme Court. . . . This practice of constitutional revision by an unelected committee of nine, always accompanied (as it is today) by extravagant praise of liberty, robs the People of the most important liberty they asserted in the Declaration of Independence and won in the Revolution of 1776: the freedom to govern themselves. . . .

These cases ask us to decide whether the Fourteenth Amendment contains a limitation that requires the States to license and recognize marriages between two people of the same sex. Does it remove that issue from the political process?

Of course not. . . . When the Fourteenth Amendment was ratified in 1868, every State limited marriage to one man and one woman, and no one doubted the constitutionality of doing so. That resolves these cases. . . . Since there is no doubt whatever that the People never decided to prohibit the limitation of marriage to opposite-sex couples, the public debate over same-sex marriage must be allowed to continue.

But the Court ends this debate, in an opinion lacking even a thin veneer of law. Buried beneath the mummeries and straining-to-be-memorable passages of the opinion is a candid and startling assertion: No matter what it was the People ratified, the Fourteenth Amendment protects those rights that the Judiciary, in its "reasoned judgment," thinks the Fourteenth Amendment ought to protect. . . .

This is a naked judicial claim to legislative—indeed, super-legislative—power; a claim fundamentally at odds with our system of government. . . . A system of government that makes the People subordinate to a committee of nine unelected lawyers does not deserve to be called a democracy.

Judges are selected precisely for their skill as lawyers; whether they reflect the policy views of a particular constituency is not (or should not be) relevant. Not surprisingly then, the Federal Judiciary is hardly a cross-section of America. Take, for example, this Court, which consists of only nine men and women, all of them successful lawyers who studied at Harvard or Yale Law School. Four of the nine are natives of New York City. Eight of them grew up in east- and west-coast States. Only one hails from the vast expanse in-between. Not a single Southwesterner or even, to tell the truth, a genuine Westerner (California does not count). Not a single evangelical Christian (a group that comprises about one quarter of Americans), or even a Protestant of any denomination. The strikingly unrepresentative character of the body voting on today's social upheaval would be irrelevant if they were functioning as judges, answering the legal question whether the American people had ever ratified a constitutional provision that was understood to proscribe the traditional definition of marriage. But of course the Justices in today's majority are not voting on that basis; they say they are not. And to allow the policy question of same-sex marriage to be considered and resolved by a select, patrician, highly unrepresentative panel of nine is to violate a principle even more fundamental than no taxation without representation: no social transformation without representation.

But what really astounds is the hubris reflected in today's judicial Putsch. The five Justices who compose today's majority are entirely comfortable concluding that every State violated the Constitution for all of the 135 years between the Fourteenth Amendment's ratification and Massachusetts' permitting of same-sex marriages in 2003. They have discovered in the Fourteenth Amendment a "fundamental right" overlooked by every person alive at the time of ratification, and almost everyone else in the time since. . . .

Hubris is sometimes defined as o'erweening pride; and pride, we know, goeth before a fall. The Judiciary is the "least dangerous" of the federal branches because it has "neither Force nor Will, but merely judgment; and must ultimately depend upon the aid of the executive arm" and the States, "even for the efficacy of its judgments." With each decision of ours that takes from the People a question properly left to them—with each decision that is unabashedly based not on law, but on the "reasoned judgment" of a bare majority of this Court—we move one step closer to being reminded of our impotence.

Justice Thomas, with whom Justice Scalia joins, dissenting . . . [omitted].

Justice Alito, with whom Justice Scalia and Justice Thomas join, dissenting. . . . [omitted].

14

Equal Protection of the Laws

[T]here is no more effective practical guaranty against arbitrary and unreasonable government than to require that the principles of law which officials would impose upon a minority must be imposed generally. Conversely, nothing opens the door to arbitrary action so effectively as to allow those officials to pick and choose only a few to whom they will apply legislation and thus to escape the political retribution that might be visited upon them if larger numbers were affected.

—JUSTICE ROBERT H. JACKSON (1949)

The Founders, James Madison in particular, were wedded to the notion that unequal distribution of wealth is the natural result in a society where individuals of differing capacities are free. Accordingly, any government action on behalf of those less fortunate, ignoring merit, was suspect. Americans today might glibly tell a pollster that they favor both "liberty" and "equality," but that response obscures an unmistakable tension between those cherished values. As the Founders recognized, emphasis on individual liberty promotes inequality among individuals; measures to promote equality constrict individual liberty.

For whatever reason, a conspicuous omission from the Constitution of 1787, as well as the Bill of Rights, is a guaranty guarding against unequal treatment under the law. This provision now so conspicuous in a wide range of Supreme Court decisions dates only from 1868, when it was made part of the Fourteenth Amendment. Along with the privileges and immunities clause and the due process clause designed to safeguard individual rights against encroachment by the states, Section 1 declares: "No State shall . . . deny to any person within its jurisdiction the equal protection of the laws." The **equal protection clause** applies when states make distinctions among similarly situated people and treat them differently. The meaning the Supreme Court gives the clause largely determines what differences among people will be allowed to matter in public policy.

The command of equal protection may sound simple enough, but its meaning continues to spark intense debate both within the Court and throughout the nation. This is partly because the word *equality* itself signifies different things to different

DOI: 10.4324/9781003164340-15

people. For some, it stands for **equality of opportunity**. Accordingly, government's duty is to remove discriminatory barriers so that all can participate. Others favor **equality of condition** and so advocate programs such as Head Start or need-based college scholarships that reduce or even eliminate handicaps that many people encounter. Still others find even those measures inadequate. The crippling effects of existing inequalities, whether of wealth, race, or gender, are too strong and pervasive, and so call for measures that promote **equality of result**. Such competing visions of equality play out in contemporary political and legal dramas.

IDENTIFYING FORBIDDEN DISCRIMINATION

Virtually all legislation *classifies*—that is, discriminates. The challenge presented by the equal protection clause, therefore, is identifying which classifications are permitted and which ones are not. When the Court first considered the clause in the **Slaughterhouse Cases** (1873) (see Chapter Eight) less than a decade after the Civil War and the end of slavery, Justice Miller doubted whether "this sweeping injunction would ever be invoked against any state action" not directed by way of discrimination against blacks as a class. "It is," he wrote, "so clearly a provision for that race and that emergency, that a strong case would be necessary for its application to any other." Indeed, until recent decades, the Supreme Court was inhospitable to litigants who sought protection under the clause to any meaningful degree, outside the contexts (and then only occasionally) of racial discrimination and state regulation of business. Decisions like *Strauder* v. *West Virginia* (1880), invalidating a law that barred blacks from jury service, and *Gulf, C. & S. R.* v. *Ellis* (1897), striking down a requirement that railroads (but not other defendants) pay attorneys' fees in certain cases, were very much the exception. Reliance on the equal protection clause, Justice Holmes observed in *Buck* v. *Bell* (1927), was the "last resort of constitutional arguments." Claims of denial of equal protection were "frequently asserted" but "rarely sustained," agreed Justice Jackson in 1949. As will be seen in the sections below, however, the Court in the past eight decades has put teeth into this part of the Fourteenth Amendment, thus suggesting a "new" equal protection. This dramatic change—from constitutional omission to constitutional nullity to constitutional prominence—carries within itself a fascinating story.

An invigorated guaranty of equal protection persists largely because, in another example of judicial power, the Court has grafted a three-tier interpretive model onto the clause. On the bottom tier is the **rational basis test**. It is the least demanding and has long been used for most classifications. The justices ask only whether the classification in question has a *rational* (or reasonable) relation to a *legitimate* state interest. In other words, is there a nexus between a lawful objective and the means chosen to achieve it? On the top tier and the most demanding is the **strict scrutiny test** that is employed for classifications such as race that the Court deems "suspect," or (as later explained) for classifications that impinge on rights the Court considers fundamental. Ironically, the Court articulated the strict scrutiny test for the first time in ***Korematsu* v. *United States*** (1944) in upholding the wartime removal of Japanese Americans from the West Coast (see Chapter Fifteen). The test of strict scrutiny asks whether the classification is *necessarily related* to a *compelling* government interest. Moreover, such classifications must be *narrowly tailored* to accomplish their purpose.

Laws judged against strict scrutiny are almost certain to fail: "'strict' in theory and fatal in fact." In contrast, laws measured by the rationality test are almost certain to pass. Occasionally, however, as in ***Romer* v. *Evans*** (1996), a case involving discrimination based on sexual orientation, even this most lenient standard appears to have teeth. Especially for gender-based classifications, the Court draws from a middle tier to apply **intermediate scrutiny**, or near-strict scrutiny. In such situations, the question is whether the challenged statute is *substantially related* to an *important* state interest. Sometimes the level of scrutiny applied is a function of which government has made the classification: State laws discriminating against aliens, for example, are usually judged by strict scrutiny; congressional acts on the same subject are not. At other times, the Court divides over the appropriate level of scrutiny to apply, as ***Cleburne* v. *Cleburne Living Center*** (1985) illustrates with respect to mental retardation.

RACIAL DISCRIMINATION

After abolition of slavery by the Thirteenth Amendment (1865) and ratification of the Fourteenth Amendment (1868), whites in some states faced a dilemma. If they wished to keep blacks in an inferior status, they would need an acceptable legal principle. The answer was found in laws requiring segregation of whites and blacks under the formula "**separate but equal**."

Legalizing Third-Class Citizenship. When the Fourteenth Amendment was invoked in ***Plessy* v. *Ferguson*** (1896) on behalf of blacks against Louisiana's law requiring racial segregation on trains, the Court refused to allow the equal protection clause to serve even the limited purpose that Justice Miller had earlier acknowledged. Justice Henry Billings Brown's majority opinion in *Plessy* drew an important distinction between political and social equality. The Fourteenth Amendment demanded only the former, and the state law merely reflected prevailing social inequality. Racially segregated facilities were reasonable (and therefore permissible) so long as they were otherwise "equal." In dissent, the Court's only ex–slave owner, Justice John Marshall Harlan (I), deplored this emasculation: "Our Constitution is color-blind, and neither knows nor tolerates classes among citizens. In respect to civil rights all citizens are equal before the law." Denouncing the majority's separate-but-equal formula, Harlan predicted that "the judgment this day rendered will in time prove to be quite as pernicious as the decision made by this tribunal in the Dred Scott case" (see Chapter Two).

In the wake of *Plessy*, three kinds of policies developed which denied African Americans their rights well into the twentieth century. First, virtually every aspect of life in the South became racially segregated by law. This fact alone is significant when one remembers that as late as 1930, 79 percent of all American blacks lived in the states of the old Confederacy. Second, laws in southern states systematically excluded blacks from the political process. Third, without the vote, blacks were shortchanged across the board in the delivery of public services such as education. Favors are rarely extended to entire groups that are permanently disfranchised. The spirit of *Plessy* was therefore honored only in part. Though separate, services and facilities (when provided at all) were only occasionally "equal" for blacks.

Although racism backed by law was most visible in the South, where most blacks lived, other regions of the country were hardly immune, as custom and private discrimination combined to perpetuate racist attitudes, segregated neighborhoods, and racially motivated violence, including riots and lynchings. True, the Court struck down an ordinance in Louisville, Kentucky, requiring racially segregated neighborhoods in 1917 (*Buchanan* v. *Warley*), yet later refused to censure judicial enforcement of **racially restrictive covenants** in deeds that accomplished the same thing (*Corrigan* v. *Buckley*, 1926). Judicial condemnation of the practice did not come until *Shelley* v. *Kraemer* (1948).

Counterattack: The Road to *Brown*. In one of the first cases in which the Court began to give serious attention to the equality requirement, the justices invalidated a law under which Gaines, a black applicant, was refused admission to the law school at the University of Missouri (*Missouri* ex rel. *Gaines* v. *Canada*, 1938). Missouri made funds available to Gaines and other black applicants to finance their legal education in schools of adjacent states that offered unsegregated educational facilities and argued that by this action it was meeting the separate-but-equal requirement. Chief Justice Hughes, for the majority of seven, disposed of the state's contention emphatically. "By the operation of the laws of Missouri a privilege has been created for white law students which is denied to negroes by reason of their race. The white resident is afforded legal education within the State; the negro resident having the same qualifications is refused it there and must go outside the State to obtain it. That is a denial of equality of legal right. . . ."

A cluster of cases between 1948 and 1950 indicated that the separate-but-equal standard would in the future be more difficult to satisfy. *Sipuel* v. *University of Oklahoma* (1948) held that blacks must be admitted to a state law school or be furnished equivalent professional education within the state. *McLaurin* v. *Oklahoma State Regents* (1950) nullified state efforts to segregate the scholastic activities *on campus* of a black student who had been admitted to the graduate school of the University of Oklahoma pursuant to a federal court order. Finally, a direct challenge to segregated education was presented in *Sweatt* v. *Painter* (1950), in which an applicant who had been denied admission to the University of Texas Law School solely on the basis of color claimed that the instruction available in the newly established state law school for blacks was markedly inferior to the instruction at the university and that equal protection of laws was thus denied. In a unanimous decision, the Supreme Court ordered his admission to the white school, indicating that it was virtually impossible in practice, at least in professional education, for a state to comply with the separate-but-equal doctrine. Taking into account professional and psychological considerations, thus anticipating the thrust of Chief Justice Warren's opinion in ***Brown* v. *Board of Education*** (1954), Chief Justice Fred Vinson of Kentucky left that judicial creation hanging by a hair.

Following the decision in *Sweatt*, the National Association for the Advancement of Colored People and other organizations pressed the fight against segregation in public elementary and secondary schools. One of the prominent black attorneys in this drive was Thurgood Marshall, later a justice on the Supreme Court from 1967 to 1991. Would the Court retract the principle of separate but equal, or, alternatively, would it construe the requirement of equality so strictly that segregation in practice would be either constitutionally impossible or prohibitively expensive? After hearing arguments in a group of public school segregation cases presented at the 1952 term, the justices were unable to reach a decision. In setting the cases for reargument during the 1953 term, the Court took the unusual step of requesting counsel to provide answers to several questions, some seeking information concerning the intention of the Congress that proposed, and the states that ratified, the Fourteenth

Amendment and others requesting advice concerning the kind of orders that the Court should issue were it to find segregated school arrangements unconstitutional.

The Court's caution, though unusual, was understandable. Its decision would affect millions of white and black children in the school systems of 17 states and the District of Columbia where segregation was required by law, and those of four states where racial segregation was permitted by local option. Even greater issues were involved: If segregation in public schools was deemed a denial of equal protection of the laws, it would be difficult if not impossible to defend segregation in other sectors of public life. The legal underpinnings of the social structure of a great part of the nation were under attack.

On May 17, 1954, the Court handed down its decision in *Brown* v. *Board of Education*. Speaking for a unanimous bench, Chief Justice Earl Warren declared that "in the field of public education the doctrine of 'separate but equal' has no place. Separate educational facilities are inherently unequal." The opinion was remarkable not only for its brevity but also for its references to sociological and psychological factors. Reduced to a footnote, these were gratuitous. Earlier decisions had eroded the constitutional foundations of the separate-but-equal formula to the vanishing point. Nor did the historical evidence, furnished at the Court's request and available to it in briefs of counsel, influence the decision. "In approaching this problem," said the chief justice, "we cannot turn the clock back to 1868, when the Amendment was adopted, or even to 1896, when *Plessy* v. *Ferguson* was written. We must consider public education in the light of its full development and its present place in American life throughout the nation."

With *Brown* from Kansas, the Court had combined cases from South Carolina, Virginia, and Delaware. ***Bolling* v. *Sharpe*** was the companion case from the District of Columbia and was decided separately on the same day. In the District of Columbia case, the Court came to a similar conclusion, finding an equal protection component within the due process clause of the Fifth Amendment. Having achieved unanimity on this difficult issue, the Court postponed formulation of a decree until the 1954–1955 term and called for additional argument.

The Law and Politics of Racial Integration. In the following term, the Court handed down its decree in the second Brown case, expressing the conclusion that desegregation in public education would necessarily take place at varying speeds and in different ways, depending on local conditions. U.S. district court judges, employing the flexible principles of equity, were given the task of determining when and how desegregation should take place. In a historic pronouncement, the Court said, "The judgments below . . . are remanded to the district courts to take such proceedings and enter such orders and decrees consistent with this opinion as are necessary and proper to admit to public schools on a racially nondiscriminatory basis *with all deliberate speed*" the parties to these cases (italics added).

Although border states showed a disposition to comply with the Supreme Court's mandate, states in the Deep South began a campaign of active and passive resistance, adopting various legal tactics and devices that delayed the implementation of *Brown*. Several legislatures passed resolutions declaring the desegregation decisions "unlawful." Almost all southern senators and representatives joined in 1956 in issuing a "Declaration of Constitutional Principles" and advocated resistance to compelled desegregation by "all lawful means."

When litigation developed, the Supreme Court staunchly upheld lower federal court decisions ordering steps toward desegregated schools, either by denying certiorari or handing down per curiam rulings. The Eisenhower administration, initially lukewarm in support of *Brown*, took strong steps (including the dispatch of troops) in 1958 to support the orders of a federal court in Arkansas, actions that were upheld by a powerful decision of the Supreme Court in ***Cooper* v. *Aaron*** (see Chapter Two). However, the Court did not issue its next significant decision on school integration until 1964 when it ordered the reopening of a public school system in Virginia that had been closed to avoid compliance with *Brown* (*Griffin* v. *School Board of Prince Edward County*). Such defiance was possible partly because most African Americans in southern states were still denied the right to vote. Not until the late 1960s, after rigorous enforcement of the Voting Rights Act (see Chapter Five) had begun, would southern representatives in Congress and local elected officials become more responsive to the needs of black citizens.

The pace of integration also quickened after 1965 because of the combination of two congressional enactments that brought both administrative and financial pressure to bear on school districts. The mid-1960s witnessed the first mass infusion of federal funds into local school coffers, and the Civil Rights Act of 1964 in several ways made continued receipt of Washington's largess conditional on integrated education. Whereas litigation often took years to effect even small changes in the schools, bureaucrats with their hands on the federal faucet could accomplish substantial changes in months. Their efforts were reinforced by the Court.

In 1968, the Court confronted a "freedom-of-choice" integration plan from New Kent County, Virginia (*Green* v. *School Board*). Here, there was no longer an official "white" or "black" label for schools, but all the white children in this rural district elected to remain in the school they had previously attended, and 85 percent of the black children chose to stay at the school they had previously attended. Labels aside, the school populations were "racially identifiable." What the Constitution required, said Justice William Brennan, was a plan that produced compliance with *Brown*—a **unitary** as opposed to a **dual school system**. "The burden on a school board today is to come forward with a plan that promises realistically to work, and promises realistically to work now."

Implications of *Green* became apparent in *Swann* v. *Charlotte-Mecklenburg Board of Education* (1971) when the Court upheld an integration plan involving widespread busing within a single metropolitan school district in North Carolina. A previous desegregation plan had left large numbers of predominantly one-race schools. Not surprisingly, this residual segregation in the schools was caused partly by racially segregated neighborhoods, themselves shaped over the years by a system of legally enforced school segregation. "The objective today," declared Chief Justice Warren Burger, "remains to eliminate from the public schools all vestiges of state-imposed segregation."

Given these judicial actions and passage of the Civil Rights Act of 1964, ***Loving* v. *Virginia*** (1967) seemed almost anti-climactic. With language later relevant to the debate over same-sex marriage, the ruling invalidated **miscegenation laws** that banned interracial marriages in some states.

Continuing Effects of *Brown*. The target of judicial efforts to apply *Brown* was **de jure segregation**—separation of the races that existed because of law and public policy. The most obvious place to find de jure segregation was in the school systems of the southern states, and through 1971, segregation cases in the Supreme Court had a southern focus. Not reached by the Constitution and not at issue in those cases was **de facto segregation**—racial separation that was a product of nongovernmental actions and practices.

In 1973, the Court's attention was drawn to the problem of school segregation outside the South. *Keyes* v. *School District* (1973) involved not statutes or other obvious official actions to create segregated schools but instead various administrative decisions in the 1960s that confined black students to schools in a section of Denver, Colorado. The Supreme Court ruled that where one part of a school system was segregated, the remedy could include busing of students from one part of the district to another to reduce the number of **racially identifiable schools** (i.e., mainly with one race). Attendance zones drawn by school boards that resulted in racial imbalances in the classroom could be a constitutional violation just as if old-style southern segregation laws had been in effect.

Although continuing to insist that a distinction be made between de facto and de jure segregation—the former being lawful, the latter unconstitutional—*Keyes* signaled northern communities that federal courts would give close scrutiny to all official decisions affecting the racial composition of schools and that absence of statutory provisions requiring segregation would not prevent judicial action. In other words, *Keyes* greatly enlarged the concept of de jure segregation and markedly shrank the concept of de facto segregation.

By this time, a much larger percentage of black pupils attended integrated schools in the South than in states outside the South. As the flight of whites to the suburbs accelerated and blacks and other racial minorities became the dominant population in cities, the question of how to achieve racially integrated schools in multidistrict metropolitan areas became acute. More and more the argument was made that the state governments should bear ultimate responsibility for achieving desegregation: If school district lines perpetuated segregation, a failure by state governments to intercede violated the Fourteenth Amendment. Thus, ***Milliken* v. *Bradley*** (1974) posed the question whether the judiciary could impose a multidistrict remedy to correct racial imbalances between districts.

Recall that the remedies the Court upheld in both *Keyes* and *Swann* did not extend beyond the bounds of the single school district involved. *Milliken* began in Detroit as litigation similar to *Keyes*. After attempting to remove racial imbalances within the city school district, the federal district judge recognized the obvious: A school district with a large black majority would still have mainly black schools, even with extensive busing within Detroit. Suburban areas, in contrast, had heavily white school populations. Because the segregation was metropolitan in scope, his remedy encompassed 53 separate suburban school districts covering an area approximately the size of the state of Delaware. By a vote of 5–4, however, the Supreme Court found the remedy excessive. It would be acceptable only on a showing that government was responsible for the racial imbalances between the school districts.

Where courts have ordered remedial measures to eliminate de jure segregation, the question of duration sooner or later arises. In *Board of Education* v. *Dowell* (1991), six justices agreed that "federal supervision of local school systems was intended as a temporary measure." If a school board has taken action in good faith to eliminate the vestiges of segregation, the district court may release the board from the integration decree, even if some **resegregation** occurs. Resegregation may have several causes, one being demographic changes within a school district. Reviewing the status of school integration in DeKalb County, Georgia, in 1992, the Court declared that officials were under no obligation to employ "heroic" measures to attain or retain racial balance when the imbalance results neither from the former de jure segregation nor from a later violation by the district, but is attributable only to independent demographic forces. Public schools, however, bear the "burden of showing that any current imbalance is not traceable, in a proximate way, to the prior violation" (*Freeman* v. *Pitts*). The effects of demographic changes on school integration patterns have been profound nationwide. Today, the public schools attended by more than half of black and Latino children have mainly nonwhite enrollments. However, ***Parents Involved* v. *Seattle School District No. 1*** (2007) severely limited the ability of public school systems to remedy racial imbalances in enrollments in the absence of de jure segregation. Struck down 5–4 were plans in Washington State and Kentucky that used race in assigning students to schools.

Higher Education. Integration has been a special problem in states that formerly maintained racially segregated colleges and universities. Before 1954, for instance, Mississippi operated five institutions for whites and three for blacks. Even though the state adopted a race-neutral admission policy after 1964, the campuses remained largely segregated. By the 1990s, 99 percent of the state's white students attending in-state public institutions were enrolled on the five historically white campuses, and 71 percent of the state's black students attending state-run colleges were enrolled in the three historically black institutions, where the racial makeup ranged from 92 to 99 percent black. As a result of litigation begun against the state in 1975, the Supreme Court acknowledged an important difference between higher education and primary and secondary education: The role that student choice plays in the former. Even so, race-neutral admission policies may not be enough to satisfy the Constitution's requirement that dual systems be eliminated. Rather, "[i]f the State perpetuates policies and practices traceable to its prior system that continue to have segregative effects—whether by influencing student enrollment decisions or by fostering segregation in other facets of the university system—and such policies are without sound educational justification and can be practicably eliminated," Justice Byron White announced, "the State has not satisfied its burden of proving that it has dismantled its prior system" (*United States* v. *Fordice*, 1992). Lower courts must now determine when previously dual systems must take measures to reduce racial disparities among students and faculty, possibly affecting the existence of degree programs and even of some institutions.

STATE ACTION

As the distinction between de jure and de facto segregation illustrates, the role of *government* in promoting segregation is crucial to a violation of the equal protection clause. Indeed, the Supreme Court made it clear well over a century ago in the **Civil Rights Cases** that the Fourteenth Amendment does not forbid racial discrimination by everyone, but only by states and their political subdivisions. This is the concept of **state action**—conduct by government, not by a private entity. Confronted in 1883 with congressional legislation guaranteeing equal access to hotels and similar places of public accommodation, the Court balked at giving the equal protection clause positive meaning. By reading the first and fifth sections of the Fourteenth Amendment to mean merely that Congress could pass legislation to supersede discriminatory state legislation and official acts (a power similar to that of judicial review), the Court preserved the existing federal system at the expense of implementing equal treatment. Justice Joseph Bradley's majority opinion naively assumed that state laws already required innkeepers and public carriers to serve all unobjectionable persons, and that anyone refused service had an adequate remedy under state law.

Private discrimination is therefore not touched by the Constitution. The line between public and private discrimination, however, is sometimes blurred. How much state involvement must there be in particular situations before the strictures of the equal protection clause apply? In recent decades, the Court has expanded the state action principle so that if a state becomes so "entwined" with private affairs that the action of private citizens becomes tantamount to "state action," the Fourteenth Amendment then applies. Thus, in 1972, *Moose Lodge* v. *Irvis* posed the question whether the Loyal Order of Moose forfeited its liquor license when it refused to admit Leroy Irvis, black majority leader of the Pennsylvania House of Representatives, as a guest of one of its members. Irvis conceded that Moose members had a constitutional right of association, permitting them to exclude him from their club. But, he argued, their club could not hold a liquor license if they did. Allowing the club to do so would amount to state licensing of racial discrimination. Six justices led by Rehnquist rejected the sweeping argument, instead resolving the case by severing the most objectionable link between the state and the lodge: The Pennsylvania Liquor Control Board's rule that private clubs adhere to their membership policy as a condition for holding a liquor license.

Ratified three years before the Fourteenth Amendment, the **Thirteenth Amendment** not only outlawed slavery and involuntary servitude but continues to have a potency of its own. Unlike the Fourteenth, the Thirteenth does not present a state action problem, as the Supreme Court demonstrated in 1968 when it construed the Civil Rights Act of 1866, enacted on the authority of the Thirteenth, to bar private discrimination in housing. **Section 1982** of that act reads, "All citizens of the United States shall have the same right, in every State and Territory, as is enjoyed by white citizens thereof to inherit, purchase, lease, sell, hold and convey real and personal property." *Jones* v. *Mayer* upheld the right of a black complainant to sue a white housing development company for refusing to sell him a house. Lower federal courts had assumed that the statute outlawed only state-required or state-authorized discrimination, but the Supreme Court found it applicable to all forms of discrimination in housing, public or private. Ironically, Congress originally proposed the Fourteenth Amendment partly to ensure the constitutionality of the 1866 act, doubting whether the Thirteenth Amendment provided a sure footing for the statute.

Jones was the basis for *Runyon* v. *McCrary* (1976), which applied **Section 1981** of the 1866 act to commercially operated, nonsectarian private schools that refused admission to black applicants solely on grounds of race. Section 1981 guarantees all persons "the same right [to] make and enforce contracts, to sue, be parties, give evidence, and to the full extent and equal benefits of all laws and proceedings for the security of persons and property as is enjoyed by white citizens."

GENDER DISCRIMINATION

Because the Constitution has been the battleground for so many years in the struggle for racial equality, one might suppose that sexual equality has occupied the attention of Congress and the courts for just as long. It has not. Until the late twentieth century, the legal (and constitutional) status of women in the United States remained one of substantial inequality, as public policies of state and federal governments routinely took gender into account. As late as 1973, some 900 sex-based federal laws were still on the books. While there have been opponents of gender-based discrimination since the earliest years of the Republic, for a long time justices of the Supreme Court were not among them.

Indeed, it was not until *Reed* v. *Reed* (1971) that the Supreme Court invalidated a gender-based statute as violative of the equal protection clause. (It was in this case that future Justice Ginsburg—then a professor at Columbia University Law School—wrote the merits brief on behalf of Sally Reed.) An Idaho law directed that males be preferred to equally qualified females in the appointment of administrators for estates. The Court acknowledged that "the objective of reducing the work load on probate courts by eliminating one class of contests is not without some legitimacy." Then, purporting to apply the traditional rationality standard, a unanimous bench held that "a mandatory preference to members of either sex over members of the other, merely to accomplish the elimination of hearings on the merits, is to work the very kind of arbitrary legislative choice forbidden by" the Fourteenth Amendment.

In 1973, in ***Frontiero* v. *Richardson***, as many as four justices were willing to consider gender a suspect classification, a position urged on the Court in *Reed*. Challenged under the equal protection component of the Fifth Amendment was a Defense Department policy that treated male and female personnel differently when obtaining support for dependent spouses. Even without the tough standard of strict scrutiny, however, four other justices probed the "rationality" of the statute and reached the same result.

Compromise between the rational basis and strict scrutiny tests accounts for Justice Brennan's opinion in ***Craig* v. *Boren*** (1976) that spelled out an intermediate level of scrutiny that emerged for gender-based distinctions. In this case, an Oklahoma statute prohibiting the sale of 3.2 percent beer to males under 21 and to females under 18 was found to fall short constitutionally. "[T]o withstand constitutional challenge, previous cases establish that classifications by gender must serve important governmental objectives and must be substantially related to achievement of those objectives." In other words, the purpose of the statute must be valid, and the justices must be convinced that another law treating the sexes equally would not do as well. As *Craig* demonstrates, gender-based distinctions today are constitutionally at high risk.

That assessment has turned out to be especially true with respect to single-sex education in state-supported institutions of higher education, a matter the Court first confronted in ***Mississippi University for Women* v. *Hogan*** (1982). Joe Hogan could have enrolled in two state-supported coeducational nursing schools in Mississippi but not the nursing school at MUW, said the state, because he was male. "Our decisions . . . establish that the party seeking to uphold a statute that classifies individuals on the basis of their gender must carry the burden of showing an 'exceedingly persuasive justification' for the classification," wrote Justice O'Connor for the majority, apparently tightening the standard in *Craig* v. *Boren*. The justices found unpersuasive the state's argument that a female-only nursing school served a substantial government interest by compensating for discrimination against women. Instead, they concluded that the Mississippi policy only tended to perpetuate the stereotyped view of nursing as exclusively a woman's job. Furthermore, even though Title IX of the Education Amendments of 1972 expressly authorized traditionally single-sex state universities to continue admitting only men or women, O'Connor explained that Congress could not permit by statute something the Fourteenth Amendment forbids. *Hogan* later determined the outcome of the six-year courtroom battle fought by Virginia Military Institute (VMI) to retain its all-male status. In 1996, with only a single dissent, the Court ordered an end to single-sex education at VMI when it invalidated an arrangement by which women seeking specialized military education could instead enroll in the state-financed Virginia Women's Institute for Leadership at nearby Mary Baldwin, an independent college for women (*United States* v. *Virginia*).

FUNDAMENTAL RIGHTS ANALYSIS

The equal protection clause can also be a far-reaching tool for judicial protection of fundamental rights specified or implicit in the Constitution, as the Court first hinted in *Skinner* v. *Oklahoma* (1942). This decision struck down a compulsory sterilization scheme mandated by Oklahoma for certain, but not all, habitual criminals. The classification threatened "marriage and procreation," wrote Justice Douglas, which "are fundamental to the very existence and survival of the race." Today, classifications that infringe on rights the Court deems fundamental are judged by the strict scrutiny test.

Shapiro* v. *Thompson (1969) illustrates how **fundamental rights analysis** (also called **substantive equal protection**) can be used to shield particular rights. Held invalid were one-year residence requirements states imposed on all persons seeking welfare assistance. Justice Brennan for the majority spoke of the "right" of freedom to travel throughout the states: "Thus, the purpose of deterring the in-migration of indigents cannot serve as justification for the classification created by the one-year waiting period, since that purpose is constitutionally impermissible. Because the classification here touches on the fundamental right of interstate movement, its constitutionality must be judged by the stricter standard—whether it promotes a compelling state interest. Under this standard, the waiting period requirement clearly violates the Equal Protection Clause."

Is education a "fundamental right"? If so, financing of public schools by a property tax stands in constitutional jeopardy because of the substantial inequalities present between property-rich and property-poor districts. But in ***San Antonio Independent School District* v. *Rodriguez*** (1973), five justices declared that education was "not among the rights afforded explicit protection under our Constitution" and did not fall within any of the categories calling for strict judicial scrutiny. Accordingly, the Texas local property tax funding law for public schools did not deny equal protection to children residing in districts with a low property tax base. The majority agreed that the tax system needed reform, but this "must come from the law makers and from the pressures of those who elect them." The Court might have held that education is a fundamental right and poverty a suspect classification. Either finding would have placed a burden on the state to show a compelling interest. Instead, the Court rejected both possible grounds in upholding the Texas scheme for financing public schools, which admittedly permitted substantial disparities in expenditures per pupil between districts.

CONGRESSIONAL PROTECTION OF CIVIL RIGHTS

Legislation has become as important as the Constitution in fighting discrimination. Indeed, because of the concept of state action, some forms of discrimination can be reached only by statute. Since the 1960s Congress has enacted a variety of laws to combat discrimination based not only on race and gender but on age, religion, and disability as well. Many have also urged Congress to add sexual orientation to the list of protected categories. Most of this legislation falls outside the scope of this book, but a few of the most important provisions merit mention here.

Probably the most comprehensive civil rights law ever passed by Congress is the **Civil Rights Act of 1964. Title II** outlawed racial discrimination in hotels, restaurants, theaters, gas stations, and other public facilities affecting interstate commerce. The statutory coverage was intended to be pervasive because "affect commerce" was defined to include both establishments serving interstate travelers and those serving or selling products that had "moved" in interstate commerce. Contrary to the Court's position in the Civil Rights Cases of 1883, Congress also claimed authority under the Fourteenth Amendment for this provision of the 1964 act. In ***Heart of Atlanta Motel* v. *United States***, the Court chose to rely only on the power to regulate interstate commerce in upholding application of the new statute to motels that catered to interstate travelers. ***Katzenbach* v. *McClung*** allowed congressional power to reach a restaurant in Birmingham which annually used about $70,000 worth of food that had moved in interstate commerce. (Both cases are reprinted in Chapter Six.) Title II was also held to apply to a 232-acre recreational facility (*Daniel* v. *Paul*, 1969) and to a community swimming pool (*Tillman* v. *Wheaton-Haven Association*, 1973). Such generous interpretation means that no facility, otherwise open to the public, may any longer discriminate on the basis of race or any of the other protected classifications.

Title VII of the same law remains the principal weapon against racial as well as gender-based and religious discrimination in employment, salary matters, promotions, and the like. In *Bostock* v. *Clayton County* (2020), the Court significantly expanded the reach of Title VII by including within its reach discrimination and harassment in the workplace based on sexual orientation and transgender status. Moreover, cases brought under Title VII differ from those brought under the Fourteenth Amendment in at least two major ways: First, the Fourteenth Amendment constrains only state governments and their political subdivisions, whereas Title VII includes the private sector too. Second, discriminatory *intent* is a necessary element of a violation of the Fourteenth Amendment; for Title VII, discriminatory *effect* is sufficient to establish a prima facie case of discrimination. According to *Griggs* v. *Duke Power Co.* (1971), Title VII "proscribes not only overt discrimination but also practices that are fair in form, but discriminatory in operation. . . . Good intent or absence of discriminatory intent does not redeem employment procedures or testing mechanisms that operate as 'built-in headwinds' for minority groups and are unrelated to measuring job capability." Under the Griggs rule, employers have the burden of showing that the questionable device is "a reasonable measure of job performance." In 1972 Congress brought local governments within the ambit of Title VII.

Significantly, legislation in 1991 insisted that the discriminatory practice not only be job related but also consistent with "business necessity." It also removed one of the major differences between suits brought under Title VII, which bans several forms of discrimination, and suits brought under Section 1981, which deals exclusively with racial discrimination. Punitive damages, albeit capped, are now allowed under Title VII. (There is no cap on punitive damages in actions brought under Section 1981.) Prior to 1991, Title VII litigants could seek compensatory damages such as back pay as well as legal fees, but the absence of punitive damages discouraged attorneys from accepting Title VII cases on a contingency fee basis.

Another significant statutory provision, especially for universities, their students, and their athletic programs, is **Title IX** of the Education Amendments of 1972, prohibiting sex discrimination in "any education program or activity receiving Federal financial assistance." (Title VI of the 1964 Civil Rights Act had already proscribed racial discrimination in such programs.) In *Grove City College* v. *Bell* (1984), the Court determined that Title IX applies to an institution with students who receive direct federal financial aid even though the institution itself accepts no funds from the government. Under the statute, institutions not in compliance with regulations written by the Department of Education implementing Title IX would be denied federal aid. The cutoff of funds would also apply, the Court said, to an institution's students receiving direct support, such as Basic Educational Opportunity Grants. Although that interpretation left virtually no American campus outside the reach of Title IX, the Court then held that federal assistance to one part of a college's program did not trigger institution-wide coverage, thus limiting the impact of institutional sanctions under Title IX. In the Civil Rights Restoration Act of 1988, Congress overturned the Court's narrow reading of Title IX, leaving no doubt that it intended the cutoff of aid to be institution-wide.

AFFIRMATIVE ACTION

If much litigation under the equal protection clause and the civil rights acts has been aimed at halting practices deemed harmful to certain minorities, what is the legal status of **affirmative action**—policies designed to help those same minorities? As the makeup of the bench has changed since the 1970s, the Supreme Court's position on such race-conscious measures has shifted from general tolerance to deep suspicion to something in between.

University Admissions. The Supreme Court first squarely confronted affirmative action in *Regents of the University of California* v. *Bakke* (1978). The medical school at the University of California at Davis operated a special admissions program in which 16 of the 100 seats in the entering class were set aside for qualifying minority students. No white had ever been admitted through the special admissions program, and the Davis medical school had no prior history of racial discrimination in its admissions policy. After his rejection in 1974, Allan Bakke, a white male, challenged the program on equal protection grounds, and the California Supreme Court ordered his admission. For those hoping for a clear, forthright, thunderbolt pronouncement by the High Court, the decision in *Bakke* was a disappointment. Bakke won (and so gained admission to medical school), but so did advocates of affirmative action. These seemingly conflicting results came about because the justices were divided into three camps.

Justices Brennan, White, Marshall, and Blackmun found no constitutional violation in the admissions program at Davis. Race-based admissions for ameliorative purposes should be judged by, at most, intermediate scrutiny, a standard that, in their view, Davis easily met. Neither did they see it as being in conflict with **Title VI** of the Civil Rights Act of 1964 that banned racial and certain other kinds of discrimination in programs receiving federal financial assistance. Four others (Stevens, Burger, Stewart, and Rehnquist) considered the Davis plan a violation of Title VI and so did not reach the constitutional question. Left was Justice Powell. The Davis plan was flawed, he thought, because the presence of the quota meant that race was used as an exclusionary factor. Race, however, could be taken into account as an illuminating factor in evaluating an applicant and to achieve racial diversity in the student body for educational reasons. Indeed, for Powell, diversity was sufficiently compelling to satisfy the strict scrutiny test.

Thus, *Bakke* pointed in two distinctly different directions. Combining Powell's concession with the Brennan group, *Bakke* suggested that one could constitutionally use race to some extent in deciding whom to admit. Combining Powell's view with the position put forth by the Stevens group, *Bakke* not only invalidated the Davis plan but also cast doubt on any admissions policy that relied on race-based quotas or percentages.

After *Bakke*, the Court did not fully revisit affirmative action in higher education until it decided two cases involving the University of Michigan in 2003: *Grutter* v. *Bollinger* and *Gratz* v. *Bollinger*. The first involved admissions at the law school, where race was used as a factor to obtain a "critical mass" of minority students; the second tested undergraduate admissions in the college of literature, science, and the arts, where a point system gave a boost to minority applicants. In both, litigants challenged the policies as a violation of equal protection and Title VI. In both, the university argued that the plans were designed to promote racial diversity and, drawing on Justice Powell's opinion in *Bakke*, that diversity was a compelling interest. While a five-justice majority in *Grutter* upheld the law school's use of race, six justices voted to strike down the undergraduate admissions system contested in *Gratz*.

In the wake of *Grutter*, however, voters in Michigan amended the state constitution to prohibit race-conscious admission policies at state universities, a ban the Supreme Court upheld in 2014 (*Schuette* v. *BAMN*).

The contrasting outcomes of the Michigan cases in 2003 may partly account for Abigail Fisher's ultimately unsuccessful challenge to the admissions policy in use at the Austin campus of the University of Texas that made two trips to the High Court and resulted in ***Fisher* v. *University of Texas at Austin*** (2016). Combined with *Grutter*, *Fisher* suggests that race may now be used as one tool to achieve a diverse student body. However, given *Bakke* and *Gratz*, academic institutions may not employ quotas or separate tracks for certain racial groups. Moreover, as illustrated earlier in this chapter by *Parents Involved* v. *Seattle School District No. 1*, the absence of individualized consideration may largely explain the rejection in that case of race-based pupil assignment plans designed to promote diversity in public schools.

Congress and Race-Conscious Measures. With cooperation of the executive branch, Congress has promoted affirmative action through a variety of programs. In *Fullilove* v. *Klutznick* (1980), six justices upheld a **set-aside**: A congressional stipulation that "absent an administrative waiver, 10 percent of the federal funds granted for local public works projects must be used by the state or local grantee to procure services or supplies from businesses owned and controlled by members of statutorily identified minority groups." Only three justices (Brennan, Marshall, and Blackmun) gave the mandate their unqualified approval. The remaining three justices in the majority (Burger, White, and Powell) went out of their way to demonstrate a very qualified approval. Their first qualification consisted of the findings by Congress and the Civil Rights Commission that the continuing effects of discrimination in the construction industry had kept minority participation to a minimum. Second was the limited nature of the set-aside itself. The figure of 10 percent fell roughly halfway between the percentage of minority contractors and the percentage of minority-group members in the nation. Moreover, the set-aside applied to less than 1 percent of all funds expended yearly in the United States on construction. The third qualification rested on Congress' unique role under the Fourteenth Amendment. No fewer than 10 times did Chief Justice Burger's plurality opinion refer specifically to Congress' authority under the enforcement clause in Section 5 of the amendment. Yet even with this unique role, the Burger three hinted that the set-aside came close to the line: The "program press[ed] the outer limits of congressional authority. . . ." The set-aside may have survived its 1980 review by a whisker.

In 1989, six justices in *Richmond* v. *J. A. Croson Co.* declared that states lacked the remedial powers enjoyed by Congress. Invalidated was a city's 30 percent minority set-aside quota for contractors. "Under Richmond's scheme," wrote O'Connor for the majority, "a successful black, Hispanic or Oriental entrepreneur from anywhere in the country enjoys an absolute preference over other citizens based solely on their race." Because the city had not established a convincing record of purposeful municipal discrimination, the Court evaluated Richmond's policy under the formidable strict scrutiny test. The ruling called into question similar policies in 36 states and at least 190 cities.

One year later, however, five justices in *Metro Broadcasting, Inc.* v. *FCC* not only reaffirmed congressional power in this area but, going beyond *Fullilove*, seemed to divorce the justification for a national affirmative action program from the need for official findings of the persistent effects of discrimination. In contrast to state and local programs, congressionally mandated affirmative action programs were subject not to strict scrutiny, but to the less demanding test of intermediate scrutiny that Justice Brennan had urged in the context of state university admissions in *Bakke*. Upholding two minority-preference policies of the Federal Communications Commission for minority-owned enterprises, the Court declared that race-conscious ameliorative programs were therefore acceptable if they served important governmental objectives and were substantially related to achieving those objectives, even if they were not intended to compensate victims of past public or private discrimination.

Adarand Constructors Co. v. *Peña* (1995) then reversed *Metro Broadcasting* outright. In a major defeat for advocates of affirmative action, federal programs containing racial classifications, like those of state and local governments, are subject to strict scrutiny, regardless of whether the classifications or preferences are invidious or benign. In dispute was a clause in a prime contractor's contract with the Department of Transportation, challenged by the low bidder, that awarded a bonus to the prime contractor for choosing as subcontractors small businesses controlled by "socially and economically disadvantaged individuals." The clause required the contractor to presume that those individuals include "Black Americans, Hispanic Americans, Native Americans, Asian Pacific Americans, and other minorities."

Affirmative action will undoubtedly continue to vex the Court. The record thus far reflects a Solomonic reluctance neither fully to embrace nor to shun race-based policies in all situations. This may be expected in view of the divisiveness and complexity of the issue. Changes in the personnel of the Court will surely keep these questions in flux.

KEY TERMS

- equal protection clause
- equality of opportunity
- equality of condition
- equality of result
- rational basis test
- strict scrutiny test
- intermediate scrutiny
- separate but equal
- racially restrictive covenants

unitary school system
dual school system
miscegenation laws
de jure segregation
de facto segregation
racially identifiable schools
resegregation
state action
Thirteenth Amendment
Section 1982
Section 1981
fundamental rights analysis
substantive equal protection
Civil Rights Act of 1964
Title II
Title VII
Title IX
affirmative action
Title VI
set-aside

QUERIES

1. In *Strauder* v. *West Virginia* (1880), Justice William Strong stated that the purpose of the Fourteenth Amendment was to grant blacks "the right to exemption from unfriendly legislation against them as distinctively colored." Measured by this standard, was the outcome in *Plessy* v. *Ferguson* correct? Are there elements of the Strauder understanding of the Fourteenth Amendment in Chief Justice Warren's opinion in *Brown* v. *Board of Education*?

2. Nearly seven decades have passed since the Court's historic decision in *Brown* v. *Board of Education*, and assessments vary considerably regarding the Court's impact on civil rights since *Brown*. At one extreme is the accolade by federal appeals judge J. Harvie Wilkinson III that *Brown* was essential to the civil rights revolution and its achievements: "Very little could have been accomplished in mid-century America without the Supreme Court. . . . *Brown* may be the most important political, social, and legal event in America's twentieth-century history." At the other is the nearly tragic despondency reflected by the 1993 statement of Kenneth Clark (whose research in psychology loomed large in the *Brown* litigation) that *Brown* and related cases accomplished little: "I look back and shudder at how naive we all were in our belief in the steady progress racial minorities would make through programs of litigation and education." What have been the effects of that decision, as well as of subsequent decisions involving school integration, on public education, on broader matters of race in American society, and on the Court and constitutional law generally?

3. What did Justice Scalia find striking about the majority's position in *Romer* v. *Evans*? Is there a link between Justice Kennedy's opinion in that case and his opinion in *Obergefell* v. *Hodges* in Chapter Thirteen?

4. Some public universities in the United States have established black-only campus housing in response to demands from African American students seeking refuge from what they consider insensitive remarks and "microaggressions" from their white classmates. Do such "safe spaces" present questions under the Fourteenth Amendment?

SELECTED READINGS

Bardolf, Richard, ed. *The Civil Rights Record: Black Americans and the Law, 1849–1970*. New York: Crowell, 1970.

Hockett, Jeffrey D. *A Storm over This Court: Law, Politics, and Supreme Court Decision Making in Brown v. Board of Education*. Charlottesville: University of Virginia Press, 2013.

Klarman, Michael J. *From Jim Crow to Civil Rights: The Supreme Court and the Struggle for Racial Equality*. New York: Oxford University Press, 2004.

Lee, Francis Graham. *Equal Protection*. Santa Barbara, CA: ABC-CLIO, 2003.

Luxenberg, Steven. *Separate: The Story of Plessy v. Ferguson and America's Journey from Slavery to Segregation*. New York: Norton, 2019.

Moses, Michelle S. *Living with Moral Disagreement: The Enduring Controversy about Affirmative Action*. Chicago: University of Chicago Press, 2016.

O'Brien, David M. *Justice Robert H. Jackson's Unpublished Opinion in Brown v. Board*. Lawrence: University Press of Kansas, 2017.

Rhode, Deborah L. *Justice and Gender*. Cambridge: Harvard University Press, 1989.

Siegel-Hawley, Genevieve. *When the Fences Come Down: Twenty-First-Century Lessons from Metropolitan School Desegregation*. Chapel Hill: University of North Carolina Press, 2016.

Vose, Clement. *Caucasians Only: The Supreme Court, the NAACP, and the Restrictive Covenant Cases*. Berkeley: University of California Press, 1959.

I. IDENTIFYING FORBIDDEN DISCRIMINATION

Korematsu v. *United States*
323 U.S. 214, 65 S.Ct. 193, 89 L.Ed. 194 (1944)

http://caselaw.findlaw.com/us-supreme-court/323/214.html

(This case is reprinted in Chapter Fifteen; see the Table of Contents.)

Cleburne v. *Cleburne Living Center*
473 U.S. 432, 105 S.Ct. 3249, 87 L.Ed. 2d 313 (1985)

http://caselaw.findlaw.com/us-supreme-court/473/432.html

The facts of this case are contained in Justice White's opinion of the Court. While all justices agreed that the city council's denial of the permit amounted to a violation of the equal protection clause, they differed over the appropriate level of scrutiny to apply. Majority: White, Blackmun, Brennan, Burger, Marshall, O'Connor, Powell, Rehnquist, Stevens.

JUSTICE WHITE delivered the opinion of the Court.

A Texas city denied a special use permit for the operation of a group home for the mentally retarded, acting pursuant to a municipal zoning ordinance requiring permits for such homes. The Court of Appeals for the Fifth Circuit held that mental retardation is a "quasi-suspect" classification and that the ordinance violated the Equal Protection Clause because it did not substantially further an important governmental purpose. We hold that a lesser standard of scrutiny is appropriate, but conclude that under that standard the ordinance is invalid as applied in this case. . . .

[W]e conclude for several reasons that the Court of Appeals erred in holding mental retardation a quasi-suspect classification calling for a more exacting standard of judicial review than is normally accorded economic and social legislation. First, it is undeniable, and it is not argued otherwise here, that those who are mentally retarded have a reduced ability to cope with and function in the everyday world. Nor are they all cut from the same pattern: as the testimony in this record indicates, they range from those whose disability is not immediately evident to those who must be constantly cared for. They are thus different, immutably so, in relevant respects, and the states' interest in dealing with and providing for them is plainly a legitimate one. How this large and diversified group is to be treated under the law is a difficult and often a technical matter, very much a task for legislators guided by qualified professionals and not by the perhaps ill-informed opinions of the judiciary. Heightened scrutiny inevitably involves substantive judgments about legislative decisions, and we doubt that the predicate for such judicial oversight is present where the classification deals with mental retardation.

Second, the distinctive legislative response, both national and state, to the plight of those who are mentally retarded demonstrates not only that they have unique problems, but also that the lawmakers have been addressing their difficulties in a manner that belies a continuing antipathy or prejudice and a corresponding need for more intrusive oversight by the judiciary. . . .

Such legislation thus singling out the retarded for special treatment reflects the real and undeniable differences between the retarded and others. That a civilized and decent society expects and approves such legislation indicates that governmental consideration of those differences in the vast majority of situations is not only legitimate but desirable. It may be, as CLC contends, that legislation designed to benefit, rather than disadvantage, the retarded would generally withstand examination under a test of heightened scrutiny. . . . The relevant inquiry, however, is whether heightened scrutiny is constitutionally mandated in the first instance. Even assuming that many of these laws could be shown to be substantially related to an important governmental purpose, merely requiring the legislature to justify its efforts in these terms may lead it to refrain from acting at all. . . .

Third, the legislative response, which could hardly have occurred and survived without public support, negates any claim that the mentally retarded are politically powerless in the sense that they have no ability to attract the attention of the lawmakers. Any minority can be said to be powerless to assert direct control over the legislature, but if that were a criterion for higher level scrutiny by the courts, much economic and social legislation would now be suspect.

Fourth, if the large and amorphous class of the mentally retarded were deemed quasi-suspect for the reasons given by the Court of Appeals, it would be difficult to find a principled way to distinguish a variety of other groups who have perhaps immutable disabilities setting them off from others, who cannot themselves mandate the desired legislative responses, and who can claim some degree of prejudice from at least part of the public at large. One need mention in this respect only the aging, the disabled, the mentally ill, and the infirm. We are reluctant to set out on that course, and we decline to do so. . . .

Our refusal to recognize the retarded as a quasi-suspect class does not leave them entirely unprotected from invidious discrimination. To withstand equal protection review, legislation that distinguishes between the mentally retarded and others must be rationally related to a legitimate governmental purpose. This standard, we believe, affords government the latitude necessary both to pursue policies designed to assist the retarded in realizing their full potential, and to freely and efficiently engage in activities that burden the retarded in what is essentially an incidental manner. The State may not rely on a classification whose relationship to an asserted goal is so attenuated as to render the distinction arbitrary or irrational. . . .

We turn to the issue of the validity of the zoning ordinance insofar as it requires a special use permit for homes for the mentally retarded. We inquire first whether requiring a special use permit for the Featherston home in the circumstances here deprives respondents of the equal protection of the laws. If it does, there will be no occasion to decide whether the special use permit provision is facially invalid where the mentally retarded are involved, or to put it another way, whether the city may never insist on a special use permit for a home for the mentally retarded in an R-3 zone. This is the preferred course of adjudication since it enables courts to avoid making unnecessarily broad constitutional judgments.

The constitutional issue is clearly posed. The City does not require a special use permit in an R-3 zone for apartment houses, multiple dwellings, boarding and lodging houses, fraternity or sorority houses, dormitories, apartment hotels, hospitals, sanitariums, nursing homes for convalescents or the aged (other than for the insane or feebleminded or alcoholics or drug addicts), private clubs or fraternal orders, and other specified uses. It does, however, insist on a special permit for the Featherston home, and it does so, as the District Court found, because it would be a facility for the mentally retarded. May the city require the permit for this facility when other care and multiple dwelling facilities are freely permitted?

It is true . . . that the mentally retarded as a group are indeed different from others not sharing their misfortune, and in this respect they may be different from those who would occupy other facilities that would be permitted in an R-3 zone without a special permit. But this difference is largely irrelevant unless the Featherston home and those who would occupy it would threaten legitimate interests of the city in a way that other permitted uses such as boarding houses and hospitals would not. Because in our view the record does not reveal any rational basis for believing that the Featherston home would pose any special threat to the city's legitimate interests, we affirm the judgment below insofar as it holds the ordinance invalid as applied in this case. . . .

The short of it is that requiring the permit in this case appears to us to rest on an irrational prejudice against the mentally retarded, including those who would occupy the Featherston facility and who would live under the closely supervised and highly regulated conditions expressly provided for by state and federal law.

The judgment of the Court of Appeals is affirmed insofar as it invalidates the zoning ordinance as applied to the Featherston home. The judgment is otherwise vacated.

It is so ordered.

JUSTICE STEVENS, with whom THE CHIEF JUSTICE joins, concurring. . . .

In my own approach to these cases, I have always asked myself whether I could find a "rational basis" for the classification at issue. The term "rational," of course, includes a requirement that an impartial lawmaker could logically believe that the classification would serve a legitimate public purpose that transcends the harm to the members of the disadvantaged class. Thus, the word "rational"—for me at least—includes elements of legitimacy and neutrality that must always characterize the performance of the sovereign's duty to govern impartially. . . .

In every equal protection case, we have to ask certain basic questions. What class is harmed by the legislation, and has it been subjected to a "tradition of disfavor" by our laws? What is the public purpose that is being served by the law? What is the characteristic of the disadvantaged class that justifies the disparate treatment? In most cases the answer to these questions will tell us whether the statute has a "rational basis." The answers will result in the virtually automatic invalidation of racial classifications and in the validation of most economic classifications, but they will provide differing results in cases involving classifications based on alienage, gender, or illegitimacy. But that is not because we apply an "intermediate standard of review" in these cases; rather it is because the characteristics of these groups are sometimes relevant and sometimes irrelevant to a valid public purpose, or, more specifically, to the purpose that the challenged laws purportedly intended to serve.

Every law that places the mentally retarded in a special class is not presumptively irrational. . . .

The discrimination against the mentally retarded that is at issue in this case is the city's decision to require an annual special use permit before property in an apartment house district may be used as a group home for persons who are mildly retarded. The record convinces me that this permit was required because of the irrational fears of neighboring property owners, rather than for the protection of the mentally retarded persons who would reside in respondent's home. . . .

JUSTICE MARSHALL, with whom JUSTICE BRENNAN and JUSTICE BLACKMUN join, concurring in the judgment in part and dissenting in part. . . .

The Court holds the ordinance invalid on rational-basis grounds and disclaims that anything special, in the form of heightened scrutiny, is taking place. Yet Cleburne's ordinance surely would be valid under the traditional rational-basis test applicable to economic and commercial regulation. . . .

I have long believed the level of scrutiny employed in an equal protection case should vary with "the constitutional and societal importance of the interest adversely affected and the recognized invidiousness of the basis upon which the particular classification is drawn." When a zoning ordinance works to exclude the retarded from all residential districts in a community, these two considerations require that the ordinance be convincingly justified as substantially furthering legitimate and important purposes. . . .

Romer v. *Evans*
517 U.S. 620, 116 S.Ct. 1620, 134 L.Ed. 2d 855 (1996)

http://caselaw.findlaw.com/us-supreme-court/517/620.html

> The facts of the case appear in Justice Kennedy's opinion below. The Colorado Supreme Court had subjected the constitutional amendment in question to strict scrutiny because it infringed the fundamental right of gays and lesbians to participate in the political process, and affirmed the trial court's decision enjoining its enforcement. Majority: Kennedy, Stevens, O'Connor, Souter, Ginsburg, Breyer. Dissenting: Scalia, Rehnquist, Thomas.

Justice Kennedy delivered the opinion of the Court.

One century ago, the first Justice Harlan admonished this Court that the Constitution "neither knows nor tolerates classes among citizens." Unheeded then, those words now are understood to state a commitment to the law's neutrality where the rights of persons are at stake. The Equal Protection Clause enforces this principle and today requires us to hold invalid a provision of Colorado's Constitution.

The enactment challenged in this case is [Amendment 2] to the Constitution of the State of Colorado, adopted in a 1992 statewide referendum. . . . The impetus for the amendment . . . came in large part from ordinances that had been passed in various Colorado municipalities . . . which banned discrimination in many transactions and activities, including housing, employment, education, public accommodations, and health and welfare services . . . by reason of . . . sexual orientation. . . .

Amendment 2 . . . does more than repeal or rescind these provisions. It prohibits all legislative, executive or judicial action at any level of state or local government designed to protect the named class, a class we shall refer to as homosexual persons or gays and lesbians. The amendment reads:

> No Protected Status Based on Homosexual, Lesbian, or Bisexual Orientation. Neither the State of Colorado, through any of its branches or departments, nor any of its agencies, political subdivisions, municipalities or school districts, shall enact, adopt or enforce any statute, regulation, ordinance or policy whereby homosexual, lesbian or bisexual orientation, conduct, practices or relationships shall constitute or otherwise be the basis of or entitle any person or class of persons to have or claim any minority status, quota preferences, protected status or claim of discrimination. . . .

. . . We . . . now affirm the judgment [of the Colorado Supreme Court], but on a rationale different from that adopted by [that] Court. The State's principal argument in defense of

Amendment 2 is that it puts gays and lesbians in the same position as all other persons. So, the State says, the measure does no more than deny homosexuals special rights. This reading of the amendment's language is implausible. . . .

Homosexuals, by state decree, are put in a solitary class with respect to transactions and relations in both the private and governmental spheres. The amendment . . . imposes a special disability upon those persons alone. Homosexuals are forbidden the safeguards that others enjoy or may seek without constraint. They can obtain specific protection against discrimination only by enlisting the citizenry of Colorado to amend the state constitution or perhaps, on the State's view, by trying to pass helpful laws of general applicability. . . . These are protections taken for granted by most people either because they already have them or do not need them; these are protections against exclusion from an almost limitless number of transactions and endeavors that constitute ordinary civic life in a free society.

The Fourteenth Amendment's promise that no person shall be denied the equal protection of the laws must co-exist with the practical necessity that most legislation classifies for one purpose or another, with resulting disadvantage to various groups or persons. We have attempted to reconcile the principle with the reality by stating that, if a law neither burdens a fundamental right nor targets a suspect class, we will uphold the legislative classification so long as it bears a rational relation to some legitimate end.

Amendment 2 fails, indeed defies, even this conventional inquiry. First, the amendment has the peculiar property of imposing a broad and undifferentiated disability on a single named group, an exceptional and, as we shall explain, invalid form of legislation. Second, its sheer breadth is so discontinuous with the reasons offered for it that the amendment seems inexplicable by anything but animus toward the class that it affects; it lacks a rational relationship to legitimate state interests.

Taking the first point, even in the ordinary equal protection case calling for the most deferential of standards, we insist on knowing the relation between the classification adopted and the object to be attained. . . .

Amendment 2 confounds this normal process of judicial review. It is at once too narrow and too broad. It identifies persons by a single trait and then denies them protection across the board. The resulting disqualification of a class of persons from the right to seek specific protection from the law is unprecedented in our jurisprudence. . . .

It is not within our constitutional tradition to enact laws of this sort. Central both to the idea of the rule of law and to our own Constitution's guarantee of equal protection is the principle that government and each of its parts remain open on impartial terms to all who seek its assistance. "Equal protection of the laws is not achieved through indiscriminate imposition of inequalities." . . . A law declaring that in general it shall be more difficult for one group of citizens than for all others to seek aid from the government is itself a denial of equal protection of the laws in the most literal sense. . . .

A second and related point is that laws of the kind now before us raise the inevitable inference that the disadvantage imposed is born of animosity toward the class of persons affected. . . .

The primary rationale the State offers for Amendment 2 is respect for other citizens' freedom of association, and in particular the liberties of landlords or employers who have personal or religious objections to homosexuality. Colorado also cites its interest in conserving resources to fight discrimination against other groups. The breadth of the Amendment is so far removed from these particular justifications that we find it impossible to credit them. . . .

We must conclude that Amendment 2 classifies homosexuals not to further a proper legislative end but to make them unequal to everyone else. This Colorado cannot do. A State cannot so deem a class of persons a stranger to its laws. Amendment 2 violates the Equal Protection Clause, and the judgment of the Supreme Court of Colorado is affirmed.

It is so ordered.

Justice Scalia, with whom The Chief Justice and Justice Thomas join, dissenting.

The Court has mistaken a Kulturkampf for a fit of spite. . . .

The only denial of equal treatment [the Court] contends homosexuals have suffered is this: They may not obtain *preferential* treatment without amending the state constitution. That is to say, the principle underlying the Court's opinion is that one who is accorded equal treatment under the laws, but cannot as readily as others obtain *preferential* treatment under the laws, has been denied equal protection of the laws. If merely stating this alleged "equal protection" violation does not suffice to refute it, our constitutional jurisprudence has achieved terminal silliness.

The central thesis of the Court's reasoning is that any group is denied equal protection when, to obtain advantage (or, presumably, to avoid disadvantage), it must have recourse to a more general and hence more difficult level of political decision-making than others. The world has never heard of such a principle, which is why the Court's opinion is so long on emotive utterance and so short on relevant legal citation. And it seems to me most unlikely that any multilevel democracy can function under such a principle. For *whenever* a disadvantage is imposed, or conferral of a benefit is prohibited, at one of the higher levels of democratic decision-making (i.e., by the state legislature rather than local government, or by the people at large in the state constitution rather than the legislature), the affected group has (under this theory) been denied equal protection. To take the simplest of examples, consider a state law prohibiting the award of municipal contracts to relatives of mayors or city councilmen. Once such a law is passed, the group composed of such relatives must, in order to get the benefit of city contracts, persuade the state legislature—unlike all other citizens, who need only persuade the municipality. It is ridiculous to consider this a denial of equal protection, which is why the Court's theory is unheard-of. . . .

I turn next to whether there was a legitimate rational basis for the substance of the constitutional amendment—for the prohibition of special protection for homosexuals. . . .

. . . The Court's opinion contains grim, disapproving hints that Coloradans have been guilty of "animus" or "animosity" toward homosexuality, as though that has been established as Unamerican. Of course it is our moral heritage that one should not hate any human being or class of human beings. But I had thought that one could consider certain conduct reprehensible—murder, for example, or polygamy, or cruelty to animals—and could exhibit even "animus" toward such conduct. Surely that is the only sort of "animus" at issue here: moral disapproval of homosexual conduct, the same sort of moral disapproval that produced the centuries-old criminal laws that we held constitutional in *Bowers [v. Hardwick]*. The Colorado amendment does not, to speak entirely precisely, prohibit giving favored status to people who are *homosexuals*; they can be favored for many reasons—for example, because they are senior citizens or members of racial minorities. But it prohibits giving them favored status *because of their homosexual conduct*—that is, it prohibits favored status *for homosexuality*.

But though Coloradans are, as I say, entitled to be hostile toward homosexual conduct, the fact is that the degree of hostility reflected by Amendment 2 is the smallest conceivable. The Court's portrayal of Coloradans as a society fallen victim to pointless, hate-filled "gay-bashing" is so false as to be comical. Colorado not only is one of the 25 States that have repealed their antisodomy laws, but was among the first to do so. . . .

There is a problem, however, which arises when criminal sanction of homosexuality is eliminated but moral and social disapprobation of homosexuality is meant to be retained. . . . The problem (a problem, that is, for those who wish to retain social disapprobation of homosexuality) is that, because those who engage in homosexual conduct tend to reside in disproportionate numbers in certain communities, . . . and of course care about homosexual-rights issues much more ardently than the public at large, they possess political power much greater than their numbers, both locally and statewide. Quite understandably, they devote this political power to achieving not merely a grudging social toleration, but full social acceptance, of homosexuality. . . .

That is where Amendment 2 came in. It sought to counter both the geographic concentration and the disproportionate political power of homosexuals by (1) resolving the controversy at the statewide level, and (2) making the election a single-issue contest for both sides. . . . [The Court's theory] is proved false every time a state law prohibiting or disfavoring certain conduct is passed, because such a law prevents the adversely affected group—whether drug addicts, or smokers, or gun owners, or motorcyclists—from changing the policy thus established in "each of [the] parts" of the State. . . .

The people of Colorado have adopted an entirely reasonable provision which does not even disfavor homosexuals in any substantive sense, but merely denies them preferential treatment. Amendment 2 is designed to prevent piecemeal deterioration of the sexual morality favored by a majority of Coloradans, and is not only an appropriate means to that legitimate end, but a means that Americans have employed before. Striking it down is an act, not of judicial judgment, but of political will. I dissent.

II. RACIAL DISCRIMINATION

Plessy v. *Ferguson*
163 U.S. 537, 16 S.Ct. 1138, 41 L.Ed. 256 (1896)

http://caselaw.findlaw.com/us-supreme-court/163/537.html

A Louisiana statute of 1890 required railroad companies carrying passengers within the state to provide "equal but separate" accommodations for white and "colored" persons, empowered train officials to enforce the law, and provided penalties for those who refused to obey segregation orders. Blacks in New Orleans promptly formed a committee to challenge the constitutionality of the separate car law through a test case. On June 7, 1892, a 34-year-old black man named Homer Plessy bought an intrastate ticket for a ride between New Orleans and Covington on the East Louisiana Railway. Apparently by prearrangement with railroad officials, who also opposed the law, Plessy was arrested for violating the law and arraigned in district court. Because Louisiana procedure did not provide for a direct appeal for minor convictions of this sort, Plessy's attorney petitioned the state supreme court to halt the trial proceedings before they began. On November 22, Chief Justice Francis Nicholls (who as governor in 1890 had signed the separate car bill into law) ordered the trial judge to show cause why the prohibition should not be made permanent. The following month, the full court found that there was no constitutional conflict between the law and the Thirteenth and Fourteenth Amendments. Plessy's attorney was then in a position to appeal the case to the U.S. Supreme Court. It was not until

January 1897, after the U.S. Supreme Court's decision in Plessy's case, that Homer Plessy entered a plea of guilty for boarding the car reserved for white passengers and paid a fine of $25. Majority: Brown, Field, Fuller, Gray, Peckham, Shiras, White. Dissenting: Harlan. Not participating: Brewer.

Mr. Justice Brown . . . delivered the opinion of the Court. . . .

The object of the [Fourteenth] amendment was undoubtedly to enforce the absolute equality of the two races before the law, but in the nature of things it could not have been intended to abolish distinctions based upon color, or to enforce social, as distinguished from political equality, or a commingling of the two races upon terms unsatisfactory to either. Laws permitting, and even requiring, their separation in places where they are liable to be brought into contact do not necessarily imply the inferiority of either race to the other, and have been generally, if not universally, recognized as within the competency of the state legislatures in the exercise of their police power. The most common instance of this is connected with the establishment of separate schools for white and colored children, which has been held to be a valid exercise of the legislative power even by courts of States where the political rights of the colored race have been longest and most earnestly enforced.

One of the earliest of these cases is that of *Roberts* v. *City of Boston* [1849], in which the Supreme Judicial Court of Massachusetts held that the general school committee of Boston had power to make provisions for the instruction of colored children in separate schools established exclusively for them, and to prohibit their attendance upon the other schools. . . .

The distinction between laws interfering with the political equality of the negro and those requiring the separation of the two races in schools, theatres, and railway carriages has been frequently drawn by this court. . . .

So far, then, as a conflict with the Fourteenth Amendment is concerned the case reduces itself to the question whether the statute of Louisiana is a reasonable regulation, and with respect to this there must necessarily be a large discretion on the part of the legislature. In determining the question of reasonableness it is at liberty to act with reference to the established usages, customs and traditions of the people, and with a view to the promotion of their comfort, and the preservation of the public peace and good order. Gauged by this standard, we cannot say that a law which authorizes or even requires the separation of the two races in public conveyances is unreasonable, or more obnoxious to the Fourteenth Amendment than the acts of Congress requiring separate schools for colored children in the District of Columbia, the constitutionality of which does not seem to have been questioned, or the corresponding acts of state legislatures.

We consider the underlying fallacy of the plaintiff's argument to consist in the assumption that the enforced separation of the two races stamps the colored race with a badge of inferiority. If this be so, it is not by reason of anything found in the act, but solely because the colored race chooses to put that construction upon it. The argument necessarily assumes that if, as has been more than once the case, and is not unlikely to be so again, the colored race should become the dominant power in the state legislature, and should enact a law in precisely similar terms, it would thereby relegate the white race to an inferior position. We imagine that the white race, at least, would not acquiesce in this assumption. The argument also assumes, that social prejudices may be overcome by legislation, and that equal rights cannot be secured to the negro except by an enforced commingling of the two races. We cannot accept this proposition. If the two races are to meet upon terms of social equality, it must be the result of natural affinities, a mutual appreciation of each other's merits and a voluntary consent of individuals. . . . Legislation is powerless to eradicate racial instincts or to abolish distinctions based upon physical differences, and the attempt to do so can only result in accentuating the difficulties of the present situation. If the civil and political rights of both races be equal, one cannot be inferior to the other civilly or politically. If one race be inferior to the other socially, the Constitution of the United States cannot put them upon the same plane. . . .

The judgment of the court below is, therefore,

Affirmed.

Mr. Justice Harlan, dissenting. . . .

It was said in argument that the statute of Louisiana does not discriminate against either race, but prescribes a rule applicable alike to white and colored citizens. But this argument does not meet the difficulty. Everyone knows that the statute . . . had its origins in the purpose, not so much to exclude white persons from railroad cars occupied by blacks, as to exclude colored people from coaches occupied by . . . white persons. . . .

[I]n view of the Constitution, in the eye of the law, there is in this country no superior, dominant, ruling class of citizens. There is no caste here. Our Constitution is color-blind, and neither knows nor tolerates classes among citizens. In respect of civil rights, all citizens are equal before the law. The humblest is the peer of the most powerful. The law regards man as man, and takes no account of his surroundings or of his color when his civil rights as guaranteed by the supreme law of the land are involved. It is, therefore, to be regretted that this high tribunal, the final expositor of the fundamental law of the land, has reached the conclusion that it is competent for a state to regulate the enjoyment by citizens of their civil rights solely upon the basis of race. . . .

In my opinion, the judgment this day rendered will, in time, prove to be quite as pernicious as the decision made by this tribunal in the Dred Scott case. . . . The present decision, it may well be apprehended, will not only stimulate aggressions, more or less brutal and irritating, upon the admitted rights of colored citizens, but will encourage the belief that it is possible, by means of state enactments, to defeat the beneficent purposes which the people of the United States had in view when they adopted the recent amendments of the Constitution, by one of which the blacks of this country were made citizens of the United States and of the States in which they respectively reside, and whose privileges and immunities, as citizens, the States are forbidden to abridge. Sixty millions of whites are in no danger from the presence here of eight millions of blacks. The destinies of the two races, in this country, are indissolubly linked together, and the interests of both require that the common government of all shall not permit the seeds of race hate to be planted under the sanction of law. . . .

If evils will result from the commingling of the two races upon public highways established for the benefit of all, they will be infinitely less than those that will surely come from state legislation regulating the enjoyment of civil rights upon the basis of race. We boast of the freedom enjoyed by our people above all other people. But it is difficult to reconcile that boast with a state of the law which, practically, puts the brand of servitude and degradation upon a large class of our fellow-citizens, our equals before the law. The thin disguise of "equal" accommodations for passengers in railroad coaches will not mislead any one, nor atone for the wrong this day done. . . .

[T]he statute of Louisiana is inconsistent with the personal liberty of citizens, white and black, in that state, and hostile to both the spirit and letter of the Constitution of the United States. If laws of like character should be enacted in the several states of the Union, the effect would be in the highest degree mischievous. Slavery as an institution . . . would, it is true, have disappeared from our country, but there would remain a power in the states, by sinister legislation, to interfere with the full enjoyment of the blessings of freedom; to regulate civil rights, common to all citizens, upon the basis of race; and to place in a condition of legal inferiority a large body of American citizens, now constituting a part of the political community, called the people of the United States, for whom and by whom, through representatives, our government is administered. Such a system is inconsistent with the guarantee given by the Constitution to each state of a republican form of government. . . .

Brown v. *Board of Education* (First Case) 347 U.S. 483, 74 S.Ct. 686, 98 L.Ed. 873 (1954)

http://caselaw.findlaw.com/us-supreme-court/347/483.html

On May 17, 1954, the Supreme Court handed down its long-awaited decision in the public school segregation cases. Although the cases directly involved only South Carolina, Virginia, Delaware, Kansas, and the District of Columbia, the answer to the question whether segregation of races was permissible under the Constitution affected a total of 17 states and the District of Columbia, which required segregation in public schools, and four states that permitted segregation at the option of local communities. The Court postponed issuing a decree until the next term. Majority: Warren, Black, Burton, Clark, Douglas, Frankfurter, Jackson, Minton, Reed.

Mr. Chief Justice Warren delivered the opinion of the court. . . .

In each of the cases, minors of the Negro race, through their legal representatives, seek the aid of the courts in obtaining admission to the public schools of their community on a nonsegregated basis. In each instance, they had been denied admission to schools attended by white children under laws requiring or permitting segregation according to race.

This segregation was alleged to deprive the plaintiffs of the equal protection of the laws under the Fourteenth Amendment. In each of the cases other than the Delaware case, a three-judge Federal District Court denied relief to the plaintiffs on the so-called "separate but equal" doctrine, announced by this court in *Plessy* v. *Ferguson*. . . .

The plaintiffs contend that segregated public schools are not "equal" and cannot be made "equal," and that, hence, they are deprived of the equal protection of the laws. Because of the obvious importance of the question presented, the Court took jurisdiction. Argument was heard in the 1952 term, and reargument was heard this term on certain questions propounded by the Court.

Reargument was largely devoted to the circumstances surrounding the adoption of the Fourteenth Amendment in 1868. It covered, exhaustively, consideration of the Amendment in Congress, ratification by the states, then existing practices in racial segregation, and the views of proponents and opponents of the Amendment.

This discussion and our own investigation convince us that, although these sources cast some light, it is not enough to resolve the problem with which we are faced.

At best, they are inconclusive. The most avid proponents of the postwar Amendments undoubtedly intended them to remove all legal distinctions among "all persons born or naturalized in the United States."

Their opponents, just as certainly, were antagonistic to both the letter and the spirit of the Amendments and wished them to have the most limited effect. What others in Congress and the State legislatures had in mind cannot be determined with any degree of certainty.

An additional reason for the illusive nature of the Amendment's history, with respect to segregated schools, is the status of public education at that time. In the South, the movement toward free common schools, supported by general taxation, had not yet taken hold. Education of white children was largely in the hands of private groups. Education of Negroes was almost nonexistent, and practically all of the race was illiterate. In fact, any education of Negroes was forbidden by law in some states. . . .

As a consequence, it is not surprising that there should be so little in the history of the Fourteenth Amendment relating to its intended effect on public education. . . .

In approaching this problem, we cannot turn the clock back to 1868, when the Amendment was adopted, or even to 1896, when *Plessy* v. *Ferguson* was written. We must consider public education in the light of its full development and its present place in American life throughout the nation. Only in this way can it be determined if segregation in public schools deprives these plaintiffs of the equal protection of the laws.

Today, education is perhaps the most important function of state and local governments. Compulsory school attendance laws and the great expenditures for education both demonstrate our recognition of the importance of education to our democratic society. It is required in the performance of our most basic public responsibilities, even service in the armed forces. It is the very foundation of good citizenship.

Today, it is a principal instrument in awakening the child to cultural values, in preparing him for later professional training, and in helping him to adjust normally to his environment. In these days, it is doubtful that any child may reasonably be expected to succeed in life if he is denied the opportunity of an education. Such an opportunity, where the state has undertaken to provide it, is a right which must be made available to all on equal terms.

We come then to the question presented: Does segregation of children in public schools solely on the basis of race, even though the physical facilities and other "tangible" factors may be equal, deprive the children of the minority group of equal educational opportunities? We believe that it does. . . .

To separate them from others of similar age and qualifications solely because of their race generates a feeling of inferiority as to their status in the community that may affect their hearts and minds in a way unlikely ever to be undone. . . .

Whatever may have been the extent of psychological knowledge at the time of *Plessy* v. *Ferguson*, this finding is amply supported by modern authority. . . . Any language in *Plessy* v. *Ferguson* contrary to this finding is rejected.

We conclude that in the field of public education the doctrine of "separate but equal" has no place. Separate educational facilities are inherently unequal. Therefore, we hold that the plaintiffs and others similarly situated for whom the actions have been brought are, by reason of the segregation complained of, deprived of the equal protection of the laws guaranteed by the Fourteenth Amendment. . . .

We have now announced that such segregation is a denial of the equal protection of the laws. In order that we may have the full assistance of the parties in formulating decrees the cases will be restored to the docket, and the parties are requested to present further argument on Questions 4 and 5 previously propounded by the court for the reargument this Term. [These pertained to the form of decree to be issued if segregated schools were outlawed.] . . .

It is so ordered.

Bolling v. *Sharpe*
347 U.S. 497, 74 S.Ct. 693, 98 L.Ed. 884 (1954)

http://caselaw.findlaw.com/us-supreme-court/347/497.html

This was the companion case to *Brown* v. *Board of Education*, decided the same day. In *Brown*, the Court held that the equal protection clause prohibited the states from maintaining racially segregated public schools. In *Bolling* v. *Sharpe*, the question was whether the due process clause of the Fifth Amendment prohibited racial segregation in the public schools of the District of Columbia. Majority: Warren, Black, Burton, Clark, Douglas, Frankfurter, Jackson, Minton, Reed.

Mr. Chief Justice Warren delivered the opinion of the Court. . . .

We have this day held that the equal protection clause of the Fourteenth Amendment prohibits the states from maintaining racially segregated public schools.

The legal problem in the District of Columbia is somewhat different, however. The Fifth Amendment, which is applicable in the District of Columbia, does not contain an equal protection clause as does the Fourteenth Amendment, which applies only to the states.

But the concepts of equal protection and due process, both stemming from our American ideal of fairness, are not mutually exclusive. The "equal protection of the laws" is a more explicit safeguard of prohibited unfairness than "due process of law," and, therefore, we do not imply that the two are always interchangeable phrases.

But, as this court has recognized, discrimination may be so unjustifiable as to be violative of due process. Classifications based solely upon race must be scrutinized with particular care, since they are contrary to our traditions and hence constitutionally suspect. . . .

Segregation in public education is not reasonably related to any proper governmental objective, and thus it imposes on Negro children of the District of Columbia a burden that constitutes an arbitrary deprivation of their liberty in violation of the Due Process Clause.

In view of our decision that the Constitution prohibits the states from maintaining racially segregated public schools, it would be unthinkable that the same Constitution would impose a lesser duty on the Federal Government. We hold that racial segregation in the public schools of the District of Columbia is a denial of the Due Process of Law guaranteed by the Fifth Amendment to the Constitution. . . .

It is so ordered.

Brown v. *Board of Education* (Second Case)
349 U.S. 294, 75 S.Ct. 753, 99 L.Ed. 1083 (1955)

http://caselaw.findlaw.com/us-supreme-court/349/294.html

In the term following the first *Brown* decision, the Court handed down its decree to guide lower courts in litigation involving desegregation. Majority: Warren, Black, Burton, Clark, Douglas, Frankfurter, Harlan, Minton, Reed.

MR. CHIEF JUSTICE WARREN delivered the opinion of the Court.

These cases were decided on May 17, 1954. The opinions of that date, declaring the fundamental principle that racial discrimination in public education is unconstitutional, are incorporated herein by reference. All provisions of federal, state, or local law requiring or permitting such discrimination must yield to this principle. There remains for consideration the manner in which relief is to be accorded. . . .

In fashioning and effectuating the decrees, the courts will be guided by equitable principles. Traditionally, equity has been characterized by a practical flexibility in shaping its remedies and by a facility for adjusting and reconciling public and private needs. These cases call for the exercise of these traditional attributes of equity power. At stake is the personal interest of the plaintiffs in admission to public schools as soon as practicable on a nondiscriminatory basis. To effectuate this interest may call for elimination of a variety of obstacles in making the transition to school systems operated in accordance with the constitutional principles set forth in our May 17, 1954, decision. Courts of equity may properly take into account the public interest in the elimination of such obstacles in a systematic and effective manner. But it should go without saying that the vitality of these constitutional principles cannot be allowed to yield simply because of disagreement with them.

While giving weight to these public and private considerations, the courts will require that the defendants make a prompt and reasonable start toward full compliance with our May 17, 1954, ruling. Once such a start has been made, the courts may find that additional time is necessary to carry out the ruling in an effective manner. The burden rests upon the defendants to establish that such time is necessary in the public interest and is consistent with good faith compliance at the earliest practicable date. To that end, the courts may consider problems related to administration, arising from the physical condition of the school plant, the school transportation system, personnel, revision of school districts and attendance areas into compact units to achieve a system of determining admission to the public schools on a nonracial basis, and revision of local laws and regulations which may be necessary in solving the foregoing problems. They will also consider the adequacy of any plans the defendants may propose to meet these problems and to effectuate a transition to a racially nondiscriminatory school system. During this period of transition, the courts will retain jurisdiction of these cases. The judgments below . . . are accordingly reversed and the cases are remanded to the District Courts to take such proceedings and enter such orders and decrees consistent with this opinion as are necessary and proper to admit to public schools on a racially nondiscriminatory basis with all deliberate speed the parties to these cases. . . .

It is so ordered.

Milliken v. *Bradley* 418 U.S. 717, 94 S.Ct. 3112, 41 L.Ed. 2d 1069 (1974)

http://caselaw.findlaw.com/us-supreme-court/418/717.html

This case began as a suit against the Detroit Board of Education seeking desegregation of the city's public schools. The district court ordered submission of desegregation plans for the city proper as well as for the three-county metropolitan area, even though the 53 suburban school districts were not parties to the action and there was no finding that they had committed any constitutional violations. The Court of Appeals, Sixth Circuit, affirmed. Many in the general public outside of the immediately affected region never learned of this highly consequential decision by the Supreme Court: It came down on July 25, 1974, the day after the ruling in *U.S. v. Nixon* that precipitated President Richard Nixon's resignation from office. Majority: Burger, Blackmun, Powell, Rehnquist, Stewart. Dissenting: Marshall, Brennan, Douglas, White.

Mr. Chief Justice Burger delivered the opinion of the Court.

We granted certiorari in these consolidated cases to determine whether a federal court may impose a multi-district, area wide remedy to a single district de jure segregation problem absent any finding that the other included school districts have failed to operate unitary school systems within their districts, absent any claim or finding that the boundary lines of any affected school district were established with the purpose of fostering racial segregation in public schools, absent any finding that the included districts committed acts which effected segregation within the other districts, and absent a meaningful opportunity for the included neighboring school districts to present evidence or be heard on the propriety of a multi-district remedy or on the question of constitutional violations by those neighboring districts. . . .

Viewing the record as a whole, it seems clear that the District Court and the Court of Appeals shifted the primary focus from a Detroit remedy to the metropolitan area only because of their conclusion that total desegregation of Detroit would not produce the racial balance which they perceived as desirable. Both courts proceeded on an assumption that the Detroit schools could not be truly desegregated—in their view of what constituted desegregation—unless the racial composition of the student body of each school substantially reflected the racial composition of the population of the metropolitan area as a whole. The metropolitan area was then defined as Detroit plus 53 of the outlying school districts. . . .

The Michigan educational structure involved in this case, in common with most States, provides for a large measure of local control and a review of the scope and character of these local powers indicates the extent to which the inter-district remedy approved by the two courts could disrupt and alter the structure of public education in Michigan. The metropolitan remedy would require, in effect, consolidation of 54 independent school districts historically administered as separate units into a vast new super school district. . . .

The controlling principle consistently expounded in our holdings is that the scope of the remedy is determined by the nature and extent of the constitutional violation. . . . Before the boundaries of separate and autonomous school districts may be set aside by consolidating the separate units for remedial purposes or by imposing a cross-district remedy, it must first be shown that there has been a constitutional violation within one district that produces a significant segregative effect in another district. Specifically it must be shown that racially discriminatory acts of the state or local school districts, or of a single school district have been a substantial cause of inter-district segregation. Thus an inter-district remedy might be in order where the racially discriminatory acts of one or more school districts caused racial segregation in an adjacent district, or where district lines have been deliberately drawn on the basis of race. In such circumstances an inter-district remedy would be appropriate to eliminate the inter-district segregation directly caused by the constitutional violation. Conversely, without an inter-district violation and inter-district effect, there is no constitutional wrong calling for an inter-district remedy. . . .

We conclude that the relief ordered by the District Court and affirmed by the Court of Appeals was based upon an erroneous standard and was unsupported by record evidence that acts of the outlying districts affected the discrimination found to exist in the schools of Detroit. Accordingly, the judgment of the Court of Appeals is reversed and the case is remanded for further proceedings consistent with this opinion leading to prompt formulation of a decree directed to eliminating the segregation found to exist in Detroit city schools, a remedy which has been delayed since 1970.

Reversed and remanded.

Mr. Justice Stewart, concurring . . . [omitted].

Mr. Justice Douglas, dissenting . . . [omitted].

Mr. Justice White, with whom Mr. Justice Douglas, Mr. Justice Brennan, and Mr. Justice Marshall join, dissenting . . . [omitted].

Mr. Justice Marshall, with whom Mr. Justice Douglas, Mr. Justice Brennan, and Mr. Justice White join, dissenting. . . .

After 20 years of small, often difficult steps toward that great end, the Court today takes a giant step backwards. . . . Ironically purporting to base its result on the principle that the scope of the remedy in a desegregation case should be determined by the nature and the extent of the constitutional violation, the Court's answer is to provide no remedy at all. . . .

Our precedents, in my view, firmly establish that where, as here, state-imposed segregation has been demonstrated, it becomes the duty of the State to eliminate root and branch all vestiges of racial discrimination and to achieve the greatest possible degree of actual desegregation. . . . [T]his duty cannot be fulfilled unless the State of Michigan involves outlying metropolitan area school districts in its desegregation remedy. . . .

We deal here with the right of all our children, whatever their race, to an equal start in life and to an equal opportunity to reach their full potential as citizens. Those children who have been denied that right in the past deserve better than to see fences thrown up to deny them that right in the future. Our Nation, I fear, will be ill served by the Court's refusal to remedy separate and unequal education, for unless our children begin to learn together, there is little hope that our people will ever learn to live together.

The great irony of the Court's opinion and, in my view, its most serious analytical flaw may be gleaned from its concluding sentence, in which the Court remands for "prompt formulation of a decree directed to eliminating the segregation found to exist in Detroit city schools, a remedy which has been delayed since 1970." . . . The majority, however, seems to have forgotten the District Court's explicit finding that a Detroit-only decree, the only remedy permitted under today's decision, "would not accomplish desegregation." . . .

Today's holding, I fear, is more a reflection of a perceived public mood that we have gone far enough in enforcing the Constitution's guarantee of equal justice than it is the product of neutral principles of law. In the short run, it may seem to be the easier course to allow our great metropolitan areas to be divided up each into two cities—one white, the other black—but it is a course, I predict, our people will ultimately regret. I dissent.

Loving v. *Virginia*
388 U.S. 1, 87 S.Ct. 1817, 18 L.Ed. 2d 1010 (1967)

http://caselaw.findlaw.com/us-supreme-court/388/1.html

When this litigation began, Virginia was one of 16 southern and border states that criminalized interracial marriages. Between 1952 and 1967, some 14 states in other parts of the United States had repealed similar anti-miscegenation laws. In June 1958 two residents of Virginia, Mildred Jeter, an African American woman, and Richard Loving, a white man, were married in the District of Columbia. They returned to Virginia and established a home in Caroline County. In October they were charged with violating Virginia's statutory ban. In January 1959, the Lovings pleaded guilty, and were sentenced to one year in jail; however, the trial judge suspended the sentence for a period of 25 years on the condition that they leave the state and not return to Virginia together for 25 years. After sentencing the Lovings moved to the District of Columbia. In 1963 they filed a motion in the Virginia trial court to vacate the judgment and set aside the sentence on the ground that the ban violated the Fourteenth Amendment. When by 1964 the state court had taken no action on their petition, the Lovings instituted a class action in the United States District Court for the Eastern District of Virginia, requesting that a three-judge court declare the Virginia restriction unconstitutional and enjoin state officials from enforcing their convictions. In early January 1965, the state trial judge denied their earlier motion to vacate the sentences, and the Lovings appealed to the Supreme Court of Appeals of Virginia which upheld the constitutionality of the law, modified the sentence, and affirmed the convictions. The U.S. Supreme Court noted probable jurisdiction. Majority: Warren, Black, Brennan, Clark, Douglas, Fortas, Harlan, Stewart, White.

MR. CHIEF JUSTICE WARREN delivered the opinion of the Court.

This case presents a constitutional question never addressed by this Court: whether a statutory scheme adopted by the State of Virginia to prevent marriages between persons solely on the basis of racial classifications violates the Equal Protection and Due Process Clauses of the Fourteenth Amendment. For reasons which seem to us to reflect the central meaning of those constitutional commands, we conclude that these statutes cannot stand consistently with the Fourteenth Amendment. . . . Penalties for miscegenation arose as an incident to slavery, and have been common in Virginia since the colonial period. The present statutory scheme dates from the adoption of the Racial Integrity Act of 1924, passed during the period of extreme nativism which followed the end of the First World War. . . .

While the state court is no doubt correct in asserting that marriage is a social relation subject to the State's police power, the State does not contend in its argument before this Court that its powers to regulate marriage are unlimited notwithstanding the commands of the Fourteenth Amendment. Nor could it do so in light of *Meyer* v. *Nebraska* (1923), and *Skinner* v. *Oklahoma* (1942). Instead, the State argues that the meaning of the Equal Protection Clause, as illuminated by the statements of the Framers, is only that state penal laws containing an interracial element as part of the definition of the offense must apply equally to whites and Negroes in the sense that members of each race are punished to the same degree. Thus, the State contends that, because its miscegenation statutes punish equally both the white and the Negro participants in an interracial marriage, these statutes, despite their reliance on racial classifications, do not constitute an invidious discrimination based upon race. The second argument advanced by the State assumes the validity of its equal application theory. The argument is that, if the Equal Protection Clause does not outlaw miscegenation statutes because of their reliance on racial classifications, the question of constitutionality would thus become whether there was any rational basis for a State to treat interracial marriages differently from other marriages. On this question, the State argues, the scientific evidence is substantially in doubt and, consequently, this Court should defer to the wisdom of the state legislature in adopting its policy of discouraging interracial marriages.

Because we reject the notion that the mere "equal application" of a statute containing racial classifications is enough to remove the classifications from the Fourteenth Amendment's proscription of all invidious racial discriminations, we do not accept the State's contention that these statutes should be upheld if there is any possible basis for concluding that they serve a rational purpose. The mere fact of equal application does not mean that our analysis of these statutes should follow the approach we have taken in cases involving no racial discrimination. . . . In these cases, involving distinctions not drawn according to race, the Court has merely asked whether there is any rational foundation for the discriminations, and has deferred to the wisdom of the state legislatures. In the case at bar, however, we deal with statutes containing racial classifications, and the fact of equal application does not immunize the statute from the very heavy burden of justification which the Fourteenth Amendment has traditionally required of state statutes drawn according to race.

The State argues that statements in the Thirty-ninth Congress about the time of the passage of the Fourteenth Amendment indicate that the Framers did not intend the Amendment to make unconstitutional state miscegenation laws. Many of the statements alluded to by the State concern the debates over the Freedmen's Bureau Bill, which President Johnson vetoed, and the Civil Rights Act of 1866, enacted over his veto. While these statements have some relevance to the intention of Congress in submitting the Fourteenth Amendment, it must be understood that they pertained to the passage of specific statutes, and not to the broader, organic purpose of a constitutional amendment. . . .

The State finds support for its "equal application" theory in the decision of the Court in *Pace* v. *Alabama* (1883). In that case, the Court upheld a conviction under an Alabama statute forbidding adultery or fornication between a white person and a Negro which imposed a greater penalty than that of a statute proscribing similar conduct by members of the same race. The Court reasoned that the statute could not be said to discriminate against Negroes because the punishment for each participant in the offense was the same. However, as recently as the 1964 Term, in rejecting the reasoning of that case, we stated "*Pace* represents a limited view of the Equal Protection Clause which has not withstood analysis in the subsequent decisions of this Court." As we there demonstrated, the Equal Protection Clause requires the consideration of whether the classifications drawn by any statute constitute an arbitrary and invidious discrimination. The clear and central purpose of the Fourteenth Amendment was to eliminate all official state sources of invidious racial discrimination in the States.

There can be no question but that Virginia's miscegenation statutes rest solely upon distinctions drawn according to race. . . . At the very least, the Equal Protection Clause demands that racial classifications, especially suspect in criminal statutes, be subjected to the "most rigid scrutiny," and, if they are ever to be upheld, they must be shown to be necessary to the accomplishment of some permissible state objective, independent of the racial discrimination which it was the object of the Fourteenth Amendment to eliminate. Indeed, two members of this Court have already stated that they cannot conceive of a valid legislative purpose . . . which makes the color of a person's skin the test of whether his conduct is a criminal offense. . . .

These statutes also deprive the Lovings of liberty without due process of law in violation of the Due Process Clause of the Fourteenth Amendment. The freedom to marry has long been recognized as one of the vital personal rights essential to the orderly pursuit of happiness by free men. . . .

To deny this fundamental freedom on so unsupportable a basis as the racial classifications embodied in these statutes, classifications so directly subversive of the principle of equality at the heart of the Fourteenth Amendment, is surely to deprive all the State's citizens of liberty without due process of law. The Fourteenth Amendment requires that the freedom of choice to marry not be restricted by invidious racial discriminations. Under our Constitution, the freedom to marry, or not marry, a person of another race resides with the individual, and cannot be infringed by the State.

These convictions must be reversed.

It is so ordered.

III. STATE ACTION

Civil Rights Cases (*United States* v. *Stanley*)
109 U.S. 3, 3 S.Ct. 18, 27 L.Ed. 835 (1883)

http://caselaw.findlaw.com/us-supreme-court/109/3.html

Five cases from Kansas, California, Missouri, New York, and Tennessee, collectively known as the Civil Rights Cases and with *United States* v. *Stanley* docketed first, involved the constitutionality of the Civil Rights Act of 1875. Resting on the Thirteenth and Fourteenth Amendments, the statute made it a misdemeanor to deny any person equal rights and privileges in inns, theaters, amusement places, and transportation facilities on the basis of color or previous condition of servitude. According to Loren Beth's biography of the first Justice Harlan, "Mallie" Harlan wrote in her memoirs that her husband had difficulty writing his dissent to Justice Bradley's opinion of the Court. As inspiration, she placed Chief Justice Taney's inkstand, a prized memento, on Harlan's desk while he was at church. When he found it upon his return, the realization that the inkstand had no doubt been used when Taney wrote his opinion in the Dred Scott case seemed "to act like magic in clarifying my husband's thoughts. . . . His pen fairly flew on that day and . . . he soon finished his dissent." Majority: Bradley, Blatchford, Field, Gray, Matthews, Miller, Waite, Woods. Dissenting: Harlan.

Mr. Justice Bradley delivered the opinion of the Court. . . .

The essence of the law is, not to declare broadly that all persons shall be entitled to the full and equal enjoyment of the accommodations, advantages, facilities, and privileges of inns, public conveyances, and theatres; but that such enjoyment shall not be subject to any conditions applicable only to citizens of a particular race or color, or who had been in a previous condition of servitude. . . .

Has congress constitutional power to make such a law? Of course, no one will contend that the power to pass it was contained in the Constitution before the adoption of the last three amendments. The power is sought, first, in the Fourteenth Amendment. . . .

It is State action of a particular character that is prohibited [by that amendment]. Individual invasion of individual rights is not the subject matter of the amendment. It has a deeper and broader scope. It nullifies and makes void all State legislation, and State action of every kind, which impairs the privileges and immunities of citizens of the United States, or which injures them in life, liberty or property without due process of law, or which denies to any of them the equal protection of the laws. It not only does this, but, in order that the national will, thus declared, may not be a mere *brutum fulmen* [empty threat], the last section of the amendment invests Congress with power to enforce it by appropriate legislation. To enforce what? To enforce the prohibition. To adopt appropriate legislation for correcting the effects of such prohibited State laws and State acts, and thus to render them effectually null, void, and innocuous. This is the legislative power conferred upon Congress, and this is the whole of it. It does not invest Congress with power to legislate upon subjects which are within the domain of State legislation; but to provide modes of relief against State legislation, or State action, of the kind referred to. It does not authorize Congress to create a code of municipal law for the regulation of private rights; but to provide modes of redress against the operation of State laws, and the action of State officers, executive or judicial, when these are subversive of the fundamental rights specified in the amendment. . . . Until some State law has been passed, or some State action through its officers or agents had been taken, adverse to the rights of citizens sought to be protected by the Fourteenth Amendment, no legislation of the United States under said amendment nor any proceeding under such legislation, can be called into activity: for the prohibitions of the amendment are against State laws and acts done under State authority. . . . Such legislation cannot properly cover the whole domain of rights appertaining to life, liberty and property, defining them and providing for their vindication. That would be to establish a code of municipal law regulative of all private rights between man and man in society. It would be to make Congress take the place of the State legislatures and to supersede them. . . .

If this legislation is appropriate for enforcing the prohibitions of the amendment, it is difficult to see where it is to stop. Why may not Congress with equal show of authority enact a code of laws for the enforcement and vindication of all rights of life, liberty, and property? . . . The truth is, that the implication of a power to legislate in this manner is based upon the assumption that if the States are forbidden to legislate or act in a particular way on a particular subject, and power is conferred upon Congress to enforce the prohibition, this gives Congress power to legislate generally upon that subject, and not merely power to provide modes of redress against such State legislation or action. The assumption is certainly unsound. It is repugnant to the Tenth Amendment of the Constitution, which declares that powers not delegated to the United States by the Constitution, nor prohibited by it to the States, are reserved to the States respectively or to the people. . . .

In this connection it is proper to state that civil rights, such as are guaranteed by the constitution against state aggression, cannot be impaired by the wrongful acts of individuals, unsupported by state authority in the shape of laws, customs, or judicial or executive proceedings. The wrongful act of an individual, unsupported by any such authority, is simply a private wrong, or a crime of that individual; an invasion of the rights of the injured party, it is true, whether they affect his person, his property, or his reputation; but if not sanctioned in some way by the state, or not done under state authority, his rights remain in full force, and may presumably be vindicated by resort to the laws of the state for redress. . . .

But the power of Congress to adopt direct and primary, as distinguished from corrective legislation, on the subject in hand, is sought, in the second place, from the Thirteenth Amendment, which abolishes slavery. This amendment declares "that neither slavery, nor involuntary servitude, except as a punishment for crime, whereof the party shall have been duly convicted, shall exist within the United States, or any place subject to their jurisdiction"; and it gives Congress power to enforce the amendment by appropriate legislation. . . .

There were thousands of free colored people in this country before the abolition of slavery, enjoying all the essential rights of life, liberty and property the same as white citizens; yet no one, at that time, thought that it was any invasion of his personal status as a freeman because he was not admitted to all the privileges enjoyed by white citizens, or because he was subjected to discriminations in the enjoyment of accommodations in inns, public conveyances and places of amusement. Mere discriminations on account of race or color were not regarded as badges of slavery. If, since that time, the enjoyment of equal rights in all these respects has become established by constitutional enactment, it is not by force of the Thirteenth Amendment (which merely abolishes slavery), but by force of the Fourteenth and Fifteenth Amendments. . . .

On the whole, we are of opinion that no countenance of authority for the passage of the law in question can be found in either the Thirteenth or Fourteenth amendment of the constitution; and . . . it must necessarily be declared void. . . . And it is so ordered.

Mr. Justice Harlan dissenting. . . .

I am of the opinion that such discrimination practiced by corporations and individuals in the exercise of their public or quasi public functions is a badge of servitude the imposition of which Congress may prevent under its power, by appropriate legislation, to enforce the Thirteenth Amendment; and, consequently, without reference to its enlarged power under the Fourteenth Amendment, the act of March 1, 1875, is not, in my judgment, repugnant to the Constitution. . . . The assumption that this amendment [the Fourteenth] consists wholly of prohibitions upon State laws and State proceedings in hostility to its provisions, is unauthorized by its language. [Its] first clause. . . . "All persons born or naturalized in the United States, and subject to the jurisdiction thereof, are citizens of the United States, and of the state wherein they reside"—is of a distinctly affirmative character. In its application to the colored race . . . it created and granted, as well as citizenship of the United States, citizenship of the State in which they respectively resided. It introduced all of that race, whose ancestors had been imported and sold as slaves, at once, into the political community known as the "People of the United States." They became, instantly, citizens of the United States, and of their respective States. Further, they were brought, by this supreme act of the nation, within the direct operation of that provision of the Constitution which declares that "the citizens of each State shall be entitled to all privileges and immunities of citizens in the several States."

The citizenship thus acquired by that race, in virtue of an affirmative grant from the nation, may be protected, not alone by the judicial branch of the government, but by congressional legislation of a primary direct character; this, because the power of Congress is not restricted to the enforcement of prohibitions upon State laws or State action. It is, in terms distinct and positive, to enforce "*the provisions of this article*" of amendment; not simply those of a prohibitive character, but the provisions all of the provisions—affirmative and prohibitive, of the amendment. . . .

It is said that any interpretation of the Fourteenth Amendment different from that adopted by the majority of the court, would imply that

Congress had authority to enact a municipal code for all the States, covering every matter affecting the life, liberty, and property of the citizens of the several States. Not so. . . . The personal rights and immunities recognized in the prohibitive clauses of the amendment were, prior to its adoption, under the protection, primarily, of the States, while rights, created by or derived from the United States, have always been, and, in the nature of things, should always be, primarily, under the protection of the general government. Exemption from race discrimination in respect of the civil rights which are fundamental in *citizenship* in a republican government, is, as we have seen, a new right, created by the nation, with express power in Congress, by legislation, to enforce the constitutional provision from which it is derived. If, in some sense, such race discrimination is, within the letter of the last clause of the first section, a denial of that equal protection of the laws which is secured against State denial to all persons, whether citizens or not, it cannot be possible that a mere prohibition upon such State denial, or a prohibition upon State laws abridging the privileges and immunities of citizens of the United States, takes from the nation the power which it has uniformly exercised of protecting, by direct primary legislation, those privileges and immunities which existed under the Constitution before the adoption of the Fourteenth Amendment, or have been created by that amendment in behalf of those thereby made *citizens* of their respective States. . . .

IV. GENDER DISCRIMINATION

Frontiero v. *Richardson*
411 U.S. 677, 93 S.Ct. 1764, 36 L.Ed. 2d 583 (1973)

http://caselaw.findlaw.com/us-supreme-court/411/677.html

A servicewoman's application for increased quarters allowances and medical and dental benefits for her husband was disallowed because she failed, as required by law, to demonstrate that her husband was dependent on her for more than one-half of his support. The servicewoman instituted action, contending that the statutes that allowed a serviceman to claim his wife as a dependent for such benefits, without regard to whether she was in fact dependent on him for any part of her support, were discriminatory on the basis of sex and in violation of the Fifth Amendment's due process clause. A three-judge district court upheld the constitutionality of the statutes. Majority: Brennan, Blackmun, Burger, Douglas, Marshall, Powell, Stewart, White. Dissenting: Rehnquist.

Mr. Justice Brennan announced the judgment of the Court in an opinion in which Mr. Justices Douglas, Marshall, and White joined.

At the outset, appellants contend that classifications based upon sex, like classifications based upon race, alienage, and national origin, are inherently suspect and must therefore be subjected to close judicial scrutiny. We agree and, indeed, find at least implicit support for such an approach in our unanimous decision only last term in *Reed* v. *Reed*. . . .

In *Reed*, the Court considered the constitutionality of an Idaho statute providing that, when two individuals are otherwise equally entitled to appointment as administrator of an estate, the male applicant must be preferred to the female. . . .

[T]he Court held the statutory preference for male applicants unconstitutional. In reaching this result, the Court implicitly rejected appellee's apparently rational explanation of the statutory scheme, and concluded that, by ignoring the individual qualifications of particular applicants, the challenged statute provided "dissimilar treatment for men and women who are . . . similarly situated." The Court therefore held that, even though the State's interest in achieving administrative efficiency "is not without some legitimacy," "[t]o give a mandatory preference to members of either sex over members of the other, merely to accomplish the elimination of hearings on the merits, is to make the very kind of arbitrary legislative choice forbidden by the [Constitution] . . . ." This departure from "traditional" rational basis analysis with respect to sex-based classification is clearly justified.

There can be no doubt that our Nation has had a long and unfortunate history of sex discrimination. . . . [I]ndeed, throughout much of the 19th century the position of women in our society was, in many respects, comparable to that of blacks under the pre-Civil War slave codes.

It is true, of course, that the position of women in America has improved markedly in recent decades. Nevertheless, it can hardly be doubted that, in part because of the high visibility of the sex characteristic, women still face pervasive, although at times more subtle, discrimination in our educational institutions, on the job market and, perhaps most conspicuously, in the political arena. . . .

Moreover, since sex, like race and national origin, is an immutable characteristic determined solely by the accident of birth, the imposition of special disabilities upon the members of a particular sex because of their sex would seem to violate "the basic concept of our system that legal burdens should bear some relationship to individual responsibility. . . ." And what differentiates sex from such nonsuspect statuses as intelligence or physical disability, and aligns it with the recognized suspect criteria, is that the sex characteristic frequently bears no relation to ability to perform or contribute to society. As a result, statutory distinctions between the sexes often have the effect of invidiously relegating the entire class of females to inferior legal status without regard to the actual capabilities of its individual members. . . .

With those considerations in mind, we can only conclude that classifications based upon sex, like classifications based upon race, alienage, or national origin, are inherently suspect, and must therefore be subjected to strict judicial scrutiny. Applying the analysis mandated by that stricter standard of review, it is clear that the statutory scheme now before us is constitutionally invalid.

The sole basis of the classification established in the challenged statutes is the sex of the individuals involved. . . . Thus . . . a female member of the uniformed services seeking to obtain housing and medical benefits for her spouse must prove his dependency in fact, whereas no such burden is imposed upon male members. In addition, the statutes operate so as to deny benefits to a female member, such as appellant Sharron Frontiero, who provides less than one-half of her spouse's support, while at the same time granting such benefits to a male member who likewise provides less than one-half of his spouse's support. Thus, to this extent at least, it may fairly be said that these statutes command "dissimilar" treatment for men and women who are. . . "similarly situated." . . .

Moreover, the Government concedes that the differential treatment accorded men and women under these statutes serves no purpose other than mere "administrative convenience." In essence, the Government maintains that, as an empirical matter, wives in our society frequently are dependent upon their husbands, while husbands rarely are dependent upon their wives. Thus, the Government argues that Congress might reasonably have concluded that it would be both cheaper and easier simply conclusively to presume that wives of male members are financially dependent upon their husbands, while burdening female members with the task of establishing dependency in fact. . . .

[A]ny statutory scheme which draws a sharp line between the sexes, solely for the purpose of achieving administrative convenience, necessarily commands "dissimilar treatment for men and women who are . . . similarly situated," and therefore involves the "very kind of arbitrary legislative choice forbidden by the [Constitution] . . . ." We therefore conclude that, by according differential treatment to male and female members of the uniformed services for the sole purpose of achieving administrative convenience, the challenged statutes violate the Due Process Clause of the Fifth Amendment insofar as they require a female member to prove the dependency of her husband.

Reversed.

MR. JUSTICE STEWART, concurring in the judgment . . . [omitted].

MR. JUSTICE POWELL, with whom the CHIEF JUSTICE and MR. JUSTICE BLACKMUN join, concurring in the judgment. . . .

It is unnecessary for the Court in this case to characterize sex as a suspect classification, with all of the far-reaching implications of such a holding. . . . In my view, we can and should decide this case on the authority of *Reed* and reserve for the future any expansion of its rationale.

There is another, and I find compelling, reason for deferring a general categorizing of sex classifications as invoking the strictest test of judicial scrutiny. The Equal Rights Amendment, which if adopted will resolve the substance of this precise question, has been approved by the Congress and submitted for ratification by the States. . . .

MR. JUSTICE REHNQUIST dissents [without opinion].

Craig v. *Boren*
429 U.S. 190, 97 S.Ct. 451, 50 L.Ed. 2d 397 (1976)

http://caselaw.findlaw.com/us-supreme-court/429/190.html

Two sections (241 and 245) of an Oklahoma statute combined to prohibit the sale of 3.2 percent beer to males under the age of 21 and to females under the age of 18. Craig (a male between 18 and 21 years of age) and Whitener (a licensed vendor of 3.2 percent beer who operated the Honk 'n' Holler convenience store) sought injunctive relief against the statute in the U.S. District Court for the Western District of Oklahoma. They contended that the gender-based differential constituted an invidious discrimination against males 18–20 years old, in violation of the equal protection clause. The three-judge panel upheld the classification and dismissed the action. In this case, unlike *Frontiero* v. *Richardson*, Justice Brennan was able to amass a majority behind his opinion, but only by settling for a slightly lower standard of review. Majority: Brennan, Blackmun, Marshall, Powell, Stevens, Stewart, White. Dissenting: Rehnquist, Burger.

MR. JUSTICE BRENNAN delivered the opinion of the Court. . . .

To withstand constitutional challenge, previous cases establish that classifications by gender must serve important governmental objectives and must be substantially related to achievement of those objectives. . . .

We accept for purposes of discussion the District Court's identification of the objective underlying § 241 and 245 as the enhancement of traffic safety. Clearly, the protection of public health and safety represents an important function of state and local governments. However, appellees' statistics in our view cannot support the conclusion that the gender-based distinction closely serves to achieve that objective and therefore the distinction cannot . . . withstand equal protection challenge.

The appellees introduced a variety of statistical surveys. . . .

Even were this statistical evidence accepted as accurate, it nevertheless offers only a weak answer to the equal protection question presented here. The most focused and relevant of the statistical surveys, arrests of 18–20-year-olds for alcohol-related driving offenses, exemplifies the ultimate unpersuasiveness of this evidentiary record. Viewed in terms of the correlation between sex and the actual activity that Oklahoma seeks to regulate—driving while under the influence of alcohol—the statistics broadly establish that 0.18 percent of females and 2 percent of males in that age group were arrested for that offense. While such a disparity is not trivial in a statistical sense, it can hardly form the basis for employment of a gender line as a classifying device. Certainly if maleness is to serve as a proxy for drinking and driving, a correlation of 2 percent must be considered an unduly tenuous "fit." . . .

There is no reason to belabor this line of analysis. It is unrealistic to expect either members of the judiciary or state officials to be well versed in the rigors of experimental or statistical technique. But this merely illustrates that proving broad sociological propositions by statistics is a dubious business, and one that inevitably is in tension with the normative philosophy that underlies the Equal Protection Clause. Suffice to say that the showing offered by the appellees does not satisfy us that sex represents a legitimate, accurate proxy for the regulation of drinking and driving. In fact, when it is further recognized that Oklahoma's statute prohibits only the selling of 3.2% beer to young males and not their drinking the beverage once acquired (even after purchase by their 18–20-year-old female companions), the relationship between gender and traffic safety becomes far too tenuous to satisfy *Reed's* requirement that the gender-based difference be substantially related to achievement of the statutory objective. . . .

We conclude that the gender-based differential . . . constitutes a denial of the equal protection of the laws to males aged 18–20 and reverse the judgment of the District Court.

It is so ordered.

MR. JUSTICE STEWART, concurring . . . [omitted].
MR. JUSTICE BLACKMUN, concurring . . . [omitted].
MR. JUSTICE POWELL, concurring . . . [omitted].
MR. JUSTICE STEVENS, concurring . . . [omitted].

MR. CHIEF JUSTICE BURGER, dissenting . . . [omitted].

MR. JUSTICE REHNQUIST, dissenting. . . .

The Court's conclusion that a law which treats males less favorably than females "must serve important governmental objectives and must be substantially related to achievement of those objectives" apparently comes out of thin air. The Equal Protection Clause contains no such language, and none of our previous cases adopt that standard. I would think we have had enough difficulty with the two standards of review which our cases have recognized—the norm of "rational basis," and the "compelling state interest" required where a "suspect classification" is involved—so as to counsel weightily against the insertion of still another "standard" between those two. How is this Court to divine what objectives are important? How is it to determine whether a particular law is "substantially" related to the achievement of such objective, rather than related in some other way to its achievement? Both of the phrases used are so diaphanous and elastic as to invite subjective judicial preferences or prejudices relating to particular types of legislation, masquerading as judgments whether such legislation is directed at "important" objectives or, whether the relationship to those objectives is "substantial" enough.

I would have thought that if this Court were to leave anything to decision by the popularly elected branches of the Government, where no constitutional claim other than that of equal protection is invoked, it would be the decision as to what governmental objectives to be achieved by law are "important," and which are not. . . .

Mississippi University for Women v. *Hogan* 458 U.S. 718, 102 S.Ct. 331, 73 L.Ed. 2d 1090 (1982)

http://caselaw.findlaw.com/us-supreme-court/458/718.html

When this litigation began in 1979, the state of Mississippi operated eight universities and 16 junior colleges. All except Mississippi University for Women in Columbus were coeducational. Joe Hogan applied for admission to the MUW School of Nursing, but was denied entrance solely because of his gender. While he could have applied to the two state coed schools of nursing in Mississippi, he preferred MUW's because it was nearest his home. He then filed an action in the U.S. District Court for the Northern District of Mississippi, claiming that MUW's single-sex admissions policy violated the equal protection clause. Applying the rational basis test, the court ruled in favor of the university. The Court of Appeals for the Fifth Circuit reversed. In its view the state had the heavier burden, which it had not met, of showing that the gender-based classification was substantially related to an important government objective. Majority: O'Connor, Brennan, White, Marshall, Stevens. Dissenting: Burger, Blackmun, Powell, Rehnquist.

Justice O'Connor delivered the opinion of the Court. . . .

We begin our analysis aided by several firmly established principles. Because the challenged policy expressly discriminates among applicants on the basis of gender, it is subject to scrutiny under the Equal Protection Clause of the Fourteenth Amendment. That this statutory policy discriminates against males rather than against females does not exempt it from scrutiny or reduce the standard of review. Our decisions also establish that the party seeking to uphold a statute that classifies individuals on the basis of their gender must carry the burden of showing an "exceedingly persuasive justification" for the classification. The burden is met only by showing at least that the classification serves "important governmental objectives and that the discriminatory means employed" are "substantially related to the achievement of those objectives." . . .

The State's primary justification for maintaining the single-sex admissions policy of MUW's School of Nursing is that it compensates for discrimination against women and, therefore, constitutes educational affirmative action. As applied to the School of Nursing, we find the State's argument unpersuasive. . . .

It is readily apparent that a State can evoke a compensatory purpose to justify an otherwise discriminatory classification only if members of the gender benefited by the classification actually suffer a disadvantage related to the classification. We considered such a situation in *Califano* v. *Webster* (1977), which involved a challenge to a statutory classification that allowed women to eliminate more low-earning years than men for purposes of computing Social Security Retirement benefits. Although the effect of the classification was to allow women higher monthly benefits than were available to men with the same earning history, we upheld the statutory scheme, noting that it took into account that women "as such have been unfairly hindered from earning as much as men" and "work[ed] directly to remedy" the resulting economic disparity. . . .

In sharp contrast, Mississippi has made no showing that women lacked opportunities to obtain training in the field of nursing or to attain positions of leadership in that field when the MUW School of Nursing opened its door or that women currently are deprived of such opportunities. In fact, in 1970, the year before the School of Nursing's first class enrolled, women earned 94 percent of the nursing baccalaureate degrees conferred in Mississippi and 98.6 percent of the degrees earned nationwide. . . .

Rather than compensate for discriminatory barriers faced by women, MUW's policy of excluding males from admission to the School of Nursing tends to perpetuate the stereotyped view of nursing as an exclusively woman's job. . . . Thus, we conclude that, although the State recited a "benign, compensatory purpose," it failed to establish that the alleged objective is the actual purpose underlying the discriminatory classification.

The policy is invalid also because it fails the second part of the equal protection test, for the State has made no showing that the gender-based classification is substantially and directly related to its proposed compensatory objective. To the contrary, MUW's policy of permitting men to attend classes as auditors fatally undermines its claim that women, at least those in the School of Nursing, are adversely affected by the presence of men. . . .

In an additional attempt to justify its exclusion of men from MUW's School of Nursing, the State contends that MUW is the direct beneficiary "of specific congressional legislation which, on its face, permits the institution to exist as it has in the past." The argument is based upon the language of § 901(a) in Title IX of the Education Amendments of 1972. Although § 901(a) prohibits gender discrimination in education programs that receive federal financial assistance, subsection 5 exempts the admissions policies of undergraduate institutions "that traditionally and continually from [their] establishment [have] had a policy of admitting only students of one sex" from the general prohibition. Arguing that Congress enacted Title IX in furtherance of its power to enforce the Fourteenth Amendment, a power granted by § 5 of that Amendment, the State would have us conclude that § 901(a)(5) is but "a congressional limitation upon the broad prohibitions of the Equal Protection Clause of the Fourteenth Amendment."

The argument requires little comment. Initially, it is far from clear that Congress intended, through § 901(a)(5), to exempt MUW from any constitutional obligation. Rather, Congress apparently intended, at most, to exempt MUW from the requirements of Title IX.

Even if Congress envisioned a constitutional exemption, the State's argument would fail. Section 5 of the Fourteenth Amendment gives Congress broad power indeed to enforce the command of the Amendment and "to secure to all persons the enjoyment of perfect equality of civil rights and the equal protection of the laws against State denial or invasion. . . ." Congress' power under § 5, however, "is limited to adopting measures to enforce the guarantees of the Amendment; § 5 grants Congress no power to restrict, abrogate, or dilute these guarantees." Although we give deference to congressional decisions and classifications, neither Congress nor a State can validate a law that denies the rights guaranteed by the Fourteenth Amendment. . . .

Because we conclude that the State's policy of excluding males from MUW's School of Nursing violates the Equal Protection Clause of the Fourteenth Amendment, we affirm the judgment of the Court of Appeals.

It is so ordered.

Chief Justice Burger, dissenting . . . [omitted].
Justice Blackmun, dissenting . . . [omitted].

Justice Powell with whom Justice Rehnquist joins, dissenting.

The Court's opinion bows deeply to conformity. Left without honor—indeed, held unconstitutional—is an element of diversity that has characterized much of American education and enriched much of American life. The Court in effect holds today that no State now may provide even a single institution of higher learning open only to women students. . . .

Coeducation, historically, is a novel educational theory. . . . At the college level, for instance, until recently some of the most prestigious colleges and universities—including most of the Ivy League—had long histories of single-sex education. As Harvard, Yale, and Princeton remained all-male colleges well into the second half of this century, the "Seven Sister" institutions established a parallel standard of excellence for women's colleges. . . .

By applying heightened equal protection analysis to this case, the Court frustrates the liberating spirit of the Equal Protection Clause. It forbids the States from providing women with an opportunity to choose the type of university they prefer. And yet it is these women whom the Court regards as the victims of an illegal, stereotyped perception of the role of women in our society. The Court reasons this way in a case in which no woman has complained, and the only complainant is a man who advances no claims on behalf of anyone else. His claim, it should be recalled, is not that he is being denied a substantive educational opportunity, or even the right to attend an all-male or a coeducational college. It is only that the colleges open to him are located at inconvenient distances.

The Court views this case as presenting a serious equal protection claim of sex discrimination. I do not and I would sustain Mississippi's right to continue MUW on a rational basis analysis. But I need not apply this "lowest tier" of scrutiny. I can accept for present purposes the standard applied by the Court: that there is a gender-based distinction that must serve an important governmental objective by means that are substantially related to its achievement. The record in this case reflects that MUW has a historic position in the State's educational system dating back to 1884. More than 2,000 women presently evidence their preference for MUW by having enrolled there. The choice is one that discriminates invidiously against no one. And the State's purpose in preserving that choice is legitimate and substantial. Generations of our finest minds, both among educators and students, have believed that single-sex college-level institutions afford distinctive benefits. . . .

V. FUNDAMENTAL RIGHTS ANALYSIS

Shapiro v. *Thompson*
394 U.S. 618, 89 S.Ct. 1322, 22 L.Ed. 2d 600 (1969)

http://caselaw.findlaw.com/us-supreme-court/394/618.html

Welfare laws in Connecticut, Pennsylvania, and the District of Columbia required applicants for benefits to show one-year residence. The rules were authorized but not required by the Social Security Act of 1935. Three-judge federal district courts held the residency provision unconstitutional. Majority: Brennan, Douglas, Fortas, Marshall, Stewart, White. Dissenting: Harlan, Black, Warren.

Mr. Justice Brennan delivered the opinion of the Court. . . .

There is no dispute that the effect of the waiting-period requirement in each case is to create two classes of needy resident families indistinguishable from each other except that one is composed of residents who have resided a year or more, and the second of residents who have resided less than a year, in the jurisdiction. On the basis of this sole difference the first class is granted and the second class is denied welfare aid upon which may depend the ability of the families to obtain the very means to subsist—food, shelter, and other necessities of life. . . .

There is weighty evidence that exclusion from the jurisdiction of the poor who need or may need relief was the specific objective of these provisions. In the Congress, sponsors of federal legislation to eliminate all residence requirements have been consistently opposed by representatives of state and local welfare agencies who have stressed the fears of the States that elimination of the requirements would result in a heavy influx of individuals into States providing the most generous benefits. . . .

We do not doubt that the one-year waiting period device is well suited to discourage the influx of poor families in need of assistance. An indigent who desires to migrate, resettle, find a new job, start a new life will doubtless hesitate if he knows that he must risk making the move without the possibility of falling back on state welfare assistance during his first year of residence when his need may be most acute. But the purpose of inhibiting migration by needy persons into the State is constitutionally impermissible.

This Court long ago recognized that the nature of our Federal Union and our constitutional concepts of personal liberty unite to require that all citizens be free to travel throughout the length and breadth of our land uninhibited by statutes, rules, or regulations which unreasonably burden or restrict this movement. . . .

We have no occasion to ascribe the source of this right to travel interstate to a particular constitutional provision. . . . "It is a right that has been firmly established and repeatedly recognized. . . ."

Appellants next advance as justification certain administrative and related governmental objectives allegedly served by the waiting-period requirement. They argue that the requirement (1) facilitates the planning of the welfare budget; (2) provides an objective test of residency; (3) minimizes the opportunity for recipients fraudulently to receive payments from more than one jurisdiction; and (4) encourages early entry of new residents into the labor force. . . .

The argument that the waiting-period requirement facilitates budget predictability is wholly unfounded. . . .

The argument that the waiting period serves as an administratively efficient rule of thumb for determining residency similarly will not withstand scrutiny. . . .

Similarly, there is no need for a State to use the one-year waiting period as a safeguard against fraudulent receipt of benefits; far less drastic means are available, and are employed, to minimize that hazard. . . .

We conclude therefore that appellants in these cases do not use and have no need to use the one-year requirement for the governmental purposes suggested. Thus, even under traditional equal protection tests a classification of welfare applicants according to whether they have lived in the State for one year would seem irrational and unconstitutional. But, of course, the traditional criteria do not apply in these cases. Since the classification here touches on the fundamental right of interstate movement, its constitutionality must be judged by the stricter standard of whether it promotes a compelling state interest. Under this standard, the waiting period requirement clearly violates the Equal Protection Clause. . . .

Affirmed.

Mr. Justice Stewart, concurring . . . [omitted].

MR. CHIEF JUSTICE WARREN, with whom MR. JUSTICE BLACK joins, dissenting . . . [omitted].

MR. JUSTICE HARLAN, dissenting. . . .

The "compelling interest" doctrine has two branches. The branch which requires that classifications based upon "suspect" criteria be supported by a compelling interest apparently had its genesis in cases involving racial classifications, which have . . . been regarded as inherently "suspect." . . .

I think that this branch of the "compelling interest" doctrine is sound when applied to racial classifications, for historically the Equal Protection Clause was largely a product of the desire to eradicate legal distinctions founded upon race. However, I believe that the more recent extensions have been unwise. . . .

The second branch of the "compelling interest" principle is even more troublesome. For it has been held that a statutory classification is subject to the "compelling interest" test if the result of the classification may be to affect a "fundamental right," regardless of the basis of the classification. . . .

I think this branch of the "compelling interest" doctrine particularly unfortunate and unnecessary. It is unfortunate because it creates an exception which threatens to swallow the standard equal protection rule. Virtually every state statute affects important rights. This Court has repeatedly held, for example, that the traditional equal protection standard is applicable to statutory classifications affecting such fundamental matters as the right to pursue a particular occupation, the right to receive greater or smaller wages or to work more or less hours, and the right to inherit property. Rights such as these are in principle indistinguishable from those involved here, and to extend the "compelling interest" rule to all cases in which such rights are affected would go far toward making this Court a "super-legislature." This branch of the doctrine is also unnecessary. When the right affected is one assured by the federal Constitution, any infringement can be dealt with under the Due Process Clause. But when a statute affects only matters not mentioned in the federal Constitution and is not arbitrary or irrational, I must reiterate that I know of nothing which entitles this Court to pick out particular human activities, characterize them as "fundamental," and give them added protection under an unusually stringent equal protection test. . . .

San Antonio Independent School District v. *Rodriguez*
411 U.S. 1, 93 S.Ct. 1278, 36 L.Ed. 2d 16 (1973)

http://caselaw.findlaw.com/us-supreme-court/411/1.html

In 1968, Demetrio Rodriguez and other parents living in Texas's Edgewood School District filed suit in the U.S. District Court for the Western District of Texas, claiming that reliance on local property taxes for the support of public education violated the equal protection clause. Edgewood had an average assessed property value of $5,960 for each of its 22,000 students. With a tax of $1.05 per $100 of assessed value (the highest in the San Antonio area), the district received less per pupil from property taxes than did the affluent Alamo Heights district, which taxed at a rate of only $0.85 but contained assessed property worth more than $49,000 for each of its 5,000 students. With state, federal, and other support included, Edgewood spent $356 and Alamo Heights $594 per pupil. These situations reflected a pattern: Property-poor districts typically taxed more and spent less for each enrolled child than did property-rich districts. Ruling that education was a fundamental constitutional right and that wealth-based distinctions in the state's system of school financing were constitutionally suspect, a three-judge panel instructed the state to adopt a system of school financing so that the amount spent per pupil would not be a function of the wealth of the district in which a child lived. Majority: Powell, Blackmun, Burger, Rehnquist, Stewart. Minority: White, Brennan, Marshall, Douglas.

MR. JUSTICE POWELL delivered the opinion of the Court. . . .

The District Court's opinion does not reflect the novelty and complexity of the constitutional questions posed by appellees' challenge to Texas' system of school financing. In concluding that strict judicial scrutiny was required, that court relied on decisions dealing with the rights of indigents to equal treatment in the criminal trial and appellate processes, and on cases disapproving wealth restrictions on the right to vote. Those cases, the District Court concluded, established wealth as a suspect classification. Finding that the local property tax system discriminated on the basis of wealth, it regarded those precedents as controlling. It then reasoned, based on decisions of this Court affirming the undeniable importance of education, that there is a fundamental right to education and that, absent some compelling state justification, the Texas system could not stand.

We are unable to agree that this case, which in significant aspects is *sui generis* [unique], may be so nearly fitted into the conventional mosaic of constitutional analysis under the Equal Protection Clause. Indeed, for the several reasons that follow, we find neither the suspect-classification nor the fundamental-interest analysis persuasive.

The wealth discrimination discovered by the District Court in this case, and by several other courts that have recently struck down school-financing laws in other States, is quite unlike any of the forms of wealth discrimination heretofore reviewed by this Court. Rather than focusing on the unique features of the alleged discrimination, the courts in these cases have virtually assumed their findings of a suspect classification through a simplistic process of analysis: since, under the traditional systems of financing public schools, some poorer people receive less expensive educations than other more affluent people, these systems discriminate on the basis of wealth. This approach largely ignores the hard threshold questions, including whether it makes a difference for purposes of consideration under the Constitution that the class of disadvantaged "poor" cannot be identified or defined in customary equal protection terms, and whether the relative—rather than absolute—nature of the asserted deprivation is of significant consequence. Before a State's laws and the justifications for the classifications they create are subjected to strict judicial scrutiny, we think these threshold considerations must be analyzed more closely than they were in the court below. . . .

First, in support of their charge that the system discriminates against the "poor," appellees have made no effort to demonstrate that it operates to the peculiar disadvantage of any class fairly definable as indigent, or as composed of persons whose incomes are beneath any designated poverty level. Indeed, there is reason to believe that the poorest families are not necessarily clustered in the poorest property districts. . . .

Second, neither appellees nor the District Court addressed the fact that . . . lack of personal resources has not occasioned an absolute deprivation of the desired benefit. The argument here is not that the children in districts having relatively low assessable property values are receiving no public education; rather, it is that they are receiving a poorer quality education than that available to children in districts having more assessable wealth. Apart from the unsettled and disputed question whether the quality of education may be determined by the amount of money expended for it, a sufficient answer to appellees' argument is that, at least where wealth is involved, the Equal Protection Clause does not require absolute equality or precisely equal advantages. . . .

For these two reasons . . . the disadvantaged class is not susceptible of identification in traditional terms. . . .

[I]t is clear that appellees' suit asks this Court to extend its most exacting scrutiny to review a system that allegedly discriminates against a large, diverse, and amorphous class, unified only by the common factor of residence in districts that happen to have less taxable wealth than other districts. The system of alleged discrimination and the class it defines have none of the traditional indicia of suspectness: the class is not saddled with such disabilities, or subjected to such a history of purposeful unequal treatment, or relegated to such a position of political powerlessness as to command extraordinary protection from the majoritarian political process.

We thus conclude that the Texas system does not operate to the peculiar disadvantage of any suspect class. . . .

Nothing this Court holds today in any way detracts from our historic dedication to public education. . . . But the importance of a service performed by the State does not determine whether it must be regarded as fundamental for purposes of examination under the Equal Protection Clause. . . . It is not the province of this Court to create substantive constitutional rights in the name of guaranteeing equal protection of the laws. . . .

Education, of course, is not among the rights afforded explicit protection under our Federal Constitution. Nor do we find any basis for saying it is implicitly so protected. . . .

Even if it were conceded that some identifiable quantum of education is a constitutionally protected prerequisite to the meaningful exercise of . . . [both the First Amendment rights and the right to vote] we have no indication that the present levels of educational expenditures in Texas provide an education that falls short. Whatever merit appellees' argument might have if a State's financing system occasioned an absolute denial of educational opportunities to any of its children, that argument provides no basis for finding any interference with fundamental rights where only relative differences in spending levels are involved and where—as is true in the present case—no charge fairly could be made that the system fails to provide each child with an opportunity to acquire the basic minimal skills necessary for the enjoyment of the rights of speech and of full participation in the political process. . . .

In sum, to the extent that the Texas system of school financing results in unequal expenditures between children who happen to reside in different districts, we cannot say that such disparities are the product of a system that is so irrational as to be invidiously discriminatory. . . . We are unwilling to assume for ourselves a level of wisdom superior to that of legislators, scholars, and educational authorities in 50 States, especially where the alternatives proposed are only recently conceived and nowhere yet tested. The constitutional standard under the Equal Protection Clause is whether the challenged state action rationally furthers a legitimate state purpose or interest. We hold that the Texas plan abundantly satisfies this standard. . . .

Reversed.

MR. JUSTICE STEWART, concurring . . . [omitted].

MR. JUSTICE BRENNAN, dissenting . . . [omitted].

MR. JUSTICE WHITE, with whom MR. JUSTICE DOUGLAS and MR. JUSTICE BRENNAN join, dissenting . . . [omitted].

MR. JUSTICE MARSHALL, with whom MR. JUSTICE DOUGLAS concurs, dissenting.

The Court today decides, in effect, that a State may constitutionally vary the quality of education which it offers its children in accordance with the amount of taxable wealth located in the school districts within which they reside. . . . More unfortunately, though, the majority's holding can only be seen as a retreat from our historic commitment to equality of educational opportunity and as unsupportable acquiescence in a system which deprives children in their earliest years of the chance to reach their full potential as citizens. The Court does this despite the absence of any substantial justification for a scheme which arbitrarily channels educational resources in accordance with the fortuity of the amount of taxable wealth within each district. . . .

The only justification offered by appellants to sustain the discrimination in educational opportunity caused by the Texas financing scheme is local educational control. Presented with this justification, the District Court concluded that "[n]ot only are defendants unable to demonstrate compelling state interests for their classifications based upon wealth, they fail even to establish a reasonable basis for these classifications." I must agree with this conclusion. . . .

[E]ven if we accept Texas' general dedication to local control in educational matters, it is difficult to find any evidence of such dedication with respect to fiscal matters. It ignores reality to suggest—as the Court does, that the local property tax element of the Texas financing scheme reflects a conscious legislative effort to provide school districts with local fiscal control. . . .[1]

VI. AFFIRMATIVE ACTION

Parents Involved in Community Schools v. *Seattle School District No. 1* 551 U.S. 701, 127 S.Ct. 2738, 168 L.Ed. 2d 508 (2007)

http://caselaw.findlaw.com/us-supreme-court/551/701.html

The background of this case follows in the Chief Justice's opinion below. Majority: Roberts, Alito, Kennedy, Scalia, Thomas. Dissenting: Breyer, Ginsburg, Souter, Stevens.

Chief Justice Roberts announced the judgment of the Court, and delivered the opinion of the Court which Justices Scalia, Thomas, and Alito joined and which Justice Kennedy joined in part.

The school districts in these cases voluntarily adopted student assignment plans that rely upon race to determine which public schools certain children may attend. The Seattle [Washington] school district classifies children as white or nonwhite; the Jefferson County school district [in metropolitan Louisville, Kentucky] as black or "other." In Seattle, this racial classification is used to allocate slots in oversubscribed high schools. In Jefferson County, it is used to make certain elementary school assignments and to rule on transfer requests. In each case, the school district relies upon an individual student's race in assigning that student to a particular school, so that the racial balance at the school falls within a predetermined range based on the racial composition of the school district as a whole. Parents of students denied assignment to particular schools under these plans solely because of their race brought suit, contending that allocating children to different public schools on the basis of race violated the Fourteenth Amendment guarantee of equal protection. The Courts of Appeals below upheld the plans. We . . . now reverse.

Both cases present the same underlying legal question—whether a public school that had not operated legally segregated schools or has been found to be unitary may choose to classify students by race and rely upon that classification in making school assignments. . . .

It is well established that when the government distributes burdens or benefits on the basis of individual racial classifications, that action is reviewed under strict scrutiny. . . . In order to satisfy this searching standard of review, the school districts must demonstrate that the use of individual racial classifications in the assignment plans here under review is "narrowly tailored" to achieve a "compelling" government interest. . . .

[O]ur prior cases, in evaluating the use of racial classifications in the school context, have recognized two interests that qualify as compelling. The first is the compelling interest of remedying the effects of past intentional discrimination. . . . The second government interest we have recognized as compelling for purposes of strict scrutiny is the interest in diversity in higher education upheld in *Grutter* . . . The diversity interest was not focused on race alone but encompassed "all factors that may contribute to student body diversity." . . .

The entire gist of the analysis in *Grutter* was that the admissions program at issue there focused on each applicant as an individual, and not simply as a member of a particular racial group. . . .

In the present cases, by contrast, race is not considered as part of a broader effort to achieve "exposure to widely diverse people, cultures, ideas, and viewpoints"; race, for some students, is determinative standing alone. The districts argue that other factors, such as student preferences, affect assignment decisions under their plans, but under each plan when race comes into play, it is decisive by itself. It is not simply one factor weighed with others in reaching a decision, as in *Grutter;* it is *the* factor. Like the University of Michigan undergraduate plan struck down in *Gratz*, the plans here "do not provide for a meaningful individualized review of applicants" but instead rely on racial classifications in a "nonindividualized, mechanical" way. Even when it comes to race, the plans here employ only a limited notion of diversity, viewing race exclusively in white/ nonwhite terms in Seattle and black/"other" terms in Jefferson County. . . .

In upholding the admissions plan in *Grutter*, though, this Court relied upon considerations unique to institutions of higher education, noting that in light of "the expansive freedoms of speech and thought associated with the university environment, universities occupy a special niche in our constitutional tradition." . . .

Perhaps recognizing that reliance on *Grutter* cannot sustain their plans, both school districts assert additional interests, distinct from the interest upheld in *Grutter*, to justify their race-based assignments. In briefing and argument before this Court, Seattle contends that its use of race helps to reduce racial concentration in schools and to ensure that racially concentrated housing patterns do not prevent nonwhite students from having access to the most desirable schools. Jefferson County has articulated a similar goal, phrasing its interest in terms of educating its students "in a racially integrated environment." Each school district argues that educational and broader socialization benefits flow from a racially diverse learning environment, and each contends that because the diversity they seek is racial diversity—not the broader diversity at issue in *Grutter*—it makes sense to promote that interest directly by relying on race alone. . . .

[I]t is clear that the racial classifications employed by the districts are not narrowly tailored to the goal of achieving the educational and social benefits asserted to flow from racial diversity. In design and operation, the plans are directed only to racial balance, pure and simple, an objective this Court has repeatedly condemned as illegitimate.

The plans are tied to each district's specific racial demographics, rather than to any pedagogic concept of the level of diversity needed to obtain the asserted educational benefits. . . .

The districts offer no evidence that the level of racial diversity necessary to achieve the asserted educational benefits happens to coincide with the racial demographics of the respective school districts—or rather the white/nonwhite or black/"other" balance of the districts, since that is the only diversity addressed by the plans. . . .

In fact, in each case the extreme measure of relying on race in assignments is unnecessary to achieve the stated goals, even as defined by the districts. . . .

This working backward to achieve a particular type of racial balance, rather than working forward from some demonstration of the level of diversity that provides the purported benefits, is a fatal flaw under our existing precedent. We have many times over reaffirmed that "[r]acial balance is not to be achieved for its own sake." . . .

Accepting racial balancing as a compelling state interest would justify the imposition of racial proportionality throughout American society, contrary to our repeated recognition that "[a]t the heart of the Constitution's guarantee of equal protection lies the simple command that the Government must treat citizens as individuals, not as simply components of a racial, religious, sexual or national class." . . . Allowing racial balancing as a compelling end in itself would "effectively assur[e] that race will always be relevant in American life. . . .

The validity of our concern that racial balancing has "no logical stopping point," is demonstrated here by the degree to which the districts tie their racial guidelines to their demographics. As the districts' demographics shift, so too will their definition of racial diversity. . . .

The districts assert, as they must, that the way in which they have employed individual racial classifications is necessary to achieve their stated ends. The minimal effect these classifications have on student assignments, however, suggests that other means would be effective. Seattle's racial tiebreaker results, in the end, only in shifting a small number of students between schools. . . .

Similarly, Jefferson County's use of racial classifications has only a minimal effect on the assignment of students. . . .

While we do not suggest that *greater* use of race would be preferable, the minimal impact of the districts' racial classifications on school enrollment casts doubt on the necessity of using racial classifications. . . .

JUSTICE BREYER's dissent . . . relies on the good intentions and motives of the school districts, stating that he has found "no case that . . . repudiated this constitutional asymmetry between that which seeks to *exclude* and that which seeks to *include* members of minority races." We have found many. Our cases clearly reject the argument that motives affect the strict scrutiny analysis. . . . This argument that different rules should govern racial classifications designed to include rather than exclude is not new; it has been repeatedly pressed in the past, . . . and has been repeatedly rejected.

The reasons for rejecting a motives test for racial classifications are clear enough. "The Court's emphasis on 'benign racial classifications' suggests confidence in its ability to distinguish good from harmful governmental uses of racial criteria. History should teach greater humility. . . . '[B]enign' carries with it no independent meaning, but reflects only acceptance of the current generation's conclusion that a politically acceptable burden, imposed on particular citizens on the basis of race, is reasonable." . . .

JUSTICE BREYER's position comes down to a familiar claim: The end justifies the means. He admits that "there is a cost in applying 'a state-mandated racial label,'" but he is confident that the cost is worth paying. Our established strict scrutiny test for racial classifications, however, insists on "detailed examination, both as to ends *and* as to means." . . .

JUSTICE BREYER also suggests that other means for achieving greater racial diversity in schools are necessarily unconstitutional if the racial classifications at issue in these cases cannot survive strict scrutiny. These other means—*e.g.*, where to construct new schools, how to allocate resources among schools, and which academic offerings to provide to attract students to certain schools—implicate different considerations than the explicit racial classifications at issue in these cases, and we express no opinion on their validity—not even in dicta. Rather, we employ the familiar and well-established analytic approach of strict scrutiny to evaluate the plans at issue today, an approach that in no way warrants the dissent's cataclysmic concerns. Under that approach, the school districts have not carried their burden of showing that the ends they seek justify the particular extreme means they have chosen—classifying individual students on the basis of their race and discriminating among them on that basis.

If the need for the racial classifications embraced by the school districts is unclear, even on the districts' own terms, the costs are undeniable. Government action dividing us by race is inherently suspect because such classifications promote "notions of racial inferiority and lead to a politics of racial hostility," "reinforce the belief, held by too many for too much of our history, that individuals should be judged by the color of their skin," and "endorse race-based reasoning and the conception of a Nation divided into racial blocs, thus contributing to an escalation of racial hostility and conflict." . . .

All this is true enough in the contexts in which these statements were made, . . . but when it comes to using race to assign children to schools, history will be heard. In *Brown* v. *Board of Education* (*Brown I*), we held that segregation deprived black children of equal educational opportunities regardless of whether school facilities and other tangible factors were equal, because government classification and separation on grounds of race themselves denoted inferiority. It was not the inequality of the facilities but the fact of legally separating children on the basis of race on which the Court relied to find a constitutional violation in 1954. . . . The next Term [in *Brown II*], we accordingly stated that "full compliance" with *Brown I* required school districts "to achieve a system of determining admission to the public schools *on a nonracial basis*" (emphasis added).

What do the racial classifications at issue here do, if not accord differential treatment on the basis of race? . . . Before *Brown*, schoolchildren were told where they could and could not go to school based on the color of their skin. The school districts in these cases have not carried the heavy burden of demonstrating that we should allow this once again—even for very different reasons. For schools that never segregated on the basis of race, such as Seattle, or that have removed the vestiges of past segregation, such as Jefferson County, the way "to achieve a system of determining admission to the public schools on a nonracial basis," is to stop assigning students on a racial basis. The way to stop discrimination on the basis of race is to stop discriminating on the basis of race. The judgments of the Courts of Appeals for the Sixth and Ninth Circuits are reversed, and the cases are remanded for further proceedings.

It is so ordered.

JUSTICE KENNEDY, concurring in part and concurring in the judgment . . . [omitted].

JUSTICE THOMAS, concurring . . . [omitted].

JUSTICE BREYER, with whom JUSTICE STEVENS, JUSTICE SOUTER, and JUSTICE GINSBURG join, dissenting. . . .

A longstanding and unbroken line of legal authority tells us that the Equal Protection Clause permits local school boards to use race-conscious criteria to achieve positive race-related goals, even when the Constitution does not compel it. Because of its importance, I shall repeat what this Court said about the matter in

Swann [v. *Charlotte Mecklenburg*] (1971). Chief Justice Burger, on behalf of a unanimous Court in a case of exceptional importance, wrote:

"School authorities are traditionally charged with broad power to formulate and implement educational policy and might well conclude, for example, that in order to prepare students to live in a pluralistic society each school should have a prescribed ratio of Negro to white students reflecting the proportion for the district as a whole. To do this as an educational policy is within the broad discretionary powers of school authorities." . . .

Swann is predicated upon a well-established legal view of the Fourteenth Amendment. That view understands the basic objective of those who wrote the Equal Protection Clause as forbidding practices that lead to racial exclusion. The Amendment sought to bring into American society as full members those whom the Nation had previously held in slavery. . . .

There is reason to believe that those who drafted an Amendment with this basic purpose in mind would have understood the legal and practical difference between the use of race-conscious criteria in defiance of that purpose, namely to keep the races apart, and the use of race-conscious criteria to further that purpose, namely to bring the races together. . . .

Sometimes Members of this Court have disagreed about the degree of leniency that the Clause affords to programs designed to include. But I can find no case in which this Court has followed [the] "colorblind" approach. And I have found no case that otherwise repudiated this constitutional asymmetry between that which seeks to *exclude* and that which seeks to *include* members of minority races.

What does the plurality say in response? First, it seeks to distinguish *Swann* and other similar cases on the ground that those cases involved remedial plans in response to *judicial findings* of *de jure* segregation. . . . [T]hat is historically untrue. . . . [T]his distinction—between court-ordered and voluntary desegregation seeks a line that sensibly cannot be drawn.

Second, the plurality downplays the importance of *Swann* and related cases by frequently describing their relevant statements as "dicta." These criticisms, however, miss the main point. *Swann* did not hide its understanding of the law in a corner of an obscure opinion or in a footnote, unread but by experts. It set forth its view prominently in an important opinion joined by all nine Justices, knowing that it would be read and followed throughout the Nation. . . . And if the plurality now chooses to reject that principle, it cannot adequately justify its retreat simply by affixing the label "dicta" to reasoning with which it disagrees. Rather, it must explain to the courts and to the Nation *why* it would abandon guidance set forth many years before, guidance that countless others have built upon over time, and which the law has continuously embodied.

Third, a more important response is the plurality's claim that later cases . . . supplanted *Swann*. . . . [N]o case . . . has ever held that the test of "strict scrutiny" means that all racial classifications—no matter whether they seek to include or exclude—must in practice be treated the same. . . .

The compelling interest at issue here, then, includes an effort to eradicate the remnants, not of general "societal discrimination," but of primary and secondary school segregation; it includes an effort to create school environments that provide better educational opportunities for all children; it includes an effort to help create citizens better prepared to know, to understand, and to work with people of all races and backgrounds, thereby furthering the kind of democratic government our Constitution foresees. If an educational interest that combines these three elements is not "compelling," what is? . . .

I recognize that the Court seeks to distinguish *Grutter* from these cases by claiming that *Grutter* arose in "the context of higher education." But that is not a meaningful legal distinction. . . . I do not believe the Constitution could possibly find "compelling" the provision of a racially diverse education for a 23-year-old law student but not for a 13-year-old high school pupil. . . . I add that one cannot find a relevant distinction in the fact that these school districts did not examine the merits of applications "individual[ly]." The context here does not involve admission by merit; a child's academic, artistic, and athletic "merits" are not at all relevant to the child's placement. These are not affirmative action plans, and hence "individualized scrutiny" is simply beside the point.

The upshot is that these plans' specific features—(1) their limited and historically-diminishing use of race, (2) their strong reliance upon other non-race-conscious elements, (3) their history and the manner in which the districts developed and modified their approach, (4) the comparison with prior plans, and (5) the lack of reasonably evident alternatives—together show that the districts' plans are "narrowly tailored" to achieve their "compelling" goals. In sum, the districts' race-conscious plans satisfy "strict scrutiny" and are therefore lawful. . . .

The wide variety of different integration plans that school districts use throughout the Nation suggests that the problem of racial segregation in schools, including *de facto* segregation, is difficult to solve. The fact that many such plans have used explicitly racial criteria suggests that such criteria have an important, sometimes necessary, role to play. The fact that the controlling opinion would make a school district's use of such criteria often unlawful (and the plurality's "colorblind" view would make such use always unlawful) suggests that today's opinion will require setting aside the laws of several States and many local communities. . . .

The last half-century has witnessed great strides toward racial equality, but we have not yet realized the promise of *Brown*. To invalidate the plans under review is to threaten the promise of *Brown*. The plurality's position, I fear, would break that promise. This is a decision that the Court and the Nation will come to regret.

Justice Stevens, dissenting . . . [omitted].

Fisher v. *University of Texas at Austin*
579 U.S. ___, 136 S.Ct. 2198, 195 L.Ed. 2d 511 (2016)

http://caselaw.findlaw.com/us-supreme-court/14–981.html

The background of this case appears in Justice Kennedy's opinion. In *Fisher I* (2013), the Court divided 7–1. Justice Kennedy wrote for a majority that included the chief justice and Justices Alito, Breyer, Scalia, Sotomayor, and Thomas. Justice Ginsburg dissented. Justice Kagan did not participate. The opinions that follow refer to *Grutter* v. *Bollinger* and *Gratz* v. *Bollinger*, both decided in 2003. In *Grutter* the Court divided 5–4 with Justices O'Connor, Breyer, Ginsburg, Souter, and Stevens in the majority, and Chief Justice Rehnquist and Justices Kennedy, Scalia, and Thomas dissenting. In *Gratz*, the Court divided 6–3 with Chief Justice Rehnquist and Justices Breyer, Kennedy, O'Connor, Scalia, and Thomas in the majority, and Justices Ginsburg, Souter, and Stevens dissenting. Majority in *Fisher II* below: Kennedy, Breyer, Ginsburg, Sotomayor. Dissenting: Alito, Roberts, Thomas. Not participating: Kagan.

Justice Kennedy delivered the opinion of the Court.

The Court is asked once again to consider whether the race-conscious admissions program at the University of Texas is lawful under the Equal Protection Clause.

The University of Texas at Austin (or University) relies upon a complex system of admissions that has undergone significant evolution over the past two decades. Until 1996, the University made its admissions decisions primarily based on a measure called "Academic Index" (or AI), which it calculated by combining an applicant's SAT score and academic performance in high school. In assessing applicants, preference was given to racial minorities.

In 1996, the Court of Appeals for the Fifth Circuit invalidated this admissions system, holding that any consideration of race in college admissions violates the Equal Protection Clause (*Hopwood* v. *Texas*). One year later the University adopted a new admissions policy. Instead of considering race, the University began making admissions decisions based on an applicant's AI and his or her "Personal Achievement Index" (PAI). The PAI was a numerical score based on a holistic review of an application. Included in the number were the applicant's essays, leadership and work experience, extracurricular activities, community service, and other "special characteristics" that might give the admissions committee insight into a student's background. Consistent with *Hopwood*, race was not a consideration in calculating an applicant's AI or PAI.

The Texas Legislature responded to *Hopwood* as well. It enacted H. B. 588, commonly known as the Top Ten Percent Law. As its name suggests, the Top Ten Percent Law guarantees college admission to students who graduate from a Texas high school in the top 10 percent of their class. Those students may choose to attend any of the public universities in the State.

The University implemented the Top Ten Percent Law in 1998. After first admitting any student who qualified for admission under that law, the University filled the remainder of its incoming freshman class using a combination of an applicant's AI and PAI scores—again, without considering race.

The University used this admissions system until 2003, when this Court decided the companion cases of *Grutter* v. *Bollinger* and *Gratz* v. *Bollinger*. In *Gratz*, this Court struck down the University of Michigan's undergraduate system of admissions, which at the time allocated predetermined points to racial minority candidates. In *Grutter*, however, the Court upheld the University of Michigan Law School's system of holistic review—a system that did not mechanically assign points but rather treated race as a relevant feature within the broader context of a candidate's application. In upholding this nuanced use of race, *Grutter* implicitly overruled *Hopwood's* categorical prohibition.

In the wake of *Grutter*, the University embarked upon a year-long study seeking to ascertain whether its admissions policy was allowing it to provide "the educational benefits of a diverse student body . . . to all of the University's undergraduate students." The University concluded that its admissions policy was not providing these benefits.

To change its system, the University submitted a proposal to the Board of Regents that requested permission to begin taking race into consideration as one of "the many ways in which [an] academically qualified individual might contribute to, and benefit from, the rich, diverse, and challenging educational environment of the University." After the board approved the proposal, the University adopted a new admissions policy to implement it. The University has continued to use that admissions policy to this day.

Although the University's new admissions policy was a direct result of *Grutter*, it is not identical to the policy this Court approved in that case. Instead, consistent with the State's legislative directive, the University continues to fill a significant majority of its class through the Top Ten Percent Plan (or Plan). Today, up to 75 percent of the places in the freshman class are filled through the Plan. As a practical matter, this 75 percent cap, which has now been fixed by statute, means that, while the Plan continues to be referenced as a "Top Ten Percent Plan," a student actually needs to finish in the top seven or eight percent of his or her class in order to be admitted under this category.

The University did adopt an approach similar to the one in *Grutter* for the remaining 25 percent or so of the incoming class. This portion of the class continues to be admitted based on a combination of their AI and PAI scores. Now, however, race is given weight as a subfactor within the PAI. The PAI is a number from 1 to 6 (6 is the best) that is based on two primary components. The first component is the average score a reader gives the applicant on two required essays. The second component is a full-file review that results in another 1-to-6 score, the "Personal Achievement Score" or PAS. The PAS is determined by a separate reader, who (1) rereads the applicant's required essays, (2) reviews any supplemental information the applicant submits (letters of recommendation, resumes, an additional optional essay, writing samples, artwork, etc.), and (3) evaluates the applicant's potential contributions to the University's student body based on the applicant's leadership experience, extracurricular activities, awards/honors, community service, and other "special circumstances."

"Special circumstances" include the socioeconomic status of the applicant's family, the socioeconomic status of the applicant's school, the applicant's family responsibilities, whether the applicant lives in a single-parent home, the applicant's SAT score in relation to the average SAT score at the applicant's school, the language spoken at the applicant's home, and, finally, the applicant's race. . . .

Therefore, although admissions officers can consider race as a positive feature of a minority student's application, there is no dispute that race is but a "factor of a factor of a factor" in the holistic-review calculus. . . . Thus, race, in this indirect fashion, considered with all of the other factors that make up an applicant's AI and PAI scores, can make a difference to whether an application is accepted or rejected.

Petitioner Abigail Fisher applied for admission to the University's 2008 freshman class. She was not in the top 10 percent of her high school class, so she was evaluated for admission through holistic, full-file review. Petitioner's application was rejected.

Petitioner then filed suit alleging that the University's consideration of race as part of its holistic-review process disadvantaged her and other Caucasian applicants, in violation of the Equal Protection Clause. The District Court entered summary judgment in the University's favor, and the Court of Appeals affirmed.

This Court granted certiorari and vacated the judgment of the Court of Appeals (*Fisher I*) because it had applied an overly deferential "good-faith" standard in assessing the constitutionality of the University's program. The Court remanded the case for the Court of Appeals to assess the parties' claims under the correct legal standard. Without further remanding to the District Court, the Court of Appeals again affirmed the entry of summary judgment in the University's favor. This Court granted certiorari for a second time, and now affirms.

Fisher I set forth three controlling principles relevant to assessing the constitutionality of a public university's affirmative-action program. First, "because racial characteristics so seldom provide a relevant basis for disparate treatment," "[r]ace may not be considered [by a university] unless the admissions process can withstand strict scrutiny." Strict scrutiny requires the university to demonstrate with clarity that its "'purpose or interest is both constitutionally permissible and substantial, and that its use of the classification is necessary . . . to the accomplishment of its purpose.'"

Second, *Fisher I* confirmed that "the decision to pursue 'the educational benefits that flow from student body diversity' . . . is, in substantial measure, an academic judgment to which some, but not complete, judicial deference is proper." A university cannot impose a fixed quota or otherwise "define diversity as 'some specified percentage of a particular group merely because of its race or ethnic origin.'" Once, however, a university gives "a reasoned, principled explanation" for its decision, deference must be given "to the University's conclusion, based on its experience and expertise, that a diverse student body would serve its educational goals."

Third, *Fisher I* clarified that no deference is owed when determining whether the use of race is narrowly tailored to achieve the university's permissible goals. A university, *Fisher I* explained, bears the burden of proving a "non-racial approach" would not promote its interest in the educational benefits of diversity "about as well and at tolerable administrative expense." Though "[n]arrow tailoring does not require exhaustion of every conceivable race-neutral alternative" or "require a university to choose between maintaining a reputation for excellence [and] fulfilling a commitment to provide educational opportunities to members of all racial groups," it does impose "on the university the ultimate burden of demonstrating" that "race-neutral alternatives" that are both "available" and "workable" "do not suffice."

Fisher I set forth these controlling principles, while taking no position on the constitutionality of the admissions program at issue in this case. The Court held only that the District Court and the Court of Appeals had "confined the strict scrutiny inquiry in too narrow a way by deferring to the University's good faith in its use of racial classifications." . . .

In seeking to reverse the judgment of the Court of Appeals, petitioner makes four arguments. First, she argues that the University has not articulated its compelling interest with sufficient clarity. . . . As this Court's cases have made clear, however, the compelling interest that justifies consideration of race in college admissions is not an interest in enrolling a certain number of minority students. Rather, a university may institute a race-conscious admissions program as a means of obtaining "the educational benefits that flow from student body diversity." As this Court has said, enrolling a diverse student body "promotes cross-racial understanding, helps to break down racial stereotypes, and enables students to better understand persons of different races." Equally important, "student body diversity promotes learning outcomes, and better prepares students for an increasingly diverse workforce and society." . . .

The record reveals that in first setting forth its current admissions policy, the University articulated concrete and precise goals. . . . The University has provided in addition a "reasoned, principled explanation" for its decision to pursue these goals. . . . Petitioner's contention that the University's goal was insufficiently concrete is rebutted by the record.

Second, petitioner argues that the University has no need to consider race because it had already "achieved critical mass" by 2003 using the Top Ten Percent Plan and race-neutral holistic review. . . . The record reveals, however, that, at the time of petitioner's application, the University could not be faulted on this score. . . .

The record itself contains significant evidence, both statistical and anecdotal, in support of the University's position. . . .

In addition to this broad demographic data, the University put forward evidence that minority students admitted under the Hopwood regime experienced feelings of loneliness and isolation. This anecdotal evidence is, in turn, bolstered by further, more nuanced quantitative data. . . .

Third, petitioner argues that considering race was not necessary because such consideration has had only a "'minimal impact' in advancing the [University's] compelling interest." Again, the record does not support this assertion. . . .

Petitioner's final argument is that "there are numerous other available race-neutral means of achieving" the University's compelling interest. A review of the record reveals, however, that, at the time of petitioner's application, none of her proposed alternatives was a workable means for the University to attain the benefits of diversity it sought. . . . Perhaps more significantly, in the wake of *Hopwood*, the University spent seven years attempting to achieve its compelling interest using race-neutral holistic review. None of these efforts succeeded, and petitioner fails to offer any meaningful way in which the

University could have improved upon them at the time of her application.

Petitioner also suggests altering the weight given to academic and socioeconomic factors in the University's admissions calculus. This proposal ignores the fact that the University tried, and failed, to increase diversity through enhanced consideration of socioeconomic and other factors. And it further ignores this Court's precedent making clear that the Equal Protection Clause does not force universities to choose between a diverse student body and a reputation for academic excellence.

Petitioner's final suggestion is to uncap the Top Ten Percent Plan, and admit more—if not all—the University's students through a percentage plan. As an initial matter, petitioner overlooks the fact that the Top Ten Percent Plan, though facially neutral, cannot be understood apart from its basic purpose, which is to boost minority enrollment. . . .

Even if, as a matter of raw numbers, minority enrollment would increase under such a regime, petitioner would be hard-pressed to find convincing support for the proposition that college admissions would be improved if they were a function of class rank alone. . . . Class rank is a single metric, and like any single metric, it will capture certain types of people and miss others. This does not imply that students admitted through holistic review are necessarily more capable or more desirable than those admitted through the Top Ten Percent Plan. It merely reflects the fact that privileging one characteristic above all others does not lead to a diverse student body. . . .

In short, none of petitioner's suggested alternatives—nor other proposals considered or discussed in the course of this litigation—have been shown to be "available" and "workable" means through which the University could have met its educational goals, as it understood and defined them in 2008. The University has thus met its burden of showing that the admissions policy it used at the time it rejected petitioner's application was narrowly tailored. . . .

The judgment of the Court of Appeals is affirmed.

It is so ordered.

JUSTICE THOMAS, dissenting . . . [omitted].

JUSTICE ALITO, with whom THE CHIEF JUSTICE and JUSTICE THOMAS join, dissenting.

Something strange has happened since our prior decision in this case. In that decision, we held that strict scrutiny requires the University of Texas at Austin to show that its use of race and ethnicity in making admissions decisions serves compelling interests and that its plan is narrowly tailored to achieve those ends. Rejecting the argument that we should defer to UT's judgment on those matters, we made it clear that UT was obligated (1) to identify the interests justifying its plan with enough specificity to permit a reviewing court to determine whether the requirements of strict scrutiny were met, and (2) to show that those requirements were in fact satisfied. On remand, UT failed to do what our prior decision demanded. The University has still not identified with any degree of specificity the interests that its use of race and ethnicity is supposed to serve. Its primary argument is that merely invoking "the educational benefits of diversity" is sufficient and that it need not identify any metric that would allow a court to determine whether its plan is needed to serve, or is actually serving, those interests. This is nothing less than the plea for deference that we emphatically rejected in our prior decision. Today, however, the Court inexplicably grants that request.

To the extent that UT has ever moved beyond a plea for deference and identified the relevant interests in more specific terms, its efforts have been shifting, unpersuasive, and, at times, less than candid. When it adopted its race-based plan, UT said that the plan was needed to promote classroom diversity. It pointed to a study showing that African-American, Hispanic, and Asian-American students were underrepresented in many classes. But UT has never shown that its race-conscious plan actually ameliorates this situation. The University presents no evidence that its admissions officers, in administering the "holistic" component of its plan, make any effort to determine whether an African-American, Hispanic, or Asian-American student is likely to enroll in classes in which minority students are underrepresented. And although UT's records should permit it to determine without much difficulty whether holistic admittees are any more likely than students admitted through the Top Ten Percent Law, to enroll in the classes lacking racial or ethnic diversity, UT either has not crunched those numbers or has not revealed what they show. Nor has UT explained why the underrepresentation of Asian-American students in many classes justifies its plan, which discriminates against those students.

At times, UT has claimed that its plan is needed to achieve a "critical mass" of African-American and Hispanic students, but it has never explained what this term means. According to UT, a critical mass is neither some absolute number of African-American or Hispanic students nor the percentage of African-Americans or Hispanics in the general population of the State. The term remains undefined, but UT tells us that it will let the courts know when the desired end has been achieved. This is a plea for deference—indeed, for blind deference—the very thing that the Court rejected in *Fisher* I.

UT has also claimed at times that the race-based component of its plan is needed because the Top Ten Percent Plan admits the wrong kind of African-American and Hispanic students, namely, students from poor families who attend schools in which the student body is predominantly African-American or Hispanic. As UT put it in its brief in *Fisher I*, the race-based component of its admissions plan is needed to admit "[t]he African-American or Hispanic child of successful professionals in Dallas."

After making this argument in its first trip to this Court, UT apparently had second thoughts, and in the latest round of briefing UT has attempted to disavow ever having made the argument. But it did, and the argument turns affirmative action on its head. Affirmative-action programs were created to help disadvantaged students.

Although UT now disowns the argument that the Top Ten Percent Plan results in the admission of the wrong kind of African-American and Hispanic students, the Fifth Circuit majority bought a version of that claim. As the panel majority put it, the Top Ten African-American and Hispanic admittees cannot match the holistic African-American and Hispanic admittees when it comes to "records of personal achievement," a "variety of perspectives" and "life experiences," and "unique skills." All in all, according to the panel majority, the Top Ten Percent students cannot "enrich the diversity of the student body" in the same way as the holistic admittees. As Judge Garza put it in dissent, the panel majority concluded that the Top Ten Percent admittees are "somehow more homogenous, less dynamic, and more undesirably stereotypical than those admitted under holistic review."

The Fifth Circuit reached this conclusion with little direct evidence regarding the characteristics of the Top Ten Percent and holistic admittees. Instead, the assumption behind the Fifth Circuit's reasoning is that most of the African-American and Hispanic students admitted under the race-neutral component of UT's plan were able to rank in the top decile of their high school classes only because they did not have to compete against white and Asian-American students. This insulting stereotype is not supported by the record. African-American and Hispanic students admitted under the Top Ten Percent Plan receive higher college grades than the African-American and Hispanic students admitted under the race-conscious program. . . .

Over the past 20 years, UT has frequently modified its admissions policies, and it has generally employed race and ethnicity in the most aggressive manner permitted under controlling precedent. Before 1997, race was considered directly as part of the general admissions process, and it was frequently a controlling factor. . . . On . . . the very day *Grutter* was handed down, UT's president announced that "[t]he University of Texas at Austin will modify its admissions procedures" in light of *Grutter*, including by "implementing procedures at the undergraduate level that combine the benefits of the Top 10 Percent Law with affirmative action programs." UT purports to have later engaged in "almost a year of deliberations," but there is no evidence that the reintroduction of race into the admissions process was anything other than a foregone conclusion following the president's announcement. . . .

UT's race-conscious admissions program cannot satisfy strict scrutiny. UT says that the program furthers its interest in the educational benefits of diversity, but it has failed to define that interest with any clarity or to demonstrate that its program is narrowly tailored to achieve that or any other particular interest. By accepting UT's rationales as sufficient to meet its burden, the majority licenses UT's perverse assumptions about different groups of minority students—the precise assumptions strict scrutiny is supposed to stamp out.

"The moral imperative of racial neutrality is the driving force of the Equal Protection Clause." "At the heart of the Constitution's guarantee of equal protection lies the simple command that the Government must treat citizens as individuals, not as simply components of a racial, religious, sexual or national class." "Race-based assignments embody stereotypes that treat individuals as the product of their race, evaluating their thoughts and efforts—their very worth as citizens—according to a criterion barred to the Government by history and the Constitution." . . .

In short, in "all contexts," racial classifications are permitted only "as a last resort," when all else has failed. . . . Here, UT has failed to define its interest in using racial preferences with clarity. As a result, the narrow tailoring inquiry is impossible, and UT cannot satisfy strict scrutiny.

When UT adopted its challenged policy, it characterized its compelling interest as obtaining a "critical mass" of underrepresented minorities. . . . But to this day, UT has not explained in anything other than the vaguest terms what it means by "critical mass." In fact, UT argues that it need not identify any interest more specific than "securing the educational benefits of diversity." UT has insisted that critical mass is not an absolute number. . . . Instead, UT prefers a deliberately malleable "we'll know it when we see it" notion of critical mass. It defines "critical mass" as "an adequate representation of minority students so that the . . . educational benefits that can be derived from diversity can actually happen," and it declares that it "will . . . know [that] it has reached critical mass" when it "see[s] the educational benefits happening." In other words: Trust us. This intentionally imprecise interest is designed to insulate UT's program from meaningful judicial review. . . .

[In] order for us to assess whether UT's program is narrowly tailored, the University must identify some sort of concrete interest. "Classifying and assigning" students according to race "requires more than . . . an amorphous end to justify it." Because UT has failed to explain "with clarity," why it needs a race-conscious policy and how it will know when its goals have been met, the narrow tailoring analysis cannot be meaningfully conducted. UT therefore cannot satisfy strict scrutiny. . . . According to the majority, however, UT has articulated the following "concrete and precise goals": "the destruction of stereotypes, the promot[ion of] cross-racial understanding, the preparation of a student body for an increasingly diverse workforce and society, and the cultivat[ion of] a set of leaders with legitimacy in the eyes of the citizenry."

These are laudable goals, but they are not concrete or precise, and they offer no limiting principle for the use of racial preferences. . . . If a university can justify racial discrimination simply by having a few employees opine that racial preferences are necessary to accomplish these nebulous goals, . . . then the narrow tailoring inquiry is meaningless. Courts will be required to defer to the judgment of university administrators, and affirmative-action policies will be completely insulated from judicial review. . . . A court cannot ensure that an admissions process is narrowly tailored if it cannot pin down the goals that the process is designed to achieve. . . .

While both the majority and the Fifth Circuit rely on UT's classroom study, they completely ignore its finding that Hispanics are better represented than Asian-Americans in UT classrooms. In fact, they act almost as if Asian-American students do not exist. Only the District Court acknowledged the impact of UT's policy on Asian-American students. But it brushed aside this impact, concluding—astoundingly—that UT can pick and choose which racial and ethnic groups it would like to favor. According to the District Court, "nothing in *Grutter* requires a university to give equal preference to every minority group," and UT is allowed "to exercise its discretion in determining which minority groups should benefit from the consideration of race."

This reasoning, which the majority implicitly accepts by blessing UT's reliance on the classroom study, places the Court on the "tortuous" path of "decid[ing] which races to favor." And the Court's willingness to allow this "discrimination against individuals of Asian descent in UT admissions is particularly troubling, in light of the long history of discrimination against Asian Americans, especially in education." . . .

Perhaps the majority finds discrimination against Asian-American students benign, since Asian-Americans are "overrepresented" at UT. "[B]enign" carries with it no independent meaning, but reflects only acceptance of the current generation's conclusion that a politically acceptable burden, imposed on particular citizens on the basis of race, is reasonable. Where, as here, the government has provided little explanation for why it needs to discriminate based on race, "'there is simply no way of determining what classifications are "benign" . . . and what classifications are in fact motivated by illegitimate notions of racial inferiority or simple racial politics.'" By accepting the classroom study as proof that UT satisfied strict scrutiny, the majority "move[s] us from 'separate but equal' to 'unequal but benign.'" . . .

UT's purported interest in intraracial diversity, or "diversity within diversity," also falls short. At bottom, this argument relies on the unsupported assumption that there is something deficient or at least radically different about the African-American and Hispanic students admitted through the Top Ten Percent Plan. . . . Ultimately, UT's intraracial diversity rationale relies on the baseless assumption that there is something wrong with African-American and Hispanic students admitted through the Top Ten Percent Plan, because they are "from the lower-performing, racially identifiable schools." . . . In effect, UT asks the Court "to assume"—without any evidence—"that minorities admitted under the Top Ten Percent Law . . . are somehow more homogenous, less dynamic, and more undesirably stereotypical than those admitted under holistic review." And UT's assumptions appear to be based on the pernicious stereotype that the African-Americans and Hispanics admitted through the Top Ten Percent Plan only got in because they did not have to compete against very many whites and Asian-Americans. These are "the very stereotypical assumptions [that] the Equal Protection Clause forbids." UT cannot satisfy its burden by attempting to "substitute racial stereotype for evidence, and racial prejudice for reason."

In addition to relying on stereotypes, UT's argument that it needs racial preferences to admit privileged minorities turns the concept of affirmative action on its head. When affirmative action programs were first adopted, it was for the purpose of helping the disadvantaged. . . . Now we are told that a program that tends to admit poor and disadvantaged minority students is inadequate because it does not work to the advantage of those who are more fortunate. This is affirmative action gone wild. . . .

Even assuming UT is correct that, under *Grutter*, it need only cite a generic interest in the educational benefits of diversity, its plan still fails strict scrutiny because it is not narrowly tailored. Narrow tailoring requires "a careful judicial inquiry into whether a university could achieve sufficient diversity without using racial classifications." . . . Here, there is no evidence that race-blind, holistic review would not achieve UT's goals at least "about as well" as UT's race-based policy. In addition, UT could have adopted other approaches to further its goals, such as intensifying its outreach efforts, uncapping the Top Ten Percent Law, or placing greater weight on socioeconomic factors.

The majority argues that none of these alternatives is "a workable means for the University to attain the benefits of diversity it sought." Tellingly, however, the majority devotes only a single, conclusory sentence to the most obvious race-neutral alternative: race-blind, holistic review that considers the applicant's unique characteristics and personal circumstances. . . . Because UT has failed to provide any evidence whatsoever that race-conscious holistic review will achieve its diversity objectives more effectively than race-blind holistic review, it cannot satisfy the heavy burden imposed by the strict scrutiny standard. . . .

Tellingly, the Court frames its analysis as if petitioner bears the burden of proof here. But it is not the petitioner's burden to show that the consideration of race is unconstitutional. To the extent the record is inadequate, the responsibility lies with UT. . . .

It is important to understand what is and what is not at stake in this case. What is not at stake is whether UT or any other university may adopt an admissions plan that results in a student body with a broad representation of students from all racial and ethnic groups. UT previously had a race-neutral plan that it claimed had "effectively compensated for the loss of affirmative action," and UT could have taken other steps that would have increased the diversity of its admitted students without taking race or ethnic background into account.

What is at stake is whether university administrators may justify systematic racial discrimination simply by asserting that such discrimination is necessary to achieve "the educational benefits of diversity," without explaining—much less proving—why the discrimination is needed or how the discriminatory plan is well crafted to serve its objectives. Even though UT has never provided any coherent explanation for its asserted need to discriminate on the basis of race, and even though UT's position relies on a series of unsupported and noxious racial assumptions, the majority concludes that UT has met its heavy burden. This conclusion is remarkable—and remarkably wrong.

Because UT has failed to satisfy strict scrutiny, I respectfully dissent.

NOTE

1. In 1984 the Mexican American Legal Defense and Education Fund challenged funding inequalities in Texas state court on behalf of the Rodriguez family and others. In *Edgewood* v. *Kirby* (1989), the Supreme Court of Texas held that the funding arrangement violated the state constitution's requirement of "an efficient system of public free schools" and directed the state legislature to redesign the financing of public education. By this time, the courts of nine other states had also relied on their state constitutions to invalidate similar property-based systems.—Ed.

15

Security and Freedom in Wartime and Pandemic

It seems to have been reserved for the people of this country, by their conduct and example, to decide the important question, whether societies of men are really capable or not of establishing good government from reflection and choice, or whether they are forever destined to depend for their political constitutions on accident and force.

—Alexander Hamilton (1787)

On the morning of September 11, 2001, members of the **al Qaeda** terrorist network commandeered four airliners to launch assaults on the United States. Two planes flew into and destroyed the twin towers of the World Trade Center in New York City. A third plane crashed into the west face of the Pentagon, headquarters of the Department of Defense, across the Potomac River from Washington, D.C. Yet another attack by the fourth plane on a third target was foiled when passengers and crew attempted to regain control of the aircraft. It crashed in Somerset County, in southwestern Pennsylvania. Together, in the bloodiest attacks on American soil since the Civil War, the 19 hijackers killed more than 3,000 persons within the span of two hours. The effects of that morning's destruction on families, society, the economy, politics—and the Constitution—have been immense.

Nineteen years after those terrorist attacks, a different menace enveloped the United States and the world in the form of the COVID-19 pandemic that with varying intensities of infection has left no state, community, or nation untouched. As of June 2021, deaths worldwide have surpassed 3.3 million, with more than 600,000 of them in the United States. These are disease-specific numbers that no living person remembers ever having witnessed. By comparison, the 1918 influenza pandemic took the lives of 675,000 Americans at a time when the national population was 103.2 million, compared to today's population of about 332 million. Worldwide deaths from the earlier pandemic are estimated to have been an overwhelming 50 million.

Aside from the enormous health impact itself, it is difficult to fathom the full extent of the virus's social and economic effects through a series of lockdowns

DOI: 10.4324/9781003164340-16

imposed by governors and mayors that closed schools, businesses, and houses of worship. Among other hardships, such measures forced thousands of people out of work and cut off their livelihoods. In a nation already polarized in numerous ways, the lockdowns revealed yet one more division: those people who could work from home and those who could not. In terms of economic loss, the pandemic has been far crueller to the latter. In a virtual address to the Federalist Society in November 2020, Justice Alito noted that the "pandemic has resulted in previously unimaginable restrictions on individual liberty," adding that the "crisis has served as a sort of constitutional stress test." In certain quarters, he continued, "religious liberty is fast becoming a disfavored right."

THE FRAGILITY OF CIVIL LIBERTIES

Both the horrific terrorist attacks and the COVID-19 pandemic coupled with the policy responses to them have again thrust to the forefront a tension that is older than the Constitution: security versus freedom. Measures designed to increase security or safety often entail a constriction of liberty. Too much insistence on maintaining liberties may jeopardize safety and security. American constitutional history is partly an attempt to find an appropriate balance between the two, although a perfect adjustment will probably forever remain out of reach. The record suggests that people are eager to embrace liberty when danger seems remote, but that officials lean in the other direction when the nation seems imperiled. There is thus a recurring pattern of under- and over-reaction. Underestimating threats to security, whether in 1860, 1941, 1946, 2001, or 2020 (to pick but five crisis-laden years), may lead to needless contractions of freedom in response. Sometimes lost amidst shifting policies is recognition that the nation's strength derives as much from the ideas and values it reflects as from the armies and munitions it deploys and restrictions it imposes. "Constitutional law," wrote Edward Corwin decades ago, "has for its primary purpose not the convenience of the state but the preservation of individual rights."

Charters of individual liberties, like a bill of rights, are commonplace today in the constitutions of many governments in the world. Yet even a casual observer of world affairs knows that civil liberties are more likely to be preserved (or suspended) in some countries than in others. Moreover, as cases in this book illustrate, American freedoms have at times expanded and contracted in accordion-like fashion. Exactly why civil liberties thrive in one place or time and not another is a complex phenomenon, but this much is certain: Civil liberties are fragile.

Civil liberties rest on at least two kinds of supports: First are rules and institutions. Federal and state statutes and constitutions carve out certain rights for protection, and courts and other bodies exist to enforce them. Second are the attitudes and values of the people generally and of opinion leaders and those entrusted with making, enforcing, and interpreting the laws. As events after September 11 and during the pandemic have demonstrated, the interplay between these two sets of supports takes place within a context where, from one month to the next, the felt needs for freedom and safety compete in shaping policy. As Justice Brandeis observed 93 years ago, the most frequent and often the most serious threats to civil liberties in American history have come not from people intent on throwing the Bill of Rights away but from well-meaning, though overzealous, people who find the Bill of Rights an inconvenience, standing in the way of objectives deemed more urgent and important. Thus, constitutional protections ironically are sometimes worth the least when they are needed the most.

THE PATRIOT AND FREEDOM ACTS

On October 26, 2001, President George W. Bush signed the **Patriot Act** into law. The statute significantly broadened the law enforcement powers of the federal government. Indeed, probably no single piece of legislation in recent decades has done more to enhance the government's crime-fighting powers. That expansion, however, has come with a price: a curtailment of some freedoms.

This response to the terrorist attacks of September 11 demonstrated once more that the scheme of separation of powers and checks and balances embedded in the Constitution can work to protect civil liberties. As the executive branch attempted to expand its authority on many fronts, legislators insisted on a more reasonable balance between security and liberty. Thus as the bill emerged from Congress, the president had secured less than he wanted, although more than many civil libertarians were prepared to give. "The Constitution is an instrument of government," once wrote the second Justice Harlan, "fundamental to which is the premise that in a diffusion of governmental authority lies the greatest promise that this Nation will realize liberty for all its citizens." Reauthorized in 2006, 2007, 2010, and 2011, the statute underwent substantial modification as the **Freedom Act** in June 2015 and was extended through December 2019. Until Congress failed to reauthorize the Freedom Act in 2020, the statute:

- Banned the bulk collection of data of Americans' telephone records and Internet metadata. (This provision was in response to publication of classified NSA [National Security Agency] memos that were leaked by Edward Snowden in June 2013, which described bulk data collection programs.)
- Limited the government's data collection to the "greatest extent reasonably practical"—which presumably meant the government was barred from collecting all data pertaining to a particular service provider or broad geographic region, such as a city or area code.
- Authorized the government—in place of broad data collection—to collect from telecom companies up to "two hops" or degrees of separation of call records related to a suspect, if the government could prove it has reasonable suspicion that the suspect is linked to a terrorist organization.
- Created new federal crimes for various terrorist acts, including misconduct at an event designated a "special event of national significance."
- Increased the maximum penalty for material support of terrorism from 15 years to 20 years.
- Created a National Security Division within the Department of Justice, headed by an assistant attorney general.
- Authorized **"sneak and peek" search warrants** that allowed agents to conduct a search without notifying the owner and to delay notification for up to 30 days (with the possibility of extensions) that a search has taken place.
- Added terrorist and computer crimes to the list of predicate offenses subject to warrant-authorized and Justice Department-approved electronic surveillance under Title III of the 1968 Omnibus Crime Control and Safe Streets Act (see Chapter Ten).
- Added electronic communications (such as email) to those communications already subject to "trap and trace" devices and pen registers. These identified the source and destination of a communication, but not its contents.

- Treated stored voicemail like email in third-party storage or communications records. Under the 1968 Crime Control Act, warrants for such material may be issued without prior Justice Department approval and in connection with *any* criminal investigation, and so are not limited to Title III's predicate offenses.
- Allowed officials to intercept communications to and from a trespasser within a computer system, with approval of the owner of the system.
- Permitted roving electronic surveillance that was not confined to a particular telephone or e-mail account but covered any electronic communications device that a suspect might use in any location.
- Authorized transitional surveillance of non-U.S. persons who come into the United States before emergency authorization for surveillance could be obtained from the attorney general, but only where a lapse in surveillance would be likely to result in death or serious bodily harm.
- Amended the **Foreign Intelligence Surveillance Act** (FISA) (see Chapter Ten) so that foreign intelligence gathering may now be a significant purpose, not *the* purpose, for conducting the electronic surveillance or other search.
- Required the FISA Court to designate a panel of "amicus curiae," or advocates, to represent the public's interest in cases that involve novel or significant legal issues.
- Subjected "lone wolf terrorists" to electronic surveillance under FISA, even though they may not be agents of a foreign power or a terrorist organization.
- Permitted judges to issue an order allowing FBI access to tangible items, such as business and education records, upon FBI certification that the items are sought "to protect against international terrorism or clandestine intelligence activities." Such orders carried with them non-disclosure requirements that prohibited the recipient of the order from informing anyone about what has been sought.
- Allowed (through **national security letters**) federal investigators to request that communication providers, financial institutions, and credit bureaus provide certain types of customer business records including information related to Internet and telephone usage. Unlike a production order for tangible items, these letters did not require prior judicial approval; however, while the letters may request telephone numbers called or email addresses used, they could not be used to access "content information" such as the substance of a telephone conversation or email message. Recipients of national security letters could be prohibited from revealing that information had been sought, provided the investigative agency has made particular certifications. According to the Congressional Research Service, public libraries providing traditional services were not subject to a national security letter.
- Allowed challenges of national security letter gag orders. These nondisclosure orders were to be based upon a danger to national security or interference with an investigation.
- Expressed the sense of Congress that the federal government should not conduct criminal investigations of Americans based solely on their membership in non-violent political organizations or their participation in other lawful political activity.

As important as these measures are, few have been judicially tested. Indeed, as of early 2021, neither the Patriot Act nor the Freedom Act had faced review in the United States Supreme Court. Congressional inaction in 2020 mainly affected four key pieces of the statute's law enforcement authority: business records (obtaining cell site and GPS location data), call details, roving wiretaps, and lone wolf. As a result, the federal government's anti-terrorism capabilities generally reverted to their status before the Patriot Act. The Congressional Research Service (CRS) has made available a report (CRS Report R40138) that examines the current status of the affected provisions.

The tension between security and freedom persists. "We know that terrorism is a problem," acknowledged Justice Breyer in 2003. "We also know we live in a country that wants to protect basic civil liberties." Courts "are fully aware of mistakes that have been made in American history," he added. "You want to know how it's going to come out? So do I."

ANTITERRORIST POLICIES IN COURT

Justice Breyer did not have long to wait. Within seven years of the 2001 attacks, the Supreme Court had rendered four significant decisions outlining constitutional limitations in the war on terrorism.

Prisoners of War or Something else? Seven days after the attacks on September 11, Congress approved Senate Joint Resolution 23 (115 Stat. 2241) on **Authorization for Use of Military Force** (AUMF) (see Chapter Three). This led to a U.S. invasion of Afghanistan to topple the Taliban government that had provided a base of operations to members of **al Qaeda**. Within a few weeks, many Taliban and al Qaeda fighters were captured, and some 600 were later transferred for detention and questioning to the U.S. naval base at Guantanamo Bay, Cuba, in a facility later known as Camp Delta. On November 13, 2001, President Bush in an executive order declared that members of al Qaeda and other terrorists, who were not U.S. citizens, were subject to trial by military tribunals. In February 2002, Bush announced that none of the captives merited the legal status of prisoners of war (POWs). They would not possess what is perhaps the most valuable right of POWs: The right not to be tried for having made war on their captors.

According to the Geneva Convention of 1949, POW status for captured combatants depends upon whether they: (1) report to a superior officer within a command-and-control structure; (2) wear a fixed insignia or uniform, visible from some distance away, that defines their identity; (3) openly bear arms; and (4) conduct their military operations according to the laws and customs of war. Al Qaeda fighters assuredly did not meet those qualifications, but blanket denial of POW status to certain Taliban soldiers appeared more questionable.

Whatever their status, could the Guantanamo detainees be held indefinitely? Did the federal judicial power extend to Guantanamo? In a lawsuit initiated by the "best friends" of 12 Kuwaitis and four other Guantanamo detainees who insisted they had done nothing wrong, the U.S. Court of Appeals for the District of Columbia Circuit ruled in 2003 that noncitizens held in such circumstances lack the rights of Americans. "The Constitution does not entitle the detainees to due process," the three-judge panel held without dissent. Given the fact that the naval base is not on American soil but on land leased from Cuba since 1903, decisions about detention and interrogation should be "left to the exclusive discretion of the executive branch . . ." (*Odah* v. *United States*). In *Rasul* v. *Bush* (2004), the Supreme Court held otherwise. Because the United States has complete control over the Guantanamo base, detainees were entitled to petition the federal courts for relief.

Military or Civilian Justice? Article I, Section 9, of the Constitution seemingly limits Congress' power to suspend the **writ of habeas corpus** to "cases of rebellion or invasion." (This writ, routinely available to civilians, is a judicial order to inquire into the legality of one's detention and, as such, is a safeguard against unlawful confinement.) Yet during the Civil War, President Lincoln suspended the writ without congressional authorization and ordered his officers to refuse service of a writ issued by Chief Justice Taney in his capacity as circuit judge (Ex parte *Merryman*, 1861). Subsequently, Congress authorized suspension in certain instances; the Supreme Court, however, refused to pass on the validity of the president's action (Ex parte *Vallandigham*, 1864), concluding that it had no jurisdiction to review directly the judgment of a military tribunal.

In another Civil War action, Lincoln imposed **martial law** on portions of the northern states and substituted trial by military commission for the judicial process in dealing with traitors and others charged with violations of wartime statutes. (Such commissions or tribunals, then as now, operate under their own rules. They are composed of military officers and are separate from courts martial that today are governed by the Uniform Code of Military Justice and adjudicate offenses involving military personnel.) **Ex parte *Milligan*** (1866) held that Lincoln had exceeded his authority. The regular courts of Indiana, where the military commission had convicted and sentenced Milligan to the gallows, were open and prepared to handle the charges against him. Five members of the Court went further and stated that martial law could never exist where civilian courts were open. Four members thought that Congress could have sanctioned what the executive could not. In World War II, a similar result followed when, following the attack on Pearl Harbor in 1941, the governor-general of Hawaii invoked martial law, which gave military commissions jurisdiction over all criminal offenses. "I do not worry about the constitutional question . . ." said President Franklin Roosevelt. "The whole matter is one of immediate and present war emergency." In 1946, the Court held such action invalid on the basis of *Milligan* (*Duncan* v. *Kahanamoku*). In both cases, final judicial decisions came after the shooting had stopped. However, **Ex parte *Quirin*** (1942), decided in the early months of World War II, upheld the trial by military commission—without the panoply of constitutional rights—of German saboteurs, including one who was probably an American citizen, who had been captured on American soil. And civilian courts were functioning.

Within a few months of the attacks on September 11, the Bush administration announced that a committee composed of the attorney general, secretary of defense, and director of central intelligence was empowered to designate suspected terrorists, U.S. citizens and noncitizens alike, as "**enemy combatants**," and to hold them in military custody indefinitely, without bringing charges and without access to judicial review. (The term referred to persons alleged to be "part of or supporting forces hostile to the United States or coalition partners.") One such person was Louisiana-born Yassar Esam Hamdi, who was captured in Afghanistan in 2001 while allegedly fighting with the Taliban and later held in the Norfolk Naval Station Brig. Could he challenge his detention in court? In *Hamdi* v. *Rumsfeld* (2004), six justices deemed the AUMF sufficient authorization for Hamdi's designation as an enemy combatant. However, the Court held that neither the AUMF nor the Constitution authorized indefinite detention for interrogation purposes without some form of judicial review to ascertain the basis of someone's incarceration. "[A] state of war," wrote Justice O'Connor, "is not a blank check when it comes to the rights of the Nation's citizens." Yet the Court left unsaid precisely what sort of procedural review was constitutionally due in such situations.

If *Hamdi* was a partial victory for the government, *Hamdan* v. *Rumsfeld* (2006) was not. A reputed personal driver for Osama bin Laden, Salim Hamdan was a detainee at Guantanamo deemed triable by a presidentially authorized military commission. After the Supreme Court had granted certiorari in Hamdan's case challenging the legality of the commission, the Detainee Treatment Act became law in 2005. Among other things, it appeared to withdraw federal court jurisdiction in cases like Hamdan's. Rejecting the government's reading of the statute, the Supreme Court assumed jurisdiction and agreed with Hamdan that the military commission was legally deficient. Furthermore, commission procedures fell short of those required by both the UCMJ and the Geneva Conventions. In response to *Hamdan*, Congress passed the Military Commissions Act in 2006. In addition to providing explicit congressional authorization for military commissions, the act barred habeas corpus actions by detainees and invocation of the Geneva Conventions during commission proceedings. In ***Boumediene* v. *Bush*** (2008), the Supreme Court struck down the jurisdiction-stripping provisions of the MCA. As for Hamdan himself, in 2008, he became the first of the Guantanamo detainees to be tried by a military commission. He was acquitted of a serious charge, convicted on a lesser charge, and was soon released to Yemeni officials to serve out his term. As of late fall 2016 most detainees had been transferred to other countries for "conditional detention" but some 61 remained at Guantanamo, despite President Obama's pledge to shut the facility by the end of his administration. Moreover, there had yet to be any judicial ruling on the legality of his administration's "**targeted killing**" program, whereby individuals far from the battlefield in Afghanistan or elsewhere, such as Islamist cleric Anwar al-Awlaki, an American citizen hiding in Yemen, have been singled out for execution (euphemistically described as being "removed from the battlefield") by a drone or other means because of their involvement in terror plots against the United States.

"INTER ARMA SILENT LEGES"

This Latin maxim, that in time of war the laws are silent, has never been applied broadly in the United States. War has never been thought to justify a wholesale suspension of constitutional rights. "We do not lose our right to condemn either measures or men because the country is at war," remarked Justice Holmes in 1919 after World War I.

Yet, although the laws are not silent in wartime, they sometimes speak with a different voice, as Chief Justice Rehnquist observed. Indeed, when Congress' legislative powers are combined with the president's already expansive powers as commander-in-chief, constitutional limitations have occasionally seemed virtually to vanish. This was certainly true in the World War II relocation case of ***Korematsu* v. *United States*** (1944), where the civil rights of thousands of persons of Japanese ancestry, including many American citizens, were abridged on an unprecedented scale. The government's policy, strongly supported by Earl Warren (California's governor at the time) was justified by supposed threats to national security on the West Coast. In 1987, toward the end of his long career, Justice Brennan acknowledged in a lecture in Israel what most by then had conceded. The national security claims were "so baseless that they would be comical if not for the serious hardships they caused." The Court tangentially reappraised *Korematsu* in ***Trump* v. *Hawaii*** (2018), reprinted in Chapter Three, leaving no doubt that the decision from World War II stands as a reminder of a colossal judicial mistake.

On the more encouraging side have been the Supreme Court's decisions in ***New York Times Company* v. *United States*** (1971) and ***United States* v. *United States District Court*** (1972). During a time of widespread domestic unrest toward the end of the Vietnam War, the Nixon administration insisted in the first case on national security grounds that the federal judiciary possessed inherent authority to block publication of classified documents (the "Pentagon Papers") that had been given to a newspaper by a third party. By a vote of 6–3, the Court upheld the newspaper's right under the First Amendment to continue publication. The second case tested the authority of the president, acting through the attorney general, to "constitutionally authorize the [warrantless] use of electronic surveillance in cases where he ha[s] determined that, in order to preserve the national security the use of such surveillance is reasonable." Asserting countervailing Fourth Amendment values, the Supreme Court rejected the claim, 8–0, at least in the context of electronic snooping on domestic groups (as opposed to agents of foreign powers) plotting sabotage and other illegal acts. At about the same time, Congress repealed the Emergency Detention Act of 1950 and substituted new language—known as the **Non-Detention Act**—that read: "No citizen shall be imprisoned or otherwise detained by the United States except pursuant to an Act of Congress."

Among other decisions, *Boumediene* suggests that with respect to the war on terrorism and in contrast to some earlier eras, the Supreme Court has decided not to be irrelevant. If this pattern holds, the executive will not be able to assume judicial deference when exigencies pit security against freedom.

THE PANDEMIC AND CONSTITUTIONAL RIGHTS

Early indications are mixed as to whether the Supreme Court will be on alert to violations of civil liberties arising from efforts to combat the COVID-19 pandemic. After all, the justices' experience with disease control efforts has been scant at best. For example, well over a century ago in *Jacobson* v. *Massachusetts* (1905), the Court in voting 7–2 upheld a state law allowing municipalities to implement compulsory smallpox vaccination. As the COVID-19 pandemic took hold in the United States in the spring of 2020, the Court, with four dissenting votes, denied an application for injunctive relief by a church in California after Governor Gavin Newsom issued an executive order on gatherings that also limited attendance at places of worship to 25 percent of building capacity or a maximum of 100 attendees (*South Bay United Pentecostal Church* v. *Newsom*). Concurring with the denial of relief, Chief Justice Roberts explained that the

> restrictions appear consistent with the Free Exercise Clause of the First Amendment. Similar or more severe restrictions apply to comparable secular gatherings, including lectures, concerts, movie showings, spectator sports, and theatrical performances, where large groups of people gather in close proximity for extended periods of time. And the Order exempts or treats more leniently only dissimilar activities, such as operating grocery stores, banks, and laundromats, in which people neither congregate in large groups nor remain in close proximity for extended periods. The precise question of when restrictions on particular social activities should be lifted during the pandemic is a dynamic and fact-intensive matter subject to reasonable disagreement. Our Constitution principally entrusts "[t]he safety and the health of the people" to the politically accountable officials of the States "to guard and protect." When those officials "undertake[] to act in areas fraught with medical and scientific uncertainties," their latitude "must be especially broad." Where those broad limits are not exceeded, they should not be subject to second-guessing by an "unelected federal judiciary," which lacks the background, competence, and expertise to assess public health and is not accountable to the people.

In a dissent joined by Justices Thomas and Gorsuch, Justice Kavanaugh insisted that

> To justify its discriminatory treatment of religious worship services, California must show that its rules are "justified by a compelling governmental interest" and "narrowly tailored to advance that interest." California undoubtedly has a compelling interest in combating the spread of COVID-19 and protecting the health of its citizens. But "restrictions inexplicably applied to one group and exempted from another do little to further these goals and do much to burden religious freedom." What California needs is a compelling justification for distinguishing between (i) religious worship services and (ii) the litany of other secular businesses that are not subject to an occupancy cap. California has not shown such a justification. The Church has agreed to abide by the State's rules that apply to comparable secular businesses. That raises important questions: "Assuming all of the same precautions are taken, why can someone safely walk down a grocery store aisle but not a pew? And why can someone safely interact with a brave deliverywoman but not with a stoic minister?" The Church and its congregants simply want to be treated equally to comparable secular businesses. California already trusts its residents and any number of businesses to adhere to proper social distancing and hygiene practices. The State cannot "assume the worst when people go to worship but assume the best when people go to work or go about the rest of their daily lives in permitted social settings."

Seven months later, ***Roman Catholic Diocese of Brooklyn* v. *Cuomo*** (2020) presented a similar request for injunctive relief. However, with Amy Coney Barrett now on the Court, the outcome now favored the claim of religious freedom. Moreover, before the end of 2020, the Court had directed federal district courts in California, Colorado, and New Jersey to reconsider restrictive rulings in light of the Brooklyn Diocese case. Such actions suggested that they would not be the High Court's last encounters with pandemic-inspired civil liberties cases.

Several decades ago, Chief Justice Warren—someone hardly bashful about wielding judicial power—once candidly acknowledged that courts are unreliable bulwarks during emergencies. Other parts of the government, he said, "must bear the primary responsibility for determining whether specific actions they are taking are consonant with our Constitution." It is "the Legislature and the elected executive who have the primary responsibility for fashioning and executing policy consistent with the Constitution." Beyond them, he added, "the day-to-day job of upholding the Constitution really lies elsewhere. It rests, realistically, on the shoulders of every citizen." Warren's assessment remains a sobering reminder that the Constitution in practice is much more than what the judges say it is.

KEY TERMS

- Authorization for Use of Military Force (AUMF)
- Patriot Act
- Freedom Act
- "sneak and peek" search warrants
- Foreign Intelligence Surveillance Act
- national security letters
- al Qaeda
- Islamic State
- writ of habeas corpus
- martial law
- enemy combatants
- targeted killing
- Non-Detention Act

QUERIES

1. On the day that the Court released its opinion in Ex parte *Quirin*, Attorney General Francis Biddle wrote a memo to President Roosevelt summarizing the main points of the decision. Noting that the Court had distinguished Ex parte *Milligan*, Biddle declared, "Practically then, the Milligan case is out of the way and should not again plague us." Did *Quirin* truly set *Milligan* "out of the way"?

2. In *Korematsu* v. *United States*, how do the opinions of Justices Black and Murphy differ in terms of the standard that must be met in order to justify an abridgement of constitutionally protected liberties? Review *Trump* v. *Hawaii* in Chapter Three. Why would Justice Sotomayor have thought it important to refer to *Korematsu*?

3. What constitutional problems are raised by the practice of "targeted killing," whereby on an order from the president, individuals perhaps far from a battlefield are singled out for execution because of their involvement in terror plots against the United States?

4. In ***Roman Catholic Diocese of Brooklyn* v. *Cuomo***, it seems safe to conclude that all nine justices favor religious freedom, just as all nine justices undoubtedly support active measures to combat COVID-19. What then leads them to divide 5–4 on the question of granting injunctive relief in this case?

SELECTED READINGS

Burnep, Gregory. *Courts at War: Executive Power, Judicial Intervention, and Enemy Combatant Policies Since 9/11*. Lawrence: University Press of Kansas, 2021.

Fisher, Louis. *Nazi Saboteurs on Trial: A Military Tribunal and American Law*. Lawrence: University Press of Kansas, 2003.

Fisher, Louis. *The Constitution and 9/11: Recurring Threats to America's Freedoms*. Lawrence: University Press of Kansas, 2008.

Nevins, Allan. "The Case of the Copperhead Conspirator." In John A. Garraty, ed. *Quarrels that Have Shaped the Constitution*, rev., exp. ed. New York: Harper & Row, 2009.

Posner, Richard A. *Not a Suicide Pact: The Constitution in a Time of National Emergency*. New York: Oxford University Press, 2006.

Rehnquist, William H. *All the Laws but One: Civil Liberties in Wartime*. New York: Knopf, 1998.

Rostow, Eugene V. "The Japanese American Cases—A Disaster." 54 *Yale Law Journal* 489, 1945.

Tushnet, Mark, ed. *The Constitution in Wartime*. Durham, NC: Duke University Press, 2005.

Ex parte *Milligan*
71 U.S. (4 Wall.) 2, 18 L.Ed. 281 (1866)

http://caselaw.findlaw.com/us-supreme-court/71/2.html

In 1864, Lambdin P. Milligan, a Southern sympathizer living in Indiana, was seized and tried on charges of disloyalty by a military commission in the military district of Indiana and sentenced to be hanged. A citizen of Indiana but not in the military, Milligan objected to the jurisdiction of the military commission and sought a writ of habeas corpus in the U.S. circuit court. In 1863 Congress had authorized suspension of the writ, but Milligan insisted that the commission had no jurisdiction of his case. Sitting as circuit judges, Justice Davis and the district judge agreed to a division in order to certify the constitutional question to the Supreme Court. Meanwhile, Davis and others convinced President Andrew Johnson to stay Milligan's execution until the Supreme Court could decide the case. Majority: Davis, Chase, Clifford, Field, Grier, Miller, Nelson, Swayne, Wayne. Note that concurring justices Chase, Swayne, Miller, and Wayne did not accept Davis's sweeping restriction on Congress.

MR. JUSTICE DAVIS delivered the opinion of the Court . . .

During the late wicked Rebellion, the temper of the times did not allow that calmness and deliberation in discussion so necessary to a correct conclusion of a purely judicial question. *Then*, considerations of safety were mingled with the exercise of power, and feelings and interests prevailed which are happily terminated. *Now* that the public safety is assured, this question, as well as all others, can be discussed and decided without passion or the admixture of any element not required to form the legal judgment. . . .

The controlling question in the case is this: . . . Had this tribunal the legal power and authority to try and punish this man?

No graver question was ever considered by this court, nor one which more nearly concerns the rights of the whole people, for it is the birthright of every American citizen when charged with crime to be tried and punished according to law. . . .

The Constitution of the United States is a law for rulers and people, equally in war and in peace, and covers with the shield of its protection all classes of men, at all times, and under all circumstances. No doctrine involving more pernicious consequences was ever intended by the wit of man than that any of its provisions can be suspended during any of the great exigencies of government. Such a doctrine leads directly to anarchy or despotism, but the theory of necessity on which it is based is false; for the government, within the Constitution, has all the powers granted to it which are necessary to preserve its existence; as has been happily proved by the result of the great effort to throw off its just authority. . . .

Every trial involves the exercise of judicial power; and from what source did the military commission that tried him derive their authority? Certainly no part of the judicial power of the country was conferred on them; because the Constitution expressly vests it "in one supreme court and such inferior courts as the Congress may from time to time ordain and establish," and it is not pretended that the commission was a court ordained and established by Congress. They cannot justify on the mandate of the President, because he is controlled by law, and has his appropriate sphere of duty, which is to execute, not to make, the laws; and there is "no unwritten criminal code to which resort can be had as a source of jurisdiction." . . .

Why was he not delivered to the Circuit Court of Indiana to be proceeded against according to law? No reason of necessity could be urged against it; because Congress had declared penalties against the offenses charged, provided for their punishment, and directed that court to hear and determine them. And soon after this military tribunal was ended, the Circuit Court met, peacefully transacted its business, and adjourned. It needed no bayonets to protect it, and required no military aid to execute its judgments. . . .

The discipline necessary to the efficiency of the army and navy required other and swifter modes of trial than are furnished by the common-law courts; and, in pursuance of the power conferred by the Constitution, Congress has declared the kinds of trial, and the manner in which they shall be conducted, for offenses committed while the party is in the military or naval service. Every one connected with these branches of the public service is amenable to the jurisdiction which Congress has created for their government, and, while thus serving, surrenders his right to be tried by the civil courts. All other persons, citizens of States where the courts are open, if charged with crime, are guaranteed the inestimable privilege of trial by jury. . . .

It is claimed that martial law covers with its broad mantle the proceedings of this military commission. The proposition is this: that in a time of war the commander of an armed force (if, in his opinion, the exigencies of the country demand it, and of which he is the judge) has the power, within the lines of his military district, to suspend all civil rights and their remedies, and subject citizens as well as soldiers to the rule of his will; and in the exercise of this lawful authority cannot be restrained, except by his superior officer or the President of the United States.

If this position is sound to the extent claimed, then when war exists, foreign or domestic, and the country is subdivided into military departments for mere convenience, the commander of one of them can, if he chooses, within his limits, on the plea of necessity, with the approval of the Executive, substitute military force for, and to the exclusion of, the laws, and punish all persons, as he thinks right and proper, without fixed or certain rules.

The statement of this proposition shows its importance; for, if true, republican government is a failure, and there is an end of liberty regulated by law. . . .

This nation, as experience has proved, cannot always remain at peace, and has no right to expect that it will always have wise and humane rulers, sincerely attached to the principles of the Constitution. Wicked men, ambitious of power, with hatred of liberty and contempt of law, may fill the place once occupied by Washington and Lincoln; and if this right is conceded, and the calamities of war again befall us, the dangers to human liberty are frightful to contemplate. . . .

The two remaining questions in this case must be answered in the affirmative. The suspension of the privilege of the writ of *habeas corpus* does not suspend the writ itself. The writ issues as a matter of course; and on the return made to it the court decides whether the party applying is denied the right of proceeding any further with it.

If the military trial of Milligan was contrary to law, then he was entitled, on the facts stated in his petition, to be discharged from custody. . . .

THE CHIEF JUSTICE [CHASE] delivered the following opinion. . . .

We think . . . that the power of Congress, in the government of the land and naval forces and of the militia, is not at all affected by the Fifth or any other amendment. . . .

We cannot doubt that, in such a time of public danger, Congress had power, under the Constitution, to provide for the organization of a military commission, and for trial by that commission of persons engaged in this conspiracy. The fact that the Federal courts were open was regarded by Congress as a sufficient reason for not exercising the power; but that fact could not deprive Congress of the right to exercise it. Those courts might be open and undisturbed in the execution of their functions, and yet wholly incompetent to avert threatened danger, or to punish, with adequate promptitude and certainty, the guilty conspirators. . . .

MR. JUSTICE WAYNE, MR. JUSTICE SWAYNE, and MR. JUSTICE MILLER concur with me in these views.

Ex parte *Quirin*
317 U.S. 1, 63 S.Ct. 2, 97 L.Ed. 3 (1942)

http://caselaw.findlaw.com/us-supreme-court/317/1.html

On June 13, 1942, a German submarine landed four saboteurs on Long Island, New York. Four days later, another German submarine landed four more saboteurs at Ponte Vedra Beach, Florida. Once ashore, all discarded their German military uniforms and assumed civilian dress. All had been born in Germany, but each had lived for several years in the United States. One was arguably an American citizen by virtue of the naturalization of his parents. After their capture in Chicago and New York City, President Roosevelt ordered that the captured saboteurs be tried by military commission, even though during 1942 the state and federal courts in all 48 states were functioning normally. Seven of the prisoners petitioned the U.S. District Court for the District of Columbia for a writ of habeas corpus. On appeal, the Supreme Court announced its judgment on July 31. Six of the prisoners were executed a few days later. The Chief Justice's opinion for the Court was issued on October 29. Majority: Stone, Black, Byrnes, Douglas, Frankfurter, Jackson, Reed, Roberts. Not participating: Murphy.

MR. CHIEF JUSTICE STONE delivered the opinion of the Court. . . .

The question for decision is whether the detention of petitioners by respondent for trial by Military Commission, appointed by Order of the President of July 2, 1942, on charges preferred against them purporting to set out their violations of the law of war and of the Articles of War, is in conformity to the laws and Constitution of the United States. . . .

Petitioners' main contention is that the President is without any statutory or constitutional authority to order the petitioners to be tried by military tribunal for offenses with which they are charged; that in consequence they are entitled to be tried in the civil courts with the safeguards, including trial by jury, which the Fifth and Sixth Amendments guarantee to all persons charged in such courts with criminal offenses. . . .

Congress and the President, like the courts, possess no power not derived from the Constitution. . . . The Constitution . . . invests the President as Commander in Chief with the power to wage war which Congress has declared, and to carry into effect all laws passed by Congress for the conduct of war and for the government and regulation of the Armed Forces, and all laws defining and punishing offences against the law of nations, including those which pertain to the conduct of war.

By the Articles of War, Congress has provided rules for the government of the Army. It has provided for the trial and punishment, by courts martial, of violations of the Articles by members of the armed forces and by specified classes of persons associated or serving with the Army. But the Articles also recognize the "military commission" appointed by military command as an appropriate tribunal for the trial and punishment of offenses against the law of war not ordinarily tried by court martial. Articles 38 and 46 authorize the President, with certain limitations, to prescribe the procedure for military commissions. . . .

It is unnecessary for present purposes to determine to what extent the President as Commander in Chief has constitutional power to create military commissions without the support of Congressional legislation. For here Congress has authorized trial of offenses against the law of war before such commissions.

By universal agreement and practice the law of war draws a distinction between the armed forces and the peaceful populations of belligerent nations and also between those who are lawful and unlawful combatants. Lawful combatants are subject to capture and detention as prisoners of war by opposing military forces. Unlawful combatants are likewise subject to capture and detention, but in addition they are subject to trial and punishment by military tribunals for acts which render their belligerency unlawful. The spy who secretly and without uniform passes the military lines of a belligerent in time of war, . . . or an enemy combatant who without uniform comes secretly through the lines for the purpose of waging war by destruction of life or property, are familiar examples of belligerents who are generally deemed not to be entitled to the status of prisoners of war, but to be offenders against the law of war subject to trial and punishment by military tribunals. . . .

Our Government, by thus defining lawful belligerents entitled to be treated as prisoners of war, has recognized that there is a class of unlawful belligerents not entitled to that privilege, including those who though combatants do not wear "fixed and distinctive emblems." And by Article 15 of the Articles of War Congress has made provision for their trial and punishment by military commission, according to "the law of war."

Citizenship in the United States of an enemy belligerent does not relieve him from the consequences of a belligerency which is unlawful because in violation of the law of war. Citizens who associate themselves with the military arm of the enemy government, and with its aid, guidance and direction enter this country bent on hostile acts are enemy belligerents within the meaning of the Hague Convention and the law of war. It is as an enemy belligerent that petitioner Haupt is charged with entering the United States, and unlawful belligerency is the gravamen of the offense of which he is accused. . . .

[P]etitioners insist that even if the offenses with which they are charged are offenses against the law of war, their trial is subject to the requirement of the Fifth Amendment that no person shall be held to answer for a capital or otherwise infamous crime unless on a presentment or indictment of a grand jury, and that such trials by Article III, § 2, and the Sixth Amendment must be by jury in a civil court. Before the Amendments, § 2 of Article III, the Judiciary Article, had provided: "The Trial of all Crimes, except in Cases of Impeachment, shall be by Jury," and had directed that "such Trial shall be held in the State where the said Crimes shall have been committed." . . .

In the light of . . . long-continued and consistent interpretation we must conclude that § 2 of Article III and the Fifth and Sixth Amendments cannot be taken to have extended the right to demand a jury to trials by military commission, or to have required that offenses against the law of war not triable by jury at common law be tried only in the civil courts. . . .

The exception from the Amendments of "cases arising in the land or naval forces" was not aimed at trials by military tribunals, without a jury, of such offenses against the law of war. Its objective was quite different—to authorize the trial by court martial of the members of our Armed Forces for all that class of crimes which under the Fifth and Sixth Amendments might otherwise have been deemed triable in the civil courts. . . .

We cannot say that Congress in preparing the Fifth and Sixth Amendments intended to extend trial by jury to the cases of alien or citizen offenders against the law of war otherwise triable by military commission, while withholding it from members of our own armed forces charged with infractions of the Articles of War punishable by death. . . . We conclude that the Fifth and Sixth Amendments did not restrict whatever authority was conferred by the Constitution to try offenses against the law of war by military commission, and that petitioners, charged with such an offense not required to be tried by jury at common law, were lawfully placed on trial by the Commission without a jury.

Petitioners, and especially petitioner Haupt, stress the pronouncement of this Court in the Milligan case, that the law of war "can never be applied to citizens in states which have upheld the authority of the government, and where the courts are open and their process unobstructed." Elsewhere in its opinion, the Court was at pains to point out that Milligan, a citizen 20 years resident in Indiana, who had never been a resident of any of the states in rebellion, was not an enemy belligerent either entitled to the status of a prisoner of war or subject to the penal ties imposed upon unlawful belligerents. We construe the Court's statement as to the inapplicability of the law of war to Milligan's case as having particular reference to the facts before it. From them the Court concluded that Milligan, not being a part of or associated with the armed forces of the enemy, was a nonbelligerent, not subject to the law of war save as—in circumstances found not there to be present and not involved here—martial law might be constitutionally established.

The Court's opinion is inapplicable to the case presented by the present record. . . . Accordingly, we conclude that [the president's] Order convening the Commission was a lawful order. . . . It follows that the orders of the District Court should be affirmed, and that leave to file petitions for habeas corpus in this Court should be denied.

Korematsu v. *United States*
323 U.S. 214, 65 S.Ct. 193, 89 L.Ed. 194 (1944)

http://caselaw.findlaw.com/us-supreme-court/323/214.html

Shortly after America entered World War II in December 1941, President Franklin Roosevelt issued an executive order authorizing creation of military areas from which persons suspected of sabotage and espionage might be excluded. This order authorized military commanders to prescribe regulations controlling the right of persons to enter, leave, or remain in the areas. In 1942 Congress provided penalties for violation of these regulations. Acting under these executive and congressional authorizations, the Western Defense Command divided the Pacific coast into two military areas and imposed restrictions on persons living in them, including a curfew that applied only to aliens and persons of Japanese ancestry. In *Hirabayashi* v. *United States* (1943), the Court unanimously upheld the curfew as a legitimate wartime measure. Soon after the curfew went into effect, the commanding general removed all Japanese, including many American citizens, to war relocation centers. Toyosaburo Korematsu, an American citizen who refused to leave his home in Alameda County, California, was convicted in U.S. district court for violation of the exclusion order. The Ninth Circuit Court of Appeals affirmed. Majority: Black, Douglas, Frankfurter, Reed, Rutledge, Stone. Dissenting: Jackson, Murphy, Roberts.

Mr. Justice Black delivered the opinion of the Court. . . .

It should be noted . . . that all legal restrictions which curtail the civil rights of a single racial group are immediately suspect. That is not to say that all such restrictions are unconstitutional. It is to say that courts must subject them to the most rigid scrutiny. Pressing public necessity may sometimes justify the existence of such restrictions; racial antagonism never can. . . .

In the light of the principles we announced in the Hirabayashi Case, we are unable to conclude that it was beyond the war power of Congress and the Executive to exclude those of Japanese ancestry from the West Coast war area at the time they did. . . . [E]xclusion from a threatened area, no less than curfew, has a definite and close relationship to the prevention of espionage and sabotage. The military authorities, charged with the primary responsibility of defending our shores, concluded that curfew provided inadequate protection and ordered exclusion. They did so, as pointed out in our Hirabayashi opinion, in accordance with congressional authority to the military to say who should, and who should not, remain in the threatened areas. . . .

Like curfew, exclusion of those of Japanese origin was deemed necessary because of the presence of an unascertained number of disloyal members of the group, most of whom we have no doubt were loyal to this country. It was because we could not reject the finding of the military authorities that it was impossible to bring about an immediate segregation of the disloyal from the loyal that we sustained the validity of the curfew order as applying to the whole group. In the instant case, temporary exclusion of the entire group was rested by the military on the same ground. The judgment that exclusion of the whole group was for the same reason a military imperative answers the contention that the exclusion was in the nature of group punishment based on antagonism to those of Japanese origin. That there were members of the group who retained loyalties to Japan has been confirmed by investigations made subsequent to the exclusion. . . .

We uphold the exclusion order as of the time it was made and when the petitioner violated it. . . . In doing so, we are not unmindful of the hardships imposed by it upon a large group of American citizens . . . Compulsory exclusion of large groups of citizens from their homes, except under circumstances of direst emergency and peril, is inconsistent with our basic governmental institutions. But when under conditions of modern warfare our shores are threatened by hostile forces, the power to protect must be commensurate with the threatened danger. . . .

Our task would be simple, our duty clear, were this a case involving the imprisonment of a loyal citizen in a concentration camp because of racial prejudice. . . . [W]e are dealing specifically with nothing but an exclusion order. To cast this case into outlines of racial prejudice, without reference to the real military dangers which were presented, merely confuses the issue. Korematsu was not excluded from the Military Area because of hostility to him or his race. He was excluded because we are at war with the Japanese Empire, because the properly constituted military authorities feared an invasion of our West Coast and felt constrained to take proper security measures, because they decided that the military urgency of the situation demanded that all citizens of Japanese ancestry be segregated from the West Coast temporarily, and finally, because Congress, reposing its confidence in this time of war in our military leaders—as inevitably it must—determined that they should have the power to do just this. . . .

We cannot—by availing ourselves of the calm perspective of hindsight—now say that at the time these actions were unjustified.

Affirmed.

MR. JUSTICE FRANKFURTER, concurring . . . [omitted].

MR. JUSTICE ROBERTS, dissenting . . . [omitted].

MR. JUSTICE MURPHY, dissenting. . . .

This exclusion of "all persons of Japanese ancestry, both alien and non-alien," from the Pacific Coast area on a plea of military necessity in the absence of martial law ought not to be approved. Such exclusion goes over "the very brink of constitutional power" and falls into the ugly abyss of racism. . . .

The judicial test of whether the Government, on a plea of military necessity, can validly deprive an individual of any of his constitutional rights is whether the deprivation is reasonably related to a public danger that is so "immediate, imminent, and impending" as not to admit of delay and not to permit the intervention of ordinary constitutional processes to alleviate the danger. . . .

[T]hat relation is lacking because the exclusion order necessarily must rely for its reasonableness upon the assumption that all persons of Japanese ancestry may have a dangerous tendency to commit sabotage and espionage and to aid our Japanese enemy in other ways. It is difficult to believe that reason, logic or experience could be marshalled in support of such an assumption. . . .

The main reasons relied upon by those responsible for the forced evacuation, therefore, do not prove a reasonable relation between the group characteristics of Japanese Americans and the dangers of invasion, sabotage and espionage. The reasons appear, instead, to be largely an accumulation of much of the misinformation, half-truths and insinuations that for years have been directed against Japanese Americans by people with racial and economic prejudices—the same people who have been among the foremost advocates of the evacuation. A military judgment based upon such racial and sociological considerations is not entitled to the great weight ordinarily given the judgments based upon strictly military considerations. . . .

I dissent, therefore, from this legalization of racism. . . .

MR. JUSTICE JACKSON, dissenting. . . .

Much is said of the danger to liberty from the Army program for deporting and detaining these citizens of Japanese extraction. But a judicial construction of the due process clause that will sustain this order is a far more subtle blow to liberty than the promulgation of the order itself. A military order, however unconstitutional, is not apt to last longer than the military emergency. Even during that period a succeeding commander may revoke it all. But once a judicial opinion rationalizes such an order to show that it conforms to the Constitution, or rather rationalizes the Constitution to show that the Constitution sanctions such an order, the Court for all time has validated the principle of racial discrimination in criminal procedure and of transplanting American citizens. The principle then lies about like a loaded weapon ready for the hand of any authority that can bring forward a plausible claim of an urgent need. Every repetition imbeds that principle more deeply in our law and thinking and expands it to new purposes. All who observe the work of the courts are familiar with what Judge Cardozo described as "the tendency of a principle to expand itself to the limit of its logic." . . . Nothing better illustrates this danger than does the Court's opinion in this case.

It argues that we are bound to uphold the conviction of Korematsu because we upheld one in *Hirabayashi* v. *United States* . . . when we sustained these orders insofar as they applied a curfew requirement to a citizen of Japanese ancestry. I think we would learn something from that experience.

In that case we were urged to consider only the curfew feature, that being all that technically was involved, because it was the only count necessary to sustain Hirabayashi's conviction and sentence. We yielded, and the Chief Justice guarded the opinion as carefully as language will do. He said: "Our investigation here does not go beyond the inquiry whether, in the light of all the relevant circumstances preceding and attending their promulgation, the challenged orders and statute *afforded a reasonable basis for the action taken in imposing the curfew*." . . . "We decide only the issue as we have defined it—we decide only that the *curfew order* as applied, and at the time it was applied, was within the boundaries of the war power." . . . And again: "It is unnecessary to consider whether or to what extent *such findings would support orders differing from the curfew order*." . . . [Italics supplied by Justice Jackson.] Now the principle of racial discrimination is pushed from support of mild measures to very harsh ones, and from temporary deprivations to indeterminate ones. And the precedent which it is said requires us to do so is *Hirabayashi*. The Court is now saying that in *Hirabayashi* we did decide the very things we there said we were not deciding. Because we said that these citizens could be made to stay in their homes during the hours of dark, it is said we must require them to leave home entirely; and if that, we are told they may also be taken into custody for deportation; and if that, it is argued they may also be held for some undetermined time in detention camps. How far the principle of this case would be extended before plausible reasons would play out, I do not know. . . .

I do not suggest that the courts should have attempted to interfere with the Army in carrying out its task. But I do not think they may be asked to execute a military expedient that has no place in law under the Constitution. I would reverse the judgment and discharge the prisoner.[1]

New York Times Co. v. *United States*
403 U.S. 713, 91 S.Ct. 2140, 29 L.Ed. 2d 822 (1971)

http://caselaw.findlaw.com/us-supreme-court/403/713.html

(This case is reprinted in Chapter Eleven; see the Table of Contents.)

United States v. *United States District Court*
407 U.S. 297, 92 S.Ct. 2125, 32 L.Ed. 2d 752 (1972)

http://caselaw.findlaw.com/us-supreme-court/407/297.html

During pretrial proceedings in a prosecution in the U.S. District Court for the Eastern District of Michigan for conspiracy to destroy government property, the court ordered the government to make full disclosure to one of the defendants of his conversations overheard by electronic surveillance instituted without a search warrant. The U.S. Court of Appeals for the Sixth Circuit denied the government's petition for a writ of mandamus to compel the district judge to vacate the disclosure order. Majority: Powell, Blackmun, Brennan, Burger, Douglas, Marshall, Stewart, White. Not participating: Rehnquist.

Mr. Justice Powell delivered the opinion of the Court.

The issue before us is an important one for the people of our country and their Government. It involves the delicate question of the President's power, acting through the Attorney General, to authorize electronic surveillance in internal security matters without prior judicial approval. Successive Presidents for more than one quarter of a century have authorized such surveillance in varying degrees, without guidance from the Congress or a definitive decision of this Court. This case brings the issue here for the first time. . . .

Title III of the Omnibus Crime Control and Safe Streets Act . . . authorizes the use of electronic surveillance for classes of crimes carefully specified. . . . The Act represents a comprehensive attempt by Congress to promote more effective control of crime while protecting the privacy of individual thought and expression. . . .

Together with the elaborate surveillance requirements in Title III, there is the following proviso, 18 USC § 2511 (3):

> Nothing contained in this chapter or in section 605 of the Communications Act of 1934 shall limit the constitutional power of the President to take such measures as he deems necessary to protect the Nation against actual or potential attack or other hostile acts of a foreign power, to obtain foreign intelligence information deemed essential to the security of the United States, or to protect national security information against foreign intelligence activities. *Nor shall anything contained in this chapter be deemed to limit the constitutional power of the President to take such measures as he deems necessary to protect the United States against the overthrow of the Government by force or other unlawful means, or against any other clear and present danger to the structure or existence of the Government.* The contents of any wire or oral communication intercepted by authority of the President in the exercise of the foregoing powers may be received in evidence in any trial hearing or other proceeding only where such interception was reasonable, and shall not be otherwise used or disclosed except as is necessary to implement that power. (Emphasis supplied [by Justice Powell]).

The Government relies on § 2511 (3). It argues that "in excepting national security surveillances from the Act's warrant requirement Congress recognized the President's authority to conduct such surveillances without prior judicial approval." . . . The section thus is viewed as a recognition or affirmance of a constitutional authority in the President to conduct warrantless domestic security surveillance such as that involved in this case.

We think the language of § 2511 (3), as well as the legislative history of the statute, refutes this interpretation. . . . At most, this is an implicit recognition that the President does have certain powers in the specified areas. Few would doubt this, as the section refers—among other things—to protection "against actual or potential attack or other hostile acts of a foreign power." But so far as the use of the president's electronic surveillance power is concerned, the language is essentially neutral.

Section 2511 (3) certainly confers no power, as the language is wholly inappropriate for such a purpose. It merely provides that the Act shall not be interpreted to limit or disturb such power as the President may have under the Constitution. In short, Congress simply left presidential powers where it found them. . . .

[N]othing in § 2511 (3) was intended to *expand* or to *contract* or to *define* whatever presidential surveillance powers existed in matters affecting the national security. If we could accept the Government's characterization of § 2511 (3) as a congressionally prescribed exception to the general requirement of a warrant, it would be necessary to consider the question of whether the surveillance in this case came within the exception and, if so, whether the statutory exception was itself constitutionally valid. But viewing § 2511 (3) as a congressional disclaimer and expression of neutrality, we hold that the statute is not the measure of the executive authority asserted in this case. Rather, we must look to the constitutional powers of the President.

It is important . . . to emphasize the limited nature of the question before the Court. This case . . . requires no judgment on the scope of the President's surveillance power with respect to the activities of foreign powers, within or without this country. . . . There is no evidence of any involvement, directly or indirectly, of a foreign power.

Our present inquiry, though important, is therefore a narrow one. . . .

History abundantly documents the tendency of Government—however benevolent and benign its motives—to view with suspicion those who most fervently dispute its policies. Fourth Amendment protections become the more necessary when the targets of official surveillance may be those suspected of unorthodoxy in their political beliefs. The danger to political dissent is acute where the Government attempts to act under so vague a concept as the power to protect "domestic security." Given the difficulty of defining the domestic security interest, the danger of abuse in acting to protect that interest becomes apparent. . . . The price of lawful public dissent must not be a dread of subjection to an unchecked surveillance power. Nor must the fear of unauthorized official eavesdropping deter vigorous citizen dissent and discussion of Government action in private conversation. For private dissent, no less than open public discourse, is essential to our free society.

Fourth Amendment freedoms cannot properly be guaranteed if domestic security surveillances may be conducted solely within the discretion of the executive branch. The Fourth Amendment does not contemplate the executive officers of Government as neutral and disinterested magistrates. Their duty and responsibility is to enforce the laws, to investigate and to prosecute. . . .

The Fourth Amendment contemplates a prior judicial judgment, not the risk that executive discretion may be reasonably exercised. This judicial role accords with our basic constitutional doctrine that individual freedoms will best be preserved through a separation of powers and division of functions among the different branches and levels of Government. . . . The independent check upon executive discretion is not satisfied, as the Government argues, by "extremely limited" post-surveillance judicial review. Indeed, post-surveillance review would never reach the surveillances which failed to result in prosecutions. Prior review by a neutral and detached magistrate is the time-tested means of effectuating Fourth Amendment rights. . . .

The Government argues that the special circumstances applicable to domestic security surveillances necessitate a further exception to the warrant requirement. It is urged that the requirement of prior judicial review would obstruct the President in the discharge of his constitutional duty to protect domestic security. We are told further that these surveillances are directed primarily to the collecting and maintaining of intelligence with respect to subversive forces and are not an attempt to gather evidence for specific criminal prosecutions. It is said that this type of surveillance should not be subject to traditional warrant requirements which were established to govern investigation of criminal activity, not on-going intelligence gathering. . . .

The Government further insists that courts "as a practical matter would have neither the knowledge nor the techniques necessary to determine whether there was probable cause to believe that surveillance was necessary to protect national security." These security problems, the Government contends, involve "a large number of complex and subtle factors" beyond the competence of courts to evaluate. . . .

But we do not think a case has been made for the requested departure from Fourth Amendment standards . . . of judicial approval prior to initiation of a search or surveillance. Although some added burden will be imposed upon the Attorney General, this inconvenience is justified in a free society to protect constitutional values. Nor do we think the Government's domestic surveillance powers will be impaired to any significant degree. A prior warrant establishes presumptive validity of the surveillance and will minimize the burden of justification in post-surveillance judicial review. By no means of least importance, will be the reassurance of the public generally that indiscriminate wiretapping and bugging of law-abiding citizens cannot occur. . . .

The judgment of the Court of Appeals is hereby

Affirmed.

Mr. Chief Justice Burger, concurring . . . [omitted].

Mr. Justice White, concurring . . . [omitted].
Mr. Justice Douglas concurring . . . [omitted].

Boumediene v. *Bush*
553 U.S. 723, 128 S.Ct. 2229, 171 L.Ed. 2d 41 (2008)

www.law.cornell.edu/supct/html/06-1195.ZS.html

This litigation began after *Rasul* v. *Bush* (2004), which allowed access to habeas corpus actions in federal court for detainees at Guantanamo Bay, and after the Department of Defense authorized Combatant Status Review Tribunals (CSRTs) in 2004 to ascertain the status of the Guantanamo detainees.

In 2005, Congress passed the Detainee Treatment Act (DTA) which professed to preclude habeas corpus petitions from Guantanamo detainees while providing for exclusive review of CSRT determinations in the United States Court of Appeals for the District of Columbia Circuit, as well as a parallel review process for detainees seeking to challenge convictions as a result of trial by military commissions. In *Hamdan* v. *Rumsfeld* (2006), the Supreme Court, among other conclusions, held that the jurisdiction-stripping provision in the DTA did not apply to pending cases and therefore found it unnecessary to address the statute's constitutional implications. In response, Congress in 2006 passed the Military Commissions Act (MCA) to bar detainee habeas petitions in all cases (pending and future).

In 2007 the Court of Appeals for the District of Columbia upheld the validity of the MCA that the Guantanamo detainees had no constitutional legal right to seek habeas corpus relief in the courts of the United States. Counsel for Lakhdar Boumediene and others filed a petition for a writ of certiorari in the U.S. Supreme Court on March 5, 2007. After denying the petition on April 2, the Court in an unusual action on June 29 vacated its earlier order and granted the writ. Majority: Kennedy, Breyer, Ginsburg, Souter, Stevens. Dissenting: Scalia, Alito, Roberts, Thomas.

Justice Kennedy delivered the opinion of the Court. . . .

Petitioners present a question not resolved by our earlier cases relating to the detention of aliens at Guantanamo: whether they have the constitutional privilege of habeas corpus, a privilege not to be withdrawn except in conformance with the Suspension Clause. . . . We hold these petitioners do have the habeas corpus privilege. Congress has enacted a statute, the Detainee Treatment Act of 2005, that provides certain procedures for review of the detainees' status. We hold that those procedures are not an adequate and effective substitute for habeas corpus. Therefore § 7 of the Military Commissions Act of 2006 (MCA) operates as an unconstitutional suspension of the writ. We do not address whether the President has authority to detain these petitioners nor do we hold that the writ must issue. These and other questions regarding the legality of the detention are to be resolved in the first instance by the District Court. . . .

The Government contends that noncitizens designated as enemy combatants and detained in territory located outside our Nation's borders have no constitutional rights and no privilege of habeas corpus. Petitioners contend they do have cognizable constitutional rights and that Congress, in seeking to eliminate recourse to habeas corpus as a means to assert those rights, acted in violation of the Suspension Clause. . . .

[T]he Suspension Clause . . . protects the rights of the detained by a means consistent with the essential design of the Constitution. It ensures that, except during periods of formal suspension, the Judiciary will have a time-tested device, the writ, to maintain the "delicate balance of governance" that is itself the surest safeguard of liberty. The Clause protects the rights of the detained by affirming the duty and authority of the Judiciary to call the jailer to account. . . . The separation-of-powers doctrine, and the history that influenced its design, therefore must inform the reach and purpose of the Suspension Clause. . . .

The Government argues the common-law writ ran only to those territories over which the Crown was sovereign. Petitioners argue that jurisdiction followed the King's officers. Diligent search by all parties reveals no certain conclusions. . . . We decline, therefore, to infer too much, one way or the other, from the lack of historical evidence on point. . . .

Drawing from its position that at common law the writ ran only to territories over which the Crown was sovereign, the Government says the Suspension Clause affords petitioners no rights because the United States does not claim sovereignty over the place of detention.

Guantanamo Bay is not formally part of the United States. And under the terms of the lease between the United States and Cuba, Cuba retains "ultimate sovereignty" over the territory while the United States exercises "complete jurisdiction and control." . . . The United States contends, nevertheless, that Guantanamo is not within its sovereign control. This was the Government's position well before the events of September 11, 2001. . . . We therefore do not question the Government's position that Cuba, not the United States, maintains sovereignty, in the legal and technical sense of the term, over Guantanamo Bay. But this does not end the analysis.

Our cases do not hold it is improper for us to inquire into the objective degree of control the Nation asserts over foreign territory. . . . Indeed, it is not altogether uncommon for a territory to be under the *de jure* sovereignty of one nation, while under the plenary control, or practical sovereignty, of another. . . . Accordingly, for purposes of our analysis, we accept the Government's position that Cuba, and not the United States, retains *de jure* sovereignty over Guantanamo Bay. As we did in *Rasul*, however, we take notice of the obvious and uncontested fact that the United States, by virtue of its complete jurisdiction and control over the base, maintains de facto sovereignty over this territory.

The Court has discussed the issue of the Constitution's extraterritorial application on many occasions. These decisions undermine the Government's argument that, at least as applied to noncitizens, the Constitution necessarily stops where *de jure* sovereignty ends. . . . Fundamental questions regarding the Constitution's geographic scope first arose at the dawn of the 20th century when the Nation acquired noncontiguous Territories: Puerto Rico, Guam, and the Philippines—ceded to the United States by Spain at the conclusion of the Spanish-American War—and Hawaii—annexed by the United States in 1898. At this point Congress chose to discontinue its previous practice of extending constitutional rights to the territories by statute. . . . In a series of opinions later known as the Insular Cases, the Court addressed whether the Constitution, by its own force, applies in any territory that is not a State. The Court held that the Constitution has independent force in these territories, a force not contingent upon acts of legislative grace. Yet it took note of the difficulties inherent in that position. . . . These considerations resulted in the doctrine of territorial incorporation, under which the Constitution applies in full in incorporated Territories surely destined for statehood but only in part in unincorporated Territories. . . .

Practical considerations weighed heavily as well in *Johnson* v. *Eisentrager* where the Court addressed whether habeas corpus jurisdiction extended to enemy aliens who had been convicted of violating the laws of war. . . . True, the Court in *Eisentrager* denied access to the writ, and it noted the prisoners "at no relevant time were within any territory over which the United States is sovereign, and [that] the scenes of their offense, their capture, their trial and their punishment were all beyond the territorial jurisdiction of any court of the United States."

The Government seizes upon this language as proof positive that the Eisentrager Court adopted a formalistic, sovereignty-based test for determining the reach of the Suspension Clause. We reject this reading. . . . [I]f the Government's reading of *Eisentrager* were correct, the opinion would have marked not only a change in, but a complete repudiation of, the Insular Cases' functional approach to questions of extraterritoriality. We cannot accept the Government's view. Nothing in *Eisentrager* says that *de jure* sovereignty is or has ever been the only relevant consideration in determining the geographic reach of the Constitution or of habeas corpus. . . . A constricted reading of *Eisentrager* overlooks what we see as a common thread. . . : the idea that questions of extraterritoriality turn on objective factors and practical concerns, not formalism.

The Government's formal sovereignty-based test raises troubling separation-of-powers concerns as well. . . . The necessary implication of the argument is that by surrendering formal sovereignty over any unincorporated territory to a third party, while at the same time entering into a lease that grants total control over the territory back to the United States, it would be possible for the political branches to govern without legal constraint. Our basic charter cannot be contracted away like this. . . . The test for determining the scope of this provision must not be subject to manipulation by those whose power it is designed to restrain. . . .

It is true that before today the Court has never held that noncitizens detained by our Government in territory over which another country maintains *de jure* sovereignty have any rights under our Constitution. But the cases before us lack any precise historical parallel. . . . The detainees, moreover, are held in a territory that, while technically not part of the United States, is under the complete and total control of our Government. Under these circumstances the lack of a precedent on point is no barrier to our holding.

We hold that Art. I, § 9, cl. 2, of the Constitution has full effect at Guantanamo Bay. If the privilege of habeas corpus is to be denied to the detainees now before us, Congress must act in accordance with the requirements of the Suspension Clause. . . . The MCA does not purport to be a formal suspension of the writ; and the Government, in its submissions to us, has not argued that it is. Petitioners, therefore, are entitled to the privilege of habeas corpus to challenge the legality of their detention.

In light of this holding the question becomes whether the statute stripping jurisdiction to issue the writ avoids the Suspension Clause mandate because Congress has provided adequate substitute procedures for habeas corpus. The Government submits there has been compliance with the Suspension Clause because the DTA review process in the Court of Appeals provides an adequate substitute. . . . The Court of Appeals, having decided that the writ does not run to the detainees in any event, found it unnecessary to consider whether an adequate substitute has been provided. . . .

Our case law does not contain extensive discussion of standards defining suspension of the writ or of circumstances under which suspension has occurred. . . . The Court of Appeals [under the DTA] has jurisdiction not to inquire into the legality of the detention generally but only to assess whether the CSRT complied with the "standards and procedures specified by the Secretary of Defense" and whether those standards and procedures are lawful. . . . This choice indicates Congress intended the Court of Appeals to have a more limited role in enemy combatant status determinations than a district court has in habeas corpus proceedings. . . .

Petitioners identify what they see as myriad deficiencies in the CSRTs. The most relevant for our purposes are the constraints upon the detainee's ability to rebut the factual basis for the Government's assertion that he is an enemy combatant. . . . Although we make no judgment as to whether the CSRTs, as currently constituted, satisfy due process standards, we agree with petitioners that, even when all the parties involved in this process act with diligence and in good faith, there is considerable risk of error in the tribunal's findings of fact. . . . [I]t suffices that the Government has not established that the detainees' access to the statutory review provisions at issue is an adequate substitute for the writ of habeas corpus. MCA § 7 thus effects an unconstitutional suspension of the writ. . . .

Our decision today holds only that the petitioners before us are entitled to seek the writ; that the DTA review procedures are an inadequate substitute for habeas corpus; and that the petitioners in these cases need not exhaust the review procedures in the Court of Appeals before proceeding with their habeas actions in the District Court. The only law we identify as unconstitutional is MCA § 7. Accordingly, both the DTA and the CSRT process remain intact.

The judgment of the Court of Appeals is reversed. The cases are remanded to the Court of Appeals with instructions that it remand the cases to the District Court for proceedings consistent with this opinion.

It is so ordered.

Justice Souter, with whom Justice Ginsburg and Justice Breyer join, concurring . . . [omitted].

Chief Justice Roberts, with whom Justice Scalia, Justice Thomas, and Justice Alito join, dissenting . . . [omitted].

Justice Scalia, with whom The Chief Justice, Justice Thomas, and Justice Alito join, dissenting. . . .

America is at war with radical Islamists. . . . The game of bait-and-switch that today's opinion plays upon the Nation's Commander in Chief will make the war harder on us. It will almost certainly cause more Americans to be killed. That consequence would be tolerable if necessary to preserve a time-honored legal principle vital to our constitutional Republic. But it is this Court's blatant abandonment of such a principle that produces the decision today. The President relied on our settled precedent in *Johnson* v. *Eisentrager* when he established the prison at Guantanamo Bay for enemy aliens. . . . Had the law been otherwise, the military surely would not have transported prisoners there, but would have kept them in Afghanistan, transferred them to another of our foreign military bases, or turned them over to allies for detention. . . .

As a court of law operating under a written Constitution, our role is to determine whether there is a conflict between [the Suspension] Clause and the Military Commissions Act. A conflict arises only if the Suspension Clause preserves the privilege of the writ for aliens held by the United States military as enemy combatants at the base in Guantanamo Bay, located within the sovereign territory of Cuba.

We have frequently stated that we owe great deference to Congress's view that a law it has passed is constitutional. That is especially so in the area of foreign and military affairs. . . . In light of those principles of deference, the Court's conclusion that "the common law [does not] yiel[d] a definite answer to the questions before us," leaves it no choice but to affirm the Court of Appeals. The writ as preserved in the Constitution could not possibly extend farther than the common law provided when that Clause was written. The Court admits that it cannot determine whether the writ historically extended to aliens held abroad, and it concedes (necessarily) that Guantanamo Bay lies outside the sovereign territory of the United States. Together, these two concessions establish that it is (in the Court's view) perfectly ambiguous whether the common-law writ would have provided a remedy for these petitioners. If that is so, the Court has no basis to strike down the Military Commissions Act, and must leave undisturbed the considered judgment of the coequal branches.

How, then, does the Court weave a clear constitutional prohibition out of pure interpretive equipoise? The Court resorts to "fundamental separation-of-powers principles" to interpret the Suspension Clause. . . .

That approach distorts the nature of the separation of powers and its role in the constitutional structure. The "fundamental separation-of-powers principles" that the Constitution embodies are to be derived not from some judicially imagined matrix, but from the sum total of the individual separation-of-powers provisions that the Constitution sets forth. Only by considering them one-by-one does the full shape of the Constitution's separation-of-powers principles emerge. It is nonsensical to interpret those provisions themselves in light of some general "separation-of-powers principles" dreamed up by the Court. Rather, they must be interpreted to mean what they were understood to mean when the people ratified them. And if the understood scope of the writ of habeas corpus was "designed to restrain" (as the Court says) the actions of the Executive, the understood limits upon that scope were (as the Court seems not to grasp) just as much "designed to restrain" the incursions of the Third Branch. "Manipulation" of the territorial reach of the writ by the Judiciary poses just as much a threat to the proper separation of powers as "manipulation" by the Executive. As I will show below, manipulation is what is afoot here. . . .

The Court purports to derive from our precedents a "functional" test for the extraterritorial reach of the writ, which shows that the Military Commissions Act unconstitutionally restricts the scope of habeas. That is remarkable because the most pertinent of those precedents, *Johnson* v. *Eisentrager*, conclusively establishes the opposite. . . . Like the petitioners here, the Germans claimed that their detentions violated the Constitution and international law, and sought a writ of habeas corpus. Writing for the Court, Justice Jackson held that American courts lacked habeas jurisdiction. . . . As Justice Black accurately said in dissent, "the Court's opinion inescapably denies courts power to afford the least bit of protection for any alien who is subject to our occupation government abroad, even if he is neither enemy nor belligerent and even after peace is officially declared." . . .

The category of prisoner comparable to these detainees are not the Eisentrager criminal defendants, but the more than 400,000 prisoners of war detained in the United States alone during World War II. Not a single one was accorded the right to have his detention validated by a habeas corpus action in federal court—and that despite the fact that they were present on U.S. soil. The Court's analysis produces a crazy result: Whereas those convicted and sentenced to death for war crimes are without judicial remedy, all enemy combatants detained during a war, at least insofar as they are confined in an area away from the battlefield over which the United States exercises "absolute and indefinite" control, may seek a writ of habeas corpus in federal court. And, as an even more bizarre implication from the Court's reasoning, those prisoners whom the military plans to try by full-dress Commission at a future date may file habeas petitions and secure release before their trials take place. . . .

What drives today's decision is neither the meaning of the Suspension Clause, nor the principles of our precedents, but rather an inflated notion of judicial supremacy. . . . But so long as there are some places to which habeas does not run—so long as the Court's new "functional" test will not be satisfied in every case—then there will be circumstances in which "it would be possible for the political branches to govern without legal constraint." Or, to put it more impartially, areas in which the legal determinations of the other branches will be (shudder!) supreme. [T]he Court's ultimate, unexpressed goal is to preserve the power to review the confinement of enemy prisoners held by the Executive anywhere in the world. . . .

Putting aside the conclusive precedent of *Eisentrager*, it is clear that the original understanding of the Suspension Clause was that habeas corpus was not available to aliens abroad. . . . It is entirely clear that, at English common law, the writ of habeas corpus did not extend beyond the sovereign territory of the Crown. . . .

What history teaches is confirmed by the nature of the limitations that the Constitution places upon suspension of the common-law writ. It can be suspended only "in Cases of Rebellion or Invasion." The latter case (invasion) is plainly limited to the territory of the United States; and while it is conceivable that a rebellion could be mounted by American citizens abroad, surely the overwhelming majority of its occurrences would be domestic. If the extraterritorial scope of habeas turned on flexible, "functional" considerations, as the Court holds, why would the Constitution limit its suspension almost entirely to instances of domestic crisis? Surely there is an even greater justification for suspension in foreign lands where the United States might hold prisoners of war during an ongoing conflict. And correspondingly, there is less threat to liberty when the Government suspends the writ's (supposed) application in foreign lands, where even on the most extreme view prisoners are entitled to fewer constitutional rights. It makes no sense, therefore, for the Constitution generally to forbid suspension of the writ abroad if indeed the writ has application there. . . . In sum, because I conclude that the text and history of the Suspension Clause provide no basis for our jurisdiction, I would affirm the Court of Appeals even if *Eisentrager* did not govern these cases. . . . The Nation will live to regret what the Court has done today. I dissent.

Roman Catholic Diocese of Brooklyn v. *Cuomo*
592 U.S. ___, 141 S.Ct. 63, 208 L.Ed. 2d 206 (2020)

The background of this request for injunctive relief is in the opinions below. Before reading this case, see the discussion of *South Bay Pentecostal Church* v. *Newsom* and *Jacobson v. Massachusetts*, near the end of the essay for Chapter Fifteen. Majority: Alito, Barrett, Gorsuch, Kavanaugh, Thomas. Dissenting: Breyer, Kagan, Roberts, Sotomayor.

Per Curiam.

The application for injunctive relief presented to JUSTICE BREYER and by him referred to the Court is granted. Respondent is enjoined from enforcing Executive Order 202.68's 10- and 25-person occupancy limits on applicant pending disposition of the appeal in the United

States Court of Appeals for the Second Circuit and disposition of the petition for a writ of certiorari, if such writ is timely sought. . . . This emergency application and another, *Agudath Israel of America* v. *Cuomo* present the same issue, and this opinion addresses both cases.

Both applications seek relief from an Executive Order issued by the Governor of New York that imposes very severe restrictions on attendance at religious services in areas classified as "red" or "orange" zones. In red zones, no more than 10 persons may attend each religious service, and in orange zones, attendance is capped at 25. The two applications . . . contend that these restrictions violate the Free Exercise Clause of the First Amendment, and they ask us to enjoin enforcement of the restrictions while they pursue appellate review. Citing a variety of remarks made by the Governor, Agudath Israel argues that the Governor specifically targeted the Orthodox Jewish community and gerrymandered the boundaries of red and orange zones to ensure that heavily Orthodox areas were included. Both the Diocese and Agudath Israel maintain that the regulations treat houses of worship much more harshly than comparable secular facilities. And they tell us without contradiction that they have complied with all public health guidance, have implemented additional precautionary measures, and have operated at 25% or 33% capacity for months without a single outbreak.

The applicants have clearly established their entitlement to relief pending appellate review. They have shown that their First Amendment claims are likely to prevail, that denying them relief would lead to irreparable injury, and that granting relief would not harm the public interest. . . . The applicants have made a strong showing that the challenged restrictions violate "the minimum requirement of neutrality" to religion. As noted by the dissent in the court below, statements made in connection with the challenged rules can be viewed as targeting the "ultra-Orthodox" [Jewish] community. But even if we put those comments aside, the regulations cannot be viewed as neutral because they single out houses of worship for especially harsh treatment.

In a red zone, while a synagogue or church may not admit more than 10 persons, businesses categorized as "essential" may admit as many people as they wish. And the list of "essential" businesses includes things such as acupuncture facilities, camp grounds, garages, as well as many whose services are not limited to those that can be regarded as essential, such as all plants manufacturing chemicals and microelectronics and all transportation facilities. The disparate treatment is even more striking in an orange zone. While attendance at houses of worship is limited to 25 persons, even nonessential businesses may decide for themselves how many persons to admit.

These categorizations lead to troubling results. At the hearing in the District Court, a health department official testified about a large store in Brooklyn that could "literally have hundreds of people shopping there on any given day." Yet a nearby church or synagogue would be prohibited from allowing more than 10 or 25 people inside for a worship service. . . . Because the challenged restrictions are not "neutral" and of "general applicability," they must satisfy "strict scrutiny," and this means that they must be "narrowly tailored" to serve a "compelling" state interest. Stemming the spread of COVID-19 is unquestionably a compelling interest, but it is hard to see how the challenged regulations can be regarded as "narrowly tailored." They are far more restrictive than any COVID-related regulations that have previously come before the Court, much tighter than those adopted by many other jurisdictions hard-hit by the pandemic, and far more severe than has been shown to be required to prevent the spread of the virus at the applicants' services. . . .

Not only is there no evidence that the applicants have contributed to the spread of COVID-19 but there are many other less restrictive rules that could be adopted to minimize the risk to those attending religious services. Among other things, the maximum attendance at a religious service could be tied to the size of the church or synagogue. Almost all of the 26 Diocese churches immediately affected by the Executive Order can seat at least 500 people, about 14 can accommodate at least 700, and 2 can seat over 1,000. Similarly, Agudath Israel of Kew Garden Hills can seat up to 400. It is hard to believe that admitting more than 10 people to a 1,000-seat church or 400-seat synagogue would create a more serious health risk than the many other activities that the State allows.

There can be no question that the challenged restrictions, if enforced, will cause irreparable harm. "The loss of First Amendment freedoms, for even minimal periods of time, unquestionably constitutes irreparable injury." If only 10 people are admitted to each service, the great majority of those who wish to attend Masson Sunday or services in a synagogue on Shabbat will be barred. And while those who are shut out may in some instances be able to watch services on television, such remote viewing is not the same as personal attendance. Catholics who watch a Mass at home cannot receive communion, and there are important religious traditions in the Orthodox Jewish faith that require personal attendance.

Finally, it has not been shown that granting the applications will harm the public. As noted, the State has not claimed that attendance at the applicants' services has resulted in the spread of the disease. And the State has not shown that public health would be imperiled if less restrictive measures were imposed. Members of this Court are not public health experts, and we should respect the judgment of those with special expertise and responsibility in this area. But even in a pandemic, the Constitution cannot be put away and forgotten. The restrictions at issue here, by effectively barring many from attending religious services, strike at the very heart of the First Amendment's guarantee of religious liberty. Before allowing this to occur, we have a duty to conduct a serious examination of the need for such a drastic measure.

The dissenting opinions argue that we should withhold relief because the relevant circumstances have now changed. After the applicants asked this Court for relief, the Governor reclassified the areas in question from orange to yellow, and this change means that the applicants may hold services at 50% of their maximum occupancy. The dissents would deny relief at this time but allow the Diocese and Agudath Israel to renew their requests if this recent reclassification is reversed.

There is no justification for that proposed course of action. It is clear that this matter is not moot. And injunctive relief is still called for because the applicants remain under a constant threat that the area in question will be reclassified as red or orange. The Governor regularly changes the classification of particular areas without prior notice. . . . The applicants have made the showing needed to obtain relief, and there is no reason why they should bear the risk of suffering further irreparable harm in the event of another reclassification. For these reasons, we hold that enforcement of the Governor's severe restrictions on the applicants' religious services must be enjoined.

It is so ordered.

Justice Gorsuch, concurring.

Government is not free to disregard the First Amendment in times of crisis. At a minimum, that Amendment prohibits government officials from treating religious exercises worse than comparable secular activities, unless they are pursuing a compelling interest and using the least restrictive means available. Yet recently, during the COVID-19 pandemic, certain States seem to have ignored these long-settled principles.

Today's case supplies just the latest example. New York's Governor has asserted the power to assign different color codes to different parts of the State and govern each by executive decree. In "red zones," houses of worship are all but closed—limited to a maximum of 10 people. In the Orthodox Jewish community that limit might operate to exclude all women, considering 10 men are necessary to establish a minyan, or a quorum. In "orange zones," it's not much different. Churches and synagogues are limited to a maximum of 25 people. These restrictions apply even to the largest cathedrals and synagogues, which ordinarily hold hundreds. And the restrictions apply no matter the precautions taken, including social distancing, wearing masks, leaving doors and windows open, forgoing singing, and disinfecting spaces between services.

At the same time, the Governor has chosen to impose no capacity restrictions on certain businesses he considers "essential." And it turns out the businesses the Governor considers essential include hardware stores, acupuncturists, and liquor stores. Bicycle repair shops, certain signage companies, accountants, lawyers, and insurance agents are all essential too. So, at least according to the Governor, it may be unsafe to go to church, but it is always fine to pick up another bottle of wine, shop for a new bike, or spend the afternoon exploring your distal points and meridians. Who knew public health would so perfectly align with secular convenience?

As almost everyone on the Court today recognizes, squaring the Governor's edicts with our traditional First Amendment rules is no easy task. People may gather inside for extended periods in bus stations and airports, in laundromats and banks, in hardware stores and liquor shops. No apparent reason exists why people may not gather, subject to identical restrictions, in churches or synagogues, especially when religious institutions have made plain that they stand ready, able, and willing to follow all the safety precautions required of "essential" businesses and perhaps more besides. The only explanation for treating religious places differently seems to be a judgment that what happens there just isn't as "essential" as what happens in secular spaces. Indeed, the Governor is remarkably frank about this: In his judgment laundry and liquor, travel and tools, are all "essential" while traditional religious exercises are not. That is exactly the kind of discrimination the First Amendment forbids. Nor is the problem an isolated one. In recent months, certain other Governors have issued similar edicts. At the flick of a pen, they have asserted the right to privilege restaurants, marijuana dispensaries, and casinos over churches, mosques, and temples. In far too many places, for far too long, our first freedom has fallen on deaf ears. . . .

It is time—past time—to make plain that, while the pandemic poses many grave challenges, there is no world in which the Constitution tolerates color-coded executive edicts that reopen liquor stores and bike shops but shutter churches, synagogues, and mosques.

JUSTICE KAVANAUGH, concurring . . . [omitted].

CHIEF JUSTICE ROBERTS, dissenting.

I would not grant injunctive relief under the present circumstances. There is simply no need to do so. . . . None of the houses of worship identified in the applications is now subject to any fixed numerical restrictions. . . .

JUSTICE BREYER, with whom JUSTICE SOTOMAYOR and JUSTICE KAGAN join, dissenting. . . .

Here, we consider severe restrictions. Those restrictions limit the number of persons who can attend a religious service to 10 and 25 congregants (irrespective of mask-wearing and social distancing). And those numbers are indeed low. But whether, in present circumstances, those low numbers violate the Constitution's Free Exercise Clause is far from clear, and, in my view, the applicants must make such a showing here to show that they are entitled to "the extraordinary remedy of injunction." . . .

JUSTICE SOTOMAYOR, with whom JUSTICE KAGAN joins, dissenting. . . .

Justices of this Court play a deadly game in second guessing the expert judgment of health officials about the environments in which a contagious virus, now infecting a million Americans each week, spreads most easily. . . .

NOTE

1. Calling the internment "part of an unfortunate episode in our nation's history," the Justice Department in 1983 successfully petitioned the U.S. district court in San Francisco to set aside Korematsu's conviction. Claiming the government exaggerated the wartime security risks on the West Coast, Korematsu and other Japanese Americans then filed a suit for damages against the government. In 1984, the District Court for the District of Columbia ruled that the Korematsu litigation was barred by a six-year statute of limitations on suits against the government. Reversing the district court, the court of appeals held 2–1 in 1986 that previously uncompensated internees could press their suit for damages. Important in the ruling was evidence that the government had concealed information that those interned did not pose a danger to national security during World War II. In *United States* v. *Hohri* (1987), the Supreme Court vacated the appeals court decision because the appeal should have been heard by the Court of Appeals for the Federal Circuit. During oral argument in *Hohri,* Solicitor General Charles Fried described the Korematsu ruling as the "greatest departure from the values for which we were fighting" during World War II. In 1988 the Supreme Court denied certiorari in *Hohri* v. *United States,* in which the Court of Appeals for the Federal Circuit had held that the statute of limitations barred the claims under the takings clause of the Fifth Amendment pressed by the interned citizens and their descendants. Congress then authorized token payments of $20,000 to surviving internees.—ED.

APPENDIX A

Justices of the Supreme Court (arranged by natural court)*

1789	Jay	Rutledge, J.	Cushing	Wilson	Blair					
1790–1791	Jay	Rutledge, J.	Cushing	Wilson	Blair	Iredell				
1792	Jay	Johnson, T.	Cushing	Wilson	Blair	Iredell				
1792–1794	Jay	Paterson	Cushing	Wilson	Blair	Iredell				
1795	Rutledge, J.	Paterson	Cushing	Wilson	Blair	Iredell				
1796–1797	Ellsworth	Paterson	Cushing	Wilson	Chase, S.	Iredell				
1798–1799	Ellsworth	Paterson	Cushing	Washington	Chase, S.	Iredell				
1800	Ellsworth	Paterson	Cushing	Washington	Chase, S.	Moore				
1801–1803	Marshall, J.	Paterson	Cushing	Washington	Chase, S.	Moore				
1804–1805	Marshall, J.	Paterson	Cushing	Washington	Chase, S.	Johnson, W.				
1806	Marshall, J.	Livingston	Cushing	Washington	Chase, S.	Johnson, W.				
1807–1810	Marshall, J.	Livingston	Cushing	Washington	Chase, S.	Johnson, W.	Todd			
1811–1822	Marshall, J.	Livingston	Story	Washington	Duvall	Johnson, W.	Todd			
1823–1825	Marshall, J.	Thompson	Story	Washington	Duvall	Johnson, W.	Todd			
1826–1828	Marshall, J.	Thompson	Story	Washington	Duvall	Johnson, W.	Trimble			
1829	Marshall, J.	Thompson	Story	Washington	Duvall	Johnson, W.	McLean			
1830–1834	Marshall, J.	Thompson	Story	Baldwin	Duvall	Johnson, W.	McLean			
1835	Marshall, J.	Thompson	Story	Baldwin	Duvall	Wayne	McLean			
1836	Taney	Thompson	Story	Baldwin	Barbour	Wayne	McLean			
1837–1840	Taney	Thompson	Story	Baldwin	Barbour	Wayne	McLean	Catron	McKinley	
1841–1844	Taney	Thompson	Story	Baldwin	Daniel	Wayne	McLean	Catron	McKinley	
1845	Taney	Nelson	Woodbury		Daniel	Wayne	McLean	Catron	McKinley	
1846–1850	Taney	Nelson	Woodbury	Grier	Daniel	Wayne	McLean	Catron	McKinley	
1850–1852	Taney	Nelson	Curtis	Grier	Daniel	Wayne	McLean	Catron	McKinley	
1853–1857	Taney	Nelson	Curtis	Grier	Daniel	Wayne	McLean	Catron	Campbell	
1858–1860	Taney	Nelson	Clifford	Grier	Daniel	Wayne	McLean	Catron	Campbell	
1861	Taney	Nelson	Clifford	Grier		Wayne	McLean	Catron	Campbell	
1862	Taney	Nelson	Clifford	Grier	Miller	Wayne	Swayne	Catron	Davis	
1863	Taney	Nelson	Clifford	Grier	Miller	Wayne	Swayne	Catron	Davis	Field
1864–1865	Chase, S. P.	Nelson	Clifford	Grier	Miller	Wayne	Swayne	Catron	Davis	Field
1866–1867	Chase, S. P.	Nelson	Clifford	Grier	Miller	Wayne	Swayne		Davis	Field
1868–1869	Chase, S. P.	Nelson	Clifford	Grier	Miller		Swayne		Davis	Field
1870–1871	Chase, S. P.	Nelson	Clifford	Strong	Miller	Bradley	Swayne		Davis	Field
1872–1873	Chase, S. P.	Hunt	Clifford	Strong	Miller	Bradley	Swayne		Davis	Field
1874–1876	Waite	Hunt	Clifford	Strong	Miller	Bradley	Swayne		Davis	Field
1877–1879	Waite	Hunt	Clifford	Strong	Miller	Bradley	Swayne	Harlan (I)	Field	
1880	Waite	Hunt	Clifford	Woods	Miller	Bradley	Swayne	Harlan (I)	Field	
1881	Waite	Hunt	Gray	Woods	Miller	Bradley	Matthews	Harlan (I)	Field	
1882–1887	Waite	Blatchford	Gray	Woods	Miller	Bradley	Matthews	Harlan (I)	Field	
1888	Fuller	Blatchford	Gray	Lamar, L.	Miller	Bradley	Matthews	Harlan (I)	Field	

1889	Fuller	Blatchford	Gray	Lamar, L.	Miller	Bradley	Brewer	Harlan (I)	Field
1890–1891	Fuller	Blatchford	Gray	Lamar, L.	Brown	Bradley	Brewer	Harlan (I)	Field
1892	Fuller	Blatchford	Gray	Lamar, L.	Brown	Shims	Brewer	Harlan (I)	Field
1893	Fuller	Blatchford	Gray	Jackson, H.	Brown	Shims	Brewer	Harlan (I)	Field
1894	Fuller	White, E.	Gray	Jackson, H.	Brown	Shims	Brewer	Harlan (I)	Field
1895–1897	Fuller	White, E.	Gray	Peckham	Brown	Shims	Brewer	Harlan (I)	Field
1898–1901	Fuller	White, E.	Gray	Peckham	Brown	Shims	Brewer	Harlan (I)	McKenna
1902	Fuller	White, E.	Holmes	Peckham	Brown	Shims	Brewer	Harlan (I)	McKenna
1903–1905	Fuller	White, E.	Holmes	Peckham	Brown	Day	Brewer	Harlan (I)	McKenna
1906–1908	Fuller	White, E.	Holmes	Peckham	Moody	Day	Brewer	Harlan (I)	McKenna
1909	Fuller	White, E.	Holmes	Lurton	Moody	Day	Brewer	Harlan (I)	McKenna
1910–1911	White, E.	Van Devanter	Holmes	Lurton	Lamar, J.	Day	Hughes	Harlan (I)	McKenna
1912–1913	White, E.	Van Devanter	Holmes	Lurton	Lamar, J.	Day	Hughes	Pitney	McKenna
1914–1915	White, E.	Van Devanter	Holmes	McReynolds	Lamar, J.	Day	Hughes	Pitney	McKenna
1916–1920	White, E.	Van Devanter	Holmes	McReynolds	Brandeis	Day	Clarke	Pitney	McKenna
1921	Taft	Van Devanter	Holmes	McReynolds	Brandeis	Day	Clarke	Pitney	McKenna
1922	Taft	Van Devanter	Holmes	McReynolds	Brandeis	Butler	Sutherland	Pitney	McKenna
1923–1924	Taft	Van Devanter	Holmes	McReynolds	Brandeis	Butler	Sutherland	Sanford	McKenna
1925–1929	Taft	Van Devanter	Holmes	McReynolds	Brandeis	Butler	Sutherland	Sanford	Stone
1930–1931	Hughes	Van Devanter	Holmes	McReynolds	Brandeis	Butler	Sutherland	Roberts	Stone
1932–1936	Hughes	Van Devanter	Cardozo	McReynolds	Brandeis	Butler	Sutherland	Roberts	Stone
1937	Hughes	Black	Cardozo	McReynolds	Brandeis	Butler	Sutherland	Roberts	Stone
1938	Hughes	Black	Cardozo	McReynolds	Brandeis	Butler	Reed	Roberts	Stone
1939	Hughes	Black	Frankfurter	McReynolds	Douglas	Butler	Reed	Roberts	Stone
1940	Hughes	Black	Frankfurter	McReynolds	Douglas	Murphy	Reed	Roberts	Stone
1941–1942	Stone	Black	Frankfurter	Byrnes	Douglas	Murphy	Reed	Roberts	Jackson, R.
1943–1944	Stone	Black	Frankfurter	Rutledge, W.	Douglas	Murphy	Reed	Roberts	Jackson, R.
1945	Stone	Black	Frankfurter	Rutledge, W.	Douglas	Murphy	Reed	Burton	Jackson, R.
1946–1948	Vinson	Black	Frankfurter	Rutledge, W.	Douglas	Murphy	Reed	Burton	Jackson, R.
1949–1952	Vinson	Black	Frankfurter	Minton	Douglas	Clark	Reed	Burton	Jackson, R.
1953–1954	Warren	Black	Frankfurter	Minton	Douglas	Clark	Reed	Burton	Jackson, R.
1955	Warren	Black	Frankfurter	Minton	Douglas	Clark	Reed	Burton	Harlan (II)
1956	Warren	Black	Frankfurter	Brennan	Douglas	Clark	Reed	Burton	Harlan (II)
1957	Warren	Black	Frankfurter	Brennan	Douglas	Clark	Whittaker	Burton	Harlan (II)
1958–1961	Warren	Black	Frankfurter	Brennan	Douglas	Clark	Whittaker	Stewart	Harlan (II)
1962–1965	Warren	Black	Goldberg	Brennan	Douglas	Clark	White, B.	Stewart	Harlan (II)
1965–1967	Warren	Black	Fortas	Brennan	Douglas	Clark	White, B.	Stewart	Harlan (II)
1967–1969	Warren	Black	Fortas	Brennan	Douglas	Marshall, T.	White, B.	Stewart	Harlan (II)
1969	Burger	Black	Fortas	Brennan	Douglas	Marshall, T.	White, B.	Stewart	Harlan (II)
1969–1970	Burger	Black		Brennan	Douglas	Marshall, T.	White, B.	Stewart	Harlan (II)
1970–1971	Burger	Black	Blackmun	Brennan	Douglas	Marshall, T.	White, B.	Stewart	Harlan (II)
1971–1975	Burger	Powell	Blackmun	Brennan	Douglas	Marshall, T.	White, B.	Stewart	Rehnquist
1975–1981	Burger	Powell	Blackmun	Brennan	Stevens	Marshall, T.	White, B.	Stewart	Rehnquist
1981–1986	Burger	Powell	Blackmun	Brennan	Stevens	Marshall, T.	White, B.	O'Connor	Rehnquist
1986–1987	Rehnquist	Powell	Blackmun	Brennan	Stevens	Marshall, T.	White, B.	O'Connor	Scalia
1987	Rehnquist		Blackmun	Brennan	Stevens	Marshall, T.	White, B.	O'Connor	Scalia
1988–1990	Rehnquist	Kennedy	Blackmun	Brennan	Stevens	Marshall, T.	White, B.	O'Connor	Scalia
1990–1991	Rehnquist	Kennedy	Blackmun	Souter	Stevens	Marshall, T.	White, B.	O'Connor	Scalia
1991–1993	Rehnquist	Kennedy	Blackmun	Souter	Stevens	Thomas	White, B.	O'Connor	Scalia

APPENDIX A (Continued)

1993–1994	Rehnquist	Kennedy	Blackmun	Souter	Stevens	Thomas	Ginsburg	O'Connor	Scalia
1994–2005	Rehnquist	Kennedy	Breyer	Souter	Stevens	Thomas	Ginsburg	O'Connor	Scalia
2005	Roberts, J.	Kennedy	Breyer	Souter	Stevens	Thomas	Ginsburg	O'Connor	Scalia
2006–2009	Roberts, J.	Kennedy	Breyer	Souter	Stevens	Thomas	Ginsburg	Alito	Scalia
2009–2010	Roberts, J.	Kennedy	Breyer	Sotomayor	Stevens	Thomas	Ginsburg	Alito	Scalia
2010–2016	Roberts, J.	Kennedy	Breyer	Sotomayor	Kagan	Thomas	Ginsburg	Alito	Scalia
2017	Roberts, J.	Kennedy	Breyer	Sotomayor	Kagan	Thomas	Ginsburg	Alito	Gorsuch
2018–2019	Roberts, J.	Kavanaugh	Breyer	Sotomayor	Kagan	Thomas	Ginsburg	Alito	Gorsuch
2020	Roberts, J.	Kavanaugh	Breyer	Sotomayor	Kagan	Thomas	Barrett	Alito	Gorsuch

Note:

* A "natural court" or "discrete court" refers to the terms or part of a term during which the Supreme Court's membership is stable.

APPENDIX B

Presidents and Justices*

President	Justices Appointed	Years of Service	Age at Start of Term
Washington (F)		1789–1797	52
	Jay (F)**	1789–1795	43
	J. Rutledge (F)[@]	1789–1791	50
	Cushing (F)	1789–1810	57
	Wilson (F)	1789–1798	47
	Blair (F)	1789–1796	57
	Iredell (F)	1790–1799	38
	Johnson (F)	1791–1793	58
	Paterson (F)	1793–1806	47
	J. Rutledge (F)**	1795	55
	S. Chase (F)	1796–1811	54
	Ellsworth (F)**	1796–1800	50
Adams, J. (F)		1797–1801	61
	Washington (F)	1798–1829	36
	Moore (F)	1799–1804	44
	J. Marshall (F)**	1801–1835	45
Jefferson (DR)		1801–1809	57
	Johnson (DR)	1804–1834	32
	Livingston (DR)	1806–1823	49
	Todd (DR)	1807–1826	42
Madison (DR)		1809–1817	57
	Duval (DR)	1812–1835	58
	Story (DR)	1812–1845	32
Monroe (DR)		1817–1825	58
	Thompson (DR)	1823–1843	55
Adams, J. Q. (DR)		1825–1829	57
	Trimble (DR)	1826–1828	49
Jackson (D)		1829–1837	61
	McLean (D)	1829–1861	43
	Baldwin (D)	1830–1844	49
	Wayne (D)	1835–1867	45
	Taney (D)**	1836–1864	58
	Barbour (D)	1836–1841	52
	Catron (D)	1837–1865	51
Van Buren (D)		1837–1841	54
	McKinley (D)	1837–1852	57

APPENDIX B (Continued)

President	Justices Appointed	Years of Service	Age at Start of Term
	Daniel (D)	1841–1860	56
Harrison, W. (W)[#]		1841	68
Tyler (W)		1841–1845	50
	Nelson (W)	1845–1872	52
Polk (D)		1845–1849	49
	Woodbury (D)	1845–1851	56
	Grier (D)	1846–1870	52
Taylor (W)[#]		1849–1850	65
Fillmore (W)		1850–1853	50
	Curtis (W)	1851–1857	42
Pierce (D)		1853–1857	48
	Campbell (D)	1853–1861	41
Buchanan (D)		1857–1861	65
	Clifford (D)	1858–1881	54
Lincoln (R)		1861–1865	52
	Swayne (R)	1862–1881	57
	Miller (R)	1862–1890	46
	Davis (R)	1862–1877	47
	Field (D)	1863–1897	46
	S. P. Chase (R)**	1864–1873	56
Johnson, A. (D)[#]		1865–1869	56
Grant (R)		1869–1877	46
	Strong (R)	1870–1880	61
	Bradley (R)	1870–1892	56
	Hunt (R)	1872–1882	62
	Waite (R)**	1874–1888	57
Hayes (R)		1877–1881	54
	Harlan, I (A)[++]	1877–1911	44
	Woods (R)	1880–1887	56
Garfield (R)		1881	49
	Matthews (R)	1881–1889	56
Arthur (R)		1881–1885	50
	Gray (R)	1881–1902	53
	Blatchford (R)	1882–1893	62
Cleveland (D)		1885–1889	47
	Lamar (D)	1888–1893	62
	Fuller (D)**	1888–1910	55
Harrison, B (R)		1889–1893	55
	Brewer (R)	1889–1910	52
	Brown (R)	1891–1906	54
	Shiras (R)	1892–1903	60
	H. Jackson (D)	1893–1895	60
Cleveland (D)		1893–1897	55
	E. White (D)[@]	1894–1910	48

President	Justices Appointed	Years of Service	Age at Start of Term
	Peckham (D)	1896–1909	57
McKinley (R)		1897–1901	54
	McKenna (R)	1898–1925	54
Roosevelt, T. (R)		1901–1909	42
	Holmes	1902–1932	61
	Day (R)	1903–1922	53
	Moody (R)	1906–1910	52
Taft (R)		1909–1913	51
	Lurton (D)	1909–1914	65
	Hughes (R)@	1910–1916	48
	E. White+ (D)**	1910–1921	65
	Van Devanter (R)	1910–1937	51
	Lamar (D)	1910–1916	53
	Pitney (R)	1912–1922	54
Wilson (D)		1913–1921	56
	McReynolds (D)	1914–1941	52
	Brandeis (R)	1916–1939	59
	Clarke (D)	1916–1922	59
Harding (R)		1921–1923	55
	Taft (R)**	1921–1930	63
	Sutherland (R)	1922–1938	60
	Butler (D)	1922–1939	56
	Sanford (R)	1923–1930	57
Coolidge (A)		1923–1929	50
	Stone (R)@	1925–1941	52
Hoover (R)		1929–1933	54
	Hughes (R)**	1930–1941	68
	Roberts (R)	1930–1945	55
	Cardozo (D)	1932–1938	61
Roosevelt, F. (D)		1933–1945	51
	Black (D)	1937–1971	51
	Reed (D)	1938–1957	53
	Frankfurter (Ind)	1939–1962	56
	Douglas (D)	1939–1975	40
	Murphy (D)	1940–1949	49
	Byrnes (D)	1941–1942	62
	Stone+ (R)**	1941–1946	68
	R. Jackson (D)	1941–1954	49
	W. Rutledge (D)	1943–1949	48
Truman (D)		1945–1953	60
	Burton (R)	1945–1958	57
	Vinson (D)**	1946–1953	56
	Clark (D)	1949–1967	49
	Minton (D)	1949–1956	58

APPENDIX B (Continued)

President	Justices Appointed	Years of Service	Age at Start of Term
Eisenhower (R)		1953–1961	62
	Warren (R)**	1953–1969	62
	Harlan, II (R)++	1955–1971	55
	Brennan (D)	1956–1990	50
	Whittaker (R)	1957–1962	56
	Stewart (R)	1958–1981	43
Kennedy (D)		1961–1963	43
	B. White (D)	1962–1993	44
	Goldberg (D)	1962–1965	54
Johnson, L. (D)		1963–1969	55
	Fortas (D)	1965–1969	55
	T. Marshall (D)	1967–1991	58
Nixon (R)		1969–1974	56
	Burger (R)**	1969–1986	61
	Blackmun (R)	1970–1994	61
	Powell (D)	1971–1987	64
	Rehnquist (R)@	1971–1986	47
Ford (R)		1974–1977	61
	Stevens (R)	1975–2010	55
Carter (D)#		1977–1981	52
Reagan (R)		1981–1989	70
	O'Connor (R)	1981–2006	51
	Rehnquist+ (R)**	1986–2005	61
	Scalia (R)	1986–2016	50
	Kennedy (R)	1988–2018	51
Bush, G.H.W. (R)		1989–1993	64
	Souter (R)	1990–2009	51
	Thomas (R)	1991–	43
Clinton (D)		1993–2001	46
	Ginsburg (D)	1993–2020	60
	Breyer (D)	1994–	55
Bush, G. W. (R)		2001–2009	54
	Roberts, J. (R)**	2005–	50
	Alito (R)	2006–	55
Obama (D)		2009–2017	47
	Sotomayor (D)	2009–	55
	Kagan (D)	2010–	50
Trump (R)		2017–2021	70
	Gorsuch (R)	2017–	49
	Kavanaugh (R)	2018–	53
	Barrett (R)	2020–	48
Biden (D)		2021–	78

Notes:
* Letter following name indicates political party affiliation: (F), Federalist; (DR), Democratic-Republican; (D), Democrat; (W), Whig; (R), Republican; (Ind), Independent.
** Denotes appointment as chief justice.
@ Later appointed as chief justice.
§ Holding a recess appointment, John Rutledge presided over the Supreme Court at the August Term, 1795, but was denied confirmation by the Senate in December 1795.
# Indicates no appointments to Supreme Court.
++ John Marshall Harlan (I) was a grandfather of John Marshall Harlan (II) and is thus far the only justice to have had a lineal descendant who also became a justice.
+ Indicates appointment from associate to chief justice.

APPENDIX C

American Constitutional Development as Reflected in a Chronology of Cases Reprinted in This Book

Presidential Terms	Judicial Decisions	Constitutionally Significant Events
Washington (1789–1797)	*Chisholm* v. *Georgia* (1793) *Hylton* v. *United States* (1796)	Judiciary Act of 1789 allows Supreme Court review of some state court decisions; ratification of the Bill of Rights (Amendments 1–10) (1791); Congress charters the first Bank of the United States (1791); Eleventh Amendment (1798) overturns Chisholm
J. Adams (1797–1801)	*Calder* v. *Bull* (1798)	Alien and Sedition Acts (1798); Kentucky and Virginia Resolutions (1798–1799)
Jefferson (1801–1809)	*Marbury* v. *Madison* (1803)	First transfer of power from one political party to another; Louisiana Purchase (1803); Twelfth Amendment (1804); the Senate fails to remove Justice Samuel Chase from office in an impeachment trial Robert Fulton's *Clermont* steams between New York City and Albany (1807).
Madison (1809–1817)		First Bank of the United States expires (1811); War of 1812 (1812–1815); Second Bank of the United States chartered (1816)
Monroe (1817–1825)	*McCulloch* v. *Maryland* (1819) *Dartmouth College* v. *Woodward* (1819) *Cohens* v. *Virginia* (1821) *Gibbons* v. *Ogden* (1824) *Eakin* v. *Raub* (1825)	John C. Calhoun, Hugh S. Legare, and others champion doctrine of states' rights
J. Q. Adams (1825–1829)		With no candidate obtaining a majority of the electoral vote, the House of Representatives elects the president (1824). Some state constitutional conventions broaden franchise to include most white adult males
Jackson (1829–1837)	*Charles River Bridge* v. *Warren Bridge* (1837)	Second Bank of the United States expires (1836) Growth of abolitionist movement
Van Buren (1837–1841)		
W. Harrison (1841)		
Tyler (1841–1845)		Women's rights movement begins

Presidential Terms	Judicial Decisions	Constitutionally Significant Events
Polk (1845–1849)		Mexican War (1846–1848); publication of Karl Marx's *Communist Manifesto* (1848)
Taylor (1849–1850)		
Fillmore (1850–1853)	*Cooley* v. *Board of Wardens* (1851)	
Pierce (1853–1857)		
Buchanan (1857–1861)	*Dred Scott* v. *Sandford* (1857)	Publication of J. S. Mill's *On Liberty* (1859); South Carolina and six other southern states secede from the Union (1860–1861)
Lincoln (1861–1865)		Southern troops fire on Fort Sumter in Charleston harbor; an additional four states secede (1861); Civil War (1861–1865); Emancipation Proclamation (1863); Lincoln assassinated (1865)
A. Johnson (1865–1869)	Ex parte *Milligan* (1866) Ex parte *McCardle* (1869) *Collector* v. *Day* (1871)	Reconstruction (1865–1877); Thirteenth Amendment (1865); Fourteenth Amendment (1868)
Grant (1869–1877)	Slaughterhouse Cases (1873) *Munn* v. *Illinois* (1877)	Transcontinental railroad completed (1869); Fifteenth Amendment (1870); special presidential election commission resolves Hayes-Tilden electoral vote dispute (1877)
Hayes (1877–1881)		American Bar Association organizes (1878); growing influence of laissez-faire economic theory and social Darwinism
Garfield (1881)		Assassination of Garfield pushes Congress to enact civil service reform
Arthur (1881–1885)	*Civil Rights Cases* (1883)	Growth of large corporations; development of Populism
Cleveland (1885–1889)		Samuel Gompers organizes the American Federation of Labor (1886); creation of the Interstate Commerce Commission (1887)
B. Harrison (1889–1893)		
Cleveland (1893–1897)	*United States* v. *E. C. Knight Co.* (1895) *Pollock* v. *Farmers' Loan & Trust Co.* (1895)	
McKinley (1897–1901)	*Plessy* v. *Ferguson* (1896)	War with Spain (1898); acquisition of territories previously belonging to Spain; McKinley assassinated (1901)
T. Roosevelt (1901–1909)	*Champion* v. *Ames* (1903) *McCray* v. *United States* (1904) *Lochner* v. *New York* (1905)	Rise of Progressivism; muckraking era; "Brandeis brief"

APPENDIX C (Continued)

Presidential Terms	Judicial Decisions	Constitutionally Significant Events
Taft (1909–1913)		
Wilson (1913–1921)	*Hammer* v. *Dagenhart* (1918) *Schenck* v. *United States* (1919) *Missouri* v. *Holland* (1920)	Establishment of the Federal Reserve System (1913); Sixteenth and Seventeenth Amendments (1913); World War I (U.S. involvement, 1917–1918); Eighteenth Amendment (1919) ushers in Prohibition era; Nineteenth Amendment (1920); "Palmer raids" (1919–1920)
Harding (1921–1923)	*Stafford* v. *Wallace* (1922) *Bailey* v. *Drexel Furniture Co.* (1922)	
Coolidge (1923–1929)	*Gitlow* v. *New York* (1925) *Myers* v. *United States* (1926) *Whitney* v. *California* (1927) *Olmstead* v. *United States* (1928)	
Hoover (1929–1933)	*Powell* v. *Alabama* (1932)	Onset of Great Depression (1929); Senate rejects nomination of John Parker to the Supreme Court; Twentieth Amendment (1933)
F. Roosevelt (1933–1945)	*Nebbia* v. *New York* (1934) *Home Bldg. & Loan Assoc.* v. *Blaisdell* (1934) *Humphrey's Executor* v. *United States* (1935) *United States* v. *Butler* (1936) *Carter* v. *Carter Coal Co.* (1936)	New Deal agenda in Congress; Twenty-First Amendment (1933) ends Prohibition
	N.L.R.B. v. *Jones & Laughlin* (1937) *West Coast Hotel* v. *Parrish* (1937) *Palko* v. *Connecticut* (1937) *Minersville School District* v. *Gobitis* (1940) *Wickard* v. *Filburn* (1941)	Court-packing fight (1937); Supreme Court's "switch-in-time"
	Ex parte *Quirin* (1942) *West Virginia Board of Education* v. *Barnette* (1943) *Korematsu* v. *United States* (1944)	World War II (U.S. involvement, 1941–1945); United States drops two atomic bombs on Japan (1945)
Truman (1945–1953)	*Southern Pacific* v. *Arizona* (1945)	

Presidential Terms	Judicial Decisions	Constitutionally Significant Events
	Adamson v. *California* (1947)	
	Dennis v. *United States* (1951)	
	Youngstown v. *Sawyer* (1952)	Cold War begins (1946); Employment Act of 1946; Americans for Democratic Action organized (1947); Democratic National Convention adopts strong civil rights plank (1948); modern civil rights movement develops; NATO established (1949); Korean War (1950–1953); height of influence of Senator Joseph McCarthy (1950–1954); Twenty-Second Amendment (1951)
Eisenhower (1953–1961)	*Brown* v. *Board of Education (I)* (1954)	
	Bolling v. *Sharpe* (1954)	
	Brown v. *Board of Education (II)* (1955)	
	Watkins v. *United States* (1957)	Civil rights movement intensifies in the wake of the Court's school integration decisions in 1954 and 1955; massive resistance to school integration begins in some southern states
	Cooper v. *Aaron* (1958)	
	Barenblatt v. *United States* (1959)	Congress enacts the first civil rights law since 1875 (1957)
Kennedy (1961–1963)	*Mapp* v. *Ohio* (1961)	
	Baker v. *Carr* (1962)	
	Ferguson v. *Skrupa* (1963)	
	Sherbert v. *Verner* (1963)	
	Gideon v. *Wainwright* (1963)	Twenty-Third Amendment (1963); U.S. commits ground forces in Vietnam; "March on Washington" for civil rights (1963); John F. Kennedy assassinated (1963)
L. Johnson (1963–1969)	*Reynolds* v. *Sims* (1964)	Great Society agenda (1964–1968); Twenty-Fourth Amendment (1964); Congress passes comprehensive Civil Rights Act (1964); conservatives seize control of Republican Party and nominate Barry Goldwater for president (1964); commitment of U.S. troops in Vietnam escalates (1964–1965); Voting Rights Act passed (1965); Twenty-Fifth Amendment (1967); Senate fails to approve nomination of Justice Abe Fortas for chief justice; Republican candidate Richard Nixon campaigns against the Supreme Court (1968)
	New York Times Co. v. *Sullivan* (1964)	
	Heart of Atlanta Motel v. *United States* (1964)	
	Katzenbach v. *McClung* (1964)	
	Griswold v. *Connecticut* (1965)	
	Miranda v. *Arizona* (1966)	
	Loving v. *Virginia* (1967)	
	Katz v. *United States* (1967)	
	Terry v. *Ohio* (1968)	

APPENDIX C (Continued)

Presidential Terms	Judicial Decisions	Constitutionally Significant Events
	Duncan v. *Louisiana* (1968) *United States* v. *O'Brien* (1968)	
Nixon (1969–1974)	*Shapiro* v. *Thompson* (1969) *Brandenburg* v. *Ohio* (1969) *Chimel* v. *California* (1969) *New York Times Co.* v. *United States* (1971) *Lemon* v. *Kurtzman* (1971) *United States* v. *U.S. District Court* (1972) *Frontiero* v. *Richardson* (1973) *Roe* v. *Wade* (1973) *San Antonio School District* v. *Rodriguez* (1973) *United States* v. *Nixon* (1974)	Justice Fortas resigns under fire (1969); Senate rejects Supreme Court nominations of J. Clement Haynsworth and Harrold Carswell (1969–1970); Twenty-Sixth Amendment (1971); Equal Rights Amendment proposed (1972); Vice President Agnew resigns and Gerald Ford is chosen vice president under Twenty-Fifth Amendment (1973); War Powers Resolution (1973); U.S. involvement in Vietnam ends (1973); Watergate scandal leads to Nixon's resignation (1974)
Ford (1974–1977)	*Craig* v. *Boren* (1976) *Gregg* v. *Georgia* (1976)	Ford pardons Nixon (1974); Congress imposes limits on campaign contributions, introduces federal financing of presidential campaigns, and creates the Federal Election Commission (1974)
Carter (1977–1981)	*Philadelphia* v. *New Jersey* (1978)	
Reagan (1981–1987)	*Nixon* v. *Fitzgerald* (1982)	Sandra Day O'Connor becomes first female justice (1981) Ratification of Equal Rights Amendment fails (1982)
	Mississippi University for Women v. *Hogan* (1982)	
	I.N.S. v. *Chadha* (1983) *United States* v. *Leon* (1984) *Cleburne* v. *Cleburne Living Center* (1985) *South Dakota* v. *Dole* (1987) *Morrison* v. *Olson* (1987) *McCleskey* v. *Kemp* (1987)	Senate rejects nomination of Robert Bork (1987)

Presidential Terms	Judicial Decisions	Constitutionally Significant Events
Bush, G. H. W. (1989–1993)	*Mistretta* v. *United States* (1989)	Cold War ends (1990)
	Texas v. *Johnson* (1989)	
	Employment Division v. *Smith* (1990)	War with Iraq (I) (1991)
	California v. *Acevedo* (1991)	Twenty-Seventh Amendment (the "lost amendment") (1992); fourteen states impose term limits on state and national legislators in 1992
	Planned Parenthood v. *Casey* (1992)	
Clinton (1993–2001)	*U.S. Term Limits* v. *Thornton* (1995)	Seven additional states enact congressional term limits (1994); Republicans take control of both houses of Congress for the first time in 40 years (1995); Supreme Court blocks state limits on congressional terms (1995)
	United States v. *Lopez* (1995)	
	Miller v. *Johnson* (1995)	
	Romer v. *Evans* (1996)	
	City of Boerne v. *Flores* (1997)	
	Clinton v. *Jones* (1997)	
	Agostini v. *Felton* (1997)	
	Minnesota v. *Carter* (1998)	
	Clinton v. *City of New York* (1998)	A limited, statutorily conferred item veto power for the president takes effect (1997); Supreme Court invalidates item veto (1998)
	Dickerson v. *United States* (2000)	House of Representatives impeaches President Clinton (1998); Senate tries and acquits the president (1999)
	California Democratic Party v. *Jones* (2000)	United States leads NATO attack on Serbia (1999)
	United States v. *Morrison* (2000)	Federal judge holds President Clinton in contempt and imposes fine because of false testimony in Jones deposition (1999)
	Boy Scouts of America v. *Dale* (2000)	
	Bush v. *Gore* (2000)	Vermont Supreme Court holds that same-sex couples are entitled to marry or to enter into marriage-equivalency unions (1999); Vermont legislature enacts provision for latter (2000); Supreme Court stops Florida hand recount and effectively picks the 43rd president of the United States
Bush, G. W. (2001–2009)	*Atwater* v. *City of Lago Vista* (2001)	Controversy over 2000 presidential election focuses attention on the variation in voting practices among the states

APPENDIX C (Continued)

Presidential Terms	Judicial Decisions	Constitutionally Significant Events
	Good News Club v. *Milford Central School* (2001)	Attacks on the United States on September 11, 2001, prompt a war on terrorism; United States invades Afghanistan; Congress passes Patriot Act (2001)
		Congress enacts major overhaul of campaign finance legislation (2002)
	Board of Education v. *Earls* (2002)	
	Zelman v. *Simmons-Harris* (2002)	
	Virginia v. *Black* (2003)	War with Iraq (II) (2003), followed by a protracted and dangerous occupation (2003–)
	Lawrence v. *Texas* (2003)	
	McConnell v. *F.E.C.* (2003) *Kelo* v. *City of New London* (2005)	Supreme Judicial Court of Massachusetts invalidates its state's ban on same-sex marriage (2003); Supreme Court rules in first cases stemming from war on terrorism (2004–); Congress extends Patriot Act (2006)
	Parents Involved v. *Seattle Sch. Dist.* (2007)	Recession is worst economic downturn since Great Depression. Financial crisis prompts unprecedented intervention by federal government
	Dist. of Columbia v. *Heller* (2008)	Sonia Sotomayor becomes first Latina justice (2009)
	Boumediene v. *Bush* (2008)	
Obama (2009–2017)	*Citizens United* v. *FEC* (2010)	Health legislation enacted. ISIL emerges as terrorist threat
	McDonald v. *Chicago* (2010)	Freedom Act replaces Patriot Act (2015)
	U.S. v. *Jones* (2012)	
	National Federation v. *Sebelius* (2012)	
	Greece v. *Galloway* (2014)	
	Riley v. *California* (2014)	
	Walker v. *Sons* (2015)	
	Obergefell v. *Hodges* (2015)	
	Fisher v. *Univ. of Texas* (2016)	
Trump	*Trump* v. *Hawaii* (2018)	#MeToo movement against sexual harassment and abuse emerges

Presidential Terms	Judicial Decisions	Constitutionally Significant Events
(2017–2021)	*Masterpiece Cakeshop* v. *Colo. Civil Rights Comm.* (2018) *South Dakota* v. *Wayfair, Inc.* (2018) *Janus* v. *AFSCME* (2018) *American Legion* v. *American Humanist Assn.* (2019) *Timbs* v. *Indiana* (2019) *Rucho* v. *Common Cause* (2019) *Chiafalo* v. *Washington* (2020) *Espinoza* v. *Montana Dept. of Revenue* (2020)	President Trump impeached on two counts (abuse of power and obstruction of Congress) by House in December 2019 and acquitted on both counts by Senate in February 2020
	June Medical Services v. *Russo* (2020) *Trump* v. *Mazars USA* (2020)	Congress fails to reauthorize Freedom Act
	Trump v. *Vance* (2020) *Roman Cath. Diocese of Brooklyn* v. *Cuomo* (2020)	Killing of George Floyd and other people of color by police highlights persisting racism in law enforcement COVID-19 pandemic sweeps through United States. Supreme Court verbally attacked by both Trump and some Democrats In an unusual challenge to civic norms, President Trump and many supporters, alleging widespread fraud, refuse to accept outcome of 2020 election. Associated Press tallies some 50 lawsuits challenging results that are either dismissed or dropped, including eventually three rebuffs at Supreme Court; remarks by President Donald Trump to distraught supporters at a "Stop the Steal" rally on the Ellipse on January 6, 2021, are quickly followed by a deadly rampage and physical breach of the United States Capitol—an assault that delayed by nearly 12 hours completion of the congressional count and certification of the electoral vote and the official end of the 2020 presidential election. On January 13, House impeaches Trump for inciting an insurrection. On February 13, after a trial where the chief justice declined to preside, the Senate vote of 57–43 fell short of the margin needed to convict the former president.
Biden (2021–)		

GLOSSARY

#MeToo movement hashtag from social media denoting an undertaking against sexual harassment and abuse, especially when perpetrated by persons of prominence and/or those in positions of power

absolute approach a view of the First Amendment associated particularly with Justice Hugo Black that tolerates no government restrictions on freedom of speech or press

absolute immunity protection from all suits for damages

accommodation one of the early ways of thinking about the proper relationship between government and religion in the United States; allows government acknowledgement of and support for religion

administrative searches category of searches where the objective is not enforcement of the criminal law; conducted under relaxed Fourth Amendment standards; see special need

advisory opinion statement by a judge or other legal officer about a hypothetical situation indicating how a court would rule were litigation to develop

affirmative action policies designed to benefit groups previously the targets of discrimination

affirming accepting or approving the decision by a lower court

Agostini test originated in *Agostini* v. *Felton* (1997); made a significant change in the Lemon test in determining whether government has violated the establishment clause; a challenged policy must have a secular purpose and a neutral effect; a policy has the impermissible effect of advancing religion if it (a) results in indoctrination of religion by government; (b) defines its recipients or beneficiaries according to religion; *or* (c) creates an excessive entanglement between government and religion

al Qaeda international terrorist organization that plotted and executed the attacks on the United States on September 11, 2001; see Islamic State

amicus (or amici) curiae literally friend (or friends) of the court; individuals, governments, or organizations not themselves parties to a case but interested in how a case will be decided

Antifederalists in the 1780s, opponents of ratification of the Constitution and a strong central government

antinomy tension or conflict between two principles or concepts

appeal generally to request a higher court to review the decision of a lower court; more specifically a part of the Supreme Court's appellate jurisdiction that is obligatory, as opposed to certiorari, which is discretionary

appellant in the narrow category of cases on appeal, the party bringing the case against the appellee

appellate jurisdiction includes cases a court receives from lower courts; the appellate jurisdiction of the Supreme Court is defined by Congress

appellee in the narrow category of cases on appeal, the party against whom a case is brought by the appellant

arraignment stage in the criminal justice process where the accused person appears before a judge to learn the nature of the charges and to enter a plea of guilty or not guilty

Article I courts also called legislative courts; established by Congress under its delegated powers in Article I in the Constitution, as opposed to its powers in Article III; Congress has greater control over the salary and tenure of judges on Article I courts

Article III courts also called constitutional courts; established by Congress under its powers in Article III in the Constitution, as opposed to its powers in Article I

Articles of Confederation first plan of national government for the 13 American states, approved in 1781 and replaced in 1788 by the Constitution; under the Articles, the states retained the bulk of political power

Ashwander rules guidelines laid out in *Ashwander* v. *TVA* (1936) suggesting when the Supreme Court will consider the constitutionality of legislative and executive actions

attitudinal model theory of judicial decision making that emphasizes the importance of a judge's values and ideology

Authorization for Use of Military Force (AUMF) passed by Congress in 2001, the principal congressional authorization for the war on terrorism

bad tendency test as applied in cases like *Gitlow* v. *New York* (1925), the most restrictive standard used in determining the boundaries of permissible speech; allows suppression of speech if the ideas expressed might lead to an evil result

balkanization situation arising from a combination of varying state regulations of commerce that raise barriers to trade among the states; term derives from the Balkan Peninsula in Europe, where the region is divided into several small countries

Bipartisan Campaign Reform Act (BCRA) significant modification in 2002 to the Federal Election Campaign Act that raised contribution limits but banned soft money contributions and certain types of issue ads and electioneering communications within a specified period prior to elections and primaries for federal office; upheld in *McConnell* v. *FEC* (2003) and partly invalidated in *Citizens United* v. *FEC* (2010)

Blaine amendment Provision in many state constitutions prohibiting use of public funds for religious purposes; named for Representative James G. Blaine of Maine, who as House speaker unsuccessfully pushed a similar amendment for the U.S. Constitution in the late nineteenth century

blanket primary party election where voters may select a candidate from any party for each office

Brady rule refers to *Brady* v. *Maryland* (1963), in which the Supreme Court held that the prosecution is obliged to share exculpatory evidence with the defense; reinforced by Due Process Act of 2020

Brandeis brief named for attorney (and later Justice) Louis D. Brandeis, describing a legal brief heavy on statistics and light on legal argument

briefing a case preparing an outline of a case in a particular format

briefs written arguments in a case that are submitted to a court

case or controversy requirement that a case represent a real, not hypothetical conflict between parties who have adverse interests

cases disputes handled by a court and so the raw material for the judicial process

certiorari Latin for "to make sure," the term refers to the category of the Supreme Court's appellate jurisdiction that is discretionary, as opposed to the appeal category, which is obligatory

cert pool labor-saving device; petitions for certiorari are first examined by a law clerk in one of the chambers who then prepares a memorandum on the case with a recommendation on whether to grant or deny review; that memorandum is then circulated to the other chambers; participation by a justice is optional

checks and balances as established for the national government by the Constitution, the system of separate institutions sharing some powers, with the purpose of keeping any one of the three branches of government from becoming too powerful

child-benefit theory application of the establishment clause in cases challenging government support for religious schools, which emphasizes the primary beneficiaries of the program, where benefits flow to those beneficiaries as a result of choices made by parents and their children

chilling effect situation where fear of possible prosecution deters people from engaging in expression that the Constitution allows

circuit riding duty of Supreme Court justices until 1891 to sit as judges on circuit courts in designated areas of the United States

civil liberty guaranty in law against unwarranted government intrusion into one's life or unwarranted government restriction of one's activities

civil right legally protected freedom to participate in society and the political system on an equal footing with others

Civil Rights Act of 1964 most comprehensive civil rights legislation ever passed by Congress, affecting voting, public accommodations, and the workplace

clear-and-present-danger test originated by Justice Holmes in *Schenck* v. *United States* (1919), a measure of freedom of speech that allows suppression only when the speech is likely to produce substantive evils that government has a right to prevent; less protective of speech than the incitement test but more protective of speech than the bad tendency test

coercion test interpretation of the establishment clause that bars government policies that oblige anyone to support a religion or to participate in a religious exercise

commercial speech expression such as advertisements that relate solely to the economic interest of the speaker and the speaker's audience

compensatory damages in tort law, awards to plaintiffs to compensate them for damages and loss because of something the defendant has done; contrasted to punitive damages

concurrent commerce doctrine interpretation of the commerce clause that allows states to regulate commerce in the absence of federal legislation

concurrent powers governing authority shared by both state and national governments

concurring opinion statement filed by a judge indicating acceptance of the court's decision but either an unwillingness to accept all of the opinion of the court or a desire to say something additional; also see regular concurrence and special concurrence

conditional spending policy embedded in congressional appropriations whereby the recipient of federal appropriations must abide by the conditions attached to those funds

conference in the Supreme Court, time set aside for discussion and decision of argued cases as well as decision on which cases to accept for review

confrontation clause part of the Sixth Amendment ordinarily requiring that witnesses against an accused person be present in court so that they may be cross-examined by defense counsel

Congressional Review Act enacted in 1996 and allows agency regulations to be negated by a joint congressional resolution of disapproval that itself is subject to presidential veto; partial and ineffective substitution for the legislative veto

constitutional interpretation the judicial process of giving meaning to words in a constitution

constitutionalism belief in limited government under a written charter

constitutional law the prevailing meaning of the U.S. Constitution, or a state constitution, as found mainly in decisions by the U.S. Supreme Court or a state supreme court.

Constitutional Revolution of 1937 response of the Supreme Court to the Court-packing plan in which the Court made significant changes to interpretation of the commerce and due process clauses, allowing legislation to stand that hitherto had been constitutionally suspect

constitutional theory a view of presidential power by which presidents must be able to justify their actions based on powers either expressly conferred or implied by the Constitution

contract clause restriction in Article I, Section 10 of the Constitution forbidding any state from "impairing the obligation of contracts"

Cooley doctrine see selective exclusiveness

countermajoritarian difficulty the apparent contradiction presented when *unelected* judges use the power of judicial review to nullify the actions of *elected* legislators or executives

Court-packing plan failed attempt by President Franklin Roosevelt in 1937 to enlarge the size of the Supreme Court in order to produce a bench more receptive to New Deal programs

criminal syndicalism belief in violence to accomplish social and political reform

de facto segregation racial segregation that results not from government policy or laws but from a combination of private discrimination and private choice; not forbidden by the Constitution

Defense of Marriage Act (DOMA) passed by Congress in 1996, providing that no state shall be required to give effect to the law of any other state with respect to same-sex marriage; for purposes of federal law defines "marriage" to mean "only a legal union between one man and one woman" and the word "spouse" to refer "only to a person of the opposite sex who is a husband or a wife"; invalidated on Fifth Amendment grounds by *United States* v. *Windsor* (2013)

de jure segregation racial segregation that is required or encouraged by law or public policy; forbidden by the Constitution

delegated powers the governing authority assigned to the national government by the Constitution

delegation the sharing by Congress of rule-making authority with administrative agencies

destructive tax extreme regulatory tax designed to destroy the entity being taxed

direct appeal provision for a narrow category of cases that allows an appeal to the Supreme Court from a decision by a three-judge district court, bypassing the court of appeals

direct taxes according to Article I, section 9 of the Constitution, a tax imposed by Congress that must be apportioned among the states by population, a limitation overcome by the Sixteenth Amendment (1913)

direct versus indirect effects approach to commerce clause interpretation by the Supreme Court prior to 1937, by which only conditions that directly affected interstate commerce lay within the legitimate powers of Congress

dissent statement filed by a member of a court in a case explaining why the majority of the court is incorrect

diversity jurisdiction allows cases ordinarily heard in state court to be tried in federal court when the parties are citizens of different states and when the dollar amount in dispute is more than $75,000

docket a court's caseload or a list of cases awaiting action by a court; also see shadow docket

dormant commerce power restraint imposed on the states by the commerce clause even in the absence of national legislation

double standard product of the fair trial rule; because states initially were required by the Fourteenth Amendment only to assure those rights essential to a fair trial, the national government, being limited by all provisions of the Bill of Rights encountered a greater list of restrictions than did state governments; hence prior to the 1960s, a double standard prevailed because a defendant's federally protected constitutional rights were typically greater in federal than in state court

dual federalism legal doctrine closely associated with Chief Justice Roger Taney, whereby the states and central government confronted each other as equals across a precise constitutional boundary dividing their respective spheres of power

dual school system public school system marked by significant numbers of one-race schools; opposite of unitary school system

due process limitation on government found in both the Fifth and Fourteenth Amendments that protects both procedural and substantive rights of individuals

due process of law see due process

due process revolution refers to a series of sweeping decisions by the Supreme Court on criminal justice between 1961 and 1969 that redefined federal constitutional restrictions on both state and federal governments mainly in favor of persons accused of crimes; see Warren Court

Eighth Amendment part of the Bill of Rights dating from 1791 that protects against excessive bail and fines and cruel and unusual punishments

Eleventh Amendment ratified in 1798, the first amendment to the Constitution to reverse a decision by the Supreme Court (*Chisholm* v. *Georgia* [1793]), denying federal court jurisdiction in suits against a state brought by a citizen of another state or a foreign country

eminent domain authority inherent in both state and federal governments to seize private property for public use following payment of just compensation as dictated by the Fifth Amendment

endorsement test interpretation of the establishment clause that bars government policies that appear to endorse religion or favor one religion over another

enemy combatants in the context of the war on terrorism, persons alleged to be part of or supporting forces hostile to the United States; those deemed unlawful enemy combatants are denied the privileges possessed by prisoners of war

enrollment process occurs after a bill or joint resolution has passed both houses of Congress in identical form. It is printed on parchment paper, signed by appropriate House and Senate officials, and submitted to the president for signature

entitlements government benefits that one is eligible to receive by law

enumerated powers the governing authority of the national government as found in the text of the Constitution

equality of condition view of equality that expects government to reduce or eliminate social and economic handicaps that many people encounter

equality of opportunity view of equality whereby government is expected to remove discriminatory barriers so that all may participate

equality of result view of equality that expects government to compensate for lingering effects of inequality by assuring equal outcomes

equal protection clause provision in the Fourteenth Amendment dating from 1868 commanding that no state deny to any person "the equal protection of the laws"

establishment clause part of the First Amendment dating from 1791 that proscribes laws "respecting an establishment of religion"

exclusion power of Congress to bar members from taking their seats

exclusionary rule judicial policy originating in *Weeks* v. *United States* (1914) whereby evidence obtained illegally by police may be suppressed or excluded from trial; applied to the states by *Mapp* v. *Ohio* (1961) with a good-faith exception in certain circumstances added by *United States* v. *Leon* (1984)

exclusive commerce doctrine interpretation of the commerce clause that allows regulation of commerce only by the national government

exclusive powers governing authority of the national government that is denied to the states

executive agreement concord between heads of state that, unlike a treaty, does not require approval by the Senate, there being no clear legal distinctions between the substance of a treaty and that of an executive agreement

executive order legally binding directive issued by the president, acting as the head of the executive branch, to persons or entities in or subject to the administration; while Congress may attempt through legislation to countermand an executive order, any such bill would itself be subject to a presidential veto; those adversely affected by an executive order may seek to challenge it judicially

executive privilege the right of certain officials in the executive branch to refuse to appear before Congress or a court and/or to produce requested materials

ex post facto laws generally retroactive laws, but within the meaning of Article I, Section 10 of the Constitution, includes only retroactive penal laws, so that all ex post facto laws are retroactive, but not all retroactive laws are ex post facto laws

expressive association conveying of a message or particular outlook through the act of association or organization; considered a right protected by the First Amendment

express powers those powers specifically delegated to the national government

expulsion power of Congress to expel members as a penalty for serious misconduct

fair trial rule interpretation of the Fourteenth Amendment that did not require states in the operation of their criminal justice systems to adhere to all procedural protections in the Bill of Rights but only to assure that a defendant received a "fair trial"; see double standard

faith-based exemption typical question in cases under the free exercise clause as to whether religious adherents will be excused from obedience to a law of general application

faithless elector a presidential elector who votes for someone other than the candidate for president and vice president who received the most votes in the elector's state or (for Maine and Nebraska) congressional district; also called a wayward elector

federal courts the courts of the United States, as opposed to the courts of the 50 states

Federal Election Campaign Act (FECA) amendments in 1974 created today's system of publicly financed presidential elections and imposed limits on campaign contributions; except for limits on expenditures, the act was upheld in *Buckley* v. *Valeo* (1976); see Bipartisan Campaign Reform Act (BCRA)

federalism division of political powers between a central and regional governments such as states or provinces, with both levels of government acting directly on the people

federal question issue involving the meaning of the U.S. Constitution, an act of Congress, or a treaty of the United States

Fifth Amendment provision in the Bill of Rights dating from 1791 that protects the right against compelled self-incrimination and the right against double jeopardy, among other safeguards

fighting words vituperative language likely to provoke a confrontation or other disturbance

First Amendment provision in the Bill of Rights dating from 1791 that specifies rights of religion, speech, press, assembly, and petition

Footnote Four appeared in *United States* v. *Carolene Products Co.* (1938) following the Constitutional Revolution of 1937, suggesting an enlarged judicial role for the protection of nonproprietarian civil liberties and civil rights

Foreign Intelligence Court of Review one of two courts created by the Foreign Intelligence Surveillance Act, it hears appeals by the government from the Foreign Intelligence Surveillance Court

Foreign Intelligence Surveillance Act passed in 1978, the statute (FISA) established the Foreign Intelligence Surveillance Court and the Foreign Intelligence Court of Review, and established the conditions for searches and electronic surveillance of U.S. persons believed to be acting on behalf of a foreign power, a foreign power, or an agent of a foreign power

Foreign Intelligence Surveillance Court one of two courts created by the Foreign Intelligence Surveillance Act; it hears requests by the executive branch for warrants to conduct secret searches and electronic surveillance of those covered by the act

Fourth Amendment provision in the Bill of Rights dating from 1791 that protects the people against "unreasonable searches and seizures"

franchise the right or privilege of voting

Freedom Act substantial modification and extension (through 2019) of the Patriot Act

free exercise clause part of the First Amendment dating from 1791 that protects the "free exercise of religion"; protects the freedom of religious practice

free government term employed by some of the American Founders to describe the combined intricate political arrangements of separation of powers and federalism

frisk permissible limited warrantless search (pat-down) of an individual for weapons by police under the conditions outlined in *Terry* v. *Ohio* (1968) and other cases; see reasonable suspicion

fundamental rights analysis use of the equal protection clause and strict scrutiny to protect rights the Supreme Court deems fundamental

gerrymandering legislative districting that deliberately enhances or diminishes the political strength of a political party or other group

governmental immunity view of federalism whereby state governments may not interfere with the operation of the national government

government speech expression that occurs when a municipality, state, or federal authority conveys messages; recognized as a significant category of speech that allows the official entity to favor viewpoints in ways otherwise prohibited by the First Amendment

grandfather clause voting requirement stipulating that a person's grandfather or other relative had to have been eligible to vote at a certain date; an element of the Jim Crow system deployed to prevent blacks from voting in the post–Civil War South

guarantee (or guaranty) clause provision in Article IV, Section 4 of the Constitution stipulating that the national government shall guarantee to each state a "Republican Form of Government"

habeas corpus Latin for "you have the body"; also called the "great writ"; a legal pleading, referenced in Article I, Section 9, Paragraph 2 of the Constitution that allows individuals to challenge the lawfulness of their imprisonment

Hamiltonian theory Alexander Hamilton's view of the spending power of Congress as a substantive independent power that allows appropriations for purposes beyond those suggested by Congress' enumerated powers

hard money financial contributions to parties, groups, or candidates that are regulated by federal law

hearsay secondhand information that is usually disallowed in court in favor of what the witness has heard or observed

Hyde Amendment so named for former Representative Henry Hyde of Illinois, it bars the expenditure of Medicaid funds on most abortions

implied contracts legally binding agreements inferred from, although not explicitly contained in, the terms of a written contract

implied powers derived from Article I, Section 8, Clause 18 of the Constitution (the necessary and proper, or elastic, clause), the discretionary governing authority of the national government to give effect to powers specifically granted; see necessary and proper clause

incitement test as applied in cases like *Brandenburg* v. *Ohio* (1969), the Supreme Court's broadest protection for freedom of speech, where speech may be suppressed only when it is very likely to provoke imminent lawless action

incorporation process by which the Supreme Court interpreted the due process clause of the Fourteenth Amendment to encompass almost all of the provisions of the Bill of Rights, thus bringing them to bear on state governments and their municipalities

independent constitutional bar a check on the taxing and spending power of Congress apart from any imposed by the text of the Constitution

independent counsel a type of special prosecutor provided by the now-expired Ethics in Government Act of 1978 to investigate and prosecute wrongdoing by high officials in the executive branch

indirect taxes levies imposed by Congress that are not subject to the apportionment requirement of direct taxes

informational privacy the right to control access to, and dissemination of, information about oneself

intermediate scrutiny middle level of scrutiny under the equal protection clause whereby the challenged statute is expected to have a close or substantial relation to an important government interest

Islamic State also known as ISIS or ISIL; displaced al Qaeda as principal instigator or inspiration for terrorist attacks in Europe and North America

item veto a provision found in some state constitutions allowing the executive to negate parts of appropriation bills

judicial activists judges more inclined than others to intervene in legal disputes and to substitute their views for those of other policymakers

judicial federalism relationships and interactions between state and federal courts

judicial restraintists judges less inclined than others to intervene in legal disputes and more inclined to defer to decisions made by other policymakers

judicial review the authority of courts to invalidate legislative or executive measures or actions as being in conflict with the Constitution

jurisdiction the authority of a court to hear a case with respect to the parties and the subject matter; the term may also refer to the geographical area in which that authority is exercised

just compensation stipulation in the takings clause of the Fifth Amendment that, when property is seized through the power of eminent domain, just compensation be paid to the owner

law clerks usually recent law school graduates who are legal assistants for judges; in the Supreme Court, most justices annually employ four law clerks

legal model theory of judicial decision making that emphasizes the influence of legal text and precedent

legislative apportionment generally the arrangement determining the distribution of seats in a legislative chamber; specifically, the allocation of seats in the U.S. House of Representatives among the states following each decennial census

legislative districting the drawing of district lines for representational purposes

legislative veto provision added to legislation allowing Congress to negate an executive initiative or rule by vote of one or two houses of Congress or even by committee vote; invalidated by the Supreme Court in *Immigration and Naturalization Service* v. *Chadha* (1983)

Lemon test originated in *Lemon* v. *Kurtzman* (1971) as a way of determining whether government has violated the establishment clause; challenged policies must have a secular purpose, an effect that neither advances nor hinders religion, and must not foster an excessive entanglement between government and religion

libel written defamation of character

liberty of contract important legal doctrine in Supreme Court decisions between 1897 and 1937 that guaranteed each person the freedom to enter into contracts without undue government interference

living wills legal documents that set the terms for the withdrawal or withholding of life-sustaining treatment for patients with incurable conditions or in situations where they are incapable of making decisions about their medical treatment

Madisonian theory James Madison's view of the spending power of Congress as an appendage of Congress' enumerated powers, not an independent or substantive power, thus limiting appropriations to those furthering enumerated powers

magistrate judges federal trial judges appointed by judges of U.S. district courts for a renewable term of eight years; these officers issue search warrants, conduct arraignments, and perform other tasks assigned by the district judges; position established by Congress in 1968 to replace the office of commissioner, which had been part of the federal judiciary since the 1790s

majority opinion see opinion of the court

majority–minority districts legislative districting plan where a racial minority constitutes the majority in the districts

martial law usually temporary rule by military authorities over a civilian population when regular law enforcement and the judicial process are not operating normally; entails a suspension of civil liberties and constitutionally prescribed procedures

Medicaid health care program set up in 1965 for people with low incomes that is jointly funded by the state and federal governments and administered by the states; in *National Federation of Independent Business*

v. *Sebelius* (2012), discussed and reprinted in Chapter Six, the Court invalidated the Affordable Care Act's expansion of Medicaid as an improper use of the spending power because it coerced the states into an expansion of Medicaid at the risk of losing federal Medicaid funding entirely

***Miranda* warnings** series of advisories, such as the right to remain silent, that must be extended by police to someone undergoing custodial interrogation in order for any confession to be admissible in court; originated in *Miranda* v. *Arizona* (1966)

miscegenation laws prohibitions of interracial marriages; invalidated by *Loving* v. *Virginia* (1967)

mootness the absence of a live dispute between parties in a legal case

national police power application of the national commerce power to give Congress broad regulatory authority parallel to the traditional police power always possessed by the states

National Popular Vote Plan an agreement among states and the District of Columbia to award all of their electoral votes to the winner of the national presidential popular vote

national security letters requests under the Patriot and/or Freedom Act from federal investigators to communication providers, financial institutions, and credit bureaus for certain types of customer business records including information related to Internet and telephone usage; unlike a production order for tangible items, these letters do not require prior judicial approval; a national security letter is most often issued by the Federal Bureau of Investigation (FBI)

national supremacy legal doctrine closely associated with Chief Justice John Marshall, whereby the states and the central government confront each other in the relationship of superior and subordinate

necessary and proper clause also called the elastic clause, Article I, Section 8, Clause 18 of the Constitution gives the national government a choice of means in implementing delegated powers; see implied powers

New Deal domestic programs of the presidency of Franklin Roosevelt between 1933 and 1938 that helped to lift the United States out of the Great Depression and transformed the role of the national government in American political and economic life

new double standard result of the new judicial federalism whereby interpretations of state constitutions by state courts have sometimes produced a more rights-friendly situation within those particular states than that produced by the Supreme Court in interpreting the federal Constitution for the nation; see new judicial federalism

new judicial federalism legal phenomenon mainly after 1970 whereby state appellate courts, applying their state constitutions, have become greater protectors of some civil liberties and civil rights than the Supreme Court in cases involving the federal Constitution; see new double standard

new property generic term applying to a person's rights in government entitlements and similar benefits, as opposed to conventional real and personal property

Non-Detention Act passed by Congress in 1971 to replace the Emergency Detention Act of 1950 and provides that "No citizen shall be imprisoned or otherwise detained by the United States except pursuant to an Act of Congress"

nonjusticiable refers to a category of cases deemed inappropriate for a court to decide; see political question doctrine

one-person, one-vote rule derived from *Wesberry* v. *Sanders* (1964) and *Reynolds* v. *Sims* (1964) that stipulates equal numbers of people in each legislative district

opinion of the court in the Supreme Court, a statement representing the consensus of the majority of the bench that explains the decision of the Court, not merely the views of the author of the opinion

oral argument occasion where the attorneys in a case present their arguments in court and answer questions from the bench

ordered liberty doctrine developed by Justice Benjamin Cardozo in *Palko* v. *Connecticut* (1937) to determine the content of Fourteenth Amendment due process of law; rights thus protected by due process were those essential to a scheme of "ordered liberty"; see total incorporation and incorporation

original jurisdiction a category of cases that originate or begin in a particular court, as opposed to cases that arrive on appeal from other courts

overbreadth doctrine guards freedom of speech against laws that sweep too broadly, encompassing laws which restrict not only that speech which might legally be proscribed but protected speech as well

Partial Birth Abortion Ban Act passed by Congress in 2003 to prohibit a particular late-term abortion procedure; upheld by the Supreme Court in *Gonzales* v. *Carhart* (2007)

Patient Self-Determination Act passed by Congress in 1991 requiring hospitals to ask all patients if they want to make a living will or to designate someone as a health-care proxy to make health-related decisions for them in the event of incapacitation

Patriot Act important anti-terrorist legislation first passed by Congress in 2001 and modified and extended in 2006 and 2010 that significantly enlarges the law enforcement powers of the national government; substantially modified and replaced in 2015 by the Freedom Act

penumbra the partial shadow surrounding the complete shadow of an eclipse

per curiam by the court

petitioner in cases reaching the Supreme Court on certiorari, the party bringing the case against the respondent

plurality opinion as opposed to a majority opinion or the opinion of the court, a statement that announces the judgment of the court and explains the views of the plurality

police power that mass of general regulatory authority that the states did not surrender to the national government

political checks nonjudicial limits on government provided by the political system itself, especially the electoral process

political question doctrine view that allows the Supreme Court to identify an issue as inappropriate for judicial decision and that instead should be left to one of the "political" or elected branches to resolve; see nonjusticiable

poll tax a levy imposed on voting, designed to reduce or prevent voting by blacks and poor people in the post–Civil War South; its use in federal elections is prohibited by the Twenty-Fourth Amendment (1964) and in state elections by *Harper* v. *Virginia Board of Elections* (1966)

popular sovereignty view that the will of the people, expressed through the ballot box, is to prevail

preemption because of the supremacy clause, a situation where a legitimate exercise of national authority supersedes any conflicting action by a state government

prerogative theory a view of presidential power that allows the president to act for the public good even if the action is illegal

prior restraint curbing of speech or publication before it occurs

privacy the right of personal autonomy to control aspects of one's life free of undue interference by government; recognized as a constitutional right in *Griswold* v. *Connecticut* (1965)

private law that part of the corpus of law that deals with the relationships of individuals to each other; distinguished from public law

probable cause stipulation of demonstrated particularity in the Fourth Amendment for the issuance of search or arrest warrants

protectionism policy that advantages domestic consumers or producers over those in neighboring states

public forum various categories of public property where people may express their views

public law that part of the corpus of law that concerns the relationship between private entities (such as businesses and individuals) and government; also includes the law governing the relationships among different kinds of government; distinguished from private law

public use stipulation in the Fifth Amendment that property seized through eminent domain be for a public use

punitive damages in tort cases, awards to plaintiffs not to compensate for damages or other loss, but to deter the defendant and others like the defendant from similar activity that would be harmful to others; contrasted with compensatory damages

qualified immunity as distinguished from absolute immunity, protection from suits in certain circumstances

racially identifiable schools public schools which are mainly one race in their enrollment

racially restrictive covenants provision inserted in deeds to promote residential segregation barring sale of property to people of certain races or ethnic groups; judicial enforcement of such covenants invalidated by *Shelley* v. *Kraemer* (1948)

ranking member on a legislative committee, ordinarily the most senior member from the minority party

rational basis test least demanding level of scrutiny applied by the Supreme Court under the equal protection clause whereby a challenged statute is expected to have a rational or reasonable relation to a legitimate state interest

reasonable suspicion measure of justification, less than probable cause, needed to support a pat-down or frisk under *Terry* v. *Ohio* (1968); see frisk

recess appointment occurs when the president fills a vacancy when the Senate is not in session; the appointment expires at the end of the next congressional session unless the Senate has confirmed the official by majority vote

reciprocal immunity view of federalism whereby neither state nor federal governments may interfere with the operations of the other

recusal the voluntary withdrawal by a judge of herself or himself from a case where there is a serious risk of actual bias

regular concurrence in the U.S. Supreme Court, a separate opinion filed by a justice who also joins the opinion of the Court; also see concurrence and special concurrence

regulatory taxation imposition of levies by government for the purpose of affecting the behavior of individuals or groups

released-time arrangement by which students are released from classes to attend religious instruction on- or off-site; the former has been judged unconstitutional, the latter constitutional

Religious Freedom Restoration Act passed by Congress under its Section 5 powers in 1993 after the Supreme Court's decision in *Employment Division* v. *Smith*, incorporating the religion-friendly interpretation of the free exercise clause from *Sherbert* v. *Verner* (1963); invalidated as applied to state governments in *Boerne* v. *Flores* (1997)

Religious Land Use and Institutionalized Persons Act passed by Congress in 2000 as a partial substitution for the Religious Freedom Restoration Act; it declares that no "government shall impose or implement a land use regulation in a manner that imposes a substantial burden on the religious exercise of a person, including a religious assembly or institution, unless the government demonstrates that imposition of the burden on that person, assembly, or institution (a) is in furtherance of a compelling governmental interest; and (b) is the least restrictive means of furthering that compelling governmental interest"; upheld in *Cutter* v. *Wilkinson* (2005)

religious test qualification or condition, based on religion, for holding public office; proscribed by Article VI of the Constitution

remand occurs when a court returns a case to a lower court for further action

resegregation the phenomenon of increased racial segregation following steps to reduce racial segregation

reservation clause provision in a contract, statute, or state constitution retaining authority for the state to alter the terms of a charter issued by the state

reserved powers governing authority not assigned to the national government and therefore retained by the states or the people

respondent in cases reaching the Supreme Court on certiorari, the party who has been brought to court by the petitioner

resulting powers authority of the national government derived from the mass of delegated powers or a group of them

retrogression a principle of the Voting Rights Act as construed by the Supreme Court that bars an electoral change which reduces black voting influence

reversing occurs when a court sets aside the ruling of a lower court

ripeness requirement that a controversy must have reached a certain stage of maturity before a court will engage it

rule of four internal rule at the Supreme Court that requires the votes of four justices before a case is accepted for review

Second Amendment the second article in the Bill of Rights, which protects a right to keep and bear arms

Section 1981 provision in the Civil Rights Act of 1866 to eliminate racial discrimination in the making of contracts, in access to the judicial system, and in other venues

Section 1982 provision in the Civil Rights Act of 1866 to eliminate discrimination against blacks in the sale, rental, and ownership of real and personal property

Section 25 provision of the Judiciary Act of 1789 conferring jurisdiction on the Supreme Court in cases from the highest court of a state involving a federal question, where the decision below was adverse to the federal claim

Sedition Act of 1798 first attempt in the United States by a political party (the Federalists) to use the criminal law to punish the opposition (the Democratic-Republicans)

selective exclusiveness interpretation of the commerce clause from *Cooley* v. *Board of Wardens* (1851) that allows regulation of commerce by the states, in the absence of federal regulation except where the regulation is one that calls for national uniformity

separate but equal legal justification for racial segregation from *Plessy* v. *Ferguson* (1896) by which government could require racially separate facilities provided the facilities were equal; overruled by *Brown* v. *Board of Education* (1954)

separation one of the early ways of thinking about the proper relationship between government and religion in the United States; stresses distance between church and state and minimal contact between the two

separation of powers division of legislative, executive, and judicial powers among separate branches of government

seriatim opinions Latin for "in a series"; as distinguished from an "opinion of the court," the practice of having each member of a court write a separate opinion expressing his or her views

set-aside stipulation in law that a certain percentage of government funds available for contracts go to minority contractors

shadow docket growing category of cases acted upon by the U.S. Supreme Court that do not receive plenary treatment; also see docket

shared-time arrangement by which students in sectarian schools receive specialized instruction (enrichment or remediation) on-site and conducted by public school employees

Sherman Anti-Trust Act passed by Congress in 1890 to restrict monopolies and other restraints of trade

Sixth Amendment provision in the Bill of Rights dating from 1791 that protects the right to assistance of counsel, jury trial, and the right to confront one's accusers, among other safeguards

Smith Act passed by Congress in 1940, this law made it a felony to advocate the violent overthrow of the government of the United States or to conspire with others to organize a group advocating such violence; upheld in *Dennis* v. *United States* (1951)

"sneak and peek" search warrants under the Patriot Act, authorization for agents to conduct a search without notifying the owner and to delay notification for up to 30 days (with the possibility of extensions) that a search has taken place

soft money financial contributions to parties, groups, or candidates that are unregulated by federal law

solicitor general official in the Department of Justice who is the lawyer for the United States in the Supreme Court, and whose approval is required in order for an appeal to be taken to any federal court in cases where the United States is a party

Solomon Amendment so named for former Representative Gerald B. H. Solomon, a congressional requirement that institutions receiving federal funds allow military recruiters on their premises; at issue in *Rumsfeld* v. *Forum for Academic and Institutional Rights* (2006)

sovereign immunity doctrine, shaped and modified by the Eleventh Amendment, federal statutes, and court decisions, that precludes a suit against a government without its consent

special concurrence in the U.S. Supreme Court, a separate opinion filed by a justice who votes with the majority but who does not join the opinion of the Court; also see concurrence and regular concurrence

special need the justification—such as airline safety or a drug-free workforce—required for administrative searches that operate under relaxed Fourth Amendment standards

special prosecutor lawyer from outside government appointed on an ad hoc basis by an attorney general at the state or federal level to investigate officials for misconduct in office

speech or debate clause provision in Paragraph 1 of Article I, Section 6, of the Constitution that protects legislative independence by immunizing members and aides against suits for protected legislative acts

standing a threshold requirement in litigation that determines whether a litigant is the proper party to initiate a case

stare decisis Latin for to stand by what has been decided; preference by courts to decide a case like similar cases in the past except in special circumstances

state action conduct by government as opposed to conduct by a private entity

state courts judicial institutions established by one of the 50 states

stewardship theory view of presidential power by which presidents may act to further the needs of the people unless forbidden by the Constitution or a statute

strategic model theory of judicial decision making that stresses the influence of the collegial environment of a Court, where judges may seek to achieve certain goals not merely by voting their own preferences but by taking the views and behavior of colleagues as well as the tribunal's internal decision-making procedures into account

strict scrutiny most rigorous standard of Supreme Court review applied to challenged official action under the equal protection clause; to withstand constitutional attack, a law or policy must be necessarily related to a compelling government interest and be narrowly tailored to further that interest

strict scrutiny test see strict scrutiny

subpoena an order compelling someone's presence in court or before a congressional committee; a subpoena *duces tecum* requires the person to produce certain documents or other material as well

substantive equal protection see fundamental rights analysis

supremacy clause sometimes called the "kingpin" clause, the provision in Paragraph 2 of Article VI in the Constitution asserting the supremacy of the national government over the states and the primacy of the Constitution and federal statutes and treaties over state law

symbolic speech activity designed to convey a message in situations where that message is likely to be understood

takings clause provision in the Fifth Amendment limiting the power of eminent domain by protecting against the taking of someone's property for public use without payment of just compensation

targeted killing policy advanced by the Obama administration whereby individuals, such as Islamist terrorists, far from the battlefield, are singled out because of their involvement in plots against the United States

Thirteenth Amendment ratified in 1865 to abolish slavery and involuntary servitude

Title II part of the Civil Rights Act of 1964 outlawing racial and religious discrimination in places of public accommodation such as hotels and restaurants

Title IX part of the Education Amendments of 1972 banning gender discrimination in educational programs receiving federal financial assistance

Title VI part of the Civil Rights Act of 1964 banning racial discrimination in programs receiving federal financial assistance

Title VII part of the Civil Rights Act of 1964 banning racial, religious, or gender discrimination in the workplace

tortfeasor in tort law, a person who commits a tort (or civil wrong)

total incorporation doctrine developed by Justice Hugo Black to determine the content of Fourteenth Amendment due process of law; rights thus protected included all provisions of the Bill of Rights; see incorporation and ordered liberty

transactional immunity complete protection from prosecution that is extended to an individual who has been compelled to testify; not considered a violation of the Fifth Amendment

undue burden standard identified with Justice Sandra Day O'Connor to mark the difference between acceptable and unacceptable regulations of abortions; regulations are acceptable unless they impose an "undue burden" on a woman's right to undergo an abortion

unitary executive theory view of presidential power under which the president not only has control over members of the executive branch, but whose authority is restricted only by the Constitution; Congress may hold the president accountable by censure, impeachment, or constitutional amendment but not by legislation that intrudes onto the chief executive's Article II domain.

unitary school system a public school system without significant numbers of heavily one-race schools; opposite of dual school system

USA Patriot Act see Patriot Act

use immunity partial protection from prosecution that is extended to an individual who has been compelled to testify, whereby the government may not later use the testimony in a prosecution against the witness; considered less generous than transactional immunity and is not considered a violation of the Fifth Amendment

vested rights legal entitlements or claims of one person that cannot be taken away by another; doctrine that stresses the sanctity of private property and insists that government regulation not unduly restrict right of ownership

viewpoint-based restrictions regulations of speech or other kinds of expression which target particular values or outlooks

void for vagueness judges may use this standard to invalidate laws that do not give individuals fair warning of prohibited conduct. A vague statute blurs the line between legal and illegal behavior

Voting Rights Act passed in 1965 and renewed most recently in 2006, the most comprehensive voting rights legislation ever enacted by Congress to combat racial discrimination in the electoral process; however, *Shelby County* v. *Holder* (2013) invalidated section 4 of the Voting Rights Act; this provision had made certain states eligible for coverage under section 5 which in turn requires pre-clearance for changes in the electoral system and practices of the affected states; without section 4, section 5 remains inoperable

War Powers Resolution passed in 1973 requiring the president to obtain congressional approval within 60 days after sending troops into combat and to consult with Congress before taking such action

warrant judicial authorization for a search or an arrest

Warren Court period of Supreme Court history (1953–1969) when Earl Warren was chief justice, notable for decisions expanding civil liberties and civil rights; see due process revolution

wayward elector see faithless elector

white primary party election in which only white people were eligible to vote

writ formal legal order issued by a judge

writ of habeas corpus see habeas corpus

writ of mandamus Latin for "we command," a judicial order to compel an organization or an individual to act; when directed to a public official, it compels performance of a ministerial or nondiscretionary act

writs of assistance general search warrants employed by the British in the years before the American Revolution; objection to their use in the colonies assured inclusion of the Fourth Amendment in the Bill of Rights; see Fourth Amendment

INDEX OF CASES

Note: **Boldface type** indicates opinions reprinted in this volume and the pages at which they may be found. *Lightface italic type* denotes cases cited in the essays, opinions, case headnotes, and case footnotes inserted by the author. ***Boldface italic type*** denotes new excerpts for this edition. *See* pages 34–37 for information on the reporting of judicial decisions.

INDEX OF SUBJECTS AND NAMES

Boldface type indicates the pages at which excerpted case opinions and other writings can be found.